ALL THE HELP, **RESOURCES**, AND PERSONAL **SUPPORT**
YOU AND YOUR STUDENTS NEED!

2-Minute Tutorials and all
of the resources you & your
students need to get started
www.wileyplus.com/firstday

Student support from an
experienced student user
Ask your local representative
for details!

Collaborate with your colleagues,
find a mentor, attend virtual and live
events, and view resources
www.WhereFacultyConnect.com

Pre-loaded, ready-to-use
assignments and presentations
www.wiley.com/college/quickstart

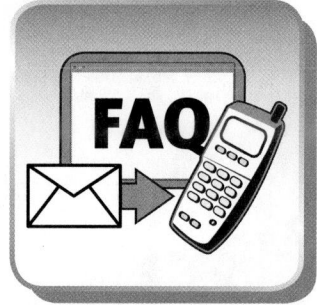

Technical Support 24/7
FAQs, online chat,
and phone support
www.wileyplus.com/support

Your *WileyPLUS*
Account Manager
Training and implementation support
www.wileyplus.com/accountmanager

www.wiley**plus**.com

MAKE IT YOURS!

BUSINESS STATISTICS

For Contemporary Decision Making

BUSINESS STATISTICS

For Contemporary Decision Making

CANADIAN EDITION

KEN BLACK

University of Houston–Clear Lake

CHUCK CHAKRAPANI

Ryerson University

IGNACIO CASTILLO

Wilfrid Laurier University

WILEY

John Wiley & Sons Canada, Ltd.

For Carolyn, Caycee, and Wendi
Ken

For Ken
For his support over the years. More than he knows
Chuck

Para mis abuelos Gonzalo y Lilián, Talo y Mamina
Ignacio

Library and Archives Canada Cataloguing in Publication

Black, Ken (Kenneth Urban)
  Business statistics : for contemporary decision making / Ken Black, Chuck Chakrapani, Ignacio Castillo. — Canadian ed.
Includes bibliographical references and index.
ISBN 978-0-470-15704-6
  1. Commercial statistics—Textbooks. I. Chakrapani, Chuck II. Castillo, Ignacio III. Title.
HF1017.B572 2010   519.502′465   C2009-907013-8

Production Credits
Acquisitions Editor: Darren Lalonde
Vice President & Publisher: Veronica Visentin
Vice President, Publishing Services: Karen Bryan
Creative Director, Publishing Services: Ian Koo
Marketing Manager: Aida Krneta
Editorial Manager: Karen Staudinger
Developmental Editor: Theresa Fitzgerald
Project and Manufacturing Coordinator: Tegan Wallace
Editorial Assistant: Laura Hwee
Permissions Coordinator: Kristiina Paul
Typesetting: Aptara Inc.
Cover Design: Interrobang Design
Cover Image: Getty Images/Photodisc/Ryan MacVay (background image), iStock/3D graph by yystorm/ Business team at meeting by Yuri Arcurs/Business woman with empty diagram by Tommi/Group at park with laptop by apomares
Printing and binding: Quad/ Graphics
Printed and bound in the United States.
2 3 4 5 QD 14 13 12 11

WILEY

John Wiley & Sons Canada, Ltd.
6045 Freemont Blvd.
Mississauga, Ontario L5R 4J3
Visit our website at: www.wiley.ca

BRIEF CONTENTS

Unit V • Special Topics

CONTENTS

UNIT II · DISTRIBUTIONS AND SAMPLING

CHAPTER 6 Continuous Distributions 208

CHAPTER 7 Sampling and Sampling Distributions 250

UNIT III • MAKING INFERENCES ABOUT POPULATION PARAMETERS

CHAPTER 8 Statistical Inference: Estimation for Single Populations 290

UNIT IV • REGRESSION ANALYSIS AND FORECASTING

Business Statistics for Contemporary Decision Making, Canadian Edition uses clear, complete, and student-friendly pedagogy to present and explain business statistics topics. The vast ancillary resources available through *WileyPLUS* complement the text in helping instructors effectively deliver this subject matter and assisting students in their learning.

We wrote the chapters in the book to help students construct their knowledge of the big picture of statistics, provide assistance as needed, and afford more opportunities to practice statistical skills. The 19 chapters in this book are organized into five units to facilitate student understanding of the bigger view of statistics. There are 17 high-quality video tutorials with Ken Black that explain difficult key topics and demonstrate how to work problems from challenging sections of the text.

This book is written and designed for a two-semester introductory undergraduate business statistics course or an MBA-level introductory course. In addition, with 19 chapters, this text lends itself nicely to adaptation for a one-semester introductory business statistics course. The text is written with the assumption that the student has a college algebra mathematical background. No calculus is used in the presentation of material in the text.

An underlying philosophical approach to the text is that every statistical tool presented in the book has some business application. While the text contains statistical rigor, it is written so that the student can readily see that the proper application of statistics in the business world goes hand-in-hand with good decision making. In this edition, statistics are presented as a means for converting data into useful information that can be used to assist the business decision maker in making more thoughtful, information-based decisions. Thus, the text presents business statistics as "value added" tools in the process of converting data into useful information.

SPECIAL FEATURES OF THIS BOOK

UNITS AND CHAPTERS

This book presents 19 chapters organized into five units. The purpose of the unit organization is to locate chapters with similar topics together, thereby increasing the likelihood that students are better able to grasp the bigger picture of statistics.

TREE DIAGRAM OF INFERENTIAL TECHNIQUES

To assist the student in sorting out the plethora of confidence intervals and hypothesis testing techniques presented in the text, tree diagrams are presented at the beginning of Unit III and Chapters 8, 9, 10, and 17. The tree diagram at the beginning of Unit III displays virtually all of the inferential techniques presented in Chapters 8–10 so that the student can construct a view of the "forest for the trees" and determine how each technique plugs into the whole. Then at the beginning of each of these three chapters, an additional tree diagram is presented to display the branch of the tree that applies to techniques in that particular chapter. Chapter 17 includes a tree diagram for just the nonparametric statistics presented in that chapter.

In determining which technique to use, there are several key questions that a student should consider. Listed here are some of the key questions (displayed in a box in the Unit III introduction) that delineate what students should ask themselves in determining the appropriate inferential technique for a particular analysis: Does the problem call for estimation (using a confidence interval) or testing (using a hypothesis test)? How many samples are being analyzed? Are you analyzing means, proportions, or variances? If means are being analyzed, is (are) the variance(s) known or not? If means from two samples are being analyzed, are the samples independent or related? If three or more samples are being analyzed, are there one or two independent variables and is there a blocking variable?

DECISION DILEMMA AND THE DECISION DILEMMA SOLVED

The Decision Dilemmas are real business vignettes that open each chapter and set the tone for the chapter by presenting a business dilemma and asking a number of managerial or statistical questions, the solutions to which require the use of techniques presented in the chapter. The Decision Dilemma Solved feature discusses and answers the managerial and statistical questions posed in the Decision Dilemma using techniques from the chapter, thus bringing closure to the chapter.

WHY STATISTICS IS RELEVANT

In keeping with our aim to make statistics relevant to students, we have included a section towards the end of each chapter, entitled "Why Statistics in Relevant". This section provides students with a link between the statistical concepts and the opportunities for application in real-life business contexts. This helps students to understand that statistics is not a purely academic subject, but something that is relevant in business decision making.

STATISTICS IN BUSINESS TODAY

This book includes one or two Statistics in Business Today features in every chapter. This feature presents a real-life example of how the statistics presented in that chapter apply in the business world today.

PROBLEMS

We examined the problems included in the text for timeliness, appropriateness, and logic before we included them in the book. Those that fell short were replaced or rewritten. While the total number of problems in the text is 925, a concerted effort has been made to include only problems that make a significant contribution to the learning process.

All demonstration problems and example problems were thoroughly reviewed and edited for effectiveness. A demonstration problem is an extra example containing both a problem and its solution and is used as an additional pedagogical tool to supplement explanations and examples in the chapters. Virtually all example and demonstration problems in this edition are business oriented and contain current data available to us.

Problems are located at the end of most sections in the chapters. A significant number of additional problems are provided at the end of each chapter in the Supplementary Problems. The Supplementary Problems are "scrambled"—problems using the various techniques in the chapter are mixed—so that students can test themselves on their ability to discriminate and differentiate ideas and concepts.

POINTS OF INTEREST

We have provided, in bite-sized pieces, interesting and pertinent information to engage the student. They can be found in the margins of each chapter.

VIDEOTAPE TUTORIALS BY KEN BLACK

An exciting feature of the package that will impact the effectiveness of student learning in business statistics and significantly enhance the presentation of course material is the series of videotape tutorials by Ken Black. With the advent of online business statistics courses, increasingly large class sizes, and the number of commuter students who have very limited access to educational resources on business statistics, it is often difficult for students to get the learning assistance that they need to bridge the gap between theory and application on their own. There are now 17 videotaped tutorial sessions on key difficult topics in business statistics delivered by Ken Black and available for all adopters on *WileyPLUS*. In addition, these tutorials can easily be uploaded for classroom usage to augment lectures and enrich classroom presentations. Each session is around 9 minutes in length. The 17 tutorials are:

1. Chapter 3: Computing Variance and Standard Deviation
2. Chapter 3: Understanding and Using the Empirical Rule
3. Chapter 4: Constructing and Solving Probability Matrices
4. Chapter 4: Solving Probability Word Problems
5. Chapter 5: Solving Binomial Distribution Problems, Part I
6. Chapter 5: Solving Binomial Distribution Problems, Part II
7. Chapter 6: Solving Problems Using the Normal Curve
8. Chapter 8: Confidence Intervals
9. Chapter 8: Determining Which Inferential Technique to Use, Part I, Confidence Intervals
10. Chapter 9: Hypothesis Testing Using the z Statistic
11. Chapter 9: Establishing Hypotheses
12. Chapter 9: Understanding p-Values
13. Chapter 9: Type I and Type II Errors
14. Chapter 9: Two-Tailed Tests
15. Chapter 9: Determining Which Inferential Technique to Use, Part II, Hypothesis Tests
16. Chapter 12: Testing the Regression Model I—Predicted Values, Residuals, and Sum of Squares of Error
17. Chapter 12: Testing the Regression Model II—Standard Error of the Estimate and r_2

FEATURES AND BENEFITS

Each chapter of the book contains sections called Learning Objectives, a Decision Dilemma, Demonstration Problems, Section Problems, Concept Checks, Statistics in Business Today, Decision Dilemma Solved, Why Statistics in Relevant, Points of Interest, Chapter Summary, Key Terms, Formulas, Key Considerations, Supplementary Problems, Analyzing the Databases, Case, and Using the Computer.

- **Learning Objectives.** Each chapter begins with a question concerning of the chapter's main learning objectives. These questions give the reader a list of key topics that will be discussed and the goals to be achieved from studying the chapter.
- **Decision Dilemma.** At the beginning of each chapter, a short case describes a real company or business situation in which managerial and statistical questions are raised. In most Decision Dilemmas, actual data are given and the student is asked to consider how the data can be analyzed to answer the questions.
- **Demonstration Problems.** Virtually every section of every chapter in the book edition contains demonstration problems. A demonstration problem contains both an example problem and its solution, and is used as an additional pedagogical tool to supplement explanations and examples.
- **Section Problems.** Problems for practice are found at the end of almost every section of the text. Most problems utilize real data gathered from a plethora of sources. Included here are two brief excerpts from some of the real-life problems in the text: "The Canadian Beef Export Federation reports that the top six destinations for Canadian beef in a recent year were the U.S. with $1,697 million, Mexico with $269 million, Japan with $171 million, South Korea with $28 million, Taiwan with $16 million, and China with $4 million." "Data accumulated by Environment Canada show that the average wind speed in kilometres per hour for Victoria International Airport, located on the Saanich Peninsula in British Columbia, is 9.3."
- **Concept Checks.** Concept checks are conceptual questions are aimed to reinforce the conceptual understanding of the material presented. They are presented following each main section of the chapter. These questions do not require students to use calculations.
- **Statistics in Business Today.** Every chapter in the book contains at least one Statistics in Business Today feature. These focus boxes contain an interesting application of how techniques of that particular chapter are used in the business world today. They are usually based on real companies, surveys, or published research.
- **Decision Dilemma Solved.** Situated at the end of the chapter, the Decision Dilemma Solved feature addresses the managerial and statistical questions raised in the Decision Dilemma. Data given in the Decision Dilemma are analyzed computationally and by computer using techniques presented in the chapter. Answers to the managerial and statistical questions raised in the Decision Dilemma are arrived at by applying chapter concepts, thus bringing closure to the chapter.
- **Why Statistics is Relevant**. This section in each chapter discusses how the material discussed in that chapter is related to real-life decision making.
- **Key Considerations.** Each chapter contains a Key Considerations feature that is very timely, given that many users of statistics are unaware of the traps that await the unwary. With the abundance of statistical data and analysis, there is also considerable potential for the misuse of statistics in business dealings. The important Key Considerations feature underscores this potential misuse by discussing such topics as lying with statistics, failing to meet statistical assumptions, and failing to include pertinent information for decision makers. Through this feature, instructors can begin to integrate the topic of ethics with applications of business statistics. Here are two excerpts from Key Considerations features:—"Invalid or spurious results can be obtained by using the parameters from one population to analyze another population. For example, a market study in Nova Scotia may result in the conclusion that the amount of fish eaten per month by adults is normally distributed with an average of 1kg of fish per month. A market researcher in Manitoba should not assume that these figures apply to her population. People in Manitoba probably have quite different fish-eating habits than people in Nova Scotia," and "In describing a body of data to an audience, it is best to use whatever statistical measures it takes to present a full picture of the data. By limiting the descriptive measures used, the business researcher may give the audience only part of the picture and skew the way the receiver understands the data."

- **Chapter Summary.** Each chapter concludes with a summary of the important concepts, ideas, and techniques of the chapter. This feature can serve as a preview of the chapter as well as a chapter review.
- **Key Terms.** Important terms are bolded and their definitions italicized throughout the text as they are discussed. At the end of the chapter, a list of the key terms from the chapter is presented. In addition, these terms appear with their definitions in an end-of-book glossary.
- **Formulas.** Important formulas in the text are highlighted to make it easy for a reader to locate them. At the end of the chapter, most of the chapter's formulas are listed together as a handy reference.
- **Supplementary Problems.** At the end of each chapter is an extensive set of additional problems. The Supplementary Problems are divided into three groups: *Calculating the Statistics*, which are strictly computational problems; *Testing Your Understanding*, which are problems for application and understanding; and *Interpreting the Output*, which are problems that require the interpretation and analysis of software output.
- **Analyzing the Databases.** There are seven major databases located on the student companion Web site that accompanies the book. The end-of-chapter Analyzing the Databases section contains several questions/problems that require the application of techniques from the chapter to data in the variables of the databases. It is assumed that most of these questions/problems will be solved using a computer.
- **Case.** Each end-of-chapter case is based on a real company, many featuring Canadian businesses. These cases give the student an opportunity to use statistical concepts and techniques presented in the chapter to solve a business dilemma. Some cases feature very large companies— such as Tim Hortons, Research in Motion, or Shell Oil. Others pertain to small businesses—such as Thermatrix, Delta Wire, or Fytokem Products Inc.—that have overcome obstacles to survive and thrive. Most cases include raw data for analysis and questions that encourage the student to use several of the techniques presented in the chapter. In many cases, the student must analyze software output in order to reach conclusions or make decisions.
- **Using the Computer.** The Using the Computer section contains directions for producing the Excel 2007 software output presented in the chapter. It is assumed that students have a general understanding of a Microsoft Windows environment. Directions include specifics about menu bars, drop-down menus, and dialogue boxes. Each dialogue box is not discussed in detail; the intent is to provide enough information for students to produce the same statistical output analyzed and discussed in the chapter.

WileyPLUS

WileyPLUS, a powerful yet easy-to-use technology solution, provides instructors and students with a suite of interactive resources, included a complete on-line version of the text and tools that allow instructors to assign and grade homework and quizzes.

WileyPLUS RESOURCES FOR STUDENTS WITHIN *WileyPLUS*

In *WileyPLUS*, students will find various helpful tools, such as an ebook, the student study manual, videos with tutorials by the author, applets, Decision Dilemma and Decision Dilemma Solved animations, learning activities, flash cards for key terms, demonstration problems, databases in both Excel and Minitab, case data in both Excel and Minitab, and problem data in both Excel and Minitab.

- **Ebook.** The complete text is available on *WileyPLUS* with learning links to various features and tools to assist students in their learning.

- **Videos.** There are 17 videos of the author explaining concepts and demonstrating how to work problems for some of the more difficult topics.
- **Applets.** Statistical applets are available, affording students the opportunity to learn concepts by iteratively experimenting with various values of statistics and parameters and observing the outcomes.
- **Learning Activities.** There are numerous learning activities to help the student better understand concepts and key terms. These activities have been developed to make learning fun, enjoyable, and challenging.
- **Data Sets.** Virtually all problems in the text along with the case problems and the databases are available to students in both Excel and Minitab format.
- **Animations.** To aid students in understanding complex interactions, selected figures from the text that involve dynamic activity have been animated using Flash technology. Students can download these animated figures and run them to improve their understanding of dynamic processes.
- **Kaddstat.** Kaddstat is an easy-to-use add-in to Excel that makes it easier to run complex statistical tests on Excel.
- **The Virtual Teaching Assistant: SPSS 16.0.** Exclusive to *WileyPLUS*, these videos are excellent for instructors who want to use SPSS 16.0 program, but do not have the class time to provide training to students. Developed under the leadership of Dr. Hannah Scott, UOIT, each video takes the student through a selected procedure; a narrator demonstrates how to interpret results of the task performed. Embedded in each video are a series of Flash® points where the video is stopped and the student is encouraged to click on an area selected by a "call-out." Each section ends with a short self test for students to apply what they have just seen.

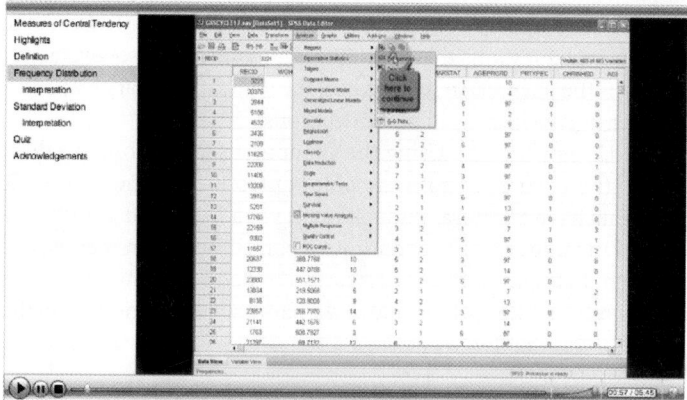

- **Flash Cards.** Key terms will be available to students in a flash card format along with their definition.
- **Student Study Guide.** Complete answers to all odd-numbered questions.
- **Demo Problems.** Step-by-step solved problems for each chapter.

ANCILLARY TEACHING AND LEARNING MATERIALS

www.wiley.com/canada/black

STUDENTS' COMPANION SITE

The student companion Web site contains:

- All databases in both Excel and Minitab formats for easy access and use.
- Excel and Minitab files of data from all text problems and all cases. Instructors and students now have the option of analyzing any of the data sets using the computer.
- A tutorial on summation theory.

INSTRUCTOR'S RESOURCE KIT

All instructor ancillaries are provided on the Instructor Resource Site. Included in this convenient format are:

- **Instructor's Manual.** Prepared by Clarence Bayne of Concordia University, this manual contains the worked out solutions to virtually all problems in the text. In addition, this manual contains chapter objectives, chapter outlines, chapter teaching strategies, and solutions to the cases.
- **PowerPoint Presentation Slides.** The presentation slides, prepared by Clarence Bayne of Concordia University, contain graphics to help instructors create stimulating lectures. The PowerPoint slides may be adapted using PowerPoint software to facilitate classroom use.
- **Test Bank.** Prepared by Svetlana Nekhai of Seneca College, the Test Bank includes multiple-choice questions for each chapter. The Test Bank is provided in Microsoft Word format.

ACKNOWLEDGMENTS

John Wiley & Sons and the authors would like to thank the reviewers who cared enough and took the time to provide us with their excellent insights and advice, which was used to shape and mold the Canadian edition. Our appreciation goes to:

Gordon Anderson, University of Toronto
Chedo Barone, University of Victoria
Walid Belassi, Athabasca University
Ellen Fowler, Simon Fraser University
Alexei Gokhman, Humber College
Norman Hill, NAIT
Stephan Kogitz, Centennial College
Jacky Li, Kwantlen Polytechnic University

Tony Mancini, Concordia University
Ata Mazaheri, University of Toronto
John Morrison, Seneca College
Tony Quon, University of Ottawa
Rob Sorensen, Camosun College
Susan Sproule, McMaster University
Brian Tozer, Conestoga College

Special thanks to our contributors for supplements and applications:

Tony Mancini, Concordia University
Jacky Li, Kwantlen Polytechnic University
Alexei Gokhman, Humber College

Ioulia Kim, Humber College
Svetlana Nekhai, Seneca College
Clarence Bayne, Concordia University

There are several people working at or with John Wiley & Sons in bringing this edition to fruition whom we would like to thank for their invaluable assistance on the project. They include Darren Lalonde, Acquisitions Editor; Aida Krneta, Marketing Manager; Karen Staudinger, Editorial Manager; Theresa Fitzgerald, Developmental Editor; Julia Cochrane, Copy Editor; and Laurel Hyatt, Proofreader.

Chuck would like to acknowledge the highly conducive environment created by Dr. Ken Jones, Dean of the Ted Rogers School of Management and by Dr. Tony Hernandez, Director for the Centre for the Study of Commercial Activity (CSCA) at Ryerson University. I would also like to thank Tony for his unfailing humour and ready support whenever I needed it. One cannot work at CSCA and not acknowledge the presence of Kathy Doddridge who makes everything happen at the Centre.

Ignacio would like to thank Dr. Erhan Erkut (Özyeğin University, Turkey) and Dr. Hamid Noori (Wilfrid Laurier University) for their support and mentorship over the years. I also would like to thank my parents Ignacio and Lilián, my brother Andrés, my sister Gabriela, my wife Ivonne, and my sons José and Emilio for their unconditional love.

Chuck Chakrapani
Ignacio Castillo

Chuck Chakrapani is President of Leger Marketing (Toronto Office), Distinguished Visiting Professor at Ted Rogers School of Management at Ryerson University, President of Standard Research Systems and Chief Knowledge Officer of the Blackstone Group in Chicago.

He was formerly the Chief Executive Officer of Millward Brown Canada, past President and Executive Director of the PMRS (now Marketing Research and Intelligence Association) and Chairman of Investors Association of Canada. Dr. Chakrapani has held academic appointments at the London Business School in England, and at universities of Liverpool, Guelph and McMaster. He was Editor-in-Chief of the *Canadian Journal of Marketing Research* for over 20 years and is currently the Editor of *Marketing Research*, a quarterly publication of the American Marketing Association. Chuck is a Fellow of the Royal Statistical Society and is elected Fellow of the Marketing Research and Intelligence Association for his "outstanding contributions to marketing research". He has been an invited speaker in England, the United States, Australia, Canada, India and the Middle East.

He is the author of more than 10 books and 500 articles on marketing research and investments. His recent books include *Statistics in Market Research* (2004) and *Marketing Research: State of the Art Perspectives* (2000), Chuck is an active academic, business consultant and seminar leader. He works internationally and his clients include several multinational companies, legal firms, marketing boards and government bodies. He can be reached at chuck.chakrapani@gmail.com or through his website ChuckChakrapani.com.

Ignacio Castillo is an associate professor of operations and decision sciences at the School of Business & Economics, Wilfrid Laurier University. He received a Ph.D. in industrial engineering from Texas A&M University, an M.S.E. in industrial engineering from Arizona State University, and a B.S. (magna cum laude) in applied sciences from Universidad San Francisco de Quito, Ecuador.

His research and teaching interests include business statistics, facility location, facility layout and material handling systems, manufacturing and service operations and logistics, and sustainable and closed-loop supply chain management. Dr. Castillo has consulted for several public and private organizations, has supervised over ten graduate theses or projects, and has produced over 20 articles that have appeared in prestigious academic journals. His research has been mainly supported by the National Research Council of Canada (NSERC).

Dr. Castillo has served as adjunct faculty at the University of Alberta and the University of Waterloo and is a member of CORS, IIE, INFORMS, POMS, Alpha Pi Mu Industrial Engineering Honor Society, The Honor Society of Phi Kappa Phi, Pinnacle Honor Society, and a former FUNDACYT/LASPAU scholar.

Ken Black is currently professor of decision sciences in the School of Business at the University of Houston–Clear Lake. Born in Cambridge, Massachusetts, and raised in Missouri, he earned a bachelor's degree in mathematics from Graceland University, a master's degree in math education from the University of Texas at El Paso, a Ph.D. in business administration in management science, and a Ph.D. in educational research from the University of North Texas.

Since joining the faculty of UHCL in 1979, Professor Black has taught all levels of statistics courses, forecasting, management science, market research, and production/operations management. In 2005, he was awarded the President's Distinguished Teaching Award for the university. He has published over 20 journal articles and 20 professional papers, as well as two textbooks: *Business Statistics: An Introductory Course* and *Business Statistics for Contemporary Decision Making*. Black has consulted for many different companies, including Aetna, the city of Houston, NYLCare, AT&T, Johnson Space Center, Southwest Information Resources, Connect Corporation, and Eagle Engineering.

Ken Black and his wife, Carolyn, have two daughters, Caycee and Wendi. His hobbies include playing the guitar, reading, traveling, and running.

Unit I

INTRODUCTION

The study of business statistics is important, valuable, and interesting. However, because it involves a new language of terms, symbols, logic, and mathematics, it can be overwhelming. For many students, this text is their first and only introduction to business statistics, which instructors often teach as a "survey course." That is, the student is presented with an overview of the subject, including many techniques, concepts, and formulas. It can be overwhelming! One of the main difficulties in studying business statistics in this way is to be able to see the forest for the trees, that is, to sort out the myriad of topics so they make sense. With this in mind, we have organized the chapters of this text into four units, with each unit containing chapters that present similar material. At the beginning of each unit, an introduction presents the overlying themes to those chapters.

Unit I is titled "Introduction" because the four chapters (1–4) contained herein introduce the study of business statistics. In Chapter 1, students will learn the many meanings of the word *statistics,* the concepts of descriptive and inferential statistics, and the levels of data measurement. In Chapter 2, students will see how raw data can be organized using various graphical and tabular techniques to facilitate their use in making better business decisions. Chapter 3 introduces some essential and basic statistics that will be used both as a way to summarize data and as tools for techniques introduced later in the text. The chapter also includes a discussion of distribution shapes and measures of association. In Chapter 4, the basic laws of probability are presented. The notion of probability underlies virtually every business statistics topic, distribution, and technique, thereby making it important to appreciate and understand the subject. In Unit I, the first four chapters, we are developing building blocks that will enable you to understand and apply statistical concepts, so you can analyze data to assist present and future business managers in making better decisions.

CHAPTER 1
INTRODUCTION TO STATISTICS

Learning Objectives

The primary objective of Chapter 1 is to introduce you to the world of statistics. We would like to answer the following questions:

1. What is statistics?
2. What is the range of applications of statistics in business?
3. What is the difference between descriptive and inferential statistics?
4. How can numbers be classified by level of data and why is doing so important?

Getty Images

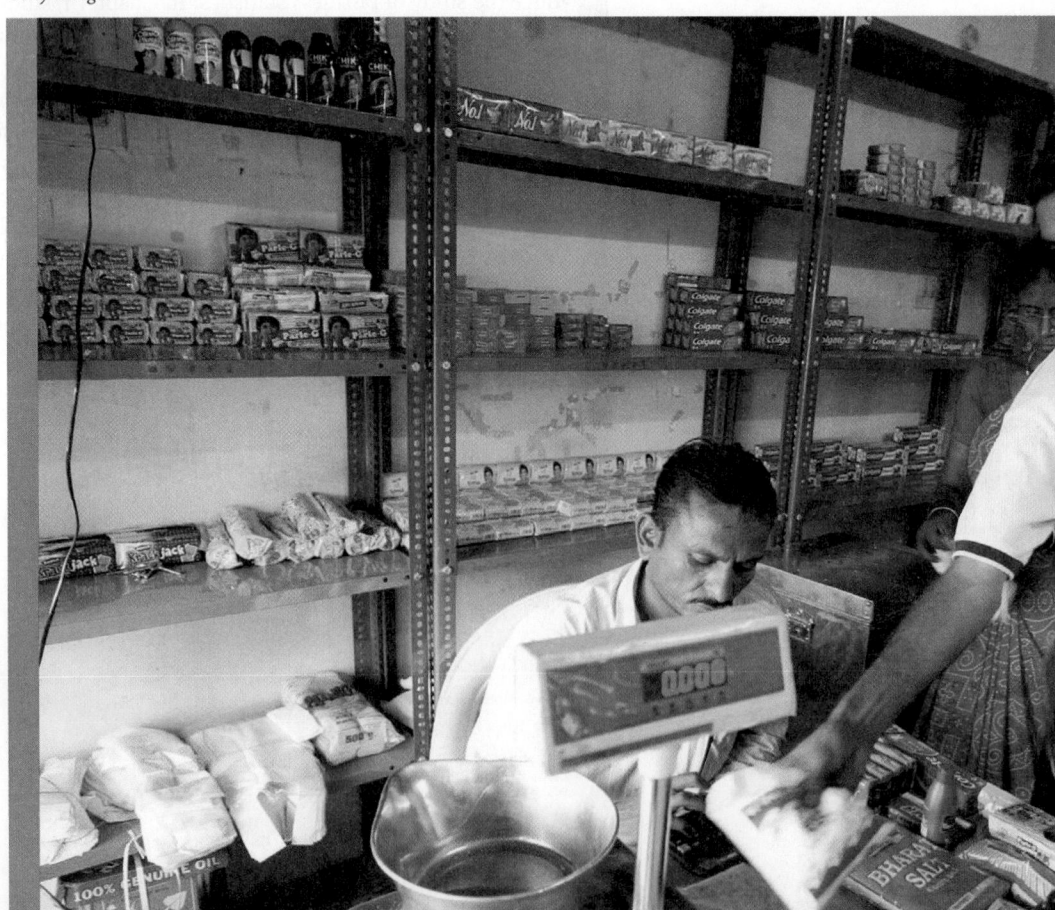

STATISTICS DESCRIBE THE STATE OF BUSINESS IN INDIA'S COUNTRYSIDE

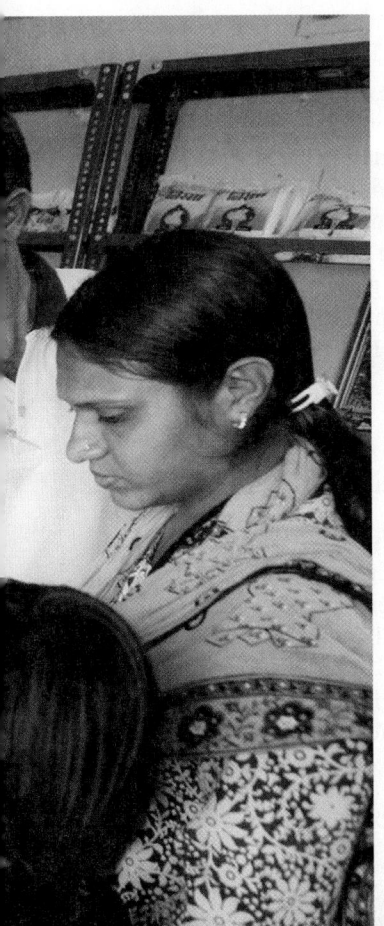

India is the second-largest country in the world, with more than a billion people. Nearly three quarters of the people live in rural areas scattered about the countryside in 600,000 villages. In fact, it may be said that more than one in every 10 people in the world live in rural India. The population in rural India can be described as poor and semiliterate. With an annual per capita income of less than $1 (U.S.) per day, rural India accounts for only about one third of total national product sales. Less than 50% of households in rural India have electricity, and many of the roads are not paved. The annual per capita consumption for toothpaste is only 30 g per person in rural India, compared to 160 g in urban India, 400 g in the United States, and 320 g as the world average.

However, in addition to the impressive size of the population, companies have other compelling reasons to market their goods and services to rural India. The market of rural India has been growing at five times the rate of the urban India market. Increasing agricultural productivity is leading to growth in disposable income, and the gap between the tastes of urban and rural customers is decreasing. The literacy level is increasing, and people are becoming more conscious of their lifestyles and of opportunities for a better life. Nearly two thirds of all middle-income households in India are in rural areas, with the number of middle- and high-income households in rural India expected to grow from 80 million to 111 million over the next three years. More than one third of all rural households now have a main source of income other than farming. Virtually every home has a radio, almost 20% have a television, and more than 30% have at least one bank account.

In the early 1990s, toothpaste consumption in rural India doubled, and the consumption of shampoo increased fourfold. Recently, other products have done well in rural India, accounting for nearly one half of all of the country's sales of televisions, fans, bicycles, bath soap, and other products. According to MART, a New Delhi-based research organization, rural India currently buys 46% of all soft drinks and 49% of motorcycles sold in India. In one year alone, the market for Coca-Cola in rural India grew by 37%, accounting for 80% of new Coke drinkers in India. Because of such factors, many global and Indian firms, such as Microsoft, General Electric, Kellogg's, Colgate-Palmolive, Hindustan-Unilever, Godrej, Nirma, and others, have entered the rural Indian market with enthusiasm. Marketing to rural customers often involves building categories by persuading them to try products that they may not have used before. Rural India is a huge, relatively untapped market for businesses. However, entering such a market is not without risks and obstacles. The dilemma facing companies is whether to enter this marketplace and, if so, to what extent and how.

Managerial and Statistical Questions

1. Are the statistics presented in this report exact figures or estimates?
2. How and where could the researchers have gathered such data?
3. In measuring the potential of the rural India marketplace, what other statistics could have been gathered?
4. What levels of data measurement are represented by data on rural India?
5. How can managers use these and other statistics to make better decisions about entering this marketplace?

Source: Adapted from Raja Ramachandran, "Understanding the Market Environment of India," *Business Horizons*, January 2000; P. Balakrishna and B. Sidharth, "Selling in Rural India," *The Hindu Business Line*—Internet Edition, February 16, 2004 <http://www.thehindubusinessline.com/bline/2004/02/16/stories/2004021600160900.htm>; Rohit Bansal and Srividya Easwaran, "Creative Marketing for Rural India," research paper <http://www.indiainfoline.com/>; Alex Steffen, "Rural India Ain't What It Used to Be," *WorldChanging* <http://www.worldchanging.com/archives/001235.html>; "Corporates Turn to Rural India for Growth," BS Corporate Bureau in New Delhi, August 21, 2003 <http://www.rediff.com/money/2003/aug/21rural.htm>; Rajesh Jain, "Tech Talk: The Discovery of India: Rural India," June 20, 2003 <http://www.emergic.org/archives/indi/005721.php>; "Marketing to Rural India: Making the Ends Meet," Knowledge@Wharton, March 8, 2007 <http://knowledge.wharton.upenn.edu/india/article.cfm?articleid=4172>.

Every minute of the working day, decisions are made by businesses around the world that determine whether companies will be profitable and grow or whether they will stagnate and die. Most of these decisions are made with the assistance of information gathered about the marketplace, the economic and financial environment, the workforce, the competition, and other factors. Such information usually comes in the form of data or is accompanied by data. Business statistics provides the tools by which such data are collected, analyzed, summarized, and presented to facilitate the decision-making process, and business statistics plays an important role in the ongoing saga of decision making within the dynamic world of business.

1.1 STATISTICS IN BUSINESS

Virtually every area of business uses statistics in decision making. Several examples follow.

MARKETING

Business statistics can be used effectively to assist companies in targeting their marketing efforts. Consider some statistics from the photographic industry that underscore gender differences in photo usage. A study conducted by the Photo Marketing Association showed that women print out 35% of digital photos compared to only 25% for men, and 19% of women use an on-line service to print their digital pictures compared to 15% for men. Kodak researchers found that 35% of all prints are given to others, and nearly 80% of the givers are women.

MANAGEMENT

A survey conducted by Open Small Business Network, American Express Company's small-business unit, asked owners of small companies how they would characterize themselves when given several options. A little more than one third described themselves as "big-picture people," who concentrate on making things run smoothly. Twenty-seven percent labelled themselves as "problem solvers," who concentrate on solving difficult company problems. Another 16% were "rainmakers," concentrating mainly on finding new business, and 11% were "artists," who were more involved in creating new products than in running the business. When the owners were asked to name their number one pet peeve about their employees, 16% replied "showing up late for work" and 15% replied "lack of initiative."

FINANCE

Which major city has the best climate as a financial centre? A study undertaken by the Association of Foreign Banks in Germany, the International Financial Services London, and the Center for the Study of Financial Innovation asked financiers in London's financial community to rate Frankfurt, London, and New York, using several criteria, as a place to do business. A 1-to-5 scale was used, with 5 denoting very good and 1 denoting very bad. For the personal and corporate taxes criterion, Frankfurt received the lowest score of the three cities, with an average rating of 2.44; both London and New York received 3.61. For the living and working environment criterion, Frankfurt received 2.62, London 3.58, and

New York 3.62. However, on housing, Frankfurt was rated 3.66, whereas London received 3.15, and New York 3.27.

OPERATIONS AND SUPPLY CHAIN MANAGEMENT

Six Sigma is a business management strategy that uses a set of quality management methods, including statistical methods built upon those discussed in this text. One of the goals of a Six Sigma program is to reduce process variation to the point where there are only 3.4 defects per million opportunities. High-profile companies that employ Six Sigma include Honeywell International, General Electric, and Motorola. Motorola has reported over $17 billion (U.S.) in savings from Six Sigma as of 2006. High-profile Canadian companies that have adopted Six Sigma include Bombardier, Noranda, Maple Leaf Foods, Air Canada, Imperial Oil, Celestica, and Ford Canada. Bombardier has realized over $83 million in savings from its Six Sigma programs, which included over 12,000 Canadian employees trained at different levels.

ECONOMICS

Statistics Canada regularly releases publications that include such business statistics as the number of housing starts, the percentage increase in the gross domestic product, the unemployment rate, and the Consumer Price Index to help investors and other decision makers track the state of the economy. These statistics and others can serve as indicators of economic and financial states to come and can be used by forecasters as they attempt to predict future business climates. Figure 1.1 is a graph of the Consumer Price Index for Canada (all items, not seasonally adjusted) for the period 1989–2007.

ACCOUNTING

The U.S. General Accounting Office conducted a study of 97 public accounting firms that reported having 10 or more Securities and Exchange Commission clients and 330 randomly selected Fortune 1000 public companies' chief financial officers and their audit committee chairpersons regarding auditor independence and audit quality issues. One of the findings was that the average length of tenure for an auditor was about 22 years for Fortune 1000 companies. The survey had many questions regarding the impact of required audit firm rotation on both the quality of the audit and the cost to audit companies. Ninety-six percent of those surveyed agreed that a public accounting firm's initial-year audit costs are likely to exceed the firm's subsequent annual audit costs, indicating that there are start-up costs to audit companies in required rotation. Seventy-nine percent generally or strongly agreed that the risk of audit failure is higher in the early years of an audit tenure period because the new firm is less likely to have a fully developed, in-depth understanding of the new client's operations and financial reporting practices. Eighty-six percent of the respondents agreed that under mandatory audit firm rotation, if public accounting firms move their most knowledgeable and experienced audit personnel from the current audit engagement to other efforts to enhance the firm's ability to attract and/ or retain clients in the future, the risk of audit failure with the current client increases to some extent.

Figure 1.1

Consumer Price Index for Canada, All Items, Not Seasonally Adjusted (1989–2007)

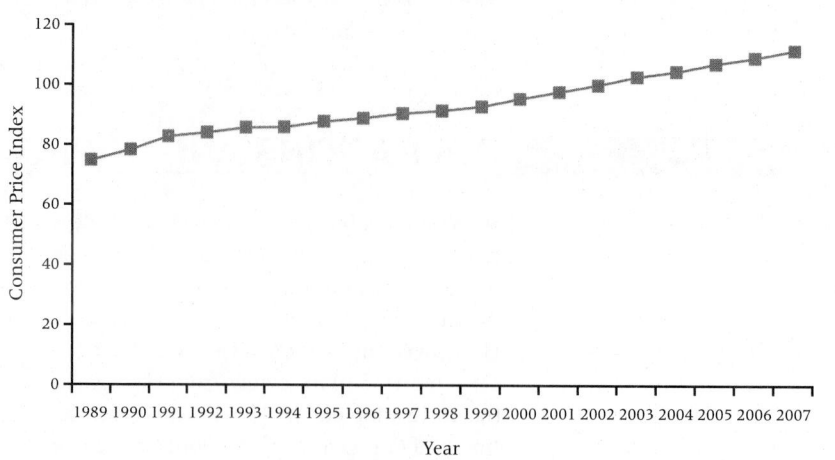

MANAGEMENT INFORMATION SYSTEMS

Management information specialists realize that on-line customer support has been a problem area for several years. Jupiter Research, a unit of Jupitermedia Corporation, conducted an on-line study of how long companies take to respond to customer questions by sending out test e-mails. They discovered that 36% of the companies took longer than three days to send a reply, if a response was received at all. Results varied by industry. For example, 56% of consumer packaged goods companies took three days or longer to respond compared to only 29% of the firms in the auto industry. On the other hand, 41% of firms in the travel industry responded within 6 hours. A study of 100 websites by E-tailing Group, a Chicago-based consulting firm, determined that the average wait time to talk on-line with a customer service representative is 12.2 minutes.

In this text, we will examine several types of graphs for depicting data as we study ways to arrange or structure data into forms that are both meaningful and useful to decision makers. We will learn about techniques for sampling from a population that allow studies of the business world to be conducted in a less expensive and more timely manner. We will explore various ways to forecast future values and we will examine techniques for predicting trends. This text also includes many statistical tools for testing hypotheses and for estimating population values. These and many other exciting statistics and statistical techniques await us on this journey through business statistics. Let us begin.

1.2 BASIC STATISTICAL CONCEPTS

Business statistics, like many areas of study, has its own language. It is important to begin our study with an introduction of some basic concepts in order to understand and communicate about the subject. We begin with a discussion of the word *statistics*. This word has many different meanings in our culture. *Webster's Third New International Dictionary* gives a comprehensive definition of **statistics** as *a science dealing with the collection, analysis, interpretation, and presentation of numerical data*. Viewed from this perspective, statistics includes all the topics presented in this text.

The study of statistics can be organized in a variety of ways. One of the main ways is to subdivide statistics into two branches: descriptive statistics and inferential statistics.

To understand the difference between descriptive and inferential statistics, definitions of *population* and *sample* are helpful. *Webster's Third New International Dictionary* defines **population** as *a collection of persons, objects, or items of interest.* The population can be a widely defined category, such as "all automobiles," or it can be narrowly defined, such as "all Ford Mustang cars produced from 2002 to 2005." A population can be a group of people, such as "all workers employed by Microsoft," or it can be a set of objects, such as "all Toyota RAV4s produced in February 2009 by Toyota Canada at the Woodstock, Ontario, plant." The researcher defines the population to be whatever he or she is studying. When researchers *gather data from the whole population for a given measurement of interest,* they call it a **census.** Most people are familiar with the Canadian Census. Every five years, the government attempts to measure all persons living in this country. If a researcher is interested in ascertaining the grade point average for all students at the University of Toronto, one way to do so is to conduct a census of all students currently enrolled at that university.

A **sample** is *a portion of the whole* and, if properly taken, is representative of the whole. For various reasons (explained in Chapter 7), researchers often prefer to work with a sample of the population instead of the entire population. For example, in conducting quality control experiments to determine the average life of light bulbs, a light bulb manufacturer might randomly sample only 75 light bulbs during a production run. Because of time and money limitations, a human resources manager might take a random sample of 40 employees instead of using a census to measure company morale.

If a business analyst is *using data gathered on a group to describe or reach conclusions about that same group,* the statistics are called **descriptive statistics.** For example, if an instructor produces statistics to summarize a class's examination results and uses those statistics to reach conclusions about that class only, the statistics are descriptive. The instructor can use these statistics to discuss class average, talk about the range of class scores, or present any other data measurements for the class based on the test.

Most athletic statistics, such as batting average, save percentages, and first downs, are descriptive statistics because they are used to describe an individual or team effort. Many of the statistical data generated by businesses are descriptive. They might include number of employees on vacation during June, average salary at the Edmonton office, corporate sales for 2009, average managerial satisfaction score on a company-wide census of employee attitudes, and average return on investment for the Lofton Company for the years 1995 through 2010.

Another type of statistics is called **inferential statistics.** If a researcher *gathers data from a sample and uses the statistics generated to reach conclusions about the population from which the sample was taken,* the statistics are inferential statistics. The data gathered from the sample are used to infer something about a larger group. Inferential statistics are sometimes referred to as *inductive statistics.* The use and importance of inferential statistics continue to grow.

One application of inferential statistics is in pharmaceutical research. Some new drugs are expensive to produce, and therefore tests must be limited to small samples of patients. Utilizing inferential statistics, researchers can design experiments with small randomly selected samples of patients and attempt to reach conclusions and make inferences about the population.

Market researchers use inferential statistics to study the impact of advertising on various market segments. Suppose a soft drink company creates an advertisement depicting a dispensing machine that talks to the buyer, and market researchers want to measure the impact of the new advertisement on various age groups. The researcher could stratify the population into age categories ranging from young to old, randomly sample each stratum, and use inferential statistics to determine the effectiveness of the advertisement for the various age groups in the population. The advantage of using inferential statistics is that they enable the researcher to effectively study a wide range of phenomena without having to conduct a census. Most of the topics discussed in this text pertain to inferential statistics.

Figure 1.2

Process of Inferential Statistics to Estimate a Population Mean (μ)

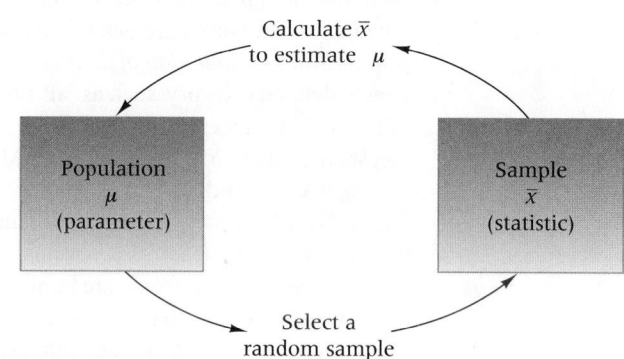

A *descriptive measure of the population* is called a **parameter.** Parameters are usually denoted by Greek letters. Examples of parameters are population mean (μ), population variance (σ^2), and population standard deviation (σ; this is the "sigma" we referred to when we briefly discussed Six Sigma earlier in this chapter). A *descriptive measure of a sample* is called a **statistic.** Statistics are usually denoted by Roman letters. Examples of statistics are sample mean ($\bar{x}$), sample variance (s^2), and sample standard deviation (s).

Differentiation between the terms *parameter* and *statistic* is important only in the use of inferential statistics. A business researcher often wants to estimate the value of a parameter or conduct tests about the parameter. However, the calculation of parameters is usually either impossible or infeasible because of the amount of time and money required to take a census. In such cases, the business researcher can take a random sample of the population, calculate a statistic on the sample, and infer by estimation the value of the parameter. The basis for inferential statistics, then, is the ability to make decisions about parameters without having to complete a census of the population.

For example, a manufacturer of washing machines would probably want to determine the average number of loads that a new machine can wash before it needs repairs. The parameter is the population mean or average number of washes per machine before repair. A company analyst takes a sample of machines, computes the number of washes before repair for each machine, averages the numbers, and estimates the population value or parameter by using the statistic, which in this case is the sample average. Figure 1.2 demonstrates the inferential process.

Inferences about parameters are made under uncertainty. Unless parameters are computed directly from the population, the statistician never knows with certainty whether the estimates or inferences made from samples are true. In an effort to estimate the level of confidence in the result of the process, statisticians use probability statements. For this and other reasons, part of this text is devoted to probability (Chapter 4).

Concept Check

Fill in the blanks.

1. The basic idea of statistics is to extrapolate from a random data _____ you have collected to make general conclusions about the larger _____ from which the random data _____ were derived.
2. Descriptive statistics can be used to _____ the data to describe a data sample either numerically or graphically.
3. Statistical inference is inference about a _____ from a random data _____ drawn from it.

1.3 DATA MEASUREMENT

Millions of numerical data are gathered in businesses every day, representing myriad items. For example, numbers represent dollar costs of items produced, geographical locations of retail outlets, masses of shipments, and rankings of employees at yearly reviews. Not all such data should be analyzed in the same way statistically because the entities represented by the numbers are different. For this reason, the business researcher needs to know the *level of data measurement* represented by the numbers being analyzed.

The disparate use of numbers can be illustrated by the numbers 40 and 80, which could represent the masses of two objects being shipped, the ratings received on a consumer test by two different products, or the hockey jersey numbers of a centre and a winger. Although 80 kg is twice as much as 40 kg, the winger is probably not twice as big as the centre! Averaging the two masses seems reasonable but averaging the hockey jersey numbers makes no sense. The appropriateness of the data analysis depends on the level of measurement of the data gathered. The phenomenon represented by the numbers determines the level of data measurement. Four common levels of data measurement are:

1. Nominal
2. Ordinal
3. Interval
4. Ratio

NOMINAL LEVEL

The *lowest level of data measurement* is the **nominal level.** Numbers representing nominal-level data (the word *level* is often omitted) can be *used only to classify or categorize.* Employee identification numbers are an example of nominal data. The numbers are used only to differentiate employees and not to make a value statement about them. Many demographic questions in surveys result in data that are nominal because the questions are used for classification only. The following is an example of a question that would result in nominal data:

Which of the following employment classifications best describes your area of work?

a. Educator
b. Construction worker
c. Manufacturing worker
d. Lawyer
e. Doctor
f. Other

Suppose that, for computing purposes, an educator is assigned a 1, a construction worker is assigned a 2, a manufacturing worker is assigned a 3, and so on. These numbers should be used only to classify respondents. The number 1 does not denote the top classification. It is used only to differentiate an educator (1) from a lawyer (4) or any other occupation.

Other types of variables that often produce nominal-level data are sex, religion, ethnicity, geographic location, and place of birth. Social insurance numbers, telephone numbers, and employee ID numbers are further examples of nominal data. Statistical techniques that are appropriate for analyzing nominal data are limited. However, some of the more widely used statistics, such as the chi-square statistic, can be applied to nominal data, often producing useful information.

ORDINAL LEVEL

Ordinal-level data measurement is higher than nominal level. In addition to having the nominal-level capabilities, ordinal-level measurement can be used to rank or order objects. For example, using ordinal data, a supervisor can evaluate three employees by ranking their productivity with the numbers 1 through 3. The supervisor could identify one employee as the most productive, one as the least productive, and one as somewhere in between by using ordinal data. However, the supervisor could not use ordinal data to establish that the intervals between the employees ranked 1 and 2 and between the employees ranked 2 and 3 are equal; that is, the supervisor could not say that the differences in the amount of productivity between the workers ranked 1, 2, and 3 are necessarily the same. With ordinal data, the distances between consecutive numbers are not always equal.

Some Likert-type scales on questionnaires are considered by many researchers to be ordinal in level. The following is an example of such a scale:

This computer tutorial is

not helpful	somewhat helpful	moderately helpful	very helpful	extremely helpful
1	2	3	4	5

When this survey question is coded for the computer, only the numbers 1 through 5 will remain, not the descriptions. Virtually everyone would agree that a 5 is higher than a 4 on this scale and that it is possible to rank responses. However, most respondents would not consider the differences between not helpful, somewhat helpful, moderately helpful, very helpful, and extremely helpful to be equal.

Mutual funds are sometimes rated in terms of investment risk by using measures of default risk, currency risk, and interest rate risk. These three measures are applied to investments by rating them as high, medium, or low risk. Suppose high risk is assigned a 3, medium risk a 2, and low risk a 1. If a fund is awarded a 3 rather than a 2, it carries more risk, and so on. However, the differences in risk between categories 1, 2, and 3 are not necessarily equal. Thus, these measurements of risk are only ordinal-level measurements. Another example of the use of ordinal numbers in business is the ranking of the 50 best employers in Canada in *Report on Business* magazine. The numbers ranking the companies are only ordinal in measurement. Certain statistical techniques are specifically suited to ordinal data, but many other techniques are not appropriate for use on ordinal data.

Because nominal and ordinal data are often derived from imprecise measurements such as demographic questions, the categorization of people or objects, or the ranking of items, *nominal and ordinal data* are **nonmetric data** and are sometimes referred to as *qualitative data*.

INTERVAL LEVEL

Interval-level data measurement is the *next to the highest level of data, in which the distances between consecutive numbers have meaning and the data are always numerical.* The distances represented by the differences between consecutive numbers are equal; that is, interval data have equal intervals. An example of interval measurement is Celsius temperature. With Celsius temperature numbers, the temperatures can be ranked, and the amounts of heat between consecutive readings, such as 20°, 21°, and 22°, are the same.

In addition, with interval-level data, the zero point is a matter of convention or convenience and not a natural or fixed zero point. Zero is just another point on the scale and does not mean the absence of the phenomenon. For example, zero degrees Celsius is not the lowest possible temperature. Some other examples of interval-level data are the percentage change in employment, the percentage return on a stock, and the dollar change in share price.

RATIO LEVEL

Ratio-level data measurement is *the highest level of data measurement*. Ratio data *have the same properties as interval data,* but ratio data have an *absolute zero* and *the ratio of two numbers is meaningful.* The notion of absolute zero means that zero is fixed, and *the zero value in the data represents the absence of the characteristic being studied.* The value of zero cannot be arbitrarily assigned because it represents a fixed point. This definition enables the statistician to create *ratios* with the data.

Examples of ratio data are height, mass, time, volume, and Kelvin temperature. With ratio data, a researcher can state that 180 kg of mass is twice as much as 90 kg or, in other words, make a ratio of 180:90. Many of the data gathered by machines in industry are ratio data.

Other examples in the business world that are ratio level in measurement are production cycle time, work measurement time, passenger distance, number of trucks sold, complaints per 10,000 fliers, and number of employees. With ratio-level data, no *b* factor is required in converting units from one measurement to another, that is, $y = ax$. As an example, in converting height from metres to feet, 1 m = 3.28 ft.

Because interval- and ratio-level data are usually gathered by precise instruments often used in production and engineering processes, in national standardized testing, or in standardized accounting procedures, they are called **metric data** and are sometimes referred to as *quantitative* data.

COMPARISON OF THE FOUR LEVELS OF DATA

Figure 1.3 shows the relationships of the usage potential among the four levels of data measurement. The concentric squares denote that each higher level of data can be analyzed by any of the techniques used on lower levels of data but, in addition, can be used in other statistical techniques. Therefore, ratio data can be analyzed by any statistical technique applicable to the other three levels of data plus some others.

Nominal data are the most limited data in terms of the types of statistical analysis that can be used with them. Ordinal data allow the researcher to perform any analysis that can be done with nominal data and some additional analyses. With ratio data, a statistician can make ratio comparisons and appropriately do any analysis that can be performed on nominal, ordinal, or interval data. Some statistical techniques require ratio data and cannot be used to analyze other levels of data.

Statistical techniques can be separated into two categories: parametric statistics and nonparametric statistics. **Parametric statistics** require that data be interval or ratio. If the data are nominal or ordinal, **nonparametric statistics** must be used. Nonparametric statistics can also be used to analyze interval or ratio data. This text focuses largely on parametric statistics, with the exception of Chapter 16 and Chapter 17, which contain nonparametric techniques. Thus, much of the material in this text requires interval or ratio data.

Figure 1.3

Usage Potential of Various Levels of Data

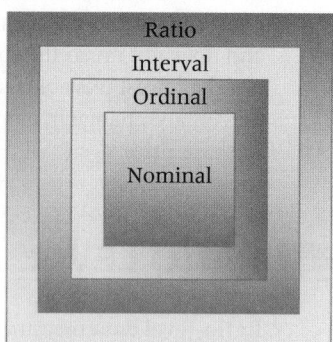

Concept Check

Match the level with the correct measurement.

1. Nominal   a. Measures with a fixed zero that means "no quantity"; a constant interval (distance on the scale)

2. Ordinal   b. Measures require a fixed distance, but the zero point is arbitrary

3. Interval   c. Measures classified by shared attributes (characteristics)

4. Ratio   d. Measures by orderings (ranks)

Demonstration Problem 1.1

Many changes continue to occur in the health-care system. Because of the increasing pressure to deliver a high level of service at increasingly lower costs and the need to determine how providers can better serve their patients, hospital administrators sometimes administer a quality satisfaction survey to their patients after release from hospital. The following types of questions are sometimes asked on such a survey. These questions will result in what level of data measurement?

1. How long ago were you released from the hospital?
2. Which type of unit were you in for most of your stay?
    ___Coronary care unit
    ___Intensive care unit
    ___Maternity care unit
    ___Medical unit
    ___Pediatric/children's unit
    ___Surgical unit
3. How serious was your condition when you were first admitted to the hospital?
    __Critical   __Serious   __Moderate   __Minor
4. Rate the skill of your doctor:
    __Excellent   __Very Good   __Good   __Fair   __Poor
5. On the following scale from one to seven, rate the nursing care:
    Poor   1   2   3   4   5   6   7   Excellent

Solution

Question 1 is a time measurement with an absolute zero and is therefore a ratio-level measurement. A person who has been out of the hospital for two weeks has been out twice as long as someone who has been out of the hospital for one week.

Question 2 yields nominal data because the patient is asked only to categorize the type of unit he or she was in. This question does not require a hierarchy or ranking of the type of unit. Questions 3 and 4 are likely to result in ordinal-level data. Suppose a number is assigned to each descriptor in each of these two questions. For question 3, "critical" might be assigned a 4, "serious" a 3, "moderate" a 2, and "minor" a 1. Certainly, the higher the number, the more serious is the patient's condition. Thus, these responses can be ranked by selection. However, the increases in importance from 1 to 2 to 3 to 4 are not necessarily equal. This same logic applies to the numeric values assigned in question 4.

Question 5 displays seven numeric choices with equal distances between the numbers shown on the scale and no adjective descriptors assigned to the numbers. Many researchers would declare this to be interval-level measurement because of the equal distance between numbers and the absence of a true zero on this scale. Some researchers might argue that because of the imprecision of the scale and the vagueness of selecting values between "poor" and "excellent," the measurement is only ordinal in level.

1.4 STATISTICAL ANALYSIS USING EXCEL

The advent of the modern computer opened many new opportunities for statistical analysis. The computer allows for storage, retrieval, and transfer of large data sets. Furthermore, computer software has been developed to analyze data by means of sophisticated statistical techniques. Some widely used statistical techniques, such as multiple regression, are so tedious and cumbersome to compute manually that they were of little practical use to researchers before computers were developed.

Business statisticians use many popular statistical software packages, including MINITAB, SAS, and SPSS. Many computer spreadsheet software packages can also analyze data statistically. In this text, when it is appropriate to use a computer, we will use Microsoft Excel for data analysis.

Excel is by far the most commonly used spreadsheet for PCs, making it the obvious choice for basic statistical analysis. Excel can perform a variety of calculations and includes a large collection of statistical functions. The Data Analysis ToolPak further provides a suite of statistical macro-functions.

We note, however, that although Excel is a fine spreadsheet, it is not a professional statistical data analysis package: there are some important limitations. Key limitations to keep in mind include the following: missing values in Excel are difficult to handle when performing data analysis; data organization differs according to analysis, sometimes forcing you to reorganize your data; some output and charts produced by Excel are of poor quality from a statistical point of view and are sometimes inadequately labelled; and there is no record of how an analysis was accomplished if the Data Analysis ToolPak is used.

Despite these limitations, Excel is the most commonly used package in the business environment and is the package you are most likely to use in your professional life.

It is important to remember that a statistical software package is not a replacement for a thorough understanding of correct statistical methods. The business analyst is responsible for determining the most appropriate statistical methods for a given business problem. Simply relying on convenient software tools that may be at hand without thinking through the most appropriate approach can lead to errors, oversights, and poor decisions. One of the goals of this text is to show you when and how to use statistical methods to provide information that can be used in business decisions.

STATISTICS IN BUSINESS TODAY

Wireless Usage

A survey conducted by Sprint of U.S. adult wireless phone subscribers produced several interesting statistics. For example, 56% of mobile phone subscribers use their phones for nonvoice functions, including 55% who use it as a camera, 48% who use it as a walkie-talkie, 43% who use it for Internet access, 38% who use it for music, and 34% who use it for games. When asked what they do with pictures taken by their phones, 67% said they personalize them and use them as their phones' background, 49% use them for Caller ID, and 42% share them with others over the Web or mobile-to-mobile. Mobile phone users sometimes turn on their phones just to use the backlight: 60% use the backlight to look for something in the dark, 43% to locate a keyhole, and 34% to guide their way in the dark. Seventy percent of mobile phone users prefer flip phones. When asked what product they most want incorporated into their phones, 27% wanted a printer/scanner/fax, 17% selected a thermometer, and 15% selected a credit card. Sixty-three percent of wireless phone users would use their phones to get maps and directions if the service was available.

Source: Adapted from The 2005 Sprint U.S. Consumer Wireless Usage Study <http://www2.sprint.com/mr/cmastaticfiles/non-landing/documents/PressKit/wirelesssurvey05.pdf>.

STATISTICS DESCRIBE THE STATE OF BUSINESS IN INDIA'S COUNTRYSIDE

Several statistics were reported in the Decision Dilemma about rural India, including the average annual consumption of toothpaste per person, the percentage of households with electricity, and the percentage of households with at least one bank account. The authors of the sources from which the Decision Dilemma was drawn never stated whether the reported statistics were based on actual data drawn from a census of rural India households or were based on estimates taken from a sample of rural households. If the data came from a census, then the totals, averages, and percentages presented in the Decision Dilemma are parameters. If, on the other hand, the data were gathered from samples, then they are statistics. Although governments do conduct censuses and at least some of the reported numbers could be parameters, more often than not, such data are gathered from samples of people or items. For example, in rural India, the government, academicians, or business researchers could have taken random samples of households, gathering consumer statistics that are then used to estimate population parameters, such as percentage of households with televisions, and so forth.

In conducting research on a topic like consumer consumption in rural India, a wide variety of statistics can be gathered that represent several levels of data. For example, ratio-level measurements on items such as income, number of children, age of household heads, number of livestock, and grams of toothpaste consumed per year might be obtained. On the other hand, if researchers use a Likert-type scale (1-to-5 measurements) to gather responses about the interests, likes, and preferences of rural India consumers, an ordinal-level measurement would be obtained, as with the ranking of products or brands in market research studies. Other variables, such as geographic location, sex, occupation, or religion, are usually measured with nominal data.

The decision to enter the rural India market is not just a marketing decision. It involves production and operations capacity, scheduling issues, transportation challenges, financial commitments, managerial growth or reassignment issues, accounting issues (accounting for rural India may differ from techniques used in urban markets), information systems, and other related areas. With so much on the line, company decision makers need as much relevant information available as possible. In this Decision Dilemma, it is obvious to the decision maker that rural India is still quite poor and illiterate. Its capacity as a market is great. The statistics on the increasing sales of a few personal-care products look promising. What are the future forecasts for the earning power of people in rural India? Will major cultural issues block the adoption of the types of products that companies want to sell there? The answers to these and many other interesting and useful questions can be obtained by the appropriate use of statistics. The approximately 750 million people living in rural India certainly make it a market segment worth studying further.

KEY CONSIDERATIONS

With the abundance and proliferation of statistical data, potential misuse of statistics in business dealings is a concern. It is, in effect, unethical business behaviour to use statistics out of context. Unethical business people might use only selective data from studies to underscore their point, omitting statistics from the same studies that argue against their case. The results of statistical studies can be misstated or overstated to gain favour.

This chapter noted that if data are nominal or ordinal, then only nonparametric statistics are appropriate for analysis. The use of parametric statistics to analyze nominal and/or ordinal data is wrong and could be considered under some circumstances to be unethical.

In this text, each chapter contains a section on ethics that discusses how businesses can misuse the techniques presented in the chapter in an unethical manner. As both users and producers, business students need to be aware of the potential ethical pitfalls that can occur with statistics.

Why Statistics Is Relevant

In the contemporary business world, good decisions are driven by data. In all areas of business, amazing amounts of diverse data are available for interpretation and quantitative insight. Business managers and professionals are increasingly required to justify decisions on the basis of data analysis. Thus, the ability to extract useful information from data is one of the most important, and marketable, skills business managers and professionals can acquire. This text is an introduction to the theory and, more importantly, the methods used to intelligently collect, analyze, and interpret data relevant to business decision making.

SUMMARY

1. In this text, the word *statistics* is defined as the science of gathering, analyzing, interpreting, and presenting data.
2. We now know that statistics is an important decision-making tool in business and is used in virtually every area of business, including the disciplines of accounting, decision sciences, operations and supply chain management, economics, finance, management, management information systems, and marketing.
3. The study of statistics can be subdivided into two main areas: *descriptive statistics* and *inferential statistics.* Descriptive statistics result from gathering data from a body, group, or population and reaching conclusions only about that group. Inferential statistics are generated from the process of gathering sample data from a group, body, or population and reaching conclusions about the larger group from which the sample was drawn.
4. The appropriate type of statistical analysis depends on the level of data measurement, which can be (1) *nominal,* (2) *ordinal,* (3) *interval,* or (4) *ratio.* Nominal is the lowest level, representing classification of only data such as geographic location, sex, or social insurance number. The next level is ordinal, which provides rank ordering measurements in which the intervals between consecutive numbers do not necessarily represent equal distances. Interval is the next to highest level of data measurement, in which the distances represented by consecutive numbers are equal. The highest level of data measurement is ratio, which has all the qualities of interval measurement, but ratio data contain an absolute zero and ratios between numbers are meaningful. Interval and ratio data are sometimes called *metric* or *quantitative* data. Nominal and ordinal data are sometimes called *nonmetric* or *qualitative* data.

Two major types of inferential statistics are (1) *parametric statistics* and (2) *nonparametric statistics.* Use of parametric statistics requires interval or ratio data and certain assumptions about the distribution of the data. The techniques presented in this text are largely parametric. If data are only nominal or ordinal in level, nonparametric statistics must be used.

KEY TERMS

census	metric data	ordinal-level data	ratio-level data
descriptive statistics	nominal-level data	parameter	sample
inferential statistics	nonmetric data	parametric statistics	statistic
interval-level data	nonparametric statistics	population	statistics

SUPPLEMENTARY PROBLEMS

1.1 Give a specific example of data that might be gathered from each of the following business disciplines: accounting, finance, human resources, marketing, operations and supply chain management, information systems, production, and management. An example in the marketing area might be "number of sales per month by each salesperson."

1.2 State examples of data that can be gathered for decision-making purposes from each of the following industries: manufacturing, insurance, travel, retailing, communications, computing, agriculture, banking, and health care. An example in the travel industry might be the cost of business travel per day in various European cities.

1.3 Give an example of *descriptive* statistics in the recorded music industry. Give an example of how *inferential* statistics could be used in the recorded music industry. Compare the two examples. What makes them different?

1.4 Suppose you are an operations manager for a plant that manufactures batteries. Give an example of how you could use *descriptive* statistics to make better managerial decisions. Give an example of how you could use *inferential* statistics to make better managerial decisions.

1.5 Classify each of the following as nominal, ordinal, interval, or ratio data.
   a. The time required to produce each tire on an assembly line
   b. The number of litres of milk a family drinks in a month
   c. The ranking of four machines in your plant after they have been designated as excellent, good, satisfactory, and poor
   d. The telephone area code of clients in Canada
   e. The age of each of your employees
   f. The dollar sales at the local pizza house each month
   g. An employee's identification number
   h. The response time of an emergency unit

1.6 Classify each of the following as nominal, ordinal, interval, or ratio data.

   a. The ranking of a company by *Report on Business* magazine's Top 1000
   b. The number of tickets sold at a movie theatre on any given night
   c. The identification number on a questionnaire
   d. Per capita income
   e. The trade balance in dollars
   f. Profit/loss in dollars
   g. A company's tax identification number
   h. The Standard & Poor's bond ratings of cities based on the following scales.

Rating	Grade
Highest quality	AAA
High quality	AA
Upper medium quality	A
Medium quality	BBB
Somewhat speculative	BB
Low quality, speculative	B
Low grade, default possible	CCC
Low grade, partial recovery possible	CC
Default, recovery unlikely	C

1.7 The Mapletech Manufacturing Company makes electric wiring, which it sells to contractors in the construction industry. Approximately 900 electrical contractors purchase wire from Mapletech annually. Mapletech's director of marketing wants to determine electrical contractors' satisfaction with Mapletech's wire. She develops a questionnaire that yields a satisfaction score of between 10 and 50 for participant responses. A random sample of 35 of the 900 contractors is asked to complete a satisfaction survey. The satisfaction scores for the 35 participants are averaged to produce a mean satisfaction score.
   a. What is the population for this study?
   b. What is the sample for this study?
   c. What is the statistic for this study?
   d. What would be a parameter for this study?

Seven major databases constructed for this text can be used to apply the techniques presented in this course. These databases are located in WileyPLUS, and each one is available in a few electronic formats for your convenience. These seven databases represent a wide variety of business areas: major league baseball, the stock market, manufacturing, international labour, finance, energy, health care, and agribusiness. Altogether, these databases contain 79 variables and 7,492 observations. The data are gathered from such reliable sources as Statistics Canada, the Toronto Stock Exchange, the Canadian Agribusiness Department, *Yahoo Finance,* the Fraser Institute, the Global Environment Outlook (GEO) Data Portal, and Major League Baseball. Four of the seven databases contain time-series data that can be especially useful in forecasting and regression analysis. Here is a description of each database, along with information that may help you to interpret outcomes.

Canadian Stock Market Database

The stock market database contains seven variables on the Toronto Stock Exchange. Weekly observations from April 2002 to September 2009 yield a total of 390 observations per variable. The variables are Composite Index, Energy Index, Financial Index, Health Index, Utility Index, I.T. Index, and Gold Index. This database was constructed from data displayed on the Internet by Yahoo Finance Canada. The original data can be accessed at the Data Library at TSX.com.

Major League Baseball Database

This database contains 19 variables taken from 30 major league baseball teams. The sources of this database are Forbes.com, MLB.com, and baseball-reference.com. The 19 variables are Division, League, Current Value, One-Year Value Change, Debt/Value, Revenues, Operating Income, Payroll, Average Attendance, Average Ticket, Percentage Change, Average Premium Ticket, Beer, Soft Drink, Hot Dog, Parking, Program, Cap, and FCI. The leagues have been condensed to a 1 to 2 scale, with 1 representing the American League and 2 representing the National League. The divisions have been condensed to the following 1 to 6 scale:

1 = American League East
2 = National League East
3 = American League Central
4 = National League Central
5 = American League West
6 = National League West

International Labour Database

This time-series database contains the civilian unemployment rates in percent from seven countries (G7) presented yearly over a 30-year period. The data are published by the Bureau of Labor Statistics of the U.S. Department of Labor. The countries are Canada, France, Germany, Italy, Japan, the United Kingdom, and the United States.

Financial Database

The financial database contains observations on 12 variables for 100 companies. The variables are Industry Group, Type of Industry, Total Revenues, Price, Average Yield, Dividend Growth, Average Price/Earnings (P/E) Ratio, Dividends per Share, Total Debt/Total Equity, Price/Cash Flow, Price/Book, and One-Year Total Return. The data were gathered from the Toronto Stock Exchange. The companies represent seven different types of industries. The variable "Type" displays a company's industry type as follows:

1 = Real Estate
2 = Financial Institutes
3 = Chemicals
4 = Mining, Electric, Oil & Gas, Pipelines
5 = Telecommunications, Retail, Commercial Services, Auto Parts & Equipment, Transportation
6 = Insurance
7 = Food, Pharmaceuticals, Electronics, Media, Aerospace/Defence, Hand/Machine Tools, Agriculture, Iron/Steel, Holding Companies, Engineering and Construction, Machinery— Diversified, Forest Products and Paper

Energy Resource Database

The energy resource database consists of data for North America and Europe on nine energy supply and emission of carbon dioxide variables over a period of 35 years. The database is adopted from the Global Environment Outlook (GEO) Data Portal. The nine variables are the seven total primary energy supplies of Solar, Wind, Tide, and Wave; Nuclear; Natural Gas; Coal and Coal Products; Crude Oil; Hydro; and Petroleum Products, plus the two sources of emissions of CO_2: Manufacturing Industries and Construction, and Transportation.

Canadian Hospitals Database

This database contains observations for nine variables on hospitals in municipalities in Alberta, British Columbia, and Ontario. These variables are Geographic Region; Acute Myocardial Infarction; Congestive Heart Failure; Acute Stroke Mortality; Hip Fracture Mortality; Failure to Rescue; Postoperative Respiratory Failure; Birth Trauma, Injury to Neonate; and Population, 2006 Census. Information for these databases is taken from the Fraser Institute's Hospital Report Cards on Alberta, British Columbia, and Ontario.

The region variable is coded from 1 to 3, representing the following regions:

1 = Alberta
2 = British Columbia
3 = Ontario

Agri-Business Canada Database

The agribusiness time-series database contains the monthly weight (in thousands of pounds) of seven different grains over an eight-year period. Each of the seven variables represents 94 months of data. The seven grains are Wheat; Wheat, Excluding Durum; Durum Wheat; Oats; Barley; Flaxseed; and Canola. The data are published by Statistics Canada under Agri-business.

Use the databases to answer the following questions.

1. In the Major League Baseball database, what is the level of data for each of the following variables?
   a. Average Attendance
   b. Parking
   c. Cap
2. In the Financial Database, what is the level of data for each of the following variables?
   a. Type of Industry
   b. Average Price
   c. Price/Cash Flow

CASE

Canadian Farmers Dealing with Stress

Over a one-year period (from 2003 to 2004), Canadian farm revenues increased from $34.2 billion to $36.8 billion. Farming is an extremely demanding job whose success depends largely on the dedication of the farmers. In order to tackle the rigorous tasks of the trade, farmers must be in good physical and mental condition. However, stress can negatively affect the productivity of any farmer, and over the last few years, the farm industry has had to face this increasingly common condition. The Canadian Agricultural Safety Association (CASA) recently sponsored research on the stress level of Canadian farmers.

Western Opinion Research Inc. conducted the research study, which was completed by 1,100 farmers across Canada. The survey asked farmers to rate their stress level ranging from "stressed" to "somewhat stressed" to "very stressed." The results varied and revealed the following: two thirds of farmers indicated feeling "stressed," 45% indicated feeling "somewhat stressed," and one in five indicated feeling "very stressed." The results of the survey also revealed that the major causes of stress among farmers were (a) financial concerns related to prices of commodities, (b) mad cow disease, and (c) finances regarding general farm expenses. The results also revealed that a large percentage of farmers (35%) were interested in having access to more stress-related resources in order to help alleviate their stress level.

This study allowed CASA to realize that stress within the farming industry is a major issue, therefore making it imperative to take action and offer stress counselling resources to farmers. These resources include (a) confidential meeting with a health care professional, (b) over-the-phone consulta-

tion with a health care professional, and (c) attending workshops such as retreats that focus on relaxation techniques and role playing with other farmers.

Over the last few years, great progress has been made by CASA in order to help reduce the stress level of Canadian farmers. For example, since 2000, successful counselling services that deal with farmers and their problems were established using phone-in lines. These include the Manitoba Farm & Rural Stress Line, the Saskatchewan Farm Line, and the Ontario Farm Line. According to CASA, more of these services will be established over the next few years. These establishments are well recognized and are having great success in helping farmers, mainly because they are staffed by paid professional counsellors who all have farming backgrounds, making the farmers feel more comfortable because they are speaking with someone who understands their work-related issues. As of 2009, an In-Person Peer Support Counselling Pilot Project has also been established that allows farmers to meet a counsellor in person and discuss their problems.

Discussion

Think of the market research that was conducted by CASA.

1. What are some of the populations that CASA might have been interested in measuring for these studies? Did CASA attempt to contact entire populations? What samples were taken? In light of these two questions, how was the inferential process used by CASA in their market research? Can you think of any descriptive statistics that might have been used by CASA in their decision-making process?

2. In the various market research efforts made by CASA for stress experienced by farmers, some of the possible measurements appear in the following list. Categorize these by level of data. Think of some other measurements that CASA researchers might have taken to help them in this research effort and categorize them by level of data.

a. Ranking of the level of stress on a stress test
b. Number of farmers who ask for professional help
c. Number of farmers that are aware of professional help resources
d. Number of farmers that try to manage stress on their own
e. Number of farmers that are interested in having access to more stress-related resources
f. Number of farmers that are close to being out of business
g. Number of farmers that would prefer dealing with stress on their own
h. Number of farmers that would prefer dealing with stress with a professional over the telephone
i. Number of farmers that would prefer dealing with stress with a professional in person
j. Age of survey respondent
k. Gender of survey respondent
l. Geographical region of survey respondent
m. Amount of time farmers spend dealing with their stress
n. Rating of the most stress-related factors on a scale from 1 to 10, where 1 is the least stress-related factor and 10 is the most stress-related factor
o. Rating of the reasons that farmers do not seek more help for stress on a scale from 1 to 10, where 1 is the least important reason and 10 is the most important reason

References

"Canadian Farm Revenue Rose on Higher Crop Output," February 26, 2005. Website for data source: <http://www.financialexpress.com/news/canadian-farm-revenue-rose-on-higher-crop-output/127159/>; "Manitoba Farm and Rural Stress Line," Annual Report, 2008, pp. 2–16. Website for data source: <http://www.ruralstress.ca/files/MFRSL_AnnualReport2008.pdf>; "National Stress and Mental Survey of Canadian Farmers," Canadian Agricultural Safety Association, February 11, 2005, pp. 2–26. Website for data source: <http://www.casa-acsa.ca/english/PDF/NationalStressSurveyResultsPublic2005.pdf>

CHARTS AND GRAPHS

Learning Objectives

The overall objective of Chapter 2 is for you to master several techniques for summarizing and depicting data. We would like to answer the following questions:

1. What is the difference between grouped and ungrouped data?

2. How can we construct a frequency distribution and what does the distribution represent?

3. How can we describe and construct a histogram, a frequency polygon, an ogive, a pie chart, a stem and leaf plot, a Pareto chart, and a scatter plot, and when should these graphs be used?

iStock

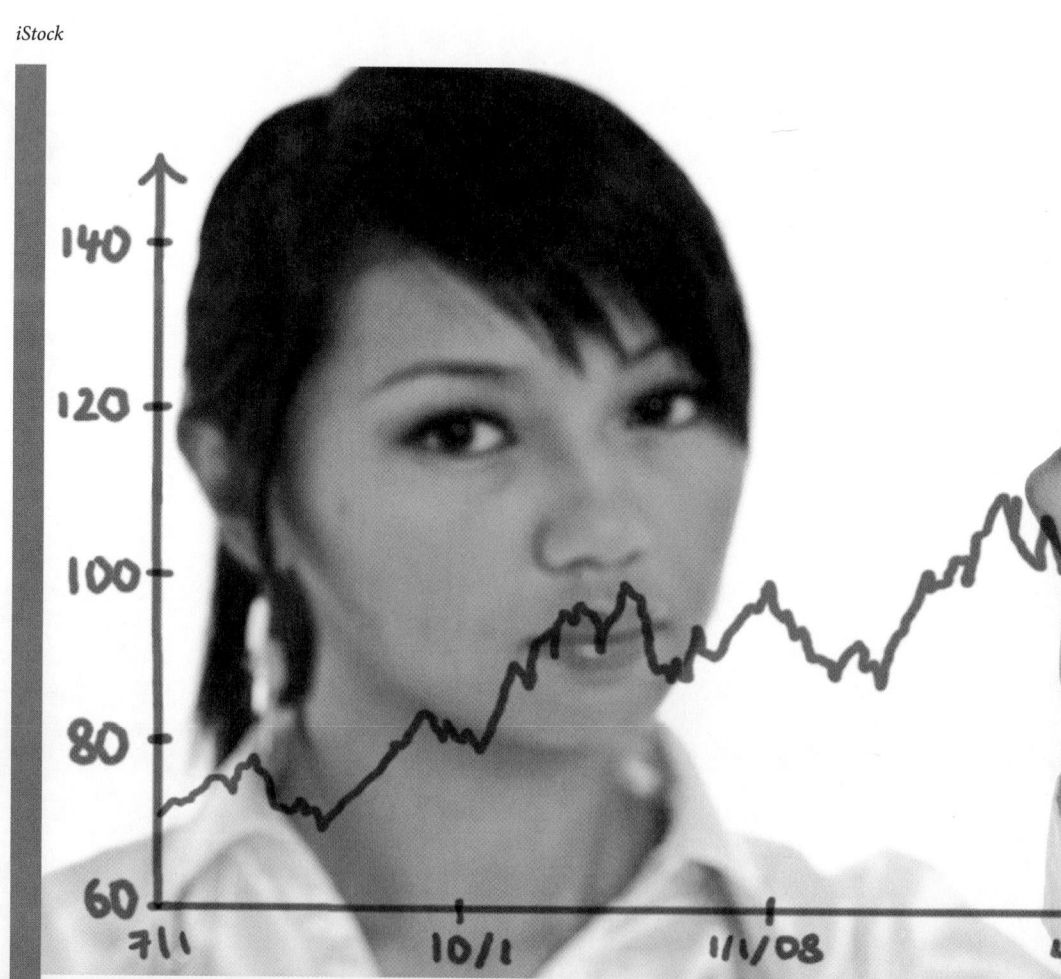

ENERGY CONSUMPTION AROUND THE WORLD

DECISION DILEMMA

As most people suspect, the United States is the number one consumer of oil in the world, followed by China, Japan, India, Russia, and Germany. (Canada ranks eighth with a consumption that is below that of South Korea and above that of Saudi Arabia.) China, however, is the world's largest consumer of coal, with the United States coming in at number two, followed by India, Japan, and South Africa. (Canada ranks 15th, below Turkey and above Kazakhstan.) The annual oil and coal consumption figures for the top six total energy-consuming nations in the world, according to figures released by the *BP Statistical Review of World Energy* for a recent year, are as follows.

Country	Oil Consumption (million tonnes)	Coal Consumption (million tonnes oil equivalent)
U.S.	943.1	573.7
China	368.0	1311.4
Japan	228.9	125.3
India	128.5	208.0
Russia	125.9	94.5
Germany	112.5	86.0

Managerial and Statistical Questions

Suppose you are an energy industry analyst and you are asked to prepare a brief report showing the leading energy-consumption countries in both oil and coal.

1. What is the best way to display the energy-consumption data in a report? Are the raw data enough? Can you effectively display the data graphically?

2. Is there a way to graphically display oil and coal figures together so that readers can visually compare countries on their consumptions of the two different energy sources?

Source: BP Statistical Review of World Energy, June 2008 <http://www.bp.com/liveassets/bp_internet/globalbp/ globalbp_uk_english/reports_and_publications/ statistical_energy_review_2008/STAGING/local_assets/ downloads/pdf/statistical_review_of_world_energy_full_ review_2008.pdf>.

In Chapters 2 and 3, many techniques are presented for reformatting or reducing data so that the data are more manageable and can be used to assist decision makers more effectively. Two techniques for grouping data are the frequency distribution and the stem and leaf plot, which are presented in this chapter. In addition, in Chapter 2 we discuss and display several graphical tools for summarizing and presenting data, including the histogram, frequency polygon, ogive, pie chart, and Pareto chart for one-variable data and the scatter plot for two-variable numerical data. By using these and other techniques, decision makers can begin to get a handle on information contained in the data and use the data to enhance the decision-making process.

Raw data, or data that have not been summarized in any way, are sometimes referred to as **ungrouped data.** Table 2.1 contains raw data of the unemployment rates for France over 40 years. *Data that have been organized into a frequency distribution* are called **grouped data.** Table 2.2 presents a frequency distribution for the data displayed in Table 2.1. The distinction between ungrouped and grouped data is important because the calculation of statistics differs between the two types of data. This chapter focuses on organizing ungrouped data into grouped data and displaying them graphically.

Table 2.1 **Unemployment Rates for France over 40 Years (Ungrouped Data)**				
1.6	2.1	4.2	6.9	9.6
1.5	2.7	4.6	10.0	10.4
1.2	2.3	5.2	10.5	11.8
1.4	2.5	5.4	10.6	12.3
1.6	2.8	6.1	10.8	11.8
1.2	2.9	6.5	10.3	12.5
1.6	2.8	7.6	9.6	12.4
1.6	2.9	8.3	9.1	11.8

Table 2.2 **Frequency Distribution of the Unemployment Rates of France (Grouped Data)**	
Class Interval	**Frequency**
1–under 3	16
3–under 5	2
5–under 7	5
7–under 9	2
9–under 11	9
11–under 13	6

2.1 FREQUENCY DISTRIBUTIONS

One particularly useful tool for grouping data is the **frequency distribution,** which is *a summary of data presented in the form of class intervals and frequencies.* How is a frequency distribution constructed from raw data? That is, how are frequency distributions like the one displayed in Table 2.2 constructed from raw data like those presented in Table 2.1? Frequency distributions are relatively easy to construct. Although some guidelines help in their construction, frequency distributions vary in final shape and design, even when the original raw data are identical. In a sense, frequency distributions are constructed according to individual business researchers' tastes.

POINTS OF INTEREST
In order to construct a frequency distribution, select between 5 and 15 classes with midpoints at convenient (ideally round) numbers.

When constructing a frequency distribution, the business researcher should first determine the range of the raw data. The **range** is often defined as *the difference between the largest and smallest numbers.* The range for the data in Table 2.1 is 11.3 (12.5 − 1.2).

The second step in constructing a frequency distribution is to determine how many classes it will contain. One guideline is to select between *5 and 15 classes.* If the frequency distribution contains too few classes, the data summary may be too general to be useful. Too many classes may result in a frequency distribution that does not aggregate the data enough to be helpful. The final number of classes is arbitrary. The business researcher arrives at a number by examining the range and determining a number of classes that will span the range adequately and be meaningful to the user. The data in Table 2.1 were grouped into six classes for Table 2.2.

After selecting the number of classes, the business researcher must determine the width of the class interval. An approximation of the class width can be calculated by dividing the range by the number of classes. For the data in Table 2.1, this approximation is 11.3/6, or 1.9. Normally, the number is rounded up to the next whole number, which in this case is 2. The frequency distribution must start at a value equal to or lower than the lowest number of the ungrouped data and end at a value equal to or higher than the highest number. The lowest unemployment rate is 1.2 and the highest is 12.5, so the business researcher starts the frequency distribution at 1 and ends it at 13. Table 2.2 contains the completed frequency distribution for the data in Table 2.1. Class endpoints are selected so that no value of the data can fit into more than one class. The class interval expression "under" in the distribution of Table 2.2 avoids this problem.

CLASS MIDPOINT

The *midpoint of each class interval* is called the **class midpoint** and is sometimes referred to as the **class mark.** It is *the value halfway across the class interval* and can be calculated as *the average of the two class endpoints.* For example, in the distribution of Table 2.2, the midpoint of the class interval 3–under 5 is 4, or $(3 + 5)/2$. A second way to obtain the class midpoint is to calculate one half the distance across the class interval (half the class width) and add it to the class beginning point, as for the unemployment rates distribution:

$$\text{Class Beginning Point} = 3$$

$$\text{Class Width} = 2$$

$$\text{Class Midpoint} = 3 + \frac{1}{2}(2) = 4$$

The class midpoint is important because it becomes the representative value for each class in most group statistics calculations. The third column in Table 2.3 contains the class midpoints for all classes of the data from Table 2.2.

Table 2.3

Class Midpoints, Relative Frequencies, and Cumulative Frequencies for Unemployment Data

Interval	Frequency	Class Midpoint	Relative Frequency	Cumulative Frequency
1–under 3	16	2	0.400	16
3–under 5	2	4	0.050	18
5–under 7	5	6	0.125	23
7–under 9	2	8	0.050	25
9–under 11	9	10	0.225	34
11–under 13	6	12	0.150	40
Totals	40		1.000	

RELATIVE FREQUENCY

Relative frequency is *the proportion of the total frequency that is in any given class interval in a frequency distribution.* Relative frequency is the individual class frequency divided by the total frequency. For example, from Table 2.3, the relative frequency for the class interval 5–under 7 is 5/40, or 0.125. We consider the relative frequency here to prepare for the study of probability in Chapter 4. Indeed, if values are selected randomly from the data in Table 2.1, the probability of drawing a number that is 5–under 7 is 0.125, the relative frequency for that class interval. The fourth column of Table 2.3 lists the relative frequencies for the frequency distribution of Table 2.2.

CUMULATIVE FREQUENCY

The **cumulative frequency** is *a running total of frequencies through the classes of a frequency distribution.* The cumulative frequency for each class interval is the frequency for that class interval added to the preceding cumulative total. In Table 2.3, the cumulative frequency for the first class is the same as the class frequency: 16. The cumulative frequency for the second class interval is the frequency of that interval (2) plus the frequency of the first interval (16), which yields a new cumulative frequency of 18. This process continues through the last interval, at which point the cumulative total equals the sum of the frequencies (40). The concept of cumulative frequency is used in many areas, including sales cumulated over a fiscal year, sports scores during a contest (cumulated points), years of service, points earned in a course, and costs of doing business over a period of time. Table 2.3 gives cumulative frequencies for the data in Table 2.2.

Demonstration Problem 2.1	

The following data are the average weekly mortgage interest rates for a 60-week period.

7.29	7.03	7.14	6.77	6.35	7.16	6.78	6.79	7.07	7.03
6.69	7.02	7.40	7.16	6.96	6.87	6.80	7.10	7.13	6.95
6.98	7.56	6.75	6.87	7.11	7.08	7.24	7.34	7.47	7.31
7.39	7.28	6.97	6.90	6.57	6.96	6.70	6.57	6.88	6.84
7.11	6.95	7.23	7.31	7.00	7.02	7.40	7.12	7.16	7.16
7.30	7.17	6.96	6.78	7.30	6.99	6.94	7.29	7.05	6.84

Construct a frequency distribution for these data. Calculate and display the class midpoints, relative frequencies, and cumulative frequencies for this frequency distribution.

Solution

How many classes should this frequency distribution contain? The range of the data is 1.21 (7.56 − 6.35). If seven classes are used, each class width is approximately:

$$\text{Class Width} = \frac{\text{Range}}{\text{Number of Classes}} = \frac{1.21}{7} = 0.173$$

If a class width of 0.20 is used, a frequency distribution can be constructed with endpoints that are more uniform looking and allow presentation of the information in categories more familiar to mortgage interest rate users.

The first class endpoint must be 6.35 or lower to include the smallest value; the last endpoint must be 7.56 or higher to include the largest value. In this case, the frequency distribution begins at 6.30 and ends at 7.70. The resulting frequency distribution, class midpoints, relative frequencies, and cumulative frequencies are listed in the following table.

Class Interval	Frequency	Class Midpoint	Relative Frequency	Cumulative Frequency
6.30–under 6.50	1	6.40	0.0167	1
6.50–under 6.70	3	6.60	0.0500	4
6.70–under 6.90	12	6.80	0.2000	16
6.90–under 7.10	18	7.00	0.3000	34
7.10–under 7.30	16	7.20	0.2666	50
7.30–under 7.50	9	7.40	0.1500	59
7.50–under 7.70	1	7.60	0.0167	60
Totals	60		1.0000	

The frequencies and relative frequencies of these data reveal the mortgage interest rate classes that are likely to occur during the period. Most of the mortgage interest rates (55 of the 60) are in the classes starting with (6.70–under 6.90) and going through (7.30–under 7.50). The rates with the greatest frequency, 18, are in the 6.90–under 7.10 class.

Concept Check

Fill in the blanks.

The value halfway across the class interval (calculated as the average of the two class endpoints) is called the class _____. For each class, the individual class frequency divided by the total frequency is called the _____ frequency. Moreover, a running total of frequencies through the classes of a frequency distribution is called the _____ frequency.

2.1 Problems

2.1 The following data represent the afternoon high temperatures for 50 construction days during a year in Toronto.

6	21	18	8	19	21	23	3	9	–4
13	29	–12	–4	7	–1	17	8	17	29
–9	4	27	–9	2	–8	4	2	7	–8
3	26	2	2	–5	18	24	12	–1	16
–1	3	11	–9	27	–11	16	6	–1	1

a. Construct a frequency distribution for the data using five class intervals.
b. Construct a frequency distribution for the data using 10 class intervals.
c. Examine the results of (a) and (b) and comment on the usefulness of the frequency distribution in terms of temperature summarization capability.

2.2 A packaging process is supposed to fill small boxes of raisins with approximately 50 raisins so that each box will have the same mass. However, the number of raisins in each box will vary. Suppose 100 boxes of raisins are randomly sampled, the raisins counted, and the following data are obtained.

57	51	53	52	50	60	51	51	52	52
44	53	45	57	39	53	58	47	51	48
49	49	44	54	46	52	55	54	47	53

49	52	49	54	57	52	52	53	49	47
51	48	55	53	55	47	53	43	48	46
54	46	51	48	53	56	48	47	49	57
55	53	50	47	57	49	43	58	52	44
46	59	57	47	61	60	49	53	41	48
59	53	45	45	56	40	46	49	50	57
47	52	48	50	45	56	47	47	48	46

Construct a frequency distribution for these data. What does the frequency distribution reveal about the box fills?

2.3   The owner of a fast-food restaurant ascertains the ages of a sample of customers. From these data, the owner constructs the frequency distribution shown. For each class interval of the frequency distribution, determine the class midpoint, the relative frequency, and the cumulative frequency.

Class Interval	Frequency
0–under 5	6
5–under 10	8
10–under 15	17
15–under 20	23
20–under 25	18
25–under 30	10
30–under 35	4

What does the relative frequency tell the fast-food restaurant owner about customer ages?

2.4   The human resources manager for a large company commissions a study in which the employment records of 500 company employees are examined for absenteeism during the past year. The business researcher conducting the study organizes the data into a frequency distribution to assist the human resources manager in analyzing the data. The frequency distribution is shown. For each class of the frequency distribution, determine the class midpoint, the relative frequency, and the cumulative frequency.

Class Interval	Frequency
0–under 2	218
2–under 4	207
4–under 6	56
6–under 8	11
8–under 10	8

2.5   List three specific uses of cumulative frequencies in business.

2.2 GRAPHICAL DEPICTION OF DATA

One of the most effective mechanisms for presenting data in a form meaningful to decision makers is graphical depiction. Through graphs and charts, the decision maker can often get an overall picture of the data and reach some useful conclusions merely by studying the chart or graph. Converting data to graphics can be creative and artistic. Often the most difficult step in this process is to reduce important and sometimes expensive data to a graphic picture that is both clear and concise and yet consistent with the message of the original data. One of the most important uses of graphical depiction in statistics is to help the researcher determine the shape of a distribution. Six types of graphic depiction are presented here: (1) histogram, (2) frequency polygon, (3) ogive, (4) pie chart, (5) stem and leaf plot, and (6) Pareto chart.

HISTOGRAMS

A **histogram** is *a type of vertical bar chart that is used to depict a frequency distribution.* Construction involves labelling the x axis (abscissa) with the class endpoints and the y axis (ordinate) with the frequencies, drawing a horizontal line segment from class endpoint to class endpoint at each frequency value, and connecting each line segment vertically from the frequency value to the x axis to form a series of rectangles. Figure 2.1 is a histogram of the frequency distribution in Table 2.2.

A histogram is a useful tool for differentiating the frequencies of class intervals. A quick glance at a histogram reveals which class intervals produce the highest frequency totals. Figure 2.1 clearly shows that the class interval 1–under 3 yields by far the highest frequency count (16). Examination of the histogram reveals where large increases or decreases occur between classes, such as from the 1–under 3 class to the 3–under 5 class, a decrease of 14, and from the 7–under 9 class to the 9–under 11 class, an increase of 7.

Note that the scales used along the x and y axes for the histogram in Figure 2.1 are almost identical. However, because ranges of meaningful numbers for the two variables being graphed often differ considerably, the histogram may have different scales on the two axes. Figure 2.2 shows what the histogram of unemployment rates would look like if the scale on the y axis were more compressed than that on the x axis. Notice that less

Figure 2.1

Histogram of French Unemployment Data

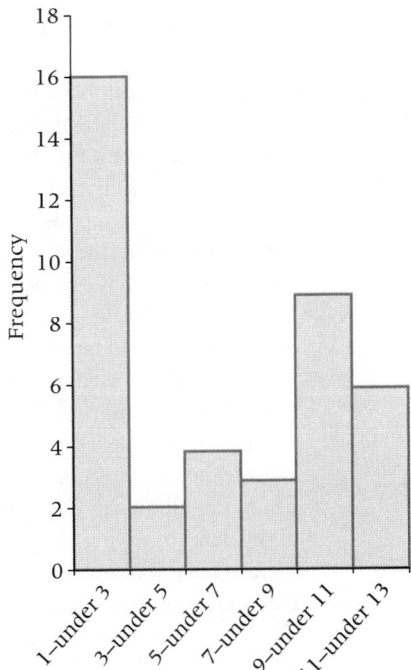

Unemployment Rates for France

Figure 2.2

Histogram of French Unemployment Data (y axis compressed)

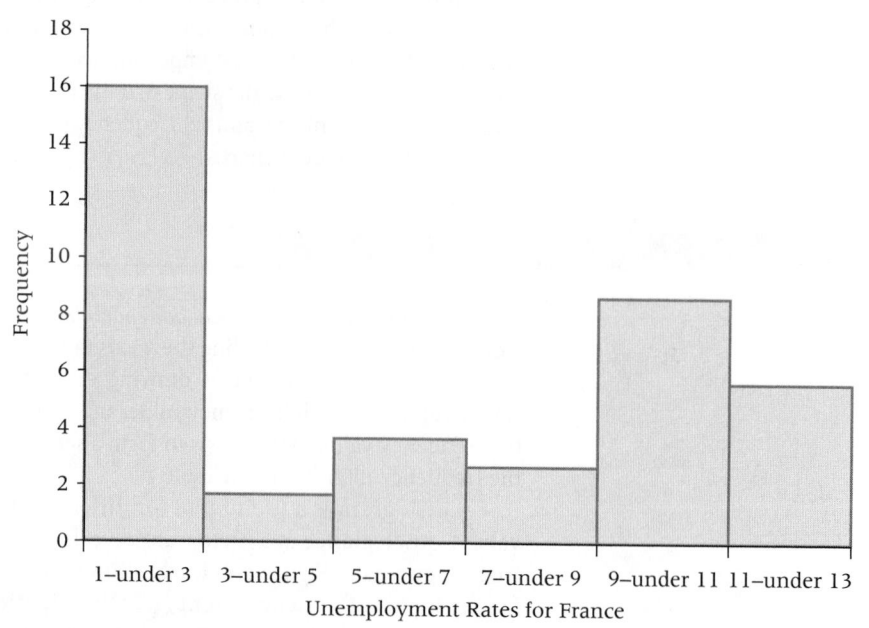

difference in the height of the rectangles appears to represent the frequencies in Figure 2.2. It is important that the user of the graph clearly understand the scales used for the axes of a histogram.

Otherwise, a graph's creator can lie with statistics by stretching or compressing a graph to make a point.*

USING HISTOGRAMS TO GET AN INITIAL OVERVIEW OF THE DATA

Because of the widespread availability of computers and statistical software packages to business researchers and decision makers, the histogram continues to grow in importance in yielding information about the shape of the distribution of a large database, the variability of the data, the central location of the data, and outlier data. Although most of these concepts are presented in Chapter 3, the notion of the histogram as an initial tool to access these data characteristics is presented here.

For example, suppose a financial decision maker wants to use data to reach some conclusions about the stock market. Figure 2.3 shows a histogram of 324 stock volume observations. What can we learn from this histogram? Virtually all stock market volumes fall between 78 million and 1 billion shares. The distribution takes on a shape that is high on the left end and tapered to the right. In Chapter 3, we will learn that the shape of this distribution is skewed toward the right end. In statistics, it is often useful to determine whether data are approximately normally distributed (bell-shaped curve), as shown in Figure 2.4. We can see by examining the histogram in Figure 2.3 that the stock market volume data are not normally distributed. Although the centre of the histogram is located near 500 million shares, a large portion of stock volume observations falls in the lower end of the data somewhere between 100 million and 400 million shares. In addition, the histogram shows some outliers in the upper end of the distribution. Outliers are data points that appear outside of the main body of observations and may represent phenomena that

---

* It should be pointed out that Excel uses the term *histogram* to refer to a frequency distribution. However, if you check Chart Output in the Excel histogram dialogue box, a graphical histogram is also created.

Figure 2.3

Histogram of Stock Volumes

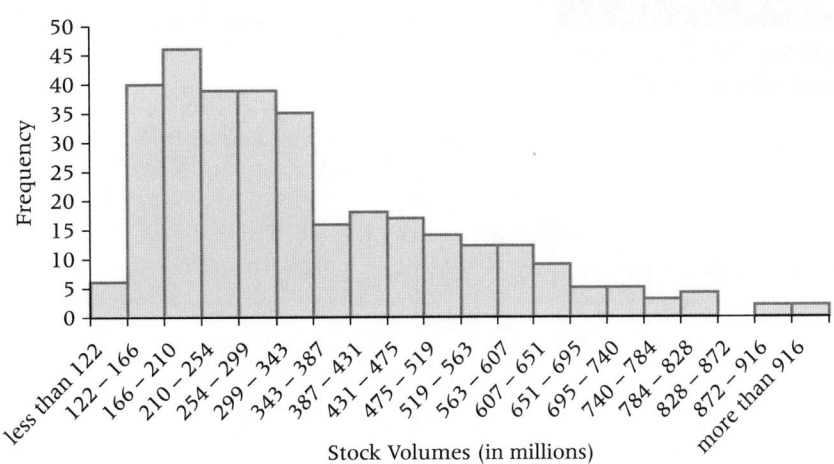

differ from those represented by other data points. By observing the histogram, we notice a few data observations near 1 billion. One could conclude that on a few stock market days an unusually large volume of shares are traded. A histogram can play an important role in the initial analysis of data due to these and other insights, which can be gleaned by examining the histogram.

FREQUENCY POLYGONS

A **frequency polygon** is *a graph in which line segments "connecting the dots" depict a frequency distribution.* Construction of a frequency polygon begins, as with a histogram, by scaling class endpoints along the *x* axis and the frequency values along the *y* axis. A dot is plotted for the frequency value at the midpoint of each class interval (class midpoint). Connecting these midpoint dots completes the graph. Figure 2.5 shows a frequency polygon of the distribution data from Table 2.2 produced in Excel. The information gleaned from frequency polygons and histograms is similar. As with the histogram, changing the scales of the axes can compress or stretch a frequency polygon, which affects the user's impression of what the graph represents.

OGIVES

An **ogive** (o-jive) is *a cumulative frequency polygon.* Again, construction begins by labelling the *x* axis with the class endpoints and the *y* axis with the frequencies. However, the use of cumulative frequency values requires that the scale along the *y* axis be great enough to include the frequency total. A dot of zero frequency is plotted at the beginning of the first class and construction proceeds by marking a dot at the *end* of each class interval for

Figure 2.4

Normal Distribution

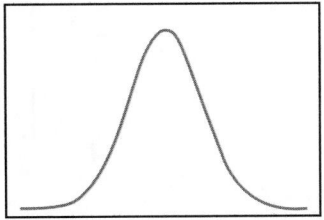

Figure 2.5

Frequency Polygon of the Unemployment Data

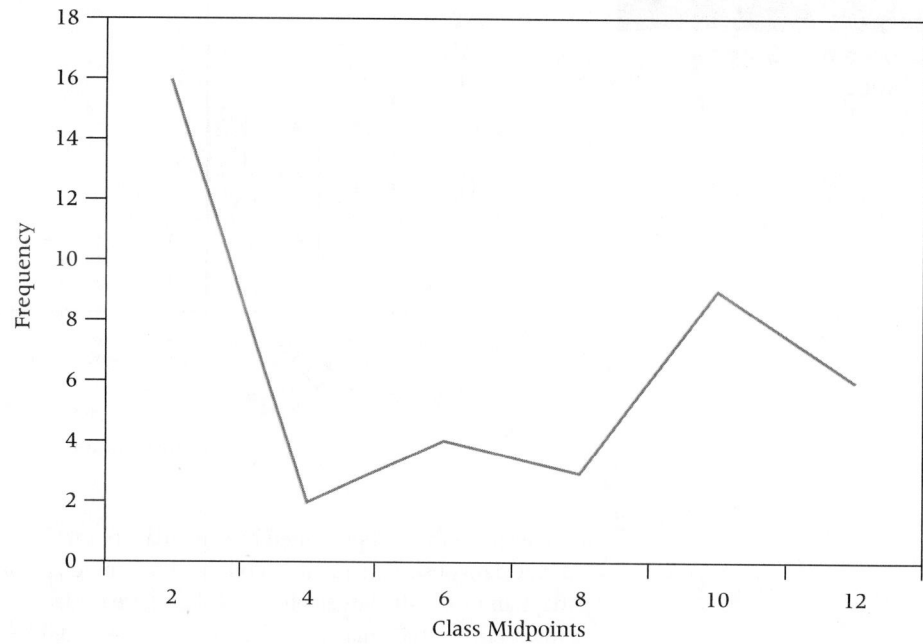

the cumulative value. Connecting the dots then completes the ogive. Figure 2.6 presents an ogive produced in Excel for the data in Table 2.2.

Ogives are most useful when the decision maker wants to see *running totals*. For example, if a comptroller is interested in controlling costs, an ogive could depict cumulative costs over a fiscal year.

Steep slopes in an ogive can be used to identify sharp increases in frequencies. In Figure 2.6, steep slopes occur in the 1–under 3 class and the 9–under 11 class, signifying large class frequency totals.

Figure 2.6

Ogive of the Unemployment Data

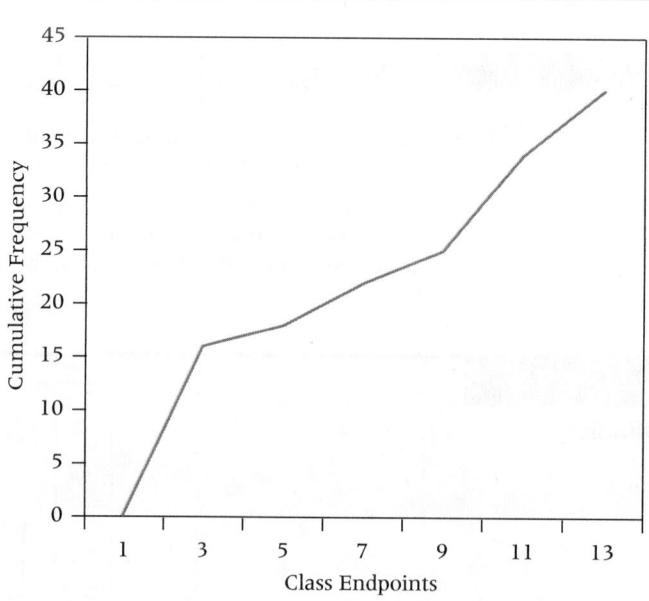

PIE CHARTS

A **pie chart** is *a circular depiction of data where the area of the whole pie represents 100% of the data and slices represent a percentage breakdown of the sublevels.* Pie charts show the relative magnitudes of parts to a whole. They are widely used in business, particularly to depict such things as budget categories, market share, and time and resource allocations. However, the use of pie charts is minimized in the sciences and technology because they can lead to less accurate judgements than are possible with other types of graphs.* Generally, it is more difficult for the viewer to interpret the relative size of angles in a pie chart than to judge the length of rectangles in a histogram or the relative distance of a frequency polygon dot from the *x* axis. In the feature Statistics in Business Today, "Where Are Soft Drinks Sold?", graphical depictions of the percentage of sales by place were displayed by both a pie chart and a vertical bar chart.

STATISTICS IN BUSINESS TODAY

Where Are Soft Drinks Sold?

Beverages that contain more than 1% by weight of flavours are considered to be soft drinks, including flavoured bottled water, soda water, seltzer water, and tonic water. Agriculture and Agri-Food Canada reports that, between 2005 and 2006, the Canadian domestic retail sales value for soft drinks decreased by 0.3%. (Interestingly, the value of retail sales of bottled water gained 21% during the same period, the largest value of growth for any non-alcoholic beverage.) Where are soft drinks sold? The following data from Sanford C. Bernstein research indicate that the four leading places for soft drink sales in the U.S. are supermarkets, fountains or snack bars, convenience/gas stores, and vending machines.

Place of Sales	Percentage
Supermarket	44
Fountain	24
Convenience stores/gas stations	16
Vending	11
Mass merchandisers	3
Drugstores	2

These data can be displayed graphically in several ways. Displayed here are a pie chart and a bar chart of the data. Some statisticians prefer the histogram or the bar chart over the pie chart because they believe it is easier to compare categories that are similar in size with the histogram or the bar chart rather than the pie chart.

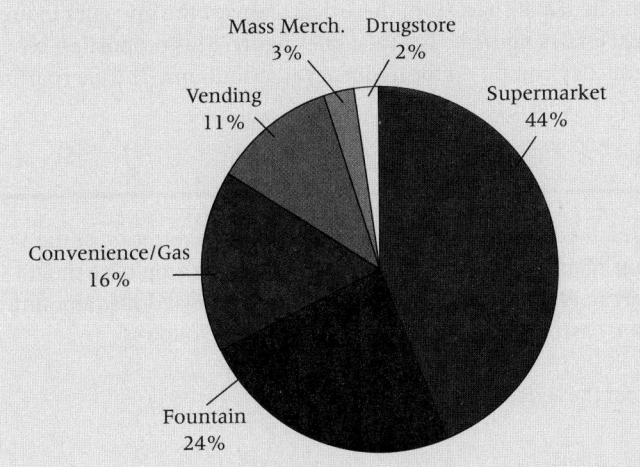

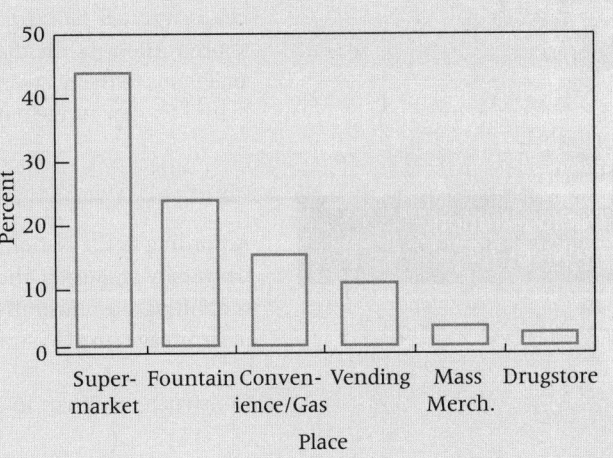

---

* William S. Cleveland, *The Elements of Graphing Data* (Monterey, CA: Wadsworth Advanced Books and Software, 1985).

Table 2.4		Annual Sales	
Leading U.S. Petroleum-Refining Companies	**Company**	**($U.S. Millions)**	**Proportion**
	Exxon Mobil	270,772	0.4232
	Chevron Texaco	147,967	0.2313
	ConocoPhillips	121,663	0.1902
	Valero Energy	53,919	0.0843
	Marathon Oil	45,444	0.0710
	Totals	639,765	1.0000

Figure 2.7

Pie Chart of Petroleum-Refining Sales by Brand

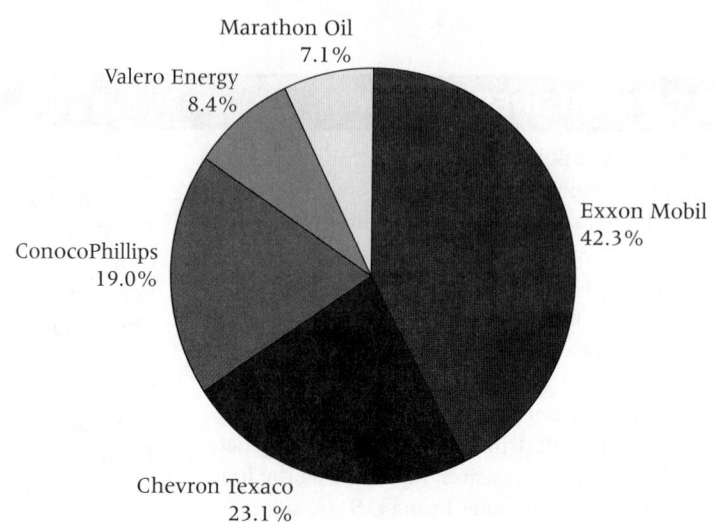

Construction of the pie chart is done by determining the proportion of the subunit to the whole. Table 2.4 contains annual sales for the top petroleum-refining companies in the U.S. in a recent year. To construct a pie chart from these data, convert the raw sales figures to proportions by dividing each sales figure by the total sales figure. This proportion is analogous to the relative frequency computed for frequency distributions. The pie chart in Figure 2.7 depicts the data from Table 2.4.

Demonstration Problem 2.2

According to the National Retail Federation and Center for Retailing Education at the University of Florida, the four main sources of inventory shrinkage are employee theft, shoplifting, administrative error, and vendor fraud. The estimated annual dollar amount in shrinkage (in $U.S. millions) associated with each of these sources follows:

Construct a pie chart to depict these data.

Employee theft	$17,918.6
Shoplifting	15,191.9
Administrative error	7,617.6
Vendor fraud	2,553.6
Total	$43,281.7

Solution

Convert each raw dollar amount to a proportion by dividing each individual amount by the total.

Employee theft	17,918.6/43,281.7	=	0.414
Shoplifting	15,191.9/43,281.7	=	0.351
Administrative error	7,617.6/43,281.7	=	0.176
Vendor fraud	2,553.6/43,281.7	=	0.059
Total			1.000

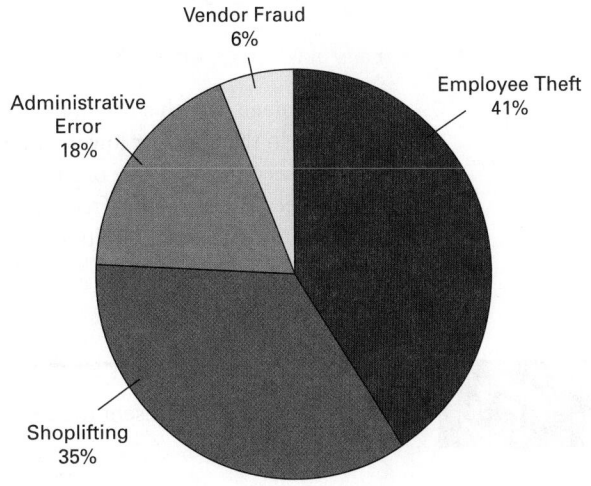

STEM AND LEAF PLOTS

POINTS OF INTEREST
Stem and leaf plots allow us to summarize data and still keep the individual data numbers.

Another way to organize raw data into groups is by a **stem and leaf plot.** This technique is simple and provides a unique view of the data. A stem and leaf plot is *constructed by separating the digits for each number of the data into two groups, a stem and a leaf.* The leftmost digits are the stem and consist of the higher-valued digits. The rightmost digits are the leaves and contain the lower values. If a set of data has only two digits, the stem is the value on the left and the leaf is the value on the right. For example, if 34 is one of the numbers, the stem is 3 and the leaf is 4. For numbers with more than two digits, division of stem and leaf is a matter of researcher preference.

Table 2.5 contains scores from an examination on plant safety policy and rules given to a group of 35 job trainees. A stem and leaf plot of these data is displayed in Table 2.6.

Table 2.5					
Safety Examination Scores for Plant Trainees	86	77	91	60	55
	76	92	47	88	67
	23	59	72	75	83
	77	68	82	97	89
	81	75	74	39	67
	79	83	70	78	91
	68	49	56	94	81

Table 2.6

Stem and Leaf Plot for Plant Safety Examination Data

Stem	Leaf								
2	3								
3	9								
4	7	9							
5	5	6	9						
6	0	7	7	8	8				
7	0	2	4	5	5	6	7	7	8	9
8	1	1	2	3	3	6	8	9	
9	1	1	2	4	7				

One advantage of such a distribution is that the instructor can readily see whether the scores are in the upper or lower end of each bracket and also determine the spread of the scores. A second advantage of stem and leaf plots is that the values of the original raw data are retained (whereas most frequency distributions and graphic depictions use the class midpoint to represent the values in a class).

Demonstration Problem 2.3

The following data represent the costs (in dollars) of a sample of 30 postal mailings by a company.

3.67	2.75	9.15	5.11	3.32	2.09
1.83	10.94	1.93	3.89	7.20	2.78
6.72	7.80	5.47	4.15	3.55	3.53
3.34	4.95	5.42	8.64	4.84	4.10
5.10	6.45	4.65	1.97	2.84	3.21

Using dollars as a stem and cents as a leaf, construct a stem and leaf plot of the data.

Solution

Stem	Leaf						
1	83	93	97				
2	09	75	78	84			
3	21	32	34	53	55	67	89
4	10	15	65	84	95		
5	10	11	42	47			
6	45	72					
7	20	80					
8	64						
9	15						
10	94						

Figure 2.8

Pareto Chart for Electric Motor Problems

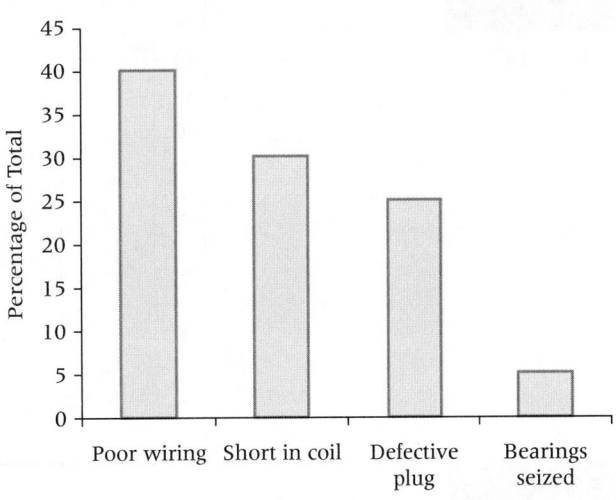

PARETO CHARTS

An important concept and movement in business is total quality management (see Chapter 18). One of the important aspects of total quality management is the constant search for causes of problems in products and processes. A graphical technique for displaying problem causes is Pareto analysis. Pareto analysis is a quantitative tallying of the number and types of defects that occur with a product or service. Analysts use this tally to produce *a vertical bar chart that displays the most common types of defects, ranked in order of occurrence from left to right.* The bar chart is called a **Pareto chart.**

Pareto charts were named after an Italian economist, Vilfredo Pareto, who observed more than 100 years ago that most of Italy's wealth was controlled by a few families who were the major drivers behind the Italian economy. Quality expert J. M. Juran applied this notion to the quality field by observing that poor quality can often be addressed by attacking a few major causes that result in most of the problems. A Pareto chart enables quality management decision makers to separate the most important defects from trivial defects, which helps them to set priorities for needed quality improvement work.

Suppose the number of electric motors being rejected by inspectors for a company has been increasing. Company officials examine the records of several hundred of the motors in which at least one defect was found to determine which defects occurred more frequently. They find that 40% of the defects involved poor wiring, 30% involved a short in the coil, 25% involved a defective plug, and 5% involved seizing of bearings. Figure 2.8 is a Pareto chart constructed from this information. It shows that the main three problems with defective motors—poor wiring, a short in the coil, and a defective plug—account for 95% of the problems. From the Pareto chart, decision makers can formulate a logical plan for reducing the number of defects.

Company officials and workers would probably begin to improve quality by examining the segments of the production process that involve the wiring. Next, they would study the construction of the coil, then examine the plugs used and the plug-supplier process.

Figure 2.9 is a different rendering of this Pareto chart. In addition to the bar chart analysis (primary axis), the Pareto analysis contains a cumulative percentage line graph (secondary axis). Observe the slopes on the line graph. The steepest slopes represent the more frequently occurring problems. As the slopes level off, the problems occur less frequently. The line graph gives the decision maker another tool for determining which problems to solve first.

Figure 2.9

Pareto Chart for Electric Motor Problems

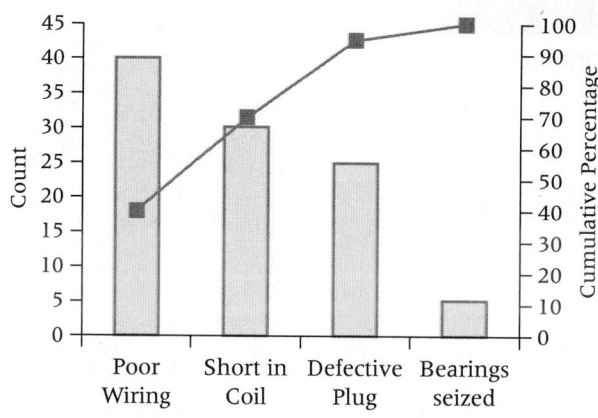

Concept Check

1. What is the first step in constructing a graph of statistical data?
2. Draw the outline of a histogram for each of the following descriptions.
   a. A set of quiz scores where the quiz was very easy
   b. The last digit of the winning lottery numbers for a year
   c. The average mass of a healthy adult measured monthly over the course of two years
3. True or false?
   Pie charts are an effective way of displaying data if the intent is to compare the size of a slice with the whole pie, rather than comparing the slices among themselves.
4. What type of chart do you think could be used to help answer the following questions?
   a. What are the main issues that our business is facing?
   b. What 20% of sources are causing 80% of our quality control problems?
   c. Where should we focus our efforts to achieve the largest improvement?

2.2 Problems

2.6   Construct a histogram and a frequency polygon for the following data.

Class Interval	Frequency
30–under 32	5
32–under 34	7
34–under 36	15
36–under 38	21
38–under 40	34
40–under 42	24
42–under 44	17
44–under 46	8

2.7   Construct a histogram and a frequency polygon for the following data.

Class Interval	Frequency
10–under 20	9
20–under 30	7
30–under 40	10
40–under 50	6
50–under 60	13
60–under 70	18
70–under 80	15

2.8   Construct an ogive for the following data.

Class Interval	Frequency
3–under 6	2
6–under 9	5
9–under 12	10
12–under 15	11
15–under 18	17
18–under 21	5

2.9   Construct a stem and leaf plot using two digits for the stem.

212	239	240	218	222	249	265	224
257	271	266	234	239	219	255	260
243	261	249	230	246	263	235	229
218	238	254	249	250	263	229	221
253	227	270	257	261	238	240	239
273	220	226	239	258	259	230	262
255	226						

2.10   Initial public offerings (IPOs) can be a risky investment; thus, in an IPO, the issuer may obtain the assistance of an underwriting firm. Shown here is a list of the top 10 Canadian underwriting firms in a recent year. Construct a pie chart to represent these data and label the slices with the appropriate percentages. Comment on the effectiveness of using a pie chart to display the revenue of these top underwriting companies.

Underwriting Firm	Amount ($ millions)
CIBC World Markets	909
RBC Capital Markets	580
Scotia Capital	551
National Bank Financial	519
BMO Nesbitt Burns	509
Merrill Lynch & Co.	508
TD Securities	482
Raymond James	362
HSBC Securities	355
Canaccord Capital	340

Source: National Post Business Magazine, Sinclair Stewart, "2001: Year of the Infrequent Public Offering," January 2002. Material reprinted with the express permission of: "The National Post Company", a Canwest Partnership.

2.11   The Canada Beef Export Federation <http://www.cbef.com> reports that the top six destinations for Canadian beef in a recent year were the U.S. with $1,697 million, Mexico with $269 million, Japan with $171 million, South Korea with $28 million, Taiwan with $16 million, and China with $4 million. Construct a pie chart to depict this information.

2.12   The following list shows the top six pharmaceutical companies in the U.S. and their sales figures (in $U.S. millions) for a recent year. Use this information to construct a pie chart to represent these six companies and their sales.

Pharmaceutical Company	Sales
Pfizer	52,921
Johnson & Johnson	47,348
Merck	22,939
Bristol-Myers Squibb	21,886
Abbott Laboratories	20,473
Wyeth	17,358

2.13   The following data represent the number of passengers per flight in a sample of 50 flights from Waterloo, Ontario, to Detroit, Michigan.

23	46	66	67	13	58	19	17	65	17
25	20	47	28	16	38	44	29	48	29
69	34	35	60	37	52	80	59	51	33
48	46	23	38	52	50	17	57	41	77
45	47	49	19	32	64	27	61	70	19

Construct a stem and leaf plot for these data. What does the stem and leaf plot tell you about the number of passengers per flight?

2.14   An airline company uses a central telephone bank and a semiautomated telephone process to take reservations. It has been receiving an unusually high number of customer complaints about its reservation system. The company conducted a survey of customers, asking them whether they had encountered any of the following problems in making reservations: busy signal, disconnection, poor connection, too long a wait to talk to someone, could not get through to an agent, connected with the wrong person. Suppose a survey of 744 complaining customers resulted in the following frequency tally.

Number of Complaints	Complaint
184	Too long a wait
10	Transferred to the wrong person
85	Could not get through to an agent
37	Got disconnected
420	Busy signal
8	Poor connection

Construct a Pareto diagram from this information to display the various problems encountered in making reservations.

2.3 GRAPHICAL DEPICTION OF TWO-VARIABLE NUMERICAL DATA: SCATTER PLOTS

In business research, it is often important to explore the relationship between two numerical variables. More detailed statistical approaches are given in Chapters 3 and 12, but here we present a graphical mechanism for examining the relationship between two numerical variables, the scatter plot (or scatter diagram). A **scatter plot** is *a two-dimensional graph plot of pairs of points from two numerical variables.*

Table 2.7		
Revenue and Total CEO Compensation for 25 Large Canadian Companies	**Revenue ($ thousands)**	**Total CEO Compensation ($ thousands)**
	327,837	442
	1,247,711	9,592
	735,276	369
	841,641	5,602
	1,206,524	2,471
	615,291	2,523
	10,604	3,485
	1,087,869	5,698
	192,895	3,424
	1,831,690	7,579
	279,064	451
	2,692,000	2,122
	3,849,552	3,586
	6,539,000	3,060
	881,437	2,238
	8,838,000	16,377
	12,664,000	4,824
	10,398,000	11,549
	849,616	308
	1,673,819	1,105
	979,496	1,218
	847,472	1,826
	1,199,866	696

Source: *National Post Business Magazine,* "CEO Score-card 2007," November 2007. Material reprinted with the express permission of: "The National Post Company", a Canwest Partnership.

As an example of two numerical variables, consider the data in Table 2.7. Displayed are the revenue and total CEO compensation for 25 large Canadian companies in a recent year. Do these two numerical variables exhibit any relationship? It might seem logical when the revenue for a company is high that the total CEO compensation would be high as well. However, the scatter plot of these data displayed in Figure 2.10 shows somewhat

Figure 2.10	
Scatter Plot of 2006 Revenue and Total CEO Compensation for 25 Large Canadian Companies	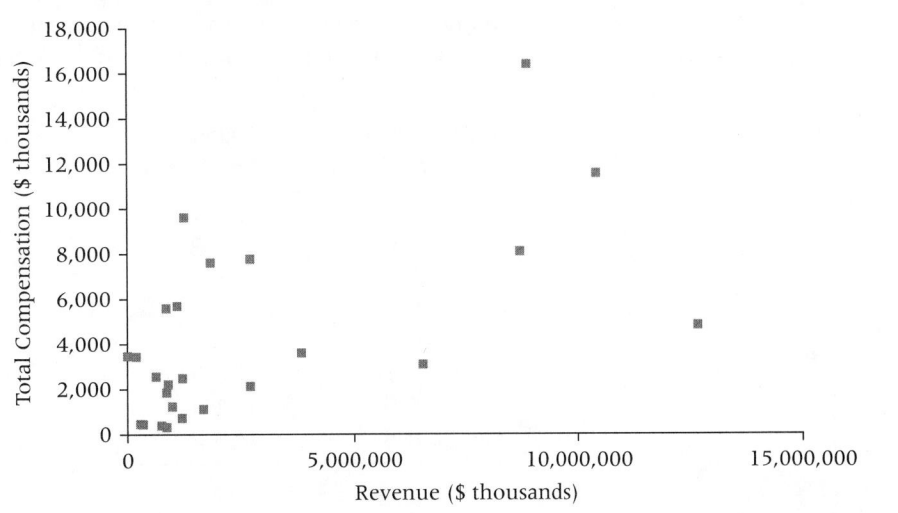

mixed results. The apparent tendency is that higher total CEO compensations occur when the companies' revenues are high and lower total CEO compensations occur when the companies' revenues are low. The scatter plot also shows that in some companies a higher total CEO compensation occurs when the revenue is rather low, and vice versa.

Concept Check

1. Draw the outline of a scatter plot for each of the following sets of two numerical variables.
   a.   The mass and height of 30 people selected at random
   b.   The mass and IQ of 30 people selected at random
   c.   The number of advertising dollars spent by a company and the total sales revenue

2.3 Problems

2.15   The U.S. National Oceanic and Atmospheric Administration, National Marine Fisheries Service, publishes data on the quantity and value of domestic fishing in the U.S. The quantity (in millions of kilograms) of fish caught and used for human food and for industrial products (oil, bait, animal food, etc.) over a decade follows. Is a relationship evident between the quantity used for human food and the quantity used for industrial products for a given year? Construct a scatter plot of the data. Examine the plot and discuss the strength of the relationship of the two variables.

Human Food	Industrial Product
1,661	1,285
1,612	1,105
1,493	1,401
1,472	1,455
1,509	1,417
1,497	1,347
1,542	1,199
1,794	1,341
2,085	1,184
2,820	1,027

2.16   Are the advertising dollars spent by a company related to total sales revenue? The following data represent the advertising dollars and the sales revenues for various companies in a given industry during a recent year. Construct a scatter plot of the data from the two variables and discuss the relationship between the two variables.

Advertising (in $ millions)	Sales (in $ millions)
4.2	155.7
1.6	87.3
6.3	135.6
2.7	99.0
10.4	168.2
7.1	136.9
5.5	101.4
8.3	158.2

ENERGY CONSUMPTION AROUND THE WORLD

The raw values as shown in the table in the Decision Dilemma are relatively easy to read and interpret. However, these numbers could also be displayed graphically in different ways to create interest and discussion among readers and to allow for more ease of comparisons.

For example, shown below are side-by-side pie charts displaying both oil and coal energy consumption figures by country. With such charts, the reader can see which countries are dominating consumption of each energy source and then can compare consumption segments across sources.

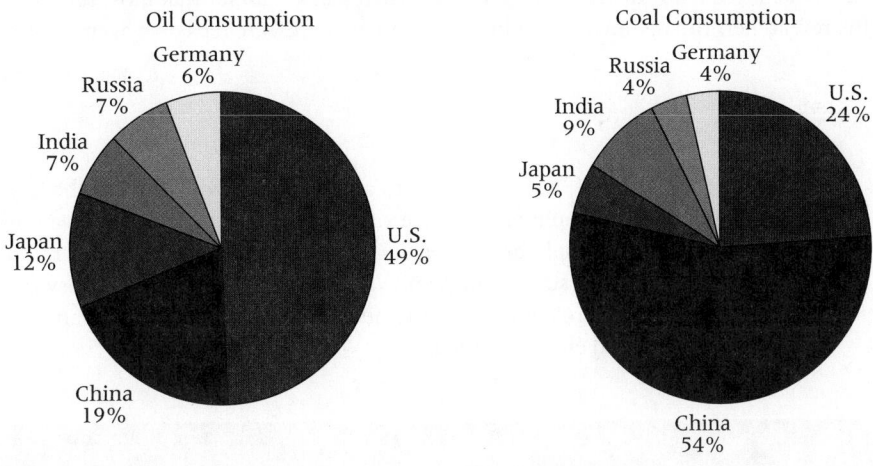

Pie Charts for World Oil and Coal Consumption (Top Six Nations)

Sometimes it is difficult for the reader to discern the relative sizes of pie slices that are close in magnitude. For that reason, a histogram might be a better way to display the data. Shown below is a histogram of the oil consumption data. It is easy to see that the U.S. dominates world oil consumption, and if the percentage figures were not there in the pie chart, it would be easier to see in the histogram than in the pie chart that Russia uses more oil than Germany.

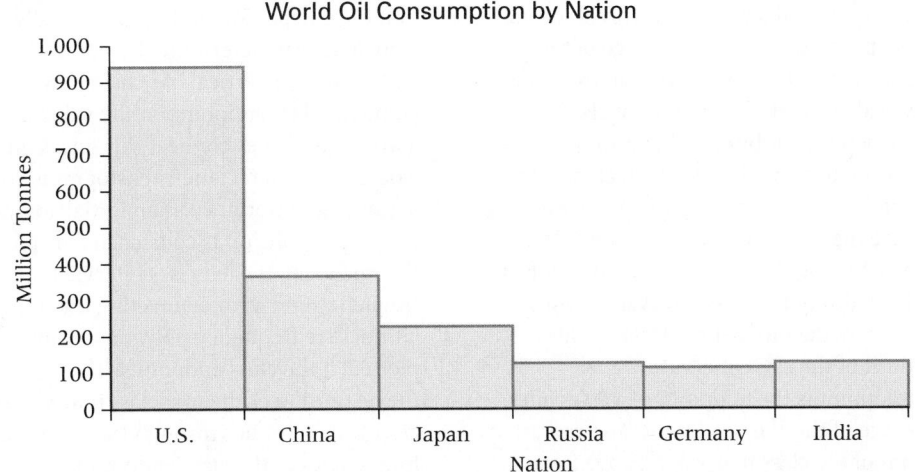

KEY CONSIDERATIONS

Ethical considerations for the techniques learned in Chapter 2 begin with the data chosen for representation. With the abundance of available data in business, the person constructing the data summary must be selective in choosing the reported variables. The potential is great for the analyst to select variables or even data within variables that are favourable to his or her own situation or that are perceived to be well received by the listener.

In Section 2.1, we noted that the number of classes and the size of the intervals in frequency distributions are usually selected by the researcher. The researcher should be careful to select values and sizes that will give an honest, accurate reflection of the situation and not a biased over- or understated case.

In Sections 2.2 and 2.3, we discussed the construction of charts and graphs. We pointed out that in many instances, it makes sense to use unequal scales on the axes. However, doing so opens the possibility of cheating with statistics by stretching or compressing the axes to underscore the researcher's or analyst's point. It is imperative that frequency distributions and charts and graphs be constructed in a manner that most reflects actual data and not merely the researcher's own agenda.

Why Statistics Is Relevant

The old cliché "a picture is worth a thousand words" is put to the test in this chapter. Charts and graphs are effective visual tools: they present information quickly and easily. Charts and graphs are powerful in business because the human mind takes the quickest route to understand reality, and visual statistics are often the answer to understanding managerial problems. It is certainly not surprising that charts and graphs are heavily used by print and electronic media.

SUMMARY

1. We now know that the two types of data are grouped and ungrouped. Most statistical analysis is performed on ungrouped or raw data. Grouped data are data organized into a frequency distribution. Differentiating between grouped and ungrouped data is important, because statistical operations on the two types are computed differently.

2. Constructing a frequency distribution involves several steps. The first step is to determine the range of the data, which is the difference between the largest value and the smallest value. Next, the number of classes is determined, which is an arbitrary choice of the researcher. However, too few classes overaggregate the data into meaningless categories, and too many classes do not summarize the data enough to be useful. The third step in constructing the frequency distribution is to determine the width of the class interval. Dividing the range of values by the number of classes yields the approximate width of the class interval.

   The class midpoint is the midpoint of a class interval. It is the average of the class endpoints and represents the halfway point of the class interval. Relative frequency is computed by dividing an individual frequency by the sum of the frequencies. Relative frequency represents the proportion of total values that is in a given class interval. The cumulative frequency is a running total frequency tally that starts with the first frequency value and adds each ensuing frequency to the total.

3. The types of graphic depictions described in this chapter are histograms, frequency polygons, ogives, pie charts, stem and leaf plots, Pareto charts, and scatter plots. When should these graphs be used? Well, graphical depiction of data is especially useful in helping statisticians to determine the shape of distributions. A histogram is a vertical bar chart in which a line segment connects class endpoints at the value of the frequency. Two vertical lines connect this line segment to the x axis, forming a rectangle. Histograms are taking on a growing importance as an initial analysis tool. A frequency polygon is constructed by plotting a dot at the midpoint of each class interval for the value of each frequency and then connecting the dots. Ogives are cumulative frequency polygons. Points on an ogive are plotted at the class endpoints. The ogive graph starts at the beginning of the first class interval with a value of zero and continues through the values of the cumulative frequencies to the class endpoints.

   A pie chart is a circular depiction of data. The amount of each category is represented as a slice of the pie proportionate to the total. The researcher is cautioned in using pie charts because it is sometimes difficult to differentiate the relative sizes of the slices. Stem and leaf plots are another way to organize data. The numbers are divided into two parts, a stem and a leaf. The stems are the leftmost digits of the numbers and the leaves are the rightmost digits. The business researcher determines how to divide the digits into stems and leaves. The stems are listed individually, with all leaf values corresponding to each stem displayed beside that stem.

A Pareto chart is a vertical bar chart that is used in total quality management to graphically display the causes of problems. The Pareto chart presents problem causes in descending order to assist the decision maker in prioritizing these problem causes. The scatter plot is a two-dimensional plot of pairs of points from two numerical variables. It is used to graphically determine whether any apparent relationship exists between the two variables.

KEY TERMS

class mark	frequency polygon	Pareto chart	scatter plot
class midpoint	grouped data	pie chart	stem and leaf plot
cumulative frequency	histogram	range	ungrouped data
frequency distribution	ogive	relative frequency	

SUPPLEMENTARY PROBLEMS

Calculating the Statistics

2.17 For the following data, construct a frequency distribution with six classes.

57	23	35	18	21
26	51	47	29	21
46	43	29	23	39
50	41	19	36	28
31	42	52	29	18
28	46	33	28	20

2.18 For each class interval of the frequency distribution given, determine the class midpoint, the relative frequency, and the cumulative frequency.

Class Interval	Frequency
20–under 25	17
25–under 30	20
30–under 35	16
35–under 40	15
40–under 45	8
45–under 50	6

2.19 Construct a histogram, a frequency polygon, and an ogive for the following frequency distribution.

Class Interval	Frequency
50–under 60	13
60–under 70	27
70–under 80	43
80–under 90	31
90–under 100	9

2.20 Construct a pie chart from the following data.

Label	Value
A	55
B	121
C	83
D	46

2.21 Construct a stem and leaf plot for the following data. Let the leaf contain one digit.

312	324	289	335	298
314	309	294	326	317
290	311	317	301	316
306	286	308	284	324

2.22 An examination of rejects shows at least 10 problems. A frequency tally of the problems follows. Construct a Pareto chart for these data.

Problem	Frequency
1	673
2	29
3	108
4	379
5	73
6	564
7	12
8	402
9	54
10	202

SUPPLEMENTARY PROBLEMS (continued)

2.23 Construct a scatter plot for the following two numerical variables.

x	y
12	5
17	3
9	10
6	15
10	8
14	9
8	8

Testing Your Understanding

2.24 Yellowknife Steel manufactures a metal ring for industrial engines that usually has a mass of about 50 g. A random sample of 50 of these metal rings produced the following masses (in grams).

51	53	56	50	44	47
53	53	42	57	46	55
41	44	52	56	50	57
44	46	41	52	69	53
57	51	54	63	42	47
47	52	53	46	36	58
51	38	49	50	62	39
44	55	43	52	43	42
57	49				

Construct a frequency distribution for these data using eight classes. What can you observe about the data from the frequency distribution?

2.25 A distribution company in Alberta surveyed 53 of its midlevel managers. The survey obtained the ages of these managers, which were later organized into the frequency distribution shown. Determine the class midpoint, relative frequency, and cumulative frequency for these data.

Class Interval	Frequency
20–under 25	8
25–under 30	6
30–under 35	5
35–under 40	12
40–under 45	15
45–under 50	7

2.26 The following data are shaped roughly like a normal distribution (discussed in Chapter 6).

61.4	27.3	26.4	37.4	30.4	47.5
63.9	46.8	67.9	19.1	81.6	47.9
73.4	54.6	65.1	53.3	71.6	58.6
57.3	87.8	71.1	74.1	48.9	60.2
54.8	60.5	32.5	61.7	55.1	48.2
56.8	60.1	52.9	60.5	55.6	38.1
76.4	46.8	19.9	27.3	77.4	58.1
32.1	54.9	32.7	40.1	52.7	32.5
35.3	39.1				

Construct a frequency distribution starting with 10 as the lowest class beginning point and using a class width of 10. Construct a histogram and a frequency polygon for this frequency distribution and observe the shape of a normal distribution. On the basis of your results from these graphs, what does a normal distribution look like?

2.27 Use the data from Problem 2.25.
  a. Construct a histogram and a frequency polygon.
  b. Construct an ogive.

2.28 In a medium-sized city, 86 houses are for sale, each having about 2,000 square feet of floor space. The asking prices vary. The frequency distribution shown contains the price categories for the 86 houses. Construct a histogram, a frequency polygon, and an ogive from these data.

Asking Price	Frequency
$80,000–under $100,000	21
100,000–under 120,000	27
120,000–under 140,000	18
140,000–under 160,000	11
160,000–under 180,000	6
180,000–under 200,000	3

2.29 A consumer group surveyed food prices at 87 stores in Atlantic Canada. Among the food prices being measured was that of sugar. From the data collected, the group constructed the frequency distribution of the prices of 2 kg of Maple Leaf's sugar in the stores surveyed. Construct a histogram, a frequency polygon, and an ogive for the following data.

Price	Frequency
$1.75–under $1.90	9
1.90–under 2.05	14
2.05–under 2.20	17
2.20–under 2.35	16
2.35–under 2.50	18
2.50–under 2.65	8
2.65–under 2.80	5

2.30 The top music genres according to SoundScan for a recent year are R&B, Alternative (Rock) Music, Rap, and Country. These and other music genres along with the number of albums sold in each (in millions) are shown.

Genre	Albums Sold
R&B	146.4
Alternative	102.6
Rap	73.7
Country	64.5
Soundtrack	56.4
Metal	26.6
Classical	14.8
Latin	14.5

Construct a pie chart for these data displaying the percentage of the whole that each of these genres represents.

2.31   It is commonly known that the Canadian-to-U.S. dollar exchange rate affects the number of Canadian travellers to the U.S. and also the number of travellers to Canada from the U.S. The following data show the number of travellers (in millions) and the exchange rate from 1991–2004. Construct a scatter plot using the exchange rate as the x axis and the number of travellers as the y axis and determine whether any relationship is apparent between the exchange rate and both numbers of travellers.

Year	Canadian Travellers to the U.S. (millions)	Travellers to Canada From U.S. (millions)	Average Canadian-to-U.S. Dollar Exchange Rate
1991	79.4	33.6	0.873
1992	76.7	32.4	0.828
1993	66.7	32.6	0.776
1994	54.3	34.9	0.732
1995	52.2	37.3	0.729
1996	52.7	38.5	0.733
1997	50.9	40.5	0.722
1998	42.8	43.9	0.675
1999	42.2	44.6	0.673
2000	42.7	44.0	0.674
2001	38.4	42.9	0.646
2002	34.6	40.9	0.637
2003	34.2	35.5	0.716
2004	35.9	34.6	0.770

Source: Data from Statistics Canada, *Canadian Economic Observer,* February 2005, Catalogue no. 11-010-XIB, F. Roy, "The Soaring Loonie and International Travel," <http://www.statcan.gc.ca/pub/11-010-x/00205/7773-eng.htm>

2.32   Shown here is a list of the 10 industrial sources with the largest air pollutant emissions in a recent year for Canada according to Environment Canada. Construct a pie chart to depict this information.

Industrial Source	Total Emissions (tonnes)
Upstream Petroleum Industry	1,859,733
Nonferrous Smelting and Refining Industry	978,235
Wood Industry	572,225
Aluminum Industry	474,087
Mining and Rock Quarrying	319,015
Pulp and Paper Industry	252,942
Downstream Petroleum Industry	217,474
Cement and Concrete Industry	200,939
Iron and Steel Industries	117,793
Chemicals Industry	97,662

2.33   A manufacturing company produces plastic bottles for the dairy industry. Some of the bottles are rejected because of poor quality. Causes of poor-quality bottles include faulty plastic, incorrect labelling, discoloration, incorrect thickness, broken handle, and others. The following data for 500 plastic bottles that were rejected include the problems and the frequency of the problems. Use these data to construct a Pareto chart. Discuss the implications of the chart.

Problem	Number
Discoloration	32
Thickness	117
Broken handle	86
Fault in plastic	221
Labelling	44

2.34   A research organization selected 50 towns with populations between 4,000 and 6,000 as a sample to represent small towns for survey purposes. The populations of these towns follow.

4420	5221	4299	5831	5750
5049	5556	4361	5737	4654
4653	5338	4512	4388	5923
4730	4963	5090	4822	4304
4758	5366	5431	5291	5254
4866	5858	4346	4734	5919
4216	4328	4459	5832	5873
5257	5048	4232	4878	5166
5366	4212	5669	4224	4440
4299	5263	4339	4834	5478

Construct a stem and leaf plot for the data, letting each leaf contain two digits.

2.35 Listed here are 30 different weekly TSX composite stock averages.

9,656	9,301	9,975	10,002	9,468
9,742	9,830	9,405	9,677	9,990
9,200	9,764	9,337	9,961	10,010
9,976	9,375	9,602	9,670	9,922
9,344	9,760	9,555	9,524	9,814
9,996	9,437	9,268	9,448	9,460

Construct a stem and leaf plot for these 30 values. Let each leaf contain two digits.

Interpreting the Output

2.36 Suppose 150 shoppers at an upscale mall are interviewed and one of the questions asked is about household income. Study the histogram of the following data and discuss what can be learned about the shoppers.

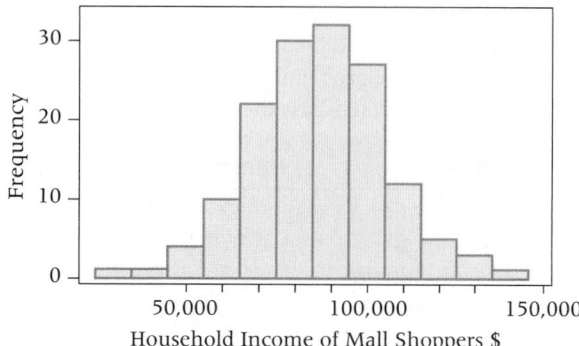

2.37 Shown here is a pie chart representing physician specialties. What does the chart tell you about the various specialties?

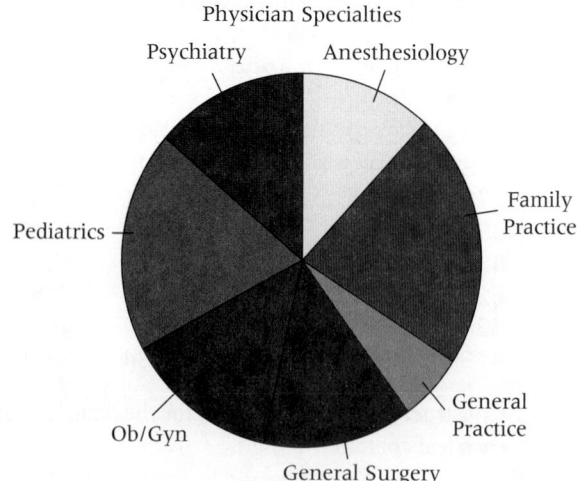

2.38 Suppose 100 CMA firms are surveyed to determine how many audits they perform over a certain time. The data are summarized using a stem and leaf plot. What can you learn about the number of audits being performed by these firms from this plot?

Character Stem and Leaf Display

Stem and Leaf of Number of Audits   N = 100
Leaf Unit = 1.0

9	1	222333333
16	1	4445555
26	1	6666667777
35	1	888899999
39	2	0001
44	2	22333
49	2	55555
(9)	2	677777777
42	2	8888899
35	3	000111
29	3	223333
23	3	44455555
15	3	67777
10	3	889
7	4	0011
3	4	222

2.39 The following ogive shows toy sales by a company over a 12-month period. What conclusions can you reach about toy sales at this company?

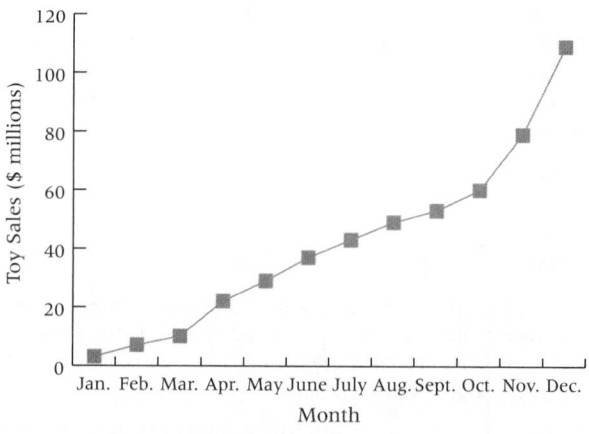

ANALYZING THE DATABASES

see www.wiley.com/canada/black

1. Using the Major League Baseball database, construct a frequency distribution for the variable Payroll. Remember that in Excel the frequency distribution is referred to as a histogram. What does the frequency distribution reveal about the payroll of each team in 2008?

2. Using the Canadian Stock Market Database, construct a histogram for the variable Energy Index. How is the histogram shaped? Is it high in the middle or near one or both of the endpoints? Is it relatively constant in size across the classes (uniform) or does it appear to have no shape? Does it appear to be normally distributed?

3. Construct an ogive for Current Value in the Major League Baseball Database. The 30 teams in this database are each categorized into one of the six divisions. These divisions are listed in Analyzing the Databases in Chapter 1. Construct a pie chart of these divisions and discuss the output. For example, which division is the most valuable and which is the least?

4. Using the International Labour Database, construct a stem and leaf plot for the United Kingdom. What does the plot show about unemployment for the United Kingdom over the past 30 years?

CASE

Soap Companies Do Battle

Procter & Gamble has been the leading soap manufacturer in the U.S. since 1879, when it introduced Ivory soap. However, late in 1991 its major rival, Lever Bros. (Unilever), overtook it by grabbing 31.5% of the $1.6 billion personal soap market, of which Procter & Gamble had a 30.5% share. Lever Bros. had trailed Procter & Gamble since it entered the soap market with Lifebuoy in 1895. In 1990, Lever Bros. introduced a new soap for the entire family, Lever 2000, into its product mix. A niche for such a soap had been created because of the segmentation of the soap market into specialty soaps for children, women, and men. Lever Bros. felt that it could sell a soap for everyone in the family. Consumer response was strong; Lever 2000 rolled up $113 million in sales in 1991, putting Lever Bros. ahead of Procter & Gamble for the first time in the personal-soap revenue contest. Procter & Gamble still sells more soap, but Lever's brands cost more, thereby resulting in greater overall sales.

Needless to say, Procter & Gamble was quick to search for a response to the success of Lever 2000. Procter & Gamble looked at several possible strategies, including repositioning Safeguard, which had been seen as a soap for men. Ultimately, Procter & Gamble responded to the challenge by introducing its Oil of Olay Moisturizing Bath Bar. In its first year of national distribution, this product was backed by a $24 million media effort. The new bath bar was quite successful and helped Procter & Gamble regain market share.

The following table gives the latest figures on the leading personal soaps in the U.S. with their respective sales figures. Each of these soaps is produced by one of four soap manufacturers: Unilever, Procter & Gamble, Dial, and Colgate-Palmolive.

Soap	Manufacturer	Sales ($U.S. millions)
Dove	Unilever	271
Dial	Dial	193
Lever 2000	Unilever	138
Irish Spring	Colgate-Palmolive	121
Zest	Procter & Gamble	115
Ivory	Procter & Gamble	94
Caress	Unilever	93
Olay	Procter & Gamble	69
Safeguard	Procter & Gamble	48
Coast	Dial	44

In 1983, the market shares for soap were Procter & Gamble with 37.1%, Lever Bros. (Unilever) with 24%, Dial with 15%, Colgate-Palmolive with 6.5%, and all others with 17.4%. By 1991, the market shares for soap were Lever Bros. (Unilever) with 31.5%, Procter & Gamble with 30.5%, Dial with 19%, Colgate-Palmolive with 8%, and all others with 11%.

Discussion

1. Suppose you are making a report for Procter & Gamble displaying its share of the market along with the share of other companies for the years 1983, 1991, and the latest figures. Produce graphs for the market shares of personal soap for each of these years. For the latest figures data, assume that the "all others" total is about $119 million. What do you observe about the market shares of the various companies by studying the graphs? In particular, how is Procter & Gamble doing relative to previous years?

2. Suppose Procter & Gamble sells about 20 million bars of soap per week, but the demand is not constant and production management would like to get a better

CASE (continued)

handle on how sales are distributed over the year. Let the following sales figures given in units of million bars represent the sales of bars per week over one year. Construct a histogram to represent these data. What do you see in the graph that might be helpful to the production (and sales) people?

17.1	19.6	15.4	17.4	15.0	18.5	20.6	18.4
20.0	20.9	19.3	18.2	14.7	17.1	12.2	19.9
18.7	20.4	20.3	15.5	16.8	19.1	20.4	15.4
20.3	17.5	17.0	18.3	13.6	39.8	20.7	21.3
22.5	21.4	23.4	23.1	22.8	21.4	24.0	25.2
26.3	23.9	30.6	25.2	26.2	26.9	32.8	26.3
26.6	24.3	26.2	23.8				

Construct a stem and leaf plot using the whole numbers as the stems. What advantages does the stem and leaf plot of these sales figures offer over the histogram? What are some disadvantages? Which would you use in discussions with production people and why?

3. A random sample of finished soap bars in their packaging is tested for quality. All defective bars are examined for problem causes. Among the problems found were improper packaging, poor labelling, bad seal, wrong shape of bar, marred bar surface, wrong bar colour, wrong bar fragrance, wrong soap consistency, and others. Some of the leading

problem causes and the number of each are given here. Use a Pareto chart to analyze these problem causes. Based on your findings, what would you recommend to the company?

Problem Cause	Frequency
Bar surface	89
Colour	17
Fragrance	2
Label	32
Shape	8
Seal	47
Labelling	5
Soap consistency	3

References

Adapted from Valerie Reitman, "Buoyant Sales of Lever 2000 Soap Bring Sinking Sensation to Procter & Gamble," *Wall Street Journal*, 19 March 1992, p. B1. Reprinted by permission of The *Wall Street Journal* © 1992, Dow Jones & Company, Inc. All rights reserved worldwide; Pam Weisz, "$40 M Extends Lever 2000 Family," *Brandweek*, vol. 36, no. 32 (21 August 1995), p. 6; Laurie Freeman, "P&G Pushes Back against Unilever in Soap," *Advertising Age*, vol. 65, no. 41 (28 September 1994), p. 21; and Jeanne Whalen and Pat Sloan, "Intros Help Boost Soap Coupons," *Advertising Age*, vol. 65, no. 19 (2 May 1994), p. 30.

USING THE COMPUTER

Excel

- Excel offers the capability of producing many of the charts and graphs presented in this chapter. Most can be accessed by clicking on the **Insert** tab found along the top of an Excel worksheet. Excel can also generate frequency distributions and histograms using the **Data Analysis** feature.

- Many of the statistical techniques presented here can be performed in Excel using a tool called **Data Analysis**. Select the **Data** tab along the top of an Excel worksheet. If the **Data Analysis** feature has been uploaded into your Excel package, it will be found in the **Analysis** section at the top right of the **Data** tab page on the far right. If **Data Analysis** does not appear in the **Analysis** section, it must be added in.

- Excel refers to frequency distributions as histograms, and to the classes of a frequency distribution as bins. If you do not specify bins (classes), Excel will automatically determine the number of bins and assign class endpoints based on a formula. If you want to specify bins, load the

class endpoints that you want to use into a column. To construct a frequency distribution, select the **Data** tab and then select the **Data Analysis** feature. If this feature does not appear, you may need to add it. Clicking on **Data Analysis**, the dialogue box features a pulldown menu of many of the statistical analysis tools presented and used in this text. Select **Histogram** from the dropdown menu in **Data Analysis**. In the **Histogram** dialogue box, place the location of the raw data values in the space beside **Input Range**. Place the location of the class endpoints (optional) in the space beside **Bin Range**. Leave this blank if you want Excel to determine the bins (classes). If you have labels, check **Labels**. If you want a histogram graph, check **Chart Output**. If you want an ogive, select **Cumulative Percentage** along with **Chart Output**. If you opt for this, Excel will yield a histogram graph with an ogive overlaid on it.

- Excel can construct many different types of charts, including column charts, line charts, pie charts, bar charts, area charts, and XY (scatter) charts. To begin, select the **Insert** tab. In the **Charts** section, there are icons for column, line, pie, bar, area, scatter, and other charts. Click on the desired icon to begin construction. Each of these types of charts allow for several versions of the chart shown in the dropdown menu. To select a particular version of a type of chart, click on the type of chart and then the version of the chart that is desired.

- To construct a pie chart, enter the categories in one column and the data values of each category in another column. Categories and data values could also be entered in rows instead of columns. Click and drag over the data for which the pie chart is to be constructed. From the **Insert** tab, select **Pie** from the **Charts** section and the select the type of pie chart to be constructed. The result is a pie chart from the data.

- Frequency polygons can be constructed in Excel 2007 by using the **Histogram** feature. Follow the directions above to construct a histogram. Then right-click on one of the "bars" of the histogram. From the dropdown menu, select **Change Series Chart Type**. Next select a line chart type. The result will be a frequency polygon.

- An ogive can be constructed at least two ways. One way is to cumulate the data manually. Enter the cumulated data in one column and the class endpoints in another column. Click and drag over both columns. Go to the **Insert** tab at the top of the worksheet. Select **Scatter** as the type of chart. Under the **Scatter** options, select the option with the solid lines. The result is an ogive. A second way is to construct a frequency distribution first using the **Histogram** feature noted above. In the **Histogram** dialogue box, enter the location of the data and enter the location of the class endpoints as bin numbers. Check **Cumulative Percentage** and **Chart Output** in the **Histogram** dialogue box. Once the chart is constructed, right-click on one of the bars and select the **Delete** option. The result will be an ogive chart with just the ogive line graph (and bars eliminated).

- Bar charts and column charts are constructed similarly to pie charts. Enter the categories in one column and the data values of each category in another column in the Excel worksheet (they could also be entered in rows instead of columns). Click and drag over the data and categories for which the chart is to be constructed. Go to the **Insert** tab at the top of the worksheet. Select **Column** or **Bar** from the **Charts** section and the select the version of the chart to be constructed. The result is a chart from the data. By right-clicking on the bars or columns, a menu appears that allows you, among other things, to label the columns or bars. This command is **Add Data Labels**. Once data labels are added, clicking on the bars or columns will allow you to modify the labels and the characteristics of the bars or columns by selecting **Format Data Labels**… or **Format Data Series**.….

- Pareto charts have categories and numbers of defects. As such, Pareto charts can be constructed as **Column** charts using the same commands. However, the user must first order the categories and their associated frequencies in descending order. In addition, there is an option in the **Histogram** dialogue box called **Pareto (sorted histogram)** in which Excel takes histogram data and presents the data with categories organized from highest frequency to lowest.

- Scatter diagrams can be constructed by entering the data for the two variables to be graphed in two separate rows or columns. You may either use a label for each variable or not. Click and drag over the data (and labels). Go to the **Insert** tab. From the **Charts** panel, select **Scatter**. From the ensuing pulldown menu of scatter plot options, select one of the versions presented. The result is the scatter chart. By right-clicking on the chart, various other chart options are available including, **Format Plot Area**…. If you also want to fit a line or curve to the data, right-click on one of the chart points. A menu pops up containing, among other options, **Add Trendline**…. From the **Trendline Options**, select the type of line or curve that you want to fit to the data. The result is a line or curve shown on the scatter plot attempting to fit to the points.

DESCRIPTIVE STATISTICS

Learning Objectives

The focus of Chapter 3 is the use of statistical techniques to describe data. Here are the key questions we would like to answer:

1. What are the measures of central tendency, measures of variability, measures of shape, and measures of association?

2. What are the meanings of *mean, median, mode, quartile, percentile,* and *range*?

3. How can we compute the mean, median, mode, percentile, quartile, range, variance, standard deviation, and mean absolute deviation on ungrouped data?

4. What is the difference between sample and population variance and standard deviation?

5. What is the meaning of standard deviation as it is applied by using the empirical rule and Chebyshev's theorem?

6. How can we compute the mean, median, mode, standard deviation, and variance on grouped data?

7. What are the definitions of *skewness* and *kurtosis* and why are they important? What are box and whisker plots and how can we construct them?

Media Bakery

LAUNDRY STATISTICS

DECISION DILEMMA

According to Procter & Gamble, 35 billion loads of laundry are run in the U.S. each year. Every second, 1,100 loads are started. Statistics show that one person in the U.S. generates about a quarter of a tonne of dirty clothing each year. Americans appear to be spending more time doing laundry than they did 40 years ago. Today, the average American spends seven to nine hours a week on laundry. However, industry research shows that the result is dirtier laundry than in other developed countries. Various companies market new and improved versions of washers and detergents. Yet, Americans seem to be resistant to manufacturers' innovations in this area. In the U.S., the average washing machine uses about 62 L of water. In Europe, the figure is about 15 L. The average wash cycle of an American wash is about 35 minutes compared to 90 minutes in Europe.

Managerial and Statistical Questions

Virtually all of the statistics cited here are gleaned from studies or surveys.

1. Suppose a study of laundry usage is done in 50 Canadian households that contain washers and dryers.

Water measurements are taken for the number of litres of water used by each washing machine in completing a cycle. The following data are the number of litres used by each washing machine during the washing cycle. Summarize the data so that study findings can be reported.

58	65	62	58	62	65	69	58	54	58
62	62	65	62	58	58	65	54	58	62
62	65	54	58	46	58	62	54	54	62
58	50	62	65	65	58	62	62	62	54
65	62	65	54	62	50	62	58	62	58

2. The average wash cycle using a top-loading machine is 35 minutes. Canadians prefer top-loading machines. Suppose the standard deviation of a wash cycle for a Canadian wash is 5 minutes. Within what range of time do most Canadian wash cycles fall?

3. Is the amount of laundry done by a household each year related in some way to the household income? Suppose eight households of two adults and two children are randomly chosen for a study. Over a year, a record is kept of the mass of clothing washed by each household, and the annual household income is ascertained. From the following study data, determine whether a relationship exists between a household's income and the mass of laundry done.

Mass of Laundry (in kilograms)	Household Income ($1,000s)
549	42
397	31
857	60
658	68
925	110
603	45
299	56
676	72
885	93

Source: Adapted from Emily Nelson, "In Doing Laundry, Americans Cling to Outmoded Ways," *Wall Street Journal*, May 16, 2002, pp. A1 & A10.

In Chapter 2, we presented graphical techniques for organizing and displaying data. For example, we attempted to summarize 40 years of unemployment rates for France with a frequency distribution, a histogram, a frequency polygon, and an ogive. Even though these graphs allow the researcher to make some general observations about the shape and spread of the data, a more complete understanding of the data can be attained by summarizing the data using statistics. This chapter presents such statistical measures, including measures of central tendency, measures of variability, and measures of shape. The computation of these measures is different for ungrouped and grouped data. Hence, we present some measures for both ungrouped and grouped data.

3.1 MEASURES OF CENTRAL TENDENCY: UNGROUPED DATA

One type of measure that is used to describe a set of data is the **measure of central tendency.** Measures of central tendency *yield information about the centre, or middle part, of a group of numbers.* Table 3.1 displays P/E ratio (price-to-earnings ratio, rounded to the nearest whole number) for 20 large Canadian companies in a recent year. For these data, measures of central tendency can yield such information as the average P/E ratio, the middle P/E ratio, and the most frequently occurring P/E ratio. Measures of central tendency do not focus on the span of the data set or how far values are from the middle numbers. The measures of central tendency presented here for ungrouped data are the mean, the median, the mode, percentiles, and quartiles.

MEAN

POINTS OF INTEREST
It is important to distinguish population parameters from sample statistics.

The **arithmetic mean** is *the average of a group of numbers* and is computed by summing all numbers and dividing by the number of numbers. Because the arithmetic mean is so widely used, most statisticians refer to it simply as the *mean.*

The population mean is represented by the Greek letter mu (μ). The sample mean is represented by $\overline{x}$. The formulas for computing the population mean and the sample mean are given in the boxes that follow.

Population Mean	$\mu = \dfrac{\sum x}{N} = \dfrac{x_1 + x_2 + x_3 + \cdots + x_N}{N}$

Sample Mean	$\overline{x} = \dfrac{\sum x}{n} = \dfrac{x_1 + x_2 + x_3 + \cdots + x_n}{n}$

The capital Greek letter sigma (Σ) is commonly used in mathematics to represent a summation of all the numbers in a grouping.* Also, N is the number of terms in the population, and n is the number of terms in the sample. The algorithm for computing a mean is to sum all the numbers in the population or sample and divide by the number of

---

* The mathematics of summations is not discussed here. A more detailed explanation is given in WileyPLUS, Chapter 3.

Table 3.1				
P/E Ratios (rounded to the nearest whole number) for 20 Large Canadian Companies in a Recent Year	12	13	13	11
	9	8	12	3
	9	12	6	20
	13	15	14	13
	27	44	8	22

terms. It is inappropriate to use the mean to analyze data that are not at least interval level in measurement.

Suppose a company has five departments with 24, 13, 19, 26, and 11 workers each. The *population mean* number of workers in each department is 18.6 workers. The computations follow:

$$\sum x = 24 + 13 + 19 + 26 + 11 = 93$$

and

$$\mu = \frac{\sum x}{N} = \frac{93}{5} = 18.6$$

The calculation of a sample mean uses the same algorithm as for a population mean and will produce the same answer if computed on the same data. However, it is inappropriate to compute a sample mean for a population or a population mean for a sample. Because both populations and samples are important in statistics, a separate symbol is necessary for the population mean and for the sample mean.

Consider the P/E ratio data in Table 3.1. The mean P/E ratio for the list of 20 large Canadian companies given in Table 3.1 is 14.2.

MEDIAN

The **median** is *the middle value in an ordered array of numbers.* For an array with an odd number of terms, the median is the middle number. For an array with an even number of terms, the median is the average of the two middle numbers. The following steps are used to determine the median.

1. Arrange the observations in an ordered data array.
2. For an odd number of terms, find the middle term of the ordered array. It is the median.
3. For an even number of terms, find the average of the middle two terms. This average is the median.

Suppose a business researcher wants to determine the median for the following numbers.

15 11 14 3 21 17 22 16 19 16 5 7 19 8 9 20 4

The researcher arranges the numbers in an ordered array.

3 4 5 7 8 9 11 14 15 16 16 17 19 19 20 21 22

Because the array contains 17 terms (an odd number of terms), the median is the middle number, or 15.

If the number 22 is eliminated from the list, the array contains only 16 terms.

3   4   5   7   8   9   11   14   15   16   16   17   19   19   20   21

Now, for an even number of terms, the statistician determines the median by averaging the two middle values, 14 and 15. The resulting median value is 14.5.

Another way to locate the median is by finding the $[(n+1)/2]$th term in an ordered array. For example, if a data set contains 77 terms, the median is the 39th term. That is,

$$\frac{n+1}{2} = \frac{77+1}{2} = \frac{78}{2} = 39\text{th term}$$

This formula is helpful when a large number of terms must be manipulated.

Consider the P/E ratio data in Table 3.1. Because this data set contains 20 values, or $n = 20$, the median for these data is located at the $[(20+1)/2]$th term, or the 10.5th term. This equation indicates that the median is located halfway between the 10th and 11th terms or the average of 12 and 13. Thus, the median P/E ratio for the list of 20 large Canadian companies given in Table 3.1 is 12.5.

The median is unaffected by the magnitude of extreme values. This characteristic is an advantage, because large and small values do not inordinately influence the median. For this reason, the median is often the best measure of location to use in the analysis of variables such as house costs, income, and age. Suppose, for example, that a real estate broker wants to determine the median selling price of 10 houses listed at the following prices.

$67,000	$105,000	$148,000	$5,250,000
91,000	116,000	167,000	
95,000	122,000	189,000	

The median is the average of the two middle terms, $116,000 and $122,000, or $119,000. This price is a reasonable representation of the prices of the 10 houses. Note that the house priced at $5,250,000 did not enter into the analysis other than to count as one of the 10 houses. If the price of the 10th house were $200,000, the results would be the same. However, if all the house prices were averaged, the resulting mean of the original 10 houses would be $635,000, higher than 9 of the 10 individual prices.

A disadvantage of the median is that not all the information from the numbers is used. For example, information about the specific asking price of the most expensive house does not really enter into the computation of the median. The level of data measurement must be at least ordinal for a median to be meaningful.

MODE

The **mode** is *the most frequently occurring value in a set of data.* For the data in Table 3.1, the mode is 13 because the P/E ratio that occurs the most times (4) is 13. Organizing the data into an ordered array (an ordering of the numbers from smallest to largest) helps to locate the mode. The following is an ordered array of the values from Table 3.1.

| 3 | 6 | 8 | 8 | 9 | 9 | 11 | 12 | 12 | 12 |
| 13 | 13 | 13 | 13 | 14 | 15 | 20 | 22 | 27 | 44 |

This grouping makes it easier to see that 13 is the most frequently occurring number.

In the case of a tie for the most frequently occurring value, two modes are listed. Then the data are said to be **bimodal.** If a set of data is not exactly bimodal but contains two values that are more dominant than others, some researchers take the liberty of referring to the data set as bimodal even without an exact tie for the mode. Data sets with more than two modes are referred to as **multimodal.**

In the world of business, the concept of mode is often used in determining sizes. For example, shoe manufacturers might produce inexpensive shoes in three widths only: small, medium, and large. Each width represents a modal width of feet. By reducing the number of sizes to a few modal sizes, companies can reduce total product costs by limiting machine setup costs. Similarly, the garment industry produces shirts, dresses, suits, and many other clothing products in modal sizes. For example, all size M men's shirts in a given lot are produced in the same size. This size is some modal size for medium-sized men.

The mode is an appropriate measure of central tendency for nominal-level data. The mode can be used to determine which category occurs most frequently.

Demonstration Problem 3.1

The number of U.S. cars in service by top car rental companies in a recent year according to *Auto Rental News* follows.

Company	Number of Cars in Service
Enterprise	460,000
Hertz	350,000
ANC Rental Group	322,000
Avis	220,000
Budget	146,000
Dollar	78,000
Thrifty	51,000
U-Save	15,000
Toyota	12,000
Rent-a-Wreck	12,000
Advantage	12,000
Payless	8,000
ACE	8,000

Compute the sample mean, the median, and the mode.

Solution

Mean: The total number of cars in service is $1,694,000 = \Sigma x$.

$$\bar{x} = \frac{\Sigma x}{n} = \frac{1,694,000}{13} = 130,307.7$$

Median: With 13 different companies in this sample, $n = 13$. The median is located at the $[(13 + 1)/2]$th = 7th position. Because the data are already ordered, the 7th term is 51,000, which is the median.

Mode: 12,000

The mean is affected by each and every value, which is an advantage. The mean uses all the data, and each data item influences the mean. It is also a disadvantage because extremely large or small values can cause the mean to be pulled toward the extreme value.

Recall the preceding discussion of the 10 house prices. If the mean is computed for the 10 houses, the mean price is higher than the prices of 9 of the houses because the $5,250,000 house is included in the calculation. The total price of the 10 houses is $6,350,000, and the mean price is $635,000.

The mean is the most commonly used measure of central tendency because it uses each data item in its computation, it is a familiar measure, and it has mathematical properties that make it attractive to use in inferential statistics analysis.

PERCENTILES

Percentiles are *measures of central tendency that divide a group of data into 100 parts.* There are 99 percentiles because it takes 99 dividers to separate a group of data into 100 parts. The *n*th percentile is the value such that at least *n* percent of the data are below that value and at most $(100 - n)$ percent are above that value. Specifically, the 87th percentile is a value such that at least 87% of the data are below the value and no more than 13% are above the value. Percentiles are "stair-step" values, as shown in Figure 3.1, because the 87th percentile and the 88th percentile have no percentile between them. If a plant operator takes a safety examination and 87.6% of the safety exam scores are below that person's score, he or she still scores at only the 87th percentile, even though more than 87% of the scores are lower.

Percentiles are widely used in reporting test results. Almost all students have taken provincial achievement tests in elementary and secondary education. In most cases, the results for these examinations are reported in percentile form and also as raw scores. Shown next is a summary of the steps used in determining the location of a percentile.

STEPS IN DETERMINING THE LOCATION OF A PERCENTILE

1. Organize the numbers into an ascending-order array.
2. Calculate the percentile location (i) by:

$$i = \frac{P}{100}(n)$$

where
P = the percentile of interest
i = percentile location
n = number in the data set
3. Determine the location by either (a) or (b).
   a. If i is a whole number, the Pth percentile is the average of the value at the ith location and the value at the $(i + 1)$th location.
   b. If i is not a whole number, the Pth percentile value is located at the whole-number part of $i + 1$.

For example, suppose you want to determine the 80th percentile of 1,240 numbers. P is 80 and n is 1,240. First, order the numbers from least to greatest. Next, calculate the

Figure 3.1

Stair-Step Percentiles

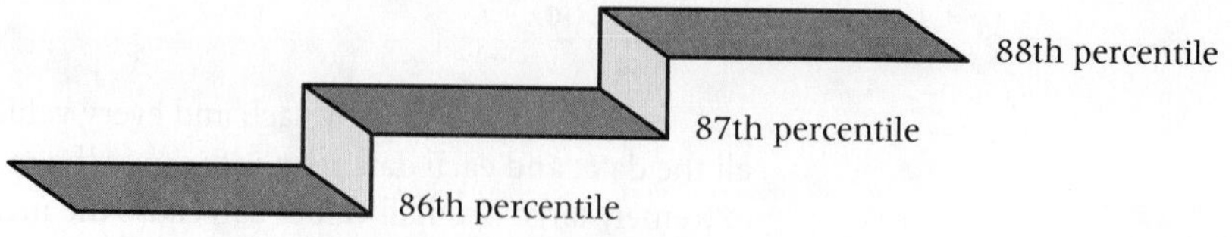

88th percentile

87th percentile

86th percentile

location of the 80th percentile.

$$i = \frac{80}{100}(1{,}240) = 992$$

Because $i = 992$ is a whole number, follow the directions in step 3(a). The 80th percentile is the average of the 992nd number and the 993rd number.

$$P_{80} = \frac{992\text{nd number} + 993\text{rd number}}{2}$$

Demonstration Problem 3.2

Determine the 30th percentile of the following eight numbers: 14, 12, 19, 23, 5, 13, 28, 17.

Solution

For these eight numbers, we want to find the value of the 30th percentile, so $n = 8$ and $P = 30$.

First, organize the data into an ascending-order array.

5	12	13	14	17	19	23	28

Next, compute the value of i.

$$i = \frac{30}{100}(8) = 2.4$$

Because i is not a whole number, use step 3(b). The value of $i + 1$ is $2.4 + 1$, or 3.4. The whole-number part of 3.4 is 3. The 30th percentile is located at the third value. The third value is 13, so 13 is the 30th percentile. Note that a percentile may or may not be one of the data values, as in P_{25}, below.

QUARTILES

Quartiles are *measures of central tendency that divide a group of data into four subgroups or parts.* The three quartiles are denoted as Q_1, Q_2, and Q_3. The first quartile, Q_1, separates the first, or lowest, one fourth of the data from the upper three fourths and is equal to the 25th percentile. The second quartile, Q_2, separates the second fourth of the data from the third fourth. Q_2 is located at the 50th percentile and equals the median of the data. The third quartile, Q_3, divides the first three fourths of the data from the last fourth and is equal to the value of the 75th percentile. These three quartiles are shown in Figure 3.2.

Suppose we want to determine the values of Q_1, Q_2, and Q_3 for the following numbers.

106	109	114	116	121	122	125	129

For this set of data, $n = 8$. The value of Q_1 is found at the 25th percentile, P_{25}, by:

$$i = \frac{25}{100}(8) = 2$$

Figure 3.2

Quartiles

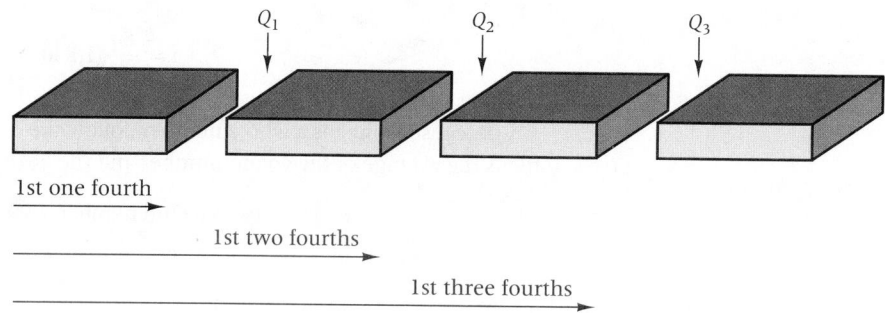

1st one fourth

1st two fourths

1st three fourths

Because i is a whole number, P_{25} is the average of the second and third numbers.

$$P_{25} = \frac{109 + 114}{2} = 111.5$$

The value of Q_1 is $P_{25} = 111.5$. Notice that one fourth, or two, of the values (106 and 109) are less than 111.5.

The value of Q_2 is equal to the median. Because the array contains an even number of terms, the median is the average of the two middle terms.

$$Q_2 = \text{median} = \frac{116 + 121}{2} = 118.5$$

Notice that exactly half of the terms are less than Q_2 and half are greater than Q_2.

The value of Q_3 is determined by P_{75} as follows:

$$i = \frac{75}{100}(8) = 6$$

Because i is a whole number, P_{75} is the average of the sixth and the seventh numbers.

$$P_{75} = \frac{122 + 125}{2} = 123.5$$

The value of Q_3 is $P_{75} = 123.5$. Notice that three fourths, or six, of the values are less than 123.5 and two of the values are greater than 123.5.

Demonstration Problem 3.3

The following shows worldwide revenue for the world's top 16 marketing organizations according to *Advertising Age*. Determine the first, the second, and the third quartiles for these data.

Marketing Organization	Headquarters	Worldwide Revenue ($U.S. millions)
Omnicom Group	New York	10,481
WPP Group	London	10,032
Interpublic Group of Cos.	New York	6,274
Publicis Groupe	Paris	5,107

(continued)

Marketing Organization	Headquarters	Worldwide Revenue ($U.S. millions)
Dentsu	Tokyo	2,889
Havas	Suresnes, France	1,808
Aegis Group	London	1,578
Hakuhodo DY Holdings	Tokyo	1,364
Asatsu-DK	Tokyo	445
MDC Partners	Toronto/New York	444
Carlson Marketing Group	Minneapolis	370
Sapient Corp.	Cambridge, MA	358
Digitas	Boston	341
aQuantive	Seattle	258
Aspen Marketing Services	West Chicago, IL	229
Media Square	London	215

Solution

For 16 marketing organizations, $n = 16$. $Q_1 = P_{25}$ is found by:

$$i = \frac{25}{100}(16) = 4$$

Because i is a whole number, Q_1 is found to be the average of the fourth and fifth values from the bottom:

$$Q_1 = \frac{341 + 358}{2} = 349.5$$

$Q_2 = P_{50}$ = median; with 16 terms, the median is the average of the eighth and ninth terms:

$$Q_2 = \frac{445 + 1,364}{2} = 904.5$$

$Q_3 = P_{75}$ is solved by:

$$i = \frac{75}{100}(16) = 12$$

Q_3 is found by averaging the 12th and 13th terms:

$$Q_3 = \frac{2,889 + 5,107}{2} = 3,998$$

Concept Check

1. Match the measure of central tendency with its correct definition.
   a. Quartiles
   b. Arithmetic mean
   c. Mode
   d. Percentiles
   e. Median

   i. The middle value in an ordered array of numbers
   ii. Measures of central tendency that divide a group of data into 100 parts
   iii. The average of a group of numbers
   iv. The most frequently occurring value in a set of data
   v. Measures of central tendency that divide a group of data into four subgroups or parts

2. What are the differences among the mean, median, and mode? What are the advantages and disadvantages of each measure?

3. Is the arithmetic mean greatly affected by any extreme value or values? Explain.

4. Can you contrive a small set of data with no mode?

3.1   Compute the mean for the following set of numbers.

| 17.3 | 44.5 | 31.6 | 40.0 | 52.8 | 38.8 | 30.1 | 78.5 |

3.2   Compute the mean for the following set of numbers.

| 7 | –2 | 5 | 9 | 0 | –3 | –6 | –7 | –4 | –5 | 2 | –8 |

3.3   Determine the median for the numbers in Problem 3.1.

3.4   Determine the median for the following set of numbers.

| 213 | 345 | 609 | 073 | 167 | 243 | 444 | 524 | 199 | 682 |

3.5   Determine the mode for the following set of numbers.

| 2 | 4 | 8 | 4 | 6 | 2 | 7 | 8 | 4 | 3 | 8 | 9 | 4 | 3 | 5 |

3.6   Compute the 35th percentile, the 55th percentile, Q_1, Q_2, and Q_3 for the following data.

| 16 | 28 | 29 | 13 | 17 | 20 | 11 | 34 | 32 | 27 | 25 | 30 | 19 | 18 | 33 |

3.7   Compute P_{20}, P_{47}, P_{83}, Q_1, Q_2, and Q_3 for the following data.

120	138	97	118	172	144
138	107	94	119	139	145
162	127	112	150	143	80
105	116	142	128	116	171

3.8   The following list shows the 15 largest banking companies in the world and their respective assets as given by *American Banker* before the financial crisis of 2008. Compute the median and the mean assets from this group. Which of these two measures do you think is most appropriate for summarizing these data and why? What is the value of Q_2? Determine the 63rd percentile for the data. Determine the 29th percentile for the data.

Bank	Assets ($U.S. billions)
UBS AG (Zurich)	1,533
Citigroup, Inc (New York)	1,484
Allianz AG (Munich)	1,357
NG Group NV (Amsterdam)	1,357
Mizuho Financial Group (Tokyo)	1,296
HSBC Holdings PLC (London)	1,277
Credit Agricole (Paris)	1,243
BNP Paribas (Paris)	1,233
JPMorgan Chase & Co. (New York)	1,157
Deutsche Bank AG (Frankfurt)	1,144
Royal Bank of Scotland Group PLC (Edinburgh)	1,119

(continued)

Bank	Assets ($U.S. billions)
Bank of America Corp. (Charlotte, NC)	1,110
Barclays PLC (London)	992
Mitsubishi Tokyo Financial Group (Tokyo)	980
Credit Suisse Group (Zurich)	963

3.9 The following lists the 12 largest automakers in the world and the number of vehicles produced by each in a recent year. Compute the median, Q_3, P_{20}, P_{60}, P_{80}, and P_{93} on these data.

Auto Manufacturer	Production
General Motors	9,349,818
Toyota	8,534,690
Volkswagen	6,267,891
Ford	6,247,506
Honda	3,911,814
PSA Peugeot Citroën	3,457,385
Nissan	3,431,398
Fiat	2,679,451
Renault	2,669,040
Hyundai	2,617,725
Suzuki	2,596,316
Chrysler	2,538,624

Source: World Motor Vehicle Production OICA correspondents survey without double counts <http://oica.net/wp-content/uploads/world-ranking-2007.pdf>.

3.10 The following lists the number of fatal accidents by scheduled commercial airlines over a 17-year period according to the Air Transport Association of America. Using these data, compute the mean, median, and mode. What is the value of the third quartile? Determine P_{11}, P_{35}, P_{58}, and P_{67}.

4 4 4 1 4 2 4 3 8 6 4 4 1 4 2 3 3

3.2 MEASURES OF VARIABILITY: UNGROUPED DATA

Measures of central tendency yield information about particular points of a data set. However, business researchers can use another group of analytic tools, **measures of variability,** to *describe the spread or the dispersion of a set of data.* Using measures of variability in conjunction with measures of central tendency makes possible a more complete numerical description of the data.

For example, a company has 25 salespeople in the field, and the median annual sales figure for these people is $1.2 million. Are the salespeople successful as a group or not? The median provides information about the sales of the person in the middle, but what about the other salespeople? Are all of them selling $1.2 million annually, or do the sales figures vary widely, with one person selling $5 million annually and another selling only $150,000 annually? Measures of variability provide the additional information necessary to answer that question.

Figure 3.3 shows three distributions in which the mean of each distribution is the same ($\mu = 50$) but the variabilities differ. Observation of these distributions shows that a measure of variability is necessary to complement the mean value in describing the data.

Figure 3.3

Three Distributions with the Same Mean but Different Dispersions

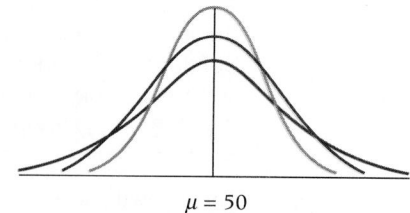

$\mu = 50$

Methods of computing measures of variability differ for ungrouped data and grouped data. This section focuses on seven measures of variability for ungrouped data: range, interquartile range, mean absolute deviation, variance, standard deviation, z scores, and coefficient of variation.

RANGE

The **range** is *the difference between the largest value of a data set and the smallest value of the set.* Although it is usually a single numeric value, some business researchers define the range of data as the ordered pair of smallest and largest numbers (smallest, largest). It is a crude measure of variability, describing the distance to the outer bounds of the data set. It reflects those extreme values because it is constructed from them. An advantage of the range is its ease of computation. One important use of the range is in quality assurance, where the range is used to construct control charts. A disadvantage of the range is that, because it is computed with the values that are on the extremes of the data, it is affected by extreme values, and its application as a measure of variability is limited.

The data in Table 3.1 represent the P/E ratios (rounded to the nearest whole number) for 20 large Canadian companies in a recent year. The lowest P/E ratio was 3 and the highest P/E ratio was 44. The range of the P/E ratios can be computed as the difference of the highest and lowest values:

$$\text{Range} = \text{Highest} - \text{Lowest} = 44 - 3 = 41$$

INTERQUARTILE RANGE

Another measure of variability is the **interquartile range.** The interquartile range is *the range of values between the first and third quartiles.* Essentially, it is the range of the middle 50% of the data and is determined by computing the value of $Q_3 - Q_1$. The interquartile range is especially useful in situations where data users are more interested in values toward the middle and less interested in extremes. In describing a real estate housing market, real estate brokers might use the interquartile range as a measure of housing prices when describing the middle half of the market for buyers who are interested in houses in the midrange. In addition, the interquartile range is used in the construction of box and whisker plots.

Interquartile Range	$Q_3 - Q_1$

The following data indicate the top 10 trading partners of Canada by Canadian exports to the country in a recent year according to Industry Canada.

Country	Exports ($ billions)
United States	377.8
United Kingdom	10.7
Japan	9.7
China	7.9
Mexico	4.6
Germany	4.2
France	3.2
Netherlands	3.2
South Korea	3.2
Belgium	2.3

What is the interquartile range for these data? The process begins by computing the first and third quartiles as follows.

Solving for $Q_1 = P_{25}$ when $n = 10$:

$$i = \frac{25}{100}(10) = 2.5$$

P_{25} is found as the third value from the bottom:

$$Q_1 = P_{25} = 3.2$$

Solving for $Q_3 = P_{75}$:

$$i = \frac{75}{100}(10) = 7.5$$

P_{75} is found as the eighth value from the bottom.

$$Q_3 = P_{75} = 9.7$$

STATISTICS IN BUSINESS TODAY

Telecommuting Statistics

In 2008, WorldatWork reported that of all flexible work arrangements, telecommuting has grown fastest in both the United States and in Canada. In 2007, 30% of American companies and 25% of Canadian companies offered telecommuting as an alternative work arrangement, growing in 2008 to 42% and 40% of the companies in the United States and Canada, respectively. This growth is attributed to rising gas prices, leading-edge technology, and increasing desire for work-life flexibility.

A 2005 study by Statistics Canada revealed that about 1.3 million Canadians are teleworking. A typical telecommuter is male, is 55 years of age or older, has a bachelor's degree or more education, and is married or common-law. The majority of teleworkers (65%) put in just a few hours of work (10 or less) at home each week. Only 3% of teleworkers put in over 40 hours. The average was 17 hours of work at home. About 29% of the telecommuters work in social sciences and education; while only 6% work in sales and service occupations.

A 2001 study by Telework America sponsored by AT&T revealed that teleworking can result in cost savings for companies due to lack of absenteeism, reduced real estate costs, and job retention. It is estimated that employees who telework can save their employers an average of $10,000 each in reduced absenteeism and job retention. Real estate costs can be reduced from 25% to 90%. AT&T saves $3,000 per teleworker annually and has saved $25 million a year in real estate costs through employees who are full-time teleworkers.

Source: Adapted from Ernest Akyeampong, "Working at Home: An Update" at <http://www.statcan.gc.ca/pub/75-001-x/10607/9973-eng.pdf>; Toni Kistner, "Annual Survey Helps Debunk Telework Myths," *Net. Worker*, October 29, 2001, at <http://www.nwfusion.com/net.worker/columnists/2001/1029kistner.html>; WorldatWork.com at <http://www.worldatwork.org/waw/adimLink?id=27072&nonav=yes>; and YouCanWorkFromAnywhere.com at <http://youcanworkfromanywhere.com/index.htm>.

The interquartile range is:

$$Q_3 - Q_1 = 9.7 - 3.2 = 6.5$$

The middle 50% of the exports for the top 10 Canadian trading partners spans a range of 6.5 ($ billions).

MEAN ABSOLUTE DEVIATION, VARIANCE, AND STANDARD DEVIATION

Three other measures of variability are the variance, the standard deviation, and the mean absolute deviation. They are obtained through similar processes and are, therefore, presented together. These measures are not meaningful unless the data are at least interval-level data. The variance and standard deviation are widely used in statistics. Although the standard deviation has some standalone potential, the importance of the variance and standard deviation lies mainly in their role as tools used in conjunction with other statistical devices.

Suppose a small company started a production line to build computers. During the first five weeks of production, the output was 5, 9, 16, 17, and 18 computers, respectively. Which descriptive statistics could the owner use to measure the early progress of production? In an attempt to summarize these figures, the owner could compute a mean.

$$\Sigma x = 5 + 9 + 16 + 17 + 18 = 65 \quad \mu = \frac{\Sigma x}{N} = \frac{65}{5} = 13$$

What is the variability in these five weeks of data? One way for the owner to begin to look at the spread of the data is to subtract the mean from each data value. *Subtracting the mean from each data value* yields the **deviation from the mean** $(x - \mu)$. Table 3.2 shows these deviations for the computer company production. Note that some deviations from the mean are positive and some are negative. Figure 3.4 shows that geometrically the negative deviations represent values that are below (to the left of) the mean and positive deviations represent values that are above (to the right of) the mean.

An examination of deviations from the mean can reveal information about the variability of data. However, the deviations are used mostly as a tool to compute other measures of variability. Note that in both Table 3.2 and Figure 3.4 these deviations total zero. This phenomenon applies to all cases. For a given set of data, the sum of all deviations from the arithmetic mean is always zero. This property requires considering alternative ways to obtain measures of variability.

Sum of Deviations from the Arithmetic Mean is Always Zero	$\Sigma(x - \mu) = 0$

Table 3.2	Number (x)	Deviations from the Mean ($x - \mu$)
Deviations from the Mean for Computer Production	5	$5 - 13 = -8$
	9	$9 - 13 = -4$
	16	$16 - 13 = +3$
	17	$17 - 13 = +4$
	18	$18 - 13 = +5$
	$\Sigma x = 65$	$\Sigma(x - \mu) = 0$

Figure 3.4

Geometric Distances from the Mean (from Table 3.2)

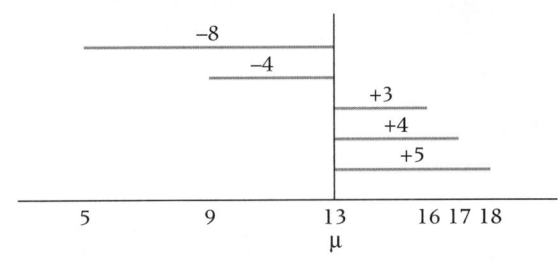

One obvious way to force the sum of deviations to have a nonzero total is to take the absolute value of each deviation around the mean. Utilizing the absolute value of the deviations about the mean makes solving for the mean absolute deviation possible.

MEAN ABSOLUTE DEVIATION

The **mean absolute deviation (MAD)** is *the average of the absolute values of the deviations around the mean for a set of numbers.*

Mean Absolute Deviation	$\text{MAD} = \dfrac{\Sigma|x - \mu|}{N}$

Using the data from Table 3.2, the computer company owner can compute a mean absolute deviation by taking the absolute values of the deviations and averaging them, as shown in Table 3.3. The mean absolute deviation for the computer production data is 4.8.

Because it is computed by using absolute values, the mean absolute deviation is less useful in statistics than other measures of dispersion. However, in the field of forecasting, it is used occasionally as a measure of error.

VARIANCE

Because absolute values are not conducive to easy manipulation, mathematicians developed an alternative mechanism for overcoming the zero-sum property of deviations from the mean. This approach utilizes the square of the deviations from the mean. The result is the variance, an important measure of variability.

Table 3.3

Mean Absolute Deviation for Computer Production Data

x	$x - \mu$	$|x - \mu|$
5	−8	+8
9	−4	+4
16	+3	+3
17	+4	+4
18	+5	+5
$\Sigma x = 65$	$\Sigma(x - \mu) = 0$	$\Sigma|x - \mu| = 24$

$$\text{MAD} = \frac{\Sigma|x - \mu|}{n} = \frac{24}{5} = 4.8$$

Table 3.4		
Computing a Variance and a Standard Deviation from the Computer Production Data		

x	$x - \mu$	$(x - \mu)^2$
5	−8	64
9	−4	16
16	+3	9
17	+4	16
18	+5	25
$\Sigma x = 65$	$\Sigma(x - \mu) = 0$	$\Sigma(x - \mu)^2 = 130$

$$SS_x = \Sigma(x - \mu)^2 = 130$$

$$\text{Variance} = \sigma^2 = \frac{SS_x}{N} = \frac{\Sigma(x - \mu)^2}{N} = \frac{130}{5} = 26.0$$

$$\text{Standard Deviation} = \sigma = \sqrt{\frac{\Sigma(x - \mu)^2}{N}} = \sqrt{\frac{130}{5}} = 5.1$$

The **variance** is *the average of the squared deviations about the arithmetic mean for a set of numbers.* The population variance is denoted by σ^2.

Population Variance	$\sigma^2 = \dfrac{\Sigma(x - \mu)^2}{N}$

Table 3.4 shows the original production numbers for the computer company, the deviations from the mean, and the squared deviations from the mean.

The sum of the squared deviations about the mean of a set of values—called the **sum of squares of x** and sometimes abbreviated as SS_x—is used throughout statistics. For the computer company, this value is 130. Dividing it by the number of data values (5 weeks) yields the variance for computer production:

$$\sigma^2 = \frac{130}{5} = 26.0$$

Because the variance is computed from squared deviations, the final result is expressed in terms of squared units of measurement. Statistics measured in squared units are problematic to interpret. Consider, for example, Mattel Toys attempting to interpret production costs in terms of squared dollars or Research in Motion (RIM) measuring production output variation in terms of squared BlackBerrys. Therefore, when used as a descriptive measure, variance can be considered as an intermediate calculation in the process of obtaining the sample standard deviation.

STANDARD DEVIATION

The standard deviation is a popular measure of variability. It is used both as a separate entity and as a part of other analyses, such as computing confidence intervals and in hypothesis testing (see Chapters 8, 9, and 10).

Population Standard Deviation	$\sigma = \sqrt{\dfrac{\Sigma(x-\mu)^2}{N}}$

The **standard deviation** is *the square root of the variance.* The population standard deviation is denoted by σ.

Like the variance, the standard deviation utilizes the sum of the squared deviations about the mean (SS_x). It is computed by averaging these squared deviations (SS_x/N) and taking the square root of that average. One feature of the standard deviation that distinguishes it from a variance is that the standard deviation is expressed in the same units as the raw data, whereas the variance is expressed in those units squared. Table 3.4 shows the standard deviation for the computer production company: $\sqrt{26}$ or 5.1.

What does a standard deviation of 5.1 mean? The meaning of standard deviation is more readily understood from its use, which is explored in the next section. Although the standard deviation and the variance are closely related and can be computed from each other, differentiating between them is important, because both are widely used in statistics.

MEANING OF STANDARD DEVIATION

What is a standard deviation? What does it do, and what does it mean? The most precise way to define standard deviation is by reciting the formula used to compute it. However, insight into the concept of standard deviation can be gleaned by viewing the manner in which it is applied. Two ways of applying the standard deviation are the empirical rule and Chebyshev's theorem.

EMPIRICAL RULE

The **empirical rule** is an important guideline that *is used to state the approximate percentage of values that lie within a given number of standard deviations from the mean of a set of data if the data are normally distributed.*

The empirical rule is used only for three numbers of standard deviations: 1σ, 2σ, and 3σ. More detailed analysis of other numbers of σ values is presented in Chapter 6. Also discussed in further detail in Chapter 6 is the normal distribution, a unimodal, symmetrical distribution that is bell (or mound) shaped. The requirement that the data be normally distributed contains some tolerance, and the empirical rule generally applies as long as the data are approximately mound shaped.

Empirical Rule*

Distance from the Mean	Values within Distance
$\mu \pm 1\sigma$	68%
$\mu \pm 2\sigma$	95%
$\mu \pm 3\sigma$	99.7%

*Based on the assumption that the data are approximately normally distributed.

If a set of data is normally distributed, or bell-shaped, approximately 68% of the data values are within one standard deviation of the mean, 95% are within two standard deviations, and almost 100% are within three standard deviations.

Figure 3.5

Empirical Rule for One and Two Standard Deviations of Gasoline Prices

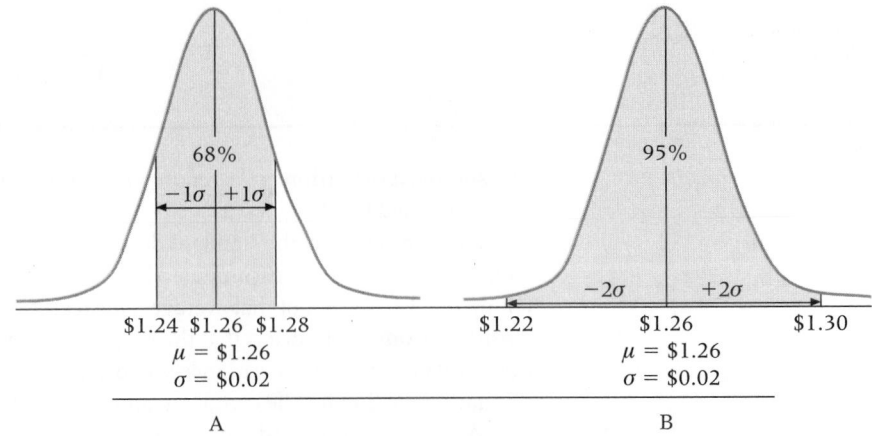

Suppose a recent report states that for Ontario, the average provincewide price of a litre of regular unleaded gasoline is $1.26. Suppose regular unleaded gasoline prices vary across the province with a standard deviation of $0.02 and are normally distributed. According to the empirical rule, approximately 68% of the prices should fall within $\mu \pm 1\sigma$, or $1.26 \pm 1(\$0.02)$. Approximately 68% of the prices should be between $1.24 and $1.28, as shown in Figure 3.5A. Approximately 95% should fall within $\mu \pm 2\sigma$ or $1.26 \pm 2(\$0.02) = \$1.26 \pm \$0.04$, or between $1.22 and $1.30, as shown in Figure 3.5B. Nearly all regular gasoline prices (99.7%) should fall between $1.20 and $1.32 ($\mu \pm 3\sigma$).

Note that with 68% of the gasoline prices falling within one standard deviation of the mean, approximately 32% are outside this range. Because the normal distribution is symmetrical, the 32% can be split in half such that 16% lie in each tail of the distribution. Thus, approximately 16% of the gasoline prices should be less than $1.24 and approximately 16% of the prices should be greater than $1.28.

Many phenomena are distributed approximately in a bell shape, including most human characteristics, such as height and mass; therefore, the empirical rule applies in many situations and is widely used.

Demonstration Problem 3.4

A company produces a lightweight valve that is specified to have a mass of 1,365 g. Unfortunately, because of imperfections in the manufacturing process not all of the valves produced have a mass of exactly 1,365 g. In fact, the masses of the valves produced are normally distributed with a mean mass of 1,365 g and a standard deviation of 294 g. Within what range of masses would approximately 95% of the valve masses fall? Approximately 16% of the masses would be more than what value? Approximately 0.15% of the masses would be less than what value?

Solution

Because the valve masses are normally distributed, the empirical rule applies. According to the empirical rule, approximately 95% of the masses should fall within $\mu \pm 2\sigma = 1,365 \pm 2(294) = 1,365 \pm 588$. Thus, approximately 95% should fall between 777 and 1,953. Approximately 68% of the masses should fall within $\mu \pm 1\sigma$ and 32% should fall outside this interval. Because the normal distribution is symmetrical, approximately 16% should lie above $\mu + 1\sigma = 1,365 + 294 = 1,659$. Approximately 99.7% of the masses should fall within $\mu \pm 3\sigma$ and 0.3% should fall outside this interval. Half of these or 0.15% should lie below $\mu - 3\sigma = 1,365 - 3(294) = 1,365 - 882 = 483$.

CHEBYSHEV'S THEOREM

The empirical rule applies only when data are known to be approximately normally distributed. What do researchers use when data are not normally distributed or when the shape of the distribution is unknown? Chebyshev's theorem applies to all distributions regardless of their shape and thus can be used whenever the data distribution shape is unknown or is nonnormal. Even though Chebyshev's theorem can in theory be applied to data that are normally distributed, the empirical rule is more widely known and is preferred whenever appropriate. Chebyshev's theorem is not a guideline, as is the empirical rule, but rather it is presented in formula format and therefore can be more widely applied. **Chebyshev's theorem** states that *at least* $1 - 1/k^2$ *values will fall within* $\pm k$ *standard deviations of the mean regardless of the shape of the distribution.*

Chebyshev's Theorem	Within k standard deviations of the mean, $\mu \pm k\sigma$, lie at least $$1 - \frac{1}{k^2}$$ proportion of the values. Assumption: $k > 1$

Specifically, Chebyshev's theorem says that at least 75% of all values are within $\pm 2\sigma$ of the mean regardless of the shape of a distribution because if $k = 2$, then $1 - 1/k^2 = 1 - 1/2^2 = 3/4 = 0.75$. Figure 3.6 provides a graphic illustration. In contrast, the empirical rule states that if the data are normally distributed, 95% of all values are within $\mu \pm 2\sigma$. According to Chebyshev's theorem, the percentage of values within three standard deviations of the mean is at least 89%, in contrast to 99.7% for the empirical rule. Because a formula is used to compute proportions with Chebyshev's theorem, any value of k greater than 1 ($k > 1$) can be used. For example, if $k = 2.5$, at least 0.84 of all values are within $\mu \pm 2.5\sigma$, because $1 - 1/k^2 = 1 - 1/(2.5)^2 = 0.84$.

Figure 3.6

Application of Chebyshev's Theorem for Two Standard Deviations

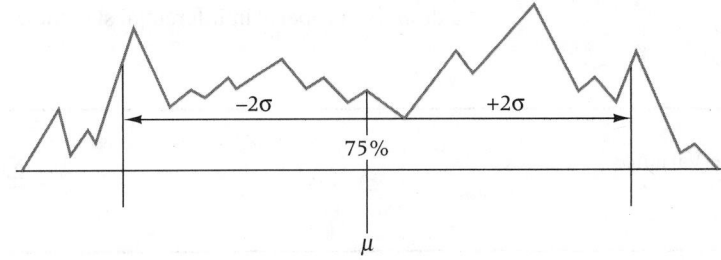

Demonstration Problem 3.5

In the computing industry, the average age of professional employees tends to be younger than in many other business professions. Suppose the average age of a professional employed by a particular computer firm is 28 with a standard deviation of 5 years. A histogram of professional employee ages with this firm reveals that the data are not normally distributed but rather are amassed in the 20s with few workers over 40. Apply Chebyshev's theorem to determine within what range of ages at least 85% of the workers' ages would fall.

Solution

Because the ages are not normally distributed, it is not appropriate to apply the empirical rule; therefore, Chebyshev's theorem must be applied to answer the question.

Chebyshev's theorem states that at least $1 - 1/k^2$ proportion of the values are within $\mu \pm k\sigma$. Because 85% of the values are within this range, let

$$1 - \frac{1}{k^2} = 0.85$$

Solving for k yields

$$0.15 = \frac{1}{k^2}$$
$$k^2 = 6.667$$
$$k = 2.58$$

Chebyshev's theorem says that at least 0.85 of the values are within $\pm 2.58\sigma$ of the mean. For $\mu = 28$ and $\sigma = 5$, at least 0.85, or 85%, of the values are within $28 \pm 2.58(5) = 28 \pm 12.9$ years of age or between 15.1 and 40.9 years old.

POPULATION VERSUS SAMPLE VARIANCE AND STANDARD DEVIATION

POINTS OF INTEREST
Note that in contrast to the population and sample means, the population and sample variances have slightly different formulas.

The sample variance is denoted by s^2 and the sample standard deviation by s. The main use for sample variances and standard deviations is as estimators of population variances and standard deviations. Because of this, computation of the sample variance and standard deviation differs slightly from computation of the population variance and standard deviation. Both the sample variance and sample standard deviation use $n - 1$ in the denominator instead of n because using n in the denominator of a sample variance results in a statistic that tends to underestimate the population variance. While discussion of the properties of *good estimators* is beyond the scope of this text, one of the properties of a good estimator is being *unbiased*. Whereas using n in the denominator of the sample variance makes it a *biased* estimator, using $n - 1$ allows it to be an *unbiased* estimator, which is a desirable property in inferential statistics.

Sample Variance	
	$s^2 = \dfrac{\sum(x - \bar{x})^2}{n - 1}$

Sample Standard Deviation	
	$s = \sqrt{\dfrac{\sum(x - \bar{x})^2}{n - 1}}$

Shown here is a sample of six of the largest accounting firms in Canada and their revenue for a recent year as reported by The Bottom Line: Annual Top 30 Survey of Accounting Firms.

3648067 .517

Firm	Revenue ($ millions)
Deloitte & Touche	1,151.00
KPMG	855.57
PricewaterhouseCoopers	878.60
Ernst & Young	788.00
Grant Thornton	361.00
BDO Dunwoody	260.89

The sample variance and sample standard deviation can be computed by:

x	$(x - \bar{x})^2$
1,151.00	189,361.32
855.57	19,523.54
878.60	26,489.73
788.00	5,206.58
361.00	125,913.79
260.89	206,982.54
$\Sigma x = 4{,}295.06$	$\Sigma(x - \bar{x})^2 = 573{,}477.51$

$$\bar{x} = \frac{4,295.06}{6} = 715.84$$

$$s^2 = \frac{\Sigma(x - \bar{x})^2}{n - 1} = \frac{573,477.51}{5} = 114,695.50$$

$$s = \sqrt{s^2} = \sqrt{114,695.50} = 338.67$$

The sample variance is 114,695.50 and the sample standard deviation is 338.67.

COMPUTATIONAL FORMULAS FOR VARIANCE AND STANDARD DEVIATION

POINTS OF INTEREST
The computational formulas for variance and standard deviation are less cumbersome when used in actual calculations. It is recommended that you use the computational versions of the formulas when you actually do your calculations.

An alternative method of computing variance and standard deviation, sometimes referred to as the computational method or shortcut method, is available. Algebraically,

$$\Sigma(x - \mu)^2 = \Sigma x^2 - \frac{(\Sigma x)^2}{N}$$

and

$$\Sigma(x - \bar{x})^2 = \Sigma x^2 - \frac{(\Sigma x)^2}{n}$$

Substituting these equivalent expressions into the original formulas for variance and standard deviation yields the following computational formulas.

Computational Formulas for Population Variance and Standard Deviation	$$\sigma^2 = \frac{\Sigma x^2 - \dfrac{(\Sigma x)^2}{N}}{N}$$ $$\sigma = \sqrt{\sigma^2}$$

Computational Formulas for Sample Variance and Standard Deviation	$$s^2 = \frac{\sum x^2 - \frac{(\sum x)^2}{n}}{n-1}$$ $$s = \sqrt{s^2}$$

These computational formulas utilize the sum of the x values and the sum of the x^2 values instead of the difference between the mean and each value and computed deviations. In the pre- calculator/computer era, this method was usually faster and easier than using the original formulas.

For situations in which the mean is already computed or is given, alternative forms of these formulas are

$$\sigma^2 = \frac{\sum x^2 - N\mu^2}{N}$$

$$s^2 = \frac{\sum x^2 - n(\bar{x})^2}{n-1}$$

Table 3.5

Computational Formula Calculations of Variance and Standard Deviation for Computer Production Data

x	x^2
5	25
9	81
16	256
17	289
18	324
$\sum x = 65$	$\sum x^2 = 975$

$$\sigma^2 = \frac{975 - \frac{65^2}{5}}{5} = \frac{975 - 845}{5} = \frac{130}{5} = 26$$

$$\sigma = \sqrt{26} = 5.1$$

Using the computational method, the owner of the start-up computer production company can compute a population variance and standard deviation for the production data, as shown in Table 3.5. (Compare these results with those in Table 3.4.)

Demonstration Problem 3.6

The effectiveness of prosecution lawyers can be measured by several variables, including the number of convictions per month, the number of cases handled per month, and the total number of years of conviction per month. A researcher uses a sample of five prosecution lawyers in a city and determines the total number of years of conviction that each lawyer won against defendants during the past month, as reported in the first column in the following tabulations. Compute the mean absolute deviation, the variance, and the standard deviation for these figures.

Solution

The researcher computes the mean absolute deviation, the variance, and the standard deviation for these data in the following manner.

x	$|x - \bar{x}|$	$(x - \bar{x})^2$
55	41	1,681
100	4	16
125	29	841
140	44	1,936
60	36	1,296
$\Sigma x = 480$	$\Sigma|x - \bar{x}| = 154$	$\Sigma(x - \bar{x})^2 = 5,770$

$$\bar{x} = \frac{\Sigma x}{n} = \frac{480}{5} = 96$$

$$\text{MAD} = \frac{154}{5} = 30.8$$

$$s^2 = \frac{5,770}{4} = 1,442.5$$

$$s = \sqrt{s^2} = 37.98$$

She then uses computational formulas to solve for s^2 and s and compares the results.

x	x^2
55	3,025
100	10,000
125	15,625
140	19,600
60	3,600
$\Sigma x = 480$	$\Sigma x^2 = 51,850$

$$s^2 = \frac{51,850 - \dfrac{480^2}{5}}{4} = \frac{51,850 - 46,080}{4} = \frac{5,770}{4} = 1,442.5$$

$$s = \sqrt{1,442.5} = 37.98$$

The results are the same. The sample standard deviation obtained by both methods is 37.98, or 38, years.

z SCORES

A **z score** represents the number of standard deviations a value (x) is above or below the mean of a set of numbers when the data are normally distributed. Using z scores allows a value's raw distance from the mean to be translated into units of standard deviations.

z Score	$$z = \frac{x - \mu}{\sigma}$$

For samples,

$$z = \frac{x - \overline{x}}{s}$$

If a z score is negative, the raw value (x) is below the mean. If the z score is positive, the raw value (x) is above the mean.

For example, for a data set that is normally distributed with a mean of 50 and a standard deviation of 10, suppose a statistician wants to determine the z score for a value of 70. This value ($x = 70$) is 20 units above the mean, so the z value is

$$z = \frac{70 - 50}{10} = +2.00$$

This z score signifies that the raw score of 70 is two standard deviations above the mean. How is this z score interpreted? The empirical rule states that 95% of all values are within two standard deviations of the mean if the data are approximately normally distributed. Figure 3.7 shows that because the value of 70 is two standard deviations above the mean ($z = +2.00$), 95% of the values are between 70 and the value ($x = 30$) that is two standard deviations below the mean, or $z = (30 - 50)/10 = -2.00$. Because 5% of the values are outside the range of two standard deviations from the mean and the normal distribution is symmetrical, 2½% (½ of the 5%) are below the value of 30. Thus 97½% of the values are below the value of 70. Because a z score is the number of standard deviations an individual data value is from the mean, the empirical rule can be restated in terms of z scores.

Between $z = -1.00$ and $z = +1.00$ are approximately 68% of the values.
Between $z = -2.00$ and $z = +2.00$ are approximately 95% of the values.
Between $z = -3.00$ and $z = +3.00$ are approximately 99.7% of the values.

The topic of z scores is discussed more extensively in Chapter 6.

COEFFICIENT OF VARIATION

The **coefficient of variation** is a statistic that is *the ratio of the standard deviation to the mean expressed in percentage* and is denoted CV.

Coefficient of Variation	$$CV = \frac{\sigma}{\mu}(100)$$

The coefficient of variation is essentially a relative comparison of a standard deviation to its mean. The coefficient of variation can be useful in comparing standard deviations that have been computed from data with different means.

Figure 3.7

**Percentage Breakdown
of Scores Two Standard
Deviations from the Mean**

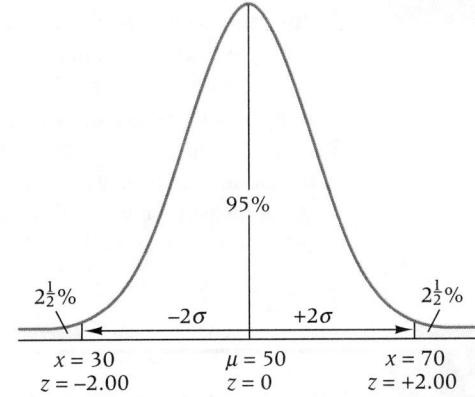

Suppose five weeks of average prices for stock A are 57, 68, 64, 71, and 62. To compute a coefficient of variation for these prices, first determine the mean and standard deviation: $\mu = 64.40$ and $\sigma = 4.84$. The coefficient of variation is:

$$CV_A = \frac{\sigma_A}{\mu_A}(100) = \frac{4.84}{64.40}(100) = 0.075 = 7.5\%$$

The standard deviation is 7.5% of the mean.

Sometimes financial investors use the coefficient of variation or the standard deviation or both as measures of risk. Imagine a stock with a price that never changes. An investor bears no risk of losing money from the price going down because no variability occurs in the price. Suppose, in contrast, that the price of the stock fluctuates wildly. An investor who buys at a low price and sells for a high price can make a nice profit. However, if the price drops below what the investor buys it for, the stock owner is subject to a potential loss. The greater the variability is, the more the potential for loss. Hence, investors use measures of variability such as standard deviation or coefficient of variation to determine the risk of a stock. What does the coefficient of variation tell us about the risk of a stock that the standard deviation does not?

Suppose the average prices for a second stock, B, over these same five weeks are 12, 17, 8, 15, and 13. The mean for stock B is 13.00 with a standard deviation of 3.03. The coefficient of variation can be computed for stock B as:

$$CV_B = \frac{\sigma_B}{\mu_B}(100) = \frac{3.03}{13}(100) = 0.233 = 23.3\%$$

The standard deviation for stock B is 23.3% of the mean.

With the standard deviation as the measure of risk, stock A is more risky over this period of time because it has a larger standard deviation. However, the average price of stock A is almost five times as much as that of stock B. Relative to the amount invested in stock A, the standard deviation of $4.84 may not represent as much risk as the standard deviation of $3.03 for stock B, which has an average price of only $13.00. The coefficient of variation reveals the risk of a stock in terms of the size of the standard deviation relative to the size of the mean (in percentage). Stock B has a coefficient of variation that is nearly three times as much as the coefficient of variation for stock A. Using the coefficient of variation as a measure of risk indicates that stock B is riskier.

The choice of whether to use a coefficient of variation or raw standard deviations to compare multiple standard deviations is a matter of preference. The coefficient of variation also provides an optional method of interpreting the value of a standard deviation.

Concept Check

1. The more dispersed the data are, the larger the range, the interquartile range, the variance, and the standard deviation will be. True or false? Explain.
2. If a set of data contains observations that are all the same, the range, the interquartile range, the variance, and the standard deviation will all be 0. True or false? Explain.
3. Can the values for the range, the interquartile range, the variance, and the standard deviation ever be negative? Explain.
4. What measure of variability can be used to compare variables when they have different units of measurement?

3.2 Problems

3.11　A data set contains the following seven values.

　　　6　　2　　4　　9　　1　　3　　5

　　　a.　Find the range.
　　　b.　Find the mean absolute deviation.
　　　c.　Find the population variance.
　　　d.　Find the population standard deviation.
　　　e.　Find the interquartile range.
　　　f.　Find the z score for each value.

3.12　A data set contains the following eight values.

　　　4　　3　　0　　5　　2　　9　　4　　5

　　　a.　Find the range.
　　　b.　Find the mean absolute deviation.
　　　c.　Find the sample variance.
　　　d.　Find the sample standard deviation.
　　　e.　Find the interquartile range.

3.13　A data set contains the following six values.

　　　12　　23　　19　　26　　24　　23

　　　a.　Find the population standard deviation using the formula containing the mean (the original formula).
　　　b.　Find the population standard deviation using the computational formula.
　　　c.　Compare the results. Which formula was faster to use? Which formula do you prefer? Why do you think the computational formula is sometimes referred to as the "shortcut" formula?

3.14　Use a calculator or a computer to find the sample variance and sample standard deviation for the following data.

57	88	68	43	93
63	51	37	77	83
66	60	38	52	28
34	52	60	57	29
92	37	38	17	67

3.15 Use a calculator or a computer to find the population variance and population standard deviation for the following data.

123	090	546	378
392	280	179	601
572	953	749	075
303	468	531	646

3.16 Determine the interquartile range for the following data.

44	18	39	40	59
46	59	37	15	73
23	19	90	58	35
82	14	38	27	24
71	25	39	84	70

3.17 According to Chebyshev's theorem, at least what proportion of the data will be within $\mu \pm k\sigma$ for each value of k?
a. $k = 2$
b. $k = 2.5$
c. $k = 1.6$
d. $k = 3.2$

3.18 Compare the variability of the following two sets of data by using both the population standard deviation and the population coefficient of variation.

Data Set 1	Data Set 2
49	159
82	121
77	138
54	152

3.19 A sample of 12 small accounting firms reveals the following numbers of professionals per office.

7	10	9	14	11	8
5	12	8	3	13	6

a. Determine the mean absolute deviation.
b. Determine the variance.
c. Determine the standard deviation.
d. Determine the interquartile range.
e. What is the z score for the firm that has six professionals?
f. What is the coefficient of variation for this sample?

3.20 The following, supplied by Marketing Intelligence Service, is a list of the companies with the most new products in a recent year.

Company	Number of New Products
Avon Products	768
L'Oreal	429

(continued)

Company	Number of New Products
Unilever U.S.	323
Revlon	306
Garden Botanika	286
Philip Morris	262
Procter & Gamble	215
Nestlé	172
Paradiso	162
Tsumura International	148
Grand Metropolitan	145

a. Find the range.
b. Find the mean absolute deviation.
c. Find the population variance.
d. Find the population standard deviation.
e. Find the interquartile range.
f. Find the z score for Nestlé.
g. Find the coefficient of variation.

3.21   A distribution of numbers is approximately bell-shaped. If the mean of the numbers is 125 and the standard deviation is 12, between what two numbers would approximately 68% of the values fall? Between what two numbers would 95% of the values fall? Between what two values would 99.7% of the values fall?

3.22   Some numbers are not normally distributed. If the mean of the numbers is 38 and the standard deviation is 6, what proportion of values would fall between 26 and 50? What proportion of values would fall between 14 and 62? Between what two values would 89% of the values fall?

3.23   According to Chebyshev's theorem, how many standard deviations from the mean would include at least 80% of the values?

3.24   The time needed to assemble a particular piece of furniture with experience is normally distributed with a mean time of 43 minutes. If 68% of the assembly times are between 40 and 46 minutes, what is the value of the standard deviation? Suppose 99.7% of the assembly times are between 35 and 51 minutes and the mean is still 43 minutes. What is the value of the standard deviation now? Suppose the time needed to assemble another piece of furniture is not normally distributed and that the mean assembly time is 28 minutes. What is the value of the standard deviation if at least 77% of the assembly times are between 24 and 32 minutes?

3.25   Environmentalists are concerned about emissions of sulphur dioxide into the air. The average number of days per year in which sulphur dioxide levels exceed 150 mg/m³ in Milan, Italy, is 29. The number of days per year in which emission limits are exceeded is normally distributed with a standard deviation of 4.0 days. What percentage of the years would average between 21 and 37 days of excess emissions of sulphur dioxide? What percentage of the years would exceed 37 days? What percentage of the years would exceed 41 days? In what percentage of the years would there be fewer than 25 days with excess sulphur dioxide emissions?

3.26   The *Runzheimer Guide* publishes a list of the most inexpensive cities in the world for the business traveller. Listed are the 10 most inexpensive cities with their respective per diem costs. Use this list to calculate the z scores for Bordeaux, Montreal, Edmonton, and Hamilton. Treat this list as a sample.

City	Per Diem ($)
Hamilton, Ontario	97
London, Ontario	109
Edmonton, Alberta	111
Jakarta, Indonesia	118
Ottawa	120
Montreal	130
Halifax, Nova Scotia	132
Winnipeg, Manitoba	133
Bordeaux, France	137
Bangkok, Thailand	137

3.3 MEASURES OF CENTRAL TENDENCY AND VARIABILITY: GROUPED DATA

Grouped data do not provide information about individual values. Hence, measures of central tendency and variability for grouped data must be computed differently from those for ungrouped or raw data.

MEASURES OF CENTRAL TENDENCY

Three measures of central tendency are presented here for grouped data: the mean, the median, and the mode.

MEAN

POINTS OF INTEREST
The class midpoint and class frequency become the relevant quantities when data have been grouped.

For ungrouped data, the mean is computed by summing the data values and dividing by the number of values. With grouped data, the specific values are unknown. What can be used to represent the data values? The midpoint of each class interval is used to represent all the values in a class interval. This midpoint is weighted by the frequency of values in that class interval. The mean for grouped data is then computed by summing the products of the class midpoint and the class frequency for each class and dividing that sum by the total number of frequencies. The formula for the mean of grouped data follows.

Mean of Grouped Data

$$\mu_{\text{grouped}} = \frac{\sum fM}{N} = \frac{\sum fM}{\sum f} = \frac{f_1 M_1 + f_2 M_2 + \cdots + f_i M_i}{f_1 + f_2 + \cdots + f_i}$$

where

i = the number of classes
f = class frequency
M = class midpoint
N = total frequencies (total number of data values)

	Class Interval	Frequency
Table 3.6		
Frequency Distribution of the Unemployment Rates of France	1–under 3	16
	3–under 5	2
	5–under 7	4
	7–under 9	3
	9–under 11	9
	11–under 13	6

Table 3.6 gives the frequency distribution of the unemployment rates of France from Table 2.2. To find the mean of these data, we need Σf and ΣfM. The value of Σf can be determined by summing the values in the frequency column. To calculate ΣfM, we must first determine the values of M, or the class midpoints. Next we multiply each of these class midpoints by the frequency in that class interval, f, resulting in fM. Summing these values of fM yields the value of ΣfM.

Table 3.7 contains the calculations needed to determine the group mean. The group mean for the unemployment data is 6.25. Remember that because each class interval was represented by its class midpoint rather than by actual values, the group mean is only approximate.

MEDIAN

The *median* for grouped data is computed as the value attributed to the 50th percentile in the distribution of observations. The formula for the median of grouped data follows.

Median of Grouped Data

$$\text{median}_{\text{grouped}} = l + \left(\frac{\frac{N}{2} - F}{f} \right) w$$

where

l = lower endpoint of the class containing the median
w = width of the class containing the median
f = frequency of the class containing the median
F = cumulative frequency of classes preceding the class containing the median
N = total frequencies (total number of data values)

Using the data from Table 3.7, we see that 18 observations are in the class interval 3–under 5 or lower, while 22 observations are in the class interval 5–under 7 or lower. The observation 20, 50% of $N = 40$, is thus in the class corresponding to 5–under 7. We need to travel $N/2 - F = 20 - 18 = 2$ out of 4 units along the interval 5–under 7. Therefore, the median is computed as $5 + (2/4) \times 2 = 5 + 1 = 6$. The median unemployment rate is 6%. Remember that this is an approximate value since we are using grouped data and not the actual observations.

MODE

The *mode* for grouped data is *the class midpoint of the modal class. The modal class is the class interval with the greatest frequency.* Using the data from Table 3.7, the 1–under 3 class

Table 3.7	Class Interval	Frequency (f)	Class Midpoint (M)	fM
Calculation of Grouped Mean	1–under 3	16	2	32
	3–under 5	2	4	8
	5–under 7	4	6	24
	7–under 9	3	8	24
	9–under 11	9	10	90
	11–under 13	6	12	72
		$\sum f = N = 40$		$\sum fm = 250$

$$\mu = \frac{\sum fM}{\sum f} = \frac{250}{40} = 6.25$$

interval contains the greatest frequency, 16. Thus, the modal class is 1–under 3. The class midpoint of this modal class is 2. Therefore, the mode for the frequency distribution shown in Table 3.7 is 2. The modal unemployment rate is 2%.

MEASURES OF VARIABILITY

Two measures of variability for grouped data are presented here: the variance and the standard deviation. Again, the standard deviation is the square root of the variance. Both measures have original and computational formulas.

Formulas for Population Variance and Standard Deviation of Grouped Data

Original Formula

$$\sigma^2 = \frac{\sum f(M - \mu)^2}{N}$$

$$\sigma = \sqrt{\sigma^2}$$

Computational Version

$$\sigma^2 = \frac{\sum fM^2 - \frac{\left(\sum fM\right)^2}{N}}{N}$$

where:

f = frequency
M = class midpoint
$N = \sum f$, or total frequencies of the population
μ = grouped mean for the population

Formulas for Sample Variance and Standard Deviation of Grouped Data

Original Formula

$$s^2 = \frac{\sum f\left(M - \bar{x}\right)^2}{n - 1}$$

$$s = \sqrt{s^2}$$

Computational Version

$$s^2 = \frac{\sum fM^2 - \frac{\left(\sum fM\right)^2}{n}}{n - 1}$$

where:

f = frequency
M = class midpoint
$N = \sum f$, or total of the frequencies of the population
μ = grouped mean for the sample

Table 3.8

Calculating Grouped Variance and Standard Deviation with the Original Formula

Class Interval	f	M	fM	$M - \mu$	$(M - \mu)^2$	$f(M - \mu)^2$
1–under 3	16	2	32	−4.25	18.063	289.008
3–under 5	2	4	8	−2.25	5.063	10.126
5–under 7	4	6	24	−0.25	0.063	0.252
7–under 9	3	8	24	1.75	3.063	9.189
9–under 11	9	10	90	3.75	14.063	126.567
11–under 13	6	12	72	5.75	33.063	198.378

$$\Sigma f = N = 40 \qquad \Sigma fm = 250 \qquad \Sigma f(M - \mu)^2 = 633.520$$

$$\mu = \frac{\Sigma fM}{\Sigma f} = \frac{250}{40} = 6.25$$

$$\sigma^2 = \frac{\Sigma f(M - m)^2}{N} = \frac{633.520}{40} = 15.838$$

$$\sigma = \sqrt{15.838} = 3.980$$

For example, let us calculate the variance and standard deviation of the French unemployment data grouped as a frequency distribution in Table 3.6. If the data are treated as a population, the computations are as follows.

For the original formula, the computations are given in Table 3.8. The method of determining σ^2 and σ by using the computational formula is shown in Table 3.9. In either case, the variance of the unemployment data is 15.838 (squared percent) and the standard deviation is 3.98%. As with the computation of the grouped mean, the class midpoint is used to represent all values in a class interval. This approach may or may not be appropriate, depending on whether the average value in a class is at the midpoint. If this situation does not occur, then the variance and the standard deviation are only approximations. Because grouped statistics are usually computed without knowledge of the actual data, the statistics computed may potentially be only approximations.

Table 3.9

Calculating Grouped Variance and Standard Deviation with the Computational Formula

Class Interval	f	M	fM	fM^2
1–under 3	16	2	32	64
3–under 5	2	4	8	32
5–under 7	4	6	24	144
7–under 9	3	8	24	192
9–under 11	9	10	90	900
11–under 13	6	12	72	864

$$f = N = 40 \qquad fM = 250 \qquad fM^2 = 2{,}196$$

$$\sigma^2 = \frac{\Sigma fM^2 - \frac{(\Sigma fM)^2}{n}}{n} = \frac{2{,}196 - \frac{250^2}{40}}{40} = \frac{2{,}196 - 1{,}562.5}{40} = \frac{633.5}{40} = 15.838$$

$$\sigma = \sqrt{15.838} = 3.980$$

Demonstration Problem 3.7

Compute the mean, median, mode, variance, and standard deviation on the following sample data.

Class Interval	Frequency
10–under 15	6
15–under 20	22
20–under 25	35
25–under 30	29
30–under 35	16
35–under 40	8
40–under 45	4
45–under 50	2

Solution

The mean is computed as follows.

Class	f	M	fM
10–under 15	6	12.5	75.0
15–under 20	22	17.5	385.0
20–under 25	35	22.5	787.5
25–under 30	29	27.5	797.5
30–under 35	16	32.5	520.0
35–under 40	8	37.5	300.0
40–under 45	4	42.5	170.0
45–under 50	2	47.5	95.0
	$\Sigma f = n = 122$		$\Sigma fM = 3{,}130.0$

$$\bar{x} = \frac{\Sigma fM}{\Sigma f} = \frac{3{,}130}{122} = 25.66$$

The grouped mean is 25.66.

Using the data from the table, we see that 28 observations are in the class interval 15–under 20 or lower. We also see that 63 observations are in the class interval 20–under 25 or lower. The observation 61 (50% of $N = 122$) is thus in the class corresponding to 20–under 25. Computing $N/2 - F$ gives $61 - 28 = 33$. Therefore, the grouped median is $20 + (33/35) \times 5 = 20 + 4.71 = 24.71$.

The grouped mode can be determined by finding the class midpoint of the class interval with the greatest frequency. The class with the greatest frequency is 20–under 25 with a frequency of 35. The midpoint of this class is 22.5, which is the grouped mode.

The variance and standard deviation can be found as shown next. First, use the original formula.

Class	f	M	$M - \bar{x}$	$(M - \bar{x})^2$	$f(M - \bar{x})^2$
10–under 15	6	12.5	−13.16	173.19	1,039.14
15–under 20	22	17.5	−8.16	66.59	1,464.98
20–under 25	35	22.5	−3.16	9.99	349.65
25–under 30	29	27.5	1.84	3.39	98.31
30–under 35	16	32.5	6.84	46.79	748.64
35–under 40	8	37.5	11.84	140.19	1,121.52
40–under 45	4	42.5	16.84	283.59	1,134.36
45–under 50	2	47.5	21.84	476.99	953.98

$$\Sigma f = n = 122 \qquad\qquad \Sigma f(M - \bar{x})^2 = 6,910.58$$

$$s^2 = \frac{\Sigma f(M - \bar{x})^2}{n - 1} = \frac{6,910.58}{121} = 57.11$$

$$s = \sqrt{57.11} = 7.56$$

Next, use the computational formula.

Class	f	M	fM	fM^2
10–under 15	6	12.5	75.0	937.50
15–under 20	22	17.5	385.0	6,737.50
20–under 25	35	22.5	787.5	17,718.75
25–under 30	29	27.5	797.5	21,931.25
30–under 35	16	32.5	520.0	16,900.00
35–under 40	8	37.5	300.0	11,250.00
40–under 45	4	42.5	170.0	7,225.00
45–under 50	2	47.5	95.0	4,512.50

$$\Sigma f = n = 122 \qquad \Sigma fM = 3,130.0 \qquad \Sigma fM^2 = 87,212.50$$

$$s^2 = \frac{\Sigma fM^2 - \frac{(\Sigma fM)^2}{n}}{n - 1} = \frac{87,212.5 - \frac{3,130^2}{122}}{121} = \frac{6,910.58}{121} = 57.11$$

$$s = \sqrt{57.11} = 7.56$$

The sample variance is 57.11 and the standard deviation is 7.56.

Concept Check

1. Are measures of central tendency and variability exact or only approximate when we are dealing with grouped data? Explain.

3.3 Problems

3.27 Compute the mean, median, and mode for the following data.

Class	f
0–under 2	39
2–under 4	27
4–under 6	16
6–under 8	15
8–under 10	10
10–under 12	8
12–under 14	6

3.28   Compute the mean, median, and mode for the following data.

Class	f
1.2–under 1.6	220
1.6–under 2.0	150
2.0–under 2.4	90
2.4–under 2.8	110
2.8–under 3.2	280

3.29   Determine the population variance and standard deviation for the following data by using the original formula.

Class	f
20–under 30	7
30–under 40	11
40–under 50	18
50–under 60	13
60–under 70	6
70–under 80	4

3.30   Determine the sample variance and standard deviation for the following data by using the computational formula.

Class	f
5–under 9	20
9–under 13	18
13–under 17	8
17–under 21	6
21–under 25	2

3.31   A random sample of voters in Regina, Saskatchewan, is classified by age group, as shown by the following data.

Age Group	Frequency
18–under 24	17
24–under 30	22
30–under 36	26
36–under 42	35
42–under 48	33
48–under 54	30
54–under 60	32
60–under 66	21
66–under 72	15

a.   Calculate the mean of the data.
b.   Calculate the median.
c.   Calculate the mode.
d.   Calculate the variance.
e.   Calculate the standard deviation.

3.32   The following data represent the number of appointments made per 15-minute interval by telephone solicitation for a lawn-care company. Assume these are population data.

Number of Appointments	Frequency of Occurrence
0–under 1	31
1–under 2	57
2–under 3	26
3–under 4	14
4–under 5	6
5–under 6	3

a.   Calculate the mean of the data.
b.   Calculate the median.
c.   Calculate the mode.
d.   Calculate the variance.
e.   Calculate the standard deviation.

3.33   NAV Canada publishes figures on the busiest airports in Canada. The following frequency distribution has been constructed from these figures for a recent year. Assume these are population data.

Number of Aircraft Movements	Number of Airports
0–under 50,000	18
50,000–under 100,000	4
100,000–under 150,000	7
150,000–under 200,000	7
200,000–under 250,000	2
250,000–under 300,000	0
300,000–under 350,000	1
350,000–under 400,000	0
400,000–under 450,000	1

a.   Calculate the mean of these data.
b.   Calculate the median.
c.   Calculate the mode.
d.   Calculate the variance.
e.   Calculate the standard deviation.

3.34   The frequency distribution shown represents the weekly mortgage interest rates for a 60-week period. Determine the average weekly rate from these data. The mean computed from the original ungrouped data was 7.04% and the standard deviation was 0.24%. How do your answers for these grouped data compare? Why might they differ?

Weekly Mortgage Interest Rate	f
6.25%–under 6.50%	1
6.50%–under 6.75%	5
6.75%–under 7.00%	21
7.00%–under 7.25%	20
7.25%–under 7.50%	12
7.50%–under 7.75%	1

3.4 MEASURES OF SHAPE

Measures of shape are *tools that can be used to describe the shape of a distribution of data.* In this section, we examine two measures of shape, skewness and kurtosis. We also look at box and whisker plots.

SKEWNESS

A distribution of data in which the right half is a mirror image of the left half is said to be *symmetrical.* One example of a symmetrical distribution is the normal distribution, or bell curve, which is presented in more detail in Chapter 6.

Skewness is when *a distribution is asymmetrical or lacks symmetry.* The distribution in Figure 3.8 has no skewness because it is symmetric. Figure 3.9 shows a distribution that is skewed left, or negatively skewed, and Figure 3.10 shows a distribution that is skewed right, or positively skewed.

The skewed portion is the long, thin part of the curve. Many researchers use skewed distribution to denote that the data are sparse at one end of the distribution and piled up at the other end. Instructors sometimes refer to a grade distribution as skewed, meaning that few students scored at one end of the grading scale, and many students scored at the other end.

Figure 3.8

Symmetrical Distribution

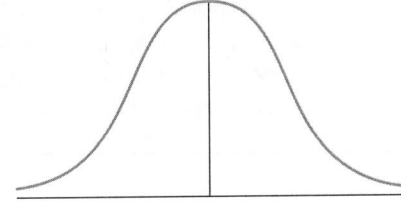

Figure 3.9

Distribution Skewed Left, or Negatively Skewed

Figure 3.10

Distribution Skewed Right, or Positively Skewed

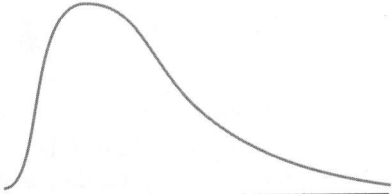

SKEWNESS AND THE RELATIONSHIP OF THE MEAN, MEDIAN, AND MODE

The concept of skewness helps us to understand the relationship of the mean, median, and mode. In a unimodal distribution (distribution with a single peak or mode) that is skewed, the mode is the apex (high point) of the curve and the median is the middle

Figure 3.11

Relationship of Mean, Median, and Mode

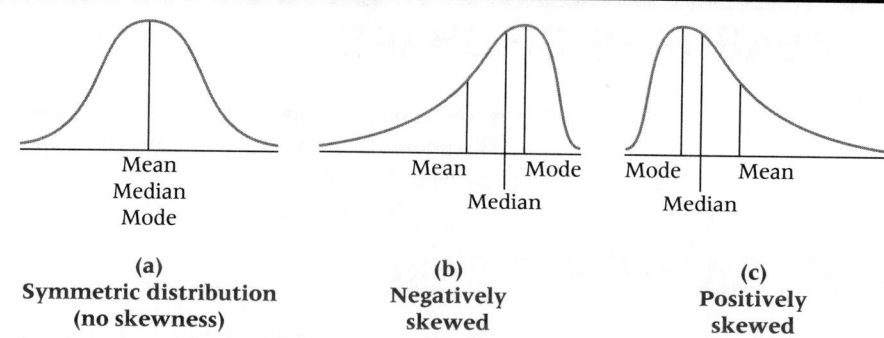

(a)	(b)	(c)
Symmetric distribution (no skewness)	**Negatively skewed**	**Positively skewed**

value. The mean tends to be located toward the tail of the distribution, because the mean is affected by all values, including the extreme ones. A bell-shaped or normal distribution with the mean, median, and mode all at the centre of the distribution has no skewness. Figure 3.11 displays the relationship of the mean, median, and mode for different types of skewness.

COEFFICIENT OF SKEWNESS

Karl Pearson (1857–1936), an English statistician, is credited with developing at least two coefficients of skewness (along with other significant statistical concepts) that can be used to determine the degree of skewness in a distribution. We present one of these coefficients here, referred to as a Pearsonian **coefficient of skewness.** This coefficient *compares the mean and median in light of the magnitude of the standard deviation.* Note that if the distribution is symmetrical, the mean and median are the same value and hence the coefficient of skewness is equal to zero.

Coefficient of Skewness

$$S_k = \frac{3(\mu - M_d)}{\sigma}$$

where
S_k = coefficient of skewness
M_d = median

Suppose, for example, that a distribution has a mean of 29, a median of 26, and a standard deviation of 12.3. The coefficient of skewness is computed as:

$$S_k = \frac{3(29 - 26)}{12.3} = +0.73$$

Because the value of S_k is positive, the distribution is positively skewed. If the value of S_k is negative, the distribution is negatively skewed. The greater the magnitude of S_k, the more skewed is the distribution.

KURTOSIS

Kurtosis *describes the amount of peakedness of a distribution.* Distributions that are tall and thin are referred to as **leptokurtic** distributions (from Greek leptós meaning thin). Distributions that are flat and spread out are referred to as **platykurtic** distributions

Figure 3.12

Types of Kurtosis

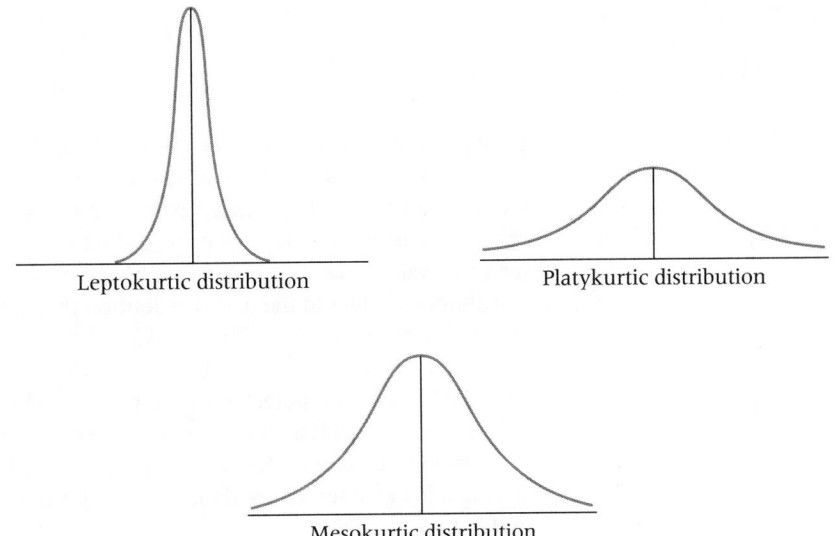

Leptokurtic distribution

Platykurtic distribution

Mesokurtic distribution

(from Greek platýs meaning flat). Between these two types are distributions that are more "normal" in shape, referred to as **mesokurtic** distributions (from Greek mésos meaning middle). These three types of kurtosis are illustrated in Figure 3.12.

BOX AND WHISKER PLOTS

Another way to describe a distribution of data is by using a box and whisker plot. A **box and whisker plot,** sometimes called a *box plot,* is *a diagram that utilizes the upper and lower quartiles along with the median and the two most extreme values to depict a distribution graphically.* The plot is constructed by using a box to enclose the median. This *box* is extended outward from the median along a continuum to the lower and upper quartiles, enclosing not only the median but also the middle 50% of the data. From the lower and upper quartiles, lines referred to as *whiskers* are extended out from the box toward the outermost data values. The box and whisker plot is determined from five specific numbers.

1. The median (Q_2)
2. The lower quartile (Q_1)
3. The upper quartile (Q_3)
4. The smallest value in the distribution
5. The largest value in the distribution

The box of the plot is determined by locating the median and the lower and upper quartiles on a continuum. A box is drawn around the median with the lower and upper quartiles (Q_1 and Q_3) as the box endpoints. These box endpoints (Q_1 and Q_3) are referred to as the *hinges* of the box.

Next, the value of the interquartile range (IQR) is computed by $Q_3 - Q_1$. The interquartile range includes the middle 50% of the data and should equal the length of the box. However, here the interquartile range is used outside the box also. At a distance of $1.5 \cdot$ IQR outward from the lower and upper quartiles are what are referred to as *inner fences*. A *whisker,* a line segment, is drawn from the lower hinge of the box outward to the smallest data value. A second whisker is drawn from the upper hinge of the box outward to the largest data value. The inner fences are established as follows:

$$Q_1 - 1.5 \cdot \text{IQR}$$
$$Q_3 + 1.5 \cdot \text{IQR}$$

If data fall beyond the inner fences, then *outer* fences can be constructed:

$$Q_1 - 3.0 \cdot IQR$$
$$Q_3 + 3.0 \cdot IQR$$

Figure 3.13 shows the features of a box and whisker plot.

Data values outside the mainstream of values in a distribution are viewed as *outliers*. Outliers can be merely the more extreme values of a data set. However, sometimes outliers occur due to measurement or recording errors. Other times they are values so unlike the other values that they should not be considered in the same analysis as the rest of the distribution. Values in the data distribution that are outside the inner fences but within the outer fences are referred to as *mild outliers*. Values that are outside the outer fences are called *extreme outliers*. Thus, one of the main uses of a box and whisker plot is to identify outliers. In some computer-produced box and whisker plots, the whiskers are drawn to the largest and smallest data values within the inner fences. An asterisk is then printed for each data value located between the inner and outer fences to indicate a mild outlier. Values outside the outer fences are indicated by a zero on the graph. These values are extreme outliers.

Figure 3.13

Box and Whisker Plot

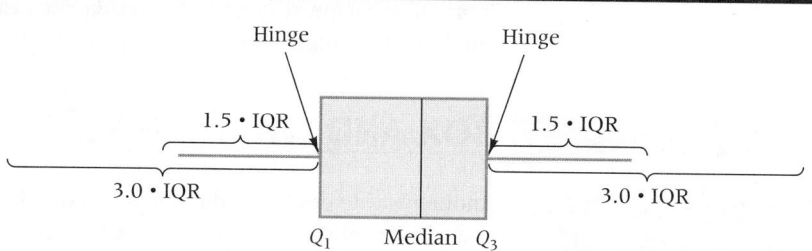

Table 3.10

Data for Box and Whisker Plot

71	87	82	64	72	75	81	69
76	79	65	68	80	73	85	71
70	79	63	62	81	84	77	73
82	74	74	73	84	72	81	65
74	62	64	68	73	82	69	71

Another use of box and whisker plots is to determine whether a distribution is skewed. The location of the median in the box can relate information about the skewness of the middle 50% of the data. If the median is located on the right side of the box, then the middle 50% are skewed to the left. If the median is located on the left side of the box, then the middle 50% are skewed to the right. By examining the length of the whiskers on each side of the box, a business researcher can make a judgement about the skewness of the outer values. If the longest whisker is to the right of the box, then the outer data are skewed to the right, and vice versa. We shall use the data given in Table 3.10 to construct a box and whisker plot.

After organizing the data into an ordered array, as shown in Table 3.11, it is relatively easy to determine the values of the lower quartile (Q_1), the median, and the upper quartile (Q_3). From these, the value of the interquartile range can be computed.

The hinges of the box are located at the lower and upper quartiles, 69 and 80.5. The median is located within the box at distances of 4 from the lower quartile and 6.5 from the upper quartile. The distribution of the middle 50% of the data is skewed right, because the median is nearer to the lower or left hinge. The inner fence is constructed by:

$$Q_1 - 1.5 \cdot IQR = 69 - 1.5(11.5) = 69 - 17.25 = 51.75$$

and

$$Q_3 + 1.5 \cdot IQR = 80.5 + 1.5(11.5) = 80.5 + 17.25 = 97.75$$

The whiskers are constructed by drawing a line segment from the lower hinge outward to the smallest data value and a line segment from the upper hinge outward to the largest data value. An examination of the data reveals that no data values in this set of numbers are outside the inner fence. The whiskers are constructed outward to the lowest value, which is 62, and to the highest value, which is 87.

To construct an outer fence, we calculate $Q_1 - 3 \cdot IQR$ and $Q_3 + 3 \cdot IQR$, as follows:

$$Q_1 - 3 \cdot IQR = 69 - 3(11.5) = 69 - 34.5 = 34.5$$
$$Q_3 + 3 \cdot IQR = 80.5 + 3(11.5) = 80.5 + 34.5 = 115.0$$

Figure 3.14 is the computer printout for this box and whisker plot.

Figure 3.14

Box and Whisker Plot

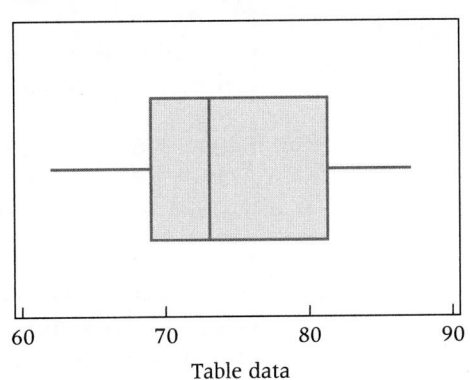

Table data

Table 3.11

Data in Ordered Array with Quartiles and Median

87	85	84	84	82	82	82	81	81	81
80	79	79	77	76	75	74	74	74	73
73	73	73	72	72	71	71	71	70	69
69	68	68	65	65	64	64	63	62	62

$Q_1 = 69$
$Q_2 = $ median $= 73$
$Q_3 = 80.5$
$IQR = Q_3 - Q_1 = 80.5 - 69 = 11.5$

Concept Check

1. What is meant by the property of the shape of a distribution of data?
2. If the mode of a data set is smaller than the median, which in turn is smaller than the mean, the distribution of data is _____ skewed.
3. Sketch a box and whisker plot for each of the following distributions of data: a) symmetric distribution, b) negatively skewed, and c) positively skewed.
4. Should the empirical rule (presented in Section 3.2) be used for data sets that are highly skewed? Explain.

3.4 Problems

3.35   On a certain day, the average closing share price of a group of stocks on the Toronto Stock Exchange is $35 (to the nearest dollar). If the median value is $33 and the mode is $21, is the distribution of these share prices skewed? If so, how?

3.36   A local hotel offers ballroom dancing on Friday nights. A researcher observes the customers and estimates their ages. Discuss the skewness of the distribution of ages if the mean age is 51, the median age is 54, and the modal age is 59.

3.37   The sales volumes for the top real estate brokerage firms in Canada for a recent year were analyzed using descriptive statistics. The mean annual dollar volume for these firms was $551 million, the median was $319 million, and the standard deviation was $959 million. Compute the value of the Pearsonian coefficient of skewness and discuss its meaning. Is the distribution skewed? If so, to what extent?

3.38   Suppose the following data are the ages of Internet users obtained from a sample. Use these data to compute a Pearsonian coefficient of skewness. What is the meaning of the coefficient?

41	15	31	25	24
23	21	22	22	18
30	20	19	19	16
23	27	38	34	24
19	20	29	17	23

3.39   Construct a box and whisker plot on the following data. Do the data contain any outliers? Is the distribution of data skewed?

540	690	503	558	490	609
379	601	559	495	562	580
510	623	477	574	588	497
527	570	495	590	602	541

3.40   Suppose a consumer group asked 18 consumers to keep a yearly log of their shopping practices and that the following data represent the number of coupons used by each consumer over the yearly period. Use the data to construct a box and whisker plot. List the median, Q_1, Q_3, the endpoints for the inner fences, and the endpoints for the outer fences. Discuss the skewness of the distribution of these data and point out any outliers.

81	68	70	100	94	47	66	70	82
110	105	60	21	70	66	90	78	85

3.5 DESCRIPTIVE STATISTICS ON THE COMPUTER

Excel yields extensive descriptive statistics. Even though Excel can compute individual statistics such as a mean or a standard deviation, it can also produce multiple descriptive statistics at one time. Excel's descriptive statistics output associated with the computer production data presented earlier in this section is displayed in Figure 3.15. The Excel output contains the mean, the median, the mode, the sample standard deviation, the sample variance, and the range. The descriptive statistics feature on this computer package yields a lot of useful information about a data set.

Figure 3.15

Excel Output for the Computer Production Problem

COMPUTER PRODUCTION DATA

	A	B
1	Mean	13
2	Standard error	2.5495
3	Median	16
4	Mode	N/A
5	Standard deviation	5.7009
6	Sample variance	32.5
7	Kurtosis	−1.7112
8	Skewness	−0.8096
9	Range	13
10	Minimum	5
11	Maximum	18
12	Sum	65
13	Count	5

LAUNDRY STATISTICS

The descriptive statistics presented in this chapter are excellent for summarizing and presenting data sets in more concise formats. For example, question 1 of the managerial and statistical questions in the Decision Dilemma reports water measurements for 50 U.S. households. Using Excel, many of the descriptive statistics presented in this chapter can be applied to these data. The result is shown in Figure 3.16.

This computer output shows that the average water usage is 59.54 L with a standard deviation of about 4.742 L. The median is 62 L with a range of 23 L (46 to 69). The first quartile is 58 L and the third quartile is 62 L. The mode is also 62 L. The skewness measures show that the data are slightly skewed to the left. Applying Chebyshev's theorem to the mean and

standard deviation shows that at least 88.9% of the measurements should fall between 45.31 L and 73.77 L. An examination of the data and the minimum and maximum reveals that 100% of the data actually fall within these limits.

According to the Decision Dilemma, the mean wash cycle time is 35 minutes with a standard deviation of 5 minutes. If the wash cycle times are approximately normally distributed, we can apply the empirical rule. According to the empirical rule, 68% of the times would fall within 30 and 40 minutes, 95% of the times would fall within 25 and 45 minutes, and 99.7% of the times would fall within 20 and 50 minutes. If the data are not normally distributed, Chebyshev's theorem reveals that at least 75% of the times should fall between 25 and 45 minutes and 88.9% should fall between 20 and 50 minutes.

Figure 3.16

Excel Descriptive Statistics

WATER USAGE

	A	B
1	Mean	59.54
2	Standard error	0.671
3	Median	62
4	Mode	62
5	Standard deviation	4.742
6	Sample variance	22.485
7	Kurtosis	0.264
8	Skewness	−0.531
9	Range	23
10	Minimum	46
11	Maximum	69
12	Sum	2977
13	Count	50

KEY CONSIDERATIONS

In describing a body of data to an audience, it is best to use whatever measures it takes to present a full picture of the data. By limiting the descriptive measures used, the business researcher may give the audience only part of the picture and can skew the way the receiver understands the data. For example, if a researcher presents only the mean, the audience will have no insight into the variability of the data; in addition, the mean might be inordinately large or small because of extreme values. Likewise, the choice of the median precludes a picture that includes the extreme values. Using the mode can cause the receiver of the information to focus only on values that occur often.

At least one measure of variability is usually needed with at least one measure of central tendency for the audience to begin to understand what the data look like. Unethical researchers might be tempted to present only the descriptive measure that will convey the picture of the data that they want the audience to see. Ethical researchers will instead use any and all methods that will present the fullest, most informative picture possible from the data.

A politician in the U.S. has been quoted as having said that "Demographers are academics who can statistically prove that the average person in Miami is born Cuban and dies Jewish…."* People are more likely to reach this type of conclusion if incomplete or misleading descriptive statistics are provided by researchers.

*Alan L. Otten, "People Patterns/Odds and Ends," *The Wall Street Journal*, June 29, 1992, p. B1. Reprinted by permission of *The Wall Street Journal* © 1992, Dow Jones & Company, Inc. All Rights Reserved Worldwide.

Why Statistics Is Relevant

Descriptive statistics are used to describe the basic features of the data under study in a manageable form. They help us to simplify large amounts of data in a sensible way and, in a sense, reduce the data to a simpler summary. Together with the charts and graphs presented in Chapter 2, descriptive statistics form the basis of virtually every quantitative analysis of data. Thus, the importance of descriptive statistics rests in their utility as tools for interpreting and analyzing data. For instance, measures of central tendency from different years can be directly compared to one another. The mean unemployment rate in 2009 can be compared to the mean unemployment rate in 2010 to see which year had a higher mean. In a similar light, means from several years may be compared to one another in order to learn how the mean unemployment rate has changed over the past 10 years. If the mean has increased, this change may be linked to significant economic changes. Measures of dispersion can also be useful in determining which provinces in Canada have unusually high unemployment rates across different years. We note that every time you try to describe a set of data with a single measure, you run the risk of distorting the original data or losing some important detail. However, even when we consider the limitations, descriptive statistics provide a powerful summary that may enable key analyses and comparisons.

SUMMARY

1. Statistical descriptive measures include measures of central tendency, measures of variability, and measures of shape. It is important to keep in mind that measures of central tendency and measures of variability are computed differently for ungrouped and grouped data.
2–4. Measures of central tendency are useful in describing data because they communicate information about the more central portions of the data. The most common measures of central tendency are the three Ms: mode, median, and mean. In addition, percentiles and quartiles are measures of central tendency.

The mode is the most frequently occurring value in a set of data. If two values tie for the mode, the data are bimodal. Data sets can be multimodal. Among other things, the mode is used in business to determine sizes.

The median is the middle term in an ordered array of numbers containing an odd number of terms. For an array with an even number of terms, the median is the average of the two middle terms. The expression $(n + 1)/2$ specifies the location of the median. A median is unaffected by the magnitude of extreme values. This characteristic makes the median a most useful and appropriate measure of location in reporting such things as income, age, and prices of houses.

The arithmetic mean is widely used and is usually what researchers are referring to when they use the word *mean*. The arithmetic mean is the average. The population mean and the sample mean are computed in the same way but are denoted by different symbols. The arithmetic mean is affected by every value and can be inordinately influenced by extreme values.

Percentiles divide a set of data into 100 groups, which means 99 percentiles are needed. Quartiles divide data into four groups. The three quartiles are Q_1, which is the lower quartile; Q_2, which is the middle quartile and equals the median; and Q_3, which is the upper quartile.

Measures of variability are statistical tools used in combination with measures of central tendency to describe data. Measures of variability provide a description of data that measures of central tendency cannot give: information about the spread of the data values. These measures include the range, mean absolute deviation, variance, standard deviation, interquartile range, z scores, and coefficient of variation for ungrouped data.

One of the most elementary measures of variability is the range. It is the difference between the largest and smallest values. Although the range is easy to compute, it has limited usefulness. The interquartile range is the difference between the third and first quartiles. It equals the range of the middle 50% of the data.

The mean absolute deviation (MAD) is computed by averaging the absolute values of the deviations from the mean. The mean absolute deviation provides the magnitude of the average deviation but without specifying its direction. The mean absolute deviation has limited use in statistics, but interest is growing for the use of MAD in the field of forecasting.

5. Variance is widely used as a tool in statistics but is used little as a standalone measure of variability. The variance is the average of the squared deviations about the mean. The square root of the variance is the standard deviation. It is also a widely used tool in statistics and is used more often than the variance as a standalone measure. Note that the formulas for computing the variance and standard deviation for a population and for a sample are slightly different.

The standard deviation is best understood by examining its applications in determining where

data are in relation to the mean. The empirical rule and Chebyshev's theorem are statements about the proportions of data values that are within various numbers of standard deviations from the mean.

The empirical rule reveals the percentage of values that are within one, two, or three standard deviations of the mean for a set of data. The empirical rule applies only if the data are in a bell-shaped distribution. According to the empirical rule, approximately 68% of all values of a normal distribution are within plus or minus one standard deviation of the mean. Ninety-five percent of all values are within two standard deviations either side of the mean, and virtually all values are within three standard deviations of the mean.

Chebyshev's theorem also delineates the proportion of values that are within a given number of standard deviations from the mean. However, it applies to any distribution. According to Chebyshev's theorem, at least $1 - 1/k^2$ values are within k standard deviations of the mean. The z score represents the number of standard deviations a value is from the mean for normally distributed data.

The coefficient of variation is the ratio of a standard deviation to its mean, given as a percentage. It is especially useful in comparing standard deviations or variances that represent data with different means.

6. Some measures of central tendency and some measures of variability are presented for grouped data, where the class midpoints and the class frequencies become the key quantities in the calculations rather than the actual data. These measures include mean, median, mode, variance, and standard deviation. Generally, these measures are only approximate for grouped data because the values of the actual raw data are unknown.

7. Two measures of shape are skewness and kurtosis. Skewness is the lack of symmetry in a distribution. If a distribution is skewed, it is stretched in one direction or the other. The skewed part of a graph is its long, thin portion. One measure of skewness is the Pearsonian coefficient of skewness. Kurtosis is the degree of peakedness of a distribution. A tall, thin distribution is referred to as leptokurtic. A flat distribution is platykurtic, and a distribution with a more normal peakedness is said to be mesokurtic.

A box and whisker plot is a graphical depiction of a distribution. The plot is constructed by using the median, the lower quartile, and the upper quartile. Box and whisker plots are rather sophisticated and can yield information about skewness and outliers.

KEY TERMS

arithmetic mean	interquartile range	median	range
bimodal	kurtosis	mesokurtic	skewness
box and whisker plot	leptokurtic	mode	standard deviation
Chebyshev's theorem	mean absolute deviation	multimodal	sum of squares of x
coefficient of skewness	(MAD)	percentiles	variance
coefficient of variation (CV)	measures of central tendency	platykurtic	z score
deviation from the mean	measures of shape	quartiles	
empirical rule	measures of variability		

FORMULAS

Population mean (ungrouped)

$$\mu = \frac{\sum x}{N}$$

Sample mean (ungrouped)

$$\bar{x} = \frac{\sum x}{n}$$

Mean absolute deviation

$$\text{MAD} = \frac{\sum |x - \mu|}{N}$$

Population variance (ungrouped)

$$\sigma^2 = \frac{\sum (x - \mu)^2}{N}$$

$$\sigma^2 = \frac{\sum x^2 - \frac{(\sum x)^2}{N}}{N}$$

$$\sigma^2 = \frac{\sum x^2 - N\mu^2}{N}$$

Population standard deviation (ungrouped)

$$\sigma = \sqrt{\sigma^2}$$

$$\sigma = \sqrt{\frac{\sum (x - u)^2}{N}}$$

$$\sigma = \sqrt{\frac{\sum x^2 - \frac{(\sum x)^2}{N}}{N}}$$

$$\sigma = \sqrt{\frac{\sum x^2 - N\mu^2}{N}}$$

Grouped mean

$$\mu_{\text{grouped}} = \frac{\sum fM}{N}$$

Population variance (grouped)

$$\sigma^2 = \frac{\sum f(M - \mu)^2}{N} = \frac{\sum fM^2 - \frac{(\sum fM)^2}{N}}{N}$$

Population standard deviation (grouped)

$$\sigma = \sqrt{\frac{\sum f(M - \mu)^2}{N}} = \sqrt{\frac{\sum fM^2 - \frac{(\sum fM)^2}{N}}{N}}$$

Sample variance

$$s^2 = \frac{\sum (x - \bar{x})^2}{n - 1}$$

$$s^2 = \frac{\sum x^2 - \frac{(\sum x)^2}{n}}{n - 1}$$

$$s^2 = \frac{\sum x^2 - n(\bar{x})^2}{n - 1}$$

Sample standard deviation

$$s = \sqrt{s^2}$$

$$s = \sqrt{\frac{\sum (x - \bar{x})^2}{n - 1}}$$

$$s = \sqrt{\frac{\sum x^2 - \frac{(\sum x)^2}{n}}{n - 1}}$$

$$s = \sqrt{\frac{\sum x^2 - n(\bar{x})^2}{n - 1}}$$

Chebyshev's theorem

$$1 - \frac{1}{k^2}$$

z score

$$z = \frac{x - \mu}{\sigma}$$

Coefficient of variation

$$cv = \frac{\sigma}{\mu}(100)$$

Interquartile range

$$IQR = Q_3 - Q_1$$

Sample variance (grouped)

$$s^2 = \frac{\sum f(M - \bar{x})^2}{n - 1} = \frac{\sum fM^2 - \frac{(\sum fM)^2}{n}}{n - 1}$$

Sample standard deviation (grouped)

$$s = \sqrt{\frac{\sum f(M - \bar{x})^2}{n - 1}} = \sqrt{\frac{\sum fM^2 - \frac{(\sum fM)^2}{n}}{n - 1}}$$

Pearsonian coefficient of skewness

$$s_k = \frac{3(\mu - M_d)}{\sigma}$$

SUPPLEMENTARY PROBLEMS

Calculating the Statistics

3.41 The latest Canadian census asked every household to report information on each person living there. Suppose for a sample of 30 households selected, the number of people living in each was reported as follows:

2 3 1 2 6 4 2 1 5 3 2 3 1 2 2
1 3 1 2 2 4 2 1 2 8 3 2 1 1 3

Compute the mean, median, mode, range, lower and upper quartiles, and interquartile range for these data.

3.42 The latest Canadian census asked every household for the age of each person living there. Suppose that a sample of 40 households taken from the census data showed the age of the first person recorded on the census form to be as follows.

42	29	31	38	55	27	28
33	49	70	25	21	38	47
63	22	38	52	50	41	19
22	29	81	52	26	35	38
29	31	48	26	33	42	58
40	32	24	34	25		

Compute P_{10}, P_{80}, Q_1, Q_3, the interquartile range, and the range for these data.

3.43 According to the National Association of Investment Clubs, PepsiCo is the most popular stock with investment clubs in the U.S., with 11,388 clubs holding

PepsiCo stock. Intel is a close second, followed by Motorola. For the following list of the most popular stocks with investment clubs, compute the mean, median, P_{30}, P_{60}, P_{90}, Q_1, Q_3, range, and interquartile range.

Company	Number of Clubs Holding Stock
PepsiCo	11,388
Intel	11,019
Motorola	9,863
Tricon Global Restaurants	9,168
Merck & Co.	8,687
AFLAC	6,796
Diebold	6,552
McDonald's	6,498
Coca-Cola	6,101
Lucent Technologies	5,563
Home Depot	5,414
Clayton Homes	5,390
RPM	5,033
Cisco Systems	4,541
General Electric	4,507
Johnson & Johnson	4,464
Microsoft	4,152
Wendy's International	4,150
Walt Disney	3,999
AT&T	3,619

3.44 Shown here are revenues of the top 10 fastest growing companies as reported by *Canadian Business* in a recent year. Use this population data to compute a mean and a standard deviation for these top 10 companies.

Company	Revenue ($ millions)
Rentcash Inc.	154.17
Digital Oilfield Inc.	11.93
Rutter Inc.	74.30
Digital Rapids Corp.	14.77
BTI Photonic Systems Inc.	12.53
Savanna Energy Services Corp.	247.08
Solium Capital Inc.	8.70
Optimal Geomatics Inc.	16.49
PEER 1 Network Enterprises Inc.	60.73
Knor Plast Inc.	6.57

3.45 We show the companies with the largest oil-refining capacity in the world according to the *Petroleum Intelligence Weekly.* Use these population data and answer the questions.

Company	Capacity (barrels per day in 1,000s)
ExxonMobil	6,300
Royal Dutch/Shell	3,791
China Petrochemical	2,867
Petroleos de Venezuela	2,437
Saudi Arabian Oil	1,970
BP Amoco	1,965
Chevron	1,661
Petrobras	1,540
Texaco	1,532
Petroleos Mexicanos (Pemex)	1,520
National Iranian Oil	1,092

a. What are the values of the mean and the median? Compare the answers and state which you prefer as a measure of location for these data and why.
b. What are the values of the range and inter-quartile range? How do they differ?
c. What are the values of the variance and standard deviation for these data?
d. What is the z score for Texaco? What is the z score for ExxonMobil? Interpret these z scores.
e. Calculate the Pearsonian coefficient of skewness and comment on the skewness of this distribution.

3.46 Following are the three-year annualized returns for the 14 leading mutual funds with a three-diamond to five-diamond risk rating in a recent year.

Fund	Three-Year Annualized Return (%)
Chou RRSP	17.10
CI Harbour Fund	13.43
CI Signature Select Canadian Seg I	21.15
Concordia Equity	13.93
Co-operators Cdn Conser Focused Eq	11.35
Dynamic Focus Plus Canadian	6.15
Empire Equity Growth	13.43
Generations Cdn Equity (Bissett)	10.16
Generations Cdn Equity (Trimark)	9.09
GWL Equity (M) DSC	9.05
Investors Canadian Equity	7.11
Investors Retirement Gwth. Port.	6.85
MLI Aggress Asset Alloc GIFe 1	5.34
Trimark Canadian SC	10.79

Source: Statistics for Managers Using Microsoft Excel, D. Levine et al., 2004, p. 111, Pearson, reprinted with permission by Pearson Education Canada Inc.

a. Calculate the mean, median, and mode.
b. Calculate the range, interquartile range, mean absolute deviation, sample variance, and sample standard deviation.
c. Compute the Pearsonian coefficient of skewness for these data.
d. Sketch a box and whisker plot.

3.47 The radio music listener market is diverse. Listener formats might include adult contemporary, album rock, top 40, oldies, rap, country and western, classical, and jazz. In targeting audiences, market researchers need to be concerned about the ages of the listeners attracted to particular formats. Suppose a market researcher surveyed a sample of 170 listeners of oldies radio stations and obtained the following age distribution.

Age	Frequency
15–under 20	9
20–under 25	16
25–under 30	27
30–under 35	44
35–under 40	42
40–under 45	23
45–under 50	7
50–under 55	2

a. What are the mean, median, and modal ages of oldies listeners?
b. What are the variance and standard deviation of the ages of oldies listeners?

3.48 A research agency administers a demographic survey to 90 telemarketing companies to determine the size of their operations. When asked to report how many employees now work in their telemarketing operation, the companies gave responses ranging from 1 to 100. The agency's analyst organizes the figures into a frequency distribution.

Number of Employees Working in Telemarketing	Number of Companies
0–under 20	32
20–under 40	16
40–under 60	13
60–under 80	10
80–under 100	19

a. Compute the mean, median, and mode for this distribution.
b. Compute the sample standard deviation for these data.

Testing Your Understanding

3.49 Financial analysts like to use the standard deviation as a measure of risk for a stock. The greater the deviation in a share price over time, the more risky it is to invest in the stock. However, the average prices of some shares are considerably higher than the average price of others, allowing for the potential of a greater standard deviation of price. For example, a standard deviation of $5.00 on a $10.00 share is considerably different from a $5.00 standard deviation on a $40.00 share. In this situation, a coefficient of variation might provide insight into risk. Suppose stock X costs an average of $32.00 per share and has shown a standard deviation of $3.45 for the past 60 days. Suppose stock Y costs an average of $84.00 per share and has shown a standard deviation of $5.40 for the past 60 days. Use the coefficient of variation to determine the variability for each stock.

3.50 The Polk Company reported that the average age of a car on U.S. roads in a recent year was 7.5 years. Suppose the distribution of ages of cars on U.S. roads is approximately bell-shaped. If 99.7% of the ages are between 1 year and 14 years, what is the standard deviation of car age? Suppose the standard deviation is 1.7 years and the mean is 7.5 years. Between what two values would 95% of the car ages fall?

3.51 According to a *Human Resources* report, a worker in the industrial countries spends on average 419 minutes a day on the job. Suppose the standard deviation of time spent on the job is 27 minutes.
a. If the distribution of time spent on the job is approximately bell-shaped, between what two times would 68% of the figures be? 95%? 99.7%?
b. If the shape of the distribution of times is unknown, approximately what percentage of the times would be between 359 and 479 minutes?
c. Suppose a worker spent 400 minutes on the job. What would that worker's z score be and what would it tell the researcher?

3.52 During the 1990s, businesses were expected to show a lot of interest in Central and Eastern European countries. As new markets began to open, Canadian business people needed a better understanding of the market potential there. The following are the per capita GDP figures (rounded to the nearest hundred) for eight of these European countries published by the International Monetary Fund. **Note:** The per capita GDP for Canada is $U.S.45,400.

Country	Per Capita GDP ($U.S.)
Albania	4,100
Bulgaria	6,900
Croatia	15,600
Czech Republic	21,000
Hungary	15,500
Poland	13,800
Romania	9,300
Bosnia/Herzegovina	4,600

a. Compute the mean and standard deviation for Albania, Bulgaria, Croatia, and Czech Republic.
b. Compute the mean and standard deviation for Hungary, Poland, Romania, and Bosnia/Herzegovina.
c. Use a coefficient of variation to compare the two standard deviations. Treat the data as population data.

3.53 According to a recent census, the average annual salary of a worker in Edmonton, Alberta, is $30,468. Suppose the median annual salary for a worker in this group is $26,721 and the mode is $25,000. Is the distribution of salaries for this group skewed? If so, how and why? Which of these measures of central tendency would you use to describe these data? Why?

3.54 The top 20 Canadian ports in a recent year, ranked by total tonnage (in millions of tonnes), were as follows.

Port	Total Tonnage
Vancouver, B.C.	80,383.4
Port Hawkesbury, N.S.	31,659.1
Come-By-Chance, N.L.	27,779.0
Montréal/Contrecoeur, Que.	24,655.3
Saint John, N.B.	23,596.9
Sept-Îles/Pointe-Noire, Que.	23,342.9
Québec/Lévis, Que.	23,076.6
Port-Cartier, Que.	17,747.3
Newfoundland Offshore, N.L.	15,172.6
Nanticoke, Ont.	13,863.8
Halifax, N.S.	13,731.5
Fraser River, B.C.	13,327.0
Hamilton, Ont.	12,642.6
Thunder Bay, Ont.	8,331.2
Prince Rupert, B.C.	7,619.5
Baie-Comeau, Que.	6,507.5
Sorel, Que.	6,288.3
Howe Sound, B.C.	5,837.1
Sault Ste. Marie, Ont.	5,748.2
Windsor, Ont.	5,517.7

Source: Data from Statistics Canada, Shipping in Canada, 2006, Catalogue no. 54-205-X, http://www.statcan.gc.ca/pub/54-205-x/54-205-x2006000-eng.pdf

a. Construct a box and whisker plot for these data.
b. Discuss the shape of the distribution from the plot.
c. Are there outliers?
d. What are they and why do you think they are outliers?

3.55 *Runzheimer International* publishes data on overseas business travel costs. They report that the average per diem total for a business traveller in Paris, France, is $349. Suppose the shape of the distribution of the per diem costs of a business traveller to Paris is unknown, but that 53% of the per diem figures are between $317 and $381. What is the value of the standard deviation? The average per diem total for a business traveller in Moscow is $415. If the shape of the distribution of per diem costs of a business

traveller in Moscow is unknown and if 83% of the per diem costs in Moscow lie between $371 and $459, what is the standard deviation?

Interpreting the Output

3.56 *American Banker* compiled a list of the top 100 banking companies in the world according to total assets. Leading the list is the Bank of Tokyo–Mitsubishi, followed by the Deutsche Bank. The following Excel descriptive statistics output lists the variable total assets ($U.S. millions) for these 100 banks. Study the output and describe in your own words what you can learn about the assets of these top 100 world banks.

	A	B
1	**Top World Banks**	
2	Mean	213496.77
3	Standard error	12972.00
4	Median	164573
5	Mode	N/A
6	Standard deviation	129720
7	Sample variance	16827278273
8	Kurtosis	1.05
9	Skewness	1.18
10	Range	615029
11	Minimum	76891
12	Maximum	691920
13	Sum	21349677
14	Count	100

3.57 *Hispanic Business, Inc.,* compiled a list of the top advertisers cultivating the Hispanic market in the U.S. These data ($U.S. millions) were entered into a spreadsheet and analyzed. Study the output and describe the expenditures of these top Hispanic market advertisers.

Variable: Media Expenditures

Mean	7.8560
Standard deviation	5.8860
Variance	34.6455
Skewness	3.6214
Kurtosis	17.7851
N	50
Minimum	3.25
1st Quartile	4.50
Median	5.75
3rd Quartile	8.625
Maximum	40.00

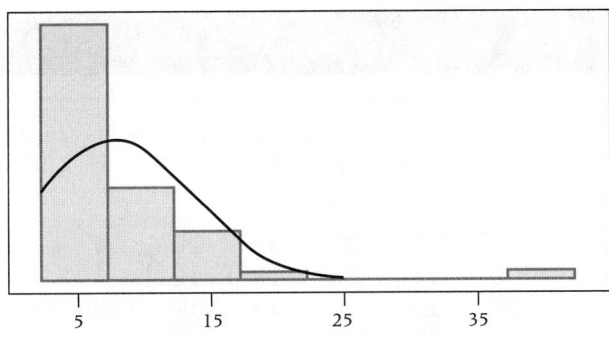

3.58 Many large companies are located around the world. The number of employees for 46 of the largest employers with headquarters outside the United States were analyzed with Excel's descriptive statistics feature. The data follow. Summarize what you have learned about the number of employees for these companies by studying this output.

	A	B
1	**Large Employers Outside of the United States**	
2	Mean	183327.1304
3	Standard error	9480.8850
4	Median	157670
5	Mode	135000
6	Standard deviation	64302.4905
7	Sample variance	4134810279
8	Kurtosis	0.8266
9	Skewness	1.2996
10	Range	256106
11	Minimum	125894
12	Maximum	382000
13	Sum	8433048
14	Count	46

3.59 The Competitive Media Reporting and Publishers Information Bureau compiled a list of the top 25 advertisers in the U.S. for a recent year. The total advertising expenditures for each company ($U.S. 1,000s) were analyzed. Study this output and summarize the expenditures of the top 25 advertisers in your own words.

Descriptive Statistics

Variable	N	Mean	Median	TrMean	StDev	SE Mean
Top 25 A	25	772702	613823	723681	436067	87213

Variable	Minimum	Maximum	Q_1	Q_3
Top 25 A	445958	2226934	484600	788256

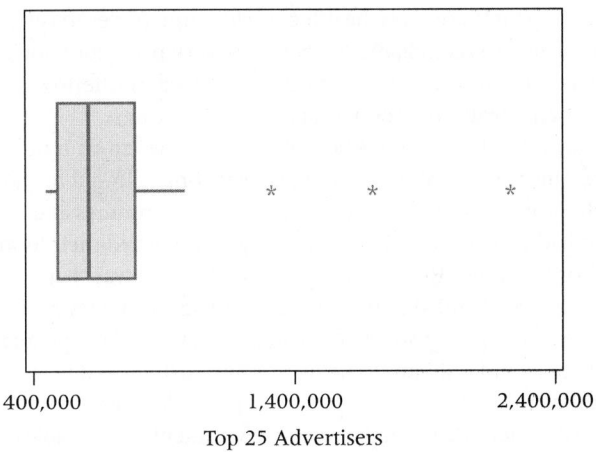

Top 25 Advertisers

ANALYZING THE DATABASES   *see* www.wiley.com/canada/black

1. Use the Major League Baseball Database. What is the mean amount of Revenues? What is the median amount of Revenues? What does comparing the mean and the median tell you about the data?

2. For the Canadian Stock Market Database, describe the Composite Index variable. Include measures of central tendency, variability, and skewness. What did you find?

3. Using the Financial Database, study Price per Share for Industry Types 2 and 7. The industry types are listed in Analyzing the Databases in Chapter 1. Compute a coefficient of variation for Type 2 and for Type 7. Compare the two coefficients and comment.

4. Use the Canadian Hospitals Database. Construct a box and whisker plot for Acute Myocardial Infarction. Thinking about geographic regions and facilities, comment on why the box and whisker plot may look the way it does.

CASE

Tim Hortons Limits Coffee Time

Tim Hortons is one of Canada's most recognizable coffee shops and is known for its tasty coffee and doughnuts. Over the last few years, Tim Hortons franchises have been appearing in numerous locations across Canada, and as of 2009, it has been able to capture 62% of the Canadian coffee market and 76% of the baked goods market, therefore making it one of the most successful Canadian franchises.

For several reasons, Tim Hortons believes that it will continue to grow and attract more customers. One of the main reasons for this added confidence is that it offers healthier products as compared to many of its competitors. This is a more important strategy for Tim Hortons than ever before because people are more health conscious and prefer to eat more sensibly. As well, many people are very price conscious, and Tim Hortons can accommodate this need by offering tastier and healthier products at affordable prices.

In 2005, Tim Hortons began enforcing the "20-minute" rule. This rule stated that customers were only allowed to stay in the store for a maximum time period of 20 minutes and then had to leave, whether or not they had finished their food and/or beverage. The reasoning behind this rule was that Tim Hortons wanted to have as much turnover as possible in order to continue growing. It wanted to serve as many people as it could and not have to turn away any customers due to insufficient store space. Recently, this policy had turned into an issue when many people (especially students) used tables for study purposes, while other people would sit for hours conducting informal business meetings. These instances led to the Tim Hortons parking lots being continuously filled to capacity, therefore deterring other potential customers from entering the establishment.

This Tim Hortons tactic may not be viewed as accommodating for many people; however, to many others it is seen as a fair solution in order to be able to successfully serve everyone who enjoys Tim Hortons fresh coffee and food. Despite backlash from some customers, Tim Hortons is still as popular as ever with 2008 revenues reaching an impressive $2.044 billion (CAD).

Discussion

1. The amount of time that customers stay at Tim Hortons will vary. Some customers may stay longer, while others stay for less time. A test is to be conducted in order to determine how close to the specified maximum time limit is the average customer's stay at Tim Hortons. Suppose the following data, collected from a random sample of 30 customers, represents the time spent (in minutes) at Tim Hortons. Use the techniques presented in this chapter to describe the sample. Consider measures of central tendency, variability, and skewness. Based on this analysis, how is the 20-minute rule working?

7	3	20	14	26	4
9	11	38	24	12	7
28	13	15	18	19	30
17	39	22	10	8	21
5	47	16	29	23	26

2. Suppose at a specific Tim Hortons store, in a remote northern region, the 20-minute rule is not enforced. A researcher randomly samples 150 customers at this specific Tim Hortons store and measures the amount of time customers spend in the store. The descriptive statistics for this sample are given below. Write a brief report to the manager of Tim Hortons summarizing what these statistics are saying.

	A	B
1	**Time Spent in Tim Hortons**	
2	Mean	20.007
3	Standard error	0.003
4	Median	20.006
5	Mode	20.005
6	Standard deviation	0.025
7	Sample variance	0.001
8	Kurtosis	1.016
9	Skewness	−0.082
10	Range	0.13
11	Minimum	19.95
12	Maximum	20.07
13	Sum	3,000.517
14	Count	150

References

"Enforcement of Tim Hortons' 20-minute Limit Could be a Source of Embarrassment and Over-identification," Hussein Warsame, March 13, 2009. Website for data source: <http://www.hiiraan.com/op2/2009/mar/enforcement_of_tim_hortons_20_minute_limit_could_be_a_source_of_embarrassment_and_over_identification.aspx; "Tim Horton's Role in the Fast Food Industry," Cassandra Cvetkovic, 2009. Website for data source: <http://www.helium.com/items/400642-tim-hortons-role-in-the-fast-food-industry>

USING THE COMPUTER

Excel

- While Excel has the capability of producing many of the statistics in this chapter piecemeal, there is one Excel feature, **Descriptive Statistics**, that produces many of these statistics in one output.
- To use the **Descriptive Statistics** feature, begin by selecting the **Data** tab on the Excel worksheet. From the **Analysis** panel at the right top of the **Data** tab worksheet, click on **Data Analysis**. If your Excel worksheet does not show the **Data Analysis** option, then you can load it as an add-in. From the **Data Analysis** pulldown menu, select **Descriptive Statistics**. In the **Descriptive Statistics** dialogue box, enter the location of the data to be analyzed in **Input Range**. Check **Labels in the First Row** if your data contains a label in the first row (cell). Check the box beside **Summary statistics.** The **Summary statistics** feature computes a wide variety of descriptive statistics. The output includes the mean, the median, the mode, the standard deviation, the sample variance, a measure of kurtosis, a measure of skewness, the range, the minimum, the maximum, the sum and the count.

- The **Rank and Percentile** feature of the **Data Analysis** tool of Excel has the capability of ordering the data, assigning ranks to the data, and yielding the percentiles of the data. To access this command, click on **Data Analysis** (see above) and select **Rank and Percentile** from the menu. In the **Rank and Percentile** dialogue box, enter the location of the data to be analyzed in **Input Range.** Check **Labels in the First Row** if your data contains a label in the first row (cell).
- Many of the individual statistics presented in this chapter can be computed using the **Insert Function** (*fx*) of Excel. To access the **Insert Function**, go to the **Formulas** tab on an Excel worksheet (top centre tab). The **Insert Function** is on the far left of the menu bar. In the **Insert Function** dialogue box at the top, there is a pulldown menu where it says **Or select a category.** From the pulldown menu associated with this command, select **Statistical.** There are 83 different statistics that can be computed using one of these commands. Select the one that you want to compute and enter the location of the data. Some of the more useful commands in this menu are **AVERAGE, MEDIAN, MODE, SKEW, STDEV,** and **VAR.**

CHAPTER 4

PROBABILITY

Learning Objectives

The focus of Chapter 4 is the basic principles of probability. Here are the key questions we would like to answer:

1. What is probability?

2. What are the different ways of assigning probability?

3. What are mutually exclusive events and how do they differ from independent events?

4. What are the techniques for counting possibilities in an experiment and when are they used?

5. What are marginal, union, joint, and conditional probabilities and how are they applied?

6. How is the appropriate law of probability selected and used in solving problems?

7. How are the laws of probability, including the law of addition, the law of multiplication, and the law of conditional probability, used to solve problems?

8. How are probabilities revised using Bayes' rule?

Digital Vision/Getty Images

EDUCATION, GENDER, AND EMPLOYMENT

Education is one of the most important determinants of employment. This has become more so since the advent of the "knowledge economy." Those with an education tend to be more easily absorbed into the workforce than those without. Closing the gender gap in education also means closing the "education gap" between men and women. For instance, gender discrimination implies the preferential treatment of members one gender over the other, other things being equal, the most important of these being education.

According to Statistics Canada, in 2004, nearly 185,000 Canadians were granted a degree, distributed as follows:

	Males	Females	Total
Basic (bachelor's/other undergraduate degree)	57,408	90,789	148,197
Master's degree	15,216	16,335	31,551
Doctoral degree	2,349	2,815	5,164
Total	74,973	109,939	184,912

Managerial and Statistical Questions

1. **a.** If an employer picks a person randomly from this pool of graduates, what is the probability of the person chosen being a woman?
   b. If an employer picks a person randomly from those with a master's degree, what is the probability of the person chosen being a woman?
2. If an employer decides to employ anyone with a basic degree (bachelor's/other undergraduate degree) and picks a person randomly, what is the probability of the person chosen being a woman? If a women is chosen, does this exhibit bias against men?
3. If an employer wants a person with a degree without regard to its level and picks a person randomly, what is the probability of the person chosen having a doctoral degree?
4. **a.** What is the probability that the person chosen in Question 3 will be a man with a master's degree?
   b. What is the probability that the person chosen is not a man with a master's degree?
   c. Suppose the person chosen is a man. What is the probability that he has a basic degree?

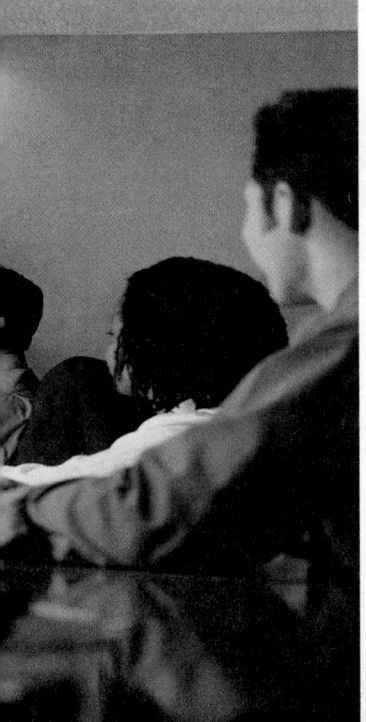

In business, most decision making involves uncertainty. For example, an operations manager does not know definitely whether a valve in the plant is going to malfunction or continue to function—or, if it continues, for how long. When should it be replaced? What is the chance that the valve will malfunction within the next week? In the banking industry, what are the new vice president's prospects for successfully turning a department around? In the case of a high-rise building, what are the chances that a fire-extinguishing system will work when needed if redundancies are built in?

The answers to these questions are uncertain. But business people must address these and thousands of similar questions daily. Because most such questions do not have definite answers, the decision making is based on uncertainty. In many of these situations, a probability can be assigned to the likelihood of an outcome. This chapter is about learning how to determine or assign probabilities.

4.1 INTRODUCTION TO PROBABILITY

In Chapter 1, we discussed the difference between descriptive and inferential statistics. Much statistical analysis is inferential, and probability is the basis for inferential statistics. Recall that inferential statistics involves taking a sample from a population, computing a statistic on the sample, and inferring from the statistic the value of the corresponding parameter of the population. We do this because the value of the parameter is unknown. Because it is unknown, the analyst conducts the inferential process under uncertainty. However, by applying rules and laws, the analyst can often assign a probability of obtaining the results. Figure 4.1 depicts this process.

Suppose a quality control inspector selects a random sample of 40 light bulbs from a population of Brand X bulbs and computes the average number of hours of luminance for the sample bulbs. By using techniques discussed later in this text, the specialist estimates the average number of hours of luminance for the *population* of Brand X light bulbs from this sample information. Because the light bulbs being analyzed are only a sample of the population, the average number of hours of luminance for the 40 bulbs may or may not accurately estimate the average for all bulbs in the population. The results are uncertain. By applying the laws presented in this chapter, the inspector can assign a value of probability to this estimate.

In addition, probabilities are used directly in certain industries and industry applications. For example, the insurance industry uses probabilities in actuarial tables to determine the likelihood of certain outcomes in order to set specific rates and coverages. The gaming industry uses probability values to establish charges and payoffs. One way to determine whether a company's hiring practices meet the government's guidelines is to compare various proportional breakdowns of their employees (by ethnicity, gender, age, etc.) to the proportions in the general population from which the employees are hired. In comparing the company figures with those of the general population, the courts could study the probabilities of a company randomly hiring a certain profile of employees from a given population. In other industries, such as manufacturing and aerospace, it is important to know the life of a mechanized part and the probability that it will malfunction at any given length of time in order to protect the firm from major breakdowns.

POINTS OF INTEREST
Descriptive statistics summarizes and describes the data on hand. But our interest is in extending our results to a larger group of subjects. The theory of probability provides the statistical basis for doing this.

Figure 4.1

Probability in the Process of Inferential Statistics

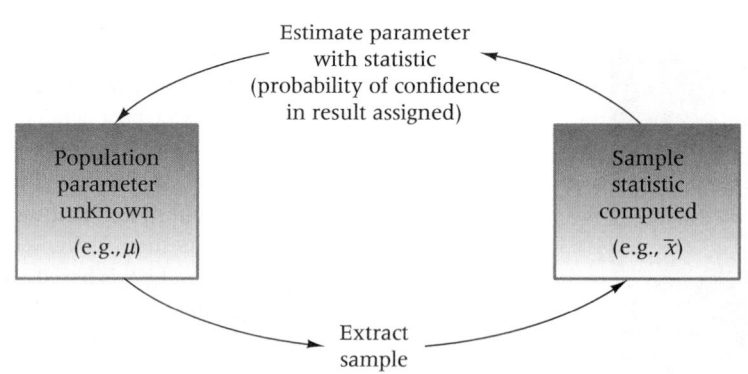

Concept Check

1. Describe what is meant by "inferential statistics."
2. Which branch of statistics is supported by probability theory?

4.2 METHODS OF ASSIGNING PROBABILITIES

The three general methods of assigning probabilities are (1) the classical method, (2) the relative frequency of occurrence method, and (3) subjective probabilities.

CLASSICAL METHOD OF ASSIGNING PROBABILITIES

When probabilities are assigned based on laws and rules, the method is referred to as the **classical method** of assigning probabilities. This method involves an experiment, which is *a process that produces outcomes,* and an event, *which is an outcome of an experiment.*

When we assign probabilities using the classical method, the probability of an individual event occurring is determined as the ratio of the number of items in a population containing the event (n_e) to the total number of items in the population (N). That is, $P(E) = n_e/N$. For example, if a company has 200 workers and 70 are female, the probability of randomly selecting a female from this company is $70/200 = 0.35$.

Classical Method of Assigning Probabilities	$$P(E) = \frac{n_e}{N}$$

where

N = total possible number of outcomes of an experiment
n_e = the number of outcomes in which the event occurs out of N outcomes

Suppose, in a particular plant, three machines make a given product. Machine A always produces 40% of the total number of this product. Ten percent of the items produced by machine A are defective. If the finished products are well mixed with regard to which machine produced them and if one of these products is randomly selected, the classical method of assigning probabilities tells us that the probability that the part was produced by machine A and is defective is 0.04. This probability can be determined even before the part is sampled because with the classical method, the probabilities can be determined **a priori;** that is, *they can be determined prior to the experiment.*

Because n_e can never be greater than N (no more than N outcomes in the population could possibly have attribute e), the highest value of any probability is 1. If the probability of an outcome occurring is 1, the event is certain to occur. The smallest possible probability is 0. If none of the outcomes of the N possibilities has the desired characteristic, e, the probability is $0/N = 0$, and the event is certain not to occur.

Range of Possible Probabilities	$$0 \leq P(E) \leq 1$$

Thus, probabilities are nonnegative proper fractions or nonnegative decimal values less than or equal to 1.

Probability values can be converted to percentages by multiplying by 100. Meteorologists often report weather probabilities in percentage form. For example, when they forecast a 60% chance of rain for tomorrow, they are saying that the probability of rain tomorrow is 0.60.

RELATIVE FREQUENCY OF OCCURRENCE

The **relative frequency of occurrence method** of assigning probabilities is based on cumulated historical data. With this method, *the probability of an event occurring is equal to the number of times the event has occurred in the past divided by the total number of opportunities for the event to have occurred.*

Probability by Relative Frequency of Occurrence	$\dfrac{\text{Number of Times an Event Occurred}}{\text{Total Number of Opportunities for the Event to Occur}}$

Relative frequency of occurrence is not based on rules or laws but on what has occurred in the past. For example, a company wants to determine the probability that its inspectors will reject the next batch of raw materials from a supplier. Data gathered from company record books show that the supplier sent the company 90 batches in the past, and inspectors rejected 10 of them. By the method of relative frequency of occurrence, the probability that the inspectors will reject the next batch is 10/90 or 0.11. If the next batch is rejected, the relative frequency of occurrence probability for the subsequent shipment would change to 11/91 = 0.12.

SUBJECTIVE PROBABILITY

The **subjective method** of *assigning probability is based on the feelings or insights of the person determining the probability.* Subjective probability comes from the person's intuition or reasoning. Although not a scientific approach to probability, the subjective method is often based on the accumulation of knowledge, understanding, and experience stored and processed in the human mind. At times it is merely a guess. At other times, subjective probability can potentially yield accurate probabilities. Subjective probability can be used to capitalize on the background of experienced workers and managers in decision making.

Suppose a director of transportation for an oil company is asked the probability of getting a shipment of oil out of Saudi Arabia to Canada within three weeks. A director who has scheduled many such shipments, has a knowledge of Saudi politics, and has an awareness of current climatological and economic conditions may be able to give an accurate probability that the shipment can be made on time.

Subjective probability can also be a potentially useful way of tapping a person's experience, knowledge, and insight and using them to forecast the occurrence of some event. An experienced airline mechanic can usually assign a meaningful probability that a particular plane will have a certain type of mechanical difficulty. Physicians sometimes assign subjective probabilities to the life expectancy of people who have cancer.

POINTS OF INTEREST
Subjective probabilities depend on a person's knowledge and experience. So, they can vary from person to person. Classical and relative frequency probabilities depend on objective conditions. So, they remain the same no matter who calculates them.

Concept Check

1. What are the three methods of assigning probabilities?
2. What's the difference between classical and relative frequency methods?
3. How is subjective probability different from the other two methods?

4.3 STRUCTURE OF PROBABILITY

In the study of probability, developing a language of terms and symbols is helpful. The structure of probability provides a common framework within which the topics of probability can be explored.

EXPERIMENT

As previously stated, an **experiment** is *a process that produces outcomes.* The following are examples of business-oriented experiments with outcomes that can be statistically analyzed:

- Interviewing 20 randomly selected consumers and asking them which brand of appliance they prefer
- Sampling every 200th bottle of ketchup from an assembly line and weighing the contents
- Testing new pharmaceutical drugs on samples of cancer patients and measuring the patients' improvement
- Auditing every 10th account to detect any errors
- Recording the Toronto Stock Exchange average on the first Monday of every month for 10 years

EVENT

Because an **event** is *an outcome of an experiment,* the experiment defines the possibilities of the event. If the experiment is to sample five bottles coming off a production line, an event could be to get one defective and four good bottles. In an experiment to roll a die, one event could be to roll an even number and another event could be to roll a number greater than two. Events are denoted by uppercase letters: italic capital letters (e.g., A and $E_1, E_2, \ldots$) represent the general or abstract case, and Roman capital letters (e.g., H and T for heads and tails) denote specific things and people.

ELEMENTARY EVENTS

Events that cannot be decomposed or broken down into other events are called **elementary events.** Elementary events are denoted by lowercase letters (e.g., $e_1, e_2, e_3, \ldots$). Suppose the experiment is to roll a die. The elementary events for this experiment are to roll a 1 or roll a 2 or roll a 3, and so on. Rolling an even number is an event, but it is not an elementary event because the even number can be broken down further into events 2, 4, and 6.

In the experiment of rolling a die, there are six elementary events {1, 2, 3, 4, 5, 6}. Rolling a pair of dice results in 36 possible elementary events (outcomes). For each of the six elementary events possible on the roll of one die, there are six possible elementary events on the roll of the second die, as depicted in the tree diagram in Figure 4.2. Table 4.1 contains a list of these 36 outcomes.

In the experiment of rolling a pair of dice, other events could include outcomes such as two even numbers, a sum of 10, a sum greater than five, and others. However, none of these events is an elementary event because each can be broken down into several of the elementary events displayed in Table 4.1.

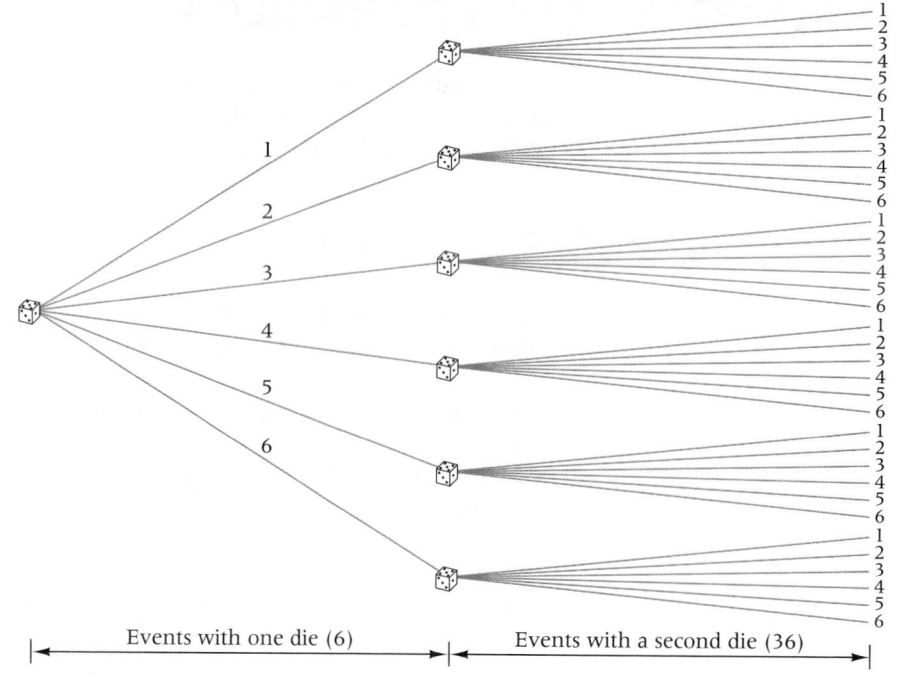

Figure 4.2

Possible Outcomes for the Roll of a Pair of Dice

Events with one die (6)   Events with a second die (36)

SAMPLE SPACE

A **sample space** is *a complete roster or listing of all elementary events for an experiment.* Table 4.1 is the sample space for the roll of a pair of dice. The sample space for the roll of a single die is {1, 2, 3, 4, 5, 6}.

Sample space can aid in finding probabilities. Suppose an experiment is to roll a pair of dice. What is the probability that the dice will sum to 7? An examination of the sample space shown in Table 4.1 reveals that there are six outcomes in which the dice sum to 7—{(1, 6), (2, 5), (3, 4), (4, 3), (5, 2), (6, 1)}—in the 36 total possible elementary events in the sample space. Using this information, we can conclude that the probability of rolling a pair of dice that sum to 7 is 6/36, or 0.1667. However, using the sample space to determine probabilities is unwieldy and cumbersome when the sample space is large. Hence, statisticians usually use other more effective methods of determining probability.

Table 4.1

All Possible Elementary Events in the Roll of a Pair of Dice (Sample Space)

(1,1)	(2,1)	(3,1)	(4,1)	(5,1)	(6,1)
(1,2)	(2,2)	(3,2)	(4,2)	(5,2)	(6,2)
(1,3)	(2,3)	(3,3)	(4,3)	(5,3)	(6,3)
(1,4)	(2,4)	(3,4)	(4,4)	(5,4)	(6,4)
(1,5)	(2,5)	(3,5)	(4,5)	(5,5)	(6,5)
(1,6)	(2,6)	(3,6)	(4,6)	(5,6)	(6,6)

Figure 4.3

A Union

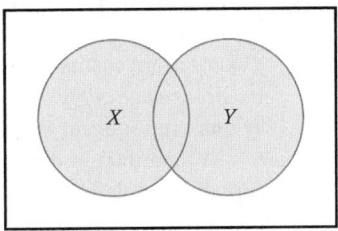

UNIONS AND INTERSECTIONS

Set notation, the use of braces to group numbers, is used as *a symbolic tool for unions and intersections* in this chapter. The **union** of X, Y is *formed by combining elements from both sets* and is denoted $X \cup Y$. An element qualifies for the union of X, Y if it is in either X or Y or in both X and Y. The union expression $X \cup Y$ can be translated to "X or Y." For example, if

$$X = \{1, 4, 7, 9\} \text{ and } Y = (2, 3, 4, 5, 6\}$$
$$X \cup Y = \{1, 2, 3, 4, 5, 6, 7, 9\}$$

Note that all the values of X and all the values of Y qualify for the union. However, none of the values is listed more than once in the union. In Figure 4.3, the shaded region of the Venn diagram denotes the union.

An intersection is denoted $X \cap Y$. To qualify for intersection, an element must be in both X and Y. The **intersection** *contains the elements common to both sets.* Thus, the intersection symbol, $\cap$, is often read as *and.* The intersection of X, Y is referred to as X and Y. For example, if

$$X = \{1, 4, 7, 9\} \text{ and } Y = \{2, 3, 4, 5, 6\}$$
$$X \cap Y = \{4\}$$

Note that only the value 4 is common to both sets X and Y. The intersection is more exclusive than and hence equal to or (usually) smaller than the union. Elements must be characteristic of both X and Y to qualify. In Figure 4.4, the shaded region denotes the intersection.

POINTS OF INTEREST
In everyday language, when we say X or Y, we mean either X or Y. In probability theory, *X or Y* means the union of X and Y. *X and Y* means the intersection of X and Y.

Figure 4.4

An Intersection

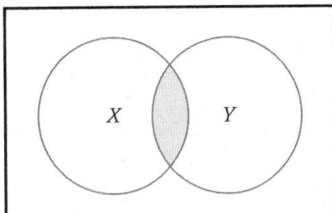

MUTUALLY EXCLUSIVE EVENTS

Two or more events are **mutually exclusive events** if *the occurrence of one event precludes the occurrence of the other event(s).* This characteristic means that mutually exclusive events cannot occur simultaneously and therefore can have no intersection.

A manufactured part is either defective or acceptable: The part cannot be both acceptable and defective at the same time because "acceptable" and "defective" are mutually exclusive categories. In a sample of the manufactured products, the event of selecting a defective part is mutually exclusive with the event of selecting a nondefective part. Suppose an office building is for sale and two different potential buyers have placed bids on the building. It is not possible for both buyers to purchase the building; therefore, the event of buyer A purchasing the building is mutually exclusive with the event of buyer B purchasing the building. In the toss of a single coin, heads and tails are mutually exclusive events. The person tossing the coin gets either a head or a tail but never both.

The probability of two mutually exclusive events occurring at the same time is zero.

Mutually Exclusive Events X and Y	$P(X \cap Y) = 0$

INDEPENDENT EVENTS

Two or more events are **independent events** if *the occurrence or nonoccurrence of one of the events does not affect the occurrence or nonoccurrence of the other event(s).* Certain experiments, such as rolling dice, yield independent events; each die is independent of the other. Whether a 6 is rolled on the first die has no influence on whether a 6 is rolled on the second die. Coin tosses are always independent of each other. The event of getting a head on the first toss of a coin is independent of getting a head on the second toss. It is generally believed that certain human characteristics are independent of other events. For example, left-handedness is probably independent of the possession of a credit card. Whether a person wears glasses or not is probably independent of the brand of milk preferred.

Many experiments using random selection can produce either independent or nonindependent events. In these experiments, the outcomes are independent if sampling is done with replacement; that is, after each item is selected and the outcome is determined, the item is restored to the population and the population is shuffled. This way, each draw becomes independent of the previous draw. Suppose an inspector is randomly selecting bolts from a bin that contains 5% defects. If the inspector samples a defective bolt and returns it to the bin, on the second draw there are still 5% defects in the bin regardless of the fact that the first outcome was a defect. If the inspector does not replace the first draw, the second draw is not independent of the first; in this case, fewer than 5% defects remain in the population. Thus, the probability of the second outcome is dependent on the first outcome.

If X and Y are independent, the following symbolic notation is used.

POINTS OF INTEREST
While it may sound counterintuitive, if two events cannot occur jointly, they are *not* independent. They are in fact dependent because the occurrence of one event is dependent on the nonoccurrence of the other event.

Independent Events X and Y	$P(X|Y) = P(X)$ and $P(Y|X) = P(Y)$

$P(X|Y)$ denotes the probability of X occurring given that Y has occurred. If X and Y are independent, then the probability of X occurring given that Y has occurred is just the probability of X occurring. Knowledge that Y has occurred does not affect the probability of X occurring because X and Y are independent. For example, P(prefers Pepsi|person is

Figure 4.5

The Complement of Event A'

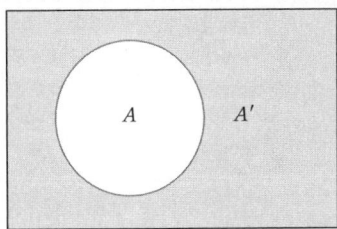

right-handed) = P(prefers Pepsi) because a person's handedness is independent of brand preference.

COLLECTIVELY EXHAUSTIVE EVENTS

A list of **collectively exhaustive events** contains *all possible elementary events for an experiment.* Thus, all sample spaces are collectively exhaustive lists. The list of possible outcomes for tossing a pair of dice contained in Table 4.1 is a collectively exhaustive list. The sample space for an experiment can be described as a list of events that are mutually exclusive and collectively exhaustive. Sample space events do not overlap or intersect, and the list is complete.

COMPLEMENTARY EVENTS

The **complement** of event A is denoted A', pronounced "not A." All *the elementary events of an experiment not in A make up its complement.* For example, if in rolling one die, event A is getting an even number, the complement of A is getting an odd number. If event A is getting a 5 on the roll of a die, the complement of A is getting a 1, 2, 3, 4, or 6. The complement of event A contains whatever portion of the sample space that event A does not contain, as the Venn diagram in Figure 4.5 shows.

Using the complement of an event can sometimes be helpful in solving for probabilities because of the following rule.

Probability of the Complement of A	$P(A') = 1 - P(A)$

POINTS OF INTEREST
The probability of the complement of an event can be computed *only* if the events are collectively exhaustive.

Suppose 32% of the employees of a company have a university degree. If an employee is randomly selected from the company, the probability that the person does not have a university degree is $1 - 0.32 = 0.68$. Suppose 42% of all parts produced in a plant are moulded by machine A and 31% are moulded by machine B. If a part is randomly selected, the probability that it was moulded by neither machine A nor machine B is $1 - 0.73 = 0.27$. (Assume that a part is only moulded on one machine.)

COUNTING THE POSSIBILITIES

In statistics, a collection of techniques and rules for counting the number of outcomes that can occur for a particular experiment can be used. Some of these rules and techniques can delineate the size of the sample space. Presented here are three of these counting methods.

THE *mn* COUNTING RULE

Suppose a customer decides to buy a certain brand of new car. Options for the car are two different engines, five different paint colours, and three interior packages. If each of these options is available with each of the others, how many different cars can the customer choose from? To determine this number, we can use the **mn counting rule.**

The *mn* Counting Rule	For an operation that can be done *m* ways and a second operation that can be done *n* ways, the two operations can then occur, in order, in *mn* ways. This rule can be extended to cases with three or more operations.

Using the *mn* counting rule, we can determine that the automobile customer has (2)(5)(3) = 30 different car combinations of engines, paint colours, and interiors available.

Suppose a scientist wants to set up a research design to study the effects of gender (M, F), marital status (single never married, divorced, married), and economic class (lower, middle, and upper) on the frequency of airline ticket purchases per year. The researcher would set up a design in which 18 different samples are taken to represent all possible groups generated from these customer characteristics.

$$\text{Number of Groups} = (\text{Gender})(\text{Marital Status})(\text{Economic Class})$$
$$= (2)(3)(3) = 18 \text{ Groups}$$

SAMPLING FROM A POPULATION WITH REPLACEMENT

In the second counting method, sampling *n* items from a population of size *N with replacement* provides

$$N^n \text{ possibilities}$$

where
 N = population size
 n = sample size

For example, each time a die, which has six sides, is rolled, the outcome is independent (with replacement) of the previous roll. If a die is rolled three times in succession, how many different outcomes can occur? That is, what is the size of the sample space for this experiment? The size of the population, N, is 6, the six sides of the die. We are sampling three dice rolls, $n = 3$. The sample space is

$$N^n = 6^3 = 216$$

Suppose in a lottery six numbers are drawn from the digits 0 through 9, with replacement (digits can be reused). How many different groupings of six numbers can be drawn? N is the population of 10 numbers (0 through 9) and n is the sample size, six numbers.

$$N^n = 10^6 = 1,000,000$$

That is, a million six-digit numbers are available!

POINTS OF INTEREST
Because the counting rule involves serial multiplication, possibilities can rapidly increase. If a car has 3 different engines, 6 different paint colours, 6 interior packages, and 2 different transmission types (automatic or manual), the number of combinations becomes 216 (3 × 6 × 6 × 2). This means that it is possible for 216 customers to buy the same car, but each with a configuration that is different from everyone else's!

COMBINATIONS: SAMPLING FROM A POPULATION WITHOUT REPLACEMENT

The third counting method uses **combinations.** Sampling n items from a population of size N without replacement provides

$$_NC_n = \binom{N}{n} = \frac{N!}{n!(N-n)!}$$

possibilities.

For example, suppose a small law firm has 16 employees and three are to be selected randomly to represent the company at the annual meeting of the Ontario Bar Association. How many different combinations of lawyers could be sent to the meeting? This situation does not allow sampling with replacement because three *different* lawyers will be selected to go. This problem is solved by using combinations. $N = 16$ and $n = 3$, so

$$_NC_n = {}_{16}C_3 = \frac{16!}{3!13!} = 560$$

A total of 560 combinations of three lawyers could be chosen to represent the firm.

COUNTING THE POSSIBLE SEQUENCES

In the above example each combination consisted of a set of three lawyers. Suppose one such set is {Amy, Bob and Bill}. This set is no different from {Bob, Bill and Amy} or {Bob, Amy and Bill} or any other sequence. But sometimes the sequences can also be important. Suppose the annual meeting is followed by a conference. The firm may decide that the first person chosen would attend the meeting and the second person would attend the conference and the third person both. Here we need to consider which three are chosen (who gets to represent the firm) and in what order (what sessions they would attend). The number of sequences in a set are called **permutations**. When we use all members of a set in every sequence, the number of permutations for a given combination equals $n!$

$$_nP_r = n!$$

In our example, each set consisted of three lawyers. Therefore the number of possible sequences or permutations is $3! = 3 * 2 * 1 = 6$. The sequences are 1. {Amy, Bill, Bob}, 2. {Amy, Bob, Bill}, 3. {Bill, Amy, Bob}, 4. {Bill, Bob, Amy}, 5. {Bob, Amy, Bill}, and 6. {Bob, Bill, Amy}.

This would indicate, for example, that while Amy's probability of representing the company is 1/560, her chances of attending both the meeting and the conference are 2/6 or 1/3, *if* she is chosen to represent the company. Therefore, Amy's probability of representing the company by attending both the meeting and the conference is

$$1/560 * 1/3 = 1/1680 = 0.0006$$

We may want to use only a part of the set as when the firm chooses a set of three as potential candidates, it may, at a later date, choose only two out of the three to actually attend the meeting. Now the problem is how many sequences of two are there in a set of three. This is given by the *generalized formula*

$$_nP_r = \frac{n!}{(n-r)!}$$

where

n = the number of elements in the set
r = the number of elements to be selected from the set

In this example, the set consists of 3 and we need select 2 out of this.

$$_nP_r = \frac{n!}{(n-r)!} = \frac{3!}{(3-2)!} = 6$$

This shows that if we take two elements from a set of three, we can order them in six different ways (coincidentally the same as taking three elements from a set of three).

Concept Check

1. Briefly explain the following terms: experiment, elementary events, sample space.
2. How would you draw a diagram to represent (a) the intersection and (b) the union of two events?
3. What is the difference between mutually exclusive events and independent events?
4. If two events can never occur together, are they mutually exclusive events or independent events?
5. What are collectively exhaustive events?
6. How would you describe the complement of an event A?
7. What is the *nm* counting rule?
8. What is meant by "combinations"?

4.3 Problems

4.1   A supplier shipped a lot of six parts to a company. The lot contained three defective parts. Suppose the customer decided to randomly select two parts and test them for defects. How large a sample space is the customer potentially working with? List the sample space. Using the sample space list, determine the probability that the customer will select a sample with exactly one defect.

4.2   Given X = {1, 3, 5, 7, 8, 9}, Y = {2, 4, 7, 9}, and Z = {1, 2, 3, 4, 7}, solve the following.
   a. $X \cup Z =$ _____
   b. $X \cap Y =$ _____
   c. $X \cap Z =$ _____
   d. $X \cup Y \cup Z =$ _____
   e. $X \cap Y \cap Z =$ _____
   f. $(X \cup Y) \cap Z =$ _____
   g. $(Y \cap Z) \cup (X \cap Y) =$ _____
   h.   X or Y = _____
   i.   Y and X = _____

4.3   If a population consists of the positive even numbers through 30 and if A = {2, 6, 12, 24}, what is A'?

4.4   A company's customer service toll-free telephone system is set up so that the caller has six options. Each of these six options leads to a menu with four options. For each of these four options, three more options are available. For each of these three options, another three options are presented. If a person calls the toll-free number for assistance, how many total options are possible?

4.5   A bin contains six parts. Two of the parts are defective and four are acceptable. If three of the six parts are selected from the bin, how large is the sample space? Which counting rule did you use and why? For this sample space, what is the probability that exactly one of the three sampled parts is defective?

4.6   A company places a seven-digit serial number on each part that is made. Each digit of the serial number can be any number from 0 through 9. Digits can be repeated in the serial number. How many different serial numbers are possible?

4.7   A small company has 20 employees. Six of these employees will be selected randomly to be interviewed as part of an employee satisfaction program.
   a.   How many different groups of six can be selected?
   b.   In how many different sequences can the six employees be selected?

4.4 MARGINAL, UNION, JOINT, AND CONDITIONAL PROBABILITIES

Four particular types of probability are presented in this chapter. The first type is **marginal probability.** Marginal probability is denoted $P(E)$, where E is some event. A marginal probability is usually *computed by dividing some subtotal by the whole.* An example of marginal probability is the probability that a person owns a Ford car. This probability is computed by dividing the number of Ford owners by the total number of car owners. The probability of a person wearing glasses is also a marginal probability. This probability is computed by dividing the number of people wearing glasses by the total number of people.

A second type of probability is the union of two events. **Union probability** is denoted $P(E_1 \cup E_2)$, where E_1 and E_2 are two events. $P(E_1 \cup E_2)$ is the probability that E_1 will occur or that E_2 will occur or that both E_1 and E_2 will occur. An example of union probability is the probability that a person owns a Ford or a Chevrolet. To qualify for the union, the person only has to have at least one of these cars. Another example is the probability of a person wearing glasses or having red hair. All people wearing glasses are included in the union, along with all redheads and all redheads who wear glasses. In a company, the probability that a person is male or a clerical worker is a union probability. A person qualifies for the union by being male or by being a clerical worker or by being both (a male clerical worker).

A third type of probability is the intersection of two events, or **joint probability.** The joint probability of events E_1 and E_2 occurring is denoted $P(E_1 \cap E_2)$. Sometimes $P(E_1 \cap E_2)$ is read as the probability of E_1 and E_2. To qualify for the intersection, both events must occur. An example of joint probability is the probability of a person owning both a Ford and a Chevrolet. Owning one type of car is not sufficient. A second example of joint probability is the probability that a person is a redhead and wears glasses.

The fourth type is **conditional probability.** Conditional probability is denoted $P(E_1|E_2)$. This expression is read as the probability that E_1 will occur given that E_2 is known to have occurred. Conditional probabilities involve knowledge of some prior information. The information that is known or given is written to the right of the vertical line in the probability statement. An example of conditional probability is the probability that a person owns a Chevrolet given that she owns a Ford. This conditional probability is only a measure of the proportion of Ford owners who have a Chevrolet—not the proportion of total car owners who own a Chevrolet. Conditional probabilities are computed

Figure 4.6

Marginal, Union, Joint, and Conditional Probabilities

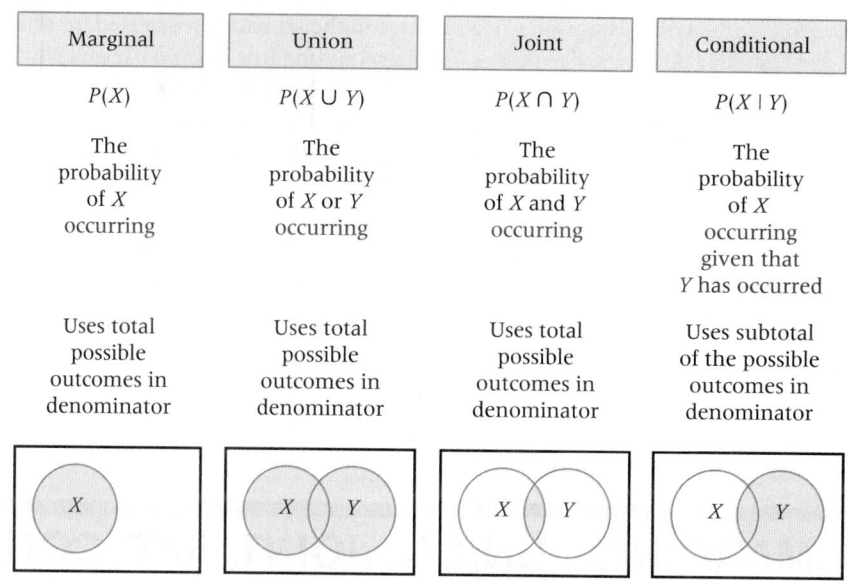

Marginal	Union	Joint	Conditional
$P(X)$	$P(X \cup Y)$	$P(X \cap Y)$	$P(X \mid Y)$
The probability of X occurring	The probability of X or Y occurring	The probability of X and Y occurring	The probability of X occurring given that Y has occurred
Uses total possible outcomes in denominator	Uses total possible outcomes in denominator	Uses total possible outcomes in denominator	Uses subtotal of the possible outcomes in denominator

by determining the number of items that have an outcome out of some subtotal of the population. In the car owner example, the possibilities are reduced to Ford owners, and then the number of Chevrolet owners out of those Ford owners is determined. Another example of a conditional probability is the probability that a worker in a company is a professional given that he is male. Of the four probability types, only conditional probability does not have the population total as its denominator. Conditional probabilities have a population subtotal in the denominator. Figure 4.6 summarizes these four types of probability.

Concept Check

1. How is union probability different from joint probability?
2. Can joint probability ever be greater than union probability? Explain.
3. How is marginal probability different from conditional probability?
4. Can conditional probability ever be greater than marginal probability? Explain.

4.5 ADDITION LAWS

Several tools are available for use in solving probability problems. These tools include sample space, tree diagrams, the laws of probability, probability matrices, and insight. Because of the individuality and variety of probability problems, some techniques apply more readily in certain situations than in others. No best method is available for solving all probability problems. In some instances, the probability matrix lays out a problem in a readily solvable manner. In other cases, setting up the probability matrix is more difficult than solving the problem in another way. The probability laws can almost always be used to solve probability problems.

Four laws of probability are presented in this chapter: the addition laws, conditional probability, the multiplication laws, and Bayes' rule. The addition laws and the multiplication laws each have a general law and a special law.

The general law of addition is used to find the probability of the union of two events, $P(X \cup Y)$. The expression $P(X \cup Y)$ denotes the probability of X occurring or Y occurring or both X and Y occurring.

General Law of Addition	$$P(X \cup Y) = P(X) + P(Y) - P(X \cap Y)$$ where X, Y are events and $(X \cap Y)$ is the intersection of X and Y.

Yankelovich Partners conducted a survey in which workers were asked which changes in office design would increase productivity. Respondents were allowed to answer more than one type of design change. The number one change, selected by 70% of the workers, was reducing noise. In second place was more storage/filing space, selected by 67%. If one of the survey respondents was randomly selected and asked which office design changes would increase worker productivity, what is the probability that this person would select reducing noise *or* more storage/filing space?

Let N represent the event "reducing noise." Let S represent the event "more storage/ filing space." The probability of a person responding with N *or* S can be symbolized statistically as a union probability by using the law of addition.

$$P(N \cup S)$$

Recall that $N \cup S$ means either N or S or both. To successfully satisfy the search for a person who responds with reducing noise *or* more storage/filing space, we need only find someone who wants *at least one* of those two events. Because 70% of the surveyed people responded that reducing noise would create more productivity, $P(N) = 0.70$. In addition, because 67% responded that increased storage space would improve productivity, $P(S) = 0.67$. Either of these would satisfy the requirement of the union. Thus, the solution to the problem seems to be

$$P(N \cup S) = P(N) + P(S) = 0.70 + 0.67 = 1.37$$

However, we have already established that probabilities cannot be more than 1.00. What is the problem here? Notice that all people who responded that *both* reducing noise *and* increasing storage space would improve productivity are included in *each* of the marginal probabilities $P(N)$ and $P(S)$. Certainly a respondent who recommends both of these improvements should be included as favouring at least one. However, because they are included in $P(N)$ *and* $P(S)$, the people who recommended both improvements are *double counted*. For that reason, the general law of addition subtracts the intersection probability, $P(N \cap S)$.

In Figure 4.7, Venn diagrams illustrate this discussion. Notice that the intersection area of N and S is double shaded in diagram A, indicating that it has been counted twice. In diagram B, the shading is consistent throughout N and S because the intersection area has been subtracted out. Thus, diagram B illustrates the proper application of the general law of addition.

So, what is the answer to the union probability question? Suppose 56% of all respondents to the survey had said that *both* noise reduction *and* increased storage/filing space would improve productivity: $P(N \cap S) = 0.56$. Then, we could use the general law of addition to solve for the probability that a person responds that *either* noise reduction *or* increased storage space would improve productivity.

$$P(N \cup S) = P(N) + P(S) - P(N \cap S) = 0.70 + 0.67 - 0.56 = 0.81$$

Hence, 81% of the workers surveyed responded that *either* noise reduction *or* increased storage space would improve productivity.

Figure 4.7

Solving for the Union in the Office Productivity Problem

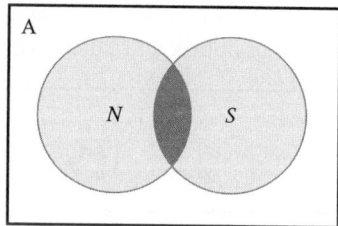

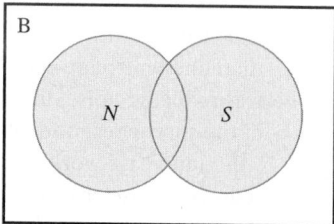

PROBABILITY MATRICES

In addition to the formulas, another useful tool in solving probability problems is a probability matrix. A **probability matrix** *displays the marginal probabilities and the intersection probabilities of a given problem.* Union probabilities and conditional probabilities must be computed from the matrix. Generally, a probability matrix is constructed as a two-dimensional table with one variable on each side of the table. For example, in the office design problem, noise reduction would be on one side of the table and increased storage space on the other. In this problem, a Yes row and a No row would be created for one variable and a Yes column and a No column would be created for the other variable, as shown in Table 4.2.

Once the matrix is created, we can enter the marginal probabilities. $P(N) = 0.70$ is the marginal probability that a person responds yes to noise reduction. This value is placed in the "margin" in the row of Yes to noise reduction, as shown in Table 4.3. If $P(N) = 0.70$, then 30% of the people surveyed did not think that noise reduction would increase productivity. Thus, $P(\text{not } N) = 1 - 0.70 = 0.30$. This value, also a marginal probability, goes in the row indicated by No under noise reduction. In the column under Yes for increased storage space, the marginal probability $P(S) = 0.67$ is recorded. Finally, the marginal probability of No for increased storage space, $P(\text{not } S) = 1 - 0.67 = 0.33$, is placed in the No column.

In this probability matrix, all four marginal probabilities are given or can be computed simply by using the probability of a complement rule, $P(\text{not } A) = 1 - P(A)$. The intersection of noise reduction and increased storage space is given as $P(N \cap S) = 0.56$. This value is entered into the probability matrix in the cell under Yes Yes, as shown in Table 4.3. The rest of the matrix can be determined by subtracting the cell values from the marginal probabilities. For example, subtracting 0.56 from 0.70 and getting 0.14 yields the value for

Table 4.2

Probability Matrix for the Office Design Problem

		Increased Storage Space	
		Yes	No
Noise Reduction	Yes		
	No		

Table 4.3

Probability Matrix for the Office Design Problem

		Increased Storage Space		
		Yes	No	
Noise Reduction	Yes	0.56	0.14	0.70
	No	0.11	0.19	0.30
		0.67	0.33	1.00

Table 4.4

Yes Row and Column for Probability Matrix of the Office Design Problem

		Increased Storage Space		
		Yes	No	
Noise Reduction	Yes	0.56	0.14	0.70
	No	0.11		
		0.67		

the cell under Yes for noise reduction and No for increased storage space. In other words, 14% of all respondents said that noise reduction would improve productivity but increased storage space would not. Filling out the rest of the matrix results in the probabilities shown in Table 4.3.

Now we can solve the union probability, $P(N \cup S)$, in at least two different ways using the probability matrix. The focus is on the Yes row for noise reduction and the Yes column for increased storage space, as displayed in Table 4.4. The probability of a person suggesting noise reduction *or* increased storage space as a solution for improving productivity, $P(N \cup S)$, can be determined from the probability matrix by adding the marginal probabilities of Yes for noise reduction and Yes for increased storage space and then subtracting the Yes Yes cell, following the pattern of the general law of probabilities.

$$P(N \cup S) = 0.70 \text{ (from Yes row)} + 0.67 \text{ (from Yes column)}$$
$$- 56 \text{ (from Yes Yes cell)} = 0.81$$

Another way to solve for the union probability from the information displayed in the probability matrix is to sum all cells in any of the Yes rows or columns. Observe the following from Table 4.4.

$$P(N \cup S) = 0.56 \text{ (from Yes Yes cell)}$$
$$+ 0.14 \text{ (from Yes on noise reduction and No on increased storage space)}$$
$$+ 0.11 \text{ (from No on noise reduction and Yes on increased storage space)}$$
$$= 0.81$$

Demonstration Problem 4.1

The data from the Decision Dilemma reveal that 184,912 students obtained one of three degrees. Shown again here is the raw values matrix (also called a contingency table) with the frequency counts for each category and for subtotals and totals containing a breakdown of these students by type of position and by gender. If a graduate is selected randomly, what is the probability that the graduate is female or obtained a master's degree?

	Males	**Females**	**Total**
Basic (bachelor's/other undergraduate degree)	57,408	90,789	148,197
Master's degree	15,216	16,335	31,551
Doctoral degree	2,349	2,815	5,164
Total	74,973	109,939	184,912

Solution

Let F denote the event of female and MD denote the event of master's degree. The question is

$$P(F \cup MD) = ?$$

By the general law of addition,

$$P(F \cup MD) = P(F) + P(MD) - P(F \cap MD)$$

Of the 184,912 graduates, 109,939 are women. Therefore, $P(F) = 109,939/184,912 = 0.5945$. The 184,912 graduates include 31,551 students who obtained a master's degree. Therefore, $P(MD) = 31,551/184,912 = 0.1706$. Because 16,335 students are both female and obtained a master's degree, $P(F \cap MD) = 16,335/184,912 = 0.0883$. The union probability is solved as

$$P(F \cup MD) = 0.5945 + 0.1706 - 0.0883 = 0.6768$$

To solve this probability using a matrix, you can either use the raw values matrix shown previously or convert the raw values matrix to a probability matrix by dividing every value in the matrix by the value of N, 184,192. The raw values matrix is used in a manner similar to that of the probability matrix. To compute the union probability of selecting a person who is either female or has a master's degree from the raw values matrix, add the number of people in the Female column (109,939) to the number of people in the Master's degree row (31,551), and then subtract the number of people in the intersection cell of Female and Master's (16,335). This step yields the value 109,939 + 31,551 − 16,335 = 125,155. Dividing this value (125,155) by the value of N (184,912) produces the union probability.

$$P(F \cup MD) = 125,155/184,912 = 0.6768$$

A second way to produce the answer from the raw values matrix is to add to the total of the Female column all those who obtained a master's degree who are not females.

$$109,939 + 15,216 = 125,155$$

and then divide by the total number of employees, $N = 184,912$, which gives

$$P(F \cup MD) = 125,155/184,912 = 0.6768$$

Demonstration Problem 4.2

Shown here are the raw values matrix and corresponding probability matrix for a survey of 200 executives from four Canadian cities. The executives were asked to identify the geographic locale of their company and their company's industry type. The executives were only allowed to select one locale and one industry type.

RAW VALUES MATRIX

		Geographic Location				
		Toronto	Calgary	Vancouver	Montreal	
		D	E	F	G	
	Finance A	24	10	8	14	56
Industry Type	Manufacturing B	30	6	22	12	70
	Communications C	28	18	12	16	74
		82	34	42	42	200

By dividing every value of the raw values matrix by the total (200), we can construct the corresponding probability matrix.

Figure 4.8

The *X* or *Y* but Not Both Case

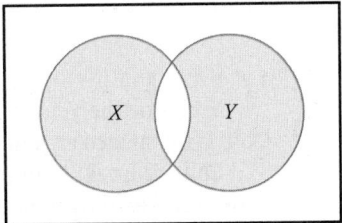

PROBABILITY MATRIX

		Geographic Location				
		Toronto	Calgary	Vancouver	Montreal	
		D	E	F	G	
	Finance A	0.12	0.05	0.04	0.07	0.28
Industry Type	Manufacturing B	0.15	0.03	0.11	0.06	0.35
	Communications C	0.14	0.09	0.06	0.08	0.37
		0.41	0.17	0.21	0.21	1.00

Suppose a respondent is selected randomly from these data.

a. What is the probability that the respondent is from Vancouver (F)?
b. What is the probability that the respondent is from the communications industry (C) or from Toronto (D)?
c. What is the probability that the respondent is from Calgary (E) or from the finance industry (A)?

Solution

a. $P(\text{Vancouver}) = P(F) = 0.21$
b. $P(C \cup D) = P(C) + P(D) - P(C \cap D) = 0.37 + 0.41 - 0.14 = 0.64$
c. $P(E \cup A) = P(E) + P(A) - P(E \cap A) = 0.17 + 0.28 - 0.05 = 0.40$

In computing the union by using the general law of addition, the intersection probability is subtracted because it is already included in both marginal probabilities. This adjusted probability leaves a union probability that properly includes both marginal values and the intersection value. If the intersection probability is subtracted out a second time, the intersection is removed, leaving the probability of X or Y but not *both*.

$$P(X \text{ or } Y \text{ but not both}) = P(X) + P(Y) - P(X \cap Y) - P(X \cap Y)$$
$$= P(X \cup Y) - P(X \cap Y)$$

Figure 4.8 is the Venn diagram for this probability.

COMPLEMENT OF A UNION

The probability of the union of two events X and Y represents the probability that the outcome is *either X or Y* or it is *both X and Y*. The union includes everything except the possibility that it is not (X or Y). Another way to state the latter is as *neither X nor Y*, which can be symbolically represented as $P(\text{not } X \cap \text{not } Y)$. Because it is the only possible case other than the union of X or Y, it is the **complement of a union.** Stated more formally,

$$P(\text{neither } X \text{ nor } Y) = P(\text{not } X \cap \text{not } Y) = 1 - P(X \cup Y)$$

Examine the Venn diagram in Figure 4.9. Note that the complement of the union of X, Y is the shaded area outside the circles. This area represents the neither X nor Y region.

In the survey about increasing worker productivity by changing the office design discussed earlier, the probability that a randomly selected worker would respond with noise reduction *or* increased storage space was determined to be

$$P(N \cup S) = P(N) + P(S) - P(N \cap S) = 0.70 + 0.67 - 0.56 = 0.81$$

The probability that a worker would respond with *neither* noise reduction *nor* increased storage space is calculated as the complement of this union.

$$P(\text{neither N nor S}) = P(\text{not N} \cap \text{not S}) = 1 - P(N \cup S) = 1 - 0.81 = 0.19$$

Thus, 19% of the workers selected neither noise reduction nor increased storage space as solutions to increasing productivity. In Table 4.3, this *neither/nor* probability is found in the No No cell of the matrix, 0.19.

SPECIAL LAW OF ADDITION

If two events are mutually exclusive, the probability of the union of the two events is the probability of the first event plus the probability of the second event. Because mutually exclusive events do not intersect, nothing has to be subtracted.

Figure 4.9

The Complement of a Union: The Neither/Nor Region

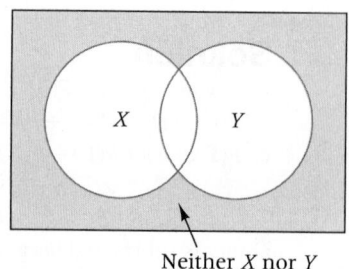

Neither X nor Y

Special Law of Addition	If X, Y are mutually exclusive, $$P(X \cup Y) = P(X) + P(Y)$$

The special law of addition is a special case of the general law of addition. The general law fits all cases; hence, if the events are mutually exclusive, the intersection of $P(X)$ and $P(Y)$ becomes zero and the general law reduces to the special law of addition.

In the survey about improving productivity by changing office design, the respondents were allowed to choose more than one possible office design change. Therefore, it is most likely that virtually none of the change choices were mutually exclusive, and the special law of addition would not apply to that example.

In another survey, however, respondents were allowed to select only one option for their answer, which made the possible options mutually exclusive. In this survey, conducted by Yankelovich Partners for William M. Mercer, Inc., workers were asked what most hinders their productivity and were given only the following selections from which to choose only one answer.

- Lack of direction
- Lack of support
- Too much work
- Inefficient process
- Not enough equipment/supplies
- Low pay/chance to advance

Lack of direction was cited by the most workers (20%), followed by lack of support (18%), too much work (18%), inefficient process (8%), not enough equipment/supplies (7%), low pay/chance to advance (7%), and a variety of other factors added by respondents. If a worker who responded to this survey is selected (or if the survey actually reflects the views of the working public and a worker in general is selected) and that worker is asked which of the given selections most hinders his or her productivity, what is the probability that the worker will respond that it is either too much work or inefficient process?

Let M denote the event "too much work" and I denote the event "inefficient process." The question is:

$$P(M \cup I) = ?$$

Because 18% of the survey respondents said "too much work,"

$$P(M) = 0.18$$

Because 8% of the survey respondents said "inefficient process,"

$$P(I) = 0.08$$

Because it was not possible to select more than one answer,

$$P(M \cap I) = 0.0000$$

Implementing the special law of addition gives

$$P(M \cup I) = P(M) + P(I) = 0.18 + 0.08 = 0.26$$

Demonstration Problem 4.3

If a student is randomly selected from among the graduates described in Demonstration Problem 4.1, what is the probability that the graduate would have obtained a master's or a doctoral degree that year? What is the probability that the student is either a basic graduate or has a master's degree?

Solution

Examine the raw values matrix of the data shown in Demonstration Problem 4.1. In many raw value and probability matrices like this one, the rows are nonoverlapping or mutually exclusive, as are the columns. In this matrix, a worker can be classified as being in only one type of position and as either male or female but not both. Thus, the categories of type of position are mutually exclusive, as are the categories of gender, and the special law of addition can be applied to the education data to determine the union probabilities.

Let G denote (basic) graduate, MD denote master's, and DD denote doctoral. The probability that a student has either a master's or a doctoral degree is

$$P(MD \cup DD) = P(MD) + P(DD) = (31{,}551/184{,}912) + (5{,}164/184{,}912)$$
$$= 36{,}715/184{,}912 = 0.1986$$

The probability that a student is either a basic graduate or has a master's degree is

$$P(G \cup MD) = P(G) + P(MD) = (148{,}197/184{,}912) + (31{,}551/184{,}912)$$
$$= 179{,}748/184{,}912 = 0.9721$$

Demonstration Problem 4.4

Use the data from the matrices in Demonstration Problem 4.2. What is the probability that a randomly selected respondent is from Calgary or Montreal?

$$P(E \cup G) = ?$$

Solution

Because geographic location is mutually exclusive (the work location is either in Calgary or in Montreal but not in both),

$$P(E \cup G) = P(E) + P(G) = 0.17 + 0.21 = 0.38$$

Concept Check

1. Under what condition can you use the special law of addition instead of the general law?
2. If you apply the general law of addition where the special law may be used, would your calculations be wrong? Explain why.
3. Give two examples of cases where you can use the special law of addition instead of the general law.
4. What is a probability matrix?
5. What is meant by the "complement of a union"?

4.5 Problems

4.8   Given $P(A) = 0.10$, $P(B) = 0.12$, $P(C) = 0.21$, $P(A \cap C) = 0.05$, and $P(B \cap C) = 0.03$, solve the following.

    a. $P(A \cup C) = $ _____
    b. $P(B \cup C) = $ _____
    c.   If A and B are mutually exclusive, $P(A \cup B) = $ _____

4.9   Use the values in the matrix to solve the equations given.

	D	E	F
A	5	8	12
B	10	6	4
C	8	2	5

    a. $P(A \cup D) = $ _____
    b. $P(E \cup B) = $ _____
    c. $P(D \cup E) = $ _____
    d. $P(C \cup F) = $ _____

4.10   Use the values in the matrix to solve the equations given.

	E	F
A	0.10	0.03
B	0.04	0.12
C	0.27	0.06
D	0.31	0.07

    a. $P(A \cup F) = $ _____
    b. $P(E \cup B) = $ _____
    c. $P(B \cup C) = $ _____
    d. $P(E \cup F) = $ _____

4.11   Suppose that 47% of all Canadians have flown in an airplane at least once and that 28% of all Canadians have ridden on a train at least once. What is the probability that a randomly selected Canadian has either ridden on a train or flown in an airplane? Can this problem be solved? Under what conditions can it be solved? If the problem cannot be solved, what information is needed to make it solvable?

4.12   Suppose that currently 75% of women 25 through 49 years of age are participating in the labour force. Suppose that 78% of the women in that age group are married. Suppose also that 61% of all women 25 through 49 years of age are married and are participating in the labour force.

    a.   What is the probability that a randomly selected woman in that age group is married or is participating in the labour force?
    b.   What is the probability that a randomly selected woman in that age group is married or is participating in the labour force but not both?
    c.   What is the probability that a randomly selected woman in that age group is neither married nor participating in the labour force?

4.13   A survey estimated that 67% of all households with television have cable TV. Seventy-four percent of all households with television have two or more TV sets. Suppose 55% of all households with television have cable TV and two or more TV sets. A household with television is randomly selected.

    a.   What is the probability that the household has cable TV or two or more TV sets?

    b.   What is the probability that the household has cable TV or two or more TV sets but not both?

    c.   What is the probability that the household has neither cable TV nor two or more TV sets?

    d.   Why does the special law of addition not apply to this problem?

4.14   A survey in the U.S. asked companies about the procedures they use in hiring. Only 54% of the responding companies review the applicant's university results as part of the hiring process, and only 44% consider faculty references. Assume that these percentages are also true for the population of companies in Canada and that 35% of all companies use both the applicant's university results and faculty references.

    a.   What is the probability that a randomly selected company uses either faculty references or university results as part of the hiring process?

    b.   What is the probability that a randomly selected company uses either faculty references or university results but not both as part of the hiring process?

    c.   What is the probability that a randomly selected company uses neither faculty references nor university results as part of the hiring process?

    d.   Construct a probability matrix for this problem and indicate the locations of your answers for parts (a), (b), and (c) on the matrix.

4.6 MULTIPLICATION LAWS

GENERAL LAW OF MULTIPLICATION

As stated in Section 4.4, the probability of the intersection of two events $(X \cap Y)$ is called the joint probability. The general law of multiplication is used to find the joint probability.

General Law of Multiplication	$P(X \cap Y) = P(X) \cdot P(Y|X) = P(Y) \cdot P(X|Y)$

Figure 4.10

Joint Probability that a Woman Is in the Labour Force and Is a Part-Time Worker

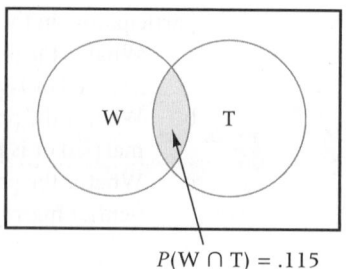

$P(W \cap T) = .115$

Table 4.5		Males	Females	Total
Probability Matrix of Gender of Graduates	Graduate	0.310	0.491	0.801
	Master's	0.082	0.088	0.171
	Doctoral	0.013	0.015	0.028
	Total	0.405	0.594	1.000

The notation $X \cap Y$ means that both X *and* Y must happen. The general law of multiplication gives the probability that *both* event X and event Y will occur at the same time.

According to Statistics Canada (CANSIM table 282-0002), in the year 2005, 47% of the Canadian labour force was female. If 25% of the women in the labour force work part time, what is the probability that a randomly selected member of the Canadian labour force is a woman *and* works part time? This question is one of joint probability, and the general law of multiplication can be applied to answer it.

Let W denote the event that the member of the labour force is a woman. Let T denote the event that the member is a part-time worker. The question is:

$$P(W \cap T) = ?$$

According to the general law of multiplication, this problem can be solved by

$$P(W \cap T) = P(W) \cdot P(T|W)$$

Since 47% of the labour force is women, $P(W) = 0.47 \cdot P(T|W)$ is a conditional probability that can be stated as the probability that a worker is a part-time worker given that the worker is a woman. This condition is what was given in the statement that 25% *of the women in the labour force* work part time. Hence, $P(T|W) = 0.25$. From there it follows that

$$P(W \cap T) = P(W) \cdot P(T|W) = (0.47)(0.25) = 0.118$$

It can be stated that 11.8% of the Canadian labour force are women *and* work part time. The Venn diagram in Figure 4.10 shows these relationships and the joint probability.

Determining joint probabilities from raw value or probability matrices is easy because every cell of these matrices is a joint probability. In fact, some statisticians refer to a probability matrix as a *joint probability table*.

For example, suppose the raw values matrix of the data from Demonstration Problem 4.1 and the Decision Dilemma is converted to a probability matrix by dividing by the total number of employees ($N = 184{,}912$), resulting in Table 4.5. Each value in the cell of Table 4.5 is an intersection, and the table contains all possible intersections (joint probabilities) for the events of gender and type of position. For example, the probability that a randomly selected student is male *and* a has a master's degree, $P(M \cap G)$, is 0.082. The probability that a randomly selected worker is female *and* has a doctorate, $P(F \cap D)$, is 0.015. Once a probability matrix is constructed for a problem, usually the easiest way to solve for the joint probability is to find the appropriate cell in the matrix and select the answer. However, sometimes because of what is given in a problem, using the formula is easier than constructing the matrix.

Demonstration Problem 4.5

A company has 140 employees, of which 30 are supervisors. Eighty of the employees are married, and 20% of the married employees are supervisors. If a company employee is randomly selected, what is the probability that the employee is married and is a supervisor?

Solution

Let M denote married and S denote supervisor. The question is:

$$P(M \cap S) = ?$$

First, calculate the marginal probability:

$$P(M) = \frac{80}{140} = 0.5714$$

Then, note that 20% of the married employees are supervisors, which is the conditional probability $P(S|M) = 0.20$. Finally, applying the general law of multiplication gives

$$P(M \cap S) = P(M) \cdot P(S|M) = (0.5714)(0.20) = 0.1143$$

Hence, 11.43% of the 140 employees are married and are supervisors.

Demonstration Problem 4.6

From the data obtained from the interviews of 200 executives in Demonstration Problem 4.2, find:

a. $P(B \cap E)$
b. $P(G \cap A)$
c. $P(B \cap C)$

PROBABILITY MATRIX

		Geographic Location				
		Toronto	Calgary	Vancouver	Montreal	
		D	E	F	G	
Industry Type	Finance A	0.12	0.05	0.04	0.07	0.28
	Manufacturing B	0.15	0.03	0.11	0.06	0.35
	Communications C	0.14	0.09	0.06	0.08	0.37
		0.41	0.17	0.21	0.21	1.00

Solution

a. From the cell of the probability matrix, $P(B \cap E) = 0.03$. To solve by the formula, $P(B \cap E) = P(B) \cdot P(E|B)$, first find $P(B)$:

$$P(B) = 0.35$$

The probability of E occurring given that B has occurred, $P(E|B)$, can be determined from the probability matrix as $P(E|B) = 0.03/0.35$. Therefore,

$$P(B \cap E) = P(B) \cdot P(E|B) = (0.35)\left(\frac{0.03}{0.35}\right) = 0.03$$

Although the formula works, finding the joint probability in the cell of the probability matrix is faster than using the formula.

An alternative formula is $P(B \cap E) = P(E) \cdot P(B|E)$, and, from the table, $P(E) = 0.17$. Then, $P(B|E)$ means the probability of B if E is given. There are 0.17 Es in the probability matrix and 0.03 Bs in these Es. Hence,

$$P(B|E) = \frac{0.03}{0.17} \quad \text{and} \quad P(B \cap E) = P(E) \cdot P(B|E) = (0.17)\left(\frac{0.03}{0.17}\right) = 0.03$$

b. To obtain $P(G \cap A)$, find the intersecting cell of G and A in the probability matrix, 0.07, or use one of the following formulas:

$$P(G \cap A) = P(G) \cdot P(A|G) = (0.21)\left(\frac{0.07}{0.21}\right) = 0.07$$

or

$$P(G \cap A) = P(A) \cdot P(G|A) = (0.28)\left(\frac{0.07}{0.28}\right) = 0.07$$

c. The probability $P(B \cap C)$ means that one respondent would have to work both in the manufacturing industry and the communications industry. The survey used to gather data from the 200 executives, however, requested that each respondent specify only one industry type for his or her company. The matrix shows no intersection for these two events. Thus, B and C are mutually exclusive. None of the respondents is in both manufacturing and communications. Hence,

$$P(B \cap C) = 0.0$$

SPECIAL LAW OF MULTIPLICATION

If events X and Y are independent, a special law of multiplication can be used to find the intersection of X and Y. This special law utilizes the fact that when two events X, Y are independent, $P(X|Y) = P(X)$ and $P(Y|X) = P(Y)$. Thus, the general law of multiplication, $P(X \cap Y) = P(X) \cdot P(Y|X)$, becomes $P(X \cap Y) = P(X) \cdot P(Y)$ when X and Y are independent.

Special Law of Multiplication	If X, Y are independent, $P(X \cap Y) = P(X) \cdot P(Y)$.

According to *Canadian Grocer,* in 2005 32% of all Canadian grocery chains had an automated banking machine and 19% had pharmacies. Is having an automated banking machine independent of the chain having a pharmacy? If they are independent, what is the probability of a randomly selected grocery chain having an automated banking machine and a pharmacy? Let A denote an automated banking machine and P denote a pharmacy.

$$P(A) = 0.32$$
$$P(P) = 0.19$$
$$P(A \cap P) = P(A) \cdot P(P) = (0.32) \cdot (0.19) = 0.061$$

Therefore, 6% of all grocery chains in Canada have both an automated banking machine *and* a pharmacy. (It is important to understand the implications of our calculation here. We are assuming that having a pharmacy and having an automated banking machine are not related to each other. This may not necessarily be true. For example, if larger outlets tended to have pharmacies *and* automated banking machines, they are not independent of each other and therefore the calculations are not valid.)

Demonstration Problem 4.7

A manufacturing firm produces pads of bound paper. Three percent of all paper pads produced are improperly bound. An inspector randomly samples two pads of paper, one at a time. Because a large number of pads are being produced during the inspection, the sampling being done, in essence, is with replacement. What is the probability that the two pads selected are both improperly bound?

Solution

Let I denote improperly bound. The problem is to determine

$$P(I_1 \cap I_2) = ?$$

The probability of $I = 0.03$, or 3% are improperly bound. Because the sampling is done with replacement, the two events are independent. Hence,

$$P(I_1 \cap I_2) = P(I_1) \cdot P(I_2) = (0.03)(0.03) = 0.0009$$

Table 4.6

Contingency Table of Data from Independent Events

	D	E	
A	8	12	20
B	20	30	50
C	6	9	15
	34	51	85

Most probability matrices contain variables that are not independent. If a probability matrix contains independent events, the special law of multiplication can be applied. If not, the special law cannot be used. In Section 4.7, we explore a technique for determining whether events are independent. Table 4.6 contains data from independent events.

Demonstration Problem 4.8

Use the data from Table 4.6 and the special law of multiplication to find $P(B \cap D)$.

Solution

$$P(B \cap D) = P(B) \cdot P(D) = \frac{50}{85} \cdot \frac{34}{85} = 0.2353$$

This approach works *only* for contingency tables and probability matrices in which the variable along one side of the matrix is *independent* of the variable along the other side of the matrix. Note that the answer obtained by using the formula is the same as the answer obtained by using the cell information from Table 4.6.

$$P(B \cap D) = \frac{20}{85} = 0.2353$$

Concept Check

1. Under what condition can you use the special law of multiplication instead of the general law?
2. Under what conditions are the general law and the special law interchangeable?

4.6 Problems

4.15 Use the values in the contingency table to solve the equations given.

	C	D	E	F
A	5	11	16	8
B	2	3	5	7

a. $P(A \cap E) =$ _____
b. $P(D \cap B) =$ _____
c. $P(D \cap E) =$ _____
d. $P(A \cap B) =$ _____

4.16 Use the values in the probability matrix to solve the equations given.

	D	E	F
A	0.12	0.13	0.08
B	0.18	0.09	0.04
C	0.06	0.24	0.06

a. $P(E \cap B) =$ _____
b. $P(C \cap F) =$ _____
c. $P(E \cap D) =$ _____

4.17 a. A batch of 50 parts contains six defects. If two parts are drawn randomly one at a time without replacement, what is the probability that both parts are defective?
   b. If this experiment is repeated, with replacement, what is the probability that both parts are defective?

4.18 Eighty-one percent of the Canadian population now lives in urban areas. Assume that about 15% of all Canadian adults care for ill relatives and that 11% of adults living in urban areas care for ill relatives.
   a. Use the general law of multiplication to determine the probability of randomly selecting an adult from the Canadian population who lives in an urban area and is caring for an ill relative.
   b. What is the probability of randomly selecting an adult from the Canadian population who lives in an urban area and does not care for an ill relative?
   c. Construct a probability matrix and show where the answers to this problem lie in the matrix.
   d. From the probability matrix, determine the probability that an adult lives in a nonurban area and cares for an ill relative.

4.19 According to the Canadian Tourism Human Resource Council, 10% of all Canadians in the labour force are employed in the tourism industry. Fifty-three percent of those who work in this sector are under 35 years of age. Statistics Canada reports that of those in the Canadian labour force not employed in the tourism industry, only 44% are under 35. Suppose you choose someone randomly from the Canadian labour force.

a. What is the probability that this person is not employed by the tourism industry?

b. What is the probability that this person is employed by the tourism industry and under 35 years of age?

c. What is the probability that this person is employed by the tourism industry and over 35 years of age?

d. What is the probability that this person is not employed by the tourism industry and under 35 years of age?

e. What is the probability that this person is not employed by the tourism industry and over 35 years of age?

f. What is the probability that this person is neither employed by the tourism industry nor over 35 years of age?

g. What is the probability that this person is not employed by the tourism industry nor under 35 years of age?

4.20 According to Statistics Canada (for 2005), 57% of all Canadian households have a dishwasher and 64% have a personal computer. Suppose 91% of all Canadian households with a dishwasher have a personal computer. A Canadian household is randomly selected.

a. What is the probability that the household has a dishwasher and a personal computer?

b. What is the probability that the household has a dishwasher or a personal computer?

c. What is the probability that the household has a dishwasher and does not have a personal computer?

d. What is the probability that the household has neither a dishwasher nor a personal computer?

e. What is the probability that the household does not have a dishwasher and does have a personal computer?

4.21 A recent study found that 30% of the travelling public said that their flight selections are influenced by perceptions of airline safety. Thirty-nine percent of the travelling public wants to know the age of the aircraft. Suppose 87% of the travelling public who say that their flight selections are influenced by perceptions of airline safety wants to know the age of the aircraft.

a. What is the probability of randomly selecting a member of the travelling public and finding out that she says that flight selection is influenced by perceptions of airline safety and she does not want to know the age of the aircraft?

b. What is the probability of randomly selecting a member of the travelling public and finding out that he says that flight selection is neither influenced by perceptions of airline safety nor does he want to know the age of the aircraft?

c. What is the probability of randomly selecting a member of the travelling public and finding out that she says that flight selection is not influenced by perceptions of airline safety and she wants to know the age of the aircraft?

4.22 Statistics Canada states that 80% of all Canadian households have CD players. In addition, 37% of all Canadian households have a truck or a van. Suppose 18% of all Canadian households have both a CD player and a truck/van. A Canadian household is randomly selected.

a. What is the probability that the household has a CD player or a truck/van?
b. What is the probability that the household has neither a CD player nor a truck/van?
c. What is the probability that the household does not have a CD player and does have a truck/van?
d. What is the probability that the household does have a CD player and does not have a truck/van?

4.7 CONDITIONAL PROBABILITY

Conditional probabilities are computed based on the prior knowledge that a business researcher has about one of the two events being studied. If X, Y are two events, the conditional probability of X occurring given that Y is known or has occurred is expressed as $P(X|Y)$ and is given in the *law of conditional probability*.

Law of Conditional Probability	$P(X \mid Y) = \dfrac{P(X \cap Y)}{P(Y)} = \dfrac{P(X) \cdot P(Y \mid X)}{P(Y)}$

The conditional probability of $(X|Y)$ is the probability that X will occur given Y. The formula for conditional probability is derived by dividing both sides of the general law of multiplication by $P(Y)$.

In the study by Yankelovich Partners to determine what changes in office design would improve productivity, 70% of the respondents believed noise reduction would improve productivity and 67% said increased storage space would improve productivity. In addition, suppose 56% of the respondents believed both noise reduction and increased storage space would improve productivity. A worker is selected randomly and asked about changes in office design. This worker believes that noise reduction would improve productivity. What is the probability that this worker believes increased storage space would improve productivity? That is, what is the probability that a randomly selected person believes storage space would improve productivity *given that* he or she believes noise reduction improves productivity? In symbols, the question is:

$$P(S|N) = ?$$

Note that the given part of the information is listed to the right of the vertical line in the conditional probability. The formula solution is

$$P(S|N) = \frac{P(S \cap N)}{P(N)}$$

but

$$P(N) = 0.70 \text{ and } P(S \cap N) = 0.56$$

so

$$P(S|N) = \frac{P(S \cap N)}{P(N)} = \frac{0.56}{0.70} = 0.80$$

Figure 4.11

Conditional Probability of Increased Storage Space Given Noise Reduction

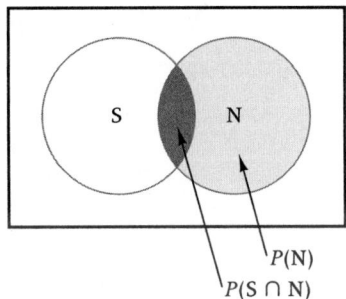

$P(N)$

$P(S \cap N)$

Eighty percent of workers who believe noise reduction would improve productivity believe increased storage space would improve productivity.

Note in Figure 4.11 that the area for N in the Venn diagram is completely shaded because it is given that the worker believes noise reduction will improve productivity. Also notice that the intersection of N and S is more heavily shaded. This portion of noise reduction includes increased storage space. It is the only part of increased storage space that is in noise reduction, and because the person is known to favour noise reduction, it is the only area of interest that includes increased storage space.

Examine the probability matrix in Table 4.7 for the office design problem. None of the probabilities given in the matrix are conditional probabilities. To reiterate what has been previously stated, a probability matrix contains only two types of probabilities, marginal and joint. The cell values are all joint probabilities and the subtotals in the margins are marginal probabilities. How are conditional probabilities determined from a probability matrix? The law of conditional probabilities shows that a conditional probability is computed by dividing the joint probability by the marginal probability. Thus, the probability matrix has all the necessary information to solve for a conditional probability.

What is the probability that a randomly selected worker believes noise reduction would not improve productivity given that the worker does believe increased storage space would improve productivity? That is,

$$P(\text{not } N | S) = ?$$

The law of conditional probability states that

$$P(\text{not } N | S) = \frac{P(\text{not } N \cap S)}{P(S)}$$

Notice that because S is given, we are interested only in the column that is shaded in Table 4.7, which is the Yes column for increased storage space. The marginal probability, $P(S)$, is the total of this column and is found in the margin at the bottom of the table as 0.67. $P(\text{not } N \cap S)$ is found as the intersection of No for noise and Yes for storage. This value is 0.11. Hence, $P(\text{not } N \cap S)$ is 0.11. Therefore,

$$P(\text{not } N | S) = \frac{P(\text{not } N \cap S)}{P(S)} = \frac{0.11}{0.67} = 0.164$$

The second version of the conditional probability law formula is:

$$P(X | Y) = \frac{P(X) \cdot P(Y | X)}{P(Y)}$$

This version is more complex than the first version, $P(X \cap Y)/P(Y)$. However, sometimes the second version must be used because of the information given in the

Table 4.7		Increased Storage Space		
Office Design Problem Probability Matrix		Yes	No	
	Noise Reduction Yes	0.56	0.14	0.70
	No	0.11	0.19	0.30
		0.67	0.33	1.00

problem—for example, when solving for $P(X|Y)$ but $P(Y|X)$ is given. The second version of the formula is obtained from the first version by substituting the formula for $P(X \cap Y) = P(X) \cdot P(Y|X)$ into the first version.

As an example, in Section 4.6, data relating to women in the Canadian labour force were presented. Included in this information was the fact that 47% of the Canadian labour force is female and the assumption that 25% of the females in the Canadian labour force work part time. If we further assume that 17.4% of all Canadian labourers are part-time workers, what is the probability that a randomly selected Canadian worker is a woman if that person is known to be a part-time worker? Let W denote the event of selecting a woman and T denote the event of selecting a part-time worker. In symbols, the question to be answered is:

$$P(W|T) = ?$$

The first form of the law of conditional probabilities is

$$P(W|T) = \frac{P(W \cap T)}{P(T)}$$

Note that this version of the law of conditional probabilities requires knowledge of the joint probability, $P(W \cap T)$, which is not given here. We therefore try the second version of the law of conditional probabilities, which is

$$P(W|T) = \frac{P(W) \cdot P(T|W)}{P(T)}$$

For this version of the formula, everything is given in the problem.

$$P(W) = 0.47$$
$$P(T) = 0.174$$
$$P(T|W) = 0.25$$

The probability of a labourer being a woman given that the person works part time can now be computed.

$$P(W|T) = \frac{P(W) \cdot P(T|W)}{P(T)} = \frac{(0.47)(0.25)}{(0.174)} = 0.675$$

Hence, 67.5% of the part-time workers are women.

In general, this second version of the law of conditional probabilities is likely to be used for solving $P(X|Y)$ when $P(X \cap Y)$ is unknown but $P(Y|X)$ is known.

Demonstration Problem 4.9

The data from the executive interviews given in Demonstration Problem 4.2 are repeated here. Use these data to find:

a. $P(B|F)$
b. $P(G|C)$
c. $P(D|F)$

RAW VALUES MATRIX

		Geographic Location				
		Toronto	Calgary	Vancouver	Montreal	
		D	E	F	G	
	Finance A	24	10	8	14	56
Industry Type	Manufacturing B	30	6	22	12	70
	Communications C	28	18	12	16	74
		82	34	42	42	200

Solution

a. $$P(B|F) = \frac{P(B \cap F)}{P(F)} = \frac{0.11}{0.21} = 0.524$$

Determining conditional probabilities from a probability matrix by using the formula is a relatively painless process. In this case, the joint probability, $P(B \cap F)$, appears in a cell of the matrix (0.11); the marginal probability, $P(F)$, appears in a margin (0.21). Bringing these two probabilities together by the formula produces the answer, $0.11/0.21 = 0.524$. This answer means that 52.4% of the Vancouver executives (the F values) are in manufacturing (the B values).

b. $$P(G|C) = \frac{P(G \cap C)}{P(C)} = \frac{0.08}{0.37} = 0.216$$

This result means that 21.6% of the responding communications industry executives (C) are from Montreal (G).

c. $$P(D|F) = \frac{P(D \cap F)}{P(F)} = \frac{0.00}{0.21} = 0.00$$

Because D and F are mutually exclusive, $P(D \cap F)$ is zero and so is $P(D|F)$. The rationale behind $P(D|F) = 0$ is that, if F is given (the respondent is known to be located in Vancouver), the respondent could not be located in D (Toronto).

INDEPENDENT EVENTS

Independent Events X, Y	If X and Y are independent events, the following must be true: $P(X|Y) = P(X)$ and $P(Y|X) = P(Y)$

In each equation, it does not matter that X or Y is given because X and Y are *independent*. When X and Y are independent, the conditional probability is solved as a marginal probability.

Sometimes it is important to test a contingency table of raw data to determine whether events are independent. If *any* combination of two events from the different sides of the matrix fail the test $P(X|Y) = P(X)$, the matrix does not contain independent events.

Demonstration Problem 4.10		Test the matrix for the 200 executive responses to determine whether industry type is independent of geographic location.

RAW VALUES MATRIX

		Geographic Location				
		Toronto	Calgary	Vancouver	Montreal	
		D	E	F	G	
	Finance A	24	10	8	14	56
Industry Type	Manufacturing B	30	6	22	12	70
	Communications C	28	18	12	16	74
		82	34	42	42	200

Solution

Select one industry and one geographic location (say, A—Finance and G—Montreal). Does $P(A|G) = P(A)$?

$$P(A|G) = \frac{14}{42} \text{ and } P(A) = \frac{56}{200}$$

Does $14/42 = 56/200$? No, $0.33 \neq 0.28$. Industry and geographic location are not independent because at least one exception to the test is present.

STATISTICS IN BUSINESS TODAY

Probabilities in the Dry Cleaning Business

According to the International Fabricare Institute, about two thirds or 67% of all dry cleaning customers are female, and 65% are married. Thirty-seven percent of dry cleaning customers use a cleaner that is within a mile (1.6 km) of their home. Do dry cleaning customers care about coupons? Fifty-one percent of dry cleaning customers say that coupons or discounts are important, and in fact, 57% would try another cleaner if a discount were offered. Converting these percentages to proportions, each could be considered to be a marginal probability. For example, if a customer is randomly selected from the dry cleaning industry, there is a 0.37 probability that he or she uses a dry cleaner within a mile of his or her home, $P(\leq 1 \text{ mile}) = 0.37$.

Suppose further analysis shows that 55% of dry cleaning customers are female and married. Converting this figure to probability results in the joint probability $P(F \cap M) = 0.55$. Subtracting this value from the 0.67 who are female, we can determine that 11% of dry cleaning customers are female and not married: $P(F \cap \text{not } M) = 0.11$. Suppose 90% of those who say that coupons or discounts are important would try another cleaner if a discount were offered. This can be restated as a conditional probability: $P(\text{try another}|\text{coupons important}) = 0.90$.

Each of the four types of probabilities discussed in this chapter can be applied to the data on consumers in the dry cleaning industry. Further breakdowns of these statistics using probabilities can offer insights into how to better serve dry cleaning customers and how to better market dry cleaning services and products.

**Demonstration
Problem 4.11**

Determine whether the contingency table shown as Table 4.6 and repeated here contains independent events.

	D	E	
A	8	12	20
B	20	30	50
C	6	9	15
	34	51	85

Solution

Check the first cell in the matrix to find whether $P(A|D) = P(A)$.

$$P(A) = \frac{8}{34} = 0.2353$$

$$P(A) = \frac{20}{85} = 0.2353$$

The checking process must continue until all the events are determined to be independent. In this matrix, all the possibilities check out. Thus, Table 4.6 contains independent events.

Concept Check

1. Explain why conditional probability provides a better estimate than unconditional probability.
2. What is the relationship between conditional probability and independent events?

4.7 Problems

4.23   Use the values in the contingency table to solve the equations given.

	E	F	G
A	15	12	8
B	11	17	19
C	21	32	27
D	18	13	12

    a. $P(G|A) =$ _____

    b. $P(B|F) =$ _____

    c. $P(C|E) =$ _____

    d. $P(E|G) =$ _____

4.24   Use the values in the probability matrix to solve the equations given.

	C	D
A	0.36	0.44
B	0.11	0.09

    a. $P(C|A) =$ _____

    b. $P(B|D) =$ _____

    c. $P(A|B) =$ _____

4.25 The results of a survey asking, "Do you have a calculator and/or a computer in your home?" follow.

Calculator

		Yes	No	
	Yes	46	3	49
Computer	No	11	15	26
		57	18	75

Is the variable "calculator" independent of the variable "computer"? Why or why not?

4.26 In 2005 and 2006 combined, 2,870,884 motor vehicles were sold in Canada. The year 2006 accounted for 1,666,327 of these vehicles. Those manufactured overseas (outside North America) accounted for 526,219 of the vehicles sold in 2006. Suppose 325,421 vehicles built overseas were sold in 2005. A vehicle is randomly selected from this list of motor vehicles.
   a. What is the probability that the vehicle was manufactured overseas?
   b. What is the probability that the vehicle was sold in 2006 or manufactured overseas?
   c. What is the probability that the vehicle was sold in 2006 if it is known that the vehicle was manufactured overseas?
   d. What is the probability that the vehicle was manufactured overseas if it is known that the vehicle was sold in 2006?
   e. What is the probability that the vehicle was not manufactured overseas if it is known that the vehicle was not sold in 2006?
   f. Given that the vehicle was sold in 2006, what is the probability that the vehicle was not manufactured overseas?

4.27 Arthur Andersen Enterprise Group/National Small Business United, Washington, conducted a survey of U.S. small-business owners to determine the challenges for growth for their businesses. The top challenge, selected by 46% of the small-business owners, was the economy. A close second was finding qualified workers (37%). Suppose 15% of the small-business owners selected both the economy and finding qualified workers as challenges for growth. A small-business owner is randomly selected.
   a. What is the probability that the owner believes the economy is a challenge for growth if the owner believes that finding qualified workers is a challenge for growth?
   b. What is the probability that the owner believes that finding qualified workers is a challenge for growth if the owner believes that the economy is a challenge for growth?
   c. Given that the owner does not select the economy as a challenge for growth, what is the probability that the owner believes that finding qualified workers is a challenge for growth?
   d. What is the probability that the owner believes neither that the economy is a challenge for growth nor that finding qualified workers is a challenge for growth?

4.28 According to a survey published by ComPsych Corporation, 54% of all workers read e-mail while they are talking on the phone. Suppose that 20% of those who read e-mail while they are talking on the phone write personal "to-do" lists during meetings. Assuming that these figures are true for all workers, if a worker is randomly selected, determine the following probabilities:

a.   The worker reads e-mail while talking on the phone and writes personal to-do lists during meetings.

b.   The worker does not write personal to-do lists given that the worker reads e-mail while talking on the phone.

c.   The worker does not write personal to-do lists and does read e-mail while talking on the phone.

4.29   Suppose that 34% of financial consultants purchase their computer hardware online and that 52% purchase their computer software on-line. Suppose that 93% of the financial consultants who purchase their computer hardware on-line purchase their computer software on-line. If a financial consultant is randomly selected, determine the following probabilities:

a.   The financial consultant does not purchase computer software on-line given that the financial consultant does purchase computer hardware on-line.

b.   The financial consultant does purchase computer software on-line given that the financial consultant does not purchase computer hardware on-line.

c.   The financial consultant does not purchase computer hardware on-line if it is known that the financial consultant does purchase computer software on-line.

d.   The financial consultant does not purchase computer hardware on-line if it is known that the financial consultant does not purchase computer software on-line.

4.30   In a study undertaken by Catalyst, 43% of women senior executives agreed or strongly agreed that a lack of role models was a barrier to their career development. In addition, 46% agreed or strongly agreed that gender-based stereotypes were barriers to their career advancement. Suppose 77% of those who agreed or strongly agreed that gender-based stereotypes were barriers to their career advancement agreed or strongly agreed that the lack of role models was a barrier to their career development. If one of these female senior executives is randomly selected, determine the following probabilities:

a.   What is the probability that the senior executive does not agree or strongly agree that a lack of role models was a barrier to her career development given that she does agree or strongly agree that gender-based stereotypes were barriers to her career development?

b.   What is the probability that the senior executive does not agree or strongly agree that gender-based stereotypes were barriers to her career development given that she does agree or strongly agree that the lack of role models was a barrier to her career development?

c.   If it is known that the senior executive does not agree or strongly agree that gender-based stereotypes were barriers to her career development, what is the probability that she does not agree or strongly agree that the lack of role models was a barrier to her career development?

4.8 REVISION OF PROBABILITIES: BAYES' RULE

An extension to the conditional law of probabilities is Bayes' rule, which was developed by and named for Thomas Bayes (1702–1761). **Bayes' rule** is *a formula that extends the use of the law of conditional probabilities to allow revision of original probabilities with new information.*

Bayes' Rule	$P(X_i \mid Y) = \dfrac{P(X_i) \cdot P(Y \mid X_i) \cdots}{P(X_1) \cdot P(Y \mid X_1) + P(X_2) \cdot P(Y \mid X_2) + \cdots + P(X_n) \cdot P(Y \mid X_n)}$

Recall that the law of conditional probability for

$$P(X_i|Y)$$

is

$$P(X_i \mid Y) = \frac{P(X_i) \cdot P(Y \mid X_i)}{P(Y)}$$

Compare Bayes' rule to this law of conditional probability. The numerators of Bayes' rule and the law of conditional probability are the same, the intersection of X_i and Y shown in the form of the general rule of multiplication. The new feature that Bayes' rule uses is found in the denominator of the rule:

$$P(X_1) \cdot P(Y|X_1) + P(X_2) \cdot P(Y|X_2) + \cdots + P(X_n) \cdot P(Y|X_n)$$

The denominator of Bayes' rule includes a product expression (intersection) for every partition in the sample space Y, including the event (X_i) itself. The denominator is thus a collectively exhaustive listing of mutually exclusive outcomes of Y. This denominator is sometimes referred to as the "total probability formula." It represents a weighted average of the conditional probabilities, with the weights being the prior probabilities of the corresponding event.

By expressing the law of conditional probabilities in this new way, Bayes' rule enables the statistician to make new and different applications using conditional probabilities. In particular, statisticians use Bayes' rule to "revise" probabilities in light of new information.

A particular formulation of an over-the-counter drug is produced by only two companies, Prairie Pharmaceuticals and Badlands Generics. Suppose Prairie produces 65% of the drug and Badlands produces 35%. Eight percent of the users of the drug produced by Prairie show some side effects and 12% of the Badlands users show similar side effects. A customer randomly picks up one of these drugs at the pharmacy. What is the probability that Prairie produced the drug? What is the probability that Badlands produced the drug? The customer uses the product and develops side effects. Now what is the probability that Prairie produced the drug? That Badlands produced the drug?

Table 4.8 **Bayesian Table for Revision of Over-the-Counter Drug Problem Probabilities**	Event	Prior Probability $P(E_i)$	Conditional Probability $P(d\|E_i)$	Joint Probability $P(E_i \cap d)$	Posterior or Revised Probability
	Prairie	0.65	0.08	0.052	$\dfrac{0.052}{0.094} = 0.553$
	Badlands	0.35	0.12	$P(\text{side effects}) = \dfrac{0.042}{0.094}$	$\dfrac{0.042}{0.094} = 0.447$

The probability was 0.65 that the drug came from Prairie and 0.35 that it came from Badlands. These are called prior probabilities because they are based on the original information.

The new information that the drug produced side effects changes the probabilities because one company's drug causes a higher incidence of side effects than the other company's drug does. How can this information be used to update or revise the original probabilities? Bayes' rule allows such updating. One way to lay out a revision of probabilities problem is to use a table. Table 4.8 shows the analysis for the over-the-counter drug problem.

The process begins with the prior probabilities: 0.65 for Prairie and 0.35 for Badlands. These prior probabilities appear in the second column of Table 4.8. Because the product is found to have side effects, the conditional probabilities, P(side effects|Prairie) and P(side effects|Badlands) should be used. Eight percent of the Prairie users experience side effects: P(side effects|Prairie) = 0.08. Twelve percent of the Badlands users experience side effects: P(side effects|Badlands) = 0.12. These two conditional probabilities appear in the third column. Eight percent of Prairie's 65% of the customers develop side effects: (0.08)(0.65) = 0.052, or 5.2% of the total. This figure appears in the fourth column of Table 4.8; it is the joint probability of getting the product that was made by Prairie and developing side effects. Because the user experienced side effects, these are the only Prairie users that are of interest. Twelve percent of Badlands' 35% of the users develop side effects. Multiplying these two percentages yields the joint probability of getting a Badlands drug leading to side effects. This figure also appears in the fourth column of Table 4.8: (0.12)(0.35) = 0.042; that is, 4.2% of the total. It is the joint probability of getting the product that was made by Badlands and developing side effects. This percentage includes the only Badlands customers of interest because the customer experienced side effects.

Column 4 is totalled to get 0.094, indicating that 9.4% of all users developed side effects (Prairie and side effects = 0.052 + Badlands and side effects = 0.042). The other 90.6% of the users are not of interest because they did not develop any side effects. To compute the fifth column, the posterior or revised probabilities, involves dividing each value in column 4 by the total of column 4. For Prairie, 0.052 of the total users used Prairie *and* experienced side effects out of the total of 0.094 who experienced side effects. Dividing 0.052 by 0.094 yields 0.553 as a revised probability that the purchased product was made by Prairie. This probability is lower than the prior or original probability of 0.65 because fewer of Prairie's users (as a percentage) experienced side effects compared to Badlands users. The product that caused side effects is now less likely to have come from Prairie than before the knowledge of the occurrence of side effects. Badlands' probability is revised by dividing the 0.042 joint probability of the product being made by Badlands *and* causing side effects by the total probability of the product causing side effects (0.094). The result is 0.042/0.094 = 0.447. The probability that side effects are caused by the Badlands drug has increased because a higher percentage of Badlands users develop side effects.

Tree diagrams are another common way to solve Bayes' rule problems. Figure 4.12 shows the solution for the over-the-counter drug problem. Note that the tree diagram contains all possibilities, including both side effect and no side effect proportions. When new information is given, only the pertinent proportions are selected and used. The joint probability values at the ends of the appropriate branches are used to revise and compute the posterior possibilities. Using the total number of users with side effects, 0.052 + 0.042 = 0.094, the calculation is as follows:

$$\text{Revised Probability: Prairie} = \frac{0.052}{0.094} = 0.553$$

$$\text{Revised Probability: Badlands} = \frac{0.042}{0.094} = 0.447$$

Figure 4.12

Tree Diagram for Over-the-Counter Drug Problem Probabilities

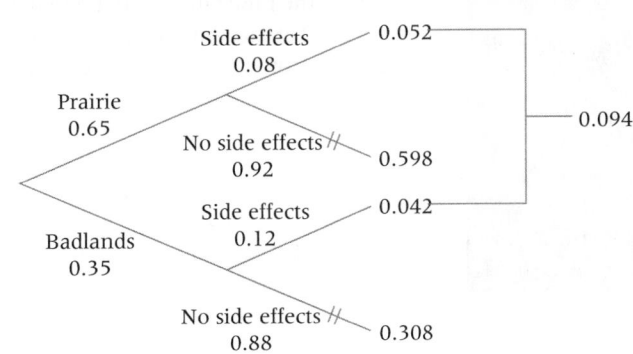

Demonstration Problem 4.12

Machines A, B, and C all produce the same two parts, X and Y. Of all the parts produced, machine A produces 60%, machine B produces 30%, and machine C produces 10%. In addition,

> 40% of the parts made by machine A are part X.
> 50% of the parts made by machine B are part X.
> 70% of the parts made by machine C are part X.

A part produced by this company is randomly sampled and is determined to be an X part. With the knowledge that it is an X part, revise the probabilities that the part came from machine A, B, or C.

Solution

The prior probability of the part coming from machine A is 0.60, because machine A produces 60% of all parts. The prior probability is 0.30 that the part came from B and 0.10 that it came from C. These prior probabilities are more pertinent if nothing is known about the part. However, the part is known to be an X part. The conditional probabilities show that different machines produce different proportions of X parts. For example, 0.40 of the parts made by machine A are X parts, but 0.50 of the parts made by machine B and 0.70 of the parts made by machine C are X parts. It makes sense that the probability of the part coming from machine C would increase and that the probability that the part was made on machine A would decrease because the part is an X part.

The following table shows how the prior probabilities; conditional probabilities; joint probabilities; and marginal probability, $P(X)$, can be used to revise the prior probabilities to obtain posterior probabilities.

Event	Prior $P(E_i)$	Conditional $P(X\|E_i)$	Joint $P(X \cap E_i)$	Posterior
A	0.60	0.40	$(0.60)(0.40) = 0.24$	$\dfrac{0.24}{0.46} = 0.52$
B	0.30	0.50	0.15	$\dfrac{0.15}{0.46} = 0.33$
C	0.10	0.70	$P(X) = \dfrac{0.07}{0.46}$	$\dfrac{0.07}{0.46} = 0.15$

After the probabilities are revised, it is apparent that the probability of the part being made at machine A decreased and that the probabilities that the part was made at machines B and C increased. A tree diagram presents another view of this problem.

Revised Probabilities: Machine A: $\dfrac{0.24}{0.46} = 0.52$

Machine B: $\dfrac{0.15}{0.46} = 0.33$

Machine C: $\dfrac{0.07}{0.46} = 0.15$

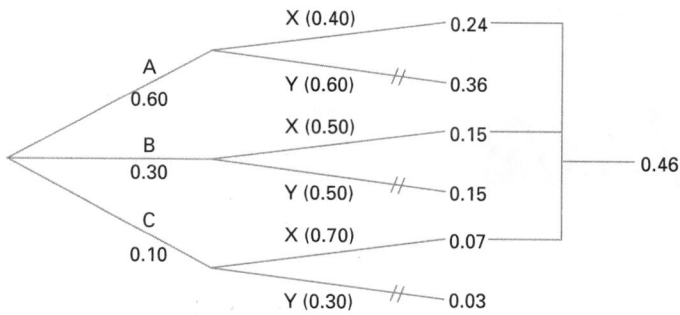

Concept Check

1. Both conditional probability and Bayes' rule incorporate in their calculations what we already know. In what way are they different?

4.8 Problems

4.31   In a manufacturing plant, machine A produces 10% of a certain product, machine B produces 40% of this product, and machine C produces 50% of this product. Five percent of machine A products are defective, 12% of machine B products are defective, and 8% of machine C products are defective. The company inspector has just sampled a product from this plant and has found it to be defective. Determine the revised probabilities that the sampled product was produced by machine A, machine B, or machine C.

4.32   Alex, Natasha, and Juan fill orders in a fast-food restaurant. Alex incorrectly fills 20% of the orders he takes. Natasha incorrectly fills 12% of the orders she takes. Juan incorrectly fills 5% of the orders he takes. Alex fills 30% of all orders, Natasha fills 45% of all orders, and Juan fills 25% of all orders. An order has just been filled.
   a.   What is the probability that Natasha filled the order?
   b.   If the order was filled by Juan, what is the probability that it was filled correctly?
   c.   Who filled the order is unknown, but the order was filled incorrectly. What are the revised probabilities that Alex, Natasha, or Juan filled the order?
   d.   Who filled the order is unknown, but the order was filled correctly. What are the revised probabilities that Alex, Natasha, or Juan filled the order?

4.33   In a small town, two lawn companies fertilize lawns during the summer. Maritime Lawn Service has 72% of the market. Thirty percent of the lawns fertilized by Maritime could be rated as very healthy one month after service. Greenchem has the other 28% of the market. Twenty percent of the lawns fertilized by Greenchem could be rated as very healthy one month after service. A lawn that has been treated with fertilizer by one of these companies within the last month is selected randomly. If the lawn is rated as very healthy, what are the revised probabilities that Maritime or Greenchem treated the lawn?

4.34   Suppose 70% of all companies are classified as small companies and the rest as large companies. Suppose further that 82% of large companies provide training to employees, but only 18% of small companies provide training. A company is randomly selected without knowing if it is a large or small company; however, it is determined that the company provides training to employees. What are the prior probabilities that the company is a large company or a small company? What are the revised probabilities that the company is large or small? Based on your analysis, what is the overall percentage of companies that offer training?

EDUCATION, GENDER, AND EMPLOYMENT

The client company data given in the Decision Dilemma are displayed in a raw values matrix. Using the techniques presented in this chapter, it is possible to statistically answer the managerial questions.

- If an employer randomly selects a person from the pool of graduates, the probability that the graduate is a woman, $P(W)$, is 109,939/184,912 or 0.595. This marginal probability indicates that roughly 59.5% of all graduates are women. Given that the graduate has a master's degree, the probability that the graduate is a woman, $P(W|MD)$, is 16,335/31,551 or 0.518.
- The proportion of basic graduates who are women is 0.613. This means that there is a 61.3% chance that a randomly picked basic graduate is female. Therefore, if a randomly picked basic graduate is a woman, it does not exhibit any bias against men.
- Suppose an employer wants a graduate and picks a graduate at random. The probability that the person has a doctoral degree is 0.027 or 2.7%, derived by dividing all doctoral graduates by the total number of graduates (5,164/184,912).
- The probability that a randomly chosen graduate is a man with a master's degree is given by

$$P(M \cap MD) = 15,216/184,912 = 0.082$$

The probability that a randomly chosen graduate is *not* a man with a master's degree is a complementary event to the above. Therefore, the probability is

$$P(M \cap MD)' = 1 - 0.082 = 0.918$$

If the chosen person is a man, the probability of his having a basic degree is given by the conditional probability

$$P(BD|M) = 57,408/74,973 = 0.766$$

Many other questions about education and employment can be answered using probabilities.

The probability approach to hiring is a factual, numerical approach to people selection taken without regard to individual talents, skills, and worth to the company. Of course, in most instances, many other considerations go into the hiring, promoting, and rewarding of workers besides the random draw of their name. However, company management should be aware that attacks on hiring, promotion, and reward practices are sometimes made using statistical analyses such as those presented here. It is not being argued here that management should base decisions merely on the probabilities within particular categories. Nevertheless, being aware of the probabilities, management can proceed to undergird their decisions with documented evidence of worker productivity and worth to the organization.

KEY CONSIDERATIONS

One of the potential misuses of probability occurs when subjective probabilities are used. Most subjective probabilities are based on a person's feelings, intuition, or experience. Almost everyone has an opinion on something and is willing to share it. As professional people, it is important that we do not give our best-guess probability of an occurrence if we are not relatively confident of what will happen. Optimistic people will tend to give higher probabilities of the likelihood of a company or client attaining some goal. Pessimistic people may tend to dampen the probability of such a goal being attained. Although such probabilities are not strictly unethical to report, they can be misleading and disastrous to other decision makers. We should be cautious in offering our subjective probabilities in decision-making situations where our opinion is highly valued. In addition, subjective probabilities leave the door open for unscrupulous people to overemphasize their point of view by manipulating the probability.

Relative frequency of occurrence probabilities are basically computed on historical figures. It is important that such historical information be accurate and valid. "Padding" the figures from the past can lead to incorrect and misleading probabilities.

The decision maker should remember that the laws and rules of probability are for the long run. If a coin is tossed, even though the probability of getting a head is 0.5, the result will be either a head or a tail. It isn't possible to get a half head. The probability of getting a head (0.5) will probably work out in the long run, but in the short run an experiment might produce 10 tails in a row. Suppose the probability of striking oil on a geological formation is 0.10. This probability means that, in the long run, if the company drills enough holes on this type of formation, it should strike oil in about 10% of the holes. However, if the company has only enough money to drill one hole, it will either strike oil or have a dry hole. The probability figure of 0.10 may mean something different to the company that can afford to drill only one hole than to the company that can drill many hundreds. Classical probabilities could be used unethically to lure a company or client into a potential short-run investment with the expectation of getting at least something in return, when in actuality the investor will either win or lose. The oil company that drills only one hole will not get 10% back from the hole. It will either win or lose on the hole. Thus, classical probabilities open the door for unsubstantiated expectations, particularly in the short run.

Why Statistics Is Relevant

Many business and personal decisions need to be made under conditions of uncertainty. For example, an organization needs to market a product without any guarantee that it will succeed in the market. A factory needs to invest in machinery without any guarantee that the factory will recuperate the costs through sales. A marketer needs to supply goods to all stores with no guarantee that they will be sold. A judge has to make a decision on the guilt or innocence of the person on evidence that is necessarily incomplete. A university has to admit students without knowing whether the students will pass or fail.

In all such conditions, probability calculations provide a means of increasing the ratio of success to failure. Probability does not eliminate risk, but it provides a numerical estimate of it. As more information becomes available, probability methods offer a way to incorporate the new information, thereby reducing the chance of making incorrect decisions.

Decisions based on probability models may not always be right. But, if used properly, probability models will ensure an increase in the proportion of right decisions, potentially saving millions of dollars for the company.

SUMMARY

1. The study of probability addresses ways of assigning probabilities, types of probabilities, and laws of probabilities. Probabilities support the notion of inferential statistics. Using sample data to estimate and test hypotheses about population parameters is done with uncertainty. If samples are taken at random, probabilities can be assigned to outcomes of the inferential process.

2. Three methods of assigning probabilities are (a) the classical method, (b) the relative frequency of occurrence method, and (c) subjective probabilities. The classical method can assign probabilities a priori, or before the experiment takes place. It relies on the laws and rules of probability. The relative frequency of occurrence method assigns probabilities based on historical data or empirically derived data. Subjective probabilities are based on the feelings, knowledge, and experience of the person determining the probability.

3. Certain special types of events necessitate amendments to some of the laws of probability: mutually exclusive events and independent events. Mutually exclusive events are events that cannot occur at the same time, so the probability of their intersection is zero. In determining the union of two mutually exclusive events, the law of addition is amended by the deletion of the intersection. With independent events, the occurrence of one has no impact or influence on the occurrence of the other. Certain experiments, such as those involving coins or dice, naturally produce independent events. Other experiments produce independent events when the experiment is conducted with replacement. If events are independent, the joint probability is computed by multiplying the individual probabilities, which is a special case of the law of multiplication.

4. Three techniques for counting the possibilities in an experiment are the mn counting rule, the N^n possibilities, and combinations. The mn counting rule is used to determine how many total possible ways an experiment can occur in a series of sequential operations. The N^n formula is applied when sampling is being done with replacement or events are independent. Combinations are used to determine the possibilities when sampling is being done without replacement.

5. Four types of probability are marginal probability, conditional probability, joint probability, and union probability. The general law of addition is used to compute the probability of a union. The general law of multiplication is used to compute joint probabilities. The conditional law is used to compute conditional probabilities.

6–7. The general law of addition is used when we need to find the probability of the union of two events (X or Y or both occurring). The general law of multiplication is used to find the probability of two events X and Y happening together (joint probability). Conditional probabilities are used when we want to incorporate prior knowledge one may have regarding the two events studied.

8. Bayes' rule is a method that can be used to revise probabilities when new information becomes available; it is a variation of the conditional law. Bayes' rule takes prior probabilities of events occurring and adjusts or revises those probabilities on the basis of information about what subsequently occurs.

KEY TERMS

a priori
Bayes' rule
classical method
collectively exhaustive events
combinations
complementary event
complement of a union

conditional probability
elementary events
event
experiment
independent events
intersection
joint probability

marginal probability
mn counting rule
mutually exclusive events
permutations
probability matrix
relative frequency of
    occurrence method

sample space
set notation
subjective method
union
union probability

FORMULAS

Counting rule

$$mn$$

Sampling with replacement

$$N^n$$

Sampling without replacement

$$_N C_n$$

Combination formula

$$_N C_n = \binom{N}{n} = \frac{N!}{n!(N-n)!}$$

Permutation formula

$$_n P_r = \frac{n!}{(n-r)!}$$

General law of addition

$$P(X \cup Y) = P(X) + P(Y) - P(X \cap Y)$$

Special law of addition

$$P(X \cup Y) = P(X) + P(Y)$$

General law of multiplication

$$P(X \cap Y) = P(X) \cdot P(Y|X) = P(Y) \cdot P(X|Y)$$

Special law of multiplication

$$P(X \cap Y) = P(X) \cdot P(Y)$$

Law of conditional probability

$$P(X \mid Y) = \frac{P(X \cap Y)}{P(Y)} = \frac{P(X) \cdot P(Y \mid X)}{P(Y)}$$

Bayes' rule

$$P(X_1 \mid Y) = \frac{P(X_1) \cdot P(Y \mid X_1)}{P(X_1) \cdot P(Y \mid X_1) + P(X_2) \cdot P(Y \mid X_2) + \cdots + P(X_n) \cdot P(Y \mid X_n)}$$

SUPPLEMENTARY PROBLEMS

Calculating the Statistics

4.35 Use the values in the contingency table to solve the equations given.

Variable 1

		D	E
	A	10	20
Variable 2	B	15	5
	C	30	15

a. $P(E) =$ _____
b. $P(B \cup D) =$ _____
c. $P(A \cap E) =$ _____
d. $P(B|E) =$ _____
e. $P(A \cup B) =$ _____
f. $P(B \cap C) =$ _____
g. $P(D|C) =$ _____
h. $P(A|B) =$ _____

4.36 Are variables 1 and 2 in Question 4.35 independent? Why or why not?

4.37 Use the values in the contingency table to solve the equations given.

	D	E	F	G
A	3	9	7	12
B	8	4	6	4
C	10	5	3	7

a. $P(F \cap A) =$ _____
b. $P(A|B) =$ _____
c. $P(B) =$ _____
d. $P(E \cap F) =$ _____
e. $P(D|B) =$ _____
f. $P(B|D) =$ _____
g. $P(D \cup C) =$ _____
h. $P(F) =$ _____

4.38 The following probability matrix contains a breakdown on the age and gender of physicians in a large city in a recent year.

PHYSICIANS IN A LARGE CITY

		Age (Years)					
		<35	35–44	45–54	55–64	>65	
Gender	*Male*	0.11	0.20	0.19	0.12	0.16	0.78
	Female	0.07	0.08	0.04	0.02	0.01	0.22
		0.18	0.28	0.23	0.14	0.17	1.00

a. What is the probability that one randomly selected physician is 35–44 years old?
b. What is the probability that one randomly selected physician is both a woman and 45–54 years old?
c. What is the probability that one randomly selected physician is a man or is 35–44 years old?
d. What is the probability that one randomly selected physician is less than 35 years old or 55–64 years old?
e. What is the probability that one randomly selected physician is a woman if the physician is 45–54 years old?
f. What is the probability that a randomly selected physician is neither a woman nor 55–64 years old?

Testing Your Understanding

4.39 Purchasing Survey asked purchasing professionals what sales traits impressed them most in a sales representative. Seventy-eight percent selected "thoroughness." Forty percent responded "knowledge of your own product." The purchasing professionals were allowed to list more than one trait. Suppose 27% of the purchasing professionals listed both "thoroughness" and "knowledge of your own product" as sales traits that impressed them most. A purchasing professional is randomly sampled.
a. What is the probability that the professional selected "thoroughness" or "knowledge of your own product"?
b. What is the probability that the professional selected neither "thoroughness" nor "knowledge of your own product"?
c. If it is known that the professional selected "thoroughness," what is the probability that the professional selected "knowledge of your own product"?
d. What is the probability that the professional did not select "thoroughness" and did select "knowledge of your own product"?

4.40 Suppose that a survey of small companies showed that 42% offer retirement plans, 61% offer life insurance, and 33% offer both retirement plans and life insurance as benefits. If a small company is randomly selected, determine the following probabilities:
a. The company offers a retirement plan given that they offer life insurance.
b. The company offers life insurance given that they offer a retirement plan.
c. The company offers life insurance or a retirement plan.
d. The company offers a retirement plan and does not offer life insurance.
e. The company does not offer life insurance if it is known that it offers a retirement plan.

4.41 According to a survey, 16% of the population is technology driven. However, these figures vary by region. For example, in B.C. the figure is 20% and in Manitoba the figure is 17%. Sixteen percent of the Canadian population in general is in B.C. and 3.7% of the Canadian population is in Manitoba. Suppose a Canadian is chosen randomly.
a. What is the probability that the person lives in B.C. and is a technology-driven person?
b. What is the probability that the person lives in Manitoba and is a technology-driven person?
c. Suppose the chosen person is known to be technology driven. What is the probability that the person lives in B.C.?
d. Suppose the chosen person is known not to be technology driven. What is the probability that the person lives in Manitoba?
e. Suppose the chosen person is known to be technology driven. What is the probability that the person lives neither in B.C. nor in Manitoba?

SUPPLEMENTARY PROBLEMS (continued)

4.42   In a certain city, 30% of the families have a MasterCard, 20% have an American Express card, and 25% have a Visa card. Eight percent of the families have both a MasterCard and an American Express card. Twelve percent have both a Visa card and a MasterCard. Six percent have both an American Express card and a Visa card. No families have all three cards.

   a.   What is the probability of selecting a family that has either a Visa card or an American Express card?

   b.   If a family has a MasterCard, what is the probability that it has a Visa card?

   c.   If a family has a Visa card, what is the probability that it has a MasterCard?

   d.   Is possession of a Visa card independent of possession of a MasterCard? Why or why not?

   e.   Is possession of an American Express card mutually exclusive of possession of a Visa card?

4.43   A few years ago, a survey commissioned by *The World Almanac* and *Maturity News* Service reported that 51% of American respondents did not believe the Social Security system will be secure in 20 years. Of the respondents who were aged 45 or older, 70% believed the system will be secure in 20 years. Of the people surveyed, 57% were under age 45. One respondent is selected randomly.

   a.   What is the probability that the person is aged 45 or older?

   b.   What is the probability that the person is younger than 45 and believes that the Social Security system will be secure in 20 years?

   c.   If the person selected believes the Social Security system will be secure in 20 years, what is the probability that the person is 45 years old or older?

   d.   What is the probability that the person is younger than age 45 or believes the Social Security system will not be secure in 20 years?

4.44   A telephone survey conducted by the Maritz Marketing Research company found that 43% of those interviewed expect to save more money next year than they saved last year. Forty-five percent of those surveyed plan to reduce debt next year. Of those who expect to save more money next year, 81% plan to reduce debt next year. A respondent is selected randomly.

   a.   What is the probability that this person expects to save more money next year and plans to reduce debt next year?

   b.   What is the probability that this person expects to save more money next year or plans to reduce debt next year?

   c.   What is the probability that this person neither expects to save more money next year nor plans to reduce debt next year?

   d.   What is the probability that this person expects to save more money next year and does not plan to reduce debt next year?

4.45   The Steelcase Workplace Index studied the types of work-related activities that employees did while on vacation in the summer. Among other things, 40% read work-related material. Thirty-four percent checked in with the boss. Respondents to the study were allowed to select more than one activity. Suppose that of those who read work-related material, 78% checked in with the boss. One of these survey respondents is selected randomly.

   a.   What is the probability that while on vacation this respondent checked in with the boss and read work-related material?

   b.   What is the probability that while on vacation this respondent neither read work-related material nor checked in with the boss?

   c.   What is the probability that while on vacation this respondent read work-related material given that the respondent checked in with the boss?

   d.   What is the probability that while on vacation this respondent did not check in with the boss given that the respondent read work-related material?

   e.   What is the probability that while on vacation this respondent did not check in with the boss given that the respondent did not read work-related material?

   f.   Construct a probability matrix for this problem.

4.46 A study on ethics in the workplace by the Ethics Resource Center and Kronos, Inc., revealed that 35% of employees admit to keeping quiet when they see coworker misconduct. Suppose 75% of employees who admit to keeping quiet when they see coworker misconduct call in sick when they are well. In addition, suppose that 40% of the employees who call in sick when they are well admit to keeping quiet when they see coworker misconduct. If an employee is randomly selected, determine the following probabilities:

a. The employee calls in sick when well and admits to keeping quiet when seeing coworker misconduct.

b. The employee admits to keeping quiet when seeing coworker misconduct or calls in sick when well.

c. Given that the employee calls in sick when well, he or she does not keep quiet when seeing coworker misconduct.

d. The employee neither keeps quiet when seeing coworker misconduct nor calls in sick when well.

e. The employee admits to keeping quiet when seeing coworker misconduct and does not call in sick when well.

4.47 In a survey, 2,400 cable company subscribers were asked to share their complaints about the cable service. The number one complaint was the time to get through to a customer representative, with 17% of the participating consumers selecting it. Several other complaints were noted including impolite customer reps (14%), customer service (14%), payment disputes (11%), incorrect billing (10%), incompetent complaint handling (8%), and indifference to customers (7%). These complaint categories are mutually exclusive. Assume that the results of this survey can be extended to all cable subscribers. If a cable subscriber is randomly selected, determine the following probabilities:

a. The subscriber complains about payment disputes or incorrect billing.

b. The subscriber complains about indifference to customers and incompetent complaint handling.

c. The subscriber complains about impolite customer reps given that the subscriber complains about incorrect billing.

d. The subscriber does not complain about incompetent complaint handling nor does the consumer complain about payment disputes.

4.48 Companies use employee training for various reasons including employee loyalty, certification, quality, and process improvement. In a survey of U.S. companies, BI Learning Systems reported that 56% of the responding companies named employee retention as a top reason for training. Suppose 36% of the companies replied that they use training for process improvement and for employee retention. In addition, suppose that of the companies that use training for process improvement, 90% use training for employee retention. A company that uses training is randomly selected.

a. What is the probability that the company uses training for employee retention and not for process improvement?

b. If it is known that the company uses training for employee retention, what is the probability that it uses training for process improvement?

c. What is the probability that the company uses training for process improvement?

d. What is the probability that the company uses training for employee retention or process improvement?

e. What is the probability that the company neither uses training for employee retention nor uses training for process improvement?

f. Suppose it is known that the company does not use training for process improvement. What is the probability that the company does use training for employee retention?

4.49 Pitney Bowes surveyed 302 directors and vice presidents of marketing at large and midsized U.S. companies to determine what they believe is the best vehicle for educating decision makers on complex issues in selling products and services. The highest percentage of companies chose direct mail/

catalogues, followed by direct sales/sales rep. Direct mail/catalogues was selected by 38% of the companies. None of the companies selected both direct mail/catalogues and direct sales/sales rep. Suppose also that 41% selected neither direct mail/catalogues nor direct sales/sales rep. If one of these companies is selected randomly and their top marketing person interviewed about this matter, determine the following probabilities:

a. The marketing person selected direct mail/catalogues and did not select direct sales/sales rep.

b. The marketing person selected direct sales/sales rep.

c. The marketing person selected direct sales/sales rep given that the person selected direct mail/catalogues.

d. The marketing person did not select direct mail/catalogues given that the person did not select direct sales/sales rep.

4.50   In a study of incentives used by companies to retain mature workers by The Conference Board, it was reported that 41% use flexible work arrangements. Suppose that of those companies that do not use flexible work arrangements, 10% give time off for volunteerism. In addition, suppose that of those companies that use flexible work arrangements, 60% give time off for volunteerism. If a company is randomly selected, determine the following probabilities:

a. The company uses flexible work arrangements or gives time off for volunteerism.

b. The company uses flexible work arrangements and does not give time off for volunteerism.

c. Given that the company does not give time off for volunteerism, the company uses flexible work arrangements.

d. The company does not use flexible work arrangements given that the company does give time off for volunteerism.

e. The company does not use flexible work arrangements or the company does not give time off or volunteerism.

4.51   A small independent physicians' practice has three doctors. Dr. Sarabia sees 41% of the patients, Dr. Tran sees 32%, and Dr. Jackson sees the rest. Dr. Sarabia requests blood tests on 5% of her patients,

Dr. Tran requests blood tests on 8% of his patients, and Dr. Jackson requests blood tests on 6% of her patients. An auditor randomly selects a patient from the past week and discovers that the patient had a blood test as a result of the physician visit. Knowing this information, what is the probability that the patient saw Dr. Sarabia? For what percentage of all patients at this practice are blood tests requested?

4.52   A survey by the Arthur Andersen Enterprise Group/ National Small Business United attempted to determine what the leading challenges are for the growth and survival of small businesses. Although the economy and finding qualified workers were the leading challenges, several others were listed in the results of the study, including regulations, listed by 30% of the companies, and the tax burden, listed by 35%. Suppose that 71% of the companies listing regulations as a challenge listed the tax burden as a challenge. Assume these percentages hold for all small businesses. If a small business is randomly selected, determine the following probabilities:

a. The small business lists both the tax burden and regulations as a challenge.

b. The small business lists either the tax burden or regulations as a challenge.

c. The small business lists either the tax burden or regulations but not both as a challenge.

d. The small business lists regulations as a challenge given that it lists the tax burden as a challenge.

e. The small business does not list regulations as a challenge given that it lists the tax burden as a challenge.

f. The small business does not list regulations as a challenge given that it does not list the tax burden as a challenge.

4.53   According to Statistics Canada figures, 31.5% of all Canadians are in the 0–24 age bracket, 13.7% are in the 25–34 age bracket, 16.1% are in the 35–44 age bracket, and 38.6% are in the 45 and older age bracket. Suppose a market research study shows that Canadians use their leisure time in different ways according to age. For example, of those who are in the 45 and older age bracket, 39% read a book or a magazine for more than 10 hours per week. Of those who are in the 0–24 age bracket, only 11% read a book or a magazine more than 10 hours per week. The percentage figures for reading a book or a magazine for more than 10 hours per week are 24% for the 25–34 age bracket and 27% for the 35–44 age bracket. Suppose a Canadian is randomly selected and it is determined that he or she reads a book or a magazine for more than 10 hours per week. Revise the probabilities that he or she is in any given age category. Using these figures, what is the overall percentage of the Canadian population that reads a book or a magazine for more than 10 hours per week?

4.54   A survey was conducted for a TV network to understand what viewers consider to be the most important thing in their lives. Twenty-nine percent said "good health," 21% responded "a happy marriage," and 40% replied "a happy family." Because they were asked which of these things is the most important thing, a respondent could not select more than one answer.

a.   What is the probability that a person replied "a happy marriage" or "a happy family"?

b.   What is the probability that a person replied "a happy marriage" or "a happy family" or "good health"?

c.   What is the probability that a person replied "a happy family" and "good health"?

d.   What is the probability that a person replied neither "a happy family" nor "good health" nor "a happy marriage"?

ANALYZING THE DATABASES

see www.wiley.com/canada/black

1. In the Major League Baseball Database, what is the probability that a randomly selected team is in Division 4? What is the probability that a randomly selected team has payroll of under $80 million? What is the probability that a randomly selected team neither is in Division 1 nor has a payroll of over $80 million?

2. Use the Major League Baseball Database. Construct a raw values matrix for Division and for League. You should have a 6×2 matrix. Using this matrix, answer the following questions. (Refer to Analyzing the Databases in Chapter 1 for category members.) What is the probability that a randomly selected team is in the East if the team is known to be in the American League? If the team is known to be in the West, what is the probability that it is a National League team?

CASE

Bluewater Recycling Association Offers Bigger Bins

The Bluewater Recycling Association is Canada's largest resource management company. It provides waste collection and recycling services. Recycling is a very important part of Bluewater's business, and in October 2008 the company implemented a new recycling system. This new system was first used in the town of St. Marys, Ontario, using new larger bins and special trucks to collect the recyclable items. This new system proved to be very popular with the residents of St. Marys as evidenced by that fact that they were putting out 27% more recyclable items than in the previous year. The new bins are very different from the previous blue bins that the residents used. They are larger and have wheels on them, which makes them easier to move. As well, they are more convenient because all the items are placed into one bin, meaning residents do not need to sort their items.

The new trucks pick up the bins from the curb every other week. These trucks are also much more efficient because they can pick up 119 bins per hour, as compared to the old trucks, which were only able to pick up 80 bins per hour.

The Bluewater Recycling Association is very pleased with the success of the new recycling system. It has improved on the time needed to collect the recyclable items, as well as on the amount of material that is actually collected. Two months after the new system was implemented, Bluewater's collection of recyclable items had significantly increased and approximately 94% of St. Marys households were using the new bins.

Discussion

1. According to Statistics Canada, approximately 22% of all St. Marys residents are in the 45–64 age range. Suppose that 97% of the people who used the new bins, once they were introduced for the first time during the initial two-month period, were in the 45–64 age category. Use this information to determine whether age is independent of the initial use of the bins during the introductory two-month time period. Explain your answer.

2. Using the probabilities given in Question 1, calculate the probability that a randomly selected resident of St. Marys is either in the 45–64 age category or used the new bin during the initial two-month period. What is the probability that a randomly selected person was in the 45–64 age category given that he or she used the new bin in the introductory two-month period?

3. Suppose 46% of all residents that recycle in St. Marys became aware of the new bins through advertising. Of those who heard the news, 62% used the bins at least once within the first two months of their introduction. Of those who did not hear about the new bins through advertising, 29% used the new bins at least once within the first two months of its introduction. Suppose a bin user is randomly selected and it is learned that he or she used the new Bluewater Recycling bin within the first two months of its introduction. Revise the probability that this person heard about the new bins through advertising and the probability that the person did not hear about the new bins through advertising. Comment on the effectiveness of the advertising campaign of the new recycling system.

References

Bluewater Recycling Association. Website for data source: <http://www.recyclexchange.com/assn/rs190234.html>; "New Recycling Bin Trial Promising," The Middlesex Banner, December 10, 2008. Website for data source: <http://www.banner.on.ca/pages/pg02.pdf>; Statistics Canada, 2009, Website for data source: <http://www12.statcan.ca/english/Profilo1/CP01/Details/Page.cfm?Lang=E&Geo1=CSD&Code1=3531016&Geo2=PR&Code2=35&Data=Count&SearchText=st.marys&SearchType=Contains&SearchPR=35&B1=All&Custom=>

Unit II

DISTRIBUTIONS AND SAMPLING

In Unit II of this textbook, we introduce the concept of statistical distribution. In lay terms, a statistical distribution is a numerical or graphical depiction of frequency counts or probabilities for the various values of a variable that can occur. Distributions are important because most of the analyses done in business statistics are based on the characteristics of a particular distribution. In Unit II, you will study eight distributions: six population distributions and two sampling distributions.

Six population distributions are presented in Chapters 5 and 6. These population distributions can be categorized as discrete distributions or continuous distributions. Discrete distributions are introduced in Chapter 5, and they include the binomial distribution, the Poisson distribution, and the hypergeometric distribution. Continuous distributions are presented in Chapter 6, and they include the uniform distribution, the normal distribution, and the exponential distribution. Information about sampling is discussed in Chapter 7 along with two sampling distributions: the sampling distribution of $\bar{x}$ and the sampling distribution of $\hat{p}$. Three more population distributions are introduced later in the text in Unit III. These include the t distribution and the chi-square distribution in Chapter 8 and the F distribution in Chapter 10.

CHAPTER 5

DISCRETE DISTRIBUTIONS

Learning Objectives

The overall learning objective of Chapter 5 is to help you understand a category of probability distributions that produces only discrete outcomes. Here are the key questions of the chapter:

1. How can we distinguish between discrete random variables and continuous random variables?

2. How can we determine the mean and variance of a discrete distribution?

3. What type of statistical experiments can be described by the binomial distribution? How should we work out such problems?

4. When should we use the Poisson distribution in analyzing statistical experiments? How should we work out such problems?

5. When is it possible to approximate binomial distribution problems by the Poisson distribution? How should we work out such problems?

6. When should we use the hypergeometric distribution and how should we work out such problems?

Bruce Laurance/The Image Bank/Getty Images

LIFE WITH A CELL PHONE

DECISION DILEMMA

As early as 1947, scientists understood the basic concept of a cell phone as a type of two-way radio. Seeing the potential of crude mobile car phones, researchers understood that by using a small range of service areas (cells) with frequency reuse, they could increase the capacity for mobile phone usage significantly even though the technology was not then available. During that same year, AT&T proposed the allocation of a large number of radio-spectrum frequencies by the U.S. Federal Communications Commission (FCC) that would thereby make widespread mobile phone service feasible. At the same time, the FCC decided to limit the amount of frequency capacity available such that only 23 phone conversations could take place simultaneously. In 1968, the FCC reconsidered its position and freed the airwaves for more phones. At about this time, AT&T and Bell Labs proposed to the FCC a system in which they would construct a series of many small, low-powered broadcast towers, each of which would broadcast to a cell covering a few miles. Taken as a whole, such cells could be used to pass phone calls from cell to cell, thereby reaching a large area.

The first company to actually produce a cell phone was Motorola, and Dr. Martin Cooper, then of Motorola and considered the inventor of the first modern portable handset, made his first call on the portable cell phone in 1973. By 1977, AT&T and Bell Labs had developed a prototype cellular phone system that was tested in Chicago by 2,000 trial customers. After the first commercial cell phone system began operation in Japan in 1979, and Motorola and American Radio developed a second U.S. cell system in 1981, the FCC authorized commercial cellular service in the U.S. in 1982. By 1987, the number of cell phone subscribers had exceeded one million in the U.S., and as frequencies were getting crowded, the FCC authorized alternative cellular technologies, opening up new opportunities for development. Since that time, researchers have developed a number of advances that have increased capacity exponentially.

Today in Canada, over 72% of households report having at least one cell phone. Provincially, this proportion ranges from a high of about 83% of households in Alberta to a low of about 63% in Quebec. The proportion of households relying solely on cell phone is about 6%, and the trend is rising.

In the U.S., there are over 140 million cell phones in use. About 5% of cell phone owners use only cellular phones and, as in Canada, the trend is rising. In addition, about 18% of Americans consider their cell phone as their primary phone number. In an Associated Press/America Online Pew poll of 1,200 cell phone users, it was discovered that two thirds of all cell phone users said that it would be hard to give up their cell phones, and 26% responded that they could not imagine life without their cell phones. In spite of this growing dependence on cell phones, not everyone is happy about their usage. Almost 9 out of 10 cell users encounter others using their phones in an annoying way. In addition, 28% claim that sometimes they do not drive as safely as they should because they are using cell phones. There are multiple uses for the cell phone, including picture taking, text messaging, and game playing. According to the study, two thirds of cell phone owners in the 18 to 29 age bracket use their cell phones to send text messages, 55% take pictures, 47% play games, and 28% surf the Internet.

Managerial and Statistical Questions

1. The study says that about 6% of Canadian households consider their cell phone as their primary phone number. Suppose you randomly select 20 households. What is the probability that more than three of your sample consider the cell phone as their primary phone number?

2. The study also reports that 9 out of 10 cell users encounter others using their phones in an annoying way. Based on this, if you were to randomly select 25 cell phone users, what is the probability that fewer than 20 would report that they encounter others using their phones in an annoying way?

3. Suppose a survey of cell phone users shows that, on average, a cell phone user receives 3.6 calls per day. If this figure is true, what is the probability that a cell phone user receives no calls in a day? What is the probability that a cell phone user receives five or more calls in a day?

Sources: Statistics Canada, *The Daily*, April 23, 2008; Mary Bellis, "Selling the Cell Phone, Part 1: History of Cellular Phones," in About Business & Finance. An America Online site; Selling The Cell Phone—History of Cellular Phones at <http://inventors.about.com/library/weekly/aa070899.htm>; *USA Today Tech,* "For Many, Their Cell Phone Has Become Their Only Phone," at <http://www.usatoday.com/tech/news/2003-03-24-cell-phones_x.htm>; and Will Lester, "A Love-Hate Relationship," *Houston Chronicle,* April 4, 2006, p. D4.

In statistical experiments involving chance, outcomes occur randomly. Suppose as an example of such an experiment, a battery manufacturer randomly selects three batteries from a large batch of batteries to be tested for quality. Each selected battery is to be rated as good or defective. The batteries are numbered from 1 to 3, a defective battery is designated with a D, and a good battery is designated with a G. All possible outcomes are shown in Table 5.1. The expression $D_1 G_2 D_3$ denotes one particular outcome in which the first and third batteries are defective and the second battery is good. In this chapter, we examine the probabilities of various outcomes that can occur with particular types of experiments.

Table 5.1			
All Possible Outcomes for the Battery Experiment	G_1	G_2	G_3
	D_1	G_2	G_3
	G_1	D_2	G_3
	G_1	G_2	D_3
	D_1	D_2	G_3
	D_1	G_2	D_3
	G_1	D_2	D_3
	D_1	D_2	D_3

5.1 DISCRETE VERSUS CONTINUOUS DISTRIBUTIONS

A **random variable** is *a variable that contains the outcomes of a chance experiment.* For example, suppose an experiment is to measure the arrivals of automobiles at a tollbooth during a 30-second period. The possible outcomes are 0 cars, 1 car, 2 cars, . . . , *n* cars. These numbers, (0, 1, 2, . . . , *n*), are the values of a random variable. Suppose another experiment is to measure the time between the completion of two tasks in a production line. The values will range from 0 seconds to *n* seconds. These time measurements are the values of another random variable. The two categories of random variables are (1) discrete random variables and (2) continuous random variables.

A random variable is a **discrete random variable** *if the set of all possible values is at most a finite or a countably infinite number of possible values.* In most statistical situations, discrete random variables produce values that are nonnegative whole numbers. For example, if six people are randomly selected from a population and how many of the six are left-handed is to be determined, the random variable produced is discrete. The only possible numbers of left-handed people in the sample of six are 0, 1, 2, 3, 4, 5, and 6. There cannot be 2.75 left-handed people in a group of six people; obtaining non-whole-number values is impossible. Other examples of experiments that yield discrete random variables are as follows:

1. Randomly selecting 25 people who consume soft drinks and determining how many people prefer diet soft drinks
2. Determining the number of defects in a batch of 50 items
3. Counting the number of people who arrive at a store during a 5-minute period
4. Sampling 100 registered voters and determining how many voted for the mayor in the last election

The battery experiment described at the beginning of the chapter produces a distribution that has discrete outcomes. Any one trial of the experiment will contain 0, 1, 2, or 3 defective batteries. It is not possible to get 1.58 defective batteries. It could be said that discrete random variables are usually generated from experiments in which things are "counted," not "measured."

Continuous random variables *take on values at every point over a given interval.* Thus, continuous random variables have no gaps or unassumed values. It could be said that continuous random variables are generated from experiments in which things are "measured," not "counted." For example, if a person is assembling a product component, the time it takes to accomplish that feat could be any value within a reasonable range such as 3 minutes 36.4218 seconds or 5 minutes 17.5169 seconds. Examples of measures for which continuous random variables might be generated are time, height, weight, and volume. Other examples of experiments that yield continuous random variables are as follows:

1. Sampling the volume of liquid nitrogen in a storage tank
2. Measuring the time between customer arrivals at a retail outlet
3. Measuring the lengths of newly designed automobiles
4. Measuring the mass of grain in a grain elevator at different points of time

Once continuous data are measured and recorded, they become discrete data because the data are rounded off to a discrete number. Thus, in actual practice virtually all business data are discrete. However, for practical reasons, data analysis is facilitated greatly by using continuous distributions on data that were continuous originally.

The outcomes for random variables and their associated probabilities can be organized into distributions. The two types of distributions are **discrete distributions,** *constructed from discrete random variables,* and **continuous distributions,** *based on continuous random variables.*

In this text, three discrete distributions are presented:

1. binomial distribution
2. Poisson distribution
3. hypergeometric distribution

In addition, six continuous distributions are discussed:

1. uniform distribution
2. normal distribution
3. exponential distribution
4. *t* distribution
5. chi-square distribution
6. *F* distribution

Concept Check

1. Characterize the following random variables as either discrete or continuous.
   - The number of heads in 25 tosses of a coin
   - The amount of gasoline you put in your car

- The duration of your phone calls
- The number of phone calls you receive per day
- The number of friends you run into during a school day

2. What is the difference between discrete and continuous variables?

5.2 DESCRIBING A DISCRETE DISTRIBUTION

How can we describe a discrete distribution? One way is to construct and study a graph of the distribution. The histogram is probably the most common graphical way to depict a discrete distribution.

Observe the discrete distribution in Table 5.2. An executive is considering out-of-town business travel for a given Friday. She recognizes that at least one crisis could occur on the day that she is gone, and she is concerned about that possibility. Table 5.2 shows a discrete distribution that contains the number of crises that could occur during the day that she is gone and the probability that each number will occur. For example, there is a 0.37 probability that no crisis will occur, a 0.31 probability of one crisis, and so on. The histogram in Figure 5.1 depicts the distribution given in Table 5.2. Notice that the x axis of the histogram contains the possible outcomes of the experiment (number of crises that might occur) and the y axis contains the probabilities of these occurring.

Table 5.2

Discrete Distribution of Occurrence of Daily Crises

Number of Crises	Probability
0	0.37
1	0.31
2	0.18
3	0.09
4	0.04
5	0.01

It is readily apparent from studying the graph of Figure 5.1 that the most likely number of crises is 0 or 1. In addition, we can see that the distribution is discrete in that no probabilities are shown for values in between the whole-number crises.

Figure 5.1

Histogram of Discrete Distribution of Crises Data

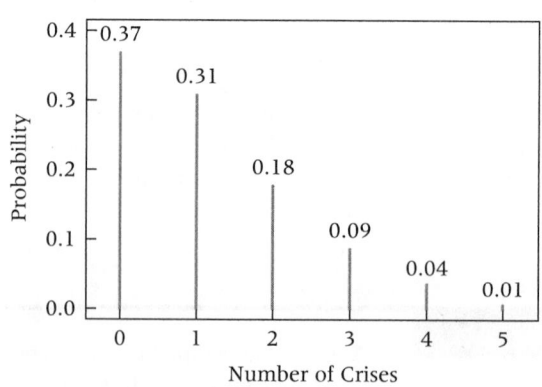

MEAN, VARIANCE, AND STANDARD DEVIATION OF DISCRETE DISTRIBUTIONS

What additional mechanisms can be used to describe discrete distributions besides depicting them graphically? The measures of central tendency and measures of variability discussed in Chapter 3 for grouped data can be applied to discrete distributions to compute a mean, a variance, and a standard deviation. Each of these three descriptive measures (mean, variance, and standard deviation) is computed on grouped data by using the class midpoint as the value to represent the data in the class interval. With discrete distributions, using the class midpoint is not necessary because the discrete value of an outcome (0, 1, 2, 3, . . .) is used to represent itself. Thus, instead of using the value of the class midpoint (M) in computing these descriptive measures for grouped data, we use the discrete experiment's outcomes (x). In computing these descriptive measures on grouped data, we use the frequency of each class interval to weight the class midpoint. With discrete distribution analysis, the probability of each occurrence is used as the weight.

MEAN OR EXPECTED VALUE

The **mean** or **expected value** of a discrete distribution is *the long-run average of occurrences*. We must realize that any one trial using a discrete random variable yields only one outcome. However, if the process is repeated enough times, the average of the outcomes is most likely to approach a long-run average, expected value, or mean value. This mean, or expected, value is computed as follows.

Mean or Expected Value of a Discrete Distribution	$$\mu = E(x) = \sum[x \cdot P(x)]$$ where $\quad E(x) = $ long-run average $\quad\quad x = $ an outcome $\quad P(x) = $ probability of that outcome

As an example, let's compute the mean or expected value of the distribution given in Table 5.2. See Table 5.3 for the resulting values. In the long run, the mean or expected number of crises on a given Friday for this executive is 1.15. Of course, the executive will never have 1.15 crises.

Table 5.3			
	x	**P(x)**	**x · P(x)**
Computing the Mean of the Crises Data	0	0.37	0.00
	1	0.31	0.31
	2	0.18	0.36
	3	0.09	0.27
	4	0.04	0.16
	5	0.01	0.05
			$\sum[x \cdot P(x)] = 1.15$
			$\mu = 1.15$ crises

VARIANCE AND STANDARD DEVIATION OF A DISCRETE DISTRIBUTION

The variance and standard deviation of a discrete distribution are solved for by using the outcomes (x) and probabilities of outcomes [$P(x)$] in a manner similar to that of computing a mean. In addition, the computations for variance and standard deviation use the mean of the discrete distribution. The formula for computing the variance follows.

Variance of a Discrete Distribution	$$\sigma^2 = \Sigma[(x - \mu)^2 \cdot P(x)]$$ where x = an outcome $P(x)$ = probability of a given outcome μ = mean

The standard deviation is then computed by taking the square root of the variance.

Standard Deviation of a Discrete Distribution	$$\sigma = \sqrt{\Sigma[(x - \mu)^2 \cdot P(x)]}$$

The variance and standard deviation of the crisis data in Table 5.2 are calculated and shown in Table 5.4. The mean of the crisis data is 1.15 crises. The standard deviation is 1.19 crises, and the variance is 1.41.

Table 5.4

Calculation of Variance and Standard Deviation on Crises Data

x	$P(x)$	$(x - \mu)^2$	$(x - \mu)^2 \cdot P(x)$
0	0.37	$(0 - 1.15)^2 = 1.32$	$(1.32)(0.37) = 0.49$
1	0.31	$(1 - 1.15)^2 = 0.02$	$(0.02)(0.31) = 0.01$
2	0.18	$(2 - 1.15)^2 = 0.72$	$(0.72)(0.18) = 0.13$
3	0.09	$(3 - 1.15)^2 = 3.42$	$(3.42)(0.09) = 0.31$
4	0.04	$(4 - 1.15)^2 = 8.12$	$(8.12)(0.04) = 0.32$
5	0.01	$(5 - 1.15)^2 = 14.82$	$(14.82)(0.01) = 0.15$
			$\Sigma[(x - \mu)^2 \cdot P(x)] = 1.41$

The variance is $\sigma^2 = \Sigma[(x - \mu)^2 \cdot P(x)] = 1.41$.

The standard deviation is $\sigma = \sqrt{1.41} = 1.19$ crises.

Demonstration Problem 5.1

Suppose the Atlantic Lottery Corporation is planning a new game for the holiday season called the Stocking Stuffer. With this game, total instant winnings of $34.8 million are to be available in 70 million $1 tickets, with ticket prizes ranging from $1 to $1,000. Shown here are the various prizes and the probability of winning each prize. Use these data to compute the expected value of the game, the variance of the game, and the standard deviation of the game.

Prize (x)	Probability P(x)
$1,000	0.00002
100	0.00063
20	0.00400
10	0.00601
4	0.02403
2	0.08877
1	0.10479
0	0.77175

Solution

The mean is computed as follows.

Prize (x)	Probability P(x)	x · P(x)
$1,000	0.00002	0.02000
100	0.00063	0.06300
20	0.00400	0.08000
10	0.00601	0.06010
4	0.02403	0.09612
2	0.08877	0.17754
1	0.10479	0.10479
0	0.77175	0.00000
		$\Sigma[x \cdot P(x)] = 0.60155$

$$\mu = E(x) = \Sigma[x \cdot P(x)] = 0.60155$$

The expected payoff for a $1 ticket in this game is 60.2 cents. If a person played the game for a long time, he or she could expect to average about 60 cents in winnings. In the long run, the participant will lose about $1.00 − $0.602 = $0.398, or about 40 cents a game. Of course, an individual will never win 60 cents in any one game.

Using this mean, $\mu = 0.60155$, the variance and standard deviation can be computed as follows.

x	P(x)	$(x - \mu)^2$	$(x - \mu)^2 \cdot P(x)$
$1,000	0.00002	998797.26190	19.97595
100	0.00063	9880.05186	6.22443
20	0.00400	376.29986	1.50520
10	0.00601	88.33086	0.53087
4	0.02403	11.54946	0.27753
2	0.08877	1.95566	0.17360
1	0.10479	0.15876	0.01664
0	0.77175	0.36186	0.27927
			$\Sigma[(x - \mu)^2 \cdot P(x)] = 28.98349$

$$\sigma^2 = \Sigma[(x - \mu)^2 \cdot P(x)] = 28.98349$$

$$\sigma = \sqrt{\sigma^2} = \sqrt{\Sigma[(x - \mu)^2 \cdot P(x)]} = \sqrt{28.98349} = 5.38363$$

The variance is 28.98349 (dollars)^2 and the standard deviation is $5.38.

Concept Check

1. What is a discrete distribution? Can you provide a rough example based on your personal experience?
2. What conditions must be satisfied by the outcome probabilities in a discrete distribution? What do these conditions mean?

5.2 Problems

5.1   Determine the mean, the variance, and the standard deviation of the following discrete distribution.

x	P(x)
1	0.238
2	0.290
3	0.177
4	0.158
5	0.137

5.2   Determine the mean, the variance, and the standard deviation of the following discrete distribution.

x	P(x)
0	0.103
1	0.118
2	0.246
3	0.229
4	0.138
5	0.094
6	0.071
7	0.001

5.3   The following data are the result of a historical study of the number of flaws found in a porcelain cup produced by a manufacturing firm. Use these data and the associated probabilities to compute the expected number of flaws and the standard deviation of flaws.

Flaws	Probability
0	0.461
1	0.285
2	0.129
3	0.087
4	0.038

5.4   Suppose 20% of the people in a city prefer Pepsi-Cola as their soft drink of choice. If a random sample of six people is chosen, the number of Pepsi drinkers can range from zero to six. Shown here are the possible numbers of Pepsi drinkers in a sample of six people and the probability of that number of Pepsi drinkers occurring in the sample. Use the data to determine the mean number of Pepsi drinkers in a sample of six people in the city and compute the standard deviation.

Number of Pepsi Drinkers	Probability
0	0.262
1	0.393
2	0.246
3	0.082
4	0.015
5	0.002
6	0.000

5.3 BINOMIAL DISTRIBUTION

Perhaps the most widely known of all discrete distributions is the **binomial distribution.** The binomial distribution has been used for hundreds of years. Several assumptions underlie the use of the binomial distribution:

Assumptions of the Binomial Distribution	<ul><li>The experiment involves n identical trials.</li><li>Each trial has only two possible outcomes denoted as success or as failure.</li><li>Each trial is independent of the previous trials.</li><li>The terms p and q remain constant throughout the experiment, where the term p is the probability of getting a success on any one trial and the term $q = 1 - p$ is the probability of getting a failure on any one trial.</li></ul>

As the word *binomial* indicates, any single trial of a binomial experiment contains only two possible outcomes. These two outcomes are labelled *success* and *failure.* Usually the outcome of interest to the researcher is labelled a success. For example, if a quality control analyst is looking for defective products, he would consider finding a defective product a success even though the company would not consider a defective product a success. If researchers are studying left-handedness, the outcome of getting a left-handed person in a trial of an experiment is a success. The other possible outcome of a trial in a binomial experiment is called a failure. The word *failure* is used only in opposition to success. In the preceding experiments, a failure could be to get an acceptable part (as opposed to a defective part) or to get a right-handed person (as opposed to a left-handed person). In a binomial distribution experiment, any one trial can have only two possible mutually exclusive outcomes (right-handed/left-handed, defective/good, male/female, etc.).

The binomial distribution is a discrete distribution. In n trials, only x successes are possible, where x is a whole number between 0 and n. For example, if five parts are randomly selected from a batch of parts, only 0, 1, 2, 3, 4, or 5 defective parts are possible in that sample. In a sample of five parts, getting 2.714 defective parts is not possible, nor is getting 8 defective parts possible.

In a binomial experiment, the trials must be independent. This constraint means that either the experiment is by nature one that produces independent trials (such as tossing coins or rolling dice) or the experiment is conducted with replacement. The effect of the independent trial requirement is that p, the probability of getting a success on one trial, remains constant from trial to trial. For example, suppose 5% of all parts in a bin are defective. The probability of drawing a defective part on the first draw is $p = 0.05$. If the first part drawn is not replaced, the second draw is not independent of the first, and the p value will change for the next draw. The binomial distribution does not allow for p to change from trial to trial within an experiment. However, if the population is large in comparison with the sample size, the effect of sampling without replacement is minimal, and the independence assumption is essentially met; that is, *p* remains relatively constant.

Generally, if the sample size, *n*, is less than 5% of the population, the independence assumption is not of great concern. Therefore, the acceptable sample size for using the binomial distribution with samples taken *without* replacement is

$$n < 5\%N$$

where

    n = sample size
    N = population size

For example, suppose 10% of the population of the world is left-handed and that a sample of 20 people is selected randomly from the world's population. If the first person selected is left-handed—and the sampling is conducted without replacement—the value of *p* = 0.10 is virtually unaffected because the population of the world is so large. In addition, with many experiments the population is continually being replenished even as the sampling is being done. This condition is often the case with quality control sampling of products from large production runs. Some examples of binomial distribution problems follow.

1. Suppose a machine producing computer chips has a 6% defective rate. If a company purchases 30 of these chips, what is the probability that none is defective?
2. One ethics study suggested that 84% of U.S. companies have an ethics code. From a random sample of 15 companies, what is the probability that at least 10 have an ethics code?
3. Suppose brand X car battery has a 35% market share. If 70 cars are selected at random, what is the probability that at least 30 cars have a brand X battery?
4. A survey found that nearly 67% of company buyers stated that their company had programs for preferred buyers. If a random sample of 50 company buyers is taken, what is the probability that 40 or more have companies with programs for preferred buyers?

SOLVING A BINOMIAL PROBLEM

A survey of relocation administrators by Runzheimer International revealed several reasons why workers reject relocation offers. Included in the list were family considerations, financial reasons, and others. Four percent of the respondents said they rejected relocation offers because they received too little relocation help. Suppose five workers who just rejected relocation offers are randomly selected and interviewed. Assuming the 4% figure holds for all workers being offered relocation, what is the probability that the first worker interviewed rejected the offer because of too little relocation help and the next four workers rejected the offer for other reasons?

Let T represent too little relocation help and R represent other reasons. The sequence of interviews for this problem is as follows:

$$T_1, R_2, R_3, R_4, R_5$$

The probability of getting this sequence of workers is calculated by using the special rule of multiplication for independent events (assuming the workers are independently selected from a large population of workers). If 4% of the workers rejecting relocation offers do so for too little relocation help, the probability of one person being randomly selected from workers rejecting relocation offers who does so for that reason is 0.04, which is the value of p. The other 96% of the workers who reject relocation offers do so for other reasons. Thus, the probability of randomly selecting a worker from those who reject relocation offers who does so for other reasons is $1 - 0.04 = 0.96$, which is the value for q. The probability of obtaining this sequence of five workers who have rejected relocation offers is

$$P(T_1 \cap R_2 \cap R_3 \cap R_4 \cap R_5) = (0.04)(0.96)(0.96)(0.96)(0.96) = 0.03397$$

Obviously, in the random selection of workers who rejected relocation offers, the worker who did so because of too little relocation help could have been the second worker or the third or the fourth or the fifth. All the possible sequences of getting one worker who rejected relocation because of too little help and four workers who did so for other reasons follow.

$$T_1, R_2, R_3, R_4, R_5$$
$$R_1, T_2, R_3, R_4, R_5$$
$$R_1, R_2, T_3, R_4, R_5$$
$$R_1, R_2, R_3, T_4, R_5$$
$$R_1, R_2, R_3, R_4, T_5$$

The probability of each of these sequences occurring is calculated as follows:

$$(0.04)(0.96)(0.96)(0.96)(0.96) = 0.03397$$
$$(0.96)(0.04)(0.96)(0.96)(0.96) = 0.03397$$
$$(0.96)(0.96)(0.04)(0.96)(0.96) = 0.03397$$
$$(0.96)(0.96)(0.96)(0.04)(0.96) = 0.03397$$
$$(0.96)(0.96)(0.96)(0.96)(0.04) = 0.03397$$

Note that in each case the final probability is the same. Each of the five sequences contains the product of 0.04 and four 0.96s. The commutative property of multiplication allows for the reordering of the five individual probabilities in any one sequence. The probabilities in each of the five sequences may be reordered and summarized as $(0.04)^1(0.96)^4$. Each sequence contains the same five probabilities, which makes recomputing the probability of each sequence unnecessary. What *is* important is to determine in how many different ways the sequences can be formed and multiply that figure by the probability of one sequence occurring. For the five sequences of this problem, the total probability of getting exactly one worker who rejected relocation because of too little relocation help in a random sample of five workers who rejected relocation offers is

$$5(0.04)^1(0.96)^4 = 0.16985$$

An easier way to determine the number of sequences than by listing all possibilities is to use *combinations* to calculate them. (The concept of combinations was introduced in Chapter 4.) Five workers are being sampled, so $n = 5$, and the problem is to get one worker who rejected a relocation offer because of too little relocation help, $x = 1$. Hence $_nC_x$ will yield the number of possible ways to get x successes in n trials. For this problem, $_5C_1$ tells the number of sequences of possibilities.

$$_5C_1 = \frac{5!}{1!(5-1)!} = 5$$

Weighting the probability of one sequence with the combination yields

$$_5C_1(0.04)^1(0.96)^4 = 0.16985$$

Using combinations simplifies the determination of how many sequences are possible for a given value of x in a binomial distribution.

Now suppose 70% of all Canadians believe cleaning up the environment is an important issue. What is the probability of randomly sampling four Canadians and having exactly two of them say that they believe cleaning up the environment is an important issue? Let E represent the success of getting a person who believes cleaning up the environment is an important issue. For this example, $p = 0.70$. Let N represent the failure of not getting a person who believes cleaning up is an important issue (N denotes not important). The probability of getting one of these people is $q = 0.30$.

The various sequences of getting two Es in a sample of four follow.

$$E_1, E_2, N_3, N_4$$
$$E_1, N_2, E_3, N_4$$
$$E_1, N_2, N_3, E_4$$
$$N_1, E_2, E_3, N_4$$
$$N_1, E_2, N_3, E_4$$
$$N_1, N_2, E_3, E_4$$

Two successes in a sample of four can occur in six ways. Using combinations, the number of sequences is

$$_4C_2 = 6 \text{ ways}$$

The probability of selecting any individual sequence is

$$(0.70)^2(0.30)^2 = 0.0441$$

Thus, the overall probability of getting exactly two people who believe cleaning up the environment is important out of four randomly selected people, when 70% of Canadians believe cleaning up the environment is important, is

$$_4C_2(0.70)^2(0.30)^2 = 0.2646$$

Generalizing from these two examples yields the binomial formula, which can be used to solve binomial problems.

Binomial Formula	
	$$P(x) = {}_nC_x \cdot p^x \cdot q^{n-x} = \frac{n!}{x!(n-x)!} \cdot p^x \cdot q^{n-x}$$

where
  n = the number of trials (or the number being sampled)
  x = the number of successes desired
  p = the probability of getting a success in one trial
  $q = 1 - p$ = the probability of getting a failure in one trial

The binomial formula summarizes the steps presented so far to solve binomial problems. The formula allows the solution of these problems quickly and efficiently.

Demonstration Problem 5.2	A Gallup survey found that 65% of all financial consumers were very satisfied with their primary financial institution. Suppose that 25 financial consumers are sampled. If the Gallup survey result still holds true today, what is the probability that exactly 19 are very satisfied with their primary financial institution?

Solution

The value of p is 0.65 (very satisfied), the value of $q = 1 - p = 1 - 0.65 = 0.35$ (not very satisfied), $n = 25$, and $x = 19$. The binomial formula yields the final answer:

$$_{25}C_{19}(0.65)^{19}(0.35)^6 = (177{,}100)(0.00027884)(0.00183827) = 0.0908$$

If 65% of all financial consumers are very satisfied, about 9.08% of the time the researcher would get exactly 19 out of 25 financial consumers who are very satisfied with their financial institution. How many very satisfied consumers would one expect to get in 25 randomly selected financial consumers? If 65% of the financial consumers are very satisfied with their primary financial institution, one would expect to get about 65% of 25 or (0.65)(25) = 16.25 very satisfied financial consumers. While in any individual sample of 25 the number of financial consumers who are very satisfied cannot be 16.25, business researchers understand the x values near 16.25 are the most likely occurrences.

Demonstration Problem 5.3	Statistics Canada reported recently that approximately 6% of all workers in Canada are unemployed. In conducting a random telephone survey, what is the probability of getting two or fewer unemployed Canadian workers in a sample of 20?

Solution

This problem must be worked as the union of three problems: (1) zero unemployed, $x = 0$; (2) one unemployed, $x = 1$; and (3) two unemployed, $x = 2$. In each problem, $p = 0.06$, $q = 0.94$, and $n = 20$. The binomial formula gives the following result:

$$
\begin{array}{ccc}
x = 0 & x = 1 & x = 2 \\
_{20}C_0(0.60)^0(0.94)^{20} + & _{20}C_1(0.60)^1(0.94)^{19} + & _{20}C_2(0.60)^2(0.94)^{18} = \\
0.2901 \quad + & 0.3703 \quad + & 0.2246 \quad = \quad 0.8850
\end{array}
$$

If 6% of the workers in Canada are unemployed, the telephone surveyor would get zero, one, or two unemployed workers 88.5% of the time in a random sample of 20 workers. The requirement of getting two or fewer is satisfied by getting zero, one, or two unemployed workers. Thus, this problem is the union of three probabilities. Whenever the binomial formula is used to solve for cumulative success (not an exact number), the probability of each x value must be solved and the probabilities summed. If an actual survey produced such a result, it would serve to validate the Statistics Canada figures.

USING THE BINOMIAL TABLE

Anyone who works enough binomial problems will begin to recognize that the probability of getting $x = 5$ successes from a sample size of $n = 18$ when $p = 0.10$ is the same no matter whether the five successes are left-handed people, defective parts, brand X purchasers, or any other variable. Whether the sample involves people, parts, or products does not matter in terms of the final probabilities. The essence of the problem is the same: $n = 18$,

Table 5.5

Excerpt from Table A.2, Appendix A

$n = 20$				Probability					
x	0.1	0.2	0.3	0.4	0.5	0.6	0.7	0.8	0.9
0	0.122	0.012	0.001	0.000	0.000	0.000	0.000	0.000	0.000
1	0.270	0.058	0.007	0.000	0.000	0.000	0.000	0.000	0.000
2	0.285	0.137	0.028	0.003	0.000	0.000	0.000	0.000	0.000
3	0.190	0.205	0.072	0.012	0.001	0.000	0.000	0.000	0.000
4	0.090	0.218	0.130	0.035	0.005	0.000	0.000	0.000	0.000
5	0.032	0.175	0.179	0.075	0.015	0.001	0.000	0.000	0.000
6	0.009	0.109	0.192	0.124	0.037	0.005	0.000	0.000	0.000
7	0.002	0.055	0.164	0.166	0.074	0.015	0.001	0.000	0.000
8	0.000	0.022	0.114	0.180	0.120	0.035	0.004	0.000	0.000
9	0.000	0.007	0.065	0.160	0.160	0.071	0.012	0.000	0.000
10	0.000	0.002	0.031	0.117	0.176	0.117	0.031	0.002	0.000
11	0.000	0.000	0.012	0.071	0.160	0.160	0.065	0.007	0.000
12	0.000	0.000	0.004	0.035	0.120	0.180	0.114	0.022	0.000
13	0.000	0.000	0.001	0.015	0.074	0.166	0.164	0.055	0.002
14	0.000	0.000	0.000	0.005	0.037	0.124	0.192	0.109	0.009
15	0.000	0.000	0.000	0.001	0.015	0.075	0.179	0.175	0.032
16	0.000	0.000	0.000	0.000	0.005	0.035	0.130	0.218	0.090
17	0.000	0.000	0.000	0.000	0.001	0.012	0.072	0.205	0.190
18	0.000	0.000	0.000	0.000	0.000	0.003	0.028	0.137	0.285
19	0.000	0.000	0.000	0.000	0.000	0.000	0.007	0.058	0.270
20	0.000	0.000	0.000	0.000	0.000	0.000	0.001	0.012	0.122

$x = 5$, and $p = 0.10$. Recognizing this fact, we have constructed a set of binomial tables containing presolved probabilities.

Two parameters, n and p, describe or characterize a binomial distribution. Binomial distributions are actually a family of distributions. Every different value of n and/or every different value of p gives a different binomial distribution, and tables are available for various combinations of n and p values. Because of space limitations, the binomial tables presented in this text are limited. Table A.2 in Appendix A contains binomial tables. Each table is headed by a value of n. Nine values of p are presented in each table of size n. In the column below each value of p is the binomial distribution for that combination of n and p. Table 5.5 contains a segment of Table A.2 with the binomial probabilities for $n = 20$.

Demonstration Problem 5.4

Solve the binomial probability for $n = 20$, $p = 0.40$, and $x = 10$ by using Table A.2, Appendix A.

Solution

To use Table A.2, first locate the value of n. Because $n = 20$ for this problem, the portion of the binomial tables containing values for $n = 20$ presented in Table 5.5 can be used. After locating the value of n, search horizontally across the top of the table for the appropriate value of p. In this problem, $p = 0.40$. The column under 0.40 contains the probabilities for the binomial distribution of $n = 20$ and $p = 0.40$. To get the probability of $x = 10$, find the value of x in the leftmost column and locate the probability in the table at the intersection of $p = 0.40$ and $x = 10$. The answer is 0.117. Working this problem by the binomial formula yields the same result:

$$_{20}C_{10}(0.40)^{10}(0.60)^{10} = 0.1171$$

Demonstration Problem 5.5

According to Information Resources, which publishes data on market share for various products, Oreos control about 10% of the market for cookie brands. Suppose 20 purchasers of cookies are selected randomly from the population. What is the probability that fewer than four purchasers choose Oreos?

Solution

For this problem, $n = 20$, $p = 0.10$, and $x < 4$. Because $n = 20$, the portion of the binomial tables presented in Table 5.5 can be used to work this problem. Search along the row of p values for 0.10. Determining the probability of getting $x < 4$ involves summing the probabilities for $x = 0$, 1, 2, and 3. The values appear in the x column at the intersection of each x value and $p = 0.10$.

x Value	Probability
0	0.122
1	0.270
2	0.285
3	0.190
	$(x < 4) = 0.867$

If 10% of all cookie purchasers prefer Oreos and 20 cookie purchasers are randomly selected, about 86.7% of the time fewer than four of the 20 will select Oreos.

USING THE COMPUTER TO PRODUCE A BINOMIAL DISTRIBUTION

Excel can be used to produce the probabilities for virtually any binomial distribution, thus offering yet another option for solving binomial problems besides using the binomial formula or the binomial tables. The advantages of using a software package for this purpose are convenience (if the binomial tables are not readily available and a computer is) and the potential for generating tables for many more values than those printed in the binomial tables.

For example, a study of bank customers stated that 64% of all financial consumers believe banks are more competitive today than they were five years ago. Suppose 23 financial consumers are selected randomly and we want to determine the probabilities of various x values occurring. Table A.2 in Appendix A could not be used because only nine different p values are included and $p = 0.64$ is not one of those values. In addition, $n = 23$ is not included in the table. Without the computer, we are left with the binomial formula as the only option for solving binomial problems for $n = 23$ and $p = 0.64$. Particularly if cumulative probability questions are asked (for example, $x < 10$), the binomial formula can be a tedious way to solve the problem.

Shown in Table 5.6 is the Excel output for the binomial distribution of $n = 23$ and $p = 0.64$. With this computer output, a researcher could obtain or calculate the probability of any occurrence within the binomial distribution of $n = 23$ and $p = 0.64$. Table 5.7 contains the output for the particular binomial problem, $P(x \leq 10)$ when $n = 23$ and $p = 0.64$, solved by using Excel's cumulative probability capability.

POINTS OF INTEREST
For example, the binomial problem $P(x = 2 \mid n = 23$ and $p = 0.64)$ will be given in Excel as =BINOMDIST (2,23,0.64,0).

Table 5.6

Excel Output for the Binomial Distribution of $n = 23$, $p = 0.64$

Probability Density Function
Binomial with $n = 23$ and $p = 0.64$

X	$P(x = X)$
0	0.000000
1	0.000000
2	0.000000
3	0.000001
4	0.000006
5	0.000037
6	0.000199
7	0.000858
8	0.003051
9	0.009040
10	0.022500
11	0.047273
12	0.084041
13	0.126420
14	0.160533
15	0.171236
16	0.152209
17	0.111421
18	0.066027
19	0.030890
20	0.010983
21	0.002789
22	0.000451
23	0.000035

Table 5.7

Excel Output for the Binomial Problem, $P(x \leq 10)$, $n = 23$, **and** $p = 0.64$

Binomial with $n = 23$ and $p = 0.64$

X	$P(x \leq X)$
10	0.035692

Shown in Table 5.8 is Excel output for all values of x that have probabilities greater than 0.000001 for the binomial distribution discussed in Demonstration Problem 5.3 ($n = 20$, $p = 0.06$) and the solution to the question posed in Demonstration Problem 5.3.

MEAN AND STANDARD DEVIATION OF A BINOMIAL DISTRIBUTION

A binomial distribution has an expected value or a long-run average, which is denoted by μ. The value of μ is determined by $n \cdot p$. For example, if $n = 10$ and $p = 0.4$, then $\mu = n \cdot p = (10)(0.4) = 4$. The long-run average or expected value means that, if n items are sampled over and over for a long time and if p is the probability of getting a success on one trial, the average number of successes per sample is expected to be $n \cdot p$. If 40% of all graduate business students at a large university are women and if random samples of 10 graduate business students are selected many times, the expectation is that, on average, 4 of the 10 students would be women.

	x	Prob(x)	
	0	0.290106	
	1	0.370348	
	2	0.224573	
	3	0.086007	
	4	0.023332	
	5	0.004766	
	6	0.000760	
	7	0.000097	
	8	0.000010	
	9	0.000001	

$P(X \leq 2 | n = 20 \text{ and } p = 0.06) = 0.885028$

Table 5.8

Output for Demonstration Problem 5.3 and the Binomial Distribution of $n = 20$, $p = 0.06$

Mean and Standard Deviation of a Binomial Distribution

$$\mu = n \cdot p$$
$$\sigma = \sqrt{n \cdot p \cdot q}$$

POINTS OF INTEREST

For example, the binomial problem $P(x \leq 10 | n = 23 \text{ and } p = 0.64)$ will be given in Excel as =BINOMDIST (10,23,0.64,1). The last parameter in the Excel function indicates that we are dealing with the cumulative probability.

Examining the mean of a binomial distribution gives an intuitive feeling about the likelihood of a given outcome.

According to one study, 64% of all financial consumers believe banks are more competitive today than they were five years ago. If 23 financial consumers are selected randomly, what is the expected number who believe banks are more competitive today than they were five years ago? This problem can be described by the binomial distribution of $n = 23$ and $p = 0.64$ given in Table 5.6. The mean of this binomial distribution yields the expected value for this problem.

$$\mu = n \cdot p = 23(0.64) = 14.72$$

In the long run, if 23 financial consumers are selected randomly over and over and if indeed 64% of all financial consumers believe banks are more competitive today, then the experiment should average 14.72 financial consumers out of 23 who believe banks are more competitive today. Realize that because the binomial distribution is a discrete distribution you will never actually get 14.72 people out of 23 who believe banks are more competitive today. The mean of the distribution does reveal the relative likelihood of any individual occurrence. Examine Table 5.6. Notice that the highest probabilities are those near $x = 14.72$: $P(x = 15) = 0.1712$, $P(x = 14) = 0.1605$, and $P(x = 16) = 0.1522$. All other probabilities for this distribution are less than these probabilities.

The standard deviation of a binomial distribution is denoted σ and is equal to $\sqrt{n \cdot p \cdot q}$. The standard deviation for the financial consumer problem described by the binomial distribution in Table 5.6 is

$$\sigma = \sqrt{n \cdot p \cdot q} = \sqrt{(23)(0.64)(0.36)} = 2.30$$

Chapter 6 shows that some binomial distributions are nearly bell-shaped and can be approximated by using the normal curve. The mean and standard deviation of a binomial distribution are the tools used to convert these binomial problems to normal curve problems.

GRAPHING BINOMIAL DISTRIBUTIONS

The graph of a binomial distribution can be constructed by using all the possible x values of a distribution and their associated probabilities. The x values are usually graphed along the horizontal axis and the probabilities are graphed along the vertical axis.

Table 5.9 lists the probabilities for three different binomial distributions: $n = 8$ and $p = 0.20$, $n = 8$ and $p = 0.50$, and $n = 8$ and $p = 0.80$. Figure 5.2 displays Excel graphs for each of these three binomial distributions. Observe how the shape of the distribution changes as the value of p increases. For $p = 0.50$, the distribution is symmetrical. For $p = 0.20$, the distribution is skewed right, and for $p = 0.80$, the distribution is skewed left. This pattern makes sense because the mean of the binomial distribution $n = 8$ and $p = 0.50$ is 4, which is in the middle of the distribution. The mean of the distribution $n = 8$ and $p = 0.20$ is 1.6, which results in the highest probabilities being near $x = 2$ and $x = 1$. This graph peaks early and stretches toward the higher values of x. The mean of the distribution $n = 8$ and $p = 0.80$ is 6.4, which results in the highest probabilities being near $x = 6$ and $x = 7$. Thus, the peak of the distribution is nearer to 8 than to 0 and the distribution stretches back toward $x = 0$.

Table 5.9

Probabilities for Three Binomial Distributions with $n = 8$

	Probabilities for		
x	$p = 0.20$	$p = 0.50$	$p = 0.80$
0	0.1678	0.0039	0.0000
1	0.3355	0.0312	0.0001
2	0.2936	0.1094	0.0011
3	0.1468	0.2187	0.0092
4	0.0459	0.2734	0.0459
5	0.0092	0.2187	0.1468
6	0.0011	0.1094	0.2936
7	0.0001	0.0312	0.3355
8	0.0000	0.0039	0.1678

In any binomial distribution, the largest x value that can occur is n and the smallest value is zero. Thus, the graph of any binomial distribution is constrained by zero and n. If the p value of the distribution is not 0.50, this constraint will result in the graph "piling up" at one end and being skewed at the other end.

Demonstration Problem 5.6

A manufacturing company produces 10,000 plastic mugs per week. This company supplies mugs to another company, which packages the mugs as part of picnic sets. The second company randomly samples 10 mugs sent from the supplier. If two or fewer of the sampled mugs are defective, the second company accepts the lot. What is the probability that the lot will be accepted if the mug manufacturing company is actually producing mugs that are 10% defective? 20% defective? 30% defective? 40% defective?

Solution

In this series of binomial problems, $n = 10$, $x \leq 2$, and p ranges from 0.10 to 0.40. From Table A.2—and cumulating the values—we have the following probability of $x \leq 2$ for each p value and the expected value ($\mu = n \cdot p$).

Figure 5.2

Excel Graphs of Three Binomial Distributions with n = 8

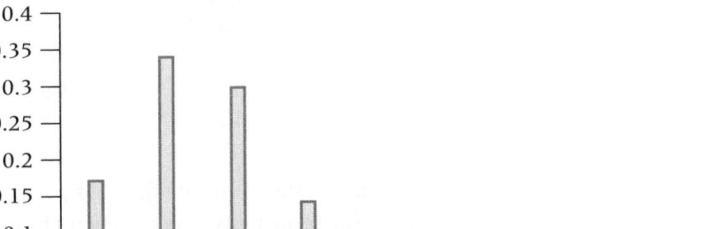

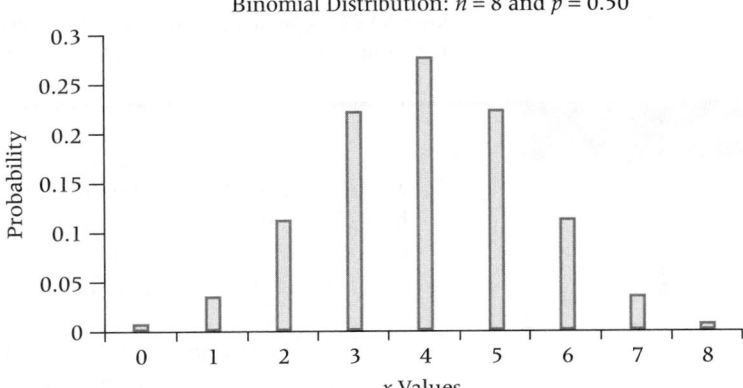

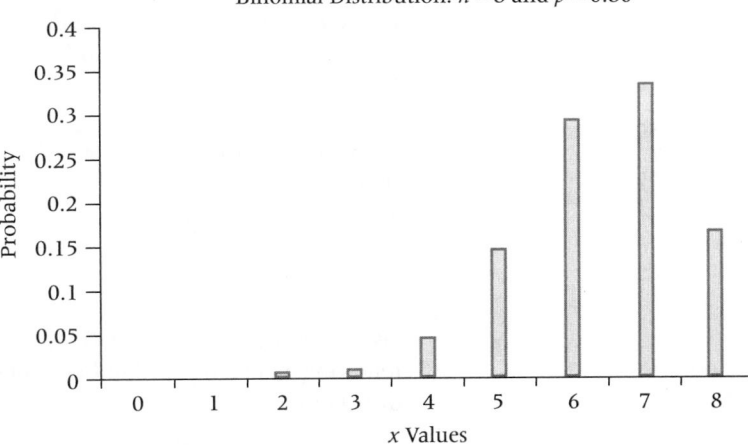

p	Lot Accepted $P(x \leq 2)$	Expected Number of Defects (μ)
0.10	0.930	1.0
0.20	0.677	2.0
0.30	0.382	3.0
0.40	0.167	4.0

These values indicate that if the manufacturing company is producing 10% defective mugs, the probability is relatively high (0.930) that the lot will be accepted by chance. For higher values of p, the probability of lot acceptance by chance decreases. In addition, as p increases, the expected value moves away from the acceptable values, $x \leq 2$. This move reduces the chances of lot acceptance.

Concept Check

1. List the key characteristics of a binomial experiment.
2. Give an example of a binomial random variable. What do the values of the variable represent? How are the values of the variable defined?

5.3 Problems

5.5   Solve the following problems by using the binomial formula.
   a.   If $n = 4$ and $p = 0.10$, find $P(x = 3)$.
   b.   If $n = 7$ and $p = 0.80$, find $P(x = 4)$.
   c.   If $n = 10$ and $p = 0.60$, find $P(x \geq 7)$.
   d.   If $n = 12$ and $p = 0.45$, find $P(5 \leq x \leq 7)$.

5.6   Solve the following problems by using the binomial tables (Table A.2).
   a.   If $n = 20$ and $p = 0.50$, find $P(x = 12)$.
   b.   If $n = 20$ and $p = 0.30$, find $P(x > 8)$.
   c.   If $n = 20$ and $p = 0.70$, find $P(x < 12)$.
   d.   If $n = 20$ and $p = 0.90$, find $P(x \leq 16)$.
   e.   If $n = 15$ and $p = 0.40$, find $P(4 \leq x \leq 9)$.
   f.   If $n = 10$ and $p = 0.60$, find $P(x \geq 7)$.

5.7   Solve for the mean and standard deviation of the following binomial distributions.
   a. $n = 20$ and $p = 0.70$
   b. $n = 70$ and $p = 0.35$
   c. $n = 100$ and $p = 0.50$

5.8   Use the probability tables in Table A.2 and sketch the graph of each of the following binomial distributions. Note on the graph where the mean of the distribution falls.
   a. $n = 6$ and $p = 0.70$
   b. $n = 20$ and $p = 0.50$
   c. $n = 8$ and $p = 0.80$

5.9   *Purchasing* magazine reported the results of a survey in which buyers were asked a series of questions with regard to Internet usage. One question asked was how they would use the Internet if security and other issues could be resolved. Seventy-eight percent said they would use it for pricing information, 75% said they would use it to send purchase orders, and 70% said they would use it for purchase order acknowledgments. Assume that these percentages hold true for all buyers. A researcher randomly samples 20 buyers and asks them how they would use the Internet if security and other issues could be resolved.

    a.   What is the probability that exactly 14 of these buyers would use the Internet for pricing information?

    b.   What is the probability that all of the buyers would use the Internet to send purchase orders?

    c.   What is the probability that fewer than 12 would use the Internet for purchase order acknowledgments?

5.10   *The Wall Street Journal* reported some interesting statistics on the job market. One statistic is that 40% of all workers say they would change jobs for "slightly higher pay." In addition, 88% of companies say that there is a shortage of qualified job candidates. Suppose 16 workers are randomly selected and asked if they would change jobs for slightly higher pay. What is the probability that nine or more say yes? What is the probability that three, four, five, or six say yes? If 13 companies are contacted, what is the probability that exactly 10 say there is a shortage of qualified job candidates? What is the probability that all of the companies say there is a shortage of qualified job candidates? What is the expected number of companies that would say there is a shortage of qualified job candidates?

5.11   An increasing number of consumers believe they have to look out for themselves in the marketplace. According to a survey conducted by the Yankelovich Partners for *USA WEEKEND* magazine, 60% of all consumers have called an information line for a product. Suppose a random sample of 25 consumers is contacted and interviewed about their buying habits.

    a.   What is the probability that 15 or more of these consumers have called an information line for a product?

    b.   What is the probability that more than 20 of these consumers have called an information line for a product?

    c.   What is the probability that fewer than 10 of these consumers have called an information line for a product?

5.12   Assume that a study has shown that about half of all Canadian workers who change jobs cash out their pension plans rather than leaving the money in the account to grow. The percentage is much higher for workers with small pension plan balances. In fact, 87% of workers with pension plan accounts less than $5,000 opt to take their balance rather than roll it over into other retirement accounts when they change jobs. Assuming that 50% of all workers who change jobs cash out their pension plans, if 16 workers who have recently changed jobs that had pension plans are randomly sampled, what is the probability that more than 10 of them cashed out their pension plan? If 10 workers who have recently changed jobs and had pension plans with accounts less than $5,000 are randomly sampled, what is the probability that exactly 6 of them cashed out?

5.13   In the past few years, outsourcing overseas has become more frequently used than ever before by Canadian and U.S. companies. However, outsourcing is not without problems. A recent survey by *Purchasing* magazine indicates that 20% of the companies that outsource overseas use a consultant. Suppose 15 companies that outsource overseas are randomly selected.

    a.   What is the probability that exactly five companies that outsource overseas use a consultant?

    b.   What is the probability that more than nine companies that outsource overseas use a consultant?

    c.   What is the probability that none of the companies that outsource overseas use a consultant?

   d.   What is the probability that between four and seven (inclusive) companies
         that outsource overseas use a consultant?
   e.   Construct a graph for this binomial distribution. In light of the graph and the
         expected value, explain why the probability results from parts (a) through
         (d) were obtained.

5.14   According to the Financial Planners Standards Council, 22% of certified financial
        planners (CFPs) earn between $100,000 and $149,999 per year. Thirty-two percent
        earn $150,000 or more. Suppose a complete list of all CFPs is available and 18 are
        randomly selected from that list.
   a.   What is the expected number of CFPs who earn between $100,000 and
         $149,999 per year? What is the expected number who earn $150,000 or more
         per year?
   b.   What is the probability that at least eight CFPs earn between $100,000 and
         $149,999 per year?
   c.   What is the probability that two, three, or four CFPs earn more than $150,000
         per year?
   d.   What is the probability that none of the CFPs earn between $100,000 and
         $149,999 per year? What is the probability that none earn $150,000 or more
         per year? Which probability is higher and why?

5.4 POISSON DISTRIBUTION

The Poisson distribution is another discrete distribution. It is named after Simeon-Denis
Poisson (1781–1840), a French mathematician, who published its essentials in a paper in
1837. The Poisson distribution and the binomial distribution have some similarities but
also several differences. The binomial distribution describes a distribution of two possible
outcomes designated as success and failure from a given number of trials. The **Poisson
distribution** *focuses only on the number of discrete occurrences over some interval or continuum.* A Poisson experiment does not have a given number of trials (*n*) as a binomial
experiment does. For example, whereas a binomial experiment might be used to determine how many cars assembled in Canada are in a random sample of 20 cars, a Poisson
experiment might focus on the number of cars randomly arriving at an automobile repair
facility during a 10-minute interval.

The Poisson distribution describes the occurrence of *rare events*. In fact, the Poisson
formula has been referred to as the *law of improbable events*. For example, serious accidents at a chemical plant are rare, and the number per month might be described by the
Poisson distribution. The Poisson distribution is often used to describe the number of random arrivals per some time interval. If the number of arrivals per interval is too frequent,
the time interval can be reduced enough so that a rare number of occurrences is expected.
Another example of a Poisson distribution is the number of random customer arrivals per
5-minute interval at a small boutique on weekday mornings.

The Poisson distribution can also be applied in the field of management science. The
models used in queuing theory (theory of waiting lines) are usually based on the assumption that the Poisson distribution is the proper distribution to describe random arrival
rates over a period of time.

The Poisson distribution has the following characteristics:

- It is a discrete distribution.
- It describes rare events.

- Each occurrence is independent of the other occurrences.
- It describes discrete occurrences over a continuum or interval.
- The occurrences in each interval can range from zero to infinity.
- The expected number of occurrences must hold constant throughout the experiment.

The following are examples of Poisson-type situations:

1. Number of telephone calls per minute at a small business
2. Number of hazardous waste sites per province in Canada
3. Number of major oil spills in the oil sands of Alberta per month
4. Number of cars entering the 407 Express Toll Route in Ontario coming from Highway 427 per minute between 3 A.M. and 4 A.M. in January
5. Number of times a 1-year-old personal computer printer breaks down per quarter (3 months)
6. Number of sewing flaws per pair of jeans during production
7. Number of times a tire blows on a commercial airplane per week
8. Number of paint spots per new automobile
9. Number of flaws per bolt of cloth
10. Number of cases of a rare blood disease per 100,000 people

Each of these examples represents a rare occurrence of events for some interval. Note that, although time is a more common interval for the Poisson distribution, *intervals* can range from a province in Canada to a pair of jeans. Some of the intervals in these examples might have zero occurrences. Moreover, the average occurrence per interval for many of these examples is probably in the single digits (1–9).

If a Poisson-distributed phenomenon is studied over a long period of time, a *long-run average* can be determined. This average is denoted **lambda (λ).** Each Poisson problem contains a lambda value from which the probabilities of particular occurrences are determined. Note that n and p are required to describe a binomial distribution; however, a Poisson distribution can be described by λ alone. The Poisson formula is used to compute the probability of occurrences over an interval for a given lambda value.

Poisson Formula	$$P(x) = \frac{\lambda^x e^{-\lambda}}{x!}$$

where
$x = 0, 1, 2, 3, \ldots$
$\lambda = $ long-run average
$e = 2.718281 \ldots$

Here, x is the number of occurrences per interval for which the probability is being computed, λ is the long-run average, and $e = 2.718281\ldots$ is the base of natural logarithms.

A word of caution about using the Poisson distribution to study various phenomena is necessary. The λ value must hold constant throughout a Poisson experiment. The researcher must be careful not to apply a given lambda to intervals for which lambda changes. For example, the average number of customers arriving at a large department store during a 1-minute interval will vary from hour to hour, day to day, and month to month. Different times of the day or week might produce different lambdas. The number of flaws per pair of jeans might vary from Monday to Friday. The researcher should be specific in describing the interval for which λ is being used.

WORKING POISSON PROBLEMS BY FORMULA

Suppose bank customers arrive randomly on weekday afternoons at an average of 3.2 customers every 4 minutes. What is the probability of exactly five customers arriving in a 4-minute interval on a weekday afternoon? The lambda for this problem is 3.2 customers per 4 minutes. The value of x is five customers per 4 minutes. The probability of five customers randomly arriving during a 4-minute interval when the long-run average has been 3.2 customers per 4-minute interval is

$$\frac{(3.2^5)(e^{-3.2})}{5!} = \frac{(335.54)(0.0408)}{120} = 0.1141$$

If a bank averages 3.2 customers every 4 minutes, the probability of five customers arriving during any one 4-minute interval is 0.1141.

Demonstration Problem 5.7	Bank customers arrive randomly on weekday afternoons at an average of 3.2 customers every 4 minutes. What is the probability of having more than seven customers in a 4-minute interval on a weekday afternoon?

Solution

$$\lambda = 3.2 \text{ customers/4 minutes}$$
$$x > 7 \text{ customers/4 minutes}$$

In theory, the solution requires obtaining the values of $x = 8, 9, 10, 11, 12, 13, 14, \ldots,$ ∞. In actuality, each x value is determined until the values are so far away from $\lambda = 3.2$ that the probabilities approach zero. The probabilities are then summed to find $P(x > 7)$.

$$P(x = 8 \mid \lambda = 3.2) = \frac{(3.2^8)(e^{-3.2})}{8!} = 0.0111$$

$$P(x = 9 \mid \lambda = 3.2) = \frac{(3.2^9)(e^{-3.2})}{9!} = 0.0040$$

$$P(x = 10 \mid \lambda = 3.2) = \frac{(3.2^{10})(e^{-3.2})}{10!} = 0.0013$$

$$P(x = 11 \mid \lambda = 3.2) = \frac{(3.2^{11})(e^{-3.2})}{11!} = 0.0004$$

$$P(x = 12 \mid \lambda = 3.2) = \frac{(3.2^{12})(e^{-3.2})}{12!} = 0.0001$$

$$P(x = 13 \mid \lambda = 3.2) = \frac{(3.2^{13})(e^{-3.2})}{13!} = 0.0000$$

$$P(x > 7) = P(x \geq 8) = 0.0169$$

If the bank has been averaging 3.2 customers every 4 minutes on weekday afternoons, it is unlikely that more than seven people would randomly arrive in any one 4-minute period. This answer indicates that more than seven people would randomly arrive in a 4-minute period only 1.69% of the time. Bank officers could use these results to help them make staffing decisions.

Demonstration Problem 5.8

A bank has an average random arrival rate of 3.2 customers every 4 minutes. What is the probability of getting exactly 10 customers during an 8-minute interval?

Solution

$$\lambda = 3.2 \text{ customers/4 minutes}$$
$$x = 10 \text{ customers/8 minutes}$$

This example is different from the first two Poisson examples in that the intervals for lambda and the sample are different. The intervals must be the same in order to use λ and x together in the probability formula. The right way to approach this dilemma is to adjust the interval for lambda so that it and x have the same interval. The interval for x is 8 minutes, so lambda should be adjusted to an 8-minute interval. Logically, if the bank averages 3.2 customers every 4 minutes, it should average twice as many, or 6.4 customers, every 8 minutes. If x were for a 2-minute interval, the value of lambda would be halved from 3.2 to 1.6 customers per 2-minute interval. The wrong approach to this dilemma is to equalize the intervals by changing the x value. Never adjust or change x in a problem. Just because 10 customers arrive in one 8-minute interval does not mean that there would necessarily have been five customers in a 4-minute interval. There is no guarantee how the 10 customers are spread over the 8-minute interval. Always adjust the lambda value. After lambda has been adjusted for an 8-minute interval, the solution is

$$\lambda = 6.4 \text{ customers/8 minutes}$$
$$x = 10 \text{ customers/8 minutes}$$

$$\frac{(6.4)^{10} e^{6.4}}{10!} = 0.0528$$

USING THE POISSON TABLES

Every value of lambda determines a different Poisson distribution. Regardless of the nature of the interval associated with a lambda, the Poisson distribution for a particular lambda is the same. Table A.3, Appendix A, contains the Poisson distributions for selected values of lambda. Probabilities are displayed in the table for each x value associated with a given lambda if the probability has a nonzero value to four decimal places. Table 5.10 presents a portion of Table A.3 that contains the probabilities of $x \le 9$ if lambda is 1.6.

Table 5.10

Poisson Table for $\lambda = 1.6$

x	Probability
0	0.2019
1	0.3230
2	0.2584
3	0.1378
4	0.0551
5	0.0176
6	0.0047
7	0.0011
8	0.0002
9	0.0000

Demonstration Problem 5.9

If a real estate office sells 1.6 houses on an average weekday and sales of houses on weekdays are Poisson distributed, what is the probability of selling exactly four houses in one day? What is the probability of selling no houses in one day? What is the probability of selling more than five houses in a day? What is the probability of selling 10 or more houses in a day? What is the probability of selling exactly four houses in two days?

Solution

$$\lambda = 1.6 \text{ houses/day}$$
$$P(x = 4 \mid \lambda = 1.6) = ?$$

Table 5.10 gives the probabilities for $\lambda = 1.6$. The left column contains the x values. The line $x = 4$ yields the probability 0.0551. If a real estate firm has been averaging 1.6 houses sold per day, only on 5.51% of the days would it sell exactly four houses and still maintain the lambda value. Line 1 of Table 5.10 shows the probability of selling no houses in a day (0.2019). That is, on 20.19% of the days, the firm would sell no houses if sales are Poisson distributed with $\lambda = 1.6$ houses per day. Table 5.10 is not cumulative. To determine $P(x > 5)$, more than five houses, find the probabilities of $x = 6$, $x = 7$, $x = 8$, $x = 9$, ..., $x = ?$. At $x = 9$, the probability to four decimal places is zero, and Table 5.10 stops when an x value zeros out at four decimal places. The answer for $x > 5$ follows.

x	Probability
6	0.0047
7	0.0011
8	0.0002
9	0.0000
$x > 5 =$	0.0060

What is the probability of selling 10 or more houses in one day? As the table zeros out at $x = 9$, the probability of $x \geq 10$ is essentially 0.0000—that is, if the real estate office has been averaging only 1.6 houses sold per day, it is virtually impossible to sell 10 or more houses in a day. What is the probability of selling exactly four houses in two days? In this case, the interval has been changed from one day to two days. Lambda is for one day, so an adjustment must be made: A lambda of 1.6 for one day converts to a lambda of 3.2 for two days. Table 5.10 no longer applies, so Table A.3 must be used to solve this problem. The answer is found by looking up $\lambda = 3.2$ and $x = 4$ in Table A.3: the probability is 0.1781.

MEAN AND STANDARD DEVIATION OF A POISSON DISTRIBUTION

The mean or expected value of a Poisson distribution is λ. It is the long-run average of occurrences for an interval if many random samples are taken. Lambda is usually not a whole number, so most of the time actually observing lambda occurrences in an interval is impossible.

For example, suppose $\lambda = 6.5$/interval for some Poisson-distributed phenomenon. The resulting numbers of x occurrences in 20 different random samples from a Poisson distribution with $\lambda = 6.5$ might be as follows.

6   9   7   4   8   7   6   6   10   6   5   5   8   4   5   8   5   4   9   10

Computing the mean number of occurrences from this group of 20 intervals gives 6.6. In theory, for infinite sampling the long-run average is 6.5. Note from the samples that, when λ is 6.5, several 5s and 6s occur. Rarely would sample occurrences of 1, 2, 3, 11, 12, 13, . . . occur when $\lambda = 6.5$. Understanding the mean of a Poisson distribution gives a feel for the actual occurrences that are likely to happen.

The variance of a Poisson distribution is also λ. The standard deviation is $\sqrt{\lambda}$. Combining the standard deviation with Chebyshev's theorem indicates the spread or dispersion of a Poisson distribution. For example, if $\lambda = 6.5$, the variance is also 6.5, and the standard deviation is 2.55. Chebyshev's theorem states that at least $1 - 1/k^2$ values are within k standard deviations of the mean. The interval $\mu \pm 2\sigma$ contains at least $1 - (1/2^2) = 0.75$ of the values. For $\mu = \lambda = 6.5$ and $\sigma = 2.55$, 75% of the values should be within the $6.5 \pm 2(2.55) = 6.5 \pm 5.1$ range. That is, the range from 1.4 to 11.6 should include at least 75% of all the values. An examination of the 20 values randomly generated for a Poisson distribution with $\lambda = 6.5$ shows that actually 100% of the values are within this range.

GRAPHING POISSON DISTRIBUTIONS

The values in Table A.3, Appendix A, can be used to graph a Poisson distribution. The x values are on the x axis and the probabilities are on the y axis. Figure 5.3 is a graph for the distribution of values for $\lambda = 1.6$.

The graph reveals a Poisson distribution skewed to the right. With a mean of 1.6 and a possible range of x from zero to infinity, the values will obviously "pile up" at 0 and 1. Consider, however, the graph of the Poisson distribution for $\lambda = 6.5$ in Figure 5.4. Note that with $\lambda = 6.5$, the probabilities are greatest for the values of 5, 6, 7, and 8. The graph has less skewness, because the probability of occurrence of values near zero is small, as are the probabilities of large values of x.

Figure 5.3

Graph of the Poisson Distribution for $\lambda = 1.6$

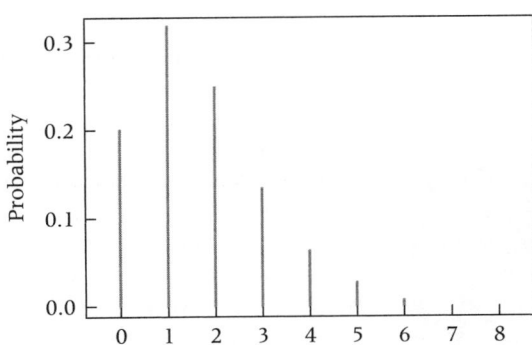

Figure 5.4

Graph of the Poisson Distribution for $\lambda = 6.5$

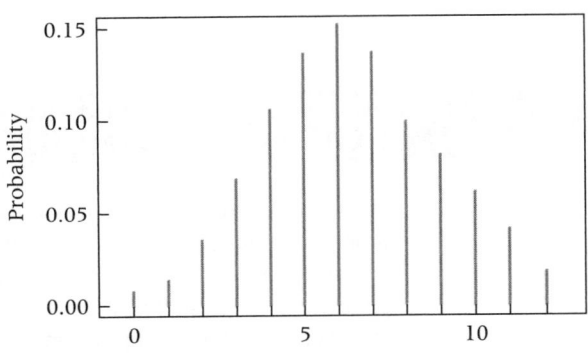

STATISTICS IN BUSINESS TODAY

Air Passengers' Complaints

In recent months, airline passengers have expressed much more dissatisfaction with airline service than ever before. It is not clear whether passengers are actually more dissatisfied with their flying experiences or they are just more vocal. Complaints include flight delays, lost baggage, long runway delays with little or no onboard service, overbooked flights, cramped space due to fuller flights, cancelled flights, and grumpy airline employees. A majority of dissatisfied fliers merely grin and bear it. However, an increasing number of passengers log complaints with the U.S. Department of Transportation. In the mid 1990s, the average number of complaints per 100,000 passengers boarded was 0.66. In ensuing years, the average rose to 0.74, 0.86, and 1.08.

In a recent year, according to the Department of Transportation, Southwest Airlines had the smallest average number of complaints per 100,000 with 0.25, followed by Alaska Airlines with 0.54, Delta Air Lines with 0.79, US Airways with 0.84, and Continental with 1.02. Within the top 10 largest U.S. airlines, Northwest had the greatest average number of complaints logged against it—2.21 complaints per 100,000 passengers.

Because these average numbers are relatively small, it appears that the actual number of complaints per 100,000 is rare and may follow a Poisson distribution. In this case, λ represents the average number of complaints and the interval is 100,000 passengers. For example, using $\lambda = 1.08$ complaints (average for all airlines), if 100,000 boarded passengers were contacted, the probability that exactly three of them logged a complaint to the Department of Transportation could be computed as

$$\frac{(1.08)^3 e^{-1.08}}{3!} = 0.01713$$

That is, if 100,000 boarded passengers were contacted over and over, 7.13% of the time exactly three would have logged complaints with the Department of Transportation.

USING THE COMPUTER TO GENERATE POISSON DISTRIBUTIONS

Using the Poisson formula to compute probabilities can be tedious when one is working problems with cumulative probabilities. The Poisson tables in Table A.3, Appendix A, are faster to use than the Poisson formula. However, Poisson tables are limited by the amount of space available, and Table A.3 only includes probability values for Poisson distributions with lambda values to the tenths place in most cases. For researchers who want to use lambda values with more precision or who feel that the computer is more convenient than textbook tables, some statistical computer software packages are an attractive option.

Excel will produce a Poisson distribution for virtually any value of lambda. For example, one study by the National Center for Health Statistics claims that, on average, an American has 1.9 acute illnesses or injuries per year. If these cases are Poisson distributed, lambda is 1.9 per year. What does the Poisson probability distribution for this lambda look like? Table 5.11 contains the Excel computer output for this distribution. Table 5.12 displays the probabilities produced by Excel for the real estate problem from Demonstration Problem 5.9 using a lambda of 1.6.

POINTS OF INTEREST
For example, the Poisson problem $P(x = 2|\lambda = 1.9)$ will be given in Excel as =POISSON(2,1.9,0).

APPROXIMATING BINOMIAL PROBLEMS BY THE POISSON DISTRIBUTION

Using the Poisson distribution can approximate certain types of binomial distribution problems. Binomial problems with large sample sizes and small values of p, which then generate rare events, are potential candidates for use of the Poisson distribution. As a guideline, if $n > 20$ and $n \cdot p \leq 7$, the approximation is close enough to use the Poisson distribution for binomial problems.

Table 5.11

Excel Output for the Poisson Distribution $\lambda = 1.9$

	Probability Density Function Poisson with Mean = 1.9
X	P(x = X)
0	0.149569
1	0.284180
2	0.269971
3	0.170982
4	0.081216
5	0.030862
6	0.009773
7	0.002653
8	0.000630
9	0.000133
10	0.000025

If these conditions are met and the binomial problem is a candidate for this process, the procedure begins with computation of the mean of the binomial distribution,

$\mu = n \cdot p$.

Because μ is the expected value of the binomial, it translates to the expected value, λ, of the Poisson distribution. Using μ as the λ value and using the x value of the binomial problem allows approximation of the probability from a Poisson table or by the Poisson formula.

Large values of n and small values of p are usually not included in binomial distribution tables, thereby precluding the use of binomial computational techniques. Using the Poisson distribution as an approximation to such a binomial problem in such cases is an attractive alternative; indeed, when a computer is not available, it can be the only alternative.

As an example, the following binomial distribution problem can be worked by using the Poisson distribution: $n = 50$ and $p = 0.03$. What is the probability that $x = 4$? That is, $P(x = 4 | n = 50$ and $p = 0.03) = ?$.

To solve this equation, first determine lambda:

$$\lambda = \mu = n \cdot p = (50)(0.03) = 1.5$$

POINTS OF INTEREST
Binomial problems with large sample sizes and small values of p are well approximated by the Poisson distribution.

Table 5.12

Excel Output for the Poisson Distribution $\lambda = 1.6$

X	P(x = X)
0	0.201897
1	0.323034
2	0.258428
3	0.137828
4	0.055131
5	0.017642
6	0.004705
7	0.001075
8	0.000215
9	0.000038

As $n > 20$ and $n \cdot p \le 7$, this problem is a candidate for the Poisson approximation. For $x = 4$, Table A.3 yields a probability of 0.0471 for the Poisson approximation. For comparison, working the problem using the binomial formula yields the following results:

$$_{50}C_4(0.03)^4(0.97)^{46} = 0.0459$$

The Poisson approximation is 0.0012 different from the result obtained by using the binomial formula to work the problem.

A graph of this binomial distribution follows.

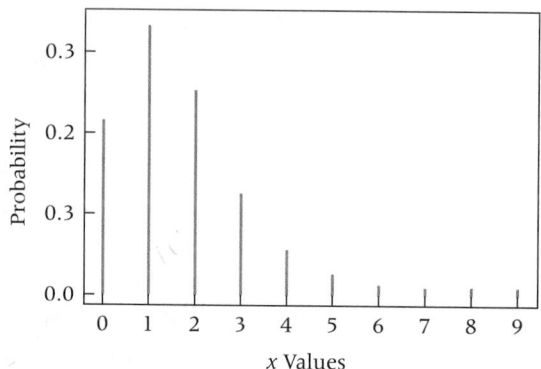

With $\lambda = 1.5$, the Poisson distribution can be generated. A graph of this Poisson distribution follows.

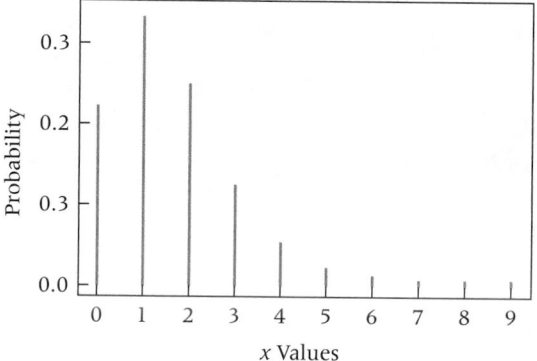

From the graphs, it is difficult to tell the difference between the binomial distribution and the Poisson distribution because the approximation of the binomial distribution by the Poisson distribution is close.

Demonstration Problem 5.10

Suppose the probability of a bank making a mistake in processing a deposit is 0.0003. If 10,000 deposits (n) are audited, what is the probability that more than six mistakes were made in processing deposits?

Solution

$$\lambda = \mu = n \cdot p = (10,000)(0.0003) = 3.0$$

Because $n > 20$ and $n \cdot p < 7$, the Poisson approximation is close enough to analyze $x > 6$. Table A.3 yields the following probabilities for $\lambda = 3.0$ and $x \geq 7$.

$\lambda = 3.0$	
x	**Probability**
7	0.0216
8	0.0081
9	0.0027
10	0.0008
11	0.0002
12	0.0001
$x > 6 = 0.0335$	

To work this problem using the binomial formula requires starting with $x = 7$:

$$_{10,000}C_7(0.0003)^7(0.9997)^{9993}$$

This process would continue for x values of 8, 9, 10, 11, . . . , until the probabilities approach zero. Obviously, this process is impractical, making the Poisson approximation an attractive alternative.

Concept Check

1. What are the key characteristics of the Poisson distribution?
2. Assume that $x = 0, 1, 2, 3, \ldots$ is a random variable that follows a Poisson distribution. What do the values of x represent?

5.4 Problems

5.15 Find the following values by using the Poisson formula.
   a. $P(x = 5 | \lambda = 2.3)$
   b. $P(x = 2 | \lambda = 3.9)$
   c. $P(x \leq 3 | \lambda = 4.1)$
   d. $P(x = 0 | \lambda = 2.7)$
   e. $P(x = 1 | \lambda = 5.4)$
   f. $P(4 < x < 8 | \lambda = 4.4)$

5.16 Find the following values by using the Poisson tables in Appendix A.
   a. $P(x = 6 | \lambda = 3.8)$
   b. $P(x > 7 | \lambda = 2.9)$
   c. $P(3 \leq x \leq 9 | \lambda = 4.2)$
   d. $P(x = 0 | \lambda = 1.9)$
   e. $P(x \leq 6 | \lambda = 2.9)$
   f. $P(5 < x \leq 8 | \lambda = 5.7)$

5.17 Sketch the graphs of the following Poisson distributions. Compute the mean and standard deviation for each distribution. Locate the mean on the graph. Note how the probabilities are graphed around the mean.
   a. $\lambda = 6.3$
   b. $\lambda = 1.3$
   c. $\lambda = 8.9$
   d. $\lambda = 0.6$

5.18   On Monday mornings, a CIBC branch has only one teller window open for deposits and withdrawals. Experience has shown that the average number of arriving customers in a 4-minute interval on Monday mornings is 2.8, and each teller can serve more than that number efficiently. The random arrivals at this bank on Monday mornings are Poisson distributed.

    a.   What is the probability that on a Monday morning exactly six customers will arrive in a 4-minute interval?

    b.   What is the probability that no one will arrive at the bank to make a deposit or withdrawal during a 4-minute interval?

    c.   Suppose the teller can serve no more than four customers in any 4-minute interval at this window on a Monday morning. What is the probability that, during any given 4-minute interval, the teller will be unable to meet the demand? What is the probability that the teller will be able to meet the demand? When demand cannot be met during any given interval, a second window is opened. What percentage of the time will a second window have to be opened?

    d.   What is the probability that exactly three people will arrive at the bank during a 2-minute period on Monday mornings to make a deposit or a withdrawal? What is the probability that five or more customers will arrive during an 8-minute period?

5.19   A restaurant manager is interested in taking a more statistical approach to predicting customer load. She begins the process by gathering data. One of the restaurant hosts or hostesses is assigned to count customers every 5 minutes from 7 P.M. until 8 P.M. every Saturday night for three weeks. The data are shown here. After the data are gathered, the manager computes lambda using the data from all three weeks as one data set as a basis for probability analysis. What value of lambda did she find? Assume that these customers randomly arrive and that the arrivals are Poisson distributed. Use the value of lambda computed by the manager and help the manager calculate the probabilities in parts (a) through (e) for any given 5-minute interval between 7 P.M. and 8 P.M. on Saturday night.

Number of Arrivals

Week 1	Week 2	Week 3
3	1	5
6	2	3
4	4	5
6	0	3
2	2	5
3	6	4
1	5	7
5	4	3
1	2	4
0	5	8
3	3	1
3	4	3

    a.   What is the probability that no customers arrive during any given 5-minute interval?

    b.   What is the probability that six or more customers arrive during any given 5-minute interval?

    c.   What is the probability that during a 10-minute interval fewer than four customers arrive?

d.   What is the probability that between three and six (inclusive) customers arrive in any 10-minute interval?

e.   What is the probability that exactly eight customers arrive in any 15-minute interval?

5.20   According to the United Nations Environment Programme and the World Health Organization, in Mumbai, India, air pollution standards for particulate matter are exceeded an average of 5.6 days in every three-week period. Assume that the distribution of number of days exceeding the standards per three-week period is Poisson distributed.

a.   What is the probability that the standard is not exceeded on any day during a three-week period?

b.   What is the probability that the standard is exceeded on exactly six days of a three-week period?

c.   What is the probability that the standard is exceeded on 15 or more days during a three-week period? If this outcome actually occurred, what might you conclude?

5.21   Suppose the average number of annual trips per family to amusement parks in Canada is Poisson distributed, with a mean of 0.6 trips per year. What is the probability of randomly selecting a Canadian family and finding the following?

a.   The family did not make a trip to an amusement park last year.

b.   The family took exactly one trip to an amusement park last year.

c.   The family took two or more trips to amusement parks last year.

d.   The family took three or fewer trips to amusement parks over a three-year period.

e.   The family took exactly four trips to amusement parks during a six-year period.

5.22   Ship collisions in the Vancouver harbour are rare. Suppose the number of collisions is Poisson distributed, with a mean of 1.2 collisions every four months.

a.   What is the probability of having no collisions occur over a four-month period?

b.   What is the probability of having exactly two collisions in a two-month period?

c.   What is the probability of having one or fewer collisions in a six-month period? If this outcome occurred, what might you conclude about harbour conditions during this period? What might you conclude about harbour safety awareness during this period? What might you conclude about weather conditions during this period? What might you conclude about lambda?

5.23   A pen company averages 1.2 defective pens per carton produced (200 pens). The number of defects per carton is Poisson distributed.

a.   What is the probability of selecting a carton and finding no defective pens?

b.   What is the probability of finding eight or more defective pens in a carton?

c.   Suppose a purchaser of these pens will stop buying from the company if a carton contains more than three defective pens. What is the probability that a carton contains more than three defective pens?

5.24   A medical researcher estimates that 0.00004 of the population has a rare blood disorder. If the researcher randomly selects 100,000 people from the population, what is the probability that seven or more people will have the rare blood disorder? What is the probability that more than 10 people will have the rare blood disorder? Suppose the researcher gets more than 10 people who have the rare blood disorder in the sample of 100,000 but that the sample was taken from a particular geographic region. What might the researcher conclude from the results?

5.25 A data firm records a large amount of data. Historically, 0.9% of the pages of data recorded by the firm contain errors. If 200 pages of data are randomly selected,
    a. what is the probability that six or more pages contain errors?
    b. what is the probability that more than 10 pages contain errors?
    c. what is the probability that none of the pages contain errors?
    d. what is the probability that fewer than five pages contain errors?

5.26 A high percentage of people who fracture or dislocate a bone see a doctor for that condition. Suppose the percentage is 99%. Consider a sample in which 300 people are randomly selected who have fractured or dislocated a bone.
    a. What is the probability that exactly five of them did not see a doctor?
    b. What is the probability that fewer than four of them did not see a doctor?
    c. What is the expected number of people who would not see a doctor?

5.5 HYPERGEOMETRIC DISTRIBUTION

Another discrete statistical distribution is the hypergeometric distribution. Statisticians often use the **hypergeometric distribution** to complement the types of analyses that can be made by using the binomial distribution. Recall that the binomial distribution applies, in theory, only to experiments in which the trials are done with replacement (independent events). The hypergeometric distribution applies only to experiments in which the trials are done without replacement.

The hypergeometric distribution, like the binomial distribution, consists of two possible outcomes: success and failure. However, the user must know the size of the population and the proportion of successes and failures in the population to apply the hypergeometric distribution. In other words, because the hypergeometric distribution is used when sampling is done without replacement, information about population makeup must be known in order to redetermine the probability of a success in each successive trial as the probability changes.

The hypergeometric distribution has the following characteristics:

- It is a discrete distribution.
- Each outcome consists of either a success or a failure.
- Sampling is done without replacement.
- The population, N, is finite and known.
- The number of successes in the population, A, is known.

Hypergeometric Formula	$$P(x) = \frac{{}_A C_x \cdot {}_{N-A} C_{n-x}}{{}_N C_n}$$

where
    N = size of the population
    n = sample size
    A = number of successes in the population
    x = number of successes in the sample; sampling is done *without* replacement

A hypergeometric distribution is characterized or described by three parameters: N, A, and n. Because of the multitude of possible combinations of these three parameters, creating tables for the hypergeometric distribution is practically impossible. Hence, the researcher who selects the hypergeometric distribution for analyzing data must use the hypergeometric formula or software to calculate each probability. Some researchers use the hypergeometric distribution as a fallback position when working binomial problems without replacement. Even though the binomial distribution theoretically applies only when sampling is done with replacement and p stays constant, recall that, if the population is large enough in comparison with the sample size, the impact of sampling without replacement on p is minimal. Thus, the binomial distribution can be used in some situations when sampling is done without replacement. Because of the tables available, using the binomial distribution instead of the hypergeometric distribution whenever possible is preferable. As a guideline, if the sample size is less than 5% of the population, use of the binomial distribution rather than the hypergeometric distribution is acceptable when sampling is done without replacement. The hypergeometric distribution yields the exact probability and the binomial distribution yields a good approximation of the probability in these situations.

In summary, the hypergeometric distribution should be used instead of the binomial distribution when the following conditions are present:

1. Sampling is being done without replacement.
2. $n \geq 5\%N$.

Hypergeometric probabilities are calculated under the assumption of equally likely sampling of the remaining elements of the sample space.

As an application of the hypergeometric distribution, consider the following problem. Twenty-four people, of whom eight are women, apply for a job. If five of the applicants are sampled randomly, what is the probability that exactly three of those sampled are women?

This problem contains a small, finite population of 24, or $N = 24$. A sample of five applicants is taken, or $n = 5$. The sampling is being done without replacement, because the five applicants selected for the sample are five different people. The sample size is 21% of the population, which is greater than 5% of the population ($n/N = 5/24 = 0.21$). The hypergeometric distribution is the appropriate distribution to use. The population breakdown is $A = 8$ women (successes) and $N - A = 24 - 8 = 16$ men. The probability of getting $x = 3$ women in the sample of $n = 5$ is

$$\frac{{}_8C_3 \cdot {}_{16}C_2}{{}_{24}C_5} = \frac{(56)(120)}{42,504} = 0.1581$$

Conceptually, the combination in the denominator of the hypergeometric formula yields all the possible ways of getting n samples from a population, N, including the ones with the desired outcome. In this problem, there are 42,504 ways of selecting 5 people from 24 people. The numerator of the hypergeometric formula computes all the possible ways of getting x successes from the A successes available and $n - x$ failures from the $N - A$ available failures in the population. There are 56 ways of getting 3 women from a pool of 8 and there are 120 ways of getting 2 men from a pool of 16. The combinations of each are multiplied in the numerator because the joint probability of getting x successes and $n - x$ failures is being computed.

POINTS OF INTEREST
If the sample size is less than 5% of the population, the use of the binomial distribution rather than the hypergeometric distribution is acceptable when sampling is done without replacement.

Demonstration Problem 5.11

Suppose 18 major computer companies operate in Canada and that 12 are located in Waterloo, Ontario. If three computer companies are selected randomly from the entire list, what is the probability that one or more of the selected companies are located in Waterloo?

Solution

$N = 18$, $n = 3$, $A = 12$, and $x \geq 1$.

This problem is actually three problems in one: $x = 1$, $x = 2$, and $x = 3$. Sampling is being done without replacement, and the sample size is 16.6% of the population. Hence, this problem is a candidate for the hypergeometric distribution. The solution follows:

$$x = 1 \qquad x = 2 \qquad x = 3$$

$$\frac{{}_{12}C_1 \cdot {}_6C_2}{{}_{18}C_3} + \frac{{}_{12}C_2 \cdot {}_6C_1}{{}_{18}C_3} + \frac{{}_{12}C_3 \cdot {}_6C_0}{{}_{18}C_3} =$$

$$0.2206 \quad + \quad 0.4853 \quad + \quad 0.2696 = 0.9755$$

An alternative solution method using the law of complements is one minus the probability that none of the companies is located in Waterloo, or

$$1 - P(x = 0 | N = 18, n = 3, A = 12)$$

Thus,

$$1 - \frac{{}_{12}C_0 \cdot {}_6C_3}{{}_{18}C_3} = 1 - 0.0245 = 0.9755$$

USING THE COMPUTER TO SOLVE FOR HYPERGEOMETRIC DISTRIBUTION PROBABILITIES

POINTS OF INTEREST
For example, the hypergeometric problem $P(x = 3 | N = 24, n = 5,$ and $A = 8)$ will be given as =HYPGEOMDIST (3,5,8,24).

Using Excel, it is possible to solve for hypergeometric distribution probabilities on the computer. Excel requires the input of N, A, n, and x. The resulting output is the exact probability for that particular value of x. The output for the example presented in this section, where $N = 24$ people of whom $A = 8$ are women, $n = 5$ are randomly selected, and $x = 3$ are women, is displayed in Table 5.13.

Table 5.13

Excel Output for a Hypergeometric Problem

	A	B	C
1	The probability of $x = 3$ when $N = 24$, $n = 5$, and $A = 8$ is: **0.158103**		

5.5 Problems

5.27 Compute the following probabilities by using the hypergeometric formula.
   a.   The probability of $x = 3$ if $N = 11$, $A = 8$, and $n = 4$
   b.   The probability of $x < 2$ if $N = 15$, $A = 5$, and $n = 6$
   c.   The probability of $x = 0$ if $N = 9$, $A = 2$, and $n = 3$
   d.   The probability of $x > 4$ if $N = 20$, $A = 5$, and $n = 7$

5.28 Shown here are the top 19 companies in the world in terms of oil-refining capacity. Some of the companies are privately owned and others are state owned. Suppose six companies are randomly selected.
   a.   What is the probability that exactly one company is privately owned?
   b.   What is the probability that exactly four companies are privately owned?
   c.   What is the probability that all six companies are privately owned?
   d.   What is the probability that none of the companies are privately owned?

Company	Ownership Status
ExxonMobil	Private
Royal Dutch/Shell	Private
BP Amoco	Private
Totalfinaelf	Private
Petroleos de Venezuela	State
Sinopec	Private
Saudi Aramco	State
China Petrochemical	State
Petroleo Brasileiro	State
Petroleo Mexicanos	State
National Iranian Oil	State
Texaco	Private
Chevron	Private
Repsol-YPF	Private
Kuwait Petroleum	State
Agip Petroli	Private
Nippon Mitsubishi Oil	Private
Marathon Ashland Petro	Private
Pertamina	State

5.29 The *Report on Business* Top 1,000 ranks 1,000 Canadian companies using various criteria. Of the top 20 companies by number of employees, 4 are banks. Suppose four companies are randomly selected.
   a. What is the probability that none of the companies are banks?
   b. What is the probability that all four companies are banks?
   c. What is the probability that exactly two are banks?

5.30 W. Edwards Deming in his red bead experiment had a box of 4,000 beads, of which 800 were red and 3,200 were white.* Suppose a researcher conducts a modified version of the red bead experiment. In her experiment, she has a bag of 20 beads, of which 4 are red and 16 are white. This experiment requires a participant to reach into the bag and randomly select five beads without replacement.
   a. What is the probability that the participant will select exactly four white beads?
   b. What is the probability that the participant will select exactly four red beads?
   c. What is the probability that the participant will select all red beads?

5.31 Shown here are the 10 Canadian provinces ranked by number of hotel rooms as compiled by the Canadian Tourism Commission for a recent year.

Rank	Province	Number of Rooms
1	Ontario	37,012
2	British Columbia	17,557
3	Alberta	17,496
4	Quebec	16,885
5	Nova Scotia	5,778
6	Saskatchewan	4,801
7	Manitoba	4,798
8	New Brunswick	3,219
9	Newfoundland and Labrador	1,892
10	Prince Edward Island	1,099

Source: Adapted from Statistics Canada, 2004. Traveller Accommodation Survey, Cat. no: Iu82-1/1-2003E, Series: Research report (Canadian Tourism Commission), p. 22.

*Mary Walton, "Deming's Parable of Red Beads," *Across the Board* (February 1987): pp. 43–48.

Suppose four of these provinces are selected randomly.
a.   What is the probability that exactly two provinces are west of Ontario?
b.   What is the probability that none of the provinces are Atlantic provinces?
c.   What is the probability that exactly three of the provinces are ones with more than 15,000 rooms?

5.32   A company produces and ships 16 personal computers knowing that 4 of them have defective wiring. The company that purchased the computers will thoroughly test three of the computers. The purchasing company can detect the defective wiring. What is the probability that the purchasing company will find the following?
a.   No defective computers
b.   Exactly three defective computers
c.   Two or more defective computers
d.   One or fewer defective computers

5.33   A western city has 18 police officers eligible for promotion. Eleven of the 18 are men. Suppose only five of the police officers are chosen for promotion and that one is a man. If the officers chosen for promotion had been selected by chance alone, what is the probability that one or fewer of the five promoted officers would have been men? What might this result indicate?

LIFE WITH A CELL PHONE

Suppose that 6% of Canadian households consider their cell phone as their primary phone number. If 20 households are randomly selected, what is the probability that more than three consider the cell phone as their primary phone number? Converting the 6% to a proportion, the value of p is 0.06, and this is a classic binomial distribution problem with $n = 20$ and $x > 3$. Because the binomial distribution probability tables (Appendix A, Table A.2) do not include $p = 0.06$, the problem will have to be solved using the binomial formula for each of $x = 4, 5, 6, 7, \ldots, 20$.

For $x = 4$: $_{20}C_4(0.06)^4(0.94)^{16} = 0.0233$

Solving for $x = 5, 6$, and 7 in a similar manner results in probabilities of 0.0048, 0.0008, and 0.0001, respectively. Since the probabilities zero out at $x = 8$, we need not proceed on to $x = 9, 10, \ldots, 20$. Summing these four probabilities ($x = 4, 5, 6, 7$) results in a total probability of 0.0290 as the answer to the posed question. To further understand

these probabilities, we calculate the expected value of this distribution as

$$\mu = n \cdot p = 20(0.06) = 1.2$$

In the long run, one would expect to average about 1.2 Canadian households out of every 20 who consider their cell phone as their primary phone number. In light of this, there is a very small probability that more than three households would do so.

The study also stated that 9 out of 10 cell users encounter others using their phones in an annoying way. Converting this to $p = 0.90$ and using $n = 25$ and $x < 20$, this, too, is a binomial problem, but it can be solved by using the binomial tables, obtaining the values shown below:

x	Probability
19	0.024
18	0.007
17	0.002
16	0.000

The total of these probabilities is 0.033. Probabilities for all other values ($x \le 15$) are displayed as 0.000 in the binomial probability table and are not included here. If 90% of all cell phone users encounter others using their phones in an annoying way, the probability is very small (0.033) that out of 25 randomly selected cell phone users fewer than 20 encounter others using their phones in an annoying way. The expected number in any random sample of 25 is (25)(0.90) = 22.5.

Suppose, on average, cell phone users receive 3.6 calls per day. Given that information, what is the probability that a cell phone user receives no calls per day? Since random telephone calls are generally thought to be Poisson distributed, this problem can be solved by using either the Poisson probability formula or the Poisson table (Table A.3, Appendix A). In this problem, $\lambda = 3.6$ and $x = 0$, and the probability associated with this is

$$\frac{\lambda^x e^{-\lambda}}{x!} = \frac{(3.6)^0 e^{-3.6}}{0!} = 0.0273$$

What is the probability that a cell phone user receives five or more calls in a day? Since this is a cumulative probability question ($x > 5$), the best option is to use the Poisson probability table (Table A.3, Appendix A) to obtain:

x	Probability
5	0.1377
6	0.0826
7	0.0425
8	0.0191
9	0.0076
10	0.0028
11	0.0009
12	0.0003
13	0.0001
14	0.0000
total	0.2936

There is a 29.36% chance that a cell phone user will receive five or more calls per day if, on average, such a cell phone user averages 3.6 calls per day.

Why Statistics Is Relevant

Distributions (both discrete and continuous) are important because most of the analyses done in business statistics are based on the characteristics of a particular distribution. Unlike data, statistical distributions are formal models that describe the likelihood of a random variable taking on a value or a range of values. Thus, statistical distributions are not only found in business statistics, they are part of the general vocabulary for communicating basic ideas. Understanding the differences between a data distribution (a histogram for example) and a statistical distribution is one of the most profound insights an analyst can have. Being able to interpret a statistical distribution and make formal, well-reasoned statements about a random variable by studying its distribution is a very important analytical skill.

SUMMARY

Probability experiments produce random outcomes. A variable that contains the outcomes of a random experiment is called a random variable. The key questions of the chapter aimed at describing these random variables in a formal and useful fashion.

1. Random variables such that the set of all possible values is at most a finite or countably infinite number of possible values are called discrete random variables. Random variables that take on values at all points over a given interval are called continuous random variables. Discrete distributions are constructed from discrete random variables. Continuous distributions are constructed from continuous random variables.

2. The measures of central tendency and measures of variability discussed in Chapter 3 for grouped data can be applied to discrete distributions to compute a mean, a variance, and a standard deviation. Important examples of discrete distributions are the binomial distribution, the Poisson distribution, and the hypergeometric distribution.

3. The binomial distribution fits experiments when only two mutually exclusive outcomes are possible. In theory, each trial in a binomial experiment must be independent of the other trials. However, if the population size is large enough in relation to the sample size ($n < 5\%N$), the binomial distribution can be used where applicable in cases where the trials are not independent. The probability of getting a desired

SUMMARY (continued)

outcome on any one trial is denoted as p, which is the probability of getting a success. The binomial distribution can be used to analyze discrete studies involving such things as heads/tails, defective/good, and male/female. The binomial formula is used to determine the probability of obtaining x outcomes in n trials. Binomial distribution problems can be solved more rapidly with the use of binomial tables than by formula. A binomial table can be constructed for every different pair of n and p values. Table A.2 of Appendix A contains binomial tables for selected values of n and p.

4–5. The Poisson distribution is usually used to analyze phenomena that produce rare occurrences. The only information required to generate a Poisson distribution is the long-run average, which is denoted by lambda (λ). The Poisson distribution pertains to occurrences over some interval. The assumptions

are that each occurrence is independent of other occurrences and that the value of lambda remains constant throughout the experiment. Examples of Poisson-type experiments are number of flaws per page of paper and number of calls per minute to a switchboard. Poisson probabilities can be determined by either the Poisson formula or the Poisson tables in Table A.3 of Appendix A. The Poisson distribution can be used to approximate binomial distribution problems when n is large ($n > 20$), p is small, and $n \cdot p < 7$.

6. The hypergeometric distribution is a discrete distribution that is usually used for binomial-type experiments when the population is small and finite and sampling is done without replacement. Because using the hypergeometric distribution is a tedious process, using the binomial distribution whenever possible is generally more advantageous.

KEY TERMS

binomial distribution
continuous distribution
continuous random
   variable

discrete distribution
discrete random variable
hypergeometric distribution
lambda (λ)

mean or expected value
Poisson distribution
random variable

FORMULAS

Mean (expected) value of a discrete distribution

$$\mu = E(x) = \Sigma[x \cdot P(x)]$$

Variance of a discrete distribution

$$\sigma^2 = \Sigma[(x - \mu)^2 \cdot P(x)]$$

Standard deviation of a discrete distribution

$$\sigma = \sqrt{\Sigma[(x - \mu)^2 \cdot P(x)]}$$

Binomial formula

$$_nC_x \cdot p^x \cdot q^{n-x} = \frac{n!}{x!(n-x)!} \cdot p^x \cdot q^{n-x}$$

Mean of a binomial distribution

$$\mu = n \cdot p$$

Standard deviation of a binomial distribution

$$\sigma = \sqrt{n \cdot p \cdot q}$$

Poisson formula

$$P(x) = \frac{\lambda^x e^{-\lambda}}{x!}$$

Hypergeometric formula

$$P(x) = \frac{_AC_x \cdot _{N-A}C_{n-x}}{_NC_n}$$

KEY CONSIDERATIONS

Several points must be emphasized about the use of discrete distributions to analyze data. The independence and/or size assumptions must be met to use the binomial distribution in situations where sampling is done without replacement. Size and λ assumptions must be satisfied to use the Poisson distribution to approximate binomial problems. In either case, failure to meet such assumptions can result in spurious conclusions.

As n increases, the use of binomial distributions to study exact x-value probabilities becomes questionable in decision making. Although the probabilities are mathematically correct, as n becomes larger, the probability of any particular x value becomes lower because there are more values among which to split the probabilities. For example, if $n = 100$ and $p = 0.50$, the probability of $x = 50$ is 0.0796. This probability of occurrence appears quite low, even though $x = 50$ is the expected value of this distribution and is also the value most likely to occur. It is more useful

to decision makers and, in a sense, probably more ethical to present cumulative values for larger sizes of n. In this example, it is probably more useful to examine $P(x > 50)$ than $P(x = 50)$.

The reader is warned in the chapter that the value of λ is assumed to be constant in a Poisson distribution experiment. Researchers may produce spurious results because the λ value changes during a study. For example, suppose the value of λ is obtained for the number of customer arrivals at a toy store between 7 P.M. and 9 P.M. in the month of December. Because December is an active month in terms of traffic volume through a toy store, the use of such a λ to analyze arrivals at the same store between noon and 2 P.M. in February is inappropriate.

It is important that statisticians and researchers adhere to assumptions and appropriate applications of these techniques. The inability or unwillingness to do so opens the way for inappropriate (and perhaps unethical) decision making.

SUPPLEMENTARY PROBLEMS

Calculating the Statistics

5.34 Solve for the probabilities of the following binomial distribution problems by using the binomial formula.
 a. If $n = 11$ and $p = 0.23$, what is the probability that $x = 4$?
 b. If $n = 6$ and $p = 0.50$, what is the probability that $x \geq 1$?
 c. If $n = 9$ and $p = 0.85$, what is the probability that $x > 7$?
 d. If $n = 14$ and $p = 0.70$, what is the probability that $x \leq 3$?

5.35 Use Table A.2, Appendix A, to find the values of the following binomial distribution problems.
 a. $P(x = 14 | n = 20 \text{ and } p = 0.60)$
 b. $P(x < 5 | n = 10 \text{ and } p = 0.30)$
 c. $P(x \geq 12 | n = 15 \text{ and } p = 0.60)$
 d. $P(x > 20 | n = 25 \text{ and } p = 0.40)$

5.36 Use the Poisson formula to solve for the probabilities of the following Poisson distribution problems.
 a. If $\lambda = 1.25$, what is the probability that $x = 4$?
 b. If $\lambda = 6.37$, what is the probability that $x \leq 1$?
 c. If $\lambda = 2.4$, what is the probability that $x > 5$?

5.37 Use Table A.3, Appendix A, to find the following Poisson distribution values.
 a. $P(x = 3 | \lambda = 1.8)$
 b. $P(x < 5 | \lambda = 3.3)$
 c. $P(x \geq 3 | \lambda = 2.1)$
 d. $P(2 < x \leq 5 | \lambda = 4.2)$

5.38 Solve the following problems by using the hypergeometric formula.
 a. If $N = 6$, $n = 4$, and $A = 5$, what is the probability that $x = 3$?
 b. If $N = 10$, $n = 3$, and $A = 5$, what is the probability that $x \leq 1$?
 c. If $N = 13$, $n = 5$, and $A = 3$, what is the probability that $x \geq 2$?

Testing Your Understanding

5.39 In a study by Peter D. Hart Research Associates for the Nasdaq Stock Market, it was determined that 20% of all stock investors are retired people. In addition, 40% of all adults invest in mutual funds. Suppose a random sample of 25 stock investors is taken. What is the probability that exactly seven are retired people? What is the probability that 10 or more are retired people? How many retired people would you expect to find in a random sample of 25 stock investors? Suppose a random sample of 20 adults is taken. What is the probability that exactly eight adults invested in mutual funds? What is the probability that fewer than six adults invested in mutual funds? What is the probability that none of the adults invested in mutual funds? What is the probability that 12 or more adults invested in mutual funds? For which exact number of adults is the probability the highest? How does this figure compare to the expected number?

5.40 A service station has a pump that distributes diesel fuel to automobiles. The station owner estimates that only about 3.2 cars use the diesel pump every 2 hours. Assume the arrivals of diesel pump users are Poisson distributed.

 a. What is the probability that three cars will arrive to use the diesel pump during a 1-hour period?

 b. Suppose the owner needs to shut down the diesel pump for half an hour to make repairs. However, the owner hates to lose any business. What is the probability that no cars will arrive to use the diesel pump during a half-hour period?

 c. What is the probability of five or more cars arriving during a 1-hour period to use the diesel pump? If this outcome actually occurred, what might you conclude?

5.41 In a particular manufacturing plant, two machines (A and B) produce a particular part. One machine (B) is newer and faster. In one 5-minute period, a lot consisting of 32 parts is produced. Twenty-two are produced by machine B and the rest by machine A. Suppose an inspector randomly samples a dozen of the parts from this lot.

 a. What is the probability that exactly three parts were produced by machine A?

 b. What is the probability that half of the parts were produced by each machine?

 c. What is the probability that all of the parts were produced by machine B?

 d. What is the probability that seven, eight, or nine parts were produced by machine B?

5.42 Suppose that, for every lot of 100 computer chips a company produces, an average of 1.4 are defective. Another company buys many lots of these chips at a time, from which one lot is selected randomly and tested for defects. If the tested lot contains more than three defects, the buyer will reject all the lots sent in

that batch. What is the probability that the buyer will accept the lots? Assume that the defects per lot are Poisson distributed.

5.43 According to the Heart and Stroke Foundation of Canada, in a recent year 17.6% of Canadians between the ages of 65 and 79 report having heart disease or stroke. Suppose you live in a province where the environment is conducive to good health and low stress and you believe these conditions promote healthy hearts. To investigate this theory, you conduct a random telephone survey of 20 persons 65 to 79 years of age in your province.

 a. On the basis of the figure from the Heart and Stroke Foundation, what is the expected number of people 65 to 79 years of age in your survey who have a chronic heart condition?

 b. Suppose only one person in your survey has a chronic heart condition. What is the probability of getting one or fewer people with a chronic heart condition in a sample of 20 if 17.6% of the population in this age bracket has this health problem? What do you conclude about your province from the sample data?

5.44 Suppose a survey reveals that 69% of Canadian workers say job stress causes frequent health problems. One in four said they expected to burn out in the job in the near future. Thirty-two percent said they thought seriously about quitting their job last year because of workplace stress. Forty-nine percent said they were required to work more than 40 hours a week very often or somewhat often.

 a. Suppose a random sample of 10 Canadian workers is selected. What is the probability that more than seven of them say job stress caused frequent health problems? What is the expected number of workers who say job stress caused frequent health problems?

 b. Suppose a random sample of 15 Canadian workers is selected. What is the expected number of these sampled workers who say they will burn out in the near future? What is the probability that none of the workers say they will burn out in the near future?

 c. Suppose a sample of seven workers is selected randomly. What is the probability that all seven say they are asked very often or somewhat often to work more than 40 hours a week? If this outcome actually happened, what might you conclude?

5.45 According to Padgett Business Services, 20% of all small-business owners say the most important advice for starting a business is to prepare for long hours and hard work. Twenty-five percent say the most important advice is to have good financing ready. Nineteen percent say having a good plan is the most important advice, 18% say studying the industry is the most important advice, and 18% list other advice. Suppose 12 small-business owners are contacted, and assume that the percentages hold for all small-business owners.

   a. What is the probability that none of the owners would say preparing for long hours and hard work is the most important advice?

   b. What is the probability that six or more owners would say preparing for long hours and hard work is the most important advice?

   c. What is the probability that exactly five owners would say having good financing ready is the most important advice?

   d. What is the expected number of owners who would say having a good plan is the most important advice?

5.46 Suppose that the probability that a passenger files a complaint with the Canadian Transportation Agency about a particular airline is 0.000014. Suppose 100,000 passengers who flew with this particular airline are randomly contacted.

   a. What is the probability that exactly five passengers filed complaints?

   b. What is the probability that none of the passengers filed complaints?

   c. What is the probability that more than six passengers filed complaints?

5.47 A hairstylist has been in business for one year. Sixty percent of his customers are walk-in business. If he randomly samples eight of the people from last week's list of customers, what is the probability that three or fewer were walk-ins? If this outcome actually occurred, what would some of the reasons be?

5.48 According to a recent census, about 63% of Manitoba residents live in cities with a population of 10,000 or more people. A catalogue sales company in Ontario just purchased a list of Manitoba consumers. Its market analyst randomly selects 25 people from this list.

   a. What is the probability that exactly 15 people live in metropolitan areas?

   b. What is the probability that the analyst would get more than 20 people in this sample who live in metropolitan areas?

   c. Suppose the analyst got more than 20 people who live in metropolitan areas from the group of 25. What might she conclude about the company's list of Manitoba consumers? What might she conclude about the census figure?

5.49 Suppose that, for every family vacation trip by car of more than 2,000 km, an average of 0.60 flat tires occurs. Suppose also that the distribution of the number of flat tires per trip of more than 2,000 km is Poisson. What is the probability that a family will take a trip of more than 2,000 km and have no flat tires? What is the probability that the family will have three or more flat tires on such a trip? Suppose trips are independent and the value of lambda holds for all trips of more than 2,000 km. If a family takes two trips of more than 2,000 km during a summer, what is the probability that the family will have no flat tires on either trip?

5.50 The Canadian Newspaper Association releases figures on the top newspapers in Canada. Shown here are the top 25 daily newspapers in Canada ranked according to circulation.

Rank	Newspaper
1	Toronto Star
2	The Globe and Mail
3	Le Journal de Montréal
4	La Presse, Montréal
5	The Toronto Sun
6	National Post
7	The Vancouver Sun
8	The Gazette, Montreal
9	Ottawa Citizen
10	Winnipeg Free Press
11	The Province, Vancouver
12	The Edmonton Journal
13	Calgary Herald
14	Le Journal de Québec
15	The Chronicle-Herald, Halifax
16	The Spectator, Hamilton
17	Le Soleil, Québec
18	The London Free Press
19	Times Colonist, Victoria
20	The Edmonton Sun
21	The Calgary Sun
22	The Windsor Star
23	The Record, Kitchener-Waterloo
24	The StarPhoenix, Saskatoon
25	The Ottawa Sun

Suppose a researcher wants to sample a portion of these newspapers and compare the sizes of the business sections of the Saturday papers. She randomly samples eight of these newspapers.

a. What is the probability that the sample contains exactly one newspaper located in Ontario?

b. What is the probability that half of the newspapers are ranked in the top 10 by circulation?

c. What is the probability that none of the newspapers are located in British Columbia?

d. What is the probability that exactly three of the newspapers are located in provinces that begin with the letter N?

5.51   An office in Calgary, Alberta, has 24 workers including management. Eight of the workers commute to work from Airdrie. Suppose six of the office workers are randomly selected.

a. What is the probability that all six workers commute from Airdrie?

b. What is the probability that none of the workers commute from Airdrie?

c. Which probability from parts (a) and (b) was greater? Why do you think this is?

d. What is the probability that half of the workers do not commute from Airdrie?

5.52   According to Statistics Canada, 16% of the workers in Calgary use public transportation. If 25 Calgary workers are randomly selected, what is the expected number to use public transportation? Graph the binomial distribution for this sample. What are the mean and the standard deviation for this distribution? What is the probability that more than eight of the selected workers use public transportation? Explain conceptually and from the graph why you would get this probability. Suppose you randomly sample 25 Calgary workers and actually get 10 who use public transportation. Is this outcome likely? How might you explain this result?

5.53   One of the earliest applications of the Poisson distribution was in analyzing incoming calls to a telephone switchboard. Analysts generally believe that random phone calls are Poisson distributed. Suppose phone

calls to a switchboard arrive at an average rate of 2.4 calls per minute.

a. Suppose an operator wants to take a 1-minute break. What is the probability that there will be no calls during a 1-minute interval?

b. If an operator can handle at most five calls per minute, what is the probability that the operator will be unable to handle the calls in any 1-minute period?

c. What is the probability that exactly three calls will arrive in a 2-minute interval?

d. What is the probability that one or fewer calls will arrive in a 15-second interval?

5.54   According to Statistics Canada, only 1% of all Canadian households do not have a colour television set. A television marketing analyst randomly selects 160 Canadian households.

a. How many households would he expect not to have a colour television set?

b. What is the probability that eight or more households do not have a colour television set?

c. What is the probability that between two and six households (inclusive) do not have a colour television set?

5.55   Suppose that in the bookkeeping operation of a large corporation the probability of a recording error on any one billing is 0.005. Suppose the probability of a recording error from one billing to the next is constant, and 1,000 billings are randomly sampled by an auditor.

a. What is the probability that fewer than four billings contain a recording error?

b. What is the probability that more than 10 billings contain a billing error?

c. What is the probability that all 1,000 billings contain no recording errors?

5.56   According to the Canadian Medical Association, about 55% of all Canadian physicians under the age of 35 are women. Your company has just hired eight physicians under the age of 35 and only two are women. If a group of women physicians under the age of 35 want to sue your company for discriminatory hiring practices, would they have a strong case based on these numbers? Use the binomial distribution to determine the probability of the company's hiring result occurring randomly and comment on the potential justification for a lawsuit.

5.57 The following table lists the 28 largest Canadian universities according to full-time undergraduate enrolment figures. The province of location is given in parentheses.

University	Enrolment
University of Toronto (Ont.)	53,500
York University (Ont.)	39,400
University of Alberta (Alta.)	28,510
Université de Montréal (Que.)	28,150
University of Ottawa (Ont.)	26,100
University of Western Ontario (Ont.)	25,800
University of British Columbia (B.C.)	25,770
University of Calgary (Alta.)	20,290
McGill University (Que.)	19,850
Université Laval (Que.)	19,600
University of Manitoba (Man.)	19,520
McMaster University (Ont.)	19,400
Université du Québec à Montréal (Que.)	18,740
University of Waterloo (Ont.)	18,700
University of Guelph (Ont.)	18,000
Concordia University (Que.)	17,150
Carleton University (Ont.)	16,500
Ryerson University (Ont.)	16,500
Queen's University (Ont.)	13,700
Memorial University of Newfoundland (N.L.)	13,110
University of Saskatchewan (Sask.)	13,040
Brock University (Ont.)	13,000
Wilfrid Laurier University (Ont.)	12,000
University of Windsor (Ont.)	11,600
Simon Fraser University (B.C.)	11,410
University of Victoria (B.C.)	11,010
Dalhousie University (N.S.)	10,250
Université de Sherbrooke (Que.)	10,160

Source: Compiled from Association of Universities and Colleges of Canada, Fall 2008 preliminary full-time and part-time enrolment at AUCC member institutions (rounded to the nearest 10), http://www.aucc.ca/publications/stats/enrol_e.html. Used by permission.

a. If five different universities are selected randomly from the list, what is the probability that three of them have enrolments of 18,000 or more?

b. If eight different universities are selected randomly from the list, what is the probability that two or fewer are universities in Quebec?

c. Suppose universities are being selected randomly from this list with replacement. If five universities are sampled, what is the probability that the sample will contain exactly two universities in British Columbia?

5.58 In one western city, the government has 14 repossessed houses, which are evaluated to be worth about the same. Ten of the houses are on the north side of town and the rest are on the west side. A local contractor submitted a bid to purchase four of the houses. Which houses the contractor will get is subject to a random draw.

a. What is the probability that all four houses selected for the contractor will be on the north side of town?

b. What is the probability that all four houses selected for the contractor will be on the west side of town?

c. What is the probability that half of the houses selected for the contractor will be on the west side and half on the north side of town?

5.59 The Public Citizen's Health Research Group studied the serious disciplinary actions that were taken during a recent year on nonfederal medical doctors in the U.S. The American average was 3.84 serious actions per 1,000 doctors. Assume that the Canadian average is the same; moreover, assume that the numbers of serious actions per 1,000 doctors is Poisson distributed.

a. What is the probability of randomly selecting 1,000 Canadian doctors and finding no serious actions taken?

b. What is the probability of randomly selecting 2,000 Canadian doctors and finding six serious actions taken?

c. Assume that British Columbia has an average of 1.6 serious actions per 1,000 doctors. What is the probability of randomly selecting 3,000 British Columbia doctors and finding fewer than seven serious actions taken?

SUPPLEMENTARY PROBLEMS (continued)

Interpreting the Output

5.60 Study the following output. Discuss the type of distribution, the mean, the standard deviation, and why the probabilities fall as they do.

Probability Density Function

Binomial with n = 15 and p = 0.36

X	P(x = X)
0	0.001238
1	0.010445
2	0.041128
3	0.100249
4	0.169170
5	0.209347
6	0.196263
7	0.141940
8	0.079841
9	0.034931
10	0.011789
11	0.003014
12	0.000565
13	0.000073
14	0.000006
15	0.000000

5.61 Study the following output. Explain the distribution in terms of shape and mean. Are these probabilities what you would expect? Why or why not?

	A	B
1	x Values	Poisson Probabilities: Lambda = 2.78
2	0	0.0620
3	1	0.1725
4	2	0.2397
5	3	0.2221
6	4	0.1544
7	5	0.0858
8	6	0.0398
9	7	0.0158
10	8	0.0055
11	9	0.0017
12	10	0.0005
13	11	0.0001

5.62 Study the following graphical output. Describe the distribution and explain why the graph takes the shape it does.

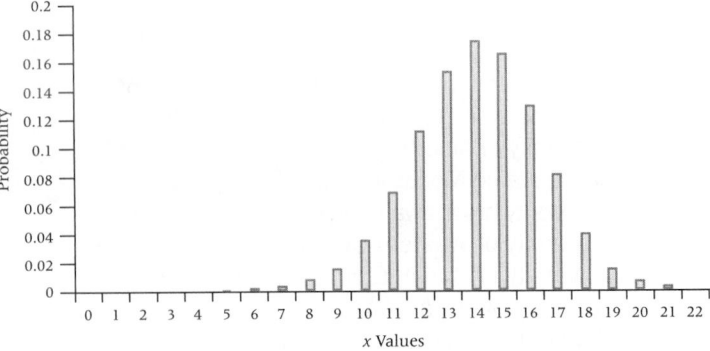

Binomial Distribution: $n = 22$ and $p = 0.64$

5.63 Study the following graph. Discuss the distribution, including type, shape, and probability outcomes.

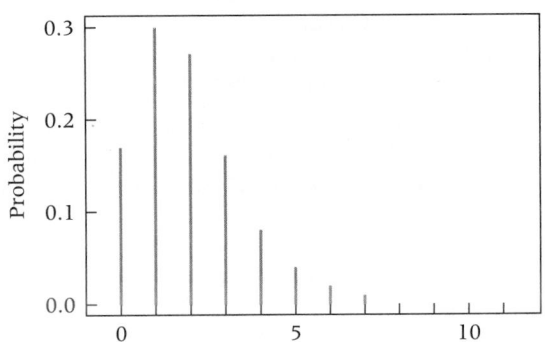

Poisson Distribution: Lambda = 1.784

1. Use the Major League Baseball Database. What is the probability that a randomly selected team is in Division 5? Use this as the p value for a binomial experiment. If you were to randomly select 10 teams, what is the probability that fewer than two would be in Division 5? If you were to randomly select 12 teams, what is the probability that exactly 2 would be in Division 5? Is the use of the binomial distribution appropriate for this problem? Why?

2. Use the Canadian Hospitals Database. In this population of 195, what is the breakdown between hospitals that are in a different geographical region? Using these figures as a breakdown of the population and the hypergeometric distribution, what is the probability of randomly selecting 16 municipalities from this database and getting exactly 9 that are in Alberta? Now use the binomial formula to determine the probability of randomly selecting 30 municipalities and getting exactly 10 that are from British Columbia.

3. Use the Financial Institutes (Type 2) variable in the Financial Database. If five of these companies are selected randomly, what is the probability that exactly three have Total Debt/Total Equity of 30% or more? What is the probability of randomly selecting eight Mining, Electric, Oil & Gas, Pipelines (Type 4) companies and getting exactly four of them with Average Yield of less than 1%?

CASE

RIM's Greatest Success—The BlackBerry

Mike Lazaridis was born in Turkey in 1961. In 1966, at the age of five, Lazaridis and his family picked up and relocated to Canada, where they would eventually call Windsor, Ontario, their hometown. Even at a very early age, Lazaridis was extremely ambitious. He would spend much of his time reading books and tinkering with various technologies in order to build radios and rockets. During his years at university, he was very motivated to make it big as soon as he possibly could. That ambition led him to leave university before he graduated and accept a position at General Motors. In 1984, however, Lazaridis made his most important business decision, changing the course of his life. At the age of 23, he established Research in Motion (RIM), allowing Lazaridis to enter the world of wireless technology and making RIM and its founder very successful.

RIM's greatest development was the BlackBerry smartphone. The BlackBerry was introduced in 1999 and today is a wireless handheld device that allows people to perform functions such as e-mailing, text messaging, surfing the Internet, and many other wireless services.

Over the years, the BlackBerry has improved tremendously and continues to introduce better features, more applications, and faster services. RIM has been able to target and successfully sell its BlackBerry smartphones to corporate customers, and its brand name and solid reputation have also allowed it to sell BlackBerry smartphones around the world: in Canada, the United States, Europe, and Asia.

According to Juniper Research, smartphone sales are increasing and are expected to rise by 95% to over 300 million by the year 2013. The demand for smartphones is a very good sign for RIM, indicating that it will continue to grow at a rapid rate. Revenues for RIM in 2008 were $6.01 billion, and this impressive number indicates that RIM is dedicated to offering quality products in order to satisfy the needs of its customers and to continuing its growth.

Discussion

Suppose you are part of a RIM team with the task of examining quality, customer satisfaction, and market issues. Using techniques presented in this chapter, analyze and discuss the following questions.

1. According to general market information, RIM is one of the top five companies in terms of smartphone sales (the other companies are Nokia, Apple, HTC, and Fujitsu). For the purpose of this discussion, assume that RIM has a market share of 20% for smartphones. Your team wants to confirm that this figure is constant for various geographical segments in Canada. In an effort to study this issue, a random sample of 40 current purchasers of smartphones is taken in each of the following provinces:

CASE (continued)

British Columbia, Saskatchewan, Manitoba, and Newfoundland and Labrador. If the 20% market share figure is constant across regions, how many of the 40 purchases of smartphones would the company expect to be RIM BlackBerry smartphones in each province? If 12 or more of the 40 purchases in British Columbia are RIM, what might that tell the team? If fewer than 7 of the 40 purchases in Newfoundland and Labrador are RIM brand, what does that mean? Suppose none of the 40 purchases in Saskatchewan are RIM-brand smartphones. Is it still possible that RIM holds 20% of the market share? Why or why not? If indeed RIM holds 20% of the market share in Manitoba, is it likely in a sample of 40 purchases that 30 or more are RIM? Explain to the team.

2. BlackBerry smartphones allow people to send e-mails and browse the Web from wherever they are—unlike with a personal computer. The BlackBerry smartphone is lightweight and easy to carry, therefore providing more ease and flexibility to its users. Suppose that the RIM team wants to ascertain if people send more or fewer e-mails with BlackBerry smartphones than they did with personal computers. Suppose in a previous study using personal computers, it was determined that, on average, corporate customers sent 3.5 e-mails per hour during their work hours. Using this figure as a guide, if the RIM team randomly samples corporate customers in various parts of Canada that are using BlackBerry smartphones, what is the probability that a corporate user sends seven or more e-mails in an hour? What might the answer to this question indicate about

the usage of BlackBerry smartphones versus regular personal computers?

3. Suppose a consumer group conducts a study of 50 recent purchasers of smartphones, of which 14 own a RIM BlackBerry. In the study, smartphone owners are asked to rate their satisfaction with their smartphones on a scale from 0 to 100. The top 10 satisfaction scores are taken and 5 of the top 10 are from owners of RIM BlackBerry smartphones. How likely would it be that two or three of the top 10 satisfaction scores come from consumers who own a RIM BlackBerry? A friend has heard that there is less than a 5% chance that none of the top 10 satisfaction scores come from consumers who own a RIM BlackBerry. How would you react to this comment? Suppose 8 of the top 10 satisfaction scores were obtained from RIM BlackBerry purchasers. What might this indicate?

References

"BlackBerry to be Sold in Europe by BT," European Telecom, January 2005. Website for data source: <http://findarticles.com/p/articles/mi_hb6534/is_200501/ai_n26360726/>; "Smartphone Sales Rise in Q1; RIM, Apple See Biggest Gains," Matt Hamblen, May 20, 2009. Website for data source: <http://www.computerworld.com/s/article/9133319/Smartphone_sales_rise_in_Q1_RIM_Apple_see_biggest_gains>; "Mike Lazaridis," European CEO, 2009. Website for data source: <http://www.europeanceo.com/news/ceo-profiles//article560.html>; "RIM Posts $6 billion Revenue for Fiscal 2008," 2008. Website for data source: <http://www.electronista.com/articles/08/04/02/rim.posts.large.profits/>

USING THE COMPUTER

Excel

- Excel can be used to compute exact or cumulative probabilities for particular values of discrete distributions including the binomial, Poisson, and hypergeometric distributions.
- Calculation of probabilities from each of these distributions begins with the **Insert Function** (*fx*). To access the **Insert Function**, go to the **Formulas** tab on an Excel worksheet (top centre tab). The **Insert Function** is on the far left of the menu bar. In the **Insert Function** dialogue box at the top, there is a pulldown menu where it says **Or select a category**. From the pulldown menu associated with this command, select **Statistical**.
- To compute probabilities from a binomial distribution, select **BINOMDIST** from the **Insert Function's Statistical** menu. In the **BINOMDIST** dialogue box, there are four lines to which you must respond. On the first line, **Number_s**, enter the value of x, the number of successes. On the second line, **Trials**, enter the number of trials (sample size, n). On the third line, **Probability_s**, enter the value of p. The fourth line, **Cumulative**, requires a logical response of either TRUE or FALSE. Place TRUE in the slot to get the cumulative probabilities

for all values from 0 to x. Place FALSE in the slot to get the exact probability of getting x successes in n trials.
- To compute probabilities from a Poisson distribution, select **POISSON** from the **Insert Function's Statistical** menu. In the **POISSON** dialogue box, there are three lines to which you must respond. On the first line, **X**, enter the value of x, the number of events. On the second line, **Mean**, enter the expected number, λ. The third line, **Cumulative**, requires a logical response of either TRUE or FALSE. Place TRUE in the slot to get the cumulative probabilities for all values from 0 to x. Place FALSE in the slot to get the exact probability of getting x successes when λ is the expected number.
- To compute probabilities from a hypergeometric distribution, select **HYPGEOMDIST** from the **Insert Function's Statistical** menu. In the **HYPGEOMDIST** dialogue box, there are four lines to which you must respond. On the first line, **Sample_s**, enter the value of x, the number of successes in the sample. On the second line, **Number_sample**, enter the size of the sample, n. On the third line, **Population_s**, enter the number of successes in the population. The fourth line, **Number_pop**, enter the size of the population, N.

CHAPTER 6
CONTINUOUS DISTRIBUTIONS

Learning Objectives

The primary learning objective of Chapter 6 is to help you understand continuous distributions. The key questions of the chapter are:

1. What are the key concepts behind the uniform distribution and its uses?

2. Why is the normal distribution so important in business statistics?

3. How can we recognize normal distribution problems and know how to solve such problems?

4. When is it possible to use the normal distribution to approximate binomial distribution problems? How should we work such problems?

5. When is it possible to use the exponential distribution to solve problems in business? How should we work such problems?

Photo Disc, Inc./Getty Images

THE COST OF HIRING A SMOKER

What is the cost of hiring a smoker? Recently, the Conference Board of Canada obtained and reviewed data from numerous sources and prepared a report in which it estimates that the average cost of hiring a smoker is $3,396 more per year than employing a non-smoker. Employing smokers increases employee absenteeism and decreases productivity, and makes smoking facilities a necessity. Several studies have shown that smokers have more absences from work, up to 20% more, than non-smokers. The Conference Board of Canada reviewed the recent Canadian Community Health Survey produced by Statistics Canada and found that smokers take two more sick-leave days per year than their non-smoking counterparts, which translates into an average cost of $323 per smoker, per year in lost revenues to the employer. Also, the average smoker takes two 20-minute unscheduled smoke breaks throughout each day. As such, the cost of lost productivity due to unscheduled smoke breaks over one year is an average of $3,053 per smoking employee. An employer also pays for accommodating smoking through the provision of commercial ashtrays and through the requirements for their maintenance and cleaning; this costs an average of $20 per smoking employee per year.

Managerial and Statistical Questions

1. The Canadian Community Health Survey reported that on average, smokers take two more sick-leave days per year than their non-smoking counterparts. Suppose that the number of sick-leave days of non-smokers and smokers is uniformly distributed across all employees and varies from 5 to 10 days per year for non-smokers, and from 6 to 13 days per year for smokers. What percentage of *non-smoking* employees will be absent between seven and nine days in one year? What percentage of *smoking* employees will be absent more than eight days in one year?

2. From numerous sources, it was estimated that, on average, it costs $3,396 to hire a smoker than to hire a non-smoker. Suppose such costs are normally distributed with a standard deviation of $500. Based on these figures, what is the probability that the hiring of one randomly selected smoker will cost more than $4,000 more than hiring a non-smoker? What percentage of smoking employees are hired for less than $3,500 more than hiring a non-smoker?

3. The same survey determined that the average smoker takes two 20-minute unscheduled smoke breaks throughout the work day. Assume that 70% of all unscheduled 20-minute breaks are taken by smokers during the day. If this is true, what is the probability of randomly sampling 150 unscheduled 20-minute breaks and finding out that less than 40 were taken by non-smokers?

Sources: "Butting Out to Raise the Bottom Line—The Benefits of Providing Support for Smoking Cessation in the Workplace," January 9, 2008, pp. 3–22. Website for data source: <www.benefitscanada.com/pdfs/smokingcessation_e_0408. pdf>; "Economics of Tobacco Use," Tobacco Basics Handbook, Third Edition, May 27, 2008, pp. 143–160. Website for data source: <www.aadac.com/documents/TBH_ThirdEdition. pdf>; "The Business Case for Tobacco-Free Workplaces in British Columbia," 2008, pp. 1–12. Website for data source <www.cancer.ca/british%20columbiayukon/prevention/ bc%20healthy%20living%20alliance/~/media/CCS/British%20 Columbia-Yukon/Files%20-%20Content%20Owners/02_ prevention/FINAL%20COPY%20-%20TFWI%20Business%20 Case.ashx>

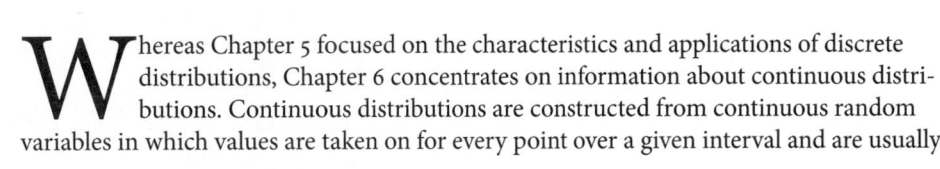

Whereas Chapter 5 focused on the characteristics and applications of discrete distributions, Chapter 6 concentrates on information about continuous distributions. Continuous distributions are constructed from continuous random variables in which values are taken on for every point over a given interval and are usually generated from experiments in which things are "measured" as opposed to "counted." With continuous distributions, probabilities of outcomes occurring between particular points are determined by calculating the area under the curve between those points. In addition, the entire area under the whole curve is equal to one. The many continuous distributions in statistics include the uniform distribution, the normal distribution, the exponential distribution, the t distribution, the chi-square distribution, and the F distribution. This chapter presents the uniform distribution, the normal distribution, and the exponential distribution.

6.1 UNIFORM DISTRIBUTION

The **uniform distribution,** sometimes referred to as the **rectangular distribution,** is a *relatively simple continuous distribution in which the same height, or $f(x)$, is obtained over a range of values.* The following probability density function defines a uniform distribution.

Probability Density Function of a Uniform Distribution	$$f(x) = \begin{cases} \dfrac{1}{b-a} & \text{for } a \le x \le b \\ 0 & \text{for all other values} \end{cases}$$

Figure 6.1 is an example of a uniform distribution. In a uniform, or rectangular, distribution, the total area under the curve is equal to the product of the length and the width of the rectangle and equals one. By definition, the distribution lies between the x values of a and b, so the length of the rectangle is $b - a$. Combining this area calculation with the fact that the area equals one, the height of the rectangle can be solved as follows.

$$\text{Area of Rectangle} = (\text{Length})(\text{Height}) = 1$$

But

$$\text{Length} = b - a$$

Therefore,

$$(b - a)(\text{Height}) = 1$$

and

$$\text{Height} = \frac{1}{b - a}$$

Figure 6.1

Uniform Distribution

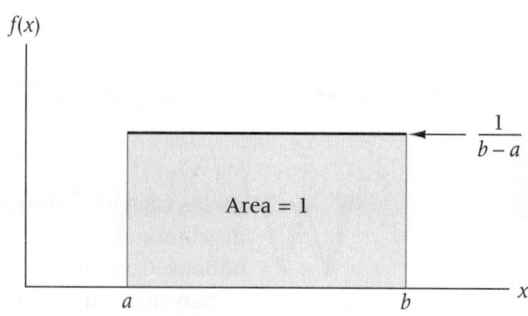

These calculations show why, between the x values of a and b, the distribution has a constant height of $1/(b - a)$.

The mean and standard deviation of a uniform distribution are given as follows.

Mean and Standard Deviation of a Uniform Distribution	$\mu = \dfrac{a + b}{2}$ $\sigma = \dfrac{b - a}{\sqrt{12}}$

Many possible situations arise in which data might be uniformly distributed. As an example, suppose a production line is set up to manufacture machine braces in lots of five per minute during a shift. When the lots are weighed, variation among the masses is detected, with lot masses ranging from 41 g to 47 g in a uniform distribution. The height of this distribution is

$$f(x) = \text{Height} = \frac{1}{b - a} = \frac{1}{47 - 41} = \frac{1}{6}$$

The mean and standard deviation of this distribution are

$$\text{Mean} = \frac{a + b}{2} = \frac{41 + 47}{2} = \frac{88}{2} = 44$$

$$\text{Standard Deviation} = \frac{b - a}{\sqrt{12}} = \frac{47 - 41}{\sqrt{12}} = \frac{6}{3.464} = 1.732$$

Figure 6.2 provides the uniform distribution for this example, with its mean, standard deviation, and the height of the distribution.

Figure 6.2

Distribution of Lot Masses

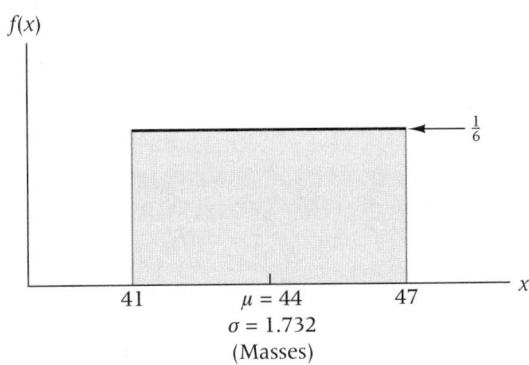

DETERMINING PROBABILITIES IN A UNIFORM DISTRIBUTION

With discrete distributions, the probability function yields the value of the probability. For continuous distributions, probabilities are calculated by determining the area over an interval of the function. With continuous distributions, there is no area under the curve for a single point. The following equation is used to determine the probabilities of x for a uniform distribution between a and b:

Probabilities in a Uniform Distribution	$$P(x) = \frac{x_2 - x_1}{b - a}$$

where:

$$a \leq x_1 \leq x_2 \leq b$$

Remember that the area between a and b is equal to one. The probability for any interval that includes a and b is 1. The probability of $x \geq b$ or of $x \leq a$ is 0 because there is no area above b or below a.

Suppose that on the machine braces problem we want to determine the probability that a lot has a mass of between 42 g and 45 g. This probability is computed as follows:

$$P(x) = \frac{x_2 - x_1}{b - a} = \frac{45 - 42}{47 - 41} = \frac{3}{6} = 0.5000$$

Figure 6.3 displays this solution.

Figure 6.3

Solved Probability in a Uniform Distribution

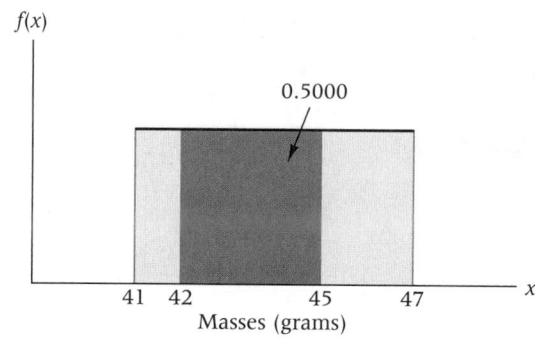

The probability that a lot has a mass of more than 48 g is zero, because $x = 48$ is greater than the upper value, $x = 47$, of the uniform distribution. A similar argument gives the probability of a lot having a mass of less than 40 g. Because 40 is less than the lowest value of the uniform distribution range, 41, the probability is zero.

Demonstration Problem 6.1

Suppose the amount of time it takes to assemble a plastic module ranges from 27 to 39 seconds and that assembly times are uniformly distributed. Describe the distribution. What is the probability that a given assembly will take between 30 and 35 seconds? Less than 30 seconds?

Solution

$$f(x) = \frac{1}{39 - 27} = \frac{1}{12}$$

$$\mu = \frac{a+b}{2} = \frac{27+39}{2} = 33$$

$$\sigma = \frac{b-a}{\sqrt{12}} = \frac{39-27}{\sqrt{12}} = \frac{12}{\sqrt{12}} = 3.464$$

The height of the distribution is 1/12. The mean time is 33 seconds with a standard deviation of 3.464 seconds.

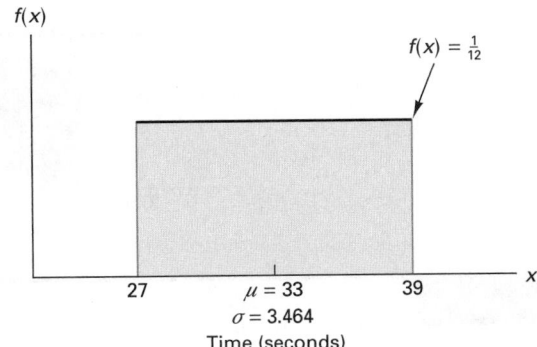

$$P(30 \leq x \leq 35) = \frac{35-30}{39-27} = \frac{5}{12} = 0.4167$$

There is a 0.4167 probability that it will take between 30 and 35 seconds to assemble the module.

$$P(x < 30) = \frac{30-27}{39-27} = \frac{3}{12} = 0.2500$$

There is a 0.2500 probability that it will take less than 30 seconds to assemble the module. Because there is no area less than 27 seconds, $P(x < 30)$ is determined by using only the interval $27 \leq x < 30$. In a continuous distribution, there is no area at any one point (only over an interval). Thus, the probability of $x < 30$ is the same as the probability of $x \leq 30$.

Demonstration Problem 6.2	According to the Insurance Bureau of Canada, the average annual cost for automobile insurance in Canada in a recent year was $945. Suppose automobile insurance costs are uniformly distributed in Canada with a range of from $275 to $1,615. What is the standard deviation of this uniform distribution? What is the height of the distribution? What is the probability that a person's annual cost for automobile insurance in Canada is between $410 and $825?

Solution

The mean is given as $945. The value of a is $275 and the value of b is $1,615.

$$\sigma = \frac{b-a}{\sqrt{12}} = \frac{1,615 - 275}{\sqrt{12}} = 386.8$$

The height of the distribution is $\dfrac{1}{1{,}615 - 275} = 0.0007$. Using $x_1 = 410$ and $x_2 = 825$, we have

$$P(410 \leq x \leq 825) = \frac{825 - 410}{1{,}615 - 275} = \frac{415}{1{,}340} = 0.3097$$

The probability that a randomly selected person pays between \$410 and \$825 annually for automobile insurance in Canada is 0.3097. That is, about 30.97% of all people in Canada pay in that range.

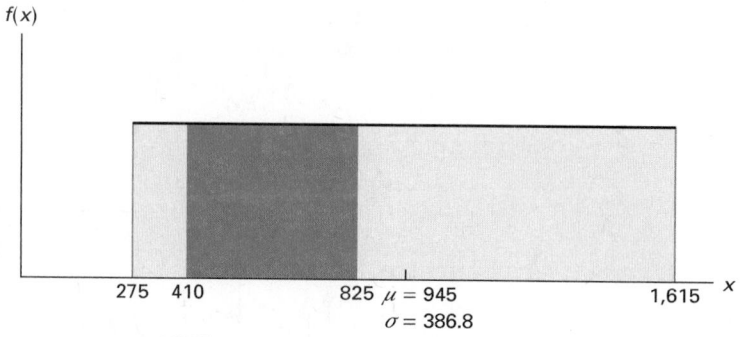

Concept Check

1. List two important properties of the uniform distribution.
2. Describe a situation (in business or otherwise) in which the use of the uniform distribution would be appropriate. Clearly define the random variable.

6.1 Problems

6.1 Values are uniformly distributed between 200 and 240.
  a. What is the value of $f(x)$ for this distribution?
  b. Determine the mean and standard deviation of this distribution.
  c. Probability of $(x > 230) =$?
  d. Probability of $(205 < x < 220) =$?
  e. Probability of $(x < 225) =$?

6.2 x is uniformly distributed over a range of values from 8 to 21.
  a. What is the value of $f(x)$ for this distribution?
  b. Determine the mean and standard deviation of this distribution.
  c. Probability of $(10 < x < 17) =$?
  d. Probability of $(x < 22) =$?
  e. Probability of $(x > 7) =$?

6.3 The retail price of a medium-sized box of a well-known brand of cornflakes ranges from \$2.80 to \$3.14. Assume these prices are uniformly distributed. What are the average price and standard deviation of prices in this distribution? If a price is randomly selected from this list, what is the probability that it will be between \$3.00 and \$3.10?

6.4 The average fill volume of a regular can of soft drink is 355 ml. Suppose the fill volume of these cans ranges from 354.0 ml to 355.8 ml and is uniformly distributed. What is the height of this distribution? What is the probability that a randomly selected can contains more than 355.2 ml of fluid? What is the probability that the fill volume is between 354.3 ml and 355.2 ml?

6.5   Suppose the average Canadian household spends \$2,100 a year on all types of insurance. Suppose the figures are uniformly distributed between the values of \$400 and \$3,800. What are the standard deviation and the height of this distribution? What proportion of households spends more than \$3,000 a year on insurance? More than \$4,000? Between \$700 and \$1,500?

6.2 NORMAL DISTRIBUTION

Probably the most widely known and used of all distributions is the **normal distribution.** It fits many human characteristics, such as height, mass, length, speed, IQ, scholastic achievement, and years of life expectancy. Like their human counterparts, living things in nature, such as trees, animals, and insects, have many normally distributed characteristics.

Many variables in business and industry are also normally distributed. Some examples of variables that could produce normally distributed measurements are the annual cost of household insurance, the cost per square foot of renting warehouse space, and managers' satisfaction with support from ownership on a five-point scale. In addition, most items produced or filled by machines are normally distributed.

Because of its many applications, the normal distribution is extremely important. Aside from the many variables mentioned above that are normally distributed, the normal distribution and its associated probabilities are an integral part of statistical process control (see Chapter 18). When large enough sample sizes are taken, many statistics are normally distributed regardless of the shape of the underlying distribution from which they are drawn (as discussed in Chapter 7). Figure 6.4 is the graphic representation of the normal distribution: the normal curve.

Figure 6.4

The Normal Curve

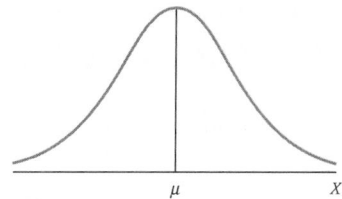

HISTORY OF THE NORMAL DISTRIBUTION

The discovery of the normal curve of errors is generally credited to mathematician and astronomer Karl Gauss (1777–1855), who recognized that the errors of repeated measurement of objects are often normally distributed.[*] Thus, the normal distribution is sometimes referred to as the *Gaussian distribution* or *the normal curve of error.* A modern-day analogy of Gauss's work might be the distribution of measurements of machine-produced parts, which often yield a normal curve of error around a mean specification.

To a lesser extent, some credit has been given to Pierre-Simon de Laplace (1749–1827) for discovering the normal distribution. However, many people now believe that Abraham de Moivre (1667–1754), a French mathematician, first understood the normal distribution. De Moivre determined that the binomial distribution approached the normal distribution as a limit. De Moivre worked with remarkable accuracy. His published table values for the normal curve are only a few ten thousandths off the values of currently published tables.[†]

---

[*]John A. Ingram and Joseph G. Monks, *Statistics for Business and Economics* (San Diego: Harcourt Brace Jovanovich, Publishers, 1989).

[†]Roger E. Kirk, *Statistical Issues: A Reader for the Behavioral Sciences* (Monterey, CA: Brooks/Cole Publishing Co., 1972).

The normal distribution exhibits the following characteristics.

* It is a continuous distribution.
* It is a symmetrical distribution about its mean.
* It is asymptotic to the horizontal axis.
* It is unimodal.
* It is a family of curves.
* The area under the curve is one.

The normal distribution is symmetrical. Each half of the distribution is a mirror image of the other half. Many normal distribution tables contain probability values for only one side of the distribution because probability values for the other side of the distribution are identical because of symmetry.

In theory, the normal distribution is asymptotic to the horizontal axis. That is, it does not touch the x axis, and it goes forever in each direction to both $-\infty$ and $+\infty$. The reality is that most applications of the normal curve are experiments that have finite limits of potential outcomes. For example, even though standardized test scores are analyzed by the normal distribution, the range of scores in a standardized test may be, for instance, from 200 to 800.

The normal curve is sometimes referred to as the *bell-shaped curve*. It is unimodal in that values *mound up* in only one portion of the graph—the centre of the curve. The normal distribution is actually a family of curves. Every unique value of the mean and every unique value of the standard deviation result in a different normal curve. In addition, *the total area under any normal distribution is one*. The area under the curve yields the probabilities, so the total of all probabilities for a normal distribution is one. Because the distribution is symmetric, the area of the distribution on each side of the mean is 0.5.

PROBABILITY DENSITY FUNCTION OF THE NORMAL DISTRIBUTION

POINTS OF INTEREST
Convince yourself that this function is a bell-shaped curve. Assume that $\mu = 0$ and $\sigma = 1$. For x far from zero, $f(x)$ is close to zero. The function is symmetrical, so $f(x) = f(-x)$, and the largest value for $f(x)$ is when $x = \mu$ (thus the function is centred on the mean).

The normal distribution is described or characterized by two parameters: the mean, μ, and the standard deviation, σ. The values of μ and σ produce a normal distribution. The density function of the normal distribution is:

$$f(x) = \frac{1}{\sigma\sqrt{2\pi}} e^{-1/2[(x-\mu)/\sigma)]^2}$$

where

μ = mean of x
σ = standard deviation of x
π = 3.14159…
e = 2.71828…

Using integral calculus to determine areas under the normal curve from this function is difficult and time-consuming; therefore, virtually all researchers use computers or table values to analyze normal distribution problems rather than this formula.

STANDARDIZED NORMAL DISTRIBUTION

Every unique pair of μ and σ values defines a different normal distribution. Figure 6.5 shows graphs of normal distributions for the following three pairs of parameters.

Figure 6.5

Normal Curves for Three Different Combinations of Means and Standard Deviations

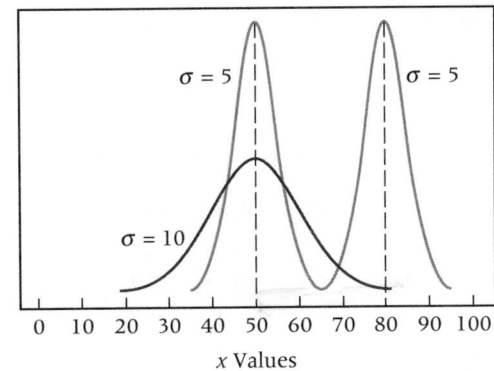

1. $\mu = 50$ and $\sigma = 5$
2. $\mu = 80$ and $\sigma = 5$
3. $\mu = 50$ and $\sigma = 10$

Note that every change in a parameter (μ or σ) determines a different normal distribution. This characteristic of the normal curve (a family of curves) could make analysis by the normal distribution tedious. Fortunately, a mechanism was developed by which all normal distributions can be converted into a single distribution: the z distribution. This process yields the **standardized normal distribution** (or curve). The conversion formula for any x value of a given normal distribution follows.

z Formula	$$z = \frac{x - \mu}{\sigma}, \quad \sigma \neq 0$$

A **z score** is *the number of standard deviations that a value, x, is above or below the mean*. If the value of x is less than the mean, the z score is negative; if the value of x is more than the mean, the z score is positive; and if the value of x equals the mean, the associated z score is 0. This formula allows conversion of the distance of any x value from its mean into standard deviation units. A standard z score table can be used to find probabilities for any normal curve problem that has been converted to z scores. The **z distribution** is *a normal distribution with a mean of 0 and a standard deviation of 1*. Any value of x at the mean of a normal curve is 0 standard deviations from the mean. Any value of x that is one standard deviation above the mean has a z value of 1. The empirical rule, introduced in Chapter 3, is based on the normal distribution in which about 68% of all values are within one standard deviation of the mean regardless of the values of μ and σ. In a z distribution, about 68% of the z values are between $z = -1$ and $z = +1$.

The z distribution probability values are given in Table A.5. Because it is so frequently used, the z distribution is also printed inside the cover of this text. For discussion purposes, a list of z distribution values is presented in Table 6.1.

Table A.5 gives the total area under the z curve between 0 and any point on the positive z axis. Since the curve is symmetric, the area under the curve between z and 0 is the same whether z is positive or negative (the sign on the z value designates whether the z score is above or below the mean). The table areas or probabilities are always positive.

SOLVING NORMAL CURVE PROBLEMS

The mean and standard deviation of a normal distribution, the z formula, and the table enable a researcher to determine the probabilities for intervals of any particular values

Table 6.1

z Distribution

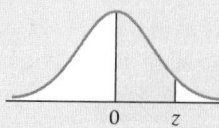

Second Decimal Place in z

z	0.00	0.01	0.02	0.03	0.04	0.05	0.06	0.07	0.08	0.09
0.0	0.0000	0.0040	0.0080	0.0120	0.0160	0.0199	0.0239	0.0279	0.0319	0.0359
0.1	0.0398	0.0438	0.0478	0.0517	0.0557	0.0596	0.0636	0.0675	0.0714	0.0753
0.2	0.0793	0.0832	0.0871	0.0910	0.0948	0.0987	0.1026	0.1064	0.1103	0.1141
0.3	0.1179	0.1217	0.1255	0.1293	0.1331	0.1368	0.1406	0.1443	0.1480	0.1517
0.4	0.1554	0.1591	0.1628	0.1664	0.1700	0.1736	0.1772	0.1808	0.1844	0.1879
0.5	0.1915	0.1950	0.1985	0.2019	0.2054	0.2088	0.2123	0.2157	0.2190	0.2224
0.6	0.2257	0.2291	0.2324	0.2357	0.2389	0.2422	0.2454	0.2486	0.2517	0.2549
0.7	0.2580	0.2611	0.2642	0.2673	0.2704	0.2734	0.2764	0.2794	0.2823	0.2852
0.8	0.2881	0.2910	0.2939	0.2967	0.2995	0.3023	0.3051	0.3078	0.3106	0.3133
0.9	0.3159	0.3186	0.3212	0.3238	0.3264	0.3289	0.3315	0.3340	0.3365	0.3389
1.0	0.3413	0.3438	0.3461	0.3485	0.3508	0.3531	0.3554	0.3577	0.3599	0.3621
1.1	0.3643	0.3665	0.3686	0.3708	0.3729	0.3749	0.3770	0.3790	0.3810	0.3830
1.2	0.3849	0.3869	0.3888	0.3907	0.3925	0.3944	0.3962	0.3980	0.3997	0.4015
1.3	0.4032	0.4049	0.4066	0.4082	0.4099	0.4115	0.4131	0.4147	0.4162	0.4177
1.4	0.4192	0.4207	0.4222	0.4236	0.4251	0.4265	0.4279	0.4292	0.4306	0.4319
1.5	0.4332	0.4345	0.4357	0.4370	0.4382	0.4394	0.4406	0.4418	0.4429	0.4441
1.6	0.4452	0.4463	0.4474	0.4484	0.4495	0.4505	0.4515	0.4525	0.4535	0.4545
1.7	0.4554	0.4564	0.4573	0.4582	0.4591	0.4599	0.4608	0.4616	0.4625	0.4633
1.8	0.4641	0.4649	0.4656	0.4664	0.4671	0.4678	0.4686	0.4693	0.4699	0.4706
1.9	0.4713	0.4719	0.4726	0.4732	0.4738	0.4744	0.4750	0.4756	0.4761	0.4767
2.0	0.4772	0.4778	0.4783	0.4788	0.4793	0.4798	0.4803	0.4808	0.4812	0.4817
2.1	0.4821	0.4826	0.4830	0.4834	0.4838	0.4842	0.4846	0.4850	0.4854	0.4857
2.2	0.4861	0.4864	0.4868	0.4871	0.4875	0.4878	0.4881	0.4884	0.4887	0.4890
2.3	0.4893	0.4896	0.4898	0.4901	0.4904	0.4906	0.4909	0.4911	0.4913	0.4916
2.4	0.4918	0.4920	0.4922	0.4925	0.4927	0.4929	0.4931	0.4932	0.4934	0.4936
2.5	0.4938	0.4940	0.4941	0.4943	0.4945	0.4946	0.4948	0.4949	0.4951	0.4952
2.6	0.4953	0.4955	0.4956	0.4957	0.4959	0.4960	0.4961	0.4962	0.4963	0.4964
2.7	0.4965	0.4966	0.4967	0.4968	0.4969	0.4970	0.4971	0.4972	0.4973	0.4974
2.8	0.4974	0.4975	0.4976	0.4977	0.4977	0.4978	0.4979	0.4979	0.4980	0.4981
2.9	0.4981	0.4982	0.4982	0.4983	0.4984	0.4984	0.4985	0.4985	0.4986	0.4986
3.0	0.4987	0.4987	0.4987	0.4988	0.4988	0.4989	0.4989	0.4989	0.4990	0.4990
3.1	0.4990	0.4991	0.4991	0.4991	0.4992	0.4992	0.4992	0.4992	0.4993	0.4993
3.2	0.4993	0.4993	0.4994	0.4994	0.4994	0.4994	0.4994	0.4995	0.4995	0.4995
3.3	0.4995	0.4995	0.4995	0.4996	0.4996	0.4996	0.4996	0.4996	0.4996	0.4997
3.4	0.4997	0.4997	0.4997	0.4997	0.4997	0.4997	0.4997	0.4997	0.4997	0.4998
3.5	0.4998									
4.0	0.49997									
4.5	0.499997									
5.0	0.4999997									
6.0	0.499999999									

of a normal curve. One example is the many possible probability values of GMAT scores examined next. The Graduate Management Aptitude Test (GMAT), produced by the Educational Testing Service in Princeton, New Jersey, is widely used by graduate schools of business in North America as an entrance requirement. Assuming that the scores are normally distributed, probabilities of achieving scores over various ranges of the GMAT can be determined. In a recent year, the mean GMAT score was 494 and the standard deviation was about 100. What is the probability that a randomly selected score from this administration of the GMAT is between 600 and the mean? That is,

$$P(494 \leq x \leq 600 | \mu = 494 \text{ and } \sigma = 100) = ?$$

Figure 6.6 is a graphical representation of this problem.

Figure 6.6

Graphical Depiction of the Area between a Score of 600 and a Mean on a GMAT

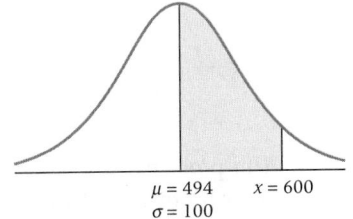

$\mu = 494$ $x = 600$
$\sigma = 100$

The z formula yields the number of standard deviations that the x value, 600, is away from the mean.

$$z = \frac{x - \mu}{\sigma} = \frac{600 - 494}{100} = \frac{106}{100} = 1.06$$

The z value of 1.06 reveals that the GMAT score of 600 is 1.06 standard deviations more than the mean. The z distribution values in Table 6.1 give the probability of a value being between this value of x and the mean. The whole-number and tenths-place portion of the z score appear in the first column of Table 6.1 (the 1.0 portion of this z score). Across the top of the table are the values of the hundredths-place portion of the z score. For this z score, the hundredths-place value is 6. The probability value in Table 6.1 for $z = 1.06$ is 0.3554. The shaded portion of the curve at the top of the table indicates that the probability value given is *always* the probability or area between an x value and the mean. In this particular example, that is the desired area. Thus, the answer is that 0.3554 of the scores on the GMAT are between a score of 600 and the mean of 494. Figure 6.7(a) graphically depicts the solution in terms of x values. Figure 6.7(b) shows the solution in terms of z values.

Figure 6.7

Graphical Solutions to the GMAT Problem

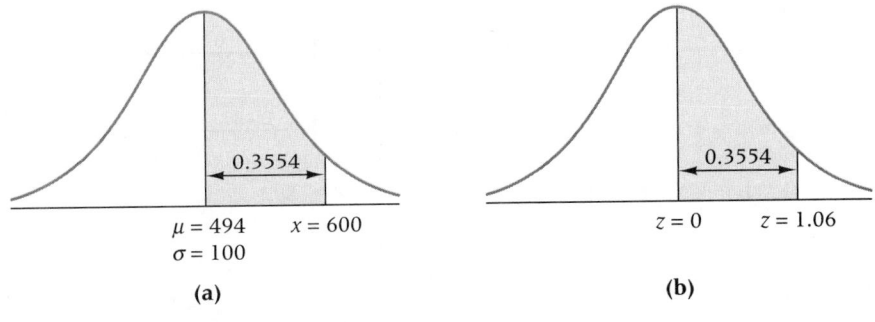

0.3554   0.3554

$\mu = 494$ $x = 600$ $z = 0$ $z = 1.06$
$\sigma = 100$

(a)   (b)

Demonstration Problem 6.3

What is the probability of obtaining a score greater than 700 on a GMAT test that has a mean of 494 and a standard deviation of 100? Assume GMAT scores are normally distributed.

$$P(x > 700 | \mu = 494 \text{ and } \sigma = 100) = ?$$

Solution

Examine the following diagram.

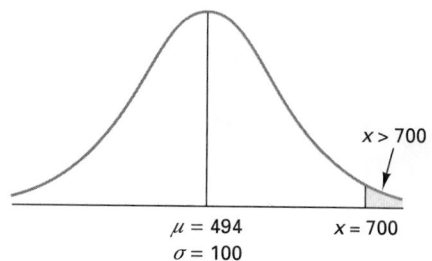

This problem calls for determining the area of the upper tail of the distribution. The z score for this problem is

$$z = \frac{x - \mu}{\sigma} = \frac{700 - 494}{100} = \frac{206}{100} = 2.06$$

Table 6.1 gives a probability of 0.4803 for this z score. This value is the probability of randomly drawing a GMAT with a score between the mean and 700. Finding the probability of getting a score greater than 700, which is the tail of the distribution, requires subtracting the probability value of 0.4803 from 0.5000, because each half of the distribution contains 0.5000 of the area. The result is 0.0197. Note that an attempt to determine the area of $x \geq 700$ instead of $x > 700$ would have made no difference because, in continuous distributions, the area under an exact number such as $x = 700$ is zero. A line segment has no width and hence no area.

$$
\begin{array}{ll}
0.5000 & \text{(probability of } x \text{ greater than the mean)} \\
-0.4803 & \text{(probability of } x \text{ between 700 and the mean)} \\
\hline
0.0197 & \text{(probability of } x \text{ greater than 700)}
\end{array}
$$

The solution is depicted graphically in (a) for x values and in (b) for z values.

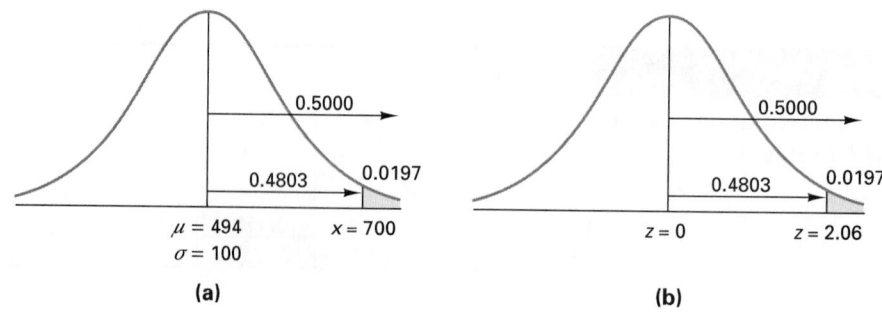

(a)   (b)

Demonstration Problem 6.4

For the same GMAT examination, what is the probability of randomly drawing a score that is 550 or less?

$$P(x \leq 550 | \mu = 494 \text{ and } \sigma = 100) = ?$$

Solution

A sketch of this problem is shown here. Determine the area under the curve for all values less than or equal to 550.

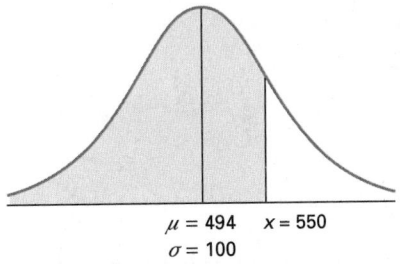

$$\mu = 494 \quad x = 550$$
$$\sigma = 100$$

The z formula yields the area between 550 and the mean.

$$z = \frac{x - \mu}{\sigma} = \frac{550 - 494}{100} = \frac{56}{100} = 0.56$$

The area under the curve for $z = 0.56$ is 0.2123, which is the probability of getting a score between 550 and the mean. However, obtaining the probability for all values less than or equal to 550 also requires including the values less than the mean. Because one half or 0.5000 of the values are less than the mean, the probability of $x \leq 550$ is found as follows.

$$\begin{aligned} &0.5000 \text{ (probability of values less than the mean)} \\ +&0.2123 \text{ (probability of values between 550 and the mean)} \\ \hline &0.7123 \text{ (probability of values} \leq 550) \end{aligned}$$

This solution is depicted graphically in (a) for x values and in (b) for z values.

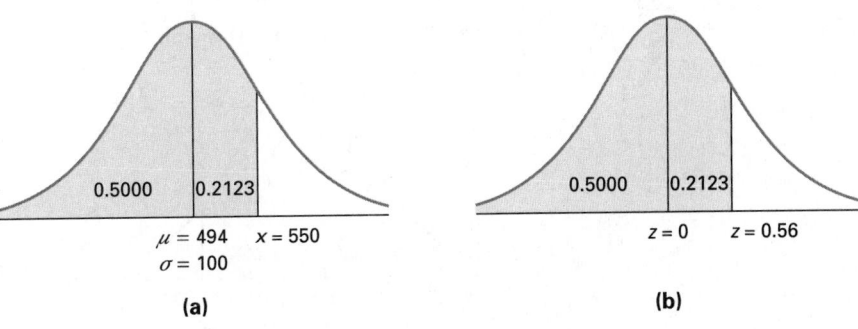

(a)   **(b)**

**Demonstration
Problem 6.5**

What is the probability of randomly obtaining a score between 300 and 600 on the GMAT exam?

$$P(300 < x < 600 \,|\, \mu = 494 \text{ and } \sigma = 100) = ?$$

Solution

The following sketch depicts the problem graphically: determine the area between $x = 300$ and $x = 600$, which spans the mean value. Because areas in the z distribution are given in relation to the mean, this problem must be worked as two separate problems and the results combined.

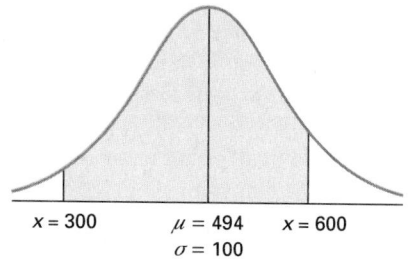

A z score is determined for each x value.

$$z = \frac{x - \mu}{\sigma} = \frac{600 - 494}{100} = \frac{106}{100} = 1.06$$

and

$$z = \frac{x - \mu}{\sigma} = \frac{300 - 494}{100} = \frac{-194}{100} = -1.94$$

Note that this z value ($z = -1.94$) is negative. A negative z value indicates that the x value is below the mean and the z value is on the left side of the distribution. None of the z values in Table 6.1 are negative. However, because the normal distribution is symmetric, probabilities for z values on the left side of the distribution are the same as for the values on the right side of the distribution. The negative sign in the z value merely indicates that the area is on the left side of the distribution. The probability is always positive.

The probability for $z = 1.06$ is 0.3554; the probability for $z = -1.94$ is 0.4738. The solution of $P(300 < x < 600)$ is obtained by summing the probabilities.

$$
\begin{array}{ll}
0.3554 & \text{(probability of a value between the mean and 600)} \\
+0.4738 & \text{(probability of a value between the mean and 300)} \\
\hline
0.8292 & \text{(probability of a value between 300 and 600)}
\end{array}
$$

Graphically, the solution is shown in (a) for x values and in (b) for z values.

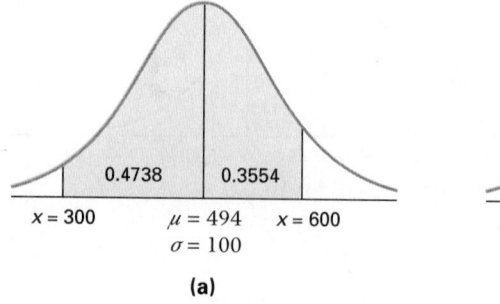

(a)

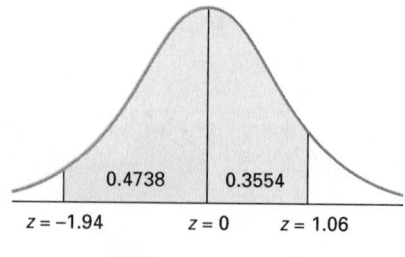

(b)

**Demonstration
Problem 6.6**

What is the probability of getting a score between 350 and 450 on the same GMAT exam?

$$P(350 < x < 450 \mid \mu = 494 \text{ and } \sigma = 100) = ?$$

Solution

The following sketch reveals that the solution to the problem involves determining the area of the shaded slice in the lower half of the curve.

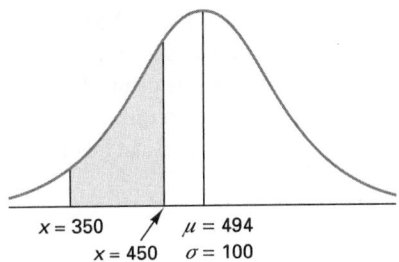

In this problem, the two x values are on the same side of the mean. The area or probability of each x value must be determined and the final probability found by determining the difference between the two areas.

$$z = \frac{x - \mu}{\sigma} = \frac{350 - 494}{100} = \frac{-144}{100} = -1.44$$

and

$$z = \frac{x - \mu}{\sigma} = \frac{450 - 494}{100} = \frac{-44}{100} = -0.44$$

The probability associated with $z = -1.44$ is 0.4251.
The probability associated with $z = -0.44$ is 0.1700.
Subtracting gives the solution.

$$
\begin{array}{l}
0.4251 \text{ (probability of a value between 350 and the mean)} \\
-0.1700 \text{ (probability of a value between 450 and the mean)} \\
\hline
0.2551 \text{ (probability of a value between 350 and 450)}
\end{array}
$$

Graphically, the solution is shown in (a) for x values and in (b) for z values.

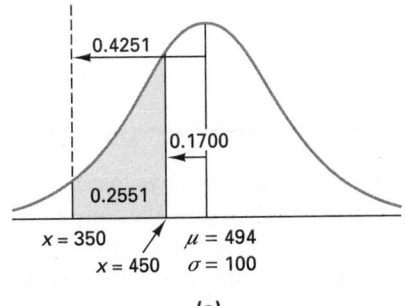

(a)

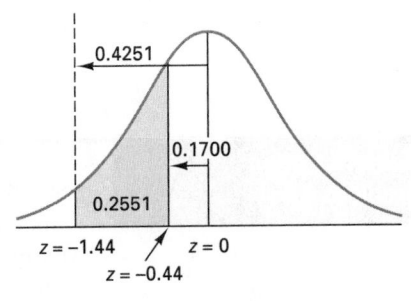

(b)

**Demonstration
Problem 6.7**

Runzheimer International publishes business travel costs for various cities throughout the world. In particular, they publish per diem totals, which represent the average costs for the typical business traveller including three meals a day in business class restaurants and single-rate lodging in business class hotels and motels. If 86.65% of the per diem costs in Buenos Aires, Argentina, are less than $449 and if the standard deviation of per diem costs is $36, what is the average per diem cost in Buenos Aires? Assume that per diem costs are normally distributed.

Solution

In this problem, the standard deviation and an x value are given; the object is to determine the value of the mean. Examination of the z score formula reveals four variables: x, μ, σ, and z. In this problem, only two of the four variables are given. Because solving one equation with two unknowns is impossible, one of the other unknowns must be determined. The value of z can be determined from the normal distribution table (Table 6.1).

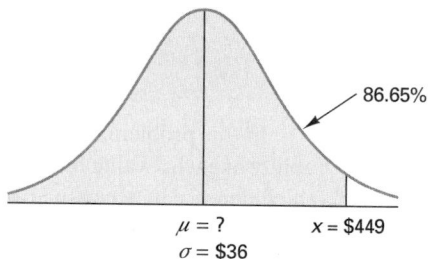

86.65%

$\mu = ?$ $x = \$449$
$\sigma = \$36$

Because 86.65% of the values are less than $x = \$449$, 36.65% of the per diem costs are between $449 and the mean. The other 50% of the per diem costs are in the lower half of the distribution. Converting the percentage to a proportion yields 0.3665 of the values between the x value and the mean. What z value is associated with this area? This area, or probability, of 0.3665 in Table 6.1 is associated with the z value of 1.11. This z value is positive, because it is in the upper half of the distribution. Using the z value of 1.11, the x value of $449, and the σ value of $36 allows us to solve for the mean algebraically.

$$z = \frac{x - \mu}{\sigma}$$

$$1.11 = \frac{\$449 - \mu}{\$36}$$

and

$$\mu = \$449 - (\$36)(1.11) = \$449 - \$39.96 = \$409.04$$

The mean per diem cost for business travel in Buenos Aires is $409.04.

**Demonstration
Problem 6.8**

Statistics Canada reports that, in a recent year, per capita solid waste generation in Canada amounted to 2.7 kg per day. Suppose the daily amount of waste generated per person is normally distributed with a mean of 2.7 kg and a standard deviation of 0.78 kg. Of the daily amounts of waste generated per person, 67.72% would be greater than what amount?

Solution

The mean and standard deviation are given, but x and z are unknown. The problem is to solve for a specific x value when 0.6772 of the x values are greater than that value.

If 0.6772 of the values are greater than x, then 0.1772 are between x and the mean (0.6772 − 0.5000). Table 6.1 shows that the probability of 0.1772 is associated with a z value of 0.46. Because x is less than the mean, the z value is actually −0.46. Whenever an x value is less than the mean, its associated z value is negative and should be reported that way.

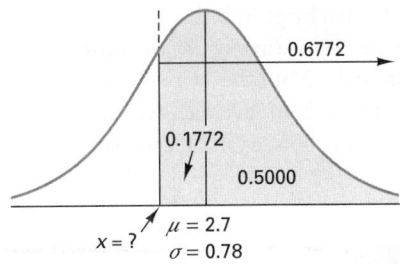

Solving the z equation yields

$$z = \frac{x - \mu}{\sigma}$$

$$-0.46 = \frac{x - 2.7}{0.78}$$

and

$$x = 2.7 + (-0.46)(0.78) = 2.34$$

Thus, 67.72% of the daily average amount of solid waste per capita has a mass of more than 2.34 kg.

USING THE COMPUTER TO SOLVE FOR NORMAL DISTRIBUTION PROBABILITIES

Excel can be used to solve for normal distribution probabilities. Excel uses μ, σ, and the value of x to compute a cumulative probability from the left. Shown in Table 6.2 is the Excel output for the probability question addressed in Demonstration Problem 6.6: $P(350 < x < 450 | \mu = 494$ and $\sigma = 100)$. Since Excel yields probabilities cumulated from the left, this problem is solved manually with the computer output by finding the difference between $P(x < 450)$ and $P(x < 350)$.

Table 6.2

Excel Normal Distribution Output for Demonstration Problem 6.6

	A	B
1	x Value	Probability < x Value
2	450	0.3300
3	350	0.0749
4		
5	P(x < 450) − P(x < 350)	**0.2550**

STATISTICS IN BUSINESS TODAY

Warehousing

Tompkins Associates conducted a study of warehousing in the U.S. The study revealed many interesting facts. Warehousing is a labour-intensive industry that presents considerable opportunity for improvement in productivity. What does the "average" warehouse look like? The construction of new warehouses is restricted by prohibitive expense. Perhaps for that reason, the average age of a warehouse is 19 years. Warehouses vary in size, but the average size is about 4,600 m². To visualize such an "average" warehouse, picture one that is square with about 65 m on each side or a rectangle that is 100 m by 46 m. The average clear height of a warehouse in the U.S. is about 6.7 m.

Suppose the ages of warehouses, the sizes of warehouses, and the clear heights of warehouses are normally distributed. Using the mean values already given and the standard deviations, techniques presented in this section could be used to determine, for example, the probability that a randomly selected warehouse is less than 15 years old, is larger than 5,500 m², or has a clear height between 6 m and 7 m.

Concept Check

1. List four important properties of the normal distribution.
2. Why are z values important when dealing with a normal distribution?
3. How does the variable x relate to the mean μ of a normal distribution given information about the z value? Match the information in column 1 with the corresponding description in column 2.
   a. The z value is zero.
   b. The z value is positive.
   c. The z value is negative.

   i. The variable x is larger than the mean μ.
   ii. The variable x is smaller than the mean μ.
   iii. The variable x is equal to the mean μ.

4. How does the normal distribution relate to the empirical rule and Chebyshev's theorem, covered in Chapter 3?

6.2 Problems

6.6   Determine the probability or area for the portions of the normal distribution described.
   a. $z \geq 1.96$
   b. $z < 0.73$
   c. $-1.46 < z \leq 2.84$
   d. $-2.67 \leq z \leq 1.08$
   e. $-2.05 < z \leq -0.87$

6.7   Determine the probabilities for the following normal distribution problems.
   a. $\mu = 604, \sigma = 56.8, x \leq 635$
   b. $\mu = 48, \sigma = 12, x < 20$
   c. $\mu = 111, \sigma = 33.8, 100 \leq x < 150$
   d. $\mu = 264, \sigma = 10.9, 250 < x < 255$
   e. $\mu = 37, \sigma = 4.35, x > 35$
   f. $\mu = 156, \sigma = 11.4, x \geq 170$

6.8   Tompkins Associates reports that the mean clear height for a Class A warehouse in the U.S. is about 6.7 m. Suppose clear heights are normally distributed and that the standard deviation is 1.2 m. A Class A warehouse in the U.S. is randomly selected.
   a.   What is the probability that the clear height is greater than 5.2 m?
   b.   What is the probability that the clear height is less than 4 m?
   c.   What is the probability that the clear height is between 7.6 and 9.4 m?

6.9   According to a report by Scarborough Research, the average monthly household cellular phone bill is $60. Suppose local monthly household cell phone bills are normally distributed with a standard deviation of $11.35.

    a.   What is the probability that a randomly selected monthly cell phone bill is more than $85?

    b.   What is the probability that a randomly selected monthly cell phone bill is between $45 and $70?

    c.   What is the probability that a randomly selected monthly cell phone bill is between $65 and $75?

    d.   What is the probability that a randomly selected monthly cell phone bill is no more than $40?

6.10   Income tax returns one year averaged $1,332 in refunds for taxpayers. One explanation of this figure is that taxpayers would rather have the government keep back too much money during the year than to owe it money at the end of the year. Suppose the average amount of tax at the end of a year is a refund of $1,332, with a standard deviation of $725. Assume that amounts owed or due on tax returns are normally distributed.

    a.   What proportion of tax returns show a refund greater than $2,000?

    b.   What proportion of the tax returns show that the taxpayer owes money to the government?

    c.   What proportion of the tax returns show a refund between $100 and $700?

6.11   Tool workers are subject to work-related injuries. One disorder, caused by strains to the hands and wrists, is called carpal tunnel syndrome. It strikes as many as 23,000 workers per year. It is estimated that the average cost of this disorder to employers and insurers is approximately $30,000 per injured worker. Suppose these costs are normally distributed, with a standard deviation of $9,000.

    a.   What proportion of the costs are between $15,000 and $45,000?

    b.   What proportion of the costs are greater than $50,000?

    c.   What proportion of the costs are between $5,000 and $20,000?

    d.   Suppose the standard deviation is unknown, but 90.82% of the costs are more than $7,000. What is the value of the standard deviation?

    e.   Suppose the mean value is unknown, but the standard deviation is still $9,000. How much is the average cost if 79.95% of the costs are less than $33,000?

6.12   Suppose you are working with a data set that is normally distributed, with a mean of 200 and a standard deviation of 47. Determine the value of x from the following information.

    a.   60% of the values are greater than x.

    b. x is less than 17% of the values.

    c.   22% of the values are less than x.

    d. x is greater than 55% of the values.

6.13   Suppose that the annual employer participation in the Canada/Quebec Pension Plan (CPP/QPP) per employee is normally distributed with a standard deviation of $625, but the mean is unknown. If 73.89% of such employer contributions are greater than $1,700, what is the mean annual employer contribution per employee? Suppose the mean annual CPP/QPP employer contribution per employee is $2,258 and the standard deviation is $625. If such employer contributions are normally distributed, 31.56% of the contributions are greater than what value?

6.14   Suppose the standard deviation for Problem 6.8 is unknown but the mean is still 6.7 m. If 72.4% of all U.S. Class A warehouses have a clear height greater than 5.6 m, what is the standard deviation?

6.15 Suppose the mean clear height of all U.S. Class A warehouses is unknown but the standard deviation is known to be 1.2 m. What is the value of the mean clear height if 29% of U.S. Class A warehouses have a clear height less than 6 m?

6.16 Data accumulated by Environment Canada show that the average wind speed in kilometres per hour for Victoria International Airport, located on the Saanich Peninsula in British Columbia, is 9.3. Suppose wind speed measurements are normally distributed for a given geographic location. If 22.45% of the time the wind speed measurements are more than 18.7 km/h, what is the standard deviation of wind speed at Victoria International Airport?

6.3 USING THE NORMAL CURVE TO APPROXIMATE BINOMIAL DISTRIBUTION PROBLEMS

For certain types of binomial distribution problems, the normal distribution can be used to approximate the probabilities. As sample sizes become large, binomial distributions approach the normal distribution in shape, regardless of the value of p. This phenomenon occurs faster (for smaller values of n) when p is near 0.50. Figures 6.8 through 6.10 show three binomial distributions. Note in Figure 6.8 that even though the sample size, n, is only 10, the binomial graph bears a strong resemblance to a normal curve.

The graph in Figure 6.9 ($n = 10$ and $p = 0.20$) is skewed to the right because of the low p value and the small size. For this distribution, the expected value is only 2 and the probabilities pile up at $x = 0$ and 1. However, when n becomes large enough, as in the binomial distribution ($n = 100$ and $p = 0.20$) presented in Figure 6.10, the graph is relatively symmetric around the mean ($\mu = n \cdot p = 20$) because enough possible outcome values to the left of $x = 20$ allow the curve to fall back to the x axis.

Figure 6.8

The Binomial Distribution for $n = 10$ and $p = 0.50$

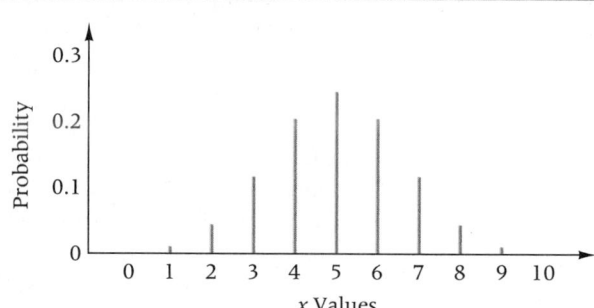

Figure 6.9

The Binomial Distribution for $n = 10$ and $p = 0.20$

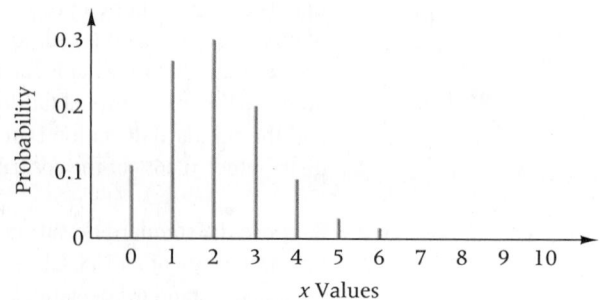

Figure 6.10

The Binomial Distribution for $n = 100$ and $p = 0.20$

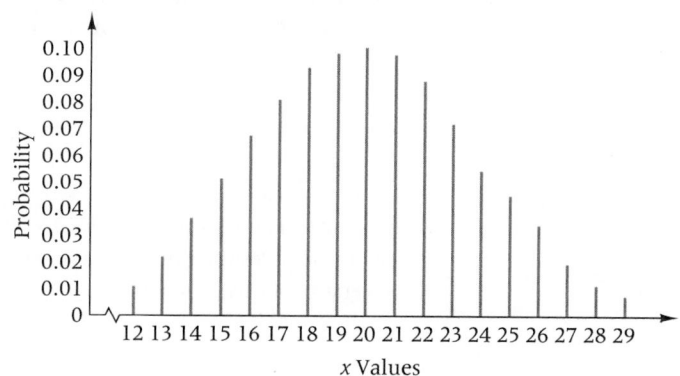

For large n values, the binomial distribution is cumbersome to analyze without a computer. Table A.2 only goes to $n = 25$. The normal distribution is a good approximation for binomial distribution problems for large values of n.

To work a binomial problem by the normal curve requires a translation process. The first part of this process is to convert the two parameters of a binomial distribution, n and p, to the two parameters of the normal distribution, μ and σ. This process utilizes formulas from Chapter 5:

$$\mu = n \cdot p \text{ and } \sigma = \sqrt{n \cdot p \cdot q}$$

After completion of this, a test must be made to determine whether the normal distribution is a good enough approximation of the binomial distribution:

Does the interval $\mu \pm 3\sigma$ lie between 0 and n?

Recall that the empirical rule states that approximately 99.7%, or almost all, of the values of a normal curve are within three standard deviations of the mean. For a normal curve approximation of a binomial distribution problem to be acceptable, all possible x values should be between 0 and n, which are the lower and upper limits, respectively, of a binomial distribution. If $\mu \pm 3\sigma$ is not between 0 and n, do *not* use the normal distribution to work a binomial problem—the approximation is not good enough. Upon demonstration that the normal curve is a good approximation for a binomial problem, the procedure continues. Another guideline for determining when to use the normal curve to approximate a binomial problem is that the approximation is good enough if both $n \cdot p > 5$ and $n \cdot q > 5$.

The process can be illustrated in the solution of the binomial distribution problem.

$$P(x \geq 25 | n = 60 \text{ and } p = 0.30) = ?$$

Note that this binomial problem contains a relatively large sample size and that none of the binomial tables in Appendix A can be used to solve the problem. This problem is a good candidate for use of the normal distribution.

Translating from a binomial problem to a normal curve problem gives

$$\mu = n \cdot p = (60)(0.30) = 18 \text{ and } \sigma = \sqrt{n \cdot p \cdot q} = 3.55$$

The binomial problem becomes a normal curve problem.

$$P(x \geq 25 | \mu = 18 \text{ and } \sigma = 3.55) = ?$$

Next, the test is made to determine whether the normal curve sufficiently fits this binomial distribution to justify the use of the normal curve.

$$\mu \pm 3\sigma = 18 \pm 3(3.55) = 18 \pm 10.65$$
$$7.35 \le \mu \pm 3\sigma \le 28.65$$

This interval is between 0 and 60, so the approximation is sufficient to allow use of the normal curve. Figure 6.11 presents a graph of this binomial distribution. Notice how closely it resembles the normal curve. Figure 6.12 is the apparent graph of the normal curve version of this problem.

Figure 6.11

Graph of the Binomial Problem: $n = 60$ and $p = 0.30$

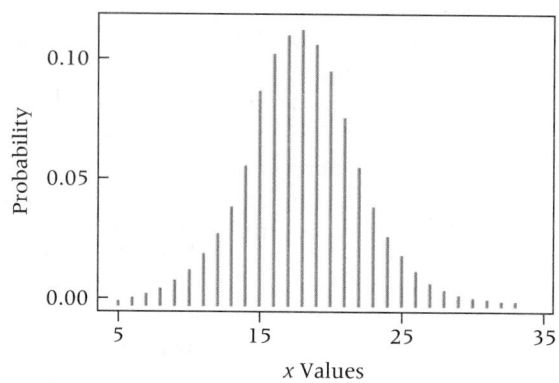

Figure 6.12

Graph of Apparent Solution of Binomial Problem Worked by the Normal Curve

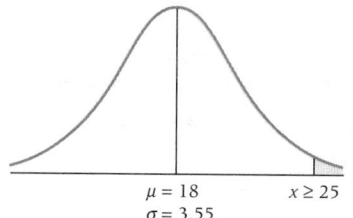

CORRECTING FOR CONTINUITY

The translation of a discrete distribution to a continuous distribution is not completely straightforward. A correction of +0.50 or −0.50 or ±0.50, depending on the problem, is required. This correction ensures that most of the binomial problem's information is correctly transferred to the normal curve analysis. This correction is called the **correction for continuity**, which is *made during conversion of a discrete distribution into a continuous distribution.*

Figure 6.13 is a portion of the graph of the binomial distribution for $n = 60$ and $p = 0.30$. Note that with a binomial distribution all the probabilities are concentrated on the whole numbers. Thus, the answers for $x \ge 25$ are found by summing the probabilities for $x = 25$, 26, 27, . . . , 60. There are no values between 24 and 25, 25 and 26, . . . , 59 and 60. Yet the normal distribution is continuous, and values are present all along the x axis. A correction must be made for this discrepancy for the approximation to be as accurate as possible.

Figure 6.13

Graph of a Portion of the Binomial Problem: $n = 60$ and $p = 0.30$

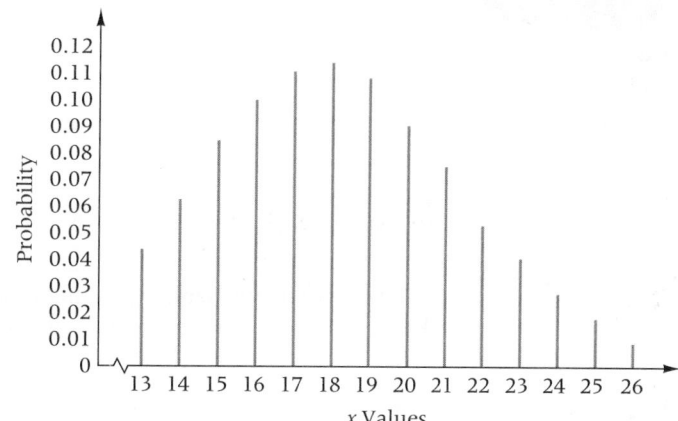

As an analogy, visualize the process of melting iron rods in a furnace. The iron rods are like the probability values on each whole number of a binomial distribution. Note that the binomial graph in Figure 6.13 looks like a series of iron rods in a line. When the rods are placed in a furnace, they melt down and spread out. Each rod melts and moves to fill the area between it and the adjacent rods. The result is a continuous sheet of solid iron (continuous iron) that looks like the normal curve. The melting of the rods is analogous to spreading the binomial distribution to approximate the normal distribution.

How far does each rod spread toward the others? A good estimate is that each rod goes about halfway toward the adjacent rods. In other words, a rod that was concentrated at $x = 25$ spreads to cover the area from 24.5 to 25.5, $x = 26$ becomes continuous from 25.5 to 26.5, and so on. For the problem $P(x \geq 25 | n = 60$ and $p = 0.30)$, conversion to a continuous normal curve problem yields $P(x \geq 24.5 | \mu = 18$ and $\sigma = 3.55)$. The correction for continuity is −0.50 because the problem called for the inclusion of the value of 25 along with all greater values; the binomial value of $x = 25$ translates to the normal curve value of 24.5 to 25.5. Had the binomial problem been to analyze $P(x > 25)$, the correction would have been +0.50, resulting in a normal curve problem of $P(x \geq 25.5)$. The latter case would begin at more than 25 because the value of 25 would not be included.

The decision as to how to correct for continuity depends on the equality sign and the direction of the desired outcomes of the binomial distribution. Table 6.3 lists some guidelines that can help in the application of the correction for continuity.

Table 6.3

Guidelines for the Correction for Continuity

For the binomial problem $P(x \geq 25 | n = 60$ and $p = 0.30)$, the normal curve becomes $P(x \geq 24.5 | \mu = 18$ and $\sigma = 3.55)$, as shown in Figure 6.14, and

$$z = \frac{x - \mu}{\sigma} = \frac{24.5 - 18}{3.55} = 1.83$$

Figure 6.14

Graph of the Solution to the Binomial Problem Worked by the Normal Curve

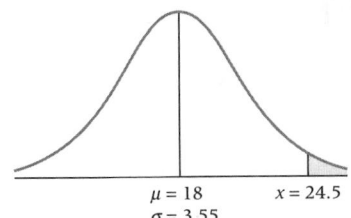

$\mu = 18$
$\sigma = 3.55$

$x = 24.5$

The probability (Table 6.1) of this *z* value is 0.4664. The answer to this problem lies in the tail of the distribution, so the final answer is obtained by subtracting.

$$\begin{array}{r} 0.5000 \\ -0.4664 \\ \hline 0.0336 \end{array}$$

Had this problem been worked using the binomial formula, the solution would have been as shown in Table 6.4. The difference between the normal distribution approximation and the actual binomial values is only 0.0025 (0.0361 − 0.0336).

Table 6.4

Probability Values for the Binomial Problem: $n = 60$, $p = 0.30$, and $x \geq 25$

x Value	Probability
25	0.0167
26	0.0096
27	0.0052
28	0.0026
29	0.0012
30	0.0005
31	0.0002
32	0.0001
33	0.0000
$x \geq 25$	0.0361

g the normal distribution.

0) = ?

2.45

Test: $\mu \pm 3\sigma = 10.0 \pm 3(2.45) = 2.65$ to 17.35

This range is between 0 and 25, so the approximation is close enough. Correct for continuity next. Because the problem is to determine the probability of *x* being exactly 12, the correction entails both −0.50 and +0.50. That is, a binomial probability at *x* = 12 translates to a continuous normal curve area that lies between 11.5 and 12.5. The graph of the problem follows:

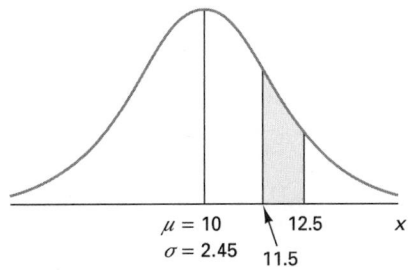

Then,

$$z = \frac{x - \mu}{\sigma} = \frac{12.5 - 10}{2.45} = 1.02$$

and

$$z = \frac{x - \mu}{\sigma} = \frac{11.5 - 10}{2.45} = 0.61$$

$z = 1.02$ produces a probability of 0.3461.
$z = 0.61$ produces a probability of 0.2291.

The difference in areas yields the following answer:

$$0.3461 - 0.2291 = 0.1170$$

Had this problem been worked using the binomial tables, the resulting answer would have been 0.114. The difference between the normal curve approximation and the value obtained by using binomial tables is only 0.003.

Demonstration Problem 6.10

Solve the following binomial distribution problem by using the normal distribution.

$$P(x < 27 | n = 100 \text{ and } p = 0.37) = ?$$

Solution

Because neither the sample size nor the p value is contained in Table A.2, working this problem using binomial distribution techniques is impractical. It is a good candidate for the normal curve. Calculating μ and σ yields

$$\mu = n \cdot p = (100)(0.37) = 37.0$$

$$\sigma = \sqrt{n \cdot p \cdot q} = \sqrt{(100)(0.37)(0.63)} = 4.83$$

Testing to determine the closeness of the approximation gives

$$\mu \pm 3\sigma = 37 \pm 3(4.83) = 37 \pm 14.49$$

The range 22.51 to 51.49 is between 0 and 100. This problem satisfies the conditions of the test. Next, correct for continuity: $x < 27$ as a binomial problem translates to $x \leq 26.5$ as a normal distribution problem. The graph of the problem follows.

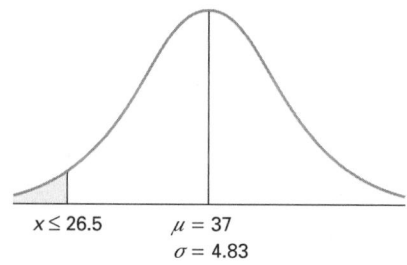

$x \leq 26.5$ $\mu = 37$
              $\sigma = 4.83$

Then,

$$z = \frac{x - \mu}{\sigma} = \frac{26.5 - 37}{4.83} = -2.17$$

Table 6.1 shows a probability of 0.4850. Solving for the tail of the distribution gives

$$0.5000 - 0.4850 = 0.0150$$

which is the answer.

Had this problem been solved by using the binomial formula, the probabilities would have been as follows:

x Value	Probability
26	0.0059
25	0.0035
24	0.0019
23	0.0010
22	0.0005
21	0.0002
20	0.0001
x < 27	0.0131

Concept Check

1. Why is it convenient to use a normal distribution to approximate a binomial distribution? Under what conditions is this approximation appropriate?
2. Explain why and how we make a continuity correction when approximating a binomial distribution with a normal distribution.

6.3 Problems

6.17   Convert the following binomial distribution problems to normal distribution problems. Use the correction for continuity.
   a. $P(x \leq 16 | n = 30 \text{ and } p = 0.70)$
   b. $P(10 < x \leq 20) | n = 25 \text{ and } p = 0.50)$
   c. $P(x = 22 | n = 40 \text{ and } p = 0.60)$
   d. $P(x > 14 | n = 16 \text{ and } p = 0.45)$

6.18   Use the test $\mu \pm 3\sigma$ to determine whether the following binomial distributions can be approximated using the normal distribution.
   a. $n = 8$ and $p = 0.50$
   b. $n = 18$ and $p = 0.80$
   c. $n = 12$ and $p = 0.30$
   d. $n = 30$ and $p = 0.75$
   e. $n = 14$ and $p = 0.50$

6.19   Where appropriate, work the following binomial distribution problems using the normal curve. Also, use Table A.2 to find the answers by using the binomial distribution and compare the answers obtained by the two methods.
   a. $P(x = 8 | n = 25$ and $p = 0.40) = ?$
   b. $P(x \geq 13 | n = 20$ and $p = 0.60) = ?$
   c. $P(x = 7 | n = 15$ and $p = 0.50) = ?$
   d. $P(x < 3 | n = 10$ and $p = 0.70) = ?$

6.20   The Zimmerman Agency conducted a study for Residence Inn by Marriott of business travellers who take trips of five nights or more. According to this study, 37% of these travellers enjoy sightseeing more than any other activity that they do not get to do as much at home. Suppose 120 randomly selected business travellers who take trips of five nights or more are contacted. What is the probability that fewer than 40 enjoy sightseeing more than any other activity that they do not get to do as much at home?

6.21   One study on managers' satisfaction with management tools reveals that 59% of all managers use self-directed work teams as a management tool. Suppose 70 managers selected randomly in Canada are interviewed. What is the probability that fewer than 35 use self-directed work teams as a management tool?

6.22   According to The Yankee Group, 53% of all cable households rate cable companies as good or excellent in quality transmission. Sixty percent of all cable households rate cable companies as good or excellent in having professional personnel. Suppose 300 cable households are randomly contacted.
   a.   What is the probability that more than 175 cable households rate cable companies as good or excellent in quality transmission?
   b.   What is the probability that between 165 and 170 (inclusive) cable households rate cable companies as good or excellent in quality transmission?
   c.   What is the probability that between 155 and 170 (inclusive) cable households rate cable companies as good or excellent in having professional personnel?
   d.   What is the probability that fewer than 200 cable households rate cable companies as good or excellent in having professional personnel?

6.23   Market researcher Liam Lahey reports that Dell Computer controls 22% of the PC market in Canada. Suppose a business researcher randomly selects 130 recent purchasers of PCs in Canada.
   a.   What is the probability that more than 36 PC purchasers bought a Dell computer?
   b.   What is the probability that between 26 and 35 PC purchasers (inclusive) bought a Dell computer?
   c.   What is the probability that fewer than 20 PC purchasers bought a Dell computer?
   d.   What is the probability that exactly 30 PC purchasers bought a Dell computer?

6.24   A study about strategies for competing in the global marketplace states that 52% of the respondents agreed that companies need to make direct investments in foreign countries. It also states that about 70% of those responding agree that it is attractive to have a joint venture to increase global competitiveness. Suppose

CEOs of 95 manufacturing companies are randomly contacted about global strategies.

a. What is the probability that between 44 and 52 (inclusive) CEOs agree that companies should make direct investments in foreign countries?

b. What is the probability that more than 56 CEOs agree with that assertion?

c. What is the probability that fewer than 60 CEOs agree that it is attractive to have a joint venture to increase global competitiveness?

d. What is the probability that between 55 and 62 (inclusive) CEOs agree with that assertion?

6.4 EXPONENTIAL DISTRIBUTION

Another useful continuous distribution is the exponential distribution. It is closely related to the Poisson distribution. Whereas the Poisson distribution is discrete and describes random occurrences over some interval, the **exponential distribution** is *continuous and describes a probability distribution of the times between random occurrences.* The following are the characteristics of the exponential distribution.

- It is a continuous distribution.
- It is a family of distributions.
- It is skewed to the right.
- The x values range from zero to infinity.
- Its apex is always at $x = 0$.
- The curve steadily decreases as x gets larger.

The exponential probability distribution is determined by the following.

Exponential Probability Density Function	$$f(x) = \lambda e^{-\lambda x}$$

where
$x \geq 0$
$\lambda > 0$
and $e = 2.71828...$

An exponential distribution can be characterized by the single parameter λ. Each unique value of λ determines a different exponential distribution, resulting in a family of exponential distributions. Figure 6.15 shows graphs of exponential distributions for four values of λ. The points on the graph are determined by using λ and various values of x in the probability density formula. The mean of an exponential distribution is $\mu = 1/\lambda$, and the standard deviation of an exponential distribution is $\sigma = 1/\lambda$.

PROBABILITIES OF THE EXPONENTIAL DISTRIBUTION

Probabilities are computed for the exponential distribution by determining the area under the curve between two points. Applying calculus to the exponential probability density

Figure 6.15

Graphs of Some Exponential Distributions

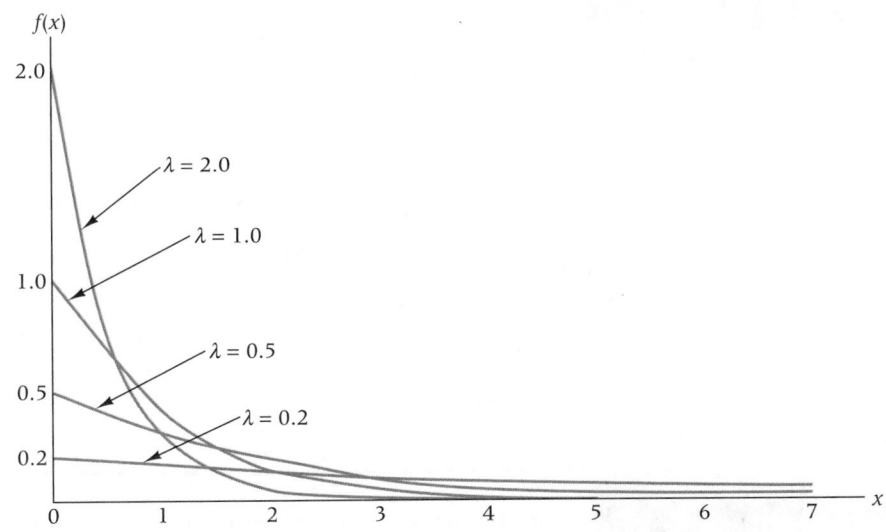

function produces a formula that can be used to calculate the probabilities of an exponential distribution.

Probabilities of the Right Tail of the Exponential Distribution	$$P(x \geq x_0) = e^{-\lambda x_0}$$ where: $x_0 \geq 0$

To use this formula requires finding values of e^{-x}. These values can be computed on most calculators or obtained from Table A.4, which contains the values of e^{-x} for selected values of x. Note that x_0 is the fraction of the interval or the number of intervals between arrivals in the probability question and λ is the average arrival rate.

For example, arrivals at a bank are Poisson distributed with a λ of 1.2 customers every minute. What is the average time between arrivals and what is the probability that at least 2 minutes will elapse between one arrival and the next arrival? Since the interval for lambda is 1 minute and we want to know the probability that at least 2 minutes elapse between arrivals (twice the lambda interval), x_0 is 2.

Interarrival times of random arrivals are exponentially distributed. The mean of this exponential distribution is $\mu = 1/\lambda = 1/1.2 = 0.833$ minutes (50 seconds). On average, 0.833 minutes, or 50 seconds, will elapse between arrivals at the bank. The probability of an interval of 2 minutes or more between arrivals can be calculated by

$$P(x \geq 2 \,|\, \lambda = 1.2) = e^{-1.2(2)} = 0.0907$$

About 9.07% of the time when the rate of random arrivals is 1.2 per minute, 2 minutes or more will elapse between arrivals, as shown in Figure 6.16.

This problem underscores the potential of using the exponential distribution in conjunction with the Poisson distribution to solve problems. In operations management and management science, these two distributions are used together to solve queuing problems (theory of waiting in lines). The Poisson distribution can be used to analyze the arrivals to the queue, and the exponential distribution can be used to analyze the interarrival time.

Figure 6.16

Exponential Distribution for $\lambda = 1.2$ and Solution for $x \geq 2$

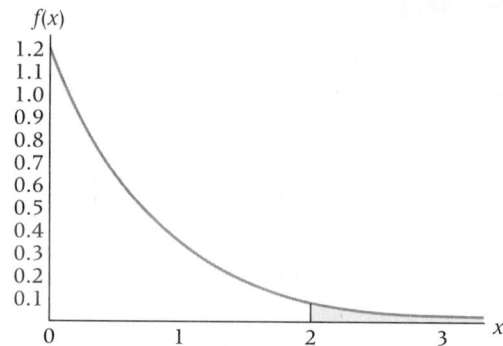

Demonstration Problem 6.11

A manufacturing firm has been involved in statistical quality control for several years. As part of the production process, parts are randomly selected and tested. From the records of these tests, it has been established that a defective part occurs in a pattern that is Poisson distributed on the average of 1.38 defects every 20 minutes during production runs. Use this information to determine the probability that less than 15 minutes will elapse between any two defects.

Solution

The value of λ is 1.38 defects per 20-minute interval. The value of μ can be determined by

$$\mu = \frac{1}{\lambda} = \frac{1}{1.38} = 0.7246$$

On the average, it is 0.7246 of the interval, or (0.7246)(20 minutes) = 14.49 minutes, between defects. The value of x_0 represents the desired number of intervals between arrivals or occurrences for the probability question. In this problem, the probability question involves 15 minutes and the interval is 20 minutes. Thus, x_0 is 15/20, or 0.75 of an interval. The question here is to determine the probability of there being less than 15 minutes between defects. The probability formula always yields the right tail of the distribution—in this case, the probability of there being 15 minutes or more between arrivals. By using the value of x_0 and the value of λ, the probability of there being 15 minutes or more between defects can be determined.

$$P(x \geq x_0) = P(x \geq 0.75) = e^{-\lambda x_0} = e^{(-1.38)(0.75)} = e^{-1035} = 0.3552$$

The probability of 0.3552 is the probability that at least 15 minutes will elapse between defects. To determine the probability of there being less than 15 minutes between defects, compute $1 - P(x)$. In this case, $1 - 0.3552 = 0.6448$. There is a probability of 0.6448 that less than 15 minutes will elapse between two defects when there is an average of 1.38 defects per 20-minute interval or an average of 14.49 minutes between defects.

USING THE COMPUTER TO DETERMINE EXPONENTIAL DISTRIBUTION PROBABILITIES

Excel can be used to solve for exponential distribution probabilities. Excel uses the values of λ and x_0. The computer yields the cumulative probability from the left (the complement of what the probability formula shown in this section yields). Table 6.5 provides the Excel output for the probability question addressed in Demonstration Problem 6.11.

Table 6.5

Excel Output for Exponential Distribution

	A	B
1	x Value	Probability < x Value
2	0.75	0.6448

Concept Check

1. List four important properties of the exponential distribution.
2. Can you think of a couple of real-life situations (in business or otherwise) where the use of the exponential distribution might be appropriate? Clearly define the random variable in each situation.

6.4 Problems

6.25 Use the probability density formula to sketch the graphs of the following exponential distributions.
  a. $\lambda = 0.1$
  b. $\lambda = 0.3$
  c. $\lambda = 0.8$
  d. $\lambda = 3.0$

6.26 Determine the mean and standard deviation of the following exponential distributions.
  a. $\lambda = 3.25$
  b. $\lambda = 0.7$
  c. $\lambda = 1.1$
  d. $\lambda = 6.0$

6.27 Determine the following exponential probabilities.
  a. $P(x \geq 5 | \lambda = 1.35)$
  b. $P(x < 3 | \lambda = 0.68)$
  c. $P(x > 4 | \lambda = 1.7)$
  d. $P(x < 6 | \lambda = 0.80)$

6.28 The average length of time between arrivals at a tollbooth is 23 seconds. Assume that the time between arrivals at the tollbooth is exponentially distributed.
   a. What is the probability that a minute or more will elapse between arrivals?
   b. If a car has just passed through the tollbooth, what is the probability that no car will show up for at least 3 minutes?

6.29 A busy restaurant determined that between 6:30 P.M. and 9:00 P.M. on Friday nights, the arrivals of customers are Poisson distributed with an average arrival rate of 2.44 per minute.
   a. What is the probability that at least 10 minutes will elapse between arrivals?
   b. What is the probability that at least 5 minutes will elapse between arrivals?
   c. What is the probability that at least 1 minute will elapse between arrivals?
   d. What is the expected amount of time between arrivals?

6.30 During the summer at a small private airport in western British Columbia, the unscheduled arrival of airplanes is Poisson distributed with an average arrival rate of 1.12 planes per hour.
   a. What is the average interarrival time between planes?
   b. What is the probability that at least 2 hours will elapse between plane arrivals?
   c. What is the probability of two planes arriving less than 10 minutes apart?

6.31 The exponential distribution can be used to solve Poisson-type problems in which the intervals are not time. According to SITA, the Geneva-based organization that provides WorldTracer and other logistical technology to the air transport industry, 32.8 million checked bags were damaged, delayed, or lost in 2008. That translates into 14.28 bags per 1,000 passengers. Assume mishandled baggage occurrences are Poisson distributed. Using the exponential distribution to analyze this problem, determine the average number of passengers between occurrences. Suppose baggage has just been mishandled. What is the probability that at least 500 passengers will have their baggage handled properly before the next mishandling occurs? What is the probability that the number will be fewer than 200 passengers?

6.32 The Foundation Corporation specializes in constructing the concrete foundations for new houses. The company knows that because of soil types, moisture conditions, variable construction, and other factors, most foundations will eventually need major repair. On the basis of its records, the company's president believes that a new house foundation on average will not need major repair for 20 years. If she wants to guarantee the company's work against major repair but wants to have to honour no more than 10% of its guarantees, for how many years should the company guarantee its work? Assume that occurrences of major foundation repairs are Poisson distributed.

6.33 During the dry month of August, one Canadian city has measurable rain on average only 2 days per month. If the arrival of rainy days is Poisson distributed in this city during the month of August, what is the average number of days that will pass between measurable rain? What is the standard deviation? What is the probability during this month that there will be a period of less than 2 days between rain?

THE COST OF HIRING A SMOKER

The Canadian Community Health Survey conducted by Statistics Canada reported that, on average, smokers take two more sick-leave days per year than their non-smoking counterparts. Suppose that the number of sick-leave days of non-smokers and smokers is uniformly distributed across all employees and varies from 5 to 10 days per year for non-smokers. Using techniques presented in Section 6.1, the uniform distribution for non-smokers can be described by $a = 5$, $b = 10$, and $\mu = 7.5$. The probability that a non-smoking employee will be absent between 7 and 9 days in one year can be determined from the following calculation assuming that $x_1 = 7$ and $x_2 = 9$:

$$P(x) = \frac{x_2 - x_1}{b - a} = \frac{9 - 7}{10 - 5} = \frac{2}{5} = 0.40$$

Thus, 40% of non-smoking employees will be absent between seven and nine days in one year.

The uniform distribution for smokers can be described by $a = 6$, $b = 13$, and $\mu = 9.5$. The probability that a smoking employee will be absent more than eight days in one year can be calculated as

$$P(x) = \frac{x_2 - x_1}{b - a} = \frac{13 - 8}{13 - 6} = \frac{5}{7} = 0.7143$$

Approximately 71.4% of smoking employees will be absent more than eight days in one year. Note that x_2 is 13 since 13 days is the upper end of the distribution.

It is estimated by some studies that, on average, it costs $3,396 to hire a smoker than to hire a non-smoker. If such costs are normally distributed with a standard deviation of $500, the probability that it will cost more than $4,000 more to hire a smoker than to hire a non-smoker is calculated using techniques from Section 6.2:

$$z = \frac{x - \mu}{\sigma} = \frac{4,000 - 3,396}{500} = 1.208$$

The area associated with this z value is 0.3869 and the tail of the distribution is 0.5000 − 0.3869 = 0.1131. That is, 11.31% of the time, it costs more than $4,000 more to hire a smoker than to hire a non-smoker. The probability that it costs less than $3,500 more to hire a smoker than to hire a non-smoker is determined in a similar manner:

$$z = \frac{x - \mu}{\sigma} = \frac{3,500 - 3,396}{500} = 0.208$$

The area associated with this z value is 0.0832, and the resulting probability is 0.5000 + 0.0832 = 0.5832. That is, 58.32% of the time, it costs less than $3,500 more to hire a smoker than to hire a non-smoker.

Seventy percent of all unscheduled 20-minute breaks are taken by smokers during the day. Using techniques presented in Section 6.3, the probability that less than 40 out of 150 unscheduled 20-minute breaks are taken by non-smoking employees can be determined. With $n = 150$, $p = 0.30$ (i.e., 1 − 0.70), and $x < 40$, this binomial distribution problem can be converted into a normal distribution problem as follows:

$$\mu = n \cdot p = (150)(0.30) = 45$$

and

$$\sigma = \sqrt{n \cdot p \cdot q} = \sqrt{(150)(0.30)(0.70)} = 5.612$$

Since $45 \pm 3(5.612)$ is in the range 0 to 150, it is appropriate to use the normal distribution to approximate this binomial problem. Applying the correction for continuity, $x \leq 39.5$, the z value is calculated as

$$z = \frac{x - \mu}{\sigma} = \frac{39.5 - 45}{5.612} = -0.98$$

The area associated with this z value is 0.3365, and the tail of the distribution is 0.5000 − 0.3365 = 0.1635. That is, 16.35% of the time, fewer than 40 out of 150 unscheduled 20-minute breaks are taken by non-smoking employees.

KEY CONSIDERATIONS

Several points must be considered in working with continuous distributions. Is the population being studied the same population from which the parameters (mean, standard deviation, λ) were determined? If not, the results may not be valid for the analysis being done. Invalid or spurious results can be obtained by using the parameters from one population to analyze another population. For example, a market study in Nova Scotia may result in the conclusion that the amount of fish eaten per month by adults is normally distributed with an average of 1 kg of fish per month. A market researcher in Manitoba should not assume that these figures apply to her population. People

KEY CONSIDERATIONS (continued)

in Manitoba probably have quite different fish-eating habits than people in Nova Scotia, and the application of Nova Scotia population parameters to Manitoba will probably result in questionable conclusions. As was true with the Poisson distribution in Chapter 5, the use of λ in the exponential distribution should be judicious because a λ for one interval in a given time period or situation may not be the same as the λ for the same interval in a different time period or situation. For example, the number of arrivals per 5-minute time period at a restaurant on Friday night is not likely to be the same as the number of arrivals in a 5-minute time period at that same restaurant from 2 P.M. to 4 P.M. on weekdays. In using established parameters such as

μ and λ, a researcher should be certain that the population from which the parameter was determined is, indeed, the same population being studied.

Sometimes a normal distribution is used to analyze data when, in fact, the data are not normal. Such an analysis can contain bias and produce false results. Certain techniques for testing a distribution of data can determine whether they are distributed a certain way. Some of the techniques are presented in Chapter 17. In general, Chapter 6 techniques can be misused if the wrong type of distribution is applied to the data or if the distribution used for analysis is the right one but the parameters (μ, σ, λ) do not fit the data of the population being analyzed.

Why Statistics Is Relevant

The normal distribution is generally considered the most user friendly, easily adaptable, and universal of the distributions. In business, the normal distribution has applications in many areas. For example, modern portfolio theory commonly assumes that the results of a diversified asset portfolio follow a normal distribution. In operations and supply chain management, process variations are often normally distributed. In human resources management, employee performance is considered to be normally distributed. In general, many of the observed variables in business are actually normally distributed. In addition, most of the test statistics (Chapters 9 and 10) are normally distributed or can be derived from the normal distribution. Moreover, the central limit theorem (Chapter 7) also relies on the normal distribution.

SUMMARY

We discussed three different continuous distributions in this chapter: the uniform distribution, the normal distribution, and the exponential distribution. With continuous distributions, the value of the probability density function does not yield the probability but instead gives the height of the curve at any given point. In fact, with continuous distributions, the probability at any discrete point is 0.0000. Probabilities are determined over an interval. In each case, the probability is the area under the curve for the interval being considered. In each distribution, the probability or total area under the curve is one.

1. Probably the simplest of these distributions is the uniform distribution, sometimes referred to as the rectangular distribution. What are the key concepts behind the uniform distribution and its uses? The uniform distribution is determined from a probability density function that contains equal values along some interval between the points a and b. Basically, the height of the curve is the same everywhere between these two

points. Probabilities are determined by calculating the portion of the rectangle between the two points a and b that is being considered.

2. The most widely used of all distributions is the normal distribution. Many phenomena are normally distributed, including characteristics of most machine-produced parts; many measurements of the biological and natural environment; and many human characteristics such as height, mass, IQ, and achievement test scores. The normal curve is continuous, symmetrical, unimodal, and asymptotic to the axis; actually, it is a family of curves.

3. The parameters necessary to describe a normal distribution are the mean and the standard deviation. For convenience, data being analyzed by the normal curve should be standardized by using the mean and the standard deviation to compute z scores. A z score is the distance that an x value is from the mean, μ, in units of standard deviations. With the z score of an x value, the probability of that value occurring by chance from a given normal distribution can be determined by using a table of z scores and their associated probabilities.

4. The normal distribution can be used to work certain types of binomial distribution problems. Doing so requires converting the n and p values of the binomial distribution to μ and σ of the normal distribution. When worked by using the normal distribution, the binomial distribution solution is only an approximation. If the values of $\mu \pm 3\sigma$ are within a range from 0 to n, the approximation is reasonably accurate. Adjusting for the fact that a discrete distribution problem is being worked using a continuous distribution requires a correction for continuity. The correction for continuity involves adding 0.50 to or subtracting 0.50 from the x value being analyzed. This correction usually improves the normal curve approximation.

5. The exponential distribution is used to compute the probabilities of times between random occurrences. The exponential distribution is a family of distributions described by the single parameter λ. The distribution is skewed to the right and always has its highest value at $x = 0$.

KEY TERMS

correction for continuity
exponential distribution
normal distribution

rectangular distribution
standardized normal
   distribution

uniform distribution
z distribution
z score

FORMULAS

Probability density function of a uniform distribution

$$f(x) = \begin{cases} \dfrac{1}{b-a} & \text{for } a \leq x \leq b \\ 0 & \text{for all other values} \end{cases}$$

Mean and standard deviation of a uniform distribution

$$\mu = \frac{a+b}{2}$$

$$\sigma = \frac{b-a}{\sqrt{12}}$$

Probability density function of the normal distribution

$$f(x) = \frac{1}{\sigma\sqrt{2\pi}} e^{-(1/2)[(x-\mu)/\sigma]^2}$$

z formula

$$z = \frac{x - \mu}{\sigma}$$

Conversion of a binomial problem to the normal curve

$$\mu = n \cdot p \quad \text{and} \quad \sigma = \sqrt{n \cdot p \cdot q}$$

Exponential probability density function

$$f(x) = \lambda e^{-\lambda x}$$

Probabilities of the right tail of the exponential distribution

$$P(x > x_0) = e^{-\lambda x_0}$$

SUPPLEMENTARY PROBLEMS

Calculating the Statistics

6.34 Data are uniformly distributed between the values of 6 and 14. Determine the value of $f(x)$. What are the mean and standard deviation of this distribution? What is the probability of randomly selecting a value greater than 11? What is the probability of randomly selecting a value between 7 and 12?

6.35 Assume a normal distribution and find the following probabilities.
   a. $P(x < 21 \mid \mu = 25 \text{ and } \sigma = 4)$
   b. $P(x \geq 77 \mid \mu = 50 \text{ and } \sigma = 9)$
   c. $P(x > 47 \mid \mu = 50 \text{ and } \sigma = 6)$
   d. $P(13 < x < 29 \mid \mu = 23 \text{ and } \sigma = 4)$
   e. $P(x \geq 105 \mid \mu = 90 \text{ and } \sigma = 2.86)$

6.36   Work the following binomial distribution problems using the normal distribution. Check your answers by using Table A.2 to solve for the probabilities.
   a. $P(x = 12 | n = 25$ and $p = 0.60)$
   b. $P(x > 5 | n = 15$ and $p = 0.50)$
   c. $P(x \leq 3 | n = 10$ and $p = 0.50)$
   d. $P(x \geq 8 | n = 15$ and $p = 0.40)$

6.37   Find the probabilities for the following exponential distribution problems.
   a. $P(x \geq 3 | \lambda = 1.3)$
   b. $P(x < 2 | \lambda = 2.0)$
   c. $P(1 \leq x \leq 3 | \lambda = 1.65)$
   d. $P(x > 2 | \lambda = 0.405)$

Testing Your Understanding

6.38   Statistics Canada reports that of people who usually work full time, the average number of hours worked per week is 42.2. Assume that the number of hours worked per week for those who usually work full time is normally distributed. Suppose 12% of these workers work more than 48 hours. Based on this percentage, what is the standard deviation of number of hours worked per week for these workers?

6.39   Statistics Canada reports that one in four people 15 years of age or older volunteers some of his or her time. If this figure holds for the entire population and if a random sample of 150 people 15 years of age or older is taken, what is the probability that more than 50 of those sampled do volunteer work?

6.40   An entrepreneur opened a small hardware store in a strip mall. During the first few weeks, business was slow, with the store averaging only one customer every 20 minutes in the morning. Assume that the random arrival of customers is Poisson distributed.
   a.   What is the probability that at least 1 hour would elapse between customers?
   b.   What is the probability that 10 to 30 minutes would elapse between customers?
   c.   What is the probability that less than 5 minutes would elapse between customers?

6.41   In a recent year, the average price of a Microsoft Windows Upgrade was $90.28, according to *PC Data*. Assume that prices of the Microsoft Windows Upgrade that year were normally distributed, with a standard deviation of $8.53. If a retailer of computer software was randomly selected that year, what is the probability that the price of a Microsoft Windows Upgrade was below $80? What is the probability that the price was above $95? What is the probability that the price was between $83 and $87?

6.42   According to Alberta Egg Producers, Alberta egg farmers produce millions of eggs every year. Suppose egg production per year in Alberta is normally distributed, with a standard deviation of 83 million eggs. If during only 3% of the years Alberta egg farmers produce more than 2,655 million eggs, what is the mean egg production by Alberta farmers?

6.43   The U.S. Bureau of Labor Statistics releases figures on the number of full-time wage and salary workers with flexible schedules. The numbers of full-time wage and salary workers in each age category are almost uniformly distributed by age, with ages ranging from 18 to 65 years. If a worker with a flexible schedule is randomly drawn from the U.S. workforce, what is the probability that he or she will be between 25 and 50 years of age? What is the mean value for this distribution? What is the height of the distribution?

6.44   A business convention holds its registration on Wednesday morning from 9:00 A.M. until 12:00 noon. Past history has shown that registrant arrivals follow a Poisson distribution at an average rate of 1.8 every 15 seconds. Fortunately, several facilities are available to register convention members.
   a.   What is the average number of seconds between arrivals to the registration area for this convention based on past results?
   b.   What is the probability that 25 seconds or more would pass between registration arrivals?
   c.   What is the probability that less than 5 seconds will elapse between arrivals?
   d.   Suppose the registration computers went down for a 1-minute period. Would this condition pose a problem? What is the probability that at least 1 minute will elapse between arrivals?

6.45   The Canada Mortgage and Housing Corporation lists average monthly apartment rates for many cities in Canada. According to its report, the average cost of renting a two-bedroom apartment in Halifax is $833. Suppose that the standard deviation of the cost of renting a two-bedroom apartment in Halifax is $84 and that two-bedroom apartment rents in Halifax are normally distributed. If a Halifax two-bedroom apartment is randomly selected, what is the probability that the price is:

a. $900 or more?

b.   Between $800 and $1,000?

c.   Between $725 and $825?

d.   Less than $600?

6.46   According to *The Wirthlin Report,* 24% of all workers say that their job is very stressful. If 60 workers are randomly selected, what is the probability that 17 or more say that their job is very stressful? What is the probability that more than 22 say that their job is very stressful? What is the probability that between 8 and 12 (inclusive) say that their job is very stressful?

6.47   Statistics Canada reports that the average annual family income in Regina is $77,900. Suppose annual family income in Regina is normally distributed, with a standard deviation of $7,077. A Regina family is randomly selected.

a.   What is the probability that the family's income is more than $83,300?

b.   What is the probability that the family's income is less than $66,500?

c.   What is the probability that the family's income is more than $58,300?

d.   What is the probability that the family's income is between $65,000 and $78,600?

6.48   Suppose interarrival times at a hospital emergency room during a weekday are exponentially distributed, with an average interarrival time of 9 minutes. If the arrivals are Poisson distributed, what is the average number of arrivals per hour? What is the probability that less than 5 minutes will elapse between any two arrivals?

6.49   Suppose the average speeds of passenger trains travelling from Winnipeg to Churchill in Manitoba are normally distributed, with a mean average speed of 142 km/h and a standard deviation of 10.3 km/h.

a.   What is the probability that a train will average less than 110 km/h?

b.   What is the probability that a train will average more than 130 km/h?

c.   What is the probability that a train will average between 145 km/h and 160 km/h?

6.50   The Conference Board published information on why companies expect to increase the number of part-time jobs and reduce full-time positions. Eighty-one percent of the companies said the reason was to get a flexible workforce. Suppose 200 companies that expect to increase the number of part-time jobs and reduce full-time positions are identified and contacted. What is the expected number of these companies that would agree that the reason is to get a flexible workforce? What is the probability that between 150 and 155 (not including the 150 or the 155) would give that reason? What is the probability that more than 158 would give that reason? What is the probability that fewer than 144 would give that reason?

6.51   According to Statistics Canada, about 71% of commuters in Canada drive to work. Suppose 150 Canadian commuters are randomly sampled.

a.   What is the probability that fewer than 105 commuters drive to work?

b.   What is the probability that between 110 and 120 (inclusive) commuters drive to work?

c.   What is the probability that more than 95 commuters drive to work?

6.52   According to the Canadian Wheat Board, mean western Canadian production of wheat and durum over a 10-year period was 22.45 million tonnes. Assume that the Canadian production of wheat over this period has been approximately uniformly distributed. If the height of this distribution is 8.94 million tonnes, what are the values of *a* and *b* for this distribution?

6.53   The U.S. Federal Reserve System publishes data on family income based on its Survey of Consumer Finances. When the head of the household has a university degree, the mean pretax family income is $85,200. Suppose that 60% of the pretax family incomes when the head of the household has a university degree are between $75,600 and $94,800 and that these incomes are normally distributed. What is the standard deviation of pretax family incomes when the head of the household has a university degree?

6.54   According to The Polk Company, a survey of households using the Internet in buying or leasing cars reported that 81% were seeking information about prices. In addition, 44% were seeking information about products offered. Suppose 75 randomly selected households who are using the Internet in buying or leasing cars are contacted.

a.   What is the expected number of households who are seeking price information?

b.   What is the expected number of households who are seeking information about products offered?

c.   What is the probability that 67 or more households are seeking information about prices?

d.   What is the probability that fewer than 23 households are seeking information about products offered?

SUPPLEMENTARY PROBLEMS (continued)

6.55   Coastal businesses in the Atlantic provinces worry about the threat of hurricanes during the season from June through October. Suppose the arrival of hurricanes during this season is Poisson distributed, with an average of three hurricanes threatening Atlantic Canada during the 5-month season. If a hurricane has just threatened the Atlantic provinces, what is the probability that at least 1 month will pass before this happens again? What is the probability that another hurricane will threaten in 2 weeks or less? What is the average amount of time between hurricanes threatening Atlantic Canada?

6.56   With the growing emphasis on technology and the changing business environment, many workers are discovering that training such as reeducation, skill development, and personal growth is of great assistance in the job marketplace. A recent Gallup survey found that 80% of Generation Xers considered the availability of company-sponsored training as a factor to weigh in taking a job. If 50 Generation Xers are randomly sampled, what is the probability that fewer than 35 consider the availability of company-sponsored training as a factor to weigh in taking a job? What is the expected number? What is the probability that between 42 and 47 (inclusive) consider the availability of company-sponsored training as a factor to weigh in taking a job?

6.57   It has been reported that the average operating cost of an MD-80 jet airliner is $2,087 per hour. Suppose the operating costs of an MD-80 jet airliner are normally distributed with a standard deviation of $175 per hour. What cost would 20% of the operating costs be less than? What cost would 65% of the operating costs be more than? What cost would be more than 85% of operating costs?

6.58   Supermarkets usually become busy at about 5 P.M. on weekdays, because many workers stop by on the way home to shop. Suppose at that time arrivals at a supermarket's express checkout station are Poisson distributed, with an average of 0.8 people/minute. If the clerk has just checked out the last person in line, what is the probability that at least 1 minute will elapse before the next customer arrives? Suppose the clerk wants to go to the manager's office to ask a quick question and needs 2.5 minutes to do so. What is the probability that the clerk will get back before the next customer arrives?

6.59   According to the Canadian Newspaper Association, the average daily circulation of *The Globe and Mail*

based on 2007 figures is 337,387. Suppose the standard deviation is 8,160. Assume the paper's daily circulation is normally distributed. On what percentage of days would it surpass a circulation of 352,000? Suppose the paper cannot support the fixed expenses of a full-production setup if the circulation drops below 320,000. If the probability of this event occurring is low, the production manager might try to keep the full crew in place and not disrupt operations. How often will this event happen, based on the historical information?

6.60   Incoming phone calls are generally thought to be Poisson distributed. If an operator averages 2.2 phone calls every 30 seconds, what is the expected (average) amount of time between calls? What is the probability that a minute or more would elapse between incoming calls? Two minutes?

Interpreting the Output

6.61   Use the output shown here and suppose the data represent the number of sales associates who are working in a department store in any given retail day. Describe the distribution, including the mean and standard deviation. Interpret the shape of the distribution and the mean in light of the data being studied. What do the probability statements mean?

Cumulative Distribution Function

Continuous uniform distribution on 11 to 32

x	$P(X \le x)$
28	0.80952
34	1.00000
16	0.23810
21	0.47619

6.62   A manufacturing company produces a metal rod. Use the Excel output shown here to describe the mass of the rod. Interpret the probability values in terms of the manufacturing process.

	A	B	C	D
1	**Normal Distribution**			
2	Mean = 227 mg.			
3	Standard Deviation = 2.3 mg			
4				
5	x Value	Probability < x Value		
6	220	0.0012		
7	225	0.1923		
8	227	0.5000		
9	231	0.9590		
10	238	1.0000		

6.63 Suppose the output shown here represents the analysis of the length in minutes of home-use cell phone calls. Describe the distribution of cell phone call lengths and interpret the meaning of the probability statements.

Cumulative Distribution Function

Normal distribution with mean = 2.35 and standard deviation = 0.11

x	$P(X \leq x)$
2.60	0.988479
2.45	0.818349
2.30	0.324718
2.00	0.000732

6.64 A restaurant averages 4.51 customers per 10 minutes during the summer in the late afternoon. Shown here is the Excel output for this restaurant. Discuss the type of distribution used to analyze the data and the meaning of the probabilities.

	A	B
1	x Values	Probability < x Value
2	0.1	0.3630
3	0.2	0.5942
4	0.5	0.8951
5	1.0	0.9890
6	2.4	1.0000

ANALYZING THE DATABASES

see www.wiley.com/canada/black

1. Select the Agri-Business Canada time-series database. Create a histogram for Barley and for Canola. Each of these variables is approximately normally distributed. Compute the mean and the standard deviation for each distribution. The data in this database represent the monthly weight (in thousands of pounds) of each grain. In terms of monthly weight, describe each grain (Barley and Canola). If a month were randomly selected from the Barley distribution, what is the probability that the weight would be more than 500,000 pounds? What is the probability that the weight would be between 250,000 and 350,000 pounds? If a month were randomly selected from the Oats distribution, what is the probability that the weight would be more than 400,000 pounds? What is the probability that the weight would be between 135,000 and 170,000 pounds?

2. Use the Energy Resource Database. The emission of CO_2 from Manufacturing Industries and Construction in the American data is nearly uniformly distributed in this database, with values from 600 to 1200. What is the height of this distribution? What is the probability of randomly selecting an emission from 800 to 1000 if the distribution is uniform? (Use the uniform distribution theory to work this problem, not the actual number from the database.)

3. Construct histograms for all variables in the Major League Baseball Database. Find at least one graph that appears to take on the shape of an exponential distribution. Compute descriptive statistics for that variable. Study the statistics and discuss what information relayed by the statistics would indicate that the shape of this distribution might be exponential.

CASE

Mercedes Goes after Younger Buyers

Mercedes and BMW have been competing head-to-head for market share in the luxury-car market for more than three decades. Back in 1959, BMW (Bayerische Motoren Werke) almost went bankrupt and nearly sold out to Daimler-Benz, the maker of Mercedes-Benz cars. BMW was able to recover to the point that in 1992 it passed Mercedes in worldwide sales. Among the reasons for BMW's success was its ability to sell models that were more luxurious than previous models but still focused on consumer quality and environmental responsibility. In particular, BMW targeted its sales pitch to the younger market, whereas Mercedes retained a more mature customer base.

In response to BMW's success, Mercedes has been trying to change its image by launching several products in an effort to attract younger buyers who are interested in sporty, performance-oriented cars. BMW, influenced by Mercedes, is pushing for more refinement and comfort. In fact, one automotive expert says that Mercedes wants to become BMW, and vice versa. However, according to other experts, the focus is still on luxury and comfort for Mercedes while BMW focuses on performance and driving dynamics. Even though each company produces many different models, two relatively comparable coupe automobiles are the BMW 335i xDrive Coupé and the Mercedes CLK 350 AMG Coupé. As of 2009, the average manufacturer's suggested retail price for a 335i xDrive was $53,100 as compared to $69,500 for a CLK 350 AMG. Fuel economy for the 335i xDrive is 7.9 L/100 km on the highway and 12.3 L/100 km in the city as compared to 7.8 L/100 km on the highway and 12.3 L/100 km in the city for the CLK 350 AMG.

Discussion

1. Suppose Mercedes is concerned that dealer prices of the CLK 350 AMG are not consistent and that even though the average price is $69,500, actual prices are normally distributed with a standard deviation of $4,528. Suppose also that Mercedes believes that at $66,800, the CLK 350 AMG is priced out of the BMW 335i xDrive market. What percentage of the dealer prices for the Mercedes CLK 350 AMG are more than $66,800 and hence priced out of the BMW 335i xDrive market? The average price for a BMW 335i xDrive is $53,100. Suppose these prices are also normally distributed with a standard deviation of $3,342. What percentage of BMW dealers are pricing the 335i xDrive at more than the average price for a CLK 350 AMG? What might this mean to BMW if dealers were pricing the 335i xDrives at this level? What percentage of Mercedes dealers are pricing the CLK 350 AMG at less than the average price of a 335i xDrive? Suppose a BMW dealer is selling a 335i xDrive for $56,500. What percentage of Mercedes dealers price the CLK 350 AMG at less than this price? In terms of the CLK 350 AMG competing with the 335i xDrive by price, what do these data tell you?

2. Suppose that fuel economy rates for various CLK 350 AMG cars are uniformly distributed over a range from 7.8 L/100 km to 9.8 L/100 km on the road. What proportion of cars fall into the 7.8 L/100 km to 9 L/100 km range? Suppose that fuel economy rates for various 335i xDrive cars are uniformly distributed over a range from 6.7 L/100 km to 9.4 L/100 km on the road. What proportion of

335i xDrive cars fall into the 7.8 L/100 km to 9 L/100 km range? How does this percentage compare to the figure for the CLK 350 AMG? What does this comparison mean? Suppose these figures were true and Mercedes wanted to appeal to environmentally conscious shoppers on the basis of fuel economy. Compute the proportion of each of the two car models that gets 7.8 L/100 km or less according to these figures, and compare the results.

3. Suppose that in one dealership an average of 1.37 CLK 350 AMGs is sold every 3 hours (during a 12-hour showroom day) and that sales are Poisson distributed. The following Excel-produced probabilities indicate the occurrence of different intersales times based on this information. Study the output and interpret it for the salespeople. For example, what is the probability that less than an hour will elapse between sales? What is the probability that more than a day (12-hour day) will pass before the next sale after a car has been sold? What can the dealership managers do with such information? How can it help in staffing? How can such information be used as a tracking device for the impact of advertising? Is there a chance that these probabilities would change during the year? If so, why?

Portion of 3-Hour Time Frame	Cumulative Exponential Probabilities from Left
0.167	0.2045
0.333	0.3663
0.667	0.5990
1	0.7459
2	0.9354
3	0.9836
4	0.9958
5	0.9989

USING THE COMPUTER

Excel

- Excel can be used to compute cumulative probabilities for particular values of x from either a normal distribution or an exponential distribution.
- Calculation of probabilities from each of these distributions begins with the **Insert Function** (*fx*). To access the **Insert Function**, go to the Formulas tab on an Excel worksheet (top centre tab). The **Insert Function** is on the far left of the menu bar. In the **Insert Function** dialogue box at the top, there is a pulldown menu where it says **Or select a category**. From the pulldown menu associated with this command, select **Statistical.**
- To compute probabilities from a normal distribution, select **NORMDIST** from the **Insert Function's Statistical** menu. In the **NORMDIST** dialogue box, there are four lines to which you must respond. On the first line, **X**, enter the value of x. On the second line, **Mean**, enter the value of the mean. On the third line, **Standard_dev**, enter the value of the standard deviation. The fourth line, **Cumulative**, requires a logical response of either TRUE or FALSE. Place TRUE in the slot to get the cumulative probabilities for all values up to x. Place FALSE in the slot to get the value of the probability density function for that combination of x, the mean, and the standard deviation. In this chapter, we are more interested in the cumulative probabilities and will enter TRUE most of the time.

- To compute probabilities from an exponential distribution, select **EXPONDIST** from the **Insert Function's Statistical** menu. In the **EXPONDIST** dialogue box, there are three lines to which you must respond. On the first line, **X**, enter the value of x. On the second line, **Lambda**, enter the value of lambda. The third line, **Cumulative**, requires a logical response of either TRUE or FALSE. Place TRUE in the slot to get the cumulative probabilities for all values up to x. Place FALSE in the slot to get the value of the probability density function for that combination of x and lambda. In this chapter, we are more interested in the cumulative probabilities and will enter TRUE most of the time.

CHAPTER 7

SAMPLING AND SAMPLING DISTRIBUTIONS

Learning Objectives

The two main objectives for Chapter 7 are to give you an appreciation for the proper application of sampling techniques and an understanding of the sampling distributions of two statistics, thereby enabling you to answer the following questions:

1. When should sampling be used instead of a census?

2. What is the difference between random and nonrandom sampling?

3. What are some of the major random sampling techniques?

4. What are some of the major nonrandom sampling techniques?

5. What different types of errors can occur in a study?

6. What is the impact of the central limit theorem on statistical analysis?

Getty Images

WHAT IS THE ATTITUDE OF MAQUILADORA WORKERS?

In 1965, Mexico initiated its widely known maquiladora program, which permits corporations from other countries to build manufacturing facilities inside the Mexican border, where the company can import supplies and materials from outside of Mexico free of duty, assemble or produce products, and then export the finished items back to the country of origin. Mexico's establishment of the maquiladora program was to promote foreign investment and jobs in the poverty-stricken country and, at the same time, provide a cheaper labour pool to the participating companies, thereby reducing labour costs so that companies could more effectively compete on the world market.

The maquiladora effort has been quite successful, with more than 3,500 registered companies participating and more than 1.1 million maquiladora workers employed in the program. It has been estimated that $50 billion has been spent by maquiladora companies with suppliers. Recently, industry exports were approaching $65 billion. About 1,600 of the maquiladora plants are located in the U.S.-Mexico border area, where about 40% manufacture electronic equipment, materi-

als, and supplies. In recent years, the maquiladora program has spread to the interior of Mexico, where maquiladora employment growth has been nearly 30%. Maquiladora companies also manufacture and assemble products from the petroleum, metal, transportation, and medical industries, among others. Whereas most maquiladora companies in the early years utilized low-skilled assembly operations, in more recent years,

maquiladoras have been moving toward sophisticated manufacturing centres. The maquiladora program now encompasses companies from all over the world, including Canada, the U.S., Japan, Korea, China, and European countries.

What are the Mexican maquiladora workers like? What are their attitudes toward their jobs and their companies? Are there cultural gaps between the company and the worker that must be bridged in order to utilize the human resources more effectively? What cultural attitudes and expectations do the maquiladora labourers bring to the work situation? How does a business researcher go about surveying workers?

Managerial and Statistical Questions

Suppose researchers decide to survey maquiladora workers to ascertain the workers' attitudes toward and expectations of the work environment and the company.

1. Should the researchers take a census of all maquiladora workers or just a sample? What are reasons for each?
2. If a sample is used, what type of sampling technique would gain the most valid information? How can the researchers be certain that the sample of workers is representative of the population?
3. How can survey questions be analyzed quantitatively?

Sources: Adapted from Cheryl I. Noll, "Mexican Maquiladora Workers: An Attitude Toward Working," *Southwest Journal of Business and Economics*, vol. IX, no. 1 (Spring 1992), pp. 1–8; Steven B. Zisser, "Maquiladora 2001 Understanding and Preparing," <http://206.251.241.31/zisser1.htm>; Maquila Portal (2004). Maquila Census-June 2004, retrieved July 14, 2004, <http://www.maquilaportal.com/cgi-bin/public/index.pl>

In this chapter, we explore the process of sampling and the sampling distributions of some statistics. How do we obtain the data used in statistical analysis? Why do researchers often take a sample rather than conduct a census? What are the differences between random and nonrandom sampling? In this chapter, we address these and other questions about sampling.

In addition to sampling theory, the distributions of two statistics—the sample mean and the sample proportion—are presented. It has been determined that statistics such as these are approximately normally distributed under certain conditions. Knowledge of the uses of the sample mean and sample proportion is important in the study of statistics and is basic to much of statistical analysis.

7.1 SAMPLING

Sampling is widely used in business as a means of gathering useful information about a population. Data are gathered from samples and conclusions are drawn about the population as a part of the inferential statistics process. In the Decision Dilemma on maquiladora workers, a random sample of workers could be taken from a wide selection of companies in several industries in many of the key border cities. A carefully constructed questionnaire that is culturally sensitive to Mexicans could be administered to the selected workers to determine work attitudes, expectations, and cultural differences between workers and companies. The researchers could compile and analyze the data gleaned from the responses. Summaries and observations could be made about worker outlook and culture in the maquiladora program. Management and decision makers could then attempt to use the results of the study to improve worker performance and motivation. Often, a sample provides a reasonable means for gathering such useful decision-making information, which might be otherwise unattainable and unaffordable.

The term *census* refers to a study of all units of the population of interest. The term *sample* refers to a study of only a portion of that population. Suppose a women's clothing manufacturer is interested in knowing how much money adult women in Montreal spend per month on clothes. A researcher who chooses to interview *all* adult women in Montreal is carrying out a census. A researcher who chooses to interview a few hundred adult women in Montreal (a far more likely scenario) to achieve the same purpose is using a sample.

REASONS FOR SAMPLING

Taking a sample instead of conducting a census offers several advantages.

1. The sample can save money.
2. The sample can save time.
3. For given resources, the sample can broaden the scope of the study.
4. Because the research process is sometimes destructive, the sample can save product.
5. If accessing the population is impossible, the sample is the only option.

A sample can be cheaper to obtain than a census for a given magnitude of questions. For example, if an 8-minute telephone interview is being undertaken, conducting the interviews with a sample of 100 customers rather than with a population of 100,000 customers is obviously less expensive. In addition to the cost savings, the significantly smaller number of interviews usually requires less total time. Thus, if obtaining the results is a matter of urgency, sampling can provide them more quickly. With the volatility of some markets and the constant barrage of new competition and new ideas, sampling has a strong advantage over a census in terms of research turnaround time.

If the resources allocated to a research project are fixed, more detailed information can be gathered by taking a sample than by conducting a census. With resources concentrated on fewer individuals or items, the study can be broadened in scope to allow for more specialized questions. One organization budgeted $100,000 for a study and opted to take a census instead of a sample by using a mail survey. The researchers mass-mailed thousands of copies of a computer card that looked like a major league baseball all-star ballot. The card contained 20 questions to which the respondent could answer Yes or No by punching out a perforated hole. The information retrieved amounted to the percentages of respondents who answered Yes and No on the 20 questions. For the same amount of money, the company could have taken a random sample from the population, held interactive one-on-one sessions with highly trained interviewers, and gathered detailed information about the process being studied. By using the money for a sample, the researchers could have spent significantly more time with each respondent and thus increased the potential for gathering useful information.

Some research processes are destructive to the product or item being studied. For example, if light bulbs are being tested to determine how long they burn or if chocolate bars are being taste tested to determine whether the taste is acceptable, the product is destroyed. If a census were conducted for this type of research, no product would be left to sell. Hence, taking a sample is the only realistic option for testing such products.

Sometimes a population is virtually impossible to access for research. For example, some people refuse to answer sensitive questions, and some telephone numbers are unlisted. Some items of interest (such as a 1957 Chevrolet) are so scattered that locating all of them would be extremely difficult. When the population is inaccessible for these or other reasons, sampling is the only option.

REASONS FOR TAKING A CENSUS

Sometimes it is preferable to conduct a census of the entire population rather than taking a sample. A business researcher may opt to take a census rather than a sample for at least two reasons, providing there is adequate time and money available to conduct such a census: (1) to eliminate the possibility that by chance a randomly selected sample may not be representative of the population and (2) for the safety of the consumer.

Even when proper sampling techniques are implemented in a study, it is possible that a sample could be selected by chance that does not represent the population. For example, if the population of interest is all truck owners in Alberta, a random sample of truck owners could yield mostly ranchers when, in fact, many of the truck owners in Alberta are urban dwellers. If the researcher or study sponsor cannot tolerate such a possibility, then taking a census may be the only option.

In addition, sometimes a census is taken to protect the safety of the consumer. For example, there are some products, such as airplanes and heart defibrillators, whose performance is so critical to the consumer that 100% of the products are tested, and sampling is not a reasonable option.

FRAME

Every research study has a target population that consists of the individuals, institutions, or entities that are the object of investigation. The sample is taken from a population *list, map, directory, or other source used to represent the population.* This list, map, or directory is called the **frame,** which can be school lists, trade association lists, or even lists sold by list brokers. Ideally, a one-to-one correspondence exists between the frame units and the population units. In reality, the frame and the target population are often different. For example, suppose the target population is all families living in Montreal.

A feasible frame would be the residential pages of the Montreal telephone book. How would the frame differ from the target population? Some families have no telephone. Other families have unlisted numbers. Still other families might have moved and/or changed numbers since the directory was printed. Some families even have multiple listings under different names.

Frames that have *overregistration* contain the target population units plus some additional units. Frames that have *underregistration* contain fewer units than does the target population. Sampling is done from the frame, not the target population. In theory, the target population and the frame are the same. In reality, a business researcher's goal is to minimize the differences between the frame and the target population.

RANDOM VERSUS NONRANDOM SAMPLING

The two main types of sampling are random and nonrandom. In **random sampling,** *every unit of the population has the same probability of being selected into the sample.* Random sampling implies that chance enters into the process of selection. For example, most people would like to believe that winners of nationwide magazine sweepstakes or numbers selected as lottery winners are selected by some random draw of numbers.

In **nonrandom sampling,** *not every unit of the population has the same probability of being selected into the sample.* Members of nonrandom samples are not selected by chance. For example, they might be selected because they are at the right place at the right time or because they know the people conducting the research.

Sometimes random sampling is called *probability sampling* and nonrandom sampling is called *nonprobability sampling.* Because every unit of the population is not equally likely to be selected, assigning a probability of occurrence in nonrandom sampling is impossible. The statistical methods presented and discussed in this text are based on the assumption that the data come from random samples. *Nonrandom sampling methods are not appropriate techniques for gathering data to be analyzed by most of the statistical methods presented in this text.* However, several nonrandom sampling techniques are described in this section, primarily to alert you to their characteristics and limitations.

RANDOM SAMPLING TECHNIQUES

The four basic random sampling techniques are simple random sampling, stratified random sampling, systematic random sampling, and cluster (or area) random sampling. Each technique offers advantages and disadvantages. Some techniques are simpler to use, some are less costly, and others show greater potential for reducing sampling error.

SIMPLE RANDOM SAMPLING

The most elementary random sampling technique is **simple random sampling.** Simple random sampling can be viewed as the basis for the other random sampling techniques. Random numbers are a sequence of numbers that lack any pattern. Each number has an equal opportunity to be included in a sample. With simple random sampling, each unit of the frame is numbered from 1 to N (where N is the size of the population). Next, a table of random numbers or a random number generator is used to select n items into the sample. A random number generator is usually a computer program that allows computer-calculated output to yield random numbers.

Table 7.1 contains a brief table of random numbers. Table A.1 in Appendix A contains a full table of random numbers. These numbers are random in all directions. The

Table 7.1

A Brief Table of Random Numbers

91567	42595	27958	30134	04024	86385	29880	99730
46503	18584	18845	49618	02304	51038	20655	58727
34914	63974	88720	82765	34476	17032	87589	40836
57491	16703	23167	49323	45021	33132	12544	41035
30405	83946	23792	14422	15059	45799	22716	19792
09983	74353	68668	30429	70735	25499	16631	35006
85900	07119	97336	71048	08178	77233	13916	47564

POINTS OF INTEREST
The word *random* does not mean *haphazard* in statistics. It means that every unit has an equal chance of being included in the sample. Random numbers are not easy to generate. Even the numbers generated by Excel are only *pseudo-random numbers*, meaning that they may contain some patterns. For this reason, if random selection is truly important, the researcher may want to use a more sophisticated random number generator, especially if it is a large-scale study.

spaces in the table are there only for ease of reading the values. For each number, any of the 10 digits (0–9) is equally likely, so getting the same digit twice or more in a row is possible.

As an example, from the population frame of companies listed in Table 7.2, we will use simple random sampling to select a sample of six companies. First, we number every member of the population. We select as many digits for each unit sampled as there are in the largest number in the population. For example, if a population has 2,000 members, we select four-digit numbers. Because the population in Table 7.2 contains 30 members, only two digits need be selected for each number. The population is numbered from 01 to 30, as shown in Table 7.3.

The object is to sample six companies, so six different two-digit numbers must be selected from the table of random numbers. Because this population contains only 30 companies, all numbers greater than 30 (31–99) must be ignored. If, for example, the number 67 is selected, the process is continued until a value between 1 and 30 is obtained. If the same number occurs more than once, we proceed to another number. For ease of understanding, we start with the first pair of digits in Table 7.1 and proceed across the first row until $n = 6$ different values between 01 and 30 are selected. If additional numbers are needed, we proceed across the second row, and so on. Often a researcher will start at some randomly selected location in the table and proceed in a predetermined direction to select numbers.

In the first row of digits in Table 7.1, the first number is 91. This number is out of range so it is cast out. The next two digits are 56. Next is 74, followed by 25, which is the first usable number. From Table 7.3, we see that 25 is the number associated with Simcoe Canada

Table 7.2

A Population Frame of 30 Companies

Acceleware Corp.	EFT Canada Inc.	Pacesetter Directional and Performance Drilling Ltd.
Apption Software (Apption Corp.)	Filemobile Inc.	PrecisionERP Inc.
Auctionwire Inc.	Hutton Forest Products Inc.	Scalar Decisions Inc.
Audability Inc.	KMA Contracting Inc.	Siamons International Inc.
b5media Inc.	League Assets Corp.	Simcoe Canada Land Development Inc.
Bond Consulting Group Inc.	Lettuce Eatery (Freshii Inc.)	Stiris Research Inc.
Cadre Staffing Inc.	LOGiQ3 Inc.	Sweetspot.ca Inc.
Direct Sales Force Inc.	MedicLINK Systems Ltd.	TAG Recruitment Group Inc.
Diversified Brands 2005 Inc.	Mortgagebrokers.com Holdings Inc.	Unity Telecom Corp.
Eagle Wake Ltd./ Ticket Gold	Rapido Trains Inc.	Vortex Mobile (Vortxt Interactive Inc.)

Table 7.3

Numbered Population of 30 Companies

01 Acceleware Corp.	11 EFT Canada Inc.	21 Pacesetter Directional and Performance Drilling Ltd.
02 Apption Software (Apption Corp.)	12 Filemobile Inc.	22 PrecisionERP Inc.
03 Auctionwire Inc.	13 Hutton Forest Products Inc.	23 Scalar Decisions Inc.
04 Audability Inc.	14 KMA Contracting Inc.	24 Siamons International Inc.
05 b5media Inc.	15 League Assets Corp.	25 Simcoe Canada Land Development Inc.
06 Bond Consulting Group Inc.	16 Lettuce Eatery (Freshii Inc.)	26 Stiris Research Inc.
07 Cadre Staffing Inc.	17 LOGiQ3 Inc.	27 Sweetspot.ca Inc.
08 Direct Sales Force Inc.	18 MedicLINK Systems Ltd.	28 TAG Recruitment Group Inc.
09 Diversified Brands 2005 Inc.	19 Mortgagebrokers.com Holdings Inc.	29 Unity Telecom Corp.
10 Eagle Wake Ltd./ Ticket Gold	20 Rapido Trains Inc.	30 Vortex Mobile (Vortxt Interactive Inc.)

Land Development Inc., so this is the first company selected into the sample. The next number is 95, unusable, followed by 27, which is usable. Twenty-seven is the number for Sweetspot.ca Inc., so this company is selected. Continuing the process, we pass over the numbers 95 and 83. The next usable number is 01, which is the value for Acceleware Corp. Thirty-four is next, followed by 04 and 02, both of which are usable. These numbers are associated with Audability Inc. and Apption Software (Apption Corp.), respectively. Continuing along the first row, the next usable number is 29, which is associated with Unity Telecom Corp. Because this selection is the sixth, the sample is complete. The following companies constitute the final sample.

> Simcoe Canada Land Development Inc.
> Sweetspot.ca Inc.
> Acceleware Corp.
> Audability Inc.
> Apption Software (Apption Corp.)
> Unity Telecom Corp.

Excel's RANDBETWEEN function offers a very simple alternative to using the table of random numbers. In our example, there are 30 companies, numbered from 1 to 30. The function RANDBETWEEN(1,30) in Excel will return a random number between 1 and 30. As with random number tables, Excel will also produce duplicates. For this reason, if a researcher has 30 items, he may want to generate many more than 30 random numbers, for example, some 150 random numbers. As with random number tables, a researcher can start at some randomly selected location in the table and proceed in a predetermined direction to select numbers. Table 7.4 shows a random number table generated by Excel. Using Excel to generate random numbers has two advantages: it is easily accessible and you can control the range of numbers that will be included in the table, so you have fewer unproductive numbers.

Simple random sampling is easier to perform on small than on large populations. The process of numbering all the members of the population and selecting items is cumbersome for large populations.

Table 7.4				
Random Numbers between 1 and 30, Generated by Excel				

12	9	26	14	9
14	26	11	10	10
10	14	8	3	28
2	18	26	10	1
28	16	27	10	26
4	22	17	8	7
1	8	6	17	5
5	18	11	17	7
29	19	21	30	26
29	22	18	28	19
8	7	20	30	29
10	3	23	4	30
29	8	23	11	23
23	26	24	23	7
24	24	16	27	23
25	12	30	27	19
10	17	1	26	5
9	23	22	16	1
29	23	6	2	30
4	8	13	5	30
21	1	6	11	1
6	16	20	12	8
8	19	25	15	23
12	8	25	17	14
7	5	28	25	11
2	30	12	12	29
9	15	10	2	4
17	23	14	29	27
11	11	21	16	5
6	4	24	5	29

STRATIFIED RANDOM SAMPLING

A second type of random sampling is **stratified random sampling,** in which the population is divided into nonoverlapping subpopulations called strata. The researcher then extracts a simple random sample from each of the subpopulations. There are many reasons for using stratified random samples. For example, stratified random samples allow the researcher to study each stratum individually by making sure that even a small stratum of interest is properly represented, and they have the potential for reducing sampling error, which is the difference between the population mean and the sample mean that occurs solely as a result of the random sampling process. However, stratified random sampling can involve additional work because each unit of the population must be assigned to a stratum before the random selection process begins.

Strata selection is usually based on available information. Such information may have been gleaned from previous censuses or surveys. Stratification benefits increase as the strata differ more. Internally, a stratum should be relatively homogeneous; externally, strata should contrast with each other. Stratification is often done by using demographic variables, such as gender, socioeconomic class, geographic region, religion, and ethnicity. For example, if a national election poll is to be conducted by a market research firm, what important variables should be stratified? The gender of the respondent might make a

Figure 7.1

Stratified Random Sampling of FM Radio Listeners

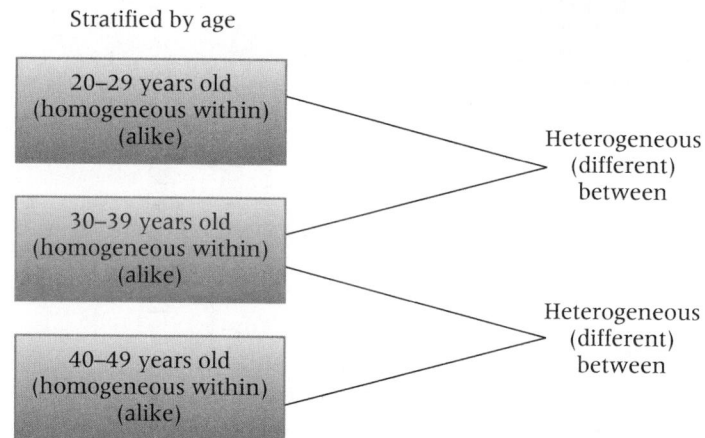

Stratified by age

difference because a gender gap in voter preference has been noted in past elections; that is, men and women tended to vote differently in national elections. Geographic region also provides an important variable in national elections because voters are influenced by local cultural values that differ from region to region. Voters in Alberta may prefer conservative candidates, while voters in the Atlantic provinces may prefer a more liberal candidate.

In FM radio markets, age of listener is an important determinant of the type of programming used by a station. Figure 7.1 contains a stratification by age with three strata, based on the assumption that age makes a difference in preference of programming. This stratification implies that listeners 20 to 29 years of age tend to prefer the same type of programming, which is different from that preferred by listeners 30 to 39 and 40 to 49 years of age. Within each age subgroup (stratum), *homogeneity* or alikeness is present; between each pair of subgroups, a difference, or *heterogeneity,* is present. Stratified random sampling can be either proportionate or disproportionate.

Proportionate stratified random sampling occurs *when the percentage of the sample taken from each stratum is proportionate to the percentage that each stratum is within the whole population.* For example, suppose voters are being surveyed in Toronto and the sample is being stratified by ethnicity. If 53% of the Toronto population is English/Irish/ Scottish and if a sample of 1,000 voters is taken, the sample would require inclusion of 53% English/Irish/Scottish people to achieve proportionate stratification. Any other number of English/Irish/Scottish would be disproportionate stratification. The sample proportion of other ethnicities such as South Asian/Indo-Caribbean (12%), Chinese (11%), black African—Caribbean (8%), and so on would also have to follow population percentages (as given in parentheses). Or consider the metropolitan area of Montreal, Quebec, where the population is approximately 65% French. If a researcher is conducting a metropolitan area poll in Montreal and if stratification is by language, a proportionate stratified random sample should contain 65% French. *Whenever the proportions of the strata in the sample are different from the proportions of the strata in the population,* **disproportionate stratified random sampling** occurs.

SYSTEMATIC SAMPLING

Systematic sampling is a third random sampling technique. Unlike stratified random sampling, systematic sampling is not done in an attempt to reduce sampling error. Rather, systematic sampling is used because of its convenience and relative ease of administration. With **systematic sampling,** *every kth item is selected to produce a sample of size n from* *a population of size N.* The value of k, sometimes called the sampling cycle, can be determined by the following formula. If k is not an integer value, the whole-number value should be used.

Determining the Value of k	$k = \dfrac{N}{n}$

where
n = sample size
N = population size
k = size of interval for selection

As an example of systematic sampling, a management information systems researcher wanted to sample the manufacturers in Canada. She had enough financial support to sample 1,000 companies (n). *Scott's National Manufacturers of Canada Directory* lists approximately 105,000 total manufacturers in Canada (N) in alphabetical order. The value of k was 105 (105,000/1,000) and the researcher selected every 105th company in the directory for her sample.

Did the researcher begin with the first company listed or the 105th or one somewhere in between? In selecting every kth value, a simple random number table should be used to select a value between 1 and k inclusive as a starting point. The second element for the sample is the starting point plus k. In the example, $k = 105$, so the researcher would have gone to a table of random numbers to determine a starting point between 1 and 105. Suppose she selected the number 5. She would have started with the 5th company, then selected the 120th (5 + 105), and then the 225th, and so on.

Besides convenience, systematic sampling has other advantages. Because systematic sampling is evenly distributed across the frame, a knowledgeable person can easily determine whether a sampling plan has been followed in a study. However, a problem with systematic sampling can occur if the data are subject to any periodicity, and the sampling interval is in syncopation with it. In such a case, the sampling would be nonrandom. For example, if a list of 150 university students is actually a merged list of five classes with 30 students in each class and if each of the lists of the five classes has been ordered with the names of top students first and bottom students last, then systematic sampling of every 30th student could cause selection of all top students, all bottom students, or all mediocre students; that is, the original list is subject to a cyclical or periodic organization. Systematic sampling methodology is based on the assumption that the source of population elements is random.

CLUSTER (OR AREA) SAMPLING

Cluster (or area) sampling is a fourth type of random sampling. **Cluster (or area) sampling** involves dividing the population into nonoverlapping areas or clusters. However, in contrast to stratified random sampling where strata are homogeneous within, cluster sampling identifies clusters that tend to be internally heterogeneous. In theory, each cluster contains a wide variety of elements, and the cluster is a miniature, or microcosm, of the population. Examples of clusters are towns, companies, homes, universities, areas of a city, and geographic regions. Often clusters are naturally occurring groups of the population and are already identified, such as provinces or cities. Although area sampling usually refers to clusters that are areas of the population, such as geographic regions and cities, the terms *cluster sampling* and *area sampling* are used interchangeably in this text.

After randomly selecting clusters from the population, the business researcher either selects all elements of the chosen clusters or randomly selects individual elements into the sample from the clusters. One example of business research that makes use of clustering is test marketing of new products. Often in test marketing, Canada is divided into clusters of test market cities, and individual consumers within the test market cities are surveyed. (A test market is a geographical area used to test potential sales or viability of a typically new product. Such test markets are typically assumed to represent the larger market.)

Sometimes the clusters are too large, and a second set of clusters is taken from each original cluster. This technique is called **two-stage sampling.** For example, a researcher could divide Canada into clusters of cities. She could then divide the cities into clusters of blocks and randomly select individual houses from the block clusters. The first stage is selecting the test cities and the second stage is selecting the blocks.

Cluster or area sampling offers several advantages. Two of the foremost advantages are convenience and cost. Clusters are usually convenient to obtain, and the cost of sampling from the entire population is reduced because the scope of the study is reduced to the clusters. The cost per element is usually lower in cluster or area sampling than in stratified sampling because of lower element listing or locating costs. The time and cost of contacting elements of the population can be reduced, especially if travel is involved, because clustering reduces the distance to the sampled elements. In addition, administration of the sample survey can be simplified. Sometimes cluster or area sampling is the only feasible approach because the sampling frames of the individual elements of the population are unavailable and therefore other random sampling techniques cannot be used.

Cluster or area sampling also has several disadvantages. If the elements of a cluster are similar, cluster sampling may be statistically less efficient than simple random sampling. In an extreme case—when the elements of a cluster are the same—sampling from the cluster may be no better than sampling a single unit from the cluster. Moreover, the costs and problems of statistical analysis are greater with cluster or area sampling than with simple random sampling.

NONRANDOM SAMPLING

Sampling techniques used to select elements from the population by any mechanism that does not involve a random selection process are called **nonrandom sampling techniques.** Because chance is not used to select items from the samples, these techniques are nonprobability techniques and are not desirable for use in gathering data to be analyzed by the methods of inferential statistics presented in this text. Sampling error cannot be determined objectively for these sampling techniques. Four nonrandom sampling techniques are presented here: convenience sampling, judgment sampling, quota sampling, and snowball sampling.

CONVENIENCE SAMPLING

In **convenience sampling,** *elements for the sample are selected for the convenience of the researcher.* The researcher typically chooses elements that are readily available, nearby, or willing to participate. The sample tends to be less variable than the population because in many environments the extreme elements of the population are not readily available. The researcher will select more elements from the middle of the population. For example, a convenience sample of homes for door-to-door interviews might include houses where people are at home, houses with no dogs, houses near the street, first-floor apartments, and houses with friendly people. In contrast, a random sample would require the researcher to gather data only from houses and apartments that have been selected randomly, no matter how inconvenient or unfriendly the location. If a research firm is located

STATISTICS IN BUSINESS TODAY

Sampling Canadian Manufacturers

Statistics Canada, Canada's national statistical agency, administers the Monthly Survey of Manufacturing (MSM), which includes information on such variables as sales of goods manufactured, inventories, and orders. The MSM data are used as indicators of the economic condition of manufacturing industries in Canada along with inputs for Canada's gross domestic product, economic studies, and econometric models. The sampling frame for the MSM is the Business Register of Statistics Canada. The target population consists of all statistical establishments on the business register that are classified as in the manufacturing sector. The frame is further reduced by eliminating the smallest units of the survey population. As a result, there

are 27,000 establishments in the sampling frame, of which approximately 10,500 units are sampled. Before the sample is taken, the sampling frame is stratified by both industry and province. Further stratification is then made within each cell by company size so that companies of similar size are grouped together. Selected establishments are required to respond to the survey and data are collected directly from the survey respondents and extracted from administrative files. Sampled companies are contacted by either mail or telephone, whichever they prefer.

Source: Statistics Canada website at <http://www.statcan.gc.ca>

in a mall, a convenience sample might be selected by interviewing only shoppers who pass the shop and look friendly.

JUDGMENT SAMPLING

Judgment sampling occurs when *elements selected for the sample are chosen by the judgment of the researcher.* Researchers often believe they can obtain a representative sample by using sound judgment, which will result in saving time and money. Ethical, professional researchers might sometimes believe they can select a more representative sample than the random process will provide. They might be right! However, some studies show that random sampling methods outperform judgment sampling in estimating the population mean even when the researcher who is administering the judgment sampling is trying to put together a representative sample. When sampling is done by judgment, calculating the probability that an element is going to be selected into the sample is not possible. The sampling error cannot be determined objectively because probabilities are based on *nonrandom* selection.

Other problems are associated with judgment sampling. The researcher tends to make errors of judgment in one direction. These systematic errors lead to what are called *biases.* The researcher is also unlikely to include extreme elements. Judgment sampling provides no objective method for determining whether one person's judgment is better than another's.

QUOTA SAMPLING

A third nonrandom sampling technique is **quota sampling,** which appears to be similar to stratified random sampling. Certain population subclasses, such as age group, gender, and geographic region, are used as strata. However, instead of randomly sampling from each stratum, the researcher uses a nonrandom sampling method to gather data from one stratum until the desired quota of samples is filled. Quotas are described by quota controls, which set the sizes of the samples to be obtained from the subgroups. Generally, a quota is based on the proportions of the subclasses in the population. In this case, the quota concept is similar to that of proportional stratified sampling.

Quotas are often filled by using available, recent, or applicable elements. For example, instead of randomly interviewing people to obtain a quota of Italian Canadians, the researcher would go to the Italian area of the city and interview there until enough responses are obtained to fill the quota. In quota sampling, an interviewer begins by asking a few filter questions; if the respondent represents a subclass whose quota has been filled, the interviewer terminates the interview.

Quota sampling can be useful if no frame is available for the population. For example, suppose a researcher wants to stratify the population into owners of different types of cars but fails to find any lists of Toyota van owners. Through quota sampling, the researcher would proceed by interviewing all car owners and casting out non-Toyota van owners until the quota of Toyota van owners is filled.

Quota sampling is less expensive than most random sampling techniques because it is essentially a technique of convenience. However, cost may not be meaningful because the quality of nonrandom and random sampling techniques cannot be compared. Another advantage of quota sampling is the speed of data gathering. The researcher does not have to call back or send out a second questionnaire if he does not receive a response; he just moves on to the next element. Also, preparatory work for quota sampling is minimal.

The main problem with quota sampling is that, when all is said and done, it is still only a *nonrandom* sampling technique. Some researchers believe that if the quota is filled by *randomly* selecting elements and discarding those not from a stratum, quota sampling is essentially a version of stratified random sampling. However, most quota sampling is carried out by the researcher going where the quota can be filled quickly. The object is to gain the benefits of stratification without the high field costs of stratification. Ultimately, it remains a nonprobability sampling method.

SNOWBALL SAMPLING

Another nonrandom sampling technique is **snowball sampling,** in which *survey subjects are selected based on referral from other survey respondents.* The researcher identifies a person who fits the profile of subjects wanted for the study. The researcher then asks this person for the names and locations of others who would also fit the profile of subjects wanted for the study. Through these referrals, survey subjects can be identified cheaply and efficiently, which is particularly useful when survey subjects are difficult to locate. It is the main advantage of snowball sampling; its main disadvantage is that it is nonrandom.

SAMPLING ERROR

Sampling error is the difference between the estimate obtained from the sample and the population parameters *as a result of the sample being only a subset of the population.* Since all samples are by definition subsets of the relevant population, sampling errors can never be completely eliminated. Whenever we take a sample, regardless of the method, it is subject to sampling errors. Many times the statistic computed on the sample may deviate from the estimate of the population parameter because of sampling error. However, with random samples, sampling error can be computed and analyzed.

NONSAMPLING ERRORS

All errors other than sampling errors are **nonsampling errors.** Nonsampling errors can introduce biases. Nonsampling errors do not arise because we used only a part of the population. They arise for many other reasons, such as missing data, recording errors, input processing errors, nonresponse (chosen respondent not being available or refusing to participate), and analysis errors. In some surveys (such as mail surveys), the respondent can choose to respond or not much more easily than in a telephone interview. This results in respondent self-selection. This introduces what is known as the selection bias. Nonsampling errors can also result from the measurement instrument, such as errors of unclear definitions, defective questionnaires, and poorly conceived concepts. Improper definition of the frame is a nonsampling error. In many cases, finding a frame that perfectly fits the population is impossible. Insofar as it does not fit, a nonsampling error can arise.

Response errors are also nonsampling errors. They occur when people do not know, will not say, or overstate. Virtually no statistical method is available to measure or control for nonsampling errors. The statistical techniques presented in this text are based on the assumption that none of these nonsampling errors were committed. The researcher should try to eliminate these errors through carefully planning and executing the research study. In many surveys, sampling error is the only part of the total survey error that is measurable. Nonsampling errors, on the other hand, can be not only numerous but for the most part very difficult to measure and, in some cases, even to identify. Therefore, one should assume that the reported error includes all possible survey errors.

POINTS OF INTEREST
In sample surveys, sampling errors are unavoidable while biases may be avoidable. Sampling errors are measurable but biases are not easily measurable.

Concept Check

1. What is the basic difference between a random and a nonrandom sample?
2. Suppose there are 100 students in your class. You are asked to pick four students at random. You look around and pick four students in a specific order. Is this a true random sample?
3. What is the only reason for sampling errors?
4. Why do nonsampling errors occur?

7.1 Problems

7.1 Develop a frame for the population of each of the following research projects.
   a. Measuring the job satisfaction of all union employees in a company
   b. Conducting a telephone survey in Edmonton, Alberta, to determine the level of interest in opening a new hunting and fishing specialty store in the West Edmonton Mall
   c. Interviewing passengers of a major airline about its food service
   d. Studying the quality control programs of boat manufacturers
   e. Attempting to measure the corporate culture of cable television companies

7.2 Make a list of 20 people you know. Include men and women, various ages, various educational levels, and so on. Number the list and then use the random number list in Table 7.1 to select six people randomly from your list. How representative of the population is the sample? Find the proportion of men in your population and in your sample. How do the proportions compare? Find the proportion of 20-year-olds in your sample and the proportion in the population. How do they compare?

7.3 Use the random numbers in Table A.1 of Appendix A to select 10 of the companies from the 30 companies listed in Table 7.2. Compare the types of companies in your sample with the types in the population. How representative of the population is your sample?

7.4 For each of the following research projects, list three variables for stratification of the sample.
   a. A nationwide study of motels and hotels is being conducted. An attempt will be made to determine the extent of the availability of on-line links for customers. A sample of motels and hotels will be taken.
   b. A consumer panel is to be formed by sampling people in Manitoba. Members of the panel will be interviewed periodically in an effort to understand current consumer attitudes and behaviours.

c. A large soft drink company wants to study the characteristics of the Canadian bottlers of its products, but the company does not want to conduct a census.

d. The business research bureau of a large university is conducting a project in which the bureau will sample paper-manufacturing companies.

7.5 In each of the following cases, the variable represents one way that a sample can be stratified in a study. For each variable, list some strata into which the variable can be divided.

a. Age of respondent (person)
b. Size of company (sales volume)
c. Size of retail outlet (square feet)
d. Geographic location
e. Occupation of respondent (person)
f. Type of business (company)

7.6 A city's telephone book lists 100,000 people. If the telephone book is the frame for a study, how large would the sample size be if systematic sampling were done on every 200th person?

7.7 If every 11th item is systematically sampled to produce a sample size of 75 items, approximately how large is the population?

7.8 If a company employs 3,500 people and if a random sample of 175 of these employees has been taken by systematic sampling, what is the value of k? The researcher would start the sample selection between which two values? Where could the researcher obtain a frame for this study?

7.9 For each of the following research projects, list at least one area or cluster that could be used in obtaining the sample.

a. A study of road conditions in the province of Nova Scotia
b. A study of Canadian offshore oil wells
c. A study of the environmental effects of petrochemical plants west of the St. Lawrence River

7.10 Give an example of how judgment sampling could be used in a study to determine how prosecutors feel about lawyers advertising on television.

7.11 Give an example of how convenience sampling could be used in a study of *Report on Business Magazine* Top 1,000 executives to measure corporate attitude toward paternity leave for employees.

7.12 Give an example of how quota sampling could be used to conduct sampling by a company test marketing a new personal computer.

7.2 SAMPLING DISTRIBUTION OF $\bar{x}$

In the inferential statistics process, a researcher selects a random sample from the population, computes a statistic on the sample, and reaches conclusions about the population parameter from the statistic. In attempting to analyze the sample statistic, it is essential to know the distribution of the statistic. So far we have studied several distributions, including the binomial distribution, the Poisson distribution, the hypergeometric distribution, the uniform distribution, the normal distribution, and the exponential distribution.

In this section, we explore the sample mean, $\bar{x}$, as the statistic. The sample mean is one of the more common statistics used in the inferential process. To compute and assign the probability of occurrence of a particular value of a sample mean, the researcher must know the distribution of the sample means. One way to examine the distribution possibilities is to take a population with a particular distribution, randomly select samples of a given size, compute the sample means, and attempt to determine how the means are distributed.

Suppose a small finite population consists of only $N = 8$ numbers:

54   55   59   63   64   68   69   70

Using an Excel-produced histogram, we can see the shape of the distribution of this population of data.

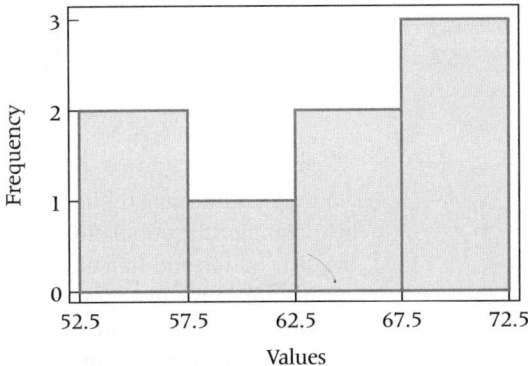

Suppose we take all possible samples of size $n = 2$ from this population with replacement. The result is the following pairs of data.

(54, 54)	(55, 54)	(59, 54)	(63, 54)
(54, 55)	(55, 55)	(59, 55)	(63, 55)
(54, 59)	(55, 59)	(59, 59)	(63, 59)
(54, 63)	(55, 63)	(59, 63)	(63, 63)
(54, 64)	(55, 64)	(59, 64)	(63, 64)
(54, 68)	(55, 68)	(59, 68)	(63, 68)
(54, 69)	(55, 69)	(59, 69)	(63, 69)
(54, 70)	(55, 70)	(59, 70)	(63, 70)
(64, 54)	(68, 54)	(69, 54)	(70, 54)
(64, 55)	(68, 55)	(69, 55)	(70, 55)
(64, 59)	(68, 59)	(69, 59)	(70, 59)
(64, 63)	(68, 63)	(69, 63)	(70, 63)
(64, 64)	(68, 64)	(69, 64)	(70, 64)
(64, 68)	(68, 68)	(69, 68)	(70, 68)
(64, 69)	(68, 69)	(69, 69)	(70, 69)
(64, 70)	(68, 70)	(69, 70)	(70, 70)

The means of all of these samples follow.

54	54.5	56.5	58.5	59	61	61.5	62
54.5	55	57	59	59.5	61.5	62	62.5
56.5	57	59	61	61.5	63.5	64	64.5
58.5	59	61	63	63.5	65.5	66	66.5
59	59.5	61.5	63.5	64	66	66.5	67
60	61.5	63.5	65.5	66	68	68.5	69
61.5	62	64	66	66.5	68.5	69	69.5
62	62.5	64.5	66.5	67	69	69.5	70

Again using an Excel-produced histogram, we can see the shape of the distribution of these sample means.

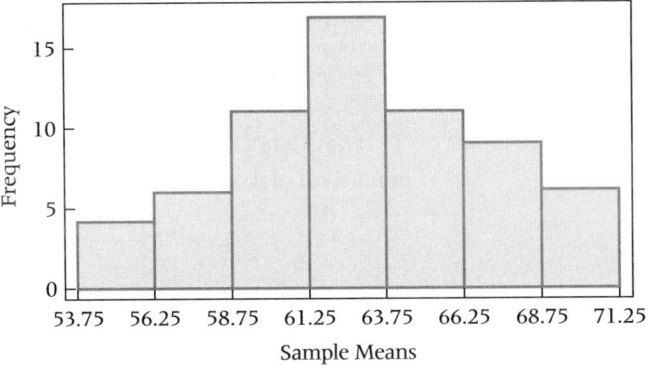

Notice that the shape of the histogram for sample means is quite unlike the shape of the histogram for the population. The sample means appear to "pile up" toward the middle of the distribution and "tail off" toward the extremes.

Figure 7.2 is a histogram of the data from a Poisson distribution of values with a population mean of 1.25. Note that the histogram is skewed to the right. Suppose 90 samples of size $n = 30$ are taken randomly from a Poisson distribution with $\lambda = 1.25$ and the means are computed on each sample. The resulting distribution of sample means is displayed in Figure 7.3. Notice that although the samples were drawn from a Poisson distribution, which is skewed to the right, the sample means form a distribution that approaches a symmetrical, nearly normal-curve-type distribution.

Suppose a population is uniformly distributed. If samples are selected randomly from a population with a uniform distribution, how are the sample means distributed? Figure 7.4 displays the histogram distributions of sample means from five different sample sizes. Each of these histograms represents the distribution of sample means from 90 samples generated randomly from a uniform distribution in which $a = 10$ and $b = 30$. Observe the shape of the distributions. Notice that even for small sample sizes, the distributions of sample means for samples taken from the uniformly distributed population begin to pile up in the middle. As sample sizes become much larger, the sample mean distributions begin to approach a normal distribution and the variation among the means decreases.

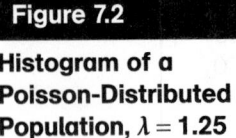

Figure 7.2

Histogram of a Poisson-Distributed Population, $\lambda = 1.25$

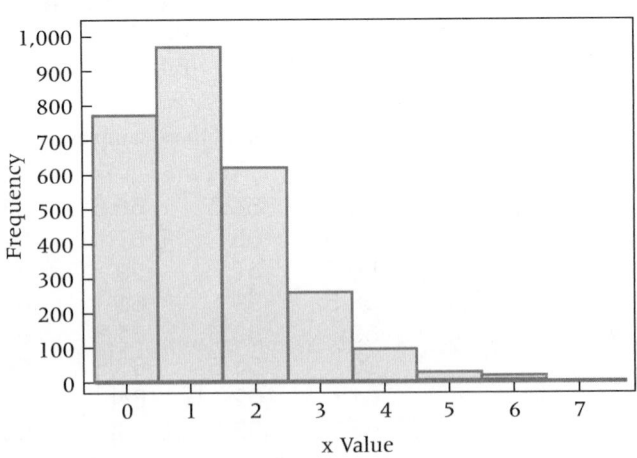

Figure 7.3

Histogram of Sample Means for the Data Shown in Figure 7.2

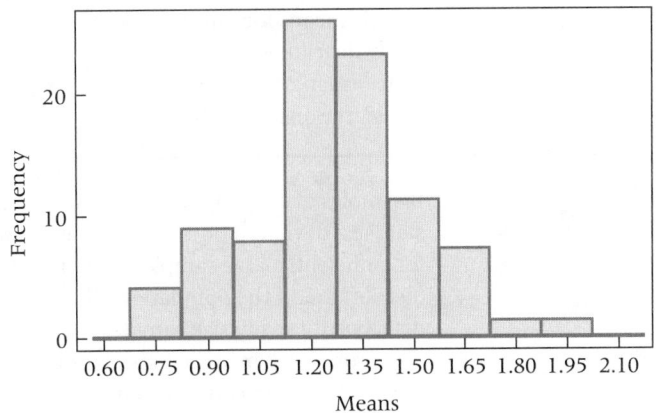

Figure 7.4

Sample Means from 90 Samples Ranging in Size from $n = 2$ to $n = 30$ from a Uniformly Distributed Population with $a = 10$ and $b = 30$

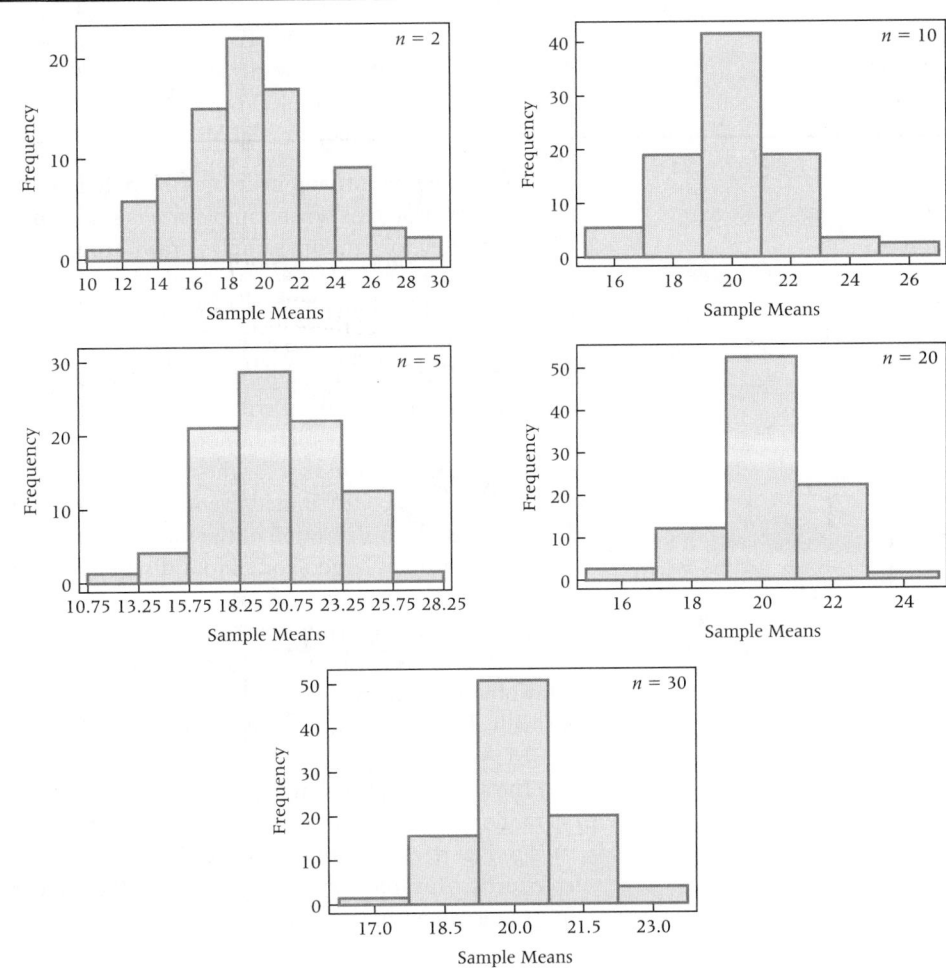

So far, we have examined three populations with different distributions. However, the sample means for samples taken from these populations appear to be approximately normally distributed, especially as the sample sizes become larger. What would happen to the distribution of sample means if we studied populations with differently shaped distributions? The answer to that question is given in the **central limit theorem.**

| Central Limit Theorem | If samples of size n are drawn randomly from a population that has a mean of μ and a standard deviation of σ, the sample means, $\bar{x}$, are approximately normally distributed for sufficiently large sample sizes ($n \geq 30^*$) regardless of the shape of the population distribution. If the population is normally distributed, the sample means are normally distributed for any size sample. |

From mathematical expectation,[†] it can be shown that the mean of the sample means is the population mean:

$$\mu_{\bar{x}} = \mu$$

and the standard deviation of the sample means (called the standard error of the mean) is the standard deviation of the population divided by the square root of the sample size:

$$\sigma_{\bar{x}} = \frac{\sigma}{\sqrt{n}}$$

The central limit theorem creates the potential for applying the normal distribution to many problems when sample size is sufficiently large. Sample means that have been computed for random samples drawn from normally distributed populations are normally distributed. However, the real advantage of the central limit theorem comes when sample data drawn from populations not normally distributed or from populations of unknown shape can also be analyzed by using the normal distribution because the sample means are normally distributed for sufficiently large sample sizes.[‡] Column 1 of Figure 7.5 shows four different population distributions. Each succeeding column displays the shape of the distribution of the sample means for a particular sample size. Note in the bottom row for the normally distributed population that the sample means are normally distributed even for $n = 2$. Note also that with the other population distributions, the distribution of the sample means begins to approximate the normal curve as n becomes larger. For all four distributions, the distribution of sample means is approximately normal for $n = 30$.

How large must a sample be for the central limit theorem to apply? The sample size necessary varies according to the shape of the population. However, in this text (as in many others), a sample of *size 30 or larger* will suffice. Recall that if the population is normally distributed, the sample means are normally distributed for sample sizes as small as $n = 1$.

The shapes displayed in Figure 7.5 coincide with the results obtained empirically from the random sampling shown in Figures 7.3 and 7.4. As shown in Figure 7.5, and as indicated in Figure 7.4, as sample size increases, the distribution narrows, or becomes more leptokurtic. This trend makes sense because the standard deviation of the mean is $\sigma/\sqrt{n}$. This value will become smaller as the size of n increases.

---

[*] Note that the central limit theorem itself does not specify what a "large sample size" is. As a guideline, it is assumed to be 30 or more, although this does not follow from the central limit theorem itself.

[†] The derivations are beyond the scope of this text and are not shown.

[‡] The actual form of the central limit theorem is a limit function of calculus. As the sample size increases to infinity, the distribution of sample means literally becomes normal in shape.

Figure 7.5

Shapes of the Distributions of Sample Means for Three Sample Sizes Drawn from Four Different Population Distributions

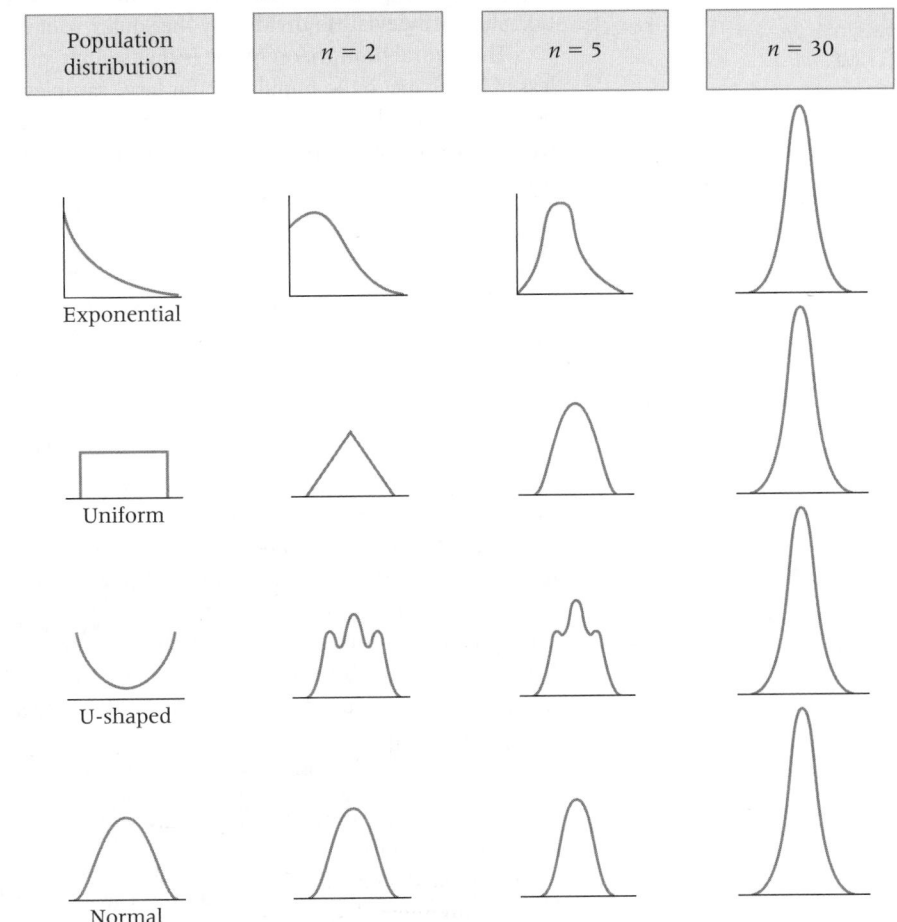

In Table 7.5, the means and standard deviations of the means are displayed for random samples of various sizes ($n = 2$ through $n = 30$) drawn from the uniform distribution of $a = 10$ and $b = 30$ shown in Figure 7.4. The population mean is 20, and the standard deviation of the population is 5.774. Note that the mean of the sample means for each sample size is approximately 20 and that the standard deviation of the sample means for each set of 90 samples is approximately equal to $\sigma/\sqrt{n}$. A small discrepancy occurs between the standard deviation of the sample means and $\sigma/\sqrt{n}$, because not all possible samples of a given size were taken from the population (only 90). In theory, if all possible samples for a given sample size are taken exactly once, the mean of the sample means will equal the

Table 7.5

$\mu_{\bar{x}}$ and $\sigma_{\bar{x}}$ of 90 Random Samples for Five Different Sizes*

Sample Size	Mean of Sample Means	Standard Deviation of Sample Means	μ	$\dfrac{\sigma}{\sqrt{n}}$
$n = 2$	19.92	3.87	20	4.08
$n = 5$	20.17	2.65	20	2.58
$n = 10$	20.04	1.96	20	1.83
$n = 20$	20.20	1.37	20	1.29
$n = 30$	20.25	0.99	20	1.05

*Randomly generated by Excel using a uniform distribution with $a = 10$ and $b = 30$.

population mean and the standard deviation of the sample means will equal the population standard deviation divided by the square root of n.

The central limit theorem states that sample means are normally distributed regardless of the shape of the population for large samples and for any sample size with normally distributed populations. Thus, sample means can be analyzed by using z scores. Recall from Chapters 3 and 6 the formula to determine z scores for individual values from a normal distribution:

$$z = \frac{x - \mu}{\sigma}$$

If sample means are normally distributed, the z score formula applied to sample means is:

$$z = \frac{\bar{x} - \mu_{\bar{x}}}{\sigma_{\bar{x}}}$$

This result follows the general pattern of z scores: the difference between the statistic and its mean divided by the statistic's standard deviation. In this formula, the mean of the statistic of interest is $\mu_{\bar{x}}$, and *the standard deviation of the statistic of interest is* $\sigma_{\bar{x}}$, sometimes referred to as the **standard error of the mean.** To determine $\mu_{\bar{x}}$, the researcher randomly draws out all possible samples of the given size from the population, computes the sample means, and averages them. This task is virtually impossible to accomplish in any realistic period of time. Fortunately, $\mu_{\bar{x}}$ equals the population mean, μ, which is easier to access. Likewise, to determine directly the value of $\sigma_{\bar{x}}$, the researcher takes all possible samples of a given size from a population, computes the sample means, and determines the standard deviation of sample means. This task is also practically impossible. Fortunately, $\sigma_{\bar{x}}$ can be computed by using the population standard deviation divided by the square root of the sample size.

As sample size increases, the standard deviation of the sample means becomes smaller and smaller because the population standard deviation is being divided by larger and larger values of the square root of n. The ultimate benefit of the central limit theorem is a practical, useful version of the z formula for sample means.

z Formula for Sample Means	$$z = \frac{\bar{x} - \mu}{\dfrac{\sigma}{\sqrt{n}}}$$

When the population is normally distributed and the sample size is 1, this formula for sample means becomes the z formula for individual values that we used in Chapter 6. The reason is that the mean of one value is that value, and when $n = 1$ the value of $\sigma/\sqrt{n} = \sigma$.

Suppose, for example, that the mean expenditure per customer at a tire store is $85.00, with a standard deviation of $9.00. If a random sample of 40 customers is taken, what is the probability that the sample average expenditure per customer for this sample will be $87.00 or more? Because the sample size is greater than 30, the central limit theorem can be used, and the sample means are normally distributed. With $\mu = \$85.00$, $\sigma = \$9.00$, and the z formula for sample means, z is computed as:

$$z = \frac{\bar{x} - \mu}{\dfrac{\sigma}{\sqrt{n}}} = \frac{\$87.00 - \$85.00}{\dfrac{\$9.00}{\sqrt{40}}} = \frac{\$2.00}{\$1.42} = 1.41$$

From the z distribution (Table A.5), $z = 1.41$ produces a probability of 0.4207. This number is the probability of getting a sample mean between $87.00 and $85.00 (the

Figure 7.6

**Graphical Solution to the
Tire Store Example**

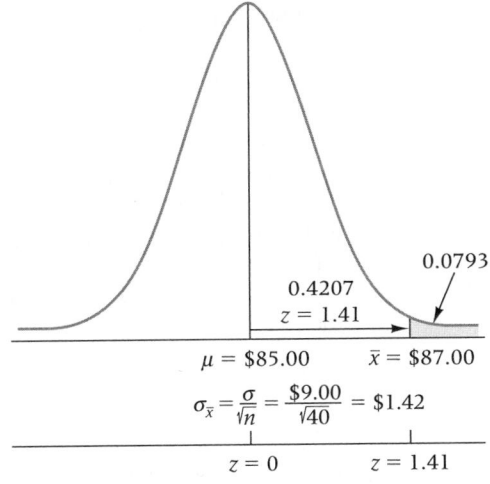

population mean). Solving for the tail of the distribution yields:

$$0.5000 - 0.4207 = 0.0793$$

which is the probability of $\bar{x} > \$87.00$. That is, 7.93% of the time, a random sample of 40 customers from this population will yield a sample mean expenditure of $87.00 or more. Figure 7.6 shows the problem and its solution.

Demonstration Problem 7.1

Suppose that during any hour in a large department store, the average number of shoppers is 448, with a standard deviation of 21 shoppers. What is the probability that a random sample of 49 different shopping hours will yield a sample mean between 441 and 446 shoppers?

Solution

For this problem, $\mu = 448$, $\sigma = 21$, and $n = 49$. The problem is to determine $P(441 \leq \bar{x} \leq 446)$. The following diagram depicts the problem.

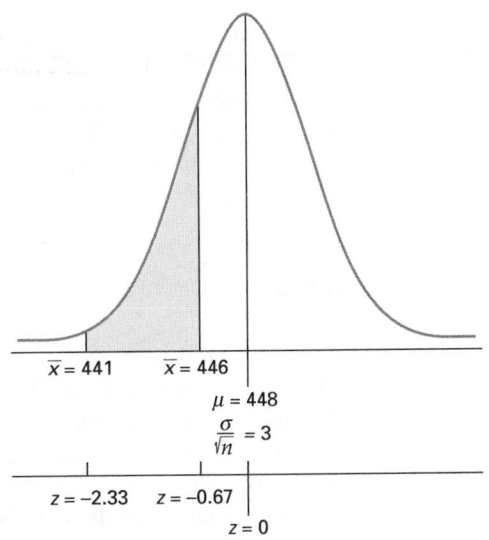

Solve this problem by calculating the z scores and using Table A.5 to determine the probabilities.

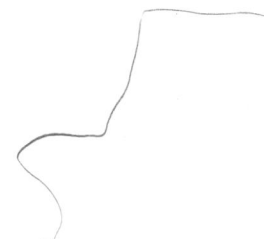

$$z = \frac{441 - 448}{\frac{21}{\sqrt{49}}} = \frac{-7}{3} = -2.33$$

and

$$z = \frac{446 - 448}{\frac{21}{\sqrt{49}}} = \frac{-2}{3} = -0.67$$

z Value	Probability
−2.33	0.4901
−0.67	−0.2486
	0.2415

The probability of a value being between $z = -2.33$ and $z = -0.67$ is 0.2415; that is, there is a 24.15% chance of randomly selecting 49 hourly periods for which the sample mean is between 441 and 446 shoppers.

SAMPLING FROM A FINITE POPULATION

The example shown in this section and Demonstration Problem 7.1 was based on the assumption that the population was infinitely or extremely large. In cases of a finite population, *a statistical adjustment can be made to the z formula for sample means.* The adjustment is called the **finite correction factor:** $\sqrt{(N - n)/(N - 1)}$. It operates on the standard deviation of sample means, $\sigma_{\bar{x}}$. Following is the z formula for sample means when samples are drawn from finite populations.

z Formula for Sample Means of a Finite Population	$z = \dfrac{\bar{x} - \mu}{\dfrac{\sigma}{\sqrt{n}} \sqrt{\dfrac{N - n}{N - 1}}}$

If a random sample of size 35 were taken from a finite population of only 500, the sample mean would be less likely to deviate from the population mean than would be the case if a sample of size 35 were taken from an infinite population. For a sample of size 35 taken from a finite population of size 500, the finite correction factor is

$$\sqrt{\frac{500 - 35}{500 - 1}} = \sqrt{\frac{465}{499}} = 0.965$$

Thus, the standard deviation of the mean—sometimes referred to as the standard error of the mean—is adjusted downward by using 0.965. As the size of the finite population becomes larger in relation to sample size, the finite correction factor approaches 1. In theory, whenever researchers are working with a finite population, they can use the finite correction factor. A rough guideline for many researchers is that, if the sample size is less than 5% of the finite population size or $n/N < 0.05$, the finite correction factor

Table 7.6

Finite Correction Factor for Some Sample Sizes

Population Size	Sample Size	Value of Correction Factor
2,000	30 (<5%N)	0.993
2,000	500	0.866
500	30	0.971
500	200	0.775
200	30	0.924
200	75	0.793

does not significantly modify the solution. Table 7.6 contains some illustrative finite correction factors.

Demonstration Problem 7.2

A production company's 350 hourly employees average 37.6 years of age, with a standard deviation of 8.3 years. If a random sample of 45 hourly employees is taken, what is the probability that the sample will have an average age of less than 40 years?

Solution

The population mean is 37.6, with a population standard deviation of 8.3; that is, $\mu = 37.6$ and $\sigma = 8.3$. The sample size is 45, but it is being drawn from a finite population of 350; that is, $n = 45$ and $N = 350$. The sample mean under consideration is 40, or $\bar{x} = 40$. The following diagram depicts the problem on a normal curve.

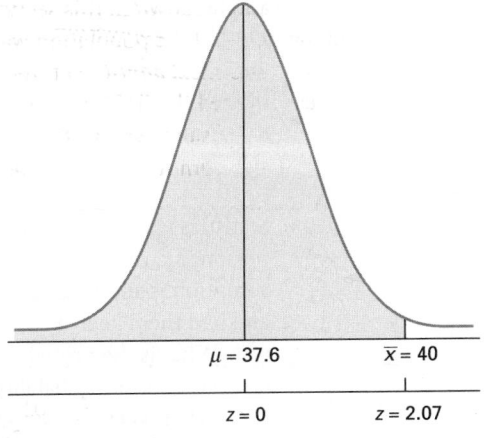

$$\mu = 37.6 \qquad \bar{x} = 40$$
$$z = 0 \qquad z = 2.07$$

Using the z formula with the finite correction factor gives

$$z = \frac{40 - 37.6}{\dfrac{8.3}{\sqrt{45}}\sqrt{\dfrac{350 - 45}{350 - 1}}} = \frac{2.4}{1.157} = 2.07$$

This z value yields a probability (Table A.5) of 0.4808. Therefore, the probability of getting a sample average age of less than 40 years is $0.4808 + 0.5000 = 0.9808$. Had the finite correction factor not been used, the z value would have been 1.94, and the final answer would have been 0.9738.

Concept Check

1. What do you understand by the central limit theorem and why is it relevant?
2. What happens to the sample mean as you increase the sample size?
3. What is a finite population? What is the finite population correction?

7.2 Problems

7.13   A population has a mean of 50 and a standard deviation of 10. If a random sample of 64 is taken, what is the probability that the sample mean is each of the following?

    a.   Greater than 52
    b.   Less than 51
    c.   Less than 47
    d.   Between 48.5 and 52.4
    e.   Between 50.6 and 51.3

7.14   A population is normally distributed, with a mean of 23.45 and a standard deviation of 3.8. What is the probability of each of the following?

    a.   Taking a sample of size 10 and obtaining a sample mean of 22 or more
    b.   Taking a sample of size 4 and getting a sample mean of more than 26

7.15   Suppose a random sample of size 36 is drawn from a population with a mean of 278. If 86% of the time the sample mean is less than 280, what is the population standard deviation?

7.16   A random sample of size 81 is drawn from a population with a standard deviation of 12. If only 18% of the time a sample mean greater than 300 is obtained, what is the mean of the population?

7.17   Find the probability in each case.

    a. $N = 1,000, n = 60, \mu = 75$, and $\sigma = 6$; $P(\bar{x} < 76.5) = ?$
    b. $N = 90, n = 36, \mu = 108$, and $\sigma = 3.46$; $P(107 < \bar{x} < 107.7) = ?$
    c. $N = 250, n = 100, \mu = 35.6$, and $\sigma = 4.89$; $P(\bar{x} \geq 36) = ?$
    d. $N = 5,000, n = 60, \mu = 125$, and $\sigma = 13.4$; $P(\bar{x} < 123) = ?$

7.18   Statistics Canada reports that the average annual consumption of fresh fruit per person in a recent year is 39.4 kg. Suppose the standard deviation of fresh fruit consumption is about 12 kg. Suppose a researcher took a random sample of 38 people and had them keep a record of the fresh fruit they ate for one year.

    a.   What is the probability that the sample average would be less than 36 kg?
    b.   What is the probability that the sample average would be between 39 kg and 42 kg?
    c.   What is the probability that the sample average would be less than 45 kg?
    d.   What is the probability that the sample average would be between 37 kg and 38 kg?

7.19   Suppose a small town in British Columbia contains 1,500 houses. A sample of 100 houses is selected randomly and evaluated by an appraiser. If the mean appraised value of a house in this town for all houses is $177,000, with a standard deviation of $8,500, what is the probability that the sample average is greater than $185,000?

7.20   Suppose the average checkout tab at a large supermarket is $65.12, with a standard deviation of $21.45. Twenty-three percent of the time when a random sample of 45 customer tabs is examined, the sample average should exceed what value?

7.21 According to Statscan, the average number of hours of TV viewing among adult females per week is is 25.6 hours. Suppose the standard deviation is 6.7 hours and a random sample of 42 Canadian households is taken.
   a. What is the probability that the sample average is more than 27 hours?
   b. What is the probability that the sample average is less than 23 hours?
   c. What is the probability that the sample average is less than 20 hours? If the sample average actually is less than 20 hours, what would it mean in this context?
   d. Suppose the population standard deviation is unknown. If 71% of all sample means are greater than 25 hours and the population mean is still 25.6 hours, what is the value of the population standard deviation?

7.3 SAMPLING DISTRIBUTION OF $\hat{p}$

Sometimes in analyzing a sample, a researcher will choose to use the sample proportion, denoted $\hat{p}$. If research produces *measurable* data such as mass, distance, time, and income, the sample mean is often the statistic of choice. However, if research results in *countable* items such as how many people in a sample choose Dr. Pepper as their favourite soft drink or how many people in a sample have a flexible work schedule, the sample proportion is often the statistic of choice. Whereas the mean is computed by averaging a set of values, the **sample proportion** is *computed by dividing the frequency with which a given characteristic occurs in a sample by the number of items in the sample.*

Sample Proportion

$$\hat{p} = \frac{x}{n}$$

where
   x = number of items in a sample that have the characteristic
   n = number of items in the sample

For example, in a sample of 100 factory workers, 30 workers might belong to a union. The value of $\hat{p}$ for this characteristic, union membership, is 30/100 = 0.30. In a sample of 500 businesses in suburban malls, if 10 are shoe stores, then the sample proportion of shoe stores is 10/500 = 0.02. The sample proportion is a widely used statistic and is usually computed on questions involving Yes or No answers. For example, do you have at least a high school education? Are you predominantly right-handed? Are you female? Do you belong to the student accounting association?

How does a researcher use the sample proportion in analysis? The central limit theorem applies to sample proportions in that the normal distribution approximates the shape of the distribution of sample proportions if $n \cdot p > 5$ and $n \cdot q > 5$ (p is the population proportion and $q = 1 - p$). The mean of sample proportions for all samples of size n randomly drawn from a population is p (the population proportion) and the standard deviation of sample proportions is $\sqrt{p \cdot q/n}$, which is sometimes referred to as the **standard error of the proportion.** Sample proportions also have a z formula.

z Formula for Sample Proportions for $n \cdot p > 5$ and $n \cdot q > 5$	$z = \dfrac{\hat{p} - p}{\sqrt{\dfrac{p \cdot q}{n}}}$

where

    $\hat{p}$ = sample proportion
    n = sample size
    p = population proportion
    $q = 1 - p$

Suppose 60% of the electrical contractors in a region use a particular brand of wire. What is the probability of taking a random sample of size 120 from these electrical contractors and finding that 0.50 or less use that brand of wire? For this problem,

$$p = 0.60 \quad \hat{p} = 0.50 \quad n = 120$$

The z formula yields

$$z = \frac{0.50 - 0.60}{\sqrt{\dfrac{(0.60)(0.40)}{120}}} = \frac{-0.10}{0.0447} = -2.24$$

From Table A.5, the probability corresponding to $z = -2.24$ is 0.4875. For $z < -2.24$ (the tail of the distribution), the answer is $0.5000 - 0.4875 = 0.0125$. Figure 7.7 shows the problem and solution graphically.

Figure 7.7

Graphical Solution to the Electrical Contractor Example

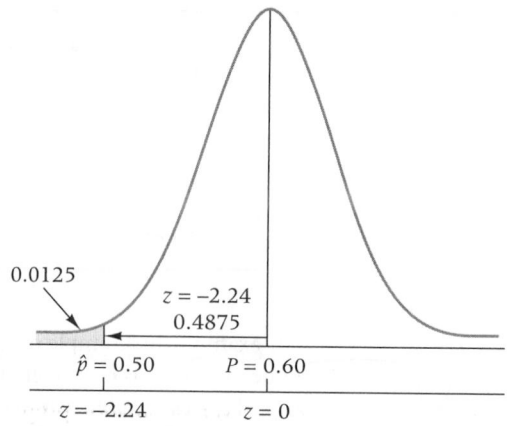

This answer indicates that a researcher would have difficulty (probability of 0.0125) finding that 50% or less of a sample of 120 contractors use a given brand of wire if indeed the population market share for that wire is 0.60. This sample result may actually occur for one of the following reasons: it is a rare chance result, the 0.60 proportion does not hold for this population, or the sampling method was not random.

Demonstration Problem 7.3

If 10% of a population of parts is defective, what is the probability of randomly selecting 80 parts and finding that 12 or more parts are defective?

Solution

Here, $p = 0.10$, $\hat{p} = 12/80 = 0.15$, and $n = 80$. Entering these values in the z formula yields:

$$z = \frac{0.15 - 0.10}{\sqrt{\dfrac{(0.10)(0.90)}{80}}} = \frac{0.05}{0.0335} = 1.49$$

Table A.5 gives a probability of 0.4319 for a z value of 1.49, which is the area between the sample proportion, 0.15, and the population proportion, 0.10. The answer to the question is:

$$P(\hat{p} \geq 0.15) = 0.5000 - 0.4319 = 0.0681$$

Thus, about 6.81% of the time, 12 or more defective parts would appear in a random sample of 80 parts when the population proportion is 0.10. If this result actually occurred, the 10% proportion for population defects would be open to question. The diagram shows the problem graphically.

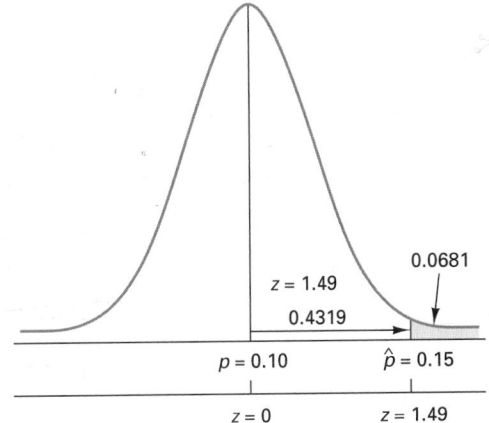

Concept Check

1. For what kind of data would you use the sampling distribution of proportions?

7.3 Problems

7.22 A given population proportion is 0.25. For the given value of n, what is the probability of getting each of the following sample proportions?
  a. $n = 110$ and $\hat{p} \leq 0.21$
  b. $n = 33$ and $\hat{p} > 0.24$
  c. $n = 59$ and $0.24 \leq \hat{p} < 0.27$
  d. $n = 80$ and $\hat{p} > 0.30$
  e. $n = 800$ and $\hat{p} > 0.30$

7.23 A population proportion is 0.58. Suppose a random sample of 660 items is sampled randomly from this population.
  a.   What is the probability that the sample proportion is greater than 0.60?
  b.   What is the probability that the sample proportion is between 0.55 and 0.65?

c. What is the probability that the sample proportion is greater than 0.57?

d. What is the probability that the sample proportion is between 0.53 and 0.56?

e. What is the probability that the sample proportion is less than 0.48?

7.24 Suppose a population proportion is 0.40, and 80% of the time when you draw a random sample from this population you get a sample proportion of 0.35 or more. How large a sample were you taking?

7.25 If a population proportion is 0.28 and if the sample size is 140, 30% of the time the sample proportion will be less than which value if you are taking random samples?

7.26 According to a study by Ipsos-Reid, 40% of Canadians rely on doctors for drug information. Suppose a random sample of 600 Canadians is taken. What is the probability that more than 150 Canadians rely on doctors for drug information?

7.27 The same study mentioned above found that 36% of Canadians rely on pharmacists for drug information. Suppose 200 Canadians are randomly surveyed.

a. What is the probability that fewer than 90 of the Canadians rely on doctors for drug information?

b. What is the probability that more than 100 Canadians rely on doctors for drug information?

c. What is the probability that more than 80 Canadians rely on doctors for drug information?

7.28 The Travel Weekly International Air Transport Association survey asked business travellers about the purpose of their most recent business trip. Nineteen percent responded that it was for an internal company visit. Suppose 950 business travellers are randomly selected.

a. What is the probability that more than 25% of the business travellers said that the reason for their most recent business trip was an internal company visit?

b. What is the probability that between 15% and 20% of the business travellers said that the reason for their most recent business trip was an internal company visit?

c. What is the probability that between 133 and 171 of the business travellers said that the reason for their most recent business trip was an internal company visit?

WHAT IS THE ATTITUDE OF MAQUILADORA WORKERS?

Because of limited resources, limited time, and a large population of workers, most work attitude and cultural studies of maquiladora workers are accomplished through the use of random sampling. To ensure the inclusion of certain groups and in an effort to reduce sampling error, a proportionate stratified sampling technique might be selected. Such a sampling plan could include as strata such things as geographic location of the plant in Mexico, type of industry, size of the plant, number of maquiladora workers at that facility, age of the worker, gender of the worker, and level of responsibility of the worker.

Lists of maquiladora companies and plants can be obtained for use as a company frame for the study. Each company is likely to have a complete list of all workers. These lists could serve as a frame for the sampling of workers. If granted permission to use the lists, the researcher could then identify strata within the lists and randomly sample workers from these lists.

Attitude and culture questions are not easy to formulate in a way that produces valid data. Experts on the measurement of such things should be consulted. However, if questions are asked in a way that produces numerical responses that can be averaged, sample means can be computed. If sample sizes are large enough, the central limit theorem can be invoked, enabling the business researcher to analyze mean sample responses as though they came from normally distributed populations.

Some of the questions asked might require only a Yes or No response. For example, the question: "Are working conditions in a maquiladora plant owned by a Canadian company considerably different from those in a plant owned by an equivalent Mexican company?" requires only a Yes or No response. These responses, when tallied, can be used to compute sample proportions. If the sample sizes are large enough, the business researcher can assume from the central limit theorem that sample proportions come from a normal distribution, which can provide the basis for analysis.

KEY CONSIDERATIONS

Considerable research is reported under the guise of random sampling when, in fact, nonrandom sampling is used. Remember, if nonrandom sampling is used, probability statements about sampling error are not appropriate. Some researchers purport to be using stratified random sampling when they are actually using quota sampling. Others claim to be using systematic random sampling when they are actually using convenience or judgment sampling.

In the process of inferential statistics, researchers use sample results to make conclusions about a population. These conclusions are disseminated to the interested public. The public often assumes that sample results truly reflect the state of the population. If the sample does not reflect the population because questionable sampling practices were used, it could be argued that unethical research behaviour occurred. Valid representative sampling is not an easy task. Researchers and statisticians should exercise extreme caution in taking samples to be sure the results obtained reflect the conditions in the population as nearly as possible.

The central limit theorem is based on large samples unless the population is normally distributed. In analyzing small-sample data, we cannot assume a sample mean is from a normal distribution unless the population can be shown with some confidence to be normally distributed. Using the normal distribution to analyze sample proportions can also be problematic if sample sizes are smaller than those recommended by the experts.

Why Statistics Is Relevant

Modern businesses, political institutions, and social institutions constantly require information that is reliable and can be gathered quickly. Is there a market for the new product that a firm is considering? Are our customers satisfied with our service? What issues are important to voters? Have the issues changed since we surveyed them last month? How many people live below the poverty line? How long will a computer last if it is used 24/7? How many beds should a maternity ward in a hospital have? We cannot collect information on, for example, every voter, every consumer, or every computer to answer these questions. Collecting information on everyone or every object can be expensive, time consuming, and in many cases not physically feasible. This necessarily means that we need to confine our information collection to a sample. The problem then is how do we know if the sample represents the population? This is where statistics comes in and provides us with a means of obtaining reliable results from just a sample, which can be a small proportion of the population. Without statistics, many business decisions (as well as decisions in many other fields) would be mostly guesswork.

SUMMARY

1. For much business research, successfully conducting a census is virtually impossible, and the sample is a feasible alternative. Other reasons for sampling are cost reduction, potential for broadening the scope of the study, and loss reduction when the testing process destroys the product. To take a sample, a population must be identified. Often the researcher cannot obtain an exact roster or list of the population and so must find some way to identify the population as closely as possible. The final list or directory used to represent the population and from which the sample is drawn is called the frame.

2. The two main types of sampling are random and nonrandom. Random sampling occurs when each unit of the population has the same probability of being selected for the sample. Nonrandom sampling is any sampling that is not random.

3. The four main types of random sampling are simple random sampling, stratified sampling, systematic sampling, and cluster or area sampling. In *simple random sampling*, every unit of the population is numbered. A table of random numbers or a random number generator is used to select n units from the population for the sample. *Stratified random sampling* uses the researcher's prior knowledge of the population to stratify the population into subgroups. Each subgroup is internally homogeneous but different from the others. Stratified random sampling is an attempt to reduce sampling error and ensure that at least some items of each of the subgroups appear in the sample. After the strata are identified, units can be sampled randomly from each stratum. If the proportions of units selected from each subgroup for the sample are the same as the proportions of the subgroups in the population, the process is called proportionate stratified sampling. If not, it is called disproportionate stratified sampling. With *systematic sampling*, every kth item of the population is sampled until n units have been selected. Systematic sampling is used because of its convenience and ease of administration. *Cluster or area sampling* involves subdividing the population into nonoverlapping clusters or areas. Each cluster or area is a microcosm of the population and is usually heterogeneous within. Individual units are then selected randomly from the clusters or areas to get the final sample. Cluster or area sampling is usually done to reduce costs. If a second set of clusters or areas is selected from the first set, the method is called two-stage sampling.

4. There are four major types of nonrandom sampling: convenience, judgment, quota, and snowball. In *convenience sampling*, the researcher selects units from the population to be in the sample for convenience. In *judgment sampling*, units are selected according to the judgment of the researcher. *Quota sampling* is similar to stratified sampling, with the researcher identifying subclasses or strata. However, the researcher selects units from each stratum by some nonrandom technique until a specified quota from each stratum is filled. With *snowball sampling*, the researcher obtains additional sample members by asking current sample members for referral information.

5. Sampling error occurs because we select only a proportion (sample) from a larger population. Random sampling methods allow us to estimate the size of the sampling error. Nonsampling errors are all other research and analysis errors that occur in a study. They include recording errors, input errors, missing data, and incorrect definition of the frame.

6. The central limit theorem states that, if a population is normally distributed, the sample means for samples taken from that population are also normally distributed regardless of sample size. The central limit theorem also says that if the sample sizes are large ($n \geq 30$), the sample mean is approximately normally distributed regardless of the distribution shape of the population. This theorem is extremely useful because it enables researchers to analyze sample data by using the normal distribution for virtually any type of study in which means are an appropriate statistic, as long as the sample size is large enough. The central limit theorem states that sample proportions are normally distributed for large sample sizes.

KEY TERMS

central limit theorem
cluster (or area) sampling
convenience sampling
disproportionate stratified
 random sampling
finite correction factor
frame

judgment sampling
nonrandom sampling
nonrandom sampling
 techniques
nonsampling errors
proportionate stratified
 random sampling

quota sampling
random sampling
sample proportion
sampling error
simple random sampling
snowball sampling
standard error of the mean

standard error of the
 proportion
stratified random sampling
systematic sampling
two-stage sampling

FORMULAS

Determining the value of k

$$k = \frac{N}{n}$$

Sample proportion

$$\hat{p} = \frac{x}{n}$$

z formula for sample means

$$z = \frac{\bar{x} - \mu}{\frac{\sigma}{\sqrt{n}}}$$

z formula for sample proportions

$$z = \frac{\hat{p} - p}{\sqrt{\frac{p \cdot q}{n}}}$$

z formula for sample means when there is a finite population

$$z = \frac{\bar{x} - \mu}{\frac{\sigma}{\sqrt{n}} \sqrt{\frac{N - n}{N - 1}}}$$

SUPPLEMENTARY PROBLEMS

Calculating the Statistics

7.29   The mean of a population is 76 and the standard deviation is 14. The shape of the population is unknown. Determine the probability of each of the following occurring from this population.
   a.   A random sample of size 35 yielding a sample mean of 79 or more
   b.   A random sample of size 140 yielding a sample mean of between 74 and 77
   c.   A random sample of size 219 yielding a sample mean of less than 76.5

7.30   Forty-six percent of a population possesses a particular characteristic. Random samples are taken from this population. Determine the probability of each of the following occurrences.
   a.   The sample size is 60 and the sample proportion is between 0.41 and 0.53.
   b.   The sample size is 458 and the sample proportion is less than 0.40.
   c.   The sample size is 1,350 and the sample proportion is greater than 0.49.

Testing Your Understanding

7.31   Suppose the age distribution in a city is as follows.

Under 18	22%
18–25	18%
26–50	36%
51–65	10%
Over 65	14%

A researcher is conducting proportionate stratified random sampling with a sample size of 250. Approximately how many people should he sample from each stratum?

7.32   Candidate Jones believes he will receive 0.55 of the total votes cast in his riding. However, in an attempt to validate this figure, his pollster contacts a random sample of 600 registered voters in the riding. The poll results show that 298 of the voters say they are committed to voting for him. If he actually has 0.55 of the total vote, what is the probability of getting a sample proportion this small or smaller? Do you think he actually has 55% of the vote? Why or why not?

7.33   Determine a possible frame for conducting random sampling in each of the following studies.
   a.   The average amount of overtime per week for production workers in a plastics company in Manitoba
   b.   The average number of employees in all Safeway supermarkets in British Columbia
   c.   A survey of commercial lobster catchers in Newfoundland

7.34   A particular automobile costs an average of $17,755 in British Columbia. The standard deviation of prices is $650. Suppose a random sample of 30 dealerships in Vancouver and Victoria is taken, and their managers are asked what they charge for this automobile. What is the probability of getting a sample average cost of less than $17,500? Assume

SUPPLEMENTARY PROBLEMS (continued)

that only 120 dealerships in all of British Columbia sell this automobile.

7.35 A company has 1,250 employees, and you want to take a simple random sample of $n = 60$ employees. Explain how you would go about selecting this sample by using the table of random numbers. Are there numbers that you cannot use? Explain.

7.36 Suppose the average client charge per hour for out-of-court work by lawyers in Saskatchewan is $125. Suppose further that a random telephone sample of 32 lawyers in Saskatchewan is taken and that the sample average charge per hour for out-of-court work is $110. If the population variance is $525, what is the probability of getting a sample mean of $110 or larger? What is the probability of getting a sample mean larger than $135 per hour? What is the probability of getting a sample mean of between $120 and $130 per hour?

7.37 A survey of 2,645 consumers by DDB Needham Worldwide showed that how a company handles a crisis when at fault is one of the top influences in consumer buying decisions, with 73% claiming it is an influence. Quality of product was the number one influence, with 96% of consumers stating that quality influences their buying decisions. How a company handles complaints was number two, with 85% of consumers reporting it as an influence in their buying decisions. Suppose a random sample of 1,100 consumers is taken and each is asked which of these three factors influence their buying decisions.
   a. What is the probability that more than 810 consumers claim that how a company handles a crisis when at fault is an influence in their buying decisions?
   b. What is the probability that fewer than 1,030 consumers claim that quality of product is an influence in their buying decisions?
   c. What is the probability that between 82% and 84% of consumers claim that how a company handles complaints is an influence in their buying decisions?

7.38 Suppose you are sending out questionnaires to a randomly selected sample of 100 managers. The frame for this study is the membership list of the Board of Trade. The questionnaire contains demographic questions about the company and its top

manager. In addition, it asks questions about the manager's leadership style. Research assistants are to score and enter the responses into the computer as soon as they are received. You are to conduct a statistical analysis of the data. Name and describe four nonsampling errors that could occur in this study.

7.39 A researcher is conducting a study of Loblaw supermarkets across the country. How can she use cluster or area sampling to take a random sample of employees of this firm?

7.40 A directory of personal computer retail outlets in Canada contains 1,208 alphabetized entries. Explain how systematic sampling could be used to select a sample of 30 outlets.

7.41 In an effort to cut costs and improve profits, many companies have been turning to outsourcing. In fact, according to *Purchasing* magazine, 54% of companies surveyed outsourced some part of their manufacturing process in the past two to three years. Suppose 565 of these companies are contacted.
   a. What is the probability that 339 or more companies outsourced some part of their manufacturing process in the past two to three years?
   b. What is the probability that 288 or more companies outsourced some part of their manufacturing process in the past two to three years?
   c. What is the probability that 50% or less of these companies outsourced some part of their manufacturing process in the past two to three years?

7.42 The average cost of a one-bedroom apartment in a town is $550 per month. What is the probability of randomly selecting a sample of 50 one-bedroom apartments in this town and getting a sample mean of less than $530 if the population standard deviation is $100?

7.43 According the International Atomic Energy Agency, electricity per-capita consumption in Canada is 16,939 kwh in 2002. A random sample of 51 households is monitored for one year to determine electricity usage. If the population standard deviation of annual usage is 3,500 kwh, what is the probability that the sample mean will be each of the following?

a. More than 18,000 kwh
b. More than 17,500 kwh
c. Between 17,000 kwh and 18,000 kwh
d. Less than 16,000 kwh
e. Less than 15,000 kwh

7.44 Use Table A.1 to select 20 three-digit random numbers. Did any of the numbers occur more than once? How is it possible for a number to occur more than once? Make a stem and leaf plot of the numbers with the stem being the left digit. Do the numbers seem to be equally distributed, or are they bunched together?

7.45 Direct marketing companies are turning to the Internet for new opportunities. A recent study by Gruppo, Levey, & Co. showed that 73% of all direct marketers conduct transactions on the Internet. Suppose a random sample of 300 direct marketing companies is taken.
   a. What is the probability that between 210 and 234 (inclusive) direct marketing companies are turning to the Internet for new opportunities?
   b. What is the probability that 78% or more of direct marketing companies are turning to the Internet for new opportunities?
   c. Suppose a random sample of 800 direct marketing companies is taken. Now what is the probability that 78% or more are turning to the Internet for new opportunities? How does this answer differ from the answer in part (b)? Why do the answers differ?

7.46 Suppose that 20% of all people 16 years of age or older do volunteer work. Further suppose that women volunteer slightly more than men, with 22% of women volunteering and 19% of men volunteering. What is the probability of randomly sampling 140 women 16 years of age or older and getting 35 or more who do volunteer work? What is the probability of getting 21 or fewer from this group? Suppose a sample of 300 men and women 16 years of age or older is selected randomly from the population. What is the probability that the sample proportion of those who do volunteer work is between 18% and 25%?

7.47 Suppose you work for a large firm that has 20,000 employees. The CEO calls you in and asks you to determine employee attitudes toward the company. She is willing to commit $100,000 to this project. What are the advantages of taking a sample versus conducting a census? What are the tradeoffs?

7.48 In a particular area in the Prairies, an estimated 75% of the homes use heating oil as the principal heating fuel during the winter. A random telephone survey of 150 homes is taken in an attempt to determine whether this figure is correct. Suppose 120 of the 150 homes surveyed use heating oil as the principal heating fuel. What is the probability of getting a sample proportion this large or larger if the population estimate is true?

7.49 According to the government of Manitoba, the average hourly wages are as follows: Alberta: $22.02, Ontario: $20.18, British Columbia: $20.05. Suppose 40 workers are selected randomly from across Alberta and asked what their hourly wage is. What is the probability that the sample average will be between $21 and $22? Suppose 35 manufacturing workers are selected randomly from across Ontario. What is the probability that the sample average will exceed $23? Suppose 50 manufacturing workers are selected randomly from across British Columbia. What is the probability that the sample average will be less than $18.90? Assume that in all three provinces, the standard deviation of hourly wages is $3.

7.50 Give a variable that could be used to stratify the population for each of the following studies. List at least four subcategories for each variable.
   a. A political party wants to conduct a poll prior to an election for the Premier of New Brunswick.
   b. A soft drink company wants to take a sample of soft drink purchases in an effort to estimate market share.
   c. A retail outlet wants to interview customers over a one-week period.
   d. An eyeglasses manufacturer and retailer wants to determine the demand for prescription eyeglasses in its marketing region.

7.51 A survey shows that a typical business traveller spends an average of $280 per day in Toronto. This cost includes hotel, meals, car rental, and incidentals. A survey of 60 randomly selected business travellers who have been to Toronto on business recently is taken. For the population mean of $280 per day, what is the probability of getting a sample average of more than $270 per day if the population standard deviation is $50?

ANALYZING THE DATABASES

see www.wiley.com/canada/black

1. Use the Major League Baseball Database. Compute the mean and standard deviation for Revenues. Take a random sample of four of the teams and compute the sample mean of Revenues on this sample. Using techniques presented in this chapter, determine the probability of getting a mean this large or larger from the population. Note that the population contains only 30 teams. Work this problem with and without the finite correction factor. Compare the results and discuss the differences in answers.

2. Use the Canadian Hospitals Database to calculate the mean and standard deviation of Failure to Rescue. Assume that these figures are true for the population of hospitals in municipalities in Canada. Suppose a random sample of 36 is taken from hospitals in municipalities in Canada. What is the probability that the sample mean of Failure to Rescue is less than 180? What is the probability that the sample mean of Failure to Rescue is between 200 and 240? What is the probability that the sample mean is between 180 and 200?

CASE

Shell Attempts to Return to Premiere Status

The Shell Oil Company, which began in about 1912, had been for decades a household name as a quality oil company in the U.S. However, by the late 1970s much of its prestige as a premiere company had disappeared. How could Shell regain its high status?

In the 1990s, Shell undertook an extensive research effort to find out what it needed to do to improve its image. As a first step, Shell hired Responsive Research and the Opinion Research Corporation to conduct a series of focus groups and personal interviews among various segments of the population. Included in these were youths, minorities, residents in neighbourhoods near Shell plants, legislators, academics, and present and past employees of Shell. The researchers learned that people believe that top companies are integral parts of the communities in which the companies are located rather than separate entities. These studies and others led to the development of materials that Shell used to explain their core values to the general public.

Next, PERT Survey Research ran a large quantitative study to determine which values were best received by the target audience. Social issues emerged as the theme with the most support. During the next few months, the advertising agency of Ogilvy & Mather, hired by Shell, developed several campaigns with social themes. Two market research companies were hired to evaluate the receptiveness of the various campaigns. The result was the "Count on Shell" campaign, which featured safety messages with useful information about what to do in various dangerous situations.

A public Count on Shell campaign was launched in February 1998 and met with considerable success: the ability to recall Shell advertising jumped from 20% to 32% among opinion influencers; more than 1 million copies of Shell's free safety brochures were distributed and activity on Shell's Internet Count on Shell site remains extremely strong. By promoting itself as a reliable company that cares, Shell seems to be regaining its premiere status.

Today, Shell continues its efforts to be community friendly. United Way of America announced Shell Oil Company as one of its three Spirit of America Summit Award winners for 2002 and commended the company for its outstanding volunteer and corporate contributions programs. Several Shell employees were recognized by the Houston Minority Business Council for their continued efforts to provide windows of opportunity for minority business owners and strengthen Shell's commitment to supplier diversity. Shell employees and retirees give back to their communities through such Shell-sponsored activities as America's WETLAND campaign, Shell's Workforce Development Initiative, and other community/quality-of-life and environmental projects. Shell is also a strong supporter of the Points of Light Foundation, which strives to engage people more effectively in volunteer community service.

Discussion

1. Suppose you were asked to develop a sampling plan to determine what a premiere company is to the general public. What sampling plan would you use? What is the target population? What would you use for a frame? Which of the four types of random sampling discussed in this chapter would you use? Could you use a combination of two or more of the types (two-stage sampling)? If so, how?

2. It appears that at least one of the research companies hired by Shell used some stratification in their sampling. What are some of the variables on which they are stratified? If you were truly interested in ascertaining opinions from a variety of segments of the population with regard to

opinions on premiere companies or about Shell, what strata might make sense? Name at least five and justify why you would include them.

3. Suppose that in 1979 only 12% of the Canadian general adult public believed that Shell was a premiere company. Suppose further that you randomly selected 350 people from the Canadian general adult public this year and 25% said that Shell was a premiere company. If only 12% of the Canadian general adult public still believes that Shell is a premiere company, how likely is it that the 25% figure is a chance result in sampling 350 people? *Hint:* Use the techniques in this chapter to determine the probability of the 25% figure occurring by chance.

4. PERT Survey Research conducted quantitative surveys in an effort to measure the effectiveness of various campaigns. Suppose they used a 1-to-5 scale, where 1 denotes that the campaign is not effective at all, 5 denotes that the campaign is extremely effective, and 2, 3, and 4 fall in between on an interval scale. Suppose also that a particular campaign received an average of 1.8 on the scale with a standard deviation of 0.7 early in the tests. Later, after the campaign had been critiqued and improved, a survey of 35 people was taken and a sample mean of 2.0 was recorded. What is the probability of this sample mean or greater occurring if the actual population mean is still just 1.8? Based on this probability, do you think that a sample mean of 2.0 is just a chance fluctuation on the 1.8 population mean, or do you think that perhaps it indicates the population mean is now greater than 1.8? Support your conclusion. Suppose a sample mean of 2.5 is attained. What is the likelihood of this result occurring by chance when the population mean is 1.8? Suppose this increase actually happens after the campaign has been improved. What does it mean?

References

Adapted from "Count on It," *American Demographics,* March 1999, p. 60; "Shell in the U.S.," 2002, available at <http://www.shellus.com/> and from Shell's website <http://www.Shell.com>.

USING THE COMPUTER

Excel

- Random numbers can be generated from Excel for several different distributions, including the binomial distribution, the Poisson distribution, the uniform distribution, and the normal distribution. To generate random numbers from a particular distribution, begin by selecting the **Data** tab on the Excel worksheet. From the **Analysis** panel at the right top of the **Data** tab worksheet, click on **Data Analysis**. If your Excel worksheet does not show the **Data Analysis** option, then you can load it as an add-in following directions given in Chapter 2. From the **Data Analysis** pulldown menu, select **Random Number Generation**.

- In the **Random Number Generation** dialogue box, enter the number of columns of values you want to produce into **Number of Variables**.
- Next, enter the number of data points to be generated in each column into **Number of Random Numbers**.
- The third line of the dialogue box, **Distribution**, contains the choices of distributions. Select from which one of the following distributions you want to generate random data: **discrete**, **uniform**, **normal**, **Bernoulli**, **binomial**, **Poisson**, and **patterned**.
- The options and required responses in the **Random Number Generation** dialogue box will change with the chosen distribution.

Unit III

MAKING INFERENCES ABOUT POPULATION PARAMETERS

The ability to estimate population parameters or to test hypotheses about population parameters using sample statistics is one of the main applications of statistics in improving and leveraging decision making in business. Whether estimating parameters or testing hypotheses about parameters, the inferential process consists of taking a random sample from a group or body (the population), analyzing data from the sample, and reaching conclusions about the population using the sample data, as shown in Figure 1.2 of Chapter 1.

One widely used technique for estimating population measures (parameters) from a sample using statistics is the confidence interval. Confidence interval estimation is generally reserved for instances where a business researcher does not know what the population value is or does not have a very clear idea of it. For example, what is the mean dollar amount spent by families per month at the movies including concession expenditures, or what proportion of workers telecommute at least one day per week? Confidence intervals can be used to estimate these values and many other useful and interesting population parameters, including means, proportions, and variances in the business world.

Sometimes a business analyst already knows the value of a population parameter or has a good idea, but would like to test to determine if the value has changed, if the value applies in other situations, or if the value is what other researchers say it is. In such cases, business researchers use hypothesis tests. In the hypothesis testing process, the known parameter is assumed to be true, data are gathered from random samples taken from the population, and the resulting data are analyzed to determine if the parameter value is still true or has changed in some way. For example, does the average worker still work 40 hours per week? Are 65% of all workers unhappy with their job? As with confidence intervals, hypothesis testing can be used to test hypotheses about means, proportions, variances, and other parameters.

Unit III of this textbook, from Chapter 8 through Chapter 11, contains a cadre of estimation and hypotheses testing techniques organized by usage and number of samples. In Chapter 8 and Chapter 10, we present confidence interval techniques for the estimation of parameters. In Chapter 8, we introduce the concept of a confidence interval and focus on one-sample analyses, while the confidence intervals in Chapter 10 are used for two-sample analyses. In Chapter 9, we introduce the concept of hypothesis testing and present one-sample hypothesis tests. Chapter 10 contains hypothesis tests for two samples, while Chapter 11 contains hypothesis tests for three or more samples.

Because there is a plethora of confidence interval and hypothesis testing techniques presented in Unit III, it is easy to lose the big picture of when to use what technique. To assist you in sorting out these techniques, a taxonomy of techniques has been created and is presented in a tree diagram both here and inside the front cover for your convenience and consideration. Note that in determining which technique to use, one should consider several key questions:

1. Are you estimating (using a confidence interval) or testing (using a hypothesis test)?
2. How many samples are you analyzing?
3. Are you analyzing means, proportions, or variances?
4. If you are analyzing means, is (are) the standard deviation(s) or variance(s) known or not?
5. If you are analyzing means from two samples, are the samples independent or related?
6. If you are analyzing three or more samples, are you studying one or two independent variables and is there a blocking variable?

Figure III-I

Tree Diagram (Confidence Interval) Taxonomy of Inferential Techniques

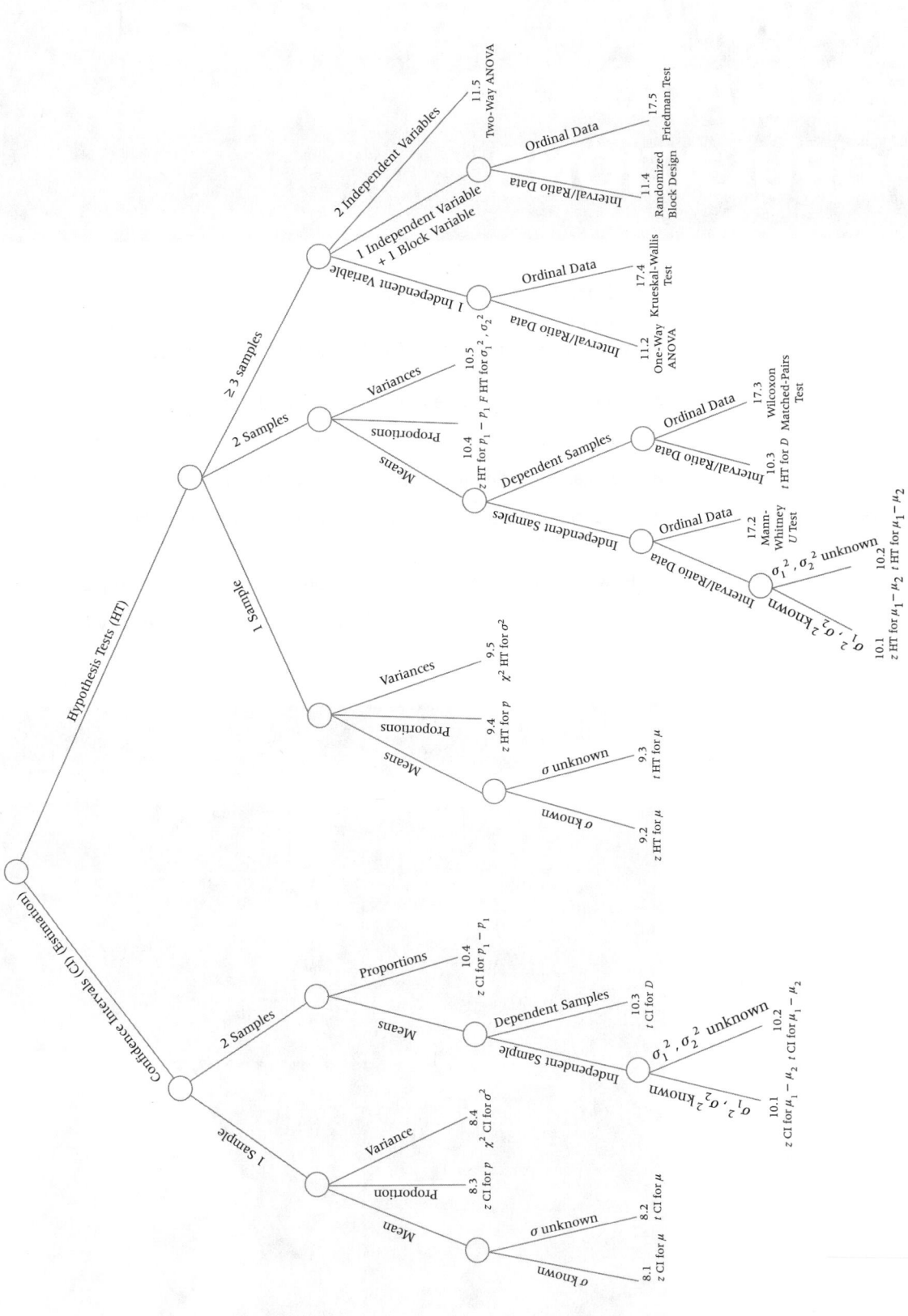

STATISTICAL INFERENCE: ESTIMATION FOR SINGLE POPULATIONS

Learning Objectives

The overall learning objective of Chapter 8 is to understand estimating parameters of single populations. The key questions of the chapter are:

1. What is the difference between point and interval estimation?

2. How can we estimate a population mean from a sample mean when σ is known?

3. How can we estimate a population mean from a sample mean when σ is unknown?

4. In terms of proportions, how can we estimate a population proportion from a sample proportion?

5. How can we estimate the population variance from a sample variance?

6. How can we estimate the minimum sample size necessary to achieve given statistical goals?

Getty Images

COMPENSATION FOR PURCHASING MANAGERS

What are purchasing managers and what types of compensation packages do they receive? In an effort to answer these questions and others, a questionnaire survey of 1,839 purchasing managers who were readers of *Purchasing* magazine or were respondents to their website was taken recently. Demographic questions about gender, age, years' experience, title, industry, company annual sales, location, and others were asked along with such compensation measures as annual salary, amount of bonus, and relationship of bonus to financial goals and quality.

The results of the survey indicated that the mean age of a purchasing manager is 46.2 years, and the mean years of experience in the field is 16. Sixty-five percent of purchasing managers are male, and 35% are female. Seventy-three percent of all respondents have a university degree or a certificate. University graduates hold the highest-paying jobs, work for the biggest companies, and hold the highest-ranking purchasing positions. Twenty-four percent of all the respondents are designated as a Certified Purchasing Manager (CPM).

Purchasing manager compensation varies with position, size of the company, industry, and company location. The mean salary for a purchasing manager is $78,500. However, salary varies according to title, with Buyers receiving a mean of $47,100 and Supplier Vice Presidents earning $159,600. Generally speaking, purchasing managers whose company's annual purchasing budget is greater than $25 million receive higher than average compensation. Respondents without supervisory responsibilities receive a less than average annual salary, whereas those with supervisory responsibilities tend to receive a higher than average annual salary. Industries with the highest purchasing salaries include computers and related equipment with a mean of $94,500 and communications equipment with a mean of $88,700. Sixty percent of all survey respondents receive bonuses as a part of their annual compensation, while 16% receive stock options.

Based on sample sizes as small as 25, mean annual salaries are broken down by U.S. region and Canada. It is estimated that the mean annual salary for a purchasing manager in Canada is $83,400. In the United States, the highest reported mean salary is in the Mid-Atlantic region with a mean of $80,900, and the lowest is in the Plains states with a mean figure of $74,300.

Managerial and Statistical Questions

1. Can the mean national salary for a purchasing manager be estimated using sample data such as that reported in this study? If so, how much error is involved and how much confidence can we have in it?

2. The study reported that the mean age of a respondent is 46.2 years and that, on average, a purchasing manager has 16 years of experience. How can these sample figures be used to estimate a mean from the population? For example, is the population mean age for purchasing managers also 46.2 years or is it different? If the population mean years of experience is estimated using such a study, what is the error of the estimate?

3. This Decision Dilemma reports that 73% of the responding purchasing managers have a university degree or certificate. Does this figure hold for all purchasing managers? Are 65% of all purchasing managers male as reported in this study? How can population proportions be estimated using sample data? How much error is involved? How confident can decision makers be in the results?

4. When survey data are broken down by U.S. region and Canada, the sample size for each subgroup is as low as 25 respondents. Does sample size affect the results of the study? If the study reports that the mean salary for a Canadian purchasing manager is $83,400 based on 25 respondents, is that information less valid than the overall mean salary of $78,500 reported by 1,839 respondents? How do business decision makers discern between study results when sample sizes vary?

Source: Adapted from Susan Avery, "2005 Salary Study: Applause Please," *Purchasing* (December 8, 2005), 134:20, pp. 29–33.

Unit III of this text (Chapters 8 to 11) presents, discusses, and applies various statistical techniques for making inferential estimations and hypothesis tests to enhance decision making in business. Figure III-l displays a Tree Diagram Taxonomy of these techniques, organizing them by usage, sample size, and level of data. Chapter 8 contains the portion of these techniques that can be used for estimating a mean, a proportion, or a variance for a population with a single sample. Displayed in Figure 8.1 is the leftmost branch of the Tree Diagram Taxonomy, presented in Figure III-l of Unit III. This branch of the tree contains all statistical techniques for constructing confidence intervals from one-sample data presented in this text. Note that at the bottom of each tree branch in Figure 8.1 the title of the statistical technique along with its respective section number is given for ease of identification and use. In Chapter 8, techniques are presented to allow a business researcher to estimate a population mean, proportion, or variance by

Figure 8.1

Chapter 8 Branch of the Tree Diagram Taxonomy of Inferential Techniques

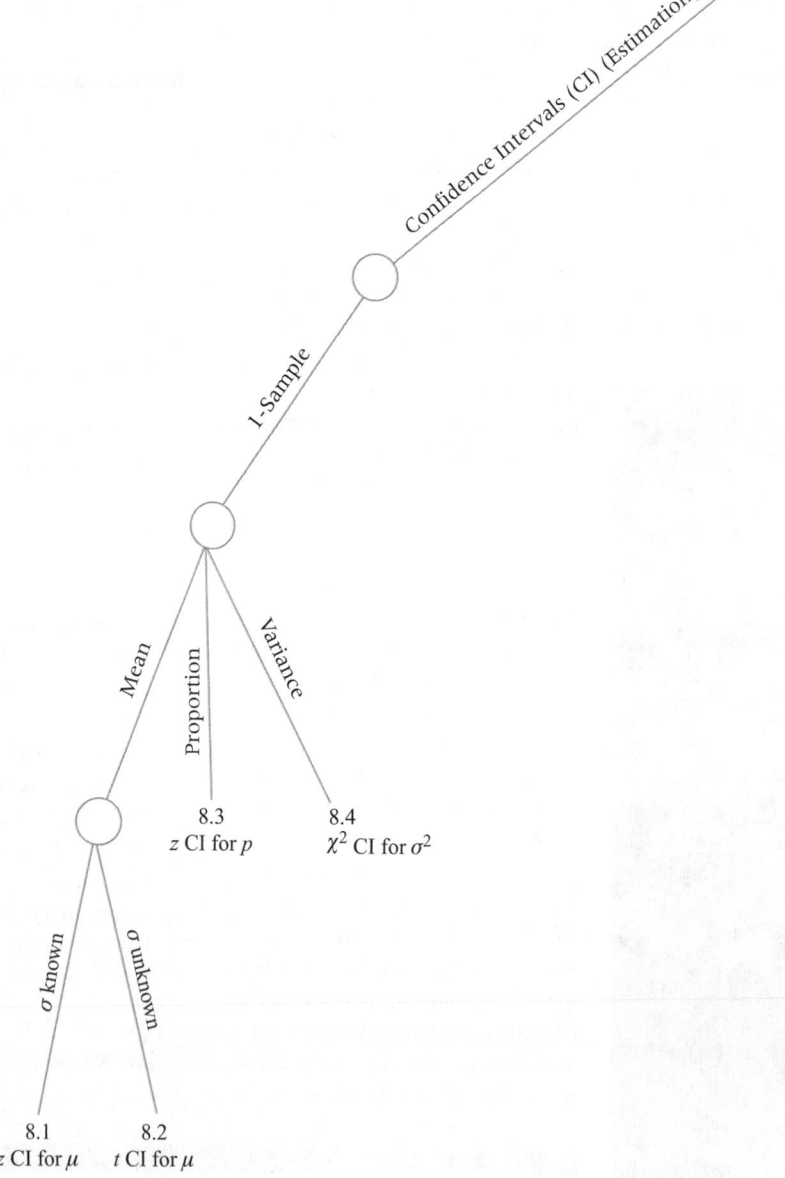

taking a sample from the population, analyzing the data from the sample, and projecting the resulting statistics back onto the population. Because it is often extremely difficult to obtain and analyze population data for a variety of reasons mentioned in Chapter 7, the importance of the ability to estimate population parameters from sample statistics cannot be underestimated. If a business researcher is estimating a population mean and the population standard deviation is known, then he will use the z confidence interval for μ contained in Section 8.1. If the population standard deviation is unknown and therefore the researcher is using the sample standard deviation, then the appropriate technique is the t confidence interval for μ contained in Section 8.2. If another business researcher is estimating a population proportion, then she will use the z confidence interval for p presented in Section 8.3. If the researcher wants to estimate a population variance with a single sample, then she will use the χ^2 confidence interval for σ^2 presented in Section 8.4. Section 8.5 contains techniques for determining how large a sample to take in order to ensure a given level of confidence within a targeted level of error.

8.1 ESTIMATING THE POPULATION MEAN USING THE z STATISTIC (σ KNOWN)

On many occasions, estimating the population mean is useful in business research. For example, the manager of human resources in a company might want to estimate the average number of days of work an employee misses per year because of illness. If the firm has thousands of employees, direct calculation of a population mean such as this may be practically impossible. Instead, a random sample of employees can be taken, and the sample mean number of sick days can be used to estimate the population mean. Suppose another company develops a new process for prolonging the shelf life of a loaf of bread. The company wants to be able to date each loaf for freshness, but company officials do not know exactly how long the bread will stay fresh. By taking a random sample and determining the sample mean shelf life, they can estimate the average shelf life for the population of bread.

As the cell phone industry matures, a cell phone company is rethinking its pricing structure. Users appear to be spending more time on the phone and are shopping around for the best deals. To plan better, the company wants to ascertain the average number of minutes of time used per month by each of its residential users but does not have the resources available to examine all monthly bills and extract the information. The company decides to take a sample of customer bills and estimate the population mean from sample data. A company researcher takes a random sample of 85 bills for a recent month and from these bills computes a sample mean of 510 minutes. This sample mean, which is a statistic, is used to estimate the population mean, which is a parameter. If the company uses the sample mean of 510 minutes as an estimate for the population mean, then the sample mean is used as a *point estimate.*

A **point estimate** is *a statistic taken from a sample that is used to estimate a population parameter.* Note that a point estimate is only as good as the representativeness of its sample. If other random samples are taken from the population, the point estimates derived from those samples are likely to vary. Because of variation in sample statistics, estimating a population parameter with an interval estimate is often preferable to using a point estimate. An **interval estimate** (confidence interval) is *a range of values within which the analyst can declare, with some confidence, that the population parameter lies.* How are confidence intervals constructed?

As a result of the central limit theorem, the following z formula for sample means can be used if the population standard deviation is known when sample sizes are large, regardless of the shape of the population distribution, or for smaller sizes if the population is normally distributed:

$$z = \frac{\bar{x} - \mu}{\frac{\sigma}{\sqrt{n}}}$$

Rearranging this formula algebraically to solve for μ gives

$$\mu = \bar{x} - z\frac{\sigma}{\sqrt{n}}$$

Because a sample mean can be greater than or less than the population mean, z can be positive or negative. Thus, the preceding expression takes the following form:

$$\bar{x} \pm z\frac{\sigma}{\sqrt{n}}$$

Rewriting this expression yields the confidence interval formula for estimating μ with large sample sizes if the population standard deviation is known.

$100(1 - \alpha)\%$ Confidence Interval to Estimate μ: σ Known (8.1)

$$\bar{x} \pm z_{\alpha/2}\frac{\sigma}{\sqrt{n}}$$

or

$$\bar{x} - z_{\alpha/2}\frac{\sigma}{\sqrt{n}} \leq \mu \leq \bar{x} + z_{\alpha/2}\frac{\sigma}{\sqrt{n}}$$

where
α = the area under the normal curve outside the confidence interval area
$\alpha/2$ = the area in one end (tail) of the distribution outside the confidence interval

---

Alpha (α) is the area under the normal curve in the tails of the distribution outside the area defined by the confidence interval. We will focus more on α in Chapter 9. Here we use α to locate the z value in constructing the confidence interval, as shown in Figure 8.2. Because the standard normal table is based on areas between a z of 0 and $z_{\alpha/2}$, the table z value is found by locating the area of $0.5000 - \alpha/2$, which is the part of the normal curve between the middle of the curve and one of the tails. Another way to locate this z value is to change the confidence level from percentage to proportion, divide it in half, and go to the table with this value. The results are the same.

The confidence interval formula 8.1 yields a range (interval) within which we feel with some confidence the population mean is located. It is not certain that the population mean is in the interval unless we have a 100% confidence interval that is infinitely wide. If we want to construct a 95% confidence interval, the level of confidence is 95% or 0.95. If 100 such intervals are constructed by taking random samples from the population, it is likely that 95 of the intervals would include the population mean and 5 would not.

As an example, in the cell phone company problem of estimating the population mean number of minutes called per residential user per month, from the sample of 85 bills

Figure 8.2

z Scores for Confidence Intervals in Relation to α

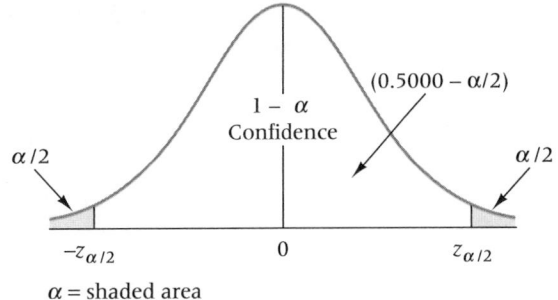

it was determined that the sample mean is 510 minutes. Using this sample mean, a confidence interval can be calculated within which the researcher is relatively confident the actual population mean is located. To make this calculation using formula 8.1, the value of the population standard deviation and the value of z (in addition to the sample mean, 510, and the sample size, 85) must be known. Suppose past history and similar studies indicate that the population standard deviation is 46 minutes.

The value of z is driven by the level of confidence. An interval with 100% confidence is so wide that it is meaningless. Some of the more common levels of confidence used by business researchers are 90%, 95%, 98%, and 99%. Why would a business researcher not just select the highest confidence and always use that level? The reason is that tradeoffs between sample size, interval width, and level of confidence must be considered. For example, as the level of confidence is increased, the interval gets wider, provided the sample size and standard deviation remain constant.

For the cell phone problem, suppose the business researcher decided on a 95% confidence interval for the results. Figure 8.3 shows a normal distribution of sample means about the population mean. When using a 95% level of confidence, the researcher selects an interval centred on μ within which 95% of all sample mean values will fall and then uses the width of that interval to create an interval around the *sample mean* within which he has some confidence the population mean will fall.

Figure 8.3

Distribution of Sample Means for 95% Confidence

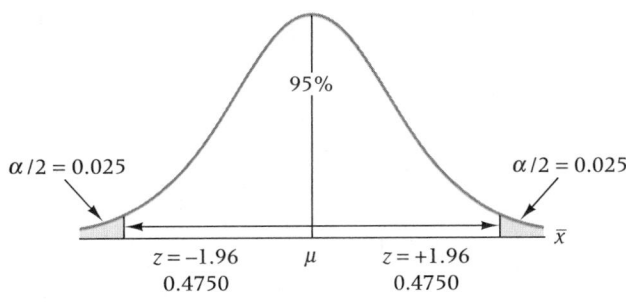

For 95% confidence, $\alpha = 0.05$ and $\alpha/2 = 0.025$. The value of $z_{\alpha/2}$ or $z_{0.025}$ is found by looking in the standard normal table under $0.5000 - 0.0250 = 0.4750$. This area in the table is associated with a z value of 1.96. The table z value can be located in another way. Because the distribution is symmetric and the intervals are equal on each side of the population mean, ½(95%), or 0.4750, of the area is on each side of the mean. Table A.5 yields a z value of 1.96 for this portion of the normal curve. Thus, the z value for a 95% confidence interval is always 1.96. In other words, of all the possible $\bar{x}$ values along the horizontal axis of the diagram, 95% of them should be within a z score of 1.96 on either side of the population mean.

The business researcher can now complete the cell phone problem. To determine a 95% confidence interval for $\bar{x} = 510$, $\sigma = 46$, $n = 85$, and $z = 1.96$, the researcher estimates the average monthly call length by including the value of z in formula 8.1:

$$510 - 1.96\frac{46}{\sqrt{85}} \leq \mu \leq 510 + 1.96\frac{46}{\sqrt{85}}$$

$$510 - 9.78 \leq \mu \leq 510 + 9.78$$

$$500.22 \leq \mu \leq 519.78$$

POINTS OF INTEREST
It is important to understand what the confidence interval actually means. See Figure 8.4 for a graphical representation.

The confidence interval is constructed from the point estimate, which in this problem is 510 minutes, and the error of this estimate (also referred to as the **error of the interval**), which is ±9.78 minutes. The resulting confidence interval is $500.22 < \mu < 519.78$. The cell phone company researcher is 95% confident that the average length of calls for the population is between 500.22 and 519.78 minutes per month.

What does being 95% confident that the population mean is in an interval actually indicate? It indicates that, if the company researcher were to randomly select 100 samples of 85 bills and use the results of each sample to construct a 95% confidence interval, approximately 95 of the 100 intervals would contain the population mean. It also indicates that 5% of the intervals would not contain the population mean. The company researcher is likely to take only a single sample and compute the confidence interval from that sample information. That interval either contains the population mean or it does not. Figure 8.4 depicts the meaning of a 95% confidence interval for the mean. Note that if 20 random samples are taken from the population, 19 of the 20 are likely to contain the population mean if a 95% confidence interval is used (19/20 = 95%). If a 90% confidence interval is constructed, only 18 of the 20 intervals are likely to contain the population mean.

Figure 8.4

Twenty 95% Confidence Intervals of μ

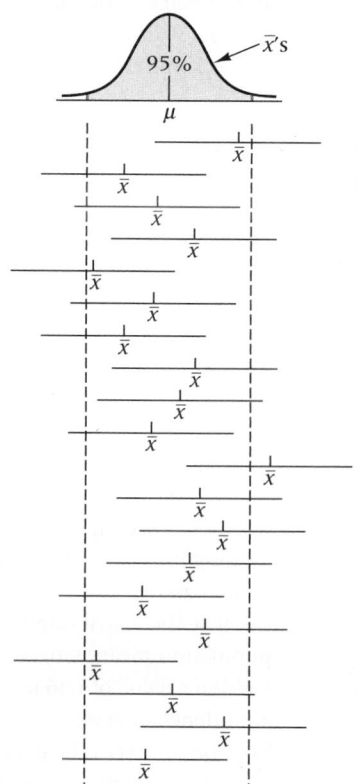

| Demonstration Problem 8.1 | A survey was taken of companies that do business with firms in India. One of the questions on the survey was, "Approximately how many years has your company been trading with firms in India?" A random sample of 44 responses to this question yielded a mean of 10.455 years. Suppose the population standard deviation for this question is 7.7 years. Using this information, construct a 90% confidence interval for the mean number of years that a company has been trading in India for the population of companies trading with firms in India. |

Solution

Here, $n = 44$, $\bar{x} = 10.455$, and $\sigma = 7.7$. To determine the value of $z_{\alpha/2}$, divide the 90% confidence in half, or take $0.5000 - \alpha/2 = 0.5000 - 0.0500$, where $\alpha = 10\%$. The z distribution of $\bar{x}$ around μ contains 0.4500 of the area on each side of μ, or $\frac{1}{2}(90\%)$. Table A.5 yields a z value of 1.645 for the area of 0.4500 (interpolating between 0.4495 and 0.4505). The confidence interval is:

$$\bar{x} - z_{\alpha/2}\frac{\sigma}{\sqrt{n}} \leq \mu \leq \bar{x} + z_{\alpha/2}\frac{\sigma}{\sqrt{n}}$$

$$10.455 - 1.645\frac{7.7}{\sqrt{44}} \leq \mu \leq 10.455 + 1.645\frac{7.7}{\sqrt{44}}$$

$$10.455 - 1.910 \leq \mu \leq 10.455 + 1.910$$

$$8.545 \leq \mu \leq 12.365$$

The analyst is 90% confident that if a census of all companies trading with firms in India were taken at the time of this survey, the actual population mean number of years a company would have been trading with firms in India would be between 8.545 and 12.365. The point estimate is 10.455 years.

For convenience, Table 8.1 contains some of the more common levels of confidence and their associated z values.

Table 8.1	Confidence Level	z Value
Values of z for Common Levels of Confidence	90%	1.645
	95%	1.96
	98%	2.33
	99%	2.575

FINITE CORRECTION FACTOR

Recall from Chapter 7 that if the sample is taken from a finite population, a finite correction factor may be used to increase the accuracy of the solution. In the case of interval estimation, the finite correction factor is used to reduce the width of the interval. As stated in Chapter 7, if the sample size is less than 5% of the population, the finite correction factor does not significantly alter the solution. If formula 8.1 is modified to include the finite correction factor, the result is formula 8.2.

Confidence Interval to Estimate μ Using the Finite Correction Factor (8.2)	$\bar{x} - z_{\alpha/2}\dfrac{\sigma}{\sqrt{n}}\sqrt{\dfrac{N-n}{N-1}} \le \mu \le \bar{x} + z_{\alpha/2}\dfrac{\sigma}{\sqrt{n}}\sqrt{\dfrac{N-n}{N-1}}$

Demonstration Problem 8.2 shows how the finite correction factor can be used.

Demonstration Problem 8.2

A study is conducted in a company that employs 800 engineers. A random sample of 50 engineers reveals that the average sample age is 34.3 years. Historically, the population standard deviation of the age of the company's engineers is approximately 8 years. Construct a 98% confidence interval to estimate the average age of all the engineers in this company.

Solution

This problem has a finite population. The sample size, 50, is greater than 5% of the population, so the finite correction factor should be used. In this case, $N = 800$, $n = 50$, $\bar{x} = 34.30$, and $\sigma = 8$. The z value for a 98% confidence interval is 2.33 (0.98 divided into two equal parts yields 0.4900; the z value is obtained from Table A.5 by using 0.4900). Substituting into formula 8.2 and solving for the confidence interval gives

$$34.30 - 2.33\frac{8}{\sqrt{50}}\sqrt{\frac{750}{799}} \le \mu \le 34.30 + 2.33\frac{8}{\sqrt{50}}\sqrt{\frac{750}{799}}$$

$$34.30 - 2.55 \le \mu \le 34.30 + 2.55$$

$$31.75 \le \mu \le 36.85$$

Without the finite correction factor, the result would have been

$$34.30 - 2.64 \le \mu \le 34.30 + 2.64$$

$$31.66 \le \mu \le 36.94$$

The finite correction factor takes into account the fact that the population is only 800 instead of being infinitely large. The sample, $n = 50$, is a greater proportion of the 800 than it would be of a larger population, and thus the width of the confidence interval is reduced.

ESTIMATING THE POPULATION MEAN USING THE z STATISTIC WHEN THE SAMPLE SIZE IS SMALL

In the formulas and problems presented so far in the section, the sample size was large ($n \ge 30$). However, quite often in the business world, sample sizes are small. While the central limit theorem applies only when the sample size is large, the distribution of sample means is approximately normal even for small sizes if the *population* is normally distributed. This is visually displayed in the bottom row of Figure 7.5 in Chapter 7. Thus, if it is known that the population from which the sample is being drawn is normally distributed and if σ is known, the z formulas presented in this section can still be used to estimate a population mean even if the sample size is small ($n < 30$).

As an example, suppose a car rental firm wants to estimate the average number of kilometres travelled per day by each of its cars rented in Alberta. A random sample of 20 cars rented in Alberta reveals that the sample mean travel distance per day is 85.5 km, with a population standard deviation of 19.3 km. Compute a 99% confidence interval to estimate μ.

Here, $n = 20$, $\bar{x} = 85.5$, and $\sigma = 19.3$. For a 99% level of confidence, a z value of 2.575 is obtained. Assume that the number of kilometres travelled per day is normally distributed in the population. The confidence interval is

$$\bar{x} - z_{\alpha/2}\frac{\sigma}{\sqrt{n}} \le \mu \le \bar{x} + z_{\alpha/2}\frac{\sigma}{\sqrt{n}}$$

$$85.5 - 2.575\frac{19.3}{\sqrt{20}} \le \mu \le 85.5 + 2.575\frac{19.3}{\sqrt{20}}$$

$$85.5 - 11.1 \le \mu \le 85.5 + 11.1$$

$$74.4 \le \mu \le 96.6$$

The point estimate indicates that the average number of kilometres travelled per day by a rental car in Alberta is 85.5. With 99% confidence, we estimate that the population mean is somewhere between 74.4 and 96.6 km per day.

USING THE COMPUTER TO CONSTRUCT z CONFIDENCE INTERVALS FOR THE MEAN

It is possible to construct a z confidence interval for the mean with Excel. Excel yields the $\pm$ error portion of the confidence interval that must be placed with the sample mean to construct the complete confidence interval. Figure 8.5 shows the Excel output for the cell phone example.

Figure 8.5

Excel Output for the Cell Phone Example

	A	B
1	The sample mean is:	510
2	The error of the interval is:	9.779
3	The confidence interval is:	510 ± 9.779
4	The confidence interval is:	500.221 ≤ μ ≤ 519.779

Concept Check

1. Explain why it is important to calculate the confidence interval in addition to calculating the point estimate of a population parameter.
2. Explain what being 95% confident that the population mean is in an interval actually indicates.

Fill in the blanks in questions 3 and 4.

3. An increase in the level of confidence will result in a _____ confidence interval for the population mean.
4. An increase in the sample size will result in a _____ confidence interval for the population mean.

8.1 Problems

8.1 Use the following information to construct the confidence intervals specified to estimate μ.
   a. 95% confidence for $\bar{x} = 25$, $\sigma = 3.5$, and $n = 60$
   b. 98% confidence for $\bar{x} = 119.6$, $\sigma = 23.89$, and $n = 75$
   c. 90% confidence for $\bar{x} = 3.419$, $\sigma = 0.974$, and $n = 32$
   d. 80% confidence for $\bar{x} = 56.7$, $\sigma = 12.1$, $N = 500$, and $n = 47$

8.2 For a random sample of 36 items and a sample mean of 211, compute a 95% confidence interval for μ if the population standard deviation is 23.

8.3 A random sample of 81 items is taken, producing a sample mean of 47. The population standard deviation is 5.89. Construct a 90% confidence interval to estimate the population mean.

8.4 A random sample of size 70 is taken from a population that has a variance of 49. The sample mean is 90.4. What is the point estimate of μ? Construct a 94% confidence interval for μ.

8.5 A random sample of size 39 is taken from a population of 200 members. The sample mean is 66 and the population standard deviation is 11. Construct a 96% confidence interval to estimate the population mean. What is the point estimate of the population mean?

8.6 A candy company fills a 550-g package of Halloween candy with individually wrapped pieces of candy. The number of pieces of candy per package varies because the package is sold by mass. The company wants to estimate the number of pieces per package. Inspectors randomly sample 120 packages of this candy and count the number of pieces in each package. They find that the sample mean number of pieces is 18.72. Assuming a population standard deviation of 0.8735, what is the point estimate of the number of pieces per package? Construct a 99% confidence interval to estimate the mean number of pieces per package for the population.

8.7 A small lawnmower company produced 1,500 lawnmowers in 1998. In an effort to determine how maintenance-free these units were, the company decided to conduct a multiyear study of the 1998 lawnmowers. A sample of 200 owners of these lawnmowers was drawn randomly from company records and contacted. The owners were given a toll-free number and asked to call the company when the first major repair was required for the lawnmowers. Owners who no longer used the lawnmower to cut their grass were disqualified. After many years, 187 of the owners had reported. The other 13 disqualified themselves. The average number of years until the first major repair was 5.3 for the 187 owners reporting. It is believed that the population standard deviation was 1.28 years. If the company wants to advertise an average number of years of repair-free lawn mowing for this lawnmower, what is the point estimate? Construct a 95% confidence interval for the average number of years until the first major repair.

8.8 The average total dollar purchase at a convenience store is less than that at a supermarket. Despite smaller-ticket purchases, convenience stores can still be profitable because of the size of operation, volume of business, and the markup. A researcher is interested in estimating the average purchase amount for convenience stores in Canmore, Alberta. To do so, she randomly sampled 24 purchases from several convenience stores in Canmore and tabulated the amounts to the nearest dollar. Use the following data to construct a 90% confidence interval for the population average amount of purchases. Assume that the population standard deviation is 3.23 and the population is normally distributed.

$2	$11	$8	$7	$9	$3
5	4	2	1	10	8
14	7	6	3	7	2
4	1	3	6	8	4

8.9   A community health association is interested in estimating the average number of maternity days women stay in the local hospital. A random sample is taken of 36 women who gave birth in the hospital during the past year. The following numbers of maternity days each woman was in the hospital are rounded to the nearest day.

3	3	4	3	2	5	3	1	4	3
4	2	3	5	3	2	4	3	2	4
1	6	3	4	3	3	5	2	3	2
3	5	4	3	5	4				

Use these data and a population standard deviation of 1.17 to construct a 98% confidence interval to estimate the average maternity stay in the hospital for all women who give birth in this hospital.

8.10   A meat-processing company in Alberta produces and markets a package of eight small sausage sandwiches. The product is nationally distributed, and the company is interested in knowing the average retail price charged for this item in stores across the country. The company cannot justify a national census to generate this information. Based on the company information system's list of all retailers that carry the product, a company researcher contacts 36 of these retailers and ascertains the selling prices for the product. Use the following price data and a population standard deviation of 0.113 to determine a point estimate for the national retail price of the product. Construct a 90% confidence interval to estimate this price.

$2.23	$2.11	$2.12	$2.20	$2.17	$2.10
2.16	2.31	1.98	2.17	2.14	1.82
2.12	2.07	2.17	2.30	2.29	2.19
2.01	2.24	2.18	2.18	2.32	2.02
1.99	1.87	2.09	2.22	2.15	2.19
2.23	2.10	2.08	2.05	2.16	2.26

8.11   Suppose that the average travel time to work in Kitchener, Ontario, is 27.4 minutes. Suppose a business researcher wants to estimate the average travel time to work in Saskatoon, Saskatchewan, using a 95% level of confidence. A random sample of 45 Saskatoon commuters is taken and the travel time to work is obtained from each. The data follow. Assuming a population standard deviation of 5.124, compute a 95% confidence interval on the data. What is the point estimate and what is the error of the interval? How do commuting times in Kitchener and Saskatoon compare?

27	25	19	21	24	27	29	34	18	29	16	28
20	32	27	28	22	20	14	14	29	28	29	33
16	29	28	28	27	23	27	20	27	25	21	18
26	14	23	27	27	21	25	28	30			

8.12   In a recent year, turkey prices increased across Ontario, the top turkey-producing province. Suppose a random sample of turkey prices is taken from across the nation in an effort to estimate the average turkey price per kilogram in Canada. Shown here is the Excel output for such a sample. Examine the output. What is the point estimate? What is the value of the assumed population standard deviation? How large is the sample? What level of confidence is being used? What table value is associated with this level of confidence? What is the confidence interval? Often the portion of the confidence interval that is added and subtracted from the mean is referred to as the error of the estimate or error of the interval. How much is the error of the estimate in this problem?

	A	B
1	The sample size is:	41
2	The assumed standard deviation is:	0.140000
3	The sample mean is:	0.576500
4	The standard error of the mean is:	0.021864
5	The confidence interval is:	0.533647 <= μ <= 0.619353

8.2 ESTIMATING THE POPULATION MEAN USING THE *t* STATISTIC (σ UNKNOWN)

POINTS OF INTEREST
This will be the case in most applications of business statistics.

In Section 8.1, we learned how to estimate a population mean by using the sample mean when the population standard deviation is known. In most instances, if a business researcher wants to estimate a population mean, the population standard deviation will be unknown and thus techniques presented in Section 8.1 will not be applicable. When the population standard deviation is unknown, the sample standard deviation must be used in the estimation process. In this section, a statistical technique is presented to estimate a population mean using the sample mean when the population standard deviation is unknown.

Suppose a business researcher is interested in estimating the average flying time of a 767 jet from Toronto to Vancouver. Since the business researcher does not know the population mean or average time, it is likely that she also does not know the population standard deviation. By taking a random sample of flights, the researcher can compute a sample mean and a sample standard deviation from which the estimate can be constructed. Another business researcher is studying the impact of movie video advertisements on consumers using a random sample of people. The researcher wants to estimate the mean response for the population but has no idea what the population standard deviation is. He will have the sample mean and sample standard deviation available to perform this analysis.

The *z* formulas presented in Section 8.1 are inappropriate for use when the population standard deviation is unknown (and is replaced by the sample standard deviation). Instead, another mechanism to handle such cases was developed by a British statistician, William S. Gosset.

William Sealy Gosset was born in 1876 in Canterbury, England. He studied chemistry and mathematics and in 1899 went to work for the Guinness Brewery in Dublin, Ireland. Gosset was involved in quality control at the brewery, studying variables such as raw materials and temperature. Because of the circumstances of his experiments, Gosset conducted many studies where the population standard deviation was unavailable. He discovered that using the standard *z* test with a sample standard deviation produced inexact and incorrect distributions. This finding led to his development of the distribution of the sample standard deviation and the *t* test.

Gosset was a student and close personal friend of Karl Pearson (who established the discipline of mathematical statistics in the early 1900s). When Gosset's first work on the *t* test was published, he used the pen name "Student." As a result, the *t* test is sometimes referred to as the Student's *t* test. Gosset's contribution was significant because it led to more exact statistical tests, which some scholars say marked the beginning of the modern era in mathematical statistics.*

THE *t* DISTRIBUTION

Gosset developed the **_t_ distribution** family, which is used instead of the *z* distribution for doing inferential statistics on the population mean when the population standard deviation is unknown and the population is normally distributed. The formula for the *t* statistic is:

$$t = \frac{\bar{x} - \mu}{\frac{s}{\sqrt{n}}}$$

This formula is essentially the same as the *z* formula, but the distribution table values are different. The *t* distribution values are contained in Table A.6 and, for convenience, inside the front cover of the text.

The *t* distribution is actually a series of distributions because every sample size has a different distribution, thereby creating the potential for many *t* tables. To make these **_t_ values** more manageable, only select key values are presented; each line in the table contains values from a different *t* distribution. An assumption underlying the use of the *t* statistic is that the population is normally distributed. If the population distribution is not normal or is unknown, nonparametric techniques (presented in Chapter 17) should be used.

ROBUSTNESS

Most statistical techniques have one or more underlying assumptions. If a statistical technique is relatively insensitive to minor violations in one or more of its underlying assumptions, the technique is said to be **robust** to that assumption (this is a desirable property). The *t* statistic for estimating a population mean is relatively robust to the assumption that the population is normally distributed.

Some statistical techniques are not robust, and a statistician should exercise extreme caution to be certain that the assumptions underlying a technique are being met before using it or interpreting statistical output resulting from its use. A business analyst should always be aware of statistical assumptions and the robustness of techniques being used in an analysis.

CHARACTERISTICS OF THE *t* DISTRIBUTION

Figure 8.6 displays two *t* distributions superimposed on the standard normal distribution. Like the standard normal curve, *t* distributions are symmetric and unimodal. The *t* distributions are flatter in the middle and have more area in their tails than the standard normal distribution.

An examination of *t* distribution values reveals that the *t* distribution approaches the standard normal curve as *n* becomes large. The *t* distribution is the appropriate distribution to use any time the population variance or standard deviation is unknown, regardless of sample size.

*Adapted from Arthur L. Dudycha and Linda W. Dudycha, "Behavioral Statistics: An Historical Perspective," in *Statistical Issues: A Reader for the Behavioral Sciences,* Roger Kirk, ed. (Monterey, CA: Brooks/Cole, 1972).

Figure 8.6

Comparison of Two *t* Distributions to the Standard Normal Curve

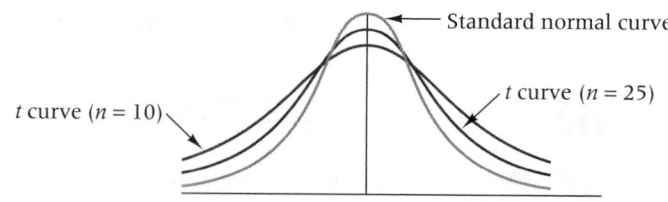

Standard normal curve

t curve (*n* = 10)

t curve (*n* = 25)

READING THE *t* DISTRIBUTION TABLE

To find a value in the *t* distribution table requires knowing the degrees of freedom; each different value of degrees of freedom (df) is associated with a different *t* distribution. The *t* distribution table used here is a compilation of many *t* distributions, with each line of the table having different degrees of freedom and containing *t* values for different *t* distributions. The degrees of freedom for the *t* statistic presented in this section are computed by $n - 1$. The term **degrees of freedom** refers to *the number of independent observations for a source of variation minus the number of independent parameters estimated in computing the variation.*[*] In this case, one independent parameter, the population mean, μ, is being estimated by $\bar{x}$ in computing *s*. Thus, the degrees of freedom formula is *n* independent observations minus one independent parameter being estimated $(n - 1)$. Because the degrees of freedom are computed differently for various *t* formulas, a degrees of freedom formula is given along with each *t* formula in the text.

In Table A.6, the degrees of freedom are located in the left column. The *t* distribution table in this text does not use the area between the statistic and the mean, as does the *z* distribution (standard normal distribution). Instead, the *t* table uses the area in the tail of the distribution. The emphasis in the *t* table is on α, and each tail of the distribution contains $\alpha/2$ of the area under the curve when confidence intervals are constructed. For confidence intervals, the table *t* value is found in the column under the value of $\alpha/2$ and in the row of the df value.

For example, if a 90% confidence interval is being computed, the total area in the two tails is 10%. Thus, α is 0.10 and $\alpha/2$ is 0.05, as indicated in Figure 8.7. The *t* distribution table shown in Table 8.2 contains only six values of $\alpha/2$ (0.10, 0.05, 0.025, 0.01, 0.005, 0.001). The *t* value is located at the intersection of the df value and the selected $\alpha/2$ value. So, if the degrees of freedom for a given *t* statistic are 24 and the desired $\alpha/2$ value is 0.05, the *t* value is 1.711.

Figure 8.7

Distribution with Alpha for 90% Confidence

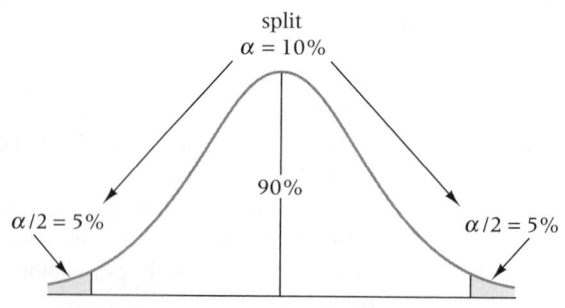

split
$\alpha = 10\%$

90%

$\alpha/2 = 5\%$

$\alpha/2 = 5\%$

---

[*]Roger E. Kirk. *Experimental Design: Procedures for the Behavioral Sciences* (Belmont, California: Brooks/Cole Publishing Company, 1968).

Table 8.2

t **Distribution**

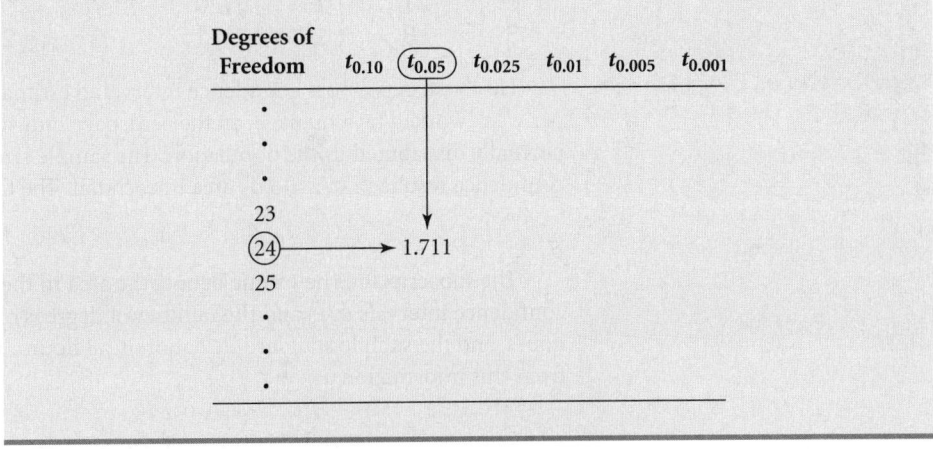

CONFIDENCE INTERVALS TO ESTIMATE THE POPULATION MEAN USING THE *t* STATISTIC

The *t* formula

$$t = \frac{\bar{x} - \mu}{\frac{s}{\sqrt{n}}}$$

can be manipulated algebraically to produce a formula for estimating the population mean when σ is unknown and the population is normally distributed. The results are the formulas given next.

Confidence Interval to Estimate μ: Population Standard Deviation Unknown and the Population Normally Distributed (8.3)	$\bar{x} \pm t_{\alpha/2,n-1}\dfrac{s}{\sqrt{n}}$ $\bar{x} - t_{\alpha/2,n-1}\dfrac{s}{\sqrt{n}} \leq \mu \leq \bar{x} + t_{\alpha/2,n-1}\dfrac{s}{\sqrt{n}}$ df $= n - 1$

Formula 8.3 can be used in a manner similar to methods presented in Section 8.1 for constructing a confidence interval to estimate μ. For example, in the aerospace industry some companies allow their employees to accumulate extra working hours beyond their 40-hour week. These extra hours are sometimes referred to as *green* time, or *comp* time. Many managers work longer than the 8-hour workday preparing proposals, overseeing crucial tasks, and taking care of paperwork. Recognition of such overtime is important. Managers are often not paid extra for this work, but a record is kept of this time and occasionally the manager is allowed to use some of this comp time as extra leave or vacation time. Suppose a researcher wants to estimate the average amount of comp time accumulated per week for managers in the aerospace industry. He randomly samples 18 managers and measures the amount of extra time they work during a specific week and obtains the results shown (in hours).

| 6 | 21 | 17 | 20 | 7 | 0 | 8 | 16 | 29 |
| 3 | 8 | 12 | 11 | 9 | 21 | 25 | 15 | 16 |

He constructs a 90% confidence interval to estimate the average amount of extra time per week worked by a manager in the aerospace industry. He assumes that comp time is normally distributed in the population. The sample size is 18, so df = 17. A 90% level of confidence results in $\alpha/2 = 0.05$ area in each tail. The table t value is:

$$t_{0.05,17} = 1.740$$

The subscripts in the t value denote the area in the right tail of the t distribution (for confidence intervals $\alpha/2$) and the number of degrees of freedom. The sample mean is 13.56 hours, and the sample standard deviation is 7.8 hours. The confidence interval is computed from this information as:

$$\bar{x} \pm t_{\alpha/2,n-1}\frac{s}{\sqrt{n}}$$

$$13.56 \pm 1.740\frac{7.8}{\sqrt{18}} = 13.56 \pm 3.20$$

$$10.36 \le \mu \le 16.76$$

The point estimate for this problem is 13.56 hours, with an error of ±3.20 hours. The researcher is 90% confident that the average amount of comp time accumulated by a manager per week in this industry is between 10.36 and 16.76 hours.

From these figures, aerospace managers could attempt to build a reward system for such extra work or evaluate the regular 40-hour week to determine how to use the normal work hours more effectively and thus reduce comp time.

Demonstration Problem 8.3

The owner of a large equipment rental company wants to make a rather quick estimate of the average number of days a piece of ditch-digging equipment is rented out per person per time. The company has records of all rentals, but the amount of time required to conduct an audit of *all* accounts would be prohibitive. The owner decides to take a random sample of rental invoices. Fourteen different rentals of ditch-diggers are selected randomly from the files, yielding the following data. The owner uses these data to construct a 99% confidence interval to estimate the average number of days that a ditch-digger is rented, assuming that the number of days per rental is normally distributed in the population.

| 3 | 1 | 3 | 2 | 5 | 1 | 2 | 1 | 4 | 2 | 1 | 3 | 1 | 1 |

Solution

Because $n = 14$, df = 13. The 99% level of confidence results in $\alpha/2 = 0.005$ area in each tail of the distribution. The table t value is:

$$t_{0.005,13} = 3.012$$

The sample mean is 2.14 and the sample standard deviation is 1.29. The confidence interval is:

$$\bar{x} \pm t_{\alpha/2,n-1}\frac{s}{\sqrt{n}}$$

$$2.14 \pm 3.012\frac{1.29}{\sqrt{14}} = 2.14 \pm 1.04$$

$$1.10 \le \mu \le 3.18$$

The point estimate of the average length of time per rental is 2.14 days, with an error of ±1.04. With a 99% level of confidence, the company's owner can estimate that the average length of time per rental is between 1.10 and 3.18 days. Combining this figure with variables such as frequency of rentals per year can help the owner estimate potential profit or loss per year for such a piece of equipment.

USING THE COMPUTER TO CONSTRUCT *t* CONFIDENCE INTERVALS FOR THE MEAN

Excel can be used to construct confidence intervals for μ using the *t* distribution. Figure 8.8 displays the Excel output for the aerospace comp time problem. The Excel output includes the mean, the standard error, the sample standard deviation, and the error of the confidence interval, referred to by Excel as the "confidence level." The standard error of the mean is computed by dividing the standard deviation (7.8006) by the square root of *n* (4.243). When using the Excel output, the confidence interval must be computed from the sample mean and the confidence level.

Figure 8.8

Excel Output for the Comp Time Example

	A	B
1	**Comp Time**	
2	Mean	13.56
3	Standard Error	1.8386
4	Standard Deviation	7.8006
5	Error of the Interval (90%)	3.20

STATISTICS IN BUSINESS TODAY

Canadian Grocery Shopping Statistics

A study of 1,000 adult Canadians was conducted by the Environics Research Group in a recent year on behalf of MasterCard Worldwide to ascertain information about Canadian shopping habits. Canadian shopping activities were divided into two categories: (1) the "quick" trip for traditional staples, convenience items, or snack foods; and (2) the "stock-up" trip that generally occurs once per week and is approximately two and a half times longer than a quick trip. As a result, many interesting statistics were reported. Canadians take a mean of 37 stock-up trips per year, spending an average of 44 minutes in the store and they take a mean of 76 quick trips per year, spending an average of 18 minutes in the store. Forty-six percent of households with kids usually take them on quick trips as

do 51% on stock-up trips. On average, Canadians spend four times more money on a stock-up trip than on a quick trip. Some other interesting statistics from this survey include: 23% often buy items that are not on their list but catch their eye, 28% often go to a store to buy an item that is on sale, 24% often switch to another check out lane to get out faster, and 45% often bring their own bag. Since these statistics are based on a sample of 1,000 shoppers, it is virtually certain that the statistics given are point estimates.

Source: 2008 MasterIndex Report: Checking out the Canadian Grocery Shopping Experience, located at: <http://www.mastercard.com/ca/wce/PDF/TRANSACTOR_REPORT_E.pdf>

Concept Check

1. When is it appropriate to use the confidence interval based on the *t* distribution for the population mean?
2. List two important properties of the *t* distribution.
3. What is the behaviour of t_α and $t_{\alpha/2}$ as the number of degrees of freedom describing a *t* distribution increases?

8.13 Suppose the following data are selected randomly from a population of normally distributed values.

40	51	43	48	44	57	54
39	42	48	45	39	43	

Construct a 95% confidence interval to estimate the population mean.

8.14 Assuming x is normally distributed, use the following information to compute a 90% confidence interval to estimate μ.

313	320	319	340	325	310
321	329	317	311	307	318

8.15 If a random sample of 41 items produces $\bar{x} = 128.4$ and $s = 20.6$, what is the 98% confidence interval for μ? Assume x is normally distributed for the population. What is the point estimate?

8.16 A random sample of 15 items is taken, producing a sample mean of 2.364 with a sample variance of 0.81. Assume x is normally distributed and construct a 90% confidence interval for the population mean.

8.17 Use the following data to construct a 99% confidence interval for μ. Assume x is normally distributed. What is the point estimate for μ?

16.4	17.1	17.0	15.6	16.2
14.8	16.0	15.6	17.3	17.4
15.6	15.7	17.2	16.6	16.0
15.3	15.4	16.0	15.8	17.2
14.6	15.5	14.9	16.7	16.3

8.18 According to Runzheimer International, the average cost of a domestic trip for business travellers in the financial industry is $1,250. Suppose another travel industry research company takes a random sample of 51 business travellers in the financial industry and determines that the sample average cost of a domestic trip is $1,192, with a sample standard deviation of $279. Construct a 98% confidence interval for the population mean from these sample data. Assume that the data are normally distributed in the population. Now go back and examine the $1,250 figure published by Runzheimer International. Does it fall into the confidence interval computed from the sample data? What does this tell you?

8.19 A valve manufacturer produces a butterfly valve composed of two semicircular plates on a common spindle that permits flow in one direction only. The semicircular plates are supplied by a vendor with specifications that the plates be 2.37 mm thick. A random sample of 20 such plates is taken. Electronic calipers are used to measure the thickness of each plate; the measurements are given here. Assuming that the thicknesses of such plates are normally distributed, use the data to construct a 95% level of confidence for the population mean thickness of these plates. What is the point estimate? How much is the error of the interval?

2.4066	2.4579	2.6724	2.1228	2.3238
2.1328	2.0665	2.2738	2.2055	2.5267
2.5937	2.1994	2.5392	2.4359	2.2146
2.1933	2.4575	2.7956	2.3353	2.2699

8.20   Some fast-food chains offer a lower-priced combination meal in an effort to attract budget-conscious customers. One chain test-marketed a burger, fries, and a drink combination for $1.71. The weekly sales volume for these meals was impressive. Suppose the chain wants to estimate the average amount its customers spent on a meal at their restaurant while this combination offer was in effect. An analyst gathers data from 28 randomly selected customers. The following data represent the sample meal totals.

$3.21	5.40	3.50	4.39	5.60	8.65	5.02	4.20	1.25	7.64
3.28	3.57	3.26	3.80	5.46	9.87	4.67	5.86	3.73	4.08
5.47	4.49	5.19	5.82	7.62	4.83	8.42	9.10		

Use these data to construct a 90% confidence interval to estimate the population mean value. Assume the amounts spent are normally distributed.

8.21   The marketing director of a large department store wants to estimate the average number of customers who enter the store every 5 minutes. She randomly selects 5-minute intervals and counts the number of arrivals at the store. She obtains the figures 58, 32, 41, 47, 56, 80, 45, 29, 32, and 78. The analyst assumes the number of arrivals is normally distributed. Using these data, the analyst computes a 95% confidence interval to estimate the mean value for all 5-minute intervals. What interval values does she get?

8.22   Runzheimer International publishes results of studies on overseas business travel costs. Suppose as a part of one of these studies the following per diem travel accounts (in dollars) are obtained for 14 business travellers staying in Johannesburg, South Africa. Use these data to construct a 98% confidence interval to estimate the average per diem expense for business people travelling to Johannesburg. What is the point estimate? Assume per diem rates for any locale are approximately normally distributed.

142.59	148.48	159.63	171.93	146.90	168.87	141.94
159.09	156.32	142.49	129.28	151.56	132.87	178.34

8.23   How much experience do supply-chain transportation managers have in their field? Suppose in an effort to estimate this, 41 supply-chain transportation managers are surveyed and asked how many years of managerial experience they have in transportation. Survey results (in years) are shown below. Use these data to construct a 99% confidence interval to estimate the mean number of years of experience in transportation. Assume that years of experience in transportation is normally distributed in the population.

5	8	10	21	20	25	14	6	19	3
1	9	11	2	3	13	2	4	9	4
5	4	21	7	6	3	28	17	32	2
25	8	13	17	27	7	3	15	4	16
6									

8.24   Cycle time in manufacturing can be viewed as the total time it takes to complete a product from the beginning of the production process. The concept of cycle time varies according to the industry and product or service being offered. Suppose a boat manufacturing company wants to estimate the mean cycle time it takes to produce a 16-foot skiff. A random sample of such skiffs is taken, and the cycle times (in hours) are recorded for each skiff in the sample. The data are analyzed using

Excel and the results are shown below in hours. What is the point estimate for cycle time? How large was the sample size? What is the level of confidence and what is the confidence interval? What is the error of the confidence interval?

	A	B
1	**Hrs. of Cycle Time**	
2	Count	26
3	Mean	25.4134
4	Standard Error	1.0467
5	Standard Deviation	5.3369
6	Confidence Interval (98%)	$22.8124 \leq \mu \leq 28.0145$

8.3 ESTIMATING THE POPULATION PROPORTION

Business decision makers and researchers often need to be able to estimate a population proportion. For most businesses, estimating market share (their proportion of the market) is important because many company decisions evolve from market share information. Companies spend thousands of dollars estimating the proportion of produced goods that are defective. Market segmentation opportunities come from knowledge of the proportion of various demographic characteristics among potential customers or clients.

Methods similar to those in Section 8.1 can be used to estimate the population proportion. The central limit theorem for sample proportions led to the following formula in Chapter 7:

POINTS OF INTEREST
As before, this formula is the basis for the calculation of the standard error of the estimate.

$$z = \frac{\hat{p} - p}{\sqrt{\dfrac{p \cdot q}{n}}}$$

where $q = 1 - p$. Recall that this formula can be applied only when $n \cdot p$ and $n \cdot q$ are greater than 5.

Algebraically manipulating this formula to estimate p involves solving for p. However, p is in both the numerator and the denominator, which complicates the resulting formula. For this reason—for confidence interval purposes only and for large sample sizes—$\hat{p}$ is substituted for p in the denominator, yielding

$$z = \frac{\hat{p} - p}{\sqrt{\dfrac{\hat{p} \cdot \hat{q}}{n}}}$$

where $\hat{q} = 1 - \hat{p}$. Solving for p results in the confidence interval in formula 8.4.*

---

*Because we are not using the true standard deviation of $\hat{p}$, the correct divisor of the standard error of $\hat{p}$ is $n - 1$. However, for large sample sizes the effect is negligible. Although technically the minimal sample size for the techniques presented in this section is $n \cdot p$ and $n \cdot q$ greater than 5, in actual practice sample sizes of several hundred are more commonly used. As an example, for $\hat{p}$ and $\hat{q}$ of 0.50 and $n = 300$ the standard error of $\hat{p}$ is 0.02887 using n and 0.02892 using $n - 1$, a difference of only 0.00005.

Confidence Interval to Estimate p (8.4)	$\hat{p} - z_{\alpha/2}\sqrt{\dfrac{\hat{p} \cdot \hat{q}}{n}} \leq p \leq \hat{p} + z_{\alpha/2}\sqrt{\dfrac{\hat{p} \cdot \hat{q}}{n}}$

where

$\hat{p}$ = sample proportion
$\hat{q} = 1 - \hat{p}$
p = population proportion
n = sample size

In this formula, $\hat{p}$ is the point estimate and $\pm z_{\alpha/2}\sqrt{\hat{p} \cdot \hat{q}/n}$ is the error of the estimate.

As an example, a study of 87 randomly selected companies with a telemarketing operation revealed that 39% of the sampled companies used telemarketing to assist them in order processing. Using this information, how could a researcher estimate the *population* proportion of telemarketing companies that use their telemarketing operation to assist them in order processing?

The sample proportion, $\hat{p}= 0.39$, is the *point estimate* of the population proportion, p. For $n = 87$ and $\hat{p} = 0.39$, a 95% confidence interval can be computed to determine the interval estimation of p. The z value for 95% confidence is 1.96. The value of $\hat{q} = 1 - \hat{p} = 1 - 0.39 = 0.61$. The confidence interval estimate is

$$0.39 - 1.96\sqrt{\frac{(0.39)(0.61)}{87}} \leq p \leq 0.39 + 1.96\sqrt{\frac{(0.39)(0.61)}{87}}$$

$$0.39 - 0.10 \leq p \leq 0.39 + 0.10$$

$$0.29 \leq p \leq 0.49$$

This interval suggests that the population proportion of telemarketing firms that use their operation to assist order processing is somewhere between 0.29 and 0.49, based on the point estimate of 0.39 with an error of ±0.10. This result has a 95% level of confidence.

Demonstration Problem 8.4

Coopers & Lybrand (now PricewaterhouseCoopers) surveyed 210 chief executives of fast-growing small companies. Only 51% of these executives had a management succession plan in place. A spokesperson for Coopers & Lybrand said that many companies do not worry about management succession unless it is an immediate problem. However, the unexpected exit of a corporate leader can disrupt and unfocus a company for long enough to cause it to lose its momentum.

Use the data given to compute a 92% confidence interval to estimate the proportion of *all* fast-growing small companies that have a management succession plan.

Solution

The point estimate is the sample proportion given to be 0.51. It is estimated that 0.51, or 51%, of all fast-growing small companies have a management succession plan. Realizing that the point estimate might change with another sample selection, we calculate a confidence interval.

The value of n is 210, $\hat{p}$ is 0.51, and $\hat{q} = 1 - \hat{p} = 0.49$. Because the level of confidence is 92%, the value of $z_{0.04} = 1.75$. The confidence interval is computed as

$$0.51 - 1.75\sqrt{\frac{(0.51)(0.49)}{210}} \leq p \leq 0.51 + 1.75\sqrt{\frac{(0.51)(0.49)}{210}}$$

$$0.51 - 0.06 \leq p \leq 0.51 + 0.06$$

$$0.45 \leq p \leq 0.57$$

It is estimated with 92% confidence that the proportion of the population of fast-growing small companies that have a management succession plan is between 0.45 and 0.57.

STATISTICS IN BUSINESS TODAY

Coffee Consumption in Canada

According to the Coffee Association of Canada, 81% of Canadians drink coffee occasionally and over 63% of Canadians over the age of 18 drink coffee on a daily basis. This makes coffee the number one beverage of choice for adult Canadians, other than tap water. Daily coffee consumption, however, varies across Canada, from a high of 70% in Quebec to a low of just over 53% in the Atlantic region. Around 60% of adults in Ontario, 67% in the Prairies, and 61% in British Columbia drink coffee on a daily basis.

Canadian coffee drinkers consume an average of 2.6 cups of coffee per day. Men and women are equally likely to be coffee consumers, with men drinking slightly more coffee than women. Nearly 51% of coffee is consumed at breakfast, 16% in the balance of the morning, 9% at lunch, 10% in the afternoon, 8% at dinner, and 7% in the evening.

Coffee is mostly consumed at home: 66%. Around 12% is consumed at work, 16% is consumed or purchased at eating establishments, and 5% is consumed in other places such as hospitals, schools, hockey rinks, and other institutions. Interestingly, drinking coffee in transit increased from 2% in 1999 to 7% in 2003.

Around 79% of the coffee consumed at home is purchased at a grocery store or supermarket, with 7% being purchased at a gourmet/specialty coffee shop. The share of total coffee consumption accounted for by instant coffee is 17%. Around 9% of coffee consumers drink decaffeinated coffee on a regular basis.

How does Canadian consumption of coffee compare to that in other countries? The Canadian per-capita consumption of coffee is 4 kg, compared to 4.2 kg in the U.S., 5.56 kg in Europe in general, and 11.4 kg in Finland.

Because much of the information presented here was gleaned from surveys, virtually all of the percentages and means are sample statistics and not population parameters. Thus, what are presented as coffee population statistics are actually point estimates. Using the sample size and a level of confidence, confidence intervals can be constructed for the proportions. Confidence intervals for means can be constructed from these point estimates if the value of the standard deviation is known or can be calculated.

Demonstration Problem 8.5

A clothing company produces men's jeans. The jeans are made and sold with either a regular cut or a boot cut. In an effort to estimate the proportion of the men's jeans market in Kingston, Ontario, that prefers boot-cut jeans, the analyst takes a random sample of 212 jeans sales from the company's two Kingston retail outlets. Only 34 of the sales were for boot-cut jeans. Construct a 90% confidence interval to estimate the proportion of the population in Kingston who prefer boot-cut jeans.

Solution

The sample size is 212, and the number preferring boot-cut jeans is 34. The sample proportion is $\hat{p} = 34/212 = 0.16$. A point estimate for boot-cut jeans in the population is 0.16, or 16%. The z value for a 90% level of confidence is 1.645, and the value of

$\hat{q} = 1 - \hat{p} = 1 - 0.16 = 0.84$. The confidence interval estimate is:

$$0.16 - 1.645\sqrt{\frac{(0.16)(0.84)}{212}} \le p \le 0.16 + 1.645\sqrt{\frac{(0.16)(0.84)}{212}}$$

$$0.16 - 0.04 \le p \le 0.16 + 0.04$$

$$0.12 \le p \le 0.20$$

The analyst estimates that the population proportion of boot-cut jeans purchases is between 0.12 and 0.20. The level of confidence in this result is 90%.

Concept Check

1. Provide a couple of business examples where the confidence interval of the population proportion might be useful.
2. Why is $n - 1$ the correct divisor of the standard error of the population proportion?
3. Explain how the standard error of the population proportion behaves as the sample size n increases.

8.3 Problems

8.25 Use the information about each of the following samples to compute the confidence interval to estimate p.
   a. $n = 44$ and $\hat{p} = 0.51$; compute a 99% confidence interval.
   b. $n = 300$ and $\hat{p} = 0.82$; compute a 95% confidence interval.
   c. $n = 1,150$ and $\hat{p} = 0.48$; compute a 90% confidence interval.
   d. $n = 95$ and $\hat{p} = 0.32$; compute an 88% confidence interval.

8.26 Use the following sample information to calculate the confidence interval to estimate the population proportion. Let x be the number of items in the sample with the characteristic of interest.
   a. $n = 116$ and $x = 57$, with 99% confidence
   b. $n = 800$ and $x = 479$, with 97% confidence
   c. $n = 240$ and $x = 106$, with 85% confidence
   d. $n = 60$ and $x = 21$, with 90% confidence

8.27 Suppose a random sample of 85 items has been taken from a population and 40 of the items contain the characteristic of interest. Use this information to calculate a 90% confidence interval to estimate the proportion of the population that has the characteristic of interest. Calculate a 95% confidence interval. Calculate a 99% confidence interval. As the level of confidence changes and the other sample information stays constant, what happens to the confidence interval?

8.28 The Universal Music Group is the music industry leader worldwide in sales according to the company website. Suppose a researcher wants to determine what market share the company holds in Burnaby, B.C., by randomly selecting 1,003 people who purchased a CD last month. In addition, suppose 25.5% of the purchases made by these people were for products manufactured and distributed by the Universal Music Group. Based on these data, construct a 99% confidence interval to estimate the proportion of the CD sales market in Burnaby that is held by the Universal Music Group. Now suppose that the survey had been taken with 10,000 people. Recompute the confidence interval and compare your results with the first confidence interval. How did they differ? What might you conclude from this about sample size and confidence intervals?

8.29 According to the Stern Marketing Group, 9 out of 10 professional women say that financial planning is more important today than it was 5 years ago. Where do these women go for help in financial planning? Forty-seven percent use a financial advisor (broker, tax consultant, financial planner). Twenty-eight percent use written sources such as magazines, books, and newspapers. Suppose these figures were obtained by taking a sample of 560 professional women who said that financial planning is more important today than it was 5 years ago. Construct a 95% confidence interval for the proportion of professional women who use a financial advisor. Use the percentage given in this problem as the point estimate. Construct a 90% confidence interval for the proportion of professional women who use written sources. Use the percentage given in this problem as the point estimate.

8.30 What proportion of pizza restaurants that are primarily for walk-in business have a salad bar? Suppose that, in an effort to determine this figure, a random sample of 1,250 of these restaurants across Canada based on the *Yellow Pages* is called. If 997 of the restaurants sampled have a salad bar, what is the 98% confidence interval for the population proportion?

8.31 The highway department wants to estimate the proportion of vehicles on Ontario's Highway 401 between the hours of midnight and 5:00 A.M. that are 18-wheel tractor trailers. The estimate will be used to determine highway repair and construction considerations and in highway patrol planning. Suppose researchers for the highway department counted vehicles at different locations on the highway for several nights during this time period. Of the 3,481 vehicles counted, 927 were 18-wheelers.
   a. Determine the point estimate for the proportion of vehicles travelling Highway 401 during this time period that are 18-wheelers.
   b. Construct a 99% confidence interval for the proportion of vehicles on Highway 401 during this time period that are 18-wheelers.

8.32 What proportion of commercial airline pilots are more than 40 years of age? Suppose a researcher has access to a list of all pilots who are members of the Air Line Pilots Association. If this list is used as a frame for the study, she can randomly select a sample of pilots, contact them, and ascertain their ages. From 89 of these pilots so selected, she learns that 48 are more than 40 years of age. Construct an 85% confidence interval to estimate the population proportion of commercial airline pilots who are more than 40 years of age.

8.33 According to Runzheimer International, in a survey of relocation administrators 63% of all workers who rejected relocation offers did so for family considerations. Suppose this figure was obtained by using a random sample of the files of 672 workers who had rejected relocation offers. Use this information to construct a 95% confidence interval to estimate the population proportion of workers who reject relocation offers for family considerations.

8.34 Suppose a survey of 275 executives is taken in an effort to determine what qualities are most important for an effective CEO to possess. The survey participants are offered several qualities as options, one of which is "communicator." One hundred twenty-one of the surveyed respondents select "communicator" as the most important quality for an effective CEO. Use these data to construct a 98% confidence interval to estimate the population proportion of executives who believe that "communicator" is the most important quality of an effective CEO.

8.4 ESTIMATING THE POPULATION VARIANCE

At times in statistical analysis, the researcher is more interested in the population variance than in the population mean or population proportion. For example, in the total quality movement, suppliers that want to earn world-class supplier status or even those that want to maintain customer contracts are often asked to show continual reduction of variation on supplied parts. Tests are conducted with samples in efforts to determine lot variation and to determine whether variability goals are being met.

Estimating the variance is important in many other instances in business. For example, variations between airplane altimeter readings need to be minimal. It is not enough just to know that, on the average, a particular brand of altimeter produces the correct altitude. It is also important for the variation between instruments to be small. Thus, measuring the variation of altimeters is critical. Parts being used in engines must fit tightly on a consistent basis. A wide variability among parts can result in a part that is too large to fit into its slots or so small that it results in too much tolerance, which causes vibrations. How can variance be estimated?

You may recall from Chapter 3 that sample variance is computed by using the formula

$$s^2 = \frac{\Sigma(x - \bar{x})^2}{n - 1}$$

Because sample variances are typically used as estimators or estimations of the population variance, as they are here, a mathematical adjustment is made in the denominator by using $n - 1$ to make the sample variance an unbiased estimator of the population variance.

Suppose a researcher wants to estimate the population variance from the sample variance in a manner that is similar to the estimation of the population mean from a sample mean. The relationship of the sample variance to the population variance is captured by the **chi-square distribution** (χ^2). The ratio of the sample variance (s^2) multiplied by $n - 1$ to the population variance (σ^2) is approximately chi-square distributed, as shown in formula 8.5, if the population from which the values are drawn is normally distributed.

Caution: Use of the chi-square statistic to estimate the population variance is extremely sensitive to violations of the assumption that the population is normally distributed. For that reason, some researchers do not include this technique among their statistical repertoire. Although the technique is still rather widely presented as a mechanism for constructing confidence intervals to estimate a population variance, you should proceed with extreme caution and apply the technique only in cases where the population is known to be normally distributed. We can say that this technique lacks robustness.

Like the t distribution, the chi-square distribution varies by sample size and contains a df value. The number of degrees of freedom for the chi-square formula 8.5 is $n - 1$.

χ^2 Formula for Single Variance (8.5)	$$\chi^2 = \frac{(n - 1)s^2}{\sigma^2}$$ $$\mathrm{df} = n - 1$$

The chi-square distribution is not symmetrical, and its shape will vary according to the degrees of freedom. Figure 8.9 shows the shape of chi-square distributions for three different degrees of freedom.

Formula 8.5 can be rearranged algebraically to produce a formula that can be used to construct confidence intervals for population variances. This new formula is shown as formula 8.6.

Figure 8.9

Three Chi-Square Distributions

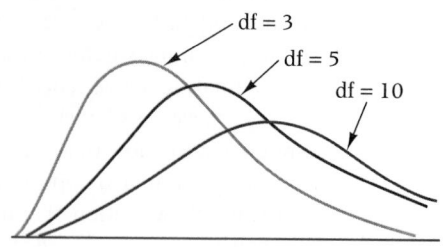

Confidence Interval to Estimate the Population Variance (8.6)

$$\frac{(n-1)s^2}{\chi^2_{\alpha/2}} \le \sigma^2 \le \frac{(n-1)s^2}{\chi^2_{1-\alpha/2}}$$

$$df = n - 1$$

The value of alpha (α) is equal to 1 – (level of confidence expressed as a proportion). Thus, if we are constructing a 90% confidence interval, alpha is 10% of the area and is expressed in proportion form: $\alpha = 0.10$.

How can this formula be used to estimate the population variance from a sample variance? Suppose eight purportedly 7-cm aluminum cylinders in a sample are measured in diameter, resulting in the following values:

6.91 cm	6.93 cm	7.01 cm	7.02 cm
7.05 cm	7.00 cm	6.98 cm	7.01 cm

In estimating a population variance from these values, the sample variance must be computed. This value is $s^2 = 0.0022125$. If a point estimate is all that is required, the point estimate is the sample variance, 0.0022125. However, realizing that the point estimate will probably change from sample to sample, we want to construct an interval estimate. To do this, we must know the degrees of freedom and the table values of the chi-squares. Because $n = 8$, the degrees of freedom are $df = n - 1 = 7$. What are the chi-square values necessary to complete the information needed in formula 8.6? Assume the population of cylinder diameters is normally distributed.

Suppose we are constructing a 90% confidence interval. The value of α is 1 – 0.90 = 0.10. It is the portion of the area under the chi-square curve that is outside the confidence interval. This outside area is needed because the chi-square table values given in Table A.8 are listed according to the area in the right tail of the distribution. In a 90% confidence

Figure 8.10

Two Table Values of Chi-Square

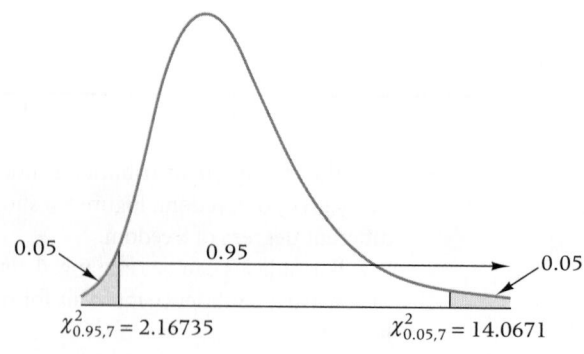

interval, $\alpha/2$ or 0.05 of the area is in the right tail of the distribution and 0.05 is in the left tail of the distribution. The chi-square value for the 0.05 area in the right tail of the distribution can be obtained directly from the table by using the degrees of freedom, which in this case are 7. Thus, the right-side chi-square, $\chi^2_{0.05,7}$, is 14.0671. Because Table A.8 lists chi-square values for areas in the right tail, the chi-square value for the left tail must be obtained by determining how much area lies to the right of the left tail. If 0.05 is to the left of the confidence interval, then $1 - 0.05 = 0.95$ of the area is to the right of the left tail. This calculation is consistent with the $1 - \alpha/2$ expression used in formula 8.6. Thus, the chi-square for the left tail is $\chi^2_{0.95,7} = 2.16735$. Figure 8.10 shows the two table values of χ^2 on a chi-square distribution.

Incorporating these values into the formula, we can construct the 90% confidence interval to estimate the population variance of the 7-cm aluminum cylinders:

$$\frac{(n-1)s^2}{\chi^2_{\alpha/2}} \leq \sigma^2 \leq \frac{(n-1)s^2}{\chi^2_{1-\alpha/2}}$$

$$\frac{7(0.0022125)}{14.0671} \leq \sigma^2 \leq \frac{7(0.0022125)}{2.16735}$$

$$0.001101 \leq \sigma^2 \leq 0.007146$$

The confidence interval says that with 90% confidence, the population variance is somewhere between 0.001101 and 0.007146.

Demonstration Problem 8.6

The U.S. Bureau of Labor Statistics publishes data on the hourly compensation costs for production workers in manufacturing for various countries. The latest figures published for Greece show that the average hourly wage for a production worker in manufacturing is $16.10. Suppose the business council of Greece wants to know how consistent this figure is. They randomly select 25 production workers in manufacturing from across the country and determine that the standard deviation of hourly wages for such workers is $1.12. Use this information to develop a 95% confidence interval to estimate the population variance for the hourly wages of production workers in manufacturing in Greece. Assume that the hourly wages for production workers across the country in manufacturing are normally distributed.

Solution

By squaring the standard deviation, $s = 1.12$, we can obtain the sample variance, $s^2 = 1.2544$. This figure provides the point estimate of the population variance. Because the sample size, n, is 25, the degrees of freedom, $n - 1$, are 24. A 95% confidence interval means that alpha is $1 - 0.95 = 0.05$. This value is split to determine the area in each tail of the chi-square distribution: $\alpha/2 = 0.025$. The values of the chi-squares obtained from Table A.8 are:

$$\chi^2_{0.025,24} = 39.3641 \quad \text{and} \quad \chi^2_{0.975,24} = 12.40115$$

From this information, the confidence interval can be determined:

$$\frac{(n-1)s^2}{\chi^2_{\alpha/2}} \leq \sigma^2 \leq \frac{(n-1)s^2}{\chi^2_{1-\alpha/2}}$$

$$\frac{24(1.2544)}{39.3641} \leq \sigma^2 \leq \frac{24(1.2544)}{12.40115}$$

$$0.7648 \leq \sigma^2 \leq 2.4276$$

The business council can estimate with 95% confidence that the population variance of the hourly wages of production workers in manufacturing in Greece is between 0.7648 and 2.4276.

Concept Check

1. Why is it that some business researchers do not include the technique presented in this section for estimating the population variance among their statistical repertoire?

8.4 Problems

8.35 For each of the following sample results, construct the requested confidence interval. Assume the data come from normally distributed populations.
 a. $n = 12$, $\bar{x} = 28.4$, $s^2 = 44.9$; 99% confidence for σ^2
 b. $n = 7$, $\bar{x} = 4.37$, $s = 1.24$; 95% confidence for σ^2
 c. $n = 20$, $\bar{x} = 105$, $s = 32$; 90% confidence for σ^2
 d. $n = 17$, $s^2 = 18.56$; 80% confidence for σ^2

8.36 Use the following sample data to estimate the population variance. Produce a point estimate and a 98% confidence interval. Assume the data come from a normally distributed population.

27	40	32	41	45	29	33	39
30	28	36	32	42	40	38	46

8.37 According to Human Resources and Skills Development Canada, in 2007 the average workweek in Canada was 36.5 hours. Suppose this figure was obtained from a random sample of 20 workers and that the standard deviation of the sample was 4.3 hours. Assume hours worked per week are normally distributed in the population. Use this sample information to develop a 98% confidence interval for the population variance of the number of hours worked per week for a worker. What is the point estimate?

8.38 A manufacturing plant produces steel rods. During one production run of 20,000 such rods, the specifications called for rods that were 46 cm in length and 3.8 cm in width. Fifteen of these rods making up a random sample were measured for length; the resulting measurements are shown here. Use these data to estimate the population variance of length for the rods. Assume rod length is normally distributed in the population. Construct a 99% confidence interval. Discuss the ramifications of the results.

44 cm	47 cm	43 cm	46 cm	46 cm
45 cm	43 cm	44 cm	47 cm	46 cm
48 cm	48 cm	43 cm	44 cm	45 cm

8.39 Suppose a random sample of 14 people 30–39 years of age produced the household incomes shown here. Use these data to determine a point estimate for the population variance of household incomes for people 30–39 years of age and construct a 95% confidence interval. Assume household income is normally distributed.

$37,500	44,800
33,500	36,900
42,300	32,400
28,000	41,200
46,600	38,500
40,200	32,000
35,500	36,800

8.5 ESTIMATING SAMPLE SIZE

In most business research that uses sample statistics to make inferences about the population, being able to *estimate the size of sample necessary to accomplish the purposes of the study* is important. The need for this **sample-size estimation** is the same for the large corporation investing tens of thousands of dollars in a massive study of consumer preference and for students undertaking a small case study and wanting to send questionnaires to local business people. In either case, such things as level of confidence, sampling error, and width of estimation interval are closely tied to sample size. If the large corporation is undertaking a market study, should it sample 40 people or 4,000 people? The question is an important one. In most cases, because of cost considerations, business researchers do not want to sample any more units or individuals than necessary.

DETERMINING SAMPLE SIZE WHEN ESTIMATING μ

In research studies when μ is being estimated, the size of the sample can be determined by using the z formula for sample means to solve for n. Consider

$$z = \frac{\bar{x} - \mu}{\dfrac{\sigma}{\sqrt{n}}}$$

The difference between $\bar{x}$ and μ is the **error of estimation** resulting from the sampling process. Let $E = \bar{x} - \mu$ be the error of estimation. Substituting E into the preceding formula yields

$$z = \frac{E}{\dfrac{\sigma}{\sqrt{n}}}$$

Solving for n yields a formula that can be used to determine sample size.

Sample Size When Estimating μ (8.7)	$n = \dfrac{z_{\alpha/2}^2 \sigma^2}{E^2} = \left(\dfrac{z_{\alpha/2} \sigma}{E} \right)^2$

Sometimes in estimating sample size the population variance is known or can be determined from past studies. Other times, the population variance is unknown and must be estimated to determine the sample size. In such cases, it is acceptable to use the following estimate to represent σ:

$$\sigma \approx \frac{1}{4}(\text{range})$$

Using formula 8.7, the business researcher can estimate the sample size needed to achieve the goals of the study before gathering data. For example, suppose a researcher wants to estimate the average monthly expenditure on bread by a family in Montreal. She wants to be 90% confident of her results. How much error is she willing to tolerate in the results? Suppose she wants the estimate to be within $1.00 of the actual figure and the standard deviation of average monthly bread purchases is $4.00. What is the sample-size estimation for this problem? The value of z for a 90% level of confidence is 1.645. Using formula 8.7 with $E = \$1.00$, $\sigma = \$4.00$, and $z = 1.645$ gives

$$n = \frac{z_{\alpha/2}^2 \sigma^2}{E^2} = \frac{(1.645)^2 (4)^2}{1^2} = 43.30$$

That is, at least $n = 43.3$ must be sampled randomly to attain a 90% level of confidence and produce an error within $1.00 for a standard deviation of $4.00. Sampling 43.3 units is impossible, so this result should be rounded up to $n = 44$ units.

In this approach to estimating sample size, we view the error of the estimate as the amount of difference between the statistic (in this case $\bar{x}$) and the parameter (in this case μ). The error could be in either direction; that is, the statistic could be over or under the parameter. Thus, the error, E, is actually $\pm E$ as we view it. So, when a problem states that the researcher wants to be within $1.00 of the actual monthly family expenditure for bread it means that the researcher is willing to allow a tolerance within $\pm \$1.00$ of the actual figure. Another name for this error is the **precision** (or bounds) of the interval.

Demonstration Problem 8.7

Suppose you want to estimate the average age of all Boeing 737-300 airplanes now in active domestic Canadian service. You want to be 95% confident, and you want your estimate to be within 2 years of the actual figure. The 737-300 was first placed in service about 24 years ago, but you believe that no active 737-300s in the Canadian domestic fleet are more than 20 years old. How large a sample should you take?

Solution

Here, $E = 2$ years, the z value for 95% is 1.96, and σ is unknown, so it must be estimated by using $\sigma \approx (1/4)(\text{range})$. As the range of ages is 0 to 20 years, $\sigma = (1/4)(20) = 5$. Use formula 8.7:

$$n = \frac{z_{\alpha/2}^2 \sigma^2}{E^2} = \frac{(1.96)^2 (5)^2}{2^2} = 24.01$$

Because you cannot sample 24.01 units, the required sample size is 25. If you randomly sample 25 airplanes, you have an opportunity to estimate the average age of active 737-300s within 2 years and be 95% confident of the results. If you want to be within 1 year for the estimate ($E = 1$), the sample-size estimate changes to

$$n = \frac{z_{\alpha/2}^2 \sigma^2}{E^2} = \frac{(1.96)^2 (5)^2}{1^2} = 96.04$$

Note that cutting the error by a factor of 1/2 increases the required sample size by a factor of 4. The reason is the squaring factor in formula 8.7. If you want to reduce the error to one half of what you used before, you must be willing to incur the cost of a sample that is four times larger, for the same level of confidence.

Note: Sample-size estimates for the population mean where σ is unknown using the t distribution are not shown here. Because a sample size must be known to determine the table value of t, which in turn is used to estimate the sample size, this procedure usually involves an iterative process.

DETERMINING SAMPLE SIZE WHEN ESTIMATING p

Determining the sample size required to estimate the population proportion, p, is also possible. The process begins with the z formula for sample proportions:

$$z = \frac{\hat{p} - p}{\sqrt{\dfrac{p \cdot q}{n}}}$$

where $q = 1 - p$.

As various samples are taken from the population, $\hat{p}$ will rarely equal the population proportion, p, resulting in an error of estimation. The difference between $\hat{p}$ and p is the error of estimation, so $E = \hat{p} - p$:

POINTS OF INTEREST
Selecting $p = 0.5$ results in the largest sample size that could be determined for a given z value and a given error value.

$$z = \frac{E}{\sqrt{\dfrac{p \cdot q}{n}}}$$

Solving for n yields the formula for determining sample size.

Sample Size When
Estimating p (8.8)

$$n = \frac{z_{\alpha/2}^2 p \cdot q}{E^2}$$

where
p = population proportion
$q = 1 - p$
E = error of estimation
n = sample size

How can the value of n be determined prior to a study if the formula requires the value of p and the study is being done to estimate p? Although the actual value of p is not known prior to the study, similar studies might have generated a good approximation for p. If no previous value is available for use in estimating p, some possible p values, as shown in Table 8.3, might be considered.

Table 8.3		p	$p \cdot q$
$p \cdot q$ for Various Selected Values of p		0.9	0.09
		0.8	0.16
		0.7	0.21
		0.6	0.24
		0.5	0.25
		0.4	0.24
		0.3	0.21
		0.2	0.16
		0.1	0.09

Note that, as $p \cdot q$ is in the numerator of the sample-size formula, $p = 0.5$ will result in the largest sample sizes. Often *if p is unknown, researchers use 0.5 as an estimate of p in* formula 8.8. This selection results in the largest sample size that could be determined from formula 8.8 for a given z value and a given error value.

**Demonstration
Problem 8.8**

Hewitt Associates conducted a national survey to determine the extent to which employers are promoting health and fitness among their employees. One of the questions asked was, "Does your company offer on-site exercise classes?" Suppose it was estimated before the study that no more than 40% of the companies would answer yes. How large a sample would Hewitt Associates have to take in estimating the population proportion to ensure a 98% confidence in the results and to be within 0.03 of the true population proportion?

Solution

The value of E for this problem is 0.03. Because it is estimated that no more than 40% of the companies would say yes, $p = 0.40$ can be used. A 98% confidence interval results in a z value of 2.33. Inserting these values into formula 8.8 yields

$$n = \frac{(2.33)^2(0.40)(0.60)}{(0.03)^2} = 1,447.7$$

Hewitt Associates would have to sample 1,448 companies to be 98% confident in the results and maintain an error of 0.03.

Concept Check

1. When calculating the sample size for estimating the population mean or the population proportion, is there ever a need to take a preliminary sample? Why?
2. Should we always round up the calculated sample size n for both the population mean and the population proportion? Why or why not?
3. Why is $p = 0.5$ used to calculate the sample size when estimating the population proportion when an approximate value of the population proportion is unknown?

8.5 Problems

8.40 Determine the sample size necessary to estimate μ for the following information.
   a. $\sigma = 36$ and $E = 5$ at 95% confidence
   b. $\sigma = 4.13$ and $E = 1$ at 99% confidence
   c.   Values range from 80 to 500, error is to be within 10, and the confidence level is 90%
   d.   Values range from 50 to 108, error is to be within 3, and the confidence level is 88%

8.41 Determine the sample size necessary to estimate p for the following information.
   a. $E = 0.02$, p is approximately 0.40, and confidence level is 96%
   b. E is to be within 0.04, p is unknown, and confidence level is 95%
   c. E is to be within 5%, p is approximately 55%, and confidence level is 90%
   d. E is to be no more than 0.01, p is unknown, and the confidence level is 99%

8.42 A bank officer wants to determine the amount of the average total monthly deposits per customer at the bank. He believes an estimate of this average amount using a confidence interval is sufficient. How large a sample should he take to be within $200 of the actual average with 99% confidence? He assumes the standard deviation of total monthly deposits for all customers is about $1,000.

8.43   Suppose you have been following the share price of a particular airline for many years. You are interested in determining the average daily price of these shares in a 10-year period and you have access to the stock reports for these years. However, you do not want to average all the daily prices over 10 years because there are several thousand data points, so you decide to take a random sample of the daily prices and estimate the average. You want to be 90% confident of your results, you want the estimate to be within $2.00 of the true average, and you believe the standard deviation of the price of these shares is about $12.50 over this period of time. How large a sample should you take?

8.44   A group of investors wants to develop a chain of fast-food restaurants. In determining potential costs for each facility, they must consider, among other expenses, the average monthly electric bill. They decide to sample some fast-food restaurants currently operating to estimate the monthly cost of electricity. They want to be 90% confident of their results and want the error of the interval estimate to be no more than $100. They estimate that such bills range from $600 to $2,500. How large a sample should they take?

8.45   Suppose a production facility purchases a particular component part in large lots from a supplier. The production manager wants to estimate the proportion of defective parts received from this supplier. She believes the defective proportion is no more than 0.20 and wants to be within 0.02 of the true proportion of defective parts with a 90% level of confidence. How large a sample should she take?

8.46   What proportion of assistants of *Report on Business Magazine* Top 1,000 companies has a personal computer at his or her workstation? You want to answer this question by conducting a random survey. How large a sample should you take if you want to be 95% confident of the results and you want the error of the confidence interval to be no more than 0.05?

8.47   What proportion of shoppers at a large appliance store actually make a big-ticket purchase? To estimate this proportion within 10% and be 95% confident of the results, how large a sample should you take?

COMPENSATION FOR PURCHASING MANAGERS

Published national management salary and demographic information, such as mean salary, mean age, and mean years' experience, is mostly likely based on random samples of data. Such is the case in the Decision Dilemma, where the salary, age, and experience parameters are actually point estimates based on a survey of 1,839 purchasing managers. For example, the study states that the average salary for a purchasing manager is $78,500. This is a point estimate of the population mean salary based on the sample mean of 1,839 purchasing managers. Suppose it is known that the population standard deviation for purchasing manager salaries is $6,000. From this information, a 95% confidence interval using the z statistic can be constructed as follows:

$$\$78,500 \pm 1.96 \frac{\$6,000}{\sqrt{1,839}} = \$78,500 \pm \$274.23$$

$$\$78,225.77 \le \mu \le \$78,774.23$$

This confidence interval, constructed to estimate the mean annual salary for purchasing managers across the U.S. and Canada, shows that the estimated mean salary is $78,500 with an error of $274.23. The reason that this error is quite small is that the sample size is very large. In fact, the sample size is so large that if the $6,000 had actually been a sample standard deviation, the table t value would have been 1.961257 (compared to the z value of 1.96), resulting in a confidence interval error of estimate of $274.41. Note that because of the large sample size, this t value is not found in Appendix Table A.6; it was obtained using Excel's TINV. Of course, in using the t statistic, one would have to assume that salaries are normally distributed in the population. Because the sample size is so large and the corresponding t table value is so close to the z value, the error using the t statistic is only 18 cents more than that produced using the z statistic. Confidence intervals for the population mean age and mean years of experience can be computed similarly.

The study also reports that the mean annual salary of a purchasing manager in Canada is $83,400, but this is based on a sample of only 25 respondents. Suppose annual salaries of purchasing managers in Canada are normally distributed and that the sample standard deviation for such managers in this study is also $6,000. A 95% confidence interval for estimating the population mean annual salary for Canadian purchasing managers can be computed using the t statistic as follows:

$$\$83,400 \pm 2.064 \frac{\$6,000}{\sqrt{25}} = \$83,400 \pm \$2,476.80$$

$$\$80,923.20 \leq \mu \leq \$85,876.80$$

Note that the point estimate mean annual salary for Canadian purchasing managers is $83,400, as reported in the study. However, the error of estimation in the interval is $2,476.80, indicating that the actual population mean annual salary could be as low as $80,923.20 or as high as $85,876.80. Observe that the error of this interval, $2,476.80, is nearly 10 times as big as the error in the confidence interval used to estimate the U.S. figure. This is due to the fact that the sample size used in the U.S. estimate is about 75 times as large. Since sample size is under the radical sign in confidence interval computation, taking the square root of the sample size (75 here) indicates that the error in the Canadian estimate is almost 9 times as large as it is in the U.S. estimate (with a slight adjustment for the fact that a t value is used in the Canadian estimate).

The study reported that 73% of the respondents have a university degree or certificate. Using methods presented in Section 8.3, a 99% confidence interval can be computed assuming that the sample size is 1,839, the table z value for a 99% confidence interval is 2.575, and $\hat{p}$ is 0.73. The resulting confidence interval is:

$$0.73 \pm 2.575 \sqrt{\frac{(0.73)(0.27)}{1,839}} = 0.73 \pm 0.027$$

$$0.703 \leq p \leq 0.757$$

While the point estimate is 0.73 or 73%, the error of the estimate is 0.027 or 2.7%, so we are 99% confident that the actual population proportion of purchasing managers who have a university degree or certificate is between 0.703 and 0.757.

KEY CONSIDERATIONS

Using sample statistics to estimate population parameters poses a couple of ethical concerns. Many survey reports and advertisers use point estimates as the values of the population parameter. Often, no error value is stated, as would have been the case if a confidence interval had been computed. These point estimates are subject to change if another sample is taken. It is probably unethical to state as a conclusion that a point estimate is the population parameter without some sort of disclaimer or explanation about what a point estimate is.

The misapplication of t formulas when data are not normally distributed in the population is also of concern. Although some studies have shown that the t formula analyses are robust, a researcher should be careful not to violate the assumptions underlying the use of the t formulas. An even greater potential for misuse lies in using the chi-square for the estimation of a population variance, because this technique is highly sensitive to violations of the assumption that the data are normally distributed.

Why Statistics Is Relevant

The descriptive statistics presented in Chapter 3 are used to describe the basic features of the data under study in a manageable form. Together with the charts and graphs presented in Chapter 2, descriptive statistics form the basis of virtually every quantitative analysis of data.

The inferential statistics presented in this chapter, on the other hand, are used to reach conclusions that extend beyond the sample data, to make claims about the population that gave rise to the sample data that we collected, and to make inferences from our sample data to more general conditions.

For instance, Statistics Canada releases information on the unemployment rate every month. In order to generate this information, Statistics Canada samples households across Canada to determine the employment status of the members of those households. Extending beyond the sample results to generate unemployment figures that apply to different regions and to the entire country is an example of applying inferential statistics.

Chapters 8 to 11 present a variety of techniques to ensure that the inferences are sound and rational, even though they may not always be correct, since we are always dealing with the uncertainty of inferring from sample data.

SUMMARY

Techniques for estimating population parameters from sample statistics are important tools for business research. Business researchers use techniques for estimating population means, techniques for estimating the population proportion and the population variance, and methodology for determining how large a sample to take.

1. At times in business research, a product is new or untested or information about the population is unknown. In such cases, gathering data from a sample and making estimates about the population is useful and can be done with a point estimate or an interval estimate. A point estimate is the use of a statistic from the sample as an estimate for a parameter of the population. Because point estimates vary with each sample, it is usually best to construct an interval estimate. An interval estimate is a range of values computed from the sample within which the researcher believes with some confidence that the population parameter lies. Certain levels of confidence seem to be used more than others: 90%, 95%, 98%, and 99%.

2–4. If the population standard deviation is known, the z statistic is used to estimate the population mean. If the population standard deviation is unknown, the t distribution should be used instead of the z distribution. It is assumed when using the t distribution that the population from which the samples are drawn is normally distributed. However,

the technique for estimating a population mean by using the t test is robust, which means it is relatively insensitive to minor violations to the assumption. Methods similar to those used to estimate a population mean when the population standard deviation is known can be used to estimate the population proportion.

5. The population variance can be estimated by using sample variance and the chi-square distribution. The chi-square technique for estimating the population variance is not robust; it is sensitive to violations of the assumption that the population is normally distributed. Therefore, extreme caution must be exercised in using this technique.

6. The formulas in Chapter 7 resulting from the central limit theorem can be manipulated to produce formulas for estimating sample size for large samples. Determining the sample size necessary to estimate a population mean, if the population standard deviation is unavailable, can be based on one fourth the range as an approximation of the population standard deviation. Determining sample size when estimating a population proportion requires the value of the population proportion. If the population proportion is unknown, the population proportion from a similar study can be used. If none is available, using a value of 0.50 will result in the largest sample-size estimation for the problem if other variables are held constant. Sample-size determination is used mostly to provide a ballpark figure to give researchers some guidance. Larger sample sizes usually result in greater costs.

KEY TERMS

chi-square distribution	error of estimation (or error	point estimate	sample-size estimation
degrees of freedom	of the interval)	precision (or bounds)	t distribution
(df)	interval estimate	robust	t value

FORMULAS

(8.1) $100(1-\alpha)\%$ confidence interval to estimate μ: population standard deviation known

$$\bar{x} - z_{\alpha/2}\frac{\sigma}{\sqrt{n}} \le \mu \le \bar{x} + z_{\alpha/2}\frac{\sigma}{\sqrt{n}}$$

(8.2) Confidence interval to estimate μ using the finite correction factor

$$\bar{x} - z_{\alpha/2}\frac{\sigma}{\sqrt{n}}\sqrt{\frac{N-n}{N-1}} \le \mu \le \bar{x} + z_{\alpha/2}\frac{\sigma}{\sqrt{n}}\sqrt{\frac{N-n}{N-1}}$$

(8.3) Confidence interval to estimate μ: population standard deviation unknown

$$\bar{x} - t_{\alpha/2,n-1}\frac{s}{\sqrt{n}} \le \mu \le \bar{x} + t_{\alpha/2,n-1}\frac{s}{\sqrt{n}}$$
$$df = n-1$$

(8.4) Confidence interval to estimate p

$$\hat{p} - z_{\alpha/2}\sqrt{\frac{\hat{p}\cdot\hat{q}}{n}} \le p \le \hat{p} + z_{\alpha/2}\sqrt{\frac{\hat{p}\cdot\hat{q}}{n}}$$

(8.5) χ^2 formula for single variance

$$\chi^2 = \frac{(n-1)s^2}{\sigma^2}$$
$$df = n-1$$

(8.6) Confidence interval to estimate the population variance

$$\frac{(n-1)s^2}{\chi^2_{\alpha/2}} \le \sigma^2 \le \frac{(n-1)s^2}{\chi^2_{1-\alpha/2}}$$

(8.7) Sample size when estimating μ

$$n = \frac{z^2_{\alpha/2}\sigma^2}{E^2} = \left(\frac{z_{\alpha/2}\sigma}{E}\right)^2$$

(8.8) Sample size when estimating p

$$n = \frac{z^2_{\alpha/2}p\cdot q}{E^2}$$

SUPPLEMENTARY PROBLEMS

Calculating the Statistics

8.48 Use the following data to construct 80%, 94%, and 98% confidence intervals to estimate μ. Assume that σ is 7.75. State the point estimate.

44	37	49	30	56	48	53	42	51
38	39	45	47	52	59	50	46	34
39	46	27	35	52	51	46	45	58
51	37	45	52	51	54	39	48	

8.49 Construct 90%, 95%, and 99% confidence intervals to estimate μ from the following data. State the point estimate. Assume the data come from a normally distributed population.

| 12.3 | 11.6 | 11.9 | 12.8 | 12.5 |
| 11.4 | 12.0 | 11.7 | 11.8 | 12.3 |

8.50 Use the following information to compute the confidence interval for the population proportion.

a. $n = 715$ and $x = 329$, with 95% confidence
b. $n = 284$ and $\hat{p} = 0.71$, with 90% confidence

c. $n = 1{,}250$ and $\hat{p} = 0.48$, with 95% confidence
d. $n = 457$ and $x = 270$, with 98% confidence

8.51 Use the following data to construct 90% and 95% confidence intervals to estimate the population variance. Assume the data come from a normally distributed population.

| 212 | 229 | 217 | 216 | 223 |
| 219 | 208 | 214 | 232 | 219 |

8.52 Determine the sample size necessary under the following conditions.

a. To estimate μ with $\sigma = 44$, $E = 3$, and 95% confidence
b. To estimate μ with a range of values from 20 to 88 with $E = 2$ and 90% confidence
c. To estimate p with p unknown, $E = 0.04$, and 98% confidence
d. To estimate p with $E = 0.03$, 95% confidence, and p thought to be approximately 0.70

Testing Your Understanding

8.53   In planning both market opportunity and production levels, being able to estimate the size of a market can be important. Suppose a diaper manufacturer wants to know how many diapers a 1-month-old baby uses during a 24-hour period. To determine this usage, the manufacturer's analyst randomly selects 17 parents of 1-month-olds and asks them to keep track of diaper usage for 24 hours. The results are shown. Construct a 99% confidence interval to estimate the average daily diaper usage of a 1-month-old baby. Assume diaper usage is normally distributed.

12	8	11	9	13	14	10
10	9	13	11	8	11	15
10	7	12				

8.54   Suppose you want to estimate the proportion of cars that are sport utility vehicles (SUVs) being driven in Regina at rush hour by standing on the corner of Victoria Avenue and Albert Street and counting SUVs. You believe the figure is no higher than 0.40. If you want the error of the confidence interval to be no greater than 0.03, how many cars should you randomly sample? Use a 90% level of confidence.

8.55   Use the data in Problem 8.53 to construct a 99% confidence interval to estimate the population variance for the number of diapers used during a 24-hour period for 1-month-olds. How could information about the population variance be used by a manufacturer or marketer in planning?

8.56   What is the average length of a company's policy book? Suppose policy books are sampled from 45 medium-sized companies. The average number of pages in the sample books is 213, and the population standard deviation is 48. Use this information to construct a 98% confidence interval to estimate the mean number of pages for the population of medium-sized company policy books.

8.57   A random sample of small-business managers was given a leadership style questionnaire. The results were scaled so that each manager received a score for initiative. Suppose the following data are a random sample of these scores:

37	42	40	39	38	31	40
37	35	45	30	33	35	44
36	37	39	33	39	40	41
33	35	36	41	33	37	38
40	42	44	35	36	33	38
32	30	37	42			

Assuming σ is 3.891, use these data to construct a 90% confidence interval to estimate the average score on initiative for all small-business managers.

8.58   A national beauty salon chain wants to estimate the number of times per year a woman has her hair done at a beauty salon if she uses one at least once a year. The chain's researcher estimates that, of those women who use a beauty salon at least once a year, the standard deviation of number of times of usage is approximately six. The national chain wants the estimate to be within one time of the actual mean value. How large a sample should the researcher take to obtain a 98% confidence level?

8.59   Is the environment a major issue with Canadians? To answer that question, a researcher conducts a survey of 1,255 randomly selected Canadians. Suppose 714 of the sampled people replied that the environment is a major issue. Construct a 95% confidence interval to estimate the proportion of Canadians who feel that the environment is a major issue. What is the point estimate of this proportion?

8.60   According to a survey by Topaz Enterprises, a travel auditing company, the average error by travel agents is $128. Suppose this figure was obtained from a random sample of 41 travel agents and the sample standard deviation is $21. What is the point estimate of the national average error for all travel agents? Compute a 98% confidence interval for the national average error based on these sample results. Assume the travel agent errors are normally distributed in the population. How wide is the interval? Interpret the interval.

8.61   A national survey on telemarketing was undertaken. One of the questions asked was, "How long has your organization had a telemarketing operation?" Suppose the following data represent some of the answers received to this question. Suppose further that only 300 telemarketing firms made up the population when this survey was taken. Use the following data to compute a 98% confidence interval to estimate the average number of years a telemarketing organization has had a telemarketing operation. The population standard deviation is 3.06.

5	5	6	3	6	7	5
5	6	8	4	9	6	4
10	5	10	11	5	14	7
5	9	6	7	3	4	3
7	5	9	3	6	8	16
12	11	5	4	3	6	5
8	3	5	9	7	13	4
6	5	8	3	5	8	7
11	5	14	4			

SUPPLEMENTARY PROBLEMS (continued)

8.62 An entrepreneur wants to open an appliance repair shop. She would like to know about what the average home repair bill is, including the charge for the service call for appliance repair in the area. She wants the estimate to be within $20 of the actual figure. She believes the range of such bills is between $30 and $600. How large a sample should the entrepreneur take if she wants to be 95% confident of the results?

8.63 A national survey of insurance offices was taken, resulting in a random sample of 245 companies. Of these 245 companies, 189 responded that they were going to purchase new software for their offices in the next year. Construct a 90% confidence interval to estimate the population proportion of insurance offices that intend to purchase new software during the next year.

8.64 A national survey of companies included a question that asked whether the company had at least one bilingual telephone operator. The sample results of 90 companies follow. (Y denotes that the company does have at least one bilingual operator; N denotes that it does not.)

N	N	N	N	Y	N	Y	N	N
Y	N	N	N	Y	Y	N	N	N
N	N	Y	N	Y	N	Y	N	Y
Y	Y	N	Y	N	N	N	Y	N
N	Y	N	N	N	N	N	N	N
Y	N	Y	Y	N	N	Y	N	Y
N	N	Y	Y	N	N	N	N	N
Y	N	N	N	N	Y	N	N	N
Y	Y	Y	N	N	Y	N	N	N
N	N	N	Y	Y	N	N	Y	N

Use this information to estimate with 95% confidence the proportion of the population that does have at least one bilingual operator.

8.65 A movie theatre has had a poor accounting system. The manager has no idea how many large containers of popcorn are sold per movie showing. He knows that the amounts vary by day of the week and hour of the day. However, he wants to estimate the overall average per movie showing. To do so, he randomly selects 12 movie performances and counts the number of large containers of popcorn sold between 30 minutes before the movie showing and 15 minutes after the movie showing. The sample average is 43.7 containers, with a variance of 228. Construct a 95% confidence interval to estimate the mean number

of large containers of popcorn sold during a movie showing. Assume the number of large containers of popcorn sold per movie is normally distributed in the population. Use this information to construct a 98% confidence interval to estimate the population variance.

8.66 According to a survey, the average cost of a fast-food meal (quarter-pound cheeseburger, large fries, medium soft drink, excluding taxes) in a certain city is $4.82. Suppose this figure was based on a sample of 27 different establishments and the standard deviation was $0.37. Construct a 95% confidence interval for the population mean cost for all fast-food meals in the city. Assume the costs of a fast-food meal in the city are normally distributed. Using the interval as a guide, is it likely that the population mean is really $4.50? Why or why not?

8.67 A survey of 77 commercial airline flights of under 2 hours resulted in a sample average late time for a flight of 2.48 minutes. The population standard deviation was 12 minutes. Construct a 95% confidence interval for the average time that a commercial flight of under 2 hours is late. What is the point estimate? What does the interval tell about whether the average flight is late?

8.68 A regional survey of 560 companies asked the vice president of operations how satisfied he or she was with the software support received from the computer staff of the company. Suppose 33% of the 560 vice presidents said they were satisfied. Construct a 99% confidence interval for the proportion of the population of vice presidents who would have said they were satisfied with the software support if a census had been taken.

8.69 A research firm has been asked to determine the proportion of all restaurants in the province of Nova Scotia that serve alcoholic beverages. The firm wants to be 98% confident of its results but has no idea of what the actual proportion is. The firm would like to report an error of no more than 0.05. How large a sample should it take?

8.70 A national magazine marketing firm attempts to win subscribers with a mail campaign that involves a contest using magazine stickers. Often when people subscribe to magazines in this manner they sign up for multiple magazine subscriptions. Suppose the marketing firm wants to estimate the average number of subscriptions per customer of those who purchase at least one subscription. To do so, the marketing firm's researcher randomly selects 65 returned contest entries. Twenty-seven contain subscription requests. Of the 27, the average number of subscriptions is 2.10, with a standard deviation of 0.86. The researcher uses this information to compute a 98% confidence interval to estimate μ and assumes that x is normally distributed. What does the researcher find?

8.71 A national survey showed that a certain brand of cold cuts were priced, on the average, at $1.15 per 100 g. Suppose a national survey of 23 retail outlets was taken and the price per 100 g of these cold cuts was ascertained. If the following data represent these prices, what is a 90% confidence interval for the population variance of these prices? Assume prices are normally distributed in the population.

1.14	1.15	1.16	1.14	$1.17
1.14	1.13	1.16	1.15	$1.13
1.11	1.14	1.16	1.15	$1.14
1.15	1.12	1.15	1.15	$1.17
1.15	1.14	1.14		

8.72 The price of a head of iceberg lettuce varies greatly with the season and the geographic location of a store. During February, a researcher contacts a random sample of 39 grocery stores across Canada and asks the produce manager of each to state the current price charged for a head of iceberg lettuce. Using the researcher's results that follow, construct a 99% confidence interval to estimate the mean price of a head of iceberg lettuce in February in Canada. Assume that σ is 0.205.

1.59	1.25	1.65	1.40	0.89
1.19	1.50	1.49	1.30	1.39
1.29	1.60	0.99	1.29	1.19
1.20	1.50	1.49	1.29	1.35
1.10	0.89	1.10	1.39	1.39
1.50	1.50	1.55	1.20	1.15
0.99	1.00	1.30	1.25	1.10
1.00	1.55	1.29	1.39	

Interpreting the Output

8.73 A soft drink company produces a cola in a 355-ml can. Even though their machines are set to fill the cans with 355 ml, variation due to calibration, operator error, and other things sometimes precludes the cans having the correct fill. To monitor the can fills, a quality team randomly selects some filled 355-ml cola cans and measures their fills in the lab. A confidence interval for the population mean is constructed from the data. Shown here is the Excel output from this effort. Discuss the output.

	A	B
1	**Soft Drink**	
2	Count	510
3	Mean	354.373
4	Standard Error	0.2071
5	Standard Deviation	1.5857
6	Confidence Interval (99%)	$353.837 \leq \mu \leq$ 354.908

8.74 A company has developed a new light bulb that seems to burn longer than most residential bulbs. To determine how long these bulbs burn, the company randomly selects a sample of these bulbs and burns them in the laboratory. The Excel output shown here is a portion of the analysis from this effort. Discuss the output.

	A	B
1	**Bulb Burn**	
2	Count	84
3	Mean	2198.217
4	Standard Deviation	152.9907
5	Confidence Level (90%)	27.76691

8.75 Suppose a researcher wants to estimate the average age of a person who is a first-time home buyer. A random sample of first-time home buyers is taken and their ages are ascertained. The Excel output shown here is an analysis of that data. Study the output and explain its implications.

<>	A	B
1	**First-Time Home Buyer**	
2	Count	21
3	Mean	27.6300
4	Standard Error	1.4271
5	Standard Deviation	6.5400
6	Confidence Interval (99%)	$24.0222 \leq \mu \leq$ 31.2378

ANALYZING THE DATABASES

see www.wiley.com/canada/black

1. Use the Canadian Hospitals Database. Construct a 90% confidence interval to estimate Congestive Heart Failure for hospitals. State the point estimate and the error of the estimate. Change the level of confidence to 99%. What happens to the interval? Did the point estimate change?

2. The Financial Database contains financial data on 100 companies. Use this database as a sample and estimate Price per Share for all corporations from these data. Select several levels of confidence and compare the results.

3. Using the tally or frequency feature of the computer software, determine the sample proportion of the Canadian Hospitals Database that is in British Columbia (Geographic Region 1). From this statistic, construct a 95% confidence interval to estimate the population proportion of hospitals that are in British Columbia. What is the point estimate? How much error is there in the interval?

CASE

Thermatrix

In 1985, a company called In-Process Technology was set up to produce and sell a thermal oxidation process that could be used to reduce industrial pollution. The initial investors acquired the rights to technology developed at the U.S. Department of Energy's Lawrence Livermore National Laboratory to more efficiently convert energy in burners, process heaters, and others. For several years, the company performed dismally and by 1991 was only earning $264,000 annually.

In 1992, the company realized that there was potential for utilizing this technology for the control and destruction of volatile organic compounds and hazardous air pollutants in improving the environment, and the company was reorganized and renamed Thermatrix. More than $20 million in private equity offerings was raised over a period of several years to produce, market, and distribute the new product. In June 1996, there was a successful public offering of Thermatrix in the financial markets. This allowed the company to expand its global presence and increase its market penetration in the United States. In 1997, as a result of research and development, the company engineers were able to develop a more effective treatment of waste streams with significantly less cost to the customer.

Thermatrix's philosophy has been to give their customers more than their competitors do without charging more. During this time period, the company targeted large corporations as customers, hoping to use its client list as a selling tool. In addition, realizing that they were a small, thinly capitalized company, Thermatrix partnered with many of its clients in developing solutions to the clients' specific environmental problems.

In April 2002, Thermatrix was acquired by Linde AG, through its subsidiary Selas Fluid Processing Corporation (SFPC) of Blue Bell, Pennsylvania. SFPC specializes in the design and engineering of fired process heaters, LNG vaporizers, and thermal oxidizers. Thermatrix offers a wide range of flameless thermal oxidizers and provides stand-alone emission devices in a variety of ways. Thermatrix is now located in Blue Bell, as a part of SFPC, where there are 90 employees.

Discussion

1. Thermatrix has grown and flourished because of its good customer relationships, which include partnering, delivering a quality product on time, and listening to the customer's needs. Suppose company management wants to formally measure customer satisfaction at least once a year and develops a brief survey that includes the following four questions. Suppose 115 customers participated in this survey with the results shown. Use techniques presented in this chapter to analyze the data to estimate population responses to these questions.

Question	Yes	No
1. In general, were deliveries on time?	63	52
2. Were the contact people at Thermatrix helpful and courteous?	86	29
3. Was the pricing structure fair to your company?	101	14
4. Would you recommend Thermatrix to other companies?	105	10

2. Now suppose Thermatrix officers want to ascertain employee satisfaction with the company. They randomly sample nine employees and ask them to complete a satisfaction survey under the supervision of an independent testing organization. As part of this survey, employees are asked to respond to questions on a five-point scale, where 1 is low satisfaction and 5 is high satisfaction. Assume the data are at least interval and that the overall responses on the questions are normally distributed.

The questions and the results of the survey follow. Analyze the results by using techniques from this chapter.

Question	Mean	Standard Deviation
1. Are you treated fairly as an employee?	3.79	0.86
2. Has the company given you the training you need to do the job adequately?	2.74	1.27
3. Does management seriously consider your input in making decisions about production?	4.18	0.63
4. Is your physical work environment acceptable?	3.34	0.81
5. Is the compensation for your work adequate and fair?	3.95	0.21

References

Adapted from "Thermatrix: Selling Products Not Technology," *Insights and Inspiration: How Businesses Succeed*, published by Nation's Business on behalf of Mass Mutual and the U.S. Chamber of Commerce in association with The Blue Chip Enterprise Initiative 1997 and Thermatrix Inc.

USING THE COMPUTER

Excel

- Excel has some capability to construct confidence intervals to estimate a population mean using the z statistic when σ is known and using the t statistic when σ is unknown.
- To construct confidence intervals of a single population mean using the z statistic (σ is known), begin with the **Insert Function (*fx*)**. To access the **Insert Function**, go to the **Formulas** tab on an Excel worksheet (top centre tab). The **Insert Function** is on the far left of the menu bar. In the **Insert Function** dialogue box at the top, there is a pulldown menu where it says **Or select a category**. From the pulldown menu associated with this command, select **Statistical**. Select **CONFIDENCE** from the **Insert Function's Statistical** menu. In the **CONFIDENCE** dialogue box, place the value of alpha (a number between 0 and 1), which equals 1 – level of confidence. (*Note:* level of confidence is given as a proportion and not as a percent.) For example, if the level of confidence is 95%, enter .05 as alpha. Insert the value of the population standard deviation in **Standard_dev**. Insert the size of the sample in **Size**. The output is the ± error of the confidence interval.
- To construct confidence intervals of a single population mean using the t statistic (σ is unknown), begin by selecting the **Data** tab on the Excel worksheet. From the **Analysis** panel at the right top of the **Data** tab worksheet, click on **Data Analysis**. If your Excel worksheet does not show the **Data Analysis** option, then you can load it as an add-in. From the **Data Analysis** pulldown menu, select **Descriptive Statistics**. In the **Descriptive Statistics** dialogue box, enter the location of the observations from the single sample in **Input Range**. Check **Labels** if you have a label for your data. Check **Summary Statistics**. Check **Confidence Level for Mean:** (required to get confidence interval output). If you want to change the level of confidence from the default value of 95%, enter it (in percent, between 0 and 100) in the box with the % sign beside it. The output is a single number that is the ± error portion of the confidence interval and is shown at the bottom of the **Descriptive Statistics** output as **Confidence Level**.

STATISTICAL INFERENCE: HYPOTHESIS TESTING FOR SINGLE POPULATIONS

Learning Objectives

The main objective of Chapter 9 is to help you to learn how to test hypotheses on single populations. The key questions in this chapter are:

1. What is the logic of hypothesis testing and how should we establish null and alternative hypotheses?

2. What are Type I and Type II errors and how can we solve for Type II errors?

3. What is the HTAB system to test hypotheses and how can we implement it?

4. How can we test hypotheses about a single population mean when σ is known?

5. How can we test hypotheses about a single population mean when σ is unknown?

6. How can we test hypotheses about a single population proportion?

7. How can we test hypotheses about a single population variance?

Shutterstock

BUSINESS REFERRALS

Word-of-mouth information about products and services is exchanged on a daily basis by millions of consumers. Many of us seek out such advice because we want to obtain product information from a third party to assist us in the market decision-making process. What we receive is often subjective opinion that is flavoured by other consumers' experiences or information they have gathered from other sources. An underlying factor in the reliance on such word-of-mouth information is trust in the source. It is important for businesses to understand the impact of such business referrals.

Research indicates that at least 90% of unhappy customers will not do business with the offending company again. In addition, each unhappy customer will share his or her displeasure with at least nine other people. According to a study by Mediamark Research, about 50% of all adults often seek the advice of others before buying services or products. In addition, almost 40% say that others seek out their advice before purchasing. Maritz Marketing Research studied adults in an effort to determine for which products or services they seek advice. Forty-six percent seek advice when selecting a physician, 44% for a mechanic, and 42% for legal advice. In looking for a restaurant in which to celebrate a special occasion, 38% of all consumers seek out advice and information from others.

Some advice givers are referred to as *influentials*. According to Chip Walker in "Word of Mouth," influentials are "trend-setting opinion leaders whose activism and expertise make them the natural source for word-of-mouth referrals." This group represents about 10% of all adults. A report issued by Roper Starch Worldwide and cosponsored by *The Atlantic Monthly* stated that influentials tend to be among the first to try new products. They are looking for new restaurants and vacation spots to try, are activists on the job and in their community,

and are self-indulgent. Businesses would do well to seek out such influentials and win them over to the company's products, thereby tapping into the word-of-mouth pipeline. On average, an influential recommends restaurants to 5.0 people a year. The following chart shows the average number of recommendations made by influentials per year on other items. These data were compiled and released by Roper Starch Worldwide.

Product or Service	Average Number of Recommendations
Office equipment	5.8
Vacation destination	5.1
TV show	4.9
Retail store	4.7
Clothing	4.5
Consumer electronics	4.5
Car	4.1
Stocks, mutual funds, etc.	3.4

Managerial and Statistical Questions

1. All of the figures enumerated in this Decision Dilemma were derived by studies conducted on samples and published as fact. If we wanted to challenge these figures by conducting surveys of our own, how would we go about testing these results? Are these studies dated now? Do they apply to all market segments (geographically, economically, etc.)? How could we test to determine whether these results apply to our market segment today?

2. The Roper Starch Worldwide study listed the mean number of recommendations made by influentials per year for different products or services. If these figures become accepted by industry users, how can we conduct our own tests to determine whether they are actually true? If we randomly sampled some influentials and our mean figures did not match these figures, could we automatically conclude that their figures are not true? How much difference would we have to obtain to reject their claims? Is there a possibility that we could make an error in conducting such research?

3. The studies by Mediamark Research and Maritz Marketing Research produced a variety of proportions about word-of-mouth advertising and advice seeking. Are these figures necessarily true? Since these figures are based on sample information and are probably point estimates, could there be error in the estimations? How can we test to determine whether figures that become accepted in the media as population parameters are actually true? Could there be differences in various population subgroups?

4. Suppose you have theories regarding word-of-mouth advertising, business referrals, or influentials. How would you test the theories to determine whether they are true?

Source: Adapted from Chip Walker, "Word of Mouth." *American Demographics* (July 1995), pp. 38–45.

One of the most important statistical mechanisms for decision making is the hypothesis test. The concept of hypothesis testing lies at the heart of inferential statistics, and the use of statistics to prove or disprove claims hinges on the concept. With **hypothesis testing,** business researchers are able *to structure problems in such a way that they can use statistical evidence to test various theories about business phenomena.* Business applications of statistical hypothesis testing run the gamut from determining whether a production line process is out of control to providing conclusive evidence that a new management leadership approach is significantly more effective than an old one.

Figure III-1 of Unit III Introduction displays a tree diagram taxonomy of inferential techniques organized by usage, number of samples, and type of statistic. While Chapter 8 contains the portion of these techniques that can be used for estimating a mean, a proportion, or a variance for a population with a single sample, Chapter 9 contains techniques used for testing hypotheses about a population mean, a population proportion, and a population variance using a single sample. The entire right side of the tree diagram taxonomy displays various hypothesis-testing techniques. The leftmost branch of this right side contains Chapter 9 techniques (for single samples), and this branch is displayed in Figure 9.1. Note that at the bottom of each tree branch in Figure 9.1 the title of the statistical technique along with its respective section number is given for ease of identification and use. If a business researcher is testing a population mean and the population standard deviation is known, she will use the z test for μ contained in Section 9.2. If the population standard deviation is unknown and therefore the researcher is using the sample standard deviation, the appropriate technique is the t test for μ contained in Section 9.3. If the business researcher is testing a population proportion, she will use the z test for p presented in Section 9.4. If the researcher desires to test a population variance from a single sample, she will use the χ^2 test for σ^2 presented in Section 9.5. Section 9.6 contains techniques for solving for Type II errors.

9.1 INTRODUCTION TO HYPOTHESIS TESTING

In the field of business, decision makers are constantly attempting to find answers to questions such as the following:

- What container shape is most economical and reliable for shipping a product?
- Which management approach best motivates employees in the retail industry?
- How can the company's retirement investment financial portfolio be diversified for optimum performance?
- What is the best way to link client databases for fast retrieval of useful information?

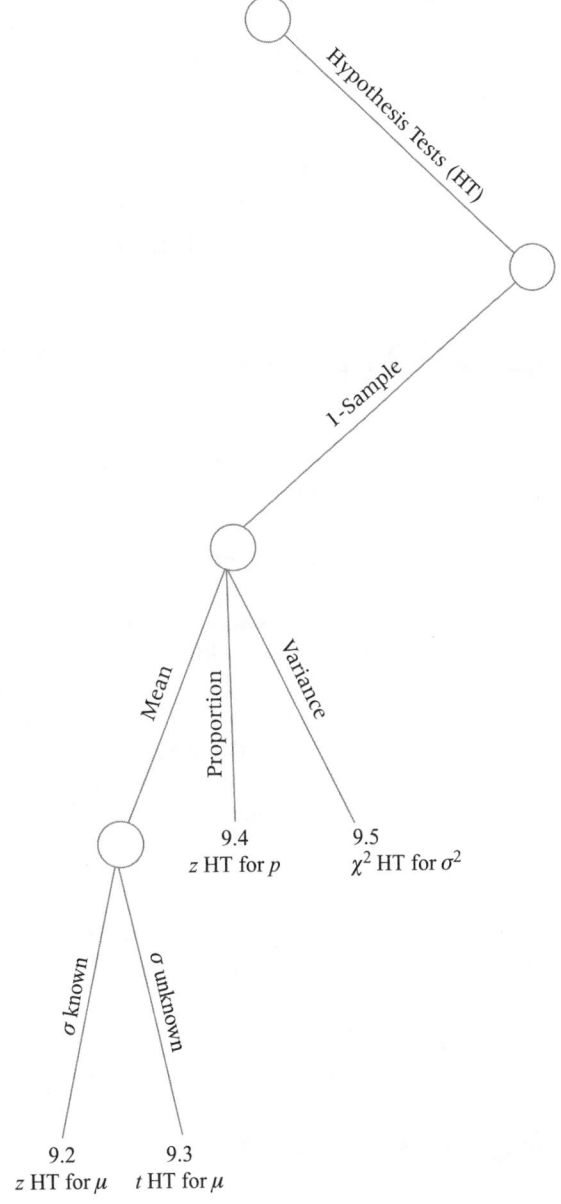

Figure 9.1

Chapter 9 Branch of the Tree Diagram Taxonomy of Inferential Techniques

- Which indicator best predicts the general state of the economy in the next six months?
- What is the most effective means of advertising in a business-to-business setting?

Business researchers are often called upon to provide insights and information to decision makers to assist them in answering such questions. In searching for answers to questions and in attempting to find explanations for business phenomena, business researchers often develop hypotheses that can be studied and explored. **Hypotheses** are *tentative explanations of a principle operating in nature.** In this text, we will explore various types of hypotheses, how to test them, and how to interpret their results so that useful information can be brought to bear on the business decision-making process.

---

* Paraphrasing of definition published in *Merriam Webster's Collegiate Dictionary*, 10th ed. (Springfield, MA: Merriam Webster Inc., 1983).

TYPES OF HYPOTHESES

Three types of hypotheses will be explored here:

1. *Research* hypotheses
2. *Statistical* hypotheses
3. *Substantive* hypotheses

Although much of the focus will be on testing statistical hypotheses, it is also important for business decision makers to understand both research and substantive hypotheses.

RESEARCH HYPOTHESES

A **research hypothesis** is *a statement of what the researcher believes will be the outcome of an experiment or a study.* Before studies are undertaken, business researchers often have some idea or theory based on experience or previous work as to how the study will turn out. These ideas, theories, or notions established before an experiment or study is conducted are research hypotheses. Some examples of research hypotheses in business are:

- Older workers are more loyal to a company.
- Companies with more than $1 billion in assets spend a higher percentage of their annual budget on advertising than do companies with less than $1 billion in assets.
- The implementation of a Six Sigma quality approach in manufacturing will result in greater productivity.
- The price of scrap metal is a good indicator of the industrial production index six months later.
- Airline company share prices are directly associated with the volume of OPEC oil production.

Virtually all inquisitive, thinking businesspeople have similar research hypotheses concerning relationships, approaches, and techniques in business. Such hypotheses can lead decision makers to new and better ways to accomplish business goals. However, to formally test research hypotheses, it is generally best to state them as statistical hypotheses.

STATISTICAL HYPOTHESES

In order to scientifically test research hypotheses, a more formal hypothesis structure needs to be set up using **statistical hypotheses.** Suppose business researchers want to prove the research hypothesis that older workers are more loyal to a company. A loyalty survey instrument is either developed or obtained. If this instrument is administered to both older and younger workers, how much higher do older workers have to score on the loyalty instrument (assuming higher scores indicate more loyalty) than younger workers to prove the research hypothesis? What is the "proof threshold"? Instead of attempting to prove or disprove research hypotheses directly in this manner, business researchers convert their research hypotheses to statistical hypotheses and then test the statistical hypotheses using standard procedures.

All statistical hypotheses consist of two parts, a null hypothesis and an alternative hypothesis. These two parts are constructed to contain all possible outcomes of the experiment or study. Generally, the **null hypothesis** *states that the "null" condition exists; that is, there is nothing new happening, the old theory is still true, the old standard is correct, and the system is in control.* The **alternative hypothesis,** on the other hand, *states that the* *new theory is true, there are new standards, the system is out of control, and/or something is happening.* As an example, suppose flour packaged by a manufacturer is sold by mass, and a particular size of package is supposed to average 1 kg. Suppose the manufacturer wants to test to determine whether its packaging process is out of control as determined by the mass of the flour packages. The null hypothesis for this experiment is that the average mass of the flour packages is 1 kg (no problem). The alternative hypothesis is that the average is not 1 kg (process is out of control).

It is common symbolism to represent the null hypothesis as H_o and the alternative hypothesis as H_a. The null and alternative hypotheses for the flour example can be restated using these symbols and μ for the population mean as:

$$H_0: \mu = 1 \text{ kg}$$
$$H_a: \mu \neq 1 \text{ kg}$$

POINTS OF INTEREST
Note that the null and alternative hypotheses contain all possible outcomes.

As another example, suppose a company has held an 18% share of the market. However, because of an increased marketing effort, company officials believe the company's market share is now greater than 18%, and the officials would like to prove it. The null hypothesis is that the market share is still 18% or perhaps it has even dropped below 18%. Converting the 18% to a proportion and using p to represent the population proportion results in the following null hypothesis:

$$H_0: p \leq 0.18$$

The alternative hypothesis is that the population proportion is now greater than 0.18:

$$H_a: p > 0.18$$

Note that the "new idea" or "new theory" that company officials want to prove is stated in the alternative hypothesis. The null hypothesis states that the old market share of 18% is still true.

Generally speaking, new hypotheses that business researchers want to prove are stated in the alternative hypothesis. Because many business researchers only undertake an experiment to determine whether their new hypothesis is correct, they are hoping that the alternative hypothesis will be proven true. However, if a manufacturer is testing to determine whether his process is out of control, as shown in the flour-packaging example, he is most likely hoping that the alternative hypothesis is not proven true, thereby demonstrating that the process is still in control.

Note in the market share example that the null hypothesis also contains the less than case (<) because between the two hypotheses (null and alternative), all possible outcomes must be included (<, >, and =). One could say that the null and alternative hypotheses are mutually exclusive (no overlap) and collectively exhaustive (all cases included). Thus, whenever a decision is made about which hypothesis is true, logically either one or the other is true but not both. Even though the company officials are not interested in proving that their market share is less than 18%, logically, it should be included as a possibility. On the other hand, many researchers and statisticians leave out the "less than" (<) portion of the null hypothesis on the market share problem because company officials are only interested in proving that the market share has increased, and the inclusion of the "less than" sign in the null hypothesis is confusing. This approach can be justified in the way that statistical hypotheses are tested. If the equal part of the null hypothesis is rejected because the market share is seemingly greater, certainly the "less than" portion of the null hypothesis is also rejected because it is farther away from "greater than" than is "equal." Using this logic, the null hypothesis for the market share problem can be written as:

$$H_0: p = 0.18$$

rather than:

$$H_0: p \leq 0.18$$

Thus, in this form, the statistical hypotheses for the market share problem can be written as

$$H_0: p = 0.18$$
$$H_a: p > 0.18$$

Even though the "less than" sign, <, is not included in the null hypothesis, it is implied that it is there. We will adopt such an approach in this book, and thus all *null* hypotheses presented in this book will be written with an equal sign only (=) rather than with a directional sign ($\leq$) or ($\geq$).

Statistical hypotheses are written so that they will produce either a one-tailed or a two-tailed test. The hypotheses shown already for the flour package manufacturing problem are two-tailed:

$$H_0: \mu = 1 \text{ kg}$$
$$H_a: \mu \neq 1 \text{ kg}$$

Two-tailed tests always use = and $\neq$ in the statistical hypotheses and are directionless in that the alternative hypothesis allows for either the greater than (>) or the less than (<) possibility. In this particular example, if the process is out of control, plant officials might not know whether machines are overfilling or underfilling packages and are interested in testing for either possibility.

The hypotheses shown for the market share problem are one-tailed:

$$H_0: p = 0.18$$
$$H_a: p > 0.18$$

One-tailed tests are always directional, and the alternative hypothesis uses either the greater than (>) or the less than (<) sign. A one-tailed test should only be used when the researcher knows for certain that the outcome of an experiment is going to occur only in one direction or the researcher is only interested in one direction of the experiment, as in the case of the market share problem. In one-tailed problems, the researcher is trying to prove that something is older, younger, higher, lower, more, less, greater, and so on. These words are considered "directional" words in that they indicate the direction of the focus of the research. Without these words, the alternative hypothesis of a one-tailed test cannot be established.

In business research, the conservative approach is to conduct a two-tailed test because sometimes study results can be obtained that are in opposition to the direction that researchers thought would occur. For example, in the market share problem, it might turn out that the company had actually lost market share; and even though company officials were not interested in proving such a case, they may need to know that it is true. It is recommended that, if in doubt, business researchers should use a two-tailed test.

POINTS OF INTEREST
It is recommended that, if in doubt, business researchers should use a two-tailed test.

SUBSTANTIVE HYPOTHESES

In testing a statistical hypothesis, a business researcher reaches a conclusion based on the data obtained in the study. If the null hypothesis is rejected and therefore the alternative hypothesis is accepted, it is common to say that a statistically significant result has been obtained. For example, in the market share problem, if the null hypothesis is rejected, the result is that the market share is "significantly greater" than 18%. The word *significant* to statisticians and business researchers merely means that the result of the experiment is unlikely due to chance and a decision has been made to reject the null hypothesis. However, in everyday business life, the word *significant* is more likely to connote "important" or "a large amount." One problem that can arise in testing statistical hypotheses is that particular characteristics of the data can result in a statistically significant outcome that is not a significant business outcome.

As an example, consider the market share study. Suppose a large sample of potential customers is taken, and a sample market share of 18.2% is obtained. Suppose further that a statistical analysis of these data results in statistical significance. We would conclude statistically that the market share is significantly higher than 18%. This finding actually means that it is unlikely that the difference between the sample proportion and the population proportion of 0.18 is due just to chance. However, to the business decision maker, a market share of 18.2% might not be significantly higher than 18%. Because of the way the word *significant* is used to denote rejection of the null hypothesis rather than an important business difference, business decision makers need to exercise caution in interpreting the outcomes of statistical tests.

In addition to understanding a statistically significant result, business decision makers need to determine what, to them, is a *substantive* result. A **substantive result** is *when the outcome of a statistical study produces results that are important to the decision maker.* The importance to the researcher will vary from study to study. As an example, in a recent year, one health care administrator was excited because patient satisfaction had significantly increased (statistically) from one year to the next. However, an examination of the data revealed that on a five-point scale, their satisfaction ratings had gone up from 3.61 to only 3.63. Is going from a 3.61 rating to a 3.63 rating in one year really a substantive increase? On the other hand, increasing the average purchase at a large, high-volume store from $55.45 to $55.50 might be substantive as well as significant if volume is large enough to drive profits higher. Both business researchers and decision makers should be aware that statistically significant results are not always substantive results.

USING THE HTAB SYSTEM TO TEST HYPOTHESES

In conducting business research, the process of testing hypotheses involves four major tasks:

- Task 1. Establishing the hypotheses
- Task 2. Conducting the test
- Task 3. Taking statistical action
- Task 4. Determining the business implications

This process, depicted in Figure 9.2, is referred to here as the HTAB system, where HTAB is an acronym for **H**ypothesize, **T**est, **A**ction, **B**usiness.

Task 1, establishing the hypotheses, encompasses all activities that lead up to the establishment of the statistical hypotheses being tested. These activities might include investigating a business opportunity or problem, developing theories about possible solutions, and establishing research hypotheses. Task 2, conducting the test, involves the selection of the proper statistical test, setting the value of alpha, establishing a decision rule, gathering sample data, and computing the statistical analysis. Task 3, taking statistical action, is making a statistical decision about whether or not to reject the null hypothesis based on the outcome of the statistical test. Task 4, determining the business implications, is deciding what the statistical action means in business terms; that is, interpreting the statistical outcome in terms of business decision making.

Figure 9.2

HTAB System of Testing Hypotheses

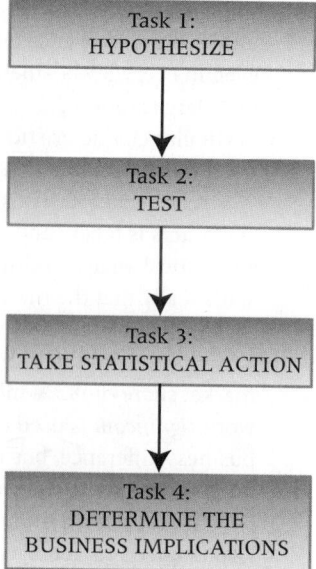

Typically, statisticians and researchers present the hypothesis-testing process in terms of an eight-step approach. These eight steps are as follows:

- Step 1. Establish a null and an alternative hypothesis.
- Step 2. Determine the appropriate statistical test.
- Step 3. Set the value of alpha, the level of significance.
- Step 4. Establish the decision rule.
- Step 5. Gather sample data.
- Step 6. Analyze the data.
- Step 7. Reach a statistical conclusion.
- Step 8. Make a business decision.

These eight steps fit nicely into the four HTAB tasks as a part of the HTAB paradigm. Figure 9.3 presents the HTAB paradigm incorporating the eight steps into the four HTAB tasks.

Task 1 of the HTAB system, hypothesizing, includes Step 1, which is establishing a null and an alternative hypothesis. In establishing the null and alternative hypotheses, it is important that the business researcher clearly identify what is being tested and whether the hypotheses are one-tailed or two-tailed. In the hypothesis-testing process, it is *always assumed that the null hypothesis is true* at the beginning of the study. In other words, it is assumed that the process is in control (no problem), that the market share has not increased, that older workers are not more loyal to a company than younger workers, and so on. This process is analogous to a trial system in which the accused is presumed innocent at the beginning of the trial.

Task 2 of the HTAB system, testing, includes Steps 2 through 6. Step 2 is to select the most appropriate statistical test to use for the analysis. In selecting such a test, the business researcher needs to consider the type, number, and level of data being used in the study along with the statistic used in the analysis (mean, proportion, variance, etc.). In addition, business researchers should consider the assumptions underlying certain statistical tests and determine whether they can be met in the study before using such tests.

At Step 3, the value of alpha is set. Alpha is the probability of committing a Type I error and will be discussed later. Common values of alpha are 0.05, 0.01, 0.10, and 0.001.

Figure 9.3

HTAB Paradigm Incorporating the Eight Steps

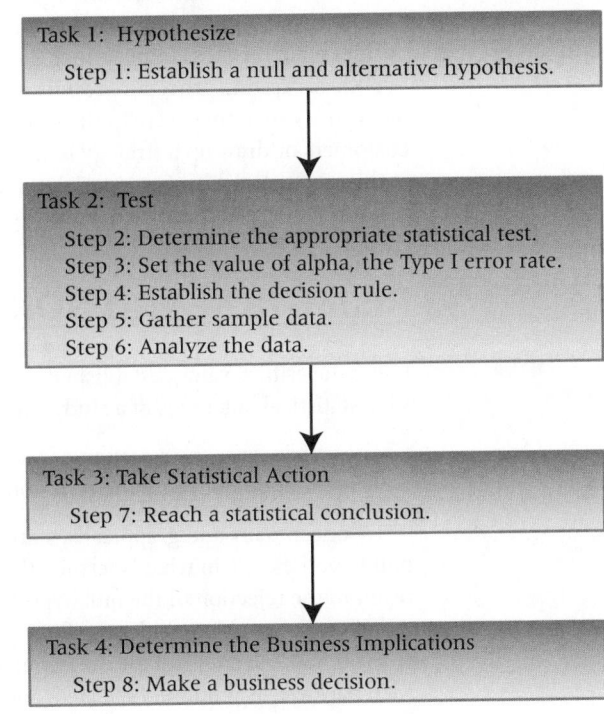

A decision rule should be established before the study is undertaken (Step 4). Using alpha and the test statistic, critical values can be determined. These **critical values** are *used at the decision step to determine whether the null hypothesis is rejected* or not. If the *p* value method (discussed later) is used, the value of alpha is used as a critical probability value. The process begins by assuming that the null hypothesis is true. Data are gathered and statistics computed. If the evidence is away from the null hypothesis, the business researcher begins to doubt that the null hypothesis is really true. If the evidence is far enough away from the null hypothesis that the critical value is surpassed, the business researcher will reject the null hypothesis and declare that a statistically significant result has been attained. Here again, the process is analogous to a trial system in which the accused is presumed innocent at the beginning of the trial. Prosecutors present evidence against the defendant (analogous to data gathered and analyzed in a study). At some point, if enough evidence is presented against the defendant such that the jury no longer believes the defendant is innocent, a critical level of evidence has been reached and the jury finds the defendant guilty. The first four steps in testing hypotheses should *always* be completed *before* the study is undertaken. It is not sound research to gather data first and then try to determine what to do with the data.

Step 5 is to gather sample data. This step might include the construction and implementation of a survey, conducting focus groups, randomly sampling items from an assembly line, or even sampling from secondary data sources (e.g., financial databases). In gathering data, the business researcher is cautioned to recall the proper techniques of random sampling (presented in Chapter 7). Care should be taken in establishing a frame, determining the sampling technique, and constructing the measurement device. A strong effort should be made to avoid all nonsampling errors. After the data are sampled, the test statistic can be calculated (Step 6).

Task 3 of the HTAB system, taking statistical action, includes Step 7. Using the previously established decision rule (in Step 4) and the value of the test statistic, the business researcher can draw a statistical conclusion. In *all* hypothesis tests, the business researcher needs to conclude whether the null hypothesis is rejected or not (Step 7).

Task 4 of the HTAB system, determining the business implications, incorporates Step 8. After a statistical decision is made, the business researcher or decision maker decides what business implications the study results contain (Step 8). For example, if the hypothesis-testing procedure results in a conclusion that train passengers are significantly older today than they were in the past, the manager may decide to cater to these older customers or draw up a strategy to make ridership more appealing to younger people. It is at this step that the business decision maker must decide whether a statistically significant result is really a substantive result.

REJECTION AND NONREJECTION REGIONS

Using the critical values established at Step 4 of the hypothesis-testing process, the possible statistical outcomes of a study can be divided into two groups:

1. Those that cause the rejection of the null hypothesis
2. Those that do not cause the rejection of the null hypothesis

Conceptually and graphically, statistical outcomes that result in the rejection of the null hypothesis lie in what is termed the **rejection region.** Statistical outcomes that fail to result in the rejection of the null hypothesis lie in what is termed the **nonrejection region.**

As an example, consider the flour package manufacturing example. The null hypothesis is that the average fill for the population of packages is 1 kg. Suppose a sample of 100 such packages is randomly selected, and a sample mean of 1.00025 kg is obtained. Because this mean is not 1 kg, should the business researcher decide to reject the null hypothesis? In the hypothesis-testing process, we are using sample statistics (in this case, the sample mean of 1.00025 kg) to make decisions about population parameters (in this case, the population mean of 1 kg). It makes sense that in taking random samples from a population with a mean of 1 kg, not all sample means will equal 1 kg. In fact, the central limit theorem (see Chapter 7) states that for large sample sizes, sample means are normally distributed around the population mean. Thus, even when the population mean is 1 kg, a sample mean might still be 1.00025 kg, 0.965 kg, or even 1.105 kg. However, suppose a sample mean of 1.25 kg is obtained for 100 packages. This sample mean may be so far from what is reasonable to expect for a population with a mean of 1 kg that the decision is made to reject the null hypothesis. This makes us want to know: when is the sample mean so far away from the population mean that the null hypothesis is rejected? The critical values established at Step 4 of the hypothesis-testing process are used to divide the means that lead to the rejection of the null hypothesis from those that do not. Figure 9.4 displays a normal distribution of sample means around a population mean of 1 kg. Note the critical values in each end (tail) of the distribution. In each direction beyond the critical values

Figure 9.4

Rejection and Nonrejection Regions

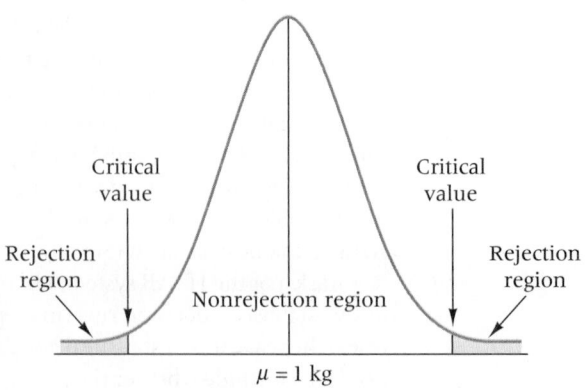

lie the rejection regions. Any sample mean that falls in that region will lead the business researcher to reject the null hypothesis. Sample means that fall between the two critical values are close enough to the population mean that the business researcher will decide not to reject the null hypothesis. These means are in the nonrejection region.

TYPE I AND TYPE II ERRORS

Because the hypothesis-testing process uses sample statistics calculated from random data to reach conclusions about population parameters, it is possible to make an incorrect decision about the null hypothesis. In particular, two types of errors can be made in testing hypotheses: Type I errors and Type II errors.

A **Type I error** is committed by *rejecting a true null hypothesis*. With a Type I error, the null hypothesis is true, but the business researcher decides that it is not. As an example, suppose the flour package process is actually in control and is averaging 1 kg of flour per package. Suppose also that a business researcher randomly selects 100 packages, weighs the contents of each, and computes a sample mean. It is possible, by chance, to randomly select 100 of the more extreme packages (mostly heavy masses or mostly light masses), resulting in a mean that falls in the rejection region. The decision is to reject the null hypothesis even though the population mean is actually 1 kg. In this case, the business researcher has committed a Type I error.

The notion of a Type I error can be used outside the realm of statistical hypothesis testing in the business world. For example, if a manager fires an employee because some evidence indicates that she is stealing from the company when she really isn't stealing from the company, the manager has committed a Type I error. As another example, suppose a worker on the assembly line of a large manufacturer hears an unusual sound and decides to shut the line down (reject the null hypothesis). If the sound turns out not to be related to the assembly line and no problems are occurring with the assembly line, the worker has committed a Type I error. When products are in great demand and production capacity is tight, workers are sometimes strongly discouraged from making such Type I errors because the production downtime could be expensive. An analogous courtroom example of a Type I error is when an innocent person is sent to jail.

In Figure 9.4, the rejection regions represent the possibility of committing a Type I error. Means that fall beyond the critical values will be considered so extreme that the business researcher chooses to reject the null hypothesis. However, if the null hypothesis is true, any mean that falls in a rejection region will result in a decision that produces a Type I error. The *probability of committing a Type I error* is called **alpha** (α) or **level of significance.** Alpha equals the area under the curve that is in the rejection region beyond the critical value(s). The value of alpha is always set before the experiment or study is undertaken. As mentioned previously, common values of alpha are 0.05, 0.01, 0.10, and 0.001.

A **Type II error** is committed when a business researcher *fails to reject a false null hypothesis*. In this case, the null hypothesis is false, but a decision is made to not reject it. Suppose in the case of the flour problem that the packaging process is actually producing a population mean of 1.025 kg even though the null hypothesis is 1 kg. A sample of 100 packages yields a sample mean of 1.005 kg, which falls in the nonrejection region. The business decision maker decides not to reject the null hypothesis. A Type II error has been committed. The packaging procedure is out of control and the hypothesis-testing process did not identify it.

Suppose in the business world an employee is stealing from the company. A manager sees some evidence that the stealing is occurring but lacks enough evidence to conclude that the employee is stealing from the company. The manager decides not to fire the employee based on theft. The manager has committed a Type II error. Consider the manufacturing line with the noise. Suppose the worker decides not enough noise is heard to shut the line down, but in actuality one of the cords on the line is unravelling, creating a dangerous situation. The worker is committing a Type II error. Manufacturers can also protect themselves against Type II errors. In many cases, it is more costly to produce bad product (e.g., scrap/rework costs and loss of market share due to poor quality) than it is to make it right the first time. Manufacturers sometimes encourage workers to shut down the line if the quality of work is seemingly not what it should be (risking a Type I error) rather than allowing poor-quality product to be shipped. In a court of law, a Type II error is committed when a guilty person is declared innocent.

The probability of committing a Type II error is **beta (β)**. Unlike alpha, beta is not usually stated at the beginning of the hypothesis-testing procedure. Actually, because beta occurs only when the null hypothesis is not true, the computation of beta varies with the many possible alternative parameters that might occur. For example, in the flour package problem, if the population mean is not 1 kg, then what is it? It could be 1.025, 0.95, or 1.05 kg. A value of beta is associated with each of these alternative means. We will cover the method of how to calculate the probability of committing a Type II error later in the chapter.

How are alpha and beta related? First of all, because alpha can only be committed when the null hypothesis is rejected and beta can only be committed when the null hypothesis is not rejected, a business researcher cannot commit both a Type I error and a Type II error at the same time on the same hypothesis test. Generally, alpha and beta are inversely related. If alpha is reduced, beta is increased, and vice versa. In terms of the manufacturing assembly line, if management makes it harder for workers to shut down the assembly line (reduce Type I error), there is a greater chance that bad product will be made or that a serious problem with the line will arise (increase Type II error). Legally, if the courts make it harder to send innocent people to jail, they have made it easier to let guilty people go free. One way to reduce both errors is to increase the sample size. If a larger sample is taken, it is more likely that the sample is representative of the population, which translates into a better chance that a business researcher will make the correct choice. Figure 9.5 shows the relationship between the two types of error. The state of nature is how things actually are and the action is the decision that the business researcher actually makes. Note that each action alternative contains only one of the errors along with the possibility that a correct decision has been made. **Power,** which is equal to $1 - \beta$, is *the probability of a statistical test rejecting the null hypothesis when the null hypothesis is false.* Figure 9.5 shows the relationship between α, β, and power.

Figure 9.5

Alpha, Beta, and Power

	State of nature	
	Null true	Null false
Fail to reject null	Correct decision	Type II error (β)
Reject null	Type I error (α)	Correct decision (power)

Action

Concept Check

1. The null hypothesis is denoted by _____, while the alternative hypothesis is denoted by _____.
2. Explain what rejection and nonrejection regions are and how they relate to hypothesis testing.
3. What is the relationship of α to the Type I error? What is the relationship of β to the Type II error? Explain.

4. Why is it possible for the null hypothesis to be rejected when it is in fact true?
5. Why is it possible to fail to reject the null hypothesis when it is in fact false?
6. What does 1 − β represent? Explain.
7. How are α and β related? Explain.

9.2 TESTING HYPOTHESES ABOUT A POPULATION MEAN USING THE *z* STATISTIC (σ KNOWN)

One of the most basic hypothesis tests is a test about a population mean. A business researcher might be interested in testing to determine whether an established or accepted mean value for an industry is still true or in testing a hypothesized mean value for a new theory or product. As an example, a computer products company sets up a telephone service to assist customers by providing technical support. The average wait time during weekday hours is 37 minutes. However, a recent hiring effort added technical consultants to the system, and management believes that the average wait time has decreased, and they want to prove it. Other business scenarios resulting in hypothesis tests of a single mean might be as follows:

- A financial investment firm wants to test to determine whether the average hourly change in the Toronto Stock Exchange over a 10-year period is +0.25.
- A manufacturing company wants to test to determine whether the average thickness of a plastic bottle is 2.4 mm.
- A retail store wants to test to determine whether the average age of its customers is less than 40 years.

Formula 9.1 can be used to test hypotheses about a single population mean when σ is known if the sample size is large ($n \geq 30$) for any population and for small samples ($n < 30$) if *x* is known to be normally distributed in the population.

z Test for a Single Mean (9.1)	$z = \dfrac{\bar{x} - \mu}{\dfrac{\sigma}{\sqrt{n}}}$

A survey of chartered accountants (CAs) found that the average net income for sole proprietor CAs is \$74,914.* Because this survey is now almost 15 years old, an accounting researcher wants to test this figure by taking a random sample of 112 sole proprietor CAs to determine whether the net income figure has changed. The researcher could use the eight steps of hypothesis testing to do so. Assume the population standard deviation of net incomes for sole proprietor CAs is \$14,530.

HYPOTHESIZE:

At Step 1, the hypotheses must be established. Because the researcher is testing to determine whether the figure has changed, the alternative hypothesis is that the mean

---

*Adapted from Daniel J. Flaherty, Raymond A. Zimmerman, and Mary Ann Murray, "Benchmarking Against the Best," *Journal of Accountancy* (July 1995), pp. 85–88.

net income is not $74,914. The null hypothesis is that the mean still equals $74,914. These hypotheses follow.

$$H_0: \mu = \$74,914$$
$$H_a: \mu \neq \$74,914$$

TEST:

Step 2 is to determine the appropriate statistical test and sampling distribution. Because the population standard deviation is known ($14,530) and the researcher is using the sample mean as the statistic, the z test in formula 9.1 is the appropriate test statistic:

$$z = \frac{\bar{x} - \mu}{\frac{\sigma}{\sqrt{n}}}$$

Step 3 is to specify the Type I error rate, or alpha, which is 0.05 in this problem. Step 4 is to state the decision rule. Because the test is two-tailed and alpha is 0.05, there is $\alpha/2$ or 0.025 area in each of the tails of the distribution. Thus, the rejection region is in the two ends of the distribution, with 2.5% of the area in each. There is a 0.4750 area between the mean and each of the critical values that separate the tails of the distribution (the rejection region) from the nonrejection region. By using this 0.4750 area and Table A.5, the critical z value can be obtained:

$$z_{\alpha/2} = \pm 1.96$$

Figure 9.6 displays the problem with the rejection regions and the critical values of z. The decision rule is that if the data gathered produce a z value greater than 1.96 or less than −1.96, the test statistic is in one of the rejection regions and the decision is to reject the null hypothesis. If the observed z value calculated from the data is between −1.96 and +1.96, the decision is to not reject the null hypothesis because the observed z value is in the nonrejection region.

Step 5 is to gather the data. Suppose the 112 CAs who respond produce a sample mean of $78,695. At Step 6, the value of the test statistic is calculated by using $\bar{x} = \$78,695$, $n = 112$, $\sigma = \$14,530$, and a hypothesized $\mu = \$74,914$:

$$z = \frac{78,695 - 74,914}{\frac{14,530}{\sqrt{112}}} = 2.75$$

Figure 9.6

CA Net Income Example

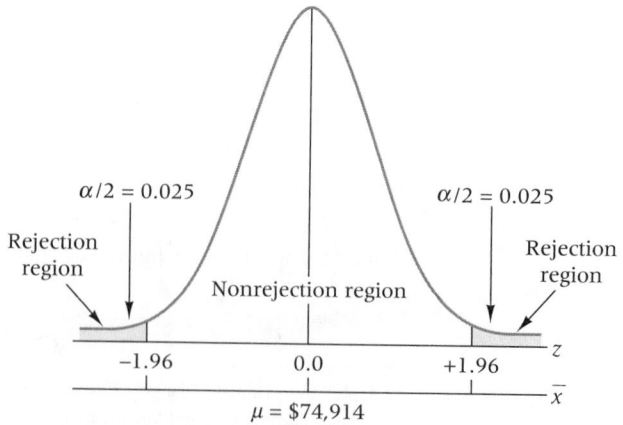

ACTION:

Because this test statistic, $z = 2.75$, is greater than the critical value of z in the upper tail of the distribution, $z = +1.96$, the statistical conclusion reached at Step 7 of the hypothesis-testing process is to reject the null hypothesis. *The calculated test statistic is often referred to as the* **observed value.** Thus, the observed value of z for this problem is 2.75 and the critical value of z for this problem is 1.96.

BUSINESS IMPLICATION:

Step 8 is to make a managerial decision. What does this result mean? Statistically, the researcher has enough evidence to reject the figure of \$74,914 as the true average net income for sole proprietor CAs. Although the researcher conducted a two-tailed test, the evidence gathered indicates that the average may have increased. The sample mean of \$78,695 is \$3,781 higher than the mean being tested. The researcher can conclude that the average is more than before, but because the \$78,695 is only a sample mean, it offers no guarantee that the average for all sole proprietor CAs is \$3,781 more. If a confidence interval were constructed with the sample data, \$78,695 would be the point estimate. Other samples might produce different sample means. Managerially, this statistical finding may mean that CAs will be more expensive to hire either as full-time employees or as consultants. It may mean that consulting services have gone up in price. For new accountants, it may mean the potential for greater earning power.

TESTING THE MEAN WITH A FINITE POPULATION

If the hypothesis test for the population mean is being conducted with a known finite population, the population information can be incorporated into the hypothesis-testing formula. Doing so can increase the potential for rejecting the null hypothesis. However, remember from Chapter 7 that if the sample size is less than 5% of the population, the finite correction factor does not significantly alter the solution. Formula 9.1 can be amended to include the population information.

Formula to Test Hypotheses About μ with a Finite Population (9.2)	$$z = \frac{\bar{x} - \mu}{\dfrac{\sigma}{\sqrt{n}} \sqrt{\dfrac{N - n}{N - 1}}}$$

In the CA net income example, suppose that a total of only 600 sole proprietor CAs are in practice. A sample of 112 CAs taken from a population of only 600 CAs is 18.67% of the population and therefore is much more likely to be representative of the population than a sample of 112 CAs taken from a population of 20,000 CAs (0.56% of the population). The finite correction factor takes this difference into consideration and allows for an increase in the observed value of z. The observed z value would change to

$$z = \frac{\bar{x} - \mu}{\dfrac{\sigma}{\sqrt{n}} \sqrt{\dfrac{N - n}{N - 1}}} = \frac{78{,}695 - 74{,}914}{\dfrac{14{,}530}{\sqrt{112}} \sqrt{\dfrac{600 - 112}{600 - 1}}} = \frac{3{,}781}{1{,}239.2} = 3.05$$

Use of the finite correction factor increased the observed z value from 2.75 to 3.05. The decision to reject the null hypothesis does not change with this new information. However, on occasion, the finite correction factor can make the difference between rejecting and failing to reject the null hypothesis.

USING THE *p* VALUE TO TEST HYPOTHESES

Another way to reach a statistical conclusion in hypothesis-testing problems is by using the *p* value, sometimes referred to as the **observed significance level.** The *p* value is growing in importance with the increasing use of statistical computer packages in business. No preset value of α is given in the *p* value method. Instead, the probability of getting a test statistic at least as extreme as the observed test statistic (computed from the data) is computed under the assumption that the null hypothesis is true. Virtually every statistical computer program yields this probability (*p* value). *The p value defines the smallest value of alpha for which the null hypothesis can be rejected.* For example, if the *p* value of a test is 0.038, the null hypothesis cannot be rejected at α = 0.01 because 0.038 is the smallest value of alpha for which the null hypothesis can be rejected. However, the null hypothesis can be rejected for α = 0.05.

Suppose a researcher is conducting a one-tailed test with a rejection region in the upper tail and obtains an observed test statistic of $z = 2.04$ from the sample data. Using the standard normal table, Table A.5, we find that the probability of randomly obtaining a *z* value this great or greater by chance is $0.5000 - 0.4793 = 0.0207$. The *p* value is 0.0207. Using this information, the researcher would reject the null hypothesis for α = 0.05 or 0.10 or any value more than 0.0207. The researcher would not reject the null hypothesis for any alpha value less than or equal to 0.0207 (in particular α = 0.01, 0.001, etc.).

For a two-tailed test, recall that we split alpha to determine the critical value of the test statistic. With the *p* value, the probability of getting a test statistic at least as extreme as the observed value is computed. This *p* value is then compared to α/2 for two-tailed tests to determine statistical significance. The business researcher should be cautioned that some statistical computer packages are programmed to double the observed probability and report that value as the *p* value when the user signifies that a two-tailed test is being requested. The researcher then compares this *p* value to alpha values to decide whether to reject the null hypothesis. The researcher must be sure she understands what the computer software package does to the *p* value for a two-tailed test before she reaches a statistical conclusion.

As an example of using *p* values with a two-tailed test, consider the CA net income problem. The observed test statistic for this problem is $z = 2.75$. Using Table A.5, we know that the probability of obtaining a test statistic at least this extreme if the null hypothesis is true is $0.5000 - 0.4970 = 0.0030$. Observe that in the Excel output in Figure 9.7 the *p* value is 0.0030. When Excel yields a *p* value in its output, it always gives the one-tailed value, which in this case is 0.0030 (see output in Figure 9.7). To reach a statistical conclusion from an Excel-produced *p* value when doing a two-tailed test, the researcher must compare the *p* value to α/2.

Figure 9.8 summarizes the decisions that can be made using various *p* values for a one-tailed test. To use this for a two-tailed test, compare the *p* value in one tail to α/2 in a similar manner. Because α = 0.10 is usually the largest value of alpha used by most researchers, if a *p* value is not less than 0.10, the decision is to fail to reject the null hypothesis. In other words, the null hypothesis cannot be rejected if *p* values are 0.579 or 0.106

Figure 9.7

Excel Output with *p* Values

	A	B
	CA Net Income Problem	
1	Sample mean	78,695
2	Standard error	1,374
3	Standard deviation	14,530
4	Observations	112
5	Hypothesized value of μ	74,914
6	*p* value	0.0030

Figure 9.8

Rejecting the Null Hypothesis Using *p* Values

Range of *p* Values	Rejection Range
p-value ≥ 0.10	Cannot reject the null hypothesis for commonly accepted values of alpha
0.05 ≤ *p* value < 0.10	Reject the null hypothesis for $\alpha = 0.10$
0.01 ≤ *p* value < 0.05	Reject the null hypothesis for $\alpha = 0.05$
0.001 ≤ *p* value < 0.01	Reject the null hypothesis for $\alpha = 0.01$
0.0001 ≤ *p* value < 0.001	Reject the null hypothesis for $\alpha = 0.001$

or 0.283, etc. If a *p* value is less than 0.10 but not less than 0.05, the null hypothesis can be rejected for $\alpha = 0.10$. If it is less than 0.05, but not less than 0.01, the null hypothesis can be rejected for $\alpha = 0.05$, and so on.

USING THE CRITICAL VALUE METHOD TO TEST HYPOTHESES

Another method of testing hypotheses is the critical value method. In the CA income example, the null hypothesis was rejected because the computed value of *z* was in the rejection zone. What mean income would it take to cause the observed *z* value to be in the rejection zone? The **critical value method** *determines the critical mean value required for z to be in the rejection region and uses it to test the hypotheses.*

This method also uses formula 9.1. However, instead of an observed *z*, a critical $\bar{x}$ value, $\bar{x}_c$, is determined. The critical table value of z_c is inserted into the formula, along with μ and σ. Thus,

$$z_c = \frac{\bar{x}_c - \mu}{\dfrac{\sigma}{\sqrt{n}}}$$

Substituting values from the CA income example gives

$$\pm 1.96 = \frac{\bar{x}_c - 74,914}{\dfrac{14,530}{\sqrt{112}}}$$

or

$$\bar{x}_c = 74,914 \pm 1.96 \frac{14,530}{\sqrt{112}} = 74,914 \pm 2,691$$

$$\text{lower } \bar{x}_c = 72,223 \text{ and upper } \bar{x}_c = 77,605$$

Figure 9.9

Rejection and Nonrejection Regions for Critical Value Method

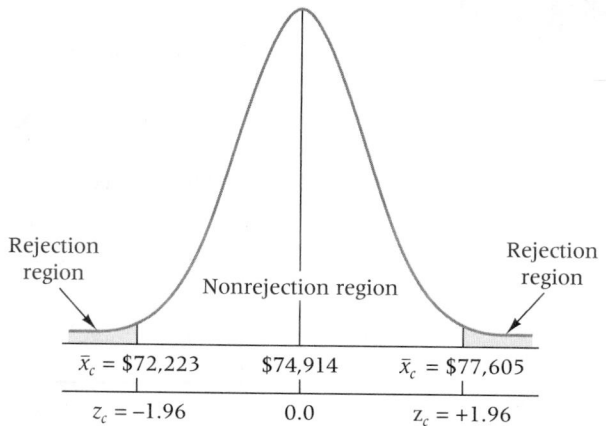

Figure 9.9 depicts graphically the rejection and nonrejection regions in terms of means instead of z scores.

With the critical value method, most of the computational work is done ahead of time. In this problem, before the sample means are computed, the analyst knows that a sample mean value of greater than $77,605 or less than $72,223 must be attained to reject the hypothesized population mean. Because the sample mean for this problem was $78,695, which is greater than $77,605, the analyst rejects the null hypothesis. This method is particularly attractive in industrial settings where standards can be set ahead of time and then quality-control technicians can gather data and compare actual measurements of products to specifications.

Demonstration Problem 9.1

In an attempt to determine why customer service is important to managers, researchers surveyed managing directors of manufacturing plants in Scotland.[*] One of the reasons proposed was that customer service is a means of retaining customers. On a scale of 1 to 5, with 1 being low and 5 being high, the survey respondents rated this reason more highly than any of the others, with a mean response of 4.30. Suppose we believe that Canadian manufacturing managers would not rate this reason as highly and conduct a hypothesis test to prove this theory. The significance level is set at 0.05. Data are gathered and the following results are obtained. Use these data and the eight steps of hypothesis testing to determine whether Canadian managers rate this reason significantly lower than the 4.30 mean ascertained in Scotland. Assume from previous studies that the population standard deviation is 0.574.

3	4	5	5	4	5	5	4	4	4	4
4	4	4	4	5	4	4	4	3	4	4
4	3	5	4	4	5	4	4	4	5	

Solution

HYPOTHESIZE:

STEP 1. Establish hypotheses. Because we are interested only in proving that the mean figure is lower in Canada, the test is one-tailed. The alternative hypothesis is that the

---

[*] William G. Donaldson, "Manufacturers Need to Show Greater Commitment to Customer Service," *Industrial Marketing Management*, vol. 24 (October 1995), pp. 421–430. The 1 to 5 scale has been reversed here for clarity of presentation.

population mean is lower than 4.30. The null hypothesis states the equality case.

$$H_0: \mu = 4.30$$
$$H_a: \mu < 4.30$$

TEST:

STEP 2. Determine the appropriate statistical test. The test statistic is:

$$z = \frac{\bar{x} - \mu}{\dfrac{\sigma}{\sqrt{n}}}$$

STEP 3. Specify the Type I error rate:

$$\alpha = 0.05$$

STEP 4. State the decision rule. Because this test is a one-tailed test, the critical z value is found by looking up $0.5000 - 0.0500 = 0.4500$ as the area in Table A.5. The critical value of the test statistic is $z_{0.05} = -1.645$. An observed test statistic must be less than -1.645 to reject the null hypothesis. The rejection region and critical value can be depicted as in the following diagram.

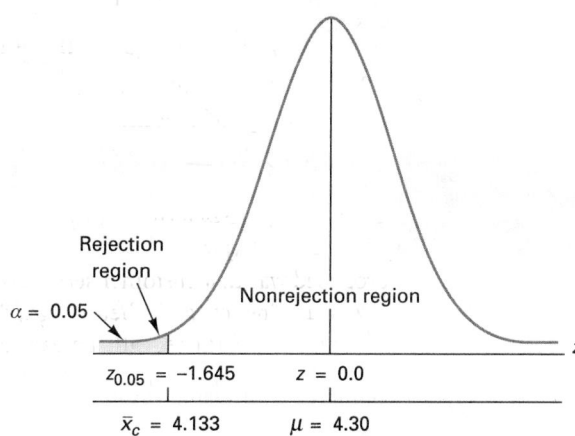

STEP 5. Gather the sample data. The data are shown.
STEP 6. Calculate the value of the test statistic:

$$\bar{x} = 4.156$$
$$\sigma = 0.574$$
$$z = \frac{4.156 - 4.30}{\dfrac{0.574}{\sqrt{32}}} = -1.42$$

ACTION:

STEP 7. State the statistical conclusion. Because the observed test statistic is not less than the critical value and is not in the rejection region, the statistical conclusion is that the null hypothesis cannot be rejected. The same result is obtained using the p value method. The observed test statistic is $z = -1.42$. From Table A.5, the probability of getting a z value at least this extreme when the null hypothesis is true is $0.5000 - 0.4222 = 0.0778$. Hence, the null hypothesis cannot be rejected at $\alpha = 0.05$ because the smallest value of alpha for which the null hypothesis can be rejected is 0.0778. Had α equalled 0.10, the decision would have been to reject the null hypothesis.

BUSINESS IMPLICATION:

STEP 8. Make a managerial decision. The test does not result in enough evidence to conclude that Canadian managers think it is less important to use customer service as a means of retaining customers than do managers in Scotland. Customer service is an important tool for retaining customers in both countries according to managers.

Using the critical value method: For what sample mean (or more extreme) value would the null hypothesis be rejected? This critical sample mean can be determined by using the critical z value associated with alpha, $z_{0.05} = -1.645$:

$$z_c = \frac{\bar{x}_c - \mu}{\dfrac{\sigma}{\sqrt{n}}}$$

$$-1.645 = \frac{\bar{x}_c - 4.30}{\dfrac{0.574}{\sqrt{32}}}$$

$$\bar{x}_c = 4.133$$

The decision rule is that a sample mean less than 4.133 would be necessary to reject the null hypothesis. Because the mean obtained from the sample data is 4.156, the researchers fail to reject the null hypothesis. The preceding diagram includes a scale with the critical sample mean and the rejection region for the critical value method.

USING THE COMPUTER TO TEST HYPOTHESES ABOUT A POPULATION MEAN USING THE z STATISTIC

Excel can be used to test hypotheses about a single population mean using the z statistic. Figure 9.10 contains output from Excel for Demonstration Problem 9.1. Note that the Excel output contains only the right-tailed p value of the z statistic. With a negative observed z for Demonstration Problem 9.1, the p value was calculated by taking 1 minus Excel's answer.

Figure 9.10

Excel Output for Demonstration Problem 9.1

	A	B
	Customer Service Problem	
1	Sample mean	4.15600
2	Standard error	0.10147
3	Standard deviation	0.57400
4	Observations	32
5	Hypothesized value of μ	4.30000
6	p value	0.07780

Concept Check

1. Explain what a p value is and how it is used in hypothesis testing.
2. Explain how a p value relates to the rejection and nonrejection regions in hypothesis testing.

9.1   a.   Use the data given to test the following hypotheses.

$$H_0: \mu = 25$$
$$H_a: \mu \neq 25$$

$$\bar{x} = 28.1, n = 57, \sigma = 8.46, \alpha = 0.01$$

     b.   Use the p value to reach a statistical conclusion.
     c.   Using the critical value method, determine the critical sample mean values.

9.2   Use the data given to test the following hypotheses. Assume the data are normally distributed in the population.

$$H_0: \mu = 7.48$$
$$H_a: \mu < 7.48$$

$$\bar{x} = 6.91, n = 24, \sigma = 1.21, \alpha = 0.01$$

9.3   a.   Use the data given to test the following hypotheses.

$$H_0: \mu = 1,200$$
$$H_a: \mu > 1,200$$

$$\bar{x} = 1,215, n = 113, \sigma = 100, \alpha = 0.10$$

     b.   Use the p value to reach a statistical conclusion.
     c.   Solve for the critical value required to reject the null hypothesis.

9.4   Assume that for the city of Hamilton, Ontario, an environmental study reported that the average number of micrograms of suspended particles per cubic metre of air is 82. Suppose Hamilton officials have been working with businesses, commuters, and industries to reduce this figure. These city officials hire an environmental company to take random measures of air soot over a period of several weeks. The resulting data are shown below. Assume that the population standard deviation is 9.184. Use these data to determine whether the urban air soot in Hamilton is significantly lower than what the environmental study reported. Let $\alpha = 0.01$. If the null hypothesis is rejected, discuss the substantive hypothesis.

81.6	66.6	70.9	82.5	58.3	71.6	72.4
96.6	78.6	76.1	80.0	73.2	85.5	73.2
68.6	74.0	68.7	83.0	86.9	94.9	75.6
77.3	86.6	71.7	88.5	87.0	72.5	83.0
85.8	74.9	61.7	92.2			

9.5   Assume that the average weekly earnings of a production worker in 2001 were $424.20. Suppose a labour researcher wants to test to determine whether this figure is still accurate today. The researcher randomly selects 54 production workers from across Canada and obtains a representative earnings statement for one week from each. The resulting sample average is $432.69. Assuming a population standard deviation of $33.90 and a 5% level of significance, determine if there is sufficient evidence to claim that the mean weekly earnings of a production worker have changed.

9.6   According to a study several years ago by the Personal Communications Industry Association, the average wireless phone user earns $62,600 per year. Suppose a researcher believes that the average annual earnings of a wireless phone user are lower now and he sets up a study in an attempt to prove his theory. He randomly samples 18 wireless phone users and finds out that the average annual salary for this sample is $58,974, with a population standard deviation of $7,810. Use $\alpha = 0.01$ to test the researcher's theory. Assume wages in this industry are normally distributed.

9.7 A manufacturing company produces valves in various sizes and shapes. One particular valve plate is supposed to have a tensile strength of 500 MPa (megapascals). The company tests a random sample of 42 such valve plates from a lot of 650 valve plates. The sample mean is a tensile strength of 506.11 MPa, and the population standard deviation is 28.03 MPa. Use $\alpha = 0.10$ and test to determine whether the lot of valve plates has an average tensile strength of 500 MPa.

9.8 A manufacturing firm has been averaging 18.2 orders per week for several years. However, during a recession, orders appeared to slow. Suppose the firm's production manager randomly samples 32 weeks and finds a sample mean of 15.6 orders. The population standard deviation is 2.3 orders. Test to determine whether the average number of orders is down by using $\alpha = 0.10$.

9.9 A study conducted by Runzheimer International showed that Paris is the most expensive place to live of 12 European Union cities. Paris ranks second in housing expense, with a rental unit of six to nine rooms costing an average of $4,292 a month. Suppose a company's CEO believes this figure is too high and decides to conduct her own survey. Her assistant contacts the owners of 55 randomly selected rental units of six to nine rooms and finds that the sample average cost is $4,008. Assume that the population standard deviation is $386. Using the sample results and $\alpha = 0.01$, test to determine whether the figure published by Runzheimer International is too high. If the null hypothesis is rejected, discuss whether the results are substantive.

9.10 The *Calgary Herald* reported on February 25, 2008, that the average daily water usage in the city for 2007 was 437 L per person. Assume that the national average daily water usage in Canada for 2007 was 492 L per person. Suppose some researchers believe that more water is being used now and want to test to determine whether it is so. They randomly select a sample of Canadians and carefully keep track of the water used by each sample member for a day, then analyze the results by using a statistical computer software package. The output is given here. Assume $\alpha = 0.05$. How many people were sampled? What was the sample mean? Was this a one- or two-tailed test? What was the result of the study? What decision could be made about the null hypothesis from these results?

One-Sample z

Test of $\mu = 492$ vs. > 492
The assumed standard deviation = 101.72

n	Mean	SE Mean	95% Lower Bound	z	p
40	529.44	17.508	500.644	2.14	0.016

9.3 TESTING HYPOTHESES ABOUT A POPULATION MEAN USING THE *t* STATISTIC (σ UNKNOWN)

Very often when a business researcher is gathering data to test hypotheses about a single population mean, the value of the population standard deviation is unknown and the researcher must use the sample standard deviation as an estimate of it. In such cases, the z test cannot be used.

Chapter 8 presented the *t* distribution, which can be used to analyze hypotheses about a single population mean when σ is unknown if the population is normally distributed for the measurement being studied. In this section, we will examine the *t* test for a single population mean. In general, this *t* test is applicable whenever the researcher is drawing a single random sample to test the value of a population mean (μ), the population standard deviation is unknown, and the population is normally distributed for the measurement of interest. Recall from Chapter 8 that the assumption that the data be normally distributed in the population is rather robust.

The formula for testing such hypotheses follows.

t Test for μ (9.3)	$$t = \frac{\bar{x} - \mu}{\frac{s}{\sqrt{n}}}$$ $$df = n - 1$$

The Maple Leaf Farmers' Production Company builds large harvesters. For a harvester to be properly balanced when operating, a 25-kg plate is installed on its side. The machine that produces these plates is set to yield plates that average 25 kg. The distribution of plates produced from the machine is normal. However, the shop supervisor is worried that the machine is out of adjustment and is producing plates that do not average 25 kg. To test this concern, he randomly selects 20 of the plates produced the day before and weighs them. Table 9.1 shows the masses obtained, along with the computed sample mean and sample standard deviation.

The test is to determine whether the machine is out of control, and the shop supervisor has not specified whether he believes the machine is producing plates that are too heavy or too light. Thus, a two-tailed test is appropriate. The following hypotheses are tested:

$$H_0: \mu = 25 \text{ kg}$$
$$H_a: \mu \neq 25 \text{ kg}$$

An α of 0.05 is used. Figure 9.11 shows the rejection regions.

Because $n = 20$, the degrees of freedom for this test are 19 (20 − 1). The *t* distribution table is a one-tailed table but the test for this problem is two-tailed, so alpha must be split, which yields $\alpha/2 = 0.025$, the value in each tail. (To obtain the table *t* value when conducting a two-tailed test, always split alpha and use $\alpha/2$.) The table *t* value for this example is 2.093. Table values such as this one are often written in the following form:

$$t_{0.025,19} = 2.093$$

Figure 9.12 depicts the *t* distribution for this example, along with the critical values, the observed *t* value, and the rejection regions. In this case, the decision rule is to reject

Table 9.1					
Masses in Kilograms of a Sample of 20 Plates	22.6	22.2	23.2	27.4	24.5
	27.0	26.6	28.1	26.9	24.9
	26.2	25.3	23.1	24.2	26.1
	25.8	30.4	28.6	23.5	23.6
		$\bar{x} = 25.51$, $s = 2.1933$, $n = 20$			

Figure 9.11

Rejection Regions for the Machine Plate Example

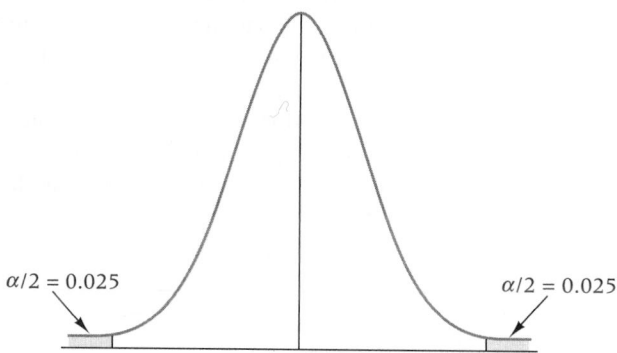

$\alpha/2 = 0.025$ $\alpha/2 = 0.025$

the null hypothesis if the observed value of t is less than -2.093 or greater than $+2.093$ (in the tails of the distribution). Computation of the test statistic yields:

$$t = \frac{\bar{x} - \mu}{\dfrac{s}{\sqrt{n}}} = \frac{25.51 - 25.00}{\dfrac{2.1933}{\sqrt{20}}} = 1.04$$

Because the observed t value is $+1.04$, the null hypothesis is not rejected. Not enough evidence is found in this sample to reject the hypothesis that the population mean is 25 kg.

Figure 9.13 shows the Excel output for this example. The Excel output contains the observed t value (1.04) plus the p value and the critical table t value for both a one-tailed

Figure 9.12

Graph of Observed and Critical t Values for the Machine Plate Example

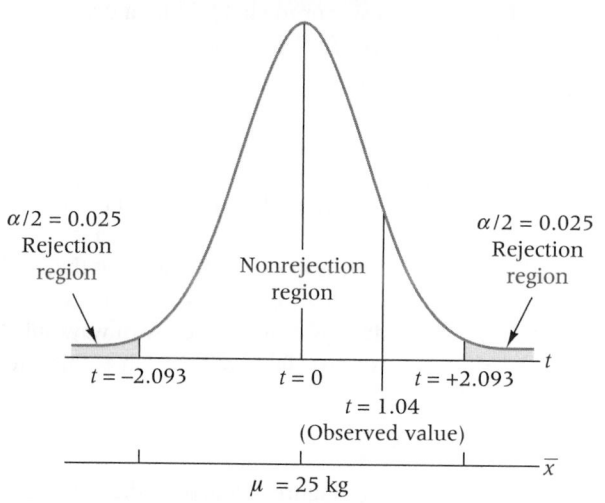

$\alpha/2 = 0.025$
Rejection region

Nonrejection region

$\alpha/2 = 0.025$
Rejection region

$t = -2.093$ $t = 0$ $t = +2.093$

$t = 1.04$
(Observed value)

$\mu = 25$ kg

Figure 9.13

Excel Output for the Machine Plate Example

	A	B
1	**t-Test: Two-Sample Assuming Unequal Variances**	
2		**Mass**
3	Mean	25.51
4	Variance	4.8104
5	df	19
6	t Stat	1.04
7	$P\,(T{<=}t)$ one-tail	0.1557
8	t Critical one-tail	1.73
9	$P\,(T{<=}t)$ two-tail	0.3114
10	t Critical two-tail	2.09

and a two-tailed test. Excel also gives the table value of $t = 2.09$ for a two-tailed test, which allows us to verify that the statistical conclusion is to fail to reject the null hypothesis because the observed t value is only 1.04, which is less than 2.09.

Demonstration Problem 9.2

Figures from Statistics Canada show that the average size of Canadian farms has increased since 1956. In 1956, the mean size of a farm was 122 ha; by 2006, the average size was 295 ha. Between those years, the number of farms decreased but the amount of tillable land remained relatively constant, so now farms are bigger. This trend might be explained, in part, by the inability of small farms to compete with the prices and costs of large-scale operations and to produce a level of income necessary to support the farmers' desired standard of living. Suppose an agribusiness researcher believes the average size of farms has now increased from the 2006 mean figure of 295 ha. To test this notion, she randomly sampled 23 farms and ascertained the size of each farm from county records. The data she gathered follow. Use a 5% level of significance to test her hypothesis. Assume that the number of hectares per farm is normally distributed in the population.

279	306	297	316	346	299	284	290	292
349	314	281	274	313	292	299	349	271
341	320	370	351	351				

Solution

HYPOTHESIZE:

STEP 1. The researcher's hypothesis is that the average size of a farm is more than 295 ha. Because this theory is unproven, it is the alternate hypothesis. The null hypothesis is that the mean is still 295 ha:

$$H_0: \mu = 295$$
$$H_a: \mu > 295$$

TEST:

STEP 2. The statistical test to be used is:

$$t = \frac{\bar{x} - \mu}{\frac{s}{\sqrt{n}}}$$

STEP 3. The value of alpha is 0.05.

STEP 4. With 23 data points, df $= n - 1 = 23 - 1 = 22$. This test is one-tailed, and the critical table t value is:

$$t_{0.05,22} = 1.717$$

The decision rule is to reject the null hypothesis if the observed test statistic is greater than 1.717.

STEP 5. The gathered data are shown.

STEP 6. The sample mean is 312.35 and the sample standard deviation is 29.44. The observed t value is:

$$t = \frac{\bar{x} - \mu}{\frac{s}{\sqrt{n}}} = \frac{312.35 - 295}{\frac{29.44}{\sqrt{23}}} = 2.83$$

ACTION:

STEP 7. The observed t value of 2.83 is greater than the table t value of 1.717, so the business researcher rejects the null hypothesis. She accepts the alternative hypothesis and concludes that the average size of a farm is now more than 295 ha. The following graph represents this analysis pictorially:

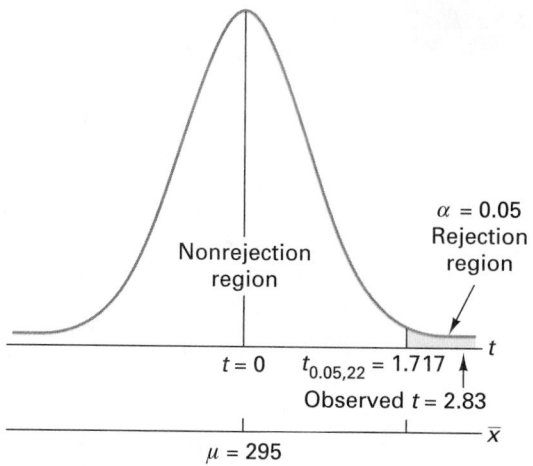

BUSINESS IMPLICATIONS:

STEP 8. Agribusiness researchers can speculate about what it means to have larger farms. If the average size of a farm has increased from 295 ha to almost 315 ha, it may represent a substantive increase.

It could mean that small farms are not financially viable. It might mean that corporations are buying out small farms and that large company farms are on the increase. Such a trend might spark legislative movements to protect the small farm. Larger farm sizes might also affect commodity trading.

USING THE COMPUTER TO TEST HYPOTHESES ABOUT A POPULATION MEAN USING THE t TEST

We note that Excel does not have a one-sample t test function. However, by using the two-sample t test for means with unequal variances, the results for a one-sample test can be obtained. This is accomplished by inputting the sample data for the first sample and the value of the parameter being tested (in this case, $\mu = 295$) for the second sample as many times as there are data in the first sample. The output includes the observed t value (2.83) and both the table t values and p values for one- and two-tailed tests. Because Demonstration Problem 9.2 was a one-tailed test, the p value of 0.0048 is used.

Figure 9.14

Excel Output for Demonstration Problem 9.2

	A	B
1	*t*-Test: Two-Sample Assuming Unequal Variances	
2		**Hectares**
3	Mean	312.348
4	Variance	866.601
5	Observations	23
6	df	0
7	*t* Stat	22
8	*P* (*T*<=*t*) one-tail	2.83
9	*t* Critical one-tail	0.0049
10	*P* (*T*<=*t*) two-tail	1.72
11	*t* Critical two-tail	0.0098

Concept Check

1. Even if σ is unknown, what is the assumption about the probability distribution of the population for the measurement being studied?
2. Under what conditions should we use a z test or a t test when testing hypotheses about a population mean?

9.3 Problems

9.11   A random sample of size 20 is taken, resulting in a sample mean of 16.45 and a sample standard deviation of 3.59. Assume x is normally distributed and use this information and $\alpha = 0.05$ to test the following hypotheses:

$$H_0: \mu = 16$$
$$H_a: \mu \neq 16$$

9.12   A random sample of 51 items is taken, with $\bar{x} = 58.42$ and $s^2 = 25.68$. Use these data to test the following hypotheses, assuming you want to take only a 1% risk of committing a Type I error and that x is normally distributed:

$$H_0: \mu = 60$$
$$H_a: \mu < 60$$

9.13   The following data were gathered from a random sample of 11 items.

1,200	1,175	1,080	1,275	1,201	1,387
1,090	1,280	1,400	1,287	1,225	

Use these data and a 5% level of significance to test the following hypotheses, assuming that the data come from a normally distributed population:

$$H_0: \mu = 1,160$$
$$H_a: \mu > 1,160$$

9.14   The following data (in kilograms), which were selected randomly from a normally distributed population of values, represent measurements of a machine part that is supposed to weigh, on average, 8.3 kg.

8.1	8.4	8.3	8.2	8.5	8.6	8.4	8.3	8.4	8.2
8.8	8.2	8.2	8.3	8.1	8.3	8.4	8.5	8.5	8.7

Use these data and $\alpha = 0.01$ to test the hypothesis that the parts average 8.3 kg.

9.15   A hole-punch machine is set to punch a hole 1.84 cm in diameter in a strip of sheet metal in a manufacturing process. The strip of metal is then creased and sent on to the next phase of production, where a metal rod is slipped through the hole. It is important that the hole be punched to the specified diameter of 1.84 cm. To test punching accuracy, technicians have randomly sampled 12 punched holes and measured the diameters. The data (in centimetres) follow. Use an alpha of 0.10 to determine whether the holes being punched have an average diameter of 1.84 cm. Assume the punched holes are normally distributed in the population.

1.81	1.89	1.86	1.83
1.85	1.82	1.87	1.85
1.84	1.86	1.88	1.85

9.16 Suppose a study reports that the average price for 1 L of self-serve regular unleaded gas is $1.07. You believe that the figure is higher in your area of the country. You decide to test this claim for your part of Canada by randomly calling gas stations. Your random survey of 25 stations produces the following prices.

$1.10	$1.11	$1.07	$1.08	$1.14
1.08	1.09	1.08	1.08	1.09
1.07	1.04	1.10	1.04	1.13
1.06	1.09	1.06	1.03	1.13
1.08	1.06	1.06	1.04	1.05

Assume gas prices for a region are normally distributed. Do the data you obtained provide enough evidence to reject the claim? Use a 1% level of significance.

9.17 Suppose that in past years the average price per square metre for warehouses in Canada has been $347.46. A national real estate investor wants to determine whether that figure has changed now. The investor hires a researcher who randomly samples 49 warehouses that are for sale across Canada and finds that the mean price per square metre is $340.89, with a standard deviation of $13.89. Assume that prices of warehouse area are normally distributed in the population. If the researcher uses a 5% level of significance, what statistical conclusion can be reached? What are the hypotheses?

9.18 Major cities around the world compete with each other in an effort to attract new businesses. Some of the criteria that businesses use to judge cities as potential locations for their headquarters might include the labour pool; the environment including work, government, and living; the tax structure; the availability of skilled/educated labour, housing, education, and medical care; and others. Suppose in a study done several years ago, the city of Calgary received a mean rating of 3.51 (on a scale of 1 to 5 and assuming an interval level of data) on housing, but that since that time, considerable residential building has occurred in the Calgary area such that city leaders feel the mean might now be higher. They hire a team of researchers to conduct a survey of businesses around the world to determine how businesses now rate the city on housing (and other variables). Sixty-one businesses take part in the new survey, with a result that Calgary receives a mean response of 3.72 on housing with a sample standard deviation of 0.65. Assuming that such responses are normally distributed, use a 1% level of significance and these data to test to determine if the mean housing rating for the city of Calgary by businesses has significantly increased.

9.19 Based on population figures and other general information on the Canadian population, suppose it has been estimated that, on average, a family of four in Canada has about $1,135 annually in dental expenditures. Suppose further that a regional dental association wants to test to determine if this figure is accurate for its area of the country. To test this, 22 families of four are randomly selected from the population in that area of the country and a log is kept of the family's dental expenditures for one year. The resulting data are given below. Assuming that dental expenditures are normally distributed in the population, use the data and an alpha of 0.05 to test the dental association's hypothesis.

1,008	812	1,117	1,323	1,308	1,415
831	1,021	1,287	851	930	730
699	872	913	944	954	987
1,695	995	1,003	994		

9.20 According to data released by The World Bank, the mean PM10 (particulate matter) concentration for the city of Kabul, Afghanistan, in 1999 was 46. Suppose that because of efforts to improve air quality in Kabul, increases in modernization, and efforts to establish environmentally friendly businesses, city leaders believe rates of particulate matter in Kabul have decreased. To test this notion, they randomly sample 12 readings over a one-year period of time with the resulting readings shown below. Do these data present enough evidence to determine that PM10 readings are significantly less now in Kabul? Assume that particulate readings are normally distributed and that $\alpha = 0.01$.

31	44	35	53	57	47
32	40	31	38	53	45

9.21 According to a survey, the average commuting time for people who commute to a city with a population of 1 to 3 million is 19.0 minutes. Suppose a researcher lives in a city with a population of 2.4 million and wants to test this claim in her city. Assume that commuter times are normally distributed in the population. She takes a random sample of commuters and gathers data. The data are analyzed using Excel and the output is shown here. What are the hypotheses? What are the results of the study?

Excel Output

	A	B
1	Mean	19.534
2	Variance	16.813
3	Observations	26
4	df	25
5	t Stat	0.66
6	$P(T<=t)$ one-tail	0.256
7	t Critical one-tail	1.71
8	$P(T<=t)$ two-tail	0.513
9	t Critical two-tail	2.06

9.4 TESTING HYPOTHESES ABOUT A PROPORTION

Data analysis used in business decision making often contains proportions to describe such aspects as market share, consumer makeup, quality defects, on-time delivery rate, and profitable stocks. Business surveys often produce information expressed in proportion form, such as 0.45 of all businesses offer flexible hours to employees or 0.88 of all businesses have websites. Business researchers conduct hypothesis tests about such proportions to determine whether they have changed in some way. As an example, suppose a company held a 26% or 0.26 share of the market for several years. Due to a massive marketing effort and improved product quality, company officials believe that the market share has increased, and they want to prove it. Other examples of hypothesis testing about a single population proportion are as follows:

- A market researcher wants to test to determine whether the proportion of new car purchasers who are female has increased.
- A financial researcher wants to test to determine whether the proportion of companies that were profitable last year in the average investment officer's portfolio is 0.60.
- A quality manager for a large manufacturing firm wants to test to determine whether the proportion of defective items in a batch is less than 0.04.

Formula 9.4 for inferential analysis of a proportion was introduced in Section 7.3 of Chapter 7. Based on the central limit theorem, this formula makes possible the testing of hypotheses about the population proportion in a manner similar to that of the formula used to test sample means. Recall that $\hat{p}$ denotes a sample proportion and p denotes the population proportion. To validly use this test, the sample size must be large enough such that $n \cdot p \geq 5$ and $n \cdot q \geq 5$.

z Test of a Population Proportion (9.4)	$$z = \frac{\hat{p} - p}{\sqrt{\dfrac{p \cdot q}{n}}}$$

where
$\hat{p}$ = sample proportion
p = population proportion
$q = 1 - p$

A manufacturer believes exactly 8% of its products contain at least one minor flaw. Suppose a company researcher wants to test this belief. The null and alternative hypotheses are:

$$H_0: p = 0.08$$
$$H_a: p \neq 0.08$$

This test is two-tailed because the hypothesis being tested is whether the proportion of products with at least one minor flaw is 0.08. Alpha is selected to be 0.10. Figure 9.15 shows the distribution, with the rejection regions and $z = 0.05$. Because α is divided for a two-tailed test, the table value for an area of $(1/2)(0.10) = 0.05$ is $z_{0.05} = \pm 1.645$.

For the business researcher to reject the null hypothesis, the observed z value must be greater than 1.645 or less than −1.645. The business researcher randomly selects a sample of 200 products, inspects each item for flaws, and determines that 33 items have at least one minor flaw. Calculating the sample proportion gives:

$$\hat{p} = \frac{33}{200} = 0.165$$

Figure 9.15

Distribution with Rejection Regions for Flawed-Product Example

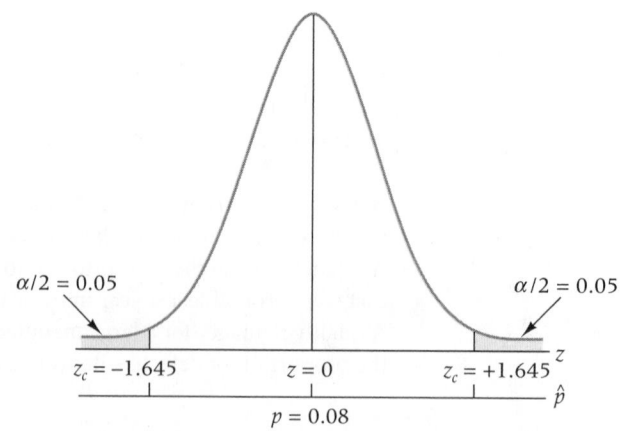

$\alpha/2 = 0.05$ $\alpha/2 = 0.05$

$z_c = -1.645$ $z = 0$ $z_c = +1.645$

$p = 0.08$

The observed z value is calculated as:

$$z = \frac{\hat{p} - p}{\sqrt{\dfrac{p \cdot q}{n}}} = \frac{0.165 - 0.080}{\sqrt{\dfrac{(0.08)(0.92)}{200}}} = \frac{0.085}{0.0192} = 4.43$$

Note that the denominator of the z formula contains the population proportion. Although the business researcher does not actually know the population proportion, he is testing a population proportion value. Hence, he uses the hypothesized population value in the denominator of the formula as well as in the numerator. This method contrasts with the confidence interval formula, where the sample proportion is used in the denominator.

The observed value of z is in the rejection region (observed $z = 4.43 >$ table $z_{0.05} = +1.645$), so the business researcher rejects the null hypothesis. He concludes that the proportion of items with at least one minor flaw in the population from which the sample of 200 was drawn is not 0.08. With $\alpha = 0.10$, the risk of committing a Type I error in this example is 0.10.

The observed value of $z = 4.43$ is outside the range of most values in virtually all z tables. Thus, if the researcher were using the p value to arrive at a decision about the null hypothesis, the probability would be approximately 0.0000, and he would reject the null hypothesis.

Suppose the researcher wanted to use the critical value method. He would enter the table value of $z_{0.05} = 1.645$ in the z formula for single-sample proportions, along with the hypothesized population proportion and n, and solve for the critical value of $\hat{p}$ denoted as $\hat{p}_c$. The result is:

$$z_{\alpha/2} = \frac{\hat{p}_c - p}{\sqrt{\dfrac{p \cdot q}{n}}}$$

$$\pm 1.645 = \frac{\hat{p}_c - 0.08}{\sqrt{\dfrac{(0.08)(0.92)}{200}}}$$

$$\hat{p}_c = 0.08 \pm 1.645 \sqrt{\frac{(0.08)(0.92)}{200}} = 0.08 \pm 0.032$$

$$= 0.048 \text{ and } 0.112$$

Using the critical value method, if the sample proportion is less than 0.048 or greater than 0.112, the decision will be to reject the null hypothesis. Since the sample proportion, $\hat{p}$, is 0.165, which is greater than 0.112, the decision here is to reject the null hypothesis. The proportion of products with at least one flaw is not 0.08. Figure 9.16 shows these critical values, the observed value, and the rejection regions.

Figure 9.16

Distribution Using Critical Value Method for the Flawed-Product Example

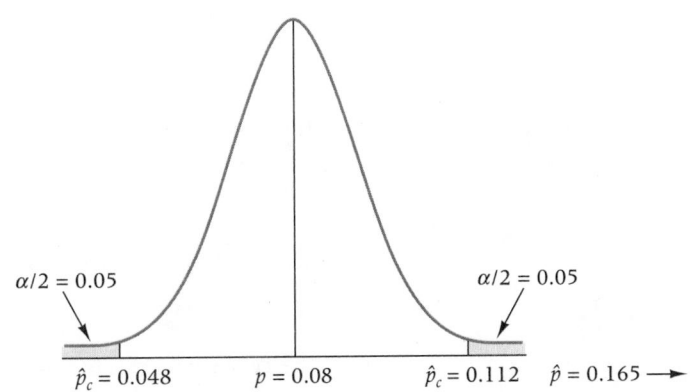

STATISTICS IN BUSINESS TODAY

Testing Hypotheses about Commuting

How do Canadians commute to work? Statistics Canada reported a few years ago that when the job is within 5 km of the city centre, 24% of commuters took public transit. However, this falls quickly to 14% when the job is between 5 km and 10 km from the city centre. Public transit take-up rates were lower still for jobs farther than 10 km from downtown. Using the hypothesis-testing methodology presented in this chapter, researchers can test whether these proportions still hold true today as well as how these figures vary by region. For example, in Toronto it is possible that the proportion of commuters using public transportation when the job is within 5 km of the city centre is higher than 24%. In other parts of the country where public transportation is not as well established, the proportion of commuters using public transportation to city centres would be close to zero.

What is the average travel time of a commute to work in Canada? According to a recent study by Statistics Canada, the average Canadian spends nearly 12 full days a year getting to and from work. Commuters spent an average of 63 minutes a day making the round trip between their place of residence and their workplace. The longest commute is in the Greater Toronto Area, where commuters take an average of 79 minutes for a round trip. In fast-growing Calgary, the round trip takes an average of 66 minutes, 14 minutes longer than it did some 10 years ago. In contrast, Vancouver workers spend no more time on average getting to work than they did some 10 years earlier. It is possible to test any of these means using the hypothesis-testing techniques presented in this chapter to either validate the figures or determine whether the figures are no longer true.

Demonstration Problem 9.3

Assume that a survey of the morning beverage market shows that the primary breakfast beverage for 17% of Canadians is milk. A milk producer in Quebec, where milk is plentiful, believes the figure is higher for Quebec. To test this idea, he contacts a random sample of 550 Quebec residents and asks which primary beverage they consumed for breakfast that day. Suppose 115 replied that milk was the primary beverage. Using a level of significance of 0.05, test the idea that the milk figure is higher for Quebec.

Solution

HYPOTHESIZE:

STEP 1. The milk producer's theory is that the proportion of Quebec residents who drink milk for breakfast is higher than the national proportion, which is the alternative hypothesis. The null hypothesis is that the proportion in Quebec does not differ from the national average. The hypotheses for this problem are:

$$H_0: p = 0.17$$
$$H_a: p > 0.17$$

TEST:

STEP 2. The test statistic is:

$$z = \frac{\hat{p} - p}{\sqrt{\dfrac{p \cdot q}{n}}}$$

STEP 3. The Type I error rate is 0.05.

STEP 4. This test is a one-tailed test, and the table value is $z_{0.05} = +1.645$. The sample results must yield an observed z value greater than 1.645 for the milk producer to reject the null hypothesis. The following diagram shows $z_{0.05}$ and the rejection region for this problem:

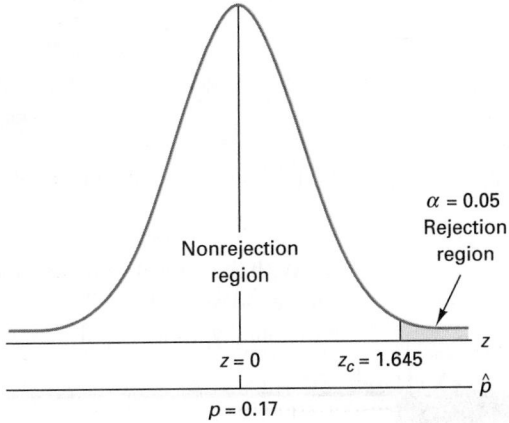

STEP 5.

$$n = 550$$

$$x = 115$$

$$\hat{p} = \frac{115}{550} = 0.209$$

STEP 6.

$$z = \frac{\hat{p} - p}{\sqrt{\dfrac{p \cdot q}{n}}} = \frac{0.209 - 0.17}{\sqrt{\dfrac{(0.17)(0.83)}{550}}} = \frac{0.039}{0.016} = 2.44$$

ACTION:

STEP 7. Because $z = 2.44$ is beyond $z_{0.05} = 1.645$ in the rejection region, the milk producer rejects the null hypothesis. The probability of obtaining $z \geq 2.44$ by chance is 0.0073. Because this probability is less than $\alpha = 0.05$, the null hypothesis is also rejected with the p value. On the basis of the random sample, the producer is ready to conclude that the proportion of Quebec residents who drink milk as the primary beverage for breakfast is higher than the national proportion.

BUSINESS IMPLICATIONS:

STEP 8. If the proportion of residents who drink milk for breakfast is higher in Quebec than in other parts of Canada, milk producers might have a market opportunity in Quebec that is not available in other parts of the country. Perhaps Quebec residents are being loyal to provincial products, in which case marketers of other Quebec products might be successful in appealing to residents to support their products. The fact that more milk is sold in Quebec might mean that if Quebec milk producers appealed to markets outside Quebec in the same way they do inside the province, they might increase their market share of the breakfast beverage market in other provinces. Is a proportion of almost 0.21 really a substantive increase over 0.17? Certainly in a market of any size at all, an increase of almost 4 percentage points in the market share could be worth millions of dollars and would be substantive.

A critical proportion can be solved for by:

$$z_{0.05} = \frac{\hat{p}_c - p}{\sqrt{\dfrac{p \cdot q}{n}}}$$

$$1.645 = \frac{\hat{p}_c - 0.17}{\sqrt{\dfrac{(0.17)(0.83)}{550}}}$$

$$\hat{p}_c = 0.17 + 1.645\sqrt{\frac{(0.17)(0.83)}{550}} = 0.17 + 0.026 = 0.196$$

With the critical value method, a sample proportion greater than 0.196 must be obtained to reject the null hypothesis. The sample proportion for this problem is 0.209, so the null hypothesis is also rejected with the critical value method.

Concept Check

1. In Demonstration Problem 9.3, how were the population for p and the sample for $\hat{p}$ defined? What is the difference between p and $\hat{p}$?

9.4 Problems

9.22 Suppose you are testing H_o: $p = 0.45$ versus H_a: $p > 0.45$. A random sample of 310 people produces a value of $\hat{p} = 0.465$. Use $\alpha = 0.05$ to test these hypotheses.

9.23 Suppose you are testing H_o: $p = 0.63$ versus H_a: $p < 0.63$. For a random sample of 100 people, $x = 55$, where x denotes the number in the sample that have the characteristic of interest. Use a 0.01 level of significance to test these hypotheses.

9.24 Suppose you are testing H_o: $p = 0.29$ versus H_a: $p \neq 0.29$. A random sample of 740 items shows that 207 have this characteristic. With a 0.05 probability of committing a Type I error, test the hypothesis. For the p value method, what is the probability of the observed z value for this problem? If you had used the critical value method, what would the two critical values be? How do the sample results compare with the critical values?

9.25 A survey of insurance consumers discovered that 48% of them always reread their insurance policies, 29% sometimes do, 16% rarely do, and 7% never do. Suppose a large insurance company invests considerable time and money in rewriting policies so that they will be more attractive and easy to read and understand. After using the new policies for a year, company managers want to determine whether rewriting the policies significantly changed the proportion of policyholders who always reread their insurance policy. They contact 380 of the company's insurance consumers who purchased a policy in the past year and ask them whether they always reread their insurance policies. One hundred and sixty-four respond that they do. Use a 1% level of significance to test the hypothesis.

9.26 A study by Hewitt Associates showed that 79% of companies offer employees flexible scheduling. Suppose a researcher believes that in accounting firms this figure is lower. The researcher randomly selects 415 accounting firms and through interviews determines that 303 of these firms have flexible scheduling. With a 1% level of significance, does the test show enough evidence to conclude that a significantly lower proportion of accounting firms offer employees flexible scheduling?

9.27 A survey was undertaken by Bruskin/Goldring Research for Quicken to determine how people plan to meet their financial goals in the next year. Respondents were allowed to select more than one way to meet their goals. Thirty-one percent said that they were using a financial planner to help them meet their goals. Twenty-four percent were using family/friends to help them meet their financial goals, followed by broker/accountant (19%), computer software (17%), and books (14%). Suppose another researcher takes a similar survey of 600 people to test these results. If 200 people respond that they are going to use a financial planner to help them meet their goals, is this proportion enough evidence to reject the 31% figure generated in the Bruskin/Goldring survey using $\alpha = 0.10$? If 158 respond that they are going to use family/friends to help them meet their financial goals, is this result enough evidence to declare that the proportion is significantly lower than Bruskin/Goldring's figure of 0.24 if $\alpha = 0.05$?

9.28   Multinational companies generally provide an allowance for personal long distance calls for executives living overseas. Assume that 18% of Canadian-based multinational companies provide such an allowance. A researcher thinks that Canadian-based multinational companies are having a more difficult time recruiting executives to live overseas and that an increasing number of these companies are providing an allowance for personal long distance calls to these executives to ease the burden of living away from home. To test this hypothesis, a study is conducted by contacting 376 multinational companies. Twenty-two percent of these surveyed companies are providing an allowance for personal long distance calls to executives living overseas. Does the test show enough evidence to declare that a significantly higher proportion of multinational companies provide a long distance call allowance? Let $\alpha = 0.01$.

9.29   A large manufacturing company investigated the service it received from suppliers and discovered that, in the past, 32% of all materials shipments were received late. However, the company recently installed a just-in-time system in which suppliers are linked more closely to the manufacturing process. A random sample of 118 deliveries since the just-in-time system was installed reveals that 22 deliveries were late. Use this sample information to test whether the proportion of late deliveries was reduced significantly. Let $\alpha = 0.05$.

9.30   Where do CFOs get their money news? According to Robert Half International, 47% get their money news from newspapers, 15% get it from communication/colleagues, 12% get it from television, 11% from the Internet, 9% from magazines, 5% from radio, and 1% don't know. Suppose a researcher wants to test these results. He randomly samples 67 CFOs and finds that 40 of them get their money news from newspapers. Does the test show enough evidence to reject the findings of Robert Half International? Use $\alpha = 0.05$.

9.5 TESTING HYPOTHESES ABOUT A VARIANCE

POINTS OF INTEREST
As mentioned in Chapter 8, testing hypotheses about a variance is extremely sensitive to violations of the assumption that the population is normally distributed.

At times a researcher needs to test hypotheses about a population variance. For example, in the area of statistical quality control, manufacturers try to produce equipment and parts that are consistent in measurement. Suppose a company produces industrial wire that is specified to be a particular thickness. Because of the production process, the thickness of the wire will vary slightly from one end to the other and from lot to lot and batch to batch. Even if the average thickness of the wire as measured from lot to lot is on specification, the variance of the measurements might be too great to be acceptable. In other words, on the average the wire is the correct thickness, but some portions of the wire might be too thin and others unacceptably thick. By conducting hypothesis tests for the variance of the thickness measurements, the quality-control people can monitor for variations in the process that are too great.

The procedure for testing hypotheses about a population variance is similar to the techniques presented in Chapter 8 for estimating a population variance from the sample variance. Formula 9.5, used to conduct these tests, assumes a normally distributed population.

Formula for Testing Hypotheses about a Population Variance (9.5)	$$\chi^2 = \frac{(n-1)s^2}{\sigma^2}$$ $$df = n - 1$$

As an example, a manufacturing firm has been working diligently to implement a just-in-time inventory system for its production line. The final product requires the installation of a pneumatic tube at a particular station on the assembly line. With the just-in-time inventory system, the company's goal is to minimize the number of pneumatic tubes that are piled up at the station waiting to be installed. Ideally, the tubes should arrive just as the operator needs them. However, because of the supplier and the variables involved in getting the tubes to the line, most of the time there will be some build-up of tube inventory. The company expects that, on average, about 20 pneumatic tubes will be at the station. However, the production superintendent does not want the variance of this inventory to be greater than 4. On a given day, the number of pneumatic tubes piled up at the workstation is determined eight different times and the following numbers of tubes are recorded.

$$23 \quad 17 \quad 20 \quad 29 \quad 21 \quad 14 \quad 19 \quad 24$$

Using these sample data, we can test to determine whether the variance is greater than 4. The hypothesis test is one-tailed. Assume the number of tubes is normally distributed. The null hypothesis is that the variance is acceptable with no problems—the variance is equal to or less than 4. The alternative hypothesis is that the variance is greater than 4.

$$H_0: \sigma^2 = 4$$
$$H_a: \sigma^2 > 4$$

Suppose alpha is 0.05. Because the sample size is eight, the degrees of freedom for the critical table chi-square value are $8 - 1 = 7$. Using Table A.8, we find the critical chi-square value:

$$\chi^2_{0.05,7} = 14.0671$$

Because the alternative hypothesis is greater than 4, the rejection region is in the upper tail of the chi-square distribution. The sample variance is calculated from the sample data to be:

$$s^2 = 20.9821$$

The observed chi-square value is calculated as:

$$\chi^2 = \frac{(8-1)(20.9821)}{4} = 36.72$$

Because this observed chi-square value, $\chi^2 = 36.72$, is greater than the critical chi-square table value, $\chi^2_{0.05,7} = 14.0671$, the decision is to reject the null hypothesis. On the basis of this sample of eight data measurements, the population variance of inventory at this workstation is greater than 4. Company production personnel and managers might want to investigate further to determine whether they can find a cause for this unacceptable

Figure 9.17

Hypothesis Test Distribution for Pneumatic Tube Example

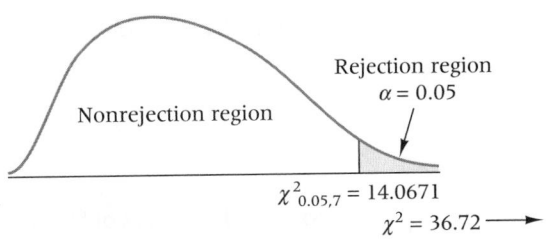

Nonrejection region

Rejection region
$\alpha = 0.05$

$\chi^2_{0.05,7} = 14.0671$

$\chi^2 = 36.72 \longrightarrow$

variance. Figure 9.17 shows a chi-square distribution with the critical value, the rejection region, the nonrejection region, the value of α, and the observed chi-square value.

Using Excel, the p value of the observed chi-square, 36.72, is determined to be 0.0000053. Because this value is less than $\alpha = 0.05$, the conclusion is to reject the null hypothesis using the p value. In fact, using this p value, the null hypothesis could be rejected for:

$$\alpha = 0.00001$$

This null hypothesis can also be tested by the critical value method. Instead of solving for an observed value of chi-square, the critical chi-square value for alpha is inserted into formula 9.5 along with the hypothesized value of σ^2 and the degrees of freedom $(n-1)$. Solving for s^2 yields a critical sample variance value, s_c^2:

$$\chi_c^2 = \frac{(n-1)s_c^2}{\sigma^2}$$

$$s_c^2 = \frac{\chi_c^2 \cdot \sigma^2}{n-1} = \frac{(14.0671)(4)}{7} = 8.038$$

The critical value of the sample variance is $s_c^2 = 8.038$. Because the observed sample variance was actually 20.9821, which is larger than the critical variance, the null hypothesis is rejected.

Demonstration Problem 9.4

A small business has 37 employees. Because of the uncertain demand for its product, the company usually pays overtime in any given week. The company assumed that about 50 total hours of overtime per week are required and that the variance on this figure is about 25. Company officials want to know whether the variance of overtime hours has changed. Given here is a sample of 16 weeks of overtime data (in hours per week). Assume hours of overtime are normally distributed. Use these data to test the null hypothesis that the variance of overtime data is 25. Let $\alpha = 0.10$.

57	56	52	44
46	53	44	44
48	51	55	48
63	53	51	50

Solution

HYPOTHESIZE:

STEP 1. This test is a two-tailed test. The null and alternative hypotheses are:

$$H_0: \sigma^2 = 25$$
$$H_a: \sigma^2 \neq 25$$

TEST:

STEP 2. The test statistic is:

$$\chi^2 = \frac{(n-1)s^2}{\sigma^2}$$

STEP 3. Because this test is two-tailed, $\alpha = 0.10$ must be split: $\alpha/2 = 0.05$.

STEP 4. The degrees of freedom are $16 - 1 = 15$. The two critical chi-square values are:

$$\chi^2_{(1-0.05),15} = \chi^2_{0.95,15} = 7.26093$$
$$\chi^2_{0.05,15} = 24.9958$$

The decision rule is to reject the null hypothesis if the observed value of the test statistic is less than 7.26093 or greater than 24.9958.

STEP 5. The data are as listed previously.

STEP 6. The sample variance is:

$$s^2 = 28.06$$

The observed chi-square value is calculated as:

$$\chi^2 = \frac{(n-1)s^2}{\sigma^2} = \frac{(15)(28.06)}{25} = 16.84$$

ACTION:

STEP 7. This observed chi-square value is in the nonrejection region because $\chi^2_{0.95,15} = 7.26094 < \chi^2_{\text{observed}} = 16.84 < \chi^2_{0.05,15} = 24.9958$. The company fails to reject the null hypothesis. There is insufficient evidence to state that the population variance is different from 25.

BUSINESS IMPLICATIONS:

STEP 8. This result indicates to the company managers that the variance of weekly overtime hours is about what they expected.

Concept Check

1. Are the conclusions from a hypothesis test about a variance useful and reliable if the population for the measurement being studied is not normally distributed?

9.5 Problems

9.31 Test each of the following hypotheses by using the given information. Assume the populations are normally distributed.

a. $H_0: \sigma^2 = 20$
$H_a: \sigma^2 > 20$
$\alpha = 0.05$, $n = 15$, $s^2 = 32$

b. $H_0: \sigma^2 = 8.5$
$H_a: \sigma^2 \neq 8.5$
$\alpha = 0.10$, $n = 22$, $s^2 = 17$

c. $H_0: \sigma^2 = 45$
$H_a: \sigma^2 < 45$
$\alpha = 0.01$, $n = 8$, $s^2 = 4.12$

d. $H_0: \sigma^2 = 5$
$H_a: \sigma^2 \neq 5$
$\alpha = 0.05$, $n = 11$, $s^2 = 1.2$

9.32   Previous experience shows the variance of a given process to be 14. Researchers are testing to determine whether this value has changed. They gather the following dozen measurements of the process. Use these data and $\alpha = 0.05$ to test the null hypothesis about the variance. Assume the measurements are normally distributed.

52	44	51	58	48	49
38	49	50	42	55	51

9.33   A manufacturing company produces bearings. One line of bearings is specified to be 1.64 cm in diameter. A major customer requires that the variance of the bearings be no more than 0.001 cm². The producer is required to test the bearings before they are shipped, and so the diameters of 16 bearings are measured with a precise instrument, resulting in the following values. Assume bearing diameters are normally distributed. Use $\alpha = 0.01$ to test the data to determine whether the null hypothesis is to be rejected because of too high a variance.

1.69	1.62	1.63	1.70
1.66	1.63	1.65	1.71
1.64	1.69	1.57	1.64
1.59	1.66	1.63	1.65

9.34   A bank averages about $100,000 in deposits per week. However, because of the way pay periods fall, seasonality, and erratic fluctuations in the local economy, deposits are subject to a wide variability. In the past, the variance for weekly deposits has been about 199,996,164. In terms that make more sense to managers, the standard deviation of weekly deposits has been $14,142. Shown here are data from a random sample of 13 weekly deposits for a recent period. Assume weekly deposits are normally distributed. Use these data and $\alpha = 0.10$ to test to determine whether the variance for weekly deposits has changed.

$93,000	$135,000	$112,000
68,000	46,000	104,000
128,000	143,000	131,000
104,000	96,000	71,000
87,000		

9.35   A company produces industrial wiring. One batch of wiring is specified to be 2.16 cm thick. A company inspects the wiring in seven locations and determines that, on the average, the wiring is about 2.16 cm thick. However, the measurements vary. It is unacceptable for the variance of the wiring to be more than 0.04 cm². The standard deviation of the seven measurements on this batch of wiring is 0.34 cm. Use $\alpha = 0.01$ to determine whether the variance on the sample wiring is too great to meet specifications. Assume wiring thickness is normally distributed.

9.6 SOLVING FOR TYPE II ERRORS

If a researcher reaches the statistical conclusion to fail to reject the null hypothesis, he makes either a correct decision or a Type II error. If the null hypothesis is true, the researcher makes a correct decision. If the null hypothesis is false, the result is a Type II error.

In business, failure to reject the null hypothesis may mean staying with the status quo, not implementing a new process, or not making adjustments. If a new process, product, theory, or adjustment is not significantly better than what is currently accepted practice, the decision maker makes a correct decision. However, if the new process, product, theory, or adjustment would significantly improve sales, the business climate, costs, or morale, the decision maker makes an error in judgment (Type II). In business, Type II errors can translate to lost opportunities, poor product quality (as a result of failure to discern a problem in the process), or failure to react to the marketplace. Sometimes the ability to react to changes, new developments, or new opportunities is what keeps a business moving and growing. The Type II error plays an important role in business statistical decision making.

Determining the probability of committing a Type II error is more complex than finding the probability of committing a Type I error. The probability of committing a Type I error is either given in a problem or stated by the researcher before proceeding with the study. A Type II error, β, varies with possible values of the alternative parameter. For example, suppose a researcher is conducting a statistical test on the following hypotheses:

$$H_0: \mu = 12 \text{ g}$$
$$H_a: \mu < 12 \text{ g}$$

A Type II error can be committed only when the researcher fails to reject the null hypothesis and the null hypothesis is false. In these hypotheses, if the null hypothesis, $\mu = 12$ g, is false, what is the true value for the population mean? Is the mean really 11.99 g or 11.90 g or 11.5 g or 10 g? For each of these possible values of the population mean, the researcher can compute the probability of committing a Type II error. Often, when the null hypothesis is false, the value of the alternative mean is unknown, so the researcher will compute the probability of committing Type II errors for several possible values. How can the probability of committing a Type II error be computed for a specific alternative value of the mean?

Suppose that, in testing the preceding hypotheses, a sample of 60 small machine parts yields a sample mean mass of 11.985 g. Assume that the population standard deviation is 0.10 g. From $\alpha = 0.05$ and a one-tailed test, the table $z_{0.05}$ value is −1.645. The observed z value from the sample data is:

$$z = \frac{11.985 - 12}{\frac{0.10}{\sqrt{60}}} = -1.16$$

From this observed value of z, the researcher determines not to reject the null hypothesis. By not rejecting the null hypothesis, the researcher either makes a correct decision or commits a Type II error. What is the probability of committing a Type II error in this problem if the population mean is actually 11.99?

The first step in determining the probability of a Type II error is to calculate a critical value for the sample mean, $\bar{x}_c$. In testing the null hypothesis by the critical value method, this value is used as the cutoff for the nonrejection region. For any sample mean obtained that is less than $\bar{x}_c$ (or greater for an upper-tail rejection region), the null hypothesis is rejected. Any sample mean greater than $\bar{x}_c$ (or less for an upper-tail rejection region) causes the researcher to fail to reject the null hypothesis. Solving for the critical value of the mean gives:

$$z_c = \frac{\bar{x}_c - \mu}{\frac{\sigma}{\sqrt{n}}}$$

$$-1.645 = \frac{\bar{x}_c - 12}{\frac{0.10}{\sqrt{60}}}$$

$$\bar{x}_c = 11.979$$

Figure 9.18

Type II Error for Machine Part Example with Alternative Mean = 11.99 g

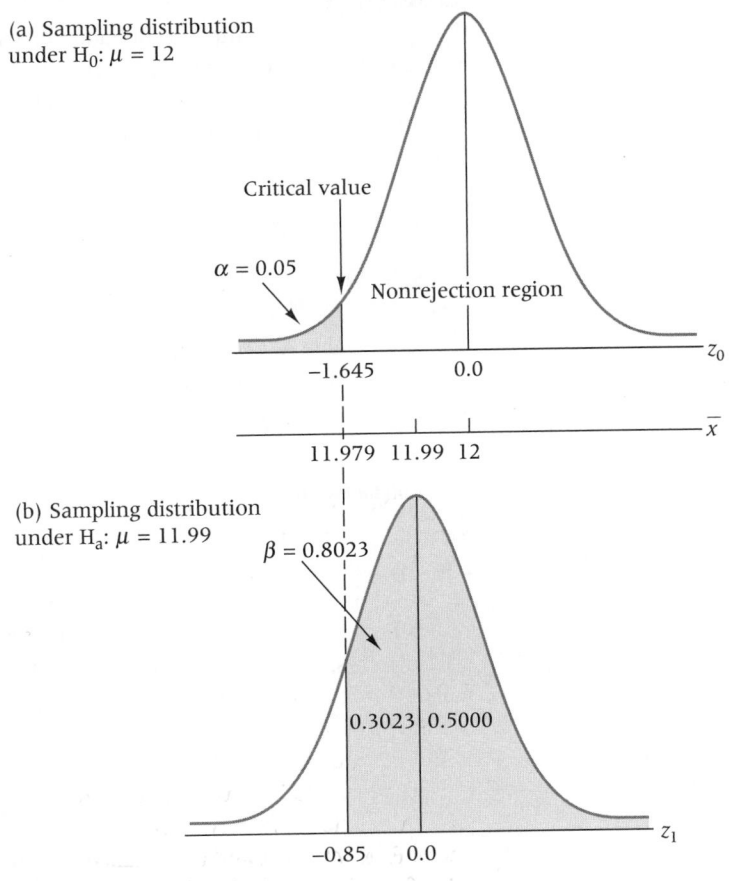

(a) Sampling distribution under H_0: $\mu = 12$

Critical value

$\alpha = 0.05$

Nonrejection region

-1.645 0.0 z_0

11.979 11.99 12 $\bar{x}$

(b) Sampling distribution under H_a: $\mu = 11.99$

$\beta = 0.8023$

0.3023 | 0.5000

-0.85 0.0 z_1

Figure 9.18(a) shows the distribution of values when the null hypothesis is true. It contains a critical value of the mean, $\bar{x}_c = 11.979$ g, below which the null hypothesis will be rejected. Figure 9.18(b) shows the distribution when the alternative mean, $\mu_a = 11.99$ g, is true. How often will the business researcher fail to reject the top distribution as true when, in reality, the bottom distribution is true? If the null hypothesis is false, the researcher will fail to reject the null hypotheses whenever $\bar{x}$ is in the nonrejection region, $\bar{x} \geq 11.979$ g. If μ actually equals 11.99 g, what is the probability of failing to reject $\mu = 12$ g when 11.979 g is the critical value? The business researcher calculates this probability by extending the critical value ($\bar{x}_c = 11.979$ g) from distribution (a) to distribution (b) and solving for the area to the right of $\bar{x}_c = 11.979$:

$$z_1 = \frac{\bar{x}_c - \mu_1}{\dfrac{\sigma}{\sqrt{n}}} = \frac{11.979 - 11.99}{\dfrac{0.10}{\sqrt{60}}} = -0.85$$

This value of z yields an area of 0.3023. The probability of committing a Type II error is all the area to the right of $\bar{x}_c = 11.979$ in distribution (b), or $0.3023 + 0.5000 = 0.8023$. Hence, there is an 80.23% chance of committing a Type II error if the alternative mean is 11.99 g.

Demonstration Problem 9.5

Recompute the probability of committing a Type II error for the example if the alternative mean is 11.96 g.

Solution

Everything in distribution (a) of Figure 9.18 stays the same. The null hypothesized mean is still 12 g, the critical value is still 11.979 g, and $n = 60$. However, distribution (b) of Figure 9.18 changes with $\mu_1 = 11.96$ g, as the diagram below shows.

The z formula used to solve for the area of distribution (b), $\mu_1 = 11.96$, to the right of 11.979 is:

$$z_1 = \frac{\bar{x}_c - \mu_1}{\frac{\sigma}{\sqrt{n}}} = \frac{11.979 - 11.96}{\frac{0.10}{\sqrt{60}}} = 1.47$$

From Table A.5, only 0.0708 of the area is to the right of the critical value. Thus, the probability of committing a Type II error is only 0.0708, as illustrated in the following diagram.

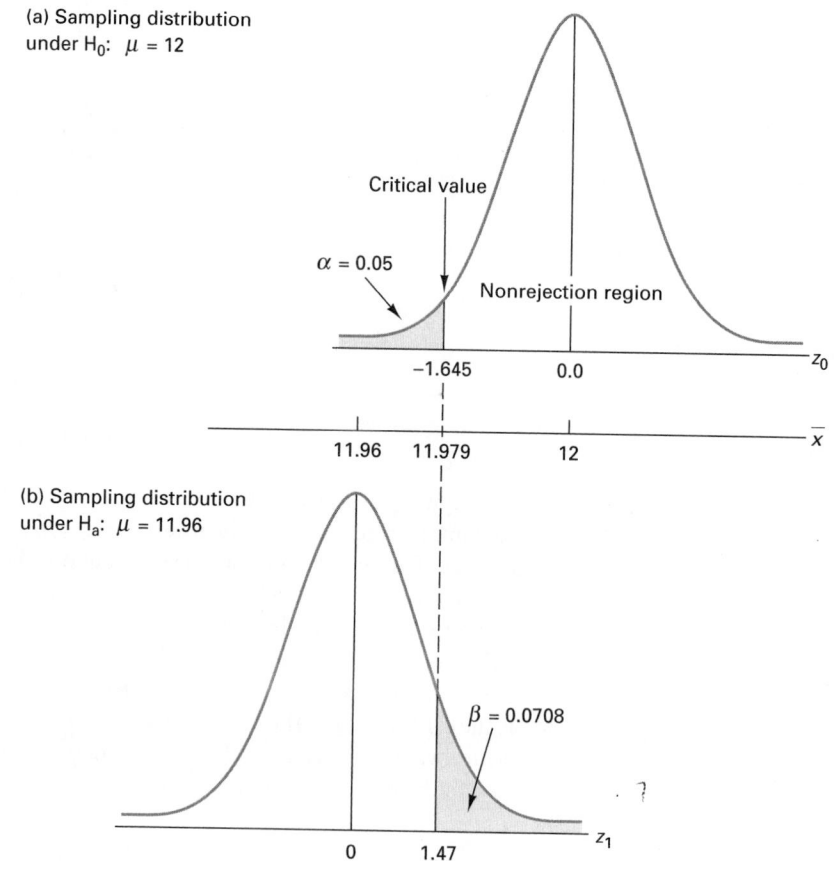

(a) Sampling distribution under H_0: $\mu = 12$

Critical value

$\alpha = 0.05$

Nonrejection region

−1.645   0.0 z_0

11.96   11.979   12 $\bar{x}$

(b) Sampling distribution under H_a: $\mu = 11.96$

$\beta = 0.0708$

0   1.47 z_1

Demonstration Problem 9.6

Suppose you are conducting a two-tailed hypothesis test of proportions. The null hypothesis is that the population proportion is 0.40. The alternative hypothesis is that the population proportion is not 0.40. A random sample of 250 produces a sample proportion of 0.44. With alpha of 0.05, the table z value for $\alpha/2$ is ±1.96. The observed z from the sample information is:

$$z = \frac{\hat{p} - p}{\sqrt{\frac{p \cdot q}{n}}} = \frac{0.44 - 0.40}{0.031} = 1.29$$

Thus, the null hypothesis is not rejected. Either a correct decision is made or a Type II error is committed. Suppose the alternative population proportion is really 0.36. What is the probability of committing a Type II error?

Solution

Solve for the critical value of the proportion:

$$z_c = \frac{\hat{p}_c - p}{\sqrt{\dfrac{p \cdot q}{n}}}$$

$$\pm 1.96 = \frac{\hat{p}_c - 0.40}{\sqrt{\dfrac{(0.40)(0.60)}{250}}}$$

$$\hat{p}_c = 0.40 \pm 0.06$$

The critical values are 0.34 on the lower end and 0.46 on the upper end. The alternative population proportion is 0.36. The following diagram illustrates these results and the remainder of the solution to this problem.

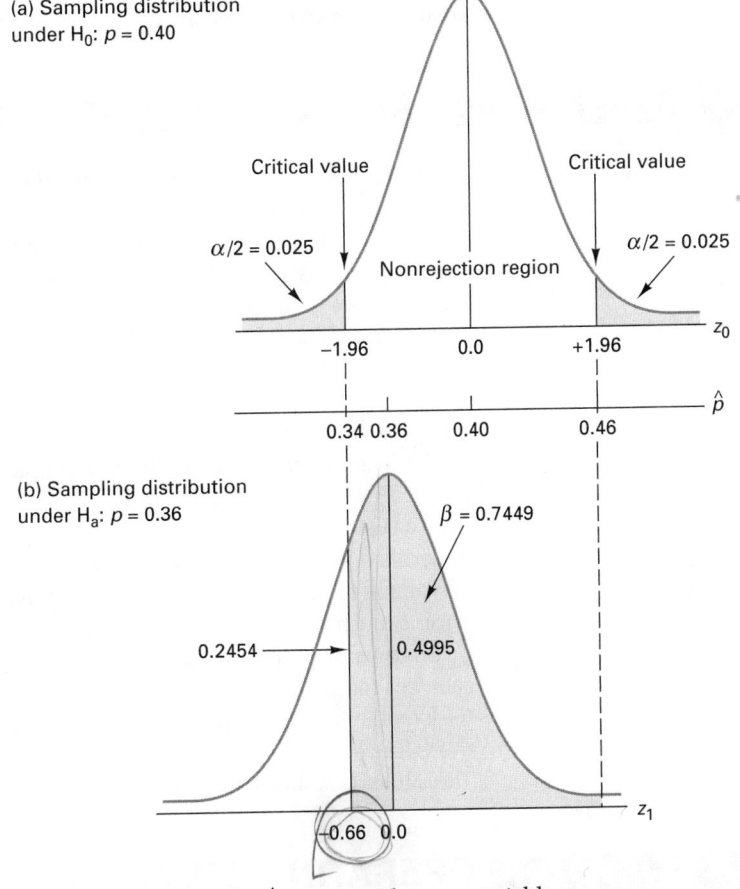

(a) Sampling distribution under H_0: $p = 0.40$

Critical value

Critical value

$\alpha/2 = 0.025$

$\alpha/2 = 0.025$

Nonrejection region

z_0

-1.96 0.0 $+1.96$

$\hat{p}$

$0.34\ 0.36$ 0.40 0.46

(b) Sampling distribution under H_a: $p = 0.36$

$\beta = 0.7449$

0.2454

0.4995

z_1

$-0.66\ \ 0.0$

Solving for the area between $\hat{p}_c = 0.34$ and $p_1 = 0.36$ yields:

$$z_1 = \frac{0.34 - 0.36}{\sqrt{\dfrac{(0.36)(0.64)}{250}}} = -0.66$$

The area associated with $z_1 = -0.66$ is 0.2454.

The area between 0.36 and 0.46 of the sampling distribution under H_a: $p = 0.36$ (graph (b)) can be solved for by using the following z value:

$$z = \frac{0.46 - 0.36}{\sqrt{\dfrac{(0.36)(0.64)}{250}}} = 3.29$$

The area from Table A.5 associated with $z = 3.29$ is 0.4995. Combining this value with the 0.2454 obtained from the left side of the distribution in graph (b) yields the total probability of committing a Type II error:

$$0.2454 + 0.4995 = 0.7449$$

With two-tailed tests, both tails of the distribution contain rejection regions. The area between the two tails is the nonrejection region and the region where Type II errors can occur. If the alternative hypothesis is true, the area of the sampling distribution under H_a between the locations where the critical values from H_o are located is β. In theory, both tails of the sampling distribution under H_a would be non-β area. However, in this problem, the right critical value is so far away from the alternative proportion ($p_1 = 0.36$) that the area between the right critical value and the alternative proportion is near 0.5000 (0.4995), and virtually no area falls in the upper right tail of the distribution (0.0005).

SOME OBSERVATIONS ABOUT TYPE II ERRORS

Type II errors are committed only when the researcher fails to reject the null hypothesis but the alternative hypothesis is true. If the alternative mean or proportion is close to the hypothesized value, the probability of committing a Type II error is high. If the alternative value is relatively far away from the hypothesized value, as in the problem with $\mu = 12$ g and $\mu_a = 11.96$ g, the probability of committing a Type II error is small. The implication is that when a value is being tested as a null hypothesis against a true alternative value that is relatively far away, the sample statistic obtained is likely to show clearly which hypothesis is true. For example, suppose a researcher is testing to determine whether a company is filling 2-L bottles of cola with an average of 2 L. If the company decides to underfill the bottles by filling them with only 1 L, a sample of 50 bottles is likely to average a quantity near the 1-L fill rather than near the 2-L fill. Committing a Type II error is highly unlikely. Even a customer could probably see by looking at the bottles on the shelf that they are underfilled. However, if the company fills 2-L bottles with 1.99 L, the bottles are close in fill volume to those filled with 2.00 L. In this case, the probability of committing a Type II error is much greater. A customer probably could not catch the underfill just by looking.

In general, if the alternative value is relatively far from the hypothesized value, the probability of committing a Type II error is smaller than it is when the alternative value is close to the hypothesized value. The probability of committing a Type II error decreases as alternative values of the hypothesized parameter move farther away from the hypothesized value. This situation is shown graphically in operating characteristic curves and power curves.

OPERATING CHARACTERISTIC AND POWER CURVES

Because the probability of committing a Type II error changes for each different value of the alternative parameter, it is best in managerial decision making to examine a series of possible alternative values. For example, Table 9.2 shows the probabilities of committing a

Table 9.2	Alternative Mean	Probability of Committing a Type II Error, β	Power
β Values and Power Values for Demonstration Problem 9.5	$\mu_a = 11.999$	0.94	0.06
	$\mu_a = 11.995$	0.89	0.11
	$\mu_a = 11.99$	0.80	0.20
	$\mu_a = 11.98$	0.53	0.47
	$\mu_a = 11.97$	0.24	0.76
	$\mu_a = 11.96$	0.07	0.93
	$\mu_a = 11.95$	0.01	0.99

Type II error (β) for several different possible alternative means for the example discussed in Demonstration Problem 9.5, in which the null hypothesis was H_o: $\mu = 12$ g and $\alpha = 0.05$.

As previously mentioned, power is the probability of rejecting the null hypothesis when it is false and represents the correct decision of selecting the alternative hypothesis when it is true. Power is equal to $1 - \beta$. Note that Table 9.2 also contains the power values for the alternative means and that the β and power probabilities sum to 1 in each case.

These values can be displayed graphically as shown in Figures 9.19 and 9.20. Figure 9.19 is an **operating characteristic (OC) curve** *constructed by plotting the β values*

Figure 9.19

OC Curve for Demonstration Problem 9.5

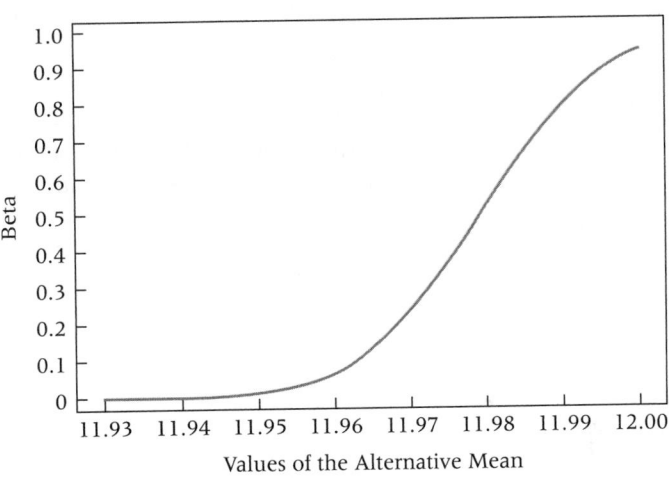

Figure 9.20

Power Curve for Demonstration Problem 9.5

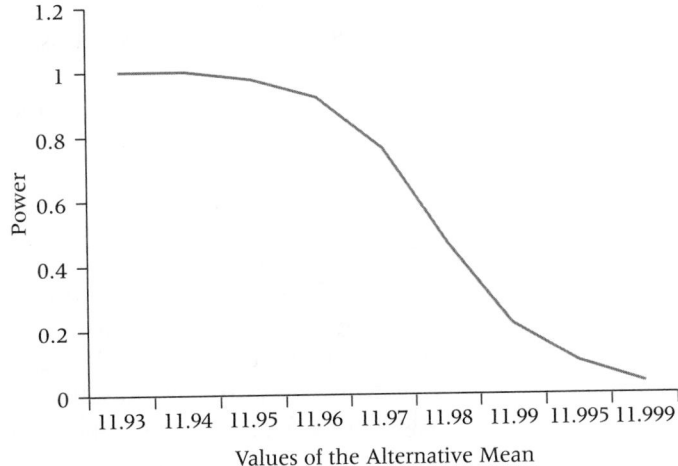

against the various values of the alternative hypothesis. Notice that when the alternative means are near the value of the null hypothesis, $\mu = 12$, the probability of committing a Type II error is high because it is difficult to discriminate between a distribution with a mean of 12 and a distribution with a mean of 11.999. However, as the values of the alternative means move away from the hypothesized value, $\mu = 12$, the values of β decrease. This visual representation underscores the notion that it is easier to discriminate between a distribution with $\mu = 12$ and a distribution with $\mu = 11.95$ than between distributions with $\mu = 12$ and $\mu = 11.999$.

Figure 9.20 is a **power curve** constructed by *plotting the power values* $(1 - \beta)$ *against the various values of the alternative hypotheses.* Note that the power increases as the alternative mean moves away from the value of μ in the null hypotheses. This relationship makes sense. As the alternative mean moves farther and farther away from the null hypothesized mean, a correct decision to reject the null hypothesis becomes more likely.

EFFECT OF INCREASING SAMPLE SIZE ON THE REJECTION LIMITS

The size of the sample affects the location of the rejection limits. Consider the example discussed in Demonstration Problem 9.5 in which we were testing the following hypotheses:

$$H_0: \mu = 12 \text{ g}$$
$$H_a: \mu < 12 \text{ g}$$

The sample size was 60 ($n = 60$) and the standard deviation was 0.10 ($\sigma = 0.10$). With $\alpha = 0.05$, the critical value of the test statistic was $z_{0.05} = -1.645$. From this information, a critical raw score value was computed:

$$z_c = \frac{\bar{x}_c - \mu}{\dfrac{\sigma}{\sqrt{n}}}$$

$$-1.645 = \frac{\bar{x}_c - 12}{\dfrac{0.10}{\sqrt{60}}}$$

$$\bar{x}_c = 11.979$$

Any sample mean obtained in the hypothesis-testing process that is less than 11.979 will result in a decision to reject the null hypothesis.

Suppose the sample size is increased to 100. The critical raw score value is:

$$-1.645 = \frac{\bar{x}_c - 12}{\dfrac{0.10}{\sqrt{100}}}$$

$$\bar{x}_c = 11.984$$

Notice that the critical raw score value is nearer to the hypothesized value ($\mu = 12$) for the larger sample size than it was for a sample size of 60. Because n is in the denominator of the standard error of the mean ($\sigma/\sqrt{n}$), an increase in n results in a decrease in the standard error of the mean, which when multiplied by the critical value of the test statistic ($z_{\alpha/2}$) results in a critical raw score that is closer to the hypothesized value. For $n = 500$, the critical raw score value for this problem is 11.993.

Figure 9.21

**Type II Error with *n*
Increased to 100**

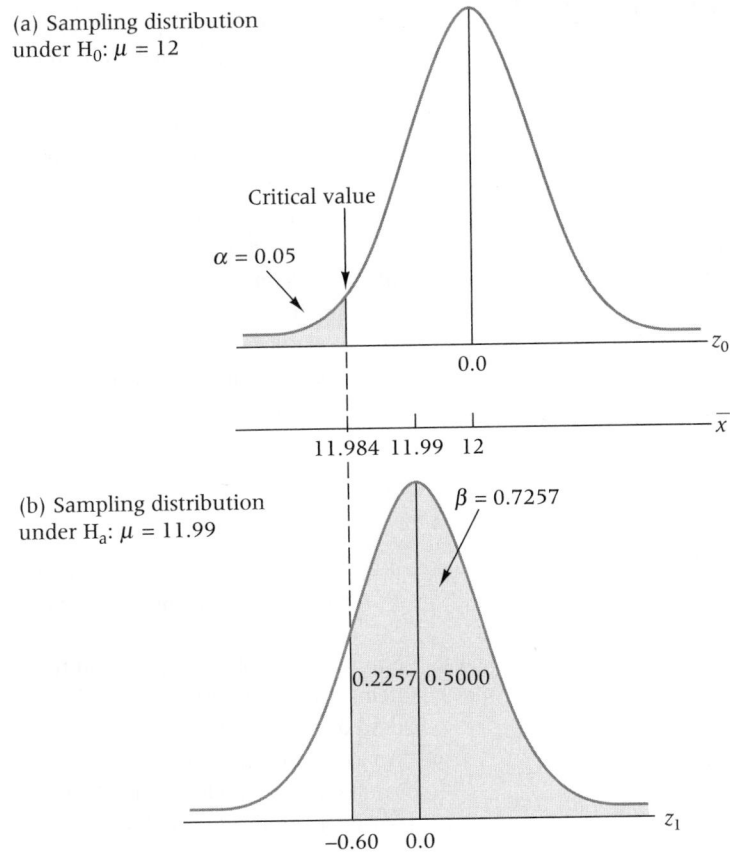

(a) Sampling distribution
under H_0: $\mu = 12$

Critical value

$\alpha = 0.05$

0.0

z_0

11.984 11.99 12

$\overline{x}$

(b) Sampling distribution
under H_a: $\mu = 11.99$

$\beta = 0.7257$

0.2257 0.5000

−0.60 0.0

z_1

Increased sample size not only affects the distance of the critical raw score value from the hypothesized value of the distribution but also can result in reducing β for a given value of α. Examine Figure 9.18. Note that the critical raw score value is 11.979 with alpha equal to 0.05 for $n = 60$. The value of β for an alternative mean of 11.99 is 0.8023. Suppose the sample size is 100. The critical raw score value (already solved) is 11.984. The value of β is now 0.7257. The computation is:

$$z = \frac{11.984 - 11.99}{\dfrac{0.10}{\sqrt{100}}} = -0.60$$

The area under the standard normal curve for $z = -0.60$ is 0.2257. Adding 0.2257 to 0.5000 (from the right half of the sampling distribution) results in a β of 0.7257. Figure 9.21 shows the sampling distributions with α and β for this problem. In addition, by increasing sample size a business researcher could reduce alpha without necessarily increasing beta. It is possible to reduce the probabilities of committing Type I and Type II errors simultaneously by increasing sample size.

Concept Check

1. What is an operating characteristic (OC) curve?
2. What is a power curve?
3. What is the relationship between sample size and the location of the rejection limits?

9.6 Problems

9.36 Suppose a null hypothesis is that the population mean is greater than or equal to 100. Suppose further that a random sample of 48 items is taken and the population standard deviation is 14.
  a. For each of the following α values, compute the probability of committing a Type II error if the population mean is actually 99.
    i. $\alpha = 0.10$
    ii. $\alpha = 0.05$
    iii. $\alpha = 0.01$
  b. Based on the answers to part (a), what happens to the value of β as α gets smaller?

9.37 a. For Problem 9.36, use $\alpha = 0.05$ and solve for the probability of committing a Type II error for the following possible true alternative means.
    i. $\mu_a = 98.5$
    ii. $\mu_a = 98$
    iii. $\mu_a = 97$
    iv. $\mu_a = 96$
  b. What happens to the probability of committing a Type II error as the alternative value of the mean gets farther from the null hypothesized value of 100?

9.38 Suppose a hypothesis states that the mean is exactly 50. If a random sample of 35 items is taken to test this hypothesis, what is the value of β if the population standard deviation is 7 and the alternative mean is 53? Use $\alpha = 0.01$.

9.39 An alternative hypothesis is that $p < 0.65$. To test this hypothesis, a random sample of size 360 is taken. What is the probability of committing a Type II error if $\alpha = 0.05$ and the alternative proportion is as follows?
  a. $p_a = 0.60$
  b. $p_a = 0.55$
  c. $p_a = 0.50$

9.40 The New York Stock Exchange recently reported that the average age of a female shareholder in the U.S. is 44 years. A broker in Vancouver wants to know whether this figure applies to the female shareholders in Vancouver. The broker secures a master list of shareholders in Vancouver and takes a random sample of 58 women. Suppose the average age for shareholders in the sample is 45.1 years, with a population standard deviation of 8.7 years. Test to determine whether the broker's sample data differ significantly enough from the 44-years figure released by the New York Stock Exchange to declare that female shareholders in Vancouver are different in age from female shareholders in the U.S. Use $\alpha = 0.05$. If no significant difference is noted, what is the broker's probability of committing a Type II error if the average age of a female Vancouver shareholder is actually 45 years? 46 years? 47 years? 48 years? Construct an OC curve for these data. Construct a power curve for these data.

BUSINESS REFERRALS

In the Decision Dilemma, many data facts are reported from numerous surveys about consumers seeking advice from others before purchasing items or services. Most of the statistics are stated as though they are facts about the population. For example, one study reports that 46% of all consumers seek advice when selecting a physician. Suppose a business researcher believes that this figure is not true, has changed over time, is not true for a particular region of the country, or is different for a particular type of medicine. Using hypothesis techniques presented in Section 9.4 of this chapter, this figure (46%) can be tested as a population proportion. Because the figures presented in the Decision Dilemma have been published and widely disseminated, the researcher who wants to test them would likely place these figures in the null hypothesis (e.g., $H_o: p = 0.46$), gather a random sample from whichever population is to be studied, and conduct a hypothesis test.

It was reported by Roper Starch Worldwide that influentials make recommendations about office equipment an average of 5.8 times per year. These and any of the other means reported in this study could be tested. The researcher would need to scientifically identify influentials in the population and randomly select a sample. A research mechanism could be set up whereby the number of referrals by each influential could be recorded for a year and averaged, thereby producing a sample mean and a sample standard deviation. Using a selected value of alpha, the sample mean could be statistically tested against the hypothetical population mean (in this case, $H_o: \mu = 5.8$). The probability of falsely rejecting a true null would be alpha. If the null was actually false ($\mu \neq 5.8$), the probability (β) of failing to reject the false null hypothesis would depend upon what the true number of mean referrals per year was for influentials on office equipment.

If a researcher has theories on influentials and these research theories can be stated as statistical hypotheses, the theory should be formulated as an alternative hypothesis, and the null hypothesis should be that the theory is not true. Samples are randomly selected. If the statistic of choice is a mean, a z test or a t test for a population mean should be used in the analysis, depending on whether or not the population standard deviation is known or unknown. In many studies, the sample standard deviation is used in the analysis instead of the unknown population standard deviation. In these cases, a t test should be used when the assumption that the population data are normally distributed can be made. If the statistic is a proportion, the z test for a population proportion is appropriate. Techniques presented in Chapter 8, Section 8.5, can be used to assist the researcher in determining how large a sample to take. Using alpha, a critical table z value can be determined and inserted into the sample size determination formulas to determine sample size.

KEY CONSIDERATIONS

The process of hypothesis testing encompasses several areas that could potentially lead to inappropriate activity, beginning with the null and alternative hypotheses. In the hypothesis-testing approach, the preliminary assumption is that the null hypothesis is true. If a researcher has a new theory or idea that he is attempting to prove, it is somewhat inappropriate to express that theory or idea as the null hypothesis. In doing so, the researcher is assuming that what he is trying to prove is true and the burden of proof is on the data to reject this idea or theory. The researcher must take great care not to assume that what he or she is attempting to prove is true.

Hypothesis testing through random sampling opens up many possible inappropriate situations that can occur in sampling, such as identifying a frame that is favourable to the outcome the researcher is seeking or using nonrandom sampling techniques to test hypotheses. In addition, the researcher should be careful to use the proper test statistic for tests of a population mean, particularly when σ is unknown. If t tests are used, or in testing a population variance, the researcher should be careful to apply the techniques only when it can be shown with some confidence that the population is normally distributed. The chi-square test of a population variance has been shown to be extremely sensitive to the assumption that the population is normally distributed. The incorrect usage of this technique occurs when the statistician does not carefully check the population distribution shape for compliance with this assumption. Failure to do so can easily result in the reporting of spurious conclusions.

It can be inappropriate from the point of view of business decision making to knowingly use the notion of statistical significance to claim business significance when the results are not substantive. Therefore, it may be unethical to intentionally attempt to mislead the business user by inappropriately using the word *significance*.

Why Statistics Is Relevant

Hypothesis testing is one of the most important tools for the application of statistics to business problems. The development of hypotheses forces the business analyst to clearly state the purpose of the research activity. This helps establish the focus and direction for the research effort. Moreover, the development of hypotheses requires the business analyst to have an operational definition of the variables of interest, thus determining what variables will be considered in the study, as well as what variables will not be considered.

It is important to have in mind that the information given by hypothesis tests like the ones described in this chapter can also be obtained from confidence intervals like the ones described in Chapter 8. For instance, if the value of the parameter specified by the null hypothesis is contained in the 95% confidence interval, the null hypothesis cannot be rejected at the 0.05 level. If the value specified by the null hypothesis is not in the interval, the null hypothesis can be rejected at the 0.05 level. The relationship between hypothesis tests and confidence intervals will be further explored in Chapters 10 and 11.

SUMMARY

Three types of hypotheses were presented in this chapter: research hypotheses, statistical hypotheses, and substantive hypotheses. Research hypotheses are statements of what the researcher believes will be the outcome of an experiment or study. In order to test hypotheses, business researchers formulate their research hypotheses into statistical hypotheses.

1. All statistical hypotheses consist of two parts, a null hypothesis and an alternative hypothesis. The null and alternative hypotheses are structured so that either one or the other is true but not both. In testing hypotheses, the researcher assumes that the null hypothesis is true. By examining the sampled data, the researcher either rejects or does not reject the null hypothesis. If the sample data are significantly in opposition to the null hypothesis, the researcher rejects the null hypothesis and accepts the alternative hypothesis by default.

Hypothesis tests can be one-tailed or two-tailed. Two-tailed tests always utilize = and ≠ in the null and alternative hypotheses. These tests are nondirectional in that significant deviations from the hypothesized value that are either greater than or less than the value are in rejection regions. The one-tailed test is directional, and the alternative hypothesis contains < or > signs. In these tests, only one end or tail of the distribution contains a rejection region. In a one-tailed test, the researcher is interested only in deviations from the hypothesized value that are either greater than or less than the value but not both.

Not all statistically significant outcomes of studies are important business outcomes. A substantive result is when the outcome of a statistical study produces results that are important to the decision maker.

2–3. When a business researcher reaches a decision about the null hypothesis, she either makes a correct decision or an error. If the null hypothesis is true, the researcher can make a Type I error by rejecting the null hypothesis. The probability of making a Type I error is alpha (α). Alpha is usually set by the researcher when establishing the hypotheses. Another expression sometimes used for the value of α is *level of significance*.

If the null hypothesis is false and the researcher fails to reject it, a Type II error is committed. Beta (β) is the probability of committing a Type II error. Type II errors must be computed from the hypothesized value of the parameter, α, and a specific alternative value of the parameter being examined. As many possible Type II errors in a problem exist as there are possible alternative statistical values.

If a null hypothesis is true and the researcher fails to reject it, no error is committed, and the researcher makes a correct decision. Similarly, if a null hypothesis is false and it is rejected, no error is committed. Power ($1 - \beta$) is the probability of a statistical test rejecting the null hypothesis when the null hypothesis is false.

An operating characteristic (OC) curve is a graphical depiction of values of β that can occur as various values of the alternative values of the parameter are explored. This graph can be studied to determine what happens to β as one moves away from the value of the null hypothesis. A power curve is used in conjunction with an OC curve. The power curve is a graphical depiction of the values of power as alternative values of the parameter are examined. The researcher can view the increase in power as values of the parameter diverge from the value of the null hypothesis.

4–7. Included in this chapter were hypothesis tests for a single mean when σ is known and when σ is unknown, a test of a single population proportion, and a test for a population variance. Three different analytic approaches were presented: (1) the standard method, (2) the p value method, and (3) the critical value method.

alpha (α)
alternative hypothesis
beta (β)
critical value
critical value method
hypothesis
hypothesis testing

level of significance
nonrejection region
null hypothesis
observed significance level
observed value
one-tailed test

operating characteristic (OC) curve
p value
power
power curve
rejection region

research hypothesis
statistical hypothesis
substantive result
two-tailed test
Type I error
Type II error

FORMULAS

z test for a single mean (9.1)

$$z = \frac{\bar{x} - \mu}{\frac{\sigma}{\sqrt{n}}}$$

Formula to test hypotheses about μ with a finite population (9.2)

$$z = \frac{\bar{x} - \mu}{\frac{\sigma}{\sqrt{n}} \sqrt{\frac{N-n}{N-1}}}$$

t test for a single mean (9.3)

$$t = \frac{\bar{x} - \mu}{\frac{s}{\sqrt{n}}}$$

$$\text{df} = n - 1$$

z test of a population proportion (9.4)

$$z = \frac{\hat{p} - p}{\sqrt{\frac{p \cdot q}{n}}}$$

Formula for testing hypotheses about a population variance (9.5)

$$\chi^2 = \frac{(n-1)s^2}{\sigma^2}$$

$$\text{df} = n - 1$$

SUPPLEMENTARY PROBLEMS

Calculating the Statistics

9.41 Use the information given and the HTAB system to test the hypotheses. Let $\alpha = 0.01$.

$$H_0: \mu = 36$$
$$H_a: \mu \neq 36$$
$$n = 63, \bar{x} = 38.4, \sigma = 5.93$$

9.42 Use the information given and the HTAB system to test the hypotheses. Let $\alpha = 0.05$. Assume the population is normally distributed.

$$H_0: \mu = 7.82$$
$$H_a: \mu < 7.82$$
$$n = 17, \bar{x} = 17.1, s = 1.69$$

9.43 For each of the following problems, test the hypotheses. Incorporate the HTAB system with its eight-step process.
   a. $H_o: p = 0.28$
      $H_a: p > 0.28$
      $n = 783, x = 230, \alpha = 0.10$
   b. $H_o: p = 0.61$
      $H_a: p \neq 0.61$
      $n = 401, \hat{p} = 0.56, \alpha = 0.05$

9.44 Test the following hypotheses by using the information given and the HTAB system. Let alpha be 0.01. Assume the population is normally distributed.

$$H_0: \sigma^2 = 15.4$$
$$H_a: \sigma^2 > 15.4$$
$$n = 18, s^2 = 29.6$$

9.45 Solve for the value of beta in each of the following problems.
   a. $H_o: \mu = 130$
      $H_a: \mu > 130$
      $n = 75, \sigma = 12, \alpha = 0.01$
      The alternative mean is actually 135.
   b. $H_o: p = 0.44$
      $H_a: p < 0.44$
      $n = 1,095, \alpha = 0.05$
      The alternative proportion is actually 0.42.

Testing Your Understanding

9.46 Assume that according to a survey, a majority of Canadian households have tried to cut long distance phone bills. Of those who have tried to cut the bills, 32% have done so by switching long distance companies. Suppose business researchers believe that this figure may be higher today. To test this theory, a researcher conducts another survey by randomly contacting 80 Canadian households who have tried to cut long distance phone bills. If 39% of the contacted households say they have tried to cut their long distance phone bills by switching long distance companies, is this result enough evidence to state that a significantly higher proportion of Canadian households are trying to cut long distance phone bills by switching companies? Let $\alpha = 0.01$.

9.47 According to Zero Population Growth, the average urban U.S. resident consumes 1.49 kg of food per day. Is this figure accurate for Canadian consumers? Suppose 64 Canadians are identi-fied by a random procedure and their average consumption per day is 1.63 kg of food. Assume a population variance of 0.59 kg of food per day. Use a 5% level of significance to determine whether the Zero Population Growth figure for urban U.S. residents is also true for Canadians on the basis of the sample data.

9.48 Brokers generally agree that bonds are a better investment during times of low interest rates than during times of high interest rates. A survey of executives during a time of low interest rates showed that 57% of them had some retirement funds invested in bonds. Assume this percentage is constant for bond market investment by executives with retirement funds. Suppose interest rates have risen lately and the proportion of executives with retirement investment money in the bond market may have dropped. To test this idea, a researcher randomly samples 210 executives who have retirement funds. Of these, 93 now have retirement funds invested in bonds. For $\alpha = 0.10$, does the test show enough evidence to declare that the proportion of executives with retirement fund investments in the bond market is significantly lower than 0.57?

9.49 Highway engineers in Alberta are painting white stripes on a highway. The stripes are supposed to be approximately 3 m long. However, because of the machine, the operator, and the motion of the vehicle carrying the equipment, considerable variation occurs among the stripe lengths. Engineers claim that the variance of stripes is not more than 0.41 m. Use the sample lengths given here from 12 measured stripes to test the variance claim. Assume stripe length is normally distributed. Let $\alpha = 0.05$.

Stripe Lengths in Metres

3.14	2.87	2.99	3.08
2.80	3.17	3.26	3.02
2.83	2.99	3.20	3.17

9.50 A computer manufacturer estimates that its line of minicomputers has, on average, 8.4 days of downtime per year. To test this claim, a researcher contacts seven companies that own one of these computers and is allowed to access company computer records. It is determined that, for the sample, the average number of downtime days is 5.6, with a sample standard deviation of 1.3 days. Assuming that number of downtime days is normally distributed, test to determine whether these minicomputers actually average 8.4 days of downtime in the entire population. Let $\alpha = 0.01$.

9.51 A life insurance salesperson claims the average worker in the city of Winnipeg has no more than $25,000 of personal life insurance. To test this claim, you randomly sample 100 workers in Winnipeg. You find that this sample of workers averages $26,650 of personal life insurance. The population standard deviation is $12,000.

a. Determine whether the test shows enough evidence to reject the null hypothesis posed by the salesperson. Assume the probability of committing a Type I error is 0.05.

b. Assuming that the actual average for this population is $30,000, what is the probability of committing a Type II error?

9.52 A financial analyst has been following the shares of a particular company for several months. The share price remained fairly stable during this time. In fact, the financial analyst claims that the variance of the share price did not exceed $4 for the entire period. Recently, the market has heated up, and the share price appears more volatile. To determine whether it is more volatile, a sample of closing share prices for eight days is randomly selected. The sample mean price is $36.25, with a sample standard deviation of $7.80. Using a level of significance of 0.10, test to determine whether the financial analyst's previous variance figure is now too low. Assume share prices are normally distributed.

9.53 A study of MBA graduates by Universum for The American Graduate Survey 1999 revealed that MBA graduates have several expectations of prospective employers beyond their base pay. In particular, according to the study, 46% expect a performance-related bonus, 46% expect stock options, 42% expect a signing bonus, 28% expect profit sharing, 27% expect extra vacation/personal days, 25% expect tuition reimbursement, 24% expect health benefits, and 19% expect guaranteed annual bonuses. Suppose a study is conducted in an ensuing year to see whether these expectations have changed. If 125 MBA graduates are randomly selected and if 66 expect stock options, does this result provide enough evidence to declare that a significantly higher proportion of MBAs expect stock options? Let $\alpha = 0.05$. If the proportion is really 0.50, what is the probability of committing a Type II error?

9.54 Suppose the number of beds filled per day in a medium-sized hospital is normally distributed.

A hospital administrator tells the board of directors that, on average, at least 185 beds are filled on any given day. One of the board members believes this figure is inflated, and she manages to secure a random sample of figures for 16 days. The data are shown here. Use $\alpha = 0.05$ and the sample data to test whether the hospital administrator's statement is false. Assume the number of filled beds per day is normally distributed in the population.

Number of Beds Occupied per Day

173	149	166	180
189	170	152	194
177	169	188	160
199	175	172	187

9.55 According to *CNN Money*, the largest share of the worldwide PC market is held by Dell Inc., with 18.2%. Suppose a market researcher believes that Dell holds a higher share of the market in Ontario. To verify this theory, he randomly selects 428 people who purchased a personal computer in the last month in Ontario. Eighty-four of these purchases were Dell computers. Using a 1% level of significance, test the market researcher's theory. What is the probability of making a Type I error? If the market share is really 0.21 in Ontario, what is the probability of making a Type II error?

9.56 A national publication reported that a university student living away from home spends, on average, no more than $15 per month on laundry. You believe this figure is too low and want to disprove this claim. To conduct the test, you randomly select 17 university students and ask them to keep track of the amount of money they spend during a given month for laundry. The sample produces an average expenditure on laundry of $19.34, with a population standard deviation of $4.52. Use these sample data to conduct the hypothesis test. Assume you are willing to take a 10% risk of making a Type I error and that spending on laundry per month is normally distributed in the population.

9.57 A local company installs natural-gas barbecues. As part of the installation, a ditch is dug to lay a small natural-gas line from the barbecue to the main line. On average, the depth of these lines seems to run about 30 cm. The company claims that the depth does not vary by more than 103.2 cm² (the variance). To test this claim, a researcher randomly took 22 depth measurements at different locations. The sample average depth was 34 cm with a standard deviation of 15.2 cm. Is this enough evidence to reject the company's claim about the variance? Assume line depths are normally distributed. Let $\alpha = 0.05$.

9.58 A study of pollutants showed that certain industrial emissions should not exceed 2.5 parts per million. You believe a particular company may be exceeding this average. To test this supposition, you randomly take a sample of nine air tests. The sample average is 3.4 parts per million, with a sample standard deviation of 0.6. Does this result provide enough evidence for you to conclude that the company is exceeding the safe limit? Use $\alpha = 0.01$. Assume emissions are normally distributed.

9.59 Suppose that the average cost per square metre for office rental space in Toronto's Bay Street business district is $23.58. A large real estate company wants to confirm this figure. The firm conducts a telephone survey of 95 offices in Toronto's Bay Street business district and asks the office managers how much they pay in rent per square metre. Suppose the sample average is $22.83 per square metre. The population standard deviation is $5.11.

a. Conduct a hypothesis test using $\alpha = 0.05$ to determine whether the cost per square metre should be rejected.

b. If the decision in part (a) is to fail to reject and if the actual average cost per square metre is $22.30, what is the probability of committing a Type II error?

9.60 The American Water Works Association reports that, on average, men use between 40 L and 60 L of water daily to shave when they leave the water running. Suppose the following data are the numbers of litres of water used in a day to shave by 12 randomly selected men. Assume that the data come from a normal distribution. Use these data and a 5% level of significance to test to determine whether the population variance for such water usage is 2.5 L.

40	32	52	68	52	60
48	52	60	64	36	28

9.61 Downtime in virtually any business can be costly. In a manufacturing setting, it means less product produced in a given time period while still having to pay the bills. This might mean late deliveries, backlogs, failure to meet orders, and even loss of market share. Suppose a manufacturing plant has been averaging 23 minutes of downtime per day for the past several years, but during the past year, there has been a

significant effort by both management and production workers to reduce downtime. In an effort to determine if downtime has been significantly reduced, company productivity researchers have randomly sampled 16 days over the past several months from company records and recorded the daily downtimes shown below in minutes. Use these data and an alpha of 0.10 to test to determine if downtime has been significantly reduced. Assume that daily downtimes are normally distributed in the population.

17 22 10 19 32 24 16 9 22 17 18 5 23 19 28 15

Interpreting the Output

9.62 According to Statistics Canada, the average Canadian generates 1.1 kg of solid waste per day. Suppose we believe that because of recycling and a greater emphasis on the environment, the figure is now lower. To test this notion, we take a random sample of Canadians and have them keep a log of their garbage for a day. We record and analyze the results by using a statistical computer package. The output follows. Describe the sample. What statistical decisions can be made on the basis of this analysis? Let alpha be 0.05. Assume that the masses of solid waste per day are normally distributed in the population. Discuss any substantive results.

One-Sample z

Test of $\mu = 2.0$ vs. < 2.0

n	Mean	StDev	SE Mean	95% Upper Bound	z	p
22	1.80031	0.39281	0.08375	1.94441	−2.38	0.087

9.63 One survey conducted by RHI Management Resources determined that the Lexus is the favourite luxury car for 25% of CFOs. Suppose a financial management association conducts its own survey of CFOs in an effort to determine whether this figure is correct. They use an alpha of 0.05. Following is the output with the results of the survey. Discuss the findings, including the hypotheses, one- or two-tailed tests, sample statistics, and the conclusion. Explain from the data why you reached the conclusion you did. Are these results substantive?

Test and CI for One Proportion

Test of $p = 0.25$ vs. p not $= 0.25$

Sample	x	n	Sample p	95% CI	Exact p value
1	79	384	0.205729	(0.166399,0.249663)	0.045

9.64   Suppose that it has been reported that the average household will spend $2,747 on home improvement projects this year. Suppose a large national home improvement company wants to test that figure in Manitoba, theorizing that the average might be lower in Manitoba. The research firm hired to conduct the study arrives at the results shown here. Analyze the data and explain the results. Comment on any substantive findings.

One-Sample z

Test of $\mu = 2747$ vs. < 2747
The assumed standard deviation = 1557

n	Mean	SE Mean	95% Upper Bound	z	p
67	2349.00	190.22	2661.88	−2.09	0.018

ANALYZING THE DATABASES

see www.wiley.com/canada/black

1. Examine the Canadian Hospital Database. Suppose you want to "prove" that the average hospital in the three provinces averages fewer than 210 failures to rescue per year. Use the hospital database as your sample and test this hypothesis. Let alpha be 0.01. On average, do hospitals in these provinces have fewer than 200 acute myocardial infarctions per year? Use the hospital database as your sample and an alpha of 0.10 to test this figure as the alternative hypothesis. Assume that the number of failures to rescue and acute myocardial infarctions in the hospitals are normally distributed in the population.

2. Consider the Financial Database. Is average P/E Ratio for companies less than 18%? Use the sample of companies represented by this database to test this hypothesis. Let $\alpha = 0.05$. Test to determine whether the average yield for all companies is equal to 2%. Use this database as the sample and $\alpha = 0.10$. Assume that the Average P/E Ration and Average Yield are normally distributed in the population.

3. Fifteen years ago, the average production in Canada for durum wheat was 270,770 pounds per month. Use the last 12 months in the Agri-Business Canada Database as a sample to test to determine whether the mean monthly production figure for durum wheat in Canada *is now different from the old figure.* Let $\alpha = 0.01$. Assume that the monthly production of durum wheat is normally distributed in the population.

CASE

McCain Frozen Pizza Targets Teens

McCain Foods Limited is one of the most recognizable and popular brand names. This company was founded in Florenceville, New Brunswick, in 1957, and today it is the world's leading producer of French fries and various frozen food items.

One of McCain's most well-known and well-liked frozen food product is its frozen pizza. In 1998, McCain introduced Crescendo Rising Crust Pizza, its first rising crust pizza. The concept of a rising crust pizza was developed in order to replicate as much as possible the taste and look of takeout pizza. However, sales for this pizza were not as McCain originally anticipated. This was due to the fact that just a few months after the Crescendo introduction, Kraft introduced its Delissio frozen pizza, and with extensive advertising, Delissio became the brand leader while McCain's Crescendo followed in second place.

In 2004, McCain's research experts concluded that the main reason for Crescendo's lagging leadership in its field was its lack of appeal and absence of a "cool factor" with the teenage market. Teenagers were not able to relate to the Crescendo

Rising Crust Pizza because they did not see it as a cool and trendy product. As such, McCain needed to change its image in order to attract the important teenage market. Research conducted in the year 2000 found that 66% of teenagers purchase a product that reflects their style and image as "hip" and trendy; therefore portraying Crescendo as "cool" would make the product more desirable to teens. At the time, McCain was focused on attracting teens, since research showed that they represented a significant growth factor in the food product industry and were the main consumers of frozen pizzas.

In order for McCain to attract teens, it had to change its advertising strategy. The first change that McCain made was to introduce more creative advertisements specifically targeted at the teenage population. These advertisements included "The Tan Lines" campaign. This was a fun and innovative ad that focused on young people and how intriguing Crescendo could be. The desired effect of the advertising was to capture sufficient interest that in turn would distract the teenagers sufficiently and make them unaware of anything else around

CASE (continued)

them. Featuring young people in the advertisements was very important to McCain so that the teenage population could easily relate to the characters portrayed. Research also indicated that television was the most powerful form of media; therefore McCain chose to advertise on both English and French channels. McCain went even further and used outdoor billboards in busy areas such as Toronto, Ottawa, Montreal, and Vancouver.

As a result of this research, McCain was able to launch its new advertisements in December 2004. Its new ads were very successful. Within the first six months of the new advertising campaign, McCain was able to double its sales goal of a 15% increase for the Crescendo Rising Crust Pizza to a 34% year-over-year increase in ex-factory sales.

Discussion

1. In the research process for McCain Foods Limited, many different numerical questions were raised regarding advertising techniques and purchase patterns among teenagers. In each of these areas, statistics, in particular hypothesis testing, plays a central role. Using the case information and the concepts of hypothesis testing, discuss the following:

a. The case information stated that 66% of teenagers purchase products that reflect their style and image as being hip and trendy. How would you test the appropriateness and validity of that percentage? In a test where 900 teens are randomly selected across Canada, 625 state that they purchase products that reflect their style and image as being hip and trendy. Test the claim made in the case regarding the purchase of products by teenagers reflecting their style and image. Use a significance level of 5% to help you reach a suitable statistical decision. What would be the probability of discrediting the claimed percentage (of 66%) if in fact it were true?

b. Historically, it has been verified that 72% of all teens that ate frozen pizza were girls. Due to apparent changes in gender tastes, it is believed that more teen boys are now eating frozen pizzas. From a random sample of 653 teens that eat frozen pizza, 513 are girls. Does this sample result provide sufficient evidence to conclude that a higher proportion of teenage girls than before eat frozen pizza?

c. What is the proportion of the teenage population that watches advertisements on television? It has been claimed by a reputable source that, historically, this proportion has been in the neighbourhood of 0.87. McCain researchers want to test whether this figure

is true. A random sample of 612 teens is selected. The results of the hypothesis-testing procedure are shown below. Analyze the results shown in the output below, and discuss and explain its contents, as well as any subsequent implications this sample study might have on the behavioural spending patterns of the teenage population as a result of television advertising viewings. To perform this analysis, use $\alpha = 0.05$.

Test and CI for One Proportion

Test of $p = 0.87$ versus $p \neq 0.87$

Sample	X	n	Sample p	95% CI	Exact p value
1	490	612	0.800654	(0.769002, 0.832306)	0.0035

2. The statistical mean can be used to measure various aspects of the teen market, including amount spent, age of teenage consumers, etc. Use techniques presented in this chapter to analyze each of the following and discuss the results in the context of the case information.

a. What is the average age of the teenage consumer of the Crescendo Rising Crust Pizza? Suppose that initial beliefs indicate that the mean age is 15. Is this figure really correct? To test whether it is, a researcher randomly contacts 30 teenage consumers of Crescendo Rising Crust Pizza, with results shown in the following output. Discuss the output in terms of a hypothesis test to determine whether the mean age is actually 15. Let α be 0.01. Assume that the distribution of the ages of all teenage consumers is mapped as a normal distribution.

	A	B
1	Mean	16.92
2	Variance	30.2963
3	Observations	30
4	df	29
5	t Stat	1.91
6	P (T>=t) one-tail	0.0348
7	t Critical one-tail	2.46
8	P (T>=t) two-tail	0.0696
9	t Critical two-tail	2.76

b. What is the average number of frozen pizzas that teens consume per year? Suppose it is hypothesized that the figure is 37 pizzas per year. A researcher who is knowledgeable of the teenage market claims that this figure is excessive and is prepared to prove it. He randomly selects 20 teens, has them keep a log of foods they eat for one year, and obtains the following figures. Analyze the data using techniques from this chapter and an alpha of 0.05. Assume that the number of frozen pizzas per end-user is a normally distributed variable in the population.

17	37	39	14
35	52	36	43
29	13	16	38
10	18	11	29
23	45	33	58

References

"Brand: McCain Crescendo Rising Crust Pizza," Cassies 2005 Cases, 2005. Website for data source: <http://www.cassies.ca/caselibrary/winners/Crescendo2005.pdf>; "Looking for a Loyal Customer? Try Generation Y," 2000. Website for data source: <http://www.cottoninc.com/lsmarticles/?articleID=181>; "The Influence of Television on Children's Gender Role Socialization," Witt, Susan D., 2000, Childhood Education Volume 76 No 5. Website for data source: <http://www2.lewisu.edu/~gazianjo/influence_of_television_on_child.htm>

USING THE COMPUTER

Excel

- Excel limited capability for conducting hypothesis testing with single samples. By piecing together various Excel commands, it is possible to compute a z test of a single population mean and a t test of a single population mean.
- To conduct a z test of a single population mean, begin with the **Insert Function** (*fx*). To access the **Insert Function**, go to the **Formulas** tab on an Excel worksheet (top center tab). The **Insert Function** is on the far left of the menu bar. In the **Insert Function** dialogue box at the top, there is a pulldown menu where it says **Or select a category**. From the pulldown menu associated with this command, select **Statistical**. Select **ZTEST** from the **Insert Function's Statistical** menu. In the **ZTEST** dialogue box, place the location of the observed values in **Array**. Place the hypothesized value of the mean in **X**. Record the value of the population standard deviation in **Sigma**. The output is the right-tailed p-value for the test statistic. If the z value is negative, subtract 1-Excel output to obtain the p-value for the left tail.

- To perform a t test of a single mean in Excel, one needs to "fool" Excel by using a two-sample t test. To do this, enter the location of the single sample observations as one of the two requested samples and enter the location of the hypothesized mean repeated as many times as there are observations as the other sample.
- Begin this t test by selecting the **Data** tab on the Excel worksheet. From the **Analysis** panel at the right top of the **Data** tab worksheet, click on **Data Analysis**. If your Excel worksheet does not show the **Data Analysis** option, then you can load it as an add-in. From the **Data Analysis** pulldown menu, select **t-Test: Two-Sample Assuming Unequal Variances** from the dialogue box. Enter the location of the observations from the single sample of data in **Variable 1 Range:**. Enter the location of the repeated hypothesized mean values in **Variable 2 Range:**. Enter the value of zero in **Hypothesized Mean Difference**. Check **Labels** if you have labels. Select **Alpha**. The output includes the observed t value, p-values for both one- and two-tailed tests, and critical t values for both one- and two-tailed tests.

CHAPTER 10

STATISTICAL INFERENCES ABOUT TWO POPULATIONS

Learning Objectives

The general focus of Chapter 10 is on testing hypotheses and constructing confidence intervals about parameters from two populations. The key questions in this chapter are:

1. How can we test hypotheses and construct confidence intervals about the difference in two population means using the z statistic?

2. How can we test hypotheses and construct confidence intervals about the difference in two population means using the t statistic?

3. How can we test hypotheses and construct confidence intervals about the mean difference in two related populations or in matched-pairs experiments from one population?

4. How can we test hypotheses and construct confidence intervals about the difference in two population proportions?

5. How can we test hypotheses and construct confidence intervals about the difference in two population variances?

Shutterstock

DECISION DILEMMA

COMPARING AUSTRIA TO FRANCE ON LABOUR STATISTICS

Labour statistics can be used to compare different countries in areas such as productivity, cost, and job satisfaction. In particular, statistics can be used to determine whether there is a difference between two countries on some measure of labour or between time periods for one country. As an example, consider Austria and France. The U.S. Bureau of Labor Statistics reports that the hourly compensation rates in U.S. dollars for manufacturing production workers in Austria in 1995 and 2004 were $25.96 and $28.29, respectively. Hourly compensation rates for France over this same period of time were $19.26 in 1995 and $23.89 in 2004. How long are the workweeks in these two countries? According to the Labor Force Survey, the hours actually worked by employees per week in Austria were 36.1 in 1995 and 35.5 in 2004. For France, the figures were 37.1 in 1995 and 35.9 in 2004.

Managerial and Statistical Questions

1. Suppose the labour data used to compute hourly labour costs for Austria and France were actually sample data. Is the 2004 hourly labour cost in Austria significantly higher than the 2004 hourly labour cost in France based on these figures?
2. The hourly labour costs for France appear to have increased from 1995 to 2004. Is this due to chance in the random sampling or has there really been a significant increase in hourly labour costs for France?
3. Has the average workweek in Austria actually declined from 36.1 to 35.5 hours or is this just a chance difference of two samples of workers taken at these two different points of time?
4. The reported average workweek in 2004 was 35.5 hours for Austria and 35.9 hours for France. If these two figures were obtained through sampling techniques, is there really a difference between the two countries' average workweek if the whole population of workers is considered?

Source: Adapted from Foreign Labor Statistics of the Bureau of Labor Statistics website, Table 2 at <http://www.bls.gov/fls/home.htm> and the International Labour Organization's website at <http://laborsta.ilo.org/>.

To this point, all discussion of confidence intervals and hypothesis tests has centred on single population parameters. That is, a single sample is randomly drawn from a population, and using data from that sample, a population mean, proportion, or variance is estimated or tested. In Chapter 8, we presented statistical techniques for constructing confidence intervals to estimate a population mean, a population proportion, or a population variance. In Chapter 9, we presented statistical techniques for testing hypotheses about a population mean, a population proportion, or a population variance. Often, it is of equal interest to make inferences about two populations. A retail analyst might want to compare per person annual expenditures on shoes in 2009 with those in 2006 to determine whether a change has occurred over time. A market researcher might want to estimate or test to determine the proportion of market share of one company in two different regions.

In this chapter, we will consider several different techniques for analyzing data that come from two samples. One technique is used with proportions, one is used with variances, and the others are used with means. The techniques for analyzing means are separated into those using the *z* statistic and those using the *t* statistic. In four of the five techniques presented in this chapter, the two samples are assumed to be **independent samples.** The samples are independent because *the items or people sampled in each group*

Figure 10.1

**Branch of the Tree
Diagram Taxonomy of
Inferential Techniques:
Confidence Intervals**

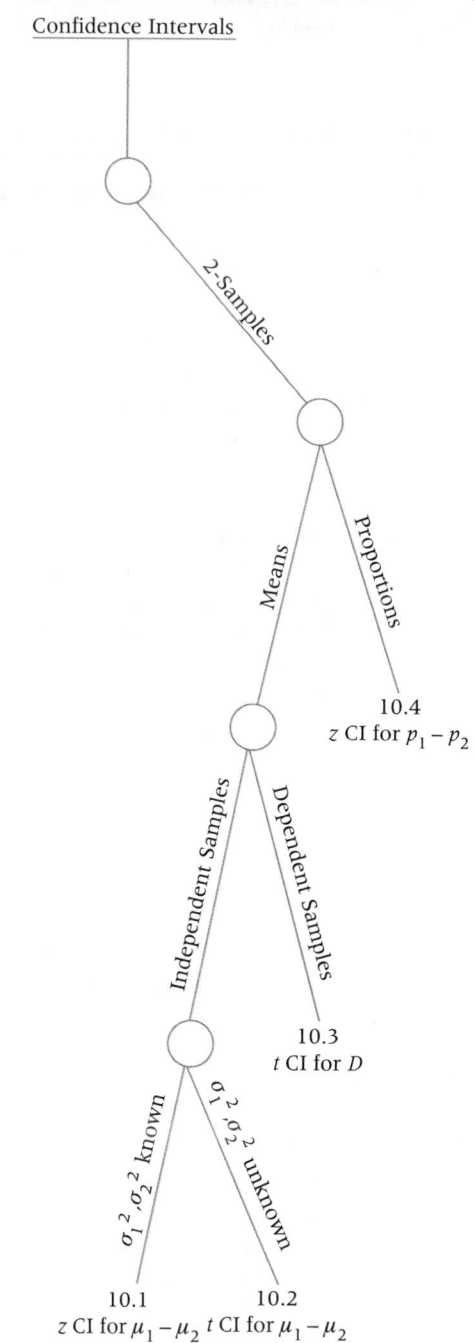

are in no way related to those in the other group. Any similarity between items or people in the two samples is coincidental and due to chance. One of the techniques presented in the chapter is for analyzing data from dependent, or related, samples in which items or persons in one sample are matched in some way with items or persons in the other sample. For four of the five techniques, we will examine both hypothesis tests and confidence intervals.

Figure III-1 of the Introduction to Unit III displays a tree diagram taxonomy of inferential techniques organized by usage, number of samples, and level of data. Chapter 10 contains techniques for constructing confidence intervals and testing hypotheses about the differences in two population means and two population proportions and, in addition, testing hypotheses about two population variances. The entire left side of the tree diagram taxonomy displays various confidence interval estimation techniques.

Figure 10.2

Branch of the Tree Diagram Taxonomy of Inference Techniques: Hypothesis Tests

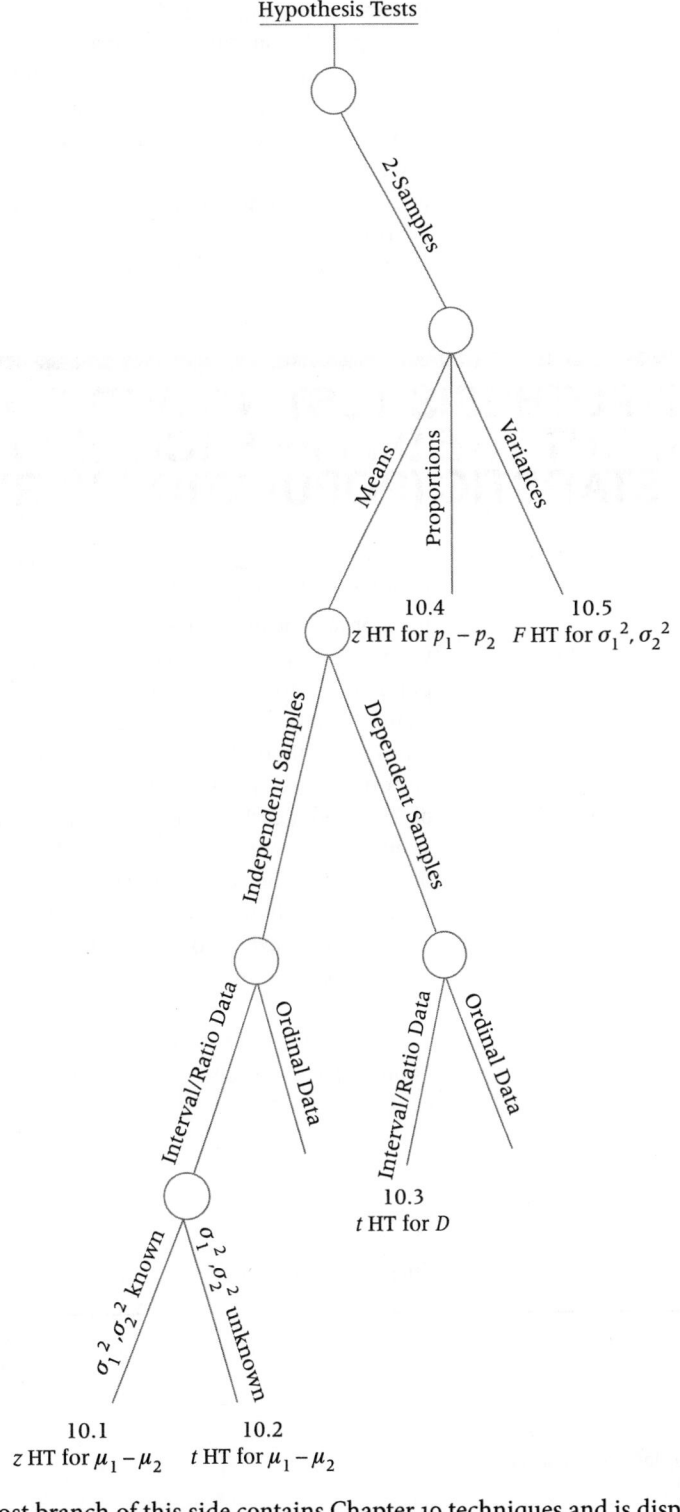

The rightmost branch of this side contains Chapter 10 techniques and is displayed in Figure 10.1. The entire right side of the tree diagram taxonomy displays various hypothesis-testing techniques. The central branch of this contains Chapter 10 techniques (2-samples) for testing hypotheses, and this branch is displayed in Figure 10.2. Note that at the bottom of each tree branch in Figures 10.1 and 10.2, the title of the statistical technique along with its respective section number is given for ease of identification and use. If a business researcher is constructing confidence intervals or testing hypotheses about the difference in two population means and the population standard deviations or variances are known, then he will use the z test for $\mu_1 - \mu_2$ contained in Section 10.1. If the population standard deviations or variances are unknown, then the appropriate technique is the t test for $\mu_1 - \mu_2$ contained in Section 10.2. If a business researcher is constructing confidence intervals or testing hypotheses about the difference in two related populations, then she will use the t test presented in Section 10.3. If a business researcher is constructing a confidence interval or testing a hypothesis about the difference in two population proportions, then he will use the z test for $p_1 - p_2$ presented in Section 10.4. If a researcher desires to test a hypothesis about two population variances, then she will use the F test presented in Section 10.5.

10.1 HYPOTHESIS TESTING AND CONFIDENCE INTERVALS ABOUT THE DIFFERENCE IN TWO MEANS USING THE z STATISTIC (POPULATION VARIANCES KNOWN)

In some research designs, the sampling plan calls for selecting two independent samples, calculating the sample means, and using the difference in the two sample means to estimate or test the difference in the two population means. The object might be to determine whether the two samples come from the same population or, if they come from different populations, to determine the amount of difference in the populations. This type of analysis can be used to determine, for example, whether the effectiveness of two brands of toothpaste differs or whether two brands of tires wear differently. Business research might be conducted to study the difference in the productivity of men and women on an assembly line under certain conditions. An engineer might want to determine differences in the strength of aluminum produced under two different temperatures. Does the average cost of a two-bedroom, one-storey house differ between Kingston, Ontario, and Edmonton, Alberta? If so, how much is the difference? These and many other interesting questions can be researched by comparing the difference in two sample means.

How does a researcher analyze the difference in two samples by using sample means? The central limit theorem states that the difference in two sample means, $\bar{x}_1 - \bar{x}_2$, is normally distributed for large sample sizes (both n_1 and $n_2 \geq 30$), regardless of the shape of the populations. It can also be shown that:

$$\mu_{\bar{x}_1 - \bar{x}_2} = \mu_1 - \mu_2$$

$$\sigma_{\bar{x}_1 - \bar{x}_2} = \sqrt{\frac{\sigma_1^2}{n_1} + \frac{\sigma_2^2}{n_2}}$$

These expressions lead to a z formula for the difference in two sample means.

z Formula for the Difference in Two Sample Means (Independent Samples and Population Variances Known) (10.1)	$z = \dfrac{(\bar{x}_1 - \bar{x}_2) - (\mu_1 - \mu_2)}{\sqrt{\dfrac{\sigma_1^2}{n_1} + \dfrac{\sigma_2^2}{n_2}}}$

where

μ_1 = mean of population 1
μ_2 = mean of population 2
n_1 = size of sample 1
n_2 = size of sample 2

This formula is the basis for statistical inferences about the difference in two means using two random independent samples.

Note: *If the populations are normally distributed on the measurement being studied and if the population variances are known, formula 10.1 can be used for small sample sizes.*

HYPOTHESIS TESTING

In many instances, business researchers want to test the differences in the mean values of two populations. As an example, a consumer organization might want to test two brands of light bulbs to determine whether one burns longer than the other. A company wanting to relocate might want to determine whether a significant difference separates the average price of a home in Kingston, Ontario, from house prices in Edmonton, Alberta. Formula 10.1 can be used to test the difference between two population means.

As a specific example, suppose we want to conduct a hypothesis test to determine whether the average annual wage of an advertising manager is different from the average annual wage of an auditing manager. Because we are testing to determine whether the means are different, it might seem logical that the null and alternative hypotheses would be:

$$H_0: \mu_1 = \mu_2$$
$$H_a: \mu_1 \neq \mu_2$$

where advertising managers are population 1 and auditing managers are population 2. However, statisticians generally construct these hypotheses as:

$$H_0: \mu_1 - \mu_2 = \delta$$
$$H_a: \mu_1 - \mu_2 \neq \delta$$

This format not only allows the business analyst to test if the population means are equal, but also affords her the opportunity to hypothesize about a particular difference in the means (δ). Thus, δ is set equal to zero, resulting in the following hypotheses, which we will use for this problem and most others:

$$H_0: \mu_1 - \mu_2 = 0$$
$$H_a: \mu_1 - \mu_2 \neq 0$$

Note, however, that a business researcher could be interested in testing to determine if there is, for example, a difference of means equal to say 10, in which case $\delta = 10$.

A random sample of 32 advertising managers from across Canada is taken. The advertising managers are contacted by telephone and asked what their annual salary is. A similar random sample is taken of 34 auditing managers. The resulting salary data are listed in Table 10.1, along with the sample means, the population standard deviations, and the population variances.

In this problem, the business analyst is testing whether there is a difference in the average wage of an advertising manager and an auditing manager; therefore, the test is two-tailed. If the business analyst had hypothesized that one was paid more than the other, the test would have been one-tailed.

Suppose $\alpha = 0.05$. Because this test is two-tailed, each of the two rejection regions has an area of 0.025, leaving 0.475 of the area in the distribution between each critical value and the mean of the distribution. The associated critical table $z_{\alpha/2}$ value for this area is $z_{0.25} = \pm 1.96$. Figure 10.3 shows the critical table z value along with the rejection regions.

Table 10.1	Advertising Managers		Auditing Managers	
Wages for Advertising Managers and Auditing Managers ($1,000s)	74.256	64.276	69.962	67.160
	96.234	74.194	55.052	37.386
	89.807	65.360	57.828	59.505
	93.261	73.904	63.362	72.790
	103.030	54.270	37.194	71.351
	74.195	59.045	99.198	58.653
	75.932	68.508	61.254	63.508
	80.742	71.115	73.065	43.649
	39.672	67.574	48.036	63.369
	45.652	59.621	60.053	59.676
	93.083	62.483	66.359	54.449
	63.384	69.319	61.261	46.394
	57.791	35.394	77.136	71.804
	65.145	86.741	66.035	72.401
	96.767	57.351	54.335	56.470
	77.242		42.494	67.814
	67.056		83.849	71.492
	$n_1 = 32$		$n_2 = 34$	
	$\bar{x}_1 = 70.700$		$\bar{x}_2 = 62.187$	
	$\sigma_1 = 16.253$		$\sigma_2 = 12.900$	
	$\sigma_1^2 = 264.164$		$\sigma_2^2 = 166.409$	

Formula 10.1 and the data in Table 10.1 yield a z value to complete the hypothesis test:

$$z = \frac{(70.700 - 62.187) - 0}{\sqrt{\dfrac{264.164}{32} + \dfrac{166.409}{34}}} = 2.35$$

The observed value of 2.35 is greater than the critical value obtained from the z table, 1.96. The business researcher rejects the null hypothesis and can say that there is a significant difference between the average annual wage of an advertising manager and the average annual wage of an auditing manager. The business researcher then examines the sample means (70.700 for advertising managers and 62.187 for auditing managers) and uses common sense to conclude that advertising managers earn more, on the average, than do auditing managers. Figure 10.4 shows the relationship between the observed z and $z_{\alpha/2}$.

Figure 10.3	
Critical Values and Rejection Regions for the Wage Example	

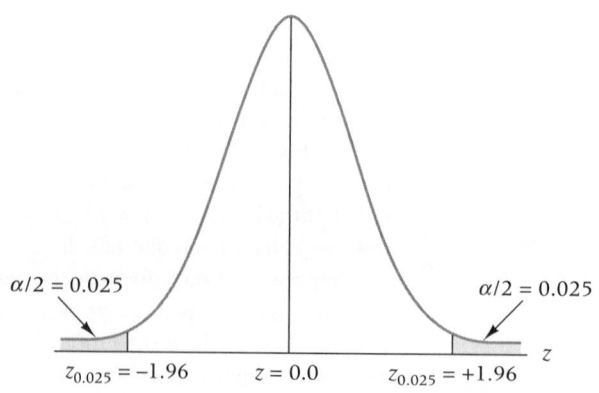

$\alpha/2 = 0.025$ $\alpha/2 = 0.025$

$z_{0.025} = -1.96$ $z = 0.0$ $z_{0.025} = +1.96$

Figure 10.4

Location of Observed z Value for the Wage Example

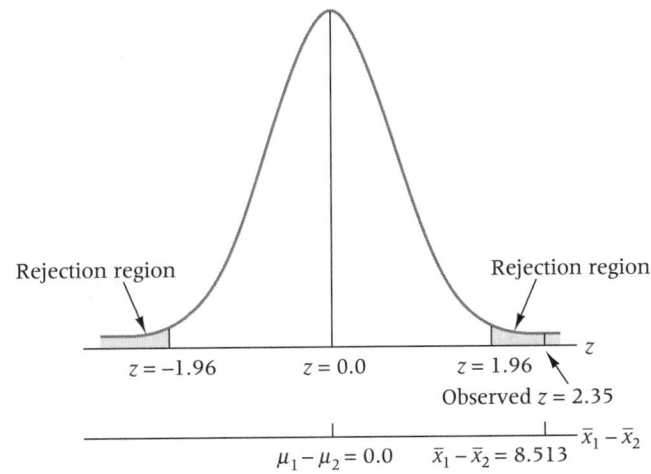

Rejection region   Rejection region

$z = -1.96$ $z = 0.0$ $z = 1.96$

Observed $z = 2.35$

$\mu_1 - \mu_2 = 0.0$ $\bar{x}_1 - \bar{x}_2 = 8.513$ $\bar{x}_1 - \bar{x}_2$

POINTS OF INTEREST
Recall that the smaller the p value, the stronger is the evidence against H_0.

This conclusion could have been reached by using the p value. Looking up the probability of $z \geq 2.35$ in the z distribution table in Appendix A.5 yields an area of $0.5000 - 0.4906 = 0.0094$. This p value (0.0094) is less than $\alpha/2 = 0.025$. The decision is to reject the null hypothesis.

Demonstration Problem 10.1

A sample of 87 professional working women showed that the average amount paid annually into a retirement fund per person was \$3,352. The population standard deviation is \$1,100. A sample of 76 professional working men showed that the average amount paid annually into a retirement fund per person was \$5,727, with a population standard deviation of \$1,700. A women's group wants to prove that women do not pay as much per year as men into retirement funds. If they use $\alpha = 0.001$ and these sample data, will they be able to reject a null hypothesis that women annually pay the same as or more than men into retirement funds? Use the eight-step hypothesis-testing process.

Solution

HYPOTHESIZE:

STEP 1. This test is one-tailed. Because the women's group wants to prove that women pay less than men into retirement funds annually, the alternative hypothesis should be $\mu_w - \mu_m < 0$, and the null hypothesis is that women pay the same as or more than men, $\mu_w - \mu_m = 0$.

TEST:

STEP 2. The test statistic is:

$$z = \frac{(\bar{x}_1 - \bar{x}_2) - (\mu_1 - \mu_2)}{\sqrt{\dfrac{\sigma_1^2}{n_1} + \dfrac{\sigma_2^2}{n_2}}}$$

STEP 3. The level of significance has been specified as 0.001.

STEP 4. By using this value of alpha, a critical $z_{0.001}$ of -3.08 can be determined. The decision rule is to reject the null hypothesis if the observed value of the test statistic, z, is less than -3.08.

STEP 5. The sample data follow.

Women	Men
$\bar{x}_1 = \$3,352$	$\bar{x}_2 = \$5,727$
$\sigma_1 = \$1,100$	$\sigma_2 = \$1,700$
$n_1 = 87$	$n_2 = 76$

STEP 6. Solving for z gives:

$$z = \frac{(3,352 - 5,727) - 0}{\sqrt{\dfrac{1,100^2}{87} + \dfrac{1,700^2}{76}}} = \frac{-2,375}{227.9} = -10.42$$

ACTION:

STEP 7. The observed z value of -10.42 is deep in the rejection region, well past the table value of $z_{0.001} = -3.08$. Even with the small $\alpha = 0.001$, the null hypothesis is rejected.

BUSINESS IMPLICATIONS:

STEP 8. The evidence is substantial that women, on average, pay less than men into retirement funds annually. The following diagram displays these results.

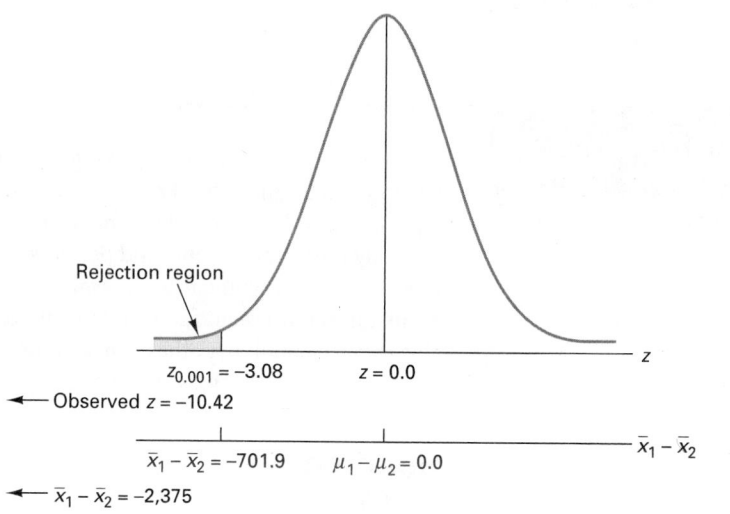

The probability of obtaining an observed z value of -10.42 by chance is virtually zero, because the value is beyond the limits of the z table. By the p value, the null hypothesis is rejected because the probability is approximately 0.0000, or less than $\alpha = 0.001$.

If this problem were worked by the critical value method, what critical value of the difference in the two means would have to be surpassed to reject the null hypothesis for a table $z_{0.001}$ value of -3.08? The answer is:

$$\bar{x}_1 - \bar{x}_2 = (\mu_1 - \mu_2) - z_{0.001}\sqrt{\frac{\sigma_1^2}{n_1} + \frac{\sigma_2^2}{n_2}}$$

$$= 0 - 3.08(227.9) = -701.9$$

The difference in sample means would need to be at least 701.9 to reject the null hypothesis. The actual sample difference in this problem was $-2,375$ ($3,352 - 5,727$), which is considerably larger than the critical value of the difference. Thus, with the critical value method, the null hypothesis is also rejected.

CONFIDENCE INTERVALS

Sometimes being able to estimate the difference in the means of two populations is valuable. By how much do two populations differ in size or mass or age? By how much do two products differ in effectiveness? Do two different manufacturing or training methods produce different mean results? The answers to these questions are often difficult to obtain through census techniques. The alternative is to take a random sample from each of the two populations and study the difference in the sample means.

Algebraically, formula 10.1 can be manipulated to produce a formula for constructing confidence intervals for the difference in two population means.

Confidence Interval to Estimate $\mu_1 - \mu_2$ (10.2)	$$(\bar{x}_1 - \bar{x}_2) - z_{\alpha/2}\sqrt{\frac{\sigma_1^2}{n_1} + \frac{\sigma_2^2}{n_2}} \le \mu_1 - \mu_2 \le (\bar{x}_1 - \bar{x}_2) + z_{\alpha/2}\sqrt{\frac{\sigma_1^2}{n_1} + \frac{\sigma_2^2}{n_2}}$$

Suppose a study is conducted to estimate the difference between middle-income shoppers and low-income shoppers in terms of the average amount saved on grocery bills per week by using coupons. Random samples of 60 middle-income shoppers and 80 low-income shoppers are taken, and their purchases are monitored for one week. The average amounts saved with coupons, as well as sample sizes and population standard deviations, are in the table below.

Middle-Income Shoppers	Low-Income Shoppers
$n_1 = 60$	$n_2 = 80$
$\bar{x}_1 = \$5.84$	$\bar{x}_2 = \$2.67$
$\sigma_1 = \$1.41$	$\sigma_2 = \$0.54$

This information can be used to construct a 98% confidence interval to estimate the difference between the mean amount saved with coupons by middle-income shoppers and the mean amount saved with coupons by low-income shoppers.

The $z_{\alpha/2}$ value associated with a 98% level of confidence is 2.33. This value, the data shown, and formula 10.2 can be used to determine the confidence interval.

$$(5.84 - 2.67) - 2.33\sqrt{\frac{1.41^2}{60} + \frac{0.54^2}{80}} \le \mu_1 - \mu_2 \le (5.84 - 2.67) + 2.33\sqrt{\frac{1.41^2}{60} + \frac{0.54^2}{80}}$$

$$3.17 - 0.45 \le \mu_1 - \mu_2 \le 3.17 + 0.45$$

$$2.72 \le \mu_1 - \mu_2 \le 3.62$$

There is a 98% level of confidence that the actual difference in the population mean coupon savings per week between middle-income and low-income shoppers is between $2.72 and $3.62. That is, the difference could be as little as $2.72 or as great as $3.62. The point estimate for the difference in mean savings is $3.17. Note that a zero difference in the population means of these two groups is unlikely, because zero is not in the 98% range.

Demonstration Problem 10.2	A consumer test group wants to determine the difference in fuel efficiency of cars using regular unleaded gas and cars using premium unleaded gas. Researchers for the group divided a fleet of 100 cars of the same make in half and tested each car on one tank of gas. Fifty of the cars were filled with regular unleaded gas and 50 were filled with premium

unleaded gas. The sample average for the regular gas group was 10.97 L/100 km, and the sample average for the premium gas group was 9.56 L/100 km. Assume that the population standard deviation of the regular unleaded gas population is 1.77 L/100 km, and that the population standard deviation of the premium unleaded gas population is 1.16 L/100 km. Construct a 95% confidence interval to estimate the difference in the mean fuel efficiency between the cars using regular gas and the cars using premium gas.

Solution

The $z_{\alpha/2}$ value for a 95% confidence interval is 1.96. The other sample information follows.

Regular	Premium
$n_1 = 50$	$n_2 = 50$
$\bar{x}_1 = 10.97$	$\bar{x}_2 = 9.56$
$\sigma_1 = 1.77$	$\sigma_2 = 1.16$

Based on this information, the confidence interval is

$$(10.97 - 9.56) - 1.96\sqrt{\frac{1.77^2}{50} + \frac{1.16^2}{50}} \le \mu_1 - \mu_2 \le (10.97 - 9.56) + 1.96\sqrt{\frac{1.77^2}{50} + \frac{1.16^2}{50}}$$

$$1.41 - 0.59 \le \mu_1 - \mu_2 \le 1.41 + 0.59$$

$$0.82 \le \mu_1 - \mu_2 \le 2.00$$

We are 95% confident that the actual difference in mean fuel efficiency between the two types of gas is between 0.82 L/100 km and 2.00 L/100 km. The point estimate is 1.41 L/100 km.

Designating one group as group 1 and another group as group 2 is an arbitrary decision. If the two groups in Demonstration Problem 10.2 were reversed, the confidence interval would be the same, but the signs would be reversed and the inequalities would be switched. Thus, the researcher must interpret the confidence interval in light of the sample information. For the confidence interval in Demonstration Problem 10.2, the population difference in mean fuel efficiency between regular and premium could be as much as 2.00 L/100 km. This result means that the premium gas could average 2.00 L/100 km less than regular gas. The other side of the interval shows that, on the basis of the sample information, the difference in favour of premium gas could be as little as 0.82 L/100 km.

If the confidence interval were being used to test the hypothesis that there is a difference in the average number of litres per 100 km between regular and premium gas, the interval would tell us to reject the null hypothesis because the interval does *not* contain zero. When both ends of a confidence interval have the same sign, zero is not in the interval. In Demonstration Problem 10.2, the interval signs are both positive. We are 95% confident that the true difference in population means is positive. Hence, we are 95% confident that there is nonzero difference in means. For such a test, $\alpha = 1 - 0.95 = 0.05$. If the signs of the confidence interval for the difference of the sample means are different, the interval includes zero, and finding no significant difference in population means is possible.

USING THE COMPUTER TO TEST HYPOTHESES ABOUT THE DIFFERENCE IN TWO POPULATION MEANS USING THE z TEST

Excel can test hypotheses about two population means using a z test. Figure 10.5 shows Excel output for the advertising manager and auditing manager wage problem. For z tests, Excel requires knowledge of the population variances. The standard output includes the sample means and population variances, the sample sizes, the hypothesized mean difference (which

Figure 10.5

Output for the Advertising Managers and Auditing Managers Wage Problem

	A	B	C
1		z Test: Two Sample for Means	
2		Ad Mgr	Auditing Mgr
3	Mean	70.700	62.187
4	Known Variance	264.164	166.411
5	Observations	32	34
6	Hypothesized Mean Difference	0	
7	z	2.35	
8	$P(Z<=z)$ one-tail	0.0094	
9	z Critical one-tail	1.64	
10	$P(Z<=z)$ two-tail	0.0189	
11	z Critical two-tail	1.96	

here, as in most cases, is zero), the observed z value, and the p values and critical table z values for both a one-tailed and a two-tailed test. Note that the p value for this two-tailed test is 0.0189, which is less than $\alpha = 0.05$ and thus indicates that the decision should be to reject the null hypothesis.

Concept Check

1. The sampling plan calls for selecting two independent samples in order to use formulas 10.1 and 10.2 about the difference in two means. Explain in your own words what it means for the two samples to be independent.
2. Explain in your own words the relationship between a hypothesis test and a confidence interval about the difference in two means.
3. Are the conclusions from a hypothesis test and a confidence interval about the difference in two means useful and reliable if the populations for the measurements being studied are not normally distributed?
4. Explain the relationship between sample sizes and the width of the confidence interval for the difference in two population means.

10.1 Problems

10.1　a.　Test the following hypotheses of the difference in population means by using the following data ($\alpha = 0.10$) and the eight-step process.

$$H_0: \mu_1 - \mu_2 = 0 \qquad\qquad H_a: \mu_1 - \mu_2 < 0$$

Sample 1	Sample 2
$\bar{x}_1 = 51.3$	$\bar{x}_2 = 53.2$
$\sigma_1^2 = 52$	$\sigma_2^2 = 60$
$n_1 = 31$	$n_2 = 32$

　　b.　Use the critical value method to find the critical difference in the mean values required to reject the null hypothesis.
　　c.　What is the p value for this problem?

10.2　Use the following sample information to construct a 90% confidence interval for the difference in the two population means.

Sample 1	Sample 2
$n_1 = 32$	$n_2 = 31$
$\bar{x}_1 = 70.4$	$\bar{x}_2 = 68.7$
$\sigma_1 = 5.76$	$\sigma_2 = 6.1$

10.3 Examine the following data. Assume the variances for the two populations are 22.74 and 26.65, respectively.

a. Use the data to test the following hypotheses ($\alpha = 0.02$).

$H_o: \mu_1 - \mu_2 = 0$ $\qquad\qquad\qquad\qquad$ $H_a: \mu_1 - \mu_2 \neq 0$

Sample 1						Sample 2					
90	88	80	88	83	94	78	85	82	81	75	76
88	87	91	81	83	88	90	80	76	83	88	77
81	84	84	87	87	93	77	75	79	86	90	75
88	90	91	88	84	83	82	83	88	80	80	74
89	95	97	95	93	97	80	90	74	89	84	79

b. Construct a 98% confidence interval to estimate the difference in population means using these data. How does your result validate the decision you reached in part (a)?

10.4 The Trade Show Bureau conducted a survey to determine why people go to trade shows. The respondents were asked to rate a series of reasons on a scale from 1 to 5, with 1 representing little importance and 5 representing great importance. One of the reasons suggested was general curiosity. The following responses for 50 people from the computers/electronics industry and 50 people from the food/beverage industry were recorded for general curiosity. Use these data and $\alpha = 0.01$ to determine whether there is a significant difference between people in these two industries on this question. Assume the variance for the computer/electronics population is 1.0188 and the variance for the food/beverage population is 0.9180.

Computers/Electronics						Food/Beverage				
1	2	1	3	2		3	3	2	4	3
0	3	3	2	1		4	5	2	4	3
3	3	1	2	2		3	2	3	2	3
3	2	2	2	2		4	3	3	3	3
1	2	3	2	1		2	4	2	3	3
1	1	3	3	2		2	4	4	4	4
2	1	4	1	4		3	5	3	3	2
2	3	0	1	0		2	0	2	2	5
3	3	2	2	3		4	3	3	2	3
2	1	0	2	3		4	3	3	3	2

10.5 Suppose you own a plumbing repair business and employ 15 plumbers. You are interested in estimating the difference in the average number of calls completed per day between two of the plumbers. A random sample of 40 days of plumber A's work results in a sample average of 5.3 calls. Historically, the variance for this plumber is known to be 1.99. A random sample of 37 days of plumber B's work results in a sample mean of 6.5 calls. Historically, the variance for this plumber is know to be 2.36. Use this information and a 95% level of confidence to estimate the difference in population mean daily efforts between plumber A and plumber B. Interpret the results. Is it possible that, for these populations of days, the average numbers of calls completed by plumber A and plumber B do not differ?

10.6   The Bureau of Labor Statistics in the U.S. shows that the average insurance cost to a company per employee per hour is $1.84 for managers and $1.99 for professional specialty workers. Suppose these figures were obtained from 35 managers and 41 professional specialty workers and that their respective population standard deviations are $0.38 and $0.51. Calculate a 98% confidence interval to estimate the difference in the mean hourly company expenditures for insurance for these two groups. What is the value of the point estimate? Test to determine whether there is a significant difference in the hourly rates employers pay for insurance between managers and professional specialty workers. Use a 2% level of significance.

10.7   A company's auditor believes the per diem cost in Windsor, Ontario, rose significantly between 1999 and 2009. To test this belief, the auditor samples 51 business trips from the company's records for 1999; the sample average was $190 per day, with a population standard deviation of $18.50. The auditor selects a second random sample of 47 business trips from the company's records for 2009; the sample average was $198 per day, with a population standard deviation of $15.60. If he uses a risk of committing a Type I error of 0.01, does the auditor find that the per diem average expense in Windsor has gone up significantly?

10.8   Suppose a market analyst wants to determine the difference in the average price of 4 L of milk in Vancouver and Montreal. To do so, he takes a telephone survey of 31 randomly selected consumers in Vancouver. He first asks whether they have purchased 4 L of milk during the past two weeks. If they say no, he continues to select consumers until he selects $n = 31$ people who say yes. If they say yes, he asks them how much they paid for the milk. The analyst undertakes a similar survey in Montreal with 31 respondents. Using the resulting sample information that follows, compute a 99% confidence interval to estimate the difference in the mean price of 4 L of milk between the two cities. Assume the population variance for Vancouver is 0.12 and the population variance for Montreal is 0.06.

Vancouver			Montreal		
$3.77	$3.48	$3.59	$5.31	$5.69	$5.69
3.94	3.30	3.59	5.50	5.50	5.69
3.71	3.77	3.53	5.21	5.40	5.31
3.83	4.12	3.65	5.69	5.21	5.40
4.59	3.83	3.77	5.69	6.16	5.97
4.24	3.77	4.01	5.40	5.69	5.21
3.71	3.89	4.36	5.21	5.31	5.78
3.65	4.01	3.89	5.78	6.16	5.50
4.06	4.01	4.12	6.16	5.31	5.97
3.89	4.18	3.94	5.69	5.40	5.59
		4.01			5.78

10.9   Employee suggestions can provide useful and insightful ideas for management. Some companies solicit and receive employee suggestions more than others, and company culture influences the use of employee suggestions. Suppose a study is conducted to determine whether there is a significant difference in mean number of suggestions a month per employee between the Manan Corporation and the Prairie Corporation. The study shows that the average number of suggestions per month is 5.8 at Manan and 5.0 at Prairie. Suppose these figures were obtained from random samples of 36 and 45 employees, respectively. If the population standard deviations of suggestions per employee are 1.7 and 1.4 for Manan and Prairie, respectively, is there a significant difference in the population means? Use $\alpha = 0.05$.

10.10 Two processes in a manufacturing line are performed manually: operation A and operation B. A random sample of 50 different assemblies using operation A shows that the sample average time per assembly is 8.05 minutes, with a population standard deviation of 1.36 minutes. A random sample of 38 different assemblies using operation B shows that the sample average time per assembly is 7.26 minutes, with a population standard deviation of 1.06 minutes. For $\alpha = 0.10$, is there enough evidence in these samples to declare that operation A takes significantly longer to perform than operation B?

10.2 HYPOTHESIS TESTING AND CONFIDENCE INTERVALS ABOUT THE DIFFERENCE IN TWO MEANS: INDEPENDENT SAMPLES WITH POPULATION VARIANCES UNKNOWN

The techniques presented in Section 10.1 are for use whenever the population variances are known. On many occasions, statisticians test hypotheses or construct confidence intervals about the difference in two population means where the population variances are not known. If the population variances are not known, the z methodology is not appropriate. This section presents methodology for handling the situation when the population variances are unknown.

HYPOTHESIS TESTING

The hypothesis test presented in this section is a test that compares the means of two samples to determine whether there is a difference in the means of two populations from which the samples come. This technique is used whenever the population variances are unknown (and hence the sample variances must be used) and the samples are independent (not related in any way). *An assumption underlying this technique is that the measurement or characteristic being studied is normally distributed for both populations.* In Section 10.1, the difference in large sample means was analyzed by formula 10.1:

$$z = \frac{(\bar{x}_1 - \bar{x}_2) - (\mu_1 - \mu_2)}{\sqrt{\dfrac{\sigma_1^2}{n_1} + \dfrac{\sigma_2^2}{n_2}}}$$

If $\sigma_1^2 = \sigma_2^2 = \sigma^2$, formula 10.1 algebraically reduces to:

$$z = \frac{(\bar{x}_1 - \bar{x}_2) - (\mu_1 - \mu_2)}{\sigma\sqrt{\dfrac{1}{n_1} + \dfrac{1}{n_2}}}$$

If σ is unknown, it can be estimated by *pooling* the two sample variances and computing a pooled sample standard deviation:

$$\sigma \approx s_p = \sqrt{\frac{s_1^2(n_1 - 1) + s_2^2(n_2 - 1)}{n_1 + n_2 - 2}}$$

s_p^2 is the weighted average of the two sample variances, s_1^2 and s_2^2. Substituting this expression for σ and changing z to t produces a formula to test the difference in means.

t Formula to Test the Difference in Means Assuming σ_1^2 and σ_2^2 are Equal (10.3)	$$t = \frac{(\bar{x}_1 - \bar{x}_2) - (\mu_1 - \mu_2)}{s_p \sqrt{\dfrac{1}{n_1} + \dfrac{1}{n_2}}}$$ $$df = n_1 + n_2 - 2$$

Formula 10.3 is constructed by assuming that the two population variances, σ_1^2 and σ_2^2, are equal. Thus, when using formula 10.3 to test hypotheses about the difference in two means for small independent samples when the population variances are unknown, we must assume that the two samples come from populations in which the variances are essentially equal. Note that if the equal variances assumption cannot be met, the following formula should be used.

t Formula to Test the Difference in Means (10.4)	$$t = \frac{(\bar{x}_1 - \bar{x}_2) - (\mu_1 - \mu_2)}{\sqrt{\dfrac{s_1^2}{n_1} + \dfrac{s_2^2}{n_2}}}$$ $$df = \frac{\left(\dfrac{s_1^2}{n_1} + \dfrac{s_2^2}{n_2}\right)^2}{\dfrac{\left(\dfrac{s_1^2}{n_1}\right)^2}{n_1 - 1} + \dfrac{\left(\dfrac{s_2^2}{n_2}\right)^2}{n_2 - 1}}$$

In formula 10.4, the population variances are not assumed to be equal. This formula clearly requires a more complex degrees-of-freedom component.

Many statistical computer software packages offer the user a choice of the "pooled" formula or the "unpooled" formula. The pooled formula in the computer packages is formula 10.3, in which equal population variances are assumed. Excel refers to this as a *t*-Test: Two-Sample Assuming Equal Variances. The unpooled formula is formula 10.4 and is used when population variances cannot be assumed to be equal. Excel refers to this as a *t*-Test: Two-Sample Assuming Unequal Variances. Again, in each of these formulas, the populations from which the two samples are drawn are assumed to be normally distributed for the phenomenon being measured.

At the Huang Manufacturing Company, an application of the test of the difference in small sample means arises. New employees are expected to attend a three-day seminar to learn about the company. At the end of the seminar, they are tested to measure their knowledge about the company. The traditional training method has been a lecture and a question-and-answer session. Management decided to experiment with a different training procedure, which processes new employees in two days by using DVDs and having no question-and-answer session. If this procedure works, it could save the company thousands of dollars over a period of several years. However, there is some concern about the effectiveness of the two-day method, and company managers would like to know whether there is any difference in the effectiveness of the two training methods.

To test the difference in the two methods, the managers randomly select one group of 15 newly hired employees to take the three-day seminar (method A) and a second group of 12 new employees for the two-day DVD method (method B). Table 10.2 shows the test scores of the two groups. Using $\alpha = 0.05$, the managers want to determine whether there is

Table 10.2

Test Scores for New Employees after Training

Training Method A					Training Method B			
56	50	52	44	52	59	54	55	65
47	47	53	45	48	52	57	64	53
42	51	42	43	44	53	56	53	57

a significant difference in the mean scores of the two groups. They assume that the scores for this test are normally distributed and that the population variances are approximately equal.

HYPOTHESIZE:

STEP 1. The hypotheses for this test follow:

$$H_0: \mu_1 - \mu_2 = 0$$
$$H_a: \mu_1 - \mu_2 \neq 0$$

TEST:

STEP 2. The statistical test to be used is formula 10.3.

STEP 3. The value of alpha is 0.05.

STEP 4. Because the hypotheses are = and ≠, this test is two-tailed. The degrees of freedom are 25 ($15 + 12 - 2 = 25$) and alpha is 0.05. The t table requires an alpha value for one tail only, and, because it is a two-tailed test, alpha is split from 0.05 to 0.025 to obtain the table t value: $t_{0.025,25} = \pm 2.060$.

The null hypothesis will be rejected if the observed t value is less than -2.060 or greater than $+2.060$.

STEP 5. The sample data are given in Table 10.2. From these data, we can calculate the sample statistics. The sample means and variances follow.

Method A	Method B
$\bar{x}_1 = 47.73$	$\bar{x}_2 = 56.5$
$s_1^2 = 19.495$	$s_2^2 = 18.273$
$n_1 = 15$	$n_2 = 12$

STEP 6. The observed value of t is:

$$t = \frac{(47.73 - 56.50) - 0}{\sqrt{\dfrac{(19.495)(14) + (18.273)(11)}{15 + 12 - 2}} \sqrt{\dfrac{1}{15} + \dfrac{1}{12}}} = -5.20$$

ACTION:

STEP 7. Because the observed value, $t = -5.20$, is less than the lower critical table value, $t = -2.06$, the observed value of t is in the rejection region. The null hypothesis is rejected. There is a significant difference in the mean scores of the two tests.

BUSINESS IMPLICATIONS:

STEP 8. Figure 10.6 shows the critical areas and the observed t value. Note that the computed t value is -5.20, which is enough to cause the managers of the Huang Manufacturing Company to reject the null hypothesis. Their conclusion is that there is a significant difference in the effectiveness of the training methods. Upon examining the sample means, they realize that method B (the two-day DVD method) actually produced an average score that was more than eight points higher than that for the group trained

Figure 10.6

***t* Values for the Training Methods Example**

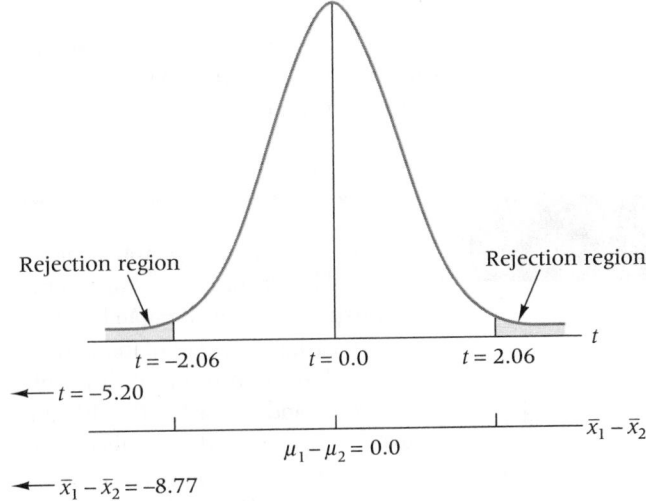

Figure 10.6

***t* Values for the Training Methods Example**

with method A. Given that training method B scores are significantly higher and that the seminar is a day shorter than method A (thereby saving both time and money), it makes business sense to adopt method B as the standard training method.

In a test of this sort, which group is group 1 and which is group 2 is an arbitrary decision. If the two samples had been designated in reverse, the observed *t* value would have been *t* = +5.20 (same magnitude but different sign), and the decision would have been the same.

USING THE COMPUTER TO TEST HYPOTHESES AND CONSTRUCT CONFIDENCE INTERVALS ABOUT THE DIFFERENCE IN TWO POPULATION MEANS USING THE *t* TEST

Excel can analyze *t* tests for the difference in two means. Figure 10.7 contains the Excel output for the Huang Manufacturing Company training methods example. Notice that the output contains the same sample means, the degrees of freedom (df = 25), the observed *t* value −5.20, and the *p* value (0.000022 as two-tailed *p*). This *p* value can be compared directly with $\alpha = 0.05$ for decision-making purposes (reject the null hypothesis).

Figure 10.7

Excel Output for the Training Methods Example

	A	B	C
1	t-Test: Two-Sample Assuming Equal Variances		
2		Method A	Method B
3	Mean	47.73	56.50
4	Variance	19.495	18.273
5	Observations	15	12
6	Pooled Variance	18.957	
7	Hypothesized Mean Difference	0	
8	df	25	
9	*t* Stat	-5.20	
10	P(*T*<=*t*) one-tail	0.0000112	
11	*t* Critical one-tail	1.71	
12	P(*T*<=*t*) two-tail	0.0000223	
13	*t* Critical two-tail	2.06	

Excel also displays the sample variances and the pooled variance and prints out p values for both a one-tailed test and a two-tailed test: the user must select the appropriate value for his or her test. Excel also prints out the critical t values for both one- and two-tailed tests. Notice that the critical t value for a two-tailed test (2.06) is the same as the critical t value obtained by using the t table (±2.060).

Demonstration Problem 10.3

Is there a difference in the way Chinese cultural values affect the purchasing strategies of industrial buyers in Taiwan and mainland China? Researchers at the National Chiao-Tung University in Taiwan attempted to determine whether there is a significant difference in the purchasing strategies of industrial buyers between Taiwan and mainland China based on the cultural dimension labelled "integration." Integration is being in harmony with one's self, family, and associates. For the study, 46 Taiwanese buyers and 26 mainland Chinese buyers were contacted and interviewed. Buyers were asked to respond to 35 items using a nine-point scale with possible answers ranging from no importance (1) to extreme importance (9). The resulting statistics for the two groups are shown in Step 5. Using $\alpha = 0.01$, test to determine whether there is a significant difference between buyers in Taiwan and buyers in mainland China on integration. Assume that integration scores are normally distributed in the population.

Solution

HYPOTHESIZE:

STEP 1. If a two-tailed test is undertaken, the hypotheses and the table t value are as follows:

$$H_0: \mu_1 - \mu_2 = 0$$
$$H_a: \mu_1 - \mu_2 \neq 0$$

TEST:

STEP 2. The appropriate statistical test is formula 10.3.

STEP 3. The value of alpha is 0.01.

STEP 4. The sample sizes are 46 and 26. Thus, there are 70 degrees of freedom. With this figure and $\alpha/2 = 0.005$, the critical table t value can be determined:

$$t_{0.005,70} = 2.648$$

STEP 5. The sample data follow.

Integration

Taiwanese Buyers	Mainland Chinese Buyers
$n_1 = 46$	$n_2 = 26$
$\bar{x}_1 = 5.42$	$\bar{x}_2 = 5.04$
$s_1^2 = 0.58^2 = 0.3346$	$s_2^2 = 0.49^2 = 0.2401$
$df = n_1 + n_2 - 2 = 46 + 26 - 2 = 70$	

STEP 6. The observed t value is:

$$t = \frac{(5.42 - 5.04) - 0}{\sqrt{\frac{(0.3364)(45) + (0.2401)(25)}{46 + 26 - 2}}\sqrt{\frac{1}{46} + \frac{1}{26}}} = 2.82$$

ACTION:

STEP 7. Because the observed value of $t = 2.82$ is greater than the critical table value of $t = 2.648$, the decision is to reject the null hypothesis.

BUSINESS IMPLICATIONS:

STEP 8. The Taiwan industrial buyers scored significantly higher than the mainland China industrial buyers on integration. Managers should keep in mind this cultural dimension when dealing with Taiwanese industrial and mainland Chinese buyers.

The following graph shows the critical *t* values, the rejection regions, the observed *t* value, and the difference in the raw means.

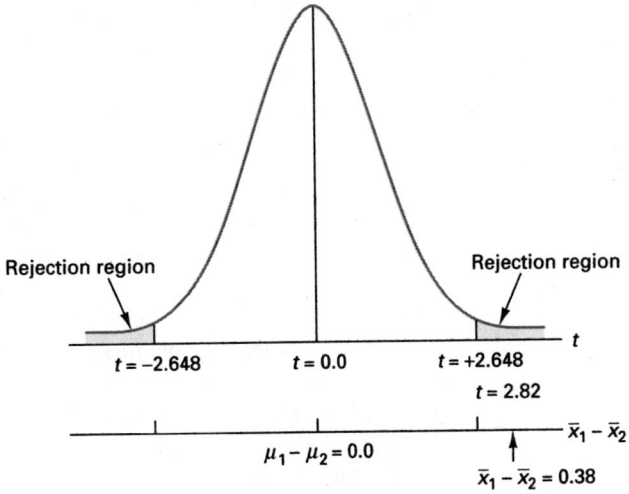

CONFIDENCE INTERVALS

Confidence interval formulas can be derived to estimate the difference in the population means for independent samples when the population variances are unknown. The focus in this section is only on confidence intervals when approximately equal population variances and normally distributed populations can be assumed.

Confidence Interval to Estimate $\mu_1 - \mu_2$ Assuming the Population Variances are Unknown and Equal (10.5)	$(\bar{x}_1 - \bar{x}_2) - t\sqrt{\dfrac{s_1^2(n_1 - 1) + s_2^2(n_2 - 1)}{n_1 + n_2 - 2}}\sqrt{\dfrac{1}{n_1} + \dfrac{1}{n_2}} \leq \mu_1 - \mu_2 \leq$ $(\bar{x}_1 - \bar{x}_2) + t\sqrt{\dfrac{s_1^2(n_1 - 1) + s_2^2(n_2 - 1)}{n_1 + n_2 - 2}}\sqrt{\dfrac{1}{n_1} + \dfrac{1}{n_2}}$ $df = n_1 + n_2 - 2$

One group of researchers set out to determine whether there is a difference between "average Canadians" and those who are "phone survey respondents."[*] Their study was based on a well-known U.S. personality survey that attempted to assess the personality

---

[*]*Source:* Data adapted from David Whitlark and Michael Geurts, "Phone Surveys: How Well Do Respondents Represent Average Americans?" *Marketing Research* (Fall 1998), pp. 13–17. Note that the results on this portion of the actual study are about the same as those shown here except that in the actual study the sample sizes were in the 500–600 range.

Table 10.3

Conscientiousness Data on Phone Survey Respondents and Average Canadians

Phone Survey Respondents	Average Canadians
35.38	35.03
37.06	33.90
37.74	34.56
36.97	36.24
37.84	34.59
37.50	34.95
40.75	33.30
35.31	34.73
35.30	34.79
	37.83
$n_1 = 9$	$n_2 = 10$
$\bar{x}_1 = 37.09$	$\bar{x}_2 = 34.99$
$s_1 = 1.727$	$s_2 = 1.253$

$$df = 9 + 10 - 2 = 17$$

profile of both average Americans and phone survey respondents. Suppose the Canadian researchers sampled nine phone survey respondents and ten average Canadians in this survey and obtained the results on one personality factor, conscientiousness, which are displayed in Table 10.3. Assume that conscientiousness scores are normally distributed in the population.

The table t value for a 99% level of confidence and 17 degrees of freedom is $t_{0.005,17} = 2.898$. The confidence interval is:

$$(37.09 - 34.99) \pm 2.898 \sqrt{\frac{(1.727)^2(8) + (1.253)^2(9)}{9 + 10 - 2}} \sqrt{\frac{1}{9} + \frac{1}{10}}$$
$$= 2.10 \pm 1.99$$
$$0.11 \leq \mu_1 - \mu_2 \leq 4.09$$

The researchers are 99% confident that the true difference in population mean personality scores for conscientiousness between phone survey respondents and average Americans is between 0.11 and 4.09. Zero is not in this interval, so they can conclude that

Figure 10.8

Output for the Phone Survey Respondent and Average Canadian Example

	A	B	C
1	t-Test: Two-Sample Assuming Equal Variances		
2		Survey Respondent	Average Canadian
3	Mean	37.09	34.99
4	Variance	2.98	1.57
5	Observations	9	10
6	Pooled Variance	2.2346	
7	Hypothesized Mean Difference	0	
8	df	17	
9	t State	3.061	
10	P (T<=t) one-tail	0.004	
11	t Critical one-tail	2.567	
12	P (T<=t) two-tail	0.007	
13	t Critical two-tail	2.898	

there is a significant difference in the average scores of the two groups. Higher scores indicate more conscientiousness. Therefore, it is possible to conclude from Table 10.3 and this confidence interval that phone survey respondents are significantly more conscientious than average Canadians. These results indicate that researchers should be careful in using phone survey results to reach conclusions about average Canadians.

Figure 10.8 contains Excel output for this problem. Note that the Excel output includes the observed *t* value (3.06) for hypothesis testing. Because the *p* value is 0.007, which is less than 0.01, the Excel hypothesis-testing information validates the conclusion reached that there is a significant difference in the scores of the two groups.

Demonstration Problem 10.4

A coffee manufacturer is interested in estimating the difference in the average daily coffee consumption of regular-coffee drinkers and decaffeinated-coffee drinkers. Its researcher randomly selects 13 regular-coffee drinkers and asks how many cups of coffee per day they drink. He randomly selects 15 decaffeinated-coffee drinkers and asks how many cups of coffee per day they drink. The average for the regular-coffee drinkers is 4.35 cups, with a standard deviation of 1.20 cups. The average for the decaffeinated-coffee drinkers is 6.84 cups, with a standard deviation of 1.42 cups. The researcher assumes, for each population, that the daily consumption is normally distributed. Construct a 95% confidence interval to estimate the difference in the averages of the two populations.

Solution

The table *t* value for this problem is $t_{0.025,26} = 2.056$. The confidence interval estimate is:

$$(4.35 - 6.84) \pm 2.056 \sqrt{\frac{(1.20)^2(12) + (1.42)^2(14)}{13 + 15 - 2}} \sqrt{\frac{1}{13} + \frac{1}{15}}$$

$$= -2.49 \pm 1.03$$

$$-3.52 \leq \mu_1 - \mu_2 \leq -1.46$$

The researcher is 95% confident that the difference in population average daily consumption of cups of coffee between regular- and decaffeinated-coffee drinkers is between 1.46 cups and 3.52 cups. The point estimate for the difference in population means is 2.49 cups, with an error of 1.03 cups.

STATISTICS IN BUSINESS TODAY

Ethical Differences between Men and Women

Is there a difference between men and women in making ethical managerial decisions? One study attempted to answer this question by studying 164 managers of a large financial conglomerate. A questionnaire was constructed using vignettes (brief, focused cases) to depict four ethical questions under two different scenarios. Vignettes dealt with (1) sale of an unsafe product, (2) bribery, (3) product misrepresentation, and (4) industrial espionage. These vignettes were to be considered under the scenarios of (a) enhancing the firm's profit position and (b) the individual's own economic gain. The questionnaire was structured to produce a score for each respondent on each ethical question without regard to scenario and a score for each

respondent on each ethical question with regard to scenario. The null hypothesis that there is no significant difference in the mean ethical scores of men and women was tested for each question using a *t* test for independent samples.

The results were mixed. In considering the responses to the four vignettes without regard to either of the two scenarios, there was a significant difference between men and women on the sale of an unsafe product at ($\alpha = 0.01$). On this question, women scored significantly higher (more ethical) than men, indicating that women are less likely to sell an unsafe product. On the questions of product misrepresentation and industrial espionage, women scored significantly higher on both ($\alpha = 0.10$). There was no significant difference between men and women on the question of bribery.

The results were somewhat different when the two scenarios were considered (firm profit position and personal economic gain). On the question of selling an unsafe product, women were significantly more ethical ($\alpha = 0.01$) when considering enhancing the firm's profit position and significantly more ethical ($\alpha = 0.05$) when considering personal economic gain. On the question of bribery, there was no significant difference in the ethics scores of men and women in light of enhancing the firm's profit position but women were significantly more ethical ($\alpha = 0.10$) when considering personal economic gain. On the question of product misrepresentation, there was no significant difference between men and women when considering personal economic gain but women were significantly more ethical than men in light of enhancing the firm's profit position ($\alpha = 0.10$). On the question of industrial espionage, women were significantly more ethical than men ($\alpha = 0.10$) in light

of enhancing the firm's profit position, and women were also significantly more ethical than men ($\alpha = 0.01$) when considering personal gain.

This study used two-sample hypothesis testing in an effort to determine whether there is a difference between men and women on ethical management issues. The results here can assist decision makers in assigning managers to various tasks that involve any of these four ethical questions. Interesting questions can be studied about why women might be more ethical than men in some managerial situations and what might be done to foster stronger ethics among men.

Source: Adapted from James J. Hoffman, "Are Women Really More Ethical Than Men? Maybe It Depends on the Situation," *Journal of Managerial Issues,* Vol. X, no. 1 (Spring 1998), pp. 60–73.

Concept Check

1. Under what conditions should we use a z formula when dealing with the difference in two means? A t formula?
2. Are the conclusions from this section useful and reliable if the populations for the measurements being studied are not normally distributed?
3. What is the key difference between the t formula 10.3 and the t formula 10.4 to test the difference in means when population variances are unknown? Explain under what conditions each formula should be used.
4. Explain the relationship between sample sizes and the width of the confidence interval for the difference in two population means when population variances are unknown and equal.

10.2 Problems

10.11   Use the data given and the eight-step process to test the following hypotheses:

$$H_0: \mu_1 - \mu_2 = 0$$
$$H_a: \mu_1 - \mu_2 < 0$$

Sample 1	Sample 2
$n_1 = 8$	$n_2 = 11$
$\bar{x}_1 = 24.56$	$\bar{x}_2 = 26.42$
$s_1^2 = 12.4$	$s_2^2 = 15.8$

Use a 1% level of significance, and assume that x is normally distributed in the populations and the variances of the populations are approximately equal.

10.12   a.   Use the following data and $\alpha = 0.10$ to test the stated hypotheses. Assume x is normally distributed in the populations and the variances of the populations are approximately equal.

$$H_0: \mu_1 - \mu_2 = 0$$
$$H_a: \mu_1 - \mu_2 \neq 0$$

Sample 1	Sample 2
$n_1 = 20$	$n_2 = 20$
$\bar{x}_1 = 118$	$\bar{x}_2 = 113$
$s_1 = 23.9$	$s_2 = 21.6$

b.   Use these data to construct a 90% confidence interval to estimate $\mu_1 - \mu_2$.

10.13 Suppose that for years the mean of population 1 has been accepted to be the same as the mean of population 2, but now population 1 is believed to have a greater mean than population 2. Letting $\alpha = 0.05$ and assuming the populations have equal variances and x is approximately normally distributed, use the following data to test this belief.

Sample 1		Sample 2	
43.6	45.7	40.1	36.4
44.0	49.1	42.2	42.3
45.2	45.6	43.1	38.8
40.8	46.5	37.5	43.3
48.3	45.0	41.0	40.2

10.14 a.   Suppose you want to determine whether the average values for populations 1 and 2 are different, and you randomly gather the following data.

Sample 1						Sample 2					
2	10	7	8	2	5	10	12	8	7	9	11
9	1	8	0	2	8	9	8	9	10	11	10
11	2	4	5	3	9	11	10	7	8	10	10

Test your conjecture, using a probability of committing a Type I error of 0.01. Assume the population variances are the same and x is normally distributed in the populations.

b.   Use these data to construct a 98% confidence interval for the difference in the two population means.

10.15 Suppose a real estate agent is interested in comparing the asking prices of single-family homes in Montreal and Halifax. The agent conducts a small telephone survey in the two cities, asking the prices of single-family homes. A random sample of 21 listings in Montreal resulted in a sample average price of $252,000, with a standard deviation of $4,900. A random sample of 26 listings in Halifax resulted in a sample average price of $243,000, with a standard deviation of $3,700. The agent assumes prices of single-family homes are normally distributed and the variance in prices in the two cities is about the same. What would he obtain for a 90% confidence interval for the difference in mean prices of single-family homes between Montreal and Halifax? Test whether there is any difference in the mean prices of single-family homes of the two cities for $\alpha = 0.10$.

10.16 According to an experiential education survey published at JobWeb.com, the average hourly wage of a university student working as a co-op is $15.64 an hour and the average hourly wage of an intern is $15.44. Assume that such wages are normally distributed in the population and that the population variances are equal. Suppose these figures were actually obtained from the data in the following table. Use these data and $\alpha = 0.10$ to test to determine if there is a significant difference in the mean hourly wage of a university co-op student and the mean hourly wage of an intern. Using these same data, construct a 90% confidence interval to estimate the difference in the population mean hourly wages of co-ops and interns.

Co-op Students	Interns
$15.34	$15.10
14.75	14.45
15.88	16.21
16.92	14.91
16.84	13.80
17.37	16.02
14.05	16.25
15.41	15.89
16.74	13.99
14.55	16.48
15.25	15.75
14.64	16.42

10.17   Based on an indication that mean daily car rental rates may be higher for Toronto than for Montreal, a survey of eight car rental companies in Toronto is taken and the sample mean car rental rate is $47, with a standard deviation of $3. Further, suppose a survey of nine car rental companies in Montreal results in a sample mean of $44 and a standard deviation of $3. Use $\alpha = 0.05$ to test to determine whether the average daily car rental rates in Toronto are significantly higher than those in Montreal. Assume car rental rates are normally distributed and the population variances are equal.

10.18   What is the difference in average daily hotel room rates between Edmonton and Quebec City? Suppose we want to estimate this difference by taking hotel rate samples from each city and using a 98% confidence level. The data for such a study follow. Use these data to produce a point estimate for the mean difference in the hotel rates for the two cities. Assume the population variances are approximately equal and hotel rates in any given city are normally distributed.

Edmonton	Quebec City
$n_E = 22$	$n_Q = 20$
$\bar{x}_E = \$112$	$\bar{x}_Q = \$122$
$s_E = \$11$	$s_Q = \$12$

10.19   A study was conducted to compare the costs of supporting a family of four Canadians for a year in different foreign cities. The lifestyle of living in Canada on an annual income of $75,000 was the standard against which living in foreign cities was compared. A comparable living standard in Perth, Australia, and Mexico City was attained for about $64,000. Suppose an executive wants to determine whether there is any difference in the average annual cost of supporting her family of four in the manner to which they are accustomed between Perth and Mexico City. She uses the following data, randomly gathered from 11 families in each city, and an alpha of 0.01 to test this difference. She assumes the annual cost is normally distributed and the population variances are equal. What does the executive find?

Perth, Australia	Mexico City
$69,000	$64,000
64,500	64,000
67,500	66,000
64,500	64,900

(continued)

Perth, Australia	Mexico City
66,700	62,000
68,000	60,500
65,000	62,500
69,000	63,000
71,000	64,500
68,500	63,500
67,500	62,400

Use the data from the table to construct a 95% confidence interval to estimate the difference in average annual costs between the two cities.

10.20 Some studies have shown that men spend more than women buying gifts and cards on Valentine's Day. Suppose a researcher wants to test this hypothesis by randomly sampling 9 men and 10 women. Each study participant is asked to keep a log beginning one month before Valentine's Day and record all purchases made for Valentine's Day during that one-month period. The resulting data are shown below. Use these data and a 1% level of significance to test to determine if, on average, men actually do spend significantly more than women on Valentine's Day. Assume that such spending is normally distributed in the population and that the population variances are equal.

Men	Women
$107.48	$125.98
143.61	45.53
90.19	56.35
125.53	80.62
70.79	46.37
83.00	44.34
129.63	75.21
154.22	68.48
93.80	85.84
	126.11

10.3 STATISTICAL INFERENCES FOR TWO RELATED POPULATIONS

In the preceding section, hypotheses were tested and confidence intervals constructed about the difference in two population means when the samples are independent. In this section, a method is presented to analyze **dependent samples** or related samples. Some researchers refer to this test as the **matched-pairs** test. Others call it the *t* **test for related measures** or the **correlated *t* test.**

What are some types of situations in which the two samples being studied are related or dependent? Let's begin with the before-and-after study. Sometimes as an experimental control mechanism, the same person or object is measured both before and after a treatment. Certainly, the after measurement is *not* independent of the before measurement because the measurements are taken on the same person or object in both cases. Table 10.4 gives data from a hypothetical study in which people were asked to rate a company before and after one week of viewing a 15-minute DVD about the company twice a day. The before scores are one sample and the after scores are a second sample, but each pair of scores is related because the two measurements apply to the same person. The before scores and the after scores are not likely to vary from each other as much as scores gathered from

Table 10.4

Rating of a Company (on a Scale from 0 to 50)

Individual	Before	After
1	32	39
2	11	15
3	21	35
4	17	13
5	30	41
6	38	39
7	14	22

independent samples because individuals bring their biases about businesses and the company to the study. These individual biases affect both the before scores and the after scores in the same way because each pair of scores is measured on the same person.

Other examples of related samples are studies in which twins, siblings, or spouses are matched and placed in two different groups. For example, a fashion merchandiser might be interested in comparing men's and women's perceptions of women's clothing. If the men and women selected for the study are spouses or siblings, a built-in relatedness to the measurements of the two groups in the study is likely. Their scores are more apt to be alike or related than those of randomly chosen independent groups of men and women because of similar backgrounds or tastes.

HYPOTHESIS TESTING

To ensure the use of the proper hypothesis-testing techniques, the researcher must determine whether the two samples being studied are dependent or independent. The approach to analyzing two *related* samples is different from the techniques used to analyze independent samples. Use of the techniques in Section 10.2 to analyze related group data can result in a loss of power and an increase in Type II errors.

The matched-pairs test for related samples requires that the two samples be the same size and that the individual related scores be matched. Formula 10.6 is used to test hypotheses about dependent populations.

---

t Formula to Test the Difference in two Dependent Populations (10.6)

$$t = \frac{\bar{d} - D}{\frac{s_d}{\sqrt{n}}}$$

$$df = n - 1$$

where

n = number of pairs
d = sample difference in pairs
D = mean population difference
s_d = standard deviation of sample difference
$\bar{d}$ = mean sample difference

This *t* test for dependent measures uses the sample difference, *d*, between individual matched sample values as the basic measurement of analysis instead of individual sample values. Analysis of the *d* values effectively converts the problem from a two-sample problem to a single sample of differences, which is an adaptation of the single-sample means formula. This test utilizes the sample mean of differences, and the standard deviation of differences, s_d, which can be computed by using formulas 10.7 and 10.8.

Formulas for $\bar{d}$ and s_d (10.7 and 10.8)	$$\bar{d} = \frac{\sum d}{n}$$ $$s_d = \sqrt{\frac{\sum (d - \bar{d})^2}{n-1}} = \sqrt{\frac{\sum d^2 - \frac{(\sum d)^2}{n}}{n-1}}$$

An assumption for this test is that the differences of the two populations are normally distributed.

Analyzing data by this method involves calculating a t value with formula 10.6 and comparing it to a critical t value obtained from the table. The critical t value is obtained from the t distribution table in the usual way, with the exception that, in the degrees of freedom $(n-1)$, n is the number of matched pairs of scores.

Suppose a stock market investor is interested in determining whether there is a significant difference in the price to earnings (P/E) ratio for companies from one year to the next. In an effort to study this question, the investor randomly samples nine companies listed on the Toronto Stock Exchange and records the P/E ratios for each of these companies at the end of year 1 and at the end of year 2. The data are shown in Table 10.5.

These data are related data because each P/E value for year 1 has a corresponding year 2 measurement on the same company. Because no prior information indicates whether P/E ratios have gone up or down, the hypothesis tested is two-tailed. Assume $\alpha = 0.01$. Assume that differences in P/E ratios are normally distributed in the population.

HYPOTHESIZE:

STEP 1.

$$H_0: D = 0$$
$$H_a: D \neq 0$$

TEST:

STEP 2. The appropriate statistical test is:

$$t = \frac{\bar{d} - D}{\frac{s_d}{\sqrt{n}}}$$

STEP 3. $\alpha = 0.01$

Table 10.5	Company	Year 1 P/E Ratio	Year 2 P/E Ratio
P/E Ratios for Nine Randomly Selected Companies	1	8.9	12.7
	2	38.1	45.4
	3	43.0	10.0
	4	34.0	27.2
	5	34.5	22.8
	6	15.2	24.1
	7	20.3	32.3
	8	19.9	40.1
	9	61.9	106.5

Table 10.6	Company	Year 1 P/E	Year 2 P/E	d
Analysis of P/E Ratio Data	1	8.9	12.7	−3.8
	2	38.1	45.4	−7.3
	3	43.0	10.0	33.0
	4	34.0	27.2	6.8
	5	34.5	22.8	11.7
	6	15.2	24.1	−8.9
	7	20.3	32.3	−12.0
	8	19.9	40.1	−20.2
	9	61.9	106.5	−44.6

$\bar{d} = -5.033$, $\quad s_d = 21.599$, $\quad n = 9$

$$\text{Observed } t = \frac{-5.033 - 0}{\dfrac{21.599}{\sqrt{9}}} = -0.70$$

STEP 4. Because $\alpha = 0.01$ and this test is two-tailed, $\alpha/2 = 0.005$ is used to obtain the table t value. With nine pairs of data, $n = 9$ and df $= n - 1 = 8$. The table t value is $t_{0.005,8} = \pm 3.355$. If the observed test statistic is greater than 3.355 or less than −3.355, the null hypothesis will be rejected.

STEP 5. The sample data are given in Table 10.5.

STEP 6. Table 10.6 shows the calculations to obtain the observed value of the test statistic, which is $t = -0.70$.

ACTION:

STEP 7. Because the observed t value is greater than the critical table t value in the lower tail ($t = -0.70 > t = -3.355$), it is in the nonrejection region.

BUSINESS IMPLICATIONS:

STEP 8. There is not enough evidence from the data to declare a significant difference in the average P/E ratio between year 1 and year 2. The graph in Figure 10.9 depicts the rejection regions, the critical values of t, and the observed value of t for this example.

Figure 10.9

Graphical Depiction of P/E Ratio Analysis

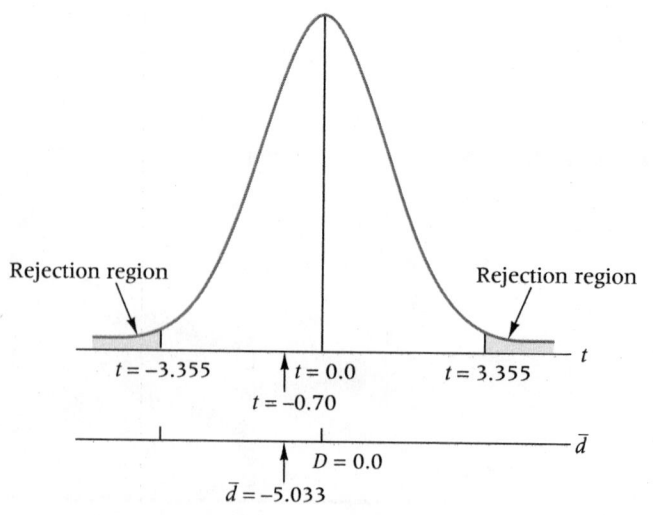

Figure 10.10

Excel Output for the P/E Ratio Example

	A	B	C
1	*t*-Test: Paired Two Sample for Means		
2		Year 1 P/E	Year 2 P/E
3	Mean	30.644	35.678
4	Variance	268.135	837.544
5	Observations	9	9
6	Pearson Correlation	0.674	
7	Hypothesized Mean Difference	0	
8	df	8	
9	*t* Stat	−0.699	
10	*P* (*T*<=*t*) one-tail	0.252	
11	*t* Critical one-tail	2.896	
12	*P* (*T*<=*t*) two-tail	0.504	
13	*t* Critical two-tail	3.355	

USING THE COMPUTER TO MAKE STATISTICAL INFERENCES ABOUT TWO RELATED POPULATIONS

Excel can be used to make statistical inferences about two related populations. Figure 10.10 shows the Excel output for the P/E ratio problem. The Excel output contains the hypothesized mean difference, the observed *t* value (−0.70), and the critical *t* values and their associated *p* values for both a one-tailed and a two-tailed test. Because the *p* value (0.504) is greater than the value of alpha (0.01), the decision is to fail to reject the null hypothesis.

Demonstration Problem 10.5

Let us revisit the hypothetical study discussed earlier in the section in which consumers are asked to rate a company both before and after viewing a video on the company twice a day for a week. The data from Table 10.4 are displayed again here. Use an alpha of 0.05 to test to determine whether there is a significant increase in the ratings of the company after the one-week DVD treatment. Assume that differences in ratings are normally distributed in the population.

Individual	Before	After
1	32	39
2	11	15
3	21	35
4	17	13
5	30	41
6	38	39
7	14	22

Solution

Because the same individuals are being used in a before-and-after study, it is a related measures study. The desired effect is to increase ratings, which means the hypothesis test is one-tailed.

HYPOTHESIZE:

Step 1.

$$H_0: D = 0$$
$$H_a: D < 0$$

Because the researchers want to prove that the ratings increase from before to after and because the difference is computed by subtracting the after ratings from the before ratings, the desired alternative hypothesis is $D < 0$.

TEST:

STEP 2. The appropriate test statistic is formula 10.6.

STEP 3. The Type I error rate is 0.05.

STEP 4. The degrees of freedom are $n - 1 = 7 - 1 = 6$. For $\alpha = 0.05$, the table t value is $t_{0.05,6} = -1.943$. The decision rule is to reject the null hypothesis if the observed value is less than -1.943.

STEP 5. The sample data and some calculations follow.

Individual	Before	After	d
1	32	39	−7
2	11	15	−4
3	21	35	−14
4	17	13	4
5	30	41	−11
6	38	39	−1
7	14	22	−8

$\bar{d} = -5.857$ $s_d = 6.0945$

STEP 6. The observed t value is:

$$t = \frac{-5.857 - 0}{\dfrac{6.0945}{\sqrt{7}}} = -2.54$$

Computer analysis of this problem reveals that the p value is 0.022.

ACTION:

STEP 7. Because the observed value of -2.54 is less than the critical table value of -1.943 and the p value (0.022) is less than alpha (0.05), the decision is to reject the null hypothesis.

BUSINESS IMPLICATIONS:

STEP 8. There is enough evidence to conclude that, on average, the ratings have increased significantly. This result might be used by managers to support a decision to continue using the DVDs or to expand the use of such DVDs in an effort to increase public support for their company.

The following graph depicts the observed value, the rejection region, and the critical t value for the problem.

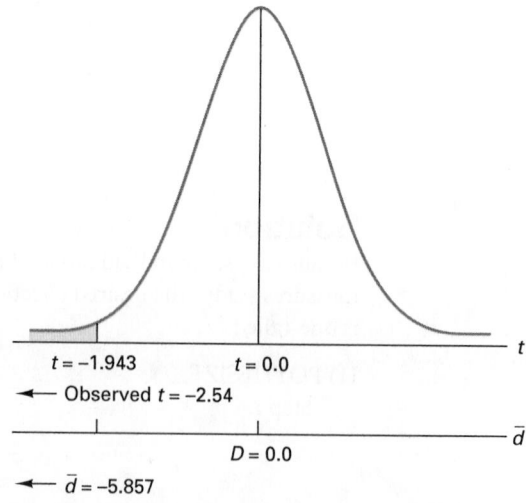

CONFIDENCE INTERVALS

Sometimes a researcher is interested in estimating the mean difference in two populations for related samples. A confidence interval for D, the mean population difference of two related samples, can be constructed by algebraically rearranging formula 10.6, which was used to test hypotheses about D. Again the assumption is that the differences are normally distributed in the population.

Confidence Interval Formula to Estimate the Difference in Related Populations, D (10.9)	$$\bar{d} - t\frac{s_d}{\sqrt{n}} \leq D \leq \bar{d} + t\frac{s_d}{\sqrt{n}}$$ $$df = n - 1$$

The following housing industry example demonstrates the application of formula 10.9. The sale of new houses apparently fluctuates seasonally. Superimposed on the seasonality are economic and business cycles that also influence the sale of new houses. In certain parts of the country, new-house sales increase in the spring and early summer and drop off in the fall. Suppose a national real estate association wants to estimate the average difference in the number of new-house sales per company in Halifax between 2008 and 2009. To do so, the association randomly selects 18 real estate firms in the Halifax area and obtains their new-house sales figures for May 2008 and May 2009. The numbers of sales per company are shown in Table 10.7. Using these data, the association's analyst estimates the average difference in the number of sales per real estate company in Halifax for May 2008 and May 2009 and constructs a 99% confidence interval. The analyst assumes that differences in sales are normally distributed in the population.

Table 10.7	Realtor	May 2008	May 2009
Number of New-House Sales in Halifax	1	8	11
	2	19	30
	3	5	6
	4	9	13
	5	3	5
	6	0	4
	7	13	15
	8	11	17
	9	9	12
	10	5	12
	11	8	6
	12	2	5
	13	11	10
	14	14	22
	15	7	8
	16	12	15
	17	6	12
	18	10	10

Realtor	May 2008	May 2009	d
1	8	11	−3
2	19	30	−11
3	5	6	−1
4	9	13	−4
5	3	5	−2
6	0	4	−4
7	13	15	−2
8	11	17	−6
9	9	12	−3
10	5	12	−7
11	8	6	2
12	2	5	−3
13	11	10	1
14	14	22	−8
15	7	8	−1
16	12	15	−3
17	6	12	−6
18	10	10	0

$$\bar{d} = -3.389 \text{ and } s_d = 3.274$$

Table 10.8

Differences in Number of New-House Sales, 2008–2009

The number of pairs, n, is 18, and the degrees of freedom are 17. For a 99% level of confidence and these degrees of freedom, the table t value is $t_{0.005,17} = 2.898$. The values for $\bar{d}$ and s_d are shown in Table 10.8.

The point estimate of the difference is $\bar{d} = -3.39$. The 99% confidence interval is:

$$\bar{d} - t\frac{s_d}{\sqrt{n}} \leq D \leq \bar{d} + t\frac{s_d}{\sqrt{n}}$$

$$-3.389 - 2.898\frac{3.274}{\sqrt{18}} \leq D \leq -3.389 + 2.898\frac{3.274}{\sqrt{18}}$$

$$-3.389 - 2.236 \leq D \leq -3.389 + 2.236$$

$$-5.625 \leq D \leq -1.153$$

The analyst estimates with a 99% level of confidence that the average difference in new-house sales for a real estate company in Halifax between 2008 and 2009 in May is somewhere between −5.625 and −1.153 houses. Because 2009 sales were subtracted from 2008 sales, the minus signs indicate more sales in 2009 than in 2008. Note that both ends of the confidence interval contain negatives. This result means that the analyst can be 99% confident that zero difference is not the average difference. If the analyst were using this confidence interval to test the hypothesis that there is no significant mean difference in average new-house sales per company in Halifax between May 2008 and May 2009, the null hypothesis would be rejected for $\alpha = 0.01$. The point estimate for this example is −3.389 houses, with an error of 2.236 houses. Figure 10.11 is the Excel computer output for the test.

Figure 10.11

Output for the New-House Sales Example

	A	B	C
1	*t*-Test: Paired Two Sample for Means		
2		May 2008	May 2009
3	Mean	8.444	11.833
4	Variance	21.556	42.735
5	Observations	18	18
6	Pearson Correlation	0.882	
7	Hypothesized Mean Difference	0	
8	df	17	
9	*t* Stat	−4.391	
10	*P* (*T*<=*t*) one-tail	0.000	
11	*t* Critical one-tail	2.567	
12	*P*(*T*<=*t*) two-tail	0.000	
13	*t* Critical two-tail	2.898	
14	Confidence Interval (99%) for D −5.626 <= D <= −1.152		

Concept Check

1. Provide a few examples of situations in which the two samples being studied are related or dependent.
2. Explain how data collection for dependent samples differs from data collection for independent samples.
3. When dealing with statistical inferences for two related populations, what is the key assumption regarding the distribution of the differences of the two populations?
4. Suppose that a nationally known supermarket wishes to compare the sales of its own brand of soft drinks before and after a two-week-long TV promotion. Explain how data could be collected to analyze such dependent samples.

10.3 Problems

10.21 Use the data given and a 1% level of significance to test the following hypotheses. Assume the differences are normally distributed in the population.

$$H_0: D = 0 \qquad H_a: D > 0$$

Pair	Sample 1	Sample 2
1	38	22
2	27	28
3	30	21
4	41	38
5	36	38
6	38	26
7	33	19
8	35	31
9	44	35

10.22 Use the data given to test the following hypotheses ($\alpha = 0.05$). Assume the differences are normally distributed in the population.

$$H_0: D = 0$$
$$H_a: D \neq 0$$

Individual	Before	After
1	107	102
2	99	98
3	110	100
4	113	108
5	96	89
6	98	101
7	100	99
8	102	102
9	107	105
10	109	110
11	104	102
12	99	96
13	101	100

10.23 Construct a 98% confidence interval to estimate D from the following sample information. Assume the differences are normally distributed in the population.

$$\bar{d} = 40.56, \ s_d = 26.58, \ n = 22$$

10.24 Construct a 90% confidence interval to estimate D from the following sample information. Assume the differences are normally distributed in the population.

Client	Before	After
1	32	40
2	28	25
3	35	36
4	32	32
5	26	29
6	25	31
7	37	39
8	16	30
9	35	31

10.25 Because of uncertainty in real estate markets, many homeowners are considering remodelling and constructing additions rather than selling. Probably the most expensive room in the house to remodel is the kitchen. In terms of resale value, is remodelling the kitchen worth the cost? Assume that the following cost and resale figures have been collected for 11 cities and that the average cost to remodel the kitchen is $23,400. Use these data to construct a 99% confidence interval for the difference between cost and added resale value of kitchen remodelling. Assume the differences are normally distributed in the population.

City	Cost	Resale
Calgary	$20,427	$25,163
Edmonton	27,255	24,625
Fredericton	22,115	12,600
Halifax	23,256	24,588
London, Ontario	21,887	19,267
Montreal	24,255	20,150
Regina	19,852	22,500
Toronto	23,624	16,667
Vancouver	25,885	26,875
Victoria	28,999	35,333
Winnipeg	20,836	16,292

10.26 The vice president of marketing brought to the attention of sales managers that most of the company's manufacturer representatives contacted clients and maintained client relationships in a disorganized, haphazard way. The sales managers brought the reps in for a three-day seminar and training session on how to use an organizer to schedule visits and recall pertinent information about each client more effectively. Sales reps were taught how to schedule visits most efficiently to maximize their efforts. Sales managers were given data on the number of site visits by sales reps on a randomly selected day both before and after the seminar. Use the following data to test whether significantly more site visits were made after the seminar ($\alpha = 0.05$). Assume the differences in the number of site visits are normally distributed.

Rep	Before	After
1	2	4
2	4	5
3	1	3
4	3	3
5	4	3
6	2	5
7	2	6
8	3	4
9	1	5

10.27 Eleven employees were put under the care of the company nurse because of high cholesterol readings. The nurse lectured them on the dangers of this condition and put them on a new diet. Shown are the cholesterol readings in millimoles per litre (mmol/L) of the 11 employees both before the new diet and one month after use of the diet began. Construct a 98% confidence interval to estimate the population mean difference of cholesterol readings for people who are involved in this program. Assume differences in cholesterol readings are normally distributed in the population.

Employee	Before	After
1	6.59	5.09
2	5.95	5.82
3	7.50	5.56
4	6.26	5.56
5	7.76	6.21
6	6.46	6.08
7	5.56	4.91
8	5.95	6.21
9	5.82	5.17
10	5.66	5.25
11	6.10	5.77

10.28 Lawrence and Glover published the results of a study in the *Journal of Managerial Issues* in which they examined the effects of accounting firm mergers on auditing delay. Auditing delay is the time between a company's fiscal year-end and the date of the auditor's report. The hypothesis is that with the efficiencies gained through mergers the length of the audit delay would decrease. Suppose that to test their hypothesis they examined the audit delays on 27 clients of four large firms from both before and after the firms merged (a span of 5 years). Suppose further that the mean difference in audit delay for these clients from before merger to after merger was a decrease of 3.71 days, and the standard deviation of difference was 5 days. Use these data and $\alpha = 0.01$ to test whether the audit delays after the merger were significantly lower than before the merger. Assume that the differences in auditing delay are normally distributed in the population.

10.29   A nationally known supermarket decided to promote its own brand of soft drinks on TV for two weeks. Before the ad campaign, the company randomly selected 21 of its stores across Canada to be part of a study to measure the campaign's effectiveness. During a specified half-hour period on a certain Monday morning, all the stores in the sample counted the number of cans of its own brand of soft drink sold. After the campaign, a similar count was made. The average difference was an increase of 75 cans, with a standard deviation of difference of 30 cans. Using this information, construct a 90% confidence interval to estimate the population average difference in soft drink sales for this company's brand before and after the ad campaign. Assume the differences in soft drink sales for the company's brand are normally distributed in the population.

10.30   Is there a significant difference in the fuel efficiency of a car for regular unleaded and premium unleaded gas? To test this question, a researcher randomly selected 15 drivers for a study. They were to drive their cars for one month on regular unleaded and for one month on premium unleaded gas. The participants drove their own cars for this experiment. The average sample difference was 1.32 L/100 km in favour of the premium unleaded, and the sample standard deviation of difference was 2.08 L/100 km. For $\alpha = 0.01$, does the test show enough evidence for the researcher to conclude that there is a significant difference in fuel efficiency between regular unleaded and premium unleaded gas? Assume the differences in fuel efficiency figures are normally distributed in the population.

10.4 STATISTICAL INFERENCES ABOUT TWO POPULATION PROPORTIONS, $p_1 - p_2$

Sometimes a researcher wishes to make inferences about the difference in two population proportions. This type of analysis has many applications in business, such as comparing the market share of a product for two different markets, studying the difference in the proportion of female customers in two different geographic regions, or comparing the proportion of defective products from one period to another. In making inferences about the difference in two population proportions, the statistic normally used is the difference in the sample proportions: $\hat{p}_1 - \hat{p}_2$. This statistic is computed by taking random samples, determining $\hat{p}$ for each sample for a given characteristic, and then calculating the difference in these sample proportions.

The central limit theorem states that for large samples (each of $n_1 \cdot \hat{p}_1$, $n_1 \cdot \hat{q}_1$, $n_2 \cdot \hat{p}_2$, and $n_2 \cdot \hat{q}_2 > 5$, where $\hat{q} = 1 - \hat{p}$), the difference in sample proportions is normally distributed with a mean difference of:

$$\mu_{\hat{p}_1 - \hat{p}_2} = p_1 - p_2$$

and a standard deviation of the difference of sample proportions of:

$$\sigma_{\hat{p}_1 - \hat{p}_2} = \sqrt{\frac{p_1 \cdot q_1}{n_1} + \frac{p_2 \cdot q_2}{n_2}}$$

From this information, a z formula for the difference in sample proportions can be developed.

POINTS OF INTEREST
In testing these types of hypotheses, we concentrate on the difference between the two population proportions ($p_1 - p_2$) and not on the actual value of the proportions.

z Formula for the Difference in Two Population Proportions (10.10)	$z = \dfrac{(\hat{p}_1 - \hat{p}_2) - (p_1 - p_2)}{\sqrt{\dfrac{p_1 \cdot q_1}{n_1} + \dfrac{p_2 \cdot q_2}{n_2}}}$

where

$\hat{p}_1$ = proportion from sample 1
$\hat{p}_2$ = proportion from sample 2
n_1 = size of sample 1
n_2 = size of sample 2
p_1 = proportion from population 1
p_2 = proportion from population 2
$q_1 = 1 - p_1$
$q_2 = 1 - p_2$

HYPOTHESIS TESTING

Formula 10.10 can be used to determine the probability of getting a particular difference in two sample proportions when given the values of the population proportions. In testing hypotheses about the difference in two population proportions, particular values of the population proportions are not usually known or assumed. Rather, the hypotheses are about the difference in the two population proportions $(p_1 - p_2)$. Note that formula 10.10 requires knowledge of the values of p_1 and p_2. Hence, a modified version of formula 10.10 is used when testing hypotheses about $p_1 - p_2$. This formula utilizes a pooled value obtained from the sample proportions to replace the population proportions in the denominator of formula 10.10.

The denominator of formula 10.10 is the standard deviation of the difference in two sample proportions and uses the population proportions in its calculations. However, the population proportions are unknown, so an estimate of the standard deviation of the difference in two sample proportions is made by using sample proportions as point estimates of the population proportions. The sample proportions are combined by using a weighted average to produce $\bar{p}$, which, in conjunction with $\bar{q}$ and the sample sizes, produces a point estimate of the standard deviation of the difference in sample proportions. The result is formula 10.11, which we shall use to test hypotheses about the difference in two population proportions.

z Formula to Test the Difference in Population Proportions (10.11)	$z = \dfrac{(\hat{p}_1 - \hat{p}_2) - (p_1 - p_2)}{\sqrt{(\bar{p} \cdot \bar{q})\left(\dfrac{1}{n_1} + \dfrac{1}{n_2}\right)}}$

where $\bar{p} = \dfrac{x_1 + x_2}{n_1 + n_2} = \dfrac{n_1 \hat{p}_1 + n_2 \hat{p}_2}{n_1 + n_2}$ and $\bar{q} = 1 - \bar{p}$

Testing the difference in two population proportions is useful whenever the researcher is interested in comparing the proportion of one population that has a certain characteristic with the proportion of a second population that has the same characteristic. For example, a researcher might be interested in determining whether the proportion of people driving new cars (less than one year old) in Windsor, Ontario, is different from the proportion in

Kingston, Ontario. A study could be conducted with a random sample of Windsor drivers and a random sample of Kingston drivers to test this idea. The results could be used to compare the new-car potential of the two markets and the propensity of drivers in these areas to buy new cars.

As another example, do consumers and CEOs have different perceptions of ethics in business? A group of researchers attempted to determine whether there was a difference in the proportion of consumers and the proportion of CEOs who believe that fear of getting caught or losing one's job is a strong influence on ethical behaviour. In their study, they found that 57% of consumers said that fear of getting caught or losing one's job was a strong influence on ethical behaviour but only 50% of CEOs felt the same way.

Suppose these data were determined from a sample of 755 consumers and 616 CEOs. Does this result provide enough evidence to declare that a significantly higher proportion of consumers than of CEOs believe fear of getting caught or losing one's job is a strong influence on ethical behaviour?

HYPOTHESIZE:

STEP 1. Suppose sample 1 is the consumer sample and sample 2 is the CEO sample. Because we are trying to prove that a higher proportion of consumers than of CEOs believe fear of getting caught or losing one's job is a strong influence on ethical behaviour, the alternative hypothesis should be $p_1 - p_2 > 0$. The following hypotheses are being tested:

$$H_0: p_1 - p_2 = 0$$
$$H_a: p_1 - p_2 > 0$$

where

p_1 is the proportion of the population of consumers who select the factor
p_2 is the proportion of the population of CEOs who select the factor

TEST:

STEP 2. The appropriate statistical test is formula 10.11.

STEP 3. Let $\alpha = 0.10$.

STEP 4. Because this test is a one-tailed test, the critical table z value is $z_\alpha = 1.28$. If an observed value of z of more than 1.28 is obtained, the null hypothesis will be rejected. Figure 10.12 shows the rejection region and the critical value for this problem.

Figure 10.12

Rejection Region for the Ethics Example

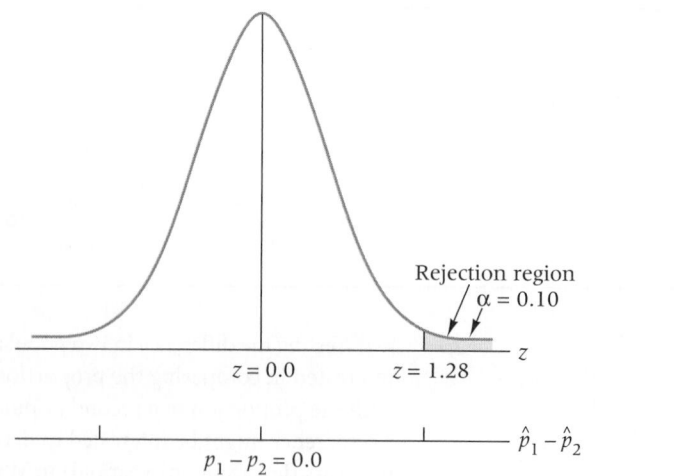

STEP 5. The sample information follows.

Consumers	CEOs
$n_1 = 755$	$n_2 = 616$
$\hat{p}_1 = 0.57$	$\hat{p}_2 = 0.50$

STEP 6.

$$\bar{p} = \frac{n_1\hat{p}_1 + n_2\hat{p}_2}{n_1 + n_2} = \frac{(755)(0.57) + (616)(0.50)}{755 + 616} = 0.539$$

If the statistics had been given as raw data instead of sample proportions, we would have used the following formula:

$$\bar{p} = \frac{x_1 + x_2}{n_1 + n_2}$$

The observed z value is:

$$z = \frac{(0.57 - 0.50) - 0}{\sqrt{(0.539)(0.461)\left(\frac{1}{755} + \frac{1}{616}\right)}} = 2.59$$

ACTION:

STEP 7. Because $z = 2.59$ is greater than the critical table z_α value of 1.28 and is in the rejection region, the null hypothesis is rejected.

BUSINESS IMPLICATIONS:

STEP 8. A significantly higher proportion of consumers than of CEOs believe fear of getting caught or losing one's job is a strong influence on ethical behaviour. CEOs might want to take another look at ways to influence ethical behaviour. If employees are more like consumers than CEOs, CEOs might be able to use fear of getting caught or losing one's job as a means of ensuring ethical behaviour on the job. By transferring the idea of ethical behaviour to the consumer, retailers might use fear of being caught and prosecuted to retard shoplifting in the retail trade.

Demonstration Problem 10.6

A study of female entrepreneurs was conducted to determine their definition of success. The women were offered choices such as happiness/self-fulfillment, sales/profit, and achievement/challenge. The women were divided into groups according to the gross sales of their businesses. A significantly higher proportion of female entrepreneurs in the $100,000 to $500,000 category than in the less than $100,000 category seemed to rate sales/profit as a definition of success.

Suppose you decide to test this result by taking a survey of your own and identify female entrepreneurs by gross sales. You interview 100 female entrepreneurs with gross sales of less than $100,000, and 24 of them define sales/profit as success. You then interview 95 female entrepreneurs with gross sales of $100,000 to $500,000, and 39 cite sales/profit as a definition of success. Use this information to test to determine whether there is a significant difference in the proportions of the two groups that define success as sales/profit. Use $\alpha = 0.01$.

Solution

HYPOTHESIZE:

STEP 1. You are testing to determine whether there is a difference between two groups of entrepreneurs, so a two-tailed test is required. The hypotheses follow:

$$H_0: p_1 - p_2 = 0$$
$$H_a: p_1 - p_2 \neq 0$$

TEST:

STEP 2. The appropriate statistical test is formula 10.11.

STEP 3. Alpha has been specified as 0.01.

STEP 4. With $\alpha = 0.01$, you obtain a critical $z_{\alpha/2}$ value from Table A.5 for $\alpha/2 = 0.005$, $z_{0.005} = \pm 2.575$. If the observed z value is more than 2.575 or less than -2.575, the null hypothesis is rejected.

STEP 5. The sample information follows.

Less than $100,000	$100,000 to $500,000
$n_1 = 100$	$n_2 = 95$
$x_1 = 24$	$x_2 = 39$
$\hat{p}_1 = \dfrac{24}{100} = 0.24$	$\hat{p}_2 = \dfrac{39}{95} = 0.41$

where

$$\bar{p} = \frac{x_1 + x_2}{n_1 + n_2} = \frac{24 + 39}{100 + 95} = \frac{63}{195} = 0.323$$

x = the number of entrepreneurs who define sales/profits as success

STEP 6. The observed z value is:

$$z = \frac{(\hat{p}_1 - \hat{p}_2) - (p_1 - p_2)}{\sqrt{(\bar{p} \cdot \bar{q})\left(\dfrac{1}{n_1} + \dfrac{1}{n_2}\right)}} = \frac{(0.24 - 0.41) - 0}{\sqrt{(0.323)(0.677)\left(\dfrac{1}{100} + \dfrac{1}{95}\right)}} = \frac{-0.17}{0.067} = -2.54$$

ACTION:

STEP 7. Although this observed value is near the rejection region, it is in the nonrejection region. The null hypothesis is not rejected. The test did not show enough evidence here to reject the null hypothesis and declare that the responses to the question by the two groups are different statistically. Note that alpha was small and that a two-tailed test was conducted. If a one-tailed test had been used, z_α would have been $z_{0.01} = -2.33$ and the null hypothesis would have been rejected. If alpha had been 0.05, $z_{\alpha/2}$ would have been $z_{0.025} = \pm 1.96$, and the null hypothesis would have been rejected. This result underscores the crucial importance of selecting alpha and determining whether to use a one-tailed or a two-tailed test in hypothesis testing.

The following diagram shows the critical values, the rejection regions, and the observed value for this problem:

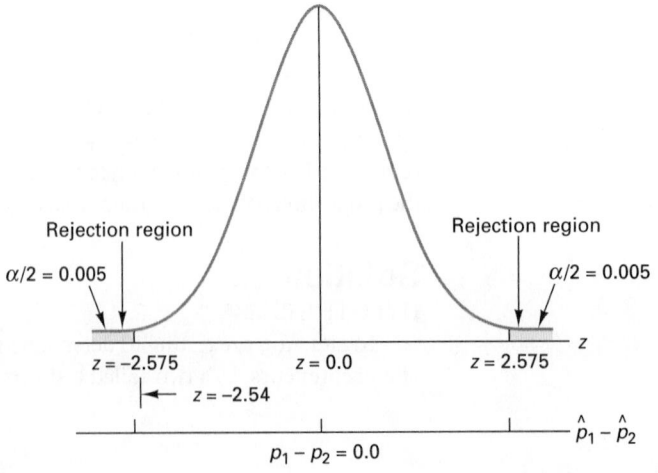

BUSINESS IMPLICATIONS:

STEP 8. We cannot statistically conclude that a greater proportion of female entrepreneurs in the higher gross sales category define success as sales/profit. One of the payoffs of such a determination is to find out what motivates the people with whom we do business. If sales/profit motivates people, offers or promises of greater sales and profits can be a means of attracting their services, their interest, or their business. If sales/profit does not motivate people, such offers would not generate the kind of response wanted and we would need to look for other ways to motivate them.

CONFIDENCE INTERVALS

Sometimes in business research the investigator wants to estimate the difference in two population proportions. For example, what is the difference, if any, in the population proportions of workers in Alberta and workers in British Columbia who favour union membership? In studying two different suppliers of the same part, a large manufacturing company might want to estimate the difference between suppliers in the proportion of parts that meet specifications. These and other situations requiring the estimation of the difference in two population proportions can be solved by using confidence intervals.

The formula for constructing confidence intervals to estimate the difference in two population proportions is a modified version of formula 10.10. Formula 10.10 for two proportions requires knowledge of each of the population proportions. Because we are attempting to estimate the difference in these two proportions, we obviously do not know their value. To overcome this lack of knowledge in constructing a confidence interval formula, we substitute the sample proportions in place of the population proportions and use these sample proportions in the estimate, as follows:

$$z = \frac{(\hat{p}_1 - \hat{p}_2) - (p_1 - p_2)}{\sqrt{\dfrac{\hat{p}_1 \cdot \hat{q}_1}{n_1} + \dfrac{\hat{p}_2 \cdot \hat{q}_2}{n_2}}}$$

Solving this equation for $p_1 - p_2$ produces the formula for constructing confidence intervals for $p_1 - p_2$.

Confidence Interval to Estimate $p_1 - p_2$ (10.12)	$(\hat{p}_1 - \hat{p}_2) - z\sqrt{\dfrac{\hat{p}_1 \cdot \hat{q}_1}{n_1} + \dfrac{\hat{p}_2 \cdot \hat{q}_2}{n_2}} \leq p_1 - p_2 \leq (\hat{p}_1 - \hat{p}_2) + z\sqrt{\dfrac{\hat{p}_1 \cdot \hat{q}_1}{n_1} + \dfrac{\hat{p}_2 \cdot \hat{q}_2}{n_2}}$

To see how this formula is used, suppose that in an attempt to target its clientele, managers of a supermarket chain want to determine the difference between the proportion of morning shoppers who are men and the proportion of after-5 p.m. shoppers who are men. Over a period of two weeks, the chain's researchers conduct a systematic random sample survey of 400 morning shoppers, which reveals that 352 are women and 48 are men. During this same period, a systematic random sample of 480 after-5 p.m. shoppers reveals that 293 are women and 187 are men. Construct a 98% confidence interval to estimate the difference in the population proportions of men.

The sample information is shown here:

Morning Shoppers	After-5 p.m. Shoppers
$n_1 = 400$	$n_2 = 480$
$x_1 = 48$ men	$x_2 = 187$ men
$\hat{p}_1 = 0.12$	$\hat{p}_2 = 0.39$
$\hat{q}_1 = 0.88$	$\hat{q}_2 = 0.61$

For a 98% level of confidence, $z_{\alpha/2} = 2.33$. Using formula 10.12 yields:

$$(0.12 - 0.39) - 2.33\sqrt{\frac{(0.12)(0.88)}{400} + \frac{(0.39)(0.61)}{480}} \leq p_1 - p_2 \leq$$

$$(0.12 - 0.39) + 2.33\sqrt{\frac{(0.12)(0.88)}{400} + \frac{(0.39)(0.61)}{480}}$$

$$-0.27 - 0.064 \leq p_1 - p_2 \leq -0.27 + 0.064$$

$$-0.334 \leq p_1 - p_2 \leq -0.206$$

There is a 98% level of confidence that the difference in population proportions is between −0.334 and −0.206. Because the after-5 P.M. shopper proportion was subtracted from the morning shopper proportion, the negative signs in the interval indicate a higher proportion of men in the after-5 P.M. shoppers than in the morning shoppers. Thus, the confidence level is 98% that the difference in proportions is at least 0.206 and may be as much as 0.334.

Concept Check

1. Why is formula 10.11 used instead of formula 10.10 when dealing with hypothesis testing about two population proportions?
2. How large should each of $n_1 \cdot \hat{p}_1$, $n_1 \cdot \hat{q}_1$, $n_2 \cdot \hat{p}_2$, and $n_2 \cdot \hat{p}_2$ be, where $\hat{q} = 1 - \hat{p}$, to be considered large samples and thus for the difference in sample proportions to be normally distributed?

10.4 Problems

10.31 Using the given sample information, test the following hypotheses.

a. $H_0: p_1 - p_2 = 0$
   $H_a: p_1 - p_2 \neq 0$

Sample 1	Sample 2
$n_1 = 368$	$n_2 = 405$
$x_1 = 175$	$x_2 = 182$

Let $\alpha = 0.05$.
Note that x is the number in the sample with the characteristic of interest.

b. $H_0: p_1 - p_2 = 0$
   $H_a: p_1 - p_2 > 0$

Sample 1	Sample 2
$n_1 = 649$	$n_2 = 558$
$\hat{p}_1 = 0.38$	$\hat{p}_2 = 0.25$

Let $\alpha = 0.10$.

10.32 In each of the following cases, calculate a confidence interval to estimate $p_1 - p_2$.
a. $n_1 = 85$, $n_2 = 90$, $\hat{p}_1 = 0.75$, $\hat{p}_2 = 0.67$; level of confidence = 90%
b. $n_1 = 1,100$, $n_2 = 1,300$, $\hat{p}_1 = 0.19$, $\hat{p}_2 = 0.17$; level of confidence = 95%
c. $n_1 = 430$, $n_2 = 399$, $x_1 = 275$, $x_2 = 275$; level of confidence = 85%
d. $n_1 = 1,500$, $n_2 = 1,500$, $x_1 = 1,050$, $x_2 = 1,100$; level of confidence = 80%

10.33 According to a study conducted for Gateway Computers, 59% of men and 70% of women say that weight is an extremely/very important factor in purchasing a laptop computer. Suppose this survey was conducted using 374 men and 481 women. Do these data show enough evidence to declare that a significantly higher proportion of women than men believe that weight is an extremely/very important factor in purchasing a laptop computer? Use a 5% level of significance.

10.34 Does age make a difference in the amount of savings a worker feels is needed to be secure at retirement? A study by CommSciences for Transamerica Asset Management found that 0.24 of workers in the 25–33 age category feel that $250,000 to $500,000 is enough to be secure at retirement. However, 0.35 of the workers in the 34–52 age category feel that this amount is enough. Suppose 210 workers in the 25–33 age category and 176 workers in the 34–52 age category were involved in this study. Use these data to construct a 90% confidence interval to estimate the difference in population proportions on this question.

10.35 Companies that had recently developed new products were asked to rate which activities are most difficult to accomplish with new products. Options included such activities as assessing market potential, market testing, finalizing the design, developing a business plan, and the like. A researcher wants to conduct a similar study to compare the results between two industries: the computer hardware industry and the banking industry. He takes a random sample of 56 computer firms and 89 banks. The researcher asks whether market testing is the most difficult activity to accomplish in developing a new product. Some 48% of the sampled computer companies and 56% of the sampled banks respond that it is the most difficult activity. Use a level of significance of 0.20 to test whether there is a significant difference in the responses to the question from these two industries.

10.36 A large production facility uses two machines to produce a key part for its main product. Inspectors have expressed concern about the quality of the finished product. Quality-control investigation has revealed that the key part made by the two machines is defective at times. The inspectors randomly sampled 35 units of the key part from each machine. Of those produced by machine A, five were defective. Seven of the 35 sampled parts from machine B were defective. The production manager is interested in estimating the difference in proportions of the populations of parts that are defective between machine A and machine B. From the sample information, compute a 98% confidence interval for this difference.

10.37 According to a CCH Unscheduled Absence survey, 9% of small businesses use telecommuting of workers in an effort to reduce unscheduled absenteeism. This proportion compares to 6% for all businesses. Is there really a significant difference between small businesses and all businesses on this issue? Use these data and an alpha of 0.10 to test this question. Assume that there were 780 small businesses and 915 other businesses in this survey.

10.38 Many adults spend time worrying about paying their bills. A survey by Fleishman-Hilliard Research for MassMutual discovered that 60% of adults with kids say that paying bills is a major concern. This proportion compares to 52% of adults without kids. Suppose 850 adults with kids and 910 without kids were contacted for this study. Use these data to construct a 95% confidence interval to estimate the difference in population proportions between adults with kids and adults without kids on this issue.

10.5 TESTING HYPOTHESES ABOUT TWO POPULATION VARIANCES

Sometimes we are interested in studying the variance of a population rather than a mean or proportion. In Section 9.5, we discussed how to test hypotheses about a single population variance, but on some occasions business researchers are interested in testing hypotheses about the difference in two population variances. In this section, we examine how to conduct such tests. When would a business researcher be interested in the variances from two populations?

In quality control, analysts often examine both a measure of central tendency (mean or proportion) and a measure of variability. Suppose a manufacturing plant made two batches of an item, produced items on two different machines, or produced items on two different shifts. It might be of interest to management to compare the variances from two batches or two machines to determine whether there is more variability in one than in another.

Variance is sometimes used as a measure of the risk of a stock in the stock market. The greater the variance, the greater is the risk. By using techniques discussed here, a financial researcher could determine whether the variances (or risks) of two stocks are the same.

In testing hypotheses about two population variances, the sample variances are used. It makes sense that if two samples come from the same population (or populations with equal variances), the ratio of the sample variances, s_1^2/s_2^2, should be about 1. However, because of sampling error, sample variances even from the same population (or from two populations with equal variances) will vary. This *ratio of two sample variances* formulates what is called an **F value:**

$$F = \frac{s_1^2}{s_2^2}$$

These ratios, if computed repeatedly for pairs of sample variances taken from a population, are distributed as an **F distribution.** The F distribution will vary by the sizes of the samples, which are converted to degrees of freedom.

With the F distribution, there are degrees of freedom associated with the numerator (of the ratio) and the denominator. An assumption underlying the F distribution is that the populations from which the samples are drawn are normally distributed for x. The F *test of two population variances is extremely sensitive to violations of the assumption that the populations are normally distributed.* The statistician should carefully investigate the shape of the distributions of the populations from which the samples are drawn to be certain the populations are normally distributed. The formula used to test hypotheses comparing two population variances follows.

F Test for Two Population Variances (10.13)	$F = \dfrac{s_1^2}{s_2^2}$ $df_{numerator} = v_1 = n_1 - 1$ $df_{denominator} = v_2 = n_2 - 1$

Table A.7 contains F distribution table values for $\alpha = 0.10, 0.05, 0.025, 0.01,$ and 0.005. Figure 10.13 shows an F distribution for $v_1 = 6$ and $v_2 = 30$. Notice that the distribution is nonsymmetric, which can be a problem when we are conducting a two-tailed test and want to determine the critical value for the lower tail. Table A.7 contains only F values for the upper tail. Since the F distribution is not symmetric, nor does it have a mean of zero as do the z and t distributions, we cannot merely place a minus sign on the upper-tail critical value and obtain the lower-tail critical value (in addition, the F ratio is always positive—it is the ratio of two variances). This dilemma can be solved by using formula 10.14, which essentially states that the critical F value for the lower tail $(1 - \alpha)$ can be solved for by taking the inverse of the F value for the upper tail (α). The degrees-of-freedom numerator for the upper-tail critical value is the degrees-of-freedom denominator for the lower-tail critical value, and the degrees-of-freedom denominator for the upper-tail critical value is the degrees-of-freedom numerator for the lower-tail critical value.

Figure 10.13

An F Distribution for $v_1 = 6$, $v_2 = 30$

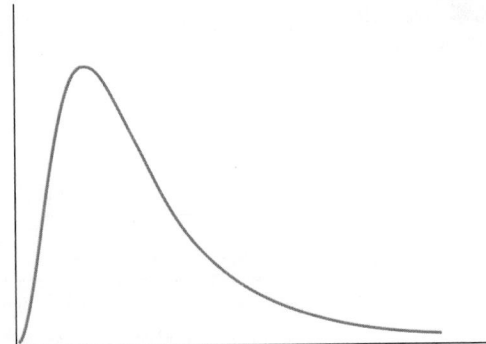

Formula for Determining the Critical Value for the Lower-Tail F (10.14)	$$F_{1-\alpha,v_1,v_2} = \frac{1}{F_{\alpha,v_1,v_2}}$$

A hypothesis test can be conducted using two sample variances and formula 10.13. The following example illustrates this process.

Suppose a machine produces metal sheets that are specified to be 22 mm thick. Because of the machine, the operator, the raw material, the manufacturing environment, and other factors, there is variability in the thickness. Two machines produce these sheets. Operators are concerned about the consistency of the two machines. To test consistency, they randomly sample 10 sheets produced by machine 1 and 12 sheets produced by machine 2. The thickness measurements of sheets from each machine are given in the table in Step 5. Assume sheet thickness is normally distributed in the population. How can we test to determine whether the variance from each sample comes from the same population variance (population variances are equal) or from different population variances (population variances are not equal)?

HYPOTHESIZE:

STEP 1. Determine the null and alternative hypotheses. In this case, we are conducting a two-tailed test (variances are the same or not), and the following hypotheses are used:

$$H_0: \sigma_1^2 = \sigma_2^2$$
$$H_a: \sigma_1^2 \neq \sigma_2^2$$

TEST:

STEP 2. The appropriate statistical test is:

$$F = \frac{s_1^2}{s_2^2}$$

STEP 3. Let $\alpha = 0.05$.

STEP 4. Because we are conducting a two-tailed test, $\alpha/2 = 0.025$. Because $n_1 = 10$ and $n_2 = 12$, the degrees-of-freedom numerator for the upper-tail critical value is $v_1 = n_1 - 1 = 10 - 1 = 9$ and the degrees-of-freedom denominator for the upper-tail critical value is $v_2 = n_2 - 1 = 12 - 1 = 11$. The critical F value for the upper tail obtained from Table A.7 is:

$$F_{0.025,9,11} = 3.59$$

Table 10.9 is a copy of the F distribution for a one-tailed $\alpha = 0.025$ (which yields equivalent values for two-tailed $\alpha = 0.05$, where the upper tail contains 0.025 of the area).

Table 10.9

A Portion of the *F* Distribution Table

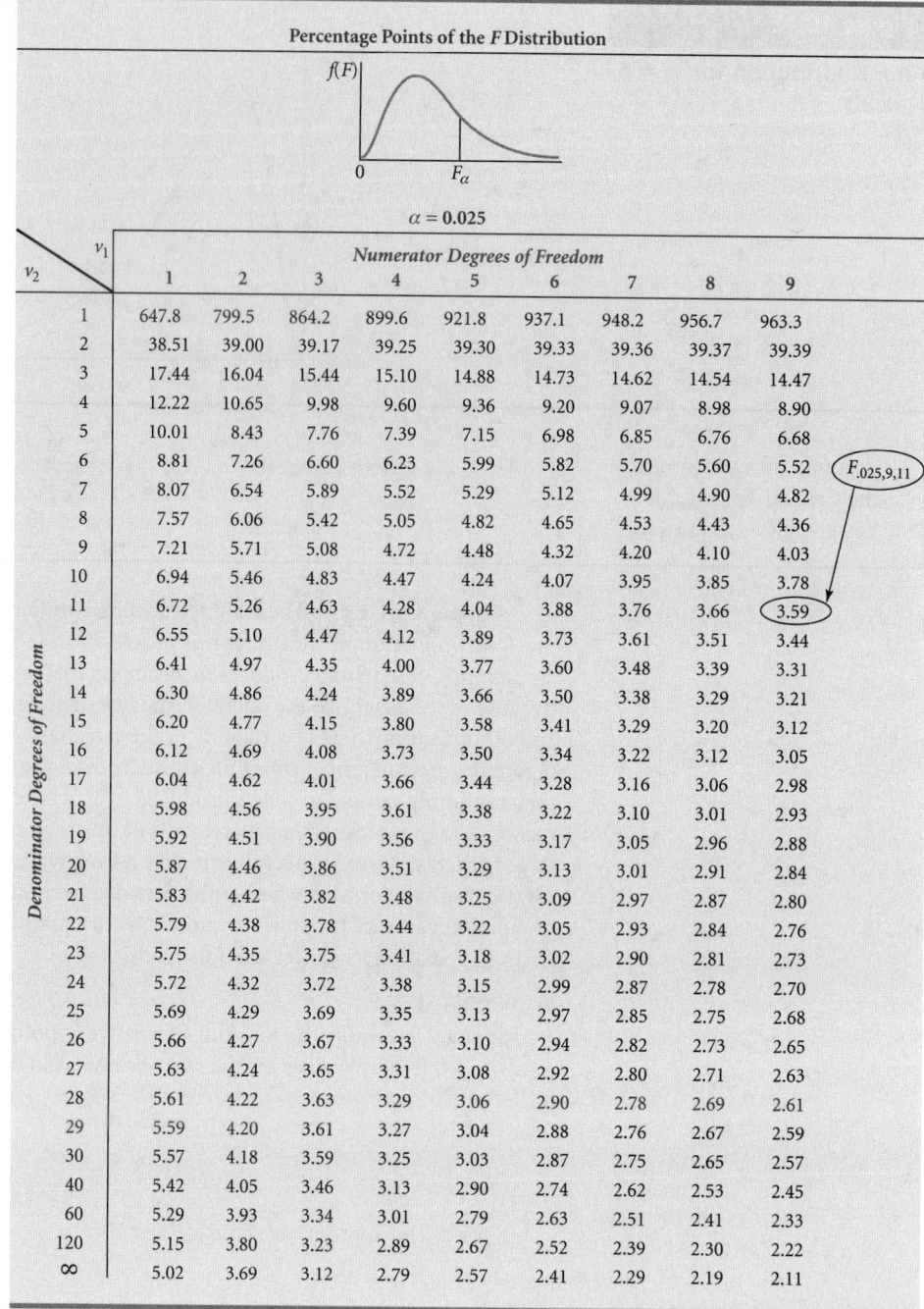

Percentage Points of the *F* Distribution

$\alpha = 0.025$

ν_2 \ ν_1	1	2	3	4	5	6	7	8	9
				Numerator Degrees of Freedom					
1	647.8	799.5	864.2	899.6	921.8	937.1	948.2	956.7	963.3
2	38.51	39.00	39.17	39.25	39.30	39.33	39.36	39.37	39.39
3	17.44	16.04	15.44	15.10	14.88	14.73	14.62	14.54	14.47
4	12.22	10.65	9.98	9.60	9.36	9.20	9.07	8.98	8.90
5	10.01	8.43	7.76	7.39	7.15	6.98	6.85	6.76	6.68
6	8.81	7.26	6.60	6.23	5.99	5.82	5.70	5.60	5.52
7	8.07	6.54	5.89	5.52	5.29	5.12	4.99	4.90	4.82
8	7.57	6.06	5.42	5.05	4.82	4.65	4.53	4.43	4.36
9	7.21	5.71	5.08	4.72	4.48	4.32	4.20	4.10	4.03
10	6.94	5.46	4.83	4.47	4.24	4.07	3.95	3.85	3.78
11	6.72	5.26	4.63	4.28	4.04	3.88	3.76	3.66	3.59
12	6.55	5.10	4.47	4.12	3.89	3.73	3.61	3.51	3.44
13	6.41	4.97	4.35	4.00	3.77	3.60	3.48	3.39	3.31
14	6.30	4.86	4.24	3.89	3.66	3.50	3.38	3.29	3.21
15	6.20	4.77	4.15	3.80	3.58	3.41	3.29	3.20	3.12
16	6.12	4.69	4.08	3.73	3.50	3.34	3.22	3.12	3.05
17	6.04	4.62	4.01	3.66	3.44	3.28	3.16	3.06	2.98
18	5.98	4.56	3.95	3.61	3.38	3.22	3.10	3.01	2.93
19	5.92	4.51	3.90	3.56	3.33	3.17	3.05	2.96	2.88
20	5.87	4.46	3.86	3.51	3.29	3.13	3.01	2.91	2.84
21	5.83	4.42	3.82	3.48	3.25	3.09	2.97	2.87	2.80
22	5.79	4.38	3.78	3.44	3.22	3.05	2.93	2.84	2.76
23	5.75	4.35	3.75	3.41	3.18	3.02	2.90	2.81	2.73
24	5.72	4.32	3.72	3.38	3.15	2.99	2.87	2.78	2.70
25	5.69	4.29	3.69	3.35	3.13	2.97	2.85	2.75	2.68
26	5.66	4.27	3.67	3.33	3.10	2.94	2.82	2.73	2.65
27	5.63	4.24	3.65	3.31	3.08	2.92	2.80	2.71	2.63
28	5.61	4.22	3.63	3.29	3.06	2.90	2.78	2.69	2.61
29	5.59	4.20	3.61	3.27	3.04	2.88	2.76	2.67	2.59
30	5.57	4.18	3.59	3.25	3.03	2.87	2.75	2.65	2.57
40	5.42	4.05	3.46	3.13	2.90	2.74	2.62	2.53	2.45
60	5.29	3.93	3.34	3.01	2.79	2.63	2.51	2.41	2.33
120	5.15	3.80	3.23	2.89	2.67	2.52	2.39	2.30	2.22
∞	5.02	3.69	3.12	2.79	2.57	2.41	2.29	2.19	2.11

Denominator Degrees of Freedom

$F_{.025,9,11}$

Locate $F_{0.025,9,11} = 3.59$ in the table. The lower-tail critical value can be calculated from the upper-tail value by using formula 10.14:

$$F_{0.975,11,9} = \frac{1}{F_{0.025,9,11}} = \frac{1}{3.59} = 0.28$$

The decision rule is to reject the null hypothesis if the observed *F* value is greater than 3.59 or less than 0.28.

Figure 10.14

Graph of F Values and Rejection Region for the Sheet Metal Example

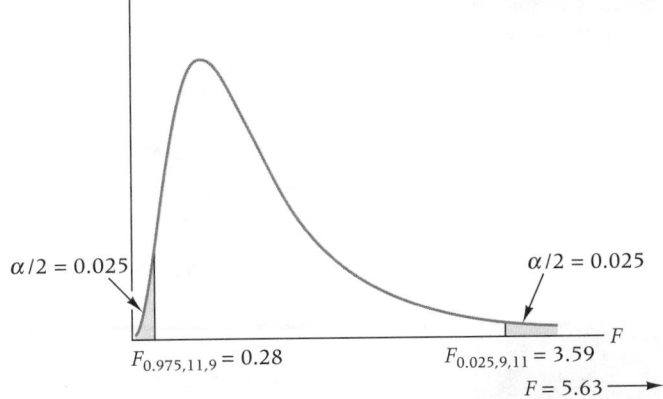

$\alpha/2 = 0.025$

$\alpha/2 = 0.025$

$F_{0.975,11,9} = 0.28$

$F_{0.025,9,11} = 3.59$

$F = 5.63 \longrightarrow$

STEP 5. Next we compute the sample variances. The data are shown here.

Machine 1		Machine 2	
22.3	21.9	22.0	21.7
21.8	22.4	22.1	21.9
22.3	22.5	21.8	22.0
21.6	22.2	21.9	22.1
21.8	21.6	22.2	21.9
		22.0	22.1
$s_1^2 = 0.11378$		$s_2^2 = 0.02023$	
$n_1 = 10$		$n_2 = 12$	

STEP 6.

$$F = \frac{s_1^2}{s_2^2} = \frac{0.11378}{0.02023} = 5.62$$

The ratio of sample variances is 5.62.

ACTION:

STEP 7. The observed F value is 5.62, which is greater than the upper-tail critical value of 3.59. As Figure 10.14 shows, this F value is in the rejection region. Thus, the decision is to reject the null hypotheses. The population variances are not equal.

BUSINESS IMPLICATIONS:

STEP 8. An examination of the sample variances reveals that the variance from machine 1 measurements is greater than that from machine 2 measurements. The operators and process managers might want to examine machine 1 further; an adjustment may be needed or something else may be causing the seemingly greater variations on that machine.

USING THE COMPUTER TO TEST HYPOTHESES ABOUT TWO POPULATION VARIANCES

POINTS OF INTEREST
Excel only reports the p value for a one-tailed test. If the actual test is two-tailed, the p value must be doubled before decision making.

Excel can directly test hypotheses about two population variances. Figure 10.15 shows the Excel output for the sheet metal example. The Excel output contains the two sample means, the two sample variances, the observed F value, the p value for a one-tailed test, and the critical F value for a one-tailed test. Because the sheet metal example is a two-tailed test, the Excel p value must be doubled to 0.0094 in order to reach a decision, or we can just compare the p value of 0.0047 to $\alpha/2 = 0.025$. Because this value is less than $\alpha = 0.05$, the decision is to reject the null hypothesis.

Figure 10.15

Excel Output for the Sheet Metal Example

	A	B	C
1	F-Test Two-Sample for Variances		
2		Machine 1	Machine 2
3	Mean	22.040	21.975
4	Variance	0.113778	0.02023
5	Observations	10	12
6	df	9	11
7	F	5.62	
8	$P(F <= f)$ one-tail	0.0047	
9	F Critical one-tail	3.59	

Demonstration Problem 10.7

Assume that a family of four in Vancouver with $60,000 annual income spends more than $22,000 a year on basic goods and services. In contrast, a family of four in Saskatoon with the same annual income spends only $15,460 on the same items. Suppose we want to test to determine whether the variance of money spent per year on the basics by families across Canada is greater than the variance of money spent on the basics by families in Vancouver—that is, whether the amounts spent by families of four in Vancouver are more homogeneous than the amounts spent by such families nationally. Suppose a random sample of eight Vancouver families produces the figures in the table below, which are given along with those reported from a random sample of seven families across Canada. Complete a hypothesis-testing procedure to determine whether the variance of values taken from across Canada can be shown to be greater than the variance of values obtained from families in Vancouver. Let $\alpha = 0.01$. Assume the amount spent on the basics is normally distributed in the population.

Amount Spent on Basics by Family of Four with $60,000 Annual Income

Across Canada	Vancouver
$18,500	$23,000
19,250	21,900
16,400	22,500
20,750	21,200
17,600	21,000
21,800	22,800
14,750	23,100
	21,300

Solution

HYPOTHESIZE:

STEP 1. This is a one-tailed test with the following hypotheses:

$$H_0: \sigma_1^2 = \sigma_2^2$$
$$H_a: \sigma_1^2 > \sigma_2^2$$

Note that what we are trying to prove—that the variance for the Canadian population is greater than the variance for families in Vancouver—is in the alternative hypothesis.

TEST:

STEP 2. The appropriate statistical test is:

$$F = \frac{s_1^2}{s_2^2}$$

STEP 3. The level of significance is 0.01.

STEP 4. This is a one-tailed test, so we will use the F distribution table in Appendix A.7 with $\alpha = 0.01$. The degrees of freedom for $n_1 = 7$ and $n_2 = 8$ are $v_1 = 6$ and $v_2 = 7$. The critical F value for the upper tail of the distribution is:

$$F_{0.01,6,7} = 7.19$$

The decision rule is to reject the null hypothesis if the observed value of F is greater than 7.19.

STEP 5. The following sample variances are computed from the data:

$$s_1^2 = 5{,}961{,}428.6$$
$$n_1 = 7$$
$$s_2^2 = 737{,}142.9$$
$$n_2 = 8$$

STEP 6. The observed F value can be determined by:

$$F = \frac{s_1^2}{s_2^2} = \frac{5{,}961{,}428.6}{737{,}142.9} = 8.09$$

ACTION:

STEP 7. Because the observed value of $F = 8.09$ is greater than the table critical F_{α,v_1,v_2} value of 7.19, the decision is to reject the null hypothesis.

BUSINESS IMPLICATIONS:

STEP 8. The variance for families in Canada is greater than the variance for families in Vancouver. Families in Vancouver are more homogeneous in amount spent on basics than families across Canada. Marketing managers need to understand this homogeneity as they attempt to find niches in the Vancouver population. Vancouver may not contain as many subgroups as can be found across Canada. The task of locating market niches may be easier in Vancouver than in the rest of the country because fewer possibilities are likely. The following graph shows the rejection region as well as the critical and calculated values of F.

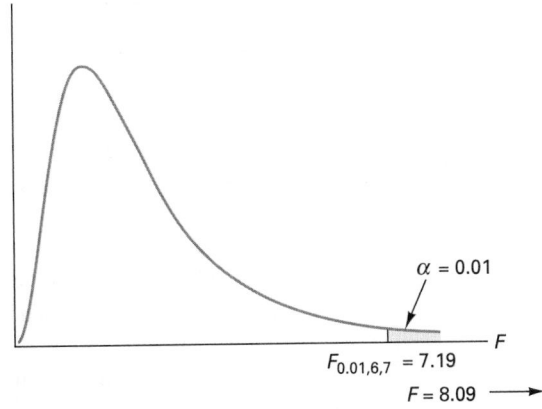

Note: *Some authors recommend the use of this F test to determine whether the data being analyzed by a t test for two population means are meeting the assumption of equal population variances. However, some statistical researchers suggest that for equal sample sizes, the t test is insensitive to the equal variance assumption, and therefore the F test is not needed in that situation. For unequal sample sizes, the F test of variances is "not generally capable of detecting assumption violations that lead to poor performance" with the t test.* This text does not present the application of the F test to determine whether variance assumptions for the t test have been met.*

---

*Carol A. Markowski and Edward P. Markowski, "Conditions for the Effectiveness of a Preliminary Test of Variance," *The American Statistician*, vol. 44 (November 1990), pp. 322–326.

Concept Check

1. Is the F test of two population variances extremely sensitive to violations of the assumption that the populations are normally distributed? What is the key implication of this?

2. Explain why we cannot merely place a minus sign on the upper-tail critical value and obtain the lower-tail critical value when using the F distribution.

10.5 Problems

10.39 Test the following hypotheses by using the given sample information and $\alpha = 0.01$. Assume the populations are normally distributed.

$$H_0: \sigma_1^2 = \sigma_2^2$$
$$H_a: \sigma_1^2 < \sigma_2^2$$
$$n_1 = 10, n_2 = 12, s_1^2 = 562, s_2^2 = 1{,}013$$

10.40 Test the following hypotheses by using the given sample information and $\alpha = 0.05$. Assume the populations are normally distributed.

$$H_0: \sigma_1^2 = \sigma_2^2$$
$$H_a: \sigma_1^2 \neq \sigma_2^2$$
$$n_1 = 5, n_2 = 19, s_1 = 4.68, s_2 = 2.78$$

10.41 Suppose the data shown here are the results of a survey to investigate gas prices. Ten service stations were selected randomly in each of two cities and the figures represent the prices of a litre of unleaded regular gas on a given day. Use the F test to determine whether there is a significant difference in the variances of the prices of unleaded regular gas between these two cities. Let $\alpha = 0.01$. Assume gas prices are normally distributed.

City 1			City 2		
1.029	0.996	1.014	0.999	0.990	1.032
1.020	1.017	1.014	1.026	1.038	1.011
1.017	1.014	0.983	1.017	1.017	1.014
1.002			1.008		

10.42 How long are resale houses on the market? Suppose that a survey reported that in Thunder Bay, resale houses are on the market an average of 112 days. Of course, the length of time varies by market. Suppose random samples of 13 houses in Thunder Bay and 11 houses in Moncton that are up for resale are traced. The data shown here represent the number of days each house was on the market before being sold. Use the given data and a 1% level of significance to determine whether the population variances for the number of days until resale are different in Thunder Bay than in Moncton. Assume the numbers of days that resale houses are on the market are normally distributed.

Thunder Bay		Moncton	
132	126	118	56
138	94	85	69
131	161	113	67
127	133	81	54
99	119	94	137
126	88	93	
134			

10.43 Suppose a recent study showed that the average annual amount spent by a Nova Scotia household on hotdog wieners was $23.84 compared with an average of $19.83 for Alberta households. Suppose a random sample of 12 Nova Scotia households showed that the standard deviation of these purchases was $7.52, whereas a random sample of 15 Alberta households resulted in a standard deviation of $6.08. Do these samples provide enough evidence to conclude that the variance of annual hotdog wiener purchases for Nova Scotia households is greater than the variance of annual hotdog wiener purchases for Alberta households? Let alpha be 0.05. Assume amounts spent per year on hotdog wieners are normally distributed. Suppose the data did show that the variance among Nova Scotia households is greater than that among Alberta households. What might this variance mean to decision makers in the hotdog wiener industry?

10.44 Assume that the average age of a male public service worker is 43.6 years and that of a male worker in the private sector is 37.3 years. Is there any difference in the variation of ages of men in the public service and men in the private sector? Suppose a random sample of 15 male public service workers is taken and the variance of their ages is 91.5. Suppose also that a random sample of 15 male private-sector workers is taken and the variance of their ages is 67.3. Use these data and $\alpha = 0.01$ to answer the question. Assume ages are normally distributed.

COMPARING AUSTRIA TO FRANCE ON LABOUR STATISTICS

Various techniques in Chapter 10 can be used to analyze the international labour data presented in the Decision Dilemma if the data are actually only sample statistics. The labour data gathered in Austria are independent of the data gathered in France. If the population variances are known, then the z test presented in Section 10.1 can be used to test if the 2004 hourly labour cost in Austria is significantly higher than the 2004 hourly labour cost in France. If, on the other hand, only sample variances are available, then the t test presented in Section 10.2 is appropriate, assuming that hourly labour costs are normally distributed. Suppose only sample data are available and the data are given below.

	Austria	France
Sample size	85	113
Sample mean	$28.29	$23.89
Sample standard deviation	$4.87	$4.64

Using $\alpha = 0.05$, a one-tailed test could be used to analyze and test these data as shown:

$$H_0: \mu_A - \mu_F = 0$$
$$H_a: \mu_A - \mu_F > 0$$

The critical t value is $t_{0.05,196} = 1.653$:

$$t = \frac{(\bar{x}_1 - \bar{x}_2) - (\mu_1 - \mu_2)}{\sqrt{\dfrac{s_1^2(n_1 - 1) + s_2^2(n_2 - 1)}{n_1 + n_2 - 2}}\sqrt{\dfrac{1}{n_1} + \dfrac{1}{n_2}}}$$

$$= \frac{(28.29 - 23.89) - 0}{\sqrt{\dfrac{(4.87)^2(84) + (4.64)^2(112)}{85 + 113 - 2}}\sqrt{\dfrac{1}{85} + \dfrac{1}{113}}}$$

$$= 6.47$$

Since the observed value of t (6.47) is greater than the critical value (1.653), the decision is to reject the null hypothesis. The 2004 hourly labour cost in Austria is significantly higher than that of France. Solving this problem using a computer results in the same observed value with a p value of approximately 0.000.

Suppose the length of the workweek in Austria was gathered from a sample of 15 companies in both 1995 and 2004 and the data are shown below. Since the data are from the same companies, the populations are related and the t test for related populations can be used to determine if there is a significant difference in the mean length of the workweek from 1995 to 2004. Assume a two-tailed test, a normally distributed population, and an alpha of 0.05.

Company	1995 Workweek	2004 Workweek	d
1	38.8	38.9	−0.1
2	35.2	34.4	0.8
3	36.7	36.5	0.2
4	34.2	33.4	0.8
5	34.7	34.1	0.6
6	38.0	38.1	−0.1
7	37.4	37.9	−0.5
8	36.4	35.7	0.7
9	36.1	34.9	1.2
10	37.7	38.0	−0.3
11	34.2	33.1	1.1
12	35.6	34.5	1.1
13	34.2	32.6	1.6
14	36.2	35.6	0.6
15	36.2	35.0	1.2

$H_0: D = 0$
$H_a: D \neq 0$

The critical t value is $t_{0.025,14} = 2.145$.

For the data, $\bar{d} = 0.593$ and $s_d = 0.625$, the observed value of t is:

$$t = \frac{\bar{d} - D}{\frac{s_d}{\sqrt{n}}} = \frac{0.593 - 0}{\frac{0.625}{\sqrt{15}}} = 3.67$$

Since the observed value of t (3.67) is greater than the critical value (2.145), the decision is to reject the null hypothesis. The 2004 workweek in Austria is significantly different from the 1995 workweek. Since the mean difference is positive, it could be concluded further that the 1995 workweek was significantly longer. Solving this problem using Excel results in the same observed value with a two-tailed p value of 0.002.

KEY CONSIDERATIONS

The statistical techniques presented in this chapter share some of the pitfalls of confidence interval methodology and hypothesis-testing techniques mentioned in preceding chapters. Included among these pitfalls are assumption violations. Remember, if small sample sizes are used in analyzing means, the z tests are valid only when the population is normally distributed and the population variances are known. If the population variances are unknown, a t test can be used if the population is normally distributed and if the population variances can be assumed to be equal. The z tests and confidence intervals for two population propor-

tions also have a minimum sample size requirement that should be met. In addition, it is assumed that both populations are normally distributed when the F test is used for two population variances.

Use of the t test for two independent populations is not unethical when the populations are related, but it is likely to result in a loss of power. As with any hypothesis-testing procedure, in determining the null and alternative hypotheses, make certain you are not assuming true what you are trying to prove.

Why Statistics Is Relevant

A market segment is a group of people or organizations that have similar product and/or service needs. Marketing activities largely focus on the identification and description of market segments. Market segment analysis often involves the identification of segment differences and statistical questions about the business implications of those differences. The material presented in this chapter targets this type of analysis whenever geographic, demographic, behavioural, etc., segmentation exists. In addition, the techniques presented in this chapter are especially important due to the crucial role of comparison in the analysis of variance and the design of experiments (Chapter 11).

SUMMARY

Business research often requires the analysis of two populations. Three types of parameters can be compared: means, proportions, and variances. Except for the F test for population variances, all techniques presented contain both confidence intervals and hypothesis tests. In each case, the two populations are studied through the use of sample data randomly drawn from each population.

1–4. The population means are analyzed by comparing two sample means. When sample sizes are large ($n \geq 30$) and population variances are known, a z test is used. When sample sizes are small, the population variances are known, and the populations are normally distributed, the z test is used to analyze the population means. If the population variances are unknown,

and the populations are normally distributed, the t test of means for independent samples is used. For populations that are related on some measure, such as twins or before-and-after, a t test for dependent measures (matched pairs) is used. The difference in two population proportions can be tested or estimated using a z test.

5. The population variances are analyzed by an F test when the assumption that the populations are normally distributed is met. The F value is a ratio of the two variances. The F distribution is a distribution of possible ratios of two sample variances taken from one population or from two populations containing the same variance.

KEY TERMS

correlated t test	F distribution	independent samples	t test for related measures
dependent samples	F value	matched-pairs test	

FORMULAS

(10.1) z test for the difference in two independent sample means

$$z = \frac{(\overline{x}_1 - \overline{x}_2) - (\mu_1 - \mu_2)}{\sqrt{\dfrac{\sigma_1^2}{n_1} + \dfrac{\sigma_2^2}{n_2}}}$$

(10.2) Confidence interval for estimating the difference in two independent population means using z

$$(\overline{x}_1 - \overline{x}_2) - z_{\alpha/2}\sqrt{\frac{\sigma_1^2}{n_1} + \frac{\sigma_2^2}{n_2}} \leq \mu_1 - \mu_2 \leq (\overline{x}_1 - \overline{x}_2) + z_{\alpha/2}\sqrt{\frac{\sigma_1^2}{n_1} + \frac{\sigma_2^2}{n_2}}$$

(10.3) t test for two independent sample means with population variances unknown but assumed to be equal (assume also that the two populations are normally distributed)

$$t = \frac{(\overline{x}_1 - \overline{x}_2) - (\mu_1 - \mu_2)}{s_p\sqrt{\dfrac{1}{n_1} + \dfrac{1}{n_2}}}$$

$$df = n_1 + n_2 - 2$$

$$\text{where } s_p = \sqrt{\frac{s_1^2(n_1 - 1) + s_2^2(n_2 - 1)}{n_1 + n_2 - 2}}$$

(10.4) t test for two independent sample means with population variances unknown and not assumed to be equal (assume also that the two populations are normally distributed)

$$t = \frac{(\overline{x}_1 - \overline{x}_2) - (\mu_1 - \mu_2)}{\sqrt{\dfrac{s_1^2}{n_1} + \dfrac{s_2^2}{n_2}}}$$

$$df = \frac{\left(\dfrac{s_1^2}{n_1} + \dfrac{s_2^2}{n_2}\right)^2}{\dfrac{\left(\dfrac{s_1^2}{n_1}\right)^2}{n_1 - 1} + \dfrac{\left(\dfrac{s_2^2}{n_2}\right)^2}{n_2 - 1}}$$

(10.5) Confidence interval for estimating the difference in two independent means with population variances unknown but assumed to be equal (assume also that the two populations are normally distributed)

$$(\overline{x}_1 - \overline{x}_2) - t\sqrt{\frac{s_1^2(n_1 - 1) + s_2^2(n_2 - 1)}{n_1 + n_2 - 2}}\sqrt{\frac{1}{n_1} + \frac{1}{n_2}} \leq \mu_1 - \mu_2 \leq$$

$$(\overline{x}_1 - \overline{x}_2) + t\sqrt{\frac{s_1^2(n_1 - 1) + s_2^2(n_2 - 1)}{n_1 + n_2 - 2}}\sqrt{\frac{1}{n_1} + \frac{1}{n_2}}$$

$$df = n_1 + n_2 - 2$$

(10.6) t test for the difference in two related samples (the differences are normally distributed in the population)

$$t = \frac{\bar{d} - D}{\frac{s_d}{\sqrt{n}}}$$

$$df = n - 1$$

(10.7 and 10.8) Formulas for $\bar{d}$ and s_d

$$\bar{d} = \frac{\sum d}{n}$$

$$s_d = \sqrt{\frac{\sum (d - \bar{d})^2}{n - 1}} = \sqrt{\frac{\sum d^2 - \frac{(\sum d)^2}{n}}{n - 1}}$$

(10.9) Confidence interval formula for estimating the difference in related samples (the differences are normally distributed in the population)

$$\bar{d} - t\frac{s_d}{\sqrt{n}} \leq D \leq \bar{d} + t\frac{s_d}{\sqrt{n}}$$

$$df = n - 1$$

(10.10) z formula for the difference in two population proportions

$$z = \frac{(\hat{p}_1 - \hat{p}_2) - (p_1 - p_2)}{\sqrt{\frac{p_1 \cdot q_1}{n_1} + \frac{p_2 \cdot q_2}{n_2}}}$$

(10.11) z formula for testing the difference in population proportions

$$z = \frac{(\hat{p}_1 - \hat{p}_2) - (p_1 - p_2)}{\sqrt{(\bar{p} \cdot \bar{q})\left(\frac{1}{n_1} + \frac{1}{n_2}\right)}}$$

where $\bar{p} = \dfrac{x_1 + x_2}{n_1 + n_2} = \dfrac{n_1\hat{p}_1 + n_2\hat{p}_2}{n_1 + n_2}$ and $\bar{q} = 1 - \bar{p}$

(10.12) Confidence interval to estimate $p_1 - p_2$

$$(\hat{p}_1 - \hat{p}_2) - z\sqrt{\frac{\hat{p}_1 \cdot \hat{q}_1}{n_1} + \frac{\hat{p}_2 \cdot \hat{q}_2}{n_2}} \leq p_1 - p_2 \leq (\hat{p}_1 - \hat{p}_2)$$
$$+ z\sqrt{\frac{\hat{p}_1 \cdot \hat{q}_1}{n_1} + \frac{\hat{p}_2 \cdot \hat{q}_2}{n_2}}$$

(10.13) F test for two population variances (assume the two populations are normally distributed)

$$F = \frac{s_1^2}{s_2^2}$$

$$df_{numerator} = v_1 = n_1 - 1$$
$$df_{denominator} = v_2 = n_2 - 1$$

(10.14) Formula for determining the critical value for the lower-tail F

$$F_{1-\alpha,v_1,v_2} = \frac{1}{F_{\alpha,v_1,v_2}}$$

SUPPLEMENTARY PROBLEMS

Calculating the Statistics

10.45 Test the following hypotheses with the data given. Let $\alpha = 0.10$.

$$H_0: \mu_1 - \mu_2 = 0$$
$$H_a: \mu_1 - \mu_2 \neq 0$$

Sample 1	Sample 2
$\bar{x}_1 = 138.4$	$\bar{x}_2 = 142.5$
$\sigma_1 = 6.71$	$\sigma_2 = 8.92$
$n_1 = 48$	$n_2 = 39$

10.46 Use the following data to construct a 98% confidence interval to estimate the difference between μ_1 and μ_2.

Sample 1	Sample 2
$\bar{x}_1 = 34.9$	$\bar{x}_2 = 27.6$
$\sigma_1^2 = 2.97$	$\sigma_2^2 = 3.50$
$n_1 = 34$	$n_2 = 31$

10.47 The following data come from independent samples drawn from normally distributed populations. Use these data to test the following hypotheses. Let the Type I error rate be 0.05. Assume that the population variances are approximately equal.

$$H_0: \mu_1 - \mu_2 = 0$$
$$H_a: \mu_1 - \mu_2 > 0$$

Sample 1	Sample 2
$\bar{x}_1 = 2.06$	$\bar{x}_2 = 1.93$
$s_1^2 = 0.176$	$s_2^2 = 0.143$
$n_1 = 12$	$n_2 = 15$

10.48 Construct a 95% confidence interval to estimate $\mu_1 - \mu_2$ by using the following data. Assume the populations are normally distributed and the population variances are approximately equal.

Sample 1	Sample 2
$\bar{x}_1 = 74.6$	$\bar{x}_2 = 70.9$
$s_1^2 = 10.5$	$s_2^2 = 11.4$
$n_1 = 18$	$n_2 = 19$

10.49 The following data have been gathered from two related samples. The differences are assumed to be normally distributed in the population. Use these data and an alpha of 0.01 to test the following hypotheses.

$$H_0: D = 0$$
$$H_a: D < 0$$
$$n = 21, \bar{d} = -1.16, s_d = 1.01$$

10.50 Use the following data to construct a 99% confidence interval to estimate D. Assume the differences are normally distributed in the population.

Respondent	Before	After
1	47	63
2	33	35
3	38	36
4	50	56
5	39	44
6	27	29
7	35	32
8	46	54
9	41	47

10.51 Test the following hypotheses by using the given data and alpha equal to 0.05.

$$H_0: p_1 - p_2 = 0$$
$$H_a: p_1 - p_2 \neq 0$$

Sample 1	Sample 2
$n_1 = 783$	$n_2 = 896$
$x_1 = 345$	$x_2 = 421$

10.52 Use the following data to construct a 99% confidence interval to estimate $p_1 - p_2$.

Sample 1	Sample 2
$n_1 = 409$	$n_2 = 378$
$\hat{p}_1 = 0.71$	$\hat{p}_2 = 0.67$

10.53 Test the following hypotheses by using the given data. Let alpha equal 0.05.

$$H_0: \sigma_1^2 = \sigma_2^2$$
$$H_a: \sigma_1^2 \neq \sigma_2^2$$
$$n_1 = 8, n_2 = 10, s_1^2 = 46, s_2^2 = 37$$

Testing Your Understanding

10.54 Suppose a large insurance company wants to estimate the difference between the average amount of term life insurance purchased per family and the average amount of whole life insurance purchased per family. To obtain an estimate, one of the company's actuaries randomly selects 27 families who have term life insurance only and 29 families who have whole life policies only. Each sample is taken from families in which the leading provider is younger than 45 years of age. Use the data obtained to construct a 95% confidence interval to estimate the difference in means for these two groups. Assume the amount of insurance is normally distributed.

Term	Whole Life
$\bar{x}_T = \$75,000$	$\bar{x}_W = \$45,000$
$s_T = \$22,000$	$s_W = \$15,500$
$n_T = 27$	$n_W = 29$

10.55 A study is conducted to estimate the average difference in bus ridership for a large city during the morning and afternoon rush hours. The transit authority's researcher randomly selects nine buses because of the variety of routes they represent. On a given day, the number of riders on each bus is counted at 7:45 A.M. and at 4:45 P.M., with the following results.

Bus	Morning	Afternoon
1	43	41
2	51	49
3	37	44
4	24	32
5	47	46
6	44	42
7	50	47
8	55	51
9	46	49

Use the data to compute a 90% confidence interval to estimate the population average difference. Assume ridership is normally distributed.

10.56 People use several methods to keep track of appointments, meetings, and deadlines. Some of these are using a desk calendar, using informal notes of scrap paper, keeping them in your head, using a day planner, using an electronic organizer, and keeping a formal to-do list. Suppose a business researcher wants to test the hypothesis that a greater proportion of marketing managers keep track of such obligations in their head than do accountants. To test this, a business researcher samples 400 marketing managers and 450 accountants. Of those sampled, 220 marketing managers keep track in their head while 216 of the accountants do so. Using a 1% level of significance, what does the business researcher find?

10.57 A study was conducted to compare the salaries of accounting clerks and data entry operators. One of the hypotheses to be tested is that the variability of salaries among accounting clerks is the same as the variability of salaries of data entry operators. To test this hypothesis, a random sample of 16 accounting clerks was taken, resulting in a sample mean salary of $26,400 and a sample standard deviation of $1,200. A random sample of 14 data entry operators was taken as well, resulting in a sample mean of $25,800 and a sample standard deviation of $1,050. Use these data and $\alpha = 0.05$ to test to determine whether the population variance of salaries is the same for accounting clerks as it is for data entry operators. Assume that salaries of data entry operators and accounting clerks are normally distributed in the population.

10.58 A study was conducted to develop a scale to measure stress in the workplace. Respondents were asked to rate 26 distinct work events. Each event was to be compared to the stress of the first week on the job, which was awarded an arbitrary score of 500. Sixty professional men and 41 professional women participated in the study. One of the stress events was "lack of support from the boss." The men's sample average rating of this event was 631 and the women's sample average rating was 848. Suppose the population standard deviations for both men and women were about 100. Construct a 95% confidence interval to estimate the difference in the population mean scores on this event for men and women.

10.59 A national grocery store chain wants to test the difference in the average mass of turkeys sold in Guelph, Ontario, and the average mass of turkeys sold in Sudbury, Ontario. According to the chain's researcher, a random sample of 20 turkeys sold at the chain's stores in Guelph yielded a sample mean of 7.97 kg, with a standard deviation of 1.5 kg. Her random sample of 24 turkeys sold at the chain's stores in Sudbury yielded a sample mean of 6.7 kg, with a standard deviation of 1.2 kg. Use a 1% level of significance to determine whether there is a difference in the mean mass of turkeys sold in these two cities. Assume the population variances are approximately the same and that the masses of turkeys sold in the stores are normally distributed.

10.60 A tree nursery has been experimenting with fertilizer to increase the growth of seedlings. A sample of 35 two-year-old pine trees is grown for three more years with a cake of fertilizer buried in the soil near the trees' roots. A second sample of 35 two-year-old pine trees is grown for three more years under identical conditions (soil, temperature, water) as the first group, but not fertilized. Tree growth is measured over the three-year period with the following results.

Trees with Fertilizer	Trees without Fertilizer
$n_1 = 35$	$n_2 = 35$
$\bar{x}_1 = 97.5$ cm	$\bar{x}_2 = 58.7$ cm
$\sigma_1 = 24.9$ cm	$\sigma_2 = 18.8$ cm

Do the data support the theory that the population of trees with the fertilizer grew significantly larger during the period in which they were fertilized than the nonfertilized trees? Use $\alpha = 0.01$.

10.61 One of the most important aspects of a store's image is the perceived quality of its merchandise. Other factors include merchandise pricing, assortment of products, convenience of location, and service. Suppose image perceptions of shoppers at specialty stores and shoppers at discount stores are being compared. A random sample of shoppers is taken at each type of store, and the shoppers are asked whether the quality of merchandise is a determining factor in their perception of the store's image. Some 75% of the 350 shoppers at the specialty stores say yes, but only 52% of the 500 shoppers at the discount store say yes. Use these data to test if there is a significant difference between the proportion of shoppers at specialty stores and the proportion of shoppers at discount stores who say that quality of merchandise is a determining factor in their perception of a store's image. Let alpha equal 0.10.

10.62 Is there more variation in the output of one shift in a manufacturing plant than in another shift? In an effort to study this question, plant managers gathered productivity reports from the 8 A.M. to 4 P.M. shift for eight days. The reports indicated that the following numbers of units were produced on each day for this shift.

5,528	4,779	5,112	5,380
4,918	4,763	5,055	5,106

Productivity information was also gathered from seven days for the 4 P.M. to midnight shift, resulting in the following data.

4,325	4,016	4,872	4,559
3,982	4,754	4,116	

Use these data and $\alpha = 0.01$ to test to determine whether the variances of productivity for the two shifts are the same. Assume productivity is normally distributed in the population.

10.63 What is the average difference between the price of name-brand soup and the price of store-brand soup? To obtain an estimate, an analyst randomly samples eight stores. Each store sells its own brand and a national name brand. The prices of a can of name-brand tomato soup and a can of the store-brand tomato soup follow.

Store	Name Brand	Store Brand
1	54¢	49¢
2	55	50
3	59	52
4	53	51
5	54	50
6	61	56
7	51	47
8	53	49

Construct a 90% confidence interval to estimate the average difference. Assume that the differences in prices of tomato soup are normally distributed in the population.

10.64 As the prices of heating oil and natural gas increase, consumers become more careful about heating their homes. Researchers want to know how warm homeowners keep their houses in January and how the results from Alberta and Saskatchewan compare. The researchers randomly called 23 Alberta households between 7 P.M. and 9 P.M. on January 15 and asked the respondent the temperature of the house according to the thermostat. The researchers then called 19 households in Saskatchewan the same night and asked the same question. The results follow.

Alberta				Saskatchewan			
21.7	21.7	18.3	20.0	22.8	23.9	23.3	21.7
21.1	16.1	19.4	20.6	23.3	22.8	23.3	21.1
23.9	20.0	21.7	22.8	22.2	21.7	20.6	22.2
23.3	20.0	19.4	20.6	23.3	22.8	21.1	22.2
20.6	22.2	19.4	22.2	20.6	21.1	19.4	
21.1	22.8	22.2					

For $\alpha = 0.01$, is the average temperature of a house in Saskatchewan significantly higher than that of a house in Alberta on the evening of January 15? Assume the population variances are equal and the house temperatures are normally distributed in each population.

10.65 In manufacturing, does worker productivity drop on Friday? In an effort to determine whether it does, a company's personnel analyst randomly selects from a manufacturing plant five workers who make the same part. He measures their output on Wednesday and again on Friday and obtains the following results.

Worker	Wednesday Output	Friday Output
1	71	53
2	56	47
3	75	52
4	68	55
5	74	58

The analyst uses $\alpha = 0.05$ and assumes the difference in productivity is normally distributed. Do the samples provide enough evidence to show that productivity drops on Friday?

10.66 A manufacturer uses two machines to drill holes in pieces of sheet metal used in engine construction. The workers who attach the sheet metal to the engine become inspectors in that they reject sheets so poorly drilled that they cannot be attached. The production manager is interested in knowing whether one machine produces more defective drillings than the other machine. As an experiment, employees mark the sheets so that the manager can determine which machine was used to drill the holes. A random sample of 191 sheets of metal drilled by machine 1 is taken, and 38 of the sheets are defective. A random sample of 202 sheets of metal drilled by machine 2 is taken, and 21 of the sheets are defective. Use $\alpha = 0.05$ to determine whether there is a significant difference in the proportion of sheets drilled with defective holes between machine 1 and machine 2.

10.67 Is there a difference in the proportion of construction workers who are under 35 years of age and the proportion of telephone repair people who are under 35 years of age? Suppose a study is conducted in Calgary using random samples of 338 construction workers and 281 telephone repair people. The sample of construction workers includes 297 people under 35 years of age and the sample of telephone repair people includes 192 people under that age. Use these data to construct a 90% confidence interval to estimate the difference in proportions of people under 35 years of age among construction workers and telephone repair people.

10.68 Executives often spend so many hours in meetings that they have relatively little time to manage their individual areas of operation. What is the difference in mean time spent in meetings by executives of the aerospace industry and executives of the automobile industry? Suppose random samples of 33 aerospace executives and 35 automobile executives are monitored for a week to determine how much time they spend in meetings. The results follow.

Aerospace	Automobile
$n_1 = 33$	$n_2 = 35$
$\bar{x}_1 = 12.4$ hours	$\bar{x}_2 = 4.6$ hours
$\sigma_1 = 2.9$ hours	$\sigma_2 = 1.8$ hours

Use the data to estimate the difference in the mean time per week executives in these two industries spend in meetings. Use a 99% level of confidence.

10.69 Various types of retail outlets sell toys during the holiday season. Among them are specialty toy stores, large discount toy stores, and other retailers that carry toys as only one part of their stock of goods. Is there any difference in the dollar amount of a customer purchase between a large discount toy store and a specialty toy store if they carry relatively comparable types of toys? Suppose in December a random sample of 60 sales slips is selected from a large discount toy outlet and a random sample of 40 sales slips is selected from a specialty toy store. The data gathered from these samples follow.

Large Discount Toy Store	Specialty Toy Store
$\bar{x}_D = \$47.20$	$\bar{x}_S = \$27.40$
$\sigma_D = \$12.45$	$\sigma_S = \$9.82$

Use $\alpha = 0.01$ and the data to determine whether there is a significant difference in the average size of purchases at these stores.

10.70 One of the new areas of quality-control management is to examine the process by which a product is produced. This approach also applies to paperwork. In industries where large long-term projects are undertaken, days and even weeks may elapse as a change order makes its way through a maze of approvals before receiving final approval. This process can result in long delays, stretching schedules to the breaking point. Suppose a quality-control consulting group claims that it can significantly reduce the number of days required for such paperwork to receive approval. In an attempt to prove its case, the group selects five jobs for which it revises the paperwork system. The following data show the number of days required for a change order to be approved before the group intervened and the number of days required for a change order to be approved after the group instituted a new paperwork system.

Before	After
12	8
7	3
10	8
16	9
8	5

Use $\alpha = 0.01$ to determine whether there was a significant drop in the number of days required to process paperwork to approve change orders. Assume that the differences in days are normally distributed.

10.71 For the two large newspapers in a certain city, you are interested in knowing whether there is a significant difference in the average number of pages in each dedicated solely to advertising. You randomly select 10 editions of newspaper A and 6 editions of newspaper B (excluding weekend editions). The data follow.

Use $\alpha = 0.01$ to test whether there is a significant difference in averages. Assume the number of pages of advertising per edition is normally distributed and the population variances are approximately equal.

A		B	
17	17	8	14
21	15	11	10
11	19	9	6
19	22		
26	16		

Interpreting the Output

10.72 A study by Colliers International presented the highest and the lowest global rental rates (in U.S. dollars) per year per square foot of office space. Among the cities with the lowest rates were Perth, Australia; Edmonton; and Calgary, with rates of $8.81, $9.55, and $9.69, respectively. At the high end were Hong Kong, Mumbai, and Tokyo, with rates over $100. Suppose a researcher conducted her own survey of businesses renting office space to determine whether one city is significantly more expensive than another. The data are tallied and analyzed using a computer. The results follow. Discuss the output. Assume that rental rates are normally distributed in the population. What cities were studied? How large were the samples? What were the sample statistics? What was the value of alpha? What were the hypotheses, and what was the conclusion?

	A	B	C
1	t-Test: Two-Sample Assuming Equal Variances		
2		Hong Kong	Mumbai
3	Mean	130.40	128.40
4	Variance	166.41	193.21
5	Observations	19	23
6	Pooled Variance	181.15	
7	Hypothesized Mean Difference	0	
8	df	40	
9	t Stat	0.48	
10	P (T<=t) two-tail	0.634	
11	Confidence Interval (98%)	$-8.11 <= \mu_1 - \mu_2 <= 12.11$	

10.73 Why do employees blow the whistle on other employees for unethical or illegal behaviour? One study conducted by the American Institute of Certified Public Accountants (AICPA) reported the likelihood that employees would blow the whistle on another employee for such things as unsafe working conditions, unsafe products, and poorly managed operations. On a scale from 1 to 7, with 1 denoting highly improbable and 7 denoting highly probable, unnecessary purchases received a 5.72 in the study. Suppose this study was administered at a company and then all employees were subjected to a one-month series of seminars on reasons to blow the whistle on fellow employees. One month later, the study was administered again to the same employees at the company in an effort to determine whether the treatment had any effect. The following Excel output shows the results of the study. What were the sample sizes? What might the hypotheses have been? If $\alpha = 0.05$, what conclusions could be made? Which of the statistical tests presented in this chapter is likely to have been used? Assume that differences in scores are normally distributed.

	A	B	C
1	t-Test: Paired Two Sample for Means		
2		Variable 1	Variable 2
3	Mean	4.357	5.214
4	Variance	1.170	0.951
5	Observations	14	14
6	Pearson Correlation	0.51	
7	Hypothesized Mean Difference	0	
8	df	13	
9	t Stat	-3.12	
10	P(T < = t) one-tail	0.0040	
11	t Critical one-tail	1.77	
12	P(T < = t) two-tail	0.0081	
13	t Critical two-tail	2.16	

SUPPLEMENTARY PROBLEMS (continued)

10.74 A large manufacturing company produces computer printers that are distributed and sold all over Canada. Due to lack of industry information, the company has a difficult time ascertaining its market share in different parts of the country. It hires a market research firm to estimate its market share in an Alberta city and an Ontario city. The company would also like to know whether there is a difference in its market shares in these two cities; if so, it wants an estimate of how much. The market research firm randomly selects printer customers from different locales across both cities and determines what brand of computer printer they purchased. The following summary shows the results from this study. Discuss the results, including sample sizes, estimation of the difference in proportions, and any significant differences determined. What hypotheses were tested?

Test and CI for Two Proportions

```
Sample    X     N     Sample p
1        147   473    0.310782
2        104   385    0.270130

Difference = p (1) − p (2)
Estimate for difference: 0.406524
99% CI for difference: (−0.0393623, 0.120667)
Test of difeerence = 0 (vs not =) 0:
z = 1.31 p-value = 0.191
```

10.75 A manufacturing company produces plastic pipes that are specified to be 25 cm long and 0.3 cm thick with an opening of 1.9 cm. These pipes are moulded on two different machines. To maintain consistency, the company periodically randomly selects pipes for testing. In one specific test, pipes were randomly sampled from each machine and the lengths were measured. A statistical test was computed using Excel in an effort to determine whether the variance for machine 1 was significantly greater than the variance for machine 2. The results are shown here. Discuss the outcome of this test along with some of the other information given in the output.

	A	B	C
1	F-Test: Two-Sample for Variances		
2		Machine 1	Machine 2
3	Mean	25.4796	25.3307
4	Variance	0.2600	0.1264
5	Observations	26	28
6	df	25	27
7	F	2.0575	
8	P (F<=f) one-tail	0.0348	
9	F Critical one-tail	1.9210	

ANALYZING THE DATABASES

see www.wiley.com/canada/black

1. Use the Major League Baseball Database to test to determine whether there is a significantly greater variance among the values of Average Ticket than among Average Premium Ticket. Let $\alpha = 0.05$.

2. Use the Financial Database to test whether there is a significant difference in the proportion of companies whose average yield is more than 1.8% and the proportion of companies whose dividends per share are more than 30%. Let $\alpha = 0.05$.

CASE

Seitz Corporation: Producing Quality Gear-Driven and Linear-Motion Products

The Seitz Corporation, a QS 9000 certified organization, is a leading designer and manufacturer of thermoplastic motion control systems and components and an industry leader in plastics and gear trains. Founded in 1949 by the late Karl F. Seitz, the company began as a small tool-making business and grew slowly. In the late 1960s, the company expanded its services to include custom injection moulding. As their customer base grew to include leading printer manufacturers, Seitz developed and patented a proprietary line of perforated-form handling tractors. Utilizing its injection-moulding technology, the company engineered an all-plastic tractor called Data Motion, which replaced costly metal versions. By the late 1970s, business was booming, and Data Motion had become the worldwide industry leader.

In the 1980s, foreign competition entered the business equipment market, and many of Seitz's customers relocated or closed shop. The ripple effect hit Seitz as sales declined and profits eroded. Employment at the company dropped from a high of 313 in 1985 to only 125 in 1987. Drastic changes had to be made at Seitz.

To meet the challenge in 1987, Seitz made a crucial decision to change the way it did business. The company implemented a formal five-year plan with measurable goals called "World-Class Excellence Through Total Quality." Senior managers devoted many hours to improving employee training and involvement. New concepts were explored and integrated into the business plan. Teams and programs were put into place to immediately correct deficiencies in Seitz's systems that were revealed in customer satisfaction surveys. All employees, from machine operators to accountants, were taught that quality means understanding customers' needs and fulfilling them correctly the first time.

Once the program started, thousands of dollars in cost savings and two new products generating almost $1 million in sales resulted. Annual sales grew from $10.8 million in 1987 to $19 million in 1990. Seitz's customer base expanded from 312 in 1987 to 550 at the end of 1990.

In the 1990s, Seitz continued its steady growth. By 1999, Seitz was shipping products to 28 countries, and customers included Xerox, Hewlett Packard, Canon, U.S. Tsubaki, and many more worldwide. By 1998, sales topped the $30 million mark. In January 2000, the company established the Seitz Motion Control Systems Co., Ltd., in Changzhou, China, about 250 km northwest of Shanghai, to provide product and tooling design engineering, sourcing and supply chain management services, and contract manufacturing. The Seitz Corporation headquarters is located in Torrington, Connecticut, in a 7,500-m² facility with over 150 associates, 50 moulding machines ranging in size from about 35 tonnes to 770 tonnes, an in-house tooling department, and a corporate staff. Seitz Motion Control Systems Co., Ltd., is a technical services centre providing both product and tooling design engineering sourcing and supply chain management services. While the primary core competency of the Seitz Corporation is rotary and linear motion control, making them an industry leader in plastics and gear trains, Seitz offers a full range of product design and tooling services.

Discussion

1. Seitz's list of several hundred business-to-business customers continues to grow. Managers would like to know whether the average dollar amount of sales per transaction per customer has changed from last year to this year. Suppose company accountants sampled 20 customers randomly from last year's records and determined that the mean sales per customer were $2,300, with a standard deviation of $500. They sampled 25 customers randomly from this year's files and determined that the mean sales per customer for this sample were $2,450, with a standard deviation of $540. Analyze these data and summarize your findings for the managers. Explain how this information can be used by decision makers. Assume that sales per customer are normally distributed.

2. One common approach to measuring a company's quality is through the use of customer satisfaction surveys. Suppose in a random sample Seitz's customers are asked whether the

CASE (continued)

plastic tractor produced by Seitz has outstanding quality (yes or no). Assume Seitz produces these tractors at two different plant locations and that the tractor customers can be divided according to where their tractors were manufactured. Suppose a random sample of 45 customers who bought tractors made at plant 1 results in 18 saying the tractors have excellent quality and a random sample of 51 customers who bought tractors made at plant 2 results in 12 saying the tractors have excellent quality. Use a confidence interval to express the estimated difference in population proportions of excellent ratings between the two groups of customers. Does it seem to matter which plant produces the tractors in terms of the quality rating received from customers? What would you report from these data?

3. Suppose the customer satisfaction survey included a question on the overall quality of Seitz measured on a five-point scale, with 1 indicating low quality and 5 indicating high quality. Company managers monitor the figures from year to year to help determine whether Seitz is improving customers' perception of its quality. Suppose random samples of the responses from 2008 customers and 2009 customers are taken and analyzed on this question, and the following analysis of the data results. Help managers interpret this analysis so that comparisons can be made between 2008 and 2009. Discuss the samples, the statistics, and the conclusions.

4. Suppose Seitz produces pulleys that are specified to be 50 mm in diameter. A large batch of pulleys is made in week 1 and another is made in week 5. Quality-control people want to determine whether there is a difference in the variance of the diameters of the two batches. Assume that a sample of six pulleys from the week 1 batch results in the following diameter measurements (in millimetres): 51, 50, 48, 50, 49, 51. Assume that a sample of seven pulleys from the week 5 batch results in the following diameter measurements (in millimetres): 50, 48, 48, 51, 52, 50, 52. Conduct a test to determine whether the variance in diameters differs between these two populations. Why would the quality-control people be interested in such a test? What results of this test would you relate to them? What about the means of these two batches? Analyze these data in terms of the means and report on the results. Assume that pulley diameters are normally distributed in the population.

References

Adapted from "Seitz Corporation," *Strengthening America's Competitiveness: Resource Management Insights for Small Business Success,* published by Warner Books on behalf of Connecticut Mutual Life Insurance Company and the U.S. Chamber of Commerce in association with the Blue Chip Enterprise Initiative, 1991. Case update based on Seitz Corporation <http://www.seitzcorp.com>.

	A	B	C
1	*t*-Test: Two-Sample Assuming Equal Variances		
2		2008	2009
3	Mean	3.268	3.322
4	Variance	0.038	0.033
5	Observations	75	93
6	Pooled Variance	0.035	
7	Hypothesized Mean Difference	0.000	
8	df	166	
9	*t* Stat	-1.85	
10	$P(T<=t)$ two-tail	0.066	
11	Confidence Interval (98%)	$-0.1116 <= \mu1 - \mu2 <= 0.0036$	

USING THE COMPUTER

Excel

- Excel has the capability of performing any of the statistical techniques presented in this chapter with the exception of testing the difference in two population proportions.

- Each of the tests presented here in Excel is accessed through the **Data Analysis** feature.

- To conduct a z test for the difference in two means, begin by selecting the **Data** tab on the Excel worksheet. From the **Analysis** panel at the right top of the **Data** tab worksheet, click on **Data Analysis**. If your Excel worksheet does not show the **Data Analysis** option, then you can load it as an add-in. From the **Data Analysis** pulldown menu, select **z-Test: Two Sample for Means** from the dialogue box. Enter the location of the observations from the first group in **Variable 1 Range**. Enter the location of the observations from the second group in **Variable 2 Range**. Enter the hypothesized value for the mean difference in **Hypothesized Mean Difference**. Enter the known variance of population 1 in **Variable 1 Variance (known)**. Enter the known variance of population 2 in **Variable 2 Variance (known)**. Check **Labels** if you have labels. Select **Alpha**.

- To conduct a t test for the difference in two means, begin by selecting the **Data** tab on the Excel worksheet. From the **Analysis** panel at the right top of the **Data** tab worksheet, click on **Data Analysis**. If your Excel worksheet does not show the **Data Analysis** option, then you can load it as an add-in. From the **Data Analysis** pulldown menu, select **t-Test: Two-Sample Assuming Equal Variances** from the dialogue box if you are assuming that the population variances are equal. Select **t-Test: Two-Sample Assuming Unequal Variances** from

the dialogue box if you are assuming that the population variances are not equal. Input is the same for either test. Enter the location of the observations from the first group in **Variable 1 Range**. Enter the location of the observations from the second group in **Variable 2 Range**. Enter the hypothesized value for the mean difference in **Hypothesized Mean Difference**. Check **Labels** if you have labels. Select **Alpha**.

- To conduct a t test for related populations, begin by selecting the **Data** tab on the Excel worksheet. From the **Analysis** panel at the right top of the **Data** tab worksheet, click on **Data Analysis**. If your Excel worksheet does not show the **Data Analysis** option, then you can load it as an add-in. From the **Data Analysis** pulldown menu, select **t-Test: Paired Two-Sample for Means** from the dialogue box. Enter the location of the observations from the first group in **Variable 1 Range**. Enter the location of the observations from the second group in **Variable 2 Range**. Enter the hypothesized value for the mean difference in **Hypothesized Mean Difference**. Check **Labels** if you have labels. Select **Alpha**.

- To conduct an F test for two population variances, begin by selecting the **Data** tab on the Excel worksheet. From the **Analysis** panel at the right top of the **Data** tab worksheet, click on **Data Analysis**. If your Excel worksheet does not show the **Data Analysis** option, then you can load it as an add-in. From the **Data Analysis** pulldown menu, select **F-Test: Two-Sample for Variances** from the dialogue box. Enter the location of the observations from the first group in **Variable 1 Range**. Enter the location of the observations from the second group in **Variable 2 Range**. Check **Labels** if you have labels. Select **Alpha**.

CHAPTER 11

ANALYSIS OF VARIANCE AND DESIGN OF EXPERIMENTS

Learning Objectives

The focus of this chapter is the design of experiments and the analysis of variance. The key questions in this chapter are:

1. What are the differences between the various experimental designs and when should each of them be used?

2. How can we compute and interpret the results of a one-way ANOVA?

3. How can we compute and interpret the results of a random block design?

4. How can we compute and interpret the results of a two-way ANOVA?

5. What is interaction and how should we interpret it?

6. When and how should we use multiple comparison techniques?

Shutterstock

DECISION DILEMMA

JOB AND CAREER SATISFACTION OF FOREIGN SELF-INITIATED EXPATRIATES

Because of worker shortages in some industries, in a global business environment, firms around the world must sometimes compete with each other for workers. This is especially true in industries and job designations where specialty skills are required. In order to fill such needs, companies sometimes turn to self-initiated expatriates. Self-initiated expatriates are defined to be workers who are hired as individuals on a contractual basis to work in a foreign country—in contrast to individuals who are given overseas transfers by a parent organization; that is, they are "guest workers" as compared to "organizational expatriates." Some examples could be computer experts from India, China, and Japan being hired by Silicon Valley companies; Canadian engineers working with Russian companies to extract oil and gas; or financial experts from England who are hired by Singapore companies to help manage the stock market. How satisfied are self-initiated expatriates with their jobs and their careers?

In an attempt to answer that question, suppose a study was conducted by randomly sampling self-initiated expatriates in five industries: information technology (IT), finance, education, health care, and consulting. Each is asked to rate his or her present job satisfaction on a seven-point Likert scale, with 7 being very satisfied and 1 being very unsatisfied. Suppose the following data are a portion of the study.

IT	Finance	Education	Health Care	Consulting
5	3	2	3	6
6	4	3	2	7
5	4	3	4	5
7	5	2	3	6
	4	2	5	
		3		

Suppose in addition, self-initiated expatriates are asked to report their overall satisfaction with their career on the same seven-point scale. The ratings are broken down by the respondent's experience in the host country and age. The resultant data are shown below.

	Time in Host Country			
	<1 year	1–2 years	3–4 years	≥5 years
30–39	3	4	3	6
	2	5	4	4
	3	3	5	5
Age 40–49	4	3	4	4
	3	4	4	6
	2	3	5	5
Over 50	4	4	5	6
	3	4	4	5
	4	5	5	6

Managerial and Statistical Questions

1. Is there a difference in the job satisfaction ratings of self-initiated expatriates by industry? If we were to use the *t* test for the difference of two independent population means presented in Chapter 10 to analyze these data, we would need to do 10 different *t* tests since there are 5 different industries. Is there a better, more efficient way to analyze these data?

Can the analysis be done simultaneously using one technique?

2. The second table in the Decision Dilemma displays career satisfaction data broken down in two different ways, age and time in country. How does a researcher analyze such data when there are two different types of groups or classifications? Suppose that one variable, such as age, acts on another variable, such as time in the country, such that there is an interaction; that is, time in the country might matter more in one category than in another. Can this effect be measured, and if so, how?

Source: Concepts adapted from Chay Hoon Lee, "A Study of Underemployment among Self-Initiated Expatriates," *Journal of World Business,* May 2005, 40, no. 2, pp. 172–187.

Sometimes business research entails more complicated hypothesis-testing scenarios than those presented to this point in the text. Instead of comparing the wear of tire tread for two brands of tires to determine whether there is a significant difference between the brands, as we could have done by using Chapter 10 techniques, a tire researcher may choose to compare three, four, or even more brands of tires at the same time. In addition, the researcher may want to include different levels of quality of tires in the experiment, such as low-quality, medium-quality, and high-quality tires. Tests may be conducted under varying conditions of temperature, precipitation, or road surface. Such experiments involve selecting and analyzing more than two samples of data.

Figure III-1 of the Introduction to Unit III displays the tree diagram taxonomy of inferential techniques organized by usage and number of samples. The entire right side of the tree diagram taxonomy contains various hypothesis-testing techniques. Techniques for testing hypotheses using a *single* sample are presented in Chapter 9, and techniques for testing hypotheses about the differences in two populations using *two* samples are presented in Chapter 10. The far right branch of the tree diagram taxonomy contains techniques for analyzing *three or more* samples. This branch, shown in Figure 11.1, represents the techniques presented in Chapter 11.

Figure 11.1

Branch of the Tree Diagram Taxonomy of Inferential Techniques

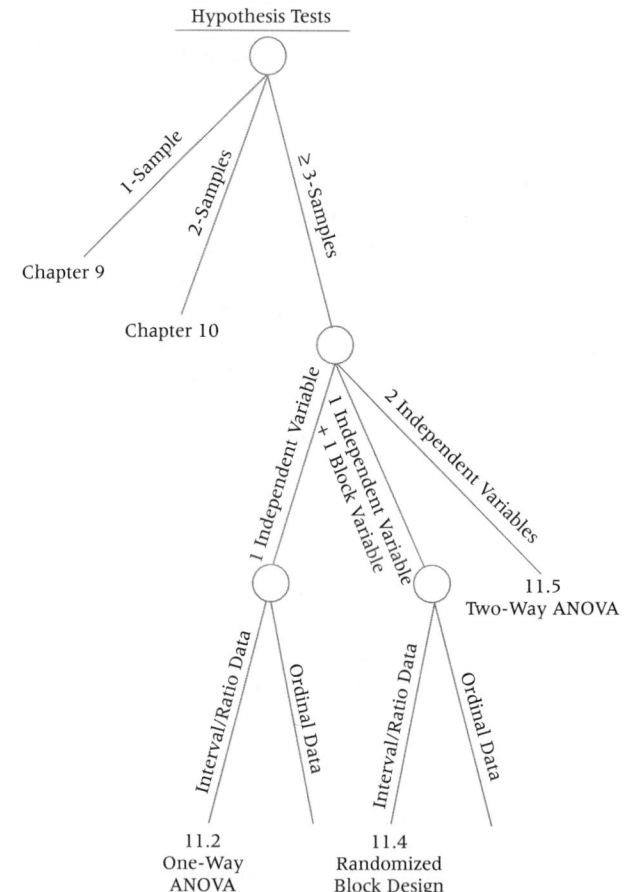

11.1 INTRODUCTION TO DESIGN OF EXPERIMENTS

An **experimental design** is *a plan and a structure to test hypotheses in which the researcher either controls or manipulates one or more variables.* It contains independent and dependent variables. In an experimental design, an **independent variable** may be either a treatment variable or a classification variable. A **treatment variable** is *a variable the experimenter controls or modifies in the experiment.* A **classification variable** is *some characteristic of the experimental subject that was present prior to the experiment and is not a result of the experimenter's manipulations or control.* Independent variables are sometimes also referred to as **factors.** Sears Canada executives might sanction an in-house study to compare daily sales volumes for a given size store in four different demographic settings: (1) inner-city stores (large city), (2) suburban stores (large city), (3) stores in a medium-sized city, and (4) stores in a small town. Managers might also decide to compare sales on the five different weekdays (Monday through Friday). In this study, the independent variables are store demographics and day of the week.

A researcher might conduct a study to determine whether there is a significant difference in application fees for higher education programs in five geographic regions of Canada and might include two different types of higher education institutions. In this study, the independent variables are geographic region and type of higher education institution. Or suppose a manufacturing organization produces a valve that is specified to have an opening with a diameter of 6.37 cm. Quality controllers within the company might decide to test to determine how the openings for produced valves vary among four different machines on three different shifts. This experiment includes the independent variables of type of machine and work shift.

Whether an independent variable can be manipulated by the researcher depends on the concept being studied. Independent variables such as work shift, gender of employee, geographic region, type of machine, and quality of tire are classification variables with conditions that existed prior to the study. The business researcher cannot change the characteristic of the variable, so he or she studies the phenomenon being explored under several conditions of the various aspects of the variable. As an example, the valve experiment is conducted under the conditions of all three work shifts.

However, some independent variables can be manipulated by the researcher. For example, in the well-known Hawthorne studies of the Western Electric Company in the 1920s, the amount of light in production areas was varied to determine its effect on productivity. In theory, this independent variable could be manipulated by the researcher to allow any level of lighting. Other examples of independent variables that can be manipulated are the size of bonuses offered workers, level of humidity, and temperature. These are examples of treatment variables.

Each independent variable has two or more levels, or classifications. **Levels,** or **classifications,** of independent variables are *the subcategories of the independent variable used by the researcher in the experimental design.* For example, the different demographic settings listed for the Sears Canada study are four levels, or classifications, of the independent variable Store Demographics: (1) inner-city store, (2) suburban store, (3) store in a medium-sized city, and (4) store in small town. In the valve experiment, four levels or classifications of machines within the independent variable Machine Type are used: machine 1, machine 2, machine 3, and machine 4.

The other type of variable in an experimental design is a **dependent variable.** A dependent variable is *the response to the different levels of the independent variables.* It is the measurement taken under the conditions of the experimental design that reflect the effects of the independent variable(s). In the Sears Canada study, the dependent variable is the dollar amount of daily total sales. For the study on loan application fees, the fee charged for a loan application is probably the dependent variable. In the valve experiment, the dependent variable is the size of the opening of the valve.

Experimental designs in this chapter are analyzed statistically by a group of techniques referred to as **analysis of variance,** or **ANOVA.** The ANOVA concept begins with the notion that individual items being studied, such as employees, machine-produced products, district offices, hospitals, and so on, are not all the same. Note the measurements for the openings of 24 valves randomly selected from an assembly line that are given in

Table 11.1				
6.26	6.19	6.33	6.26	6.50
6.19	6.44	6.22	6.54	6.23
6.29	6.40	6.23	6.29	6.58
6.27	6.38	6.58	6.31	6.34
6.21	6.19	6.36	6.56	

Valve Opening Measurements (in centimetres) for 24 Valves Produced on an Assembly Line

$\bar{x} = 6.34$

Total Sum of Squares Deviation = SST = $\Sigma(x_i - \bar{x})^2 = 0.3915$

Table 11.1. The mean opening is 6.34 cm. Only one of the 24 valve opening measurements is actually the mean. Why do the valve openings vary? The total sum of squares of deviation of these valve openings around the mean is 0.3915 cm². Why is this value not zero? Using various types of experimental designs, we can explore some possible reasons for this variance with ANOVA techniques. As we explore each of the experimental designs and their associated analysis, note that the statistical technique is attempting to break down the total variance among the objects being studied into possible causes. In the case of the valve openings, this variance of measurements might be due to such variables as machine, operator, shift, supplier, and production conditions.

Many different types of experimental designs are available to researchers. In this chapter, we will present and discuss three specific types of experimental designs: completely randomized design, randomized block design, and factorial experiments.

Concept Check

1. Explain in your own words the meaning of an experimental design.
2. Define the terms *treatment variable, classification variable, factor, level,* and *dependent variable.*

11.1 Problems

11.1   Some New York Stock Exchange analysts believe that 24-hour trading on the stock exchange is the wave of the future. As an initial test of this idea, the New York Stock Exchange opened two after-hours "crossing sections" in the early 1990s and studied the results of these extra-hour sessions for one year.
   a.   State an independent variable that could have been used for this study.
   b.   List at least two levels, or classifications, for this variable.
   c.   Give a dependent variable for this study.

11.2   WestJet Airlines is able to keep fares low in part because of relatively low maintenance costs on its airplanes. One of the main reasons for the low maintenance costs is that WestJet flies only one type of aircraft, the Boeing 737. However, WestJet flies three different versions of the 737. Suppose WestJet decides to conduct a study to determine whether there is a significant difference in the average annual maintenance costs for the three types of 737s used.
   a.   State an independent variable for such a study.
   b.   What are some of the levels or classifications that might be studied under this variable?
   c.   Give a dependent variable for this study.

11.3   A large multinational banking company wants to determine whether there is a significant difference in the average dollar amounts purchased by users of different types of credit cards. Among the credit cards being studied are MasterCard, Visa, and American Express.

a.   If an experimental design were set up for such a study, what are some possible independent variables?

b.   List at least three levels, or classifications, for each independent variable.

c.   What are some possible dependent variables for this experiment?

11.4   Is there a difference in the family demographics of people who stay at hotels? Suppose a study is conducted in which three categories of hotels are used: economy hotels, modestly priced chain hotels, and exclusive hotels. One of the dependent variables studied might be the number of children in the family of the person staying in the hotel. Name three other dependent variables that might be used in this study.

11.2 THE COMPLETELY RANDOMIZED DESIGN (ONE-WAY ANOVA)

One of the simplest experimental designs is the completely randomized design. In the **completely randomized design,** *subjects are assigned randomly to treatments.* The completely randomized design contains only one independent variable, with two or more treatment levels, or classifications. If only two treatment levels, or classifications, of the independent variable are present, the design is the same one used to test the difference in means of two independent populations presented in Chapter 10, which used the *t* test to analyze the data.

In this section, we will focus on completely randomized designs with three or more classification levels. ANOVA will be used to analyze the data that result from the treatments.

A completely randomized design could be structured for a tire-quality study in which tire quality is the independent variable and the treatment levels are low, medium, and high quality. The dependent variable might be the number of kilometres driven before the tread fails provincial inspection. A study of daily sales volumes for Sears Canada stores could be undertaken by using a completely randomized design with demographic setting as the independent variable. The treatment levels, or classifications, would be inner-city stores, suburban stores, stores in medium-sized cities, and stores in small towns. The dependent variable would be sales dollars.

As an example of a completely randomized design, suppose a researcher decides to analyze the effects of the machine operator on the valve opening measurements of valves produced in a manufacturing plant, like those shown in Table 11.1. The independent variable in this design is the machine operator. Suppose further that four different operators operate the machines. These four machine operators are the levels of treatment, or classification, of the independent variable. The dependent variable is the opening measurement of the valve. Figure 11.2 shows the structure of this completely randomized design. Is there a significant difference in the mean valve openings of 24 valves produced by the four operators? Table 11.2 contains the valve opening measurements for valves produced under each operator.

ONE-WAY ANOVA

In the machine operator example, is it possible to analyze the four samples by using a *t* test for the difference in two sample means? These four samples would require $_4C_2 = 6$ individual

Figure 11.2

Completely Randomized Design

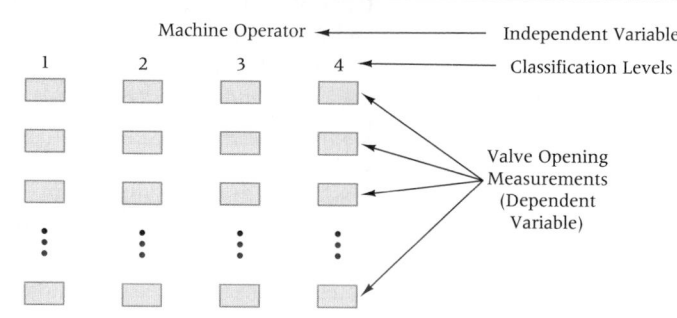

Table 11.2

Valve Opening Measurements by Operator

1	2	3	4
6.33	6.26	6.44	6.29
6.26	6.36	6.38	6.23
6.31	6.23	6.58	6.19
6.29	6.27	6.54	6.21
6.40	6.19	6.56	
	6.50	6.34	
	6.19	6.58	
	6.22		

t tests to accomplish the analysis of two groups at a time. Recall that if $\alpha = 0.05$ for a particular test, there is a 5% chance of rejecting a null hypothesis that is true (i.e., committing a Type I error). If enough tests are done, eventually one or more null hypotheses will be falsely rejected by chance. Hence, $\alpha = 0.05$ is valid only for one t test. In this problem, with six t tests, the error rate compounds, so when the analyst is finished with the problem there is a much greater than 0.05 chance of committing a Type I error. Fortunately, a technique has been developed that analyzes all the sample means at one time and thus precludes the build-up of error rate: ANOVA. A completely randomized design is analyzed by a **one-way ANOVA.**

In general, if k samples are being analyzed, the following hypotheses are being tested in a one-way ANOVA:

$$H_0: \mu_1 = \mu_2 = \mu_3 = \cdots = \mu_k$$
$$H_a: \text{At least one of the means is different from the others.}$$

The null hypothesis states that the population means for all treatment levels are equal. Because of the way the alternative hypothesis is stated, if even one of the population means is different from the others, the null hypothesis is rejected.

Testing these hypotheses by using one-way ANOVA is accomplished by partitioning the total variance of the data into the following two variances:

1. The variance resulting from the treatment (columns)
2. The error variance, or that portion of the total variance unexplained by the treatment

As part of this process, the total sum of squares of deviation of values around the mean can be divided into two additive and independent parts.

$$\text{SST} \quad = \quad \text{SSC} \quad + \quad \text{SSE}$$
$$\sum_{i=1}^{n_j}\sum_{j=1}^{C}(x_{ij} - \overline{x})^2 = \sum_{j=1}^{C}n_j(\overline{x}_j - \overline{x})^2 + \sum_{i=1}^{n_j}\sum_{j=1}^{C}(x_{ij} - \overline{x}_j)^2$$

POINTS OF INTEREST
Even if only one of the population means is different from the others, the null hypothesis is still rejected.

Figure 11.3

Partitioning Total Sum of Squares of Variation

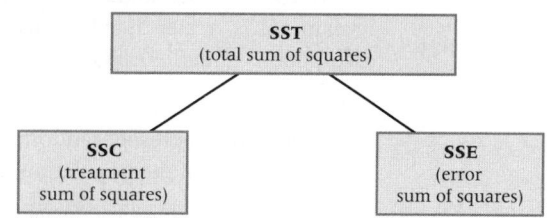

where

SST = total sum of squares

SSC = sum of squares of column (treatment)

SSE = sum of squares of error

   i = particular member of a treatment level

   j = a treatment level

  C = number of treatment levels

  n_j = number of observations in a given treatment level

  $\bar{x}$ = grand mean

  $\bar{x}_j$ = mean of a treatment group or level

  x_{ij} = individual value

This relationship is shown in Figure 11.3. Observe that the total sum of squares of variation is partitioned into the sum of squares of treatment (columns) and the sum of squares of error.

The formulas used to accomplish one-way ANOVA are developed from this relationship. The double summation sign indicates that the values are summed within a treatment level and across treatment levels. Basically, ANOVA compares the relative sizes of the *treatment* variation and the *error* variation (within-group variation). The error variation is unaccounted for and can be viewed at this point as due to individual differences within treatment groups. If a significant difference in treatments is present, the treatment variation should be large relative to the error variation.

Figure 11.4 displays the data from the machine operator example in terms of treatment level. Note the variation of values (x) *within* each treatment level. Now examine the variation between levels 1 through 4 (the difference in the machine operators). In particular, note that values for treatment level 3 seem to be located differently from those of levels 2 and 4. This difference is also underscored by the mean values for each treatment level:

$$\bar{x}_1 = 6.3180 \quad \bar{x}_2 = 6.2775 \quad \bar{x}_3 = 6.488571 \quad \bar{x}_4 = 6.23$$

Figure 11.4

Location of Mean Valve Openings by Operator

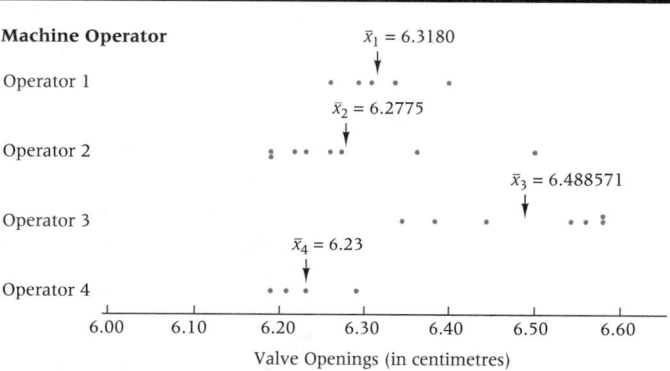

ANOVA is used to determine statistically whether the variance between the treatment level means is greater than the variances within levels (error variance). Several important assumptions underlie ANOVA:

1. Observations are drawn from normally distributed populations.
2. Observations represent random samples from the populations.
3. The variances of the populations are equal.

These assumptions are similar to those for using the *t* test for independent samples in Chapter 10. It is assumed that the populations are normally distributed and that the population variances are equal. These techniques should be used only with random samples.

An ANOVA is computed with the three sums of squares: total, treatment (columns), and error. Shown here are the formulas to compute a one-way ANOVA. SS represents sum of squares and MS represents mean square. SSC is the sum of squares of columns, which yields the sum of squares between treatments. It measures the variation between columns or between treatments since the independent variable treatment levels are presented as columns. SSE is the sum of squares of error, which yields the variation within treatments (or columns). Some say that it is a measure of the individual differences unaccounted for by the treatments. SST is the total sum of squares and is a measure of all variation in the dependent variable. As shown previously, SST contains both SSC and SSE and can be partitioned into SSC and SSE. MSC, MSE, and MST are the mean squares of column, error, and total, respectively. Mean square is an average and is computed by dividing the sum of squares by the degrees of freedom. Finally, the *F* value is determined by dividing the treatment variance (MSC) by the error variance (MSE). As discussed in Chapter 10, the *F* value is a ratio of two variances. In the ANOVA situation, the **F value** is *a ratio of the treatment variance to the error variance.*

> **POINTS OF INTEREST**
> These calculations are tedious. In general, we leave the detailed numerical analysis to the computer.

Formulas for Computing a One-Way ANOVA

$$SSC = \sum_{j=1}^{C} n_j (\bar{x}_j - \bar{x})^2$$

$$SSE = \sum_{i=1}^{n_j} \sum_{j=1}^{C} (x_{ij} - \bar{x}_j)^2$$

$$SST = \sum_{i=1}^{n_j} \sum_{j=1}^{C} (x_{ij} - \bar{x})^2$$

$$df_C = C - 1$$

$$df_E = N - C$$

$$df_T = N - 1$$

$$MSC = \frac{SSC}{df_C}$$

$$MSE = \frac{SSE}{df_E}$$

$$F = \frac{MSC}{MSE}$$

where

i = a particular member of a treatment level
j = a treatment level
C = number of treatment levels
n_j = number of observations in a given treatment level
$\bar{x}$ = grand mean
$\bar{x}_j$ = column mean
x_{ij} = individual value

Performing these calculations for the machine operator example yields the following:

Machine Operator

1	2	3	4
6.33	6.26	6.44	6.29
6.26	6.36	6.38	6.23
6.31	6.23	6.58	6.19
6.29	6.27	6.54	6.21
6.40	6.19	6.56	
	6.50	6.34	
	6.19	6.58	
	6.22		

T_j:	$T_1 = 31.59$	$T_2 = 50.22$	$T_3 = 45.42$	$T_4 = 24.92$	$T = 152.15$
n_j:	$n_1 = 5$	$n_2 = 8$	$n_3 = 7$	$n_4 = 4$	$N = 24$
$\bar{x}_j$:	$\bar{x}_1 = 6.318$	$\bar{x}_2 = 6.2775$	$\bar{x}_3 = 6.488571$	$\bar{x}_4 = 6.230$	$\bar{x} = 6.339583$

$$SSC = \sum_{j=1}^{C} n_j (\bar{x}_j - \bar{x})^2 = [5(6.318 - 6.339583)^2 + 8(6.2775 - 6.339583)^2$$

$$+ 7(6.488571 - 6.339583)^2 + 4(6.230 - 6.339583)^2]$$

$$= 0.00233 + 0.03083 + 0.15538 + 0.04803$$

$$= 0.23657$$

$$SSE = \sum_{i=1}^{n_j} \sum_{j=1}^{C} (x_{ij} - \bar{x}_j)^2 = [(6.33 - 6.318)^2 + (6.26 - 6.318)^2 + (6.31 - 6.318)^2$$

$$+ (6.29 - 6.318)^2 + (6.40 - 6.318)^2 + (6.26 - 6.2775)^2$$

$$+ (6.36 - 6.2775)^2 + \cdots + (6.19 - 6.230)^2 + (6.21 - 6.230)^2]$$

$$= 0.15492$$

$$SST = \sum_{i=1}^{n_j} \sum_{j=1}^{C} (x_{ij} - \bar{x})^2 = [(6.33 - 6.339583)^2 + (6.26 - 6.339583)^2$$

$$+ (6.31 - 6.339583)^2 + \cdots + (6.19 - 6.339583)^2$$

$$+ (6.21 - 6.339583)^2$$

$$= 0.39150$$

$$df_C = C - 1 = 4 - 1 = 3$$
$$df_E = N - C = 24 - 4 = 20$$
$$df_T = N - 1 = 24 - 1 = 23$$
$$MSC = \frac{SSC}{df_C} = \frac{0.23657}{3} = 0.078857$$
$$MSE = \frac{SSE}{df_E} = \frac{0.15492}{20} = 0.007746$$
$$F = \frac{0.078857}{0.007746} = 10.18$$

From these computations, an ANOVA chart can be constructed, as shown in Table 11.3. The observed F value is 10.18. It is compared to a critical value from the F table to determine whether there is a significant difference in treatment or classification.

Table 11.3

ANOVA for the Machine Operator Example

Source of Variance	df	SS	MS	F
Between	3	0.23657	0.078857	10.18
Error	20	0.15492	0.007746	
Total	23	0.39150		

READING THE *F* DISTRIBUTION TABLE

The **F distribution** table is in Table A.7. Associated with every F value in the table are two unique df values: degrees of freedom in the numerator (df_C) and degrees of freedom in the denominator (df_E). To look up a value in the F distribution table, the researcher must know both degrees of freedom. Because each F distribution is determined by a unique pair of degrees of freedom, many F distributions are possible. Space constraints limit Table A.7 to F values for only $\alpha = 0.005, 0.01, 0.025, 0.05,$ and 0.10. However, statistical computer software packages for computing ANOVAs usually give a probability for the F value, which allows a hypothesis-testing decision for any alpha based on the p value method.

In the one-way ANOVA, the df_C values are the treatment (column) degrees of freedom, $C - 1$. The df_E values are the error degrees of freedom, $N - C$. Table 11.4 contains an abbreviated F distribution table for $\alpha = 0.05$. For the machine operator example, $df_C = 3$ and $df_E = 20$. $F_{0.05,3,20}$ from Table 11.4 is 3.10. This value is the critical value of the F test. ANOVA tests are always one-tailed tests with the rejection region in the upper tail. The decision rule is to reject the null hypothesis if the observed F value is greater than the critical F value ($F_{0.05,3,20} = 3.10$). For the machine operator problem, the observed F value of 10.18 is larger than the table F value of 3.10. The null hypothesis is rejected. Not all means are equal, so there is a significant difference in the mean valve opening measurements by machine operator. Figure 11.5 is a graph of an F distribution showing the critical F value

Table 11.4

An Abbreviated *F* Table for $\alpha = 0.05$

Denominator Degrees of Freedom	Numerator Degrees of Freedom								
	1	2	3	4	5	6	7	8	9
⋮									
19	4.38	3.52	3.13	2.90	2.74	2.63	2.54	2.48	2.42
20	4.35	3.49	3.10	2.87	2.71	2.60	2.51	2.45	2.39
21	4.32	3.47	3.07	2.84	2.68	2.57	2.49	2.42	2.37

Figure 11.5

Graph of *F* Values for the Machine Operator Example

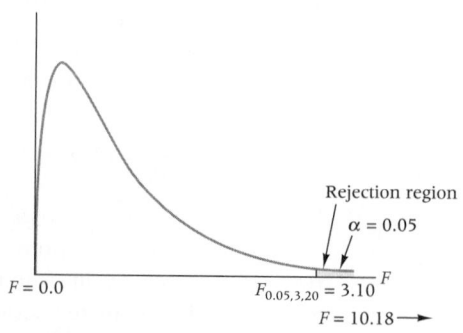

Rejection region
$\alpha = 0.05$

$F = 0.0$

$F_{0.05,3,20} = 3.10$

$F = 10.18 \longrightarrow$

for this example and the rejection region. Note that the F distribution begins at zero and contains no negative values because the F value is the ratio of two variances, and variances are always positive.

USING THE COMPUTER FOR ONE-WAY ANOVA

Most researchers use the computer to analyze data with a one-way ANOVA. Figure 11.6 shows the Excel output of the ANOVA computed for the machine operator example. The output includes the ANOVA table presented in Table 11.3. Excel ANOVA tables display the observed F value, mean squares, sum of squares, degrees of freedom, and a value of p. The value of p is the probability of an F value of 10.18 occurring by chance in an ANOVA with this structure (same degrees of freedom) even if there is no difference between means of the treatment levels. Using the p value method of testing hypotheses presented in Chapter 9, we can easily see that because this p value is only 0.000279, the null hypothesis would be rejected using $\alpha = 0.05$. Most computer output yields the value of p, so there is no need to look up a table value of F against which to compare the observed F value. The Excel output also includes the critical table F value for this problem, $F_{0.05,3,20} = 3.10$.

Figure 11.6

Excel Analysis of the Machine Operator Problem

	A	B	C	D	E	F	G
1	Anova: Single Factor						
2							
3	SUMMARY						
4	*Groups*	*Count*	*Sum*	*Average*	*Variance*		
5	Operator 1	5	31.59	6.3180	0.0028		
6	Operator 2	8	50.22	6.2775	0.0111		
7	Operator 3	7	45.42	6.4886	0.0101		
8	Operator 4	4	24.92	6.2300	0.0019		
9							
10							
11	ANOVA						
12	*Source of Variation*	*SS*	*df*	*MS*	*F*	*P-value*	*F crit*
13	Between Groups	0.2366	3	0.0789	10.1810	0.0003	3.0984
14	Within Groups	0.1549	20	0.0077			
15							
16	Total	0.3915	23				

COMPARISON OF F AND t VALUES

ANOVA can be used to test hypotheses about the difference in two means. Analysis of data from two samples by both a t test and an ANOVA shows that the observed F value equals the observed t value squared:

$$F = t^2 \quad \text{for} \quad df_C = 1$$

The t test of independent samples is actually a special case of one-way ANOVA when there are only two treatment levels ($df_C = 1$). The t test is computationally simpler than ANOVA for two groups. However, some statistical computer software packages do not contain a t test. In these cases, the researcher can perform a one-way ANOVA and then either take the square root of the F value to obtain the value of t or use the generated probability with the p value method to reach conclusions.

Demonstration Problem 11.1

A company has three manufacturing plants, and company officials want to determine whether there is a difference in the average age of workers at the three locations. The following data are the ages of five randomly selected workers at each plant. Perform a one-way ANOVA to determine whether there is a significant difference in the mean ages of the workers at the three plants. Use $\alpha = 0.01$ and note that the sample sizes are equal.

Solution

HYPOTHESIZE:

STEP 1. The hypotheses follow.

$$H_0: \mu_1 = \mu_2 = \mu_3$$
$$H_a: \text{At least one of the means is different from the others.}$$

TEST:

STEP 2. The appropriate test statistic is the F test calculated from ANOVA.

STEP 3. The value of α is 0.01.

STEP 4. The degrees of freedom for this problem are $3 - 1 = 2$ for the numerator and $15 - 3 = 12$ for the denominator. The critical F value is $F_{0.01,2,12} = 6.93$.

Because ANOVAs are always one-tailed with the rejection region in the upper tail, the decision rule is to reject the null hypothesis if the observed value of F is greater than 6.93.

STEP 5.

Plant (Employee Ages)

1	2	3
29	32	25
27	33	24
30	31	24
27	34	25
28	30	26

STEP 6.

T_j: $T_1 = 141$ $T_2 = 160$ $T_3 = 124$ $T = 425$

n_j: $n_1 = 5$ $n_2 = 5$ $n_3 = 5$ $N = 15$

$\bar{x}_j$: $\bar{x}_1 = 28.2$ $\bar{x}_2 = 32.0$ $\bar{x}_3 = 24.8$ $\bar{x} = 28.33$

$\text{SSC} = 5(28.2 - 28.33)^2 + 5(32.0 - 28.33)^2 + 5(24.8 - 28.33)^2 = 129.73$

$\text{SSE} = (29 - 28.2)^2 + (27 - 28.2)^2 + \cdots + (25 - 24.8)^2 + (26 - 24.8)^2 = 19.60$

$\text{SST} = (29 - 28.33)^2 + (27 - 28.33)^2 + \cdots + (25 - 28.33)^2 + (26 - 28.33)^2 = 149.33$

$\text{df}_C = 3 - 1 = 2$

$\text{df}_E = 15 - 3 = 12$

$\text{df}_T = 15 - 1 = 14$

Source of Variance	SS	df	MS	F
Between	129.73	2	64.87	39.80
Error	19.60	12	1.63	
Total	149.33	14		

ACTION:

STEP 7. The decision is to reject the null hypothesis because the observed F value of 39.80 is greater than the critical table F value of 6.93.

BUSINESS IMPLICATIONS:

STEP 8. There is a significant difference in the mean ages of workers at the three plants. This difference can have hiring implications. Company leaders should understand that because motivation, discipline, and experience may differ with age, the differences in ages may call for different managerial approaches in each plant.

The following chart displays the dispersion of the ages of workers from the three samples, along with the mean age for each plant sample. Note the difference in group means. The significant F value says that the difference between the mean ages is relatively greater than the differences of ages within each group.

Plant 1 $\bar{x}_1 = 28.2$

Plant 2 $\bar{x}_2 = 32.0$

Plant 3 $\bar{x}_3 = 24.8$

23 24 25 26 27 28 29 30 31 32 33 34

Age

Following is the Excel output for this problem.

Excel Output

	A	B	C	D	E	F	G
1	Anova: Single Factor						
2							
3	SUMMARY						
4	*Groups*	*Count*	*Sum*	*Average*	*Variance*		
5	Plant 1	5	141	28.20	1.70		
6	Plant 2	5	160	32.00	2.50		
7	Plant 3	5	124	24.80	0.70		
8							
9							
10	ANOVA						
11	*Source of Variation*	*SS*	*df*	*MS*	*F*	*P-value*	*F crit*
12	Between Groups	129.73	2	64.87	39.71	0.00	6.93
13	Within Groups	19.60	12	1.63			
14							
15	Total	149.33	14				

Concept Check

1. Explain the difference between the *treatment* variation and the *error* variation.
2. What are the three assumptions that underlie ANOVA?
3. How is the F value conceptually defined in the ANOVA situation?

11.2 Problems

11.5   Compute a one-way ANOVA on the following data.

1	2	3
2	5	3
1	3	4
3	6	5
3	4	5
2	5	3
1		5

Determine the observed F value. Compare the observed F value with the critical table F value and decide whether to reject the null hypothesis. Use $\alpha = 0.05$.

11.6   Compute a one-way ANOVA on the following data.

1	2	3	4	5
14	10	11	16	14
13	9	12	17	12
10	12	13	14	13
	9	12	16	13
	10		17	12
				14

Determine the observed F value. Compare the observed F value with the critical table F value and decide whether to reject the null hypothesis. Use $\alpha = 0.01$.

11.7   Develop a one-way ANOVA on the following data.

1	2	3	4
113	120	132	122
121	127	130	118
117	125	129	125
110	129	135	125

Determine the observed F value. Compare it to the critical F value and decide whether to reject the null hypothesis. Use a 1% level of significance.

11.8   Compute a one-way ANOVA on the following data.

1	2
27	22
31	27
31	25
29	23
30	26
27	27
28	23

Determine the observed F value. Compare it to the critical table F value and decide whether to reject the null hypothesis. Perform a t test for independent measures on the data. Compare the t and F values. Are the results different? Use $\alpha = 0.05$.

11.9   Suppose you are using a completely randomized design to study some phenomenon. There are five treatment levels and a total of 55 people in the study. Each treatment level has the same sample size. Complete the following ANOVA.

Source of Variance	SS	df	MS
Treatment	583.39		
Error	972.18		
Total	1555.57		

11.10   Suppose you are using a completely randomized design to study some phenomenon. There are three treatment levels and a total of 17 people in the study. Complete the following ANOVA table. Use $\alpha = 0.05$ to find the table F value and use the data to test the null hypothesis.

Source of Variance	SS	df	MS	F
Treatment	29.64			
Error	68.42			
Total				

11.11 A milk company has four machines that fill 4-L jugs with milk. The quality control manager is interested in determining whether the average fill for these machines is the same. The following data represent random samples of fill measure (in litres) for 19 jugs of milk filled by the different machines. Use $\alpha = 0.01$ to test the hypothesis. Discuss the business implications of your findings.

Machine 1	Machine 2	Machine 3	Machine 4
4.05	3.99	3.97	4.00
4.01	4.02	3.98	4.02
4.02	4.01	3.97	3.99
4.04	3.99	3.95	4.01
	4.00	4.00	
	4.00		

11.12 That the starting salaries of new accounting graduates would differ according to geographic regions of Canada seems logical. A random selection of accounting firms is taken from three provinces, and each is asked to state the starting salary for a new accounting graduate who is going to work in auditing. The data obtained follow. Use a one-way ANOVA to analyze these data. Note that the data can be restated to make the computations more reasonable (example: $\$42,500 = 4.25$). Use a 1% level of significance. Discuss the business implications of your findings.

Nova Scotia	Ontario	British Columbia
$40,500	$51,000	$45,500
41,500	49,500	43,500
40,000	49,000	45,000
41,000	48,000	46,500
41,500	49,500	46,000

11.13 A management consulting company presents a three-day seminar on project management to various clients. The seminar is basically the same each time it is given. However, sometimes it is presented to high-level managers, sometimes to midlevel managers, and sometimes to low-level managers. The seminar facilitators believe evaluations of the seminar may vary with the audience. Suppose the following data are some randomly selected evaluation scores from different levels of managers who attended the seminar. The ratings are on a scale from 1 to 10, with 10 being the highest. Use a one-way ANOVA to determine whether there is a significant difference in the evaluations according to manager level. Assume $\alpha = 0.05$. Discuss the business implications of your findings.

High Level	Midlevel	Low Level
7	8	5
7	9	6
8	8	5
7	10	7
9	9	4
	10	8
	8	

11.14 Family transportation costs are usually higher than most people believe because those costs include car payments, insurance, fuel costs, repairs, parking, and public transportation. Twenty randomly selected families in four major cities are asked to use their records to estimate a monthly figure for transportation cost. Use the data obtained and ANOVA to test whether there is a significant difference in monthly transportation costs for families living in these cities. Assume that $\alpha = 0.05$. Discuss the business implications of your findings.

Edmonton	Toronto	Vancouver	Halifax
$650	$250	$850	$540
480	525	700	450
550	300	950	675
600	175	780	550
675	500	600	600

11.15 Shown here is the Excel output for a one-way ANOVA. Analyze the results. Include the number of treatment levels, the sample sizes, the F value, the overall statistical significance of the test, and the values of the means.

	A	B	C	D	E	F	G
1	Anova: Single Factor						
2							
3	SUMMARY						
4	*Groups*	*Count*	*Sum*	*Average*	*Variance*		
5	C1	18	4081.14	226.73	184.69		
6	C2	15	3581.85	238.79	88.55		
7	C3	21	4884.18	232.58	147.87		
8	C4	11	2638.02	239.82	20.96		
9							
10							
11	ANOVA						
12	*Source of Variation*	*SS*	*df*	*MS*	*F*	*P*-value	*F*-crit
13	Between Groups	1701.00	3	567.00	2.95	0.04	2.7555
14	Within Groups	11728.00	61	192.00			
15							
16	Total	13429.00	64				

11.16 Business is very good for a chemical company. In fact, it is so good that workers are averaging more than 40 hours per week at each of the chemical company's five plants. However, management is not certain whether there is a difference between the five plants in the average number of hours worked per week per worker. Random samples of data are taken at each of the five plants. The data are analyzed using Excel. The results follow. Explain the design of the study and determine whether there is an overall significant difference between the means at $\alpha = 0.05$. Why or why not? What are the values of the means? What are the business implications of this study to the chemical company?

	A	B	C	D	E	F	G
1	Anova: Single Factor						
2							
3	SUMMARY						
4	*Groups*	*Count*	*Sum*	*Average*	*Variance*		
5	Plant 1	11	636.5577	57.87	63.5949		
6	Plant 2	12	601.7648	50.15	62.4813		
7	Plant 3	8	491.7352	61.47	47.4772		
	Plant 4	5	246.0172	49.20	65.6072		
	Plant 5	7	398.6368	56.95	140.3540		
8							
9							
10	ANOVA						
11	*Source of Variation*	SS	df	MS	F	*P*-value	F crit
12	Between Groups	900.0863	4	225.0216	3.10	0.026595	2.62
13	Within Groups	2760.136	38	72.63516			
14							
15	Total	3660.223	42				

11.3 MULTIPLE COMPARISON TESTS

ANOVA techniques are particularly useful in testing hypotheses about the differences of means in multiple groups because ANOVA utilizes only one single overall test. The advantage of this approach is that the probability of committing a Type I error, α, is controlled. As noted in Section 11.2, if four groups are tested two at a time, it takes six t tests ($_4C_2$) to analyze hypotheses between all possible pairs. In general, if k groups are tested two at a time, $_kC_2 = k(k-1)/2$ paired comparisons are possible.

Suppose alpha for an experiment is 0.05. If two different pairs of comparisons are made in the experiment using alpha of 0.05 in each, there is a 0.95 probability of not making a Type I error in each comparison. This approach results in a 0.9025 probability of not making a Type I error in either comparison (0.95 × 0.95), and a 0.0975 probability of committing a Type I error in at least one comparison (1 − 0.9025). Thus, the probability of committing a Type I error for this experiment is not 0.05 but 0.0975. In an experiment where the means of four groups are being tested two at a time, six different tests are conducted. If each is analyzed using $\alpha = 0.05$, the probability that no Type I error will be committed in any of the six tests is 0.95 × 0.95 × 0.95 × 0.95 × 0.95 × 0.95 = 0.735 and the probability of committing at least one Type I error in the six tests is 1 − 0.735 = 0.265. If an ANOVA is computed on all groups simultaneously using $\alpha = 0.05$, the value of alpha is maintained in the experiment.

Sometimes the researcher is satisfied with conducting an overall test of differences in groups such as the one ANOVA provides. However, when it is determined that there is an overall difference in population means, it is often desirable to go back to the groups and determine from the data which pairs of means are significantly different. Such pairwise analyses can lead to the build-up of the Type I experimental error rate, as mentioned. Fortunately, several techniques, referred to as **multiple comparisons,** have been developed to handle this problem.

Multiple comparisons are to be used only when an overall significant difference between groups has been obtained by using the F value of the ANOVA. Some of these techniques protect more for Type I errors and others protect more for Type II errors. Some multiple comparison techniques require equal sample sizes. There seems to be some difference of opinion in the literature about which techniques are most appropriate. Here we will consider only a posteriori or post hoc pairwise comparisons.

A posteriori or **post hoc** pairwise comparisons are made *after the experiment when the researcher decides to test for any significant differences in the samples based on a significant overall F value.* In contrast, **a priori** comparisons are made when the researcher *determines before the experiment which comparisons are to be made.* The error rates for these two types of comparisons are different, as are the recommended techniques. In this text, we consider only pairwise (two-at-a-time) multiple comparisons. Other types of comparisons are possible but belong in a more advanced presentation. The two multiple comparison tests discussed here are Tukey's HSD test for designs with equal sample sizes and the Tukey-Kramer procedure for situations in which sample sizes are unequal.

TUKEY'S HONESTLY SIGNIFICANT DIFFERENCE (HSD) TEST: THE CASE OF EQUAL SAMPLE SIZES

Tukey's honestly significant difference (HSD) test, sometimes known as Tukey's T method, is a popular test for pairwise a posteriori multiple comparisons. This test, developed by John W. Tukey and presented in 1953, is somewhat limited by the fact that it requires equal sample sizes.

Tukey's HSD test takes into consideration the number of treatment levels, the value of the mean square error, and the sample size. Using these values and a table value, q, the HSD determines the critical difference necessary between the means of any two treatment levels for the means to be significantly different. Once the HSD is computed, the researcher can examine the absolute value of any or all differences between pairs of means from treatment levels to determine whether there is a significant difference. The formula to compute a Tukey's HSD test follows.

Tukey's HSD Test

$$HSD = q_{\alpha,C,N-C}\sqrt{\frac{MSE}{n}}$$

where

$\quad$ MSE = mean square error

$\quad$ n = sample size

$\quad$ $q_{\alpha,C,N-C}$ = critical value of the studentized range distribution from Table A.10

In Demonstration Problem 11.1, an ANOVA test was used to determine that there was an overall significant difference in the mean ages of workers at the three different plants, as evidenced by the F value of 39.8. The sample data for this problem follow.

	Plant		
	1	**2**	**3**
	29	32	25
	27	33	24
	30	31	24
	27	34	25
	28	30	26
Group Means	28.2	32.0	24.8
n_j	5	5	5

Table 11.5

q Values for $\alpha = 0.01$

Degrees of Freedom	Number of Populations				
	2	**3**	**4**	**5**	**...**
1	90	135	164	186	
2	14	19	22.3	24.7	
3	8.26	10.6	12.2	13.3	
4	6.51	8.12	9.17	9.96	
.					
.					
.					
11	4.39	5.14	5.62	5.97	
12	4.32	5.04	5.50	5.84	

Because the sample sizes are equal in this problem, Tukey's HSD test can be used to compute multiple comparison tests between groups 1 and 2, 2 and 3, and 1 and 3. To compute the HSD, the values of MSE, n, and q must be determined. From the solution presented in Demonstration Problem 11.1, the value of MSE is 1.63. The sample size, n_j, is 5. The value of q is obtained from Table A.10 by using

$$\text{Number of Populations} = \text{Number of Treatment Means} = C$$

along with $\text{df}_E = N - C$.

In this problem, the values used to look up q are:

$$C = 3$$
$$\text{df}_E = N - C = 12$$

Table A.10 has a q table for $\alpha = 0.05$ and one for $\alpha = 0.01$. In this problem, $\alpha = 0.01$. Shown in Table 11.5 is a portion of Table A.10 for $\alpha = 0.01$.

For this problem, $q_{0.01,3,12} = 5.04$. HSD is computed as

$$\text{HSD} = q_{\alpha,C,N-C}\sqrt{\frac{\text{MSE}}{n}} = 5.04\sqrt{\frac{1.63}{5}} = 2.88$$

Using this value of HSD, the business researcher can examine the differences between the means from any two groups of plants. Any of the pairs of means that differ by more than 2.88 are significantly different at $\alpha = 0.01$. Here are the differences for all three possible pairwise comparisons:

$$|\bar{x}_1 - \bar{x}_2| = |28.2 - 32.0| = 3.8$$
$$|\bar{x}_1 - \bar{x}_3| = |28.2 - 24.8| = 3.4$$
$$|\bar{x}_2 - \bar{x}_3| = |32.0 - 24.8| = 7.2$$

All three comparisons are greater than the value of HSD, which is 2.88. Thus, the mean ages between any and all pairs of plants are significantly different.

USING THE COMPUTER TO DO MULTIPLE COMPARISONS

Although we mostly use Excel for statistical calculations in this book, Excel does not have a tool for performing Tukey's HSD test. MINITAB, another widely used statistical software program, does contain this tool. Table 11.6 shows the MINITAB output for computing a Tukey's HSD test. The computer output contains the confidence intervals for the differences in pairwise means for pairs of treatment levels. If the confidence interval includes zero, there is no significant difference in the pair of means. (If the interval contains zero, there is a possibility of no difference in the means.) Note in Table 11.6 that all three pairs of confidence intervals contain the same sign throughout the interval. For example, the confidence interval for estimating the difference in means from 1 and 2 is $0.914 \leq \mu_1 - \mu_2 \leq 6.686$. This interval does not contain zero, so we are confident that there is more than a zero difference in the two means. The same holds true for levels 1 and 3 and levels 2 and 3.

Table 11.6

Output for Tukey's HSD

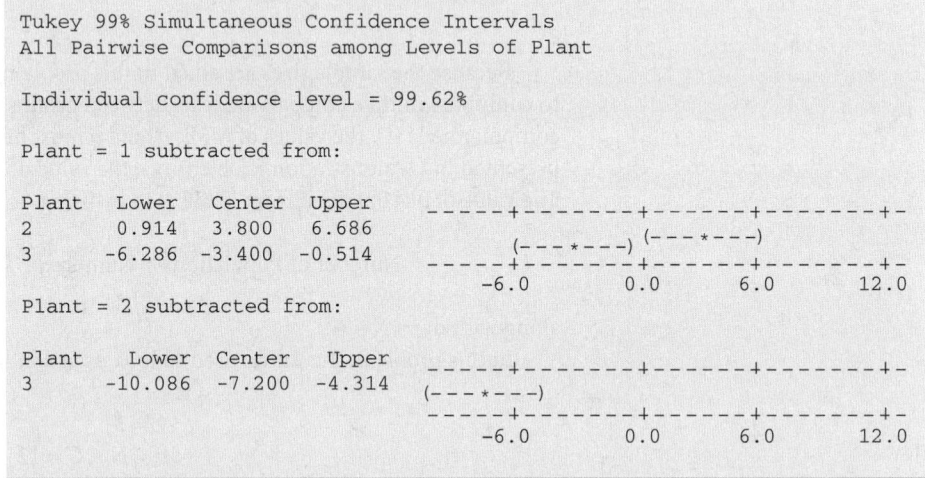

```
Tukey 99% Simultaneous Confidence Intervals
All Pairwise Comparisons among Levels of Plant

Individual confidence level = 99.62%

Plant = 1 subtracted from:

Plant    Lower    Center    Upper
2        0.914    3.800     6.686
3       -6.286   -3.400    -0.514

Plant = 2 subtracted from:

Plant    Lower    Center    Upper
3      -10.086   -7.200    -4.314
```

Demonstration Problem 11.2

A metal-manufacturing firm wants to test the tensile strength of a given metal under varying conditions of temperature. Suppose that in the design phase, the metal is processed under five different temperature conditions and that random samples of size five are taken under each temperature condition. The data follow.

Tensile Strength of Metal Produced Under Five Different Temperature Settings

1	2	3	4	5
2.46	2.38	2.51	2.49	2.56
2.41	2.34	2.48	2.47	2.57
2.43	2.31	2.46	2.48	2.53
2.47	2.40	2.49	2.46	2.55
2.46	2.32	2.50	2.44	2.55

A one-way ANOVA is performed on these data by using MINITAB, with the resulting analysis shown here.

One-way ANOVA: Tensile Strength versus Temp Setting

Source	DF	SS	MS	F	p
Temp Setting	4	0.108024	0.027006	43.70	0.000
Error	20	0.012360	0.000618		
Total	24	0.120384			

Note from the ANOVA table that the *F* value of 43.70 is statistically significant at $\alpha = 0.01$. There is an overall difference in the population means of metal produced under the five temperature settings. Use the data to compute a Tukey's HSD to determine which of the five groups are significantly different from the others.

Solution

From the ANOVA table, the value of MSE is 0.000618. The sample size, n_j, is 5. The number of treatment means, *C*, is 5 and the df_E are 20. With these values and $\alpha = 0.01$, the value of *q* can be obtained from Table A.10:

$$q_{0.01,5,20} = 5.29$$

HSD can be computed as:

$$\text{HSD} = q_{\alpha,C,N-C}\sqrt{\frac{\text{MSE}}{n}} = 5.29\sqrt{\frac{0.000618}{5}} = 0.0588$$

The treatment group means for this problem follow:

Group 1 = 2.446
Group 2 = 2.350
Group 3 = 2.488
Group 4 = 2.468
Group 5 = 2.552

Computing all pairwise differences between these means (in absolute values) produces the following data.

	Group				
	1	**2**	**3**	**4**	**5**
1	—	0.096	0.042	0.022	0.106
2	0.096	—	0.138	0.118	0.202
3	0.042	0.138	—	0.020	0.064
4	0.022	0.118	0.020	—	0.084
5	0.106	0.202	0.064	0.084	—

Comparing these differences to the value of HSD = 0.0588, we can determine that the differences between groups 1 and 2 (0.096), 1 and 5 (0.106), 2 and 3 (0.138), 2 and 4 (0.118), 2 and 5 (0.202), 3 and 5 (0.064), and 4 and 5 (0.084) are significant at $\alpha = 0.01$. Not only is there an overall significant difference in the treatment levels as shown by the ANOVA results, but there is a significant difference in the tensile strength of metal between seven pairs of levels. By studying the magnitudes of the individual treatment levels' means, the steel-manufacturing firm can determine which temperatures result in the greatest tensile strength. The MINITAB output for this Tukey's HSD is shown next. Note that the computer analysis shows significant differences between pairs 1 and 2, 1 and 5, 2 and 3, 2 and 4, 2 and 5, 3 and 5, and 4 and 5 because these confidence intervals do not contain zero. These results are consistent with the manual calculations.

```
Tukey 99% Simultaneous Confidence Intervals
All Pairwise Comparisons among Levels of Temp Setting

Individual confidence level = 99.87%

Temp Setting = 1 subtracted from:
Temp
Setting     Lower      Center     Upper     -----+---------+-------+-------+-
2         -0.15481   -0.09600   -0.03719          (-- *-- )
3         -0.01681    0.04200    0.10081                    (-- *-- )
4         -0.03681    0.02200    0.08081                 (-- *-- )
5          0.04719    0.10600    0.16481                     (-- *-- )
                                            -----+---------+-------+-------+-
                                               -0.15     0.00    0.15     0.30

Temp Setting = 2 subtracted from:
Temp
Setting     Lower      Center     Upper     -----+---------+-------+-------+-
3          0.07919    0.13800    0.19681                     (-- *-- )
4          0.05919    0.11800    0.17681                   (-- *-- )
5          0.14319    0.20200    0.26081                         (-- *-- )
                                            -----+---------+-------+-------+-
                                               -0.15     0.00    0.15     0.30

Temp Setting = 3 subtracted from:
Temp
Setting     Lower      Center     Upper     -----+---------+-------+-------+-
4         -0.07881   -0.02000    0.03881               (-- *-- )
5          0.00519    0.06400    0.12281                   (-- *-- )
                                            -----+---------+-------+-------+-
                                               -0.15     0.00    0.15     0.30

Temp Setting = 4 subtracted from:
Temp
Setting     Lower      Center     Upper     -----+---------+-------+-------+-
5          0.02519    0.08400    0.14281                  (-- *-- )
                                            -----+---------+-------+-------+-
                                               -0.15     0.00    0.15     0.30
```

TUKEY-KRAMER PROCEDURE: THE CASE OF UNEQUAL SAMPLE SIZES

Tukey's HSD was modified by C. Y. Kramer in the mid-1950s to handle situations in which the sample sizes are unequal. The modified version of HSD is sometimes referred to as the **Tukey-Kramer procedure.** The formula for computing the significant differences with this procedure is similar to that for the equal sample sizes, with the exception that the mean square error is divided in half and weighted by the sum of the inverses of the sample sizes under the root sign.

Tukey-Kramer
Formula

$$q_{\alpha,C,N-C}\sqrt{\frac{MSE}{2}\left(\frac{1}{n_r}+\frac{1}{n_s}\right)}$$

where

MSE = mean square error
n_r = sample size for rth sample
n_s = sample size for sth sample
$q_{\alpha,C,N-C}$ = critical value of the studentized range distribution from Table A.10

	Operator	Sample Size	Mean
Table 11.7	1	5	6.3180
Means and Sample Sizes	2	8	6.2775
for the Valves Produced by	3	7	6.4886
Four Operators	4	4	6.2300

As an example of the application of the Tukey-Kramer procedure, consider the machine operator example in Section 11.2. A one-way ANOVA was used to test for any difference in the mean valve opening measurements produced by four different machine operators. An overall F of 10.18 was computed, which was significant at $\alpha = 0.05$. Because the ANOVA hypothesis test is significant and the null hypothesis is rejected, this problem is a candidate for multiple comparisons. Because the sample sizes are not equal, Tukey's HSD cannot be used to determine which pairs are significantly different. However, the Tukey-Kramer procedure can be applied. Shown in Table 11.7 are the means and sample sizes for the valve openings for valves produced by the four different operators.

The mean square error for this problem, MSE, is shown in Table 11.3 as 0.007746. The four operators in the problem represent the four levels of the independent variable. Thus, $C = 4$, $N = 24$, and $N - C = 20$. The value of alpha in the problem is 0.05. With this information, the value of $q_{\alpha,C,N-C}$ is obtained from Table A.10 as:

$$q_{0.05,4,20} = 3.96$$

The distance necessary for the difference in the means of two samples to be statistically significant must be computed by using the Tukey-Kramer procedure for each pair because the sample sizes differ. In this problem with $C = 4$, there are $C(C - 1)/2$ or six possible pairwise comparisons. The computations follow.

For operators 1 and 2:

$$3.96\sqrt{\frac{0.007746}{2}\left(\frac{1}{5} + \frac{1}{8}\right)} = 0.1405$$

The difference between the means of operator 1 and operator 2 is:

$$6.3180 - 6.2775 = 0.0405$$

Because this result is less than the critical difference of 0.1405, there is no significant difference between the average valve openings of valves produced by machine operators 1 and 2.

Table 11.8 reports the critical differences for each of the six pairwise comparisons as computed by using the Tukey-Kramer procedure, along with the absolute value of the actual distances between the means. Any actual distance between means that is greater than the critical distance is significant. As shown in the table, the means of three pairs of samples, operators 1 and 3, operators 2 and 3, and operators 3 and 4, are significantly different.

Table 11.9 shows the MINITAB output for this problem. MINITAB uses the Tukey-Kramer procedure for unequal values of n. As before with the HSD test, MINITAB produces a confidence interval for the differences in means for pairs of treatment levels. If the confidence interval includes zero, there is no significant difference in the pairs of means.

Table 11.8

Results of Pairwise Comparisons for the Machine Operators Example Using the Tukey-Kramer Procedure

Pair	Critical Difference	Actual Difference
1 and 2	0.1405	0.0405
1 and 3	0.1443	0.1706*
1 and 4	0.1653	0.0880
2 and 3	0.1275	0.2111*
2 and 4	0.1509	0.0475
3 and 4	0.1545	0.2586*

*Significant at $\alpha = 0.05$.

Table 11.9

MINITAB Multiple Comparisons in the Machine Operator Example Using the Tukey-Kramer Procedure

```
Tukey 95% Simultaneous Confidence Intervals
All Pairwise Comparisons

Individual confidence level = 98.89%

Operator 1 subtracted from:

              Lower       Center      Upper
Operator 2   -0.18099    -0.04050    0.09999
Operator 3    0.02627     0.17057    0.31487
Operator 4   -0.25332    -0.08800    0.07732


             -----+-------+-------+-------+-
Operator 2             (----*----)
Operator 3                   (----*----)
Operator 4          (----*-----)
             -----+-------+-------+-------+-
               -0.25    0.00     0.25    0.50


Operator 2 subtracted from:
              Lower       Center      Upper
Operator 3    0.08353     0.21107    0.33862
Operator 4   -0.19841    -0.04750    0.10341


             -----+-------+-------+-------+-
Operator 3                   (---·*---)
Operator 4             (---·*---)
             -----+-------+-------+-------+-
               -0.25    0.00     0.25    0.50
Operator 3 subtracted from:

              Lower       Center      Upper
Operator 4   -0.41304    -0.25857   -0.10411


             -----+-------+-------+-------+-
Operator 4  (-----*----)
             -----+-------+-------+-------+-
               -0.25    0.00     0.25    0.50
```

If the signs over the interval are the same (zero is not in the interval), there is a significant difference in the means. Note that the signs over the intervals for pairs (1, 3), (2, 3), and (3, 4) are the same, indicating a significant difference in the means of those three pairs. This conclusion agrees with the results determined through the calculations reported in Table 11.8.

Concept Check

1. Explain why we conduct multiple comparison tests between groups.
2. What can be done to handle multiple comparison tests when the sample sizes are unequal?

11.3 Problems

11.17　Suppose an ANOVA has been performed on a completely randomized design containing six treatment levels. The mean for group 3 is 15.85, and the sample size for group 3 is eight. The mean for group 6 is 17.21, and the sample size for group 6 is seven. MSE is 0.3352. The total number of observations is 46. Compute the significant difference for the means of these two groups by using the Tukey-Kramer procedure. Let $\alpha = 0.05$.

11.18　A completely randomized design has been analyzed by using a one-way ANOVA. There are four treatment groups in the design, and each sample size is six. MSE is equal to 2.389. Using $\alpha = 0.05$, compute Tukey's HSD for this ANOVA.

11.19　Using the results of Problem 11.5, compute a critical value by using the Tukey-Kramer procedure for groups 1 and 2. Use $\alpha = 0.05$. Determine whether there is a significant difference between these two groups.

11.20　Use the Tukey-Kramer procedure to determine whether there is a significant difference between the means of groups 2 and 5 in Problem 11.6. Let $\alpha = 0.01$.

11.21　Using the results from Problem 11.7, compute a Tukey's HSD to determine whether there are any significant differences between group means. Let $\alpha = 0.01$.

11.22　Using Problem 11.8, compute Tukey's HSD and determine whether there is a significant difference in means by using this methodology. Let $\alpha = 0.05$.

11.23　Use the Tukey-Kramer procedure to do multiple comparisons for Problem 11.11. Let $\alpha = 0.01$. State which pairs of machines, if any, produce significantly different mean fills.

11.24　Use Tukey's HSD test to compute multiple comparisons for the data in Problem 11.12. Let $\alpha = 0.01$. State which regions, if any, are significantly different from other regions in mean starting salary figures.

11.25　Using $\alpha = 0.05$, compute critical values using the Tukey-Kramer procedure for the pairwise groups in Problem 11.13. Determine which pairs of groups are significantly different, if any.

11.26　Do multiple comparisons on the data in Problem 11.14 using Tukey's HSD test and $\alpha = 0.05$. State which pairs of cities, if any, have significantly different mean costs.

11.27　Problem 11.16 analyzed the number of weekly hours worked per person at five different plants. An F value of 3.10 was obtained with a probability of 0.0266. Because the probability is less than 0.05, the null hypothesis is rejected at $\alpha = 0.05$. There is an overall difference in the mean weekly hours worked by plant. Which pairs of plants have significant differences in the means, if any? To answer this question, a

MINITAB computer analysis was done. The data follow. Study the output in light of Problem 11.16 and discuss the results.

```
Tukey 95% Simultaneous Confidence Intervals
All Pairwise Comparisons

Individual confidence level = 99.32%

Plant 1 subtracted from:

            Lower    Center   Upper    -----+---------+---------+---------+-
Plant 2   -17.910   -7.722   2.466           (----*-----)
Plant 3    -7.743    3.598  14.939                  (----*-----)
Plant 4   -21.830   -8.665   4.499        (------*-------)
Plant 5   -12.721   -0.921  10.880              (-----*-----)
                                         -----+---------+---------+---------+-
Plant 2 subtracted from:                    -15        0        15        30

            Lower    Center   Upper    -----+---------+---------+---------+-
Plant 3     0.180   11.320  22.460                    (------*----)
Plant 4   -13.935   -0.944  12.048           (------*------)
Plant 5    -4.807    6.801  18.409                (-----*------)
                                         -----+---------+---------+---------+-
Plant 3 subtracted from:                    -15        0        15        30

            Lower    Center   Upper    -----+---------+---------+---------+-
Plant 4   -26.178  -12.263   1.651    (-------*--------)
Plant 5   -17.151   -4.519   8.113         (------*------)
                                         -----+---------+---------+---------+-
Plant 4 subtracted from:                    -15        0        15        30

            Lower    Center   Upper    -----+---------+---------+---------+-
Plant 5    -6.547    7.745  22.036               (------*------)
                                         -----+---------+---------+---------+-
                                            -15        0        15        30
```

Does Regional Ideology Affect a Firm's Definition of Success?

One researcher, G. C. Lodge, proposed that companies pursue different performance goals based on the ideology of their regional culture. L. Thurow went further by suggesting that such regional ideologies drive North American firms to be short-term profit maximizers, Japanese firms to be growth maximizers, and European firms to be a mix of the two.

Three other researchers, J. Katz, S. Werner, and L. Brouthers, decided to test these suggestions by studying 114 international banks from the U.S., the European Union (EU), and Japan listed in the Global 1,000. Specifically, there were 34 banks from the U.S., 45 banks from the EU, and 35 banks from Japan in the study. Financial and market data were gathered and averaged on each bank over a five-year period to limit the effect of single-year variations. All statistics were converted by Morgan Stanley Capital International to U.S. dollar denominations on the same day of each year to ensure consistency of measurement.

The banks were compared on general measures of success such as profitability, capitalization, growth, size, risk, and earnings distribution by specifically examining 11 mea-sures. Eleven one-way ANOVA designs were computed, one for each dependent variable. These included return on equity, return on assets, yield, capitalization, assets, market value, growth, Tobin's Q, price-to-earnings ratio, payout ratio, and risk. The independent variable in each ANOVA was region, with three levels: U.S., EU, and Japan.

In all 11 ANOVAs, there was a significant difference between banks in the three regions ($\alpha = 0.01$), supporting the theme of different financial success goals for different regional cultures. Because of the overall significant differ-ence attained in the ANOVAs, each ANOVA was followed by a Duncan's multiple range test (multiple comparison) to determine which, if any, of the pairs were significantly dif-ferent. These comparisons revealed that U.S. and EU banks maintained significantly higher levels than Japanese banks on return on equity, return on assets, and yield. This result underscores the notion that U.S. and EU banks have more of a short-term profit orientation than do Japanese banks. There was a significant difference in banks from each of the three regions on amount of capitalization. U.S. banks had the highest level of capitalization, followed by EU banks and then Japanese banks. This result may reflect the cultural attitude about how much capital is needed to ensure a sound economy, with U.S. banks maintaining higher levels of capital.

The study found that Japanese banks had significantly higher levels on growth, Tobin's Q, and price-to-earnings ratio than did the other two entities. This result confirms the hypothesis that Japanese firms are more interested in growth. In addition, Japanese banks had a significantly higher asset size and market value of equity than did U.S. banks. The researchers had hypothesized that EU

banks would have a greater portfolio risk than that of U.S. or Japanese banks. They found that EU banks did have significantly higher risk and paid out significantly higher dividends than did either Japanese or U.S. banks.

Source: Adapted from Jeffrey P. Katz, Steve Werner, and Lance Brouthers, "Does Winning Mean the Same Thing around the World? National Ideology and the Performance of Global Competitors," *Journal of Business Research,* vol. 44, no. 2 (February 1999), pp. 117–126.

11.4 THE RANDOMIZED BLOCK DESIGN

POINTS OF INTEREST
This method accounts for and reduces natural variability.

A second research design is the **randomized block design.** The randomized block design is similar to the completely randomized design in that it focuses on one independent variable (treatment variable) of interest. However, the randomized block design also includes a second variable, referred to as a blocking variable, that can be used to control for confounding or concomitant variables.

Confounding variables, or **concomitant variables,** are *variables that are not being controlled by the researcher in the experiment but can have an effect on the outcome of the treatment being studied.* For example, Demonstration Problem 11.2 showed how a completely randomized design could be used to analyze the effects of temperature on the tensile strengths of metal. However, other variables not being controlled by the researcher in this experiment may affect the tensile strength of metal, such as humidity, raw materials, machine, and shift. One way to control for these variables is to include them in the experimental design. The randomized block design can add one of these variables into the analysis as a blocking variable. A **blocking variable** is *a variable that the researcher wants to control but is not the treatment variable of interest.*

One of the first people to use the randomized block design was Sir Ronald A. Fisher. He applied the design to the field of agriculture, where he was interested in studying the growth patterns of varieties of seeds for a given type of plant. The seed variety was his independent variable. However, he realized that as he experimented on different plots of ground, the "block" of ground might make some difference in the experiment. Fisher designated several different plots of ground as blocks, which he controlled as a second variable. Each of the seed varieties was planted on each of the blocks. The main thrust of his study was to compare the seed varieties (independent variable). He merely wanted to control for the difference in plots of ground (blocking variable).

In Demonstration Problem 11.2, examples of blocking variables might be machine number (if several machines are used to make the metal), worker, shift, or day of the week. The researcher probably already knows that different workers or different machines will produce at least slightly different metal tensile strengths because of individual differences. However, designating the variable (machine or worker) as the blocking variable and computing a randomized block design affords the potential for a more powerful analysis. In other experiments, some other possible variables that might be used as blocking variables are gender of subject, age of subject, intelligence of subject, economic level of subject, brand, supplier, or vehicle.

A special case of the randomized block design is the repeated measures design. The **repeated measures design** is *a randomized block design in which each block level is an individual item or person, and that person or item is measured across all treatments.* Thus, where a block level in a randomized block design is night shift, and items produced under different treatment levels on the night shift are measured, in a repeated measures design, a block level might be an individual machine or person; items produced by that person or machine are then randomly chosen across all treatments. Thus, a repeated measure of the person or machine is made across all treatments. This repeated measures design is an extension of the t test for dependent samples presented in Section 10.3.

The sum of squares in a completely randomized design is:

$$SST = SSC + SSE$$

In a randomized block design, the sum of squares is:

$$SST = SSC + SSR + SSE$$

where
SST = sum of squares total
SSC = sum of squares columns (treatment)
SSR = sum of squares rows (blocking)
SSE = sum of squares error

SST and SSC are the same for a given analysis whether a completely randomized design or a randomized block design is used. For this reason, the SSR (blocking effects) comes out of the SSE; that is, some of the error variation in the completely randomized design is accounted for in the blocking effects of the randomized block design, as shown in Figure 11.7. If the error term is reduced, it is possible that the value of F for treatment will increase (the denominator of the F value is decreased). However, if there is not sufficient difference between levels of the blocking variable, the use of a randomized block design can lead to a less powerful result than would a completely randomized design computed on the same problem. Thus, the researcher should seek out blocking variables that he or she believes are significant contributors to variation among measurements of the dependent variable. Figure 11.8 shows the layout of a randomized block design.

In each of the intersections of independent variable and blocking variable in Figure 11.8, one measurement is taken. In the randomized block design, one measurement is given for each treatment level under each blocking level.

The null and alternative hypotheses for the treatment effects in the randomized block design are:

H_0: $\mu_{.1} = \mu_{.2} = \mu_{.3} = \ldots = \mu_{.C}$
H_a: At least one of the treatment means is different from the others.

For the blocking effects, the hypotheses are:

H_0: $\mu_{1.} = \mu_{2.} = \mu_{3.} = \ldots = \mu_{R.}$
H_a: At least one of the blocking means is different from the others.

Figure 11.7

Partitioning the Total Sum of Squares in a Randomized Block Design

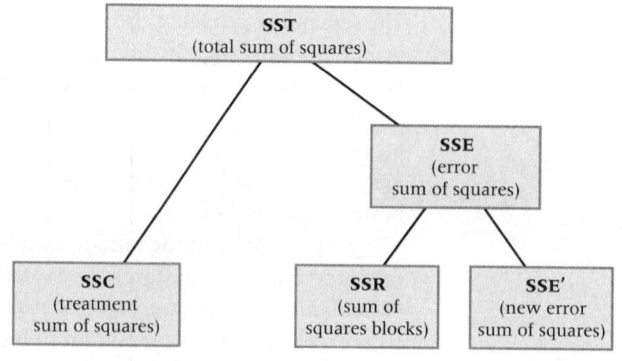

Figure 11.8

A Randomized Block Design

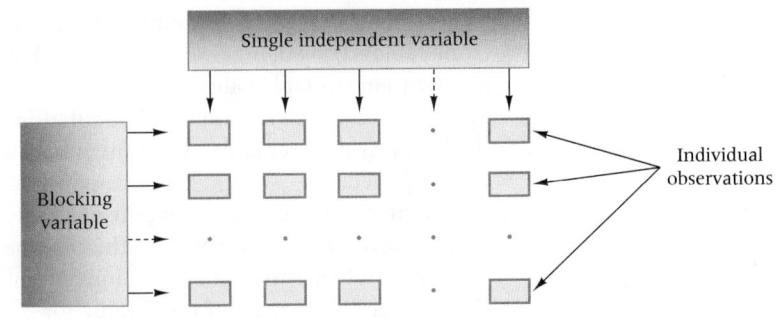

Essentially, we are testing the null hypothesis that the population means of the treatment groups are equal. If the null hypothesis is rejected, at least one of the population means does not equal the others.

The formulas for computing a randomized block design follow.

Formulas for Computing a
Randomized Block Design

$$SSC = n\sum_{j=1}^{C} (\bar{x}_j - \bar{x})^2$$

$$SSR = C\sum_{i=1}^{n} (\bar{x}_i - \bar{x})^2$$

$$SSE = \sum_{i=1}^{n}\sum_{j=1}^{C} (x_{ij} - \bar{x}_j - \bar{x}_i + \bar{x})^2$$

$$SST = \sum_{i=1}^{n}\sum_{j=1}^{C} (x_{ij} - \bar{x})^2$$

where
    i = block group (row)
    j = treatment level (column)
    C = number of treatment levels (columns)
    n = number of observations in each treatment level (number of blocks or rows)
    x_{ij} = individual observation
    $\bar{x}_j$ = treatment (column) mean
    $\bar{x}_i$ = block (row) mean
    $\bar{x}$ = grand mean
    N = total number of observations

$$df_C = C - 1$$

$$df_R = n - 1$$

$$df_E = (C-1)(n-1) = N - n - C + 1$$

$$MSC = \frac{SSC}{C-1}$$

$$MSR = \frac{SSR}{n-1}$$

$$MSE = \frac{SSE}{N-n-C+1}$$

$$F_{treatments} = \frac{MSC}{MSE}$$

$$F_{blocks} = \frac{MSR}{MSE}$$

The observed F value for treatments computed using the randomized block design formula is tested by comparing it to a table F value, which is ascertained from Table A.7 by using α, df_C (treatment), and df_E (error). If the observed F value is greater than the table value, the null hypothesis is rejected for that alpha value. Such a result would indicate that not all population treatment means are equal. At this point, the business researcher can compute multiple comparisons if the null hypothesis has been rejected.

Some researchers also compute an F value for blocks even though the main emphasis in the experiment is on the treatments. The observed F value for blocks is compared to a critical table F value determined from Table A.7 by using α, df_R (blocks), and df_E (error). If the F value for blocks is greater than the critical F value, the null hypothesis that all block population means are equal is rejected. This result tells the business researcher that including the blocking in the design was probably worthwhile and that a significant amount of variance was drawn off from the error term, thus increasing the power of the treatment test. In this text, we have omitted F_{blocks} from the normal presentation and problem solving. We leave the use of this F value to the discretion of the reader.

As an example of the application of the randomized block design, consider a tire company that developed a new tire. The company conducted tread wear tests on the tire to determine whether there is a significant difference in tread wear if the average speed with which the automobile is driven varies. The company set up an experiment in which the independent variable was speed of automobile. There were three treatment levels: slow speed (car is driven at 30 km/h), medium speed (car is driven at 65 km/h), and high speed (car is driven at 100 km/h). Company researchers realized that several possible variables could confound the study. One of these variables was supplier. The company uses five suppliers to provide a major component of the rubber from which the tires are made. To control for this variable experimentally, the researchers used supplier as a blocking variable. Fifteen tires were randomly selected for the study, three from each supplier. Each of the three was assigned to be tested under a different speed condition. The data are given here, along with treatment and block totals. These figures represent tire wear in units of 10,000 km.

Supplier	Speed			Block Means $\bar{x}_i$
	Slow	Medium	Fast	
1	3.7	4.5	3.1	3.77
2	3.4	3.9	2.8	3.37
3	3.5	4.1	3.0	3.53
4	3.2	3.5	2.6	3.10
5	3.9	4.8	3.4	4.03
Treatment Means $\bar{x}_j$	3.54	4.16	2.98	$\bar{x} = 3.56$

To analyze this randomized block design using $\alpha = 0.01$, the computations are as follows.

$$C = 3$$
$$n = 5$$
$$N = 15$$

$$SSC = n\sum_{j=1}^{C}(\bar{x}_j - \bar{x})^2$$
$$= 5[(3.54 - 3.56)^2 + (4.16 - 3.56)^2 + (2.98 - 3.56)^2]$$
$$= 3.484$$

$$\mathrm{SSR} = C \sum_{i=1}^{n} (\bar{x}_i - \bar{x})^2$$

$$= 3[(3.77 - 3.56)^2 + (3.37 - 3.56)^2 + (3.53 - 3.56)^2 + (3.10 - 3.56)^2$$

$$+ (4.03 - 3.56)^2]$$

$$= 1.549$$

$$\mathrm{SSE} = \sum_{i=1}^{n} \sum_{j=1}^{C} (x_{ij} - \bar{x}_j - \bar{x}_i + \bar{x})^2$$

$$= (3.7 - 3.54 - 3.77 + 3.56)^2 + (3.4 - 3.54 - 3.37 + 3.56)^2$$

$$+ \cdots + (2.6 - 2.98 - 3.10 + 3.56)^2 + (3.4 - 2.98 - 4.03 + 3.56)^2$$

$$= 0.143$$

$$\mathrm{SST} = \sum_{i=1}^{n} \sum_{j=1}^{C} (x_{ij} - \bar{x})^2$$

$$= (3.7 - 3.56)^2 + (3.4 - 3.56)^2 + \cdots + (2.6 - 3.56)^2 + (3.4 - 3.56)^2$$

$$= 5.176$$

$$\mathrm{MSC} = \frac{\mathrm{SSC}}{C - 1} = \frac{3.484}{2} = 1.742$$

$$\mathrm{MSR} = \frac{\mathrm{SSR}}{n - 1} = \frac{1.549}{4} = 0.38725$$

$$\mathrm{MSE} = \frac{\mathrm{SSE}}{N - n - C + 1} = \frac{0.143}{8} = 0.017875$$

$$F = \frac{\mathrm{MSC}}{\mathrm{MSE}} = \frac{1.742}{0.017875} = 97.45$$

Source of Variation	SS	df	MS	F
Treatment	3.484	2	1.742	97.45
Block	1.549	4	0.38725	
Error	0.143	8	0.017875	
Total	5.176	14		

For alpha of 0.01, the critical F value is:

$$F_{0.01,2,8} = 8.65$$

Because the observed value of F for treatment (97.45) is greater than this critical F value, the null hypothesis is rejected. At least one of the population means of the treatment levels is not the same as the others; that is, there is a significant difference in tread wear for cars driven at different speeds. If this problem had been set up as a completely randomized design, the SSR would have been part of the SSE. The degrees of freedom for the blocking effects would have been combined with the degrees of freedom of error. Thus, the value of SSE would have been 1.549 + 0.143 = 1.692, and df_E would have been 4 + 8 = 12. These would then have been used to recompute MSE = 1.692/12 = 0.141. The value of F for treatments would have been:

$$F = \frac{\mathrm{MSC}}{\mathrm{MSE}} = \frac{1.742}{0.141} = 12.35$$

Thus, the F value for treatment with the blocking was 97.45 and *without* the blocking was 12.35. By using the random block design, a much larger observed F value was obtained.

Table 11.10

Excel Output for the Tread Wear Example

	A	B	C	D	E	F	G
1	Anova: Two-Factor Without Replication						
2							
3	SUMMARY	Count	Sum	Average	Variance		
4	Row 1	3	11.3000	3.7667	0.4933		
5	Row 2	3	10.1000	3.3667	0.3033		
6	Row 3	3	10.6000	3.5333	0.3033		
7	Row 4	3	9.3000	3.1000	0.2100		
8	Row 5	3	12.1000	4.0333	0.5033		
9							
10	Column 1	5	17.7000	3.5400	0.0730		
11	Column 2	5	20.8000	4.1600	0.2580		
12	Column 3	5	14.9000	2.9800	0.0920		
13							
14							
15	ANOVA						
16	Source of Variation	SS	df	MS	F	P-value	F crit
17	Rows	1.5493	4	0.3873	21.7196	0.0002	7.0061
18	Columns	3.4840	2	1.7420	97.6822	0.0000	8.6491
19	Error	0.1427	8	0.0178			
20							
21	Total	5.1760	14				

USING THE COMPUTER TO ANALYZE RANDOMIZED BLOCK DESIGNS

Excel can analyze a randomized block design. The computer output for the tire tread wear example is displayed in Table 11.10. Excel treats a randomized block design like a two-way ANOVA (Section 11.5) that has only one observation per cell. The Excel output includes sums, averages, and variances for each row and column. The Excel ANOVA table displays the observed F values for the treatment (columns) and the blocks (rows). An important inclusion in the Excel output is the p value for each F, along with the critical (table) F values.

Demonstration Problem 11.3

Suppose a national travel association studied the cost of premium unleaded gas in Canada during a recent summer. From experience, association directors believed there was a significant difference in the average cost of a litre of premium gas among urban areas in different parts of the country. To test this belief, they placed random calls to gas stations in five different cities. In addition, the researchers realized that the brand of gas might make a difference. They were mostly interested in the differences between cities, so they made city their treatment variable. To control for the fact that pricing varies with brand, the researchers included brand as a blocking variable and selected six different brands to participate. The researchers randomly telephoned one gas station for each brand in each city, resulting in 30 measurements (five cities and six brands). Each station operator was asked to report the current cost of a litre of premium unleaded gas at that station. The data are shown here. Test these data by using a randomized block design analysis to determine whether there is a significant difference in the average cost of premium unleaded gas by city. Let $\alpha = 0.01$.

Geographic Region

Brand	Vancouver	Toronto	Montreal	Saskatoon	Calgary	$\bar{x}_i$
A	0.868	0.850	0.845	0.830	0.875	0.854
B	0.858	0.853	0.855	0.838	0.860	0.853
C	0.860	0.853	0.858	0.840	0.863	0.855
D	0.865	0.863	0.850	0.825	0.863	0.853
E	0.865	0.850	0.848	0.848	0.870	0.856
F	0.860	0.858	0.855	0.848	0.873	0.859
$\bar{x}_j$	0.863	0.854	0.852	0.838	0.867	$\bar{x} = 0.855$

Solution

HYPOTHESIZE:

STEP 1. The hypotheses follow.
For treatments:

$H_0: \mu_{.1} = \mu_{.2} = \mu_{.3} = \mu_{.4} = \mu_{.5}$
H_a: At least one of the treatment means is different from the others.

For blocks:

$H_0: \mu_{1.} = \mu_{2.} = \mu_{3.} = \mu_{4.} = \mu_{5.}$
H_a: At least one of the blocking means is different from the others.

TEST:

STEP 2. The appropriate statistical test is the F test in the ANOVA for randomized block designs.

STEP 3. Let $\alpha = 0.01$.

STEP 4. There are four degrees of freedom for the treatment ($C - 1 = 5 - 1 = 4$), five degrees of freedom for the blocks ($n - 1 = 6 - 1 = 5$), and 20 degrees of freedom for error [$(C - 1)(n - 1) = (4)(5) = 20$]. Using these, $\alpha = 0.01$, and Table A.7, we find the critical F values:

$$F_{0.01,4,20} = 4.43 \text{ for treatments}$$
$$F_{0.01,5,20} = 4.10 \text{ for blocks}$$

The decision rule is to reject the null hypothesis for treatments if the observed F value for treatments is greater than 4.43 and to reject the null hypothesis for blocking effects if the observed F value for blocks is greater than 4.10.

STEP 5. The sample data including row and column means and the grand mean are given in the preceding table.

STEP 6.

$$SSC = n\sum_{j=1}^{C}(\bar{x}_j - \bar{x})^2$$
$$= 6[(0.863 - 0.855)^2 + (0.854 - 0.855)^2 + \cdots + (0.867 - 0.855)^2]$$
$$= 0.003032$$

$$SSR = C\sum_{i=1}^{n}(\bar{x}_i - \bar{x})^2$$
$$= 5[(0.854 - 0.855)^2 + (0.853 - 0.855)^2 + \cdots + (0.859 - 0.855)^2]$$
$$= 0.000127$$

$$SSE = \sum_{i=1}^{n} \sum_{j=1}^{C} (x_{ij} - \overline{x}_j - \overline{x}_i + \overline{x})^2$$

$$= (0.868 - 0.863 - 0.854 + 0.855)^2 + (0.858 - 0.863 - 0.853 + 0.855)^2 + \cdots$$

$$+ (0.870 - 0.867 - 0.856 + 0.855)^2 + (0.873 - 0.867 - 0.859 + 0.855)^2$$

$$= 0.000800$$

$$SST = \sum_{i=1}^{n} \sum_{j=1}^{C} (x_{ij} - \overline{x})^2$$

$$= (0.868 - 0.855)^2 + (0.858 - 0.855)^2 + \cdots$$

$$+ (0.870 - 0.855)^2 + (0.873 - 0.855)^2$$

$$= 0.003959$$

$$MSC = \frac{SSC}{C-1} = \frac{0.003032}{4} = 0.000758$$

$$MSR = \frac{SSR}{n-1} = \frac{0.000127}{5} = 0.000025$$

$$MSE = \frac{SSE}{(C-1)(n-1)} = \frac{0.000800}{20} = 0.000040$$

$$F = \frac{MSC}{MSE} = \frac{0.000758}{0.000040} = 18.94$$

Source of Variance	SS	df	MS	F
Treatment	0.003032	4	0.000758	18.94
Block	0.000127	5	0.000025	
Error	0.000800	20	0.000040	
Total	0.003959	29		

ACTION:

STEP 7. Because $F_{treat} = 18.94 > F_{0.01,4,20} = 4.43$, the null hypothesis is rejected for the treatment effects. There is a significant difference in the average price of a litre of premium unleaded gas in various cities.

A glance at the MSR reveals that there appears to be relatively little blocking variance. The result of determining an F value for the blocking effects is:

$$F = \frac{MSR}{MSE} = \frac{0.000025}{0.000040} = 0.63$$

The value of F for blocks is not significant at $\alpha = 0.01$ ($F_{0.01,5,20} = 4.10$). This result indicates that the blocking portion of the experimental design did not contribute significantly to the analysis. If the blocking effects (SSR) are added back into SSE and the df_R are included with df_E, the MSE becomes 0.000037 instead of 0.000040. Using the value 0.000037 in the denominator for the treatment F increases the observed treatment F value to 20.44. Thus, including nonsignificant blocking effects in the original analysis caused a loss of power.

Shown here is the Excel ANOVA table output for this problem.

	A	B	C	D	E	F	G
1	ANOVA						
2	*Source of Variation*	SS	df	MS	F	*P*-value	F crit
3	Rows	0.000127	5	0.000025	0.633004	0.676888	4.102685
4	Columns	0.003032	4	0.000758	18.940656	0.000001	4.430690
5	Error	0.000800	20	0.000040			
6							
7	Total	0.003959	29				

BUSINESS IMPLICATIONS:

STEP 8. The fact that there is a significant difference in the price of gas in different parts of the country can be useful information to decision makers. For example, companies in the ground transportation business are greatly affected by increases in the cost of fuel. Knowledge of price differences in fuel can help these companies plan strategies and routes. Fuel price differences can sometimes be indications of cost-of-living differences or distribution problems, which can affect a company's relocation decision or cost-of-living increases given to employees who transfer to the higher-priced locations. Knowing that the price of gas varies around the country can generate interest among market researchers who might want to study why the differences are there and what drives them. This information can sometimes result in a better understanding of the marketplace.

Concept Check

1. Explain in your own words what a blocking variable is.
2. Consider Problem 11.12. Provide three examples of blocking variables that can be used for that particular experiment.

11.4 Problems

11.28 Use ANOVA to analyze the data from the randomized block design given here. Let $\alpha = 0.05$. State the null and alternative hypotheses and determine whether the null hypothesis is rejected.

		Treatment Level			
		1	2	3	4
	1	23	26	24	24
	2	31	35	32	33
Block	3	27	29	26	27
	4	21	28	27	22
	5	18	25	27	20

11.29 The following data were gathered from a randomized block design. Use $\alpha = 0.01$ to test for a significant difference in the treatment levels. Establish the hypotheses and reach a conclusion about the null hypothesis.

		Treatment Level		
		1	2	3
	1	1.28	1.29	1.29
Block	2	1.40	1.36	1.35
	3	1.15	1.13	1.19
	4	1.22	1.18	1.24

11.30 A randomized block design has a treatment variable with six levels and a blocking variable with 10 blocks. Using this information and $\alpha = 0.05$, complete the following table and reach a conclusion about the null hypothesis.

Source of Variance	SS	df	MS	F
Treatment	2,477.53			
Blocks	3,180.48			
Error	11,661.38			
Total				

11.31   A randomized block design has a treatment variable with four levels and a blocking variable with seven blocks. Using this information and $\alpha = 0.01$, complete the following table and reach a conclusion about the null hypothesis.

Source of Variance	SS	df	MS	F
Treatment	199.48			
Blocks	265.24			
Error	306.59			
Total				

11.32   Safety in motels and hotels is a growing concern among travellers. Suppose a survey was conducted by the National Motel and Hotel Association to determine Canadian travellers' perception of safety in various motel chains. The association chose four different national chains from the economy lodging sector and randomly selected 10 people who had stayed overnight in a motel in each of the four chains in the past two years. Each selected traveller was asked to rate each motel chain on a scale from 0 to 100 to indicate how safe he or she felt at that motel. A score of 0 indicates completely unsafe and a score of 100 indicates perfectly safe. The scores follow. Test this randomized block design to determine whether there is a significant difference in the safety ratings of the four motels. Use $\alpha = 0.05$.

Traveller	Motel 1	Motel 2	Motel 3	Motel 4
1	40	30	55	45
2	65	50	80	70
3	60	55	60	60
4	20	40	55	50
5	50	35	65	60
6	30	30	50	50
7	55	30	60	55
8	70	70	70	70
9	65	60	80	75
10	45	25	45	50

11.33   In recent years, the debate over the Canadian economy has been constant. The electorate seems somewhat divided as to whether the economy is in a recovery or not. Suppose a survey was undertaken to ascertain whether the perception of economic recovery in Nova Scotia differs according to political affiliation. People were selected for the survey from the Liberal party, the PC party, and the NDP. A 25-point scale was developed in which respondents gave a score of 25 if they felt the economy was definitely in complete recovery, a 0 if the economy was definitely not in a recovery, and some value in between for more uncertain responses. To control for differences in socioeconomic class, a blocking variable was maintained using five different socioeconomic categories. The data are given here in the form of a randomized block design. Use $\alpha = 0.01$ to determine whether there is a significant difference in mean responses according to political affiliation.

| Socioeconomic Class | Political Affiliation | | |
	Liberal	PC	NDP
Upper	11	5	8
Upper middle	15	9	8
Middle	19	14	15
Lower middle	16	12	10
Lower	9	8	7

11.34 As part of a manufacturing process, a plastic container is supposed to be filled with 46 ml of saltwater solution. The plant has three machines that fill the containers. Managers are concerned that the machines might not be filling the containers with the same amount of saltwater solution, so they set up a randomized block design to test this concern. A pool of five machine operators operates each of the three machines at different times. Company technicians randomly select five containers filled by each machine (one container for each of the five operators). The measurements are gathered and analyzed. The output from this analysis follows. What was the structure of the design? How many blocks were there? How many treatment classifications? Is there a statistical difference in the treatment means? Are the blocking effects significant? Discuss the implications of the output.

Two-way ANOVA: Measurement versus Machine, Operator

Source	df	SS	MS	F	p
Machine	2	78.30	39.15	6.72	0.019
Operator	4	5.09	1.27	0.22	0.807
Error	8	46.66	5.83		
Total	14	130.06			

11.35 The comptroller of a company is interested in determining whether the average length of long distance calls by managers varies according to type of telephone. A randomized block design experiment is set up in which a long distance call by each of five managers is sampled for four different types of telephones: cellular, computer, regular, and cordless. The treatment is type of telephone and the blocks are the managers. The results of the analysis by Excel are shown here. Discuss the results and any implications they might have for the company.

ANOVA: Two-Factor without Replication

	A	B	C	D	E	F	G
1	ANOVA						
2							
3	*Source of Variation*	SS	df	MS	F	P-value	F crit
4	Managers	11.3346	4	2.8336	12.74	0.00028	3.26
5	Phone Type	10.6043	3	3.5348	15.89	0.00018	3.49
6	Error	2.6696	12	0.2225			
7	Total	24.6085	19				

11.5 A FACTORIAL DESIGN (TWO-WAY ANOVA)

Some experiments are designed so that *two or more treatments* (independent variables) *are explored simultaneously.* Such experimental designs are referred to as **factorial designs.** In factorial designs, *every level of each treatment is studied under the conditions of every level of all other treatments.* Factorial designs can be arranged such that three, four, or *n* treatments or independent variables are studied simultaneously in the same experiment. As an example, consider the valve opening data in Table 11.1. The mean valve opening for the 24 measurements is 6.34 cm. However, every valve but one in the sample measures something other than the mean. Why? Company management realizes that valves at this firm are made on different machines, by different operators, on different shifts, on different days, with raw materials from different suppliers. Business researchers who are interested in finding the sources of variation might decide to set up a factorial design that incorporates all five of these independent variables in one study. In this text, we explore the factorial designs with two treatments only.

ADVANTAGES OF THE FACTORIAL DESIGN

POINTS OF INTEREST
In factorial design, the total variability is allocated among the different sources at the same time, saving time and effort.

If two independent variables are analyzed by using a completely randomized design, the effects of each variable are explored separately (one per design). Thus, it takes two completely randomized designs to analyze the effects of the two independent variables. By using a factorial design, the business researcher can analyze both variables at the same time in one design, saving the time and effort of doing two different analyses and minimizing the experimentwise error rate.

Some business researchers use the factorial design as a way to control confounding or concomitant variables in a study. By building variables into the design, the researcher attempts to control for the effects of multiple variables in the experiment. With the completely randomized design, the variables are studied in isolation. With the factorial design, there is potential for increased power over the completely randomized design because the additional effects of the second variable are removed from the error sum of squares.

The researcher can explore the possibility of interaction between the two treatment variables in a two-factor factorial design if multiple measurements are taken under every combination of levels of the two treatments. Interaction will be discussed later.

Factorial designs with two treatments are similar to randomized block designs. However, whereas randomized block designs focus on one treatment variable and *control* for a blocking effect, a two-treatment factorial design focuses on the effects of both variables. Because the randomized block design contains only one measure for each (treatment-block) combination, interaction cannot be analyzed in randomized block designs.

FACTORIAL DESIGNS WITH TWO TREATMENTS

The structure of a two-treatment factorial design is featured in Figure 11.9. Note that there are two independent variables (two treatments) and that there is an intersection of each level of each treatment. These intersections are referred to as *cells*. One treatment is arbitrarily designated as the *row* treatment (forming the rows of the design), and the other treatment is designated as the *column* treatment (forming the columns of the design). Although it is possible to analyze factorial designs with unequal numbers of items in the cells, the analysis of unequal cell designs is beyond the scope of this text. All factorial designs discussed here have cells of equal size.

Treatments (independent variables) of factorial designs must have at least two levels each. The simplest factorial design is a 2×2 factorial design, where each treatment has

Figure 11.9

Two-Way Factorial Design

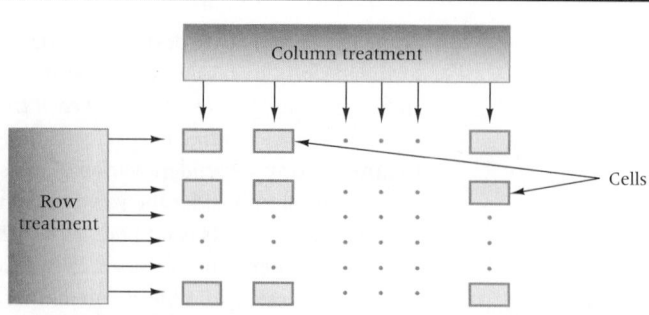

two levels. If such a factorial design were diagrammed in the manner of Figure 11.9, it would include two rows and two columns, forming four cells.

In this section, we study only factorial designs with $n > 1$ measurements for each combination of treatment levels (cells). This approach allows us to attempt to measure the interaction of the treatment variables. As with the completely randomized design and the randomized block design, a factorial design contains only *one* dependent variable.

APPLICATIONS

Many applications of the factorial design are possible in business research. For example, the natural gas industry can design an experiment to study usage rates and how they are affected by temperature and precipitation. Theorizing that the outside temperature and type of precipitation make a difference in natural gas usage, industry researchers can gather usage measurements for a given community over a variety of temperature and precipitation conditions. At the same time, they can make an effort to determine whether certain types of precipitation, combined with certain temperature levels, affect usage rates differently than other combinations of temperature and precipitation (interaction effects).

Stock market analysts can select a company from an industry such as the construction industry and observe the behaviour of its shares under different conditions. A factorial design can be set up by using volume of the stock market and prime interest rate as two independent variables. For volume of the market, business researchers can select some days when the volume is up from the day before, some days when the volume is down from the day before, and some days when the volume is essentially the same as on the preceding day. These groups of days would constitute three levels of the independent variable, market volume. Business researchers can do the same thing with prime rate. Levels can be selected such that the prime rate is (1) up, (2) down, or (3) essentially the same. For the dependent variable, the researchers would measure how much the company's share price rises or falls on those randomly selected days (share price change). Using the factorial design, the business researcher can determine whether share price changes are different under various levels of market volume, whether share price changes are different under various levels of the prime interest rate, and whether share price changes react differently under various combinations of volume and prime rate (interaction effects).

STATISTICALLY TESTING THE FACTORIAL DESIGN

ANOVA is used to analyze data gathered from factorial designs. For factorial designs with two factors (independent variables), a **two-way ANOVA** is used to test hypotheses statistically. The following hypotheses are tested by a two-way ANOVA.

Row effects:	H_o: Row means are all equal.
	H_a: At least one row mean is different from the others.
Column effects:	H_o: Column means are all equal.
	H_a: At least one column mean is different from the others.
Interaction effects:	H_o: Interaction effects are zero.
	H_a: An interaction effect is present.

Formulas for computing a two-way ANOVA are given in the box below. These formulas are computed in a manner similar to computations for the completely randomized design and the randomized block design. F values are determined for three effects:

1. Row effects
2. Column effects
3. Interaction effects

The row effects and the column effects are sometimes referred to as the main effects. Although F values are determined for these main effects, an F value is also computed for interaction effects. Using these observed F values, the researcher can make a decision about the null hypotheses for each effect.

Each of these observed F values is compared to a table F value. The table F value is determined by α, df_{num}, and df_{denom}. The degrees of freedom for the numerator (df_{num}) are determined by the effect being studied. If the observed F value is for columns, the degrees of freedom for the numerator are $C - 1$. If the observed F value is for rows, the degrees of freedom for the numerator are $R - 1$. If the observed F value is for interaction, the degrees of freedom for the numerator are $(R - 1)(C - 1)$. The number of degrees of freedom for the denominator of the table value for each of the three effects is the same: the error degrees of freedom, $RC(n - 1)$. The table F values (critical F) for a two-way ANOVA follow.

Table F Values for a Two-Way ANOVA		
	Row effects:	$F_{\alpha, R-1, RC(n-1)}$
	Column effects:	$F_{\alpha, C-1, RC(n-1)}$
	Interaction effects:	$F_{\alpha, (R-1)(C-1), RC(n-1)}$

Formulas for Computing a Two-Way ANOVA

$$SSR = nC \sum_{i=1}^{R} (\bar{x}_i - \bar{x})^2$$

$$SSC = nR \sum_{j=1}^{C} (\bar{x}_j - \bar{x})^2$$

$$SSI = n \sum_{i=1}^{R} \sum_{j=1}^{C} (\bar{x}_{ij} - \bar{x}_i - \bar{x}_j + \bar{x})^2$$

$$SSE = \sum_{i=1}^{R} \sum_{j=1}^{C} \sum_{k=1}^{n} (x_{ijk} - \bar{x}_{ij})^2$$

$$SST = \sum_{i=1}^{R} \sum_{j=1}^{C} \sum_{k=1}^{n} (x_{ijk} - \bar{x})^2$$

$$df_R = R - 1$$

$$df_C = C - 1$$

$$df_I = (R - 1)(C - 1)$$

$$df_E = RC(n - 1)$$

$$df_T = N - 1$$

$$MSR = \frac{SSR}{R - 1}$$

$$MSC = \frac{SSC}{C - 1}$$

$$MSI = \frac{SSI}{(R - 1)(C - 1)}$$

$$MSE = \frac{SSE}{RC(n - 1)}$$

$$F_R = \frac{MSR}{MSE}$$

$$F_C = \frac{MSC}{MSE}$$

$$F_I = \frac{MSI}{MSE}$$

where

n = number of observations per cell
C = number of column treatments
R = number of row treatments
i = row treatment level
j = column treatment level
k = cell member
x_{ijk} = individual observation
$\bar{x}_{ij}$ = cell mean
$\bar{x}_i$ = row mean
$\bar{x}_j$ = column mean
$\bar{x}$ = grand mean

INTERACTION

POINTS OF INTEREST
Measuring interaction effects between treatments is one of the key features in factorial design.

As noted before, along with testing the effects of the two treatments in a factorial design, it is possible to test for the interaction effects of the two treatments whenever multiple measures are taken in each cell of the design. **Interaction** occurs *when the effects of one treatment vary according to the levels of treatment of the other effect.* For example, in a study examining the impact of temperature and humidity on a manufacturing process, it is possible that temperature and humidity will interact in such a way that the effect of temperature on the process varies with the humidity. Low temperatures might not be a significant manufacturing factor when humidity is low but might be a factor when humidity is high. Similarly, high temperatures might be a factor with low humidity but not with high humidity.

As another example, suppose a business researcher is studying the amount of red meat consumed by families per month and is examining economic class and religion as two independent variables. Class and religion might interact in such a way that with certain religions, economic class does not matter in the consumption of red meat, but with other religions, class does make a difference.

In terms of the factorial design, interaction occurs when the pattern of cell means in one row (going across columns) varies from the pattern of cell means in other rows. This variation indicates that the differences in column effects depend on which row is being examined. Hence, an interaction of the rows and columns occurs. The same thing can happen when the pattern of cell means within a column is different from the pattern of cell means in other columns.

Interaction can be depicted graphically by plotting the cell means within each row (and can also be done by plotting the cell means within each column). The means within each row (or column) are then connected by a line. If the broken lines for the rows (or columns) are parallel, no interaction is indicated.

Figure 11.10 is a graph of the means for each cell in each row in a 2 × 3 (2 rows, 3 columns) factorial design with interaction. Note that the lines connecting the means in each

Figure 11.10

A 2 × 3 Factorial Design with Interaction

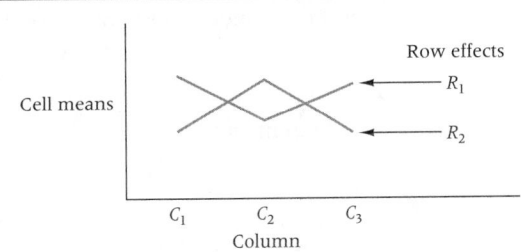

Figure 11.11

A 2 × 3 Factorial Design with Some Interaction

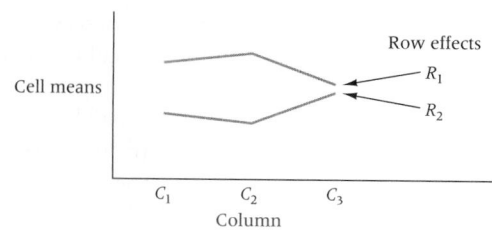

Figure 11.12

A 2 × 3 Factorial Design with No Interaction

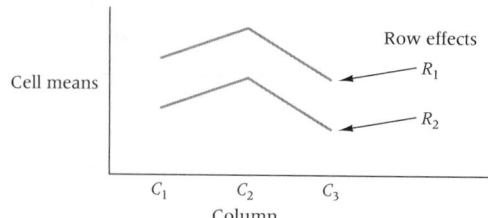

row cross each other. In Figure 11.11, the lines converge, indicating the likely presence of some interaction. Figure 11.12 depicts a 2 × 3 factorial design with no interaction.

When the interaction effects are significant, the main effects (row and column) are confounded and should not be analyzed in the usual manner. In this case, it is not possible to state unequivocally that the row effects or the column effects are significantly different because the difference in means of one main effect varies according to the level of the other main effect (interaction is present). Some specific procedures are recommended for examining main effects when significant interaction is present. However, these techniques are beyond the scope of material presented here. Hence, in this text, whenever interaction effects are present (F_{inter} is significant), the researcher should *not* attempt to interpret the main effects (F_{row} and F_{col}).

As an example of a factorial design, consider the fact that at the end of a financially successful fiscal year, CEOs must often decide whether to award a dividend to stockholders or to make a company investment. One factor in this decision might be whether attractive investment opportunities are available.* To determine whether this factor is important, business researchers randomly select 24 CEOs and ask them to rate how important "availability of profitable investment opportunities" is in deciding whether to pay dividends or invest. The CEOs are requested to respond to this item on a scale from 0 to 4, where 0 = no importance, 1 = slight importance, 2 = moderate importance, 3 = great importance, and 4 = maximum importance. The 0–4 response is the dependent variable in the experimental design.

The business researchers are concerned that where the company's shares are traded (New York Stock Exchange, Toronto Stock Exchange, and over the counter) might make a difference in the CEOs' response to the question. In addition, the business researchers believe that how shareholders are informed of dividends (annual reports versus presentations) might affect the outcome of the experiment. Thus, a two-way ANOVA is set up with "where the company's shares are traded" and "how shareholders are informed of dividends" as the two independent variables. The variable "how shareholders are informed of dividends" has two treatment levels, or classifications.

1. Annual/quarterly reports
2. Presentations to analysts

*Adapted from H. Kent Baker, "Why Companies Pay No Dividends," *Akron Business and Economic Review*, vol. 20 (Summer 1989), pp. 48–61.

The variable "where company shares are traded" has three treatment levels, or classifications.

1. New York Stock Exchange
2. Toronto Stock Exchange
3. Over the counter

This factorial design is a 2 × 3 design (2 rows, 3 columns) with four measurements (ratings) per cell, as shown in the following table.

		Where Company Shares Are Traded			
		New York Stock Exchange	Toronto Stock Exchange	Over the Counter	$\bar{x}_i =$
How Shareholders Are Informed of Dividends	Annual/Quarterly Reports	2 1 2 1 $\bar{x}_{11} = 1.5$	2 3 3 2 $\bar{x}_{12} = 2.5$	4 3 4 3 $\bar{x}_{13} = 3.5$	2.5
	Presentations to Analysts	2 3 1 2 $\bar{x}_{21} = 2.0$	3 3 2 4 $\bar{x}_{22} = 3.0$	4 4 3 4 $\bar{x}_{23} = 3.75$	2.9167
	$\bar{x}_j =$	1.75	2.75	3.625	
				$\bar{x} = 2.7083$	

These data are analyzed by using a two-way ANOVA and $\alpha = 0.05$:

$$SSR = nC\sum_{i=1}^{R}(\bar{x}_i - \bar{x})^2$$
$$= 4(3)[(2.5 - 2.7083)^2 + (2.9167 - 2.7083)^2] = 1.0418$$

$$SSC = nR\sum_{j=1}^{C}(\bar{x}_j - \bar{x})$$
$$= 4(2)[(1.75 - 2.7083)^2 + (2.75 - 2.7083)^2 + (3.625 - 2.7083)^2 = 14.0833$$

$$SSI = \sum_{i=1}^{R}\sum_{j=1}^{C}(\bar{x}_{ij} - \bar{x}_i - \bar{x}_j + \bar{x})^2$$
$$= 4[(1.5 - 2.5 - 1.75 + 2.7083)^2 + (2.5 - 2.5 - 2.75 + 2.7083)^2$$
$$+ (3.5 - 2.5 - 3.625 + 2.7083)^2 + (2.0 - 2.9167 - 1.75 + 2.7083)^2$$
$$+ (3.0 - 2.9167 - 2.75 + 2.7083)^2 + (3.75 - 2.9167 - 3.625 + 2.7083)^2] = 0.0833$$

$$SSE = \sum_{i=1}^{R}\sum_{j=1}^{C}\sum_{k=1}^{n}(x_{ijk} - \bar{x}_{ij})^2$$
$$= (2 - 1.5)^2 + (1 - 1.5)^2 + \cdots + (3 - 3.75)^2 + (4 - 3.75)^2 = 7.7500$$

$$SST = \sum_{i=1}^{R}\sum_{j=1}^{C}\sum_{k=1}^{n}(x_{ijk} - \bar{x})^2$$
$$= (2 - 2.7083)^2 + (1 - 2.7083)^2 + \cdots + (3 - 2.7083)^2 + (4 - 2.7083)^2 = 22.9583$$

$$MSR = \frac{SSR}{R-1} = \frac{1.0418}{1} = 1.0418$$

$$MSC = \frac{SSC}{C-1} = \frac{14.0833}{2} = 7.0417$$

$$MSI = \frac{SSI}{(R-1)(C-1)} = \frac{0.0833}{2} = 0.0417$$

$$MSE = \frac{SSE}{RC(n-1)} = \frac{7.7500}{18} = 0.4306$$

$$F_R = \frac{MSR}{MSE} = \frac{1.0418}{0.4306} = 2.42$$

$$F_C = \frac{MSC}{MSE} = \frac{7.0417}{0.4306} = 16.35$$

$$F_I = \frac{MSI}{MSE} = \frac{0.0417}{0.4306} = 0.10$$

Source of Variation	SS	df	MS	F
Row	1.0418	1	1.0418	2.42
Column	14.0833	2	7.0417	16.35*
Interaction	0.0833	2	0.0417	0.10
Error	7.7500	18	0.4306	
Total	22.9583	23		

*Denotes significance at $\alpha = 0.01$.

The critical F value for the interaction effects at $\alpha = 0.05$ is:

$$F_{0.05,2,18} = 3.55$$

The observed F value for interaction effects is 0.10. Because this value is less than the critical table value (3.55), no significant interaction effects are evident. Because no significant interaction effects are present, it is possible to examine the main effects.

The critical F value of the row effects at $\alpha = 0.05$ is $F_{0.05,1,18} = 4.41$. The observed F value of 2.42 is less than the table value. Hence, no significant row effects are present.

The critical F value of the column effects at $\alpha = 0.05$ is $F_{0.05,2,18} = 3.55$. This value is coincidently the same as the critical table value for interaction because in this problem the degrees of freedom are the same for interaction and column effects. The observed F value for columns (16.35) is greater than this critical value. Hence, a significant difference in row effects is evident at $\alpha = 0.05$.

A significant difference is noted in the CEOs' mean ratings of the item "availability of profitable investment opportunities" according to where the company's shares are traded. A cursory examination of the means for the three levels of the column effects (where shares are traded) reveals that the lowest mean rating was from CEOs whose company traded shares on the New York Stock Exchange. The highest mean rating was from CEOs whose company traded shares over the counter. Using multiple comparison techniques, the business researchers can statistically test for differences in the means of these three groups.

Because the sample sizes within each column are equal, Tukey's HSD test can be used to compute multiple comparisons. The value of MSE is 0.431 for this problem. In testing the column means with Tukey's HSD test, the value of n is the number of items in a column, which is eight. The number of treatments is $C = 3$ for columns and $N - C = 24 - 3 = 21$.

With these two values and $\alpha = 0.05$, a value for $q_{\alpha, C, N-C}$ can be determined from Table A.10:

$$q_{\alpha, C, N-C} = 3.58$$

From these values, the HSD can be computed:

$$\text{HSD} = q_{\alpha, C, N-C}\sqrt{\frac{\text{MSE}}{n}} = 3.58\sqrt{\frac{0.431}{8}} = 0.831$$

The mean ratings for the three columns are:

$$\bar{x}_1 = 1.75, \; \bar{x}_2 = 2.75, \; \bar{x}_3 = 3.625$$

The absolute value of the differences between means are as follows:

$$|\bar{x}_1 - \bar{x}_2| = |1.75 - 2.75| = 1.00$$

$$|\bar{x}_1 - \bar{x}_3| = |1.75 - 3.625| = 1.875$$

$$|\bar{x}_2 - \bar{x}_3| = |2.75 - 3.625| = 0.875$$

All three differences are greater than 0.831 and are therefore significantly different at $\alpha = 0.05$ by the HSD test. Where a company's shares are traded makes a difference in the way a CEO responds to the question.

USING A COMPUTER TO DO A TWO-WAY ANOVA

A two-way ANOVA can be computed using Excel. The Excel output for two-way ANOVA with replications on the CEO dividend example is included in Figure 11.13. The Excel

Figure 11.13

Excel Output for the CEO Dividend Problem

	A	B	C	D	E	F	G
1	Anova: Two-Factor with Replication						
2							
3	SUMMARY	NYSE	TSE	OTC	Total		
4	A.Q. Reports						
5	Count	4	4	4	12		
6	Sum	6	10	14	30		
7	Average	1.5	2.5	3.5	2.5		
8	Variance	0.3333	0.3333	0.3333	1		
9							
10	Pres. to Analysts						
11	Count	4	4	4	12		
12	Sum	8	12	15	35		
13	Average	2	3	3.75	2.9167		
14	Variance	0.6667	0.6667	0.25	0.9924		
15							
16	Total						
17	Count	8	8	8			
18	Sum	14	22	29			
19	Average	1.75	2.75	3.6350			
20	Variance	0.5	0.5	0.2679			
21							
22	ANOVA						
23	*Source of Variation*	SS	df	MS	F	P-value	F crit
24	Sample	1.04167	1	1.04167	2.42	0.13725	4.41
25	Columns	14.0833	2	7.04167	16.35	8.9E-05	3.55
26	Interaction	0.08333	2	0.04167	0.10	0.90823	3.55
27	Within	7.75	18	0.43056			
28							
29	Total	22.9583	23				

output contains cell, column, and row means along with observed F values for rows (sample), columns, and interaction. The Excel output also contains p values and critical F values for each of these F's. Note that the output here is virtually identical to the findings obtained by the manual calculations.

Demonstration Problem 11.4

Some theorists believe that training warehouse workers can reduce absenteeism.* Suppose an experimental design is structured to test this belief. Warehouses in which training sessions have been held for workers are selected for the study. The four types of warehouses are (1) general merchandise, (2) commodity, (3) bulk storage, and (4) cold storage. The training sessions are differentiated by length. Researchers identify three levels of training sessions according to the length of sessions: (1) 1–20 days, (2) 21–50 days, and (3) more than 50 days. Three warehouse workers are selected randomly for each particular combination of type of warehouse and session length. The workers are monitored for the next year to determine how many days they are absent. The resulting data are in the following 4×3 design (4 rows, 3 columns) structure. Using this information, calculate a two-way ANOVA to determine whether there are any significant differences in effects. Use $\alpha = 0.05$.

Solution

HYPOTHESIZE:

STEP 1. The following hypotheses are being tested.
For row effects:

$$H_0: \mu_{1.} = \mu_{2.} = \mu_{3.} = \mu_{4.}$$
$$H_a: \text{At least one of the row means is different from the others.}$$

For column effects:

$$H_0: \mu_{.1} = \mu_{.2} = \mu_{.3}$$
$$H_a: \text{At least one of the column means is different from the others.}$$

For interaction effects:

$$H_0: \text{The interaction effects are zero.}$$
$$H_a: \text{There is an interaction effect.}$$

TEST:

STEP 2. The two-way ANOVA with the F test is the appropriate statistical test.
STEP 3. $\alpha = 0.05$
STEP 4.

$$df_{rows} = 4 - 1 = 3$$
$$df_{columns} = 3 - 1 = 2$$
$$df_{interacton} = (3)(2) = 6$$
$$df_{error} = (4)(3)(2) = 24$$

For row effects, $F_{0.05,3,24} = 3.01$; for column effects, $F_{0.05,2,24} = 3.40$; and for interaction effects, $F_{0.05,6,24} = 2.51$. For each of these effects, if any observed F value is greater than its associated critical F value, the respective null hypothesis will be rejected.

---

*Adapted from Paul R. Murphy and Richard F. Poist, "Managing the Human Side of Public Warehousing: An Overview of Modern Practices," *Transportation Journal*, vol. 31 (Spring 1992), pp. 54–63.

STEP 5.

		Length of Training Session (Days)		
		1–20	21–50	More than 50	$\bar{x}_r$
	General Merchandise	3 4.5 4	2 2.5 2	2.5 1 1.5	2.5556
	Commodity	5 4.5 4	1 3 2.5	0 1.5 2	2.6111
Types of Warehouses	Bulk Storage	2.5 3 3.5	1 3 1.5	3.5 3.5 4	2.8333
	Cold Storage	2 2 3	5 4.5 2.5	4 4.5 5	3.6111
	$\bar{x}_c$	3.4167	2.5417	2.75	

$$\bar{x} = 2.9028$$

STEP 6. The Excel (ANOVA table only) output for this problem follows:

	A	B	C	D	E	F	G
1	ANOVA						
2	Source of Variation	SS	df	MS	F	P-value	F crit
3	Sample	6.409722	3	2.136574	3.46	0.032205	3.01
4	Columns	5.013889	2	2.506944	4.06	0.030372	3.40
5	Interaction	33.15278	6	5.525463	8.94	0.000035	2.51
6	Within	14.83333	24	0.618056			
7							
8	Total	59.40972	35				

ACTION:

STEP 7. Looking at the source of variation table, we must first examine the interaction effects. The observed F value for interaction is 8.94. The observed F value for interaction is greater than the critical F value. The interaction effects are statistically significant at $\alpha = 0.05$. The p value for interaction shown in Excel is 0.000035. The interaction effects are significant at $\alpha = 0.0001$. The business researcher should not bother to examine the main effects because the significant interaction confounds the main effects.

BUSINESS IMPLICATIONS:

STEP 8. The significant interaction effects indicate that certain warehouse types in combination with certain lengths of training session result in different absenteeism rates than do other combinations of levels for these two variables. Using the cell means shown here, we can depict the interactions graphically.

	Length of Training Session (Days)		
	1–20	21–50	More than 50
General Merchandise	3.8	2.2	1.7
Commodity	4.5	2.2	1.2
Bulk Storage	3.0	1.8	3.7
Cold Storage	2.3	4.0	4.5

Types of Warehouses (row label)

The following is a graph of the interaction.

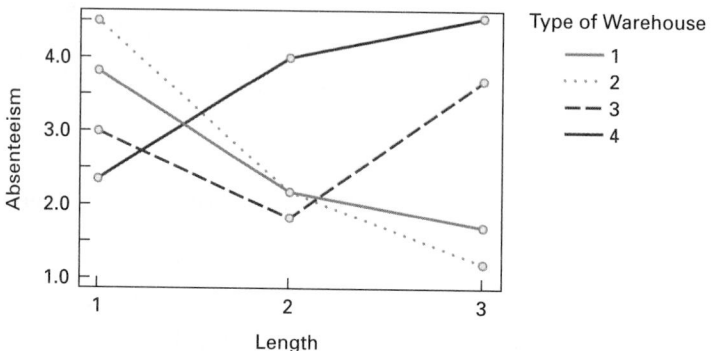

Note the intersecting and crossing lines, which indicate interaction. Under the short-length training sessions (1), cold storage workers had the lowest rate of absenteeism and workers at commodity warehouses had the highest. However, for medium-length sessions (2), cold storage workers had the highest rate of absenteeism and bulk storage had the lowest. For the longest training sessions (3), commodity warehouse workers had the lowest rate of absenteeism, even though these workers had the highest rate of absenteeism for short-length sessions. Thus, the rate of absenteeism for workers at a particular type of warehouse depended on length of session. There was an interaction between type of warehouse and length of session. This graph could be constructed with the row levels along the bottom axis instead of the column levels.

Concept Check

1. When are factorial designs used?
2. Describe a business research situation where a factorial design application is possible.
3. Draw a 2 × 3 factorial design graph where interaction is present. What do we mean when we say that interaction does exist?
4. Draw a 2 × 3 factorial design graph where interaction is not present. What do we mean when we say that interaction does not exist?

11.5 Problems

11.36   Describe the following factorial design. How many independent and dependent variables are there? How many levels are there for each treatment? If the data were known, could interaction be determined from this design? Compute all degrees of freedom. Each data value is represented by an x.

Variable 1

x_{111}	x_{121}	x_{131}	x_{141}
x_{112}	x_{122}	x_{132}	x_{142}
x_{113}	x_{123}	x_{133}	x_{143}

Variable 2

x_{211}	x_{221}	x_{231}	x_{241}
x_{212}	x_{222}	x_{232}	x_{242}
x_{213}	x_{223}	x_{233}	x_{243}

11.37 Describe the following factorial design. How many independent and dependent variables are there? How many levels are there for each treatment? If the data were known, could interaction be determined from this design? Compute all degrees of freedom. Each data value is represented by an x.

Variable 1

x_{111}	x_{121}	x_{131}
x_{112}	x_{122}	x_{132}
x_{211}	x_{221}	x_{231}
x_{212}	x_{222}	x_{232}

Variable 2

x_{311}	x_{321}	x_{331}
x_{312}	x_{322}	x_{332}
x_{411}	x_{421}	x_{431}
x_{412}	x_{422}	x_{432}

11.38 Complete the following two-way ANOVA table. Determine the critical table F values and reach conclusions about the hypotheses for effects. Let $\alpha = 0.05$.

Source of Variance	SS	df	MS	F
Row	126.98	3		
Column	37.49	4		
Interaction	380.82			
Error	733.65	60		
Total				

11.39 Complete the following two-way ANOVA table. Determine the critical table F values and reach conclusions about the hypotheses for effects. Let $\alpha = 0.05$.

Source of Variance	SS	df	MS	F
Row	1.047	1		
Column	3.844	3		
Interaction	0.773			
Error	_____	__		
Total	12.632	23		

11.40 The data gathered from a two-way factorial design follow. Use the two-way ANOVA to analyze these data. Let $\alpha = 0.01$.

	Treatment 1		
Treatment 2	**A**	**B**	**C**
A	23	21	20
	25	21	22
B	27	24	26
	28	27	27

11.41 Suppose the following data have been gathered from a study with a two-way factorial design. Use $\alpha = 0.05$ and a two-way ANOVA to analyze the data. State your conclusions.

		Treatment 2		
Treatment 1	**A**	**B**	**C**	**D**
A	1.2 1.3 1.3 1.5	2.2 2.1 2.0 2.3	1.7 1.8 1.7 1.6	2.4 2.3 2.5 2.4
B	1.9 1.6 1.7 2.0	2.7 2.5 2.8 2.8	1.9 2.2 1.9 2.0	2.8 2.6 2.4 2.8

11.42 Children are generally believed to have considerable influence over their parents in the purchase of certain items, particularly food and beverage items. To study this notion further, a study is conducted in which parents are asked to report how many food and beverage items purchased by the family per week are purchased mainly because of the influence of their children. Because the age of the child may have an effect on the study, parents are asked to focus on one particular child in the family for the week, and to report the age of the child. Four age categories are selected for the children: 4–5 years, 6–7 years, 8–9 years, and 10–12 years. Also, because the number of children in the family might make a difference, three different sizes of families are chosen for the study: families with one child, families with two children, and families with three or more children. Suppose the following data represent the reported number of child-influenced buying incidents per week. Use the data to compute a two-way ANOVA. Let $\alpha = 0.05$.

		Number of Children in Family		
		1	**2**	**3 or more**
Age of Child (years)	4–5	2	1	1
		4	2	1
	6–7	5	3	2
		4	1	1
	8–9	8	4	2
		6	5	3
	10–12	7	3	4
		8	5	3

11.43 A shoe retailer conducted a study to determine whether there is a difference in the number of pairs of shoes sold per day by stores according to the number of competitors within a 2-km radius and the location of the store. The company researchers selected three types of stores for consideration in the study: standalone suburban stores, mall stores, and downtown stores. These stores vary in the numbers of competing stores within a 2-km radius, which have been reduced to four categories: 0 competitors, 1 competitor, 2 competitors, and 3 or more competitors. Suppose the following data represent the number of pairs of shoes sold per day for each of these types of stores with the given number of competitors. Use $\alpha = 0.05$ and a two-way ANOVA to analyze the data.

		Number of Competitors			
		0	**1**	**2**	**3 or more**
	Standalone	41	38	59	47
		30	31	48	40
Store Location		45	39	51	39
	Mall	25	29	44	43
		31	35	48	42
		22	30	50	53
		18	22	29	24
	Downtown	29	17	28	27
		33	25	26	32

11.44 Study the following ANOVA table. Describe the design (number of treatments, sample sizes, etc.). Are there any significant effects? Discuss the output. The graph that follows the ANOVA table was produced on these same data. Analyze the graph.

Two-way ANOVA: Dependent Variable versus Row Effect, Column Effect

Source	df	SS	MS	F	p
RowEffect	2	92.31	46.156	13.23	0.000
ColEffect	4	998.8	249.7	71.57	0.000
Interaction	8	442.13	55.267	15.84	0.000
Error	30	104.67	3.489		
Total	44	1637.91			

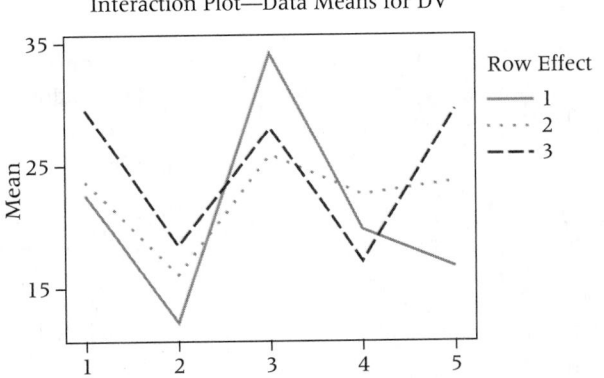

Interaction Plot—Data Means for DV

11.45 Consider the valve opening data displayed in Table 11.1. Suppose the data represent valves produced on four different machines on three different shifts and that the quality controllers want to know whether there is any difference in the mean measurements of valve openings by shift or by machine. The data are given here, organized by machine and shift. In addition, Excel has been used to analyze the data with a two-way ANOVA. What are the hypotheses for this problem? Study the output in terms of significant differences. Discuss the results obtained. What conclusions might the quality controllers reach from this analysis?

Valve Openings (cm)

		Shift 1	Shift 2	Shift 3
	1	6.56	6.38	6.29
		6.40	6.19	6.23
	2	6.54	6.26	6.19
Machine		6.34	6.23	6.33
	3	6.58	6.22	6.26
		6.44	6.27	6.31
	4	6.36	6.29	6.21
		6.50	6.19	6.58

ANOVA: Two-Factor With Replication

	A	B	C	D	E	F	G
1	ANOVA						
2							
3	*Source of Variation*	SS	df	MS	F	P-value	F crit
4	Sample	0.00538	3	0.00179	0.14	0.9368	3.49
5	Columns	0.19731	2	0.09865	7.47	0.0078	3.89
6	Interaction	0.03036	6	0.00506	0.38	0.8760	3.00
7	Within	0.15845	12	0.01320			
8	Total	0.39150	23				

11.46 Finish the computations in the ANOVA table shown next and determine the critical table *F* values. Interpret the analysis. Examine the associated graph and interpret the results. Discuss this problem, including the structure of the design, the sample sizes, and decisions about the hypotheses. Assume that $\alpha = 0.05$.

Two-way ANOVA: Dependent Variable versus Row, Column

Source	df	SS	MS
Row	2	0.296	0.148
Column	4	1.852	0.926
Interaction	8	4.370	1.093
Error	18	14.000	0.778
Total	26	20.519	

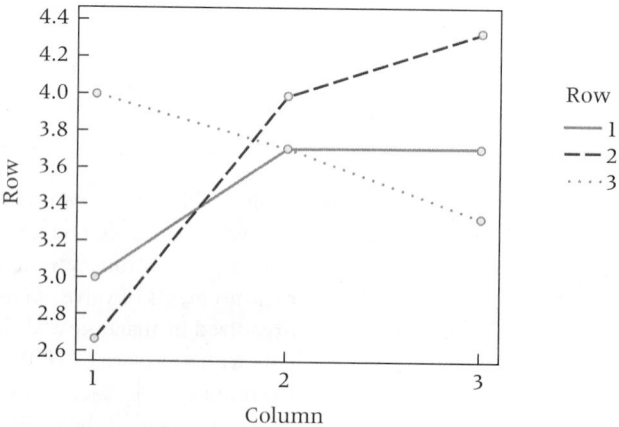

JOB AND CAREER SATISFACTION OF FOREIGN SELF-INITIATED EXPATRIATES

Is there a difference in the job satisfaction ratings of self-initiated expatriates by industry? The data presented in the Decision Dilemma to study this question represent responses on a seven-point Likert scale by 24 self-initiated expatriates from five different industries. The Likert scale score is the dependent variable. There is only one independent variable, industry, with five classification levels: IT, finance, education, health care, and consulting. If a series of t tests for the difference of two means from independent populations were used to analyze these data, there would be $_5C_2$ or 10 different t tests on this one problem. Using $\alpha = 0.05$ for each test, the probability of at least one of the 10 tests being significant by chance when the null hypothesis is true is $1 - (0.95)^{10} = 0.4013$. That is, performing 10 t tests on this problem could result in an overall probability of committing a Type I error equal to 0.4013, not 0.05. In order to control the overall error, a one-way ANOVA is used on this completely randomized design to analyze these data by producing a single value of F and holding the probability of committing a Type I error at 0.05. Excel can analyze these data, and its output is shown next.

	A	B	C	D	E	F	G
1	Anova: Single Factor						
2							
3	SUMMARY						
4	*Groups*	*Count*	*Sum*	*Average*	*Variance*		
5	IT	4	23	5.750	0.917		
6	Finance	5	20	4.000	0.500		
7	Education	6	15	2.500	0.300		
8	Health Care	5	17	3.400	1.300		
9	Consulting	4	24	6.000	0.667		
10							
11							
12	ANOVA						
13	*Source of Variation*	*SS*	*df*	*MS*	*F*	*P-value*	*F* crit
14	Between Groups	43.175	4	10.794	15.248	0.000	2.895
15	Within Groups	13.450	19	0.708			
16							
17	Total	56.625	23				

With an F value of 15.25 and a p value of 0.000, the results of the one-way ANOVA show that there is an overall significant difference in job satisfaction between the five industries. Examining the average and the associated variances suggests that there might be a significant difference between some pairs of industries. Because there was an overall significant difference in the industries, it is appropriate to use Tukey's HSD test to determine which of the pairs of industries are significantly different. Tukey's test controls for the overall error so that the problem mentioned previously arising from computing 10 t tests is avoided. The MINITAB output for Tukey's test is:

```
Tukey 95% Simultaneous Confidence Intervals
All Pairwise Comparisons

Individual confidence level = 99.27%

IT subtracted from:
              Lower     Center    Upper    -----+---------+--------+--------+-
Finance      -3.4462   -1.7500   -0.0538          (----*----)
Education    -4.8821   -3.2500   -1.6179   (----*----)
Health care  -4.0462   -2.3500   -0.6538       (-----*-----)
Consulting   -1.5379    0.2500    2.0379                (-----*-----)
                                           -----+---------+--------+--------+-
                                              -3.0      0.0      3.0      6.0


Finance subtracted from:
              Lower     Center    Upper    -----+---------+--------+--------+-
Education    -3.0311   -1.5000    0.0311          (----*----)
Health care  -2.1991   -0.6000    0.9991             (----*----)
Consulting    0.3038    2.0000    3.6962                   (----*---)
                                           -----+---------+--------+--------+-
                                              -3.0      0.0      3.0      6.0
```

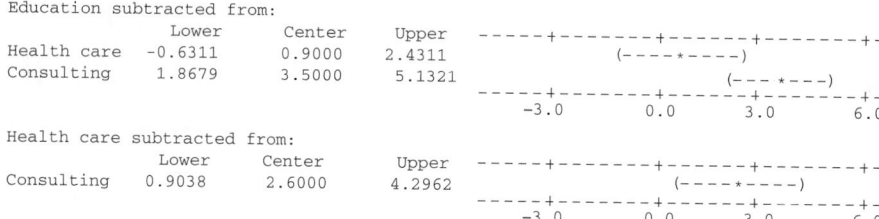

```
Education subtracted from:
               Lower      Center     Upper    -----+--------+------+-------+-
Health care  -0.6311      0.9000    2.4311              (----*---)
Consulting    1.8679      3.5000    5.1321                      (--- *---)
                                             -----+--------+------+-------+-
                                                 -3.0      0.0    3.0    6.0

Health care subtracted from:
               Lower      Center     Upper    -----+--------+------+-------+-
Consulting    0.9038      2.6000    4.2962               (----*----)
                                             -----+--------+------+-------+-
                                                 -3.0      0.0    3.0    6.0
```

Any confidence interval in which the sign of the value for the lower end of the interval is the same as the sign of the value for the upper end indicates that zero is not in the interval and that there is a significant difference between the items in the pair in that case. Examining the output reveals that IT and finance, IT and education, IT and health care, finance and consulting, education and consulting, and health care and consulting are all significantly different pairs of industries.

In analyzing career satisfaction, self-initiated expatriates were sampled from three age categories and four categories of time in the host country. This experimental design is a two-way factorial design with age and time in the host country as independent variables and individual scores on the seven-point Likert scale as the dependent variable. There are three classification levels under the independent variable Age: 30–39, 40–49, and over 50. There are four classifications under the independent variable Time in Host Country: <1 year, 1 to 2 years, 3 to 4 years, and 5 or more years. Because there is more than one score per cell, interaction can be analyzed. A two-way ANOVA with replication is run in Excel to analyze the data, and the result is shown below:

Excel Output: ANOVA

Source of Variation	SS	df	MS	F	p value	F crit
Age	3.5556	2	1.7778	2.91	0.073920	3.40
Time in Host Country	20.9722	3	6.9907	11.44	0.000075	3.01
Interaction	1.1111	6	0.1852	0.30	0.929183	2.51
Within	14.6667	24	0.6111			
Total	40.3056	35				

An examination of this output reveals no significant interaction effects (p value of 0.929183). Since there are no significant interaction effects, it is appropriate to examine the main effects. Because of a p value of 0.000075, there is a significant difference in Time in Host Country using an alpha of 0.0001. Multiple comparison analysis could be done to determine which, if any, pairs of Time in Host Country are significantly different. The p value for Age is 0.073920, indicating that there is a significant difference between age classifications at $\alpha = 0.10$ but not at $\alpha = 0.05$.

KEY CONSIDERATIONS

In theory, any phenomenon that affects the dependent variable in an experiment should be either entered into the experimental design or controlled in the experiment. Researchers will sometimes report statistical findings from an experiment and fail to mention the possible concomitant variables that were controlled by neither the experimental setting nor the experimental design. The findings from such studies are highly questionable and often lead to spurious conclusions. Scientifically, the researcher needs to conduct the experiment in an environment such that as many concomitant variables are controlled as possible. To the extent that they are not controlled, the researcher has an ethical responsibility to report that fact in the findings.

Other key considerations enter into conducting research with experimental designs. Selection of treatment levels should be done with fairness or even randomness in cases where the treatment has several possibilities for levels. A researcher can build in skewed views of the treatment effects by erroneously selecting treatment levels to be studied. Some researchers believe that reporting significant main effects from a factorial design when there are confounding interaction effects is unethical or at least misleading.

Another key consideration is the levelling of sample sizes. Some designs, such as the two-way factorial design or completely randomized design with Tukey's HSD, require equal sample sizes. Sometimes unequal sample sizes arise either through the selection process or through attrition. A number of techniques for approaching this problem are not presented in this book. It remains highly unethical to make up data values or to eliminate values arbitrarily to produce equal sample sizes.

Why Statistics Is Relevant

The relevance of ANOVA and design of experiments has increased during the past few years as essential tools for improving the quality of both products and services. In particular, the use of ANOVA and design of experiments has been linked to the successful design of robust products and services; that is, products and services that are rather insensitive to environmental fluctuations and changes.

One of the key managerial implications of ANOVA and design of experiments is that properly designed and executed experiments will generate more precise data while requiring substantially fewer experimental runs than other, perhaps more traditional approaches. A rather traditional approach to experimentation is to evaluate only one factor at a time, while holding all other factors constant during test runs. This approach reveals the effect of the chosen factor under a set of conditions, but it does not show what would happen if the other factors also changed (the interactions). Thus, carefully planned experiments offer a clear advantage over one-factor-at-a-time approaches.

In addition, the experimental designs can be configured to block out extraneous factors or expanded to cover more advanced response surface methodologies.

SUMMARY

Sound business research requires that the researcher plan and establish a design for the experiment before a study is undertaken. The design of the experiment should encompass the treatment variables to be studied, manipulated, and controlled. These variables are often referred to as the independent variables. It is possible to study several independent variables and several levels, or classifications, of each of the variables in one design. In addition, the researcher selects one measurement to be taken from sample items under the conditions of the experiment. This measurement is referred to as the dependent variable because if the treatment effect is significant, the measurement of the dependent variable will "depend" on the independent variable(s) selected. In this chapter, we explored three types of experimental designs: completely randomized design, randomized block design, and factorial experimental designs.

1. The completely randomized design is the simplest of the experimental designs presented in this chapter. It has only one independent, or treatment, variable. With the completely randomized design, subjects are assigned randomly to treatments. If the treatment variable has only two levels, the design becomes identical to the one used to test the difference in means of independent populations presented in Chapter 10. The data from a completely randomized design are analyzed by a one-way ANOVA.

2. A one-way ANOVA produces an F value that can be compared to table F values in Table A.7 to determine whether the ANOVA F value is statistically significant. If it is, the null hypothesis that all population means are equal is rejected and at least one of the means is different from the others. ANOVA does not tell the researcher which means, if any, are significantly different from others. Although the researcher can visually examine means to determine which ones are greater and lesser, statistical techniques called multiple comparisons must be used to determine statistically whether pairs of means are significantly different.

Two types of multiple comparison techniques are presented and used in this chapter: Tukey's HSD test and the Tukey-Kramer procedure. Tukey's HSD test requires that equal sample sizes be used. It utilizes the mean square of error from the ANOVA, the sample size, and a q value that is obtained from Table A.10 to solve for the least difference between a pair of means that would be significant (HSD). The absolute value of the difference in sample means is compared to the HSD value to determine statistical significance. The Tukey-Kramer procedure is used in the case of unequal sample sizes.

3. A second experimental design is the randomized block design. This design contains a treatment variable (independent variable) and a blocking variable. The independent variable is the main variable of interest in this design. The blocking variable is a variable the researcher is interested in controlling rather than studying. A special case of randomized block design is the repeated measures design, in which the blocking variable represents subjects or items for which repeated measures are taken across the full range of treatment levels.

In randomized block designs, the variation of the blocking variable is removed from the error variance. This approach can potentially make the test of treatment effects more powerful. If the blocking variable contains no significant differences, the blocking can make the treatment effects test less powerful. Usually an F is computed only for the treatment effects in a randomized block design. Sometimes an F value is computed for blocking effects to determine whether the blocking was useful in the experiment.

4–6. A third experimental design is the factorial design. A factorial design enables the researcher to test the effects of two or more independent variables simultaneously. In complete factorial designs, every treatment level of each independent variable is studied under the conditions of every other treatment level for all independent variables. This chapter focused only on factorial designs with two independent variables. Each independent variable can have two or more treatment levels. These two-way factorial designs are analyzed by two-way ANOVA. This analysis produces an F value for each of the two treatment effects and for interaction. Interaction is present when the results of one treatment vary significantly according to the levels of the other treatment. At least two measurements per cell must be present in order to compute interaction. If the F value for interaction is statistically significant, the main effects of the experiment are confounded and should not be examined in the usual manner.

KEY TERMS

a posteriori	concomitant variables	factors	randomized block design
a priori	confounding variables	independent variable	repeated measures design
analysis of variance (ANOVA)	dependent variable	interaction	treatment variable
blocking variable	experimental design	levels	Tukey-Kramer procedure
classification variable	F distribution	multiple comparisons	Tukey's HSD test
classifications	F value	one-way ANOVA	two-way ANOVA
completely randomized design	factorial design	post hoc	

FORMULAS

Formulas for computing a one-way ANOVA

$$SSC = \sum_{j=1}^{C} n_j (\bar{x}_j - \bar{x})^2$$

$$SSE = \sum_{i=1}^{n_j} \sum_{j=1}^{C} (x_{ij} - \bar{x}_j)^2$$

$$SST = \sum_{i=1}^{n_j} \sum_{j=1}^{C} (x_{ij} - \bar{x})^2$$

$$df_C = C - 1$$

$$df_E = N - C$$

$$df_T = N - 1$$

$$MSC = \frac{SSC}{df_C}$$

$$MSE = \frac{SSE}{df_E}$$

$$F = \frac{MSC}{MSE}$$

Tukey's HSD test

$$HSD = q_{\alpha,C,N-C} \sqrt{\frac{MSE}{n}}$$

Tukey-Kramer formula

$$q_{\alpha,C,N-C} \sqrt{\frac{MSE}{2} \left(\frac{1}{n_r} + \frac{1}{n_s} \right)}$$

Formulas for computing a randomized block design

$$df_C = C - 1$$
$$df_R = R - 1$$
$$df_E = (C-1)(n-1) = N - n - C + 1$$

$$MSC = \frac{SSC}{C-1}$$

$$SSC = n\sum_{j=1}^{C}(\overline{x}_j - \overline{x})^2$$

$$MSR = \frac{SSR}{n-1}$$

$$SSR = C\sum_{i=1}^{n}(\overline{x}_i - \overline{x})^2$$

$$MSE = \frac{SSE}{N-n-C+1}$$

$$SSE = \sum_{i=1}^{n}\sum_{j=1}^{C}(x_{ij} - \overline{x}_j - \overline{x}_i + \overline{x})^2 \qquad F_{treatments} = \frac{MSC}{MSE}$$

$$SST = \sum_{i=1}^{n}\sum_{j=1}^{C}(x_{ij} - \overline{x})^2 \qquad F_{blocks} = \frac{MSR}{MSE}$$

Formulas for computing a two-way ANOVA

$$df_R = R - 1$$
$$df_C = C - 1$$
$$df_I = (R-1)(C-1)$$
$$df_E = RC(n-1)$$
$$df_T = N - 1$$

$$MSR = \frac{SSR}{R-1}$$

$$MSC = \frac{SSC}{C-1}$$

$$SSR = nC\sum_{i=1}^{R}(\overline{x}_i - \overline{x})^2$$

$$MSI = \frac{SSI}{(R-1)(C-1)}$$

$$SSC = nR\sum_{j=1}^{C}(\overline{x}_j - \overline{x})^2$$

$$MSE = \frac{SSE}{RC(n-1)}$$

$$SSI = n\sum_{i=1}^{R}\sum_{j=1}^{C}(\overline{x}_{ij} - \overline{x}_i - \overline{x}_j + \overline{x})^2 \qquad F_R = \frac{MSR}{MSE}$$

$$SSE = \sum_{i=1}^{R}\sum_{j=1}^{C}\sum_{k=1}^{n}(x_{ijk} - \overline{x}_{ij})^2 \qquad F_C = \frac{MSC}{MSE}$$

$$SST = \sum_{i=1}^{R}\sum_{j=1}^{C}\sum_{k=1}^{n}(x_{ijk} - \overline{x})^2 \qquad F_I = \frac{MSI}{MSE}$$

SUPPLEMENTARY PROBLEMS

Calculating the Statistics

11.47 Compute a one-way ANOVA on the following data. Use $\alpha = 0.05$. If there is a significant difference in treatment levels, use Tukey's HSD to compute multiple comparisons. Let $\alpha = 0.05$ for the multiple comparisons.

Treatment			
1	**2**	**3**	**4**
10	9	12	10
12	7	13	10
15	9	14	13
11	6	14	12

SUPPLEMENTARY PROBLEMS (continued)

11.48   Complete the following ANOVA table.

Source of Variance	SS	df	MS	F
Treatment				
Error	249.61	19		
Total	317.80	25		

11.49   You are asked to analyze a completely randomized design that has six treatment levels and a total of 42 measurements. Complete the following table, which contains some information from the study.

Source of Variance	SS	df	MS	F
Treatment	210			
Error	655			
Total				

11.50   Compute a one-way ANOVA of the following data. Let $\alpha = 0.01$. Use the Tukey-Kramer procedure to conduct multiple comparisons for the means.

Treatment

1	2	3
7	11	8
12	17	6
9	16	10
11	13	9
8	10	11
9	15	7
11	14	10
10	18	
7		
8		

11.51   Examine the structure of the following experimental design. Determine which of the three designs presented in the chapter would be most likely to characterize this structure. Discuss the variables and the levels of variables. Determine the degrees of freedom.

Methodology

Person	Method 1	Method 2	Method 3
1	x_{11}	x_{12}	x_{13}
2	x_{21}	x_{22}	x_{23}
3	x_{31}	x_{32}	x_{33}
4	x_{41}	x_{42}	x_{43}
5	x_{51}	x_{52}	x_{53}
6	x_{61}	x_{62}	x_{63}

11.52   Complete the following ANOVA table and determine whether there is any significance in treatment effects. Let $\alpha = 0.05$.

Source of Variance	SS	df	MS	F
Treatment	20,994	3		
Blocking		9		
Error	33,891			
Total	71,338			

11.53   Analyze the following data, gathered from a randomized block design using $\alpha = 0.05$. If there is a significant difference in the treatment effects, use Tukey's HSD test to do multiple comparisons.

		Treatment			
		A	B	C	D
	1	17	10	9	21
	2	13	9	8	16
Blocking	3	20	17	18	22
Variable	4	11	6	5	10
	5	16	13	14	22
	6	23	19	20	28

11.54   A two-way ANOVA has been computed on a factorial design. Treatment 1 has five levels and treatment 2 has two levels. Each cell contains four measures. Complete the following ANOVA table. Use $\alpha = 0.05$ to test to determine the significance of the effects. Comment on your findings.

Source of Variance	SS	df	MS	F
Treatment 1	29.13			
Treatment 2	12.67			
Interaction	73.49			
Error	110.38			
Total				

11.55   Compute a two-way ANOVA on the following data ($\alpha = 0.01$).

		Treatment 1		
		A	B	C
		5	2	2
A		3	4	3
		6	4	5
		11	9	13
B		8	10	12

(continued)

		A	B	C
Treatment 2		12	8	10
		6	7	4
	C	4	6	6
		5	7	8
		9	8	8
	D	11	12	9
		9	9	11

Testing Your Understanding

11.56 A company conducted a consumer research project to ascertain customer service ratings from its customers. The customers were asked to rate the company on a scale from 1 to 7 on various quality characteristics. One question was the promptness of company response to a repair problem. The following data represent customer responses to this question. The customers were divided by geographic region and by age. Use ANOVA to analyze the responses. Let $\alpha = 0.05$. Compute multiple comparisons where they are appropriate. Graph the cell means and observe any interaction.

		Geographic Region			
		West	**North**	**Central**	**Atlantic**
		3	2	3	2
	21–35	2	4	3	3
		3	3	2	2
		5	4	5	6
Age	**36–50**	5	4	6	4
		4	6	5	5
		3	2	3	3
	Over 50	1	2	2	2
		2	3	3	1

11.57 A major automobile manufacturer wants to know whether there is any difference in the average distance until failure of four different brands of tires (A, B, C, and D), because the manufacturer is trying to select the best supplier in terms of tire durability. The manufacturer selects comparable levels of tires from each company and tests some on comparable cars. The maximum distance results (in kilometres) follow.

A	**B**	**C**	**D**
31,000	24,000	30,500	24,500
25,000	25,500	28,000	27,000
28,500	27,000	32,500	26,000
29,000	26,500	28,000	21,000
32,000	25,000	31,000	25,500
27,500	28,000		26,000
	27,500		

Use $\alpha = 0.05$ to test whether there is a significant difference in the mean maximum distance of these four brands. Assume maximum tire distance is normally distributed.

11.58 Agricultural researchers are studying three different ways of planting wheat to determine whether significantly different levels of production yield will result. The researchers have access to a large farm on which to conduct their tests. They identify six blocks of land. In each block of land, wheat is planted in each of the three different ways. At the end of the growing season, the wheat is harvested and the average number of tonnes per hectare is determined for wheat planted under each method in each block. Using the following data and $\alpha = 0.01$, test to determine whether there is a significant difference in yields among the planting methods.

Block	**Method 1**	**Method 2**	**Method 3**
1	3.57	2.71	1.86
2	3.44	2.79	2.49
3	3.45	2.60	1.60
4	3.25	2.49	1.93
5	3.12	2.38	1.69
6	3.53	2.53	2.08

11.59 The Construction Labor Research Council lists a number of construction labour jobs that seem to pay approximately the same wages per hour. Some of these are bricklaying, iron working, and crane operation. Suppose a labour researcher takes a random sample of workers from each of these types of construction jobs and from across the country and asks what their hourly wages are. If this survey yields the following data, is there a significant difference in mean hourly wages for these three jobs? If there is a significant difference, use the Tukey-Kramer procedure to determine which pairs, if any, are also significantly different. Let $\alpha = 0.05$.

	Job Type	
Bricklaying	**Iron Working**	**Crane Operation**
19.25	26.45	16.20
17.80	21.10	23.30
20.50	16.40	22.90
24.33	22.86	19.50
19.81	25.55	27.00
22.29	18.50	22.95
21.20		25.52
		21.20

11.60 Why are mergers attractive to CEOs? One of the reasons might be the potential increase in market share that can come with the pooling of company markets. Suppose a random survey of CEOs is taken, and they are asked to respond on a scale from 1 to 5 (5 representing strongly agree) whether increase in market share is a good reason to consider merging their company with another. Suppose also that the data are as given here and that CEOs have been categorized by size of company and years they have been with their company. Use a two-way ANOVA to determine whether there are any significant differences in the responses to this question. Let $\alpha = 0.05$.

		Company Size ($ million per year in sales)			
		0–5	**6–20**	**21–100**	**>100**
		2	2	3	3
		3	1	4	4
	0–2	2	2	4	4
		2	3	5	3
Years		2	2	3	3
with the		1	3	2	3
Company	**3–5**	2	2	4	3
		3	3	4	4
		2	2	3	2
		1	3	2	3
	Over 5	1	1	3	2
		2	2	3	3

11.61 Are some office jobs viewed as having more status than others? Suppose a study is conducted in which eight unemployed people are interviewed. The people are asked to rate each of five positions on a scale from 1 to 10 to indicate the status of the position, with 10 denoting most status and 1 denoting least status. The resulting data are given below. Use $\alpha = 0.05$ to analyze the repeated measures randomized block design data.

		Job				
		Mail Clerk	**Typist**	**Recep- tionist**	**Secre- tary**	**Telephone Operator**
	1	4	5	3	7	6
	2	2	4	4	5	4
	3	3	3	2	6	7
Respondent	4	4	4	4	5	4
	5	3	5	1	3	5
	6	3	4	2	7	7
	7	2	2	2	4	4
	8	3	4	3	6	6

Interpreting the Output

11.62 Analyze the following output. Describe the design of the experiment. Using $\alpha = 0.05$, determine whether there are any significant effects; if so, explain why. Discuss any other ramifications of the output.

```
One-way ANOVA: Dependent Variable versus Factor
Analysis of Variance
Source          DF        SS       MS      F      p
Factor           3     876.6    292.2   3.01  0.045
Error           32    3107.5     97.1
Total           35    3984.1
                              Individual 95% CIs for
                              Mean  Based  on  Pooled
                              StDev
Level   N    Mean    StDev  -+----+----+----+--
C1      8   307.73    5.98  (----*----)
C2      7   313.20    9.71          (----*----)
C3     11   308.60    9.78      (----*----)
C4     10   319.74   12.18                  (---*---)
                            -+----+----+----+--
Pooled StDev = 9.85    301.0 308.0 315.0 322.0
```

11.63 Following is Excel output for an ANOVA problem. Describe the experimental design. The given value of alpha was 0.05. Discuss the output in terms of significant findings.

ANOVA: Two-Factor without Replication

	A	B	C	D	E	F	G
1	ANOVA						
2	*Source of Variation*	SS	df	MS	F	P-value	F crit
3	Rows	48.278	5	9.656	3.16	0.057	3.33
4	Columns	10.111	2	5.056	1.65	0.239	4.10
5	Error	30.556	10	3.056			
6	Total	88.944	17				

11.64 Study the following output and graph. Discuss the meaning of the output.

Two-way ANOVA: Dependent Variable versus Row Effects, Column Effects

Source	df	SS	MS	F	P
Row Eff	4	4.70	1.17	0.98	0.461
Col. Eff	1	3.20	3.20	2.67	0.134
Interaction	4	22.30	5.57	4.65	0.022
Error	10	12.00	1.20		
Total	19	42.20			

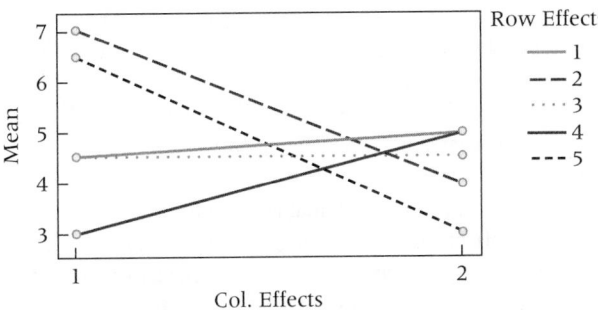

Row Effects
— 1
-- 2
···· 3
— 4
--- 5

Col. Effects

11.65 Interpret the following Excel output. Discuss the structure of the experimental design and any significant effects. Alpha is 0.01.

ANOVA: Two-Factor with Replication

	A	B	C	D	E	F	G
1	ANOVA						
2	*Source of Variation*	SS	df	MS	F	P-value	F crit
3	Sample	2913.889	3	971.296	4.30	0.0146	3.01
4	Columns	240.389	2	120.194	0.53	0.5940	3.40
5	Interaction	1342.944	6	223.824	0.99	0.4533	2.51
6	Within	5419.333	24	225.806			
7	Total	9916.556	35				

11.66 Study the following output. Determine whether there are any significant effects and discuss the results. Assume that $\alpha = 0.05$. What kind of design was used and what was its size?

Two-way Analysis of Variance

Source	DF	SS	MS
Blocking	4	41.44	10.36
Treatment	4	143.93	35.98
Error	16	117.82	7.36
Total	24	303.19	

11.67 Discuss the following output.

```
One-Way Analysis of Variance
Source        df      SS      MS      F       P
Treatment      3    138.0    46.0    3.51    0.034
Error         20    262.2    13.1
Total         23    400.3
Individual 95% CIs For Mean Based on Pooled
StDev
Level  N    Mean    StDev  ----+----+----+----+
1      6   53.778   5.470  (----*----)
2      6   54.665   1.840  (----*----)
3      6   59.911   3.845           (----*----)
4      6   57.293   2.088       (----*----)
                           ----+----+----+----+
Pooled StDev = 3.621       52.5  56.0  59.5  63.0
```

```
Tukey's pairwise comparisons
Family error rate = 0.0500
Individual error rate = 0.0111
Critical value = 3.96
Intervals for (column level mean) - (row level
mean)
           1         2         3
2      -6.741
        4.967
3     -11.987   -11.100
       -0.279     0.608
4      -9.369    -8.482    -3.236
        2.339     3.225     8.472
```

ANALYZING THE DATABASES

see www.wiley.com/canada/black

Let $\alpha = 0.05$ for all problems.

1. Do various financial indicators differ significantly according to type of company? Use a one-way ANOVA and the Financial Database to answer this question. Let Type of Company be the independent variable with seven levels (as listing in Analyzing the Databases in Chapter 1). Compute three one-way ANOVAs, one for each of the following dependent variables: Average Yield, Dividend per Share, and Average P/E Ratio. On each ANOVA, if there is a significant overall difference between Type of Industry, compute multiple comparisons to determine which pairs of types of industries, if any, are significantly different.

2. Use the Canadian Stock Market Database to determine whether there is any difference in stock market statistics for different weeks of the month. Use a one-way ANOVA with Composite Index as the dependent variable and Week of the Month as the independent variable with five levels. Compute a second ANOVA with I.T. Index as the dependent variable and Week of the Month

as the independent variable. Is there a significant difference in Week of the Month on either of these variables? If there is, compute multiple comparisons to determine which weeks of the month, if any, are significantly different from the others.

3. In the Major League Baseball Database, group the current value of each team into three classifications, less than 400, 400 to 599, 600 and over. Let this value be the independent variable with three levels of classifications. Compute a one-way ANOVA to determine whether there is any significant difference in classification of

the Payroll (dependent variable). Now change the independent variable to Operating Income and use four classifications, less than 0, 0 to 19.9, 20 to 39.9, and 40 to 60. Perform first a one-way ANOVA using Payroll as the dependent variable and then a one-way ANOVA using Revenues as the dependent variable.

4. The Canadian Hospital Database contains data on hospitals from three different geographic regions. Let this variable be the independent variable. Determine whether there is a significant difference in Failure to Rescue for these geographic regions using a one-way ANOVA.

CASE

ASCO Valve Canada Introduces New Red Hat Valve

With headquarters located in Brantford, Ontario, ASCO Valve Canada is one of Canada's top producers of solenoid valves. The company was founded in 1965, and since that time it has emerged as a very successful industrial company that currently employs 75 people across Canada. ASCO offers an array of products to its clients. These products range from valves that are used in the gas pipeline industry to valves that are used in medical procedures.

One of ASCO's goals was to develop a valve that could minimize the cost to consumers, including cost of operations and the amount of power consumed. In 2005, ASCO achieved its goal by developing and introducing its new Red Hat Next Generation valves. Today, these valves are well recognized and respected in many different countries due to their exceptional performance in difficult conditions. These valves are also very energy efficient because they are able to use a mere 2 watts of power rather than the 17 watts of power that the typical solenoid valves use. This is a very important cost benefit for any company using valves because these new products can decrease the total cost of ownership by almost 14% over the installed life of the valve.

The Red Hat Next Generation valves have many advantages, for example, (1) better and more reliable functionality, (2) reduced usage of power, and (3) modular design. These advantages have allowed ASCO to provide consumers with better quality valves, at reasonable prices, and ensure fast delivery. Recently, ASCO has made it very clear that one of its objectives was to reduce lead times in order to satisfy customer demand. Within a short period of time, it has already accomplished this and can deliver products to its customers at a much faster rate.

Discussion

1. The new Red Hat Next Generation valves are durable and reliable. They can operate with high air pressure of up to 2200 psi (pounds per square inch). Suppose ASCO develops a new and stronger version of the Red Hat Next Generation valve. They want to set up an experimental design to test the strength of the new valve, but they want to conduct the tests under three different temperature conditions, 23°C, 49°C, and 68°C. In addition, suppose ASCO uses two different suppliers (supplier 1 and supplier 2) for the synthetic materials that are used to manufacture the valves. Some valves are made primarily of raw materials supplied by supplier 1, and some are made primarily of raw materials from supplier 2. Consequently, a 2×3 factorial design is appropriate for the experiment, with temperature and supplier as the independent variables and air pressure (measured in psi) as the dependent variable. An appropriate sampling frame has produced the data shown below. Analyze the data and discuss the business implications of the findings. If you were conducting the study, what conclusions would you report to the company?

	Temperature		
	23°C	**49°C**	**68°C**
Supplier 1	2257	2207	2201
	2479	2491	2173
	2361	2314	2192
Supplier 2	2215	2230	2229
	2308	2359	2088
	2511	2488	2287

2. It is estimated that these Red Hat energy-efficient valves can save a great deal of power usage and lower the total cost of ownership by up to 14% over the installed life of the valve, therefore making the Red Hat valves more attractive. ASCO does business with pipeline companies globally. In an attempt to position itself as a market leader across the world, ASCO is keen on finding out whether the cost saved over the installed life of the valve is significantly different among the different countries in which it does business. Four countries, Canada, Spain, Japan, and the United States, are chosen for the study. Pipeline companies are selected from each country. The companies keep a log of valve power usage. A random sample of the data is shown below. Test whether there is a difference in relative cost savings in each of these countries. Justify your answer and prepare a short report to present to the management of ASCO in which your conclusions are explained, with support from the statistical test that you performed.

Canada	Spain	Japan	U.S.
12%	9%	14%	13%
14	10.5	14	12.5
11.5	11	13	14
10	14	13.5	11.5
14	8.5	12	14
13	12	12.5	13

3. As previously mentioned, ASCO has been able to reduce its lead time. Suppose ASCO's original lead time averaged 10 weeks and that the reduction is in the neighbourhood of 80%. As such, most lead times now average slightly below two weeks. ASCO is interested in knowing whether lead times differ significantly according to the type of Red Hat

valve it is manufacturing. To control the experiment, they will use as a blocking variable the day of the week the valve was ordered. One lead time was selected per valve per day of the week. The sample data are given below in weeks. Analyze the data and discuss your findings.

	Type of Red Hat Valve		
	Two-way	**Three-way**	**Four-way**
Monday	1.7	1.9	2.2
Tuesday	1.9	1.8	1.9
Wednesday	1.0	2.3	2.4
Thursday	1.4	1.5	1.8
Friday	2.1	2.0	2.5

References

ASCO Valve Canada, 2009. Website for data source: <http://www.processcontrols.ca/Asco/>; ASCO Introduces Red Hat Next Generation Solenoid Valve, 2005. Website for data source: <http://www.ascovalve.com/Applications/News/NewsRedHatNextGeneration.aspx>; ASCO Dynamic Solution, 2009. Website for data source: <http://www.ascovalvenet.com/pdf/LiteratureRequest/DynamicSolutions_V7368R3.pdf>; Frasers.com—Canada's Online Industrial Directory, "ASCO," 2009. Website for data source: <http://www.frasers.com/public/extendedListingDetails.jsf?listingId=14701&cmoid=6>; ASCO Red Hat Next Generation, 2009. Website for data source: <http://www.ascovalve.com/Applications/Products/ElectronicallyEnhancedSolenoidValves.aspx>; "ASCO Red Hat Next Generation Solenoid Valves," The RHFS Pulse, June 2007, Volume 1, Number 1. Website for data source: <http://www.rhfspulse.com/files/RyanHerco_PulseNwslttr_June07.pdf>

USING THE COMPUTER

Excel

- Excel has the capability of performing a completely randomized design (one-way ANOVA), a randomized block design, and a two-way factorial design (two-way ANOVA).
- Each of the tests presented here in Excel is accessed through the **Data Analysis** feature.
- To conduct a one-way ANOVA, begin by selecting the **Data** tab on the Excel worksheet. From the **Analysis** panel at the right top of the **Data** tab worksheet, click on **Data Analysis**. If your Excel worksheet does not show the **Data Analysis** option, then you can load it as an add-in. From

the **Data Analysis** pulldown menu, select **Anova: Single Factor**. Click and drag over the data and enter in **Input Range**. Check **Labels in the First Row** if you included labels in the data. Insert the value of alpha in **Alpha**.

- To conduct a randomized block design, load the treatment observations into columns. Data may be loaded either with or without labels. Select the **Data** tab on the Excel worksheet. From the **Analysis** panel at the right top of the **Data** tab worksheet, click on **Data Analysis**. If your Excel worksheet does not show the **Data Analysis** option, then you can load it as an add-in.

USING THE COMPUTER (continued)

From the **Data Analysis** pulldown menu, select **Anova: Two-Factor Without Replication**. Click and drag over the data under **Input Range**. Check **Labels in the First Row** if you have included labels in the data. Insert the value of alpha in **Alpha**.

- To conduct a two-way ANOVA, load the treatment observations into columns. Excel is quite particular about how the data are entered for a two-way ANOVA. Data must be loaded in rows and columns as with most two-way designs. However, two-way ANOVA in Excel requires labels for both rows and columns; and if labels are not supplied, Excel will incorrectly use some of the data for labels. Since cells will have multiple values, there need only be a label for each new row (cell). Select the **Data** tab on the Excel worksheet. From the **Analysis** panel at the right top of the **Data** tab worksheet, click on **Data Analysis**. If your Excel worksheet does not show the **Data Analysis** option, then you can load it as an add-in. From the **Data Analysis** pulldown menu, select **Anova: Two-Factor With Replication**. Click and drag over the data under **Input Range**. Enter the number of values per cell in **Rows per sample**. Insert the value of alpha in **Alpha**.

Unit IV

REGRESSION ANALYSIS AND FORECASTING

In the first three units of the text, you were introduced to basic statistics, distributions, and how to make inferences through confidence interval estimation and hypothesis testing. In Unit IV, we explore relationships between variables through regression analysis and learn how to develop models that can be used to predict one variable by another variable or even multiple variables. You will examine a cadre of statistical techniques that can be used to forecast values from time series data and then learn how to measure how good the forecast is.

CHAPTER 12

CORRELATION AND SIMPLE REGRESSION ANALYSIS

Learning Objectives

The overall objective of this chapter is to give you an understanding of bivariate linear regression analysis. The key questions in this chapter are:

1. What is correlation and when is it used?

2. What is simple regression and what is it used for?

3. How can we interpret the slope and intercept of the equation?

4. How can we use residual analysis to examine the fit of the regression line and to test the assumptions underlying regression analysis?

5. How can we compute and interpret the standard error of the estimate?

6. How can we compute and interpret the coefficient of determination?

7. How can we test hypotheses and interpret the results about the slope of the regression model?

8. How can we estimate values of y by using the regression model?

9. How can we develop a linear trend line and use it to make forecasts?

Shutterstock

PREDICTING INTERNATIONAL HOURLY WAGES BY THE PRICE OF A BIG Mac™

The McDonald's Corporation is the leading global foodservice retailer with more than 30,000 local restaurants serving nearly 50 million people in more than 119 countries each day. This global presence, in addition to its consistency in food offerings and restaurant operations, makes McDonald's a unique and attractive setting for economists to make salary and price comparisons around the world. Because the Big Mac™ hamburger is a standardized hamburger produced and sold in virtually every McDonald's around the world, *The Economist,* a weekly newsmagazine focusing on international politics and business news and opinion, as early as 1986, was compiling information about Big Mac prices as an indicator of exchange rates. Building on this idea, researchers Ashenfelter and Jurajda proposed comparing wage rates and the price of a Big Mac hamburger across countries. Shown at right are Big Mac prices and net hourly wage figures (in U.S. dollars) for 27 countries. Note that net hourly wages are based on a weighted average of 12 professions.

Country	Big Mac Price ($U.S.)	Net Hourly Wage ($U.S.)
Argentina	1.42	1.70
Australia	1.86	7.80
Brazil	1.48	2.05
Britain	3.14	12.30
Canada	2.21	9.35
Chile	1.96	2.80
China	1.20	2.40
Czech Republic	1.96	2.40
Denmark	4.09	14.40
Euro area	2.98	9.59
Hungary	2.19	3.00
Indonesia	1.84	1.50
Japan	2.18	13.60
Malaysia	1.33	3.10
Mexico	2.18	2.00
New Zealand	2.22	6.80
Philippines	2.24	1.20
Poland	1.62	2.20
Russia	1.32	2.60
Singapore	1.85	5.40
South Africa	1.85	3.90
South Korea	2.70	5.90
Sweden	3.60	10.90
Switzerland	4.60	17.80
Thailand	1.38	1.70
Turkey	2.34	3.20
United States	2.71	14.30

Sources: McDonald's home website at <http://www.aboutmcdonalds.com/mcd/our_company.html>; Michael R. Pakko and Patricia S. Pollard, "Burgernomics: A Big Mac™ Guide to Purchasing Power Parity," research publication by the St. Louis Federal Reserve Bank at <http://research.stlouisfed.org/publications/review/03/11/pakko.pdf>; Orley Ashenfelter and Štěpán Jurajda, "Cross-Country Comparisons of Wage Rates: The Big Mac Index," unpublished manuscript, Princeton University and CERGEEI/Charles University, October 2001; *The Economist*, at <http://www.economist.com/index.html>.

Managerial and Statistical Questions

1. Is there a relationship between the price of a Big Mac™ and the net hourly wages of workers around the world? If so, how strong is the relationship?
2. Is it possible to develop a model to predict or determine the net hourly wage of a worker anywhere around the world by the price of a Big Mac hamburger in that country? If so, how good is the model?
3. If a model can be constructed to determine the net hourly wage of a worker anywhere around the world by the price of a Big Mac hamburger, what is the predicted net hourly wage of a worker in a country if the price of a Big Mac hamburger is $3.00?

In business, the key to decision making often lies in understanding the relationships between two or more variables. For example, a company in the distribution business may determine that there is a relationship between the price of crude oil and its own transportation costs. Financial experts, in studying the behaviour of the bond market, might find it useful to know if the interest rates on bonds are related to the prime interest rate set by the Bank of Canada. A marketing executive might want to know how strong the relationship is between advertising dollars and sales dollars for a product or a company.

In this chapter, we will study the concept of correlation and how it can be used to estimate the relationship between two variables. We will also explore simple regression analysis, through which mathematical models can be developed to predict one variable by another. We will examine tools for testing the strength and predictability of regression models and we will learn how to use regression analysis to develop forecasting trend lines.

12.1 CORRELATION

Correlation *is a measure of the degree of relatedness of variables.* It can help a business researcher determine, for example, whether the share prices of two airlines rise and fall in any related manner. For a sample of pairs of data, correlation analysis can yield a numerical value that represents the degree of relatedness of the two share prices over time. In the transportation industry, is a correlation evident between the price of transportation and the mass of the object being shipped? If so, how strong is the correlation? In economics, how strong is the correlation between the producer price index and the unemployment rate? In retail sales, are sales related to population density, number of competitors, size of the store, amount of advertising, or other variables?

Table 12.1	Day	Interest Rate	Futures Index
Data for the Economics Example	1	7.43	221
	2	7.48	222
	3	8.00	226
	4	7.75	225
	5	7.60	224
	6	7.63	223
	7	7.68	223
	8	7.67	226
	9	7.59	226
	10	8.07	235
	11	8.03	233
	12	8.00	241

Several measures of correlation are available, the selection of which depends mostly on the level of data being analyzed. Ideally, researchers would like to solve for ρ, the population coefficient of correlation. However, because researchers virtually always deal with sample data, this section introduces a widely used sample **coefficient of correlation, r**. This measure is applicable only if both variables being analyzed have at least an interval level of data.

The statistic r is the **Pearson product-moment correlation coefficient,** named after Karl Pearson. The term r is a *measure of the linear correlation of two variables*. It is a number that ranges from -1 to 0 to $+1$, representing the strength of the relationship between the variables. An r value of $+1$ denotes a perfect positive relationship between two sets of numbers. An r value of -1 denotes a perfect negative correlation, which indicates an inverse relationship between two variables: as one variable gets larger, the other gets smaller, and vice versa. An r value of 0 means no linear relationship is present between the two variables.

Pearson Product-Moment Correlation Coefficient (12.1)

$$r = \frac{\sum(x-\bar{x})(y-\bar{y})}{\sqrt{\sum(x-\bar{x})^2\sum(y-\bar{y})^2}} = \frac{\sum xy - \frac{(\sum x \sum y)}{n}}{\sqrt{\left[\sum x^2 - \frac{(\sum x)^2}{n}\right]\left[\sum y^2 - \frac{(\sum y)^2}{n}\right]}}$$

Figure 12.1 depicts five different degrees of correlation: (a) represents strong negative correlation, (b) represents moderate negative correlation, (c) represents moderate positive correlation, (d) represents strong positive correlation, and (e) contains no correlation.

What is the measure of correlation between the interest rate of federal funds and the commodities futures index? With data such as those shown in Table 12.2, which represent the values for interest rates of federal funds and commodities futures indexes for a sample of 12 days, a correlation coefficient, r, can be computed.

Table 12.2		Interest	Futures Index			
Computation of r for the Economics Example	Day	x	y	x^2	y^2	xy
	1	7.43	221	55.205	48,841	1,642.03
	2	7.48	222	55.950	49,284	1,660.56
	3	8.00	226	64.000	51,076	1,808.00
	4	7.75	225	60.063	50,625	1,743.75
	5	7.60	224	57.760	50,176	1,702.40
	6	7.63	223	58.217	49,729	1,701.49
	7	7.68	223	58.982	49,729	1,712.64
	8	7.67	226	58.829	51,076	1,733.42
	9	7.59	226	57.608	51,076	1,715.34
	10	8.07	235	65.125	55,225	1,896.45
	11	8.03	233	64.481	54,289	1,870.99
	12	8.00	241	64.000	58,081	1,928.00
		$\sum x = 92.93$	$\sum y = 2,725$	$\sum x^2 = 720.220$	$\sum y^2 = 619,207$	$\sum xy = 21,115.07$

$$r = \frac{21,115.07 - \frac{(92.93)(2,725)}{12}}{\sqrt{\left[720.22 - \frac{92.93^2}{12}\right]\left[619,207 - \frac{2,725^2}{12}\right]}} = 0.815$$

Figure 12.1

Five Correlations

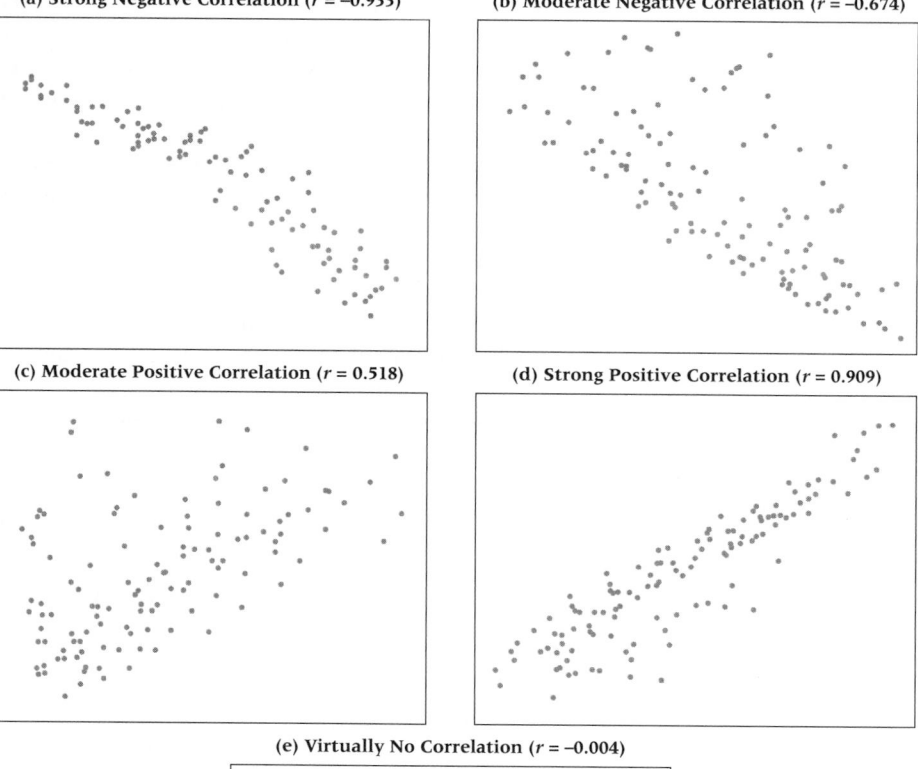

(a) Strong Negative Correlation ($r = -0.933$)

(b) Moderate Negative Correlation ($r = -0.674$)

(c) Moderate Positive Correlation ($r = 0.518$)

(d) Strong Positive Correlation ($r = 0.909$)

(e) Virtually No Correlation ($r = -0.004$)

POINTS OF INTEREST
When two things are related to each other, they will be correlated. However, if two things are correlated they are not necessarily related to each other. For example, two unrelated businesses can grow equally fast showing a strong correlation in growth. This does not mean that the two businesses are related. One of the major pitfalls in business is assuming that two variables are related just because they are correlated. Correlation does not mean causation.

Examination of the formula for computing a Pearson product-moment correlation coefficient reveals that the following values must be obtained to compute r: Σx, Σx^2, Σy, Σy^2, Σxy, and n. In correlation analysis, it does not matter which variable is designated x and which is designated y. For this example, the correlation coefficient is computed as shown in Table 12.2. The r value obtained ($r = 0.815$) represents a relatively strong positive relationship between interest rates and commodities futures index over this 12-day period.

Figure 12.2 shows Excel output for this problem.

Figure 12.2

Excel Output for the Economics Example

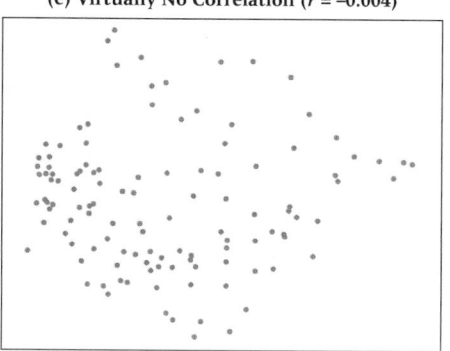

	A	B	C
1		Interest Rate	Futures Index
2	Interest Rate	1	
3	Futures Index	0.815	1

Concept Check

1. In statistics, the phrase "correlation does not imply causation" is used to emphasize that correlation between two variables does not automatically imply that one causes the other. Can you think of two variables (in the world of business or otherwise) that are correlated, yet one does not cause the other; that is, there is no cause-and-effect relationship between the variables?

12.1 Problems

12.1 Determine the value of the correlation coefficient, r, for the following data.

x	4	6	7	11	14	17	21
y	18	12	13	8	7	7	4

12.2 Determine the value of r for the following data.

x	158	296	87	110	436
y	349	510	301	322	550

12.3 In an effort to determine whether any correlation exists between the share prices of airlines, an analyst sampled six days of activity on the stock market. Using the following share prices of Air Canada and WestJet, compute the coefficient of correlation. Share prices have been rounded off to the nearest hundredth for ease of computation.

Air Canada	WestJet
0.75	11.92
0.76	12.09
0.84	12.25
0.85	11.85
0.86	11.78
0.86	11.74

12.4 The following data are the revenue and total CEO compensation for 23 large Canadian companies.

Revenue ($1,000s)	Total CEO Compensation ($1,000s)
327,837	442
1,247,711	9,592
735,276	369
841,641	5,602
1,206,524	2,471
615,291	2,523
10,604	3,485
1,087,869	5,698
192,895	3,424
1,831,690	7,579
279,064	451
2,692,000	2,122

(continued)

Revenue ($1,000s)	Total CEO Compensation ($1,000s)
3,849,552	3,586
6,539,000	3,060
881,437	2,238
8,838,000	16,377
12,664,000	4,824
10,398,000	11,549
849,616	308
1,673,819	1,105
979,496	1,218
847,472	1,826
1,199,866	696

Source: National Post Business Magazine, "CEO Scorecard 2007," November 2007. Material reprinted with the express permission of: "The National Post Company", a Canwest Partnership.

Use the data to compute a correlation coefficient, r, to determine the correlation between company revenue and total CEO compensation.

12.5 The National Safety Council of the U.S. released the following data on the incidence rates for fatal or lost-worktime injuries per 100 employees for several industries in three recent years.

Industry	Year 1	Year 2	Year 3
Textile	0.46	0.48	0.69
Chemical	0.52	0.62	0.63
Communication	0.90	0.72	0.81
Machinery	1.50	1.74	2.10
Services	2.89	2.03	2.46
Nonferrous metals	1.80	1.92	2.00
Food	3.29	3.18	3.17
Government	5.73	4.43	4.00

Compute r for each pair of years and determine which years are most highly correlated.

12.2 INTRODUCTION TO SIMPLE REGRESSION ANALYSIS

Regression analysis is *a mathematical model or function that can be used to predict or determine one variable by another variable or other variables.* The most elementary regression model is called **simple regression** or **bivariate regression** and involves two variables in which one variable is predicted by another variable. In simple regression, *the variable to be predicted* is called the **dependent variable** and is designated as y. The *predictor* is called the **independent variable**, or *explanatory variable,* and is designated as x. In the simple regression analysis that is described here, only a straight-line relationship between two variables is examined. Nonlinear relationships and regression models with more than one independent variable can be explored by using multiple regression models, which are presented in Chapters 13 and 14.

Table 12.3

Airline Cost Data

Number of Passengers	Cost ($1,000s)
61	4.28
63	4.08
67	4.42
69	4.17
70	4.48
74	4.30
76	4.82
81	4.70
86	5.11
91	5.13
95	5.64
97	5.56

POINTS OF INTEREST

The term *regression* was coined by Francis Galton, a cousin of Charles Darwin, to describe the phenomenon that taller parents tend to produce children who are somewhat shorter. Conversely, shorter parents tend to produce children who are somewhat taller. Thus, height "regresses" toward the mean. The term *regression* has become a general statistical term mostly meaning "least-squares curve fitting" (explained later in this chapter).

Can the cost of flying a commercial airliner be predicted using regression analysis? If so, what variables are related to this cost? A few of the many variables that can potentially contribute are type of plane, distance, number of passengers, amount of luggage/freight, weather conditions, direction of destination, and perhaps even pilot skill. Suppose a study is conducted using only Boeing 737s travelling 800 km on comparable routes during the same season of the year. Can the number of passengers predict the cost of flying such routes? It seems logical that more passengers result in more mass and more baggage, which could, in turn, result in increased fuel consumption and other costs. Suppose the data displayed in Table 12.3 are the costs and associated number of passengers for twelve 800-km commercial airline flights using Boeing 737s during the same season of the year. We will use these data to develop a regression model to predict cost by number of passengers.

Usually, the first step in simple regression analysis is to construct a **scatter plot** (or scatter diagram), discussed in Chapter 2. Graphing the data in this way yields preliminary information about the shape and spread of the data. Figure 12.3 is an Excel scatter plot of the data in Table 12.3. Figure 12.4 is a close-up view of the scatter plot. Try to imagine a line passing through the points. Is a linear fit possible? Would a curve fit the data better? The scatter plot gives some idea of how well a regression line fits the data. Later in the chapter, we present statistical techniques that can be used to determine more precisely how well a regression line fits the data.

Figure 12.3

Excel Scatter Plot of Airline Cost Data

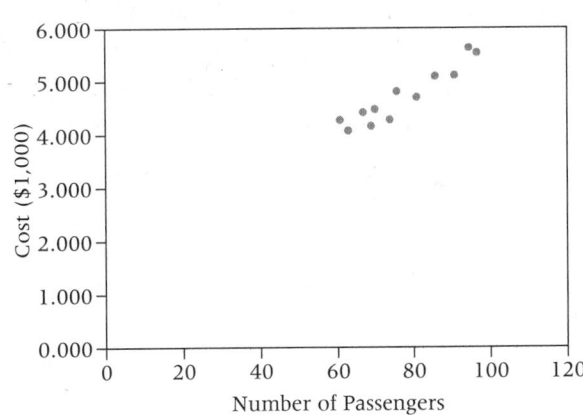

Figure 12.4

**Close-Up Scatter Plot of
Airline Cost Data**

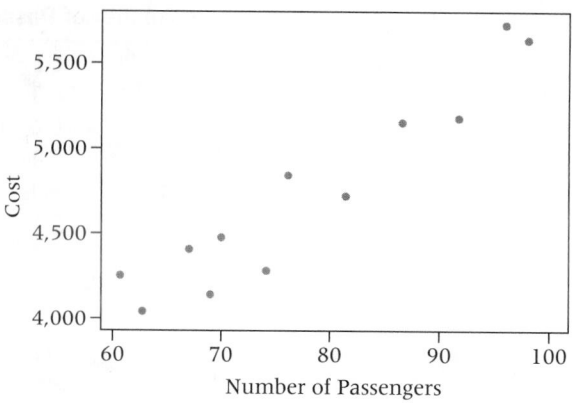

Concept Check

1. What is regression analysis?
2. You know the price and sales history of a product. You need to predict the effect of next year's price on sales. Do you think regression analysis is the right technique to use? Explain.

12.3 DETERMINING THE EQUATION OF THE REGRESSION LINE

The first step in determining the equation of the regression line that passes through the sample data is to establish the equation's form. Several different types of equations of lines are discussed in algebra, finite math, and analytic geometry courses. Recall that among these equations of a line are the two-point form, the point-slope form, and the slope-intercept form. In regression analysis, researchers use the slope-intercept equation of a line. In math courses, the slope-intercept form of the equation of a line often takes the form:

$$y = mx + b$$

where
m = slope of the line
b = y intercept of the line

In statistics, the slope-intercept form of the equation of the regression line through the population points is:

$$\hat{y} = \beta_0 + \beta_1 x$$

where
$\hat{y}$ = the predicted value of y
β_0 = the population y intercept
β_1 = the population slope

For any specific dependent variable value, y_i,

$$y_i = \beta_0 + \beta_1 x_i + \epsilon_i$$

where

x_i = the value of the independent variable for the ith value
y_i = the value of the dependent variable for the ith value
β_0 = the population y intercept
β_1 = the population slope
ϵ_i = the error of prediction for the ith value

Unless the points being fitted by the regression equation are in perfect alignment, the regression line will miss at least some of the points. In the preceding equation, ϵ_i represents the error of the regression line in fitting these points. If a point is on the regression line, $\epsilon_i = 0$.

These mathematical models can be either deterministic models or probabilistic models. **Deterministic models** are *mathematical models that produce an "exact" output for a given input.* For example, suppose the equation of a regression line is:

$$y = 1.68 + 2.40x$$

For a value of $x = 5$, the exact predicted value of y is:

$$y = 1.68 + 2.40(5) = 13.68$$

We recognize, however, that most of the time the values of y will not exactly equal the values yielded by the equation. Random error will occur in the prediction of the y values for values of x because it is likely that the variable x does not explain all the variability of the variable y. For example, suppose we are trying to predict the volume of sales (y) for a company through regression analysis by using the annual dollar amount of advertising (x) as the predictor. Although sales are often related to advertising, other factors related to sales are not accounted for by amount of advertising. Hence, a regression model to predict sales volume by amount of advertising probably involves some error. For this reason, in regression, we present the general model as a probabilistic model. A **probabilistic model** is *one that includes an error term that allows for the y values to vary for any given value of x.* A deterministic regression model is:

$$y = \beta_0 + \beta_1 x$$

The probabilistic regression model is:

$$y_i = \beta_0 + \beta_1 x_i + \epsilon$$

$\beta_0 + \beta_1 x$ is the deterministic portion of the probabilistic model, $\beta_0 + \beta_1 x_i + \epsilon$. In a deterministic model, all points are assumed to be on the line and in all cases ϵ is zero.

Virtually all regression analyses of business data involve sample data, not population data. As a result, β_0 and β_1 are unattainable and must be estimated by using the sample statistics, b_0 and b_1. Hence, the equation of the regression line contains the sample y intercept, b_0, and the sample slope, b_1.

Equation of the Simple Regression Line	$\hat{y} = b_0 + b_1 x$

where

b_0 = the sample intercept
b_1 = the sample slope

Figure 12.5

Plot of a Regression Line

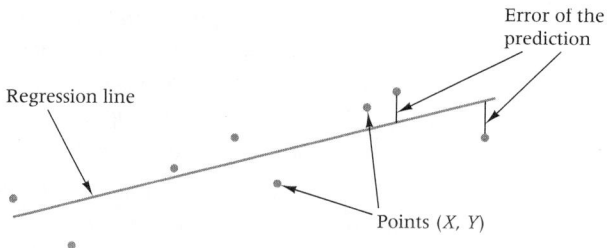

To determine the equation of the regression line for a sample of data, the researcher must determine the values for b_0 and b_1. This process is sometimes referred to as least squares analysis. **Least squares analysis** is *a process whereby a regression model is developed by producing the minimum sum of the squared error values.* On the basis of this premise and calculus, a particular set of equations has been developed to produce components of the regression model.*

Examine the regression line fit through the points in Figure 12.5. Observe that the line does not actually pass through any of the points. The vertical distance from each point to the line is the error of the prediction. In theory, an infinite number of lines could be constructed to pass through these points in some manner. The least squares regression line is the regression line that results in the smallest sum of errors squared.

Formula 12.2 is an equation for computing the value of the sample slope. Several versions of the equation are given to afford latitude in doing the computations.

Slope of the Regression Line (12.2)

$$b_1 = \frac{\sum(x - \bar{x})(y - \bar{y})}{\sum(x - \bar{x})^2} = \frac{\sum xy - n\bar{x}\bar{y}}{\sum x^2 - n\bar{x}^2} = \frac{\sum xy - \frac{(\sum x)(\sum y)}{n}}{\sum x^2 - \frac{(\sum x)^2}{n}}$$

The expression in the numerator of the slope formula 12.2 appears frequently in this chapter and is denoted as SS_{xy}:

$$SS_{xy} = \sum(x - \bar{x})(y - \bar{y}) = \sum xy - \frac{(\sum x)(\sum y)}{n}$$

The expression in the denominator of the slope formula 12.2 also appears frequently in this chapter and is denoted as SS_{xx}:

$$SS_{xx} = \sum(x - \bar{x})^2 = \sum x^2 - \frac{(\sum x)^2}{n}$$

With these abbreviations, the equation for the slope can be expressed as in formula 12.3.

Alternative Formula for Slope (12.3)

$$b_1 = \frac{SS_{xy}}{SS_{xx}}$$

---

*Derivation of these formulas is beyond the scope of information being discussed here, but is presented in Wiley PLUS.

Formula 12.4 is used to compute the sample y intercept. The slope must be computed before the y intercept.

y Intercept of the Regression Line (12.4)	$b_0 = \bar{y} - b_1\bar{x} = \dfrac{\sum y}{n} - b_1\dfrac{(\sum x)}{n}$

Formulas 12.2, 12.3, and 12.4 show that the following data are needed from sample information to compute the slope and intercept: $\sum x$, $\sum y$, $\sum x^2$, and $\sum xy$, unless sample means are used. Table 12.4 contains the results of solving for the slope and intercept and determining the equation of the regression line for the data in Table 12.3.

The least squares equation of the regression line for this problem is:

$$\hat{y} = 1.57 + 0.0407x$$

The slope of this regression line is 0.0407. Because the x values were recoded for ease of computation and are actually in $1,000 denominations, the slope is actually

Table 12.4

Solving for the Slope and the y Intercept of the Regression Line for the Airline Cost Example

Number of Passengers	Cost ($1,000s)		
x	y	x²	xy
61	4.280	3,721	261.080
63	4.080	3,969	257.040
67	4.420	4,489	296.140
69	4.170	4,761	287.730
70	4.480	4,900	313.600
74	4.300	5,476	318.200
76	4.820	5,776	366.320
81	4.700	6,561	380.700
86	5.110	7,396	439.460
91	5.130	8,281	466.830
95	5.640	9,025	535.800
97	5.560	9,409	539.320
$\sum x = 930$	$\sum y = 56.690$	$\sum x^2 = 73,764$	$\sum xy = 4,462.220$

$$SS_{xy} = \sum xy - \frac{(\sum x)(\sum y)}{n} = 4,462.22 - \frac{(930)(56.69)}{12} = 68.745$$

$$SS_{xx} = \sum x^2 - \frac{(\sum x^2)}{n} = 73.764 - \frac{930^2}{12} = 1,689$$

$$b_1 = \frac{SS_{xy}}{SS_{xx}} = \frac{68.745}{1,689} = 0.0407$$

$$b_0 = \frac{\sum y}{n} - b_1\frac{\sum x}{n} = \frac{56.69}{12} - (0.0407)\frac{930}{12} = 1.57$$

$$\hat{y} = 1.57 + 0.0407x$$

Figure 12.6

Excel Graph of Regression Line for the Airline Cost Example

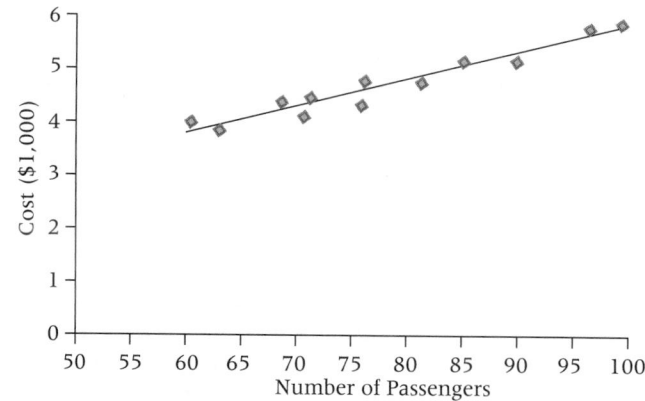

$40.70. One interpretation of the slope in this problem is that for every unit increase in x (every person added to the flight of the airplane), there is a $40.70 increase in the cost of the flight. The y intercept is the point where the line crosses the y axis (where x is zero). Sometimes in regression analysis, the y intercept is meaningless in terms of the variables studied. However, in this problem, one interpretation of the y intercept, which is 1.570 or $1,570, is that even if there were no passengers on the commercial flight, it would still cost $1,570. In other words, there are costs associated with a flight that carries no passengers.

Superimposing the line representing the least squares equation for this problem on the scatter plot indicates how well the regression line fits the data points, as shown in the Excel graph in Figure 12.6. The next several sections explore mathematical ways of testing how well the regression line fits the points.

Demonstration Problem 12.1

A specialist in hospital administration stated that the number of full-time employees (FTEs) in a hospital can be estimated by counting the number of beds in the hospital (a common measure of hospital size). A health care business researcher decided to develop a regression model in an attempt to predict the number of FTEs of a hospital by the number of beds. She surveyed 12 hospitals and obtained the following data. The data are presented in sequence, according to the number of beds.

Number of Beds	FTEs	Number of Beds	FTEs
23	69	50	138
29	95	54	178
29	102	64	156
35	118	66	184
42	126	76	176
46	125	78	225

Solution

The following graph is a scatter plot of these data. Note the linear appearance of the data.

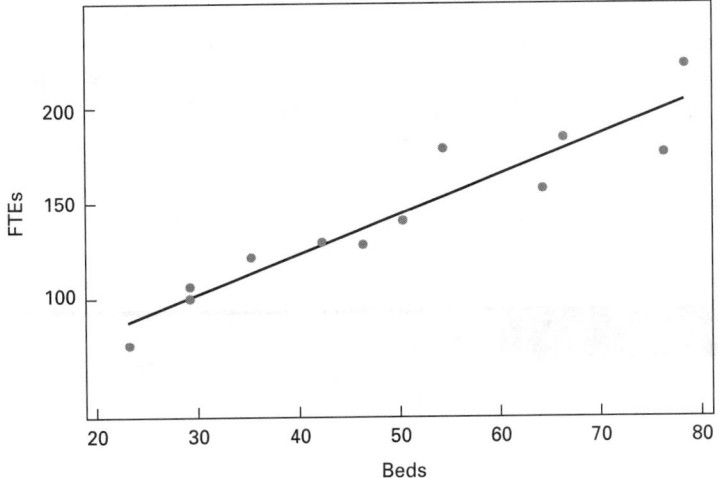

Next, the researcher determined the values of Σx, Σy, Σx^2, and Σxy.

Hospital	Number of Beds x	FTEs y	x^2	xy
1	23	69	529	1,587
2	29	95	841	2,755
3	29	102	841	2,958
4	35	118	1,225	4,130
5	42	126	1,764	5,292
6	46	125	2,116	5,750
7	50	138	2,500	6,900
8	54	178	2,916	9,612
9	64	156	4,096	9,984
10	66	184	4,356	12,144
11	76	176	5,776	13,376
12	78	225	6,084	17,550
	$\Sigma x = 592$	$\Sigma y = 1,692$	$\Sigma x^2 = 33,044$	$\Sigma xy = 92,038$

Using these values, the researcher solved for the sample slope (b_1) and the sample y intercept (b_0):

$$SS_{xy} = \Sigma xy - \frac{(\Sigma x)(\Sigma y)}{n} = 92,038 - \frac{(592)(1,692)}{12} = 8,566$$

$$SS_{xx} = \Sigma x^2 - \frac{(\Sigma x)^2}{n} = 33,044 - \frac{592^2}{12} = 3,838.667$$

$$b_1 = \frac{SS_{xy}}{SS_{xx}} = \frac{8,566}{3,838.667} = 2.232$$

$$b_0 = \frac{\Sigma y}{n} - b_1 \frac{\Sigma x}{12} = \frac{1,692}{12} - (2.232)\frac{592}{12} = 30.888$$

The least squares equation of the regression line is:

$$\hat{y} = 30.888 + 2.232x$$

POINTS OF INTEREST
The fundamental question answered by regression analysis is this: How much increase in the y variable can we expect for a unit increase in the x variable? For instance, how much increase in sales can a company expect for each $1 spent on advertising?

The slope of the line, $b_1 = 2.232$, means that for every unit increase of x (every bed), y (number of FTEs) is predicted to increase by 2.232. Even though the y intercept helps the researcher sketch the graph of the line by being one of the points on the line $(0, 30.888)$, it has limited usefulness in terms of this solution because $x = 0$ denotes a hospital with no beds. On the other hand, it could be interpreted that a hospital has to have at least 31 FTEs to open its doors even with no patients—a sort of "fixed cost" of personnel.

Concept Check

1. What does *slope* mean in regression analysis?

2. What does *intercept* mean in regression analysis?

12.3 Problems

12.6   Sketch a scatter plot from the following data, and determine the equation of the regression line.

x	12	21	28	8	20
y	17	15	22	19	24

12.7   Sketch a scatter plot from the following data, and determine the equation of the regression line.

x	140	119	103	91	65	29	24
y	25	29	46	70	88	112	128

12.8   A corporation owns several companies. The strategic planner for the corporation believes dollars spent on advertising can to some extent be a predictor of total sales dollars. As an aid in long-term planning, she gathers the following sales and advertising information from several of the companies for 2009 ($ millions).

Advertising	Sales
12.5	148
3.7	55
21.6	338
60.0	994
37.6	541
6.1	89
16.8	126
41.2	379

Develop the equation of the simple regression line to predict sales from advertising expenditures using these data.

12.9   Investment analysts generally believe the interest rate on bonds is inversely related to the prime interest rate for loans; that is, bonds perform well when lending rates are down and perform poorly when interest rates are up. Can the bond rate be predicted by the prime interest rate? Use the following data to construct a least squares regression line to predict bond rates by the prime interest rate.

Bond Rate	Prime Interest Rate
5%	16%
12	6
9	8
15	4
7	7

12.10 Is it possible to predict the annual number of business bankruptcies by the number of firm births (business starts)? The following table shows the number of business bankruptcies (1,000s) and the number of firm births (10,000s) for a six-year period. Use these data to develop the equation of the regression model to predict the number of business bankruptcies by the number of firm births. Discuss the meaning of the slope.

Business Bankruptcies (1,000s)	Firm Births (10,000s)
34.3	58.1
35	55.4
38.5	57
40.1	58.5
35.5	57.4
37.9	58

12.11 It appears that over the past 50 years, the number of farms in Canada declined while the average size of farms (in hectares) increased. The following data show five-year interval data for Canadian farms. Use these data to develop the equation of a regression line to predict the average size of a farm by the number of farms. Discuss the slope and y intercept of the model.

Year	Number of Farms	Average Size (ha)
1956	574,993	122
1961	480,877	145
1966	430,503	164
1971	366,110	188
1976	338,552	202
1981	318,361	207
1986	293,089	231
1991	280,043	242
1996	276,548	246
2001	246,923	273
2006	229,373	295

Source: Adapted from Statistics Canada, *Canada at a Glance 2008,* Chart 11 (data) Number and area of farms, Canada, http://www45.statcan.gc.ca/2008/cgco_2008_011a-eng.htm

12.12 Can the annual new orders for manufacturing be predicted by raw steel production? Shown here are the annual new orders for 10 years and the raw steel production for the same 10 years. Use these data to develop a regression model to predict annual new orders by raw steel production. Construct a scatter plot and draw the regression line through the points.

Raw Steel Production (100,000s of net tonnes)	New Orders ($U.S. trillions)
90.6	2.74
88.8	2.87
89.7	2.93
79.7	2.87
84.3	2.98
88.8	3.09
91.3	3.36
95.2	3.61
95.5	3.75
98.5	3.95

12.4 RESIDUAL ANALYSIS: TESTING THE REGRESSION MODEL I–PREDICTED VALUES, RESIDUALS, AND SUM OF SQUARES OF ERROR

How does a business researcher test a regression line to determine whether the line is a good fit for the data other than by observing the fitted line plot (regression line fit through a scatter plot of the data)? One particularly popular approach is to use the *historical data* (x and y values used to construct the regression model) to test the model. With this approach, the values of the independent variable (x values) are inserted into the regression model and a predicted value ($\hat{y}$) is obtained for each x value. These predicted values ($\hat{y}$) are then compared to the actual y values to determine how much error the equation of the regression line produced. *Each difference between the actual y values and the predicted y values is the error of the regression line at a given point, $y - \hat{y}$, and is referred to as the* **residual.** It is the sum of squares of these residuals that is minimized to find the least squares line.

Table 12.5 shows $\hat{y}$ values and the residuals for each pair of data for the airline cost regression model developed in Section 12.3. The predicted values are calculated by inserting

Table 12.5

Predicted Values and Residuals for the Airline Cost Example

Number of Passengers x	Cost ($1,000s) y	Predicted Value $\hat{y}$	Residual $y - \hat{y}$
61	4.280	4.053	0.227
63	4.080	4.134	−0.054
67	4.420	4.297	0.123
69	4.170	4.378	−0.208
70	4.480	4.419	0.061
74	4.300	4.582	−0.282
76	4.820	4.663	0.157
81	4.700	4.867	−0.167
86	5.110	5.07	0.04
91	5.130	5.274	−0.144
95	5.640	5.436	0.204
97	5.560	5.518	0.042
			$\Sigma(y - \hat{y}) = -0.001$

Figure 12.7

Close-Up Scatter Plot with Residuals for the Airline Cost Example

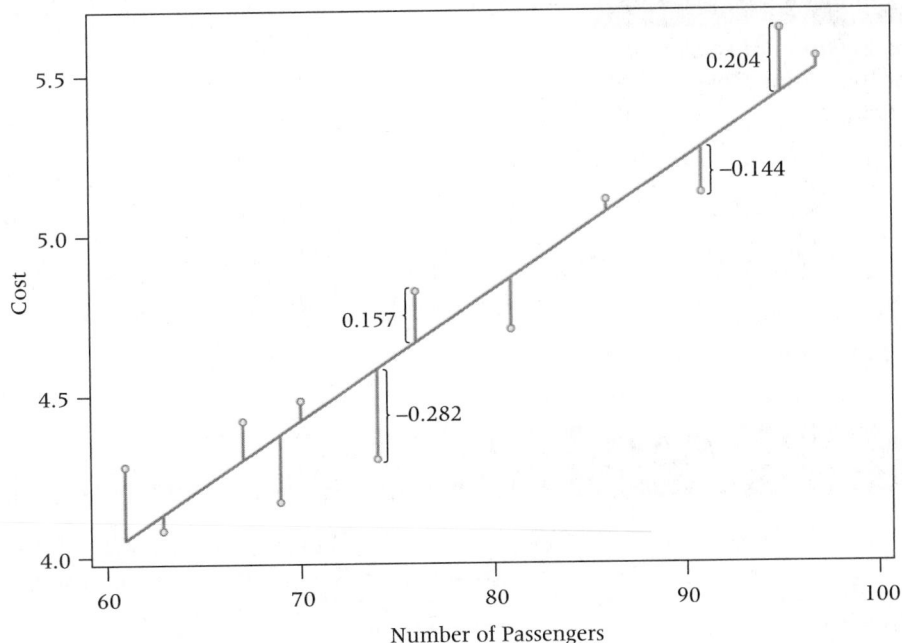

an x value into the equation of the regression line and solving for $\hat{y}$. For example, when $x = 61$, $\hat{y} = 1.57 + 0.0407(61) = 4.053$, as displayed in column 3 of the table. Each of these predicted y values is subtracted from the actual y value to determine the error, or residual. For example, the first y value listed in the table is 4.280 and the first predicted value is 4.053, resulting in a residual of $4.280 - 4.053 = 0.227$. The residuals for this problem are given in column 4 of the table.

Note that the sum of the residuals is approximately zero. Except for rounding error, the sum of the residuals is *always zero*. The reason is that a residual is geometrically the vertical distance from the regression line to a data point. The equations used to solve for the slope and intercept place the line geometrically in the middle of all points. Therefore, vertical distances from the line to the points will cancel each other and sum to zero. Figure 12.7 is a scatter plot of the data and the residuals for the airline cost example.

An examination of the residuals may give the researcher an idea of how well the regression line fits the historical data points. The largest residual for the airline cost example is −0.282, and the smallest is 0.040. Because the objective of the regression analysis was to predict the cost of a flight in thousands of dollars, the regression line produces an error of $282 when there are 74 passengers and an error of only $40 when there are 86 passengers. This result presents the *best* and *worst* cases for the residuals. The researcher must examine other residuals to determine how well the regression model fits other data points.

Sometimes residuals are used to locate outliers. **Outliers** are *data points that lie apart from the rest of the points.* Outliers can produce residuals with large magnitudes and are usually easy to identify on scatter plots. Outliers can be the result of misrecorded or miscoded data, or they may simply be data points that do not conform to the general trend. The equation of the regression line is influenced by every data point used in its calculation in a manner similar to the arithmetic mean. Therefore, outliers can sometimes unduly influence the regression line by "pulling" the line toward the outliers. The origin of outliers must be investigated to determine whether they should be retained or whether the regression equation should be recomputed without them.

Residuals are usually plotted against the x axis, which reveals a view of the residuals as x increases. Figure 12.8 shows the residuals plotted by Excel against the x axis for the airline cost example.

Figure 12.8

Excel Graph of Residuals for the Airline Cost Example

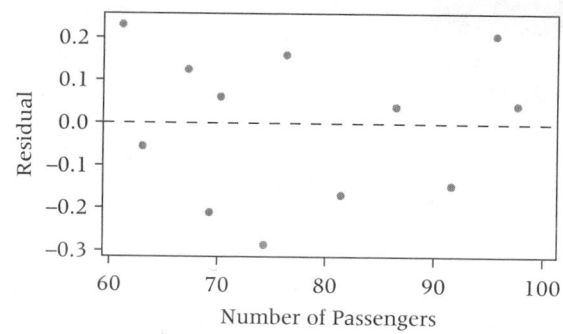

USING RESIDUALS TO TEST THE ASSUMPTIONS OF THE REGRESSION MODEL

One of the major uses of residual analysis is to test some of the assumptions underlying regression. The following are the assumptions of simple regression analysis:

1. The model is linear.
2. The error terms have constant variances.
3. The error terms are independent.
4. The error terms are normally distributed.

A particular method for studying the behaviour of residuals is the residual plot. The **residual plot** is *a type of graph in which the residuals for a particular regression model are plotted along with their associated value of x as an ordered pair (x, y − ŷ)*. Information about how well the regression assumptions are met by the particular regression model can be gleaned by examining the plots. Residual plots are more meaningful with larger sample sizes. For small sample sizes, residual plot analyses can be problematic and subject to overinterpretation. Hence, because the airline cost example is constructed from only 12 pairs of data, one should be cautious in reaching conclusions from Figure 12.8. The residual plots in Figures 12.9, 12.10, and 12.11, however, represent large numbers of data points and therefore are more likely to depict overall trends accurately.

If a residual plot such as the one in Figure 12.9 appears, the assumption that the model is linear does not hold. Note that the residuals are negative for low and high values of x and are positive for middle values of x. The graph of these residuals is parabolic, not linear. The residual plot does not have to be shaped like this for a nonlinear relationship to exist. Any significant deviation from an approximately linear residual plot may mean that a nonlinear relationship exists between the two variables.

The assumption of constant *error variance* is sometimes called **homoscedasticity.** If *the error variances are not constant* (called **heteroscedasticity**), the residual plots might look like one of the two plots in Figure 12.10. Note in Figure 12.10(a) that the error variance is greater for small values of x and smaller for large values of x. The situation is reversed in Figure 12.10(b).

Figure 12.9

Nonlinear Residual Plot

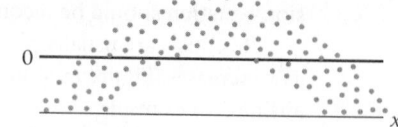

Figure 12.10

Nonconstant Error Variance

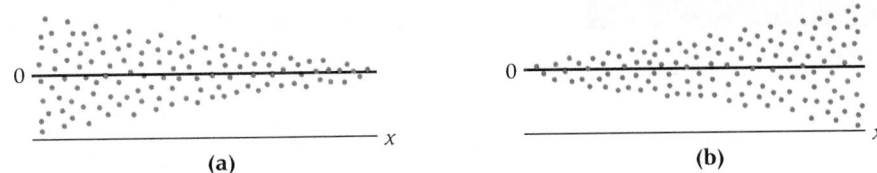

If the error terms are not independent, the residual plots could look like one of the graphs in Figure 12.11. According to these graphs, instead of each error term being independent of the one next to it, the value of the residual is a function of the residual value next to it. For example, a large positive residual is next to a large positive residual and a small negative residual is next to a small negative residual.

Figure 12.11

Graphs of Nonindependent Error Terms

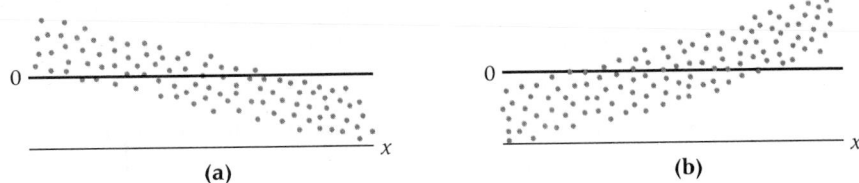

The graph of the residuals from a regression analysis that meets the assumptions—a *healthy residual graph*—might look like the graph in Figure 12.12. The plot is relatively linear; the variances of the errors are about equal for each value of x, and the error terms do not appear to be related to adjacent terms.

Figure 12.12

Healthy Residual Graph

USING THE COMPUTER FOR RESIDUAL ANALYSIS

Many computer programs contain mechanisms for analyzing residuals for violations of the regression assumptions. Figure 12.13 displays residual graphic analyses for a regression model developed to predict the production of carrots per month by the total production of sweet corn. The data were gathered over a time period of 168 consecutive months.

The graph on the upper right is a plot of the residuals versus the fits. Note that this residual plot flares out as x gets larger. This pattern is an indication of heteroscedasticity, which is a violation of the assumption of constant variance for error terms. The graph in the upper left is a normal probability plot of the residuals. A straight line indicates that the residuals are normally distributed. Observe that this normal plot is relatively close to being a straight line, indicating that the residuals are nearly normal in shape. This normal distribution is confirmed by the graph on the lower left, which is a histogram of the residuals. The histogram groups residuals in classes so the researcher can observe where groups of the residuals lie without having to rely on the residual plot or to validate the notion that the residuals are approximately normally distributed. In this problem, the pattern is indicative of at least a mound-shaped distribution of residuals.

Figure 12.13

Residual Analyses

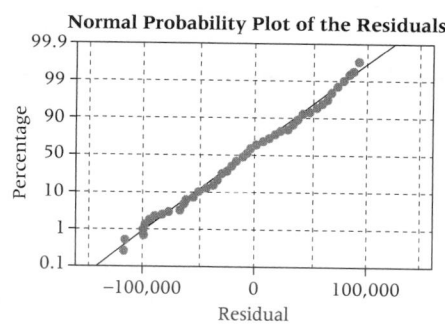

Normal Probability Plot of the Residuals

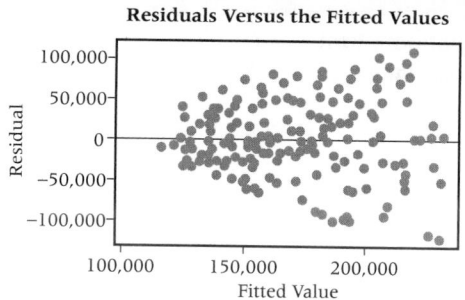

Residuals Versus the Fitted Values

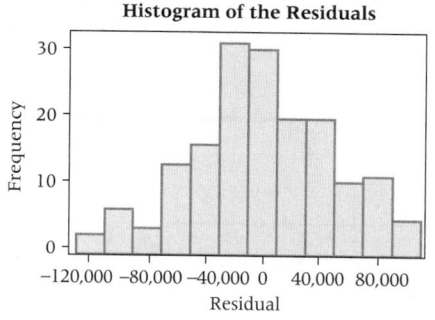

Histogram of the Residuals

Demonstration Problem 12.2

Compute the residuals for Demonstration Problem 12.1 in which a regression model was developed to predict the number of full-time equivalent workers (FTEs) by the number of beds in a hospital. Analyze the residuals by using graphic diagnostics.

Solution

The data and computed residuals are shown in the following table.

Hospital	Number of Beds x	FTEs y	Predicted Value $\hat{y}$	Residuals $y - \hat{y}$
1	23	69	82.22	−13.22
2	29	95	95.62	−0.62
3	29	102	95.62	6.38
4	35	118	109.01	8.99
5	42	126	124.63	1.37
6	46	125	133.56	−8.56
7	50	138	142.49	−4.49
8	54	178	151.42	26.58
9	64	156	173.74	−17.74
10	66	184	178.20	5.80
11	76	176	200.52	−24.52
12	78	225	204.98	20.02

$$\Sigma(y - \hat{y}) = -0.01$$

Note that the regression model fits these particular data well for hospitals 2 and 5, as indicated by residuals of −0.62 and 1.37 FTEs, respectively. For hospitals 1, 8, 9, 11, and 12, the residuals are relatively large, indicating that the regression model does not fit the data for these hospitals well. The Residuals Versus the Fitted Values graph below indicates that the residuals seem to increase as *x* increases, indicating a potential problem with heteroscedasticity. The normal plot of residuals indicates that the residuals are nearly normally distributed. The histogram of residuals shows that the residuals pile up in the middle but are somewhat skewed toward the larger positive values.

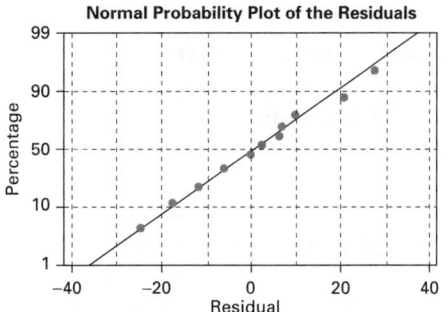

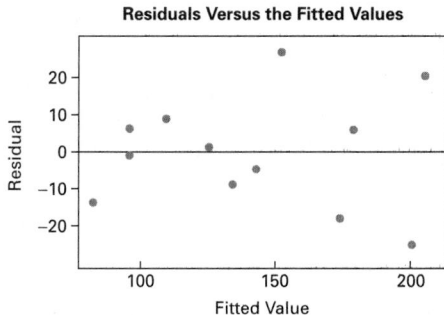

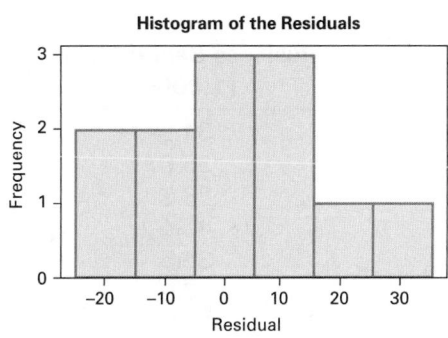

Concept Check

1. What are residuals in regression analysis?
2. Why is it important to analyze the residuals?
3. How would you identify nonlinear residuals?
4. How would you identify heteroscedasticity using residuals?
5. How would you identify nonindependent error terms using residuals?

12.4 Problems

12.13   Determine the equation of the regression line for the following data, and compute the residuals.

x	15	8	19	12	5
y	47	36	56	44	21

12.14   Solve for the predicted values of *y* and the residuals for the data in Problem 12.6. The data are provided here again:

x	12	21	28	8	20
y	17	15	22	19	24

12.15   Solve for the predicted values of *y* and the residuals for the data in Problem 12.7. The data are provided here again:

x	140	119	103	91	65	29	24
y	25	29	46	70	88	112	128

12.16   Solve for the predicted values of y and the residuals for the data in Problem 12.8. The data are provided here again:

Advertising	12.5	3.7	21.6	60.0	37.6	6.1	16.8	41.2
Sales	148	55	338	994	541	89	126	379

12.17   Solve for the predicted values of y and the residuals for the data in Problem 12.9. The data are provided here again:

Bond Rate	5%	12%	9%	15%	7%
Prime Interest Rate	16%	6%	8%	4%	7%

12.18   In Problem 12.10, you were asked to develop the equation of a regression model to predict the number of business bankruptcies by the number of firm births. Using this regression model and the data given in Problem 12.10 (and provided here again), solve for the predicted values of y and the residuals. Comment on the size of the residuals.

Business Bankruptcies (1,000s)	Firm Births (10,000s)
34.3	58.1
35.0	55.4
38.5	57.0
40.1	58.5
35.5	57.4
37.9	58.0

12.19   The equation of a regression line is:

$$\hat{y} = 50.506 - 1.646x$$

The data are as follows.

x	5	7	11	12	19	25
y	47	38	32	24	22	10

Solve for the residuals and graph a residual plot. Do these data seem to violate any of the assumptions of regression?

12.20   Suppose milk is produced in a certain area. Some people might argue that because of transportation costs, the cost of milk increases with the distance of markets from that area. Suppose the milk prices in eight cities are as follows.

Cost of Milk (per 2 L)	Distance from Milk-Producing Area (km)
$2.64	1,245
2.31	425
2.45	1,346
2.52	973
2.19	255
2.55	865
2.40	1,080
2.37	296

Use the prices along with the distance of each city from the milk-producing area to develop a regression line to predict the price of 2 L of milk by the number of kilometres the city is from the milk-producing area. Use the data and the regression equation to compute residuals for this model. Sketch a graph of the residuals in the order of the x values. Comment on the shape of the residual graph.

12.21 Graph the following residuals, and indicate which of the assumptions underlying regression appear to be in jeopardy on the basis of the graph.

x	$y - \hat{y}$
213	−11
216	−5
227	−2
229	−1
237	6
247	10
263	12

12.22 Graph the following residuals, and indicate which of the assumptions underlying regression appear to be in jeopardy on the basis of the graph.

x	$y - \hat{y}$	x	$y - \hat{y}$
10	6	14	−3
11	3	15	2
12	−1	16	5
13	−11	17	8

12.23 Study the following residuals versus fits graphic for a simple regression analysis. Comment on the residual evidence of lack of compliance with the regression assumptions.

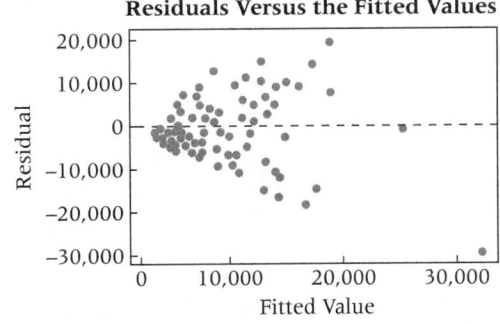

Residuals Versus the Fitted Values

12.5 STANDARD ERROR OF THE ESTIMATE: TESTING THE REGRESSION MODEL II—STANDARD ERROR OF THE ESTIMATE AND *r* SQUARED

Residuals represent errors of estimation for individual points. With large samples of data, residual computations become laborious. Even with computers, a researcher sometimes has difficulty working through pages of residuals in an effort to understand the error of the regression model. An alternative way of examining the error of the model is the standard error of the estimate, which provides a single measurement of the regression error.

Table 12.6

Determining SSE for the Airline Cost Example

Number of Passengers x	Cost ($1,000s) y	Residual $y - \hat{y}$	$(y - \hat{y})^2$
61	4.280	0.227	0.05153
63	4.080	−0.054	0.00292
67	4.420	0.123	0.01513
69	4.170	−0.208	0.04326
70	4.480	0.061	0.00372
74	4.300	−0.282	0.07952
76	4.820	0.157	0.02465
81	4.700	−0.167	0.02789
86	5.110	0.040	0.00160
91	5.130	−0.144	0.02074
95	5.640	0.204	0.04162
97	5.560	0.042	0.00176

$$\Sigma(y - \hat{y}) = -0.001 \quad \Sigma(y - \hat{y})^2 = 0.31434$$

Sum of squares of error = SSE = 0.31434

Because the sum of the residuals is zero, attempting to determine the total amount of error by summing the residuals is fruitless. This zero-sum characteristic of residuals can be avoided by squaring the residuals and then summing them.

Table 12.6 contains the airline cost data from Table 12.3, along with the residuals and the residuals squared. The *total of the residuals squared* column is called the **sum of squares of error (SSE)**.

Sum of Squares of Error

$$SSE = \Sigma(y - \hat{y})^2$$

In theory, infinitely many lines can be fit to a sample of points. However, formulas 12.2 and 12.4 produce a line of best fit for which the SSE is the smallest for any line that can be fit to the sample data. This result is guaranteed, because formulas 12.2 and 12.4 are derived from calculus to minimize SSE. For this reason, the regression process used in this chapter is called *least squares* regression.

The meaning of the computational version of the equation for computing SSE is less obvious in terms of interpretation than $\Sigma(y - \hat{y})^2$, but it is usually easier to compute when calculations are carried out manually. As computers have become universal in business, computational formulas have lost their importance and are seldom used in practice. The computational formula for SSE follows.

Computational Formula for SSE

$$SSE = \Sigma y^2 - b_0 \Sigma y - b_1 \Sigma xy$$

For the airline cost example:

$$\Sigma y^2 = \Sigma[(4.280)^2 + (4.080)^2 + (4.420)^2 + (4.170)^2 + (4.480)^2 + (4.300)^2 + (4.820)^2 + (4.700)^2$$
$$+ (5.110)^2 + (5.130)^2 + (5.640)^2 + (5.560)^2] = 270.9251$$

$$b_0 = 1.5697928$$
$$b_1 = 0.0407016*$$
$$\Sigma y = 56.69$$
$$\Sigma xy = 4,462.22$$
$$\text{SSE} = \Sigma y^2 - b_0 \Sigma y - b_1 \Sigma xy$$
$$= 270.9251 - (1.5697928)(56.69) - (0.0407016)(4,462.22) = 0.31405$$

The slight discrepancy between this value and the value computed in Table 12.6 is due to rounding error.

The sum of squares is in part a function of the number of pairs of data being used to compute the sum, which lessens the value of SSE as a measurement error. A more useful measurement of error is the **standard error of the estimate,** denoted s_e, which is the estimated standard deviation of the error of the regression model and has a more practical use than SSE. The formula for the standard error of the estimate follows.

Standard Error of the Estimate	$s_e = \sqrt{\dfrac{\text{SSE}}{n-2}}$

The standard error of the estimate for the airline cost example is:

$$s_e = \sqrt{\frac{\text{SSE}}{n-2}} = \sqrt{\frac{0.31434}{10}} = 0.1773$$

How is the standard error of the estimate used? As previously mentioned, the standard error of the estimate is a standard deviation of error. Recall from Chapter 3 that if data are approximately normally distributed, the empirical rule states that about 68% of all values are within $\mu \pm 1\sigma$ and about 95% of all values are within $\mu \pm 2\sigma$. One of the assumptions for regression states that for a given x the error terms are normally distributed. Because the error terms are normally distributed, s_e is the standard deviation of error, and the average error is zero, approximately 68% of the error values (residuals) should be within $0 \pm 1s_e$ and 95% of the error values (residuals) should be within $0 \pm 2s_e$. By having knowledge of the variables being studied and by examining the value of s_e, the researcher can often make a judgement about the fit of the regression model to the data by using s_e. How can the s_e value for the airline cost example be interpreted?

The regression model in that example is used to predict airline cost by number of passengers. Note that the range of the airline cost data in Table 12.3 is from 4.08 to 5.64 ($4,080 to $5,640). The regression model for the data yields an s_e of 0.1773. An interpretation of s_e is that the standard deviation of error for the airline cost example is $177.30. If the error terms were normally distributed about the given values of x, approximately 68% of the error terms would be within $\pm\$177.30$ and 95% would be within $\pm 2(\$177.30) = \pm\$354.60$. Examination of the residuals reveals that 100% of the residuals are within $2s_e$. The standard error of the estimate provides a single measure of error, which, if the researcher has enough background in the area being analyzed, can be used to understand the magnitude of errors in the model. In addition, some researchers use the standard error of the estimate to identify outliers. They do so by looking for data that are outside $\pm 2s_e$ or $\pm 3s_e$.

POINTS OF INTEREST
Because SSE is divided by $n - 2$ in calculating the standard deviation of the error (also known as the *standard error*), the larger the n, the smaller will be the standard deviation of the error. This means you can decrease the standard deviation of the error by simply increasing the sample size.

---

*In previous sections, the values of the slope and intercept were rounded off for ease of computation and interpretation. They are shown here with more precision in an effort to reduce rounding error.

Demonstration Problem 12.3

Compute the sum of squares of error and the standard error of the estimate for Demonstration Problem 12.1, in which a regression model was developed to predict the number of FTEs at a hospital by the number of beds.

Solution

Hospital	Number of Beds x	FTEs y	Residuals $y - \hat{y}$	$(y - \hat{y})^2$
1	23	69	−13.22	174.77
2	29	95	−0.62	−0.38
3	29	102	6.38	40.70
4	35	118	8.99	80.82
5	42	126	1.37	1.88
6	46	125	−8.56	73.27
7	50	138	−4.49	20.16
8	54	178	26.58	706.50
9	64	156	−17.74	314.71
10	66	184	5.80	33.64
11	76	176	−24.52	601.23
12	78	225	20.02	400.80

$$\Sigma x = 592 \qquad \Sigma y = 1{,}692 \qquad \Sigma(y - \hat{y}) = -0.01 \qquad \Sigma(y - \hat{y})^2 = 2{,}448.86$$

$$\text{SSE} = 2{,}448.86$$

$$s_e = \sqrt{\frac{\text{SSE}}{n - 2}} = \sqrt{\frac{2{,}448.86}{10}} = 15.65$$

POINTS OF INTEREST
The larger the standard error in relation to the mean, the greater is the variability in the data and the poorer is the fit of the model.

The standard error of the estimate is 15.65 FTEs. An examination of the residuals for this problem reveals that 8 of 12 (67%) are within $\pm 1 s_e$ and 100% are within $\pm 2 s_e$. Is this size of error acceptable? Hospital administrators can probably best answer that question.

Concept Check

1. What does the standard error of the estimate mean in regression analysis?
2. Does the standard error of the estimate tell us anything about the predictive accuracy of the regression model? Explain your answer.

12.5 Problems

12.24   Determine the sum of squares of error (SSE) and the standard error of the estimate (s_e) for Problem 12.6. Determine how many of the residuals computed in Problem 12.14 (for Problem 12.6) are within one standard error of the estimate. If the error terms are normally distributed, approximately how many of these residuals should be within $\pm 1 s_e$?

12.25   Determine the SSE and s_e for Problem 12.7. Use the residuals computed in Problem 12.15 (for Problem 12.7) and determine how many of them are within $\pm 1 s_e$ and $\pm 2 s_e$. How do these numbers compare with what the empirical rule says should occur if the error terms are normally distributed?

12.26   Determine the SSE and s_e for Problem 12.8. Think about the variables being analyzed by regression in this problem and comment on the value of s_e.

12.27 Determine the SSE and s_e for Problem 12.9. Examine the variables being analyzed by regression in this problem and comment on the value of s_e.

12.28 In Problem 12.10, you were asked to develop the equation of a regression model to predict the number of business bankruptcies by the number of firm births. For this regression model, solve for the standard error of the estimate and comment on it.

12.29 Use the data from Problem 12.19 and determine s_e.

12.30 Determine the SSE and s_e for Problem 12.20. Comment on the size of s_e for this regression model, which is used to predict the cost of milk.

12.31 Determine the equation of the regression line to predict annual sales of a company from the yearly stock market volume of shares sold in a recent year. Compute the standard error of the estimate for this model. Does volume of shares sold appear to be a good predictor of a company's sales? Why or why not?

Company	Annual Sales ($ billions)	Annual Volume (millions of shares)
Merck	10.5	728.6
Philip Morris	48.1	497.9
IBM	64.8	439.1
Eastman Kodak	20.1	377.9
Bristol-Myers Squibb	11.4	375.5
General Motors	123.8	363.8
Ford Motors	89.0	276.3

12.6 COEFFICIENT OF DETERMINATION: TESTING THE REGRESSION MODEL II–STANDARD ERROR OF THE ESTIMATE AND *r* SQUARED

A widely used measure of fit for regression models is the **coefficient of determination,** or r^2. The coefficient of determination is *the proportion of variability of the dependent variable (y) accounted for or explained by the independent variable (x).*

The coefficient of determination ranges from 0 to 1. An r^2 of zero means that the predictor accounts for none of the variability of the dependent variable and that there is no regression prediction of y by x. An r^2 of 1 means perfect prediction of y by x and that 100% of the variability of y is accounted for by x. Of course, most r^2 values are between the extremes. The researcher must interpret whether a particular r^2 is high or low, depending on the use of the model and the context within which the model was developed.

In exploratory research where the variables are less understood, low values of r^2 are likely to be more acceptable than they are in areas of research where the parameters are more developed and understood. A NASA researcher who uses vehicular mass to predict mission cost might want to search for a regression model with an r^2 of 0.90 or higher. However, a business researcher who is trying to develop a model to predict the motivation level of employees might be pleased to get an r^2 near 0.50 in the initial research.

The dependent variable, y, being predicted in a regression model has a variation that is measured by the sum of squares of y (SS$_{yy}$):

$$SS_{yy} = \Sigma(y - \bar{y})^2 = \Sigma y^2 - \frac{(\Sigma y)^2}{n}$$

This is the sum of the squared deviations of the y values from the mean value of y. This variation can be broken into two additive variations: the *explained variation*, measured by the sum of squares of regression (SSR or SS_{reg}), and the *unexplained variation*, measured by the sum of squares of error (SSE or SS_{err}). This relationship can be expressed in equation form as:

$$SS_{yy} = SSR + SSE$$

If each term in the equation is divided by SS_{yy}, the resulting equation is:

$$1 = \frac{SSR}{SS_{yy}} + \frac{SSE}{SS_{yy}}$$

The term r^2 is the proportion of the y variability that is explained by the regression model and represented here as:

$$r^2 = \frac{SSR}{SS_{yy}}$$

Substituting this equation into the preceding relationship gives:

$$1 = r^2 + \frac{SSE}{SS_{yy}}$$

Solving for r^2 yields formula 12.5.

Coefficient of Determination (12.5)

$$r^2 = 1 - \frac{SSE}{SS_{yy}} = 1 - \frac{SSE}{\sum y^2 - \frac{(\sum y)^2}{n}}$$

Note: $0 \le r^2 \le 1$

The value of r^2 for the airline cost example is solved as follows:

$$SSE = 0.31434$$

$$SS_{yy} = \sum y^2 - \frac{(\sum y)^2}{n} = 270.9251 - \frac{56.69^2}{12} = 3.11209$$

$$r^2 = 1 - \frac{SSE}{SS_{yy}} = 1 - \frac{0.31434}{3.11209} = 0.899$$

That is, 89.9% of the variability of the cost of flying a Boeing 737 airplane on a commercial flight is explained by variations in the number of passengers. This result also means that 11.1% of the variance in airline flight cost, y, is unaccounted for by x or unexplained by the regression model.

The coefficient of determination can be solved for directly by using:

$$r^2 = \frac{SSR}{SS_{yy}}$$

It can be shown through algebra that:

$$SSR = b_1^2 SS_{xx}$$

From this equation, a computational formula for r^2 can be developed.

Computational Formula for r^2	$r^2 = \dfrac{b_1^2 \, SS_{xx}}{SS_{yy}}$

For the airline cost example, $b_1 = 0.0407016$, $SS_{xx} = 1,689$, and $SS_{yy} = 3.11209$. Using the computational formula for r^2 yields:

$$r^2 = \frac{(0.0407016)^2 (1,689)}{3.11209} = 0.899$$

Demonstration Problem 12.4

Compute the coefficient of determination (r^2) for Demonstration Problem 12.1, in which a regression model was developed to predict the number of FTEs of a hospital by the number of beds.

Solution

$$SSE = 2,448.86$$

$$SS_{yy} = 260,136 - \frac{1,692^2}{12} = 21,564$$

$$r^2 = 1 - \frac{SSE}{SS_{yy}} = 1 - \frac{2,448.6}{21,564} = 0.886$$

POINTS OF INTEREST
r^2 is often expressed as a percentage. If $r = 0.4$, then r^2 is 0.16. This translates to "16% of the variance in one variable is accounted for by the variance in the other variable." While r is not on a linear scale (an r of 0.4 is not twice as strong as an r of 0.2), r^2 is.

This regression model accounts for 88.6% of the variance in FTEs, leaving only 11.4% unexplained variance.

Using $SS_{xx} = 3,838.667$ and $b_1 = 2.232$ from Demonstration Problem 12.1, we can solve for r^2 with the computational formula:

$$r^2 = \frac{b_1^2 SS_{xx}}{SS_{yy}} = \frac{(2.232)^2 (3,838.667)}{21,564} = 0.886$$

RELATIONSHIP BETWEEN r AND r^2

Is r, the coefficient of correlation (Section 12.1), related to r^2, the coefficient of determination in linear regression? The answer is yes: r^2 equals $(r)^2$. The coefficient of determination is the square of the coefficient of correlation. In Demonstration Problem 12.1, a regression model was developed to predict FTEs by number of hospital beds. The r^2 value for the model was 0.886. Taking the square root of this value yields $r = 0.941$, which is the correlation between the sample number of beds and FTEs. A word of caution here: Solving for r by taking $\sqrt{r^2}$ gives the correct magnitude of r but may give the wrong sign. The researcher must examine the sign of the slope of the regression line to determine whether a positive or negative relationship exists between the variables and then assign the appropriate sign to the correlation value.

Concept Check

1. What is the coefficient of determination?
2. How would you interpret a given value of the coefficient of determination?

12.6 Problems

12.32   Compute r^2 for Problem 12.24 (Problem 12.6). Discuss the value of r^2 obtained.

12.33   Compute r^2 for Problem 12.25 (Problem 12.7). Discuss the value of r^2 obtained.

12.34   Compute r^2 for Problem 12.26 (Problem 12.8). Discuss the value of r^2 obtained.

12.35   Compute r^2 for Problem 12.27 (Problem 12.9). Discuss the value of r^2 obtained.

12.36   In Problem 12.10, you were asked to develop the equation of a regression model to predict the number of business bankruptcies by the number of firm births. For this regression model, solve for the coefficient of determination and comment on it.

12.37   The growth of a country's Gross Domestic Product (GDP) refers to the strength of the economy. Long-term interest rates, on the other hand, reflect the outlook for inflation in the future. It is said the economic growth often fuels inflation or inflationary expectations. Given below are the Canadian long-term interest rates and Canadian GDP growth rates (as percentages). Determine the equation of the regression line to predict the long-term interest rates from the GDP growth. Compute the standard error of the estimate for this model. Compute the value of r^2. Does GDP growth appear to be a good predictor of the long-term interest rate? Why or why not?

Year	Long-term Interest Rates (%)	Real GDP Growth (%)
1997	6.14	4.2
1998	5.28	4.1
1999	5.54	5.5
2000	5.93	5.2
2001	5.48	1.8
2002	5.30	2.9
2003	4.80	1.8
2004	4.58	3.3
2005	4.07	2.9

Source: Data extracted from *OECD Fact book 2007*

12.7 HYPOTHESIS TESTS FOR THE SLOPE OF THE REGRESSION MODEL AND TESTING THE OVERALL MODEL

TESTING THE SLOPE

A hypothesis test can be conducted on the sample slope of the regression model to determine whether the population slope is significantly different from zero. This test is another way to determine how well a regression model fits the data. Suppose a researcher decides that it is not worth the effort to develop a linear regression model to predict y from x. An alternative approach might be to average the y values and use $\bar{y}$ as the predictor of y for all values of x. For the airline cost example, instead of using number of passengers as the predictor, the researcher would use the average value of airline cost, $\bar{y}$, as the predictor. In this case, the average value of y is:

$$\bar{y} = \frac{56.69}{12} = 4.7242, \text{ or } \$4,724.20$$

Using this result as a model to predict y, if the number of passengers is 61, 70, or 95—or any other number—the predicted value of y is still 4.7242. Essentially, this approach fits the line of $\bar{y} = 4.7242$ through the data, which is a horizontal line with a slope of zero. Would a regression analysis offer anything more than the $\bar{y}$ model? Using this nonregression model (the $\bar{y}$ model) as a worst case, the researcher can analyze the regression line to determine whether it adds a more significant amount of predictability of y than does the $\bar{y}$ model. Because the slope of the $\bar{y}$ line is zero, one way to determine whether the regression line adds significant predictability is to test the population slope of the regression line to find out whether the slope is different from zero. As the slope of the regression line diverges from zero, the regression model is adding predictability that the $\bar{y}$ line is not generating. For this reason, testing the slope of the regression line to determine whether the slope is different from zero is important. If the slope is not different from zero, the regression line is doing nothing more than the $\bar{y}$ line in predicting y.

How does the researcher go about testing the slope of the regression line? Why not just examine the observed sample slope? For example, the slope of the regression line for the airline cost data is 0.0407. This value is obviously not zero. The problem is that this slope is obtained from a sample of 12 data points, and if another sample were taken, it is likely that a different slope would be obtained. For this reason, the population slope is statistically tested using the sample slope. The question is: If all the pairs of data points for the population were available, would the slope of that regression line be different from zero? Here the sample slope, b_1, is used as evidence to test whether the population slope is different from zero. The hypotheses for this test follow:

$$H_0: \beta_1 = 0$$
$$H_a: \beta_1 \neq 0$$

Note that this test is two-tailed. The null hypothesis can be rejected if the slope is either negative or positive. A negative slope indicates an inverse relationship between x and y. That is, larger values of x are related to smaller values of y, and vice versa. Both negative and positive slopes can be different from zero. To determine whether there is a significant *positive* relationship between two variables, the hypotheses would be one-tailed, or:

$$H_0: \beta_1 = 0$$
$$H_a: \beta_1 > 0$$

To test for a significant negative relationship between two variables, the hypotheses would also be one-tailed, or:

$$H_0: \beta_1 = 0$$
$$H_a: \beta_1 < 0$$

In each case, testing the null hypothesis involves a t test of the slope.

t Test of Slope

$$t = \frac{b_1 - \beta_1}{s_b}$$

where

$$s_b = \frac{s_e}{\sqrt{SS_{xx}}}$$

$$s_e = \sqrt{\frac{SSE}{n-2}}$$

$$SS_{xx} = \sum x^2 - \frac{(\sum x)^2}{n}$$

β_1 = the hypothesized slope

df = $n - 2$

The test of the slope of the regression line for the airline cost regression model for $\alpha = 0.05$ follows. The regression line derived for the data is:

$$\hat{y} = 1.57 + 0.0407x$$

The sample slope is $0.0407 = b_1$. The value of s_e is 0.1773, $\sum x = 930$, $\sum x^2 = 73,764$, and $n = 12$. The hypotheses are:

$$H_0: \beta_1 = 0$$
$$H_a: \beta_1 \neq 0$$

The df = $n - 2 = 12 - 2 = 10$. As this test is two-tailed, $\alpha/2 = 0.025$. The table *t* value is $t_{0.025,10} = \pm 2.228$. The observed *t* value for this sample slope is:

$$t = \frac{0.0407 - 0}{\dfrac{0.1773}{\sqrt{73,764 - \dfrac{930^2}{12}}}} = 9.43$$

As shown in Figure 12.14, the *t* value calculated from the sample slope falls in the rejection region and the *p* value is 0.00000014. The null hypothesis that the population slope is zero is rejected. This linear regression model adds significantly more predictive information to the $\overline{y}$ model (no regression).

Figure 12.14

t **Test of Slope from Airline Cost Example**

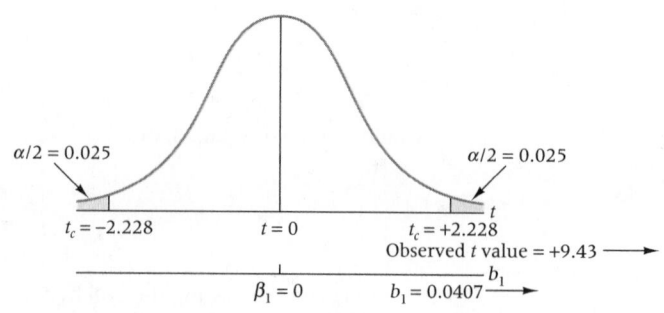

It is desirable to reject the null hypothesis in testing the slope of the regression model. In rejecting the null hypothesis of a zero population slope, we are stating that the regression model adds something to the explanation of the variation of the dependent variable that the average value of y model does not. Failure to reject the null hypothesis in this test causes the researcher to conclude that the regression model has no predictability of the dependent variable, and the model, therefore, has little or no use.

STATISTICS IN BUSINESS TODAY

Predicting the Price of an SUV

Vehicle Make	Vehicle Model	Sales (Jan.–June 2009)	Base Price	Weight (base model in kg)
Ford	Escape	18,143	$24,024	1,503
Toyota	Rav4	12,619	$24,295	1,579
Hyundai	Santa Fe	10,992	$25,995	1,690
Honda	CRV	9,617	$27,790	1,544
Chevrolet	Equinox	5,164	$25,995	2,300

What variables are good predictors of the base price of a new car? Let us consider five variables on five different makes of SUVs: base price, engine horsepower, mass (in kilograms), towing capacity (in kilograms), and city fuel efficiency. The SUV makes are Ford Escape, Toyota Rav4, Hyundai Santa Fe, Honda CRV, and Chevrolet Equinox. The base prices of these five models ranged from $24,024 to $27,790. Suppose a business researcher wanted to develop a regression model to predict the base price of these cars. What variable would be the strongest predictor and how strong would the prediction be?

Using a correlation matrix constructed from the data for the five variables, it was determined that mass was most correlated with base price and had the greatest potential as a predictor. Towing capacity had the second highest correlation with base price, followed by city fuel efficiency, and horsepower. City fuel efficiency was negatively related to base price, indicating that the more expensive SUVs tended to use more gas.

A regression model was developed using mass as a predictor of base price, and the results are shown at right.

Regression Analysis: Base Price versus Mass

The regression equation is:

Base Price $= 10,140 + 5.77$(Mass)

Predictor	Coef	SE Coef	t	p
Constant	18831	2437	7.7	0.004
Mass	3.939	1.394	2.83	0.066

$S = 919$ $R\text{-Sq} = 72.7\%$ $R\text{-Sq(adj)} = 63.4\%$

Note that the r^2 for this model is over 70% and that the t statistic is significant at $\alpha = 0.05$. In the regression equation, the slope indicates that for every kilogram of mass increase there is a $3.94 increase in the price, although the relationship just fell short of significance required for the 0.05 level. The y intercept indicates that if the SUV weighed nothing at all, it would still cost $18,831. (A more reasonable interpretation of the intercept in this context would be that factors other than the mass of the car contributed to the price indicated by the intercept.)

Source: Adapted from Jonathan Welsh, "The Biggest Station Wagon of Them All," *The Wall Street Journal*, 7 June 2002, p. W15C.

Demonstration Problem 12.5

Test the slope of the regression model developed in Demonstration Problem 12.1 to predict the number of FTEs in a hospital from the number of beds to determine whether there is a significant positive slope. Use $\alpha = 0.01$.

Solution

The hypotheses for this problem are:

$$H_0: \beta_1 = 0$$
$$H_a: \beta_1 > 0$$

The level of significance is 0.01. With 12 pairs of data, df = 10. The critical table t value is $t_{0.01,10} = 2.764$. The regression line equation for this problem is:

$$\hat{y} = 30.888 + 2.232x$$

The sample slope, b_1, is 2.232, and $s_e = 15.65$, $\Sigma x = 592$, $\Sigma x^2 = 33,044$, and $n = 12$. The observed t value for the sample slope is:

$$t = \frac{2.232 - 0}{\dfrac{15.65}{\sqrt{33,044 - \dfrac{592^2}{12}}}} = 8.84$$

The observed t value (8.84) is in the rejection region because it is greater than the critical table t value of 2.764 and the p value is 0.0000024. The null hypothesis is rejected. The population slope for this regression line is significantly different from zero in the positive direction. This regression model adds significant predictability over the y model.

TESTING THE OVERALL MODEL

It is common in regression analysis to compute an F test to determine the overall significance of the model. Most computer software packages include the F test and its associated ANOVA table as standard regression output. In multiple regression (Chapters 13 and 14), this test determines whether at least one of the regression coefficients (from multiple predictors) is different from zero. Simple regression provides only one predictor and only one regression coefficient to test. Because the regression coefficient is the slope of the regression line, the F test for overall significance tests the same thing as the t test in simple regression. The hypotheses being tested in simple regression by the F test for overall significance are:

$$H_0: \beta_1 = 0$$
$$H_a: \beta_1 \neq 0$$

In the case of simple regression analysis, $F = t^2$. Thus, for the airline cost example, the F value is:

$$F = t^2 = 9.43^2 = 88.92$$

The F value is computed directly by:

$$F = \frac{SS_{reg}/df_{reg}}{SS_{err}/df_{err}} = \frac{MS_{reg}}{MS_{err}}$$

where
$$df_{reg} = k$$
$$df_{err} = n - k - 1$$
$$k = \text{the number of independent variables}$$

The values of the sum of squares (SS), degrees of freedom (df), and mean squares (MS) are obtained from the ANOVA table, which is produced with other regression statistics as standard output from statistical software packages. Shown here is the ANOVA table produced by Excel for the airline cost example.

ANOVA

	df	SS	MS	F
Regression	1	2.7980	2.7980	89.08
Residual	10	0.3141	0.0314	
Total	11	3.1121		

	Coefficients	Standard Error	t Stat	p value
Intercept	1.5698	0.3381	4.6432	0.0009
Number of Passengers	0.0407	0.0043	9.4389	0.0000

The F value for the airline cost example is calculated from the ANOVA table information as:

$$F = \frac{2.7980/1}{0.3141/10} = \frac{2.7980}{0.03141} = 89.08$$

The difference between this value (89.08) and the value obtained by squaring the t statistic (88.92) is due to rounding error. The probability of obtaining an F value this large or larger by chance if there is no regression prediction in this model is 0.000 according to the ANOVA output (the p value). This output value means it is highly unlikely that the population slope is zero and that there is no prediction due to regression from this model given the sample statistics obtained. Hence, it is highly likely that this regression model adds significant predictability of the dependent variable.

Note from the ANOVA table that the degrees of freedom due to regression are equal to 1. Simple regression models have only one independent variable; therefore, $k = 1$. The degrees of freedom error in simple regression analysis is always $n - k - 1 = n - 1 - 1 = n - 2$. With the degrees of freedom due to regression (1) as the numerator degrees of freedom and the degrees of freedom due to error ($n - 2$) as the denominator degrees of freedom, Table A.7 can be used to obtain the critical F value ($F_{\alpha,1,n-2}$) to help make the hypothesis-testing decision about the overall regression model if the p value of F is not given in the computer output. This critical F value is always found in the right tail of the distribution. In simple regression, the relationship between the critical t value to test the slope and the critical F value of overall significance is:

$$t^2_{\alpha/2, n-2} = F_{\alpha, 1, n-2}$$

For the airline cost example with a two-tailed test and $\alpha = 0.05$, the critical value of $t_{0.025,10}$ is ± 2.228 and the critical value of $F_{0.05,1,10}$ is 4.96. $t^2_{0.025,10} = (\pm 2.228)^2 = 4.96 = F_{0.05,1,10}$.

Concept Check

1. Why should you check the slope and the overall model before using the sample regression model you have developed?

12.7 Problems

12.38 Test the slope of the regression line determined in Problem 12.6. Use $\alpha = 0.05$.

12.39 Test the slope of the regression line determined in Problem 12.7. Use $\alpha = 0.01$.

12.40 Test the slope of the regression line determined in Problem 12.8. Use $\alpha = 0.10$.

12.41 Test the slope of the regression line determined in Problem 12.9. Use a 5% level of significance.

12.42 Test the slope of the regression line developed in Problem 12.10. Use a 5% level of significance.

12.43 Study the following ANOVA table, which was generated from a simple regression analysis. Discuss the F test of the overall model. Determine the value of t and test the slope of the regression line.

Analysis of Variance

Source	DF	SS	MS	F	p
Regression	1	116.65	116.65	8.26	0.021
Error	8	112.95	14.12		
Total	9	229.60			

12.8 ESTIMATION

One of the main uses of regression analysis is as a prediction tool. If the regression function is a good model, the researcher can use the regression equation to determine values of the dependent variable from various values of the independent variable. For example, financial brokers would like to have a model with which they could predict the selling price of a stock on a certain day by a variable such as unemployment rate or producer price index. Marketing managers would like to have a site location model with which they could predict the sales volume of a new location by variables such as population density or number of competitors. The airline cost example presents a regression model that has the potential to predict the cost of flying an airplane by the number of passengers.

In simple regression analysis, a point estimate prediction of y can be made by substituting the associated value of x into the regression equation and solving for y. From the airline cost example, if the number of passengers is $x = 73$, the predicted cost of the airline flight can be computed by substituting the x value into the regression equation determined in Section 12.3:

$$\hat{y} = 1.57 + 0.0407x = 1.57 + 0.0407(73) = 4.5411$$

The point estimate of the predicted cost is 4.5411 or \$4,541.10.

CONFIDENCE INTERVALS TO ESTIMATE THE CONDITIONAL MEAN OF y: $\mu_{y|x}$

Although a point estimate is often of interest to the researcher, the regression line is determined by a sample set of points, and if a different sample is taken, a different line will result, yielding a different point estimate. Hence, computing a *confidence interval* for the estimation is often useful. Because for any value of x (independent variable) there can be many values of y (dependent variable), one type of **confidence interval** is *an estimate of the average value of y for a given x*. This average value of y is denoted $E(y_x)$—the expected value of y—and can be computed using formula 12.6.

| Confidence Interval to Estimate $E(y_x)$ for a Given Value of x (12.6) | $\hat{y} \pm t_{\alpha/2, n-2} s_e \sqrt{\dfrac{1}{n} + \dfrac{(x_0 - \bar{x})^2}{SS_{xx}}}$ |

where

x_0 = a particular value of x

$$SS_{xx} = \sum x^2 - \frac{(\sum x)^2}{n}$$

The application of this formula can be illustrated with the construction of a 95% confidence interval to estimate the average value of y (airline cost) for the airline cost example when x (number of passengers) is 73. For a 95% confidence interval, $\alpha = 0.05$ and $\alpha/2 = 0.025$. The df $= n - 2 = 12 - 2 = 10$. The table t value is $t_{0.025,10} = 2.228$. Other needed values for this problem, which were solved for previously, are:

$$s_e = 0.1773 \quad \sum x = 930 \quad \bar{x} = 77.5 \quad \sum x^2 = 73,764$$

For $x_0 = 73$, the value of $\hat{y}$ is 4.5411. The computed confidence interval for the average value of y, $E(y_{73})$, is:

$$4.5411 \pm (2.228)(0.1773) \sqrt{\frac{1}{12} + \frac{(73 - 77.5)^2}{73,764 - \dfrac{930^2}{12}}} = 4.5411 \pm 0.1220$$

$$4.4191 \leq E(y_{73}) \leq 4.6631$$

That is, with 95% confidence the average value of y for $x = 73$ is between 4.4191 and 4.6631.

Table 12.7 shows confidence intervals computed for the airline cost example for several values of x to estimate the average value of y. Note that as the x values get farther from the mean x value (77.5), the confidence intervals get wider; as the x values get closer to the mean, the confidence intervals narrow. The reason is that the numerator of the second term under the radical sign approaches zero as the value of x nears the mean and increases as x departs from the mean.

Table 12.7	x	Confidence Interval	
Confidence Intervals to Estimate the Average Value of y for Some x Values in the Airline Cost Example	62	4.0934 ± 0.1876	3.9058 to 4.2810
	68	4.3376 ± 0.1461	4.1915 to 4.4837
	73	4.5411 ± 0.1220	4.4191 to 4.6631
	85	5.0295 ± 0.1349	4.8946 to 5.1644
	90	5.2230 ± 0.1656	5.0574 to 5.3886

PREDICTION INTERVALS TO ESTIMATE A SINGLE VALUE OF y

A second type of interval in regression estimation is a **prediction interval** to *estimate a single value of y for a given value of x.*

Prediction Interval to Estimate y for a Given Value of x (12.7)

$$\hat{y} \pm t_{\alpha/2,n-2} s_e \sqrt{1 + \frac{1}{n} + \frac{(x_0 - \bar{x})^2}{SS_{xx}}}$$

where

x_0 = a particular value of x

$$SS_{xx} = \Sigma x^2 - \frac{\left(\Sigma x\right)^2}{n}$$

Formula 12.7 is virtually the same as formula 12.6, except for the additional value of 1 under the radical. This additional value widens the prediction interval to estimate a single value of y from the confidence interval to estimate the average value of y. This result seems logical because the average value of y is toward the middle of a group of y values. Thus, the confidence interval to estimate the average need not be as wide as the prediction interval produced by formula 12.7, which takes into account all the y values for a given x.

A 95% prediction interval can be computed to estimate the single value of y for $x = 73$ from the airline cost example by using formula 12.7. The same values used to construct the confidence interval to estimate the average value of y are used here:

$$t_{0.025,10} = 2.228 \qquad s_e = 0.1773 \qquad \Sigma x = 930 \qquad \bar{x} = 77.5 \qquad \Sigma x^2 = 73,764$$

For $x_0 = 73$, the value of $\hat{y} = 4.5411$. The computed prediction interval for the single value of y is:

$$4.5411 \pm (2.228)(0.1773) \sqrt{1 + \frac{1}{12} + \frac{(73 - 77.5)^2}{73,764 - \dfrac{930^2}{12}}} = 4.5411 \pm 0.4134$$

$$4.1277 \le y \le 4.9545$$

Prediction intervals can be obtained by using the computer. Shown in Figure 12.15 is the computer output for the airline cost example. The output displays the predicted value for $x = 73$ ($\hat{y} = 4.5411$), a 95% confidence interval for the average value of y for $x = 73$, and a 95% prediction interval for a single value of y for $x = 73$. Note that the resulting values are virtually the same as those calculated in this section.

Figure 12.16 displays confidence intervals for various values of x for the average y value and the prediction intervals for a single y value for the airline example. Note that the intervals flare out toward the ends as the values of x depart from the average x value. Note also that the intervals for a single y value are always wider than the intervals for the average y value for any given value of x.

An examination of the prediction interval formula to estimate y for a given value of x explains why the intervals flare out:

$$\hat{y} \pm t_{\alpha/2,n-2} s_e \sqrt{1 + \frac{1}{n} + \frac{(x_0 - \bar{x})^2}{SS_{xx}}}$$

Figure 12.15

Prediction Intervals

Fit	StDev Fit	95.0% CI	95.0% PI
4.5410	0.0547	(4.4191, 4.6629)	(4.1278, 4.9543)

Figure 12.16

Intervals for Estimation

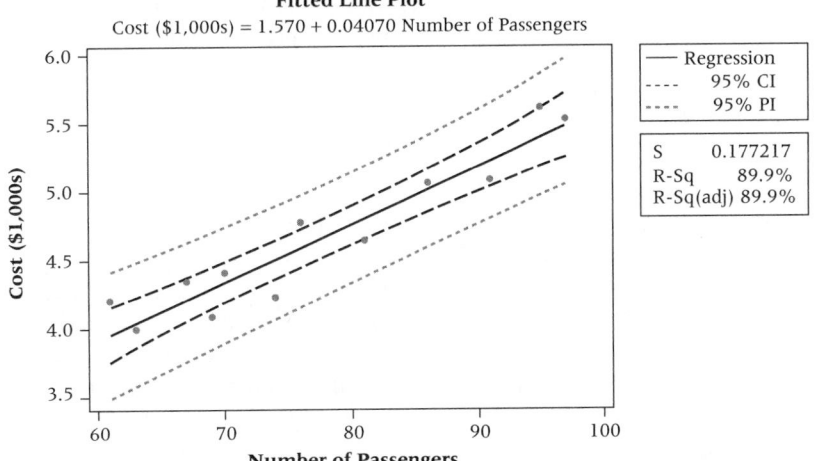

Fitted Line Plot
Cost ($1,000s) = 1.570 + 0.04070 Number of Passengers

As we enter different values of x_o from the regression analysis into the equation, the only thing that changes in the equation is $(x_o - \bar{x})^2$. This expression increases as individual values of x_o get farther from the mean, resulting in an increase in the width of the interval. The interval is narrower for values of x_o nearer $\bar{x}$ and wider for values of x_o farther from $\bar{x}$. A comparison of formulas 12.6 and 12.7 reveals them to be identical except that formula 12.7—to compute a prediction interval to estimate y for a given value of x—contains a 1 under the radical sign. This distinction ensures that formula 12.7 will yield wider intervals than formula 12.6 for otherwise identical data.

Caution: *A regression line is determined from a sample of points. The line, the r², the s_e, and the confidence intervals change for different sets of sample points. That is, the linear relationship developed for a set of points does not necessarily hold for values of x outside the domain of those used to establish the model. In the airline cost example, the domain of x values (number of passengers) varied from 61 to 97. The regression model developed from these points may not be valid for flights of say 40, 50, or 100 because the regression model was not constructed with x values of those magnitudes. However, decision makers sometimes extrapolate regression results to values of x beyond the domain of those used to develop the formulas (often in time-series sales forecasting). Understanding the limitations of this use of regression analysis is essential.*

Demonstration Problem 12.6

Construct a 95% confidence interval to estimate the average value of y (FTEs) for Demonstration Problem 12.1 when $x = 40$ beds. Then, construct a 95% prediction interval to estimate the single value of y for $x = 40$ beds.

Solution

For a 95% confidence interval, $\alpha = 0.05$, n = 12, and df = 10. The table t value is $t_{0.025,10} = 2.228$; $s_e = 15.65$, $\Sigma x = 592$, $\bar{x} = 49.33$, and $\Sigma x^2 = 33,044$. For $x_o = 40$, $\hat{y} = 120.17$. The computed confidence interval for the average value of y is:

$$120.17 \pm (2.228)(15.65)\sqrt{\frac{1}{12} + \frac{(40 - 49.33)^2}{33,044 - \frac{592^2}{12}}} = 120.17 \pm 11.35$$

$$108.82 \leq E(y_{40}) \leq 131.52$$

With 95% confidence, the statement can be made that the average number of FTEs for a hospital with 40 beds is between 108.82 and 131.52.

The computed prediction interval for the single value of y is

$$120.17 \pm (2.228)(15.65) \sqrt{1 + \frac{1}{12} + \frac{(40 - 49.33)^2}{33,044 - \frac{592^2}{12}}} = 120.17 \pm 36.67$$

$$83.5 \le y \le 156.84$$

With 95% confidence, the statement can be made that a single number of FTEs for a hospital with 40 beds is between 83.5 and 156.84. Obviously this interval is much wider than the 95% confidence interval for the average value of y for $x = 40$.

The following graph depicts the 95% interval bands for both the average y value and the single y values for all 12 x values in this problem. Note once again the flaring out of the bands near the extreme values of x.

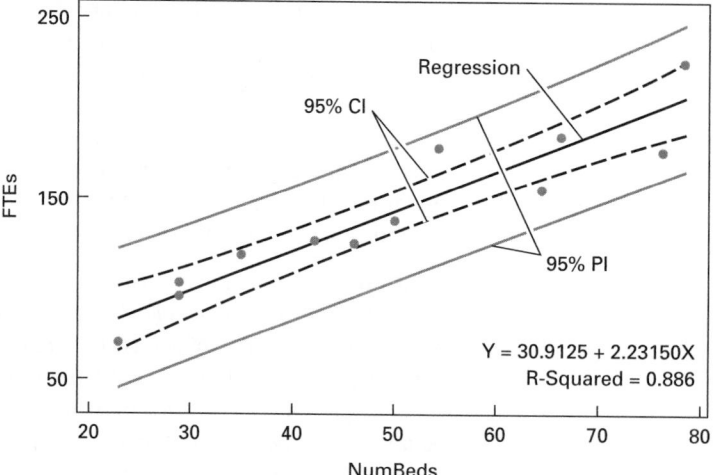

1. What is a confidence interval?

2. A regression equation gives the value of y given the value of x. Do we then need to construct a confidence interval around predicted values?

12.8 Problems

12.44 Construct a 95% confidence interval for the average value of y for Problem 12.6. Use $x = 25$.

12.45 Construct a 90% prediction interval for a single value of y for Problem 12.7 using $x = 100$. Construct a 90% prediction interval for a single value of y for Problem 12.7 using $x = 130$. Compare the results. Which prediction interval is greater? Why?

12.46 Construct a 98% confidence interval for the average value of y for Problem 12.8 using $x = 20$. Construct a 98% prediction interval for a single value of y for Problem 12.8 using $x = 20$. Which is wider? Why?

12.47 Construct a 99% confidence interval for the average bond rate in Problem 12.9 for a prime interest rate of 10%. Discuss the meaning of this confidence interval.

12.9 USING REGRESSION TO DEVELOP A FORECASTING TREND LINE

Business researchers often use historical data with measures taken over time in an effort to forecast what might happen in the future. A particular type of data that often lends itself well to this analysis is **time-series data,** which is defined as *data gathered on a particular character-istic over a period of time at regular intervals.* Some examples of time-series data are 10 years of weekly Toronto Stock Exchange averages, 12 months of daily oil production, or monthly consumption of coffee over a two-year period. To be useful to forecasters, time-series measurements need to be made in regular time intervals and arranged according to time of occurrence. As an example, consider the time-series sales data over a 10-year time period for the Huntsville Chemical Company shown in Table 12.8. Note that the measurements (sales) are taken over time and that the sales figures are given on a yearly basis. Time-series data can also be reported daily, weekly, monthly, quarterly, semiannually, or for other defined time periods.

Table 12.8	Year	Sales ($ millions)
Ten-Year Sales Data for Huntsville Chemical Company	2000	7.84
	2001	12.26
	2002	13.11
	2003	15.78
	2004	21.29
	2005	25.68
	2006	23.80
	2007	26.43
	2008	29.16
	2009	33.06

It is generally believed that time-series data contain any one or combination of four elements: trend, cyclicality, seasonality, and irregularity. While each of these four elements will be discussed in greater detail in Chapter 15, Time-Series Forecasting and Index Numbers, here we examine **trend** and define it as *the long-term general direction of data.* Observing the scatter plot of the Huntsville Chemical Company's sales data shown in Figure 12.17, it is

Figure 12.17

Scatter Plot of Huntsville Chemical Company Data

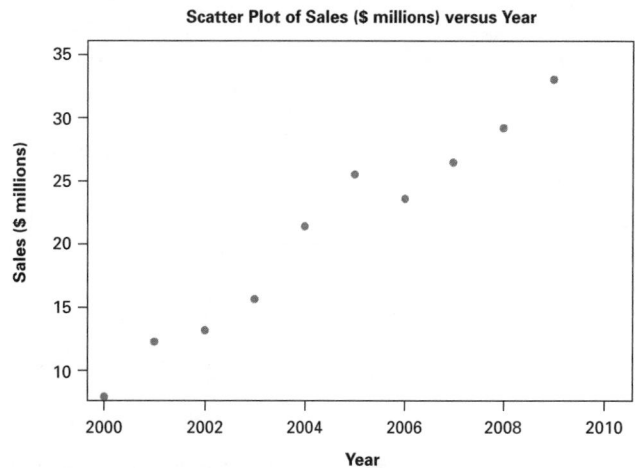

apparent that there is a positive trend in the data. That is, there appears to be a long-term upward general direction of sales over time. How can trend be expressed in mathematical terms? In the field of forecasting, it is common to attempt to fit a trend line through time-series data by determining the equation of the trend line and then using the equation of the trend line to predict future data points. How does one go about developing such a line?

DETERMINING THE EQUATION OF THE TREND LINE

Developing the equation of a linear trend line in forecasting is actually a special case of simple regression where the y or dependent variable is the variable of interest that a business analyst wants to forecast and for which a set of measurements has been taken over a period of time. For example, with the Huntsville Chemical Company data, if company forecasters want to predict sales for the year 2012 using these data, sales would be the dependent variable in the simple regression analysis. In linear trend analysis, the time period is used as the x, the independent or predictor variable, in the analysis to determine the equation of the trend line. In the case of the Huntsville Chemical Company, the x variable represents the years 2000–2009.

Using sales as the y variable and time (year) as the x variable, the equation of the trend line can be calculated in the usual way, as shown in Table 12.9, and is determined to be $\hat{y} = -5,320.56 + 2.6687x$. The slope, 2.6687, means that for every yearly increase in time, sales increase by an average of \$2.6687 (million). The intercept would represent company sales in the year 0, which, of course, in this problem has no meaning since the Huntsville Chemical Company was not in existence in the year 0. Figure 12.18 is a display of the Huntsville sales data with the fitted trend line. Note that the output contains the equation of the trend line along with the values of s (standard error of the estimate) and

Table 12.9				
Determining the Equation of the Trend Line for the Huntsville Chemical Company Sales Data	**Year** x	**Sales** y	x^2	xy
	2000	7.84	4,000,000	15,680.00
	2001	12.26	4,004,001	24,532.26
	2002	13.11	4,008,004	26,246.22
	2003	15.78	4,012,009	31,607.34
	2004	21.29	4,016,016	42,665.16
	2005	25.68	4,020,025	51,488.40
	2006	23.80	4,024,036	47,742.80
	2007	26.43	4,028,049	53,045.01
	2008	29.16	4,032,064	58,553.28
	2009	33.06	4,036,081	66,417.54

$\Sigma x = 20{,}045 \quad \Sigma y = 208.41 \quad \Sigma x^2 = 40{,}180{,}285 \quad \Sigma xy = 417{,}978.01$

$$b_1 = \frac{\Sigma xy - \dfrac{(\Sigma x)(\Sigma y)}{n}}{\Sigma x^2 - \dfrac{(\Sigma x)^2}{n}} = \frac{417{,}978.01 - \dfrac{(20{,}045)(208.41)}{10}}{40{,}180{,}285 - \dfrac{20{,}045^2}{10}} = \frac{220.165}{82.5} = 2.6687$$

$$b_0 = \frac{\Sigma y}{n} - b_1 \frac{\Sigma x}{n} = \frac{208.41}{10} - (2.6687)\frac{20{,}045}{10} = -5{,}328.57$$

Equation of the Trend Line: $\hat{y} = -5{,}328.57 + 2.6687x$

Figure 12.18

Figure 12.18

Huntsville Sales Data with a Fitted Trend Line

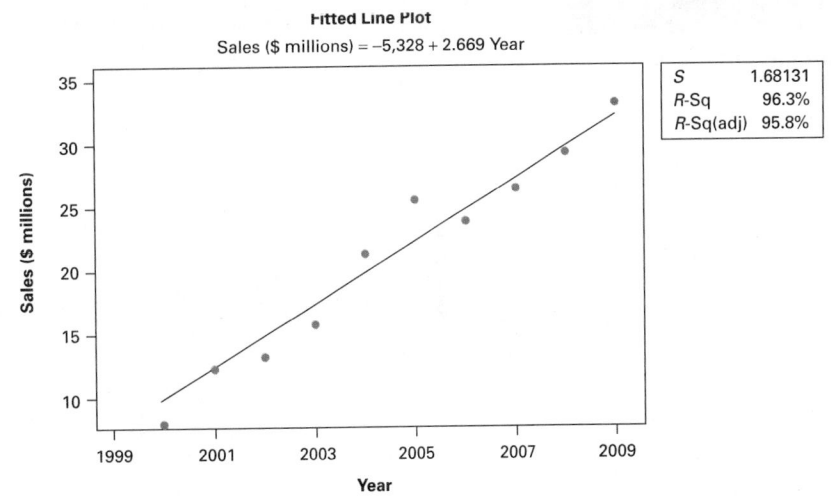

R-Sq (r^2). As is typical with data that have a relatively strong trend, the r^2 value (0.963) is quite high.

FORECASTING USING THE EQUATION OF THE TREND LINE

The main use of the equation of a trend line by business analysts is for forecasting outcomes for time periods in the future. Recall the caution from Section 12.8 that using a regression model to predict y values for x values outside the domain of those used to develop the model may not be valid. Despite this caution and understanding the potential drawbacks, business forecasters nevertheless extrapolate trend lines beyond the most current time periods of the data and attempt to predict outcomes for time periods in the future. To forecast for future time periods using a trend line, insert the time period of interest into the equation of the trend line and solve for $\hat{y}$. For example, suppose forecasters for the Huntsville Chemical Company want to predict sales for the year 2012 using the equation of the trend line developed from their historical time-series data. Replacing x in the equation of the sales trend line with 2012 results in a forecast of $40.85 (million):

$$\hat{y}(2012) = -5,328.57 + 2.6687(2012) = 40.85$$

Figure 12.19 shows the Huntsville Chemical Company data with the trend line through the data and graphical forecasts for the next three periods (2010, 2011, and 2012). Observe from the graph that the forecast for 2012 is about $41 (million).

ALTERNATIVE CODING FOR TIME PERIODS

If you manually calculate the equation of a trend line when the time periods are years, you will notice that the calculations can get quite large and cumbersome (observe Table 12.9). However, if the years are consecutive, they can be recoded using many different possible schemes and still produce a meaningful trend line equation (albeit a different y intercept value). For example, instead of using the years 2000–2009, suppose we use the years 1 to 10. That is, 2000 = 1 (first year), 2001 = 2, 2002 = 3, and so on, to 2009 = 10. This recoding scheme produces the trend line equation of $\hat{y} = 6.1632 + 2.6687x$, as shown in Table 12.10. Notice that the slope of the trend line is the same whether the years 2000 through 2009

Figure 12.19

Trend Line and Forecasts

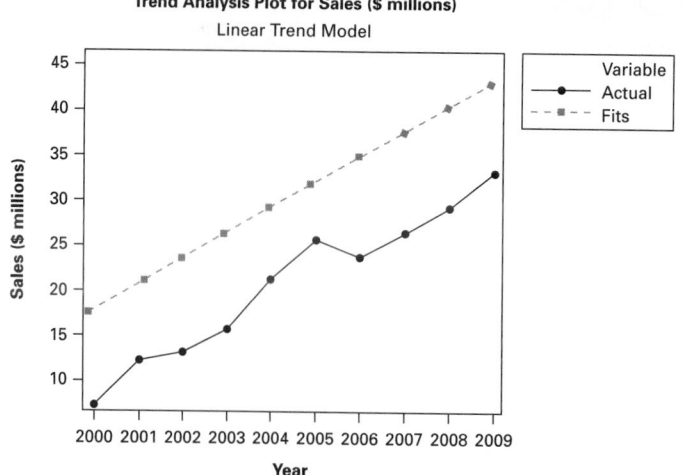

are used or the recoded years of 1 through 10, but the y intercept (6.1632) is different. This needs to be taken into consideration when using the equation of the trend line for forecasting. Since the new trend equation was derived from recoded data, forecasts will also need to be made using recoded data. For example, using the recoded system of 1 through 10 to represent years, the year 2012 is recoded as 13 (2009 = 10, 2010 = 11, 2011 = 12, and 2012 = 13). Inserting this value into the trend line equation results in a forecast of \$40.86, the same as the value obtained using raw years as time:

$$\hat{y} = 6.1632 + 2.6687x = 6.1632 + 2.6687(13) = \$40.86 \text{ (million)}$$

Table 12.10

Using Recoded Data to Calculate the Trend Line Equation

| Year | Sales | | |
x	y	x^2	xy
1	7.84	1	7.84
2	12.26	4	24.52
3	13.11	9	39.33
4	15.78	16	63.12
5	21.29	25	106.45
6	25.68	36	154.08
7	23.80	49	166.6
8	26.43	64	211.44
9	29.16	81	262.44
10	33.06	100	330.6
$\Sigma x = 55$	$\Sigma y = 208.41$	$\Sigma x^2 = 385$	$\Sigma xy = 1{,}366.42$

$$b_1 = \frac{\Sigma xy - \dfrac{(\Sigma x)(\Sigma y)}{n}}{\Sigma x^2 - \dfrac{(\Sigma x)^2}{n}} = \frac{1{,}366.42 - \dfrac{(55)(208.41)}{10}}{385 - \dfrac{55^2}{10}} = \frac{220.165}{82.5} = 2.6687$$

$$b_0 = \frac{\Sigma y}{n} - b_1 \frac{\Sigma x}{n} = \frac{208.41}{10} - (2.6687)\frac{55}{10} = 6.1632$$

Equation of the Trend Line: $\hat{y} = 6.1632 + 2.6687x$

Similar time recoding schemes can be used in the calculating of trend line equations when the time variable is something other than years. For example, in the case of monthly time series data, the time periods can be recoded as:

January = 1, February = 2, March = 3, …, December = 12

In the case of quarterly data over a two-year period, the time periods can be recoded with a scheme such as:

	Time Period	Recoded Time Period
Year 1:	Quarter 1	1
	Quarter 2	2
	Quarter 3	3
	Quarter 4	4
Year 2:	Quarter 1	5
	Quarter 2	6
	Quarter 3	7
	Quarter 4	8

Demonstration Problem 12.7

Shown below are the sales figures of an international company during a recent year over an eight-month period ($ millions). Develop the equation of a trend line through these data and use the equation to forecast sales for October.

Month	Sales ($ millions)
January	32,569
February	32,274
March	32,583
April	32,304
May	32,149
June	32,077
July	31,989
August	31,977

Solution

Shown here is a scatter diagram of these time series data:

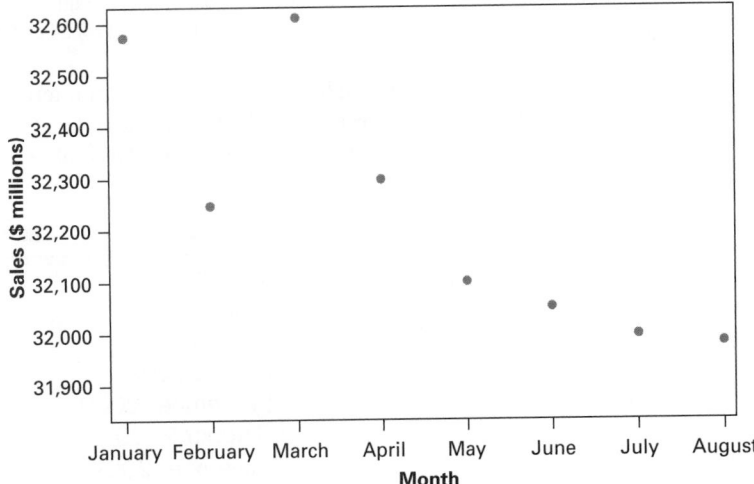

The months of January through August can be coded using the numbers 1 through 8. The analysis shown below uses these numbers as the time period values (x) and sales as the dependent variable (y).

Regression Analysis: Sales versus Month

	Coefficients	Standard Error	t Stat	p Value
Intercept	32,628.2	93.3	349.8	0.000
Month	−86.21	18.47	−4.67	0.003

POINTS OF INTEREST

Trend line construction is one of the most common applications of regression analysis.

The equation of the trend line is $\hat{y} = 32{,}628.2 - 86.21x$. A slope of −86.21 indicates that there is a downward trend in sales over this period of time at a rate of $86.21 (million) per month. The y intercept of 32,628.2 represents what the trend line would estimate the sales to have been in period 0 or December of the previous year. The sales figure for October can be forecast by inserting $x = 10$ into this model and obtaining:

$$\hat{y}(10) = 32{,}628.2 - 86.21(10) = 31{,}766.1$$

Concept Check

1. How would you use regression analysis to predict future values? What type of data is used for this purpose?

12.9 Problems

12.48 Determine the equation of the trend line for the data shown below on Canadian exports of wheat over a five-year period provided by Statistics Canada. Using the trend line equation, forecast the value for the year 2010.

Year	Exports ($ millions)
2004	3,481.4
2005	2,697.2
2006	3,609.2
2007	4,637.7
2008	6,867.9

Source: Statistics Canada, Summary Tables, Exports of goods on a balance-of-payments basis, by product; http://www40.statcan.gc.ca/l01/cst01/gblec04-eng.htm?sdi=exports

12.49 Shown below are the long term interest rates in Canada over a 7-month period according to OECD. Use these data to construct a trend line and to forecast the long-term interest rate for December 2009.

Month	Long-Term Interest Rates
May 2009	3.22
June 2009	3.47
July 2009	3.42
August 2009	3.473
September 2009	3.366
October 2009	3.423
November 2009	3.41

12.50 Canada's new housing prices index has been steadily increasing over the years. Given below are data for Canada's new housing pricing index between 1994 and 2004. Use these data to determine the equation of a trend line for new housing prices index. Use the trend model you developed to forecast new housing prices for 2005.

Year	New Housing Prices Index
1994	102.0
1995	101.2
1996	99.3
1997	100.0
1998	101.0
1999	101.9
2000	104.1
2001	107.0
2002	111.3
2003	116.7
2004	123.2

Source: Data excerpted from Market Research Handbook 2005, published by Statistics Canada.

12.10 INTERPRETING THE OUTPUT

Most regression problems are analyzed by using a computer. In this section, computer output from Excel will be presented and discussed.

The Excel regression output is shown in Figure 12.20 for Demonstration Problem 12.1. The regression equation is found under Coefficients at the bottom of ANOVA. The

Figure 12.20

Excel Regression Output for Demonstration Problem 12.1

	A	B	C	D	E	F
1	SUMMARY OUTPUT					
2	Regression Statistics					
3	Multiple *R*	0.942				
4	*R* Square	0.886				
5	Adjusted *R* Square	0.875				
6	Standard Error	15.6491				
7	Observations	12				
8						
9	ANOVA					
10		df	SS	MS	F	Significance F
11	Regression	1	19115.0632	19115.0632	78.05	.000005
12	Residual	10	2448.9368	244.8937		
13	Total	11	21564			
14						
15		Coefficients	Standard Error	*t* Stat	*p* Value	
16	Intercepts	30.9125	13.2542	2.33	0.041888	
17	Beds	2.2315	0.2526	8.83	0.000005	
18						
19	RESIDUAL OUTPUT					
20	Observation	Predicted FTEs	Residuals			
21	1	82.237	−13.237			
22	2	95.626	−0.626			
23	3	95.626	6.374			
24	4	109.015	8.985			
25	5	124.636	1.364			
26	6	133.562	−8.562			
27	7	142.488	−4.488			
28	8	151.414	26.586			
29	9	173.729	−17.729			
30	10	178.192	5.808			
31	11	200.507	−24.507			
32	12	204.970	20.030			

slope or coefficient of x is 2.2315 and the y intercept is 30.9125. The standard error of the estimate for the hospital problem is given as the fourth statistic under Regression Statistics at the top of the output, Standard Error = 15.6491. The r^2 value is given as 0.886 on the second line. The t test for the slope is found under t Stat near the bottom of the ANOVA section in the "Number of beds" (x variable) row, $t = 8.83$. Adjacent to the t Stat is the p value, which is the probability of the t statistic occurring by chance if the null hypothesis is true. For this slope, the probability shown is 0.000005. The ANOVA table is in the middle of the output with the F value having the same probability as the t statistic, 0.000005, and equalling t^2. The predicted values and the residuals are shown in the Residual Output section.

PREDICTING INTERNATIONAL HOURLY WAGES BY THE PRICE OF A BIG Mac™

In the Decision Dilemma, questions were raised about the relationship between the price of a Big Mac hamburger and net hourly wages around the world and whether a model could be developed to predict net hourly wages by the price of a Big Mac. Data were given for a sample of 27 countries. In exploring the possibility that there is a relationship between these two variables, a Pearson product-moment correlation coefficient, r, was computed to be 0.812. This r value indicates that there is a relatively high correlation between the two variables and that developing a regression model to predict one variable by the other has potential. Designating Net Hourly Wages as the y or dependent variable and the price of a Big Mac as the x or predictor variable, the following regression output was obtained for these data using Excel.

Regression Statistics

Multiple R	0.812
R Square	0.660
Adjusted R Square	0.646
Standard Error	2.934
Observations	27

ANOVA

	df	SS	MS	F	Significance F
Regression	1	416.929	416.929	48.45	0.0000003
Residual	25	215.142	8.606		
Total	26	632.071			

	Coefficients	Standard Error	t Stat	p Value
Intercept	−4.545	1.626	−2.79	0.009828805
Big Mac Price	4.741	0.681	6.96	0.0000003

Taken from this output, the regression model is:

Net Hourly Wage = −4.545 + 4.741 (Price of Big Mac)

While the y intercept has virtually no practical meaning in this analysis, the slope indicates that for every dollar increase in the price of a Big Mac, there is an incremental increase of $4.741 in Net Hourly Wages for a country. It is worth underscoring here that just because there is a relationship between two variables, it does not mean there is a cause-and-effect relationship. That is, McDonald's cannot raise net hourly wages in a country just by increasing the cost of a Big Mac!

Using this regression model, the net hourly wage for a country with a $3.00 Big Mac can be predicted by substituting $x = 3$ into the model:

Net Hourly Wage = −4.545 + 4.741(3) = $9.68

That is, the model predicts that the net hourly wage for a country is $9.68 when the price of a Big Mac is $3.00.

How good a fit is the regression model to the data? Observe from the Excel output that the F value for testing the overall significance of the model (48.45) is highly significant with a p value of 0.0000003, and that the t statistic for testing to determine if the slope is significantly different from zero is

6.96 with a *p* value of 0.0000003. In simple regression, the *t* statistic is the square root of the *F* value, so these statistics relate essentially the same information—that there are significant regression effects in the model. The r^2 value is 66.0%, indicating that the model has moderate predictability. The standard error of the model, $s_e = 2.934$, indicates that if the error terms are approximately normally distributed, about 68% of the predicted net hourly wages would fall within ±$2.93.

Shown here is an Excel-produced line fit plot. Note from the plot that there generally appears to be a linear relationship between the variables but that many of the data points fall considerably away from the fitted regression line, indicating that the price of a Big Mac only partially accounts for net hourly wages.

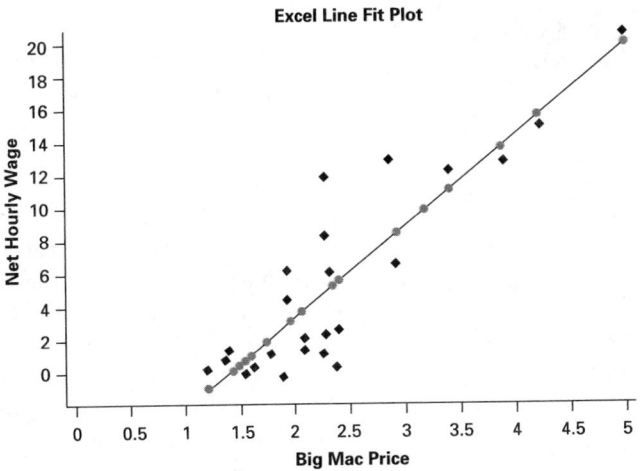

Excel Line Fit Plot

KEY CONSIDERATIONS

Regression analysis offers several opportunities for misleading interpretations. One way is to present a regression model in isolation from information about the fit of the model. That is, the regression model is represented as a valid tool for prediction without any regard for how well it actually fits the data. While it is true that least squares analysis can produce a line of best fit through **virtually any set of points, it does not necessarily follow that the regression model is a good** predictor of the dependent variable. For example, sometimes business consultants sell regression models to companies as forecasting tools or market predictors without disclosing to the client that the r^2 value is very low, the slope of the regression line is not significant, the residuals are large, and the standard error of the estimate is large. This can be misleading and so the analyst should be cautious.

Another inappropriate use of simple regression analysis is stating or implying a cause-and-effect relationship between two variables just because they are highly correlated and produce a high r^2 in regression. The Decision Dilemma presents a good example of this with the regression analysis of the price of a Big Mac™ hamburger and the net hourly wages in a country. While the coefficient of determination is 66.0% and there appears to be a modest fit of the regression line to the data, that does not mean that increasing the price of a Big Mac in a given country will increase the country's net hourly wages. Often, two correlated variables are related to a third variable that drives the two of them but is not included in the regression analysis. In the Decision Dilemma example, both Big Mac prices and net hourly wages may be related to exchange rates or a country's economic condition.

Regression analysis is based on several assumptions, such as equal error variance, independent error terms, and error terms being normally distributed. Through the use of residual plots and other statistical techniques, a business researcher can test these assumptions. It is inappropriate to present a regression model as fact when the assumptions underlying it are being grossly violated, since this can mislead the user.

It is important to remember that since regression models are developed from sample data, when an *x* value is entered into a simple regression model, the resulting prediction is only a point estimate. While business people often use regression models as predicting tools, it should be kept in mind that the prediction value is an estimate, not a guaranteed outcome. By utilizing or at least pointing out confidence intervals and prediction intervals, such as those presented in Section 12.8, the business researcher places the predicted point estimate within the context of inferential estimation and thereby provides sufficient warning to the user.

Lastly, another issue we should be concerned about is using the regression model to predict values of the independent variable that are outside the domain of values used to develop the model. The airline cost model used in this chapter was built with between 61 and 97 passengers. A linear relationship appeared to be evident between flight costs and number of passengers over this domain. This model is not guaranteed to fit values outside the domain of 61 to 97 passengers, however. In fact, either a nonlinear relationship or no relationship may be present between flight costs and number of passengers if values from outside this domain are included in the model-building process. It is a mistake to make claims for a regression model outside the purview of the domain of values for which the model was developed.

Why Statistics Is Relevant

In a business context, you are constantly required to make decisions. To make effective decisions, you need to know how things work: Is the price of a product related to how many people would buy it? If you raise the salary of an employee, is he or she likely to stay with the company longer? Is customer satisfaction related to customer loyalty? Will inflation reduce your profit margin? Regression analysis can answer questions like these and provide input into making effective decisions.

Decision makers also need to understand what is likely to happen in the future so they can plan for it. They need to predict such things as the effect of current investments on future sales and the effect of increased investments in machinery on future profitability. Regression analysis provides a method by which predictions can be carried out in a systematic manner.

A third reason why regression analysis is important is this. Sometimes, decision makers need to assess the effect of alternative scenarios. For example, a decision maker may predict the sales next year to be $150 million, given an inflation rate of 3%. But what would happen if the inflation rate turned out to be 4%? Regression analysis can be used to understand the effect of alternative scenarios on business decisions.

SUMMARY

1. Correlation is a measure that can be used to understand the existence and the strength of the relationship between two variables. The measure of correlation known as the correlation coefficient can range from −1.0 through 0 to +1.0. If the correlation coefficient is negative, as the value of one variable goes up (down), the value of the other variable goes down (up). If the correlation coefficient is positive, as the value of one variable goes up (down), the value of the other variable goes up (down) as well. A zero correlation indicates that the two variables under consideration are not related to each other.

2. Simple regression is a mathematical model that can be used to predict the value of one variable given the value of another variable, such as predicting how much a consumer would spend in a year on clothing, given that person's income during that year. Simple regression is bivariate (two variables) and linear (only a line fit is attempted). Simple regression analysis produces a model that attempts to predict a y variable, referred to as the dependent variable, by an x variable, referred to as the independent variable. The general form of the equation of the simple regression line is the slope-intercept equation of a line. The equation of the simple regression model consists of the slope of the line as the coefficient of x and the y intercept value as the constant.

3. The slope of the line (b) is an estimate of the effect of a one-unit increase in the independent variable on the dependent variable. For example, simple regression can answer the question of how much a consumer is likely to spend on clothing for each dollar increase in income.

4. After the equation of the line has been developed, several statistics are available that can be used to determine how well the line fits the data. Using the historical data values of x, predicted values of y (denoted as $\hat{y}$) can be calculated by inserting values of x into the regression equation. The predicted values can then be compared to the actual values of y to determine how well the regression equation fits the known data. The difference between a specific y value and its associated predicted $\hat{y}$ value is called the residual or error of prediction. Examination of the residuals can offer insight into the magnitude of the errors produced by a model. In addition, residual analysis can be used to help determine whether the assumptions underlying the regression analysis have been met. Specifically, graphs of the residuals can reveal (1) lack of linearity, (2) lack of homogeneity of error variance, and (3) independence of error terms. Geometrically, the residuals are the vertical distances from the y values to the regression line. Because the equation that yields the regression line is derived in such a way that the line is in the geometric middle of the points, the sum of the residuals is zero.

5. The standard error of the estimate is the standard deviation of error of a model. A single value of error measurement called the standard error of the estimate, s_e, can be computed using the formula described. The value of s_e can be used as a single guide to the magnitude of the error produced by the regression model as opposed to examining all the residuals.

6. The coefficient of determination is simply the square of the correlation coefficient. The coefficient of

determination is the proportion of the total variance of the y variable accounted for or predicted by x. The coefficient of determination ranges from 0 to 1. The higher the r^2 value is, the stronger is the predictability of the model.

7. Testing to determine whether the slope of the regression line is different from zero is another way to judge the fit of the regression model to the data. If the population slope of the regression line is not different from zero, the regression model is not adding significant predictability to the dependent variable. A t statistic is used to test the significance of the slope. The overall significance of the regression model can be tested using an F statistic. In simple regression, because only one predictor is present, this test accomplishes the same thing as the t test of the slope, and $F = t^2$.

8. One of the most prevalent uses of a regression model is to predict the values of y for given values of x. Recognizing that the predicted value is often not the same as the actual value, a confidence interval has been developed to yield a range within which the mean y value for a given x should fall. A prediction interval for a single y value for a given x value is also specified. This second interval is wider because it allows for the wide diversity of individual values, whereas the confidence interval for the mean y value reflects only the range of average y values for a given x.

9. Time-series data are data that are gathered over a period of time at regular intervals. Developing the equation of a forecasting trend line for time-series data is a special case of simple regression analysis where the time factor is the predictor variable. The time variable can be in units of years, months, weeks, quarters, and others.

KEY TERMS

bivariate regression
coefficient of correlation (r)
coefficient of determination (r^2)
confidence interval
correlation
dependent variable

deterministic model
heteroscedasticity
homoscedasticity
independent variable
least squares analysis
outliers

Pearson product-moment correlation coefficient
prediction interval
probabilistic model
regression analysis
residual
residual plot

scatter plot
simple regression
standard error of the estimate (s_e)
sum of squares of error (SSE)
time-series data
trend

FORMULAS

(12.1) Pearson product-moment correlation coefficient

$$r = \frac{\sum(x - \bar{x})(y - \bar{y})}{\sqrt{\sum(x - \bar{x})^2 \sum(y - \bar{y})^2}}$$

$$= \frac{\sum xy - \dfrac{\sum x \sum y}{n}}{\sqrt{\left[\sum x^2 - \dfrac{(\sum x)^2}{n}\right]\left[\sum y^2 - \dfrac{(\sum y)^2}{n}\right]}}$$

Equation of the simple regression line

$$\hat{y} = \beta_0 + \beta_1 x$$

Sum of squares

$$SS_{xx} = \sum x^2 - \frac{(\sum x)^2}{n}$$

$$SS_{yy} = \sum y^2 - \frac{(\sum y)^2}{n}$$

$$SS_{xy} = \sum xy - \frac{(\sum x)(\sum y)}{n}$$

(12.2) Slope of the regression line

$$b_1 = \frac{\sum(x - \bar{x})(y - \bar{y})}{\sum(x - \bar{x})^2} = \frac{\sum xy - n\bar{x}\bar{y}}{\sum x^2 - n\bar{x}^2}$$

$$= \frac{\sum xy - \dfrac{(\sum x)(\sum y)}{n}}{\sum x^2 - \dfrac{(\sum x)^2}{n}}$$

(12.3) Alternative formula for slope

$$b_1 = \frac{SS_{xy}}{SS_{xx}}$$

(12.4) y intercept of the regression line

$$b_0 = \bar{y} - b_1\bar{x} = \frac{\sum y}{n} - b_1\frac{(\sum x)}{n}$$

Sum of squares of error

$$SSE = \Sigma(y - \hat{y})^2 = \Sigma y^2 - b_0 \Sigma y - b_1 \Sigma xy$$

Standard error of the estimate

$$s_e = \sqrt{\frac{SSE}{n-2}}$$

(12.5) Coefficient of determination

$$r^2 = 1 - \frac{SSE}{SS_{yy}} = 1 - \frac{SSE}{\Sigma y^2 - \dfrac{(\Sigma y)^2}{n}}$$

Computational formula for r^2

$$r^2 = \frac{b_1^2 SS_{xx}}{SS_{yy}}$$

t test of slope

$$t = \frac{b_1 - \beta_1}{s_b}$$

$$s_b = \frac{s_e}{\sqrt{SS_{xx}}}$$

(12.6) Confidence interval to estimate $E(y_x)$ for a given value of x

$$y \pm t_{\alpha/2, n-2} s_e \sqrt{\frac{1}{n} + \frac{(x_0 - \bar{x})^2}{SS_{xx}}}$$

(12.7) Prediction interval to estimate y for a given value of x

$$\hat{y} \pm t_{\alpha/2, n-2} s_e \sqrt{1 + \frac{1}{n} + \frac{(x_0 - \bar{x})^2}{SS_{xx}}}$$

SUPPLEMENTARY PROBLEMS

Calculating the Statistics

12.51 Determine the Pearson product-moment correlation coefficient for the following data.

x	1	10	9	6	5	3	2
y	8	4	4	5	7	7	9

12.52 Use the following data for parts (a) through (f).

x	5	7	3	16	12	9
y	8	9	11	27	15	13

a. Determine the equation of the least squares regression line to predict y by x.
b. Using the x values, solve for the predicted values of y and the residuals.
c. Solve for s_e.
d. Solve for r^2.
e. Test the slope of the regression line. Use $\alpha = 0.01$.
f. Comment on the results determined in parts (b) through (e), and make a statement about the fit of the line.

12.53 Use the following data for parts (a) through (g).

x	53	47	41	50	58	62	45	60
y	5	5	7	4	10	12	3	11

a. Determine the equation of the simple regression line to predict y from x.
b. Using the x values, solve for the predicted values of y and the residuals.
c. Solve for SSE.
d. Calculate the standard error of the estimate.
e. Determine the coefficient of determination.
f. Test the slope of the regression line. Assume $\alpha = 0.05$. What do you conclude about the slope?
g. Comment on parts (d) and (e).

12.54 If you were to develop a regression line to predict y by x, what value would the coefficient of determination have?

x	213	196	184	202	221	247
y	76	65	62	68	71	75

12.55 Determine the equation of the least squares regression line to predict y from the following data.

x	47	94	68	73	80	49	52	61
y	14	40	34	31	36	19	20	21

a. Construct a 95% confidence interval to estimate the mean y value for $x = 60$.

b. Construct a 95% prediction interval to estimate an individual y value for $x = 70$.

c. Interpret the results obtained in parts (a) and (b).

12.56 Determine the equation of the trend line through the following cost data. Use the equation of the line to forecast cost for year 7.

Year	Cost ($ millions)
1	56
2	54
3	49
4	46
5	45

Testing Your Understanding

12.57 A manager of a car dealership believes there is a relationship between the number of salespeople on duty and the number of cars sold. Suppose the following sample is used to develop a simple regression model to predict the number of cars sold by the number of salespeople. Solve for r^2 and explain what r^2 means in this problem.

Week	Number of Cars Sold	Number of Salespeople
1	79	6
2	64	6
3	49	4
4	23	2
5	52	3

12.58 Executives of a video rental chain want to predict the success of a potential new store. The company's researcher begins by gathering information on number of rentals and average family income from several of the chain's outlets.

Rentals	Average Family Income ($1,000s)
710	65
529	43
314	29
504	47

(continued)

Rentals	Average Family Income ($1,000s)
619	52
428	50
317	46
205	29
468	31
545	43
607	49
694	64

Develop a regression model to predict the number of rentals per day by the average family income. Comment on the output.

12.59 It seems logical that restaurant chains with more units (restaurants) would have greater sales. This assumption is mitigated, however, by several possibilities: some units may be more profitable than others, some units may be larger, some units may serve more meals, some units may serve more expensive meals, and so on. The data shown here were published by Technomic. Perform a simple regression analysis to predict a restaurant chain's sales by its number of units. How strong is the relationship?

Chain	Sales ($ billions)	Number of Units (1,000s)
McDonald's	17.1	12.4
Burger King	7.9	7.5
Taco Bell	4.8	6.8
Pizza Hut	4.7	8.7
Wendy's	4.6	4.6
KFC	4.0	5.1
Subway	2.9	11.2
Dairy Queen	2.7	5.1
Hardy's	2.7	2.9

12.60 Shown here are the total employment labour force figures for Romania over a 13-year period published in LABORSTA. Develop the equation of a trend line through these data and use the equation to predict the total employment labour force of Romania for the year 2011.

Year	Total Employment (1,000s)
1995	11,152
1996	10,935
1997	11,050
1998	10,845
1999	10,776
2000	10,764

(continued)

Year	Total Employment (1,000s)
2001	10,697
2002	9,234
2003	9,223
2004	9,158
2005	9,147
2006	9,313
2007	9,353

12.61 How strong is the correlation between the inflation rate and the unemployment rate? The following data are given as pairs of inflation rates and unemployment rates for the month of May for 2000 to 2009.

Inflation Rate (%)	Unemployment Rate (%)
2.4	6.7
3.9	7.0
1.1	7.8
2.8	7.9
2.4	7.2
1.6	6.9
2.8	6.1
2.2	6.0
2.2	6.1
0.1	8.4

Compute the Pearson product-moment correlation coefficient to determine the strength of the correlation between these two variables. Comment on the strength and direction of the correlation.

12.62 The table below shows the shipments (in millions of dollars) of consumer durables and nondurables in Canada. Is there a linear relationship between the shipments of durables and nondurables? In other words, if we know the value of nondurables shipped in any one year, can we predict the value of durables during that year? (Hint: Make the value of nondurables the independent variable.) According to the model, if at any given year the nondurables shipment is $200,000 million, what would the predicted amount for durables shipment be for the same year? Construct a confidence interval for the average y value for $200,000 million. Use the t statistic to test to

determine whether the slope is significantly different from zero. Use $\alpha = 0.05$.

Year	Nondurables	Durables
1992	130,650	149,868
1993	134,896	169,047
1994	148,431	198,509
1995	167,586	222,194
1996	169,912	230,173
1997	176,276	250,243
1998	174,169	266,984
1999	201,678	308,872
2000	227,038	334,263
2001	231,082	312,190
2002	238,218	321,684
2003	247,606	314,945
2004	258,600	328,180
2005	272,814	333,440
2006	278,473	332,571
2007	280,065	333,406

12.63 People in the aerospace industry believe the cost of a space project is a function of the mass of the major object being sent into space. Use the following data to develop a regression model to predict the cost of a space project by the mass of the space object. Determine r^2 and s_e.

Mass (tonnes)	Cost ($U.S. millions)
1.721	$53.6
2.739	184.9
0.411	6.4
0.896	23.5
0.960	33.4
1.905	110.4
2.165	104.6

12.64 Canada's trade balance with the rest of the world has been steadily increasing over the past several years. It is well known that the U.S. is Canada's leading trade partner. Is there a predictable linear relationship between our total trade balance and our trade balance with the U.S.? Develop a regression model to predict the trade balance with the U.S. by our trade balance in total. Comment on the strength of the model. Develop a time-series trend line for Total Trade Balance using the time periods given. Forecast Total Trade Balance for 2008 using this equation.

	Balance	
Year	**Total**	**U.S.**
1998	23,763	35,541
1999	42,009	59,632
2000	67,036	92,510
2001	70,659	97,834
2002	57,311	91,819
2003	56,413	88,627
2004	65,848	100,538
2005	62,346	109,066
2006	49,480	96,417
2007	48,046	86,342

12.65   Is the amount of money spent by companies on advertising a function of the total sales of the company? Shown are sales income and advertising cost data for seven companies, published by *Advertising Age*.

Company	**Advertising ($ millions)**	**Sales ($ billions)**
Procter & Gamble	4,898	68.2
AT&T	3,345	63.1
General Motors	3,296	207.3
Verizon	2,822	93.2
Ford Motor	2,577	160.1
Wal-Mart	1,073	351.1
Hewlett-Packard	829	91.7

Use the data to develop a regression line to predict the amount of advertising by sales. Compute s_e and r^2. Assuming $\alpha = 0.05$, test the slope of the regression line. Comment on the strength of the regression model.

12.66   Can the consumption of water in a city be predicted by temperature? The following data represent a sample of a day's water consumption and the high temperature for that day.

Water Use (millions of litres)	**Temperature (degrees Celsius)**
829	39
212	4
405	25
488	26
257	10
697	36
568	32
424	24

Develop a least squares regression line to predict the amount of water used in a day in a city by the high temperature for that day. What would the predicted water usage be for a temperature of 38°? Evaluate the regression model by calculating s_e, by calculating r^2, and by testing the slope. Let $\alpha = 0.01$.

Interpreting the Output

12.67   Study the following Excel regression output for an analysis attempting to predict the number of union members by the size of the labour force for selected years over a 30-year period. Analyze the computer output. Discuss the strength of the model in terms of the proportion of variation accounted for, slope, and overall predictability. Using the equation of the regression line, attempt to predict the number of union members when the labour force is 100,000. Note that the model was developed with data already recorded in 1,000 units. Use the data in the model as is.

	A	B	C	D	E	F
1	SUMMARY OUTPUT					
2	Regression Statistics					
3	Multiple R	0.610				
4	R Square	0.372				
5	Adjusted R Square	0.320				
6	Standard Error	982.219				
7	Observations	14				
8						
9	ANOVA					
10		df	SS	MS	F	Significance F
11	Regression	1	6868285.79	6868286	7.12	0.0205
12	Residual	12	11577055.64	967455		
13	Total	13	18445341.43			
14						
15		Coefficients	Standard Error	t Stat	p value	
16	Intercept	22348.97	1846.37	12.10	.000000044	
17	X Variable 1	−0.0524	0.02	−2.67	0.0205	
18						
19	RESIDUAL OUTPUT					
20	Observation	Predicted Y	Residuals			
21	1	19161.39	−1862.39			
22	2	18631.75	749.25			
23	3	18315.95	1295.05			
24	4	17602.12	2240.88			
25	5	17516.68	−176.68			
26	6	17394.71	−398.71			
27	7	17269.86	−294.86			
28	8	17144.07	−231.07			
29	9	17033.79	−31.79			
30	10	16925.13	34.87			
31	11	16902.86	−162.86			
32	12	16961.51	−393.51			
33	13	16914.23	−524.23			
34	14	16841.95	−243.95			

SUPPLEMENTARY PROBLEMS (continued)

12.68 Study the following residual diagnostic graphs. Comment on any possible violations of regression assumptions.

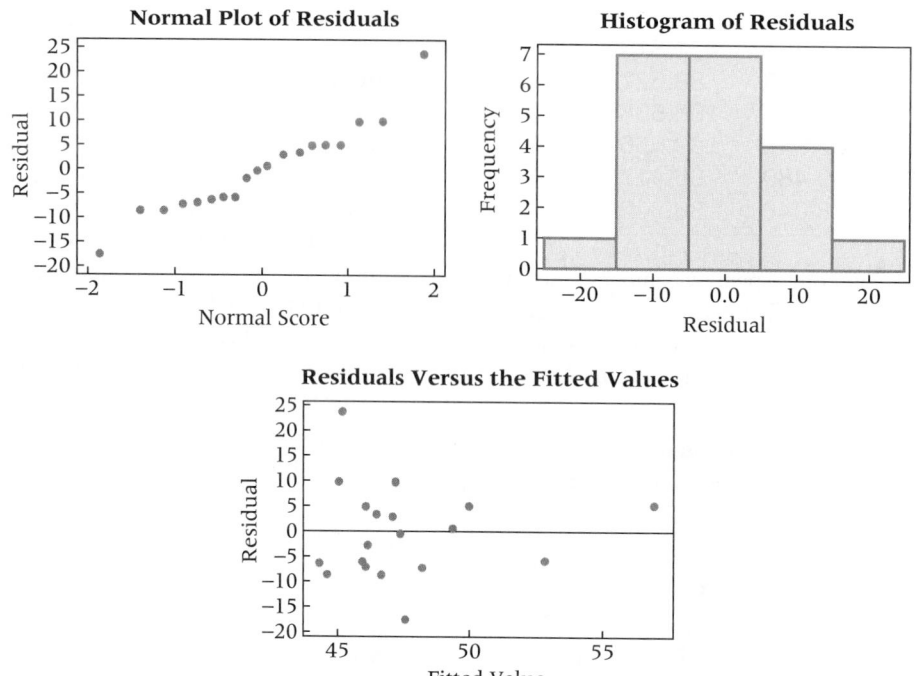

ANALYZING THE DATABASES

see www.wiley.com/canada/black

1. Use the Major League Baseball Database. Develop a regression model from the manufacturing database to predict Current Value from Average Attendance per home game. Discuss the model and its strength on the basis of indicators presented in this chapter. Does it seem logical that the Current Value of the team could be predicted by Average Attendance per home game?

2. Using the Canadian Hospital Database, develop a regression model to predict the number of Congestive Heart Failure by the Population of the municipality. Now develop a regression model to predict number of Acute Stroke Mortality from the Population of the municipality. Examine the regression output. Which type of mortality is more strongly associated with the Population? Explain why, using techniques presented in this chapter. Use the second regression model to predict the number of Acute Stroke Mortality in municipalities that have a Population of 24,000 or more. Construct a 90% confidence interval around this prediction for the average value of y, where x is the population of the municipality.

3. Analyze the variables in columns D, E, F, G, H, J, and K of the Financial Database by using a correlation matrix. These seven variables are capable of producing 21 pairs of correlations. Which are most highly correlated? Select the variable that is most highly correlated with Average Price/Earnings (P/E) ratio and use it as a predictor to develop a regression model to predict P/E ratio. How did the model do?

4. Use the Canadian Stock Market Database to develop a regression model to predict the Utility Index by the Composite Index. How well did the model perform? Did it perform as you expected? Why or why not? Construct a correlation matrix for the variables of this database (excluding Week of the Month) so that you can explore the stock market. Did you discover any apparent relationships between variables?

CASE

Delta Wire Uses Training as an Advantage

The Delta Wire Corporation manufactures high-carbon specialty steel wire for global markets and employs about 100 people. For the past few years, sales have increased each year.

A few years ago, however, things did not look as bright for Delta Wire because it was caught in a potentially disastrous bind. With the U.S. dollar declining in value, foreign competition was becoming a growing threat to Delta's market position. In addition to the growing foreign competition, industry quality requirements were becoming tougher each year.

Delta officials realized that some conditions, such as the value of the dollar, were beyond their control. However, one area that they could improve upon was employee education. The company worked with training programs developed by the state of Mississippi and a local community college to set up its own school. Delta employees were introduced to statistical process control and other quality-assurance techniques. Delta reassured its customers that the company was working hard on improving quality and staying competitive. Customers were invited to sit in on the educational sessions. Because of this effort, Delta has been able to weather the storm and continues to sustain a leadership position in the highly competitive steel wire industry.

Delta continued its training and education program. In the 1990s, Delta instituted a basic skills training program that eventually led to a decrease in nonconforming material from 6% to 2% and a productivity increase from 70,000 to 90,000 pounds (about 32,000 kg to 41,000 kg) per week. In addition, this initiative resulted in a "best in class" award from Goodyear, its largest customer.

Although acquired by Bekaert of Belgium in January of 2006, the Delta Wire Corporation, a major supplier of bead wire for tire reinforcement and other specialized wire products for the North American market, continues to operate in its current capacity. Bekaert wants to support Delta Wire's market share growth and ensure adequate product availability to its customers.

Discussion

1. Delta Wire prides itself on its efforts in the area of employee education. Employee education can pay off in many ways. Discuss some of them. One payoff can be the renewed interest and excitement generated toward the job and the company. Some people theorize that because of a more positive outlook and interest in implementing things learned, the more education received by a worker, the less likely he or she is to miss work days. Suppose the following data represent the number of days of sick leave taken by 20 workers last year along with the number of contact hours of employee education/training they each received in the past year. Use the techniques learned in this chapter to analyze the data. Include both regression and correlation techniques. Discuss the strength of the relationship and any models that are developed.

Employee	Hours of Education	Sick Days	Employee	Hours of Education	Sick Days
1	24	5	11	8	8
2	16	4	12	60	1
3	48	0	13	0	9
4	120	1	14	28	3
5	36	5	15	15	8
6	10	7	16	88	2
7	65	0	17	120	1
8	36	3	18	15	8
9	0	12	19	48	0
10	12	8	20	5	10

2. Many companies find that the implementation of total quality management eventually results in improved sales. Companies that fail to adopt quality efforts lose market share in many cases or go out of business. One measure of the effect of a company's quality improvement efforts is customer satisfaction. Suppose Delta Wire hired a research firm to measure customer satisfaction each year. The research firm developed a customer satisfaction scale in which totally satisfied customers can award a score as high as 50 and totally unsatisfied customers can award a score as low as 0. The scores are measured across many different industrial customers and averaged for a yearly mean customer score. Do sales increase with increases in customer satisfaction scores? To study this notion, suppose the average customer satisfaction score each year for Delta Wire is paired with the company's total sales of that year for the last 15 years, and a regression analysis is run on the data. Assume the following Excel output is the result. Suppose you were asked by Delta Wire to analyze the data and summarize the results. What would you find?

CASE (continued)

Excel Output

	A	B	C	D	E	F
1	SUMMARY OUTPUT					
2	Regression Statistics					
3	Multiple R	0.949				
4	R Square	0.901				
5	Adjusted R Square	0.894				
6	Standard Error	0.411				
7	Observations	15				
8						
9	ANOVA					
10		df	SS	MS	F	Significance F
11	Regression	1	20.098	20.098	118.8	0.000
12	Residual	13	2.199	0.169		
13	Total	14	22.297			
14						
15		Coefficients	Standard	t Stat	p Value	
16	Intercept	1.733	0.436	3.97	0.0016	
17	CustSat	0.162	0.015	10.9	0.000	

3. Delta Wire increased productivity from 70,000 to 90,000 pounds (about 32,000 kg to 41,000 kg) per week during a time when it instituted a basic skills training program. Suppose this program was implemented over an 18-month period and that the following data are the number of total cumulative basic skills hours of training and the per week productivity figures taken once a month over this time. Use techniques from this chapter to analyze the data and make a brief report to Delta about the predictability of productivity from cumulative hours of training.

Cumulative Hours of Training	Productivity (in pounds per week)
0	70,000
100	70,350
250	70,500
375	72,600
525	74,000
750	76,500
875	77,000
1,100	77,400
1,300	77,900
1,450	77,200
1,660	78,900
1,900	81,000
2,300	82,500
2,600	84,000
2,850	86,500
3,150	87,000
3,500	88,600
4,000	90,000

References

Adapted from "Delta Wire Corporation," *Strengthening America's Competitiveness: Resource Management Insights for Small Business Success.* Published by Warner Books on behalf of Connecticut Mutual Life Insurance Company and the U.S. Chamber of Commerce in association with The Blue Chip Enterprise Initiative, 1991; International Monetary Fund; Terri Bergman, "TRAINING: The Case for Increased Investment," *Employment Relations Today,* Winter 1994–1995, pp. 381–391, available at <http://www.ed.psu.edu/nwac/document/train/invest.html>; Bekaert website at <http://www.bekaert.com/en/About us/Press and Media/Press archive/2006/2006-01-31.aspx>.

USING THE COMPUTER

Excel

- Excel has the capability of doing simple regression analysis. For a more inclusive analysis, use the **Data Analysis** tool. For a more "a la carte" approach, use Excel's **Insert Function**.
- To use the **Data Analysis** tool for a more inclusive analysis, begin by selecting the **Data** tab on the Excel worksheet. From the **Analysis** panel at the right top of the **Data** tab worksheet, click on **Data Analysis**. If your Excel worksheet does not show the **Data Analysis** option, then you can load it as an add-in. From the **Data Analysis** pulldown menu, select **Regression**. In the **Regression** dialogue box, input the location of the y values in **Input Y Range**. Input the location of the x values in **Input X Range**. Input **Labels** and input **Confidence Level**. To pass the line through the origin, check **Constant is Zero**. To print out the raw residuals, check **Residuals**. To print out residuals converted to z scores, check **Standardized Residuals**. For a plot of the residuals, check **Residual Plots**. For a plot of the line through the points, check **Line Fit Plots**. Standard output includes r, r^2, s_e, and an ANOVA table with the F test, the slope and intercept, t statistics with associated p-values, and any optionally requested output such as graphs or residuals.

- To use the **Insert Function** (*fx*) go to the **Formulas** tab on an Excel worksheet (top center tab). The **Insert Function** is on the far left of the menu bar. In the **Insert Function** dialogue box at the top, there is a pulldown menu where it says **Or select a category**. From the pulldown menu associated with this command, select **Statistical**. Select **INTERCEPT** from the **Insert Function's Statistical** menu to solve for the y-intercept, **RSQ** to solve for r 2, **SLOPE** to solve for the slope, and **STEYX** to solve for the standard error of the estimate.

A NOTE ON SOME COMPUTER OUTPUTS IN CHAPTERS 12–18

Please note that some of the exhibits in this and some subsequent chapters are produced using Minitab rather than Excel. Strictly speaking, they are to illustrate the points made in the text and are not necessary to follow the material presented. While there are many excellent add-ons to Excel that would perform complex analyses and graphics, the basic Excel program itself does not contain all the readymade functionalities of dedicated statistical software. More information on Minitab can be found on Wiley's website. [www.wiley.com/canada/black]

CHAPTER 13

MULTIPLE REGRESSION ANALYSIS

Learning Objectives

This chapter presents the potential of multiple regression analysis as a tool in business decision making, as well as its applications. The key questions in this chapter are:

1. What is multiple regression analysis?

2. How can we specify a multiple regression model?

3. How can we interpret the results of the model?

4. How can we assess the statistical significance of the regression model and its coefficients?

5. How can we compute and interpret residuals, the standard error of the estimate, and the coefficient of multiple determination?

Digital Vision/Getty Images

DECISION DILEMMA

WILL YOU LIKE YOUR NEW JOB?

Getting a new job can be an exciting and energizing event in your life.

But what if you discover after a short time on the job that you hate it? Is there any way to determine ahead of time whether you will love or hate your job? Sue Shellenbarger of *The Wall Street Journal* discusses some of the things to look for when interviewing for a position that may provide clues as to whether you will be happy there.

Among other things, work cultures vary from hip, freewheeling start-ups to old-school organizational-driven domains. Some organizations place pressure on workers, causing them to feel tense and to work long hours, while others place more emphasis on creativity and the bottom line. Shellenbarger suggests that job interviewees should pay close attention to how they are treated in an interview. Are you just another cog in the wheel or are you valued as an individual? Is a work-life balance apparent within the company? Ask what a typical workday is like at that firm. Inquire about the values that undergird the management by asking questions such as, "What is your proudest accomplishment?" Ask about flexible schedules and how job

training is managed. For example, would you have to go to job training on your own time?

A "Work Trends" survey undertaken by the John J. Heldrich Center for Workforce Development at Rutgers University and the Center for Survey Research and Analysis at the University of Connecticut posed several questions to employees in a survey to ascertain their job satisfaction. Some of the themes included in these questions were relationship with your supervisor, overall quality of the work environment, total hours worked each week, and opportunities for advancement at the job.

Suppose another researcher gathered survey data from 19 employees on these questions and also asked the employees to rate their job satisfaction on a scale from 0 to 100 (with 100 being perfectly satisfied). Suppose the following data represent the results of this survey. Assume that Relationship with Supervisor is rated on a scale from 1 to 5 (1 represents a poor relationship and 5 represents an excellent relationship), Overall Quality of Work Environment is rated on a scale from 0 to 10 (0 represents a poor work environment and 10 represents an excellent work environment), and Opportunities for Advancement is rated on a scale from 1 to 5 (1 represents no opportunities and 5 represents excellent opportunities).

Job Satisfaction	Relationship with Supervisor	Overall Quality of Work Environment	Total Hours Worked per Week	Opportunities for Advancement
55	3	6	55	4
20	1	1	60	3
85	4	8	45	1
65	4	5	65	5
45	3	4	40	3
70	4	6	50	4
35	2	2	75	2
60	4	7	40	3
95	5	8	45	5
65	3	7	60	1
85	3	7	55	3
10	1	1	50	2
75	4	6	45	4
80	4	8	40	5
50	3	5	60	5
90	5	10	55	3
75	3	8	70	4
45	2	4	40	2
65	3	7	55	1

Managerial and Statistical Questions

1. Several variables are presented that may be related to job satisfaction. Which variables are stronger predictors of job satisfaction? Might other variables not mentioned here be related to job satisfaction?

2. Is it possible to develop a mathematical model to predict job satisfaction using the data given? If so, how strong is the model? With four independent variables, will we need to develop four different simple regression models and compare their results?

Source: Adapted from Sue Shellenbarger, "How to Find Out If You're Going to Hate a New Job Before You Agree to Take It," *The Wall Street Journal,* 13 June 2002, p. D1.

Simple regression analysis (discussed in Chapter 12) is bivariate linear regression in which one **dependent variable,** y, is predicted by one **independent variable,** x. Examples of simple regression applications include models to predict retail sales by population density, Toronto Stock Exchange averages by prime interest rates, crude oil production by energy consumption, and CEO compensation by quarterly sales. However, in many cases, other independent variables, taken in conjunction with these variables, can make the regression model a better fit in predicting the dependent variable. For example, sales could be predicted by size of store and number of competitors in addition to population density. A model to predict the Toronto Stock Exchange average could include, in addition to the prime interest rate, such predictors as yesterday's volume, the bond interest rate, and the producer price index. A model to predict CEO compensation could be developed by using variables such as company earnings per share, age of CEO, and size of company in addition to quarterly sales. A model could perhaps be developed to predict the cost of outsourcing by such variables as unit price, export taxes, cost of money, damage in transit, and other factors. Each of these examples contains only one dependent variable, y, as with simple regression analysis. However, multiple independent x variables (predictors) are involved. *Regression analysis with two or more independent variables* is called **multiple regression** analysis.

13.1 THE MULTIPLE REGRESSION MODEL

Multiple regression analysis is similar in principle to simple regression analysis. However, it is more complex conceptually and computationally. Recall from Chapter 12 that the equation of the probabilistic simple regression model is:

$$y = \beta_0 + \beta_1 x + \in$$

where

y = the value of the dependent variable
β_0 = the population y intercept
β_1 = the population slope
$\in$ = the error of prediction

Extending this notion to multiple regression gives the general equation for the probabilistic multiple regression model:

$$y = \beta_0 + \beta_1 x_1 + \beta_2 x_2 + \beta_3 x_3 + \cdots + \beta_k x_k + \in$$

where

y = the value of the dependent variable
β_0 = the regression constant

$\beta_1 =$ the partial regression coefficient for independent variable 1
$\beta_2 =$ the partial regression coefficient for independent variable 2
$\beta_3 =$ the partial regression coefficient for independent variable 3
$\beta_k =$ the partial regression coefficient for independent variable k
$k =$ the number of independent variables

In multiple regression analysis, the dependent variable, y, is sometimes referred to as the **response variable.** The **partial regression coefficient** of an independent variable, β_i, *represents the increase that will occur in the value of y from a one-unit increase in that independent variable if all other variables are held constant.* The "full" (versus partial) regression coefficient of an independent variable is a coefficient obtained from the bivariate model (simple regression) in which the independent variable is the sole predictor of y. The partial regression coefficients occur because more than one predictor is included in a model. The partial regression coefficients are analogous to β_1, the slope of the simple regression model in Chapter 12.

In actuality, the partial regression coefficients and the regression constant of a multiple regression model are population values and are unknown. In virtually all research, these values are estimated by using sample information. Shown here is the form of the equation for estimating with sample information:

$$\hat{y} = b_0 + b_1 x_1 + b_2 x_2 + b_3 x_3 + \cdots + b_k x_k$$

where

$\hat{y} =$ the predicted value of y
$b_0 =$ the estimate of the regression constant
$b_1 =$ the estimate of regression coefficient 1
$b_2 =$ the estimate of regression coefficient 2
$b_3 =$ the estimate of regression coefficient 3
$b_k =$ the estimate of regression coefficient k
$k =$ the number of independent variables

MULTIPLE REGRESSION MODEL WITH TWO INDEPENDENT VARIABLES (FIRST ORDER)

The simplest multiple regression model is one constructed with two independent variables, where the highest power of either variable is 1 (first-order regression model). The regression model is:

$$y = \beta_0 + \beta_1 x_1 + \beta_2 x_2 + \in$$

The constant and coefficients are estimated from sample information, resulting in the following model:

$$\hat{y} = b_0 + b_1 x_1 + b_2 x_2$$

Figure 13.1 is a three-dimensional graph of a series of points (x_1, x_2, y) representing values from three variables used in a multiple regression model to predict the sales price of a house by the number of square feet in the house and the age of the house. Simple regression models yield a line that is fit through data points in the xy plane. In multiple regression analysis, the resulting model produces a **response surface.** In the multiple regression model shown here with two independent first-order variables, the response surface is a **response plane.** The response plane for such a model is fit in a three-dimensional space (x_1, x_2, y).

Figure 13.1

Points in a Sample Space

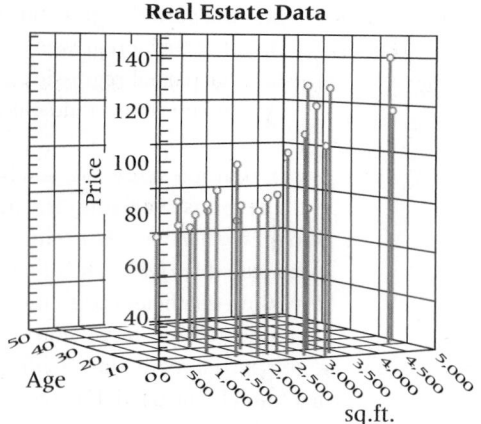

If such a response plane is fit into the points shown in Figure 13.1, the result is the graph in Figure 13.2. Notice that most of the points are not on the plane. As in simple regression, an error in the fit of the model in multiple regression is usually present. The distances shown in the graph from the points to the response plane are the errors of fit, or residuals $(y - \hat{y})$. Multiple regression models with three or more independent variables involve more than three dimensions and are difficult to depict geometrically.

Observe in Figure 13.2 that the regression model attempts to fit a plane into the three-dimensional plot of points. Notice that the plane intersects the y axis. Figure 13.2 depicts some values of y for various values of x_1 and x_2. The error of the response plane $(\in)$ in predicting or determining the y values is the distance from the points to the plane.

DETERMINING THE MULTIPLE REGRESSION EQUATION

The simple regression equations for determining the sample slope and intercept given in Chapter 12 are the result of using methods of calculus to minimize the sum of squares of error for the regression model. The procedure for developing these equations involves solving two simultaneous equations with two unknowns, b_0 and b_1. Finding the sample slope and intercept from these formulas requires the values of Σx, Σy, Σxy, and Σx^2.

Figure 13.2

Response Plane for a First-Order Two-Predictor Multiple Regression Model

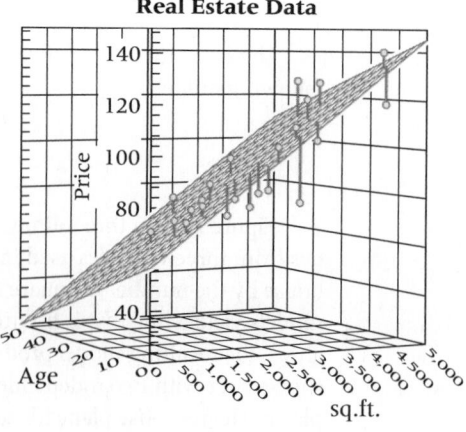

The procedure for determining formulas to solve for multiple regression coefficients is similar. The formulas are established to meet an objective of *minimizing the sum of squares of error for the model.* Hence, the regression analysis shown here is referred to as **least squares analysis.** Methods of calculus are applied, resulting in $k + 1$ equations with $k + 1$ unknowns (b_0 and k values of b_i) for multiple regression analyses with k independent variables. Thus, a regression model with six independent variables will generate seven simultaneous equations with seven unknowns (b_0, b_1, b_2, b_3, b_4, b_5, b_6).

For multiple regression models with two independent variables, the result is three simultaneous equations with three unknowns (b_0, b_1, and b_2):

$$b_0 n + b_1 \sum x_1 + b_2 \sum x_2 = \sum y$$
$$b_0 \sum x_1 + b_1 \sum x_1^2 + b_2 \sum x_1 x_2 = \sum x_1 y$$
$$b_0 \sum x_2 + b_1 \sum x_1 x_2 + b_2 \sum x_2^2 = \sum x_2 y$$

The process of solving these equations by hand is tedious and time consuming. Solving for the regression coefficients and regression constant in a multiple regression model with two independent variables requires $\sum x_1$, $\sum x_2$, $\sum y$, $\sum x_1^2$, $\sum x_2^2$, $\sum x_1 x_2$, $\sum x_1 y$, and $\sum x_2 y$. In actuality, virtually all business researchers use computer statistical software packages to solve for the regression coefficients, the regression constant, and other pertinent information. In this chapter, we will discuss computer output and assume little or no hand calculation. The emphasis will be on the interpretation of the computer output.

A MULTIPLE REGRESSION MODEL

A real estate study was conducted in a Canadian rural town to determine what variables, if any, are related to the market price of a home. Several variables were explored, including the number of bedrooms, the number of bathrooms, the age of the house, the number of square feet of living space, the total number of square feet of space, and the number of garages. Suppose the researcher wants to develop a regression model to predict the market price of a home by two variables, total number of square feet in the house and age of the house. Listed in Table 13.1 are the data for these three variables.

A number of statistical software packages can perform multiple regression analysis, including Excel. The output for the Excel multiple regression analysis on the real estate data is given in Figure 13.3. The values of b_0, b_1, and b_2 are given under Coefficients near the bottom of the output. From Figure 13.3, the regression equation for the real estate data in Table 13.1 is:

$$\hat{y} = 57.4 + 0.0177x_1 - 0.666x_2$$

The regression constant, 57.4, is the y intercept. The y intercept is the value of $\hat{y}$ if both x_1 (number of square feet) and x_2 (age) are zero. In practical terms, it may make little sense to say that a brand new or not yet built ($x_2 = 0$) house containing no square feet ($x_1 = 0$) would cost $57,400. (Note in Figure 13.2 that the response plane crosses the y (price) axis at 57.4.) However, one could presumably interpret this to mean that $57,400 is the value of the land with a house yet to be built. Even so, an interpretation such as this can pose challenges to the analyst: there is no clear interpretation of the size of the land that this value refers to. In general, it is a good idea to consider the intercept as the *theoretical* value of y when $x = 0$, which may or may not have a practical interpretation. This is particularly true when one does not expect x to equal 0 for the problem being considered.

The coefficient of x_1 (total number of square feet in the house) is 0.0177, which means that a one-unit increase in square footage would result in a predicted increase of 0.0177($1,000) = $17.70 in the price of the home if age were held constant. All other

Table 13.1

Real Estate Data

Market Price ($1,000s) y	Total Number of Square Feet x_1	Age of House (Years) x_2
63.0	1,605	35
65.1	2,489	45
69.9	1,553	20
76.8	2,404	32
73.9	1,884	25
77.9	1,558	14
74.9	1,748	8
78.0	3,105	10
79.0	1,682	28
83.4	2,470	30
79.5	1,820	2
83.9	2,143	6
79.7	2,121	14
84.5	2,485	9
96.0	2,300	19
109.5	2,714	4
102.5	2,463	5
121.0	3,076	7
104.9	3,048	3
128.0	3,267	6
129.0	3,069	10
117.9	4,765	11
140.0	4,540	8

Figure 13.3

Excel Output of Regression for the Real Estate Example

	A	B	C	D	E	F
1	Summary Output					
2	Regression Statistics					
3	Multiple R	0.861				
4	R Square	0.741				
5	Adjusted R Square	0.715				
6	Standard Error	11.960				
7	Obervations	22				
8						
9	ANOVA					
10		df	SS	MS	F	Significance F
11	Regression	2	8189.7	4094.9	28.63	0.000
12	Residual	20	2861.0	143.1		
13	Total	22	11050.7			
14						
15		Coefficients	Standard Error	t Stat	p Value	
16	Intercept	57.35	10.01	5.73	0.000	
17	Square Feet	0.017718	0.003146	5.63	0.000	
18	Age	−0.6663	0.228	−2.92	0.008	

variables being held constant, the addition of one square foot of space in the house results in a predicted increase of $17.70 in the price of the house.

The coefficient of x_2 (age) is -0.666. The negative sign on the coefficient denotes an inverse relationship between the age of a house and the price of the house: the older the house, the lower the price. In this case, if the total number of square feet in the house is kept constant, a one-unit increase in the age of the house (one year) will result in $-0.666(\$1,000) = -\$666$, a predicted $666 drop in the price.

In examining the regression coefficients, it is important to remember that the independent variables are often measured in different units. It is usually not wise to compare the regression coefficients of predictors in a multiple regression model and decide that the variable with the largest regression coefficient is the best predictor. In this example, the two variables are in different units, square feet and years. Just because x_2 has the larger coefficient (0.666) does not necessarily make x_2 the strongest predictor of y.

This regression model can be used to predict the price of a house in this Canadian rural town. If the house has 2,500 square feet total and is 12 years old, $x_1 = 2,500$ and $x_2 = 12$. Substituting these values into the regression model yields:

$$\hat{y} = 57.4 + 0.0177x_1 - 0.666x_2$$
$$= 57.4 + 0.0177(2,500) - 0.666(12) = 93.658$$

The predicted price of the house is $93,658. Figure 13.2 is a graph of these data with the response plane and the residual distances.

Demonstration Problem 13.1

Much of the freight cargo in the world is transported over roads. The volume of freight cargo shipped over roads varies from country to country depending on the size of the country, the amount of commerce, the wealth of the country, and other factors. Shown here are seven of the top 10 countries in which freight cargo is shipped over roads, along with the number of kilometres of roads and the number of commercial vehicles (trucks and buses) for each country. Use these data to develop a multiple regression model to predict the volume of freight cargo shipped over roads by the length of roads and the number of commercial vehicles. Determine the predicted volume of freight cargo over roads if the length of roads is 600,000 km and the number of commercial vehicles is 3 million.

Country	Freight Cargo Shipped by Road (millions of tonne-kilometres)	Length of Roads (kilometres)	Number of Commercial Vehicles
China	407,057	1,083,473	5,010,000
Brazil	260,404	1,660,349	1,371,127
India	210,240	2,159,740	1,980,000
Germany	202,904	636,282	2,923,000
Italy	182,750	303,517	2,745,500
Spain	154,503	331,961	2,859,438
Mexico	140,232	252,725	3,758,034

Source: World Data; World Road Statistics; George Thomas Kurian, *The Illustrated Book of World Rankings* (Armonk, NY: M.E. Sharpe, Inc., 1997).

Solution

The following output shows the results of analyzing the data by using the regression portion of Excel.

	A	B	C	D	E	F
1	Summary Output					
2	Regression Statistics					
3	Multiple R	0.812				
4	R Square	0.659				
5	Adjusted R Square	0.488				
6	Standard Error	64639.80005				
7	Observations	7				
8						
9	ANOVA					
10		df	SS	MS	F	Significance F
11	Regression	2	32290723884	16145361942	3.86	0.116
12	Residual	4	16713215001	4178303750		
13	Total	6	49003938885			
14						
15		Coefficients	Standard Error	t Stat	p Value	
16	Intercept	–38581.02552	98732.340	–0.39	0.7161	
17	Length	0.092371903	0.0395	2.34	0.079	
18	Vehicles	0.05978497	0.0250	2.39	0.075	

The regression equation is

$$\hat{y} = -38{,}581.03 + 0.0924x_1 + 0.0598x_2$$

where

$\hat{y}$ = volume of freight cargo shipped
x_1 = length of roads
x_2 = number of commercial vehicles

The model indicates that for every one-unit (1-km) increase in length of roads, the predicted volume of freight cargo shipped increases by 0.0924 million tonne-kilometres, or 92,400 tonne-kilometres, if the number of commercial vehicles is held constant. If the number of commercial vehicles is increased by one unit, the predicted volume of freight cargo shipped increases by 0.0598 million tonne-kilometres, or 59,800 tonne-kilometres, if the length of roads is held constant.

If x_1 (length of roads) is 600,000 and x_2 (number of commercial vehicles) is 3 million, the model predicts that the volume of freight cargo shipped will be 196,259 million tonne-kilometres:

$$\hat{y} = -38{,}581.03 + 0.0924(600{,}000) + 0.0598(3{,}000{,}000) = 196{,}258.97$$

POINTS OF INTEREST
Multiple regression avoids double counting the effects of inter-correlated variables. Each coefficient in a multiple regression equation tells us how much an x variable affects the y variable, when all other x variables in the equation are held constant.

Concept Check

1. What is the difference between simple regression analysis and multiple regression analysis?
2. What is a partial regression coefficient and how is it different from a full regression coefficient?
3. How would you interpret the partial regression coefficient?

13.1 Use a computer to develop the equation of the regression model for the following data. Comment on the regression coefficients. Determine the predicted value of y for $x_1 = 200$ and $x_2 = 7$.

y	x_1	x_2
12	174	3
18	281	9
31	189	4
28	202	8
52	149	9
47	188	12
38	215	5
22	150	11
36	167	8
17	135	5

13.2 Use a computer to develop the equation of the regression model for the following data. Comment on the regression coefficients. Determine the predicted value of y for $x_1 = 33$, $x_2 = 29$, and $x_3 = 13$.

y	x_1	x_2	x_3
114	21	6	5
94	43	25	8
87	56	42	25
98	19	27	9
101	29	20	12
85	34	45	21
94	40	33	14
107	32	14	11
119	16	4	7
93	18	31	16
108	27	12	10
117	31	3	8

13.3 Using the following data, determine the equation of the regression model. How many independent variables are there? Comment on the meaning of these regression coefficients.

Predictor	Coefficient
Constant	121.62
x_1	−0.174
x_2	6.02
x_3	0.00026
x_4	0.0041

13.4 Use the following data to determine the equation of the multiple regression model. Comment on the regression coefficients.

Predictor	Coefficient
Constant	31,409.5
x_1	0.08425
x_2	289.62
x_3	−0.0947

13.5 Is there a particular product that is an indicator of per capita personal consumption for countries around the world? Shown below are data on per capita personal consumption, paper consumption, fish consumption, and gasoline consumption for 11 countries. Use the data to develop a multiple regression model to predict per capita personal consumption by paper consumption, fish consumption, and gasoline consumption. Discuss the meaning of the partial regression weights.

Country	Per Capita Personal Consumption ($U.S.)	Paper Consumption (kilograms per person)	Fish Consumption (kilograms per person)	Gasoline Consumption (litres per person)
Bangladesh	836	1	10	2
Greece	3,145	85	24	394
Italy	21,785	204	22	368
Japan	37,931	250	64	447
Kenya	276	4	5	16
Norway	1,913	156	51	477
Philippines	2,195	19	30	43
Portugal	3,154	116	60	257
U.K.	19,539	207	20	460
U.S.	109,521	308	21	1,624
Venezuela	622	27	18	528

13.6 Jensen, Solberg, and Zorn investigated the relationship of insider ownership, debt, and dividend policies in companies. One of their findings was that firms with high insider ownership choose lower levels of both debt and dividends. Shown here is a sample of data of these 3 variables for 11 different industries. Use the data to develop the equation of the regression model to predict insider ownership by debt ratio and dividend payout. Comment on the regression coefficients.

Industry	Insider Ownership	Debt Ratio	Dividend Payout
Mining	8.2	14.2	10.4
Food and beverage	18	20.8	14.3
Furniture	12	18.6	12.1
Publishing	28	18.5	11.8
Petroleum refining	7.4	28.2	10.6
Glass and cement	15	24.7	12.6
Motor vehicle	16	15.6	12.6
Department store	18	21.7	7.2
Restaurant	13	23	11.3
Amusement	18	46.7	4.1
Hospital	10	35.8	9

13.2 SIGNIFICANCE TESTS OF THE REGRESSION MODEL AND ITS COEFFICIENTS

Multiple regression models can be developed to fit almost any data set if the level of measurement is adequate and enough data points are available. Once a model has been constructed, it is important to test the model to determine whether it fits the data well and whether the assumptions underlying regression analysis are met. Assessing the adequacy of the regression model can be done in several ways, including testing the overall significance of the model, studying the significance tests of the regression coefficients, computing the residuals, examining the standard error of the estimate, and observing the coefficient of determination. In this section, we examine significance tests of the regression model and of its coefficients.

TESTING THE OVERALL MODEL

With simple regression, a t test of the slope of the regression line is used to determine whether the population slope of the regression line is different from zero; that is, whether the independent variable contributes statistically significantly in linearly predicting the dependent variable.

The hypotheses for this test, presented in Chapter 12, are:

$$H_0: \beta_1 = 0$$
$$H_a: \beta_1 \neq 0$$

For multiple regression, an analogous test makes use of the F statistic. The overall significance of the multiple regression model is tested with the following hypotheses.

$$H_0: \beta_1 = \beta_2 = \beta_3 = \cdots = \beta_k = 0$$

H_a: At least one of the regression coefficients is not equal to 0.

If we fail to reject the null hypothesis, we are stating that the regression model has no significant predictability for the dependent variable. A rejection of the null hypothesis indicates that at least one of the independent variables adds significant predictability for y.

This F test of overall significance is often printed as a part of the standard multiple regression output from statistical software packages. The output appears as an analysis of variance (ANOVA) table. Shown here is the ANOVA table for the real estate example taken from the Excel output in Figure 13.3.

	A	B	C	D	E	F
1	ANOVA					
2		df	SS	MS	F	Significance F
3	Regression	2	32290723884	16145361942	3.86	0.116
4	Residual	4	16713215001	4178303750		
5	Total	6	49003938885			
6						
7		Coefficients	Standard Error	t Stat	p Value	
8	Intercept	–38581.02552	98732.34	–0.39	0.7161	
9	Length	0.092371903	0.0395	2.34	0.079	
10	Vehicles	0.05978497	0.025	2.39	0.075	

The F value is 28.63; because $p = 0.000$ (from Figure 13.3), the F value is significant at $\alpha = 0.001$. The null hypothesis is rejected, and there is at least one significant predictor of house price in this analysis.

The F value is calculated by the following equation:

$$F = \frac{MS_{reg}}{MS_{err}} = \frac{SS_{reg}/df_{reg}}{SS_{err}/df_{err}} = \frac{SSR/k}{SSE/(N-k-1)}$$

where
MS = mean square
SS = sum of squares
df = degrees of freedom
k = number of independent variables
N = number of observations

Note that in the ANOVA table for the real estate example, $df_{reg} = 2$. The degrees-of-freedom formula for regression is the number of regression coefficients plus the regression constant minus 1. The net result is the number of regression coefficients, which equals the number of independent variables, k. The real estate example uses two independent variables, so $k = 2$. Degrees-of-freedom error in multiple regression equals the total number of observations minus the number of regression coefficients minus the regression constant, or $N - k - 1$. For the real estate example, $N = 23$; thus, $df_{err} = 23 - 2 - 1 = 20$.

As shown in Chapter 11, $MS = SS/df$. The F ratio is formed by dividing MS_{reg} by MS_{err}. In using the F distribution table to determine a critical value against which to test the observed F value, the degrees-of-freedom numerator is df_{reg} and the degrees-of-freedom denominator is df_{err}. The table F value is obtained in the usual manner, as presented in Chapter 11. With $\alpha = 0.01$ for the real estate example, the table value is:

$$F_{0.01, 2, 20} = 5.85$$

Comparing the observed F of 28.63 to this table value shows that the decision is to reject the null hypothesis. This same conclusion was reached using the p value method from the computer output.

If a regression model has only one linear independent variable, it is a simple regression model. In that case, the F test for the overall model is the same as the t test for significance of the population slope. The F value displayed in the regression ANOVA table is related to the t test for the slope in the simple regression case as follows:

$$F = t^2$$

In simple regression, the F value and the t value give redundant information about the overall test of the model.

Most researchers who use multiple regression analysis will observe the value of F and its p value rather early in the process. If F is not significant, then no population regression coefficient is significantly different from zero, and the regression model has no predictability for the dependent variable.

SIGNIFICANCE TESTS OF THE REGRESSION COEFFICIENTS

In multiple regression, individual significance tests can be computed for each regression coefficient using a t test. Each of these t tests is analogous to the t test for the slope used in Chapter 12 for simple regression analysis. The hypotheses for testing the regression coefficient of each independent variable take the following form:

$$H_0: \beta_1 = 0$$
$$H_a: \beta_1 \neq 0$$

$$H_0: \beta_2 = 0$$
$$H_a: \beta_2 \neq 0$$
$$\cdot$$
$$\cdot$$
$$\cdot$$
$$H_0: \beta_k = 0$$
$$H_a: \beta_k \neq 0$$

Most multiple regression computer packages yield observed t values to test the individual regression coefficients as standard output. Shown here are the t values and their associated probabilities for the real estate example as displayed with the multiple regression output in Figure 13.3.

Variable	t	p
Square feet	5.63	0
Age	−2.92	0.008

At $\alpha = 0.05$, the null hypothesis is rejected for both variables because the probabilities (p) associated with their t values are less than 0.05. If the t ratios for any predictor variable are not significant (fail to reject the null hypothesis), the researcher might decide to drop that variable from the analysis as a nonsignificant predictor. Other factors can enter into this decision. In Chapter 14, we will explore techniques for model building in which some variable sorting is required.

The degrees of freedom for each of these individual tests of regression coefficients are $n - k - 1$. In this particular example, because there are $k = 2$ predictor variables, the degrees of freedom are $23 - 2 - 1 = 20$. With $\alpha = 0.05$ and a two-tailed test, the critical table t value is:

$$t_{0.025,20} = \pm 2.086$$

Notice from the t ratios shown here that if this critical table t value had been used as the hypothesis test criterion instead of the p value method, the results would have been the same. Testing the regression coefficients not only gives the researcher some insight into the fit of the regression model but also helps in the evaluation of how worthwhile individual independent variables are in predicting y.

Concept Check

1. Why is it important to test the multiple regression model once it is developed? What would you test it for?

13.2 Problems

13.7   Examine the results shown here for a multiple regression analysis. How many predictors were there in this model? Comment on the overall significance of the regression model. Discuss the t ratios of the variables and their significance.

	Coefficient	Standard Error	T	p
Constant	4.096	1.2884	3.24	0.006
X_1	−5.111	1.87	2.73	0.011
X_2	2.662	2.0796	1.28	0.212
X_3	1.557	1.2811	1.22	0.235
X_4	1.141	1.4712	0.78	0.445
X_5	1.65	1.4994	1.1	0.281
X_6	−1.248	1.2735	0.98	0.336
X_7	0.436	0.3617	1.21	0.239
X_8	0.962	1.1896	0.81	0.426
X	1.289	1.9182	0.67	0.508
	$S = 3.503$ R-sq $= 40.8\%$ R-sq(adj.) $= 20.3\%$			

ANOVA	DF	SS	MS	F	p
Regression	9	219.746	24.416	1.99	0.0825
Residual	26	319.004	12.269		
Total	35	538.750			

13.8   Displayed here is another output for a multiple regression analysis. Study the ANOVA table and the t ratios and use these to discuss the strengths of the regression model and the predictors. Does this model appear to fit the data well? From the information here, what recommendations would you make about the predictor variables in the model?

	Coefficient	Standard Error	T	p
Constant	34.672	5.256	6.6	0
X_1	0.07629	0.02234	3.41	0.005
X_2	0.000259	0.001031	0.25	0.805
X_3	−1.1212	0.9955	−1.13	0.23

S = 9.722   R-sq = 51.5%   R-sq(adj) = 40.4%

ANOVA	DF	SS	MS	F	p
Regression	3	1306.99	435.66	4.61	0.021
Residual	13	1228.78	94.52		
Total	16	2535.77			

13.9   Using the data in Problem 13.5, develop a multiple regression model to predict per capita personal consumption by the consumption of paper, fish, and gasoline. Discuss the output and pay particular attention to the F test and the t tests.

13.10   Using the data from Problem 13.6, develop a multiple regression model to predict insider ownership from debt ratio and dividend payout. Comment on the strength of the model and the predictors by examining the ANOVA table and the t tests.

13.11   Develop a multiple regression model to predict y from x_1, x_2, and x_3 using the following data. Discuss the values of F and t.

y	x_1	x_2	x_3
5.3	44	11	401
3.6	24	40	219
5.1	46	13	394
4.9	38	18	362
7.0	61	3	453
6.4	58	5	468
5.2	47	14	386
4.6	36	24	357
2.9	19	52	206
4.0	31	29	301
3.8	24	37	243
3.8	27	36	228
4.8	36	21	342
5.4	50	11	421
5.8	55	9	445

13.12   Use the following data to develop a regression model to predict y from x_1 and x_2. Comment on the output. Develop a regression model to predict y from x_1 only.

Compare the results of this model with those of the model using both predictors. What might you conclude by examining the output from both regression models?

y	x_1	x_2
28	12.6	134
43	11.4	126
45	11.5	143
49	11.1	152
57	10.4	143
68	9.6	147
74	9.8	128
81	8.4	119
82	8.8	130
86	8.9	135
101	8.1	141
112	7.6	123
114	7.8	121
119	7.4	129
124	6.4	135

13.13 Study the following Excel multiple regression output. How many predictors are in this model? How many observations? What is the equation of the regression line? Discuss the strength of the model in terms of F. Which predictors, if any, are significant? Why or why not? Comment on the overall effectiveness of the model.

	A	B	C	D	E	F
1	Summary Output					
2	Regression Statistics					
3	Multiple R	0.842				
4	R Square	0.710				
5	Adjusted R Square	0.630				
6	Standard Error	109.430				
7	Observations	15				
8						
9	ANOVA					
10		df	SS	MS	F	Significance F
11	Regression	3	321946.82	107315.6	8.96	0.0027
12	Residual	11	131723.20	11974.8		
13	Total	14	453670			
14						
15		Coefficients	Standard Error	t Stat	p Value	
16	Intercept	657.053	167.460	3.92	.0024	
17	X Variable 1	5.7103	1.792	3.19	.0087	
18	X Variable 2	−0.4169	0.322	−1.29	.2222	
19	X Variable 3	−3.4715	1.443	−2.41	.0349	

13.3 RESIDUALS, STANDARD ERROR OF THE ESTIMATE, AND R^2

Three more statistical tools for examining the strength of a regression model are the residuals, the standard error of the estimate, and the coefficient of multiple determination.

RESIDUALS

The **residual,** or error, of the regression model is *the difference between the y value and the predicted value, $\hat{y}$:*

$$\text{Residual} = y - \hat{y}$$

The residuals for a multiple regression model are solved for in the same manner as they are with simple regression. First, a predicted value, $\hat{y}$, is determined by entering the value for each independent variable for a given set of observations into the multiple regression equation and solving for $\hat{y}$. Next, the value of $y - \hat{y}$ is computed for each set of observations. Shown here are the calculations for the residuals of the first set of observations from Table 13.1. The predicted value of y for $x_1 = 1,605$ and $x_2 = 35$ is:

$$\hat{y} = 57.4 + 0.0177(1,605) - 0.666(35) = 62.50$$
$$\text{Actual value of } y = 63.0$$
$$\text{Residual} = y - \hat{y} = 63.0 - 62.50 = 0.50$$

All residuals for the real estate data and the regression model displayed in Table 13.1 and Figure 13.3 are displayed in Table 13.2.

An examination of the residuals in Table 13.2 can reveal some information about the fit of the real estate regression model. The business researcher can observe the residuals and decide whether the errors are small enough to support the accuracy of the model. The house price figures are in units of $1,000. Two of the 23 residuals are more

Table 13.2			
Residuals for the Real Estate Regression Model	**y**	**$\hat{y}$**	**$y - \hat{y}$**
	63.0	62.499	0.501
	65.1	71.485	−6.385
	69.9	71.568	−1.668
	76.8	78.639	−1.839
	73.9	74.097	−0.197
	77.9	75.653	2.247
	74.9	83.012	−8.112
	78.0	105.699	−27.699
	79.0	68.523	10.477
	83.4	81.139	2.261
	79.5	88.282	−8.782
	83.9	91.335	−7.435
	79.7	85.618	−5.918
	84.5	95.391	−10.891
	96.0	85.456	10.544
	109.5	102.774	6.726
	102.5	97.665	4.835
	121.0	107.183	13.817
	104.9	109.352	−4.452
	128.0	111.230	16.770
	129.0	105.061	23.939
	117.9	134.415	−16.515
	140.0	132.430	7.570

Figure 13.4

Residual Diagnosis for the Real Estate Example

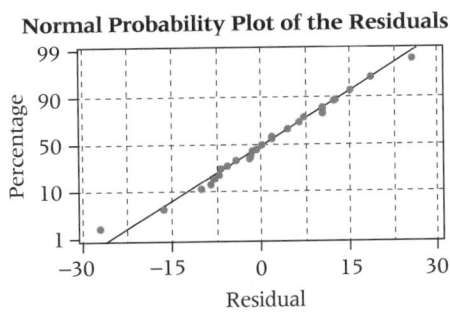

Normal Probability Plot of the Residuals

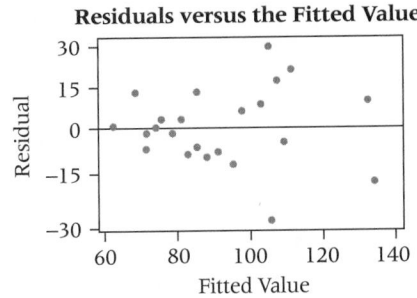

Residuals versus the Fitted Values

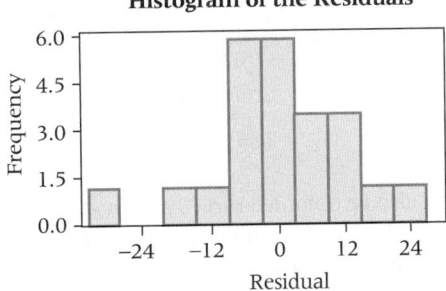

Histogram of the Residuals

than 20.00, meaning that the model is more than $20,000 off in its prediction. On the other hand, two residuals are less than 1, meaning that the model is less than $1,000 off in its prediction.

Residuals are also helpful in locating outliers. **Outliers** are *data points that are apart, or far, from the mainstream of the other data.* They are sometimes data points that were mistakenly recorded or measured. Because every data point influences the regression model, outliers can exert an overly important influence on the model based on their distance from other points. In Table 13.2, the eighth residual listed is −27.699. This error indicates that the regression model was not nearly as successful in predicting house price on this particular house as it was with others (an error of more than $27,000). For whatever reason, this data point stands somewhat apart from other data points and may be considered an outlier.

Residuals are also useful in testing the assumptions underlying regression analysis. Figure 13.4 displays the residuals for the real estate example. In the top right is a graph of the residuals. Notice that residual variance seems to increase in the right half of the plot, indicating potential heteroscedasticity. As discussed in Chapter 12, one of the assumptions underlying regression analysis is that the error terms have homoscedasticity or homogeneous variance. That assumption might be violated in this example. The normal plot of residuals is nearly a straight line, indicating that the assumption of normally distributed error terms has probably not been violated.

SSE AND STANDARD ERROR OF THE ESTIMATE

One of the properties of a regression model is that the residuals sum to zero. As pointed out in Chapter 12, this property precludes the possibility of computing an "average" residual as a single measure of error. In an effort to compute a single statistic that can represent the error in a regression analysis, the zero-sum property can be overcome by *squaring the residuals and then summing the squares.* Such an operation produces the sum of squares of error (SSE).

The formula for computing SSE for multiple regression is the same as it is for simple regression:

$$SSE = \Sigma(y - \hat{y})^2$$

For the real estate example, SSE can be computed by squaring and summing the residuals displayed in Table 13.2:

$$
\begin{aligned}
SSE = [&(0.501)^2 + (-6.385)^2 + (-1.668)^2 + (-1.839)^2 \\
& + (-0.197)^2 + (2.247)^2 + (-8.112)^2 + (-27.699)^2 \\
& + (10.477)^2 + (2.261)^2 + (-8.782)^2 + (-7.435)^2 \\
& + (-5.918)^2 + (-10.891)^2 + (10.544)^2 + (6.726)^2 \\
& + (4.835)^2 + (13.817)^2 + (-4.452)^2 + (16.770)^2 \\
& + (23.939)^2 + (-16.515)^2 + (7.570)^2] \\
= &\, 2{,}861.0
\end{aligned}
$$

SSE can also be obtained directly from the multiple regression computer output by selecting the value of SS (sum of squares) listed beside error. Shown here is the ANOVA portion of the output displayed in Figure 13.3, which is the result of a multiple regression analysis model developed to predict house prices. Note that the SS for error shown in the ANOVA table equals the value of $\Sigma(y - \hat{y})^2$ just computed (2,861.0).

```
ANOVA
                                          /SSE

                                                  Significance
                df      SS    /    MS       F        F
Regression       2    8189.7  /  4094.9   28.63    0.000
Error           20   (2861.0)    143.1
Total           22   11050.7
```

SSE has limited usage as a measure of error. However, it is a tool used to solve for other more useful measures. One of these is the **standard error of the estimate, s_e,** which is essentially *the standard deviation of residuals (error) for the regression model.* As explained in Chapter 12, an assumption underlying regression analysis is that the error terms are approximately normally distributed with a mean of zero. With this information and by the empirical rule, approximately 68% of the residuals should be within $\pm 1 s_e$ and 95% should be within $\pm 2 s_e$. This property makes the standard error of the estimate a useful tool in estimating how accurately a regression model fits the data.

The standard error of the estimate is computed by dividing SSE by the degrees of freedom of error for the model and taking the square root:

$$s_e = \sqrt{\frac{SSE}{n - k - 1}}$$

where

n = number of observations
k = number of independent variables

The value of s_e can be computed for the real estate example as follows:

$$s_e = \sqrt{\frac{SSE}{n - k - 1}} = \sqrt{\frac{2{,}861.0}{23 - 2 - 1}} = 11.96$$

The standard error of the estimate, s_e, is usually given as standard output from regression analysis by computer software packages. The output displayed in Figure 13.3 contains the standard error of the estimate for the real estate example:

$$s_e = 11.96$$

By the empirical rule, approximately 68% of the residuals should be within $\pm 1 s_e = \pm 1(11.96) = \pm 11.96$. Because house prices are in units of \$1,000, approximately 68% of the predictions are within $\pm 11.96(\$1,000)$, or $\pm\$11,960$. Examining the output displayed in Table 13.2, 18/23, or about 78%, of the residuals are within this span. According to the empirical rule, approximately 95% of the residuals should be within $\pm 2 s_e$, or $\pm 2(11.96) = \pm 23.92$. Further examination of the residual values in Table 13.2 shows that 21 of 23, or 91%, fall within this range. The business researcher can study the standard error of the estimate and these empirical rule-related ranges and decide whether the error of the regression model is sufficiently small to justify further use of the model.

COEFFICIENT OF MULTIPLE DETERMINATION (R^2)

The **coefficient of multiple determination (R^2)** is analogous to the coefficient of determination (r^2) discussed in Chapter 12. R^2 represents *the proportion of variation of the dependent variable, y, accounted for by the independent variables in the regression model.* As with r^2, the range of possible values for R^2 is from 0 to 1. An R^2 of 0 indicates no relationship between the predictor variables in the model and y. An R^2 of 1 indicates that 100% of the variability of y has been accounted for by the predictors. Of course, it is desirable for R^2 to be high, indicating the strong predictability of a regression model. The coefficient of multiple determination can be calculated by the following formula:

$$R^2 = \frac{SSR}{SS_{yy}} = 1 - \frac{SSE}{SS_{yy}}$$

R^2 can be calculated in the real estate example by using the sum of squares regression (SSR), the sum of squares of error (SSE), and the sum of squares total (SS_{yy}) from the ANOVA portion of Figure 13.3.

ANOVA

	df	SS		MS	F	Significance F
Regression	2	8189.7	SSR	4094.9	28.63	0.000
Error	20	2861.0	SSE	143.1		
Total	22	11050.7	SS_{yy}			

$$R^2 = \frac{SSR}{SS_{yy}} = \frac{8{,}189.7}{11{,}050.7} = 0.741$$

or

$$R^2 = 1 - \frac{SSE}{SS_{yy}} = 1 - \frac{2{,}861.0}{11{,}050.7} = 0.741$$

In addition, virtually all statistical software packages print out R^2 as standard output with multiple regression analysis. A re-examination of Figure 13.3 reveals that R^2 is given as:

R Square   0.741

or $R^2 = 74.1\%$. This result indicates that a relatively high proportion of the variation of the dependent variable house price is accounted for by the independent variables in this regression model.

ADJUSTED R^2

As additional independent variables are added to a regression model, the value of R^2 cannot decrease, and in most cases it will increase. In the formulas for determining R^2:

$$R^2 = \frac{SSR}{SS_{yy}} = 1 - \frac{SSE}{SS_{yy}}$$

The value of SS_{yy} for a given set of observations will remain the same as independent variables are added to the regression analysis because SS_{yy} is the sum of squares for the dependent variable. Because additional independent variables are likely to increase SSR at least by some amount, the value of R^2 will probably increase for any additional independent variables.

However, sometimes additional independent variables add no *significant* information to the regression model, yet R^2 increases. R^2 therefore may yield an inflated figure. Statisticians have developed an **adjusted R^2** *to take into consideration both the additional information each new independent variable brings to the regression model and the changed degrees of freedom of regression.* Many standard statistical computer packages now compute and report adjusted R^2 as part of the output. The formula for computing adjusted R^2 is:

$$\text{Adjusted } R^2 = 1 - \frac{SSE/(n-k-1)}{SS_{yy}/(n-1)}$$

The value of adjusted R^2 for the real estate example can be solved by using information from the ANOVA portion of the computer output in Figure 13.3.

$$\text{Adjusted } R^2 = 1 - \left[\frac{2,861/20}{11,050.7/22} \right] = 1 - 0.285 = 0.715$$

The regression output in Figure 13.3 contains the value of the adjusted R^2 already computed. For the real estate example, this value is shown as:

Adjusted R Square   0.715

or 71.5%. A comparison of R^2 (0.741) with the adjusted R^2 (0.715) for this example shows that the adjusted R^2 reduces the overall proportion of variation of the dependent variable accounted for by the independent variables by a factor of 0.026, or 2.6%. The gap between R^2 and adjusted R^2 tends to increase as nonsignificant independent variables are added to the regression model. As n increases, the difference between R^2 and adjusted R^2 becomes less.

STATISTICS IN BUSINESS TODAY

Using Regression Analysis to Help Select a Robot

Several factors contribute to the success of a manufacturing firm in the world markets. Some examples are creating more efficient plants, lowering labour costs, increasing the quality of products, improving the standards of supplier materials, and learning more about international markets. Basically, success boils down to producing a better product for less cost.

One way to achieve that goal is to improve the technology of manufacturing facilities. Many companies are now using robots in plants to increase productivity and reduce labour costs. The use of such technology is relatively new. The science of selecting and purchasing robots is imperfect and often involves considerable subjectivity.

Two researchers, Moutaz Khouja and David Booth, devised a way to use multiple regression to assist decision makers in robot selection. After sorting through 20 of the more promising variables, they found that the most important variables related to robot performance are repeatability, accuracy, load capacity, and velocity. Accuracy is measured by the distance between where the robot goes on a single trial and the centre of all points to which it goes on repeated trials. Repeatability is the radius of the circle that just includes all points to which the robot goes on repeated trials. Repeatability is of most concern to decision makers because it is hardest to correct. Accuracy can be viewed as bias and is easier to correct. Load capacity is the maximum mass that the robot can handle, and velocity is the maximum tip velocity of the robot arm.

Khouja and Booth used data gathered from 27 robots and regression analysis to develop a multiple regression model that attempts to predict repeatability of robots (the variable of most concern for decision makers) by the velocity and load capacity of robots. Using the resulting regression model and the residuals of the fit, they developed a ranking system for selecting robots that takes into account repeatability, load capacity, velocity, and cost.

Source: Adapted from Moutaz Khouja and David E. Booth, "A Decision Model for the Robot Selection Problem Using Robust Regression," *Decision Sciences,* 22, no. 3 (July/August 1991), pp. 656–662. The *Decision Sciences* journal is published by the Decision Sciences Institute, located at Georgia State University.

Concept Check

1. What are residuals?
2. Describe what you can learn by analyzing the residuals.
3. Explain the term *standard error of the estimate.*
4. What is the coefficient of determination and what does it tell us?
5. What is the difference between R^2 and adjusted R^2?

13.3 Problems

13.14 Study the output shown in Problem 13.7. Comment on the overall strength of the regression model in light of S, R^2, and adjusted R^2.

13.15 Study the output shown in Problem 13.8. Comment on the overall strength of the regression model in light of S, R^2, and adjusted R^2.

13.16   Using the regression output obtained by working Problem 13.5, comment on the overall strength of the regression model using S, R^2, and adjusted R^2.

13.17   Using the regression output obtained by working Problem 13.6, comment on the overall strength of the regression model using S, R^2, and adjusted R^2.

13.18   Using the regression output obtained by working Problem 13.11, comment on the overall strength of the regression model using S, R^2, and adjusted R^2.

13.19   Using the regression output obtained by working Problem 13.12, comment on the overall strength of the regression model using S, R^2, and adjusted R^2.

13.20   Study the Excel output shown in Problem 13.13. Comment on the overall strength of the regression model in light of S, R^2, and adjusted R^2.

13.21   Study the residual diagnostics that follow. Discuss any potential problems with meeting the regression assumptions for this regression analysis based on the residual graphics.

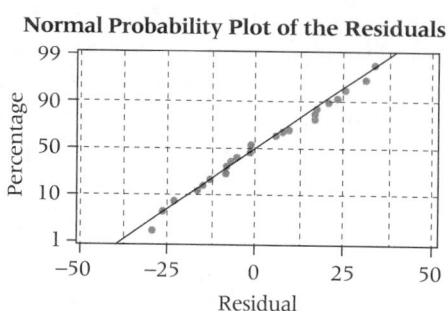

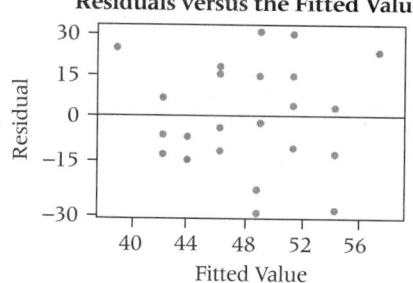

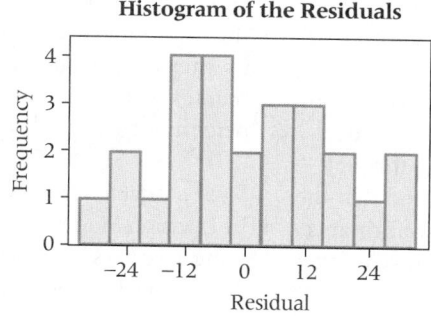

13.4 INTERPRETING MULTIPLE REGRESSION COMPUTER OUTPUT

A RE-EXAMINATION OF THE MULTIPLE REGRESSION OUTPUT

Figure 13.5 shows again the multiple regression output for the real estate example. Many of the concepts discussed thus far in the chapter are highlighted. Note the following items:

1. The equation of the regression model
2. The ANOVA table with the F value for the overall test of the model
3. The t ratios, which test the significance of the regression coefficients
4. The value of SSE
5. The value of s_e
6. The value of R^2
7. The value of adjusted R^2

Figure 13.5

Annotated Version of the Excel Output of Regression for the Real Estate Example

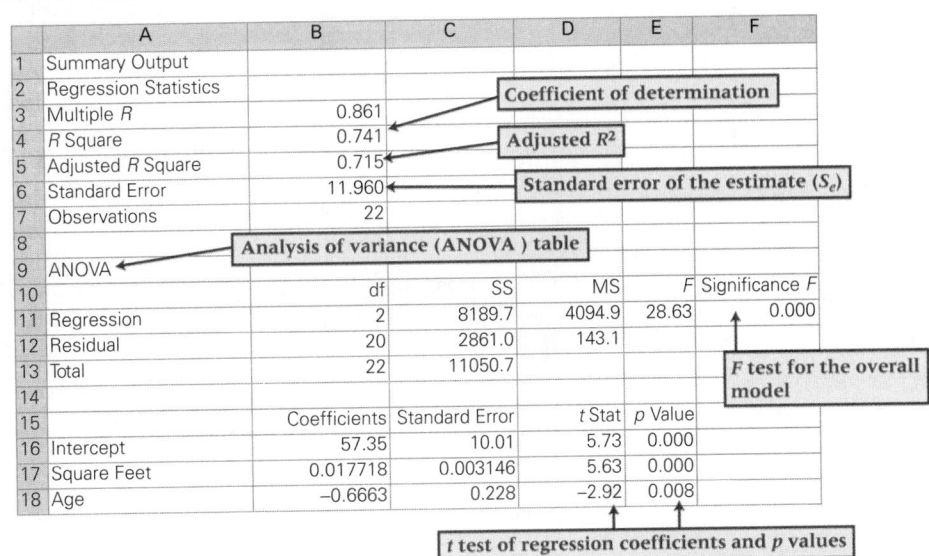

From the data in the table, as shown under "Coefficients" the regression equation is
$\hat{y} = 57.4 + 0.0177x_1 - 0.666x_2$.

Demonstration Problem 13.2

Discuss the Excel multiple regression output for Demonstration Problem 13.1. Comment on the F test for the overall significance of the model, the t tests of the regression coefficients, and the values of s_e, R^2, and adjusted R^2.

Solution

This regression analysis was done to predict the volume of freight cargo shipped annually in a country by road using the predictors Length of Roads and Number of Commercial Vehicles. The equation of the regression model was presented in the solution of Demonstration Problem 13.1. Shown here is the complete multiple regression output from the Excel analysis of the data.

The value of F for this problem is 3.86, with a p value of 0.1163, which is not significant at $\alpha = 0.05$. On the basis of this information, the null hypothesis would not be rejected for the overall test of significance. None of the regression coefficients are significantly different from zero, and no statistically significant predictability of the volume of freight cargo shipped by road is given from this regression model.

An examination of the t ratios supports this conclusion using an alpha of 0.05. The t ratio for Length of Roads is 2.34 with an associated p value of 0.0793, and the t ratio for Number of Commercial Vehicles is 2.39 with an associated p value of 0.0750. Neither p value is less than 0.05.

The standard error of the estimate is $s_e = 64{,}639.80$, indicating that approximately 68% of the residuals are within $\pm 64{,}639.80$. An examination of the Excel-produced residuals shows that actually five out of seven, or 71.4%, of the residuals fall in this interval. Approximately 95% of the residuals should be within $\pm 2(64{,}639.80) = \pm 129{,}279.60$, and an examination of the Excel-produced residuals shows that seven out of seven, or 100%, of the residuals are within this interval. Shipping industry researchers could examine the value of the standard error of the estimate to determine whether this model produces results with small enough error to suit their needs.

	A	B	C	D	E	F
1	Summary Output					
2	Regression Statistics					
3	Multiple R	0.812				
4	R Square	0.659				
5	Adjusted R Square	0.488				
6	Standard Error	64639.80005				
7	Observations	7				
8						
9	ANOVA					
10		df	SS	MS	F	Significance F
11	Regression	2	32290723884	16145361942	3.86	0.116
12	Residual	4	16713215001	4178303750		
13	Total	6	49003938885			
14						
15		Coefficients	Standard Error		t Stat	p Value
16	Intercept	–38581.02552	98732.340		–0.39	0.7161
17	Length	0.092371903	0.0395		2.34	0.079
18	Vehicles	0.05978497	0.0250		2.39	0.075
19						
20	Residual Output					
21	Observation	Predicted Tonne-Kilometres	Residuals			
22	1	361,024.15	46,032.85			
23	2	196,761.36	63,642.64			
24	3	279,292.51	–69,052.51			
25	4	194,945.03	7,958.97			
26	5	153,595.06	29,154.94			
27	6	163,034.27	–8,531.27			
28	7	209,437.62	–69,205.62			

R^2 for this regression analysis is 0.659 or 65.9%; that is, 65.9% of the variation in the volume of freight cargo is accounted for by these two independent variables. Conversely, 34.1% of the variation is unaccounted for by this model. The adjusted R^2 is only 0.488 or 48.8%, indicating that the value of R^2 is considerably inflated. Thus, it could be that the two predictors of the regression model actually account for less than half of the variation of the dependent variable when R^2 is adjusted.

This problem highlights the notion that a regression model can be developed for data and not really fit the data in a significant way. By examining the values of F, t, s_e, R^2, and adjusted R^2, the business researcher can begin to understand whether the regression model provides any significant predictability for y.

Concept Check

1. What can we learn from the ANOVA table in a multiple regression analysis output?

13.4 Problems

13.22 Study the regression output that follows. How many predictors are there? What is the equation of the regression model? Using the key statistics discussed in this chapter, discuss the strength of the model and the predictors.

Regression Analysis: y versus x_1, x_2, x_3, x_4

Summary Output

Regression Statistics	
R Square	0.802
Adjusted R Square	0.787
Standard Error	9.025
Observations	60

ANOVA	DF	SS	MS	F	p
Regression	2	18,088.5	4,522.1	55.52	0.000
Residual	55	4,479.7	81.4		
Total	59	22,568.2			

	Coefficient	Standard Error	t Stat	p Value
Constant	−55.93	24.22	−2.31	0.025
x_1	0.01049	0.021	0.5	0.619
x_2	−0.1072	0.03503	−3.06	0.003
x_3	0.57922	0.07633	7.59	0.000
x_4	−0.8695	0.1498	−5.81	0.000

13.23   Study the Excel regression output that follows. How many predictors are there? What is the equation of the regression model? Using the key statistics discussed in this chapter, discuss the strength of the model and its predictors.

	A	B	C	D	E	F
1	Summary Output					
2	Regression Statistics					
3	Multiple R	0.814				
4	R Square	0.663				
5	Adjusted R Square	0.636				
6	Standard Error	51.761				
7	Observations	28				
8						
9	ANOVA					
10		df	SS	MS	F	Significance F
11	Regression	2	131567.0243	65783.5121	24.55	0.0000013
12	Residual	25	66979.6543	2679.1862		
13	Total	27	198546.6786			
14						
15		Coefficients	Standard Error	t Stat	p Value	
16	Intercept	203.3937	67.5177	3.01	0.0059	
17	x_1	1.1151	0.5278	2.11	0.0448	
18	x_2	−2.2115	0.5667	−3.90	0.0006	

WILL YOU LIKE YOUR NEW JOB?

In the Decision Dilemma, several variables are considered in attempting to determine whether a person will like his or her new job. Four predictor (independent) variables are given with the data set: relationship with supervisor, overall quality of work environment, total hours worked per week, and opportunities for advancement. Other possible variables might include openness of work culture, amount of pressure, how the interviewee is treated during the interview, availability of flexible scheduling, size of office, amount of time allotted for lunch, availability of management, and interesting work.

Using the data that are given, a multiple regression model can be developed to predict job satisfaction from the four independent variables. Such an analysis allows the business researcher to study the entire data set in one model rather than constructing four different simple regression models, one for each independent variable. In the multiple regression model, job satisfaction is the dependent variable. There are 19 observations. The Excel regression output for this problem follows.

	A	B	C	D	E	F
1	Summary Output					
2	Regression					
3	Multiple R	0.952				
4	R Square	0.906				
5	Adjusted R Square	0.880				
6	Standard Error	8.03				
7	Observations	19				
8						
9	ANOVA					
10		df	SS	MS	F	Significance F
11	Regression	4	8748.967	2187.242	33.89	0.00000046
12	Residual	14	903.664	64.547		
13	Total	18	9652.632			
14						
15		Coefficients	Standard Error		t Stat	p Value
16	Intercept	−2.6961	13.0047		−0.21	0.8387
17	Relationship with Supervisior	6.9211	3.7741		1.83	0.0880
18	Overall Quality of Work Environment	6.0814	1.5499		3.92	0.0015
19	Total Hours Worked per Week	0.1063	0.1925		0.55	0.5895
20	Opportunities for Advancement	0.3881	1.6322		0.24	0.8155

The test for overall significance of the model produced an F of 33.89 with a p value of 0.00000046 (significant at $\alpha = 0.000001$). The R^2 of 0.906 and adjusted R^2 of 0.880 indicate strong predictability in the model. The standard error of the estimate, 8.03, can be viewed in light of the job satisfaction values, which ranged from 10 to 95, and the residuals, which are not shown here. Sixteen of the 19 residuals (over 84%) are within the standard error of the estimate. Examining the t statistics and their associated p values reveals that only one independent variable, Overall Quality of Work Environment ($t = 3.92$, p value = 0.0015), is significant at $\alpha = 0.01$. Using a more generous α of 0.10, one could argue that Relationship with Supervisor is also a significant predictor of job satisfaction. Judging by their large p values, it appears that Total Hours Worked per Week and Opportunities for Advancement are not good predictors of job satisfaction.

KEY CONSIDERATIONS

Multiple regression analysis can be used either intentionally or unintentionally in questionable ways. When the degrees of freedom are small, an inflated value of R^2 can be obtained, leading to overenthusiastic expectations about the predictability of a regression model. To prevent this type of reliance, a researcher should take into account the nature of the data, the variables, and the value of the adjusted R^2.

Another misleading aspect of multiple regression can be the tendency of researchers to assume cause-and-effect relationships between the dependent variable and predictors. Just because independent variables produce a significant R^2 does not necessarily mean those variables are causing the deviation of the y values. Indeed, some other force not in the model may be driving both the independent variables and the dependent variable over the range of values being studied.

Some people use the estimates of the regression coefficients to compare the worth of the predictor variables: the larger the coefficient, the greater is its worth. At least two problems can be found in this approach. The first is that most variables are measured in different units. Thus, regression coefficient weights are partly a function of the unit of measurement of the variable. Second, if multicollinearity (discussed in Chapter 14) is present, the interpretation of the regression coefficients is questionable. In addition, the presence of multicollinearity raises several issues about the interpretation of other regression output. Researchers who ignore this problem are at risk of presenting spurious results.

Another danger in using regression analysis is in the extrapolation of the model to values beyond the range of values used to derive the model. A regression model that fits data within a given range does not necessarily fit data outside that range. One of the uses of regression analysis is in the area of forecasting. Users need to be aware that what has occurred in the past is not guaranteed to continue to occur in the future. Unscrupulous and sometimes even well-intentioned business decision makers can use regression models to project conclusions about the future that have little or no basis. The receiver of such messages should be cautioned that regression models may lack validity outside the range of values in which the models were developed.

Why Statistics Is Relevant

Any business variable is affected by a number of factors. For example:

- Sales of a product can be affected by its quality, price, availability, and packaging.
- The productivity of an employee may be the result of job satisfaction, financial compensation, working atmosphere, and encouragement from superiors.
- A computer purchase decision may depend on the technological features of the computer, the available alternatives, and the suitability of the computer that is currently being used.

Whenever we have a number of variables affecting a single variable, it is important for us to know which variables are really influential and to what extent. Without a technique like multiple regression, we cannot identify the exact nature of such relationships and make informed decisions.

SUMMARY

1. Multiple regression analysis is a statistical tool in which a mathematical model is developed in an attempt to predict a dependent variable by two or more independent variables or in which at least one predictor is nonlinear.

2. Because doing multiple regression analysis by hand is extremely tedious and time consuming, it is almost always done on a computer. However, the model is specified by the analyst. The specification should consist of one dependent variable (y) and several independent variables ($x_1, x_2, x_3, x_4, \ldots$).

3. The standard output from a multiple regression analysis is similar to that of simple regression analysis. A regression equation is produced with a constant that is analogous to the y intercept in simple regression and with estimates of the regression coefficients that are analogous to the estimate of the slope in simple regression.

4. An F test for the overall model is computed to determine whether at least one of the regression coefficients is significantly different from zero. This F value is usually displayed in an ANOVA table, which

is part of the regression output. The ANOVA table also contains the sum of squares of error and sum of squares of regression, which are used to compute other statistics in the model. Most multiple regression computer output contains t values, which are used to determine the significance of the regression coefficients. Using these t values, statisticians can make decisions about including or excluding variables from the model.

5. Residuals, standard error of the estimate, and R^2 are also standard computer regression output with multiple regression. The coefficient of determination for simple regression models is denoted r^2, whereas for multiple regression it is R^2. The interpretation of residuals, standard error of the estimate, and R^2 in multiple regression is similar to that in simple regression. Because R^2 can be inflated with nonsignificant variables in the mix, an adjusted R^2 is often computed. Unlike R^2, adjusted R^2 takes into account the degrees of freedom and the number of observations.

KEY TERMS

adjusted R^2
coefficient of multiple
   determination (R^2)
dependent variable

independent variable
least squares analysis
multiple regression
outliers

partial regression coefficient
residual
response plane
response surface

response variable
standard error of the
   estimate (s_e)

FORMULAS

The F value

$$F = \frac{MS_{reg}}{MS_{err}} = \frac{SS_{reg}/df_{reg}}{SS_{err}/df_{err}} = \frac{SSR/k}{SSE/(N-k-1)}$$

Sum of squares of error

$$SSE = \sum(y - \hat{y})^2$$

Standard error of the estimate

$$s_e = \sqrt{\frac{SSE}{n-k-1}}$$

Coefficient of multiple determination

$$R^2 - \frac{SSR}{SS_{yy}} = 1 - \frac{SSE}{SS_{yy}}$$

Adjusted R^2

$$\text{Adjusted } R^2 = 1 - \frac{SSE/(n-k-1)}{SS_{yy}/(n-1)}$$

SUPPLEMENTARY PROBLEMS

Calculating the Statistics

13.24 Use the following data to develop a multiple regression model to predict y from x_1 and x_2. Discuss the output, including comments about the overall strength of the model, the significance of the regression coefficients, and other indicators of model fit.

y	x_1	x_2
198	29	1.64
214	71	2.81
211	54	2.22
219	73	2.7
184	67	1.57
167	32	1.63
201	47	1.99
204	43	2.14
190	60	2.04
222	32	2.93
197	34	2.15

13.25 Given here are the data for a dependent variable, y, and independent variables. Use these data to develop a regression model to predict y. Discuss the output.

y	x_1	x_2	x_3
14	51	16.4	56
17	48	17.1	64
29	29	18.2	53
32	36	17.9	41
54	40	16.5	60
86	27	17.1	55
117	14	17.8	71
120	17	18.2	48
194	16	16.9	60
203	9	18.0	77
217	14	18.9	90
235	11	18.5	67

Testing Your Understanding

13.26 Shown here are the average prices per year for several minerals over a decade. Use these data and multiple regression to produce a model to predict the average price of gold from the other variables.

Gold ($ per ounce)	Copper (cents per pound)	Silver ($ per ounce)	Aluminum (cents per pound)
161.1	64.2	4.4	39.8
308.0	93.3	11.1	61.0
613.0	101.3	20.6	71.6
460.0	84.2	10.5	76.0
376.0	72.8	8.0	76.0
424.0	76.5	11.4	77.8
361.0	66.8	8.1	81.0
318.0	67.0	6.1	81.0
368.0	66.1	5.5	81.0
448.0	82.5	7.0	72.3
438.0	120.5	6.5	110.1
382.6	130.9	5.5	87.8

13.27 Can we predict the interest rate of the 90-day treasury bill rate on the basis of the prime rate and the bank rate? The table below gives the Canadian prime rate, the bank rate, and the treasury bill rate for seven years. Use the data to develop a regression model to predict the treasury bill rate from the other two rates (bank rate and prime rate). Comment on the regression model and its strengths and its weaknesses.

Year	Bank Rate	Prime Rate	Treasury Rate
2001	4.31	5.81	3.85
2002	2.71	4.21	2.55
2003	3.19	4.69	2.87
2004	2.50	4.00	2.23
2005	2.92	4.42	2.71
2006	4.31	5.81	4.02
2007	4.60	6.10	4.17

13.28 Statistics Canada produces consumer price indexes for several different categories. Shown here are the percentage changes in consumer price indexes over a period of 22 years for durable goods, semidurable goods, and nondurable goods. Also displayed are the percentage changes in total goods price index. Use these data and multiple regression to develop a model that attempts to predict the total goods index by the other three variables. Comment on the result of this analysis.

Consumer Price Indexes (2002 = 100)

Year	Total Goods	Durable Goods	Semi-durable Goods	Non-durable Goods
1986	69.8	79.5	71.6	65.5
1987	72.6	82.0	74.5	68.4
1988	75.2	85.1	78.2	70.5
1989	78.4	88.9	81.7	73.9
1990	81.6	89.5	84.0	78.5
1991	85.7	89.4	91.9	83.2
1992	86.4	90.4	92.5	83.8
1993	87.8	92.5	93.4	85.2
1994	86.8	96.0	94.2	81.6
1995	88.4	99.0	94.9	82.9
1996	89.9	100.8	95.4	84.4
1997	91.2	101.6	97.0	86.0
1998	91.4	101.5	97.7	86.1
1999	93.1	101.5	99.2	88.4
2000	96.0	100.8	99.6	93.3
2001	98.4	100.1	100.3	97.4
2002	100	100	100	100
2003	101.9	99.2	98.6	104.3
2004	103.4	97.5	98.2	107.9
2005	105.8	96.9	97.7	112.6
2006	107.1	96.2	96.2	115.9
2007	108.0	94.7	96.0	118.4

13.29 The table on next page shows Canada's exchange rate for 1 US$ for a 14-year period. Use these data and multiple regression analysis to predict the exchange rate from the different variables like price index in relation to OECD countries, relative unit labour cost, manufacturing producer price index and CPI. Comment on the results.

Year	Cdn$ per US$	Price Index (OECD = 100)	Relative Unit Labour Cost	PPI-Mfg	CPI
1992	1.209	93	120.1	78.6	88.1
1993	1.29	89	108.6	81.5	89.7
1994	1.366	82	101.1	86.4	89.8
1995	1.373	78	101.9	92.8	91.8
1996	1.364	82	108.6	93.2	93.2
1997	1.385	86	107.5	93.9	94.7
1998	1.484	82	103.2	94.2	95.7
1999	1.486	81	101.7	95.9	97.3
2000	1.485	88	100	100	100
2001	1.548	88	100.2	101	102.2
2002	1.57	87	101.9	101	104.8
2003	1.4	91	115.8	99.7	107.7
2004	1.301	94	122	102.8	109.7
2005	1.212	101	129.9	104.3	112.2

Source: Data extracted from *OECD Fact book 2007.*

13.30 The table below shows the growth of new car dealers between 1991 and 2007. Use the data to predict the number of new car dealers on the basis of the amount spent on used vehicles and parts, total excluding vehicles and parts, and gasoline stations. Discuss the results, highlighting both the significant and nonsignificant predictors.

Year	New Car Dealers	Used Vehicles and Parts	Total Excluding Used Vehicles and Parts	Gas Stations
1991	31,817	6,853	146,390	17,139
1992	32,737	6,931	149,995	17,009
1993	35,600	7,457	156,278	17,202
1994	41,166	8,492	164,334	17,251
1995	44,037	8,810	168,231	17,872
1996	46,821	9,444	172,174	20,105
1997	52,879	10,722	183,217	20,380
1998	54,308	11,038	191,149	19,607
1999	58,721	11,393	201,418	21,535
2000	61,031	12,872	213,935	26,676
2001	63,518	14,009	222,920	26,986
2002	69,161	14,303	236,061	28,138
2003	68,184	14,394	248,566	29,951
2004	68,141	14,559	264,021	33,364
2005	71,516	15,301	279,354	38,357
2006	74,531	17,286	297,667	41,753
2007	76,884	18,674	316,479	46,388

Interpreting the Results

13.31   Shown here are the data for y and three predictors, x_1, x_2, and x_3. A multiple regression analysis has been done on these data. Comment on the outcome of the analysis in light of the data.

y	x_1	x_2	x_3
94	21	1	204
97	25	0	198
93	22	1	184
95	27	0	200
90	29	1	182
91	20	1	159
91	18	1	147
94	25	0	196
98	26	0	228
99	24	0	242
90	28	1	162
92	23	1	180
96	25	0	219

Summary Output

Regression Statistics	
Multiple R	0.9699
R Square	0.9407
Adjusted R Square	0.9209
Standard Error	0.8503
Observations	13

ANOVA	df	SS	MS	F	Significance F
Regression	3	103.185	34.395	47.571	0.000
Residual	9	6.507	0.723		
Total	12	109.692			

	Coefficients	Standard Error	t Stat	p Value
Intercept	87.890	3.445	25.51	0.000
x_1	−0.256	0.083	−3.08	0.013
x_2	−2.714	0.731	−3.71	0.005
x_3	0.071	0.014	5.22	0.001

13.32   The residual diagnostics for the multiple regression analysis for the data given in Problem 13.30 follow. Discuss any potential problems with meeting the regression assumptions for this regression analysis based on the residual graphics.

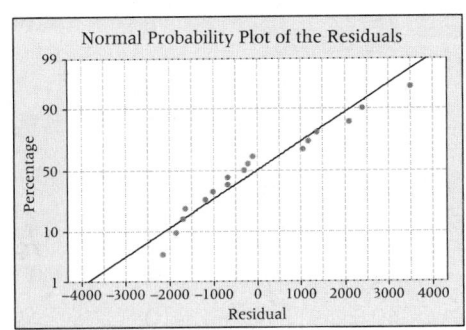

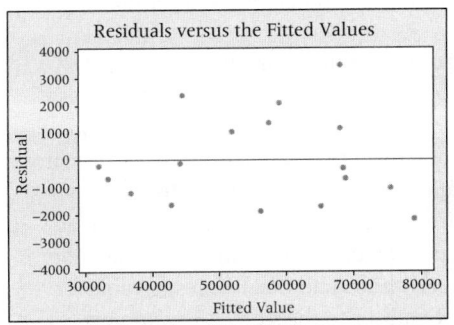

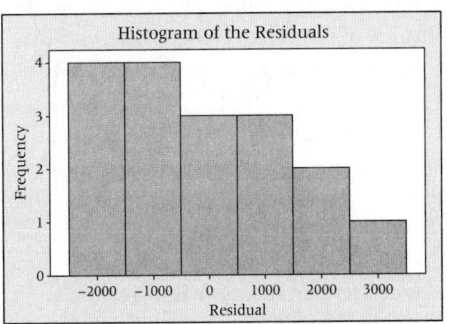

ANALYZING THE DATABASES

see www.wiley.com/canada/black

1. Use the Major League Baseball Database to develop a multiple regression model to predict Payroll (independent variable), Current Value, Revenues and Average Attendance (dependent variables) per home game. Discuss the results of the analysis.

2. Develop a regression model using the Financial Database. Use Total Revenues, Average Yield, Dividend Growth, and Dividend per Share to predict the Average P/E Ratio for a company. How strong is the model? Which variables seem to be the best predictors?

CASE

Starbucks Introduces Debit Card

Starbucks is a resounding restaurant success story. Beginning with its first coffee house in 1971, Starbucks has grown to more than 15,000 locations. Opening up its first international outlet in the mid-1990s, Starbucks now operates in more than 40 countries outside of North America. Besides selling beverages, pastries, confections, and coffee-related accessories and equipment at its retail outlets, Starbucks also purchases and roasts high-quality coffee beans in several locations. The company's objective is to become the most recognized and respected brand in the world. Starbucks maintains a strong environmental orientation and is committed to taking a leadership position environmentally. In addition, the company has won awards for corporate social responsibility through its community-building programs, its strong commitment to its origins (coffee producers, family, community), and the Starbucks Foundation, which is dedicated to creating hope, discovery, and opportunity in the communities where Starbucks resides.

In November 2001, Starbucks launched its prepaid (debit) Starbucks Card. The card, which holds between $5 and $500, can be used at virtually any Starbucks location. The card was so popular when it was first released that many stores ran out. By mid-2002, Starbucks had activated more than 5 million of these cards. It is believed that the card accounted for a large portion of the company's 7% same-store increase in sales in early 2002 and that it is responsible for attracting many new patrons to the store. As customers "reload" the cards, it appears they are placing more money on them than the initial value of the card.

Starbucks has gone on to promote its Starbucks Card as a flexible marketing tool that can be used by individuals as a gift of thanks and appreciation for friendship or service and can be used by companies to reward loyal customers and as an incentive to employees.

Discussion

1. Starbucks enjoyed considerable success with its debit cards, which it sells for $5 to $500. Since the card was introduced in November 2001, sales revenues increased. Suppose Starbucks management wants to study the reasons some people purchase debit cards with higher

prepaid amounts than do other people. Suppose a study of 25 randomly selected prepaid card purchasers is taken. Respondents are asked the amount of the prepaid card, the customer's age, the number of days per month the customer makes a purchase at Starbucks, the number of cups of coffee the customer drinks per day, and the customer's income. The data follow. Using these data, develop a multiple regression model to study how well the amount of the prepaid card can be predicted by the other variables and which variables seem to be more promising in making the prediction. What sales implications might be evident from this analysis?

Amount of Prepaid Card ($)	Age	Days per Month at Starbucks	Cups of Coffee per Day	Income ($1,000s)
5	25	4	1	20
25	30	12	5	35
10	27	10	4	30
5	42	8	5	30
15	29	11	8	25
50	25	12	5	60
10	50	8	3	30
15	45	6	5	35
5	32	16	7	25
5	23	10	1	20
20	40	18	5	40
35	35	12	3	40
40	28	10	3	50
15	33	12	2	30
200	40	15	5	80
15	37	3	1	30
40	51	10	8	35
5	20	8	4	25
30	26	15	5	35
100	38	19	10	45
30	27	12	3	35
25	29	14	6	35
25	34	10	4	45
50	30	6	3	55
15	22	8	5	30

2. Suppose marketing wants to be able to profile frequent visitors to a Starbucks store. Using the same data set already provided, develop a multiple regression model to predict Days per Month at Starbucks by age, income, and number of cups of coffee per day. How strong is the model? Which particular independent variables seem to have more promise in predicting how many days per month a customer visits Starbucks? What marketing implications might be evident from this analysis?

3. Over the past decade or so, Starbucks has grown quite rapidly. As it adds stores and increases the number of drinks, its sales revenues increase. In reflecting about this growth, think about some other variables that might be related to the increase in Starbucks sales revenues. Some data for the past seven years on the number of Starbucks stores (worldwide), approximate sales revenue (in $U.S. millions), number of different drinks sold, and average weekly earnings of U.S. production workers are given here. Most figures are approximate. Develop a multiple regression model to predict sales revenue by number of drinks sold, number of stores, and average weekly earnings. How strong is the model? What are the key predictors, if any? How might this analysis help

Starbucks management in attempting to determine what drives sales revenues?

Sales Year	Revenue	Number of Stores	Number of Drinks	Average Weekly Earnings
1	400	676	15	386
2	700	1,015	15	394
3	1,000	1,412	18	407
4	1,350	1,886	22	425
5	1,650	2,135	27	442
6	2,200	3,300	27	457
7	2,600	4,709	30	474

References

Adapted from Shirley Leung, "Starbucks May Indeed Be a Robust Staple," *The Wall Street Journal*, July 26, 2002, p. B4; Starbucks, available at <http://www.starbucks.com/aboutus>; James Peters, "Starbucks' Growth Still Hot; Gift Card Jolts Chain's Sales," *Nation's Restaurant News*, February 11, 2002, pp. 1–2. Starbucks' website (June 2009) at <http://www/starbucks.com/aboutus/company_factsheet.pdf>.

USING THE COMPUTER

Excel

- Excel has the capability of doing multiple regression analysis. The commands are essentially the same as those for simple regression except that the *x* range of data may include several columns. Excel will determine the number of predictor variables from the number of columns entered in to **Input X Range**.

- Begin by selecting the **Data** tab on the Excel worksheet. From the **Analysis** panel at the right top of the **Data** tab worksheet, click on **Data Analysis**. If your Excel worksheet does not show the **Data Analysis** option, then you can load it as an add-in. From the **Data Analysis** pulldown menu, select **Regression**. In the **Regression** dialogue box, input the location of the *y* values in **Input Y Range**. Input the location of the *x* values in **Input X Range**. Input **Labels** and input **Confidence Level**. To pass the line through the origin, check **Constant is Zero**. To printout the raw residuals, check **Residuals**. To printout residuals converted to *z* scores, check **Standardized Residuals**. For a plot of the residuals, check **Residual Plots**. For a plot of the line through the points check **Line Fit Plots**.

- Standard output includes R, R^2, s_e, and an ANOVA table with the F test, the slope and intercept, t statistics with associated p-values, and any optionally requested output, such as graphs or residuals.

CHAPTER 14

BUILDING MULTIPLE REGRESSION MODELS

Learning Objectives

1. How can we analyze and interpret nonlinear variables in multiple regression analysis?

2. What is the role of qualitative variables in multiple regression analysis and how can we incorporate them in the analysis?

3. How can we build and evaluate multiple regression models?

4. What is multicollinearity and how can we deal with it?

iStock Photo

DETERMINING COMPENSATION FOR CEOs

Chief executive officers for large companies receive widely varying amounts of compensation for their work. Why is the range so wide? What are some of the variables that seem to contribute to the diversity of CEO compensation packages?

As a starting place, one might examine the role of company size as measured by sales volume, number of employees, number of plants, and so on in driving CEO compensation. It could be argued that CEOs of larger companies carry larger responsibilities and hence should receive higher compensation. Some researchers believe CEO compensation is related to such things as industry performance of the firm, percentage of shares with outside ownership, and proportion of insiders on the board. At least a significant proportion of CEOs are likely to be compensated according to the performance of their companies during the fiscal period preceding compensation. Company performance can be measured by such variables as earnings per share, percentage change in profit, sales, and

profit. In addition, some theorize that companies with outside ownership are more oriented toward declaring dividends to shareholders than toward large CEO compensation packages.

Do CEOs' individual and family characteristics play a role in their compensation? Do such things as CEO age, degrees obtained, marital status, military experience, and number of children matter in compensation? Do type of industry and geographic location of the company matter? What are the significant factors in determining CEO compensation?

What follow are CEO compensation data generated by using management compensation models published by Wyatt Data Services. In the first column on the left are cash compensation figures (in $U.S. thousands) for 20 CEOs. These figures represent salary, bonuses, and any other cash remuneration given to the CEO as part of compensation. The four columns to the right contain data on four variables associated with each CEO's company: sales, number of employees, capital investment, and whether the company is in manufacturing. Sales figures and capital investment figures are given in millions of U.S. dollars.

Cash Compensation	Sales	Number of Employees	Capital Investment	Manufacturing
212	35.0	248.00	10.5	1
226	27.2	156.00	3.8	0
237	49.5	348.00	14.9	1
239	34.0	196.00	5.0	0
242	52.8	371.00	15.9	1
245	37.6	216.00	5.7	0
253	60.7	425.00	18.3	1
262	49.2	285.00	8.0	0
271	75.1	524.00	22.6	1
285	69.0	401.00	12.3	0
329	137.2	947.00	41.4	1
340	140.1	825.00	30.3	0
353	162.9	961.00	36.7	0
384	221.7	1,517.00	67.1	1
405	261.6	1,784.00	79.2	1
411	300.1	1,788.00	79.8	0
456	455.5	2,733.00	135.7	0
478	437.6	2,957.00	132.7	1
525	802.1	4,857.00	278.4	0
564	731.5	4,896.00	222.2	1

Managerial and Statistical Questions

1. Can a model be developed to predict CEO compensation?
2. If a model is developed, how can the model be evaluated to determine whether it is valid?
3. Is it possible to sort out variables that appear to be related to CEO compensation and determine which variables are more significant predictors?
4. Are some of the variables related to CEO compensation in a nonlinear manner?
5. Are some variables highly interrelated and redundant in their potential for determining CEO compensation?

Sources: Adapted from Jeffrey L. Kerr and Leslie Kren, "Effect of Relative Decision Monitoring on Chief Executive Compensation," *Academy of Management Journal*, vol. 35, no. 2 (June 1992). Used with permission. Robin L. Bartlett, James H. Grant, and Timothy I. Miller, "The Earnings of Top Executives: Compensating Differentials for Risky Business," *Quarterly Review of Economics and Finance*, vol. 32, no. 1 (Spring 1992). Used with permission. Database derived using models published in *1993/1994 Top Management Compensation Regression Analysis Report*, 44th ed. (Fort Lee, NJ: Wyatt Data Services/ECS, December 1994).

14.1 NONLINEAR MODELS: MATHEMATICAL TRANSFORMATION

The regression models presented thus far are based on the general linear regression model, which has the form:

$$y = \beta_0 + \beta_1 x_1 + \beta_2 x_2 + \cdots + \beta_k x_k + \varepsilon \tag{14.1}$$

where

β_0 = the regression constant

$\beta_1, \beta_2, \ldots, \beta_k$ are the partial regression coefficients for the k independent variables

$x_1, \ldots, x_k$ are the independent variables

k = the number of independent variables

In this general linear model, the parameters, β_i, are linear. This does not mean, however, that the dependent variable, y, is necessarily linearly related to the predictor variables. Scatter plots sometimes reveal a curvilinear relationship between x and y. Multiple regression response surfaces are not restricted to linear surfaces and may be curvilinear.

To this point, the variables, x_i, have represented different predictors. For example, in the real estate example presented in Chapter 13, the variables, x_1, x_2, represented two predictors: number of square feet in the house and the age of the house, respectively. Certainly, regression models can be developed for more than two predictors. For example, a marketing site location model could be developed in which sales, as the response variable, is predicted by population density, number of competitors, size of the store, and number of salespeople. Such a model could take the form:

$$y = \beta_0 + \beta_1 x_1 + \beta_2 x_2 + \beta_3 x_3 + \beta_4 x_4 + \varepsilon$$

This regression model has four x_i variables, each of which represents a different predictor.

The general linear model also applies to situations in which some x_i represent recoded data from a predictor variable already represented in the model by another independent variable. In some models, x_i represents variables that have undergone a mathematical transformation to allow the model to follow the form of the general linear model.

In this section of this chapter, we explore some of these other models, including polynomial regression models, regression models with interaction, and models with transformed variables.

POLYNOMIAL REGRESSION

Regression models in which the highest power of any predictor variable is 1 and in which there are no interaction terms—cross products ($x_i \cdot x_j$)—are referred to as *first-order models*. Simple regression models like those presented in Chapter 12 are *first-order models with one independent variable*. The general model for simple regression is:

$$y = \beta_0 + \beta_1 x_1 + \varepsilon$$

If a second independent variable is added, the model is referred to as a first-order model with two independent variables and appears as:

$$y = \beta_0 + \beta_1 x_1 + \beta_2 x_2 + \varepsilon$$

Polynomial regression models are regression models that are second- or higher-order models. They contain squared, cubed, or higher powers of the predictor variable(s) and contain response surfaces that are curvilinear. Yet they are still special cases of the general linear model given in formula 14.1.

Consider a regression model with one independent variable where the model includes a second predictor, which is the independent variable squared. Such a model is referred to as a second-order model with one independent variable because the highest power among the predictors is 2, but there is still only one independent variable. This model takes the following form:

$$y = \beta_0 + \beta_1 x_1 + \beta_2 x_1^2 + \varepsilon$$

This model can be used to explore the possible fit of a quadratic model in predicting a dependent variable. A **quadratic model** is *a multiple regression model in which a variable and the square of that variable are the predictors*. How can this be a special case of the general linear model? Let x_2 of the general linear model be equal to x_1^2. Then, $y = \beta_0 + \beta_1 x_1 + \beta_2 x_1^2 + \varepsilon$ becomes $y = \beta_0 + \beta_1 x_1 + \beta_2 x_2 + \varepsilon$. What process does a researcher go through to develop the regression constant and coefficients for a curvilinear model such as this one?

Multiple regression analysis assumes a linear fit of the regression coefficients and regression constant but not necessarily a linear relationship of the independent variable values (x). Hence, a researcher can often accomplish curvilinear regression by recoding the data before the multiple regression analysis is attempted.

As an example, consider the data given in Table 14.1. This table contains sales volumes (in $ millions) for 13 manufacturing companies along with the number of

Table 14.1			
Sales Data for 13 Manufacturing Companies	**Manufacturer**	**Sales ($ millions)**	**Number of Manufacturer's Representatives**
	1	2.1	2
	2	3.6	1
	3	6.2	2
	4	10.4	3
	5	22.8	4
	6	35.6	4
	7	57.1	5
	8	83.5	5
	9	109.4	6
	10	128.6	7
	11	196.8	8
	12	280.0	10
	13	462.3	11

Figure 14.1

Excel Simple Regression Output for Manufacturing Example

	A	B	C	D	E	F
1	SUMMARY OUTPUT					
2	Regression Statistics					
3	Multiple R	0.933				
4	R Square	0.870				
5	Adjusted R Square	0.858				
6	Standard Error	51.098				
7	Observations	13				
8						
9	ANOVA					
10		df	SS	MS	F	Significant F
11	Regression	1	192,395.416	192,395.416	73.69	0.0000033
12	Residual	11	28,721.452	2,611.041		
13	Total	12	221,116.868			
14						
15		Coefficients	Standard Error	t Stat	p Value	
16	Intercept	−107.029	28.7373	−3.72	0.0033561	
17	Reps	41.026	4.7794	8.58	0.0000033	

manufacturer's representatives associated with each firm. A simple regression analysis to predict sales by the number of manufacturer's representatives results in the Excel output in Figure 14.1.

This regression output shows a regression model with an r^2 of 87.0%, a standard error of the estimate equal to 51.10, a significant overall F test for the model, and a significant t ratio for the predictor number of manufacturer's representatives.

Figure 14.2(a) is a scatter plot of the data in Table 14.1. Notice that the plot of number of representatives and sales is not a straight line and is an indication that the relationship between the two variables may be curvilinear. To explore the possibility that a quadratic relationship may exist between sales and number of representatives, the business researcher creates a second predictor variable, (number of manufacturer's representatives)^2, to use in the regression analysis to predict sales along with number of manufacturer's representatives, as shown in Table 14.2. Thus, a variable can be created to explore second-order parabolic relationships by squaring the data from the independent variable of the linear model and entering it into the analysis. Figure 14.2(b) is a scatter plot of sales with (number of manufacturer's reps)^2. Note that this graph, with the squared term, more closely approaches a straight line than does the graph in Figure 14.2(a). By recoding the predictor variable, the researcher creates a potentially better regression fit.

With these data, a multiple regression model can be developed. Figure 14.3 shows the Excel output for the regression analysis to predict sales by number of manufacturer's representatives and (number of manufacturer's representatives)^2.

Figure 14.2

Scatter Plots of Manufacturing Data

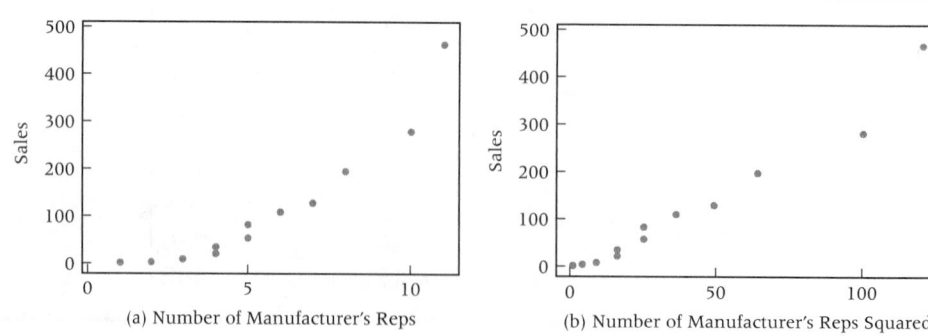

(a) Number of Manufacturer's Reps

(b) Number of Manufacturer's Reps Squared

Table 14.2

Display of Manufacturing Data with Newly Created Variable

Manufacturer	Sales ($ millions) y	Number of Manufacturer Reps x_1	Number of (Manufacturer Reps)^2 $x_2 = (x_1)^2$
1	2.1	2	4
2	3.6	1	1
3	6.2	2	4
4	10.4	3	9
5	22.8	4	16
6	35.6	4	16
7	57.1	5	25
8	83.5	5	25
9	109.4	6	36
10	128.6	7	49
11	196.8	8	64
12	280.0	10	100
13	462.3	11	121

Examine the output in Figure 14.3 and compare it with the output in Figure 14.1 for the simple regression model. The R^2 for this model is 97.3%, which is an increase from the r^2 of 87.0% for the single linear predictor model. The standard error of the estimate for this model is 24.59, which is considerably lower than the 51.10 value obtained from simple regression model. Remember, the sales figures were in millions of dollars. The quadratic model reduced the standard error of the estimate by 26.51($1,000,000$), or $26,510,000. It appears that the quadratic model is a better model for predicting sales.

An examination of the t statistic for the squared term and its associated probability in Figure 14.3 shows that it is statistically significant at $\alpha = 0.001$ ($t = 6.12$ with a probability of 0.0001). If this t statistic were not significant, the researcher would most likely drop the squared term and revert to the first-order model (simple regression model).

Figure 14.3

Excel Output for Quadratic Model of Manufacturing Example

	A	B	C	D	E	F
1	SUMMARY OUTPUT					
2	Regression Statistics					
3	Multiple R	0.986				
4	R Square	0.973				
5	Adjusted R Square	0.967				
6	Standard Error	24.593				
7	Observations	13				
8						
9	ANOVA					
10		df	SS	MS	F	Significance F
11	Regression	2	215068.6001	107534.3	177.79	0.000000015
12	Residual	10	6048.3	604.8		
13	Total	12	221116.8677			
14						
15		Coefficients	Standard Error	t Stat	p Value	
16	Intercept	18.067	24.673	0.73	0.4808	
17	Reps	−15.723	9.550	−1.65	0.1307	
18	RepsSq	4.750	0.776	6.12	0.0001	

In theory, third- and higher-order models can be explored. Generally, business researchers tend to utilize first- and second-order regression models more than higher-order models. Remember that most regression analysis is used in business to aid decision making. Higher-power models (third, fourth, etc.) become difficult to interpret and difficult to explain to decision makers. In addition, the business researcher is usually looking for trends and general directions. The higher the order in regression modelling, the more the model tends to follow irregular fluctuations rather than meaningful directions.

TUKEY'S LADDER OF TRANSFORMATIONS

As just shown with the manufacturing example, recoding data can be a useful tool in improving the regression model fit. Many other ways of recoding data can be explored in this process. Nonlinear data can be recoded to make them linear. When $x > 1$, powers less than 1, such as $1/x^2$, $1/x^3$, $1/x^4$, will reduce the high values relative to the low values, as in positively skewed data. Powers greater than 1 (x^2, x^3, x^4, …) will have the opposite effect of stretching out high values relative to low ones, as in negatively skewed data. The type of recoding (or transformations) required depend on the nature and extent of nonlinearity and may need some experimentation to identify the most appropriate transformation.

John W. Tukey[*] presents a "ladder of expressions" that can be explored to straighten out a plot of x and y, thereby offering potential improvement in the predictability of the regression model. **Tukey's ladder of transformations** gives the following expressions for both x and y.

Ladder for x

$\leftarrow$up Ladder $\qquad$ $\downarrow$Neutral $\qquad$ Down Ladder $\rightarrow$

$$\ldots \quad x^4 \quad x^3 \quad x^2 \qquad x \quad \sqrt{x} \quad x \qquad \log x \quad -\frac{1}{\sqrt{x}} \quad -\frac{1}{x} \quad -\frac{1}{x^2} \quad -\frac{1}{x^3} \quad -\frac{1}{x^4} \quad \ldots$$

Ladder for y

$\leftarrow$up Ladder $\qquad$ $\downarrow$Neutral $\qquad$ Down Ladder $\rightarrow$

$$\ldots \quad y^4 \quad y^3 \quad y^2 \qquad y \quad \sqrt{y} \quad y \qquad \log y \quad -\frac{1}{\sqrt{y}} \quad -\frac{1}{y} \quad -\frac{1}{y^2} \quad -\frac{1}{y^3} \quad -\frac{1}{y^4} \quad \ldots$$

These ladders suggest to the user potential ways to recode the data. Tukey published a **four-quadrant approach** to determining which expressions on the ladder are more appropriate for a given situation. This approach is based on the shape of the scatter plot of x and y. Figure 14.4 shows the four quadrants and the associated recoding expressions. For example, if the scatter plot of x and y indicates a shape like that shown in the upper left quadrant, recoding should move "down the ladder" for the x variable toward:

$$\log x, -\frac{1}{\sqrt{x}}, -\frac{1}{x}, -\frac{1}{x^2}, -\frac{1}{x^3}, -\frac{1}{x^4}, \ldots$$

or "up the ladder" for the y variable toward:

$$y^2, y^3, y^4, \ldots$$

Or, if the scatter plot of x and y indicates a shape like that of the lower right quadrant, the recoding should move "up the ladder" for the x variable toward:

$$x^2, x^3, x^4, \ldots$$

[*]John W. Tukey, *Exploratory Data Analysis* (Reading, MA: Addison-Wesley, 1977).

Figure 14.4

Tukey's Four-Quadrant Approach

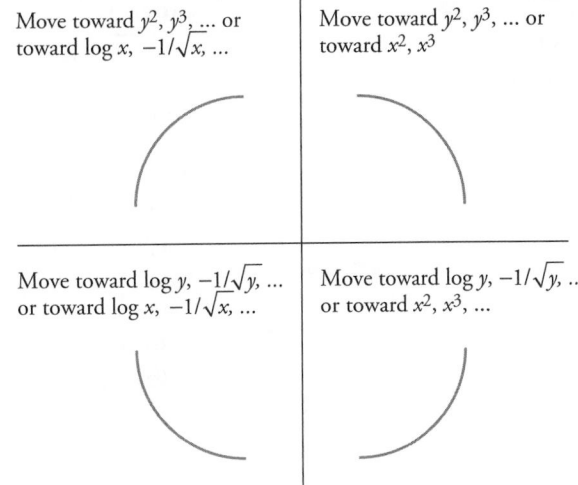

or "down the ladder" for the y variable toward:

$$\log y, -\frac{1}{\sqrt{y}}, -\frac{1}{y}, -\frac{1}{y^2}, -\frac{1}{y^3}, -\frac{1}{y^4}, \ldots$$

In the manufacturing example, the graph in Figure 14.2(a) is shaped like the curve in the lower right quadrant of Tukey's four-quadrant approach. His approach suggests that the business researcher move "up the ladder" on x as was done by using the squared term. The researcher could have explored other options such as continuing on up the ladder of x or going down the ladder of y. Tukey's ladder is a continuum and leaves open other recoding possibilities between the expressions. For example, between x^2 and x^3 are many possible powers of x that can be explored, such as $x^{2.1}$, $x^{2.5}$, or $x^{2.86}$.

REGRESSION MODELS WITH INTERACTION

Often when two different independent variables are used in a regression analysis, an *interaction* occurs between the two variables. This interaction was discussed in Chapter 11 in two-way analysis of variance (ANOVA), where one variable will act differently over a given range of values for the second variable than it does over another range of values for the second variable. For example, in a manufacturing plant, temperature and humidity might interact in such a way as to have an effect on the hardness of the raw material. The humidity of the air may affect the raw material differently at different temperatures.

In regression analysis, interaction can be examined as a separate independent variable. An interaction predictor variable can be designed by multiplying the data values of one variable by the values of another variable, thereby creating a new variable. A model that includes an interaction variable is:

$$y = \beta_0 + \beta_1 x_1 + \beta_2 x_2 + \beta_3 x_1 x_2 + \varepsilon$$

The interaction term β_3 can now be tested with the null hypothesis:

$$\beta_3 = 0 \ (\text{no interaction between } x_1 \text{ and } x_2)$$

and the alternative hypothesis:

$$\beta_3 \neq 0 \ (x_1 \text{ and } x_2 \text{ interact})$$

	Stock 1	Stock 2	Stock 3
Table 14.3	41	36	35
	39	36	35
Share Prices of Three Stocks over a 15-Month Period	38	38	32
	45	51	41
	41	52	39
	43	55	55
	47	57	52
	49	58	54
	41	62	65
	35	70	77
	36	72	75
	39	74	74
	33	83	81
	28	101	92
	31	107	91

The x_1x_2 term is the interaction term. Even though this model has 1 as the highest power of any one variable, it is considered to be a second-order equation because of the x_1x_2 term.

Suppose the data in Table 14.3 represent the closing share prices for three corporations over a period of 15 months. An investment firm wants to use the prices for stocks 2 and 3 to develop a regression model to predict the price of stock 1. The form of the general linear regression equation for this model is:

$$y = \beta_0 + \beta_1 x_1 + \beta_2 x_2 + \varepsilon$$

where

y = price of stock 1
x_1 = price of stock 2
x_2 = price of stock 3

Using Excel to develop this regression model, the firm's researcher obtains the first output displayed in Figure 14.5. This regression model is a first-order model with two predictors, x_1 and x_2. This model produced a modest R^2 of 0.472. Both of the t ratios are small and statistically nonsignificant ($t = -0.62$ with a p value of 0.549 and $t = -0.36$ with a p value of 0.728). Although the overall model is statistically significant, $F = 5.37$ with probability of 0.022, neither predictor is significant.

Sometimes the effects of two variables are not additive because of the interacting effects between the two variables. In such a case, the researcher can use multiple regression analysis to explore the interaction effects by including an interaction term in the equation:

$$y = \beta_0 + \beta_1 x_1 + \beta_2 x_2 + \beta_3 x_1 x_2 + \varepsilon$$

The equation fits the form of the general linear model:

$$y = \beta_0 + \beta_1 x_1 + \beta_2 x_2 + \beta_3 x_3 + \varepsilon$$

where $x_3 = x_1 x_2$. Each individual observation of x_3 is obtained through a recoding process by multiplying the associated observations of x_1 and x_2.

Figure 14.5

Two Excel Regression Outputs—Without and with Interaction

	A	B	C	D	E	F
1	SUMMARY OUTPUT					
2	Regression Statistics					
3	Multiple R	0.687213				
4	R Square	0.472262				
5	Adjusted R Square	0.384306				
6	Standard Error	4.570196				
7	Observations	15				
8						
9	ANOVA					
10		df	SS	MS	F	Significance F
11	Regression	2	224.2931	112.1465	5.369282	0.021603
12	Residual	12	250.6403	20.88669		
13	Total	14	474.9333			
14						
15		Coefficients	Standard Error	t Stat	p Value	
16	Intercept	50.85548	3.790993	13.41482	1.38E–08	
17	x_1	–0.119	0.193082	–0.61632	0.549199	
18	x_2	–0.07076	0.198985	–0.35561	0.728302	
19						
20						
21						
22	SUMMARY OUTPUT					
23	Regression Statistics					
24	Multiple R	0.896661				
25	R Square	0.804001				
26	Adjusted R Square	0.750546				
27	Standard Error	2.909024				
28	Observations	15				
29						
30	ANOVA					
31		df	SS	MS	F	Significance F
32	Regression	3	381.8467	127.2822	15.04088	0.00033
33	Residual	11	93.08662	8.46242		
34	Total	14	474.9333			
35						
36		Coefficients	Standard Error	t Stat	p Value	
37	Intercept	12.04618	9.3124	1.293563	0.22232	
38	x_1	0.878778	0.261873	3.355738	0.006412	
39	x_2	0.220493	0.143522	1.5363	0.152715	
40	Interaction	–0.00998	0.002314	–4.31486	0.001225	

Applying this procedure to the stock example, the researcher uses the interaction term to obtain the second regression output shown in Figure 14.5. This output contains x_1; x_2; and the interaction term, $x_1 x_2$. Observe the R^2, which equals 0.804 for this model. The introduction of the interaction term caused the R^2 to increase from 47.2% to 80.4%. In addition, the standard error of the estimate decreased from 4.570 in the first model to 2.909 in the second model. The t ratios for both the x_1 term and the interaction term are statistically significant in the second model ($t = 3.36$ with a p value of 0.006 for x_1 and $t = -4.31$ with a probability of 0.001 for $x_1 x_2$). The inclusion of the interaction term helped the regression model account for a substantially greater amount of the dependent variable and is a significant contributor to the model.

Figure 14.6(a) is the response surface for the first regression model presented in Figure 14.5 (the model without interaction). As you observe the response plane with stock 3 as the point of reference, you see the plane moving upward with increasing values of stock 1 as the plane moves away from you toward smaller values of stock 2. Now examine Figure 14.6(b), the response surface for the second regression model presented in Figure 14.5 (the model with interaction). Note how the response plane is twisted, with

Figure 14.6

Response Surfaces for the Stock Example–Without and with Interaction

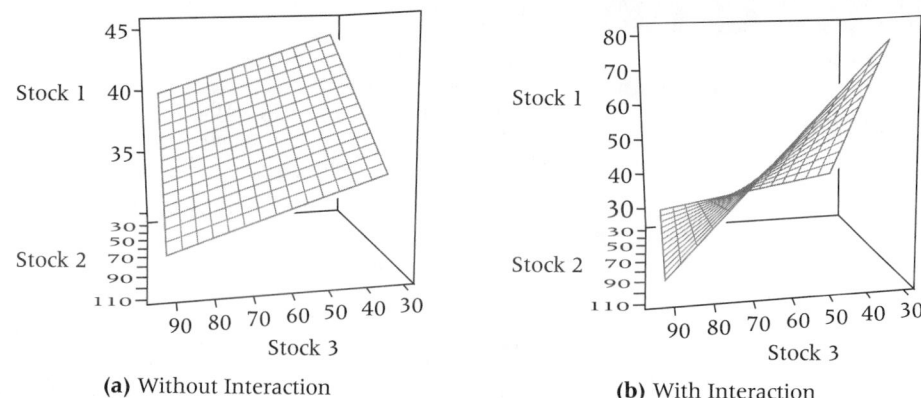

(a) Without Interaction

(b) With Interaction

its slope changing as it moves along stock 2. This pattern is caused by the interaction effects of stock 2 prices and stock 3 prices. A cross-section of the plane taken from left to right at any given stock 2 price produces a line that attempts to predict the price of stock 3 from the price of stock 1. As you move back through different prices of stock 2, the slope of that line changes, indicating that the relationship between stock 1 and stock 3 varies according to stock 2.

A researcher could also develop a model using two independent variables with their squares and interaction. Such a model would be a second-order model with two independent variables. The model would look like this:

$$y = \beta_0 + \beta_1 x_1 + \beta_2 x_2 + \beta_3 x_1^2 + \beta_4 x_2^2 + \beta_5 x_1 x_2 + \varepsilon$$

MODEL TRANSFORMATION

To this point in examining polynomial and interaction models, the focus has been on recoding values of x variables. Some multiple regression situations require that the dependent variable, y, be recoded. To examine different relationships between x and y, Tukey's four-quadrant analysis and ladder of transformations can be used to explore ways to recode x or y in attempting to construct regression models with more predictability. Included on the ladder are such y transformations as $\log y$ and $1/y$.

Suppose the following data represent the annual sales and annual advertising expenditures for seven companies. Can a regression model be developed from these figures that can be used to predict annual sales by annual advertising expenditures?

Company	Sales ($ millions/year)	Advertising ($ millions/year)
1	2,580	1.2
2	11,942	2.6
3	9,845	2.2
4	27,800	3.2
5	18,926	2.9
6	4,800	1.5
7	14,550	2.7

One mathematical model that is a good candidate for fitting these data is an exponential model of the form:

$$y = \beta_0 \beta_1^x \varepsilon$$

This model can be transformed (by taking the log of each side) so that it is in the form of the general linear equation:

$$\log y = \log \beta_0 + x \log \beta_1$$

This transformed model requires a recoding of the y data through the use of logarithms. Notice that x is not recoded but that the regression constant and coefficient are in logarithmic scale. If we let $y' = \log y$, $\beta_0' = \log \beta_0$, and $\beta_1' = \log \beta_1$, the exponential model is in the form of the general linear model:

$$y' = \beta_0' + \beta_1' x$$

The process begins by taking the log of the y values. The data used to build the regression model and the Excel regression output for these data follow.

Log Sales (y)	Advertising (x)
3.4116	1.2
4.0771	2.6
3.9932	2.2
4.4440	3.2
4.2771	2.9
3.6812	1.5
4.1629	2.7

	A	B	C	D	E	F
1	SUMMARY OUTPUT					
2	Regression Statistics					
3	Multiple R	0.990				
4	R Square	0.980				
5	Adjusted R Square	0.977				
6	Standard Error	0.0543				
7	Observations	7				
8						
9	ANOVA					
10		df	SS	MS	F	Significance F
11	Regression	1	0.739215	0.739215	250.36	0.000018
12	Residual	5	0.014763	0.002953		
13	Total	6	0.753979			
14						
15		Coefficients	Standard Error	t Stat	p Value	
16	Intercept	2.9003	0.0729	39.80	0.00000019	
17	Advertising (x)	0.4751	0.0300	15.82	0.00001834	

A simple regression model (without the log recoding of the y variable) yields an R_2 of 87%, whereas the exponential model R^2 is 98%. The t statistic for advertising is 15.82 with a p value of 0.00001834 in the exponential model and 5.77 with a p value of 0.00219 in the simple regression model. Thus, the exponential model gives a better fit than does the simple regression model. An examination of (x^2, y) and (x^3, y) models reveals R^2 of 0.930 and 0.969, respectively, which are quite high but still not as good as the R^2 yielded by the exponential model. The resulting equation of the exponential regression model is:

$$y = 2.9003 + 0.4751x$$

In using this regression equation to determine predicted values of y for x, remember that the resulting predicted y value is in logarithmic form, and the antilog of the predicted y must be taken to get the predicted y value in raw units. For example, to get the predicted y value (sales) for an advertising figure of 2.0 ($ millions), substitute $x = 2.0$ into the regression equation:

$$y = 2.9003 + 0.4751x = 2.9003 + 0.4751(2.0) = 3.8505$$

The log of sales is 3.8505. Taking the antilog of 3.8505 results in the predicted sales in raw units:

$$\text{antilog } (3.8505) = 7{,}087.61(\$ \text{ millions})$$

Thus, the exponential regression model predicts that $2.0 million of advertising will result in $7,087.61 million of sales.

Other ways can be used to transform mathematical models so that they can be treated like the general linear model. One example is an inverse model such as:

$$y = \frac{1}{\beta_0 + \beta_1 x_1 + \beta_2 x_2 + \varepsilon}$$

Such a model can be manipulated algebraically into the form:

$$\frac{1}{y} = \beta_0 + \beta_1 x_1 + \beta_2 x_2 + \varepsilon$$

Substituting $y' = 1/y$ into this equation results in an equation that is in the form of the general linear model:

$$y' = \beta_0 + \beta_1 x_1 + \beta_2 x_2 + \varepsilon$$

To use this "inverse" model, recode the data values for y by using $1/y$. The regression analysis is done on the $1/y$, x_1, and x_2 data. To get predicted values of y from this model, enter the raw values of x_1 and x_2. The resulting predicted value of y from the regression equation will be the inverse of the actual predicted y value.

Demonstration Problem 14.1

In the aerospace and defence industry, some cost estimators predict the cost of new space projects by using mathematical models that take the form:

$$y = \beta_0 x^{\beta_1} \varepsilon$$

These cost estimators often use the weight of the object being sent into space as the predictor (x) and the cost of the object as the dependent variable (y). Quite often β_1 turns out to be a value between 0 and 1, resulting in the predicted value of y equalling some root of x.

Using the sample cost data given here, develop a cost regression model in the form just shown to determine the equation for the predicted value of y. Use this regression equation to predict the value of y for $x = 3{,}000$.

y ($ billions)	x (mass in tonnes)
1.2	450
9.0	20,200
4.5	9,060
3.2	3,500
13.0	75,600
0.6	175
1.8	800
2.7	2,100

Solution

The equation:

$$y = \beta_0 x^{\beta_1} \varepsilon$$

is not in the form of the general linear model, but it can be transformed by using logarithms:

$$\log y = \log \beta_0 + \beta_1 \log x + \log \varepsilon$$

which takes on the general linear form:

$$y' = \beta_0' + \beta_1 x'$$

where

$y' = \log y$
$\beta_0' = \log \beta_0 + \log \varepsilon$
$x' = \log x$

This equation requires that both x and y be recoded by taking the logarithm of each.

log y	log x
0.0792	2.6532
0.9542	4.3054
0.6532	3.9571
0.5051	3.5441
1.1139	4.8785
−0.2218	2.2430
0.2553	2.9031
0.4314	3.3222

Using these data, the computer produces the following regression constant and coefficient:

$$b_0' = -1.25292 \quad b_1 = 0.49606$$

From these values, the equation of the predicted y value is determined to be:

$$\log \hat{y} = -1.25292 + 0.49606 \log x$$

If $x = 3{,}000$, $\log x = 3.47712$, and

$$\log \hat{y} = -1.25292 + 0.49606(3.47712) = 0.47194$$

then

$$\hat{y} = \text{antilog}(\log \hat{y}) = \text{antilog}(0.47194) = 2.9644$$

The predicted value of y is $2.9644 billion for $x = 3{,}000$ tonnes. Taking the antilog of $b_0' = -1.25292$ yields 0.055857. From this and $b_1 = 0.49606$, the model can be written in the original form:

$$y = (0.055857)x^{0.49606}$$

Substituting $x = 3{,}000$ into this formula also yields $2.9645 billion for the predicted value of y.

POINTS OF INTEREST
Not all business data are linear in nature. When you encounter nonlinear data, you can either use a nonlinear regression procedure or transform the relevant variables to make them suitable for linear regression. In general, it is simpler to work with transformed variables than with nonlinear regression. Many statistical programs provide procedures for transforming nonlinear data.

1. What are first-order models and how are they different from second-order models?
2. What is a quadratic model?
3. In what context would you use the ladder of transformation?
4. What is Tukey's four-quadrant approach? When is it useful?

14.1   Use the following data to develop a quadratic model to predict y from x. Develop a simple regression model from the data and compare the results of the two models. Does the quadratic model seem to provide any better predictability? Why or why not?

x	y	x	y
14	200	15	247
9	74	8	82
6	29	5	21
21	456	10	94
17	320		

14.2   Develop a multiple regression model of the form:

$$y = b_0 b_1^x \varepsilon$$

using the following data to predict y from x. From a scatter plot and Tukey's ladder of transformation, explore ways to recode the data and develop an alternative regression model. Compare the results.

y	x	y	x
2,485	3.87	740	2.83
1,790	3.22	4,010	3.62
874	2.91	3,629	3.52
2,190	3.42	8,010	3.92
3,610	3.55	7,047	3.86
2,847	3.61	5,680	3.75
1,350	3.13	1,740	3.19

14.3   The Publishers Information Bureau in New York City released magazine advertising expenditure data compiled by leading national advertisers. The data were organized by product type over several years. Shown here are data on total magazine advertising expenditures and household equipment and supplies advertising expenditures. Using these data, develop a regression model to predict total magazine advertising expenditures by household equipment and supplies advertising expenditures and by (household equipment and supplies advertising expenditures)^2. Compare this model to a regression model to predict total magazine advertising expenditures by only household equipment and supplies advertising expenditures. Construct a scatter plot of the data. Does the shape of the plot suggest some alternative models in light of Tukey's four-quadrant approach? If so, develop at least one other model and compare the model to the other two previously developed.

Total Magazine Advertising Expenditures ($ millions)	Household Equipment and Supplies Expenditures ($ millions)
1,193	34
2,846	65
4,668	98
5,120	93
5,943	102
6,644	103

14.4   Dun & Bradstreet reports, among other things, information about new business incorporations and number of business failures over the years. Shown here are data on business failures and current liabilities of the failing companies over several years. Use these data and the following model to predict current liabilities of the failing companies by the number of business failures:

$$y = b_0 b_1^x \varepsilon$$

Discuss the strength of the model. Now develop a different regression model by recoding x. Use Tukey's four-quadrant approach as a resource. Compare your models.

Rate of Business Failures Since 1970 (10,000)	Current Liabilities of Failing Companies ($ millions)
44	1,888
43	4,380
42	4,635
61	6,955
88	15,611
110	16,073
107	29,269
115	36,937
120	44,724
102	34,724
98	39,126
65	44,261

14.5   Use the following data to develop a curvilinear model to predict y. Include both x_1 and x_2 in the model in addition to x_1^2 and x_2^2 and the interaction term $x_1 x_2$. Comment on the overall strength of the model and the significance of each predictor. Develop a regression model with the same independent variables as the first model but without the interaction variable. Compare this model to the model with interaction.

y	x_1	x_2
47.8	6	7.1
29.1	1	4.2
81.8	11	10.0
54.3	5	8.0
29.7	3	5.7
64.0	9	8.8
37.4	3	7.1

(continued)

y	x_1	x_2
44.5	4	5.4
42.1	4	6.5
31.6	2	4.9
78.4	11	9.1
71.9	9	8.5
17.4	2	4.2
28.8	1	5.8
34.7	2	5.9
57.6	6	7.8
84.2	12	10.2
63.2	8	9.4
39.0	3	5.7
47.3	5	7.0

14.6   What follows is Excel output from a regression model to predict y using x_1, x_2, x_1^2, x_2^2, and the interaction term, $x_1 x_2$. Comment on the overall strength of the model and the significance of each predictor. The data follow the Excel output. Develop a regression model with the same independent variables as the first model but without the interaction variable. Compare this model to the model with interaction.

	A	B	C	D	E	F
1	SUMMARY OUTPUT					
2	Regression Statistics					
3	Multiple R	0.954				
4	R Square	0.910				
5	Adjusted R Square	0.878				
6	Standard Error	7.544				
7	Observations	20				
8						
9	ANOVA					
10		df	SS	MS	F	Significance F
11	Regression	5	8089.275	1617.855	28.43	0.00000073
12	Residual	14	796.725	56.909		
13	Total	19	8886			
14						
15		Coefficients	Standard Error	t Stat	p Value	
16	Intercept	464.4433	503.0955	0.92	0.3716	
17	x_1	−10.5101	6.0074	−1.75	0.1021	
18	x_2	−1.2212	1.9791	−0.62	0.5471	
19	x_1^2	0.0357	0.0195	1.84	0.0876	
20	x_2^2	−0.0002	0.0021	−0.08	0.9394	
21	$x_1 x_2$	0.0243	0.0107	2.28	0.0390	

y	x_1	x_2	y	x_1	x_2
34	120	190	45	96	245
56	105	240	34	79	288
78	108	238	23	66	312
90	110	250	89	88	315
23	78	255	76	80	320
34	98	230	56	73	335
45	89	266	43	69	335
67	92	270	23	75	250
78	95	272	45	63	372
65	85	288	56	74	360

14.2 INDICATOR (DUMMY) VARIABLES

Some variables are referred to as **qualitative variables** (as opposed to *quantitative* variables) because qualitative variables do not yield quantifiable outcomes. Instead, *qualitative variables yield nominal- or ordinal-level information,* which is used more to categorize items. These variables have a role in multiple regression and are referred to as indicator, or dummy, variables. In this section, we will examine the role of **indicator** or **dummy variables** as predictors or independent variables in multiple regression analysis.

Indicator variables arise in many ways in business research. Mail questionnaire or personal interview demographic questions are prime candidates because they tend to generate qualitative measures on such items as gender, geographic region, occupation, marital status, level of education, economic class, political affiliation, religion, management/nonmanagement status, buying/leasing a home, method of transportation, or type of broker. In one business study, business researchers were attempting to develop a multiple regression model to predict the distances shoppers drive to malls in the greater Toronto area. One independent variable was whether the mall was located near the 401 highway. In a second study, a site location model for pizza restaurants included indicator variables for (1) whether the restaurant served beer and (2) whether the restaurant had a salad bar.

These indicator variables are qualitative in that no interval or ratio level measurement is assigned to a response. For example, if a mall is located near the 401 a score of 20 or 30 or 75 because of its location makes no sense. In terms of gender, what value would you assign to a man or a woman in a regression study? Yet these types of indicator, or dummy, variables are often useful in multiple regression studies and can be included if they are coded in the proper format.

Most researchers code indicator variables by using 0 or 1. For example, in the shopping mall study, malls located near the 401 could be assigned a 1, and all other malls would then be assigned a 0. The assignment of 0 or 1 is arbitrary, with the number merely holding a place for the category. For this reason, the coding is referred to as "dummy" coding; the number represents a category by holding a place and is not a measurement.

Many indicator, or dummy, variables are dichotomous, such as male/female, salad bar/no salad bar, employed/not employed, and lease/own. For these variables, a value of 1 is arbitrarily assigned to one category and a value of 0 is assigned to the other category. Some qualitative variables contain several categories, such as the variable type of job, which might have the categories assembler, painter, and inspector. In this case, it is tempting to use a coding of 1, 2, and 3, respectively. However, that type of coding creates problems for multiple regression analysis. For one thing, the category inspector would receive a value that is three times that of painter. In addition, the values of 1, 2, and 3 indicate a hierarchy of job types: assembler < painter < inspector. The proper way to code such indicator variables is with the 0, 1 coding. Two separate independent variables should be used to code the three categories of type of job. The first variable is assembler, where a 1 is recorded if the person's job is assembler and a 0 is recorded if it is not. The second variable is painter, where a 1 is recorded if the person's job is painter and a 0 is recorded if it is not. A variable should not be assigned to inspector, because all workers in the study for whom a 1 was not recorded either for the assembler variable or the painter variable must be inspectors. Thus, coding the inspector variable would result in redundant information and is not necessary. This reasoning holds for all indicator variables with more than two categories. If an indicator variable has c categories, then $c - 1$ dummy variables must be created and inserted into the regression analysis in order to include the indicator variable in the multiple regression.[*]

---

[*]If c indicator variables are included in the analysis, no unique estimator of the regression coefficients can be found. [J. Neter, M. H. Kuter, W. Wasserman, and C. Nachtsheim. *Applied Linear Regression Models*, 3rd ed. (Chicago: Richard D. Irwin, 1996).]

Table 14.4

Coding for the Indicator Variable of Geographic Location for Regression Analysis

Atlantic x_1	Quebec x_2	Ontario x_3
1	0	0
0	0	0
1	0	0
0	0	1
0	1	0
0	1	0
0	0	0
0	0	1
1	0	0
1	0	0
0	0	0
0	1	0
0	0	1

An example of an indicator variable with more than two categories is the result of the following question taken from a typical questionnaire.

Your office is located in which region of the country?

_____ Atlantic _____ Quebec _____ Ontario _____ West

Suppose a researcher is using a multiple regression analysis to predict the cost of doing business and believes geographic location of the office is a potential predictor. How does the researcher insert this qualitative variable into the analysis? Because $c = 4$ for this question, three dummy variables are inserted into the analysis. Table 14.4 shows one possible way this process works with 13 respondents. Note that rows 2, 7, and 11 contain all zeros, which indicate that those respondents have offices in the West. Thus, a fourth dummy variable for the West region is not necessary and, indeed, should not be included because the information contained in such a fourth variable is contained in the other three variables.

A word of caution is in order. Because of degrees of freedom and interpretation considerations, it is important that a multiple regression analysis have enough observations to adequately handle the number of independent variables entered. Some researchers recommend as a guideline at least three observations per independent variable. If a qualitative variable has multiple categories, resulting in several dummy independent variables, and if several qualitative variables are being included in an analysis, the number of predictors can rather quickly exceed the limit of recommended number of variables per number of observations. Nevertheless, dummy variables can be useful and are a way in which nominal or ordinal information can be recoded and incorporated into a multiple regression model.

As an example, consider the issue of sex discrimination in the salary earnings of workers in some industries. In examining this issue, suppose a random sample of 15 workers is drawn from a pool of employed labourers in a particular industry and the workers' average monthly salaries are determined, along with their age and gender. The data are shown in Table 14.5. As gender can be only male or female, this variable is a dummy variable requiring 0, 1 coding. Suppose we arbitrarily let 1 denote male and 0 denote female. Figure 14.7 is the multiple regression model developed from the data of Table 14.5 to predict the dependent variable, monthly salary, by two independent variables, age and gender.

Table 14.5

Data for the Monthly Salary Example

Monthly Salary ($1,000s)	Age (10 years)	Gender (1 = male, 0 = female)
1.548	3.2	1
1.629	3.8	1
1.011	2.7	0
1.229	3.4	0
1.746	3.6	1
1.528	4.1	1
1.018	3.8	0
1.190	3.4	0
1.551	3.3	1
0.985	3.2	0
1.610	3.5	1
1.432	2.9	1
1.215	3.3	0
0.990	2.8	0
1.585	3.5	1

Figure 14.7

Regression Analysis for the Monthly Salary Example

	A	B	C	D	E	F
1	SUMMARY OUTPUT					
2	Regression Statistics					
3	Multiple R	0.943391				
4	R Square	0.889987				
5	Adjusted R Square	0.871652				
6	Standard Error	0.096792				
7	Observations	15				
8						
9	ANOVA					
10			df	SS	MS	F	Significance F
11	Regression	2	0.909488	0.454744	48.53914	1.77E–06
12	Residual	12	0.112423	0.009369		
13	Total	14	1.021912			
14						
15		Coefficients	Standard Error	t Stat	p Value	
16	Intercept	0.732061	0.235584	3.107425	0.009064	
17	Age (10 years)	0.11122	0.072083	1.542937	0.148796	
18	Gender (1= male, 0 = female)	0.458684	0.053458	8.58019	1.82E–06	

The Excel computer output in Figure 14.7 contains the regression equation (under Coefficients) for this model:

$$\text{Salary} = 0.732 + 0.111(\text{age}) + 0.459(\text{gender})$$

An examination of the t ratios reveals that the dummy variable gender has a regression coefficient that is significant at $\alpha = 0.001$ ($t = 8.58, p = 0.000$). The overall model is significant at $\alpha = 0.001$ ($F = 48.54, p = 0.000$). The standard error of the estimate, $s_e = 0.09679$, indicates that approximately 68% of the errors of prediction are within ±$96.79 (0.09679 × $1,000). The R^2 is relatively high at 89.0%, and the adjusted R^2 is 87.2%.

The t value for gender indicates that it is a significant predictor of monthly salary in this model. This significance is apparent when one looks at the effects of this dummy variable in another way. Figure 14.8 shows the graph of the regression equation when

Figure 14.8

Regression Model for Male and Female Gender

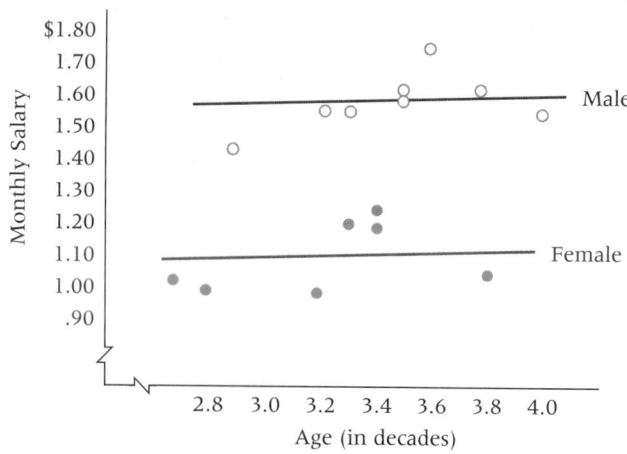

gender = 1 (male) and the graph of the regression equation when gender = 0 (female). When gender = 1 (male), the regression equation becomes:

$$0.732 + 0.111(\text{age}) + 0.459(1) = 1.191 + 0.111(\text{age})$$

When gender = 0 (female), the regression equation becomes:

$$0.732 + 0.111(\text{Age}) + 0.459(0) = 0.732 + 0.111(\text{Age})$$

The full regression model (with both predictors) has a response surface that is a plane in a three-dimensional space. However, if a value of 1 is entered for gender into the full regression model, as just shown, the regression model is reduced to a line passing through the plane formed by monthly salary and age. If a value of 0 is entered for gender, as shown, the full regression model also reduces to a line passing through the plane formed by monthly salary and age. Figure 14.8 displays these two lines. Notice that the only difference in the two lines is the y intercept. Observe the monthly salary with male gender, as depicted by ○, versus the monthly salary with female gender, depicted by ●. The difference in the y intercepts of these two lines is 0.459, which is the value of the regression coefficient for gender. This intercept figure signifies that, on average, men earn $459 per month more than women for this population.

POINTS OF INTEREST
Dummy variables are not automatically recognized by computer programs. They need to be specified. If you forget to specify a dummy variable the way it should be, the variable will be treated as a metric variable, resulting in erroneous analysis.

STATISTICS IN BUSINESS TODAY

Predicting Export Intensity of Chinese Manufacturing Firms Using Multiple Regression Analysis

According to business researchers Hongxin Zhao and Shaoming Zou, little research has been done on the impact of external or uncontrollable variables on the export performance of a company. These two researchers conducted a study of Chinese manufacturing firms and used multiple regression to determine whether both domestic market concentration and firm location are good predictors of a firm's export intensity. The study included 999 Chinese manufacturing firms that exported. The dependent variable was export intensity, defined to be the proportion of production output that is exported and computed by dividing the firm's export value by its production output value. The higher the proportion, the higher was the export intensity.

Zhao and Zou used covariate techniques (beyond the scope of this text) to control for the fact that companies in the study varied by size, capital intensity, innovativeness, and industry. The independent variables were industry concentration and location. Industry concentration was computed as a ratio, with higher values indicating more concentration in the industry. The location variable was a composite index taking into account total freight volume, available modes of transportation, number of telephones, and size of geographic area.

The multiple regression model produced an R^2 of approximately 52%. Industry concentration was a statistically significant predictor at $\alpha = 0.01$, and the sign on the regression coefficient indicated that a negative relationship may exist between industry concentration and export intensity. This means that export intensity is lower in highly concentrated industries and higher in lower concentrated industries. The researchers believe that in a more highly concentrated industry, the handful of firms dominating the industry will stifle the export competitiveness of firms. In the absence of dominating firms in a more fragmented setting, more competition and an increasing tendency to export are noted. The location variable was also a significant predictor at $\alpha = 0.01$. Firms located in coastal areas had higher export intensities than did those located in inland areas.

Source: Hongxin Zhao and Shaoming Zou, "The Impact of Industry Concentration and Firm Location on Export Propensity and Intensity: An Empirical Analysis of Chinese Manufacturing Firms," *Journal of International Marketing*, vol. 10, no. 1 (2002), pp. 52–71.

Concept Check

1. What is an indicator or a dummy variable? Give three examples.
2. How would you code a dummy variable with three categories?

14.2 Problems

14.7　Analyze the following data by using a multiple regression computer software package to predict y using x_1 and x_2. Notice that x_2 is a dummy variable. Discuss the output from the regression analysis; in particular, comment on the predictability of the dummy variable.

y	x_1	x_2
16.8	27	1
13.2	16	0
14.7	13	0
15.4	11	1
11.1	17	0
16.2	19	1
14.9	24	1
13.3	21	0
17.8	16	1
17.1	23	1
14.3	18	0
13.9	16	0

14.8　Given here are the data from a dependent variable and two independent variables. The second independent variable is an indicator variable with several categories.

Hence, this variable is represented by x_2, x_3, and x_4. How many categories are needed in total for this independent variable? Use a computer to perform a multiple regression analysis on this data to predict y from the x values. Discuss the output and pay particular attention to the dummy variables.

y	x_1	x_2	x_3	x_4
11	1.9	1	0	0
3	1.6	0	1	0
2	2.3	0	1	0
5	2.0	0	0	1
9	1.8	0	0	0
14	1.9	1	0	0
10	2.4	1	0	0
8	2.6	0	0	0
4	2.0	0	1	0
9	1.4	0	0	0
11	1.7	1	0	0
4	2.5	0	0	1
6	1.0	1	0	0
10	1.4	0	0	0
3	1.9	0	1	0
4	2.3	0	1	0
9	2.2	0	0	0
6	1.7	0	0	1

14.9 The output displayed here is the result of a multiple regression analysis with three independent variables. Variable x_1 is a dummy variable. Discuss the computer output and the role x_1 plays in this regression model.

```
The regression equation is
Y = 121 + 13.4 X₁ -0.632 X₂ + 1.42 X₃
Predictor        Coef      Stdev        T            p
Constant        121.31     11.56      10.50       .000
X₁               13.355     4.714       2.83       .014
X₂               -0.6322    0.2270     -2.79       .015
X₃                1.421     3.342       0.43       .678
S = 7.041    R-sq =79.5%          R-sq(adj) = 74.7%

Analysis of Variance
Source           df         SS         MS          F        p
Regression        3      2491.98     830.66      16.76     .000
Error            13       644.49      49.58
Total            16      3136.47
```

14.10 Given here is Excel output for a multiple regression model that was developed to predict y from two independent variables, x_1 and x_2. Variable x_2 is a dummy variable. Discuss the strength of the multiple regression model on the basis of the output. Focus on the contribution of the dummy variable. Plot x_1 and y with x_2 as 0, and then plot x_1 and y with x_2 as 1. Compare the two lines and discuss the differences.

	A	B	C	D	E	F
1	SUMMARY OUTPUT					
2	Regression Statistics					
3	Multiple R	0.623				
4	R Square	0.388				
5	Adjusted R Square	0.341				
6	Standard Error	11.744				
7	Observations	29				
8						
9	ANOVA					
10		df	SS	MS	F	Significance F
11	Regression	2	2270.11	1135.05	8.23	0.0017
12	Residual	26	3585.75	137.91		
13	Total	28	5855.86			
14						
15		Coefficients	Standard Error	t Stat	p Value	
16	Intercept	41.225	6.380	6.46	0.00000076	
17	x_1	1.081	1.353	0.80	0.4316	
18	x_2	−18.404	4.547	−4.05	0.0004	

14.11 A researcher developed a multiple regression model to predict the average price of a meal at a restaurant in a western city. After exploring several variables that might affect the average price, the researcher decides the three most important variables that decide the price of a meal are (1) how long the restaurant is open (i.e., how many hours in a week), (2) how likely you are to be seated when you get to the restaurant, and (3) whether the restaurant is downtown or not. Use the following data and a computer to develop such a model. Comment on the output.

Price	Hours	Probability of Being Seated	Downtown*
$5.55	72	0.37	0
7.76	55	0.64	0
12.26	48	0.51	1
15.00	60	0.32	1
9.15	52	0.62	0
6.48	62	0.83	0
8.49	65	0.62	0
20.95	48	0.43	1
15.90	50	0.58	1
6.23	68	0.74	0
11.99	55	0.19	1
24.86	56	0.49	1
14.00	62	0.80	0
19.05	70	0.75	1

*0 = not located in downtown; 1 = located in downtown

14.12 A researcher gathered 155 observations on four variables: job satisfaction, occupation, industry, and marital status. She wants to develop a multiple regression model to predict job satisfaction by the other three variables. All three predictor variables are qualitative variables with the following categories.

1. Occupation: accounting, management, marketing, finance (3)
2. Industry: manufacturing, health care, transportation (2)
3. Marital status: married, single (1)

How many variables will be in the regression model? Delineate the number of predictors needed in each category and discuss the total number of predictors.

14.3 MODEL-BUILDING: SEARCH PROCEDURES

To this point in the chapter, we have explored various types of multiple regression models. We evaluated the strengths of regression models and learned more about the output from multiple regression computer packages. In this section, we examine procedures for developing several multiple regression model options to aid in the decision-making process.

Suppose a researcher wants to develop a multiple regression model to predict the world production of crude oil. The researcher realizes that much of the world crude oil market is driven by variables related to usage and production in the U.S. The researcher decides to use as predictors the following five independent variables:

1. U.S. energy consumption
2. Gross U.S. nuclear electricity generation
3. U.S. coal production
4. Total U.S. dry gas (natural gas) production
5. Fuel rate of U.S.-owned automobiles

The researcher measured data for each of these variables for the year preceding each data point of world crude oil production, figuring that the world production is driven by the previous year's activities in the U.S. It would seem that as the energy consumption of the U.S. increased, so would world production of crude oil. In addition, it makes sense that as nuclear electricity generation, coal production, dry gas production, and fuel rates increased, world crude oil production would decrease if energy consumption stayed approximately constant. Table 14.6 shows data for the five independent variables along with the dependent variable, world crude oil production. Using the data presented in Table 14.6, the researcher attempted to develop a multiple regression model using five different independent variables. The result of this process was the output in Figure 14.9. Examining the output, the researcher can reach some conclusions about that particular model and its variables.

Figure 14.9

Excel Output of Regression for Crude Oil Production Example

	A	B	C	D	E	F
1	SUMMARY OUTPUT					
2	Regression Statistics					
3	Multiple R	0.959674				
4	R Square	0.920975				
5	Adjusted R Square	0.901218				
6	Standard Error	1.214705				
7	Observations	26				
8						
9	ANOVA					
10		df	SS	MS	F	Significance F
11	Regression	5	343.9264	68.78328	46.61668	2.41E–10
12	Residual	20	29.51015	1.475508		
13	Total	25	373.4265			
14						
15		Coefficients	Standard Error	t Stat	p Value	
16	Intercept	2.708474	8.90876	0.304024	0.76425	
17	EnCons	0.83567	0.180234	4.636595	0.000159	
18	NclrElec	−0.00654	0.009854	−0.66412	0.514197	
19	CoalProd	0.009815	0.007286	1.348422	0.192596	
20	DryGas	−0.14321	0.448408	−0.31938	0.752753	
21	FuelRate	−0.73414	0.548823	−1.33767	0.196018	

Table 14.6

Data for Multiple Regression Model to Predict Crude Oil Production

World Crude Oil Production (million barrels per day)	U.S. Energy Consumption (quadrillion BTUs generation per year)	U.S. Nuclear Electricity (billion kilowatt-hours)	U.S. Coal Gross Production (million short-tons)	U.S. Total Dry Gas Production (trillion cubic feet)	U.S. Fuel Rate for Automobiles (miles per gallon)
55.7	74.3	83.5	598.6	21.7	13.4
55.7	72.5	114.0	610.0	20.7	13.6
52.8	70.5	172.5	654.6	19.2	14.0
57.3	74.4	191.1	684.9	19.1	13.8
59.7	76.3	250.9	697.2	19.2	14.1
60.2	78.1	276.4	670.2	19.1	14.3
62.7	78.9	255.2	781.1	19.7	14.6
59.6	76.0	251.1	829.7	19.4	16.0
56.1	74.0	272.7	823.8	19.2	16.5
53.5	70.8	282.8	838.1	17.8	16.9
53.3	70.5	293.7	782.1	16.1	17.1
54.5	74.1	327.6	895.9	17.5	17.4
54.0	74.0	383.7	883.6	16.5	17.5
56.2	74.3	414.0	890.3	16.1	17.4
56.7	76.9	455.3	918.8	16.6	18.0
58.7	80.2	527.0	950.3	17.1	18.8
59.9	81.4	529.4	980.7	17.3	19.0
60.6	81.3	576.9	1,029.1	17.8	20.3
60.2	81.1	612.6	996.0	17.7	21.2
60.2	82.2	618.8	997.5	17.8	21.0
60.2	83.9	610.3	945.4	18.1	20.6
61.0	85.6	640.4	1,033.5	18.8	20.8
62.3	87.2	673.4	1,033.0	18.6	21.1
64.1	90.0	674.7	1,063.9	18.8	21.2
66.3	90.6	628.6	1,089.9	18.9	21.5
67.0	89.7	666.8	1,109.8	18.9	21.6

The output contains an R^2 value of 92.1%, a standard error of the estimate of 1.215, and an overall significant F value of 46.62. Notice from Figure 14.9 that the t ratios indicate that the regression coefficients of four of the predictor variables, nuclear, coal, dry gas, and fuel rate, are not significant at $\alpha = 0.05$. If the researcher were to drop these four variables out of the regression analysis and rerun the model with the other predictor only, what would happen to the model? What if the researcher ran a regression model with only three predictors? How would these models compare to the full model with all five predictors? Are all the predictors necessary?

Developing regression models for business decision making involves at least two considerations. The first is to develop a regression model that accounts for the most variation of the dependent variable—that is, develop models that maximize the explained proportion of the deviation of the y values. At the same time, the regression model should be as parsimonious (simple and economical) as possible. The more complicated a quantitative model becomes, the harder it is for managers to understand and implement the model. In addition, as more variables are included in a model, it becomes more expensive to gather historical data or update present data for the model. These two considerations (dependent variable explanation and parsimony of the model) are quite often in opposition to each other. Hence, the business researcher, as the model builder, often needs to explore many model options.

In the world crude oil production regression model, if three variables explain the deviation of world crude oil production nearly as well as five variables, the simpler model is more attractive. How might researchers conduct regression analysis so that they can examine several models and then choose the most attractive one? The answer is to use search procedures.

SEARCH PROCEDURES

Search procedures are *processes whereby more than one multiple regression model is developed for a given database, and the models are compared and sorted by different criteria,* depending on the given procedure. Virtually all search procedures are done on a computer. Several search procedures are discussed in this section, including all possible regressions, stepwise regression, forward selection, and backward elimination.

ALL POSSIBLE REGRESSIONS

The **all possible regressions** search procedure *computes all possible linear multiple regression models from the data using all variables.* If a data set contains k independent variables, all possible regressions will determine $2^k - 1$ different models.

For the crude oil production example, the procedure of all possible regressions would produce $2^5 - 1 = 31$ different models from the $k = 5$ independent variables. With $k = 5$ predictors, the procedure produces all single-predictor models, all models with two predictors, all models with three predictors, all models with four predictors, and all models with five predictors, as shown in Table 14.7.

The all possible regressions procedure enables the business researcher to examine every model. In theory, this method eliminates the chance that the business researcher will not consider some models, as can be the case with other search procedures. On the other hand, the search through all possible models can be tedious, time-consuming, inefficient, and perhaps overwhelming.

STEPWISE REGRESSION

Perhaps the most widely known and used of the search procedures is stepwise regression. **Stepwise regression** is *a step-by-step process that begins by developing a regression model with a single predictor variable and adds and deletes predictors one step at a time,* examining

Table 14.7	Single Predictor	Two Predictors	Three Predictors	Four Predictors	Five Predictors
Predictors for All Possible Regressions with Five Independent Variables	X_1	X_1, X_2	X_1, X_2, X_3	X_1, X_2, X_3, X_4	X_1, X_2, X_3, X_4, X_5
	X_2	X_1, X_3	X_1, X_2, X_4	X_1, X_2, X_3, X_5	
	X_3	X_1, X_4	X_1, X_2, X_5	X_1, X_2, X_4, X_5	
	X_4	X_1, X_5	X_1, X_3, X_4	X_1, X_3, X_4, X_5	
	X_5	X_2, X_3	X_1, X_3, X_5	X_2, X_3, X_4, X_5	
		X_2, X_4	X_1, X_4, X_5		
		X_2, X_5	X_2, X_3, X_4		
		X_3, X_4	X_2, X_3, X_5		
		X_3, X_5	$\underline{X_2}, X_4, X_5$		
		X_4, X_5	X_3, X_4, X_5		

the fit of the model at each step until no more significant predictors remain outside the model.

STEP 1. In Step 1 of a stepwise regression procedure, the k independent variables are examined one at a time by developing a simple regression model for each independent variable to predict the dependent variable. The model containing the largest absolute value of t for an independent variable is selected, and the independent variable associated with the model is selected as the "best" single predictor of y at the first step. Some computer software packages use an F value instead of a t value to make this determination. Most of these computer programs allow the researcher to predetermine critical values for t or F but also contain a default value as an option. If the first independent variable selected at step 1 is denoted x_1, the model appears in the form:

$$\hat{y} = b_0 + b_1 x_1$$

If, after examining all possible single-predictor models, it is concluded that none of the independent variables produces a t value that is significant at α, then the search procedure stops at Step 1 and recommends no model.

STEP 2. In Step 2, the stepwise procedure examines all possible two-predictor regression models with x_1 as one of the independent variables in the model and determines which of the other $k - 1$ independent variables in conjunction with x_1 produces the highest absolute t value in the model. If this other variable selected from the remaining independent variables is denoted x_2 and is included in the model selected at Step 2 along with x_1, the model appears in the form:

$$\hat{y} = b_0 + b_1 x_1 + b_2 x_2$$

At this point, stepwise regression pauses and examines the t value of the regression coefficient for x_1. Occasionally, the regression coefficient for x_1 will become statistically nonsignificant when x_2 is entered into the model. In that case, stepwise regression will drop x_1 out of the model and go back and examine which of the other $k - 2$ independent variables, if any, will produce the largest significant absolute t value when that variable is included in the model along with x_2. If no other variables show significant t values, the procedure halts. It is worth noting that the regression coefficients are likely to change from step to step to account for the new predictor being added in the process. Thus, if x_1 stays in the model at Step 2, the value of b_1 at Step 1 will probably be different from the value of b_1 at Step 2.

STEP 3. Step 3 begins with independent variables x_1 and x_2 (the variables that were finally selected at Step 2) in the model. At this step, a search is made to determine which of the $k - 2$ remaining independent variables in conjunction with x_1 and x_2 produces the largest significant absolute t value in the regression model. Let us denote the one that is selected as x_3. If no significant t values are acknowledged at this step, the process stops here and the model determined in Step 2 is the final model. At Step 3, the model appears in the form:

$$\hat{y} = b_0 + b_1 x_1 + b_2 x_2 + b_3 x_3$$

In a manner similar to Step 2, stepwise regression now goes back and examines the t values of the regression coefficients of x_1 and x_2 in this Step 3 model. If either or both of the t values are now nonsignificant, the variables are dropped out of the model and the process calls for a search through the remaining $k - 3$ independent variables to determine which, if any, in conjunction with x_3 produce the largest significant t values in this model. The stepwise regression process continues step by step until no significant independent variables remain that are not in the model.

In the crude oil production example, recall that Table 14.6 contained data that can be used to develop a regression model to predict world crude oil production from as many as five different independent variables. Figure 14.9 displayed the results of a multiple regression analysis to produce a model using all five predictors. Suppose the researcher were to use a stepwise regression search procedure on these data to find a regression model. Recall that the following independent variables were being considered:

1. U.S. energy consumption
2. U.S. nuclear generation
3. U.S. coal production
4. U.S. dry gas production
5. U.S. fuel rate

STEP 1. Each of the independent variables is examined one at a time to determine the strength of each predictor in a simple regression model. The results are reported in Table 14.8.

Table 14.8

Step 1: Results of Simple Regression Using Each Independent Variable to Predict Oil Production

Dependent Variable	Independent Variable	t Ratio	R^2
Oil production	Energy consumption	11.77	85.2%
Oil production	Nuclear	4.43	45.0
Oil production	Coal	3.91	38.9
Oil production	Dry gas	1.08	4.6
Oil production	Fuel rate	3.54	34.2

→ Variable selected to serve as x_1

Note that the independent variable energy consumption was selected as the predictor variable, x_1, in Step 1. An examination of Table 14.8 reveals that energy consumption produced the largest absolute t value (11.77) of the single predictors. By itself, energy consumption accounted for 85.2% of the variation of the y values (world crude oil production). The regression equation taken from the computer output for this model is:

$$y = 13.075 + 0.580x_1$$

where

y = world crude oil production
x_1 = U.S. energy consumption

STEP 2. In Step 2, x_1 was retained initially in the model and a search was conducted among the four remaining independent variables to determine which of those variables in conjunction with x_1 produced the largest significant t value. Table 14.9 reports the results of this search.

Table 14.9

Step 2: Regression Results with Two Predictors

Dependent Variable y	Independent Variable x_1	Independent Variable x_2	t Ratio of x_2	R^2
Oil production	Energy consumption	Nuclear	−3.60	90.6%
Oil production	Energy consumption	Coal	−2.44	88.3
Oil production	Energy consumption	Dry gas	2.23	87.9
Oil production	Energy consumption	Fuel rate	−3.75	90.8

→ Variables selected at step 2

The information in Table 14.9 shows that the model selected in Step 2 includes the independent variables energy consumption and fuel rate. Fuel rate has the largest absolute t value (-3.75), and it is significant at $\alpha = 0.05$. Other variables produced varying sizes of t values. The model produced at Step 2 has an R^2 of 90.8%. These two variables taken together account for almost 91% of the variation of world crude oil production in this sample.

From other computer information, it is ascertained that the t value for the x_1 variable in this model is 11.91, which is even higher than in Step 1. Therefore, x_1 will not be dropped from the model by the stepwise regression procedure. The Step 2 regression model from the computer output is:

$$y = 7.14 + 0.772x_1 - 0.517x_2$$

where

 y = world crude oil production
 x_1 = U.S. energy consumption
 x_2 = U.S. fuel rate

Note that the regression coefficient for x_1 changed from 0.580 at Step 1 in the model to 0.772 at Step 2.

The R^2 for the model in Step 1 was 85.2%. Notice that none of the R^2 values produced from Step 2 models is less than 85.2%. The reason is that x_1 is still in the model, so the R^2 at this step must be at least as high as it was in Step 1, when only x_1 was in the model. In addition, by examining the R^2 values in Table 14.9, you can get a feel for how much the prospective new predictor adds to the model by seeing how much R^2 increases from 85.2%. For example, with x_2 (fuel rate) added to the model, the R^2 goes up to 90.8%. However, adding the variable dry gas to x_1 increases R^2 very little (it goes up to 87.9%).

STEP 3. In Step 3, the search procedure continues to look for an additional predictor variable from the three independent variables remaining out of the solution. Variables x_1 and x_2 are retained in the model. Table 14.10 reports the result of this search.

Table 14.10 **Step 3: Regression Results with Three Predictors**	Dependent Variable y	Independent Variable x_1	Independent Variable x_2	Independent Variable x_3	t Ratio of x_3	R^2
	Oil Production	Energy consumption	Fuel rate	Nuclear	-0.43	90.9%
	Oil Production	Energy consumption	Fuel rate	Coal	1.71	91.9
	Oil Production	Energy consumption	Fuel rate	Dry gas	-0.46	90.9
	No t ratio is significant at $\alpha = 0.05$. No new variables are added to the model.					

In this step, regression models are explored that contain x_1 (energy consumption) and x_2 (fuel rate) in addition to one of the three remaining variables. None of the three models produce t ratios that are significant at $\alpha = 0.05$. No new variables are added to the model produced in Step 2. The stepwise regression process ends.

Figure 14.10 shows the stepwise regression output for the world crude oil production example. The results printed in the table are virtually identical to the step-by-step results discussed in this section, but are in a different format.

Figure 14.10

Stepwise Regression Output for the Crude Oil Production Example

```
Stepwise Regression: CrOilPrd versus USEnCons, USNucGen, ...

Alpha-to-Enter: 0.1 Alpha-to-Remove: 0.1

Response is CrOilPrd on 5 predictors, with N =   26

Step               1       2
Constant      13.075   7.140

USEnCons       0.580   0.772
T-Value        11.77   11.91
P-Value        0.000   0.000

FuelRate               -0.52
T-Value                -3.75
P-Value                0.001

S               1.52    1.22
R-Sq           85.24   90.83
R-Sq(adj)      84.62   90.03
```

Each column in Figure 14.10 contains information about the regression model at each step. Thus, column 1 contains data on the regression model for Step 1. In each column at each step you can see the variables in the model. As an example, at Step 2, energy consumption and fuel rate are in the model. The numbers above the t ratios are the regression coefficients. The coefficients and the constant in column 2, for example, yield the regression model equation values for Step 2:

$$\hat{y} = 7.140 + 0.772x_1 - 0.52x_2$$

The values of R^2 (R-Sq) and the standard error of the estimate (S) are displayed on the bottom row of the output along with the adjusted value of R^2.

FORWARD SELECTION

Another search procedure is forward selection. **Forward selection** is essentially the same as stepwise regression, but once a variable is entered into the process, it is never dropped out. Forward selection begins by finding the independent variable that will produce the largest absolute value of t (and largest R^2) in predicting y. The selected variable is denoted here as x_1 and is part of the model:

$$\hat{y} = b_0 + b_1x_1$$

Forward selection proceeds to Step 2. While retaining x_1, it examines the other $k - 1$ independent variables and determines which variable in the model with x_1 produces the highest absolute value of t that is significant. To this point, forward selection is the same as stepwise regression. If this second variable is designated x_2, the model is:

$$\hat{y} = b_0 + b_1x_1 + b_2x_2$$

At this point, forward selection does not reexamine the t value of x_1. Both x_1 and x_2 remain in the model as other variables are examined and included. When independent variables are correlated in forward selection, the overlapping of information can limit the potential predictability of two or more variables in combination. Stepwise regression takes this into account, in part, when it goes back to reexamine the t values of predictors already in the model to determine whether they are still significant predictors of y given the variables that have now entered the process. In other words, stepwise regression acknowledges that the strongest single predictor of y that is selected at Step 1 may not be a significant predictor of y when taken in conjunction with other variables.

Using a forward selection procedure to develop multiple regression models for the world crude oil production example would result in the same outcome as that provided by stepwise regression because neither x_1 nor x_2 was removed from the model in that particular stepwise regression. The difference in the two procedures is more apparent in examples where variables selected at earlier steps in the process are removed during later steps in stepwise regression.

BACKWARD ELIMINATION

The **backward elimination** search procedure is a *step-by-step process that begins with the "full" model (all k predictors).* Using the t values, a search is made to determine whether any nonsignificant independent variables are in the model. If no nonsignificant predictors are found, the backward process ends with the full model. If nonsignificant predictors are found, the predictor with the smallest absolute value of t is eliminated and a new model is developed with $k - 1$ independent variables.

This model is then examined to determine whether it contains any independent variables with nonsignificant t values. If it does, the predictor with the smallest absolute t value is eliminated from the process and a new model is developed for the next step.

This procedure of identifying the smallest nonsignificant t value and eliminating that variable continues until all variables left in the model have significant t values. Sometimes this process yields results similar to those obtained from forward selection and other times it does not. A word of caution is in order. Backward elimination always begins with all possible predictors in the model. Sometimes the sample data do not provide enough observations to justify the use of all possible predictors at the same time in the model. In this case, backward elimination is not a suitable option with which to build regression models.

The following steps show how the backward elimination process can be used to develop multiple regression models to predict world crude oil production using the data and five predictors displayed in Table 14.6.

STEP 1. A full model is developed with all predictors. The results are shown in Table 14.11. The R^2 for this model is 92.1%. A study of Table 14.11 reveals that the predictor dry gas has the smallest absolute value of a nonsignificant t ($t = -0.32$, $p = 0.753$). In Step 2, this variable will be dropped from the model.

	Predictor	Coefficient	t Ratio	p
Table 14.11	Energy consumption	0.8357	4.64	0.000
	Nuclear	−0.00654	−0.66	0.514
Step 1: Backward Elimination, Full Model	Coal	0.00983	1.35	0.193
	Dry gas	−0.1432	−0.32	0.753
	Fuel rate	−0.7341	−1.34	0.196
	Variable to be dropped from the model			

STEP 2. A second regression model is developed with $k - 1 = 4$ predictors. Dry gas has been eliminated from consideration. The results of this multiple regression analysis are presented in Table 14.12. The computer results in Table 14.12 indicate that the variable nuclear has the smallest absolute value of a nonsignificant t of the variables remaining in the model ($t = -0.64$, $p = 0.528$). In Step 3, this variable will be dropped from the model.

Table 14.12

Step 2: Backward Elimination, Four Predictors

Predictor	Coefficient	t Ratio	p
Energy consumption	0.7843	9.85	0.000
Nuclear	−0.004261	−0.64	0.528
Coal	0.010933	1.74	0.096
Fuel rate	−0.8253	−1.80	0.086

Variable to be dropped from the model

STEP 3. A third regression model is developed with $k - 2 = 3$ predictors. Both nuclear and dry gas variables have been removed from the model. The results of this multiple regression analysis are reported in Table 14.13. The computer results in Table 14.13 indicate that the variable coal has the smallest absolute value of a nonsignificant t of the variables remaining in the model ($t = 1.71$, $p = 0.102$). In Step 4, this variable will be dropped from the model.

Table 14.13

Step 3: Backward Elimination, Three Predictors

Predictor	Coefficient	t Ratio	p
Energy consumption	0.75394	11.94	0.000
Coal	0.010479	1.71	0.102
Fuel rate	−1.0283	−3.14	0.005

Variable to be dropped from the model

STEP 4. A fourth regression model is developed with $k - 3 = 2$ predictors. Nuclear, dry gas, and coal variables have been removed from the model. The results of this multiple regression analysis are reported in Table 14.14. Observe that all p values are less than $\alpha = 0.05$, indicating that all t values are significant, so no additional independent variables need to be removed. The backward elimination process ends with two predictors in the model. The final model obtained from this backward elimination process is the same model as that obtained by using stepwise regression.

Table 14.14

Step 4: Backward Elimination, Two Predictors

Predictor	Coefficient	t Ratio	p
Energy consumption	0.77201	11.91	0.000
Fuel rate	−0.5173	−3.75	0.001

All variable are significant at $\alpha = 0.05$.
No variables will be dropped from this model.
The process stops.

Concept Check

1. What does the term *search procedures* mean in regression analysis?
2. Name some commonly used search procedures in regression analysis and briefly describe them.

14.3 Problems

14.13 Use a stepwise regression procedure and the following data to develop a multiple regression model to predict y. Discuss the variables that enter at each step, commenting on their t values and on the value of R^2.

y	x_1	x_2	x_3	y	x_1	x_2	x_3
21	5	108	57	22	13	105	51
17	11	135	34	20	10	111	43
14	14	113	21	16	20	140	20
13	9	160	25	13	19	150	14
19	16	122	43	18	14	126	29
15	18	142	40	12	21	175	22
24	7	93	52	23	6	98	38
17	9	128	38	18	15	129	40

14.14 Given here are data for a dependent variable and four potential predictors. Use these data and a stepwise regression procedure to develop a multiple regression model to predict y. Examine the values of t and R^2 at each step and comment on those values. How many steps did the procedure use? Why do you think the process stopped?

y	x_1	x_2	x_3	x_4
101	2	77	1.2	42
127	4	72	1.7	26
98	9	69	2.4	47
79	5	53	2.6	65
118	3	88	2.9	37
114	1	53	2.7	28
110	3	82	2.8	29
94	2	61	2.6	22
96	8	60	2.4	48
73	6	64	2.1	42
108	2	76	1.8	34
124	5	74	2.2	11
82	6	50	1.5	61
89	9	57	1.6	53
76	1	72	2	72
109	3	74	2.8	36
123	2	99	2.6	17
125	6	81	2.5	48

14.15 The computer output given here is the result of a stepwise multiple regression analysis to predict a dependent variable by using six predictor variables. The number of observations was 108. Study the output and discuss the results. How many predictors ended up in the model? Which predictors, if any, did not enter the model?

```
STEPWISE REGRESSION OF Y ON 6 PREDICTORS, WITH N = 108
```

STEP	1	2	3	4
CONSTANT	8.71	6.82	6.57	5.96
X_3	-2.85	-4.92	-4.97	-5.00
T-RATIO	2.11	2.94	3.04	3.07
X_1		4.42	3.72	3.22
T-RATIO		2.64	2.20	2.05
X_2			1.91	1.78
T-RATIO			2.07	2.02
X_6				1.56
T-RATIO				1.98
S	3.81	3.51	3.43	3.36
R-SQ	29.20	49.45	54.72	59.29

14.16 Study the output given here from a stepwise multiple regression analysis to predict y from four variables. Comment on the output at each step.

```
STEPWISE REGRESSION OF Y ON 4 PREDICTORS, WITH N = 63
```

STEP	1	2
CONSTANT	27.88	22.3
X_3	0.89	
T-RATIO	2.26	
X_2		12.38
T-RATIO		2.64
X_4		0.0047
T-RATIO		2.01
S	16.52	9.47
R-SQ	42.39	68.2

14.17 A marketing researcher carries out a survey to assess whether the amount of money a customer spends in a clothing store depends on how the customer feels about the value he receives, the perceived durability of the material, and the service provided by the retail outlet. Customers are asked to rate value, durability, and service on a 10-point scale (the higher the better). Given below is a part of the data so collected. Use stepwise regression to assess if these variables influence the amount spent and, if so, determine the relationship.

Amount Spent ($)	Value	Durability	Service
37	3	4	2
49	4	3	2
38	4	3	2
50	4	3	2
29	3	2	4
60	6	3	5
21	3	2	4
77	5	6	7
46	6	4	5
16	3	2	3
55	4	5	4
23	2	1	5
48	5	4	6

(continued)

Amount Spent ($)	Value	Durability	Service
66	5	4	7
15	3	2	2
62	5	6	7
53	6	7	5
76	3	5	4
22	4	6	3
34	5	3	6

14.18 The U.S. Energy Information Administration releases figures in its publication, *Monthly Energy Review,* about the cost of various fuels and electricity. Shown here are the figures for four different energy items over a 12-year period. Use the data and stepwise regression to predict the cost of residential electricity from the cost of residential natural gas, residual fuel oil, and regular gasoline. Examine the data and discuss the output.

Residential Electricity (kWh)	Residential Natural Gas (1,000 ft³)	Residual Fuel Oil (gal)	Regular Gasoline (gal)
2.54	1.29	0.21	0.39
3.51	1.71	0.31	0.57
4.64	2.98	0.44	0.86
5.36	3.68	0.61	1.19
6.2	4.29	0.76	1.31
6.86	5.17	0.68	1.22
7.18	6.06	0.65	1.16
7.54	6.12	0.69	1.13
7.79	6.12	0.61	1.12
7.41	5.83	0.34	.86
7.41	5.54	0.42	.90
7.49	4.49	0.33	.90

14.4 MULTICOLLINEARITY

One problem that can arise in multiple regression analysis is multicollinearity. **Multicollinearity** is *when two or more of the independent variables of a multiple regression model are highly correlated.* Technically, if two of the independent variables are correlated, we have collinearity; when three or more independent variables are correlated, we have multicollinearity. However, the two terms are frequently used interchangeably.

The reality of business research is that most of the time some correlation between predictors (independent variables) will be present. The problem of multicollinearity arises when the intercorrelation between predictor variables is high. This relationship causes several other problems, particularly in the interpretation of the analysis.

1. It is difficult, if not impossible, to interpret the estimates of the regression coefficients.
2. Inordinately small t values for the regression coefficients may result.
3. The standard deviations of regression coefficients are overestimated.
4. The algebraic sign of estimated regression coefficients may be the opposite of what would be expected for a particular predictor variable.

Table 14.15		**Energy Consumption**	**Nuclear**	**Coal**	**Dry Gas**	**Fuel Rate**
Correlations among Oil Production Predictor Variables	Energy Consumption	1	0.856	0.791	0.057	0.791
	Nuclear	0.856	1	0.952	−0.404	0.972
	Coal	0.791	0.952	1	−0.448	0.968
	Dry gas	0.057	−0.404	−0.448	1	−0.423
	Fuel rate	0.796	0.972	0.968	−0.423	1

The problem of multicollinearity can arise in regression analysis in a variety of business research situations. For example, suppose a model is being developed to predict salaries in a given industry. Independent variables such as years of education, age, years in management, experience on the job, and years of tenure with the firm might be considered as predictors. It is obvious that several of these variables are correlated (virtually all of these variables have something to do with number of years, or time) and yield redundant information. Suppose a financial regression model is being developed to predict bond market rates by such independent variables as TSX average, prime interest rates, GNP, producer price index, and consumer price index. Several of these predictors are likely to be intercorrelated.

In the world crude oil production example used in Section 14.3, several of the independent variables are intercorrelated, leading to the potential of multicollinearity problems. Table 14.15 gives the correlations of the predictor variables for this example. Note that r values are quite high ($r > 0.90$) for fuel rate and nuclear (0.972), fuel rate and coal (0.968), and coal and nuclear (0.952).

Table 14.15 shows that fuel rate and coal production are highly correlated. Using fuel rate as a single predictor of crude oil production produces the following simple regression model:

$$\hat{y} = 44.869 + 0.7838(\text{fuel rate})$$

Notice that the estimate of the regression coefficient, 0.7838, is positive, indicating that as fuel rate increases, oil production increases. Using coal as a single predictor of crude oil production yields the following simple regression model:

$$\hat{y} = 45.072 + 0.0157(\text{coal})$$

The multiple regression model developed using both fuel rate and coal to predict crude oil production is:

$$\hat{y} = 45.806 + 0.0227(\text{coal}) - 0.3934(\text{fuel rate})$$

Observe that this regression model indicates a negative relationship between fuel rate and oil production (−0.3934), which is in opposition to the *positive* relationship shown in the regression equation for fuel rate as a single predictor. Because of the multicollinearity between coal and fuel rate, these two independent variables interact in the regression analysis in such a way as to produce regression coefficient estimates that are difficult to interpret. Extreme caution should be exercised before interpreting these regression coefficient estimates.

The problem of multicollinearity can also affect the t values that are used to evaluate the regression coefficients. Because the problems of multicollinearity among predictors can result in an overestimation of the standard deviation of the regression coefficients, the t values tend to be underrepresentative when multicollinearity is present. In some regression models containing multicollinearity in which all t values are nonsignificant, the overall F value for the model is highly significant. In Section 14.1, an example was given of how including interaction when it is significant strengthens a regression model. The computer output for the regression models both with and without the interaction term was shown in Figure 14.5. The model without interaction produced a statistically significant F value but neither predictor variable was significant. Further investigation of this model reveals that the correlation between the two predictors, x_1 and x_2, is 0.945. This extremely high correlation indicates a strong collinearity between the two predictor variables.

This collinearity may explain the fact that the overall model is significant but neither predictor is significant. It also underscores one of the problems with multicollinearity: underrepresented t values. The t values test the strength of the predictor given the other variables in the model. If a predictor is highly correlated with other independent variables, it will appear not to add much to the explanation of y and produce a low t value. However, had the predictor not been in the presence of these other correlated variables, the predictor might have explained a high proportion of variation of y.

Many of the problems created by multicollinearity are interpretation problems. The business researcher should be alert to and aware of multicollinearity potential with the predictors in the model and view the model outcome in light of such potential.

The problem of multicollinearity is not a simple one to overcome. However, several methods offer an approach to the problem. One way is to examine a correlation matrix like the one in Table 14.15 to search for possible intercorrelations among potential predictor variables. If several variables are highly correlated, the researcher can select the variable that is most correlated to the dependent variable and use that variable to represent the others in the analysis. One problem with this idea is that correlations can be more complex than simple correlation among variables. In other words, simple correlation values do not always reveal multiple correlation between variables. In some instances, variables may not appear to be correlated as pairs, but one variable is a linear combination of several other variables. This situation is also an example of multicollinearity, and a cursory observation of the correlation matrix will probably not reveal the problem.

Other techniques are available to attempt to detect the problem of multicollinearity. One is called a **variance inflation factor (VIF),** in which a regression analysis is conducted to predict an independent variable by the other independent variables. In this case, the independent variable being predicted becomes the dependent variable. As this process is done for each of the independent variables, it is possible to determine whether any of the independent variables are functions of the other independent variables, yielding evidence of multicollinearity. By using the results from such a model, a VIF can be computed to determine whether the standard errors of the estimates are inflated:

$$\text{VIF} = \frac{1}{1 - R_i^2}$$

where R_i^2 is the coefficient of determination for any of the models, used to predict an independent variable by the other $k - 1$ independent variables. Some researchers follow a guideline that any VIF greater than 10 or R_i^2 value greater than 0.90 for the largest VIFs indicates a severe multicollinearity problem.[*]

[*]William Mendenhall and Terry Sincich, *A Second Course in Business Statistics: Regression Analysis* (San Francisco: Dellen Publishing Company, 1989); John Neter, William Wasserman, and Michael H. Kutner, *Applied Linear Regression Models*, 2nd ed. (Homewood, IL: Richard D. Irwin, 1989).

POINTS OF INTEREST
Multiple regression is designed to work with correlated independent variables. The problem of multicollinearity occurs when the intercorrelation is very high (such as 0.8 or 0.9). Multicollinearity can result in models that are unstable. You should always check for the presence of multicollinearity before finalizing the model.

Concept Check

1. What is multicollinearity and why is it a problem?
2. What procedures would you use to detect multicollinearity?

14.4 Problems

14.19 Develop a correlation matrix for the independent variables in Problem 14.13. Study the matrix and make a judgment as to whether substantial multicollinearity is present among the predictors. Explain your judgment.

14.20 Construct a correlation matrix for the four independent variables for Problem 14.14 and search for possible multicollinearity. What did you find and why?

14.21 In Problem 14.17, you were asked to use stepwise regression to predict amount spent by value, durability, and service. Study the stepwise results, including the regression coefficients, to determine whether there may be a problem with multicollinearity. Construct a correlation matrix of the three variables to aid you in this task.

14.22 Study the three predictor variables in Problem 14.18 and attempt to determine whether substantial multicollinearity is present between the predictor variables. If there is a problem of multicollinearity, how might it affect the outcome of the multiple regression analysis?

DETERMINING COMPENSATION FOR CEOs

One statistical tool that can be used to study CEO compensation is multiple regression analysis. Regression models can be developed using predictor variables, such as age, years of experience, and worth of company, for analyzing CEO compensation. Search procedures such as stepwise regression can be used to sort out the more significant predictors of CEO compensation.

The researcher prepares for the multiple regression analysis by conducting a study of CEOs and gathering data on several variables. The data presented in the Decision Dilemma could be used for such an analysis. It seems reasonable to believe that CEO compensation is related to the size and worth of a company; therefore, it makes sense to attempt to develop a regression model or models to predict CEO compensation by the variables company sales, number of employees in the company, and the capital investment of a company. Qualitative or dummy variables can also be used in such an analysis. In the database given in the Decision Dilemma, one variable indicates whether a company is a manufacturing company. One way to recode this variable for regression analysis is to assign a 1 to companies that are manufacturers and a 0 to others.

A stepwise regression procedure can sort out the variables that seem to be more important predictors of CEO compensation. A stepwise regression analysis was conducted on the Decision Dilemma database using sales, number of employees, capital investment, and whether a company is in manufacturing as the four independent variables. The result of this analysis follows.

```
Stepwise Regression: Cash Compen versus Sales,
No. of Emp., ...
Alpha-to-Enter: 0.15 Alpha-to-Remove: 0.15
Response is Cash Com on 4 predictors, with N = 20
```

Step	1	2	3	4
Constant	243.9	232.2	223.8	223.3
No. of E	0.0696	0.1552	0.0498	
T-Value	13.67	4.97	0.98	
P-Value	0.000	0.000	0.343	
Cap. Inv		-1.66	-2.92	-3.06
T-Value		-2.77	-3.97	-4.27
P-Value		0.013	0.001	0.001
Sales			1.08	1.45
T-Value			2.46	6.10
P-Value			0.026	0.000
S	32.6	27.9	24.5	24.5
R-Sq	91.22	93.95	95.61	95.34
R-Sq(adj)	90.73	93.24	94.78	94.80

The stepwise regression analysis produces a single predictor model at Step 1 with a high R^2 value of 0.9122. The number of employees variable used in a simple regression model accounts for over 91.2% of the variation of CEO compensation data. An examination of the regression coefficient of number of employees at the first step (0.0696) indicates that a one-employee increase results in a predicted increase of (0.0696 × $1,000) or about $70 in the CEO's compensation.

At Step 2, the company's capital investment enters the model. Notice that the R^2 increases only by 0.0273 and that the regression coefficient on capital investment is negative.

This result seems counterintuitive because we would expect that the more capital investment a company has, the more the CEO should be compensated for the responsibility. A simple regression analysis using only capital investment produces the following model:

Cash compensation = 257 + 1.29(capital investment)

Notice that the regression coefficient in this model is positive as we would suppose. Multicollinearity is likely. In fact, multicollinearity is evident among sales, number of employees, and capital investment. Each is a function or determiner of company size. Examine the following correlation matrix.

Correlations

	Sales	Number of Employees
Number of Employees	0.997	1
Capital Investment	0.995	0.999

Notice that these three predictors are highly interrelated. Therefore, the interpretation of the regression coefficients and the order of entry of these variables in the stepwise regression become more difficult. Nevertheless, number of employees is most highly related to CEO compensation in these data. Observe also in the stepwise regression output that number of employees actually drops out of the model at Step 4. The t ratio for number of employees is not significant ($t = 0.98$) at Step 3. However, the R^2 actually drops slightly when number of employees is removed. In searching for a model that is both parsimonious and explanatory, the researcher could do worse than to merely select the model at Step 1.

Researchers might want to explore more complicated nonlinear models. Some of the independent variables might be related to CEO compensation but in some nonlinear manner.

A brief study of the predictor variables in the Decision Dilemma database reveals that as compensation increases, the values of the data in the independent variables do not increase at a linear rate. Scatter plots of sales, number of employees, and capital investment with CEO compensation confirm this suspicion. Shown here is a scatter plot of sales with cash compensation.

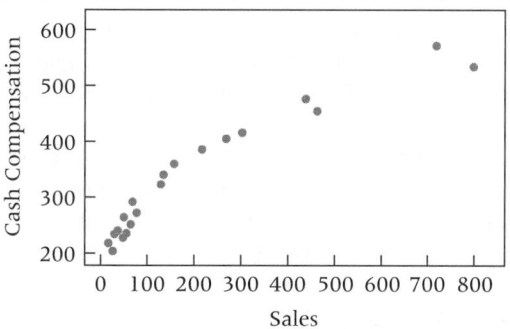

Observe that the graph suggests more of a logarithmic fit than a linear one. We can use recoding techniques presented in the chapter to conduct a multiple regression analysis to predict compensation using the log of each of these variables. In the analysis, the compensation figures remain the same, but each of the three quantitative independent variables is recoded by taking the log of each value and entering the resultant variable in the model. A second stepwise regression analysis is undertaken with the log variables in the mix along with the original variables. The results follow:

```
Stepwise Regression: Cash Compen versus Sales,
No. of Emp., ...
Alpha-to-Enter: 0.1 Alpha-to-Remove: 0.1
Response is Cash Com on 7 predictors, with N = 20
```

Step	1	2	3	4	5
Constant	-129.61	-13.23	-122.53	-147.22	-120.74
Log Sale	224.3	152.2	281.4	307.8	280.8
T-Value	22.22	8.75	11.08	32.75	26.81
P-Value	0.000	0.000	0.000	0	0
No. Emp		0.0251	0.0233	0.0903	0.0828
T-Value		4.53	6.97	13.94	15.52
P-Value		0.000	0.000	0.000	0.000
Log Cap			-106.4	-126	-109.8
T-Value			-5.58	-17.87	-15.56
P-Value			0.000	0.000	0.000
Sales				-0.434	-0.250
T-Value				-10.52	-4.11
P-Value				0.000	0.001
Cap. Inv					-0.37
T-Value					-3.51
P-Value					0.003
S	20.7	14.3	8.59	3.07	2.32
R-Sq	96.48	98.41	99.46	99.94	99.97
R-Sq(adj)	96.29	98.22	99.36	99.92	99.95

Note that in this stepwise regression analysis, the variable log sales has the highest single predictability of compensation producing an R^2 of 0.9648, which is higher than the value at Step 1 in the first stepwise regression analysis. Number of employees enters at Step 2 and log of capital investment at Step 3. However, such a high R^2 at Step 1 leaves little room for improved predictability. Our search through the variables may well end with the decision to use the log of sales as the efficient, predictable model of compensation. The final model might be:

CEO compensation = −129.61 + 224.3 log (sales)

Human resource managers sometimes use compensation tables to assist them in determining ranges and ballparks for salary offers. Company boards of directors can use such models as the one developed here to assist them in negotiations with possible candidates for CEO positions or to aid them in determining whether a presently employed CEO is over- or undercompensated. In addition, candidates who are searching for new CEO opportunities can use models like these to determine the potential compensation for a new position and to help them be more adequately prepared for salary negotiations should they be offered a CEO position.

Some of the variables in this study will undoubtedly produce redundant information. The use of a correlation matrix and a stepwise regression process can protect the analysis from some of the problems of multicollinearity. The use of multiple regression analysis on a large sample of CEO compensation data with many independent variables could provide some interesting and exciting results.

KEY CONSIDERATIONS

Some business researchers misuse the results of search procedures by using the order in which variables come into a model (on stepwise and forward selection) to rank the variables in importance. They state that the variable entered at Step 1 is the most important predictor of y, the variable entering at Step 2 is second most important, and so on. In actuality, variables entering the analysis after Step 1 are being analyzed by how much of the unaccounted-for variation (residual variation) they are explaining, not how much they are related to y by themselves. A variable that comes into the model at the fourth step is the variable that most greatly accounts for the variation of the y values left over after the first three variables have explained the rest. However, the fourth variable taken by itself might explain more variation of y than the second or third variable when seen as single predictors. In multiple regression, unlike in simple regression, the variance explained should be interpreted in the context of other variables involved in the regression equation.

Some people use the estimates of the regression coefficients (b) to compare the worth of the predictor variables; the larger the coefficient is, the greater its worth. However, the unstandardized regression b coefficients do not necessarily reflect the relative importance of the variables. Because different variables may have been measured in different units, regression coefficient weights are partly a function of the unit of measurement of the variable. Interpretation of multiple regression coefficients would also require that we have accounted for external distortions such as multicollinearity. Researchers who ignore these problems are at risk of presenting spurious results.

Why Statistics Is Relevant

Businesses are constantly affected by a multiplicity of variables. For example, what influences customer loyalty to our products? Is it our customer service, product quality, product pricing, or the product's wide availability? Once we can hypothesize what such variables might be, we can use multiple regression analysis to test our hypothesis. However, the relationships can be more complex. Some of them may be nonlinear: customers may be less price sensitive up to a certain point, but much more sensitive after that. They may reject poor-quality products but may also not assign value to products that exceed certain quality standards. Procedures described in this chapter show how to identify such complex relationships in order to make proper business decisions.

SUMMARY

1. Even when our independent variables are nonlinear, we can use multiple regression analysis to analyze the data. One way to accommodate this issue is to recode the data and enter the variables into the analysis in the normal way. Other nonlinear regression models, such as exponential models, require that the entire model be transformed. Often the transformation involves the use of logarithms. In some cases, the resulting value of the regression model is in logarithmic form and the antilogarithm of the answer must be taken to determine the predicted value of y.

2. Indicator, or dummy, variables are qualitative variables used to represent categorical data in the multiple regression model. These variables are coded as 0, 1 and are often used to represent nominal or ordinal classification data that the researcher wants to include in the regression analysis. If a qualitative variable contains more than two categories, it generates multiple dummy variables. In general, if a qualitative variable contains c categories, $c - 1$ dummy variables should be created.

3. You can build regression models in many ways. Search procedures are used to help sort through the independent variables as predictors in the examination of various possible models. Several search procedures are available, including all possible regressions, stepwise regression, forward selection, and backward elimination. The all possible regressions procedure computes every possible regression model for a set of data. The drawbacks of this procedure include the time and energy required to compute all possible regressions and the difficulty of deciding which models are most appropriate. The stepwise regression procedure involves selecting and adding one independent variable at a time to the regression process after beginning with a one-predictor model. Variables are added to the model at each step if they contain the most significant t value associated with the remaining variables. If no additional t value is statistically significant at any given step, the procedure stops. With stepwise regression, at each step the process examines the variables already in the model to determine whether their t values are still significant. If not, they are dropped from the model, and the process searches for other independent variables with large, significant t values to replace the variable(s) dropped. The forward selection procedure is the same as stepwise regression but does not drop variables out of the model once they have been included. The backward elimination procedure begins with a "full" model, a model that contains all the independent variables. The sample size must be large enough to justify a full model, which can be a limiting factor. Backward elimination drops out the least important predictors one at a time until only significant predictors are left in the regression model. The variable with the smallest absolute t value of the statistically nonsignificant t values is the independent variable that is dropped out of the model at each step.

4. One of the problems in using multiple regression is multicollinearity, or correlations among the predictor variables. This problem can cause overinflated estimates of the standard deviations of regression coefficients, misinterpretation of regression coefficients, undersized t values, and misleading signs on the regression coefficients. It can be lessened by using an intercorrelation matrix of independent variables to help recognize bivariate correlation, by using stepwise regression to sort the variables one at a time, or by using statistics such as a VIF.

KEY TERMS

all possible regressions	multicollinearity	stepwise regression	variance inflation factor
backward elimination	nonlinear regression model	Tukey's four-quadrant	(VIF)
dummy variable	quadratic regression model	approach	
forward selection	qualitative variable	Tukey's ladder of transfor-	
indicator variable	search procedures	mations	

FORMULAS

(14.1) variance inflation factor

$$VIF = \frac{1}{1 - R_i^2}$$

SUPPLEMENTARY PROBLEMS

Calculating the Statistics

14.23 Given here are the data for a dependent variable, y, and independent variables. Use these data to develop a regression model to predict y. Discuss the output. Which variable is an indicator variable? Was it a significant predictor of y?

x_1	x_2	x_3	y
0	51	16.4	14
0	48	17.1	17

(continued)

x_1	x_2	x_3	y
1	29	18.2	29
0	36	17.9	32
0	40	16.5	54
1	27	17.1	86
1	14	17.8	117
0	17	18.2	120
1	16	16.9	194
1	9	18	203
1	14	18.9	217
0	11	18.5	235

14.24 Use the following data and a stepwise regression analysis to predict y. In addition to the two independent variables given here, include three other predictors in your analysis: the square of each x as a predictor and an interaction predictor. Discuss the results of the process.

x_1	x_2	y	x_1	x_2	y
10	3	2,002	5	12	1,750
5	14	1,747	6	8	1,832
8	4	1,980	5	18	1,795
7	4	1,902	7	4	1,917
6	7	1,842	8	5	1,943
7	6	1,883	6	9	1,830
4	21	1,697	5	12	1,786
11	4	2,021			

14.25 Use the x_1 values and the log of the x_1 values given here to predict the y values by using a stepwise regression procedure. Discuss the output. Were either or both of the predictors significant?

y	x_1	y	x_1
20.4	850	13.2	204
11.6	146	17.5	487
17.8	521	12.4	192
15.3	304	10.6	98
22.4	1,029	19.8	703
21.9	910	17.4	394
16.4	242	19.4	647

Testing Your Understanding

14.26 Shown here are the volume trading figures for grain, oilseeds, and livestock products over a period of several years in the U.S. commodity futures exchanges. Use these data to develop a multiple regression model to predict grain futures volume of trading from oilseeds volume and livestock products volume. All figures are given in units of millions. Graph each of these predictors separately with the response variable and use Tukey's four-quadrant approach to explore possible recoding schemes for nonlinear relationships. Include any of these in the regression model. Comment on the results.

Grain	Oilseeds	Livestock
2.2	3.7	3.4
18.3	15.7	11.8
19.8	20.3	9.8
14.9	15.8	11
17.8	19.8	11.1
15.9	23.5	8.4
10.7	14.9	7.9
10.3	13.8	8.6
10.9	14.2	8.8
15.9	22.5	9.6
15.9	21.1	8.2

14.27 Shown here are the average prices per year for several minerals over a decade. Use these data and a stepwise regression procedure to produce a model to predict the average price of gold from the other variables. Comment on the results of the process.

Gold ($ per oz)	Copper (¢ per lb)	Silver ($ per oz)	Aluminum (¢ per lb)
161.1	64.2	4.4	39.8
308.0	93.3	11.1	61.0
613.0	101.3	20.6	71.6
460.0	84.2	10.5	76.0
376.0	72.8	8.0	76.0
424.0	76.5	11.4	77.8
361.0	66.8	8.1	81.0
318.0	67.0	6.1	81.0
368.0	66.1	5.5	81.0
448.0	82.5	7.0	72.3
438.0	120.5	6.5	110.1
382.6	130.9	5.5	87.8

14.28 Given below is the population, number of households, and market income for 10 Canadian cities. Use the data to develop a regression model to predict market income from population and number of households. Graph each of these predictors separately with the response variable and use Tukey's four-quadrant approach to explore possible recoding schemes for nonlinear relationships. Include any of these in the regression model. Comment on the regression model and its strengths and its weaknesses.

	2001		
	Market Income	**Households**	**Population (1,000s)**
Toronto	125.0	1,635	4,683
Montreal	76.1	1,417	3,426
Vancouver	47.8	759	1,987
Ottawa-Hull	29.5	416	1,064
Calgary	26.4	356	951
Edmonton	22.0	357	938
Hamilton	16.2	253	662
Quebec	14.8	295	683
Winnipeg	14.6	270	661
London	10.2	173	433

14.29 Given below is the consumer price index for a Canadian city over a period of 30 months. Also displayed are some of the major components of the index: bread, coffee, beef, chicken, and eggs. Use these data and a stepwise regression procedure to develop a model that attempts to predict price index by the other five variables. Construct scatter plots of each of these variables with the price index. Examine the graphs in light of Tukey's four-quadrant approach. Develop any other appropriate predictor variables by recoding data, and include them in the analysis. Comment on the result of this analysis.

Month	Price Index	Bread	Coffee	Beef	Chicken	Eggs
1	118.033	8.915	2.075	3.123	2.515	1.405
2	118.165	9.077	2.053	3.076	2.546	1.412
3	118.580	9.317	2.083	3.237	2.572	1.370
4	118.757	9.461	2.094	3.164	2.635	1.404
5	118.908	9.595	2.091	3.172	2.629	1.421
6	119.127	9.711	2.098	3.247	2.647	1.426
7	118.761	9.537	2.025	3.172	2.625	1.403
8	119.077	9.829	2.004	3.162	2.672	1.409
9	119.130	9.884	2.040	3.179	2.629	1.399
10	119.354	10.103	2.046	3.155	2.652	1.398
11	119.565	10.243	2.048	3.153	2.717	1.403
12	119.625	10.361	2.025	3.058	2.771	1.409
13	120.121	10.702	2.034	3.011	2.906	1.469
14	120.799	11.118	2.066	3.106	3.044	1.464
15	120.880	11.217	2.058	3.122	3.010	1.472
16	120.843	11.260	2.050	3.086	2.980	1.468
17	121.061	11.436	2.061	3.161	2.904	1.499
18	121.169	11.510	2.085	3.140	2.914	1.520
19	120.774	11.287	2.039	3.063	2.942	1.443
20	120.636	11.249	2.044	2.984	2.897	1.460
21	120.949	11.418	2.057	3.112	2.887	1.475
22	121.294	11.642	2.080	3.113	2.962	1.497
23	121.134	11.558	2.051	3.108	2.936	1.481
24	121.010	11.528	2.025	3.073	2.905	1.478
25	120.631	11.309	1.997	3.012	2.876	1.437
26	120.805	11.488	1.999	3.009	2.880	1.429
27	121.589	11.904	2.057	3.282	2.920	1.426
28	121.625	12.005	2.043	3.173	2.962	1.443
29	121.805	12.081	2.060	3.243	2.957	1.465
30	122.659	12.642	2.108	3.472	2.965	1.472

14.30 Shown here are the unit production figures for three farm products for 10 years. Use these data and a stepwise regression analysis to predict corn production by the production of soybeans and wheat. Comment on the results.

Corn (million bushels)	Soybeans (million bushels)	Wheat (million bushels)
4,152	1,127	1,352
6,639	1,798	2,381
4,175	1,636	2,420
7,672	1,861	2,595
8,876	2,099	2,424
8,226	1,940	2,091
7,131	1,938	2,108
4,929	1,549	1,812
7,525	1,924	2,037
7,933	1,922	2,739

14.31 A Canadian supermarket carried out a survey among its customers to predict the factors that influenced the visit frequency to the store. Number of visits refers to the number of times a consumer visited the store in the past 30 days. All the remaining ratings are on a seven-point scale. For example, 7 on satisfaction means that the consumer is very satisfied with the supermarket while 1 means the customer is not at all satisfied with the supermarket. Use the data to develop a regression model to predict the number of visits to the supermarket on the basis of consumer ratings on the remaining variables. Discuss the results, highlighting both the significant and nonsignificant predictors.

Consumer ID	Number of Visits	Familiarity	Satisfaction	Proximity
1	8	7	7	6
2	2	2	3	3
3	3	3	4	3
4	3	3	7	5
5	7	7	7	7
6	6	4	5	4
7	2	2	4	5
8	6	3	5	4
9	6	3	6	4
10	8	9	7	6

Consumer ID	Number of Visits	Familiarity	Satisfaction	Proximity
11	3	4	4	3
12	4	5	6	4
13	9	6	6	5
14	8	6	3	2
15	5	6	5	4
16	3	4	4	3
17	9	6	5	3
18	4	4	5	4
19	7	7	6	6
20	6	6	6	4
21	9	6	4	2
22	5	5	5	4
23	2	3	4	2
24	9	7	6	6
25	6	6	5	3
26	8	6	6	6
27	4	5	5	5
28	2	4	3	2
29	4	4	5	3
30	3	3	7	5

Interpreting the Output

14.32 A stepwise regression procedure was used to analyze a set of 20 observations taken on four predictor variables to predict a dependent variable. The results of this procedure are given next. Discuss the results.

```
STEPWISE REGRESSION OF Y ON 4
PREDICTORS, WITH N = 20
STEP              1        2
CONSTANT        152.2    124.5
X₁              -50.6    -43.4
T-RATIO          7.42     6.13
X₂                        1.36
T-RATIO                   2.13
S                15.2     13.9
R-SQ             75.39    80.59
```

14.33 Shown here are the data for y and three predictors, x_1, x_2, and x_3. A stepwise regression procedure has been done on these data; the results are also given. Comment on the outcome of the stepwise analysis in light of the data.

(continued)

y	x_1	x_2	x_3
94	21	1	204
97	25	0	198
93	22	1	184
95	27	0	200
90	29	1	182
91	20	1	159
91	18	1	147
94	25	0	196
98	26	0	228
99	24	0	242
90	28	1	162
92	23	1	180
96	25	0	219

STEP	1	2	3
CONSTANT	74.81	82.18	87.89
X_3	0.099	0.067	0.071
T-RATIO	6.90	3.65	5.22
X_2		-2.26	-2.71
T-RATIO		-2.32	-3.71
X_1			-0.256
T-RATIO			-3.08
S	1.37	1.16	0.850
R-SQ	81.24	87.82	94.07

14.34 Shown below is output from two Excel regression analyses on the same problem. The first output was done on a "full" model. In the second output, the variable with the smallest absolute t value has been removed, and the regression has been rerun like the second step of a backward elimination process. Examine the two outputs. Explain what happened, what the results mean, and what might happen in a third step.

	A	B	C	D	E	F
1	FULL MODEL:					
2	Regression Statistics					
3	Multiple R	0.567				
4	R Square	0.321				
5	Adjusted R Square	0.208				
6	Standard Error	159.681				
7	Observations	29				
8						
9	ANOVA					
10		df	SS	MS	F	Significance F
11	Regression	4	289856.08	72464.02	2.84	0.046
12	Residual	24	611955.23	25498.13		
13	Total	28	901811.31			
14		Coefficients	Standard Error	Stat	p Value	
15	Intercept	336.79	124.08	2.71	0.012	
16	x_1	1.65	1.78	0.93	0.363	
17	x_2	-5.63	13.47	-0.42	0.680	
18	x_3	0.26	1.68	0.16	0.878	
19	x_4	185.50	66.22	2.80	0.010	
20						
21	SECOND MODEL:					
22	Regression Statistics					
23	Multiple R	0.566				
24	R Square	0.321				
25	Adjusted R Square	0.239				
26	Standard Error	156.534				
27	Observations	29				
28						
29	ANOVA					
30		df	SS	MS	F	Significance F
31	Regression	3	289238.1	96412.7	3.93	0.020
32	Residual	25	612573.2	24502.9		
33	Total	28	901811.3			
34		Coefficients	Standard Error	Stat	p Value	
35	Intercept	342.919	115.34	2.97	0.006	
36	x_1	1.834	1.31	1.40	0.174	
37	x_2	-5.749	13.18	-0.44	0.667	
38	x_4	181.220	59.05	3.07	0.005	

ANALYZING THE DATABASES

see www.wiley.com/canada/black

1. Develop a regression model using the Financial Database. Use Total Revenues, Average Yield, and Dividends per Share to predict Average P/E Ratio for a company. How strong is the model? Use stepwise regression to help sort out the variables. Several of these variables may be measuring similar things. Construct a correlation matrix to explore the possibility of multicollinearity among the predictors.

2. Use the Canadian Stock Market Database to develop a regression model to predict Composite Index from Week of the Month. You will need to treat Week of the Month as a qualitative variable with four subcategories (only use four since not every month has fifth week). Drop out the least significant variable if it is not significant at $\alpha = 0.05$ and rerun the model. How much did R^2 drop? Continue this process until only significant predictors are left. Describe the final model.

CASE

Fytokem Products Inc. Introduces New Tyrostat

Fytokem Products Inc. is a Saskatchewan-based company that was established in 1994. This company produces products by using plant extracts from the Canadian prairies and sells them to cosmetic, pharmaceutical, and personal care companies. From its inception, the number of Fytokem domestic customers was limited and not very enthusiastic about the products that Fytokem offered, leading to poor sales. Fytokem realized that in order to increase its sales, it needed to introduce a new and innovative product and offer it to the larger international market.

Fytokem conducted research and realized that one of the most demanded products in the international market was skin-lightening lotions. The skin-lightening lotion market is very lucrative, worth billions of dollars. For example, Japan used approximately $5.6 billion worth of lotions that contained skin-lightening ingredients in 2001 alone.

In March of 1998, Fytokem unveiled one of its most original and successful products—the Tyrostat. The Tyrostat is a skin-lightening ingredient that is placed in lotions. It can be used to lighten a person's skin and remove age spots.

The Tyrostat was introduced in various countries, and as of 2003, it has been used in approximately 30 cosmetic products and one pharmaceutical product worldwide, including a lotion in Italy and a skin-whitening deodorant in the Thai market. In 2005, the Indian company Unimarck Pharma Ltd. was also interested in the Tyrostat ingredient and signed an agreement with Fytokem to use it in its skin-lightening lotions.

Since Fytokem introduced Tyrostat, the financial health and position of the company has improved significantly. Customer purchases of the Tyrostat ingredient have increased, and, consequently, 2006 year-over-year sales increased by 31% over 2005. This is a very good sign because between 2004 and 2006, sales for Fytokem have increased by an average of 22% annually. Fytokem has seen excellent results over the last few years with the introduction of its Tyrostat product into the international market. Fytokem's continued investment in R&D and improvements in new products has allowed it to develop one of the safest and most effective all-natural skin-lightening ingredients.

Discussion

1. With every business, it is important to evaluate what components are relevant to the size of a customer's purchase. Fytokem's management is interested in determining this information. Suppose its research team is able to obtain appropriate and relevant data on several customer companies. These data will allow Fytokem to analyze what variables may be predictors of the size of the purchase. The data that Fytokem collected from 15 companies include four variables: the total size of the purchase, the size of the purchasing company, the cost of delivery, and the number of similar products that the purchasing company has. Use the techniques learned in this chapter to obtain a multiple regression model to predict the size of the purchase on the basis of all or some of the other variables mentioned above. Determine the goodness of fit of the regression model, and determine which variables (if any) contribute significantly to the prediction of size of purchase.

Size of Purchase ($1,000s)	Company Size ($ millions sales)	Cost of Delivery ($)	Similar Products
26.3	26.3	200	3
87.9	108.1	710	4
11.8	39.7	180	2
33.7	15.3	1120	1
406.5	280.6	2130	1
175.4	98.1	1100	3
104.1	102.7	810	2
512.3	137.4	430	0
381.4	209.1	400	0
85.3	25.3	120	1
101.2	14.1	240	3
28.5	5.9	570	4
233.8	85.5	930	0
465.8	179.2	1980	1
307.2	133.4	770	2

2. Fytokem has been able to gather the following data for the past 10 years regarding average sales, average hours worked per week by a full-time employees, and the number of customers that purchase Fytokem's skin-whitening products. Analyze the average hours worked per week and the number of customers, and interpret how these two variables are relevant to the sales figures. In order to address this, construct scatter plots to analyze the possibility of a relationship between the sales and hours worked per week and the sales and the number of customers. Would it be possible to recode the data by using Tukey's four-quadrant approach? If yes, use and explain the approach. The relationship between these variables may also be examined by using stepwise regression analysis; therefore, let the response variable be the sales figures and allow the predictors to be average number of hours worked per week, number of customers, and any new variables that have been developed through the recoding process. With all the information you have collected, you can now analyze the quadratic relationships, interaction, and any other relationships by using stepwise regression.

Average Sales ($ million)	Hours Worked per Week	Number of Customers
16.4	45	56
16.1	41	51
15.7	42	55
13.8	39	53
12.3	41	38
9.2	40	26
9.9	44	42
10.1	37	59
12.6	33	70
13.8	38	188

CASE (continued)

3. Fytokem is doing well and is growing. However, there is always a risk of reverting back to being the financially unstable company it once was if it does not continue to invest in R&D and develop new products. Fytokem's sales have been increasing significantly over the last few years; however, these sales will eventually begin to flatten out and settle. What if, at this point, Fytokem still continues to hire employees? Below are the data indicating how these figures might look over a 10-year period. By using the sales as the response variable and the number of employees as the predictor, graph the information and then use Tukey's four-quadrant approach to analyze the graph. Now, construct and explore a regression model in order to predict sales by using the number of employees. Analyze the information that you find and determine whether there is any need for concern or any need to contact top management to inform them of any critical issues.

Sales ($ millions)	Number of Employees
21.3	125
23.8	119
29.6	135
32.5	130
36.1	143
35.3	150
37.8	161
34.4	157
37.9	185
35.8	213

References

"Fytokem Announces Record Sales in 2006," TSX Venture Exchange: FYT, April 30, 2007. Website for data source: <http://www.canadanewswire.ca/fr/releases/archive/May2007/01/c3403.html>; "Fytokem Announces Record Second Quarter Financial Results," TSX Venture Exchange: FYT, August 29, 2006, pp. 1–6. Website for data source: <http://www.fytokem.com/news/PR-2006-08-29.pdf>; "Fytokem Announces Second Quarter 2005 Financial Results," TSX Venture Exchange: FYT, August 29, 2005, pp. 1–4. Website for data source: <http://www.fytokem.com/news/PR-2005-08-29.pdf>; "Fytokem—Building on the Science of Nature," Annual Report, 2000, pp. 1–16. Website for data source: <http://www.fytokem.com/investors/annual2000.pdf>; "Fytokem—Company Overview," 2009. Website for data source: <http://www.fytokem.com/company/overview.php>; "Fytokem Introduces New Skin Toner Products," May 5, 1998. Website for data source: <http://findarticles.com/p/articles/mi_m0EIN/is_1998_May_5/ai_n27527160/>; "Fytokem Products Inc. ASE:FYT—First Quarter Report Period Ending March 31, 1998," 1998, pp. 1–6. Website for data source: <http://www.fytokem.com/investors/Q1-1998.pdf>; "Fytokem—Skin Whitening Patent Is Issued to Fytokem," February 26, 2003, p. 1. Website for data source: <http://www.fytokem.com/news/PR-2003-02-26.pdf>; "Lightening in a Bottle," Andy Holloway, March 31, 2003, Canadian Business Online, Website for data source: <http://www.canadianbusiness.com/article.jsp?content=20030331_52810_52810>; "Tyrostat," Skin-Whitening-Products.com, 2009. Website for data source: <http://www.skin-whitening-product.com/skin-whitening-ingredients.html>; "Unimarck Gets Rights to Tyrostat and Canadian Willowherb Product Lines," Biotech Business Week, June 20, 2005. Website for data source: <http://www.newsrx.com/newsletters/Biotech-Business-Week/2005-06-20/06202005333106BB.html>

USING THE COMPUTER

Excel

- Excel does not have model-building search procedure capability. However, Excel can perform multiple regression analysis. The commands are essentially the same as those for simple regression except that the x range of data may include several columns. Excel will determine the number of predictor variables from the number of columns entered into **Input X Range.**
- Begin by selecting the **Data** tab on the Excel worksheet. From the **Analysis** panel at the right top of the **Data** worksheet, click on **Data Analysis.** If your Excel worksheet does not show the **Data Analysis** option, then you can load it as an add-in. From the **Data Analysis** pull-down menu,

select **Regression.** In the **Regression** dialogue box, input the location of the y values in **Input Y Range.** Input the location of the x values in **Input X Range.** Input **Labels** and input **Confidence Level.** To pass the line through the origin, check **Constant is Zero.** To print out the raw residuals, check **Residuals.** To print out residuals converted to z scores, check **Standardized Residuals.** For a plot of the residuals, check **Residual Plots.** For a plot of the line through the points, check **Line Fit Plots.**

- Standard output includes R, R^2, and s_e; an ANOVA table with the F test, the slope and intercept, t-statistics, and associated p values; and any optionally requested output such as graphs or residuals.

CHAPTER 15

TIME-SERIES FORECASTING AND INDEX NUMBERS

Learning Objectives

1. How can we understand time-series forecasting techniques?

2. What are the four possible components of time-series data?

3. What are stationary forecasting techniques?

4. How can we use regression models for trend analysis?

5. How can we establish the validity of forecasts?

6. What are the different forms of smoothing techniques?

7. How can we decompose time-series data into their various elements and how can we forecast by using decomposition techniques?

8. What is autocorrelation and how can we test for it?

9. What is autoregression?

10. What are index numbers?

Photodisc/Getty Images

FORECASTING AIR POLLUTION

For the past two decades, there has been heightened awareness of and increased concern over pollution in various forms in different countries around the world. One of the main areas of environmental concern is air pollution. Environment Canada regularly monitors the quality of air around the country. Some of the air pollutants monitored are carbon monoxide emissions, nitrogen oxide emissions, volatile organic compounds, sulphur dioxide emissions, particulate matter, fugitive dust, and lead emissions. Shown below are emission data for two of these air pollution variables, carbon monoxide and nitrogen oxides, over a 19-year period reported by the U.S. Environmental Protection Agency in millions of tonnes.

Year	Carbon Monoxide	Nitrogen Oxides
1985	160.43	23.37
1986	157.55	23.06
1987	156.92	23.21
1988	158.23	23.65
1989	145.62	23.02
1990	139.88	23.16
1991	133.47	22.84
1992	127.82	22.92
1993	123.29	23.01
1994	121.16	23.00
1995	115.01	22.64
1996	116.90	22.49
1997	106.97	22.42
1998	104.67	22.09
1999	103.91	20.73
2000	103.85	20.50
2001	96.43	19.55
2002	101.65	19.14
2003	96.97	18.81

Managerial and Statistical Questions

1. Is it possible to forecast the emissions of carbon monoxide or nitrogen oxides for 2008, 2012, or even 2020 using these data?

2. What techniques best forecast the emissions of carbon monoxide or nitrogen oxides for future years from these data?

Source: Adapted from statistics published as National Transportation Statistics by the Bureau of Transportation Statistics (U.S. Government) at <http://www.bts.gov/publications/national_transportation_statistics/>.

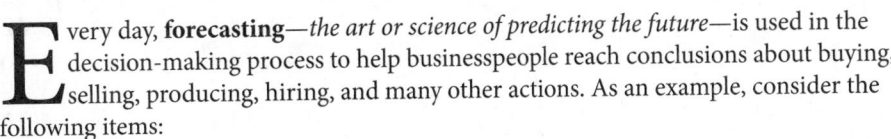

Every day, **forecasting**—*the art or science of predicting the future*—is used in the decision-making process to help businesspeople reach conclusions about buying, selling, producing, hiring, and many other actions. As an example, consider the following items:

- Market watchers predict a resurgence of stock values next year.
- Planners predict a crisis in fish stocks off the coast of Newfoundland.
- Future brightens for solar power.

- Energy minister sees rising demand for oil.
- CEO says difficult times won't be ending soon for the Canadian airline industry.
- Life insurance outlook fades.
- Increased competition from overseas businesses will result in significant layoffs in the Canadian software industry.

How are these and other conclusions reached? What forecasting techniques are used? Are the forecasts accurate? In this chapter, we discuss several forecasting techniques, how to measure the error of a forecast, and some of the problems that can occur in forecasting. In addition, this chapter will focus only on data that occur over time; that is, time-series data.

Time-series data are *data gathered on a given characteristic over a period of time at regular intervals.* Time-series forecasting techniques attempt to account for changes over time by examining patterns, cycles, or trends, or using information about previous time periods to predict the outcome for a future time period. Time-series methods include naive methods, averaging, smoothing, regression trend analysis, and the decomposition of the possible time-series factors, all of which are discussed in subsequent sections.

15.1 INTRODUCTION TO FORECASTING

Virtually all areas of business, including production, sales, employment, transportation, distribution, and inventory, produce and maintain time-series data. Table 15.1 provides an example of time-series data containing the bond yield rates of three-month treasury bills for a 17-year period. Why does the average yield differ from year to year? Is it possible to use these time series data to predict average yields for year 18 or ensuing years? Figure 15.1 is a graph of these data over time. A graphical depiction of time-series data can often give a clue about any trends, cycles, or relationships that might exist there. Does the graph in

Table 15.1		
Bond Yields of Three-Month Treasury Bills	**Year**	**Average Yield**
	1	14.03%
	2	10.69
	3	8.63
	4	9.58
	5	7.48
	6	5.98
	7	5.82
	8	6.69
	9	8.12
	10	7.51
	11	5.42
	12	3.45
	13	3.02
	14	4.29
	15	5.51
	16	5.02
	17	5.07

Figure 15.1

Excel Graph of Bond Yield Time-Series Data

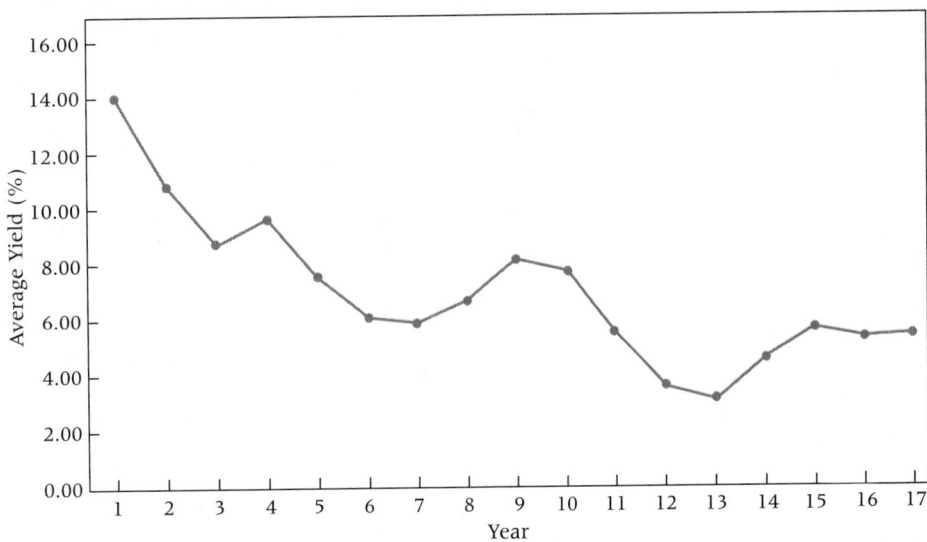

Figure 15.1 show that bond yields are decreasing? Will next year's yield rate be lower or is a cycle occurring in these data that will result in an increase?

Time-series data have several implications for businesses. For example, retail sales may surge during the holiday season and may show a slump in the period that follows the holiday season. Businesses need to identify this pattern to control inventory. Customer calls to a call centre may go up or down depending on the time of the day. Businesses need to know this pattern for appropriate staffing. Thus, we need to be able to answer many questions with regard to time series. To answer such questions, it is sometimes helpful to determine which of the four components of time-series data exist in the data being studied.

TIME-SERIES COMPONENTS

It is generally believed that time-series data are composed of four elements: trend, cyclicality, seasonality, and irregularity. Not all time-series data have all these elements. Consider Figure 15.2, which shows the effects of these time-series elements on data over a period of 13 years.

Figure 15.2

Time-Series Effects

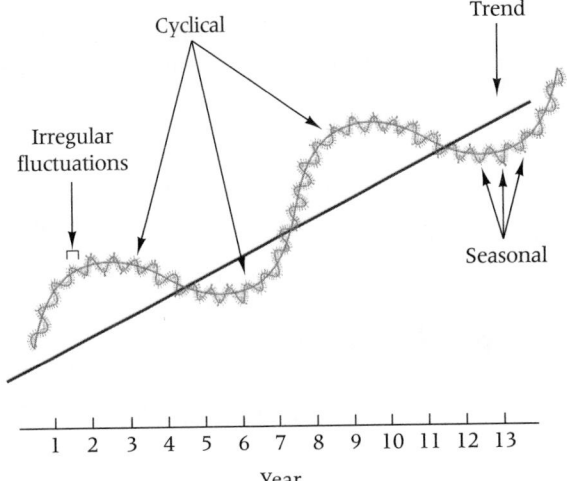

The long-term general direction of data is referred to as **trend.** Notice that even though the data depicted in Figure 15.2 move through upward and downward periods, the general direction or trend is increasing (denoted in Figure 15.2 by the line). **Cycles** are *patterns of highs and lows through which data move over time periods usually of more than a year.* Notice that the data in Figure 15.2 seemingly move through two periods or cycles of highs and lows over a 13-year period. Time-series data that do not extend over a long period of time may not have enough "history" to show **cyclical effects. Seasonal effects,** on the other hand, are *shorter cycles, which usually occur in time periods of less than one year.* Often seasonal effects are measured by the month, but they may occur by quarter, or may be measured in as small a time frame as a week or even a day. Note the seasonal effects shown in Figure 15.2 as up and down cycles, many of which occur during a one-year period. **Irregular fluctuations** are *rapid changes or "blips" in the data, which occur in even shorter time frames than seasonal effects.* Irregular fluctuations can happen as often as day to day. They are subject to momentary change and are often unexplained. Note the irregular fluctuations in the data of Figure 15.2.

Observe again the bond yield data depicted in Figure 15.1. The general trend seems to move downward and contain two cycles. Each of the cycles traverses approximately five to eight years. It is possible, although not displayed here, that seasonal periods of highs and lows within each year result in seasonal bond yields. In addition, irregular daily fluctuations of bond yield rates may occur but are unexplainable.

Time-series data that contain no trend, cyclical, or seasonal effects are said to be **stationary.**

Techniques used to forecast stationary data analyze only the irregular fluctuation effects.

THE MEASUREMENT OF FORECASTING ERROR

In this chapter, several forecasting techniques will be introduced that typically produce different forecasts. How does a decision maker know which forecasting technique is doing the best job in predicting the future? One way is to compare forecast values with actual values and determine the amount of **forecasting error** a technique produces. An examination of individual errors gives some insight into the accuracy of the forecasts. However, this process can be tedious, especially for large data sets, and often a single measurement of overall forecasting error is needed for the entire set of data under consideration. Any of several methods can be used to compute error in forecasting. The choice depends on the forecaster's objective, the forecaster's familiarity with the technique, and the method of error measurement used by the computer forecasting software. Several techniques can be used to measure overall error, including mean error (ME), mean absolute deviation (MAD), mean square error (MSE), mean percentage error (MPE), and mean absolute percentage error (MAPE). Here we will consider the mean absolute deviation (MAD) and the mean square error (MSE).

ERROR

The **error of an individual forecast** is *the difference between the actual value and the forecast of that value.*

Error of an Individual Forecast	$e_t = x_t - F_t$
	where
	e_t = the error of the forecast
	x_t = the actual value
	F_t = the forecast value

MEAN ABSOLUTE DEVIATION (MAD)

One measure of overall error in forecasting is the mean absolute deviation, MAD. The **mean absolute deviation (MAD)** is *the mean, or average, of the absolute values of the errors.*

Table 15.2 presents the nonfarm partnership tax returns in the U.S. over an 11-year period along with the forecast for each year and the error of the forecast. An examination of these data reveals that some of the forecast errors are positive and some are negative. In summing these errors in an attempt to compute an overall measure of error, the negative and positive values offset each other, resulting in an underestimation of the total error. The mean absolute deviation overcomes this problem by taking the absolute value of the error measurement, thereby analyzing the magnitude of the forecast errors without regard to direction.

Mean Absolute Deviation	$$\text{MAD} = \frac{\sum |e_i|}{\text{Number of Forecasts}}$$

The mean absolute error can be computed for the forecast errors in Table 15.2 as follows:

$$\text{MAD} = \frac{|56.0| + |111.8| + |93.5| + |91.0| + |106.3| + |83.9| + |42.2| + |14.7| + |-41.6| + |-33.5|}{10} = 67.45$$

Table 15.2

Nonfarm Partnership Tax Returns

Year	Actual	Forecast	Error
1	1,402	—	—
2	1,458	1,402	56.0
3	1,553	1,441.2	111.8
4	1,613	1,519.5	93.5
5	1,676	1,585.0	91.0
6	1,755	1,648.7	106.3
7	1,807	1,723.1	83.9
8	1,824	1,781.8	42.2
9	1,826	1,811.3	14.7
10	1,780	1,821.6	−41.6
11	1,759	1,792.50	−33.5

MEAN SQUARE ERROR (MSE)

The **mean square error (MSE)** is another way to circumvent the problem of the cancelling effects of positive and negative forecast errors. The MSE is *computed by squaring each error (thus creating a positive number) and averaging the squared errors*. The following formula states it more formally.

Mean Square Error	$$MSE = \frac{\sum e_i^2}{\text{Number of Forecasts}}$$

The mean square error can be computed for the errors shown in Table 15.2 as follows:

$$MSE = \left[\frac{56.0^2 + 111.8^2 + 93.5^2 + 91.0^2 + 106.3^2 + 83.9^2 + 42.2^2 + 14.7^2 + (-41.6)^2 + (-33.5)^2}{10} \right]$$
$$= 5,584.7$$

Selection of a particular mechanism for computing error is up to the forecaster. It is important to understand that different error techniques will yield different information. The business researcher should be informed enough about the various error measurement techniques to make an educated evaluation of the forecasting results.

15.1 Problems

15.1 Use the forecast errors given here to compute MAD and MSE. Discuss the information yielded by each type of error measurement.

Period	e
1	2.3
2	1.6
3	−1.4
4	1.1
5	0.3
6	−0.9
7	−1.9
8	−2.1
9	0.7

15.2 Determine the error for each of the following forecasts. Compute MAD and MSE.

Period	Value	Forecast	Error
1	202	—	—
2	191	202	
3	173	192	

(continued)

Period	Value	Forecast	Error
4	169	181	
5	171	174	
6	175	172	
7	182	174	
8	196	179	
9	204	189	
10	219	198	
11	227	211	

15.3   Using the following data, determine the values of MAD and MSE. Which of these measurements of error seems to yield the best information about the forecasts? Why?

Period	Value	Forecast
1	19.4	16.6
2	23.6	19.1
3	24.0	22.0
4	26.8	24.8
5	29.2	25.9
6	35.5	28.6

15.4   Figures for acres of tomatoes harvested from an 11-year period follow. With these data, forecasts have been made by using techniques presented later in this chapter. Compute MAD and MSE on these forecasts. Comment on the errors.

Year	Number of Acres	Forecast
1	140,000	—
2	141,730	140,000
3	134,590	141,038
4	131,710	137,169
5	131,910	133,894
6	134,250	132,704
7	135,220	133,632
8	131,020	134,585
9	120,640	132,446
10	115,190	125,362
11	114,510	119,259

15.2 SMOOTHING TECHNIQUES

Several techniques are available to forecast time-series data that are stationary, or that include no significant trend, cyclical, or seasonal effects. These techniques are often referred to as **smoothing techniques** because they *produce forecasts based on "smoothing out" the irregular fluctuation effects in the time-series data.* Three general categories of smoothing techniques are presented here: (1) naive forecasting models, (2) averaging models, and (3) exponential smoothing.

NAIVE FORECASTING MODELS

Naive forecasting models are *simple models in which it is assumed that the more recent time periods of data represent the best predictions or forecasts for future outcomes.* Naive models do not take into account data trend, cyclical effects, or seasonality. For this reason, naive models seem to work better with data that are reported on a daily or weekly basis or in situations that show no trend or seasonality. The simplest of the naive forecasting methods is the model in which the forecast for a given time period is the value for the previous time period:

$$F_t = x_{t-1}$$

where

F_t = the forecast value for time period t

x_{t-1} = the value for time period $t - 1$

As an example, if 532 pairs of shoes were sold by a retailer last week, this naive forecasting model would predict that the retailer will sell 532 pairs of shoes this week. With this naive model, the actual sales for this week will be the forecast for next week.

Table 15.3 presents the average price of lettuce in Canada for a given year. Figure 15.3 presents an Excel graph of the prices over the 12-month period. From these data, we can make a naive forecast of the price of lettuce for January of the next year by using the figure for December, which is 0.823.

Another version of the naive forecast might be to use the price in January of the previous year as the forecast for January of next year, because the business researcher may believe a relationship exists between lettuce prices and the month of the year. In this case, the naive forecast for next January from Table 15.3 is 0.876 (January of the previous year). The forecaster is free to be creative with the naive forecast model method and search for other relationships or rationales within the limits of the time-series data that would seemingly produce a valid forecast.

AVERAGING MODELS

Many naive model forecasts are based on the value of one time period. Often such forecasts become a function of irregular fluctuations of the data; as a result, the forecasts are "oversteered." Using averaging models, a forecaster enters information from several time

Table 15.3		
Average Price of Lettuce in Canada	**Month**	**Average Price ($)**
	January	0.876
	February	0.805
	March	0.813
	April	0.801
	May	0.710
	June	0.751
	July	0.737
	August	0.808
	September	0.771
	October	0.830
	November	0.849
	December	0.823

Figure 15.3

Excel Graph of Lettuce Prices over a 12-Month Period

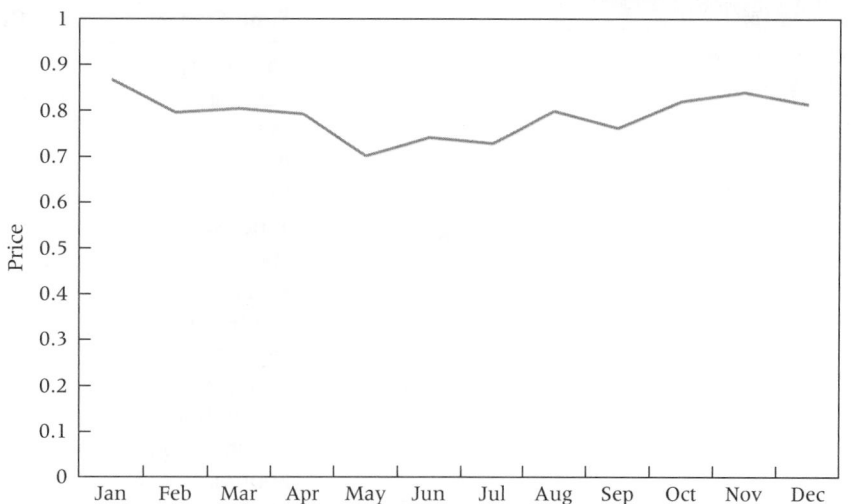

periods into the forecast and "smooths" the data. **Averaging models** are computed by *averaging data from several time periods and using the average as the forecast for the next time period.*

SIMPLE AVERAGES

The most elementary of the averaging models is the **simple average model.** With this model, *the forecast for time period t is the average of the values for a given number of previous time periods,* as shown in the following equation:

$$F_t = \frac{X_{t-1} + X_{t-2} + X_{t-3} + \cdots + X_{t-n}}{n}$$

The data in Table 15.4 provide the costs of residential heating oil for three years. Figure 15.4 displays a graph of these data.

A simple 12-month average could be used to forecast the cost of residential heating oil for September of year 3 from the data in Table 15.4 by averaging the values for September of year 2 through August of year 3 (the preceding 12 months):

$$F_{\text{Sept, year 3}} = \frac{55.7 + 56.7 + 57.2 + 58.0 + 58.2 + 58.3 + 57.7 + 56.7 + 56.8 + 55.5 + 53.8 + 52.8}{12} = 56.45$$

With this **simple average,** the forecast for year 3 September heating oil cost is 56.45¢. Note that none of the previous 12-month figures equal this value and that this average is not necessarily more closely related to values early in the period than to those late in the period. The use of the simple average over 12 months tends to smooth the variations, or fluctuations, that occur during this time.

MOVING AVERAGES

Suppose we were to attempt to forecast the heating oil cost for October of year 3 by using averages as the forecasting method. Would we still use the simple average for September of year 2 through August of year 3 as we did to forecast for September of year 3? Instead of using the same 12 months' average used to forecast September of year 3, it would seem to make sense to use the 12 months prior to October of year 3 (October of year 2 through September of year 3) to average for the new forecast. Suppose in

Table 15.4

Cost of Residential Heating Oil (cents per litre)

Time Frame	Cost of Heating Oil
January (year 1)	66.1
February	66.1
March	66.4
April	64.3
May	63.2
June	61.6
July	59.3
August	58.1
September	58.9
October	60.9
November	60.7
December	59.4
January (year 2)	61.3
February	63.3
March	62.1
April	59.8
May	58.4
June	57.6
July	55.7
August	55.1
September	55.7
October	56.7
November	57.2
December	58.0
January (year 3)	58.2
February	58.3
March	57.7
April	56.7
May	56.8
June	55.5
July	53.8
August	52.8

Figure 15.4

Graph of Heating Oil Cost Data

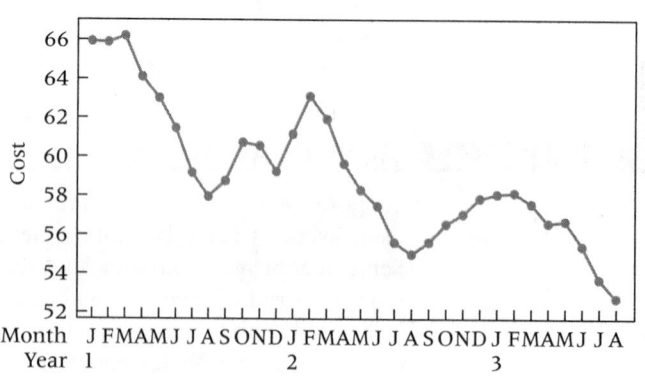

September of year 3 the cost of heating oil is 53.3¢. We could forecast October of year 3 with a new average that includes the same months used to forecast September of year 3, but without the value for September of year 2 and with the value of September of year 3 added:

$$F_{\text{Sept, year 3}} = \frac{56.7 + 57.2 + 58.0 + 58.2 + 58.3 + 57.7 + 56.7 + 56.8 + 55.5 + 53.8 + 52.8 + 53.3}{12}$$

$$= 56.25$$

Computing an average of the values from October of year 2 through September of year 3 produces a moving average, which can be used to forecast the cost of heating oil for October of year 3. In computing this moving average, the earliest of the previous 12 values, September of year 2, is dropped and the most recent value, September of year 3, is included.

A **moving average** is *an average that is updated or recomputed for every new time period being considered.* The most recent information is utilized in each new moving average. This advantage is offset by the disadvantages that (1) it is difficult to choose the optimal length of time for which to compute the moving average, and (2) moving averages do not usually adjust for such time-series effects as trend, cycles, or seasonality. To determine the more optimal lengths for which to compute the moving averages, we would need to forecast with several different average lengths and compare the errors produced by them.

Demonstration Problem 15.1

Shown here are shipments (in $ millions) for electric lighting and wiring equipment over a 12-month period. Use these data to compute a 4-month moving average for all available months.

Month	Shipments
January	1,056
February	1,345
March	1,381
April	1,191
May	1,259
June	1,361
July	1,110
August	1,334
September	1,416
October	1,282
November	1,341
December	1,382

Solution

The first moving average is:

$$\text{4-Month Moving Average} = \frac{1,056 + 1,345 + 1,381 + 1,191}{4} = 1,243.25$$

This first 4-month moving average can be used to forecast the shipments in May. Because 1,259 shipments were actually made in May, the error of the forecast is:

$$\text{Error}_{\text{May}} = 1,259 - 1,243.25 = 15.75$$

Shown next, along with the monthly shipments, are the 4-month moving averages and the errors of forecast when using the 4-month moving averages to predict the next month's shipments. The first moving average is displayed beside the month of May because it is computed by using January, February, March, and April and because it is being used to forecast the shipments for May. The rest of the 4-month moving averages and errors of forecast are as shown.

4-Month Moving Forecast

Month	Shipments	Average	Error
January	1,056	—	—
February	1,345	—	—
March	1,381	—	—
April	1,191	—	—
May	1,259	1,243.25	15.75
June	1,361	1,294.00	67.00
July	1,110	1,298.00	−188.00
August	1,334	1,230.25	103.75
September	1,416	1,266.00	150.00
October	1,282	1,305.25	−23.25
November	1,341	1,285.50	55.50
December	1,382	1,343.25	38.75

The following graph shows the actual shipment values and the forecasted shipment values based on the 4-month moving averages. Notice that the moving averages are "smoothed" in comparison with the individual data values. They appear to be less volatile and seem to be attempting to follow the general trend of the data.

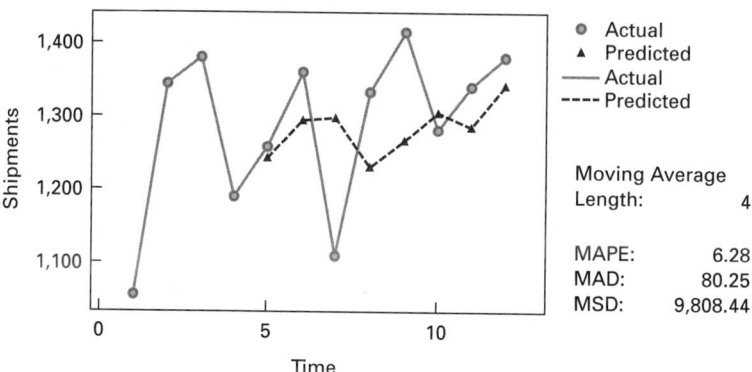

WEIGHTED MOVING AVERAGES

A forecaster may want to place more weight on certain periods of time than on others. For example, a forecaster might believe that the previous month's value is three times as important in forecasting as other months. *A moving average in which some time periods are weighted differently than others* is called a **weighted moving average.**

As an example, suppose a 3-month weighted average is computed by weighting last month's value by 3, the value for the previous month by 2, and the value for the month before that by 1. This weighted average is computed as:

$$\overline{x}_{\text{weighted}} = \frac{3(M_{t-1}) + 2(M_{t-2}) + 1(M_{t-3})}{6}$$

where

M_{t-1} = last month's value

M_{t-2} = value for the previous month

M_{t-3} = value for the month before the previous month

Notice that the divisor is 6. With a weighted average, the divisor always equals the total number of weights. In this example, the value of M_{t-1} counts three times as much as the value for M_{t-3}.

Demonstration Problem 15.2

Compute a 4-month weighted moving average for the electric lighting and wiring data from Demonstration Problem 15.1, using weights of 4 for last month's value, 2 for the previous month's value, and 1 for each of the values from the two months prior to that.

Solution

The first weighted average is:

$$\frac{4(1,191) + 2(1,381) + 1(1,345) + 1(1,056)}{8} = 1,240.875$$

This moving average is recomputed for each ensuing month. Displayed next are the monthly values, the weighted moving averages, and the forecast error for the data.

Month	Shipments	4-Month Weighted Moving Average Forecast	Error
January	1,056	—	—
February	1,345	—	—
March	1,381	—	—
April	1,191	—	—
May	1,259	1,240.9	18.1
June	1,361	1,268.0	93.0
July	1,110	1,316.8	−206.8
August	1,334	1,201.5	132.5
September	1,416	1,272.0	144.0
October	1,282	1,350.4	−68.4
November	1,341	1,300.5	40.5
December	1,382	1,334.8	47.2

Note that in this problem the errors obtained by using the 4-month weighted moving average were greater than most of the errors obtained by using an unweighted 4-month moving average, as shown here.

Forecast Error Unweighted 4-Month Moving Average	Forecast Error, Weighted 4-Month Moving Average
—	—
—	—
—	—
—	—
15.8	18.1
67.0	93.0

(continued)

Forecast Error Unweighted 4-Month Moving Average	Forecast Error, Weighted 4-Month Moving Average
−188.0	−206.8
103.8	132.5
150.0	144.0
−23.3	−68.4
55.5	40.5
38.8	47.2

Larger errors are not always associated with weighted moving averages. The forecaster can experiment with different weights in using the weighted moving average as a technique. Many possible weighting schemes can be used.

EXPONENTIAL SMOOTHING

Another forecasting technique, **exponential smoothing**, is *used to weight data from previous time periods with exponentially decreasing importance in the forecast*. Exponential smoothing is accomplished by multiplying the actual value for the present time period, X_t, by a value between 0 and 1 (the exponential smoothing constant) referred to as α (not the same α used for a Type I error) and adding that result to the product of $(1 - \alpha)$ and the present time period's forecast, F_t. The following is a more formalized version.

Exponential Smoothing	$$F_{t+1} = \alpha \cdot X_t + (1 - \alpha) \cdot F_t$$

where

F_{t+1} = the forecast for the next time period $(t + 1)$
F_t = the forecast for the present time period (t)
X_t = the actual value for the present time period
α = a value between 0 and 1 referred to as the exponential smoothing constant

The value of α is determined by the forecaster. The essence of this procedure is that the new forecast is a combination of the present forecast and the present actual value. If α is chosen to be less than 0.5, less weight is placed on the actual value than on the forecast of that value. If α is chosen to be greater than 0.5, more weight is placed on the actual value than on the forecast value.

As an example, suppose the prime interest rate for a time period is 5% and the forecast of the prime interest rate for this time period was 6%. If the forecast of the prime interest rate for the next period is determined by exponential smoothing with $\alpha = 0.3$, the forecast is:

$$F_{t+1} = (0.3)(5\%) + (1.0 - 0.3)(6\%) = 5.7\%$$

Notice that the forecast value of 5.7% for the next period is weighted more toward the previous forecast of 6% than toward the actual value of 5% because α is 0.3. Suppose we use $\alpha = 0.7$ as the exponential smoothing constant. Then:

$$F_{t+1} = (0.7)(5\%) + (1.0 - 0.7)(6\%) = 5.3\%$$

This value is closer to the actual value of 5% than the previous forecast of 6% because the exponential smoothing constant, α, is greater than 0.5.

To see why this procedure is called exponential smoothing, examine the formula for exponential smoothing again:

$$F_{t+1} = \alpha \cdot X_t + (1 - \alpha) \cdot F_t$$

If exponential smoothing has been used over a period of time, the forecast for F_t will have been obtained by:

$$F_t = \alpha \cdot X_{t-1} + (1 - \alpha) \cdot F_{t-1}$$

Substituting this forecast value, F_t, into the preceding equation for F_{t+1} produces:

$$F_{t+1} = \alpha \cdot X_t + (1 - \alpha)[\alpha \cdot X_{t-1} + (1 - \alpha) \cdot F_{t-1}]$$
$$= \alpha \cdot X_t + \alpha(1 - \alpha) \cdot X_{t-1} + (1 - \alpha)^2 F_{t-1}$$

but:

$$F_{t-1} = \alpha \cdot X_{t-2} + (1 - \alpha)F_{t-2}$$

Substituting this value of F_{t-1} into the preceding equation for F_{t+1} produces:

$$F_{t+1} = \alpha \cdot X_t + \alpha(1 - \alpha) \cdot X_{t-1} + (1 - \alpha)^2 F_{t-1}$$
$$= \alpha \cdot X_t + \alpha(1 - \alpha) \cdot X_{t-1} + (1 - \alpha)^2[\alpha \cdot X_{t-2} + (1 - \alpha)F_{t-2}]$$
$$= \alpha \cdot X_t + \alpha(1 - \alpha) \cdot X_{t-1} + \alpha(1 - \alpha)^2 \cdot X_{t-2} + (1 - \alpha)^3 F_{t-2}$$

Continuing this process shows that the weights on previous-period values and forecasts include $(1 - \alpha)^n$ (exponential values). The following chart shows the values of α, $(1 - \alpha)$, $(1 - \alpha)^2$, and $(1 - \alpha)^3$ for three different values of α. Included is the value of $\alpha(1 - \alpha)^3$, which is the weight of the actual value for three time periods back. Notice the rapidly decreasing emphasis on values for earlier time periods. Exponential smoothing on time-series data places much more emphasis on recent time periods. The choice of α determines the amount of emphasis.

α	$1 - \alpha$	$(1 - \alpha)^2$	$(1 - \alpha)^3$	$\alpha(1 - \alpha)^3$
0.2	0.8	0.64	0.512	0.1024
0.5	0.5	0.25	0.125	0.0625
0.8	0.2	0.04	0.008	0.0064

Some forecasters use the computer to analyze time-series data for various values of α. By setting up criteria with which to judge the forecasting errors, forecasters can select the value of α that best fits the data.

The exponential smoothing formula:

$$F_{t+1} = \alpha \cdot X_t + (1 - \alpha) \cdot F_t$$

can be rearranged algebraically as:

$$F_{t+1} = F_t + \alpha(X_t - F_t)$$

This form of the equation shows that the new forecast, F_{t+1}, equals the old forecast, F_t, plus an adjustment based on α times the error of the old forecast $(X_t - F_t)$. The smaller α is, the less impact the error has on the new forecast and the more the new forecast is like the old. This demonstrates the damping effect of α on the forecasts.

**Demonstration
Problem 15.3**

The total value of Canadian exports over a recent 16-year period as reported by Statistics Canada is given here. Use exponential smoothing to forecast the values for each ensuing time period. Work the problem using $\alpha = 0.2$, 0.5, and 0.8.

Year	Total Exports
1	163,464
2	190,213
3	228,167
4	265,334
5	280,079
6	303,378
7	327,162
8	369,035
9	429,372
10	420,730
11	414,038
12	399,122
13	429,006
14	450,150
15	453,732
16	463,051

Solution

An Excel graph of these data is shown here.

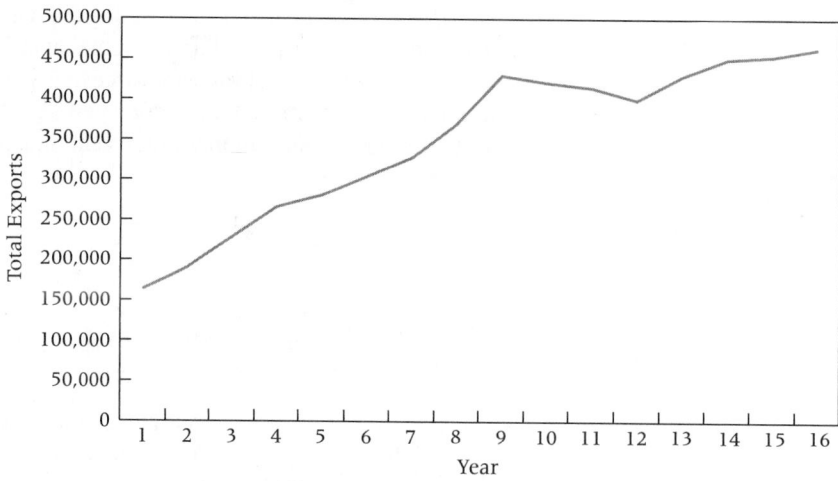

The following table provides the forecasts with each of the three values of alpha. Note that because no forecast is given for the first time period, we cannot compute a forecast based on exponential smoothing for the second period. Instead, we use the actual value for the first period as the forecast for the second period to get started. As examples, the forecasts for the third, fourth, and fifth periods are computed for $\alpha = 0.2$ as follows:

$$F_3 = 0.2(190,213) + 0.8(163,464) = 168,814$$
$$F_4 = 0.2(228,177) + 0.8(168,814) = 180,684$$
$$F_5 = 0.2(265,334) + 0.8(180,684) = 197,614$$

	$\alpha = 0.2$	$\alpha = 0.5$	$\alpha = 0.8$
MAD	83,087	80,530	29,648
MSE	7,769,409,900	7,340,352,772	1,490,164,142

Which value of alpha works best on the data? At the bottom of the preceding analysis are the values of two different measurements of error for each of the three different values of alpha. With each measurement of error, $\alpha = 0.8$ produces the largest measurement of error. Observe from the Excel graph of the original data that the data do not vary up and down considerably. In exponential smoothing, the value of alpha is multiplied by the actual value and $1 - \alpha$ is multiplied by the forecast value to get the next forecast. Because the actual values are not varying considerably, the exponential smoothing value with the smallest alpha seems to be forecasting the best.

STATISTICS IN BUSINESS TODAY

Forecasting the Economy by Scrap Metal Prices?

Economists are constantly on the lookout for valid indicators of a country's economy. Forecasters have sifted through oil indicators, the price of gold on the world markets, stock exchange averages, government-published indexes, and practically anything else that might seem related in some way to the state of the economy.

Would you believe that the price of scrap metal is a popular indicator of economic activity in the U.S.? Several well-known and experienced economic forecasters believe that the price of scrap metal is a good indicator of the industrial economy.

Scrap metal is leftover copper, steel, aluminum, and other metals. Scrap metal is a good indicator of industrial activity because as manufacturing increases, the demand for scrap metals increases, as does the price of scrap metal. Market analyst Donald Fine says that "scrap metal is the beginning of the production chain"; hence, an increasing demand for it is an indicator of increasing manufacturing production. Mr. Fine goes on to say that scrap metal is sometimes a better indicator of the future direction of the economy than many governmental statistics. In some cases, scrap metal correctly predicted no economic recovery when some government measures indicated that a recovery was underway.

Source: Anita Raghavan and David Wessel, "In Scraping Together Economic Data, Forecasters Turn to Scrap-Metal Prices," *The Wall Street Journal*, April 27, 1992, C1.

Concept Check

1. What is a time series? Would you say that data collected at random intervals over a number of years may be called a time series? Why or why not?
2. What are the four components of time-series data? Do all time-series data have all four components?
3. Name two methods of measuring forecasting errors. Why do these methods avoid simply averaging positive and negative errors?
4. What are smoothing techniques and when would you use them?
5. What is the basic assumption behind naive forecasting models?
6. Describe the differences between simple averages, moving averages, and weighted moving averages.
7. Exponential smoothing is a form of weighted average. How is weighting done in exponential smoothing?

15.5 Use the following time-series data to answer the given questions.

Time Period	Value	Time Period	Value
1	27	6	66
2	31	7	71
3	58	8	86
4	63	9	101
5	59	10	97

a. Develop forecasts for periods 5 through 10 using 4-month moving averages.
b. Develop forecasts for periods 5 through 10 using 4-month weighted moving averages. Weight the most recent month by a factor of 4, the previous month by 2, and the other months by 1.
c. Compute the errors of the forecasts in parts (a) and (b) and observe the differences in the errors forecast by the two different techniques.

15.6 Following are time-series data for eight different periods. Use exponential smoothing to forecast the values for periods 3 through 8. Use the value for the first period as the forecast for the second period. Compute forecasts using two different values of alpha, $\alpha = 0.1$ and $\alpha = 0.8$. Compute the errors for each forecast and compare the errors produced by using the two different exponential smoothing constants.

Time Period	Value	Time Period	Value
1	211	5	242
2	228	6	227
3	236	7	217
4	241	8	203

15.7 Following are time-series data for nine time periods. Use exponential smoothing with constants of 0.3 and 0.7 to forecast time periods 3 through 9. Let the value for time period 1 be the forecast for time period 2. Compute additional forecasts for time periods 4 through 9 using a 3-month moving average. Compute the errors for the forecasts and discuss the size of the errors under each method.

Time Period	Value	Time Period	Value
1	9.4	6	11
2	8.2	7	10.3
3	7.9	8	9.5
4	9	9	9.1
5	9.8		

15.8 Shown here are the average after-tax income for household with two or people.
a. Use these data to develop forecasts for the year 2004 using a 5-year moving average.
b. Use these data to develop forecasts for the year 2004 using a 5-year weighted moving average. Weight the most recent year by 6, the previous year by 4, the year before that by 2, and the other years by 1.
c. Compute the errors of the forecasts in parts (a) and (b) and observe the differences in the errors of the forecasts.

Year	Avg After-tax Income (HH 2 or more)
1991	52
1992	52
1993	51.2
1994	51.5
1995	51.6
1996	51.9
1997	52.9
1998	54.7
1999	56.3
2000	58.1
2001	60.4
2002	60.4
2003	59.9

Source: Data excerpted from *Market Research Handbook 2005*, published by Statistics Canada.

15.9   The following data show the number of issues from initial public offerings (IPOs) for a 13-year period released by the Securities Data Company. Use these data to develop forecasts for the years 3 through 13 using exponential smoothing techniques with alpha values of 0.2 and 0.9. Let the forecast for year 2 be the value for year 1. Compare the results by examining the errors of the forecasts.

Year	Number of Issues
1	332
2	694
3	518
4	222
5	209
6	172
7	366
8	512
9	667
10	571
11	575
12	865
13	609

15.3 TREND ANALYSIS

There are several ways to determine trend in time-series data, and one of the more prominent is regression analysis. In Section 12.9, we explored the use of simple regression analysis in determining the equation of a trend line. In time-series regression trend analysis, the response variable, Y, is the variable being forecast, and the independent variable, X, represents time.

Many possible trend fits can be explored with time-series data. In this section, we examine only the linear model and the quadratic model because they are the easiest to understand and simplest to compute. Because seasonal effects can confound trend analysis, it is assumed here that no seasonal effects occur in the data or they were removed prior to determining the trend.

LINEAR REGRESSION TREND ANALYSIS

The data in Table 15.5 represent 35 years of data on the average length of the workweek in Canada for factory workers. A regression line can be fit to these data by using the time periods as the independent variable and length of workweek as the dependent variable. Because the time periods are consecutive, they can be renumbered from 1 to 35 and entered as X along with the time-series data (Y) into a regression analysis. The linear model explored in this example is:

$$Y_i = \beta_0 + \beta_1 X_{ti} + \varepsilon_i$$

where

Y_i = data value for period i
X_{ti} = ith time period

Figure 15.5 shows the Excel regression output for this example. By using the coefficients of the X variable and intercept, the equation of the trend line can be determined to be

$$\hat{Y} = 37.4161 - 0.0614X_t$$

The slope indicates that for every unit increase in time period, X_t, a predicted decrease of 0.0614 occurs in the length of the average workweek in manufacturing. Because the workweek is measured in hours, the length of the average workweek decreases

Table 15.5	Time Period	Hours	Time Period	Hours
	1	37.2	19	36.0
Average Hours per Week in Manufacturing by Factory Workers	2	37.0	20	35.7
	3	37.4	21	35.6
	4	37.5	22	35.2
	5	37.7	23	34.8
	6	37.7	24	35.3
	7	37.4	25	35.6
	8	37.2	26	35.6
	9	37.3	27	35.6
	10	37.2	28	35.9
	11	36.9	29	36.0
	12	36.7	30	35.7
	13	36.7	31	35.7
	14	36.5	32	35.5
	15	36.3	33	35.6
	16	35.9	34	36.3
	17	35.8	35	36.5
	18	35.9		

Source: Data prepared by the U.S. Bureau of Labor Statistics, Office of Productivity and Technology.

Figure 15.5

Excel Regression Output for Hours Worked Using Linear Trend

	A	B	C	D	E	F
1	SUMMARY OUTPUT					
2	Regression Statistics					
3	Multiple R	0.782				
4	R Square	0.611				
5	Adjusted R Square	0.600				
6	Standard Error	0.5090				
7	Observations	35				
8						
9	ANOVA					
10		df	SS	MS	F	Significance F
11	Regression	1	13.4467	13.4467	51.91	0.000000029
12	Residual	33	8.5487	0.2591		
13	Total	34	21.9954			
14						
15		Coefficients	Standard Error	t Stat	p Value	
16	Intercept	37.4161	0.1758	212.81	0.00000000	
17	Year	−0.0614	0.0085	−7.20	0.00000003	

by an average of $(0.0614)(60 \text{ minutes}) = 3.7$ minutes each year in manufacturing. The Y intercept, 37.4161, indicates that in the year prior to the first period of these data the average workweek was 37.4161 hours.

The probability of the t ratio (0.00000003) indicates that significant linear trend is present in the data. In addition, $R^2 = 0.611$ indicates considerable predictability in the model. Inserting the various period values (1, 2, 3, ..., 35) into the preceding regression equation produces the predicted values of Y that are the trend. For example, for period 23 the predicted value is:

$$\hat{Y} = 37.4161 - 0.0614(23) = 36.0 \text{ hours}$$

The model was developed with 35 periods (years). From this model, the average workweek in manufacturing for period 41 (the 41st year) can be forecast:

$$\hat{Y} = 37.4161 - 0.0614(41) = 34.9 \text{ hours}$$

Figure 15.6 presents an Excel scatter plot of the average workweek lengths over the 35 periods (years). In this Excel plot, the trend line has been fitted through the points.

Figure 15.6

Excel Graph of Manufacturing Data with Trend Line

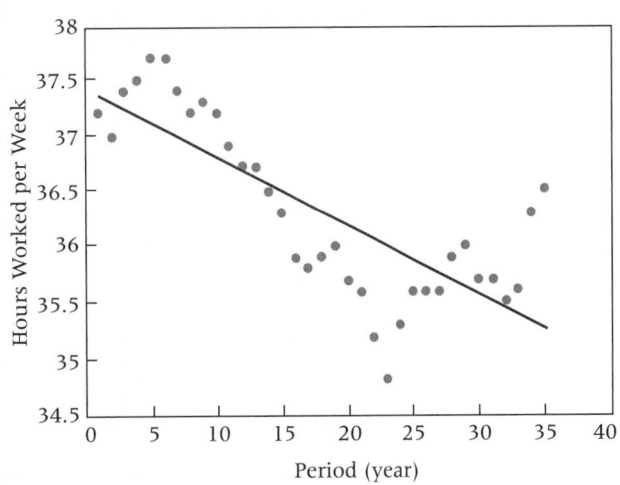

Observe the general downward trend of the data, but also note the somewhat cyclical nature of the points. Because of this pattern, a forecaster might want to determine whether a quadratic model is a better fit for trend.

REGRESSION TREND ANALYSIS USING QUADRATIC MODELS

In addition to linear regression, forecasters can explore using quadratic regression models to predict data by using the time-series periods. The quadratic regression model is:

$$Y_i = \beta_0 + \beta_1 X_{ti} + \beta_2 X_{ti}^2 + \varepsilon_i$$

where

Y_i = the time-series data value for period i

X_{ti} = the ith period

X_{ti}^2 = the square of the ith period

This model can be implemented in time-series trend analysis by using the time periods squared as an additional predictor. Thus, in the hours worked example, besides using $X_t = 1$, 2, 3, 4, …, 35 as a predictor, we would also use $X_{ti}^2 = 1, 4, 9, 16, …, 1,225$ as a predictor.

Table 15.6 provides the data needed to compute a quadratic regression trend model on the manufacturing workweek data. Note that the table includes the original data, the time periods, and the time periods squared.

The Excel computer output for this quadratic trend regression analysis is shown in Figure 15.7. We see that the quadratic regression model produces an R^2 of 0.761 with both X_t and X_t^2 in the model. The linear model produced an R^2 of 0.611 with X_t alone. The quadratic regression seems to add some predictability to the trend model. Figure 15.8 displays an Excel scatter plot of the workweek data with a second-degree polynomial fit through the data.

Table 15.6					
Time Period	**(Time Period)²**	**Hours**	**Time Period**	**(Time Period)²**	**Hours**
1	1	37.2	19	361	36.0
2	4	37.0	20	400	35.7
3	9	37.4	21	441	35.6
4	16	37.5	22	484	35.2
5	25	37.7	23	529	34.8
6	36	37.7	24	576	35.3
7	49	37.4	25	625	35.6
8	64	37.2	26	676	35.6
9	81	37.3	27	729	35.6
10	100	37.2	28	784	35.9
11	121	36.9	29	841	36.0
12	144	36.7	30	900	35.7
13	169	36.7	31	961	35.7
14	196	36.5	32	1,024	35.5
15	225	36.3	33	1,089	35.6
16	256	35.9	34	1,156	36.3
17	289	35.8	35	1,225	36.5
18	324	35.9			

Data for Quadratic Fit of Manufacturing Workweek Example

Figure 15.7

Excel Regression Output for Manufacturing Example with Quadratic Trend

	A	B	C	D	E	F
1	SUMMARY OUTPUT					
2	Regression Statistics					
3	Multiple R	0.873				
4	R Square	0.761				
5	Adjusted R Square	0.747				
6	Standard Error	0.4049				
7	Observations	35				
8						
9	ANOVA					
10		df	SS	MS	F	Significance F
11	Regression	2	16.7483	8.3741	51.07	0.0000000001
12	Residual	32	5.2472	0.1640		
13	Total	34	21.9954			
14						
15		Coefficients	Standard Error	t Stat	p Value	
16	Intercept	38.1644	0.2177	175.34	0.0000000	
17	Year	−0.1827	0.0279	−6.55	0.0000002	
18	YearSq	0.0034	0.0008	4.49	0.0000876	

Figure 15.8

Excel Graph of Manufacturing Data with a Second-Degree Polynomial Fit

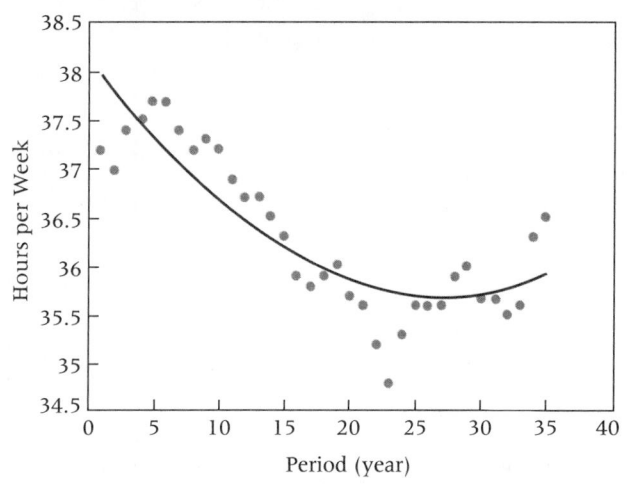

Demonstration Problem 15.4

Following are data on the gross national per capita income of Canadians for 1992 through 2005, as reported by OECD. Use regression analysis to fit a trend line through the data. Explore a quadratic regression trend also. Does either model do well? Compare the two models.

Year	Gross National Income Per Capita ($)
1992	19,288
1993	20,005
1994	21,137
1995	21,968
1996	22,544
1997	23,713
1998	24,704
1999	26,217
2000	27,708
2001	28,506

(continued)

Year	Gross National Income Per Capita ($)
2002	29,154
2003	30,083
2004	31,751
2005	33,435

Source: Data extracted from *OECD Fact book 2007*.

Solution

Recode the time periods as 1 through 14 and let that be X. Run the regression analysis with Per Capita Income as Y, the dependent variable, and the time period as the independent variable. Now square all the X values, resulting in 1, 4, 9, …, 144, 169, 196 and let those formulate a second predictor (X^2). Run the regression analysis to predict the GNI per capita with both the time period variable (X) and the (time period)^2 variable. The results for each of these regression analyses follow.

Linear Trend Analysis

	A	B	C	D	E	F	G
1	SUMMARY OUTPUT						
2	*Regression Statistics*						
3	Multiple *R*	0.996077					
4	*R* Square	0.992169					
5	Adjusted *R* Square	0.991516					
6	Standard Error	414.2495					
7	Observations	14					
8							
9	ANOVA						
10		df	SS	MS	F	Significance F	
11	Regression	1	2.61E+08	2.61E+08	1520.276	5.22E–14	
12	Residual	12	2059231	171602.6			
13	Total	13	2.63E+08				
14							
15		Coefficients	Standard Error	*t* Stat	*p* Value	Lower 95%	Upper 95%
16	Intercept	17698.05	233.8516	75.68072	1.89E–17	17188.54	18207.57
17	Year	1070.859	27.46447	38.99071	5.22E–14	1011.019	1130.699

Quadratic Trend Analysis

	A	B	C	D	E	F	G
1	SUMMARY OUTPUT						
2	*Regression Statistics*						
3	Multiple *R*	0.997757					
4	*R* Square	0.995518					
5	Adjusted *R* Square	0.994703					
6	Standard Error	327.311					
7	Observations	14					
8							
9	ANOVA						
10		df	SS	MS	F	Significance F	
11	Regression	2	2.62E+08	1.31E+08	1221.684	1.21E–13	
12	Residual	11	1178457	107132.5			
13	Total	13	2.63E+08				
14							
15		Coefficients	Standard Error	*t* Stat	*p* Value	Lower 95%	Upper 95%
16	Intercept	18393.71	304.9674	60.31371	3.22E–15	17722.49	19064.94
17	Year	809.9871	93.53428	8.659789	3.05E–06	604.1195	1015.855
18	Year Sqrd	17.39148	6.065476	2.867291	0.015316	4.041461	30.74151

A comparison of the models shows that the linear model accounts for 99.6% of the variability in Per Capita Income, and the quadratic model increases that predictability to 99.8%, a very marginal improvement at best. Even the standard errors of both models are approximately the same. When a more complex model (such as the quadratic model here) does not improve predictability by much, the simpler model should be preferred.

HOLT'S TWO-PARAMETER EXPONENTIAL SMOOTHING METHOD

POINTS OF INTEREST
Trend analysis is a specialized topic and can be quite complex. However, multiple regression analysis provides a means of analyzing trends that is both prominent and intuitive.

The exponential smoothing technique presented in Section 15.2 (single exponential smoothing) is appropriate to use in forecasting stationary time-series data but is ineffective in forecasting time-series data with a trend because the forecasts will lag behind the trend. However, another exponential smoothing technique, Holt's two-parameter exponential smoothing method, can be used for trend analysis. Holt's technique uses weights (β) to smooth the trend in a manner similar to the smoothing used in single exponential smoothing (α). Using these two weights and several equations, Holt's method is able to develop forecasts that include both a smoothing value and a trend value. A more detailed explanation of Holt's two-parameter exponential smoothing method, along with examples and practice problems, can be accessed at Wiley PLUS and at the Wiley website for this text.

Concept Check

1. When you use linear regression to do trend analysis, what is the independent variable?
2. It is known that seasonal effects can confound regression analysis. What would you do if you knew that there were seasonal effects?
3. How do quadratic models differ from linear models in regression analysis?

15.3 Problems

15.10 Shown here are the figures for new manufacturers' orders over a 21-year period. Use a computer to develop a regression model to fit the trend effects for these data. Use a linear model and then try a quadratic model. How well does either model fit the data?

Year	Total Number of New Orders	Year	Total Number of New Orders
1	55,022	12	168,025
2	55,921	13	162,140
3	64,182	14	175,451
4	76,003	15	192,879
5	87,327	16	195,706
6	85,139	17	195,204
7	99,513	18	209,389
8	115,109	19	227,025
9	131,629	20	240,758
10	147,604	21	243,643
11	156,359		

15.11 The table below shows the Consumer Price Index (CPI) for food in a Canadian city for the years 1983 to 2003. Using regression techniques discussed in this section, analyze the data for trend. Develop a scatter plot of the data and fit the trend line through the data. Discuss the strength of the model.

Year	Food
1983	72.8
1984	76.8
1985	79.8
1986	82.7
1987	87.4
1988	88.9
1989	92.1
1990	96.8
1991	100.5
1992	100.0
1993	101.8
1994	102.2
1995	104.4
1996	105.8
1997	107.8
1998	109.5
1999	110.9
2000	111.9
2001	116.9
2002	120.8
2003	122.9

15.12 Shown below is the part-time employment incidence (as a percentage of total employment) in Canada between 1997 and 2005, according to the Organisation for Economic Co-operation and Development (OECD). Plot the data, fit a trend line, and discuss the strength of the regression model. In addition, explore a quadratic trend and compare the results of the two models.

Year	Part-Time Employment (%)
1 (1997)	19.1
2	18.8
3	18.4
4	18.1
5	18.1
6	18.8
7	18.9
8	18.5
9 (2005)	18.3

15.4 SEASONAL EFFECTS

Earlier in the chapter, we discussed the notion that time-series data consist of four elements: trend, cyclical effects, seasonality, and irregularity. In this section, we examine techniques for identifying seasonal effects. Seasonal effects are *patterns of data behaviour that occur in periods of time of less than one year*. How can we separate out the seasonal effects?

DECOMPOSITION

One of the main techniques for isolating the effects of seasonality is **decomposition.** The decomposition methodology presented here uses the multiplicative model as its basis. The multiplicative model is:

$$T \cdot C \cdot S \cdot I$$

where
- T = trend
- C = cyclicality
- S = seasonality
- I = irregularity

To illustrate the decomposition process, we will use the 5-year quarterly time-series data on shipments of household appliances given in Table 15.7. Figure 15.9 provides a graph of these data.

Table 15.7

Shipments of Household Appliances

Year	Quarter	Shipments
1	1	4,009
	2	4,321
	3	4,224
	4	3,944
2	1	4,123
	2	4,522
	3	4,657
	4	4,030
3	1	4,493
	2	4,806
	3	4,551
	4	4,485
4	1	4,595
	2	4,799
	3	4,417
	4	4,258
5	1	4,245
	2	4,900
	3	4,585
	4	4,533

Figure 15.9

Time-Series Graph of Household Appliance Data

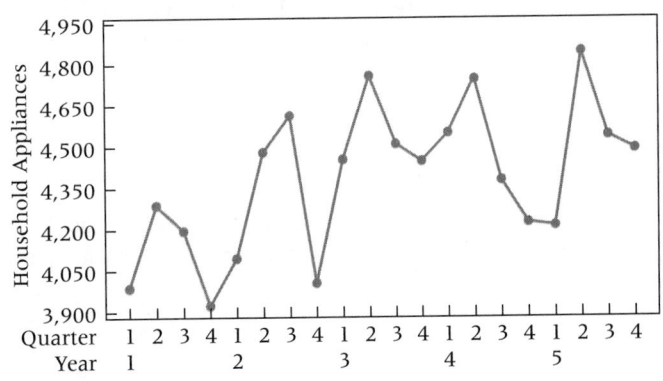

According to the multiplicative time-series model, $T \cdot C \cdot S \cdot I$, the data can contain the elements of trend, cyclical effects, seasonal effects, and irregular fluctuations. The process of isolating the seasonal effects begins by determining $T \cdot C$ for each value and dividing the time-series data $(T \cdot C \cdot S \cdot I)$ by $T \cdot C$. The result is:

$$\frac{T \cdot C \cdot S \cdot I}{T \cdot C} = S \cdot I$$

The resulting expression contains seasonal effects along with irregular fluctuations. After reducing the time-series data to the effects of SI (seasonality and irregularity), a method for eliminating the irregular fluctuations can be applied, leaving only the seasonal effects.

Suppose we start with time-series data that cover several years and are measured in quarterly increments. If we average the data over four quarters, we will have "damped" the seasonal effects of the data because the rise and fall of values during the quarterly periods will have been averaged out over the year.

We begin by computing a 4-quarter moving average for quarter 1 through quarter 4 of year 1, using the data from Table 15.7.

$$\text{4-quarter average} = \frac{4{,}009 + 4{,}321 + 4{,}224 + 3{,}944}{4} = 4{,}124.5$$

The 4-quarter moving average for quarter 1 through quarter 4 of year 1 is 4,124.5 (\$ millions) worth of shipments. Because the 4-quarter average is in the middle of the four quarters, it would be placed in the decomposition table between quarter 2 and quarter 3.

Quarter 1
Quarter 2
   — 4,124.5
Quarter 3
Quarter 4

To remove seasonal effects, we need to determine a value that is "centred" with each month. To find this value, instead of using a 4-quarter moving average, we use 4-quarter moving totals and then sum two consecutive moving totals. This 8-quarter total value is divided by 8 to produce a "centred" 4-quarter moving average that lines up across from a quarter. Using this method is analogous to computing two consecutive 4-quarter moving averages and averaging them, thus producing a value that falls in line with a quarter, in between the two averages. The results of using this procedure on the data from Table 15.7 are shown in Table 15.8 in column 5.

A 4-quarter moving total can be computed on these data starting with quarter 1 of year 1 through quarter 4 of year 1 as follows:

First Moving Total = $4{,}009 + 4{,}321 + 4{,}224 + 3{,}944 = 16{,}498$

In Table 15.8, 16,498 is between quarter 2 and quarter 3 of year 1. The 4-month moving total for quarter 2 of year 1 through quarter 1 of year 2 is:

Second Moving Total = $4{,}321 + 4{,}224 + 3{,}944 + 4{,}123 = 16{,}612$

Table 15.8
Development of 4-Quarter Moving Averages for the Household Appliance Data

Quarter	Actual Values $(T \cdot C \cdot S \cdot I)$	4-Quarter Moving Total	8-Quarter 2-Year Moving Total	4 th Quarter Centred Moving Average	Values to Moving Averages $(S \cdot I) \cdot (100)$
1 (year 1)	4,009				
2	4,321				
		16,498			
3	4,224		33,110	4,139	102.05
		16,612			
4	3,944		33,425	4,178	94.4
		16,813			
1 (year 2)	4,123		34,059	4,257	96.85
		17,246			
2	4,522		34,578	4,322	104.63
		17,332			
3	4,657		35,034	4,379	106.35
		17,702			
4	4,030		35,688	4,461	90.34
		17,986			
1 (year 3)	4,493		35,866	4,483	100.22
		17,880			
2	4,806		36,215	4,527	106.16
		18,335			
3	4,551		36,772	4,597	99
		18,437			
4	4,485		36,867	4,608	97.33
		18,430			
1 (year 4)	4,595		36,726	4,591	100.09
		18,296			
2	4,799		36,365	4,546	105.57
		18,069			
3	4,417		35,788	4,474	98.73
		17,719			
4	4,258		35,539	4,442	95.86
		17,820			
1 (year 5)	4,245		35,808	4,476	94.84
		17,988			
2	4,900		36,251	4,531	108.14
		18,263			
3	4,585				
4	4,533				

In Table 15.8, this value is between quarter 3 and quarter 4 of year 1. The 8-quarter (2-year) moving total is computed for quarter 3 of year 1 as:

$$\text{8-Quarter Moving Total} = 16{,}498 + 16{,}612 = 33{,}110$$

Notice that in Table 15.8 this value is centred with quarter 3 of year 1 because it is between the two adjacent 4-quarter moving totals. Dividing this total by 8 produces the

4-quarter moving average for quarter 3 of year 1 shown in column 5 of Table 15.8:

$$\frac{33{,}110}{8} = 4{,}139$$

Column 3 contains the uncentred 4-quarter moving totals, column 4 contains the 2-year centred moving totals, and column 5 contains the 4-quarter centred moving averages.

The 4-quarter centred moving averages shown in column 5 of Table 15.8 represent $T \cdot C$. Seasonal effects have been removed from the original data (actual values) by summing across the 4-quarter periods. Seasonal effects are removed when the data are summed across the time periods that include the seasonal periods and the irregular effects are smoothed, leaving only trend and cycle.

Column 2 of Table 15.8 contains the original data (actual values), which include all effects ($T \cdot C \cdot S \cdot I$). Column 5 contains only the trend and cyclical effects, $T \cdot C$. If column 2 is divided by column 5, the result is $S \cdot I$, which is displayed in column 6 of Table 15.8.

The values in column 6, sometimes called ratios of actuals to moving average, have been multiplied by 100 to index the values. These values are thus seasonal indexes. An **index number** is *a ratio of a measure taken during one time frame to that same measure taken during another time frame, usually denoted as the time period.* Often the ratio is multiplied by 100 and expressed as a percentage. Index numbers will be discussed more fully in Section 15.6. Column 6 contains the effects of seasonality and irregular fluctuations. Now we must remove the irregular effects.

Table 15.9 contains the values from column 6 of Table 15.8 organized by quarter and year. Each quarter in these data has four seasonal indexes. Throwing out the high and low index for each quarter eliminates the extreme values. The remaining two indexes are averaged as follows for quarter 1:

Quarter 1: 96.85   100.22   100.09   94.84
Eliminate: 94.84 and 100.22
Average the Remaining Indexes:

$$\overline{X}_{\text{Q1 index}} = \frac{96.85 + 100.09}{2} = 98.47$$

Table 15.9	Quarter	Year 1	Year 2	Year 3	Year 4	Year 5
Seasonal Indexes for the Household Appliance Data	1	—	96.85	100.22	100.09	94.84
	2	—	104.63	106.16	105.57	108.14
	3	102.05	106.35	99.00	98.73	—
	4	94.4	90.34	97.33	95.86	—

Table 15.10 gives the final seasonal indexes for all the quarters of these data.

Table 15.10	Quarter	Index
Final Seasonal Indexes for the Household Appliance Data	1	98.47
	2	105.87
	3	100.53
	4	95.13

After the final adjusted seasonal indexes are determined, the original data can be **deseasonalized.** The deseasonalization of actual values is relatively common with data published by the government and other agencies. Data can be deseasonalized by dividing the actual values, which consist of $T \cdot C \cdot S \cdot I$, by the final adjusted seasonal effects:

$$\text{Deseasonalized Data} = \frac{T \cdot C \cdot S \cdot I}{S} = T \cdot C \cdot I$$

Because the seasonal effects are in terms of index numbers, the seasonal indexes must be divided by 100 before deseasonalization. Shown here are the computations for deseasonalizing the household appliance data from Table 15.7 for quarter 1 of year 1:

$$\text{Year 1 Quarter 1 Actual} = 4{,}009$$
$$\text{Year 1 Quarter 1 Seasonal Index} = 98.47$$
$$\text{Year 1 Quarter 1 Deseasonalized Value} = \frac{4{,}009}{0.9847} = 4{,}017.3$$

Table 15.11 gives the deseasonalized data for this example for all years. Figure 15.10 is a graph of the deseasonalized data.

		Table 15.11		
Deseasonalized Household Appliance Data				

Year	Quarter	Shipments Actual Values $(T \cdot C \cdot S \cdot I)$	Seasonal Indexes S	Deseasonalized Data $T \cdot C \cdot I$
1	1	4,009	98.47	4,071
	2	4,321	105.87	4,081
	3	4,224	100.53	4,202
	4	3,944	95.13	4,146
2	1	4,123	98.47	4,187
	2	4,522	105.87	4,271
	3	4,657	100.53	4,632
	4	4,030	95.13	4,236
3	1	4,493	98.47	4,563
	2	4,806	105.87	4,540
	3	4,551	100.53	4,527
	4	4,485	95.13	4,715
4	1	4,595	98.47	4,666
	2	4,799	105.87	4,533
	3	4,417	100.53	4,394
	4	4,258	95.13	4,476
5	1	4,245	98.47	4,311
	2	4,900	105.87	4,628
	3	4,585	100.53	4,561
	4	4,533	95.13	4,765

Figure 15.10

Graph of the Deseasonalized Household Appliance Data

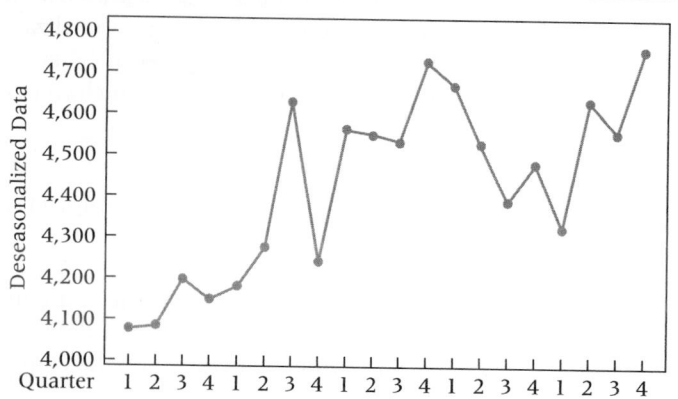

WINTERS' THREE-PARAMETER EXPONENTIAL SMOOTHING METHOD

POINTS OF INTEREST
Understanding seasonality is critical to businesses. It affects many factors, such as inventory levels, staffing requirements, and even sale periods.

Holt's two-parameter exponential smoothing method can be extended to include seasonal analysis. This technique, referred to as Winters' method, not only smoothes observations and trend but also smoothes the seasonal effects. In addition to the single exponential smoothing weight of α and the trend weight of β, Winters' method introduces γ, a weight for seasonality. Using these three weights and several equations, Winters' method is able to develop forecasts that include a smoothing value for observations, a trend value, and a seasonal value. A more detailed explanation of Winters' three-parameter exponential smoothing method along with examples and practice problems is presented in WileyPLUS and at the Wiley website for this text.

Concept Check

1. What are seasonal effects? What is the main technique used to isolate seasonality?
2. Briefly describe Winters' three-parameter exponential smoothing method.

15.4 Problems

15.13   Given below are the monthly prices of orange juice for 24 months. Use these data to compute 12-month centred moving averages ($T \cdot C$). Using these computed values, determine the seasonal effects ($S \cdot I$).

		Orange Juice Price ($)
Year 1	January	1.847
	February	1.881
	March	1.808
	April	1.785
	May	1.731
	June	1.825
	July	1.836
	August	1.887
	September	1.899
	October	1.972

(continued)

		Orange Juice Price ($)
	November	1.906
	December	1.836
Year 2	January	1.958
	February	1.877
	March	1.826
	April	1.865
	May	1.816
	June	1.917
	July	1.879
	August	1.874
	September	1.818
	October	1.939
	November	1.928
	December	1.969

15.14 The following table shows shipment data for paperboard containers and boxes. The shipment figures are given in millions of dollars. Use the data to analyze the effects of seasonality, trend, and cycle. Develop the trend model with a linear model only.

Month	Shipments	Month	Shipments
January (year 1)	1,891	January (year 3)	2,183
February	1,986	February	2,230
March	1,987	March	2,222
April	1,987	April	2,319
May	2,000	May	2,369
June	2,082	June	2,529
July	1,878	July	2,267
August	2,074	August	2,457
September	2,086	September	2,524
October	2,045	October	2,502
November	1,945	November	2,314
December	1,861	December	2,277
January (year 2)	1,936	January (year 4)	2,336
February	2,104	February	2,474
March	2,126	March	2,546
April	2,131	April	2,566
May	2,163	May	2,473
June	2,346	June	2,572
July	2,109	July	2,336
August	2,211	August	2,518
September	2,268	September	2,454
October	2,285	October	2,559
November	2,107	November	2,384
December	2,077	December	2,305

(continued)

Month	Shipments	Month	Shipments
January (year 5)	2,389	January (year 6)	2,377
February	2,463	February	2,381
March	2,522	March	2,268
April	2,417	April	2,407
May	2,468	May	2,367
June	2,492	June	2,446
July	2,304	July	2,341
August	2,511	August	2,491
September	2,494	September	2,452
October	2,530	October	2,561
November	2,381	November	2,377
December	2,211	December	2,277

15.5 AUTOCORRELATION AND AUTOREGRESSION

Data values gathered over time are often correlated with values from past time periods. This characteristic can cause problems in the use of regression in forecasting and at the same time can open some opportunities. One of the problems that can occur in regressing data over time is autocorrelation.

AUTOCORRELATION

Autocorrelation, or **serial correlation,** occurs in data *when the error terms of a regression forecasting model are correlated.* The likelihood of this occurring with business data increases over time, particularly with economic variables. Autocorrelation can be a problem in using regression analysis as the forecasting method because one of the assumptions underlying regression analysis is that the error terms are independent or random (not correlated). In most business analysis situations, the correlation of error terms is likely to occur as positive autocorrelation (positive errors are associated with positive errors of comparable magnitude and negative errors are associated with negative errors of comparable magnitude).

When autocorrelation occurs in a regression analysis, several possible problems might arise. First, the estimates of the regression coefficients no longer have the minimum variance property and may be inefficient. Second, the variance of the error terms may be greatly underestimated by the mean square error value. Third, the true standard deviation of the estimated regression coefficient may be seriously underestimated. Fourth, the confidence intervals and tests using the t and F distributions are no longer strictly applicable.

First-order autocorrelation results from correlation between the error terms of adjacent time periods (as opposed to two or more previous periods). If first-order autocorrelation is present, the error for one time period, e_t, is a function of the error of the previous time period, e_{t-1}, as follows:

$$e_t = \rho e_{t-1} + v_t$$

The first-order autocorrelation coefficient, ρ, measures the correlation between the error terms. It is a value that lies between -1 and 0 and $+1$, as does the coefficient of correlation discussed in Chapter 12. v_t is a normally distributed independent error term. If positive autocorrelation is present, the value of ρ is between 0 and +1. If the value of ρ is 0, $e_t = v_t$, which means there is no autocorrelation and e_t is just a random, independent error term.

One way to test to determine whether autocorrelation is present in a time-series regression analysis is by using the **Durbin-Watson test** for autocorrelation. Shown next is the formula for computing a Durbin-Watson test for autocorrelation.

Durbin-Watson Test	
	$$D = \frac{\sum_{t=2}^{n}(e_t - e_{t-1})^2}{\sum_{t=1}^{n}e_t^2}$$

where
n = the number of observations

Note from the formula that the Durbin-Watson test involves finding the difference between successive values of error $(e_t - e_{t-1})$. If errors are positively correlated, this difference will be smaller than with random or independent errors. Squaring this term eliminates the cancellation effects of positive and negative terms.

The null hypothesis for this test is that there is no autocorrelation. For a two-tailed test, the alternative hypothesis is that there is autocorrelation:

$$H_0: \rho = 0$$
$$H_a: \rho \neq 0$$

As mentioned before, most business forecasting autocorrelation is positive autocorrelation. In most cases, a one-tailed test is used:

$$H_0: \rho = 0$$
$$H_a: \rho > 0$$

In the Durbin-Watson test, D is the observed value of the Durbin-Watson statistic using the residuals from the regression analysis. A critical value for D can be obtained from the values of α, n, and k by using Table A.9 in the appendix, where α is the level of significance, n is the number of data items, and k is the number of predictors. Two Durbin-Watson tables are given in the appendix. One table contains values for $\alpha = 0.01$ and the other for $\alpha = 0.05$. The Durbin-Watson tables in Appendix A include values for d_U and d_L. These values range from 0 to 4. If the observed value of D is above d_u, we fail to reject the null hypothesis and there is no significant autocorrelation. If the observed value of D is below d_L, the null hypothesis is rejected and there is autocorrelation. Sometimes the observed statistic, D, is between the values of d_u and d_L. In this case, the Durbin-Watson test is inconclusive.

As an example, consider Table 15.12, which contains crude oil production and natural gas withdrawal data for the U.S. over a 25-year time period published by the U.S. Energy Information Administration in its Annual Energy Review. A regression line can be fit through these data to determine whether the amount of natural gas withdrawals can be predicted by the amount of crude oil production. The resulting errors of prediction can be tested by the Durbin-Watson statistic for the presence of significant positive autocorrelation by using $\alpha = 0.05$. The hypotheses are:

$$H_0: \rho = 0$$
$$H_a: \rho > 0$$

Table 15.12

U.S. Crude Oil Production and Natural Gas Withdrawals over a 25-Year Time Period

Year	Crude Oil Production (1,000s)	Natural Gas Withdrawals from Natural Gas Wells (1,000s)
1	8.597	17.573
2	8.572	17.337
3	8.649	15.809
4	8.688	14.153
5	8.879	15.513
6	8.971	14.535
7	8.680	14.154
8	8.349	14.807
9	8.140	15.467
10	7.613	15.709
11	7.355	16.054
12	7.417	16.018
13	7.171	16.165
14	6.847	16.691
15	6.662	17.351
16	6.560	17.282
17	6.465	17.737
18	6.452	17.844
19	6.252	17.729
20	5.881	17.590
21	5.822	17.726
22	5.801	18.129
23	5.746	17.795
24	5.681	17.819
25	5.430	17.739

The following regression equation was obtained:

$$\text{Natural Gas Withdrawals} = 22.7372 - 0.8507 \, (\text{Crude Oil Production})$$

Using the values for crude oil production (X) from Table 15.12 and the regression equation shown here, predicted values of Y (natural gas withdrawals) can be computed. From the predicted values and the actual values, the errors of prediction for each time interval, e_t, can be calculated. Table 15.13 shows the values of $\hat{Y}$, e_t, e_t^2, $(e_t - e_{t-1})$, and $(e_t - e_{t-1})^2$ for this example. Note that the first predicted value of Y is:

$$\hat{Y}_1 = 22.7372 - 0.8507(8.597) = 15.4237$$

The error for year 1 is:

$$\text{Actual}_1 - \text{Predicted}_1 = 17.573 - 15.4237 = 2.1493$$

The value of $e_t - e_{t-1}$ for year 1 and year 2 is computed by subtracting the error for year 1 from the error for year 2:

$$e_{\text{year2}} - e_{\text{year1}} = 1.8920 - 2.1493 = -0.2573$$

Year	$\hat{Y}$	e_t	e_t^2	$e_t - e_{t-1}$	$(e_t - e_{t-1})^2$
1	15.4237	2.1493	4.6195	—	—
2	15.445	1.892	3.5797	0.2573	0.0662
3	15.3795	0.4295	0.1845	1.4625	2.1389
4	15.3463	−1.1933	1.4240	1.6228	2.6335
5	15.1838	0.3292	0.1084	1.5225	2.3180
6	15.1056	−0.5706	0.3256	0.8998	0.8096
7	15.3531	−1.1991	1.4378	0.6285	0.3950
8	15.6347	−0.8277	0.6851	0.3714	0.1379
9	15.8125	−0.3455	0.1194	0.4822	0.2325
10	16.2608	−0.5518	0.3045	0.2063	0.0426
11	16.4803	−0.4263	0.1817	0.1255	0.0158
12	16.4276	−0.4096	0.1678	0.0167	0.0003
13	16.6368	−0.4718	0.2226	0.0622	0.0039
14	16.9125	−0.2215	0.0491	0.2503	0.0627
15	17.0698	0.2812	0.0791	0.5027	0.2527
16	17.1566	0.1254	0.0157	0.1558	0.0243
17	17.2374	0.4996	0.2496	0.3742	0.1400
18	17.2485	0.5955	0.3546	0.0959	0.0092
19	17.4186	0.3104	0.0963	0.2851	0.0813
20	17.7342	−0.1442	0.0208	0.4546	0.2067
21	17.7844	−0.0584	0.0034	0.0858	0.0074
22	17.8023	0.3267	0.1067	0.3851	0.1483
23	17.8491	−0.0541	0.0029	0.3808	0.1450
24	17.9044	−0.0854	0.0073	0.0313	0.0010
25	18.1179	−0.3789	0.1436	0.02935	0.0861
			$\Sigma e_t^2 = 14.4897$		$\Sigma(e_t - e_{t-1})^2 = 9.9589$

Table 15.13

Predicted Values and Error Terms for the Crude Oil Production and Natural Gas Withdrawal Data

The Durbin-Watson statistic can now be computed:

$$D = \frac{\sum_{t=2}^{n}(e_t - e_{t-1})^2}{\sum_{t=1}^{n} e_t^2} = \frac{9.9589}{14.4897} = 0.6873$$

Because we used a simple linear regression, the value of k is 1. The sample size, n, is 25, and $\alpha = 0.05$. The critical values in Table A.9 are:

$$d_U = 1.45 \text{ and } d_L = 1.29$$

Because the computed D statistic, 0.6873, is less than the value of $d_L = 1.29$, the null hypothesis is rejected. A positive autocorrelation is present in this example.

WAYS TO OVERCOME THE AUTOCORRELATION PROBLEM

Several approaches to data analysis can be used when autocorrelation is present. One uses additional independent variables and another transforms the independent variable.

ADDITION OF INDEPENDENT VARIABLES

Often the reason autocorrelation occurs in regression analyses is that one or more important predictor variables have been left out of the analysis. For example, suppose a researcher develops a regression forecasting model that attempts to predict sales of new homes by sales of used homes over some period of time. Such a model might contain significant autocorrelation. The exclusion of the variable prime mortgage interest rate might be a factor driving the autocorrelation between the other two variables. Adding this variable to the regression model might significantly reduce the autocorrelation.

TRANSFORMING VARIABLES

When the inclusion of additional variables is not helpful in reducing autocorrelation to an acceptable level, transforming the data in the variables may help to solve the problem. One such method is the **first-differences approach.** With the first-differences approach, each value of X is subtracted from each succeeding time period value of X; these "differences" become the new and transformed X variable. The same process is used to transform the Y variable. The regression analysis is then computed on the transformed X and transformed Y variables to compute a new model that is hopefully free of significant autocorrelation effects.

Another way is to generate new variables by using the percentage changes from period to period and regressing these new variables. A third way is to use autoregression models.

AUTOREGRESSION

A forecasting technique that takes advantage of the relationship of values (Y_t) to previous period values (Y_{t-1}, Y_{t-2}, Y_{t-3}, …) is called autoregression. **Autoregression** is a multiple regression technique in which the independent variables are time-lagged versions of the dependent variable, which means we try to predict a value of Y from values of Y from previous time periods. The independent variable can be lagged for one, two, three, or more time periods. An autoregressive model containing independent variables for three time periods looks like this:

$$\hat{Y} = b_0 + b_1 Y_{t-1} + b_2 Y_{t-2} + b_3 Y_{t-3}$$

> **POINTS OF INTEREST**
> Autocorrelation and autoregression can distort the underlying relationships among business variables and exaggerate the impact of one business variable on another, leading to incorrect business decisions. Therefore, in doing time-series analysis one should always check for autocorrelation and autoregression.

As an example, we shall attempt to predict the volume of natural gas withdrawal, displayed in Table 15.12, by using data lagged for both one and two time periods. The data used in this analysis are displayed in Table 15.14. Using Excel, a multiple regression model is developed to predict the values of Y_t by the values of Y_{t-1} and Y_{t-2}. The results appear in Figure 15.11. Note that the regression analysis does not use data from years 1 and 2 of Table 15.14 because there are no values for the two lagged variables for one or both of those years.

The autoregression model is:

$$Y_t = 2.4081 + 0.9678 Y_{t-1} - 0.1128 Y_{t-2}$$

The relatively high value of R^2 (74.6%) and relatively small value of s_e (0.693) indicate that this regression model has fairly strong predictability. Interestingly, the one-period lagged variable is quite significant ($t = 4.36$ with a p value of 0.000306), but the two-period lagged variable is not significant ($t = -0.50$ with a p value of 0.62), indicating the presence of first-order autocorrelation.

Table 15.14

Time-Lagged Natural Gas Data

Year	Natural Gas Withdrawal Y_t	One Period Lagged $Y_{t-1}(X_1)$	Two Periods Lagged $Y_{t-2}(X_2)$
1	17.573	—	—
2	17.337	17.573	—
3	15.809	17.337	17.573
4	14.153	15.809	17.337
5	15.513	14.153	15.809
6	14.535	15.513	14.153
7	14.154	14.535	15.513
8	14.807	14.154	14.535
9	15.467	14.807	14.154
10	15.709	15.467	14.807
11	16.054	15.709	15.467
12	16.018	16.054	15.709
13	16.165	16.018	16.054
14	16.691	16.165	16.018
15	17.351	16.691	16.165
16	17.282	17.351	16.691
17	17.737	17.282	17.351
18	17.844	17.737	17.282
19	17.729	17.844	17.737
20	17.590	17.729	17.844
21	17.726	17.590	17.729
22	18.129	17.726	17.590
23	17.795	18.129	17.726
24	17.819	17.795	18.129
25	17.739	17.819	17.795

Figure 15.11

Excel Autoregression Results for Natural Gas Withdrawal Data

	A	B	C	D	E	F
1	SUMMARY OUTPUT					
2	Regression Statistics					
3	Multiple R	0.864				
4	R Square	0.746				
5	Adjusted R Square	0.721				
6	Standard Error	0.693				
7	Observations	23				
8						
9	ANOVA					
10		df	SS	MS	F	Significance F
11	Regression	2	28.3203	14.1602	29.44	0.0000011
12	Residual	20	9.6187	0.4809		
13	Total	22	37.9390			
14						
15		Coefficients	Standard Error	t Stat	p Value	
16	Intercept	2.4081	1.9608	1.23	0.233658	
17	Lagged 1	0.9678	0.2221	4.36	0.000306	
18	Lagged 2	−0.1128	0.2239	−0.50	0.620075	

Autoregression can be a useful tool in locating seasonal or cyclical effects in time series data. For example, if the data are given in monthly increments, autoregression using variables lagged by as much as 12 months can search for the predictability of previous monthly time periods. If data are given in quarterly time periods, autoregression of up to four periods removed can be a useful tool in locating the predictability of data from previous quarters. When the time periods are in years, lagging the data by yearly periods and using autoregression can help in locating cyclical predictability.

Concept Check

1. What is autocorrelation and why does it pose a problem in regression analysis?
2. What statistic is commonly used to measure autocorrelation?
3. Name and describe two methods by which you can overcome the autocorrelation problem.
4. Autocorrelation can be a problem in trend analysis. What about autoregression: what does it do? Is it a problem or a solution?

15.5 Problems

15.15 The following table shows the percentage savings rates in Canada and in the U.S. from 1980 to 2005. Use these data to develop a linear regression model to forecast the percentage change in the Canadian savings rate by the percentage change in the U.S. savings rate. Compute a Durbin-Watson statistic to determine whether significant autocorrelation is present in the model. Let $\alpha = 0.05$.

	1980	1981	1982	1983	1984	1985	1986	1987	1988	1989
Canada	16	17.9	20.7	17.2	17	16	13.7	12.1	12.6	13.3
U.S.	10.3	11.2	11.5	9.2	11.2	9.3	8.5	7.2	7.5	7.4

	1990	1991	1992	1993	1994	1995	1996	1997	1998	1999
Canada	13.3	13.6	13.3	12.1	9.6	9.4	7.2	5	4.9	4.1
U.S.	7.2	7.5	7.6	6.1	5.3	5.1	4.2	3.7	4.5	2.5

	2000	2001	2002	2003	2004	2005
Canada	4.8	5.3	3.5	2.8	2.7	1.2
U.S.	2.4	1.8	2.5	2.4	1.9	−0.4

Source: OECD, 2007.

15.16 Use the data from Problem 15.15 to create a regression forecasting model using the first-differences data transformation. How do the results from this model differ from those obtained in Problem 15.15?

15.17 Given below are the Canadian Producer Price Index (PPI) and the Consumer Price Index (CPI) for the years 1988 to 2005. Use these data to develop a simple regression forecasting model that attempts to predict CPI from PPI. Compute a Durbin-Watson statistic for this regression model and determine whether significant autocorrelation is present. Let $\alpha = 0.05$.

	1988	**1989**	**1990**	**1991**	**1992**	**1993**	**1994**	**1995**	**1996**
PPI	77.3	78.8	79.1	78.2	78.6	81.5	86.4	92.8	93.2
CPI All Items	74.7	78.4	82.1	86.8	88.1	89.7	89.8	91.8	93.2

	1997	**1998**	**1999**	**2000**	**2001**	**2002**	**2003**	**2004**	**2005**
PPI	93.9	94.2	95.9	100	101	101	99.7	102.8	104.4
CPI All Items	94.7	95.7	97.3	100	102.5	104.8	107.7	109.7	112.2

Source: OECD, 2007.

15.18   Use the data in Problem 15.17 to compute a regression model after recoding the data by the first-differences approach. Compute a Durbin-Watson statistic to determine whether significant autocorrelation is present in this first-differences model. Compare this model with the model determined in Problem 15.17, and compare the significance of the Durbin-Watson statistics for the two problems. Let $\alpha = 0.05$.

15.19   Given below is the crude oil production (millions of tonnes) in Canada between 1979 and 2005. Use these time-series data to develop an autoregression model with a one-period lag. Now try an autoregression model with a two-period lag. Discuss the results and compare the two models.

Crude oil production in Canada (million tonnes)

1979	**1980**	**1981**	**1982**	**1983**	**1984**	**1985**	**1986**	**1987**	**1988**	**1989**
84.4	81.4	73.7	73.5	77.3	83.3	84.1	85.5	90.3	93.9	91.8

1990	**1991**	**1992**	**1993**	**1994**	**1995**	**1996**	**1997**	**1998**	**1999**	**2000**
91.6	92	96.4	101.3	105.3	110.3	113.5	119	124.7	119.9	124.8

2001	**2002**	**2003**	**2004**	**2005**
126.6	132.9	140.4	145.8	143.4

Source: OECD, 2007.

15.20   Shown here is the contribution of renewables to energy supply in Canada, shown as a percentage of the total primary energy supply. Use these data to develop an autoregression forecasting model with a two-period lag. Discuss the results of this analysis.

1971	**1972**	**1973**	**1974**	**1975**	**1976**	**1977**	**1978**	**1979**	**1980**	**1981**	**1982**
15.2	15.2	15.4	15.9	14.2	14.3	14.3	14.9	14.7	15.2	16	16.2

1983	**1984**	**1985**	**1986**	**1987**	**1988**	**1989**	**1990**	**1991**	**1992**	**1993**	**1994**
17.1	17.2	17.9	18.1	17.8	16.7	15.4	16.1	16.6	16.6	16.3	16.6

1995	**1996**	**1997**	**1998**	**1999**	**2000**	**2001**	**2002**	**2003**	**2004**	**2005**
16.7	17.1	16.7	16.3	16.7	16.9	16.1	16.7	15.5	15.4	16.4

Source: OECD, 2007.

15.6 INDEX NUMBERS

One particular type of descriptive measure that is useful in allowing comparisons of data over time is the index number. An index number is, in part, a ratio of a measure taken during one time frame to that same measure taken during another time frame, usually denoted as the base period. Often the ratio is multiplied by 100 and is expressed as a percentage. When expressed as a percentage, index numbers serve as an alternative to comparing raw numbers. Index number users become accustomed to interpreting measures for a given time period in light of a base period on a scale in which the base period has an index of 100(%). Index numbers are used to compare phenomena from one time period to another and are especially helpful in highlighting interperiod differences.

Index numbers are widely used around the world to relate information about stock markets, inflation, sales, exports and imports, agriculture, and many other things. Some examples of specific indexes are the employment cost index, price index for construction, index of manufacturing capacity, producer price index, consumer price index, Dow Jones industrial average, index of output, and TSX average. This section, although recognizing the importance of stock indexes and others, will focus on price indexes.

The motivation for using an index number is to reduce data to an easier-to-use, more convenient form. As an example, examine the per capita income in Canada from 1992 through 2005 as shown in Table 15.15. An analyst can describe these data by observing that, in general, Canadian per capita income has been increasing since 1992. How does per capita income in 1997 compare to 1992? How does per capita income in 2000 compare to 1990 or 1992? To answer these questions without index numbers, a business researcher would probably resort to subtracting the per capita income for the years of interest and comparing the corresponding increases or decreases. This process can be tedious and frustrating for decision makers who must maximize their effort in minimal time. Using simple index numbers, the business researcher can transform these data into values that are more usable and make it easier to compare other years to one particular key year.

Table 15.15		
Per Capita Income in Canada	**Year**	**Per Capita Income ($)**
	1992	27,850
	1993	27,600
	1994	27,820
	1995	28,020
	1996	27,900
	1997	28,300
	1998	29,090
	1999	29,670
	2000	30,710
	2001	30,900
	2002	30,650
	2003	30,650
	2004	31,280
	2005	31,850

SIMPLE INDEX NUMBERS AND UNWEIGHTED AGGREGATE PRICE INDEXES

How are index numbers computed? The equation for computing a **simple index number** follows.

Simple Index Number	$$I_i = \frac{X_i}{X_0}(100)$$
	where
	X_0 = the quantity, price, or cost in the base year
	X_i = the quantity, price, or cost in the year of interest
	I_i = the index number for the year of interest

Suppose cost-of-living researchers examining the data from Table 15.15 decide to compute per capita income using 1992 as the base year. The index number for the year 2000 is:

$$I_{2000} = \frac{X_{2000}}{X_{1992}}(100) = \frac{30{,}710}{27{,}850}(100) = 110.3$$

Table 15.16 displays all the index numbers for the data in Table 15.15, with 1992 as the base year, along with the raw data. A cursory glance at these index numbers reveals that the per capita income of Canadians was quite static between 1992 and 1996 and showed faster growth between 1998 and 2000. Because most people are easily able to understand the concept of 100%, it is likely that decision makers can make quick judgments on the per capita income of Canadians from one year relative to another by examining the index numbers over this period.

Table 15.16			
Per Capita Income in Canada: In Dollars and as an Index	**Year**	**$**	**Index**
	1992	27,850	100
	1993	27,600	99.1
	1994	27,820	99.9
	1995	28,020	100.6
	1996	27,900	100.2
	1997	28,300	101.6
	1998	29,090	104.5
	1999	29,670	106.5
	2000	30,710	110.3
	2001	30,900	111.0
	2002	30,650	110.1
	2003	30,650	110.1
	2004	31,280	112.3

UNWEIGHTED AGGREGATE PRICE INDEX NUMBERS

The use of simple index numbers makes possible the conversion of prices, costs, quantities, and so on for different time periods into a number scale with the base year equalling 100%. One of the drawbacks of simple index numbers, however, is that each time period is represented by only one item or commodity. When multiple items are involved, multiple sets of index numbers are possible. Suppose a decision maker is interested in combining or pooling the prices of several items, creating a "market basket" in order to compare the prices for several years. Fortunately, a technique does exist for combining several items and determining index numbers for the total (aggregate). Because this technique is used mostly in determining price indexes, the focus in this section is on developing aggregate price indexes. The formula for constructing the **unweighted aggregate price index number** follows.

Unweighted Aggregate Price Index Number	$$I_i = \frac{\sum P_i}{\sum P_0}(100)$$

where

P_i = the price of an item in the year of interest (i)
P_0 = the price of an item in the base year (o)
I_i = the index number for the year of interest (i)

Suppose a researcher wants to compare the cost of family food buying over the years. The researcher decides that instead of using a single food item to do this comparison, she will use a food basket that consists of five items: eggs, milk, bananas, potatoes, and sugar. She gathered price information on these five items for the years 1995, 2000, and 2008. The items and the prices are listed in Table 15.17.

From the data in Table 15.17 and the formula, the unweighted aggregate price indexes for the years 1995, 2000, and 2008 can be computed by using 1995 as the base year. The first step is to add together, or aggregate, the prices for all the food basket items in a given year. These totals are shown in the last row of Table 15.17. The index numbers are constructed by using these totals (not individual item prices): $\sum P_{1995} = 3.90$, $\sum P_{2000} = 4.63$, and $\sum P_{2005} = 5.21$. From these figures, the unweighted aggregate price index for 2000 is computed as follows:

$$\text{For 2000: } I_{2000} = \frac{\sum P_{2000}}{\sum P_{1995}}(100) = \frac{4.63}{3.90}(100) = 118.7$$

Table 15.17

Prices for a Basket of Food Items

Item	1995	2000	2008
Eggs (dozen)	0.78	0.86	1.06
Milk (2 L)	1.14	1.39	1.59
Bananas (per kg)	0.72	0.92	0.98
Potatoes (per kg)	0.56	0.62	0.72
Sugar (per kg)	0.70	0.84	0.86
Total of Items	3.90	4.63	5.21

WEIGHTED AGGREGATE PRICE INDEX NUMBERS

A major drawback to unweighted aggregate price indexes is that they are *unweighted*—that is, equal weight is put on each item by assuming the market basket contains only one of each item. This assumption may or may not be true. For example, a household may consume 5 kg of bananas per year but drink 200 L of milk. In addition, unweighted aggregate index numbers depend on the units selected for various items. For example, if milk is measured in 2-L instead of 4-L containers, the price of milk used in determining the index numbers is considerably lower. A class of index numbers that can be used to avoid these problems is weighted aggregate price index numbers.

Weighted aggregate price index numbers are *computed by multiplying quantity weights and item prices in determining the market basket worth for a given year*. Sometimes when price and quantity are multiplied to construct index numbers, the index numbers are referred to as *value indexes*. Thus, weighted aggregate price index numbers are also value indexes.

Including quantities eliminates the problems caused by how many of each item are consumed per time period and the units of items. If 200 L of milk but only 5 kg of bananas are consumed, weighted aggregate price index numbers will reflect those weights. If the business researcher switches from 4-L to 2-L containers, the prices will change downward but the quantity will increase twofold.

In general, weighted aggregate price indexes are constructed by multiplying the price of each item by its quantity and then summing these products for the market basket over a given time period (often a year). The ratio of this sum for one time period of interest (year) to a base time period of interest (base year) is multiplied by 100. The following formula reflects a weighted aggregate price index computed by using quantity weights from each time period (year):

$$I_i = \frac{\sum P_i Q_i}{\sum P_0 Q_0}(100)$$

One of the problems with this formula is the implication that new and possibly different quantities apply for each time period. However, business researchers expend much time and money ascertaining the quantities used in a market basket. Redetermining quantity weights for each year is therefore often prohibitive for most organizations (even the government). Two particular types of weighted aggregate price indexes offer a solution to the problem of which quantity weights to use. The first and most widely used is the Laspeyres price index. The second and less widely used is the Paasche price index.

LASPEYRES PRICE INDEX

The Laspeyres price index is *a weighted aggregate price index computed by using the quantities of the base period (year) for all other years*. The advantages of this technique are that the price indexes for all years can be compared, and new quantities do not have to be determined for each year. The formula for constructing the Laspeyres price index follows.

Laspeyres Price Index	$I_L = \dfrac{\sum P_i Q_0}{\sum P_0 Q_0}(100)$

Table 15.18				

Food Basket Items with Quantity Weights

Item	Quantity	Price 1995	Price 2008
Eggs (dozen)	45	0.78	1.06
Milk (2 L)	60	1.14	1.59
Bananas (per kg)	12	0.72	0.98
Potatoes (per kg)	55	0.56	0.72
Sugar (per kg)	36	0.70	0.86

Notice that the formula requires the base period quantities (Q_0) in both the numerator and the denominator.

In Table 15.17, a food basket is presented in which aggregate price indexes are computed. This food basket consisted of eggs, milk, bananas, potatoes, and sugar. The prices of these items were combined (aggregated) for a given year and the price indexes were computed from these aggregate figures. The unweighted aggregate price indexes computed on these data gave all items equal importance. Suppose that the business researchers realize that applying equal weight to these five items is probably not a representative way to construct this food basket and consequently ascertain quantity weights on each food item for one year's consumption. Table 15.18 lists these five items, their prices, and their quantity usage weights for the base year (1995). From these data, the business researchers can compute Laspeyres price indexes.

The Laspeyres price index for 2008 with 1995 as the base year is calculated as follows:

$$\sum P_i Q_0 = \sum P_{2008} Q_{1995}$$
$$= \sum[(1.06)(45) + (1.59)(60) + (0.98)(12) + (0.72)(55) + (0.86)(36)]$$
$$= 47.70 + 95.40 + 11.76 + 39.6 + 30.96 = 225.42$$

$$\sum P_0 Q_0 = \sum P_{1995} Q_{1995}$$
$$= \sum[(0.78)(45) + (1.14)(60) + (0.72)(12) + (0.56)(55) + (0.70)(36)]$$
$$= 35.10 + 68.40 + 8.64 + 30.80 + 25.20 = 168.14$$

$$I_{2008} = \frac{\sum P_{2008} Q_{1995}}{\sum P_{1995} Q_{1995}}(100) = \frac{225.42}{168.14}(100) = 134.1$$

PAASCHE PRICE INDEX

The **Paasche price index** is *a weighted aggregate price index computed by using the quantities for the year of interest in computations for a given year.* The advantage of this technique is that it incorporates current quantity figures in the calculations. One disadvantage is that ascertaining quantity figures for each time period is expensive. The formula for computing Paasche price indexes follows.

Paasche Price Index	$I_p = \dfrac{\sum P_i Q_i}{\sum P_0 Q_i}(100)$

Table 15.19				
Food Basket Items with Yearly Quantity Weights for 1995 and 2008				

Item	P_{1995}	Q_{1995}	P_{2008}	Q_{2008}
Eggs (dozen)	0.78	45	1.06	42
Milk (2-L)	1.14	60	1.59	57
Bananas (per kg)	0.72	12	0.98	13
Potatoes (per kg)	0.56	55	0.72	52
Sugar (per kg)	0.70	36	0.86	36

Suppose the yearly quantities for the basket of food items listed in Table 15.18 are determined. The result is the quantities and prices shown in Table 15.19 for the years 1995 and 2008 that can be used to compute Paasche price index numbers.

The Paasche price index numbers can be determined for 2008 by using a base year of 1995 as follows:

For 2008:

$$\sum P_{2008}Q_{2008} = \sum[(1.06)(42) + (1.59)(57) + (0.98)(13) + (0.72)(52) + (0.86)(36)]$$
$$= 44.52 + 90.63 + 12.74 + 37.44 + 30.96 = 216.29$$

$$\sum P_{1995}Q_{2008} = [(0.78)(42) + (1.14)(57) + (0.72)(13) + (0.56)(52) + (0.70)(36)]$$
$$= 32.76 + 64.98 + 9.36 + 29.12 + 25.20 = 161.42$$

$$I_{2008} = \frac{\sum P_{2008}Q_{2008}}{\sum P_{1995}Q_{2008}}(100) = \frac{216.29}{161.42}(100) = 134.0$$

Demonstration Problem 15.5	

The Arapaho Valley Pediatrics Clinic has been in business for 18 years. The office manager noticed that prices of clinic materials and office supplies fluctuate over time. To get a handle on the price trends for running the clinic, the office manager examined prices of six items the clinic uses as part of its operation. Shown here are the items, their prices, and the quantities for the years 2008 and 2009. Use these data to develop unweighted aggregate price indexes for 2009 with a base year of 2008. Compute the Laspeyres price index for the year 2009 using 2008 as the base year. Compute the Paasche index number for 2009 using 2008 as the base year.

	2008		2009	
Item	Price	Quantity	Price	Quantity
Syringes (dozen)	6.70	150	6.95	135
Cotton swabs (box)	1.35	60	1.45	65
Patient record forms (pad)	5.10	8	6.25	12
Children's Tylenol (bottle)	4.50	25	4.95	30
Computer paper (box)	11.95	6	13.20	8
Thermometers	7.90	4	9.00	2
Totals	37.50		41.80	

Solution

Unweighted Aggregate Index for 2009:

$$I_{2009} = \frac{\sum P_{2009}}{\sum P_{2008}}(100) = \frac{41.80}{37.50}(100) = 111.5$$

POINTS OF INTEREST
Index numbers are to time series data what percentages are to polls. Without index numbers, it is not easy to make comparisons. Index numbers, even the more complicated ones, are easy to calculate and to understand, yet immensely useful.

Laspeyres Index for 2009:

$$\sum P_{2009}Q_{2008} = [(6.95)(150) + (1.45)(60) + (6.25)(8) + (4.95)(25) + (13.20)(6) + (9.00)(4)]$$
$$= 1,042.50 + 87.00 + 50.00 + 123.75 + 79.20 + 36.00 = 1,418.45$$

$$\sum P_{2008}Q_{2008} = [(6.70)(150) + (1.35)(60) + (5.10)(8) + (4.50)(25) + (11.95)(6) + (7.90)(4)]$$
$$= 1,005.00 + 81.00 + 40.80 + 112.50 + 71.70 + 31.60 = 1,342.6$$

$$I_{2009} = \frac{\sum P_{2009}Q_{2008}}{\sum P_{2008}Q_{2008}}(100) = \frac{1,418.45}{1,342.6}(100) = 105.6$$

Passache Index for 2009:

$$\sum P_{2009}Q_{2009} = [(6.95)(135) + (1.45)(65) + (6.25)(12) + (4.95)(30) + (13.20)(8) + (9.00)(2)]$$
$$= 938.25 + 94.25 + 75.00 + 148.50 + 105.60 + 18.00 = 1,379.60$$

$$\sum P_{2008}Q_{2009} = [(6.70)(135) + (1.35)(65) + (5.10)(12) + (4.50)(30) + (11.95)(8) + (7.90)(2)]$$
$$= 904.50 + 87.75 + 61.20 + 135.00 + 95.60 + 15.80 = 1,299.85$$

$$I_{2009} = \frac{\sum P_{2009}Q_{2009}}{\sum P_{2008}Q_{2009}}(100) = \frac{1,379.60}{1,299.85}(100) = 106.1$$

Concept Check

1. Why are index numbers necessary? Why can't we compare raw numbers directly with each other?
2. How do unweighted aggregate price index numbers differ from weighted aggregate price index numbers?
3. Why do weighted aggregate price index numbers provide a more realistic picture than unweighted aggregate price index numbers? Give an example to explain your answer.

15.6 Problems

15.21 Suppose the following data represent the price of 20 reams (10,000 sheets) of office paper over a 50-year time frame. Find the simple index numbers for the data.
   a.   Let 1950 be the base year.
   b.   Let 1980 be the base year.

Year	Price	Year	Price
1950	$22.45	1980	$69.75
1955	31.40	1985	73.44
1960	32.33	1990	80.05
1965	36.50	1995	84.61
1970	44.90	2000	87.28
1975	61.24	2005	89.56

15.22 Following are the numbers of patents issued for Canadian research and development (R&D) by three sources: Japan Patent Office, European Patent Office, and the U.S. Patent and Trademark Office (Triadic Patent Families). Using these data and a base year of 1990, determine the simple index numbers for each year.

Triadic Patent Families for Canadian R&D

1990	1991	1992	1993	1994	1995	1996	1997	1998	1999	2000	2001	2002	2003
290	275	270	285	353	380	436	543	532	595	643	661	685	710

Source: OECD, 2007.

15.23 Using the data that follow, compute the aggregate index numbers for the four types of meat. Let 1995 be the base year for this market basket of goods.

Items	1995	2002	2009
Ground beef (per kg)	3.37	3.08	4.77
Sausage (per kg)	4.86	4.73	5.52
Bacon (per kg)	4.22	5.90	5.72
Round steak (per kg)	7.44	6.82	8.80

15.24 Suppose the following data are prices of market goods involved in household transportation for the years 2001 through 2009. Using 2003 as a base year, compute aggregate transportation price indexes for this data.

	Year								
Items	2001	2002	2003	2004	2005	2006	2007	2008	2009
Gasoline (per gal.)	1.1	1.16	1.23	1.23	1.08	1.56	1.85	2.59	2.89
Oil (per qt.)	1.58	1.61	1.78	1.77	1.61	1.71	1.9	2.05	2.08
Transmission fluid (per qt.)	1.8	1.82	1.98	1.96	1.94	1.9	1.92	1.94	1.96
Radiator coolant (per gal.)	7.95	7.96	8.24	8.21	8.19	8.05	8.12	8.1	8.24

15.25 Calculate Laspeyres price indexes for 2007 to 2009 from the following data. Use 2000 as the base year.

	Quantity	Price			
Item	2000	2000	2007	2008	2009
1	21	$0.50	$0.67	$0.68	$0.71
2	6	1.23	1.85	1.90	1.91
3	17	0.84	0.75	0.75	0.80
4	43	0.15	0.21	0.25	0.25

15.26 Calculate Paasche price indexes for 2008 and 2009 using the following data and 2000 as the base year.

		2008		2009	
Item	2000 Price	Price	Quantity	Price	Quantity
1	$22.50	$27.80	13	$28.11	12
2	10.90	13.10	5	13.25	8
3	1.85	2.25	41	2.35	44

FORECASTING AIR POLLUTION

In searching for the most effective forecasting technique to use to forecast either carbon monoxide or nitrogen oxide emission, it is useful to determine whether a trend is evident in either set of time-series data. The trend analysis is presented below for nitrogen oxides.

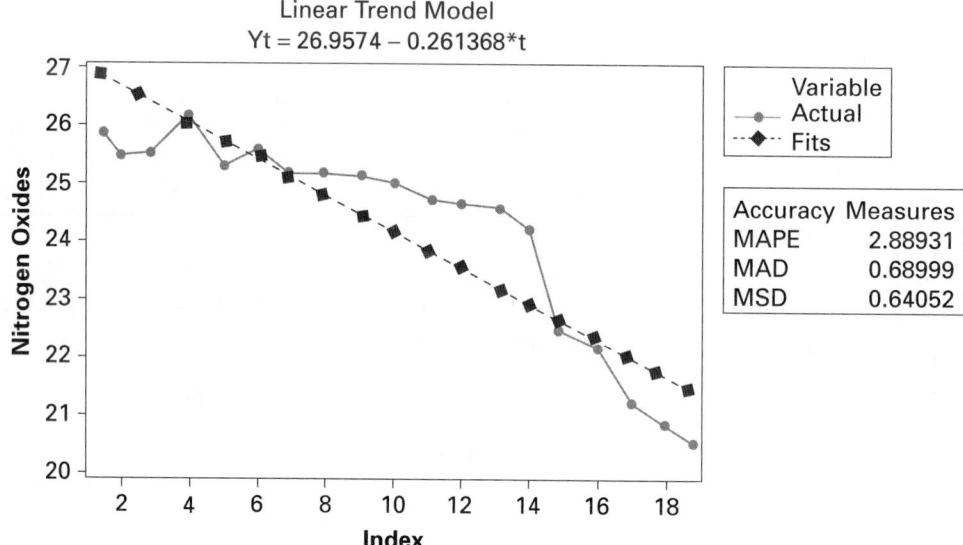

In observing the fit of this trend line and the time-series plot, more of a quadratic trend than a linear trend appears to be evident. Therefore, a quadratic trend model was applied and the results are presented below. Note that the error measures are all smaller for the quadratic model and that the curve fits the data much better than does the linear model.

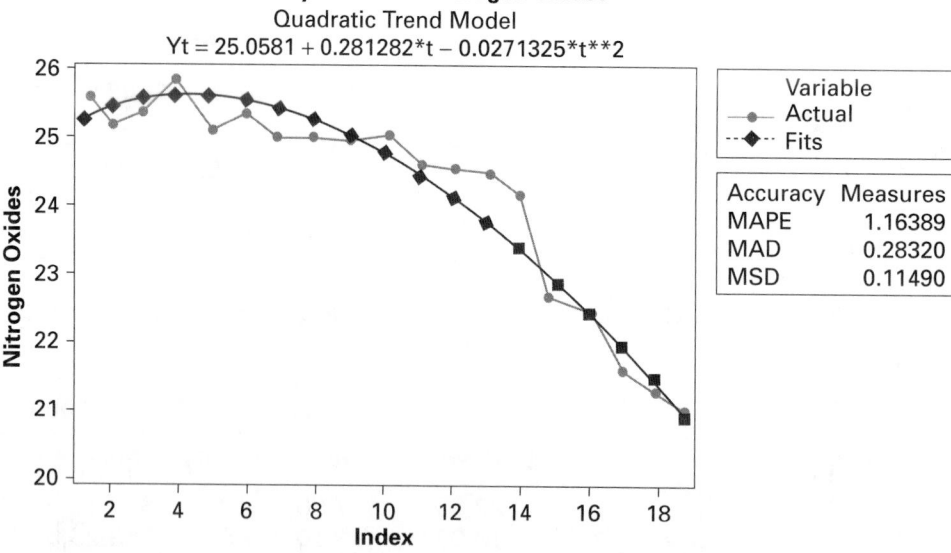

Various smoothing techniques can be used to forecast time-series data. After exploring several moving average models to predict carbon monoxide emissions, it was determined that a 3-year moving average fits the data relatively well. The results of a 3-year moving average graphical analysis of carbon monoxide are shown below. Note that the forecasts shadow the actual values quite well and actually intersect them in two locations.

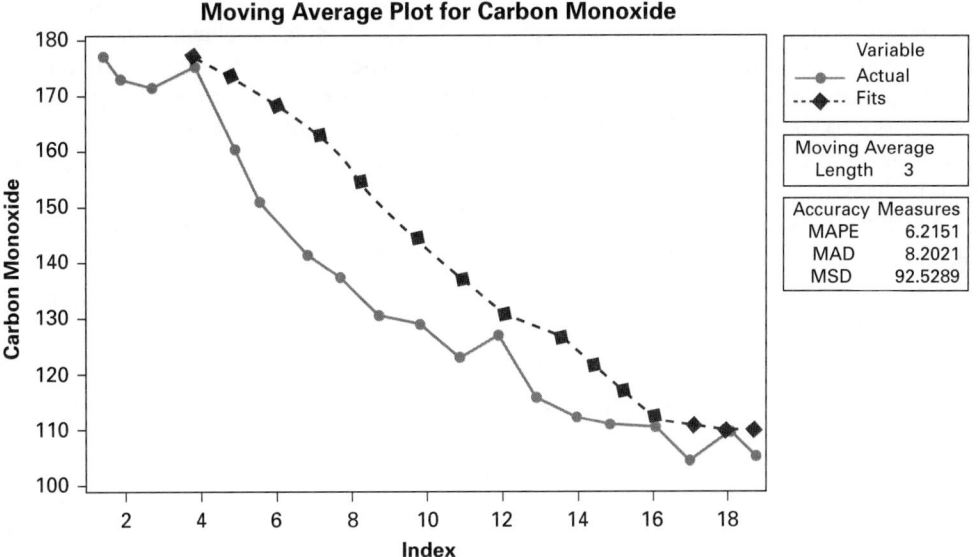

The effectiveness of exponential smoothing as a forecasting tool for nitrogen oxide emissions was tested for several values of α. Through this analysis, it was determined that the best forecasts were obtained for values of α near 1, indicating that the actual value for the previous time period was a much stronger contributor to the forecast than the previous time period's forecast. Shown below is a graphical analysis of an exponential smoothing forecast of the nitrogen oxide data using an alpha of 0.95. You are encouraged to explore other methods for forecasting nitrogen oxide and carbon monoxide emissions.

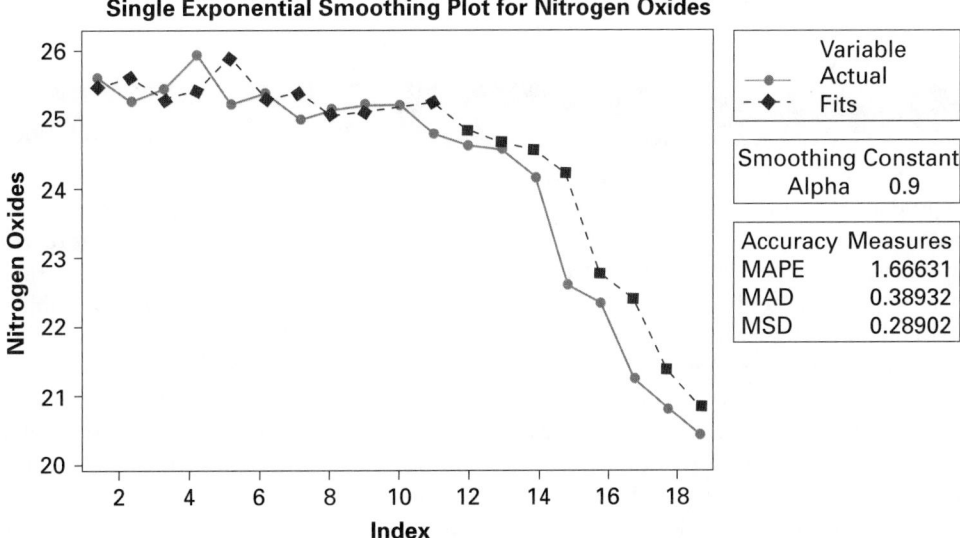

KEY CONSIDERATIONS

The true test of a forecast is the accuracy of the prediction. Until the actual value is obtained for a given time period, the accuracy of the forecast is unknown. Many forecasters make predictions in society, including card readers, religious leaders, and self-proclaimed prophets. The proof of the forecast is in the outcome. The same holds true in the business world. Forecasts are made about everything from market share to interest rates to number of international air travellers. Many businesses fail because of faulty forecasts.

Forecasting is perhaps as much an art as a science. To keep forecasting ethical, the consumer of the forecast should be given the caveats and limitations of the forecast. The forecaster should be honestly cautious in selling the predictions to a client. In addition, the forecaster should be constantly on the lookout for changes in the business setting being modelled and quickly translate and incorporate these changes into the forecasting model.

Methodological problems can occur in forecasting when particular data are selected to develop a model that has been predetermined to produce certain results. As mentioned previously, statistics can be used to "prove" almost anything. The ethical forecaster lets the data drive the model and is constantly seeking honest input from new variables to revise the forecast. He or she strives to communicate the limitations of both the forecasts and the models to clients.

Why Statistics Is Relevant

Businesses need to forecast sales for the next year so they can budget for resources and personnel. Governments need to know how the population will grow in the next few years so they can plan for taxation and amenities. Hospitals need to know the demographic trends so they know how to allocate their resources for hospital beds and staffing. Airlines need to know the trend in air traffic so they can increase flights to destinations that are becoming popular and cut back flights to destinations that are becoming less popular.

If businesses naively assume that nothing will change, businesses may be under-resourced and unable to take advantage of opportunities, governments may be unable to meet the needs of citizens, hospitals may not be ready to provide the required services, and planes may be overbooked or go to the destination practically empty.

Again, without the help of statistics we cannot understand how much the cost of living has gone up after accounting for inflation, how much of a spurt in sales can be attributed to our marketing efforts, and how much to pay attention to seasonal effects. Thus, statistics have real-life implications that provide guidelines for future planning that is realistic and cost effective.

SUMMARY

1. Time-series forecasting refers to analysis techniques designed to produce estimates or predictions based on historical data collected at regular time intervals.

2. Generally speaking, time-series data are composed of four elements—trend, cyclical effects, seasonality, and irregularity. Trend is the long-term general direction of the time-series data. Cyclical effects are the business and economic cycles that occur over periods of more than one year. Seasonal effects are patterns or cycles of data behaviour that occur over time periods of less than one year. Irregular fluctuations are unaccounted-for "blips" or variations that occur over short periods of time.

3. Time-series data that contain no trend, cyclical, or seasonal effects are said to be **stationary.** Techniques used to forecast stationary data analyze only the irregular fluctuation effects.

4. Regression analysis with either linear or quadratic models can be used to explore trend. Regression trend analysis is a special case of regression analysis in which the dependent variable is the data to be forecast and the independent variable is the time periods numbered consecutively from 1 to k, where k is the number of time periods. For the quadratic model, a second independent variable is constructed by squaring the values in the first independent variable, and both independent variables are included in the analysis.

5. One way to establish the validity of a forecast is to examine the forecasting error. The error of a forecast is the difference between the actual value and the forecast value. Computing a value to measure forecasting error can be done in several different ways.

This chapter presents mean absolute deviation (MAD) and mean square error (MSE) for this task.

6. One group of time-series forecasting methods contains smoothing techniques. Among these techniques are naive models, averaging techniques, and simple exponential smoothing. These techniques do much better if the time-series data are stationary or show no significant trend or seasonal effects. Naive forecasting models are models in which it is assumed that the more recent time periods of data represent the best predictions or forecasts for future outcomes.

Simple averages use the average value for some given length of previous time periods to forecast the value for the next period.

Moving averages are time period averages that are revised for each time period by including the most recent value(s) in the computation of the average and deleting the value or values that are farthest away from the present time period. A special case of the moving average is the weighted moving average, in which different weights are placed on the values from different time periods.

Simple (single) exponential smoothing is a technique in which data from previous time periods are weighted exponentially to forecast the value for the present time period. The forecaster can select how much to weight more recent values versus those of previous time periods.

7. Decomposition is a method for isolating the four possible effects in time-series data: trend, cyclical effects, seasonality, and irregular fluctuations.

8. Autocorrelation or serial correlation occurs when the error terms from forecasts are correlated over time. In regression analysis, this effect is particularly disturbing because one of the assumptions is that the error terms are independent. One way to test for autocorrelation is to use the Durbin-Watson test. A number of methods attempt to overcome the effects of autocorrelation on the data. One way is to determine whether at least one independent variable is missing and, if so, include it or them in the model. Another way is to transform the variables. One transformation technique is the first-differences approach, in which each value of X is subtracted from the succeeding time period value of X and the differences are used as the values of the X variable. The same approach is used to transform the Y variable. The forecasting model is then developed from the transformed variables.

9. Autoregression is a forecasting technique in which time-series data are predicted by independent variables that are lagged versions of the original dependent variable data. A variable that is lagged one period is derived from values of the previous time period. Other variables can be lagged two or more periods.

10. Index numbers can be used to translate raw data into numbers that are more readily comparable. Simple index numbers are constructed by creating the ratio of the raw data value for a given time period to the raw data value for the base period and multiplying the ratio by 100. The index number for the base time period is designated to be 100.

Unweighted aggregate price index numbers are constructed by summing the prices of several items for a time period and comparing that sum to the sum of the prices of the same items during a base time period and multiplying the ratio by 100. Weighted aggregate price indexes are index numbers utilizing the prices of several items, and the items are weighted by their quantity usage.

The Laspeyres price index uses the quantity weights from the base year in all calculations. The Paasche price index uses the quantity weights for the current time period for both the current time period and the base time period in calculations.

KEY TERMS

autocorrelation	exponential smoothing	mean square error (MSE)	smoothing techniques
autoregression	first-differences approach	moving average	stationary
averaging models	forecasting	naive forecasting models	time-series data
cycles	forecasting error	Paasche price index	trend
cyclical effects	index number	seasonal effects	unweighted aggregate price
decomposition	irregular fluctuations	serial correlation	index number
deseasonalized data	Laspeyres price index	simple average	weighted aggregate price
Durbin-Watson test	mean absolute deviation	simple average model	index numbers
error of an individual forecast	(MAD)	simple index number	weighted moving average

FORMULAS

Individual forecast error

$$e_t = X_t - F_t$$

Mean absolute deviation

$$\text{MAD} = \frac{\Sigma |e_i|}{\text{Number of Forecasts}}$$

Mean square error

$$\text{MSE} = \frac{\Sigma e_i^2}{\text{Number of Forecasts}}$$

Exponential smoothing

$$F_{t+1} = \alpha \cdot X_t + (1 - \alpha) \cdot F_t$$

Durbin-Watson test

$$D = \frac{\displaystyle\sum_{t=2}^{n}(e_t - e_{t-1})^2}{\displaystyle\sum_{t=1}^{n} e_t^2}$$

SUPPLEMENTARY PROBLEMS

Calculating the Statistics

15.27 Following are the average yields of long-term new corporate bonds over a several-month period.

Month	Yield	Month	Yield
1	10.08	13	7.91
2	10.05	14	7.73
3	9.24	15	7.39
4	9.23	16	7.48
5	9.69	17	7.52
6	9.55	18	7.48
7	9.37	19	7.35
8	8.55	20	7.04
9	8.36	21	6.88
10	8.59	22	6.88
11	7.99	23	7.17
12	8.12	24	7.22

a. Explore trends in these data by using regression trend analysis. How strong are the models? Is the quadratic model significantly stronger than the linear trend model?

b. Use a 4-month moving average to forecast values for each of the ensuing months.

c. Use simple exponential smoothing to forecast values for each of the ensuing months. Let $\alpha = 0.3$ and then let $\alpha = 0.7$. Which weight produces better forecasts?

d. Compute MAD for the forecasts obtained in parts (b) and (c) and compare the results.

e. Determine seasonal effects using decomposition on these data. Let the seasonal effects have four periods. After determining the seasonal indexes, deseasonalize the data.

15.28 Compute index numbers for the following data using 2002 as the base year.

Year	Quantity	Year	Quantity
2002	2,073	2010	2,520
2003	2,290	2011	2,529
2004	2,349	2012	2,483
2005	2,313	2013	2,467
2006	2,456	2014	2,397
2007	2,508	2015	2,351
2008	2,463	2016	2,308
2009	2,499		

15.29 Compute unweighted aggregate price index numbers for each of the given years, using 2005 as the base year.

Item	2005	2006	2007	2008	2009
1	3.21	3.37	3.8	3.73	3.65
2	0.51	0.55	0.68	0.62	0.59
3	0.83	0.9	0.91	1.02	1.06
4	1.3	1.32	1.33	1.32	1.3
5	1.67	1.72	1.9	1.99	1.98
6	0.62	0.67	0.7	0.72	0.71

15.30 Using the following data and 2006 as the base year, compute the Laspeyres price index for 2009 and the Paasche price index for 2008.

Item	2006 Price	2006 Quantity	2007 Price	2007 Quantity
1	$2.75	12	$2.98	9
2	0.85	47	0.89	52
3	1.33	20	1.32	28

Item	2008 Price	2008 Quantity	2009 Price	2009 Quantity
1	$3.10	9	$3.21	11
2	0.95	61	0.98	66
3	1.36	25	1.4	32

Testing Your Understanding

15.31 The following table contains the annual data for CO_2 emissions in Canada over a 34-year period as published by the OECD.

a. Use a 3-year moving average to forecast the CO_2 emissions for the years 1974 through 2004 for these data. Compute the error of each forecast and then determine the mean absolute deviation of error for the forecast.

b. Use exponential smoothing and $\alpha = 0.2$ to forecast the data from 1974 through 2004. Let the forecast for 1972 equal the actual value for 1971. Compute the error of each forecast and then determine the mean absolute deviation of error for the forecast.

c. Compare the results obtained in parts (a) and (b) using MAD. Which technique seems to perform better? Why?

CO_2 Emissions from Energy Use in Canada (millions of tonnes)

1971	1972	1973	1974	1975	1976
340	358	376	386	378	393

1977	1978	1979	1980	1981	1982
406	409	423	428	411	393

1983	1984	1985	1986	1987	1988
385	402	403	394	406	437

1989	1990	1991	1992	1993	1994
453	429	423	435	435	450

1995	1996	1997	1998	1999	2000
461	476	493	498	508	530

2001	2002	2003	2004		
523	531	556	551		

15.32 Given below are the sales (in $'000) of a regional department store in Canada, monthly from January 2005 through December 2009. Use time-series decomposition methods to develop the seasonal indexes for these data.

Monthly Sales

2005	$'000	2006	$'000
January	1591	January	1478
February	1337	February	2031
March	2122	March	2220
April	2781	April	3436
May	2216	May	3917
June	1518	June	2913
July	1167	July	2415
August	1998	August	3165
September	2565	September	2504
October	2702	October	2994
November	2224	November	3732
December	2477	December	2887

2007	$'000	2008	$'000
January	1715	January	3044
February	2862	February	2128
March	2324	March	2726
April	4191	April	3760
May	2500	May	3805
June	2488	June	3829
July	4344	July	2209
August	3004	August	4482
September	3632	September	3021
October	4121	October	3698
November	3626	November	3888
December	2963	December	3215

2009	$'000
January	4097
February	2511
March	3064
April	3879
May	3555
June	3505
July	4715
August	4088
September	3179
October	4210
November	4226
December	2776

15.33 Use the seasonal indexes computed to deseasonalize the data in Problem 15.32.

15.34 Determine the trend for the data in Problem 15.32 using the deseasonalized data from Problem 15.33. Explore both a linear and a quadratic model in an attempt to develop the better trend model.

SUPPLEMENTARY PROBLEMS (continued)

15.35 Shown here are retail price figures and quantity estimates for five different food commodities over three years. Use these data and a base year of 2007 to compute unweighted aggregate price indexes for this market basket of food. Using a base year of 2007, calculate Laspeyres price indexes and Paasche price indexes for 2008 and 2009.

Item	Price	Quantity
2007		
Margarine (500 g)	1.26	21
Shortening (500 g)	0.94	5
Milk (2 L)	1.43	70
Cola (2 litres)	1.05	12
Potato chips (750 g)	2.81	27
2008		
Margarine (500 g)	1.32	23
Shortening (500 g)	0.97	3
Milk (2 L)	1.56	68
Cola (2 litres)	1.02	13
Potato chips (750 g)	2.86	29
2009		
Margarine (500 g)	1.39	22
Shortening (500 g)	1.12	4
Milk (2 L)	1.62	65
Cola (2 litres)	1.25	11
Potato chips (750 g)	2.99	28

15.36 Given below are data on the number of business establishments (millions) and the self-employment rate (%). Develop a regression model to predict the self-employment rate by the number of business establishments. Use this model to predict the self-employment rate for a year in which there are 7.0 (million) business establishments. Discuss the strength of the regression model. Use these data and the regression model to compute a Durbin-Watson test to determine whether significant autocorrelation is present. Let alpha be 0.05.

Number of Establishments (millions)	Self-Employment Rate (%)
4.54317	8.1
4.58651	8.0
4.63396	8.1
5.30679	8.2
5.51772	8.2
5.70149	8.0

(continued)

Number of Establishments (millions)	Self-Employment Rate (%)
5.80697	7.9
5.93706	8.0
6.01637	8.2
6.10692	8.1
6.17556	8.0
6.20086	8.1
6.31930	7.8
6.40123	8.0
6.50907	8.1
6.61272	7.9
6.73848	7.8
6.89487	7.7
6.94182	7.5
7.00844	7.2
7.07005	6.9

15.37 Shown here are the monthly Canadian total consumer price indexes (CPIs) for the years 2005 through 2007. Use the data to answer the following questions.
a. Compute the 4-month moving average to forecast the CPIs from May 2005 to December 2007.
b. Compute the 4-month weighted moving average to forecast the CPIs from May 2005 to December 2007. Weight the most recent year by 4, the next most recent year by 3, the next year by 2, and the last year of the four by 1.
c. Determine the errors for parts (a) and (b). Compute MSE for parts (a) and (b). Compare the MSE values and comment on the effectiveness of the moving average versus the weighted moving average for these data.

Year	Month	CPI
2005	January	104.5
	February	104.8
	March	105.2
	April	105.2
	May	105.4
	June	105.4
	July	105.4
	August	105.6
	September	105.9
	October	105.9
	November	106.3
	December	106.2

(continued)

Year	Month	CPI
2006	January	106.2
	February	106.6
	March	107
	April	106.9
	May	107.5
	June	107.2
	July	107.5
	August	107.7
	September	108.3
	October	108.4
	November	108.6
	December	108.4
2007	January	108.6
	February	109.1
	March	109.5
	April	109.6
	May	109.9
	June	109.9
	July	110
	August	110.1
	September	110.5
	October	110.3
	November	110.3
	December	110

15.38 In the *Survey of Current Business,* the U.S. Department of Commerce publishes data on farm commodity prices. Given are the cotton prices from November of year 1 through February of year 4. The prices are indexes with a base of 100 from the period of 1910 through 1914. Use these data to develop autoregression models for a 1-month lag and a 4-month lag. Compare the results of these two models. Which model seems to yield better predictions? Why?

Time Period	Cotton Prices
November (year 1)	552
December	519
January (year 2)	505
February	512
March	541
April	549
May	552
June	526
July	531
August	545
September	549
October	570
November	576
December	568

(continued)

Time Period	Cotton Prices
January (year 3)	571
February	573
March	582
April	587
May	592
June	570
July	560
August	565
September	547
October	529
November	514
December	469
January (year 4)	436
February	419

15.39 The U.S. Department of Commerce publishes data on industrial machinery and equipment. Shown here are the shipments (in $ billions) of industrial machinery and equipment from the first quarter of year 1 through the fourth quarter of year 6. Use these data to determine the seasonal indexes for the data through time-series decomposition methods. Use the four-quarter centred moving average in the computations.

Time Period	Industrial Machinery and Equipment Shipments
1st quarter (year 1)	54.019
2nd quarter	56.495
3rd quarter	50.169
4th quarter	52.891
1st quarter (year 2)	51.915
2nd quarter	55.101
3rd quarter	53.419
4th quarter	57.236
1st quarter (year 3)	57.063
2nd quarter	62.488
3rd quarter	60.373
4th quarter	63.334
1st quarter (year 4)	62.723
2nd quarter	68.380
3rd quarter	63.256
4th quarter	66.446
1st quarter (year 5)	65.445
2nd quarter	68.011
3rd quarter	63.245
4th quarter	66.872
1st quarter (year 6)	59.714
2nd quarter	63.590
3rd quarter	58.088
4th quarter	61.443

SUPPLEMENTARY PROBLEMS (continued)

15.40 Use the seasonal indexes computed to deseasonalize the data in Problem 15.39.

15.41 Use both a linear and a quadratic model to explore trends in the deseasonalized data from Problem 15.40. Which model seems to produce a better fit for the data?

15.42 OECD publishes data on inflows of foreign direct investments in different countries including Canada, which is given below. Use these data to develop an autoregression model with a 1-period lag. Discuss the strength of the model.

Year	US $ millions
1994	8204
1995	9255
1996	9633
1997	11,522
1998	22,803
1999	24,747
2000	66,796
2001	27,670
2002	22,146
2003	7619
2004	1533
2005	33,824

15.43 The data shown here, from the OECD, show the inflows and outflows of foreign direct investments in Canada. Use these data to develop a regression model to forecast the foreign inflows by foreign outflows. Conduct a Durbin-Watson test on the data and the regression model to determine whether significant autocorrelation is present. Let $\alpha = .01$.

Year	US $ millions Inflows	US $ millions Outflows
1994	8204	9294
1995	9255	11,482
1996	9633	13,094
1997	11,522	23,059
1998	22,803	34,349
1999	24,747	17,250
2000	66,796	44,678
2001	27,670	36,037
2002	22,146	26,761
2003	7619	21,526
2004	1533	43,248
2005	33,824	34,084

15.44 The purchasing-power value figures for the minimum wage in year 18 dollars for the years 1 through 18 are shown here. Use these data and exponential smoothing to develop forecasts for the years 2 through 18. Try $\alpha = 0.1$, 0.5, and 0.8, and compare the results using MAD. Discuss your findings. Select the value of alpha that worked best and use your exponential smoothing results to predict the figure for year 19.

Year	Purchasing Power	Year	Purchasing Power
1	$6.04	10	$4.34
2	5.92	11	4.67
3	5.57	12	5.01
4	5.40	13	4.86
5	5.17	14	4.72
6	5.00	15	4.60
7	4.91	16	4.48
8	4.73	17	4.86
9	4.55	18	5.15

Interpreting the Output

15.45 Shown below is the Excel output for a regression analysis to predict the number of business bankruptcy filings over a 16-year period by the number of consumer bankruptcy filings. How strong is the model? Note the residuals. Compute a Durbin-Watson statistic from the data and discuss the presence of autocorrelation in this model.

	A	B	C	D	E	F
1	SUMMARY OUTPUT					
2	Regression Statistics					
3	Multiple *R*	0.529				
4	*R* Square	0.280				
5	Adjusted *R* Square	0.228				
6	Standard Error	8179.84				
7	Observations	16				
8						
9	ANOVA					
10		df	SS	MS	*F*	Significance *F*
11	Regression	1	364069877.4	364069877.4	5.44	0.0351
12	Residual	14	936737379.6	66909812.8		
13	Total	15	1300807257			
14						
15		Coefficients	Standard Error	*t* Stat	*p* Value	
16	Intercept	75532.43621	4980.08791	15.17	0.0000	
17	Consumer Bankruptcies	−0.01574	0.00675	−2.33	0.0351	
18						
19	RESIDUAL OUTPUT					
20	Observation	Predicted Bus. Bankruptcies	Residuals			
21	1	70638.58	−1338.6			
22	2	71024.28	−8588.3			
23	3	71054.61	−7050.6			
24	4	70161.99	1115.0			
25	5	68462.72	12772.3			
26	6	67733.25	14712.8			
27	7	66882.45	−3029.4			
28	8	65834.05	−2599.1			
29	9	64230.61	622.4			
30	10	61801.70	9747.3			
31	11	61354.16	9288.8			
32	12	62738.76	−434.8			
33	13	63249.36	−10875.4			
34	14	61767.01	−9808.0			
35	15	57826.69	−4277.7			
36	16	54283.80	−256.8			

ANALYZING THE DATABASES

see **www.wiley.com/canada/black**

1. Use the Agri-Business Canada Database and the variable Total Wheat to forecast Total Wheat for the period 95 by using the following techniques.
   a. Five-period moving average
   b. Simple exponential smoothing with $\alpha = 0.6$
   c. Time-series linear trend model
   d. Decomposition

2. Use decomposition on Canola in the Agri-Business Canada Database to determine the seasonal indexes. These data actually represent 7 years of 10-month data. Do the seasonal indexes indicate the presence of some seasonal effects? Run an autoregression model to predict Canola by a 1-month lag and another by a 12-month lag. Compare the two models. Because crops are somewhat seasonal, is the 12-month lag model significant?

3. Use the Energy Resource Database to forecast 2004 North America energy production through Hydro by using simple exponential smoothing of previous energy production through Hydro. Let $\alpha = 0.2$ and $\alpha = 0.8$. Compare the forecast with the actual figure. Which of the two models produces the forecast with the least error? Repeat the same test using the European data set. Is there any difference between North America and Europe in energy production through Hydro?

4. Use the International Labour Database to develop a regression model to predict the Unemployment Rate for Germany by the Unemployment Rate for Italy. Test for autocorrelation and discuss its presence or absence in this regression analysis using 0.05 level of significance.

CASE

Dofasco Changes its Style

Dofasco Inc. was founded in 1912 in Hamilton, Ontario, by Clifton W. Sherman. Dofasco provides steel to various industries, including the automotive and pipe industries, and today is considered one of Canada's leading steel makers. Originally, its strategy was based on producing as much steel as it could in order to be able to grow as much and as fast as possible. Financially, Dofasco was doing very well. However, in the late 1980s, things took an unexpected turn and Dofasco was left in a difficult position. The demand for steel was decreasing, competition was getting fiercer, and costs (operational and capital) were continuously increasing, negatively affecting Dofasco's sales and profitability. Between 1990 and 1992, Dofasco reported a total net loss of $900 million. The executive of the company understood that it had to take charge and restructure its operations if it were to survive this financial crisis. Dofasco's first order of business in restructuring the company was to sell off some of its assets, which included many of its divisions. It then went even further and cut its non-unionized labour force from 13,000 to 7,000 employees. The final step that Dofasco took in its restructuring process was to enter into joint ventures, allowing it to work with companies from different countries. These actions allowed Dofasco to begin its slow climb to the top once again.

Dofasco realized that it was extremely important during the restructuring process to focus on its core: its employees. Dofasco made it its mission to engage the employees by recognizing their needs and opinions. This change in organizational setting and human resources represented a significant shift of strategy. Human capital was now becoming Dofasco's most valuable resource, hence opening the road to financial recovery. Dofasco realized that its workforce was hard-working and motivated and ready to take on challenging work. Dofasco therefore accommodated these needs and provided employees with resources and encouragement to have a more hands-on approach with their clients. The new responsibilities gave employees the ability to get involved in everyday decisions and allowed them to work in teams and cross-functional groups, providing them with a broader view of the overall company process. This made the employees an integral part of the company and made them understand that they were vital to the success of the business.

Dofasco believed that empowering employees was one effective way of improving the company, but it also realized that the employees needed to be healthy and safe in order to be more productive. Therefore, in its restructuring process, Dofasco also began health initiatives such as offering information sessions on how to sleep better, weekly Weight Watchers meetings, CPR and first aid demonstrations, yoga and workout sessions, and sessions on how to deal with stress.

Since its restructuring program in the early 1990s, Dofasco has made major strides and has successfully managed to overcome its financial crisis. Its main goal was to change its business strategy and focus on employee engagement in order to improve its sales and profitability. The results of fiscal year 2000 showed the degree of success of the change in business strategy, as sales and net profit reached $3.2 billion and $188 million, respectively.

Discussion

1. Dofasco realized that the most effective way to improve its business and increase its sales was through a restructuring process. After this process was implemented, Dofasco's productivity and sales figures began to improve, allowing the company to overcome the financial crisis that it was facing. Dofasco's impressive sales figures from January 1998 to December 2005 (in billions) are reported below. When analyzing these figures, are any trends apparent? Are there any signs that indicate that Dofasco's sales may be seasonally influenced? Use the sales figures to perform a decomposition analysis using 12-month seasonality. Following this analysis, determine the trend line and a graphical display using Excel. Take a close look at all this information and put together a brief analysis of Dofasco sales. In this analysis, focus on any specific direction that Dofasco sales may be headed towards.

Month	1998	1999	2000	2001	2002	2003	2004	2005
January	142.1	166.7	178.6	229.3	267.3	432.5	382.0	432.9
February	112.5	175.2	202.7	253.0	315.4	456.1	405.7	443.8
March	102.7	175.2	229.6	267.8	369.1	456.1	432.4	496.3
April	154.9	205.3	277.4	341.8	430.2	483.9	456.3	531.2
May	213.1	239.7	319.2	356.7	458.1	532.7	496.2	559.9
June	230.6	280.5	329.1	405.1	570.2	623.8	583.9	645.2
July	214.8	292.0	369.4	445.0	546.9	659.4	608.8	675.4
August	191.8	318.6	354.1	432.1	482.0	521.4	559.6	658.6
September	175.3	202.2	243.5	329.6	432.7	509.0	507.0	610.5
October	140.4	178.4	211.9	329.6	407.5	482.1	497.3	582.5
November	140.4	164.9	216.3	305.7	392.8	458.2	442.7	522.9
December	150.8	177.9	201.9	291.9	407.6	430.9	421.6	481.7

2. It is very important to be able to analyze the cost of steel on a per-unit basis. Assume that Dofasco's financial team was able to calculate this cost for each year between 1995 and 2008. The result of these calculations is shown below. By using information learned in this chapter, such as smoothing techniques, moving averages, and trend analysis, forecast the per-unit labour costs for each year. How would you compute the error of the forecasts and determine which forecasting method is the most effective in reducing error?

Year	Per-Unit Labour Cost	Year	Per-Unit Labour Cost
1995	$81.25	2002	$58.44
1996	84.11	2003	59.67
1997	86.72	2004	56.71
1998	62.86	2005	57.83
1999	65.49	2006	56.12
2000	60.56	2007	56.99
2001	61.38	2008	56.12

References

"Dofasco's Healthy Lifestyle Program," Gordon DiGiacomo, March 2002, Case Study. Website for data source: <http://www.clbc.ca/files/CaseStudies/dofasco.pdf>; "Dofasco Inc.," 1997. Website for data source: <http://www.fundinguniverse.com/company-histories/Dofasco-Inc-Company-History.html>

USING THE COMPUTER

- Excel has the capability of forecasting using several of the techniques presented in this chapter. Two of the forecasting techniques are accessed using the **Data Analysis** tool, and two other forecasting techniques are accessed using the **Insert Function**.
- To use the **Data Analysis** tool, begin by selecting the **Data** tab on the Excel worksheet. From the **Analysis** panel at the right top of the **Data** tab worksheet, click on **Data Analysis**. If your Excel worksheet does not show the **Data Analysis** option, then you can load it as an add-in.
- To do exponential smoothing, select **Exponential Smoothing** from the **Data Analysis** pull-down menu. In the dialog box, input the location of the data to be smoothed in **Input Range**. Input the value of the dampening factor in **Damping factor**. Excel will default to .3. Input the location of the upper left cell of the output table in the **Output Range** space. The output consists of forecast values of the data. If you check **Standard Errors**, a second column of output will be given of standard errors.
- To compute moving averages, select **Moving Average** from the **Data Analysis** pull-down menu. In the dialogue box, input the location of the data for which the moving averages are to be computed in **Input Range**. Record how many values you want to include in computing the moving average in **Interval**. The default number is three values. Input the location of the upper left cell of the output table in **Output Range**. The output consists of the moving averages. If you check **Standard Errors**, a second column of output will be given of standard errors.

- To use the **Insert Function (f_x)** to compute forecasts and/or to fit a trend line, go to the **Formulas** tab on an Excel worksheet (top centre tab). The **Insert Function** is on the far left of the menu bar. In the **Insert Function** dialogue box at the top, there is a pull-down menu where it says **Or select a category**. From the pulldown menu associated with this command, select **Statistical**.
- To compute forecasts using linear regression, select **FORECAST** from the **Insert Function's Statistical** menu. In the first line of the **FORECAST** dialogue box, place the value of x for which you want a predicted value in **X**. An entry here is required. On the second line, place the location of the values to be used in the development of the regression model in **Known_y's**. On the third line, place the location of the x values to be used in the development of the regression model in **Known_x's**. The output consists of the predicted value.
- To fit a trend line to data, select **TREND** from the **Insert Function's Statistical** menu. On the first line of the **TREND** dialogue box, place the location of the y values to be used in the development of the regression model in **Known_y's**. On the second line, place the location of the x values to be used in the development of the regression model in **Known_x's**. Note that the x values can consist of more than one column if you want to fit a polynomial curve. To accomplish this, place squared values of x, cubed values of x, and so on as desired in other columns, and include those columns in **Known_x**. On the third line, place the values for which you want to return corresponding y values in **New_x's**. In the fourth line, place **TRUE in Const** if you want to get a value for the constant as usual (default option). Place **FALSE** if you want to set b_o to zero.

Unit V

SPECIAL TOPICS

This fifth and final unit of the text includes chapters 16, 17, 18, and 19. Chapter 16, Analysis of Categorical Data, presents two well-known chi-square techniques for analyzing frequency data that have been organized into nominal or ordinal categories—the chi-square goodness-of-fit test and the chi-square test of independence. Chapter 17, Nonparametric Statistics, contains some of the more well-known nonparametric statistics for analyzing nominal and ordinal data. These techniques include the runs test, the Mann-Whitney U test, the Wilcoxon matched-pairs signed rank test, the Kruskal-Wallis test, the Friedman test, and Spearman's rank correlation. In Chapter 18, Statistical Quality Control, we learn about the concept of quality as it is viewed in the business world and how statistics can be used in continuous quality improvement. Chapter 19, Decision Analysis, deals with managerial decision making. Managers are often required to make decisions with incomplete information. Statistical techniques provide quantitative means for arriving at optimal decisions under uncertain conditions while minimizing risks associated with wrong decisions.

CHAPTER 16
ANALYSIS OF CATEGORICAL DATA

Learning Objectives

The overall objective of this chapter is to give you an understanding of two statistical techniques used to analyze categorical data. The key questions of the chapter are:

1. What are categorical data?

2. What are chi-square tests?

3. When can you use the chi-square goodness-of-fit test and when can you use the chi-square test of independence?

4. What minimum sample size will you need in each cell to use chi-square tests?

PhotoDisc/Getty Images

SELECTING SUPPLIERS IN THE ELECTRONICS INDUSTRY

What criteria are used in the electronics industry to select a supplier? In years past, price was the dominant criterion of suppliers in many industries, and the supplier with the low bid often got the job. In more recent years, companies have been forced by global competition and a marked increase in quality to examine other aspects of potential suppliers.

Pearson and Ellram investigated the techniques used by firms in the electronics industry to select suppliers to determine if there is a difference between small and large firms in supplier selection. They sent out a survey instrument with questions about criteria used to select and evaluate suppliers, the participation of various functional areas in the selection process, and the formality of methods used in the selection. Of the 210 survey responses received, 87 were from small companies and 123 were from large companies. The average sales were $33 million for the small companies and $583 million for the large companies.

Survey questions were stated in such a way as to generate frequencies. The respondents were given a series of supplier selection and evaluation criteria such as quality, cost, current technology, design capabilities, speed to market, manufacturing process, and location. They were asked to check off the criteria used in supplier selection and evaluation and to rank the criteria that they checked. As part of the analysis, the researchers recorded how many of each of the small and large company respondents ranked a criterion first, how many ranked it second, and how many ranked it third. The results are shown in the following table of raw numbers for the criteria of quality, cost, and current technology.

Quality	Company Size	
	Small	Large
1	48	70
2	17	27
3	7	6

Cost	Company Size	
	Small	Large
1	8	14
2	29	36
3	26	37

Current Technology	Company Size	
	Small	Large
1	5	13
2	8	11
3	5	12

In addition, in some companies in the study, departments such as research/development or engineering were involved in the supplier search process. For example, 41.38% of the small companies in the study included research/development in the supplier search process versus 48.78% of the large companies.

Managerial and Statistical Questions

1. Is there a difference between small and large companies in the ranking of criteria for the evaluation and selection of suppliers in the electronics industry?
2. The authors of the study used frequencies to measure the relative rankings of criteria. What is the appropriate statistical technique to analyze these data?
3. In comparing the participation of company employees in the process of selection and evaluation of suppliers by function and by company size, the researchers reported percentages. Are the differences in percentages merely chance differences from samples or is there a significant difference between small and large companies in the extent to which they involve people from various functional areas in the supplier selection and evaluation process? What statistical technique is appropriate for analyzing these data?

Source: Adapted from John N. Pearson and Lisa M. Ellram, "Supplier Selection and Evaluation in Small Versus Large Electronics Firms," *Journal of Small Business Management,* vol. 33, no. 4 (October 1995), pp. 53–65.

In this chapter, we explore techniques for analyzing categorical data. **Categorical data** are *nonnumerical data that can be summarized as frequency counts.* For example, it is determined that of the 790 people attending a convention, 240 are engineers, 160 are managers, 310 are sales reps, and 80 are information technologists. The variable is position in company with four categories: engineers, managers, sales reps, and information technologists. The data are not ratings or sales figures but rather frequency counts of how many of each position attended. Research questions producing this type of data are often analyzed using chi-square techniques. The chi-square distribution was introduced in Chapters 8 and 9. The techniques presented here for analyzing categorical data, the *chi-square goodness-of-fit test* and *the chi-square test of independence,* are an outgrowth of the binomial distribution and the inferential techniques for analyzing population proportions.

16.1 CHI-SQUARE GOODNESS-OF-FIT TEST

In Chapter 5, we studied the binomial distribution, in which only two possible outcomes could occur on a single trial in an experiment. An extension of the binomial distribution is a multinomial distribution in which more than two possible outcomes can occur in a single trial. The **chi-square goodness-of-fit test** is *used to analyze probabilities of multinomial distribution trials along a single dimension.* For example, if the variable being studied is economic class with three possible outcomes of lower income class, middle income class, and upper income class, the single dimension is economic class and the three possible outcomes are the three classes. On each trial, one and only one of the outcomes can occur. In other words, a family unit must be classified as lower income class, middle income class, or upper income class and cannot be in more than one class.

The chi-square goodness-of-fit test compares the *expected,* or theoretical, *frequencies* of categories from a population distribution to the *observed,* or actual, *frequencies* from a distribution to determine whether there is a difference between what was expected and what was observed. For example, airline industry officials might theorize that the ages of airline ticket purchasers are distributed in a particular way. To validate or reject this expected distribution, an actual sample of ticket purchaser ages can be gathered randomly, and the observed results can be compared to the expected results with the chi-square goodness-of-fit test. This test can also be used to determine whether the observed arrivals at teller windows at a bank are Poisson distributed, as might be expected. In the paper industry, manufacturers can use the chi-square goodness-of-fit test to determine whether the demand for paper follows a uniform distribution throughout the year.

Formula 16.1 is used to compute a chi-square goodness-of-fit test.

Chi-Square Goodness-of-Fit Test (16.1)	$$\chi^2 = \sum \frac{(f_o - f_e)^2}{f_e}$$ $$\mathrm{df} = k - 1 - c$$

where

f_o = frequency of observed values
f_e = frequency of expected values
k = number of categories
c = number of parameters being estimated from the sample data

This formula compares the frequency of observed values to the frequency of the expected values across the distribution. The test loses one degree of freedom because the total number of expected frequencies must equal the number of observed frequencies; that is, the observed total taken from the sample is used as the total for the expected frequencies. In addition, in some instances a population parameter, such as λ, μ, or σ, is estimated from the sample data to determine the frequency distribution of expected values. Each time this estimation occurs, an additional degree of freedom is lost. As a rule, if a uniform distribution is being used as the expected distribution or if an expected distribution of values is given, $k - 1$ degrees of freedom are used in the test. In testing to determine whether an observed distribution is Poisson, the degrees of freedom are $k - 2$ because an additional degree of freedom is lost in estimating λ. In testing to determine whether an observed distribution is normal, the degrees of freedom are $k - 3$ because two additional degrees of freedom are lost in estimating both μ and σ from the observed sample data.

Karl Pearson introduced the chi-square test in 1900. The **chi-square distribution** is *the sum of the squares of k independent random variables* and therefore can never be less than zero; it extends indefinitely in the positive direction. Actually the chi-square distributions constitute a family, with each distribution defined by the degrees of freedom (df) associated with it. For small df values the chi-square distribution is skewed considerably to the right (positive values). As the degrees of freedom increase, the chi-square distribution begins to approach the normal curve. Table values for the chi-square distribution are given in Appendix A. Because of space limitations, chi-square values are listed only for certain probabilities.

How can the chi-square goodness-of-fit test be applied to business situations? Suppose that a large-scale benchmark study done by the hospitality industry has shown that across Canada, this is how consumers rate their hospitality experience.

Excellent	8%
Pretty good	47%
Only fair	34%
Poor	11%

Suppose a hotel manager wants to find out whether the hotel deviates significantly from this benchmark. To determine this, she interviews 207 randomly selected guests who stayed at the hotel in a given week. The response categories, as in the benchmark study, are excellent, pretty good, only fair, and poor. The observed responses from this study are given in Table 16.1. Now the manager can use a chi-square goodness-of-fit test to determine whether the observed frequencies of responses from this survey are the same as the frequencies that would be expected on the basis of the national survey.

HYPOTHESIZE:

STEP 1. The hypotheses for this example follows:

H_o: The observed distribution is the same as the expected distribution.
H_a: The observed distribution is not the same as the expected distribution.

Table 16.1		
Results of a Local Survey of Consumer Satisfaction with the Hospitality Industry	**Response**	**Frequency (f_o)**
	Excellent	21
	Pretty good	109
	Only fair	62
	Poor	15

Table 16.2	Response	Expected Proportion	Expected Frequency (f_e) (proportion × sample total)
Construction of Expected Values for Hospitality Study	Excellent	0.08	(0.08)(207) = 16.56
	Pretty good	0.47	(0.47)(207) = 97.29
	Only fair	0.34	(0.34)(207) = 70.38
	Poor	0.11	(0.11)(207) = 22.77
			207.00

TEST:

STEP 2. The statistical test being used is:

$$\chi^2 = \sum \frac{(f_o - f_e)^2}{f_e}$$

STEP 3. Let $\alpha = 0.05$.

STEP 4. Chi-square goodness-of-fit tests are one-tailed because a chi-square of zero indicates perfect agreement between distributions. Any deviation from zero difference occurs in the positive direction only because chi-square is determined by a sum of squared values and can never be negative. With four categories in this example (excellent, pretty good, only fair, and poor), $k = 4$. The degrees of freedom are $k - 1$ because the expected distribution is given: $k - 1 = 4 - 1 = 3$. For $\alpha = 0.05$ and df = 3, the critical chi-square value is:

$$\chi^2_{0.05,3} = 7.8147$$

After the data are analyzed, an observed chi-square greater than 7.8147 must be computed in order to reject the null hypothesis.

STEP 5. The observed values gathered in the sample data from Table 16.1 sum to 207. Thus, $n = 207$. The expected proportions are given, but the expected frequencies must be calculated by multiplying the expected proportions by the sample total of the observed frequencies, as shown in Table 16.2.

STEP 6. The chi-square goodness-of-fit can then be calculated, as shown in Table 16.3.

ACTION:

STEP 7. Because the observed value of chi-square of 6.25 is not greater than the critical table value of 7.8147, the hotel manager will not reject the null hypothesis.

POINTS OF INTEREST
Chi-square tests indicate whether two distributions are the same are not. They do not tell you in what specific way they are different.

Table 16.3	Response	f_o	f_e	$\dfrac{(f_o - f_e)^2}{f_e}$
Calculation of Chi-Square for Hospitality Example	Excellent	21	16.56	1.19
	Pretty good	109	97.29	1.41
	Only fair	62	70.38	1.00
	Poor	15	22.77	2.65
		207	207.00	6.25

BUSINESS IMPLICATIONS:

STEP 8. The data gathered in the sample of 207 hotel customers indicate that the distribution of responses of hotel customers is not significantly different from the distribution of responses to the benchmark national survey.

The hotel manager may conclude that her customers do not appear to have attitudes different from those people who took the benchmark survey.

Demonstration Problem 16.1

Dairies would like to know whether the sales of milk are distributed uniformly over a year so they can plan for milk production and storage. A uniform distribution means that the frequencies are the same in all categories. In this situation, the producers are attempting to determine whether the amounts of milk sold are the same for each month of the year. They ascertain the number of litres of milk sold by sampling one large supermarket each month during a year, obtaining the following data. Use $\alpha = 0.01$ to test whether the data fit a uniform distribution.

Month	Amount (L)	Month	Amount (L)
January	1,610	August	1,350
February	1,585	September	1,495
March	1,649	October	1,564
April	1,590	November	1,602
May	1,540	December	1,655
June	1,397	Total	18,447
July	1,410		

Solution

HYPOTHESIZE:

STEP 1. The hypotheses follow.

H_0: The monthly figures for milk sales are uniformly distributed.
H_a: The monthly figures for milk sales are not uniformly distributed.

TEST:

STEP 2. The statistical test used is:

$$\chi^2 = \sum \frac{(f_o - f_e)^2}{f_e}$$

STEP 3. Alpha is 0.01.

STEP 4. There are 12 categories and a uniform distribution is the expected distribution, so the degrees of freedom are $k - 1 = 12 - 1 = 11$. For $\alpha = 0.01$, the critical value is $\chi^2_{0.01,11} = 24.725$. An observed chi-square value of more than 24.725 must be obtained to reject the null hypothesis.

STEP 5. The data are given in the preceding table.

STEP 6. The first step in calculating the test statistic is to determine the expected frequencies. The total for the expected frequencies must equal the total for the observed frequencies (18,447). If the frequencies are uniformly distributed, the same number of litres of milk is expected to be sold each month. The expected monthly figure is:

$$\frac{18,447}{12} = 1,537.25 \text{ L}$$

The following table shows the observed frequencies, the expected frequencies, and the chi-square calculations for this problem.

Month	f_o	f_e	$\dfrac{(f_o - f_e)^2}{f_e}$
January	1,610	1,537.25	3.44
February	1,585	1,537.25	1.48
March	1,649	1,537.25	8.12
April	1,590	1,537.25	1.81
May	1,540	1,537.25	0.00
June	1,397	1,537.25	12.80
July	1,410	1,537.25	10.53
August	1,350	1,537.25	22.81
September	1,495	1,537.25	1.16
October	1,564	1,537.25	0.47
November	1,602	1,537.25	2.73
December	1,655	1,537.25	9.02
Total	18,447	18,447.00	$\chi^2 = 74.37$

ACTION:

STEP 7. The observed χ^2 value of 74.37 is greater than the critical table value of $\chi^2_{0.01,11} = 24.725$, so the decision is to reject the null hypothesis. This problem provides enough evidence to indicate that the distribution of milk sales is not uniform.

BUSINESS IMPLICATIONS:

STEP 8. Because retail milk demand is not uniformly distributed, sales and production managers need to generate a production plan to cope with uneven demand. In times of heavy demand, more milk will need to be processed or on reserve; in times of less demand, provision for milk storage or for a reduction in the purchase of milk from dairy farmers will be necessary.

Demonstration Problem 16.2

Chapter 5 indicated that, quite often in the business world, random arrivals are Poisson distributed. This distribution is characterized by an average arrival rate, λ, per some interval. Suppose a customer service representative (CSR) supervisor believes the distribution of random arrivals at a local bank is Poisson and sets out to test this hypothesis by gathering information. The following data represent a distribution of frequency of arrivals during one-minute intervals at the bank. Use $\alpha = 0.05$ to test these data in an effort to determine whether they are Poisson distributed.

Number of Arrivals	Observed Frequencies
0	7
1	18
2	25
3	17
4	12
≥ 5	5

Solution

HYPOTHESIZE

STEP 1. The hypotheses follow.

H_o: The frequency distribution is Poisson.
H_a: The frequency distribution is not Poisson.

TEST:

STEP 2. The appropriate statistical test for this problem is:

$$\chi^2 = \sum \frac{(f_o - f_e)^2}{f_e}$$

STEP 3. Alpha is 0.05.

STEP 4. The degrees of freedom are $k - 1 - 1 = 6 - 2 = 4$ because the expected distribution is Poisson. An extra degree of freedom is lost because the value of lambda must be calculated by using the observed sample data. For $\alpha = 0.05$, the critical table value is $\chi^2_{0.05,4} = 9.4877$. The decision rule is to reject the null hypothesis if the observed chi-square is greater than $\chi^2_{0.05,4} = 9.4877$.

STEP 5. To determine the expected frequencies, the supervisor must obtain the probability of each category of arrivals and then multiply each by the total of the observed frequencies. These probabilities are obtained by determining lambda and then using the Poisson table. As it is the mean of a Poisson distribution, lambda can be determined from the observed data by computing the mean of the data. In this case, the supervisor computes a weighted average by summing the product of the number of arrivals and the frequency of those arrivals and dividing that sum by the total number of observed frequencies.

Number of Arrivals	Observed Frequencies	Arrival Observed
0	7	0
1	18	18
2	25	50
3	17	51
4	12	48
≥5	5	25
	84	192

$$\lambda = \frac{192}{84} = 2.3$$

With this value of lambda and the Poisson distribution table in Appendix A, the supervisor can determine the probabilities of the number of arrivals in each category. The expected probabilities are determined from Table A.3 by looking up the values of $x = 0, 1, 2, 3,$ and 4 in the column under $\lambda = 2.3$, shown in the following table as expected probabilities. The probability for $x \geq 5$ is determined by summing the probabilities for the values of $x = 5, 6, 7, 8,$ and so on. Using these probabilities and the total of 84 from the observed data, the supervisor computes the expected frequencies by multiplying each expected probability by the total (84).

Arrivals	Expected Probabilities	Expected Frequencies
0	0.1003	8.42
1	0.2306	19.37
2	0.2652	22.28
3	0.2033	17.08
4	0.1169	9.82
≥5	0.0837	7.03
		84.00

STEP 6. The supervisor uses these expected frequencies and the observed frequencies to compute the observed value of chi-square.

Arrivals	Observed Frequencies	Expected Frequencies	$\dfrac{(f_o - f_e)^2}{f_e}$
0	7	8.42	0.24
1	18	19.37	0.10
2	25	22.28	0.33
3	17	17.08	0.00
4	12	9.82	0.48
≥5	5	7.03	0.59
	84	84.00	$\chi^2 = 1.74$

ACTION:

STEP 7. The observed value is not greater than the critical chi-square value of 9.4877, so the supervisor's decision is to not reject the null hypothesis. In other words, he fails to reject the hypothesis that the distribution of bank arrivals is Poisson.

BUSINESS IMPLICATIONS:

STEP 8. The supervisor can use the Poisson distribution as the basis for other types of analysis, such as queuing modelling.

Caution: *When the expected value of a category is small, a large chi-square value can be obtained erroneously, leading to a Type I error. To control for this potential error, the chi-square goodness-of-fit test should not be used when any of the expected frequencies is less than 5. If the observed data produce expected values of less than 5, combining adjacent categories (when meaningful) to create larger frequencies may be possible.*

TESTING A POPULATION PROPORTION BY USING THE CHI-SQUARE GOODNESS-OF-FIT TEST AS AN ALTERNATIVE TECHNIQUE TO THE z TEST

In Chapter 9, we discussed a technique for testing the value of a population proportion. When sample size is large enough ($n \cdot p \geq 5$ and $n \cdot q \geq 5$), sample proportions are normally distributed and the following formula can be used to test hypotheses about p:

$$z = \frac{\hat{p} - p}{\sqrt{\dfrac{p \cdot q}{n}}}$$

The chi-square goodness-of-fit test can also be used to conduct tests about p; this situation can be viewed as a special case of the chi-square goodness-of-fit test where the number of classifications equals two (binomial distribution situation). The observed chi-square is computed in the same way as in any other chi-square goodness-of-fit test, but because the test contains only two classifications (success or failure), $k = 2$ and the degrees of freedom are $k - 1 = 2 - 1 = 1$.

As an example, we will work two problems from Section 9.4 by using chi-square methodology. The first example in Section 9.4 tests the hypothesis that exactly 8% of a manufacturer's products are defective. The following hypotheses are being tested:

$$H_0: p = 0.08$$
$$H_a: p \neq 0.08$$

The value of alpha was given to be 0.10. To test these hypotheses, a business researcher randomly selected a sample of 200 items and determined that 33 of the items had at least one flaw.

Working this problem by the chi-square goodness-of-fit test, we view it as a two-category expected distribution in which we expect 0.08 defects and 0.92 nondefects. The observed categories are 33 defects and $200 - 33 = 167$ nondefects. Using the total observed items (200), we can determine an expected distribution as $0.08(200) = 16$ and $0.92(200) = 184$. Shown here are the observed and expected frequencies.

	f_o	f_e
Defects	33	16
Nondefects	167	184

Alpha is 0.10 and the degrees of freedom are 1. (Note that, because this is apparently a two-tailed test, if we use the z test to solve this problem, we need to use the value corresponding to $\alpha/2 = 0.05$. For the chi-square test, this step is not necessary.) The critical table chi-square value is:

$$\chi^2_{0.1,1} = 2.7055$$

An observed chi-square value greater than this value must be obtained to reject the null hypothesis. The chi-square for this problem is calculated as follows.

$$\chi^2 = \sum \frac{(f_o - f_e)^2}{f_e} = \frac{(33-16)^2}{16} + \frac{(167-184)^2}{184} = 18.06 + 1.57 = 19.63$$

Notice that this observed value of chi-square, 19.63, is greater than the critical table value, 2.7055. The decision is to reject the null hypotheses. The manufacturer does not produce 8% defects according to this analysis. Observing the actual sample result, in which 0.165 of the sample was defective, indicates that the proportion of the population that is defective might be greater than 8%.

The results obtained are approximately the same as those computed in Chapter 9, in which an observed z value of 4.43 was determined and compared to a critical z value of 1.645, causing us to reject the null hypothesis. This result is not surprising to researchers who understand that when the degrees of freedom equal 1, the value of χ^2 equals z^2.

Demonstration Problem 16.3

Rework Demonstration Problem 9.3 using the chi-square goodness-of-fit technique.

Solution

In this problem, we tested to determine whether the residents of Quebec consume a significantly higher proportion of milk as their primary breakfast beverage than the 0.17 figure for Canada. The hypotheses were:

$$H_0: p = 0.17$$
$$H_a: p > 0.17$$

The value of alpha was 0.05, and it is a one-tailed test. The degrees of freedom are $k - 1 = 2 - 1 = 1$, as there are $k = 2$ categories (milk or not milk). The critical table value for chi-square is:

$$\chi^2_{0.05,1} = 3.8415$$

To test these hypotheses, a sample of 550 people were contacted. Of these, 115 declared that milk was their primary breakfast beverage. The observed categories are 115 and $550 - 115 = 435$. The expected categories are determined by multiplying 0.17 and 0.83 by the observed total number (550). Thus, the expected categories are $0.17(550) = 93.5$ and $0.83(550) = 456.5$. These frequencies follow.

	f_o	f_e
Milk	115	93.5
Not milk	435	456.5

The observed chi-square is determined by:

$$\chi^2 = \sum \frac{(f_o - f_e)^2}{f_e} = \frac{(115 - 93.5)^2}{93.5} + \frac{(435 - 456.5)^2}{456.5} = 4.94 + 1.01 = 5.95$$

This observed chi-square, 5.95, is greater than the critical chi-square value of 3.8415. The decision is to reject the null hypothesis. The proportion of residents who drink milk as their primary breakfast beverage is higher in Quebec than in Canada as a whole. In Demonstration Problem 9.3, an observed z value of 2.44 was obtained, which was greater than the critical value of 1.645, allowing us to reject the null hypothesis. The results obtained by the two different methods (χ^2 and z) are essentially the same, with the observed value of χ^2 approximately equal to z^2 ($z = 2.44$, $z^2 = 5.95 = \chi^2$).

16.1 Problems

16.1 Use a chi-square goodness-of-fit test to determine whether the observed frequencies are distributed the same as the expected frequencies ($\alpha = 0.05$).

Category	f_o	f_e
1	53	68
2	37	42
3	32	33
4	28	22
5	18	10
6	15	8

16.2 Use the following data and $\alpha = 0.01$ to determine whether the observed frequencies represent a uniform distribution.

Category	f_o
1	19
2	17
3	14
4	18
5	19
6	21
7	18
8	18

16.3 Are the following data Poisson distributed? Use $\alpha = 0.05$ and the chi-square goodness-of-fit test to answer this question. What is your estimated lambda?

Number of Arrivals	f_0
0	28
1	17
2	11
≥3	5

16.4 Use the chi-square goodness-of-fit to test to determine if the following observed data are normally distributed. Let $\alpha = 0.05$. What are your estimated mean and standard deviation?

Category	Observed
10–under 20	6
20–under 30	14
30–under 40	29
40–under 50	38
50–under 60	25
60–under 70	10
70–under 80	7

16.5 In one survey, successful female entrepreneurs were asked to state their personal definition of success in terms of several categories from which they could select. Thirty-nine percent responded that happiness was their definition of success, 12% said that sales/profit was their definition, 18% responded that helping others was their definition, and 31% responded that achievements/challenge was their definition. Suppose you wanted to determine whether male entrepreneurs felt the same way and took a random sample of men, resulting in the following data. Use the chi-square goodness-of-fit test to determine whether the observed frequency distribution of data for men is the same as the distribution for women. Let $\alpha = 0.05$.

Definition	f_0
Happiness	42
Sales/profit	95
Helping others	27
Achievements/challenge	63

16.6 The following percentages come from a national survey of the ages of recorded-music shoppers. A local survey produced the observed values. Does the evidence in the observed data indicate that we should reject the national survey distribution for local recorded-music shoppers? Use $\alpha = 0.01$.

Age	Percentage from Survey	f_0
10–14	9	22
15–19	23	50
20–24	22	43
25–29	14	29
30–34	10	19
≥35	22	49

16.7 The general manager of a major league baseball team believes the ages of purchasers of game tickets are normally distributed. The following data represent the distribution of ages for a sample of observed purchasers of major league baseball game tickets. Use the chi-square goodness-of-fit test to determine whether this distribution is significantly different from the normal distribution. Assume that $\alpha = 0.05$.

Age of Purchaser	Frequency
10–under 20	16
20–under 30	44
30–under 40	61
40–under 50	56
50–under 60	35
60–under 70	19

16.8 A 911 service keeps records of emergency telephone calls. A study of 150 five-minute time intervals resulted in the distribution of number of calls as follows. For example, during 18 of the five-minute intervals, no calls occurred. Use the chi-square goodness-of-fit test and $\alpha = 0.01$ to determine whether this distribution is Poisson.

Number of Calls (per 5-minute interval)	Frequency
0	18
1	28
2	47
3	21
4	16
5	11
6 or more	9

16.9 According to an extensive survey conducted for *Business Marketing* by Leo J. Shapiro & Associates, 66% of all computer companies were planning to spend more on marketing in a certain year than in previous years. Only 33% of other information technology companies and 28% of non–information technology companies were planning to spend more. Suppose a researcher wanted to conduct a survey of her own to test the claim that 28% of all non–information technology companies were planning to spend more on marketing next year than this year. She randomly selects 270 companies and determines that 62 of the companies do plan to spend more on marketing next year. Use $\alpha = 0.05$, the chi-square goodness-of-fit test, and the sample data to test to determine whether the 28% figure holds for all non–information technology companies.

16.10 Cross-cultural training is rapidly becoming a popular way to prepare executives for foreign management positions within their company. This training includes such aspects as foreign language, previsit orientations, meetings with former expatriates, and cultural background information on the country. According to Runzheimer International, 30% of all major companies provide formal cross-cultural programs to their executives being relocated in foreign countries. Suppose a researcher wants to test this figure for companies in the communications industry to determine whether the figure is too high for that industry. In a random sample, 180 communications firms are contacted; 42 provide such a program. Let $\alpha = 0.05$ and use the chi-square goodness-of-fit test to determine whether the 0.30 proportion for all major companies is too high for this industry.

16.2 CONTINGENCY ANALYSIS: CHI-SQUARE TEST OF INDEPENDENCE

The chi-square goodness-of-fit test is used to analyze the distribution of frequencies for categories of *one* variable, such as age or number of bank arrivals, to determine whether the distribution of these frequencies is the same as some hypothesized or expected distribution. However, the goodness-of-fit test cannot be used to analyze *two* variables simultaneously. A different chi-square test, the **chi-square test of independence,** can be *used to analyze the frequencies of two variables with multiple categories to determine whether the two variables are independent.* There are many cases in which this type of analysis is desirable. For example, a market researcher might want to determine whether the type of soft drink preferred by a consumer is independent of the consumer's age. An organizational behaviourist might want to know whether absenteeism is independent of job classification. Financial investors might want to determine whether the type of preferred stock investment is independent of the region where the investor resides.

The chi-square test of independence can be used to analyze any level of data measurement, but it is particularly useful in analyzing nominal data. Suppose a business researcher is interested in determining whether geographic region is independent of type of financial investment. On a questionnaire, the following two questions might be used to measure geographic region and type of financial investment.

1. Where do you reside?
    A. A large town (or city)   B. A medium town   C. A small town   D. A rural area

2. Which type of financial investment are you most likely to make today?
    E. Stocks   F. Bonds   G. Treasury Bills

The business researcher would *tally the frequencies of responses* to these two questions into a two-way table called a **contingency table.** Because the chi-square test of independence uses a contingency table, this test is sometimes referred to as **contingency analysis.**

Depicted in Table 16.4 is a contingency table for these two variables. Variable 1, geographic type, uses four categories: A, B, C, and D. Variable 2, type of financial investment, uses three categories: E, F, and G. The observed frequency for each cell is denoted as o_{ij}, where i is the row and j is the column. Thus, o_{13} is the observed frequency for the cell in the first row and third column. The expected frequencies are denoted in a similar manner.

Table 16.4

Contingency Table for the Investment Example

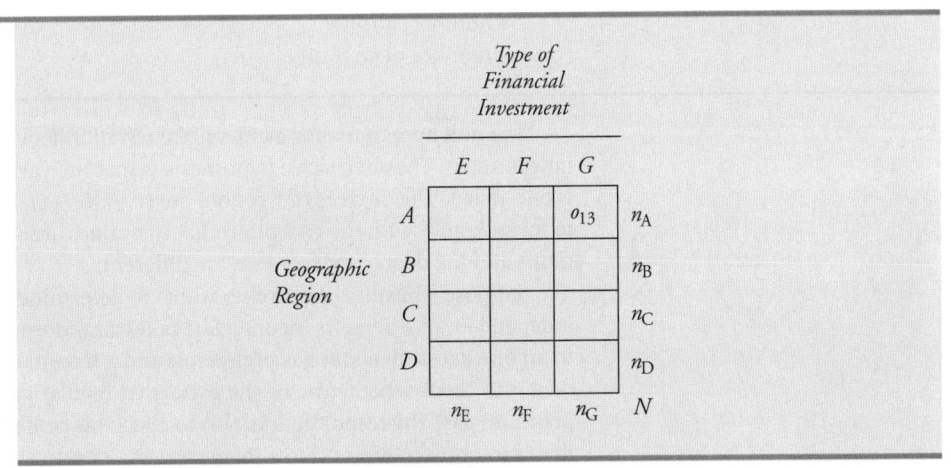

If the two variables are independent, they are not related. In a sense, the chi-square test of independence is a test of whether the variables are related. The null hypothesis for a chi-square test of independence is that the two variables are independent (not related). If the null hypothesis is rejected, the conclusion is that the two variables are not independent and are related.

Assume at the beginning that variable 1 and variable 2 are independent. The probability of the intersection of two of their respective categories, A and F, can be found by using the multiplicative law for independent events presented in Chapter 4:

$$P(A \cap F) = P(A) \cdot P(F)$$

If A and F are independent, then:

$$P(A) = \frac{n_A}{N}, \ P(F) = \frac{n_F}{N}, \text{ and } P(A \cap F) = \frac{n_A}{N} \cdot \frac{n_F}{N}.$$

If $P(A \cap F)$ is multiplied by the total number of frequencies, N, the expected frequency for the cell of A and F can be determined:

$$e_{AF} = \frac{n_A}{N} \cdot \frac{n_F}{N}(N) = \frac{n_A \cdot n_F}{N}$$

In general, if the two variables are independent, the expected frequency values of each cell can be determined by:

$$e_{ij} = \frac{n_i \cdot n_j}{N}$$

where:
  i = the row
  j = the column
  n_i = the total of row i
  n_j = the total of column j
  N = the total of all frequencies

Using these expected frequency values and the observed frequency values, we can compute a chi-square test of independence to determine whether the variables are independent. Formula 16.2 is the formula for accomplishing this test.

Chi-Square Test of Independence (16.2)

$$\chi^2 = \sum \sum \frac{(f_o - f_e)^2}{f_e}$$
$$df = (r-1)(c-1)$$

where:
  r = number of rows
  c = number of columns

The null hypothesis for a chi-square test of independence is that the two variables are independent. The alternative hypothesis is that the variables are not independent. This test is one-tailed. The degrees of freedom are $(r-1)(c-1)$. Note that formula 16.2 is similar to formula 16.1, with the exception that the values are summed across both rows and columns and the degrees of freedom are different.

Suppose a business researcher wants to determine whether type of gas preferred is independent of a person's income. She takes a random survey of gas purchasers, asking them one question about gas preference and a second question about income. The respondent is to check whether he or she prefers (1) regular gas, (2) premium gas, or (3) extra premium gas. The respondent is also to check his or her income bracket as being (1) less than $30,000, (2) $30,000 to $49,999, (3) $50,000 to $99,999, or (4) more than $100,000.

Table 16.5			*Type of Gas*			
Contingency Table for the Gas Consumer Example			Regular	Premium	Extra Premium	
		Less than $30,000	85	16	6	107
		$30,000 to $49,999	102	27	13	142
	Income	$50,000 to $99,999	36	22	15	73
		More than $100,000	15	23	25	63
			238	88	59	385

The business researcher tallies the responses and obtains the results in Table 16.5. Using $\alpha = 0.01$, she can use the chi-square test of independence to determine whether type of gas preferred is independent of income level.

HYPOTHESIZE:

STEP 1. The hypotheses follow.

H_0: Type of gas is independent of income.
H_a: Type of gas is not independent of income.

TEST:

STEP 2. The appropriate statistical test is:

$$\chi^2 = \sum\sum \frac{(f_o - f_e)^2}{f_e}$$

STEP 3. Alpha is 0.01.

STEP 4. Here, there are four rows ($r = 4$) and three columns ($c = 3$). The degrees of freedom are $(4 - 1)(3 - 1) = 6$. The critical value of chi-square for $\alpha = 0.01$ is $\chi^2_{0.01,6} = 16.8119$. The decision rule is to reject the null hypothesis if the observed chi-square is greater than 16.8119.

STEP 5. The observed data appear in Table 16.5.

STEP 6. To determine the observed value of chi-square, the researcher must compute the expected frequencies. The expected values for this example are calculated as follows, with the first term in the subscript (and numerator) representing the row and the second term in the subscript (and numerator) representing the column:

$$e_{11} = \frac{(n_{1.})(n_{.1})}{N} = \frac{(107)(238)}{385} = 66.15 \quad e_{21} = \frac{(n_{2.})(n_{.1})}{N} = \frac{(142)(238)}{385} = 87.78$$

$$e_{12} = \frac{(n_{1.})(n_{.2})}{N} = \frac{(107)(88)}{385} = 24.46 \quad e_{22} = \frac{(n_{2.})(n_{.2})}{N} = \frac{(142)(88)}{385} = 32.46$$

$$e_{13} = \frac{(n_{1.})(n_{.3})}{N} = \frac{(107)(59)}{385} = 16.40 \quad e_{23} = \frac{(n_{2.})(n_{.3})}{N} = \frac{(142)(59)}{385} = 21.76$$

$$e_{31} = \frac{(n_{3.})(n_{.1})}{N} = \frac{(73)(238)}{385} = 45.13 \quad e_{41} = \frac{(n_{4.})(n_{.1})}{N} = \frac{(63)(238)}{385} = 38.95$$

$$e_{32} = \frac{(n_{3.})(n_{.2})}{N} = \frac{(73)(88)}{385} = 16.69 \quad e_{42} = \frac{(n_{4.})(n_{.2})}{N} = \frac{(63)(88)}{385} = 14.40$$

$$e_{33} = \frac{(n_{3.})(n_{.3})}{N} = \frac{(73)(59)}{385} = 11.19 \quad e_{43} = \frac{(n_{4.})(n_{.3})}{N} = \frac{(63)(59)}{385} = 9.65$$

Table 16.6

Contingency Table of Observed and Expected Frequencies for Gas Consumer Example

		Type of Gas			
		Regular	*Premium*	*Extra Premium*	
	Less than $30,000	(66.15) 85	(24.46) 16	(16.40) 6	107
	$30,000 to $49,999	(87.78) 102	(32.46) 27	(21.76) 13	142
Income	*$50,000 to $99,999*	(45.13) 36	(16.69) 22	(11.19) 15	73
	More than $100,000	(38.95) 15	(14.40) 23	(9.65) 25	63
		238	88	59	385

The researcher then lists the expected frequencies in the cells of the contingency tables along with the observed frequencies. In this text, expected frequencies are enclosed in parentheses. Table 16.6 provides the contingency table for this example.

Next, the researcher computes the chi-square value by summing $(f_o - f_e)^2/f_e$ for all cells:

$$\chi^2 = \frac{(85 - 66.15)^2}{66.15} + \frac{(16 - 24.46)^2}{24.46} + \frac{(6 - 16.40)^2}{16.40} + \frac{(102 - 87.78)^2}{87.78} + \frac{(27 - 32.46)^2}{32.46}$$

$$+ \frac{(13 - 21.76)^2}{21.76} + \frac{(36 - 45.13)^2}{45.13} + \frac{(22 - 16.69)^2}{16.69} + \frac{(15 - 11.19)^2}{11.19} + \frac{(15 - 38.95)^2}{38.95}$$

$$+ \frac{(23 - 14.40)^2}{14.40} + \frac{(25 - 9.65)^2}{9.65}$$

$$= 5.37 + 2.93 + 6.60 + 2.30 + 0.92 + 3.53 + 1.85 + 1.69 + 1.30 + 14.73 + 5.14 + 24.42$$

$$= 70.78$$

ACTION:

STEP 7. The observed value of chi-square, 70.78, is greater than the critical value of chi-square, 16.8119, obtained from Table A.8. The business researcher's decision is to reject the null hypothesis; that is, type of gas preferred is not independent of income.

BUSINESS IMPLICATIONS:

STEP 8. Having established that conclusion, the business researcher can then examine the outcome to determine which people, by income brackets, tend to purchase which type of gas and use this information in market decisions.

Demonstration Problem 16.4

Is the type of beverage ordered with lunch at a restaurant independent of the age of the consumer? A random poll of 309 lunch customers is taken, resulting in the following contingency table of observed values. Use $\alpha = 0.01$ to determine whether the two variables are independent.

Preferred Beverage

		Coffee/Tea	Soft Drink	Other (Milk, etc.)	
	21–34	26	95	18	139
Age	35–55	41	40	20	101
	>55	24	13	32	69
		91	148	70	309

Solution

HYPOTHESIZE:

STEP 1. The hypotheses follow.

H_o: Type of beverage preferred is independent of age.
H_a: Type of beverage preferred is not independent of age.

TEST:

STEP 2. The appropriate statistical test is:

$$\chi^2 = \sum\sum \frac{(f_o - f_e)^2}{f_e}$$

STEP 3. Alpha is 0.01.

STEP 4. The degrees of freedom are $(3-1)(3-1) = 4$, and the critical value is $\chi^2_{0.01,4} = 13.2767$. The decision rule is to reject the null hypothesis if the observed value of chi-square is greater than 13.2767.

STEP 5. The sample data were shown previously.

STEP 6. The expected frequencies are the product of the row and column totals divided by the grand total. The contingency table, with expected frequencies, follows.

Preferred Beverage

		Coffee/Tea	Soft Drink	Other (Milk, etc.)	
	21–34	(40.94) 26	(66.58) 95	(31.49) 18	1:
Age	35–55	(29.74) 41	(48.38) 40	(22.88) 20	1(
	>55	(20.32) 24	(33.05) 13	(15.63) 32	(
		91	148	70	3(

For these values, the observed χ^2 is:

$$\chi^2 = \frac{(26-40.94)^2}{40.94} + \frac{(95-66.58)^2}{66.58} + \frac{(18-31.49)^2}{31.49} + \frac{(41-29.74)^2}{29.74} + \frac{(40-48.38)^2}{48.38}$$
$$+ \frac{(20-22.88)^2}{22.88} + \frac{(24-20.32)^2}{20.32} + \frac{(13-33.05)^2}{33.05} + \frac{(32-15.63)^2}{15.63}$$
$$= 5.45 + 12.13 + 5.78 + 4.26 + 1.45 + 0.36 + 0.67 + 12.16 + 17.15$$
$$= 59.41$$

POINTS OF INTEREST
The chi-square test of independence indicates whether two variables (such as preferred beverage and age) are dependent or not. But it does not tell you in which way they are dependent. In the Demonstration Problem, the chi-square test shows that beverage preference and age are dependent. But it does not tell the nature of the relationship between different beverages and age groups.

ACTION:

STEP 7. The observed value of chi-square, 59.41, is greater than the critical value, 13.2767, so the null hypothesis is rejected.

BUSINESS IMPLICATIONS:

STEP 8. The two variables—preferred beverage and age—are not independent. The type of beverage that a customer orders with lunch is related to or dependent on age. Examination of the categories reveals that younger people tend to prefer soft drinks and older people prefer other types of beverages. Managers of eating establishments and marketers of beverage products can utilize such information in targeting their market and in providing appropriate products.

Caution: *As with the chi-square goodness-of-fit test, small expected frequencies can lead to inordinately large chi-square values with the chi-square test of independence. Hence, contingency tables should not be used with expected cell values of less than 5. One way to avoid small expected values is to collapse (combine) columns or rows whenever possible and whenever doing so makes sense.*

STATISTICS IN BUSINESS TODAY

Risk-Taking by Ad Agencies

A study was conducted by Douglas C. West to examine under what conditions, if any, advertising agencies take more risk. The primary statistical technique used to analyze the data in the study was the chi-square test of independence. Although several studies previously examined risk on the part of advertisers, little research addresses the willingness of advertising agencies to take risks on behalf of their clients. West theorized that people are more apt to take risks when the outcome affects someone else's livelihood and income rather than their own; consequently, advertising agencies might be more willing to take risks than advertisers. In addition, he theorized that advertising agencies might be more willing to take risks with smaller clients rather than large clients and that newer agencies might tend to be more willing to take risks than older agencies.

The study involved 64 account directors and/or heads of creative departments of advertising agencies selected from a standard directory. Respondents were presented with two advertising options under a plan to launch a new product. Plan A was a standard plan with an average rate of return (risk-averse), and Plan B was an uncertain plan in which there is a 50% chance of getting a lower rate of return than the client's worst forecast and a 50% chance of getting a better rate of return than the client's highest forecast (risk-seeking). Using a chi-square test of independence, the percentages of respondents selecting each plan were compared to percentages produced in a similar study with advertisers. The result was that the proportions of agency respondents that were risk-averse/risk-seeking were not significantly different from the proportions of advertisers that were risk-averse/risk-seeking ($\chi^2 = 3.165$, $p = 0.076$). Agencies and advertisers were also compared on four

degrees of risk in light of the risk taken with their most recent client. The result showed no significant difference between agencies and advertisers on the amount of risk taken with their most recent client ($\chi^2 = 3.165$, $p = 0.076$, $\alpha = 0.05$). Thus, on two questions, there was no difference in the risk-taking between agencies and advertisers.

Are there circumstances under which an advertising agency might be more willing to take risks? Respondents were asked to what degree they were willing to take risks if the client is their smallest client versus if the client is their largest client. A 4×2 contingency table was constructed with four degrees of risk and the two client sizes. Analysis of these data produced a significant chi-square of 9.819 ($p = 0.021$), showing that agencies tended to be more risk-taking with smaller clients than with large clients.

The effect of agency age on participant selection of Plan A versus Plan B was analyzed using a 2×2 contingency table. Agencies were separated into two age categories (3–19 years versus 20–135 years) with Plan A and Plan B as the risk options. Using a chi-square test of independence, it was determined that a significantly higher proportion of the younger agencies were more risk-seeking than of the older agencies ($\chi^2 = 6.75$, $p = 0.01$).

In this study, the chi-square test of independence allowed for categorical comparisons between agencies and advertisers, between small clients and large clients, and between young and old agencies. In many other studies, chi-square categorical statistics can be used to study business phenomena.

Source: Adapted from Douglas C. West, "360° of Creative Risk," *Journal of Advertising Research*, vol. 39, no. 1 (January/February 1999), pp. 39–50.

1. Under what conditions would you consider using chi-square tests?
   a.   The data are in a categorical form.
   b.   The data are ranked.
   c.   The data are continuous.
   d.   The type of data is not relevant.

2. A researcher asks 1,000 consumers across Canada to rate five major banks on a 10-point scale of reliability. Here are the average ratings of the five banks.

	Bank 1	Bank 2	Bank 3	Bank 4	Bank 5
Average Rating	8.5	7.8	8.1	4.4	6.7

The researcher would like to know what type of analysis would be appropriate here. What would you suggest and why?

3. This chapter discussed chi-square tests in relation to two major purposes. List the two purposes and illustrate each with an example.

4. What restrictions apply to sample size while using chi-square analysis?

16.11   Use the following contingency table to test whether variable 1 is independent of variable 2. Let $\alpha = 0.01$.

Variable 2

Variable 1	203	326
	68	110

16.12   Use the following contingency table to determine whether variable 1 is independent of variable 2. Let $\alpha = 0.01$.

Variable 2

Variable 1	24	13	47	58
	93	59	187	244

16.13   Use the following contingency table and the chi-square test of independence to determine whether social class is independent of number of children in a family. Let $\alpha = 0.05$.

		Social Class		
		Lower	Middle	Upper
	0	7	18	6
Number of Children	1	9	38	23
	2 or 3	34	97	58
	More than 3	47	31	30

16.14 A group of 30-year-olds is interviewed to determine whether the type of music most listened to by people in their age category is independent of the geographic location of their residence. Use the chi-square test of independence, $\alpha = 0.01$, and the following contingency table to determine whether music preference is independent of geographic location.

| | | Type of Music Preferred | | | |
		Rock	R & B	Country	Classical
Geographic Region	Ontario/Quebec	140	32	5	18
	Alberta/Prairies	134	41	52	8
	British Columbia	154	27	8	13

16.15 Is the transportation mode used to ship goods independent of type of industry? Suppose the following contingency table represents frequency counts of types of transportation used by the publishing and the computer hardware industries. Analyze the data by using the chi-square test of independence to determine whether type of industry is independent of transportation mode. Let $\alpha = 0.05$.

| | | Transportation Mode | | |
		Air	Train	Truck
Industry	Publishing	32	12	41
	Computer Hardware	5	6	24

16.16 According to a survey of new homes, there is an almost 50–50 split between one-storey and two-storey homes. In addition, more than half of all new homes have three bedrooms. Suppose a study is done to determine whether the number of bedrooms in a new home is independent of the number of storeys. Use $\alpha = 0.10$ and the following contingency table to conduct a chi-square test of independence to determine whether, in fact, the number of bedrooms is independent of the number of storeys.

| | | Number of Bedrooms | | |
		≤2	3	≥4
Number of Storeys	1	116	101	57
	2	90	325	160

16.17 A study was conducted to assess the magnitude of business that Canadian border retailers were doing with U.S. residents. Forty-one shoppers of border city department stores were interviewed; 24 were U.S. residents, and the rest were Canadian residents. Thirty-five discount store shoppers were interviewed, as were 30 hardware store and 60 shoe store customers. In these three groups, 20, 11, and 32 were U.S. residents, and the remaining shoppers were Canadian residents. Use a chi-square contingency analysis to determine whether the shoppers' residence (Canada versus U.S.) is independent of type of border city retailer (department, discount, hardware, shoe) for these data. Let $\alpha = 0.05$.

SELECTING SUPPLIERS IN THE ELECTRONICS INDUSTRY

Pearson and Ellram examined the comparative rankings of selection and evaluation criteria for suppliers of small and large electronics firms. These researchers chose to analyze the relative rankings by using frequency counts for various categories of rankings. The three tables of data displayed in the Decision Dilemma contain frequencies for small and large company respondents on three of these criteria: quality, cost, and current technology. Because each of these tables contains categorical data with two variables, company size and rank category, a contingency analysis (chi-square test of independence) is an appropriate statistical technique for analyzing the data. The null hypothesis is that company size is independent of category of rank for each criterion. The alternative hypothesis is that category of rank for each criterion is not independent of company size (company size makes a difference in how the criterion is ranked). Excel chi-square analysis produced the following results. For quality:

$$Chi\text{-}Sq = 0.991, \quad df = 2, \quad p \text{ Value} = 0.609$$

The p value of 0.609 indicates that we fail to reject the null hypothesis. On quality as a criterion, rankings of small-company respondents are independent of rankings of large-company respondents. There appears to be no difference between small- and large-company respondents on the importance of quality as a selection and evaluation criterion. Observe in looking at the table that more than half of the respondents for both small and large companies ranked quality as the number 1 criterion.

For cost:

$$Chi\text{-}Sq = 0.483, \quad df = 2, \quad p \text{ Value} = 0.785$$

The p value of 0.785 indicates failure to reject the null hypothesis. Company size is independent of the ranking of this criterion as a supplier selection and evaluation tool. In

perusing the raw data, it is evident that about one third of the respondents in both large and small companies ranked cost as either the second or the third most important criterion.

For current technology:

$$Chi\text{-}Sq = 1.026, \quad df = 2, \quad p \text{ Value} = 0.599$$

The p value of 0.599 indicates failure to reject the null hypothesis. Company size is independent of the ranking of this criterion as a supplier selection and evaluation tool.

Pearson and Ellram also found that of small companies' responses to the question of what functional areas are involved in the selection and evaluation of suppliers, 41.38% included research and development versus 48.78% for large companies. Because sample statistics are used, is enough evidence provided to declare that there is a significant difference in proportions between small and large companies? Techniques presented in Chapter 10 can be used to statistically test this hypothesis. However, the chi-square test of independence can also be used. The two variables are company size (small, large) and whether or not the functional area is included (Yes, No), producing a 2 × 2 table:

	Company Size	
	Small	*Large*
Yes	36	60
No	51	63

Recall that 87 small companies and 123 large companies took part in the study. The raw numbers are obtained by multiplying the sample sizes by the percentages (e.g., sample size for small companies = 87 and 87(0.4138) = 36). Excel gives a chi-square value of 1.125 with a p value of 0.289. Based on this result, there is no significant difference between small and large companies on the inclusion of research and development in the supplier selection and evaluation process.

KEY CONSIDERATIONS

The usage of chi-square goodness-of-fit tests and chi-square tests of independence becomes an issue when the expected frequencies are too small. Considerable debate surrounds the discussion of how small is too small. In this chapter, we used an expected frequency of less than 5 as too small. As an example, suppose an expected frequency is 2. If the observed value is 6, then the calculation of $(f_o - f_e)^2/f_e$

results in $(6 - 2)^2/2 = 8$ just for this pair of observed and expected frequencies. Such a contribution to the overall computed chi-square can inordinately affect the total chi-square value and skew the analysis. Researchers should exercise caution in using small expected frequencies with chi-square tests lest they arrive at an incorrect statistical outcome.

Why Statistics Is Relevant

A considerable amount of data comes to us in categorical form: How many would vote Conservative, Liberal, or NDP? How many students are enrolled in different majors? Do more consumers prefer Brand A than prefer Brand B, C, or D? In all such cases, chi-square provides a way of analyzing the data and understanding the implications. For example:

- An industrial engineer is testing three machines for their accuracy. He counts the number of defective parts produced by each machine. Chi-square analysis can assess whether these three machines are equally accurate (i.e., whether they produce similar levels of nondefective parts produced).
- A company's call centre has 30 employees. The manager gets the impression that on certain days of the week the lines are so busy that many calls go unanswered. On other days, there are so few calls that employees are underutilized. Knowing for sure that there is a higher call volume on certain days of the week would help the manager to deploy the resources more productively. A chi-square test would indicate whether there is any difference in call volume on different days of the week.
- A pollster would like to know whether a voter's religion influences his or her voting preference. The pollster obtains the religious affiliation and the voting preference of 1,000 randomly selected Canadians. Chi-square analysis can tell us whether religious affiliation is associated with voting preferences or not.
- An employer would like to understand if productivity of blue-collar workers goes down toward the end of the day. The employer keeps a record of the number of items produced by the workers each hour. Chi-square can indicate whether there is a relationship between time of day and productivity.
- A professor would like to know whether the number of questions asked by her students relates to their grades. So, she decides to keep a record of the number of questions asked by each respondent during a semester and tabulates it against the grades (A, B, C, …). A chi-square analysis could indicate if the two are related.

SUMMARY

1. Categorical data are nonnumerical data that can be summarized as frequency counts of one or more categories. For example, business can be categorized into small, medium or large.

2. Chi-square tests analyze categorical data. The two techniques presented for analyzing categorical data are the chi-square goodness-of-fit test and the chi-square test of independence. These techniques are an outgrowth of the binomial distribution and the inferential techniques for analyzing population proportions.

3. The chi-square goodness-of-fit test is used to compare a theoretical or expected distribution of measurements for several categories of a variable with the actual or observed distribution of measurements. It can be used to determine whether a distribution of values fits a given distribution, such as the Poisson or normal distribution.

If only two categories are used, the test offers the equivalent of a z test for a single proportion.

The chi-square test of independence is used to analyze frequencies for categories of two variables to determine whether the two variables are independent. The data used in analysis by a chi-square test of independence are arranged in a two-dimensional table called a contingency table. For this reason, the test is sometimes referred to as contingency analysis. A chi-square test of independence is computed in a manner similar to that used with the chi-square goodness-of-fit test. Expected values are computed for each cell of the contingency table and then compared to observed values with the chi-square statistic.

4. Both the chi-square test of independence and the chi-square goodness-of-fit test require that expected values be greater than or equal to 5.

KEY TERMS

categorical data	chi-square goodness-of-fit	chi-square test of indepen-	contingency analysis
chi-square distribution	test	dence	contingency table

FORMULAS

χ^2 goodness-of-fit test (16.1)

$$\chi^2 = \sum \frac{(f_o - f_e)^2}{f_e}$$

$$df = k - 1 - c$$

χ^2 test of independence (16.2)

$$\chi^2 = \sum \sum \frac{(f_o - f_e)^2}{f_e}$$

$$df = (r - 1)(c - 1)$$

SUPPLEMENTARY PROBLEMS

Calculating the Statistics

16.18 Use a chi-square goodness-of-fit test to determine whether the following observed frequencies are distributed the same as the expected frequencies. Let $\alpha = 0.01$.

Category	f_o	f_e
1	214	206
2	235	232
3	279	268
4	281	284
5	264	268
6	254	232
7	211	206

16.19 Use a chi-square contingency analysis to test to determine whether variable 1 is independent of variable 2. Use a 5% level of significance.

	Variable 2		
Variable 1	12	23	21
	8	17	20
	7	11	18

Testing Your Understanding

16.20 Is a manufacturer's geographic location independent of the type of customer? Use the following data for companies with primarily industrial customers and companies with primarily retail customers to test this question. Let $\alpha = 0.10$.

		Geographic Location		
		Ontario/ Quebec	West	Atlantic Provinces
Customer Type	Industrial	230	115	68
	Retail	185	143	89

16.21 A national youth organization sells six different kinds of cookies during its annual cookie campaign. A local leader is curious about whether national sales of the six kinds of cookies are uniformly distributed. He randomly selects the amounts of each kind of cookies sold from five youths and combines them into the observed data that follow. Use $\alpha = 0.05$ to determine whether the data indicate that sales for these six kinds of cookies are uniformly distributed.

Kind of Cookie	Observed Frequency
Chocolate chip	189
Peanut butter	168
Oatmeal raisin	155
Lemon	161
Chocolate mint	216
Vanilla filled	165

16.22 A researcher interviewed 2,067 people and asked whether they were the primary decision makers in the household when buying a new car last year. Two hundred seven were men and had bought a new car last year. Sixty-five were women and had bought a new car last year. Eight hundred eleven of the responses were from men who did not buy a car last year. Nine hundred eighty-four were from women who did not buy a car last year. Use these data to determine whether gender is independent of being a major decision maker in purchasing a car last year. Let $\alpha = 0.05$.

16.23 Are random arrivals at a shoe store at the local mall Poisson distributed? Suppose a mall employee researches this question by gathering data for arrivals during one-minute intervals on a weekday be-

SUPPLEMENTARY PROBLEMS (continued)

tween 6:30 P.M. and 8:00 P.M. The data obtained follow. Use $\alpha = 0.05$ to determine whether the observed data seem to be from a Poisson distribution.

Arrivals per Minute	Observed Frequency
0	26
1	40
2	57
3	32
4	17
5	12
6	8

16.24 According to Beverage Digest/Maxwell Report, the distribution of market share in the U.S. for the top seven soft drinks was as follows: Coca-Cola Classic 17.9%, Pepsi-Cola 11.5%, Diet Coke 9.7%, Mountain Dew 6.3%, Diet Pepsi 6.1%, Sprite 5.7%, and Dr. Pepper 5.6%. Suppose a marketing analyst wants to determine whether this distribution fits that of her geographic region. She randomly surveys 1,726 people and asks them to name their favourite soft drink. The responses are as follows: Classic Coke 314, Pepsi 219, Diet Coke 212, Mountain Dew 121, Diet Pepsi 98, Sprite 93, Dr. Pepper 88, and others 581. She then tests to determine whether the local distribution of soft drink preferences is the same or different from the national figures, using $\alpha = 0.05$. What does she find?

16.25 Are the types of professional jobs held in the computing industry independent of the number of years a person has worked in the industry? Suppose 246 workers are interviewed. Use the results obtained to determine whether type of professional job held in the computer industry is independent of years worked in the industry. Let $\alpha = 0.01$.

		Professional Position			
		Manager	*Programmer*	*Operator*	*Systems Analyst*
Years	*0–3*	6	37	11	13
	4–8	28	16	23	24
	More than 8	47	10	12	19

16.26 A study by Market Facts/TeleNation for Personnel Decisions International (PDI) found that the average workweek is getting longer for U.S. full-time workers. Forty-three percent of the responding workers in the survey cited "more work, more business" as the number one reason for this increase in workweek. Suppose you want to test this figure in Canada to determine whether Canadian workers feel the same way. A random sample of 315 Canadian full-time workers whose workweek has been getting longer is chosen. They are offered a selection of possible reasons for this increase and 120 pick "more work, more business." Use techniques presented in this chapter and an alpha of 0.05 to test to determine whether the 43% U.S. figure for this reason holds true in Canada.

16.27 Is the number of children that a post-secondary student currently has independent of the type of college or university being attended? Suppose students were randomly selected from three types of colleges and universities and the data shown represent the results of a survey of those students. Use a chi-square test of independence of answer the question. Let $\alpha = 0.05$.

		Type of College or University		
		Community College	*Large University*	*Small University*
Number of Children	*0*	25	178	31
	1	49	141	12
	2	31	54	8
	3 or more	22	14	6

Interpreting the Output

16.28 A survey by Ipsos-Reid showed that given a $1,000 windfall, 36% of recipients would spend the money on home improvement, 24% on leisure travel/vacation, 15% on clothing, 15% on home entertainment or electronic products, and 10% on local entertainment including restaurants and movies. Suppose a researcher believes that these results would not be the same if posed to adults between 21 and 30 years of age. The researcher conducts a new survey interviewing 200 adults between 21 and 30 years of age asking these same questions. A chi-square goodness-of-fit test is conducted to compare the results of the new survey to the one taken by Ipsos-Reid. The

Excel results follow. The observed and expected values are for the categories as already listed and appear in the same order. Discuss the findings. How did the distribution of results from the new survey compare to the old? Discuss the business implications of this outcome.

21–30 Years of Age	General Population
Observed	Expected
36	72
64	48
42	30
38	30
20	20

The *p* value for the chi-square goodness-of-fit test is 0.0000043. The observed chi-square for the goodness-of-fit test is 30.18.

16.29 Do men and women prefer the same colours of cars? That is, is gender independent of colour preference for cars? Suppose a study is undertaken to address this question. A random sample of men and women are asked which of five colours (silver, white, black, green, blue) they prefer in a car. The results of a chi-square test of independence are shown here. Discuss the test used, the hypotheses, the findings, and the business implications.

```
Chi-Square Test: Men, Women

Expected counts are printed below ob-
served counts.
Chi-square contributions are printed
below expected counts.
           Men       Women      Total
Silver      90        52         142
           85.20     56.80
            0.270     0.406
White       75        58         133
           79.80     53.20
            0.289     0.433
Black       63        30          93
           55.80     37.20
            0.929     1.394
Green       39        33          72
           43.20     28.80
            0.408     0.612
Blue        33        27          60
           36.00     24.00
            0.250     0.375
Total      300       200         500

Chi-Sq = 5.366, df = 4, p Value = 0.252
```

ANALYZING THE DATABASES

see www.wiley.com/canada/black

Let $\alpha = 0.05$ for both problems.

1. The Financial Database contains companies in seven different types of industries. These seven are denoted by the variable Type. Use a chi-square goodness-of-fit test to determine whether the seven types of industries are uniformly distributed in this database.

2. Use a chi-square test of independence to determine whether Region is independent of Birth Trauma Injury to the Neonate in the Canadian Hospitals Database. Comment on the results of this test.

CASE

Foot Locker in the Shoe Mix

Foot Locker, Inc., is the world's number one retailer of athletic footwear and apparel. The company has approximately 3,800 retail stores in 20 countries across North America and Europe, and in Australia under various brand names. Foot Locker estimates that it controls about 18% of the $U.S. 15 billion athletic footwear market. The company intends to increase its share of the worldwide market by adding stores and by growing its Internet and catalogue business.

In recent years, Foot Locker officials have been rethinking the company's retail mix. Determining the shoe mix that will maximize profits is an important decision for Foot Locker. By the year 2002, in an effort to stock more lower-priced footwear, the company had reduced its inventory of sneakers priced at $120 or more by 50%.

Discussion

Suppose the data presented below represented the number of unit sales (millions of U.S. dollars) for athletic footwear in the years 2000 and 2009. Use techniques presented in this chapter to analyze these data, and discuss the business implications for Foot Locker.

Price Category	2000	2009
Less than $30	115	126
$30–less than $40	38	40
$40–less than $50	37	35
$50–less than $60	30	27
$60–less than $70	22	20
$70–less than $85	21	20
$85–less than $100	11	11
$100 or more	17	18

Suppose Foot Locker strongly encourages its employees to make formal suggestions to improve the store, the product, and the working environment. Suppose a quality auditor keeps records of the suggestions, the people who submitted them, and the geographic region from which they come. A possible breakdown of the number of suggestions over a three-year period by employee gender and geographic location follows. Is there any relationship between the gender of the employee and the geographic location in terms of number of suggestions? If they are related, what does this relationship mean to the company? What business implications might there be for such an analysis?

Location	Gender Male	Gender Female
U.S. West	29	43
U.S. South	48	20
U.S. East	52	61
U.S. North	28	25
Europe	78	32
Australia	47	29

According to Wells Fargo Securities and the NPD-Fashionworld Consumer Panel, Foot Locker holds 19.4% of the sneaker market. Suppose that due to its relationship with Nike and Nike's presence in the U.S. West region, Foot Locker believes that its share of the market in that region is higher than it is in the rest of the country. Foot Locker hires a market research company to test this notion. The research company randomly samples 1,000 people in the U.S. West who have just purchased a pair of sneakers, and 230 of the sampled shoppers purchased their sneakers at Foot Locker. Is this result enough evidence to declare that Foot Locker's share of the market in the U.S. West is significantly higher than it is otherwise? Use techniques from this chapter to test this hypothesis. What business implications might there be for Foot Locker if this market share information is true?

References

Adapted from Christopher Lawton and Maureen Tkacik, "Foot Locker Changes Mix of Sneakers," *Wall Street Journal*, July 22, 2002, p. B3; Foot Locker, Inc., available at <http://www.footlocker-inc.com>; "Venator Group, Inc. Announces Name Change to Foot Locker, Inc.," *PR NEWSWIRE*, November 1, 2001, p. 1; <http://www.footlockerinc.com/>.

USING THE COMPUTER

Excel

- Excel can compute the chi-square goodness-of-fit test but not the chi-square test of independence.
- To compute the chi-square goodness-of-fit test, begin with **Insert Function (f_x)**. To access **Insert Function** go to the **Formulas** tab on an Excel worksheet (top centre tab). The Insert Function tab is on the far left of the menu bar. In the **Insert Function** dialogue box at the top, there is a pull-down menu where it says **Or select a category.** From the pull-down menu associated with this command, select **Statistical**. Select **CHITEST** from the **Insert Function's Statistical** menu. In the **CHITEST** dialogue box, place the location of the observed values in **Actual_range.** Place the location of the expected values in **Expected_range.** The output will consist of a p value. To determine the observed chi-square from this p value, go back to **Insert Function (f_x)** and select **Statistical.** Then, in the **CHIINV** dialogue box, place the p value in **Probability** and the degrees of freedom in **Deg_freedom.** The output is the chi-square value.

CHAPTER 17

NONPARAMETRIC STATISTICS

Learning Objectives

This chapter presents several nonparametric statistics that can be used to analyze data. The key questions of the chapter are:

1. What are the advantages and disadvantages of nonparametric statistics?

2. What is the runs test to test for randomness and how can we use it?

3. When and how should we use the Mann-Whitney U test, the Wilcoxon matched-pairs signed rank test, the Kruskal-Wallis test, and the Friedman test?

4. How can we measure correlation by using Spearman's rank correlation measurement?

Richard Levine/Alamy

HOW IS THE DOUGHNUT BUSINESS DOING?

DECISION DILEMMA

By investing $5,000, William Rosenberg founded the Industrial Luncheon Services company in 1946 to deliver meals and coffee break snacks to customers. Building on his success in this venture, Rosenberg opened his first coffee and doughnut shop, called the Open Kettle, in 1948. In 1950, Rosenberg changed the name of his shop to Dunkin' Donuts, and thus the first Dunkin' Donuts shop was established. The first Dunkin' Donuts franchise was awarded in 1955, and by 1963, there were 100 Dunkin' Donuts shops. In 1970, the first overseas Dunkin' Donuts shop was opened in Japan, and by 1979, there were 1,000 Dunkin' Donuts shops.

Today, there are over 8,800 Dunkin' Donuts worldwide in 31 countries. In the U.S. alone, there are over 6,400 Dunkin' Donuts locations. In Canada, there are over 70 locations, with plans for 1,500 new stores through 2017. In Canada and parts of the Great Lakes region of the U.S., Tim Hortons is a major competitor. Dunkin' Donuts is the world's largest coffee and baked goods chain, serving more than 3 million customers per day. Dunkin' Donuts sells 52 varieties of doughnuts and more than a dozen coffee beverages, as well as an array of bagels, breakfast sandwiches, and other baked goods. Dunkin' Donuts is a brand of Dunkin' Brands, Inc., based in Canton, Massachusetts.

Suppose researchers at Dunkin' Donuts are studying several manufacturing and marketing questions in an effort to improve the consistency of their products and understand their market. Manufacturing engineers want to ensure that the various machines produce a consistent doughnut size. In an effort to test this issue, four machines are selected for a study. Each machine is set to produce a doughnut that is supposed to be about 7.62 cm in diameter. A random sample of doughnuts is taken from each machine and the diameters of the doughnuts are measured. The result is the data shown.

Machine 1	Machine 2	Machine 3	Machine 4
7.58	7.41	7.56	7.72
7.52	7.44	7.55	7.65
7.5	7.42	7.5	7.67
7.52	7.38	7.58	7.7
7.48	7.45	7.53	7.69
	7.4		7.71
			7.73

Suppose Dunkin' Donuts implements a national advertising campaign in Canada. Marketing researchers want to determine whether the campaign has increased the number of doughnuts sold at various outlets around the country. Ten stores are randomly selected and the number of doughnuts sold between 8 and 9 A.M. on a Tuesday is measured both before and after the campaign is implemented. The data follow.

Outlet	Before	After
1	301	374
2	198	187
3	278	332
4	205	212
5	249	243
6	410	478
7	360	386
8	124	141
9	253	251
10	190	264

Do bigger stores have greater sales? To test this question, suppose sales data were gathered from seven Dunkin' Donuts stores along with store size. These figures are used to rank the seven stores on each variable. The ranked data follow.

Store	Sales Rank	Size Rank
1	6	7
2	2	2
3	3	6
4	7	5
5	5	4
6	1	1
7	4	3

Managerial and Statistical Questions

1. The manufacturing researchers who are testing to determine whether there is a difference in the size of doughnuts by machine want to run a one-way ANOVA, but they have serious doubts that the ANOVA assumptions can be met by these data. Is it still possible to analyze the data using statistics?

2. The market researchers are uncertain that normal distribution assumptions underlying the matched-pairs *t* test can be met with the number of doughnuts data. How can the before-and-after data still be used to test the effectiveness of the advertisements?

3. If the sales and store size data are given as ranks, how do we compute a correlation to answer the research question about the relationship of sales and store size? The Pearson product-moment correlation coefficient requires at least interval-level data, and these data are given as ordinal level.

Source: Adapted from information presented on the Dunkin' Donuts' website at <http://www.dunkindonuts.com/aboutus/company/>. Please note that the data set forth in the problem are fictional, were not supplied by Dunkin' Donuts, and do not necessarily represent Dunkin' Donuts' experience.

Except for the chi-square analyses presented in Chapter 16, all statistical techniques presented in the text thus far have been parametric techniques. **Parametric statistics** are *statistical techniques based on assumptions about the population from which the sample data are selected.* For example, if a *t* statistic is being used to conduct a hypothesis test about a population mean, the assumption is that the data being analyzed are randomly selected from a *normally* distributed population. The name *parametric statistics* refers to the fact that an assumption (here, normally distributed data) is being made about the data used to test or estimate the parameter (in this case, the population mean). In addition, the use of parametric statistics requires quantitative measurements that yield interval- or ratio-level data.

For data that do not meet the assumptions made about the population, or when the level of data being measured is qualitative, statistical techniques called nonparametric, or distribution-free, techniques are used. **Nonparametric statistics** are *based on fewer assumptions about the population and the parameters than are parametric statistics.* Sometimes they are referred to as *distribution-free* statistics because many of them can be used regardless of the shape of the population distribution. A variety of nonparametric statistics are available for use with nominal or ordinal data. Some require at least ordinal-level data, but others can be specifically targeted for use with nominal-level data. Nonparametric techniques have the following advantages.

1. Sometimes there is no parametric alternative to the use of nonparametric statistics.
2. Certain nonparametric tests can be used to analyze nominal data.
3. Certain nonparametric tests can be used to analyze ordinal data.
4. The computations on nonparametric statistics are usually less complicated than those for parametric statistics, particularly for small samples.
5. Probability statements obtained from most nonparametric tests are exact probabilities.

Using nonparametric statistics also has some disadvantages.

1. Nonparametric tests can be wasteful of data if parametric tests are available for use with the data.
2. Nonparametric tests are usually not as widely available and well known as parametric tests.
3. For large samples, the calculations for many nonparametric statistics can be tedious.

Entire courses and texts are dedicated to the study of nonparametric statistics. This text presents only some of the more important techniques: the runs test, the Mann-Whitney *U* test, the Wilcoxon matched-pairs signed rank test, the Kruskal-Wallis test, the Friedman test, Spearman's rank correlation coefficient, the chi-square test of goodness-of-fit, and the chi-square test of independence. The chi-square goodness-of-fit test and the chi-square test of independence were presented in Chapter 16. The others are presented in this chapter.

Figure 17.1

Branch of the Tree Diagram Taxonomy of Inferential Techniques

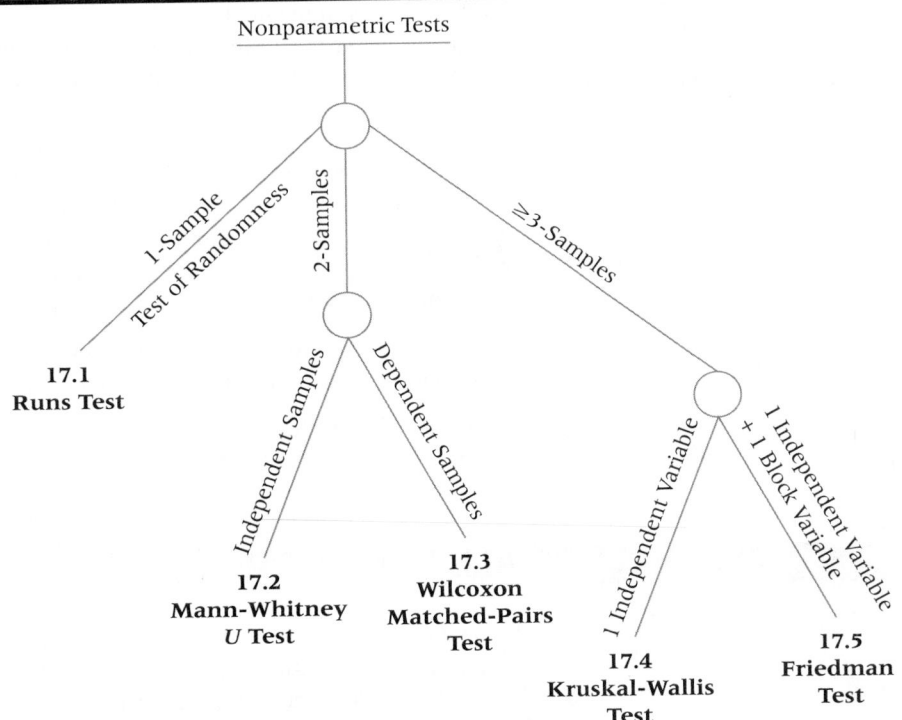

Figure 17.1 contains a tree diagram that displays all of the nonparametric techniques presented in this chapter with the exception of Spearman's rank correlation, which is used to analyze the degree of association of two variables. As you peruse the tree diagram, you will see that it includes a test of randomness, the runs test; two tests of the differences of two populations, the Mann-Whitney *U* test and the Wilcoxon matched-pairs signed rank test; and two tests of the differences of three or more populations, the Kruskal-Wallis test and the Friedman test.

17.1 RUNS TEST

The one-sample **runs test** is *a nonparametric test of randomness*. The runs test is *used to determine whether the order or sequence of observations in a sample is random*. The runs test examines the number of "runs" of each of two possible characteristics that sample items may have. A *run* is a succession of observations that have a particular one of the characteristics. For example, if a sample of people contains both men and women, one run could be a continuous succession of women. In tossing coins, the outcome of three heads in a row constitutes a run, as does a succession of seven tails.

Suppose a researcher takes a random sample of 15 people who arrive at a Canadian Tire store to shop. Eight of the people are women and seven are men. If these people arrive randomly at the store, it makes sense that the sequence of arrivals would have some mix of men and women, but probably not a perfect mix. That is, it seems unlikely (although possible) that the sequence of a random sample of such shoppers would be first eight women and then seven men. In such a case, there are two runs. Suppose, however, the sequence of shoppers is woman, man, woman, man, woman, and so on all the way through the sample. This would result in 15 runs. Each of these cases is possible, but neither is highly likely in a random scenario. In fact, if there are just two runs, it seems possible that a group of women came shopping together followed by a group of men who did likewise. In that case, the observations would not be random. Similarly, a pattern of woman-man all the way through may make the business researcher suspicious that what has been observed is not really individual random arrivals, but actually random arrivals of couples consisting of a man and a woman.

In a random sample, the number of runs is likely to be somewhere between these extremes. What number of runs is reasonable? The one-sample runs test takes into consideration the size of the sample, n; the number observations in the sample having each characteristic, n_1, n_2 (man, woman for instance); and the number of runs in the sample, R, to reach conclusions about hypotheses of randomness. The following hypotheses are tested by the one-sample runs test:

H_0: The observations in the sample are randomly generated.
H_a: The observations in the sample are not randomly generated.

The one-sample runs test is conducted differently for small samples than it is for large samples. Each test is presented here. First, we consider the small-sample case.

SMALL-SAMPLE RUNS TEST

If both n_1 and n_2 are less than or equal to 20, the small-sample runs test is appropriate. In the example of shoppers with $n_1 = 7$ men and $n_2 = 8$ women, the small-sample runs test could be used to test for randomness. The test is carried out by comparing the observed number of runs, R, to critical values of runs for the given values of n_1 and n_2. The critical values of R are given in Tables A.11 and A.12 in the Appendix for $\alpha = 0.05$. Table A.11 contains critical values of R for the lower tail of the distribution in which so few runs occur that the probability of that many runs or fewer occurring is less than 0.025 ($\alpha/2$). Table A.12 contains critical values of R for the upper tail of the distribution in which so many runs occur that the probability of that many runs or more occurring is less than 0.025 ($\alpha/2$). Any observed value of R that is less than or equal to the critical value of the lower tail (Table A.11) results in the rejection of the null hypothesis and the conclusion that the sample data are not random. Any observed value of R that is equal to or greater than the critical value in the upper tail (Table A.12) also results in the rejection of the null hypothesis and the conclusion that the sample data are not random.

As an example, suppose 26 cola drinkers are sampled randomly to determine whether they prefer regular cola or diet cola. The random sample contains 18 regular cola drinkers and 8 diet cola drinkers. Let C denote regular cola drinkers and D denote diet cola drinkers. Suppose the sequence of sampled cola drinkers is DCCCCCDCCDCCCCDCDCCCDDDCCC. Is this sequence of cola drinkers evidence that the sample is not random? Applying the HTAB system of hypothesis testing to this problem results in the following analysis.

HYPOTHESIZE:

STEP 1. The hypotheses tested follow.

H_0: The observations in the sample were generated randomly.
H_a: The observations in the sample were not generated randomly.

TEST:

STEP 2. Let n_1 denote the number of regular cola drinkers and n_2 denote the number of diet cola drinkers. Because $n_1 = 18$ and $n_2 = 8$, the small-sample runs test is the appropriate test.

STEP 3. Alpha is 0.05.

STEP 4. With $n_1 = 18$ and $n_2 = 8$, Table A.11 yields a critical value of 7 and Table A.12 yields a critical value of 17. If there are 7 or fewer runs or 17 or more runs, the decision rule is to reject the null hypothesis.

Figure 17.2

Output for the Cola Example

```
Runs Test: Cola
Runs above and below K = 1.69231
The observed number of runs = 12
The expected number of runs = 12.0769
18 observations above K; 8 below
* N Small, so following approximation may be invalid.
p value = 0.971
```

STEP 5. The sample data are given as:

DCCCCCDCCDCCCCDCDCCCDDDCCC

STEP 6. Tally the number of runs in this sample.

1	2	3	4	5	6	7	8	9	10	11	12
D	CCCCC	D	CC	D	CCCC	D	C	D	CCC	DDD	CCC

The number of runs, R, is 12.

ACTION:

STEP 7. Because the value of R falls between the critical values of 7 and 17, the decision is to not reject the null hypothesis. Not enough evidence is provided to declare that the data are not random.

BUSINESS IMPLICATION:

STEP 8. The cola researcher can proceed with the study under the assumption that the sample represents randomly selected cola drinkers.

Excel cannot analyze data by using the runs test; however, Minitab can. Figure 17.2 is the Minitab output for the cola example runs test. Notice that the output includes the number of runs, 12, and the significance level of the test. For this analysis, diet cola was coded as a 1 and regular cola as a 2. The Minitab runs test is a two-tailed test and the reported significance of the test is equivalent to a p value. Because the significance is 0.9710, the decision is to not reject the null hypothesis.

LARGE-SAMPLE RUNS TEST

POINTS OF INTEREST
When samples are large, they start looking like samples that come from normal distributions.

Tables A.11 and A.12 do not contain critical values for n_1 and n_2 greater than 20. Fortunately, the sampling distribution of R is approximately normal with a mean and standard deviation of:

$$\mu_R = \frac{2n_1 n_2}{n_1 + n_2} + 1$$

and

$$\sigma_R = \sqrt{\frac{2n_1 n_2 (2n_1 n_2 - n_1 - n_2)}{(n_1 + n_2)^2 (n_1 + n_2 - 1)}}$$

The test statistic is a z statistic computed as:

$$z = \frac{R - \mu_R}{\sigma_R} = \frac{R - \left(\dfrac{2n_1 n_2}{n_1 + n_2} + 1\right)}{\sqrt{\dfrac{2n_1 n_2 (2n_1 n_2 - n_1 - n_2)}{(n_1 + n_2)^2 (n_1 + n_2 - 1)}}}$$

The following hypotheses are being tested.

H_o: The observations in the sample were generated randomly.
H_a: The observations in the sample were not generated randomly.

The critical z values are obtained in the usual way by using alpha and Table A.5.

Consider the following manufacturing example. A machine occasionally produces parts that are flawed. When the machine is working in adjustment, flaws still occur but seem to happen randomly. A quality control person randomly selects 50 of the parts produced by the machine today and examines them one at a time in the order that they were made. The result is 40 parts with no flaws and 10 parts with flaws. The sequence of no flaws (denoted by N) and flaws (denoted by F) is shown on the next page. Using an alpha of 0.05, the quality controller tests to determine whether the machine is producing randomly (the flaws are occurring randomly):

NNNFNNNNNNNFNNFFNNNNNNNFNNNNNFNNNNNN
FFFFNNNNNNNNNNNNN

HYPOTHESIZE:

STEP 1. The hypotheses follow.

H_o: The observations in the sample were generated randomly.
H_a: The observations in the sample were not generated randomly.

TEST:

STEP 2. The appropriate statistical test is the large-sample runs test. The test statistic is:

$$z = \frac{R - \mu_R}{\sigma_R} = \frac{R - \left(\dfrac{2n_1 n_2}{n_1 + n_2} + 1 \right)}{\sqrt{\dfrac{2n_1 n_2 (2n_1 n_2 - n_1 - n_2)}{(n_1 + n_2)^2 (n_1 + n_2 - 1)}}}$$

STEP 3. The value of alpha is 0.05.

STEP 4. This test is two-tailed. Too few or too many runs could indicate that the machine is not producing flaws randomly. With $\alpha = 0.05$ and $\alpha/2 = 0.025$, the critical values are $z_{0.025} = \pm 1.96$. The decision rule is to reject the null hypothesis if the observed value of the test statistic is greater than 1.96 or less than -1.96.

STEP 5. The preceding sequence provides the sample data. The value of n_1 is 40 and the value of n_2 is 10. The number of runs (R) is 13:

STEP 6.

$$\mu_R = \frac{2(40)(10)}{40 + 10} + 1 = 17$$

$$\sigma_R = \sqrt{\frac{2(40)(10)[2(40)(10) - 40 - 10]}{(40 + 10)^2 (40 + 10 - 1)}} = 2.213$$

$$z = \frac{13 - 17}{2.213} = -1.81$$

ACTION:

STEP 7. Because the observed value of the test statistic, $z = -1.81$, is greater than the lower-tail critical value, $z = -1.96$, the decision is to not reject the null hypothesis.

BUSINESS IMPLICATION:

STEP 8. There is no evidence that the machine is not producing flaws randomly. If the null hypothesis had been rejected, there might be concern that the machine is producing flaws systematically and thereby is in need of inspection or repair.

Figure 17.3

Output for the Flawed Parts Example

```
Runs Test For Flaws
Runs above and below K = 0.2
The observed number of runs = 13
The expected number of runs = 17
10 Observations above K; 40 below
* N is small, so the following approximation may be invalid.
p value = 0.071
```

Figure 17.3 is the Minitab output for this example. The value of K is the average of the observations. The data were entered into Minitab with a nonflaw coded as a 0 and a flaw as a 1. The value $K = 0.20$ is merely the average of these coded values. In Minitab, a run is a sequence of observations above or below this mean, which effectively yields the same thing as the number of 0s in a row (nonflaws) or number of 1s in a row (flaws). The non-flaws and flaws could have been coded as any two different numbers and the same results would have been achieved. The output shows the number of runs as 13 (the same number obtained manually) and a test significance (p value) equal to 0.071. The test statistic is not significant at $\alpha = 0.05$ because the p value is greater than 0.05.

Concept Check

1. In your own words, describe the meaning of nonparametric statistics.
2. List two advantages and two disadvantages of nonparametric statistics.
3. State the null and the alternative hypotheses in a runs test.

17.1 Problems

17.1 Test the following sequence of observations by using the runs test and $\alpha = 0.05$ to determine whether the process produced random results.

$$XXXYXXYYYXYXYXYXAXYYYX$$

17.2 Test the following sequence of observations by using the runs test and $\alpha = 0.05$ to determine whether the process produced random results.

$$MMNNNNNMMMMMMNNMMMMMNMM$$
$$NNNNNNNNNNNNNMMMMMMMMMMM$$

17.3 A process produced good parts and defective parts. A sample of 60 parts was taken and inspected. Eight defective parts were found. The sequence of good and defective parts was analyzed by using Minitab. The output is given here. With a two-tailed test and $\alpha = 0.05$, what conclusions can be reached about the randomness of the sample?

Runs Test: Defects
  Defects
  $K = 0.1333$
  The observed number of runs = 11
  The expected number of runs = 14.8667
  8 observations above K; 52 below
  The test is significant at 0.0264.

17.4 Assume that a survey showed that 58% of all working Canadians are satisfied with their salary. Suppose a researcher randomly samples 27 Canadian workers and asks whether they are satisfied with their salary with the result that 15 say yes. The sequence of Yes and No responses is recorded and tested for randomness using

Minitab. The output follows. Using an alpha of 0.05 and a two-tailed test, what could you conclude about the randomness of the sample?

Runs Test: Yes/No
   Yes/No
   $K = 0.5556$
   The observed number of runs $= 18$
   The expected number of runs $= 14.3333$
   15 observations above K; 12 below
   The test is significant at 0.1452.
   Cannot reject at alpha $= 0.05$

17.5 An opinion poll by Roper Starch found that more than 70% of the women interviewed believe they have had more opportunity to succeed than their parents. Suppose a researcher in your province or territory conducts a similar poll and asks the same question with the result that of 64 women interviewed, 40 believe they have had more opportunity to succeed than their parents. The sequence of responses to this question is given below with Y denoting yes and N denoting no. Use the runs test and $\alpha = 0.05$ to test this sequence and determine whether the responses are random.

YYNYYNNYYYNNYNNYYYYYNYYYYNNYYNNNYYY
NNYYYYNYNYYYNNNYNNYYYYYNNYYYY

17.6 A survey conducted by the Ethics Resource Center discovered that 35% of all workers say that coworkers have committed some kind of office theft. Suppose a survey is conducted in your large company to ask the same question of 13 randomly selected employees. The results are that five of the sample say coworkers have committed some kind of office theft and eight say they are not aware of such infractions. The sequence of responses follows (Y denotes yes and N denotes no.) Use $\alpha = 0.05$ to test to determine whether this sequence represents a random sample.

NNNNYYYNNNNYY

17.2 MANN-WHITNEY *U* TEST

The **Mann-Whitney *U* test** is a *nonparametric counterpart of the* t *test used to compare the means of two independent populations.* This test was developed by Henry B. Mann and D. R. Whitney in 1947. Recall that the *t* test for independent samples presented in Chapter 10 can be used when data are at least interval in measurement and the populations are normally distributed. However, if the assumption of a normally distributed population is invalid or if the data are only ordinal in measurement, the *t* test should not be used. In such cases, the Mann-Whitney *U* test is an acceptable option for analyzing the data. The following assumptions underlie the use of the Mann-Whitney *U* test.

1. The samples are independent.
2. The level of data is at least ordinal.

The two-tailed hypotheses being tested with the Mann-Whitney *U* test are as follows:

   H_o: The two populations are identical.
   H_a: The two populations are not identical.

Computation of the *U* test begins by arbitrarily designating two samples as group 1 and group 2. The data from the two groups are combined into one group, with each data value retaining a group identifier of its original group. The pooled values are then ranked from 1 to *n*, with the smallest value being assigned a rank of 1. The sum of the ranks of values from group 1 is computed and designated as W_1 and the sum of the ranks of values from group 2 is designated as W_2.

The Mann-Whitney U test is implemented differently for small samples than for large samples. If both $n_1 \leq 10$ and $n_2 \leq 10$, the samples are considered small. If either n_1 or n_2 is greater than 10, the samples are considered large.

SMALL-SAMPLE CASE

With small samples, the next step is to calculate a U statistic for W_1 and for W_2 as:

$$U_1 = n_1 n_2 + \frac{n_1(n_1 + 1)}{2} - W_1$$

and:

$$U_2 = n_1 n_2 + \frac{n_2(n_2 + 1)}{2} - W_2$$

The test statistic is the smallest of these two U values. Both values do not need to be calculated; instead, one value of U can be calculated and the other can be found by using the transformation:

$$U' = n_1 n_2 - U$$

Table A.13 contains p values for U. To determine the p value for a U from the table, let n_1 denote the size of the smaller sample and n_2 the size of the larger sample. Using the particular table in Table A.13 for n_1, n_2, locate the value of U in the left column. At the intersection of the U and n_1 is the p value for a one-tailed test. For a two-tailed test, double the p value shown in the table.

Demonstration Problem 17.1

Is there a difference between health service workers and educational service workers in the amount of compensation employers pay them per hour? Suppose a random sample of seven health service workers is taken along with a random sample of eight educational service workers from different parts of the country. Each of their employers is interviewed and figures are obtained on the amount paid per hour for employee compensation for these workers. The data below indicate total compensation per hour. Use a Mann-Whitney U test to determine whether these two populations are different in employee compensation.

Health Service Worker	Educational Service Worker
$20.10	$26.19
19.80	23.88
22.36	25.50
18.75	21.64
21.90	24.85
22.96	25.30
20.75	24.12
	23.45

Solution

HYPOTHESIZE:

STEP 1. The hypotheses are as follows.

H_o: The health service population is identical to the educational service population on employee compensation.

H_a: The health service population is not identical to the educational service population on employee compensation.

TEST:

STEP 2. Because we cannot be certain the populations are normally distributed, we choose a nonparametric alternative to the f test for independent populations: the small-sample Mann-Whitney U test.

STEP 3. Let alpha be 0.05.

STEP 4. If the final p value from Table A.13 (after doubling for a two-tailed test here) is less than 0.05, the decision is to reject the null hypothesis.

STEP 5. The sample data were already provided.

STEP 6. We combine scores from the two groups and rank them from smallest to largest while retaining group identifier information.

Total Employee Compensation	Rank	Group
$18.75	1	H
19.80	2	H
20.10	3	H
20.75	4	H
21.64	5	E
21.90	6	H
22.36	7	H
22.96	8	H
23.45	9	E
23.88	10	E
24.12	11	E
24.85	12	E
25.30	13	E
25.50	14	E
26.19	15	E

$W_1 = 1 + 2 + 3 + 4 + 6 + 7 + 8 = 31$

$W_2 = 5 + 9 + 10 + 11 + 12 + 13 + 14 + 15 = 89$

$$U_1 = (7)(8) + \frac{(7)(8)}{2} - 31 = 53$$

$$U_2 = (7)(8) + \frac{(8)(9)}{2} - 89 = 3$$

Because U_2 is the smaller value of U, we use $U = 3$ as the test statistic for Table A.13. Because it is the smallest size, let $n_1 = 7$ and $n_2 = 8$.

ACTION:

STEP 7. Table A.13 yields a p value of 0.0011. Because this test is two-tailed, we double the table p value, producing a final p value of 0.0022. Because the p value is less than $\alpha = 0.05$, the null hypothesis is rejected. The statistical conclusion is that the populations are not identical.

Figure 17.4

Output for Demonstration Problem 17.1

```
Mann-Whitney Test and CI: Health, Education
Health N = 7 Median = 20.750
Education N = 8 Median = 24.485
Point estimate for ETA1-ETA2 is -3.385
95.7 Percent CI for ETA1-ETA2 is (-5.370, -1.551)
W = 31.0
Test of ETA1 = ETA2  versus  ETA1 ≠ ETA2 is significant at 0.0046
```

BUSINESS IMPLICATIONS:

STEP 8. An examination of the total compensation figures from the samples indicates that employers pay educational service workers more per hour than they pay health service workers.

As shown in Figure 17.4, Minitab can compute a Mann-Whitney *U* test. The output includes a *p* value of 0.0046 for the two-tailed test for Demonstration Problem 17.1. The decision based on the computer output is to reject the null hypothesis, which is consistent with what we computed. The difference in *p* values is due to rounding error in the table.

LARGE-SAMPLE CASE

For large sample sizes, the value of *U* is approximately normally distributed. Using an average expected *U* value for groups of this size and a standard deviation of *U*'s allows computation of a *z* score for the *U* value. The probability of yielding a *z* score of this magnitude, given no difference between the groups, is computed. A decision is then made whether to reject the null hypothesis. A *z* score can be calculated from *U* by the following formulas.

Large-Sample Formulas for Mann-Whitney *U* Test (17.1)

$$\mu_U = \frac{n_1 n_2}{2}$$

$$\sigma_U = \sqrt{\frac{n_1 n_2 (n_1 + n_2 + 1)}{12}}$$

$$z = \frac{U - \mu_U}{\sigma_U}$$

For example, the Mann-Whitney *U* test can be used to determine whether there is a difference in the average income of families who watch CBC television and families who do not watch CBC television. Suppose a sample of 14 families that have identified themselves as CBC television viewers and a sample of 13 families that have identified themselves as non-CBC television viewers are selected randomly.

HYPOTHESIZE:

STEP 1. The hypotheses for this example are as follows.

H_0: The incomes of CBC and non-CBC viewers are identical.
H_a: The incomes of CBC and non-CBC viewers are not identical.

TEST:

STEP 2. Use the Mann-Whitney *U* test for large samples.

STEP 3. Let $\alpha = 0.05$.

STEP 4. Because this test is two-tailed with $\alpha = 0.05$, the critical values are $z_{0.025} = \pm 1.96$. If the test statistic is greater than 1.96 or less than −1.96, the decision is to reject the null hypothesis.

STEP 5. The average annual reported income for each family in the two samples is given in Table 17.1.

Table 17.1

Income of CBC and Non-CBC Viewers

CBC	Non-CBC
$24,500	$41,000
39,400	32,500
36,800	33,000
43,000	21,000
57,960	40,500
32,000	32,400
61,000	16,000
34,000	21,500
43,500	39,500
55,000	27,600
39,000	43,500
62,500	51,900
61,400	27,800
53,000	
$n_1 = 14$	$n_2 = 13$

STEP 6. The first step in computing a Mann-Whitney U test is to combine these two columns of data into one group and rank the data from lowest to highest, while maintaining the identification of each original group. Table 17.2 shows the results of this step.

Note that in the case of a tie, the ranks associated with the tie are averaged across the values that tie. For example, two incomes of $43,500 appear in the sample. These incomes represent ranks 19 and 20. Each value is therefore awarded a ranking of 19.5, or the average of 19 and 20.

If CBC viewers are designated as group 1, W_1 can be computed by summing the ranks of all the incomes of CBC viewers in the sample:

$$W_1 = 4 + 7 + 11 + 12 + 13 + 14 + 18 + 19.5 + 22 + 23 + 24 + 25 + 26 + 27 = 245.5$$

Then, W_1 is used to compute the U value. Because $n_1 = 14$ and $n_2 = 13$, then:

$$U = n_1 n_2 + \frac{n_1(n_1 + 1)}{2} - W_1 = (14)(13) + \frac{(14)(15)}{2} - 245.5 = 41.5$$

Table 17.2

Ranks of Incomes from Combined Groups of CBC and Non-CBC Viewers

Income	Rank	Group	Income	Rank	Group
$16,000	1	Non-CBC	39,500	15	Non-CBC
21,000	2	Non-CBC	40,500	16	Non-CBC
21,500	3	Non-CBC	41,000	17	Non-CBC
24,500	4	CBC	43,000	18	CBC
27,600	5	Non-CBC	43,500	19.5	CBC
27,800	6	Non-CBC	43,500	19.5	Non-CBC
32,000	7	CBC	51,900	21	Non-CBC
32,400	8	Non-CBC	53,000	22	CBC
32,500	9	Non-CBC	55,000	23	CBC
33,000	10	Non-CBC	57,960	24	CBC
34,000	11	CBC	61,000	25	CBC
36,800	12	CBC	61,400	26	CBC
39,000	13	CBC	62,500	27	CBC
39,400	14	CBC			

Figure 17.5

Output for the CBC Viewer Example

```
Mann-Whitney Test and CI: CBC, NON-CBC
CBC: N = 14, Median = 43,250
Non-CBC: N = 13, Median = 32,500
Point estimate for ETA1-ETA2 is 12,500.
95.1 percent CI for ETA1-ETA2 is (3,000, 22,000).
W = 245.5
Test of ETA1 = ETA2 versus ETA1 ≠ ETA2 is significant at 0.0174.
The test is significant at 0.0174 (adjusted for ties).
```

Because n_1, $n_2 > 10$, U is approximately normally distributed, with a mean of:

$$\mu_U = \frac{n_1 n_2}{2} = \frac{(14)(13)}{2} = 91$$

and a standard deviation of:

$$\sigma_U = \sqrt{\frac{n_1 n_2 (n_1 + n_2 + 1)}{12}} = \sqrt{\frac{(14)(13)(28)}{12}} = 20.6$$

A z value can now be computed to determine the probability of the sample U value coming from the distribution with $\mu_U = 91$ and $\sigma_U = 20.6$ if there is no difference in the populations:

$$z = \frac{U - \mu_U}{\sigma_U} = \frac{41.5 - 91}{20.6} = \frac{-49.5}{20.6} = -2.40$$

ACTION:

STEP 7. The observed value of z is −2.40, which is less than $z_{\alpha/2} = -1.96$, so the results are in the rejection region. That is, there is a difference between the income of a CBC viewer and that of a non-CBC viewer. Examination of the sample data confirms that, in general, the income of a CBC viewer is higher than that of a non-CBC viewer.

BUSINESS IMPLICATIONS:

STEP 8. The fact that CBC viewers have higher average income can affect the type of programming on CBC in terms of both trying to please present viewers and offering programs that might attract viewers of other income levels. In addition, advertising can be sold to appeal to viewers with higher incomes.

Assignment of CBC viewers to group 1 was arbitrary. If non-CBC viewers had been designated as group 1, the results would have been the same but the observed z value would have been positive.

Figure 17.5 is the Minitab output for this example. Note that Minitab does not produce a z value but rather yields the value of W and the probability of the test results occurring by chance (0.0174). Because the p value (0.0174) is less than $\alpha = 0.05$, the decision based on the computer output is to reject the null hypothesis. The p value of the observed test statistic ($z = -2.40$) is 0.0164. The difference is likely to be due to rounding error.

Demonstration Problem 17.2

Do construction workers who purchase lunch from street vendors spend less per meal than construction workers who go to restaurants for lunch? To test this question, a researcher selects two random samples of construction workers, one group that purchases lunch from street vendors and one group that purchases lunch from restaurants. Workers are asked to record how much they spend on lunch that day. The data follow.

Use the data and a Mann-Whitney U test to analyze the data to determine whether street-vendor lunches are significantly cheaper than restaurant lunches. Let $\alpha = 0.01$.

Vendor	Restaurant
$2.75	$4.10
3.29	4.75
4.53	3.95
3.61	3.50
3.10	4.25
4.29	4.98
2.25	5.75
2.97	4.10
4.01	2.70
3.68	3.65
3.15	5.11
2.97	4.80
4.05	6.25
3.60	3.89
	4.80
	5.50
$n_1 = 14$	$n_2 = 16$

Solution

HYPOTHESIZE:

STEP 1. The hypotheses follow.

H_o: The populations of construction-worker spending for lunch at vendors and lunch at restaurants are the same.

H_a: The population of construction-worker spending at vendors is shifted to the left of the population of construction-worker spending at restaurants.

TEST:

STEP 2. The large-sample Mann-Whitney U test is appropriate. The test statistic is z.

STEP 3. Alpha is 0.01.

STEP 4. If the p value of the sample statistic is less than 0.01, the decision is to reject the null hypothesis.

STEP 5. The sample data are given.

STEP 6. Determine the value of W_1 by combining the groups, while retaining group identification, and ranking all the values from 1 to 30 (14 + 16), with 1 representing the smallest value.

Value	Rank	Group	Value	Rank	Group
$2.25	1	V	$3.61	11	V
2.70	2	R	3.65	12	R
2.75	3	V	3.68	13	V
2.97	4.5	V	3.89	14	R
2.97	4.5	V	3.95	15	R
3.10	6	V	4.01	16	V
3.15	7	V	4.05	17	V
3.29	8	V	4.10	18.5	R
3.50	9	R	4.10	18.5	R
3.60	10	V	4.25	20	R

(continued)

Value	Rank	Group	Value	Rank	Group
4.29	21	V	4.98	26	R
4.53	22	V	5.11	27	R
4.75	23	R	5.50	28	R
4.80	24.5	R	5.75	29	R
4.80	24.5	R	6.25	30	R

Summing the ranks for the vendor sample gives:

$$W_1 = 1 + 3 + 4.5 + 4.5 + 6 + 7 + 8 + 10 + 11 + 13 + 16 + 17 + 21 + 22 = 144$$

Solving for U, μ_U, and σ_U yields:

$$U = (14)(16) + \frac{(14)(15)}{2} - 144 = 185$$

$$\mu_U = \frac{(14)(15)}{2} = 112$$

$$\sigma_U = \sqrt{\frac{(14)(16)(31)}{12}} = 24.1$$

Solving for the observed z value gives:

$$z = \frac{185 - 112}{24.1} = 3.03$$

ACTION:
STEP 7. The p value associated with $z = 3.03$ is 0.0012. The null hypothesis is rejected.

BUSINESS IMPLICATIONS:
STEP 8. The business researcher concludes that construction-worker spending at vendors is less than spending at restaurants for lunches.

Concept Check

1. In your own words, describe the Mann-Whitney U test.
2. What are the two key assumptions of the Mann-Whitney U test?

17.2 Problems

17.7   Use the Mann-Whitney U test and the following data to determine whether there is a significant difference between the values of group 1 and group 2. Let $\alpha = 0.05$.

Group 1	Group 2
15	23
17	14
26	24
11	13
18	22
21	23
13	18
29	21

17.8   The data shown represent two random samples gathered from two populations. Is there sufficient evidence in the data to determine whether the values of population 1 are significantly larger than the values of population 2? Use the Mann-Whitney U test and $\alpha = 0.01$.

Sample 1	Sample 2
224	203
256	218
231	229
222	230
248	211
283	230
241	209
217	223
240	219
255	236
216	227
	208
	214

17.9   A survey indicated that people between 65 and 74 years of age contact a physician an average of 9.8 times per year. People 75 and older contact physicians an average of 12.9 times per year. Suppose you want to validate these results by taking your own samples. The following data represent the number of annual contacts people make with a physician. The samples are independent. Use a Mann-Whitney U test to determine whether the number of contacts with physicians by people 75 and older is greater than the number by people 65 to 74 years old. Let $\alpha = 0.01$.

65 to 74	75 and Older
12	16
13	15
8	10
11	17
9	13
6	12
11	14
	9
	13

17.10   Suppose 12 urban households and 12 rural households are selected randomly and each family is asked to report the amount spent on food at home annually. The results follow. Use a Mann-Whitney U test to determine whether there is a significant difference between urban and rural households in the amounts spent for food at home. Use $\alpha = 0.05$.

Urban	Rural	Urban	Rural
$2,110	$2,050	$1,950	$2,770
2,655	2,800	2,480	3,100
2,710	2,975	2,630	2,685
2,540	2,075	2,750	2,790
2,200	2,490	2,850	2,995
2,175	2,585	2,850	2,995

17.11   Does the male stock market investor earn significantly more than the female stock market investor? One study by the New York Stock Exchange showed that the male investor has an income of $46,400 and that the female investor has an income of $39,400. Suppose an analyst wanted to prove that the male investor earns more than the female investor. Suppose the following data represent random samples of male and female investors from across Canada. The analyst uses the Mann-Whitney U test to determine whether the male investor earns significantly more than the female investor for $\alpha = 0.01$. What does the analyst find?

Male	Female
$50,100	$41,200
47,800	36,600
45,000	44,500
51,500	47,800
55,000	42,500
53,850	47,500
51,500	40,500
63,900	28,900
57,800	48,000
61,100	42,300
51,000	40,000
	31,400

17.12   In one month in 2009, the median price of a single-family home in Calgary was $380,737 and the median price of a single-family home in Halifax was $282,499. Suppose a survey of 13 randomly selected single-family homes is taken in Calgary and a survey of 15 randomly selected single-family homes is taken in Halifax, with the resulting prices shown here. Use a Mann-Whitney U test to determine whether there is a significant difference in the price of a single-family home in these two cities. Let $\alpha = 0.05$.

Calgary	Halifax
$374,157	$283,947
378,057	274,127
375,062	275,238
377,016	277,359
375,940	280,031
376,981	279,114
380,479	282,012
380,102	284,500
379,638	276,419
381,861	277,867
381,408	277,741
372,405	274,514
381,730	282,136
	276,333
	283,968

17.3 WILCOXON MATCHED-PAIRS SIGNED RANK TEST

The Mann-Whitney U test presented in Section 17.2 is a nonparametric alternative to the t test for two *independent* samples. If the two samples are *related*, the U test is not applicable. A test that does handle related data is the **Wilcoxon matched-pairs signed rank test,** which serves as *a nonparametric alternative to the* t *test for two related samples.* Developed by Frank Wilcoxon in 1945, the Wilcoxon test, like the *t* test for two related samples, is used to analyze several different types of studies when the data of one group are related to the data in the other group, including before-and-after studies, studies in which measures are taken on the same person or object under two different conditions, and studies of twins or other relatives.

The Wilcoxon test utilizes the differences of the scores of the two matched groups in a manner similar to that of the *t* test for two related samples. After the difference scores have been computed, the Wilcoxon test ranks all differences regardless of whether the difference is positive or negative. The values are ranked from smallest to largest, with a rank of 1 assigned to the smallest difference. If a difference is negative, the rank is given a negative sign. The sum of the positive ranks is tallied along with the sum of the negative ranks. Zero differences representing ties between scores from the two groups are ignored, and the value of n is reduced accordingly. When ties occur between ranks, the ranks are averaged over the values. The smallest sum of ranks (either $+$ or $-$) is used in the analysis and is represented by T. The Wilcoxon matched-pairs signed rank test procedure for determining statistical significance differs with sample size. When the number of matched pairs, n, is greater than 15, the value of T is approximately normally distributed and a z score is computed to test the null hypothesis. When the sample size is small, $n \leq 15$, a different procedure is followed.

Two assumptions underlie the use of this technique.

1. The paired data are selected randomly.
2. The underlying distributions are symmetrical.

The following hypotheses are being tested.

For two-tailed tests:

$$H_0: M_d = 0$$
$$H_a: M_d \neq 0$$

For one-tailed tests:

$$H_0: M_d = 0$$
$$H_a: M_d > 0$$

or:

$$H_0: M_d = 0$$
$$H_a: M_d < 0$$

where M_d is the median.

SMALL-SAMPLE CASE ($n \leq 15$)

When sample size is small, a critical value against which to compare T can be found in Table A.14 to determine whether the null hypothesis should be rejected. The critical value is located by using n and α. Critical values are given in the table for $\alpha = 0.05$, 0.025, 0.01, and 0.005 for two-tailed tests and $\alpha = 0.10$, 0.05, 0.02, and 0.01 for one-tailed tests. If the observed value of T is less than or equal to the critical value of T, the decision is to reject the null hypothesis.

As an example, consider a survey that estimated the average annual household spending on movie rentals. The national average was $1,800. Suppose six families in Toronto are matched demographically with six families in Montreal, and their amounts of household spending on movie rentals for last year are obtained. The data follow.

Family Pair	Toronto	Montreal
1	$1,950	$1,760
2	1,840	1,870
3	2,015	1,810
4	1,580	1,660
5	1,790	1,340
6	1,925	1,765

An analyst uses $\alpha = 0.05$ to test to determine whether there is a significant difference in annual household movie rental spending between these two cities.

HYPOTHESIZE:

STEP 1. The following hypotheses are being tested.

$$H_0: M_d = 0$$
$$H_a: M_d \neq 0$$

TEST:

STEP 2. Because the sample size of pairs is six, the small-sample Wilcoxon matched-pairs signed rank test is appropriate if the underlying distributions are assumed to be symmetrical.

STEP 3. Alpha is 0.05.

STEP 4. From Table A.14, if the observed value of T is less than or equal to 1, the decision is to reject the null hypothesis.

STEP 5. The sample data were listed earlier.

STEP 6.

Family Pair	Toronto	Montreal	d	Rank
1	$1,950	$1,760	+190	+4
2	1,840	1,870	−30	−1
3	2,015	1,810	+205	+5
4	1,580	1,660	−80	−2
5	1,790	1,340	+450	+6
6	1,925	1,765	+160	+3

$$T = \text{minimum of } (T_+, T_-)$$
$$T_+ = 4 + 5 + 6 + 3 = 18$$
$$T_- = 1 + 2 = 3$$
$$T = \text{minimum of } (18, 3) = 3$$

ACTION:

STEP 7. Because $T = 3$ is greater than critical $T = 1$, the decision is to not reject the null hypothesis.

BUSINESS IMPLICATIONS:

STEP 8. Not enough evidence is provided to declare that Toronto and Montreal differ in annual household spending on movie rentals. This information may be useful to movie rental services and stores in the two cities.

LARGE-SAMPLE CASE ($n > 15$)

For large samples, the T statistic is approximately normally distributed and a z score can be used as the test statistic. Formula 17.2 contains the necessary formulas to complete this procedure.

Wilcoxon Matched-Pairs Signed Rank Test (17.2)	$$\mu_T = \frac{n(n+1)}{4}$$ $$\sigma_T = \sqrt{\frac{n(n+1)(2n+1)}{24}}$$ $$z = \frac{T - \mu_T}{\sigma_T}$$

where

n = number of pairs

T = total ranks for either + or − differences, whichever is less in magnitude

This technique can be applied to the airline industry, where an analyst might want to determine whether there is a difference in the cost per mile of airfares in Canada between 1979 and 2009 for various cities. Suppose the data in Table 17.3 represent the costs per mile of airline tickets for a sample of 17 cities for both 1979 and 2009.

HYPOTHESIZE:

STEP 1: The analyst states the hypotheses as follows.

$$H_0: M_d = 0$$
$$H_a: M_d \neq 0$$

TEST:

STEP 2. The analyst applies a Wilcoxon matched-pairs signed rank test to the data to test the difference in cents per mile for the two periods of time. She assumes the underlying distributions are symmetrical.

Table 17.3

Airline Ticket Costs for Various Cities

City	1979	2009	d	Rank
1	20.3	22.8	−2.5	−8
2	19.5	12.7	+6.8	+17
3	18.6	14.1	+4.5	+13
4	20.9	16.1	+4.8	+15
5	19.9	25.2	−5.3	−16
6	18.6	20.2	−1.6	−4
7	19.6	14.9	+4.7	+14
8	23.2	21.3	+1.9	+6.5
9	21.8	18.7	+3.1	+10
10	20.3	20.9	−0.6	−1
11	19.2	22.6	−3.4	−11.5
12	19.5	16.9	+2.6	+9
13	18.7	20.6	−1.9	−6.5
14	17.7	18.5	−0.8	−2
15	21.6	23.4	−1.8	−5
16	22.4	21.3	+1.1	+3
17	20.8	17.4	+3.4	+11.5

STEP 3. Use $\alpha = 0.05$.

STEP 4. Because this test is two-tailed, $\alpha/2 = 0.025$ and the critical values are $z = \pm 1.96$. If the observed value of the test statistic is greater than 1.96 or less than -1.96, the null hypothesis is rejected.

STEP 5. The sample data are given in Table 17.3.

STEP 6. The analyst begins the process by computing a difference score, d. Which year's data are subtracted from the other does not matter as long as consistency in direction is maintained. For the data in Table 17.3, the analyst subtracts the 2009 figures from the 1979 figures. The sign of the difference is left on the difference score. Next, she ranks the differences without regard to sign, but the sign is left on the rank as an identifier. Note the tie for ranks 6 and 7; each is given a rank of 6.5, the average of the two ranks. The same applies to ranks 11 and 12.

After the analyst ranks all difference values regardless of sign, she sums the positive ranks (T_+) and the negative ranks (T_-). She then determines the T value from these two sums as the smaller of T_+ and T_-:

$$T = \text{minimum of } (T_+, T_-)$$
$$T_+ = 17 + 13 + 15 + 14 + 6.5 + 10 + 9 + 3 + 11.5 = 99$$
$$T_- = 8 + 16 + 4 + 1 + 11.5 + 6.5 + 2 + 5 = 54$$
$$T = \text{minimum of } (99, 54) = 54$$

The T value is normally distributed for large sample sizes, with a mean and standard deviation of:

$$\mu_T = \frac{n(n+1)}{4} = \frac{(17)(18)}{4} = 76.5$$

$$\sigma_T = \sqrt{\frac{n(n+1)(2n+1)}{24}} = \sqrt{\frac{(17)(18)(35)}{24}} = 21.1$$

The observed z value is:

$$z = \frac{T - \mu_T}{\sigma_T} = \frac{54 - 76.5}{21.1} = -1.07$$

ACTION:

STEP 7. The critical z value for this two-tailed test is $z_{0.025} = \pm 1.96$. The observed $z = -1.07$, so the analyst fails to reject the null hypothesis. There is no significant difference in the cost of airline tickets between 1979 and 2009.

BUSINESS IMPLICATIONS:

STEP 8. Promoters in the airline industry can use this type of information (the fact that ticket prices have not increased significantly in 30 years) to sell their product as a good buy. In addition, industry managers could use it as an argument for raising prices.

Demonstration Problem 17.3

During the 1980s and 1990s, North American businesses increasingly emphasized quality control. One of the arguments in favour of quality control programs is that quality control can increase productivity. Suppose a company implemented a quality control program and has been operating under it for two years. The company's president wants to determine whether worker productivity has significantly increased since installation of the program. Company records contain the figures for items produced per worker during a sample of production runs two years ago. Productivity figures on the same workers are gathered now and compared to the previous figures. The following data represent items produced per hour. The company's statistical analyst uses the Wilcoxon matched-pairs signed rank test to determine whether there is a significant increase in per worker production for $\alpha = 0.01$.

Worker	Before	After	Worker	Before	After
1	5	11	11	2	6
2	4	9	12	5	10
3	9	9	13	4	9
4	6	8	14	5	7
5	3	5	15	8	9
6	8	7	16	7	6
7	7	9	17	9	10
8	10	9	18	5	8
9	3	7	19	4	5
10	7	9	20	3	6

Solution

HYPOTHESIZE:

STEP 1. The hypotheses are as follows.

$$H_0: M_d = 0$$
$$H_a: M_d < 0$$

TEST:

STEP 2. The analyst applies a Wilcoxon matched-pairs signed rank test to the data to test the difference in productivity from before to after. He assumes the underlying distributions are symmetrical.

STEP 3. Use $\alpha = 0.01$.

STEP 4. This test is one-tailed. The critical value is $z = -2.33$. If the observed value of the test statistic is less than -2.33, the null hypothesis is rejected.

STEP 5. The sample data are as already given.

STEP 6. The analyst computes the difference values, and, because zero differences are to be eliminated, deletes worker 3 from the study. This reduces n from 20 to 19. He then ranks the differences regardless of sign. The differences that are the same (ties) receive the average rank for those values. For example, the differences for workers 4, 5, 7, 10, and 14 are the same. The ranks for these five are 7, 8, 9, 10, and 11, so each worker receives the rank of 9, the average of these five ranks.

Worker	Before	After	d	Rank
1	5	11	−6	−19
2	4	9	−5	−17
3	9	9	0	delete
4	6	8	−2	−9
5	3	5	−2	−9
6	8	7	+1	+3.5
7	7	9	−2	−9
8	10	9	+1	+3.5

(continued)

Worker	Before	After	d	Rank
9	3	7	−4	−14.5
10	7	9	−2	−9
11	2	6	−4	−14.5
12	5	10	−5	−17
13	4	9	−5	−17
14	5	7	−2	−9
15	8	9	−1	−3.5
16	7	6	+1	+3.5
17	9	10	−1	−3.5
18	5	8	−3	−12.5
19	4	5	−1	−3.5
20	3	6	−3	−12.5

The analyst determines the values of T_+, T_-, and T to be:

$$T_+ = 3.5 + 3.5 + 3.5 = 10.5$$
$$T_- = 19 + 17 + 9 + 9 + 9 + 14.5 + 9 + 14.5 + 17 + 17 + 9$$
$$+ 3.5 + 3.5 + 12.5 + 3.5 + 12.5 = 179.5$$
$$T = \text{minimum of } (10.5, 179.5) = 10.5$$

The mean and standard deviation of T are:

$$\mu_T = \frac{n(n+1)}{4} = \frac{(19)(20)}{4} = 95$$
$$\sigma_T = \sqrt{\frac{n(n+1)(2n+1)}{24}} = \sqrt{\frac{(19)(20)(39)}{24}} = 24.8$$

The observed z value is:

$$z = \frac{T - \mu_T}{\sigma_T} = \frac{10.5 - 95}{24.8} = -3.41$$

ACTION:

STEP 7. The observed z value (−3.41) is in the rejection region, so the analyst rejects the null hypothesis. The productivity is significantly greater after the implementation of quality control at this company.

BUSINESS IMPLICATIONS:

STEP 8. Managers, the quality team, and any consultants can point to the figures as validation of the efficacy of the quality program. Such results could be used to justify further activity in the area of quality.

Figure 17.6 is Minitab output for Demonstration Problem 17.3. Minitab does not produce a z test statistic for the Wilcoxon matched-pairs signed rank test. Instead, it calculates a

Figure 17.6
Output for Demonstration Problem 17.3

```
Wilcoxon Signed Rank Test: difference

Test of median = 0.000000 versus median < 0.000000

                 N for  Wilcoxon  Estimated
            N    Test   Statistic    P       Median
difference  20    19      10.5     0.0000    -2.000
```

Wilcoxon statistic that is equivalent to T. A p value of 0.000 is produced for this T value. The p value of the observed $z = -3.41$ determined in Demonstration Problem 17.3 is 0.0003.

Concept Check

1. In your own words, describe the Wilcoxon matched-pairs signed rank test.
2. What are the two key assumptions underlying the Wilcoxon matched-pairs signed rank test?

17.3 Problems

17.13 Use the Wilcoxon matched-pairs signed rank test to determine whether there is a significant difference between the two groups of related data given. Use $\alpha = 0.10$. Assume the underlying distributions are symmetrical.

1	2	1	2
212	179	220	223
234	184	218	217
219	213	234	208
199	167	212	215
194	189	219	187
206	200	196	198
234	212	178	189
225	221	213	201

17.14 Use the Wilcoxon matched-pairs signed rank test and $\alpha = 0.05$ to analyze the before-and-after measurements given. Assume the underlying distributions are symmetrical.

Before	After
49	43
41	29
47	30
39	38
53	40
51	43
51	46
49	40
38	42
54	50
46	47
50	47
44	39
49	49
45	47

17.15 A corporation owns a chain of several hundred gas stations in the Atlantic provinces. The marketing director wants to test a proposed marketing campaign by running ads on some local television stations and determining whether gas sales at a sample of the company's stations increase after the advertising. The following data represent gas sales for a day before and a day after the advertising campaign. Use the Wilcoxon matched-pairs signed rank test to determine whether sales increased significantly after the advertising campaign. Let $\alpha = 0.05$. Assume the underlying distributions are symmetrical.

Station	Before	After
1	$10,500	$12,600
2	8,870	10,660
3	12,300	11,890
4	10,510	14,630
5	5,570	8,580
6	9,150	10,115
7	11,980	14,350
8	6,740	6,900
9	7,340	8,890
10	13,400	16,540
11	12,200	11,300
12	10,570	13,330
13	9,880	9,990
14	12,100	14,050
15	9,000	9,500
16	11,800	12,450
17	10,500	13,450

17.16   Most supermarkets across Canada have invested heavily in optical scanner systems to expedite customer checkout, increase checkout productivity, and improve product accountability. These systems are not 100% effective, and items often have to be scanned several times. Sometimes items are manually entered into the cash register because the scanner cannot read the item number. In general, do optical scanners register significantly more items than manual entry systems do? The following data are from an experiment in which a supermarket selected 14 of its best checkers and measured their productivity both when using a scanner and when working manually. The data show the number of items checked per hour by each method. Use a Wilcoxon matched-pairs signed rank test and $\alpha = 0.05$ to test the difference. Assume the underlying distributions are symmetrical.

Checker	Manual	Scanner
1	426	473
2	387	446
3	410	421
4	506	510
5	411	465
6	398	409
7	427	414
8	449	459
9	407	502
10	438	439
11	418	456
12	482	499
13	512	517
14	402	437

17.17   Attitudes toward big business change over time and are probably cyclical. Suppose the following data represent a survey of 20 Canadian adults taken in 1990 and again in 2009 in which each adult was asked to rate Canadian big business overall on a scale from 1 to 100 in terms of positive opinion. A response of 1 indicates a low opinion and a response of 100 indicates a high opinion. Use a Wilcoxon matched-pairs signed rank test to determine whether the scores from 2009 are significantly higher than the scores from 1990. Use $\alpha = 0.10$. Assume the underlying distributions are symmetrical.

Person	1990	2009
1	49	54
2	27	38
3	39	38
4	75	80
5	59	53
6	67	68
7	22	43
8	61	67
9	58	73
10	60	55
11	72	58
12	62	57
13	49	63
14	48	49
15	19	39
16	32	34
17	60	66
18	80	90
19	55	57
20	68	58

17.18 Suppose 16 people in various industries are contacted in 2008 and asked to rate business conditions on several factors. The ratings of each person are tallied into a "business optimism" score. The same people are contacted in 2009 and asked to do the same thing. The higher the score, the more optimistic the person is. Shown here are the 2008 and 2009 scores for the 16 people. Use a Wilcoxon matched-pairs signed rank test to determine whether people were less optimistic in 2009 than in 2008. Assume the underlying distributions are symmetrical and that alpha is 0.05.

Industry	April 2008	April 2009
1	63.1	57.4
2	67.1	66.4
3	65.5	61.8
4	68.0	65.3
5	66.6	63.5
6	65.7	66.4
7	69.2	64.9
8	67.0	65.2
9	65.2	65.1
10	60.7	62.2
11	63.4	60.3
12	59.2	57.4
13	62.9	58.2
14	69.4	65.3
15	67.3	67.2
16	66.8	64.1

17.4 KRUSKAL-WALLIS TEST

The *nonparametric alternative to the one-way analysis of variance* (ANOVA) is the **Kruskal-Wallis test,** developed in 1952 by William H. Kruskal and W. Allen Wallis. Like the one-way ANOVA, the Kruskal-Wallis test is used to determine whether $c \geq 3$ samples come from the same or different populations. Whereas the one-way ANOVA is based on the assumptions of normally distributed populations, independent groups, at least interval level data, and equal population variances, the Kruskal-Wallis test can be used to analyze ordinal data and is not based on any assumption about population shape. The Kruskal-Wallis test is based on the assumption that the c groups are independent and that individual items are selected randomly.

The hypotheses tested by the Kruskal-Wallis test follow.

H_o: The c populations are identical.
H_a: At least one of the c populations is different.

This test determines whether all of the groups come from the same or equal populations or whether at least one group comes from a different population.

The process of computing a Kruskal-Wallis K statistic begins with ranking the data in all the groups together, as though they were from one group. The smallest value is awarded a 1. As usual, for ties, each value is given the average rank for those tied values. Unlike one-way ANOVA, in which the raw data are analyzed, the Kruskal-Wallis test analyzes the ranks of the data.

Formula 17.3 is used to compute a Kruskal-Wallis K statistic.

Kruskal-Wallis Test (17.3)	$$K = \frac{12}{n(n+1)} \left(\sum_{j=1}^{c} \frac{T_j^2}{n_j} \right) - 3(n+1)$$

where
    c = number of groups
    n = total number of items
    T_j = total of ranks in a group
    n_j = number of items in a group
    $K \approx \chi^2$, with df $= c - 1$

The K value is approximately chi-square distributed, with $c - 1$ degrees of freedom as long as n_j is not less than 5 for any group.

Suppose a researcher wants to determine whether the number of physicians in an office produces significant differences in the number of office patients seen by each physician per day. She takes a random sample of physicians from practices in which (1) there are only two partners, (2) there are three to five partners, or (3) the office has more than five partners. Table 17.4 shows the data she obtained.

Three groups are targeted in this study, so $c = 3$, and $n = 18$ physicians, with the numbers of patients ranked for these physicians. The researcher sums the ranks within each column to obtain T_j, as shown in Table 17.5.

Table 17.4		Two Partners	Three to Five Partners	More than Five
Number of Office Patients per Physician		13	24	26
		15	16	22
		20	19	31
		18	22	27
		23	25	28
			14	33
			17	

The Kruskal-Wallis K is:

$$K = \frac{12}{18(18 + 1)}(1{,}897) - 3(18 + 1) = 9.56$$

The critical chi-square value is $\chi^2_{\alpha,df}$. If $\alpha = -0.05$ and df is $c - 1 = 3 - 1 = 2$, $\chi^2_{0.05,2} = 5.9915$. This test is always one-tailed, and the rejection region is always in the right tail of the distribution. Because $K = 9.56$ is larger than the critical χ^2 value, the researcher rejects the null hypothesis. The number of patients seen in the office by a physician is not the same in these three sizes of offices. Examination of the values in each group reveals that physicians in two-partner offices see fewer patients per physician in the office, and physicians in more-than-five-partner offices see more patients per physician in the office.

Figure 17.7 is the Minitab computer output for this example. The statistic H printed in the output is equivalent to the K statistic calculated here (both K and H are 9.56).

Table 17.5		Two Partners	Three to Five Partners	More than Five
Kruskal-Wallis Analysis of Physicians' Patients		1	12	14
		3	4	9.5
		8	7	17
		6	9.5	15
		11	13	16
			2	18
			5	
		$T_1 = 29$	$T_2 = 52.5$	$T_3 = 89.5$
		$n_1 = 5$	$n_2 = 7$	$n_3 = 6$ $n = 18$

$$\sum_{j=1}^{3} \frac{T_j^2}{n_j} = \frac{29^2}{5} + \frac{52.5^2}{7} + \frac{89.5^2}{6} = 1{,}897$$

Figure 17.7

Output for the Physicians' Patients Example

```
Kruskal-Wallis Test on Patients
                        Average
Type      N   Median     Rank       Z
1         5    18.00      5.8     -1.82
2         7    19.00      7.5     -1.27
3         6    27.50     14.9      3.04
Overall  18               9.5
```

$H = 9.56$ df $= 2$ $p = 0.008$
$H = 9.57$ df $= 2$ $p = 0.008$ (adjusted for ties)

Demonstration Problem 17.4

Agribusiness researchers are interested in determining the conditions under which Christmas trees grow fastest. A random sample of seedlings of equivalent size is divided into four groups. The trees are all grown in the same field. One group is left to grow naturally, one group is given extra water, one group is given fertilizer spikes, and one group is given fertilizer spikes and extra water. At the end of one year, the seedlings are measured for growth (in height). These measurements are shown for each group. Use the Kruskal-Wallis test to determine whether there is a significant difference in the growth of trees in these groups. Use $\alpha = 0.01$.

Group 1 (natural)	Group 2 (+ water)	Group 3 (+ fertilizer)	Group 4 (+ water and fertilizer)
20 cm	25 cm	28 cm	46 cm
13	30	36	51
18	28	25	41
28	23	41	38
23	33	43	36
15	30	30	56

Solution

Here, $n = 24$, and $n_j = 6$ in each group.

HYPOTHESIZE:

STEP 1. The hypotheses follow.

H_0: group 1 = group 2 = group 3 = group 4
H_a: At least one group is different.

TEST:

STEP 2. The Kruskal-Wallis K is the appropriate test statistic.

STEP 3. Alpha is 0.01.

STEP 4. The degrees of freedom are $c - 1 = 4 - 1 = 3$. The critical value of chi-square is $\chi^2_{0.01,3} = 11.3449$. If the observed value of K is greater than 11.3449, the decision is to reject the null hypothesis.

STEP 5. The data are as shown previously.

STEP 6. Ranking all group values yields the following.

1	2	3	4
4	7.5	10	22
1	13	16.5	23
3	10	7.5	19.5
10	5.5	19.5	18
5.5	15	21	16.5
2	13	13	24

$$T_1 = 25.5 \quad T_2 = 64.0 \quad T_3 = 87.5 \quad T_4 = 123.0$$
$$n_1 = 6 \quad\quad n_2 = 6 \quad\quad n_3 = 6 \quad\quad n_4 = 6 \quad\quad\quad n = 24$$

$$\sum_{i=1}^{c} \frac{T_i^2}{n_i} = \frac{25.5^2}{6} + \frac{64.0^2}{6} + \frac{87.5^2}{6} + \frac{123.0^2}{6} = 4{,}588.6$$

$$K = \frac{12}{24(24+1)}(4{,}588.6) - 3(24) = 16.77$$

ACTION:

STEP 7. The observed K value is 16.77 and the critical $\chi^2_{0.01,3} = 11.3449$. Because the observed value is greater than the table value, the null hypothesis is rejected. There is a significant difference in the way the trees grow.

BUSINESS IMPLICATIONS:

STEP 8. From the increased heights in the original data, the trees with both water and fertilizer seem to be doing the best. However, these are sample data; without analyzing the pairs of samples with nonparametric multiple comparisons (not included in this text), it is difficult to conclude whether the water/fertilizer group is actually growing faster than the others. It appears that the trees under natural conditions are growing more slowly than the others. The following diagram shows the relationship of the observed K value and the critical chi-square value.

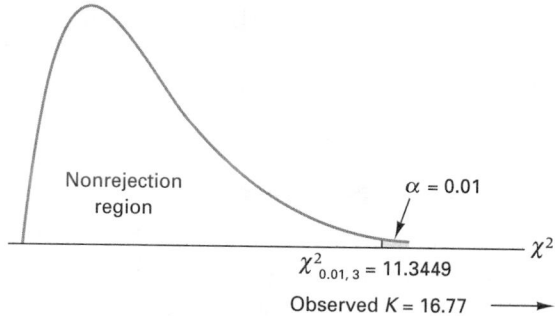

STATISTICS IN BUSINESS TODAY

Heavy Internet Users: Who Are They?

The penetration rate of the Web in Canada was around 40% in the year 2000. Since less than half of the population was regularly using the Web, it was important for marketers to profile who these people were and to determine their particular needs and wants. However, by the year 2005, the Web penetration rate was approaching 68%, thus closing the gap between this particular market segment and the Canadian population in general. Today's Web penetration in Canada is over 84%.

Henry Assael, a researcher at the Stern School of Business at New York University, conducted a study focusing on the demographic and psychographic profiles of heavy Internet users—those who use the Web for at least 20 hours a week—instead of studying Web users in general. Although these heavy users probably represent only about 20% of Web users, they account for possibly as much as 50% of all usage.

Based on a survey of 5,000 respondents, Assael discovered that heavy users are 40% more likely to be in the 18- to 34-year age bracket and 20% more likely to be in the 35- to

44-year age bracket than the general population of Web users. Although 12% more females than males use the Web in general, the gap is only 2% for heavy users. The percentage of Web users who have never been married is 60% higher for heavy users than for the general population of users. There is a higher percentage of heavy users in the $50,000 to $99,999 and the $100,000 to $150,000 income brackets than in the general population of Web users. Thirty-seven percent of heavy Web users have a bachelor's degree compared to 28% of all Web users. Heavy Web users tend to work more hours per week. The study showed that 39% of heavy Web users work more than 40 hours per week compared to only 27% of all Web users. Another study showed that the heaviest Internet users are also watching the most TV.

Nonparametric techniques can be used in studies similar to this one. For example, one study published in the year 2001 found that males average over 1,300 minutes per month online compared to about 1,200 for females. If the distributions of online usage are unknown, the Mann-Whitney U test could be used to test to determine if there is a significant difference in online usage between males and females in today's market. Furthermore, suppose the demographics of online users can be broken down by income levels such as under $25,000, $25,000 to under $50,000, $50,000 to $99,999, and more than $100,000. A Kruskal-Wallis test could be used to determine if there is a significant difference in online usage by income level. In addition, a Wilcoxon matched-pairs signed rank test could be used to determine if online usage has significantly increased from one year to the next for the same set of users.

Source: Henry Assael, "A Demographic and Psychographic Profile of Heavy Internet Users and Users by Type of Internet Usage," *Journal of Advertising Research*, vol. 45, no. 1, March 2005, pp. 93–123; "Who Goes There?" *The Wall Street Journal*, October 29, 2001, p. R4; <http://blog.nielsen.com/nielsenwire/online-mobile/heavy-internet-users-also-watch-more-tv/>.

Concept Check

1. What can we use the Kruskal-Wallis test to determine?

2. State the null and alternative hypotheses of the Kruskal-Wallis test.

17.4 Problems

17.19 Use the Kruskal-Wallis test to determine whether groups 1 through 5 come from different populations. Let $\alpha = 0.01$.

1	2	3	4	5
157	165	219	286	197
188	197	257	243	215
175	204	243	259	235
174	214	231	250	217
201	183	217	279	240
203		203		233
				213

17.20 Use the Kruskal-Wallis test to determine whether there is a significant difference in the following groups. Use $\alpha = 0.05$.

Group 1	19	21	29	22	37	42
Group 2	30	38	35	24	29	
Group 3	39	32	41	44	30	27	33

17.21 Is there a difference in the amount of customers' initial deposits when they open savings accounts according to geographic region of Canada? To test this question, an analyst selects banks of equal size from four regions of Canada. The banks selected are located in areas having similar economic and population characteristics. The analyst randomly selects adult customers who are opening their first savings account and obtains the following dollar amounts. Use the Kruskal-Wallis test to determine whether there is a significant difference between geographic regions. Use $\alpha = 0.05$.

Region 1	Region 2	Region 3	Region 4
$1,200	$225	$675	$1,075
450	950	500	1,050
110	100	1,100	750
800	350	310	180
375	275	660	330
200			680
			425

17.22 Does the asking price of a new car vary according to whether the dealership is in a small town, a city, or a suburban area? To test this question, a researcher randomly selects dealerships selling Hondas in the province of Ontario. The researcher goes to these dealerships posing as a prospective buyer and makes a serious inquiry as to the asking price of a new Honda Civic sedan (all with the same equipment). The following data represent the results of this sample. Is there a significant difference between prices according to the area in which the dealership is located? Use the Kruskal-Wallis test and $\alpha = 0.05$.

Small Town	City	Suburb
$21,800	$22,300	$22,000
22,500	21,900	22,600
21,750	21,900	22,800
22,200	22,650	22,050
21,600	21,800	21,250
		22,550

17.23 A survey showed that a higher percentage of people travel to the ocean/beach for vacation than to any other destination. Much farther behind in the survey, and virtually tied for second place, were the mountains and small/rural towns. How long do people stay at vacation destinations? Does the length of stay differ according to location? Suppose the following data were taken from a survey of vacationers who were asked how many nights they stay at a destination when on vacation. Use a Kruskal-Wallis test to determine whether there is a significant difference in the duration of stay by type of vacation destination. Let $\alpha = 0.05$.

Amusement Park	Lake Area	City	National Park
0	3	2	2
1	2	2	4
1	3	3	3
0	5	2	4
2	4	3	3
1	4	2	5
0	3	3	4
	5	3	4
	2	1	
		3	

17.24 Do workers on different shifts get different amounts of sleep per week? Some people believe that shift workers who regularly work the graveyard shift (12:00 A.M. to 8:00 A.M.) or swing shift (4:00 P.M. to 12:00 A.M.) are unable to get the same amount of sleep as day workers because of family schedules, noise, amount of daylight, and other factors. To test this theory, a researcher samples workers from day, swing, and graveyard shifts and asks each worker to keep a sleep journal for one week. The following data represent the number of hours of sleep per week per worker for the different shifts. Use the Kruskal-Wallis test to determine whether there is a significant difference in the number of hours of sleep per week for workers on these shifts. Use $\alpha = 0.05$.

Day Shift	Swing Shift	Graveyard Shift
52	45	41
57	48	46
53	44	39
56	51	49
55	48	42
50	54	35
51	49	52
	43	

17.5 FRIEDMAN TEST

The **Friedman test,** developed by M. Friedman in 1937, is *a nonparametric alternative to the randomized block design* discussed in Chapter 11. The randomized block design has the same assumptions as other ANOVA procedures, one of which is that observations are drawn from normally distributed populations. When this assumption cannot be met or when the researcher has ranked data, the Friedman test provides a nonparametric alternative.

Three assumptions underlie the Friedman test.

1. The blocks are independent.
2. No interaction is present between blocks and treatments.
3. Observations within each block can be ranked.

The hypotheses being tested are as follows.

H_0: The treatment populations are equal.
H_a: At least one treatment population yields larger values than at least one other treatment population.

The first step in computing a Friedman test is to convert all raw data to ranks (unless the data are already ranked). However, unlike the Kruskal-Wallis test, where all data are ranked together, the data in a Friedman test are ranked *within* each block from smallest (1) to largest (*c*). Each block contains *c* ranks, where *c* is the number of treatment levels. Using these ranks, the Friedman test will test to determine whether it is likely that the different treatment levels (columns) came from the same population. Formula 17.4 is used to calculate the test statistic, which is approximately chi-square distributed with df $= c - 1$ if $c > 4$ or when $c = 3$ and $b > 9$, or when $c = 4$ and $b > 4$.

Friedman Test (17.4)
$$\chi_r^2 = \frac{12}{bc(c+1)} \sum_{j=1}^{c} R_j^2 - 3b(c+1)$$

where
    c = number of treatment levels (columns)
    b = number of blocks (rows)
    R_j = total of ranks for a particular treatment level (column)
    j = particular treatment level (column)
$\chi_r^2 \approx \chi^2$, with df $= c - 1$

As an example, suppose a manufacturing company assembles microcircuits that contain a plastic housing. Managers are concerned about an unacceptably high number of the products that sustained housing damage during shipment. The housing component is made by four different suppliers. Managers have decided to conduct a study of the plastic housing by randomly selecting five housings made by each of the four suppliers. To determine whether a supplier is consistent during the production week, one housing is selected for each day of the week. That is, for each supplier, a housing made on Monday is selected, one made on Tuesday is selected, and so on.

In analyzing the data, the treatment variable is supplier and the treatment levels are the four suppliers. The blocking effect is day of the week, with each day representing a block level. The quality control team wants to determine whether there is any significant difference in the tensile strength of the plastic housing by supplier. The data are given here (in megapascals (MPa)).

Day	Supplier 1	Supplier 2	Supplier 3	Supplier 4
Monday	62	63	57	61
Tuesday	63	61	59	65
Wednesday	61	62	56	63
Thursday	62	60	57	64
Friday	64	63	58	66

HYPOTHESIZE:

STEP 1. The hypotheses follow.

H_0: The supplier populations are equal.
H_a: At least one supplier population yields larger values than at least one other supplier population.

TEST:

STEP 2. The quality researchers do not feel they have enough evidence to conclude that the observations come from normally distributed populations. Because they are analyzing a randomized block design, the Friedman test is appropriate.

STEP 3. Let $\alpha = 0.05$.

STEP 4. For four treatment levels (suppliers), $c = 4$ and df $= 4 - 1 = 3$. The critical value is $\chi^2_{0.01,3} = 7.8147$. If the observed chi-square is greater than 7.8147, the decision is to reject the null hypothesis.

STEP 5. The sample data are as given.

STEP 6. The calculations begin by ranking the observations in each row, with 1 designating the rank of the smallest observation. The ranks are then summed for each column, producing R_j. The values of R_j are squared and then summed. Because the study is concerned with five days of the week, five blocking levels are used and $b = 5$. The value of R_j is computed as shown in the following table.

Day	Supplier 1	Supplier 2	Supplier 3	Supplier 4
Monday	3	4	1	2
Tuesday	3	2	1	4
Wednesday	2	3	1	4
Thursday	3	2	1	4
Friday	3	2	1	4
R_j	14	13	5	18
R_j^2	196	169	25	324

$$\sum_{j=1}^{c} R_j^2 = 196 + 169 + 25 + 324 = 714$$

$$\chi_r^2 = \frac{12}{bc(c+1)} \sum_{j=1}^{c} R_j^2 - 3b(c+1) = \frac{12}{5(4)(4+1)}(714) - 3(5)(4+1) = 10.68$$

ACTION:

STEP 7. Because the observed value of $\chi_r^2 = 10.68$ is greater than the critical value, $\chi_{0.05,3}^2 = 7.8147$, the decision is to reject the null hypothesis.

BUSINESS IMPLICATIONS:

STEP 8. Statistically, there is a significant difference in the tensile strength of housings made by different suppliers. The sample data indicate that supplier 3 is producing housings with a lower tensile strength than those made by other suppliers and that supplier 4 is producing housings with a higher tensile strength. Further study by managers and a quality team may result in attempts to bring supplier 3 up to standard on tensile strength or perhaps cancellation of the contract.

Figure 17.8 displays the chi-square distribution for df = 3 along with the critical value, the observed value of the test statistic, and the rejection region. Figure 17.9 is the Minitab output for the Friedman test. The computer output contains the value of χ_r^2, referred to as S, along with the p value of 0.014, which informs the researcher that the null hypothesis is rejected at an alpha of 0.05. Additional information is given about the medians and the column sum totals of ranks.

Figure 17.8

Distribution for Tensile Strength Example

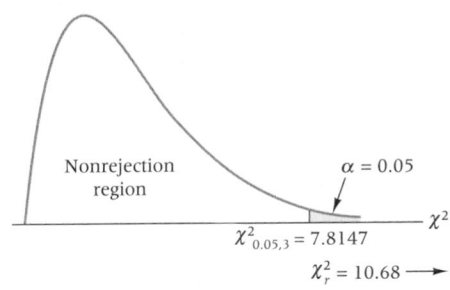

Figure 17.9

Output for the Tensile Strength Example

```
Friedman Test: Rank Versus Supplier Blocked by Day

S = 10.68   df = 3   p = 0.014

                          Sum
              Estimated    of
Supplier  N    Median    Ranks
1         5    62.125     14.0
2         5    61.375     13.0
3         5    56.875      5.0
4         5    64.125     18.0

Grand median = 61.125
```

Demonstration Problem 17.5

A market research company wants to determine brand preference for refrigerators. Five companies contracted with the research company to have their products included in the study. As part of the study, the research company randomly selects 10 potential refrigerator buyers and shows them one of each of the five brands. Each survey participant is then asked to rank the refrigerator brands from 1 to 5. The results of these rankings are given in the table below. Use the Friedman test and $\alpha = 0.01$ to determine whether there are any significant differences between the rankings of these brands.

Solution

HYPOTHESIZE:

STEP 1. The hypotheses are as follows.

H_o: The brand populations are equal.
H_a: At least one brand population yields larger values than at least one other brand population.

TEST:

STEP 2. The market researchers collected ranked data that are ordinal in level. The Friedman test is the appropriate test.

STEP 3. Let $\alpha = 0.01$.

STEP 4. Because the study uses five treatment levels (brands), $c = 5$ and df $= 5 - 1 = 4$. The critical value is $\chi^2_{0.01,4} = 13.2767$. If the observed chi-square is greater than 13.2767, the decision is to reject the null hypothesis.

STEP 5. The sample data follow.

STEP 6. The ranks are totalled for each column, squared, and then summed across the column totals. The results are shown in the table.

Individual	Brand A	Brand B	Brand C	Brand D	Brand E
1	3	5	2	4	1
2	1	3	2	4	5
3	3	4	5	2	1
4	2	3	1	4	5
5	5	4	2	1	3
6	1	5	3	4	2
7	4	1	3	2	5
8	2	3	4	5	1
9	2	4	5	3	1
10	3	5	4	2	1
R_j	26	37	31	31	25
R_j^2	676	1,369	961	961	625

$$\sum R_j^2 = 4{,}592$$

The value of χ_r^2 is:

$$\chi_r^2 = \frac{12}{bc(c+1)}\sum_{j=1}^{c} R_j^2 - 3b(c+1) = \frac{12}{10(5)(5+1)}(4{,}592) - 3(10)(5+1) = 3.68$$

ACTION:

STEP 7. Because the observed value of $\chi_r^2 = 3.68$ is not greater than the critical value, $\chi^2_{0.01,4} = 13.2767$, the researchers fail to reject the null hypothesis.

BUSINESS IMPLICATIONS:

STEP 8. Potential refrigerator purchasers appear to have no significant brand preference. Marketing managers for the various companies might want to develop strategies for positively distinguishing their product from the others.

The chi-square distribution for four degrees of freedom, produced by Minitab, is shown with the observed test statistic and the critical value. In addition, Minitab output for the Friedman test is shown. Note that the p value is 0.451, which underscores the decision not to reject the null hypothesis at $\alpha = 0.01$.

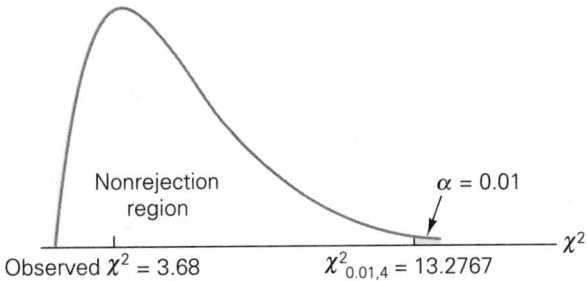

Observed $\chi^2 = 3.68$ $\chi^2_{0.01,4} = 13.2767$

Friedman Output:

```
Friedman Test: Rank versus Brand Blocked by Individual
S = 3.68  df = 4  p = 0.451
```

			Estimated
Brand	N	Median	Sum of Ranks
1	10	2.300	26.0
2	10	4.000	37.0
3	10	3.000	31.0
4	10	3.000	31.0
5	10	1.700	25.0

Grand median = 2.800

Concept Check

1. What is the parametric alternative to the Friedman test?
2. What are the key assumptions underlying the Friedman test?
3. State the null and alternative hypotheses of the Friedman test.

17.5 Problems

17.25   Use the following data to test to determine whether there are any differences between treatment levels. Let $\alpha = 0.05$.

		Treatment				
		1	2	3	4	5
	1	200	214	212	215	208
	2	198	211	214	217	206
Block	3	207	206	213	216	207
	4	213	210	215	219	204
	5	211	209	210	221	205

17.26   Use the Friedman test and $\alpha = 0.05$ to test the following data to determine whether there is a significant difference between treatment levels.

		Treatment					
		1	**2**	**3**	**4**	**5**	**6**
	1	29	32	31	38	35	33
	2	33	35	30	42	34	31
	3	26	34	32	39	36	35
	4	30	33	35	41	37	32
Block	5	33	31	32	35	37	36
	6	31	34	33	37	36	35
	7	26	32	35	43	36	34
	8	32	29	31	38	37	35
	9	30	31	34	41	39	35

17.27 An experiment is undertaken to study the effects of four different medical treatments on the recovery time for a medical disorder. Six physicians are involved in the study. One patient with the disorder is sampled for each physician under each treatment, resulting in 24 patients in the study. Recovery time in days is the observed measurement. The data are given here. Use the Friedman test and $\alpha = 0.01$ to determine whether there is a significant difference in recovery times for the four different medical treatments.

		Treatment			
		1	**2**	**3**	**4**
	1	3	7	5	4
	2	4	5	6	3
Physician	3	3	6	5	4
	4	3	6	7	4
	5	2	6	7	3
	6	4	5	7	3

17.28 Does the configuration of the workweek have any impact on productivity? This question is raised by a researcher who wants to compare the traditional five-day workweek with a four-day workweek and a workweek with three 12-hour days and one 4-hour day. The researcher conducts the experiment in a factory making small electronic parts. He selects 10 workers who spend a month working under each type of workweek configuration. The researcher randomly selects one day from each of the three months (three workweek configurations) for each of the 10 workers. The observed measurement is the number of parts produced per day by each worker. Use the Friedman test and $\alpha = 0.05$ to determine whether there is a difference in productivity by workweek configuration.

		Workweek Configuration		
		Five Days	**Four Days**	**Three-and-a-Half Days**
	1	37	33	28
	2	44	38	36
	3	35	29	31
	4	41	40	36
Worker	5	38	39	35
	6	34	27	23
	7	43	38	39
	8	39	35	32
	9	41	38	37
	10	36	30	31

17.29   Shown here is Minitab output from a Friedman test. What is the size of the experimental design in terms of treatment levels and blocks? Discuss the outcome of the experiment in terms of any statistical conclusions.

FRIEDMAN TEST

```
Friedman Test of Observations by Treatment Blocked by Block
S = 2.04     df = 3     p = 0.564
Treatment          N     Estimated Median     Sum of Ranks
    1              5          3.250                15.0
    2              5          2.000                10.0
    3              5          2.750                11.0
    4              5          4.000                14.0
Grand median = 3.000
```

17.30   Shown here is Minitab output for a Friedman test. Discuss the experimental design and the outcome of the experiment.

FRIEDMAN TEST

```
Friedman Test of Observations by Treatment Blocked by Block
S = 13.71    df = 4     p = 0.009
Treatment          N     Estimated Median     Sum of Ranks
    1              7         21.000                12.0
    2              7         24.000                14.0
    3              7         29.800                30.0
    4              7         27.600                26.0
    5              7         27.600                23.0
Grand median = 26.000
```

17.6 SPEARMAN'S RANK CORRELATION

In Chapter 12, the Pearson product-moment correlation coefficient, r, was presented and discussed as a technique to measure the amount or degree of association between two variables. The Pearson r requires at least interval level of measurement for the data. When only ordinal-level data or ranked data are available, **Spearman's rank correlation,** r_s, can be used to analyze the degree of association of two variables. Charles E. Spearman (1863–1945) developed this correlation coefficient.

The formula for calculating a Spearman's rank correlation is as follows.

Spearman's Rank Correlation (17.5)	$$r_s = 1 - \frac{6\sum d^2}{n(n^2 - 1)}$$

where

n = number of pairs being correlated
d = the difference in the ranks of each pair

The Spearman's rank correlation formula is derived from the Pearson product-moment formula and utilizes the ranks of the n pairs instead of the raw data. The value of d is the difference in the ranks of each pair.

Table 17.6		
Choice Spring Lamb and Choice Heifer Prices over a 10-Year Period		

Year	Choice Spring Lamb Prices ($/100 lb)	Choice Heifer Prices ($/100 lb)
1	77.91	65.46
2	82.00	64.18
3	89.20	65.66
4	74.37	59.23
5	66.42	65.68
6	80.10	69.55
7	69.78	67.81
8	72.09	67.39
9	92.14	82.06
10	96.31	84.40

The process begins by the assignment of ranks within each group. The difference in ranks between each group (d) is calculated by subtracting the rank of a member of one group from the rank of its associated member of the other group. The differences (d) are then squared and summed. The number of pairs in the groups is represented by n.

The interpretation of r_s values is similar to the interpretation of r values. Positive correlations indicate that high values of one variable tend to be associated with high values of the other variable, and low values of one variable tend to be associated with low values of the other variable. Correlations near +1 indicate high positive correlations, and correlations near −1 indicate high negative correlations. Negative correlations indicate that high values of one variable tend to be associated with low values of the other variable, and vice versa. Correlations near zero indicate little or no association between variables.

Listed in Table 17.6 are the average prices in dollars per 100 pounds (about 45 kg) for choice spring lambs and choice heifers over a 10-year period. Suppose we want to determine the strength of association of the prices between these two commodities by using Spearman's rank correlation.

The lamb prices are ranked and the heifer prices are ranked. The difference in ranks is computed for each year. The differences are squared and summed, producing $\Sigma d^2 = 108$. The number of pairs, n, is 10. The value of $r_s = 0.345$ indicates that there is a very modest positive correlation between lamb and heifer prices. The calculations for this Spearman's rank correlation are shown in Table 17.7.

Table 17.7		
Calculations for Spearman's Rank Correlation for Lamb and Heifer Prices over a 10-Year Period		

Year	Rank: Lamb	Rank: Heifer	d	d^2
1	5	3	2	4
2	7	2	5	25
3	8	4	4	16
4	4	1	3	9
5	1	5	−4	16
6	6	8	−2	4
7	2	7	−5	25
8	3	6	−3	9
9	9	9	0	0
10	10	10	0	0
				$\Sigma d^2 = 108$

$$r_s = 1 - \frac{6 \sum d^2}{n(n^2 - 1)} = 1 - \frac{6(108)}{10(10^2 - 1)} = 0.345$$

Demonstration Problem 17.6

How strong is the correlation between crude oil prices and prices of gas at the pump? In an effort to estimate this association, an oil company analyst gathered the data shown over a period of several months. She lets crude oil prices be represented by the market value of a barrel of West Texas intermediate crude and gas prices be the estimated average price of a litre of regular unleaded gas in a certain city. She computes a Spearman's rank correlation for these data.

Crude Oil	Gas
$14.60	$0.813
10.50	0.815
12.30	0.820
15.10	0.815
18.35	0.830
22.60	0.860
28.90	0.890
31.40	0.900
26.75	0.885

Solution

Here, $n = 9$. When the analyst ranks the values within each group and computes the values of d and d^2, she obtains the following.

Crude Oil	Gas	d	d^2
3	1	+2	4
1	2.5	−1.5	2.25
2	4	−2	4
4	2.5	+1.5	2.25
5	5	0	0
6	6	0	0
8	8	0	0
9	9	0	0
7	7	0	0
			$\sum d^2 = 12.5$

$$r_s = 1 - \frac{6\sum d^2}{n(n^2 - 1)} = 1 - \frac{6(12.5)}{9(9^2 - 1)} = 0.896$$

A high positive correlation is computed between the price of a barrel of West Texas intermediate crude and a litre of regular unleaded gas.

Concept Check

1. What technique can be used to analyze the degree of association of two variables when only ordinal-level data or ranked data are available?
2. In the Spearman's rank correlation technique, how are ranks assigned within each group?

17.6 Problems

17.31   Compute a Spearman's rank correlation for the following variables to determine the degree of association between the two variables.

x	y
23	201
41	259
37	234
29	240
25	231
17	209
33	229
41	246
40	248
28	227
19	200

17.32   The following data are the ranks for values of the two variables x and y. Compute a Spearman's rank correlation to determine the degree of relation between the two variables.

x	y	x	y
4	6	3	2
5	8	1	3
8	7	2	1
11	10	9	11
10	9	6	4
7	5		

17.33   Compute a Spearman's rank correlation for the following data.

x	y	x	y
99	108	80	124
67	139	57	162
82	117	49	145
46	168	91	102

17.34   Over a period of a few months, is there a strong correlation between the value of the Canadian dollar (in U.S. dollars) and the prime interest rate? The following data represent a sample of these quantities over a period of time. Compute a Spearman's rank correlation to determine the strength of the relationship between prime interest rates and the value of the dollar.

Dollar Value ($U.S.)	Prime Rate (%)	Dollar Value ($U.S.)	Prime Rate (%)
0.92	9.3	0.88	8.4
0.96	9.0	0.84	8.1
0.91	8.5	0.81	7.9
0.89	8.0	0.83	7.2
0.91	8.3		

17.35 Shown here are the percentages of consumer loans with payments that are 30 days or more overdue for both bank credit cards and home equity loans over a 14-year period according to the American Bankers Association. Compute a Spearman's rank correlation to determine the degree of association between these two variables.

Year	Bank Credit Card	Home Equity Loan
1	2.51%	2.07%
2	2.86	1.95
3	2.33	1.66
4	2.54	1.77
5	2.54	1.51
6	2.18	1.47
7	3.34	1.75
8	2.86	1.73
9	2.74	1.48
10	2.54	1.51
11	3.18	1.25
12	3.53	1.44
13	3.51	1.38
14	3.11	1.30

17.36 Shown here are the net tonnage figures for total pig iron and raw steel output as reported by the American Iron and Steel Institute over a 12-year period. Use these data to calculate a Spearman's rank correlation to determine the degree of association between production of pig iron and raw steel over this period. Was the association strong? Comment on the results.

Year	Total Pig Iron (net tons)	Raw Steel (net tons)
1	43,952,000	81,606,000
2	48,410,000	89,151,000
3	55,745,000	99,924,000
4	55,873,000	97,943,000
5	54,750,000	98,906,000
6	48,637,000	87,896,000
7	52,224,000	92,949,000
8	53,082,000	97,877,000
9	54,426,000	100,579,000
10	56,097,000	104,930,000
11	54,485,000	105,309,478
12	54,679,000	108,561,182

17.37 Is there a correlation between the number of companies listed on the New York Stock Exchange in a given year and the number of equity issues on the American Stock Exchange? Shown below are the values for these two variables over an 11-year period. Compute a Spearman's rank correlation to determine the degree of association between these two variables.

Year	Number of Companies on NYSE	Number of Equity Issues on AMEX
1	1,774	1,063
2	1,885	1,055
3	2,088	943
4	2,361	1,005
5	2,570	981
6	2,675	936
7	2,907	896
8	3,047	893
9	3,114	862
10	3,025	769
11	2,862	765

DECISION
DILEMMA
SOLVED

HOW IS THE DOUGHNUT BUSINESS DOING?

The Dunkin' Donuts researchers' dilemma is that in each of the three studies presented, the assumptions underlying the use of parametric statistics are in question or have not been met. The distribution of the data is unknown, bringing into question the normal distribution assumption. Also, the level of data is only ordinal. For each study, a nonparametric technique presented in this chapter could appropriately be used to analyze the data.

The differences in doughnut sizes according to machine can be analyzed using the Kruskal-Wallis test. The independent variable is machine with four levels of classification. The dependent variable is size of doughnut in centimetres. The Kruskal-Wallis test is not based on any assumption about population shape. The following Minitab output is from a Kruskal-Wallis test on the machine data presented in the Decision Dilemma.

```
Kruskal-Wallis Test: Size versus Machine
Kruskal-Wallis Test on Size
```

Machine	N	Median	Average Rank	z
1	5	7.520	10.4	−0.60
2	6	7.415	3.5	−3.57
3	5	7.550	12.6	0.22
4	7	7.700	20.0	3.74
Overall	23		12.0	

$H = 19.48$ df $= 3$ $p = 0.000$
$H = 19.51$ df $= 3$ $p = 0.000$ (adjusted for ties)

Because the H statistic (Minitab's equivalent to the K statistic) has a p value of 0.000, there is a significant difference in the diameter of the doughnut according to machine at $\alpha = 0.001$. An examination of median values reveals that machine 4 is producing the largest doughnuts and machine 2 the smallest.

How well did the advertising work? One way to address this question is to perform a before-and-after test of the number of doughnuts sold. The nonparametric alternative to the matched-pairs t test is the Wilcoxon matched-pairs signed rank test. The analysis for these data is as follows.

Before	After	d	Rank
301	374	−73	−9
198	187	11	4
278	332	−54	−7
205	212	−7	−3
249	243	6	2
410	478	−68	−8
360	386	−26	−6
124	141	−17	−5
253	251	2	1
190	264	−74	−10

$T_+ = 4 + 2 + 1 = 7$
$T_- = 9 + 7 + 3 + 8 + 6 + 5 + 10 = 48$
observed $T = \min(T_+, T_-) = 7$
critical T for 0.025 and $n = 10$ is 8

Using a two-sided test and $\alpha = 0.05$, the critical T value is 8. Because the observed T is 7, the decision is to reject the null hypothesis. There is a significant difference between the before and after numbers of donuts sold. An observation of the ranks and raw data reveals that a majority of the stores experienced an increase in sales after the advertising campaign.

Do bigger stores have greater sales? Because the data are given as ranks, it is appropriate to use Spearman's rank correlation to determine the extent of the correlation between these two variables. Shown below are the calculations of a Spearman's rank correlation for this problem.

Sales	Size	d	d²
6	7	−1	1
2	2	0	0
3	6	−3	9
7	5	2	4
5	4	1	1

(continued)

Sales	Size	d	d²
1	1	0	0
4	3	1	1
			$\sum d^2 = 16$

$$r_s = 1 - \frac{6\sum d^2}{n(n^2 - 1)} = 1 - \frac{6(16)}{7(49 - 1)} = 0.714$$

There is a relatively strong correlation (0.714) between sales and size of store. It is not, however, a perfect correlation, which leaves room for other factors that may determine a store's sales such as location, attractiveness of store, population density, number of employees, management style, and others.

KEY CONSIDERATIONS

The researcher should be aware of all assumptions underlying the usage of statistical techniques. Many parametric techniques have level-of-data requirements and assumptions about the distribution of the population or assumptions about the parameters. Inasmuch as these assumptions and requirements are not met, the researcher sets herself or himself up for misuse of statistical analysis. Spurious results can follow, and misguided conclusions can be reached. Nonparametric statistics can be used in many cases to avoid such pitfalls. In addition, some nonparametric statistics require at least ordinal-level data.

Why Statistics Is Relevant

Is income distributed normally in the population? Most likely not. Can we always verify the popular normality assumption for tests with small samples? Very often we cannot. These are examples of situations where nonparametric statistics are quite relevant. In general, nonparametric techniques allow us to work with data from small samples and/or on variables about which very little is known regarding their distribution. Recently, several successful applications of nonparametric techniques to market research have been reported. An example is corporate planning situations where a new product or service is being introduced and no (or little) prior data are available. Also, these techniques can be applied in situations in which an unprecedented event has occurred (such as airline or power deregulation), thus changing the way in which corporations do business.

SUMMARY

1. Nonparametric tests offer several advantages. Sometimes the nonparametric test is the only technique available, with no parametric alternative. Nonparametric tests can be used to analyze nominal- or ordinal-level data. Computations from nonparametric tests are usually simpler than those used with parametric tests. Probability statements obtained from most nonparametric tests are exact probabilities. Nonparametric techniques also have some disadvantages. They are wasteful of data whenever a parametric technique can be used. Nonparametric tests are not as widely available as parametric tests. For large sample sizes, the calculations of nonparametric statistics can be tedious.

SUMMARY (continued)

Many of the parametric techniques presented in this text have corresponding nonparametric techniques. The six nonparametric statistical techniques presented here are the runs test, the Mann-Whitney U test, the Wilcoxon matched-pairs signed rank test, the Kruskal-Wallis test, the Friedman test, and Spearman's rank correlation.

2. The runs test is a nonparametric test of randomness. It is used to determine whether the order of sequence of observations in a sample is random. A run is a succession of observations that have a particular characteristic. If data are truly random, neither a very high number of runs nor a very small number of runs is likely to be present.

3. The Mann-Whitney U test is a nonparametric version of the t test of the means from two independent samples. When the assumption of normally distributed data cannot be met or if the data are only ordinal in level of measurement, the Mann-Whitney U test can be used in place of the t test. The Mann-Whitney U test—like many nonparametric tests—works with the ranks of data rather than the raw data.

The Wilcoxon matched-pairs signed rank test is used as an alternative to the t test for related measures when assumptions cannot be met or if the data are ordinal in measurement. In contrast to the Mann-Whitney U test, the Wilcoxon test is used when the data are related in some way. The Wilcoxon test is used to analyze the data by ranks of the differences of the raw data.

The Kruskal-Wallis test is a nonparametric one-way ANOVA technique. It is particularly useful when the assumptions underlying the F test of the parametric one-way ANOVA cannot be met. The Kruskal-Wallis test is usually used when the researcher wants to determine whether three or more groups or samples are from the same or equivalent populations. This test is based on the assumption that the sample items are selected randomly and that the groups are independent. The raw data are converted to ranks and the Kruskal-Wallis test is used to analyze the ranks with the equivalent of a chi-square statistic.

The Friedman test is a nonparametric alternative to the randomized block design. Friedman's test is computed by ranking the observations within each block and then summing the ranks for each treatment level. The resulting test statistic χ^2 is approximately chi-square distributed.

4. If two variables contain data that are ordinal in level of measurement, a Spearman's rank correlation can be used to determine the amount of relationship or association between the variables. Spearman's rank correlation coefficient is a nonparametric alternative to Pearson's product-moment correlation coefficient. Spearman's rank correlation coefficient is interpreted in a manner similar to the Pearson r.

KEY TERMS

Friedman test
Kruskal-Wallis test
Mann-Whitney U test

nonparametric statistics
parametric statistics

runs test
Spearman's rank correlation

Wilcoxon matched-pairs
  signed rank test

FORMULAS

Large-sample runs test

$$\mu_R = \frac{2n_1 n_2}{n_1 + n_2} + 1$$

$$\sigma_R = \sqrt{\frac{2n_1 n_2 (2n_1 n_2 - n_1 - n_2)}{(n_1 + n_2)^2 (n_1 + n_2 - 1)}}$$

$$z = \frac{R - \mu_R}{\sigma_R} = \frac{R - \left(\frac{2n_1 n_2}{n_1 + n_2} + 1\right)}{\sqrt{\frac{2n_1 n_2 (2n_1 n_2 - n_1 - n_2)}{(n_1 + n_2)^2 (n_1 + n_2 - 1)}}}$$

Mann-Whitney U test (small sample)

$$U_1 = n_1 n_2 + \frac{n_1 (n_1 + 1)}{2} - W_1$$

$$U_2 = n_1 n_2 + \frac{n_2 (n_2 + 1)}{2} - W_2$$

$$U' = n_1 n_2 - U$$

Mann-Whitney U test (large sample) (17.1)

$$\mu_U = \frac{n_1 n_2}{2}$$

$$\sigma_U = \sqrt{\frac{n_1 n_2 (n_1 + n_2 + 1)}{12}}$$

$$z = \frac{U - \mu_U}{\sigma_U}$$

Wilcoxon matched-pairs signed rank test (17.2)

$$\mu_T = \frac{(n)(n+1)}{4}$$

$$\sigma_T = \sqrt{\frac{(n)(n+1)(2n+1)}{24}}$$

$$z = \frac{T - \mu_T}{\sigma_T}$$

Kruskal-Wallis test (17.3)

$$K = \frac{12}{n(n+1)}\left(\sum_{j=1}^{c} \frac{T_j^2}{n_j}\right) - 3(n+1)$$

Friedman test (17.4)

$$\chi_r^2 = \frac{12}{bc(c+1)}\sum_{j=1}^{c} R_j^2 - 3b(c+1)$$

Spearman's rank correlation (17.5)

$$r_s = 1 - \frac{6\sum d^2}{n(n^2-1)}$$

SUPPLEMENTARY PROBLEMS

Calculating the Statistics

17.38 Use the runs test to determine whether the sample is random. Let alpha be 0.05.

1 1 1 1 2 2 2 2 2 2 2 2 1 1 1 2 2 2
2 2 2 2 2 1 2 1 2 2 1 1 1 1 2 2 2

17.39 Use the Mann-Whitney U test and $\alpha = 0.01$ to determine whether there is a significant difference between the populations represented by the two samples given here.

Sample 1	Sample 2
573	547
532	566
544	551
565	538
540	557
548	560
536	557
523	547

17.40 Use the Wilcoxon matched-pairs signed rank test to determine whether there is a significant difference between the related populations represented by the matched pairs given here. Assume $\alpha = 0.05$.

Group 1	Group 2
5.6	6.4
1.3	1.5
4.7	4.6
3.8	4.3
2.4	2.1

(continued)

Group 1	Group 2
5.5	6.0
5.1	5.2
4.6	4.5
3.7	4.5

17.41 Use the Kruskal-Wallis test and $\alpha = 0.01$ to determine whether the four groups come from different populations.

Group 1	Group 2	Group 3	Group 4
6	4	3	1
11	13	7	4
8	6	7	5
10	8	5	6
13	12	10	9
7	9	8	6
10	8	5	7

17.42 Use the Friedman test to determine whether the treatment groups come from different populations. Let alpha be 0.05.

Block	Group 1	Group 2	Group 3	Group 4
1	16	14	15	17
2	8	6	5	9
3	19	17	13	18
4	24	26	25	21
5	13	10	9	11
6	19	11	18	13
7	21	16	14	15

17.43 Compute a Spearman's rank correlation to determine the degree of association between the two variables.

Variable 1	Variable 2
101	87
129	89
133	84
147	79
156	70
179	64
183	67
190	71

Testing Your Understanding

17.44 Commercial fish raising is a growing industry in North America. What makes fish raised commercially grow faster and larger? Suppose that a fish industry study is conducted over the three summer months in an effort to determine whether the amount of water allotted per fish makes any difference in the speed with which the fish grow. The following data represent the amount of growth (in centimetres) of marked catfish in fish farms for different volumes of water per fish. Use $\alpha = 0.01$ to test whether there is a significant difference in fish growth by volume of allotted water.

4 L per Fish	20 L per Fish	40 L per Fish
2.8	7.4	7.9
3.6	6.4	6.1
4.3	6.6	7.6
3.3	5.6	5.8
4.8	5.3	7.4
3.6	5.1	4.8
5.3	6.9	

17.45 Manchester Partners International claims that 60% of the banking executives who lose their job stay in banking whereas 40% leave banking. Suppose 40 people who have lost their job as banking executives are contacted and asked whether they are still in banking. The results follow. Test to determine whether this sample appears to be random on the basis of the sequence of those who have left banking and those who have not. Let L denote "left banking" and S denote "stayed in banking." Let $\alpha = 0.05$.

SSLSLLSSSSSLSSLLLSSL
LLLSSLSSSSSSLLSLSSLS

17.46 Three machines produce the same part. Ten different machine operators work these machines. A quality team wants to determine whether the machines are producing parts that are significantly different from each other in mass. The team devises an experimental design in which a random part is selected from each of the 10 machine operators on each machine. The results follow.

Using an alpha of 0.05, test to determine whether there is a difference in machines.

Operator	Machine 1	Machine 2	Machine 3
1	231	229	234
2	233	232	231
3	229	233	230
4	232	235	231
5	235	228	232
6	234	237	231
7	236	233	230
8	230	229	227
9	228	230	229
10	237	238	234

17.47 In some firefighting organizations, you must serve as a firefighter for some period of time before you can become part of the emergency medical service arm of the organization. Does that mean EMS workers are older, on average, than traditional firefighters? Use the data shown and $\alpha = 0.05$ to test whether EMS workers are significantly older than firefighters. Assume the two groups are independent and you do not want to use a t test to analyze the data.

Firefighters	EMS Workers	Firefighters	EMS Workers
23	27	32	39
37	29	24	33
28	30	21	30
25	33	27	28
41	28		27
36	36		30

17.48 Automobile dealers usually advertise in the Yellow Pages. Sometimes they have to pay to be listed in the white pages, and some dealerships opt to save money by omitting that listing, assuming most people will use the yellow pages to find the telephone number. A two-year study is conducted with 20 car dealerships where in one year the dealer is listed in the white pages and the other year it is not. Ten of the dealerships are listed in the white pages the first year and the other 10 are listed there in the second year in an attempt to control for economic cycles. The following data represent the numbers of units sold per year. Is there a significant difference between the number of units sold when the dealership is listed in the white pages and the number sold when it is not listed? Assume all companies are continuously listed in the yellow pages, that the t test is not appropriate, and that $\alpha = 0.01$.

Dealer	With Listing	Without Listing
1	1,180	1,209
2	874	902
3	1,071	862
4	668	503
5	889	974
6	724	675
7	880	821
8	482	567
9	796	602
10	1,207	1,097
11	968	962
12	1,027	1,045
13	1,158	896
14	670	708
15	849	642
16	559	327
17	449	483
18	992	978
19	1,046	973
20	852	841

17.49 Suppose you want to take a random sample of the Graduate Management Admission Test (GMAT) scores to determine whether there is any significant difference between the GMAT scores for the test given in March and the scores for the test given in June. You gather the following data from a sample of people who took each test. Use the Mann-Whitney U test to determine whether there is a significant difference in the two test results. Let $\alpha = 0.10$.

March	June
540	350
570	470
600	630
430	590

(continued)

March	June
500	610
510	520
530	460
560	550
550	530
490	570

17.50 Does impulse buying really increase sales? A market researcher is curious to find out whether the location of packages of chewing gum in a grocery store really has anything to do with volume of gum sales. As a test, gum is moved to a different location in the store every Monday for four weeks (four locations). To control the experiment for type of gum, six different brands are moved around. Sales representatives keep track of how many packs of each type of gum are sold every Monday for the four weeks. The results follow. Test to determine whether there are any differences in the volume of gum sold at the various locations. Let $\alpha = 0.05$.

		Location			
		1	2	3	4
	A	176	58	111	120
	B	156	62	98	117
Brand	C	203	89	117	105
	D	183	73	118	113
	E	147	46	101	114
	F	190	83	113	115

17.51 Does perfume sell better in a box or without additional packaging? An experiment in a large store is designed in which, for one month, all perfumes are sold packaged in a box and, during a second month, all perfumes are removed from the box and sold without packaging. Is there a significant difference in the number of units of perfume sold with and without the additional packaging? Let $\alpha = 0.05$.

Perfume	Box	No Box
1	185	170
2	109	112
3	92	90
4	105	87
5	60	51
6	45	49
7	25	11
8	58	40
9	161	165

(continued)

SUPPLEMENTARY PROBLEMS (continued)

Perfume	Box	No Box
10	108	82
11	89	94
12	123	139
13	34	21
14	68	55
15	59	60
16	78	52

17.52 Some people drink coffee to relieve stress on the job. Is there a correlation between the number of cups of coffee consumed on the job and perceived job stress? Suppose the data shown represent the number of cups of coffee consumed per week and a stress rating for the job on a scale of 0 to 100 for nine managers in the same industry. Determine the correlation between these two variables, assuming you do not want to use the Pearson product-moment correlation coefficient.

Cups of Coffee per Week	Job Stress
25	80
41	85
16	35
0	45
11	30
28	50
34	65
18	40
5	20

17.53 A Gallup/Air Transport Association survey showed that in a recent year, 52% of all air trips were for pleasure/personal and 48% were for business. Suppose the organization randomly samples 30 air travellers and asks them to state the purpose of their trip. The results are shown here, with B denoting business and P denoting personal. Test the sequence of these data to determine whether the data are random. Let $\alpha = 0.05$.

BPBPBBPBPPBPBPP
PBPBBPBPPBBPPBB

17.54 Does a statistics course improve a student's mathematics skills, as measured by a national test? Suppose a random sample of 13 students takes the same national mathematics examination just prior to enrolling in a statistics course and just after completing the course. Listed are the students' quantitative scores from both examinations. Use $\alpha = 0.01$ to determine whether the scores after the statistics

course are significantly higher than the scores before.

Student	Before	After
1	430	465
2	485	475
3	520	535
4	360	410
5	440	425
6	500	505
7	425	450
8	470	480
9	515	520
10	430	430
11	450	460
12	495	500
13	540	530

17.55 Should male managers wear a tie during the workday to command respect and demonstrate professionalism? Suppose a measurement scale has been developed that generates a management professionalism score. A random sample of managers in a high-tech industry is selected for the study, some of whom wear ties at work and others of whom do not. One subordinate is selected randomly from each manager's department and asked to complete the scale on their boss's professionalism. Analyze the data taken from these independent groups to determine whether the managers with the ties received significantly higher professionalism scores. Let $\alpha = 0.05$.

With Tie	Without Tie
27	22
23	16
25	25
22	19
25	21
26	24
21	20
25	19
26	23
28	26
22	17

17.56 Many fast-food restaurants have soft drink dispensers with preset amounts, so that when the operator pushes a button for the desired drink the cup is automatically filled. This method apparently saves time and seems to increase worker productivity. To test this conclusion, a researcher randomly selects

18 workers from the fast-food industry, 9 from a restaurant with automatic soft drink dispensers, and 9 from a comparable restaurant with manual soft drink dispensers. The samples are independent. During a comparable hour, the amount of sales rung up by the worker is recorded. Assume that $\alpha = 0.01$ and that a t test is not appropriate. Test whether workers with automatic dispensers are significantly more productive (higher sales per hour).

Automatic Dispenser	Manual Dispenser
$153	$105
128	118
143	129
110	114
152	125
168	117
144	106
137	92
118	126

17.57 A particular metal part can be produced at different temperatures (in degrees Celsius). All other variables being equal, a company would like to determine whether the strength of the metal part is significantly different for different temperatures. Given are the strengths of random samples of parts produced under different temperatures. Use $\alpha = 0.01$ and determine whether there is a significant difference in the strength of the part for different temperatures.

5°	15°	20°	30°
216	228	219	218
215	224	220	216
218	225	221	217
216	222	223	221
219	226	224	218
214	225		217

17.58 Is there a strong correlation between the number of kilometres driven by a salesperson and sales volume achieved? Data were gathered from nine salespeople who worked territories of similar size and potential. Determine the correlation coefficient for these data. Assume the data are ordinal in level of measurement.

Sales	Kilometres per Month
$150,000	1,500
210,000	2,100
285,000	3,200

(continued)

Sales	Kilometres per Month
301,000	2,400
335,000	2,200
390,000	2,500
400,000	3,300
425,000	3,100
440,000	3,600

17.59 Workers in three different but comparable companies were asked to rate the use of quality control techniques in their firms on a 50-point scale. A score of 50 represents nearly perfect implementation of quality control techniques and 0 represents no implementation. Workers are divided into three independent groups. One group worked in a company that had required all its workers to attend a three-day seminar on quality control one year ago. A second group worked in a company in which each worker was part of a quality circle group that had been meeting at least once a month for a year. The third group of workers was employed by a company in which management had been actively involved in the quality control process for more than a year. Use $\alpha = 0.10$ to determine whether there is a significant difference between the three groups, as measured by the ratings.

Attended Three-Day Seminar	Quality Circles	Management Involved
9	27	16
11	38	21
17	25	18
10	40	28
22	31	29
15	19	20
6	35	31

17.60 The scores given are husband-wife scores on a marketing measure. Use the Wilcoxon matched-pairs signed rank test to determine whether the wives' scores are significantly higher on the marketing measure than the husbands'. Assume that $\alpha = 0.01$.

Husbands	Wives
27	35
22	29
28	30
19	20

(continued)

SUPPLEMENTARY PROBLEMS (continued)

Husbands	Wives
28	27
29	31
18	22
21	19
25	29
18	28
20	21
24	22
23	33
25	38
22	34
16	31
23	36
30	31

Interpreting the Output

17.61 Study the following Minitab output. What statistical test was run? What type of design was it? What was the result of the test?

```
Friedman Test of Observations by
Treatment Blocked by Block
S = 11.31   df = 3   p = 0.010
S = 12.16   df = 3   p = 0.007 (adjusted
                                 for ties)
```

Treatment	N	Estimated Median	Sum of Ranks
1	10	20.125	17.0
2	10	25.875	33.0
3	10	24.500	30.5
4	10	22.500	19.5

Grand median = 23.250

17.62 Examine the following Minitab output. Discuss the statistical test, its intent, and its outcome.

```
Runs Test
K = 1.4200
The observed number of runs = 28
The expected number of runs = 25.3600
21 observations above K; 29 below
The test is significant at 0.4387.
Cannot reject an alpha = 0.05
```

17.63 Study the following Minitab output. What statistical test was being computed by Minitab? What are the results of this analysis?

```
Mann-Whitney Confidence Interval and Test
C₁  N = 16     Median = 37.000
C₂  N = 16     Median = 46.500
Point estimate for ETA1 – ETA2 is –8.000.
95.2 Percent C.I. For ETA1 – ETA2 is
    (–13.999, –2.997).
W = 191.5
Test of ETA1 = ETA2 versus ETA1 ≅
    ETA2 is significant at 0.0067.
The test is significant at 0.0066
    (adjusted for ties).
```

17.64 Study the following Minitab output. What type of statistical test was done? What were the hypotheses and what was the outcome? Discuss the results.

```
Kruskal-Wallis Test on Observations
```

Group	N	Median	Average Rank	z
1	5	35.00	14.8	0.82
2	6	25.50	4.2	–3.33
3	7	35.00	15.0	1.11
4	6	35.00	16.0	1.40
Overall	24		12.5	

$H = 11.21$ df = 3 p_5 0.011
$H = 11.28$ df = 3 p_5 0.010 (adjusted
                                 for ties)

ANALYZING THE DATABASES

see www.wiley.com/canada/black

Let $\alpha = 0.05$ for all problems.

1. Compute a Spearman's rank correlation of Current Value and Payroll in the Major League Baseball Database. Is the amount spent annually on Payroll related to the Current Value of the team? Are these two variables highly correlated? Explain.

2. Use a Kruskal-Wallis test to determine whether there is a significant difference between the six different divisions and Average Attendance per Game for the Major League Baseball Database. Discuss the results.

3. Use the Canadian Hospitals Database. Use a Mann-Whitney U test to determine whether there is a significant difference between hospitals that are located in Alberta and those that are located in Ontario on Hip Fracture Mortality. Discuss the results.

4. Use the Canadian Stock Market Database and the Kruskal-Wallis test to determine whether there is a significant difference in Composite Index by Week of the Month.

Schwinn

In 1895, Ignaz Schwinn and his partner, Adolph Arnold, incorporated Arnold, Schwinn & Company to produce bicycles. In the early years with bicycle products such as the "Roadster," a single-speed bike that weighed 19 pounds (about 9 kg), Schwinn products appealed to people of all ages as a means of transportation. By 1900, bicycles could go as fast as 100 km/h. Because of the advent of the automobile in 1909, the use of bicycles as a means of transportation waned. In that same year, Schwinn developed manufacturing advances that allowed bicycles to be made more cheaply and sturdily. These advances opened a new market to the company as they manufactured and sold bicycles for children for the first time. Meanwhile, Ignaz Schwinn bought out Arnold to become the sole owner of the company. Over the next 20 years, Schwinn bought out two motorcycle companies and developed mudguards as its major technological achievement. In the 1930s, Schwinn developed a series of quality, appearance, and technological breakthroughs including the balloon tire, which some say was the biggest innovation in mountain bike technology; the forewheel brake; the cantilever frame; and the spring fork. In 1946, built-in kickstands were added to their bikes. In the 1950s, Schwinn began an authorized dealer network and expanded its parts and accessory programs.

In the 1960s, Schwinn expanded into the fitness arena with in-home workout machines. In 1967, the company became the Schwinn Bicycle Company. The company introduced the Airdyne stationary bike in the late 1970s. In 1993, the company filed for bankruptcy and in 1994 it was moved to Boulder, Colorado, to be nearer the mountain bike scene. In the next several years, Schwinn's mountain bike products won accolades and awards. In 2001, Pacific Cycle, the U.S.'s largest importer of quality bicycles, purchased Schwinn and united Schwinn bicycle lines with Pacific Cycle's other brands. Under new management in 2002, Schwinn bicycles began being featured, along with Pacific Cycle's other bikes, at mass retail outlets in North America. In 2004, Dorel Industries, Inc., a global consumer products company based in Montreal, purchased Pacific Cycle and made it a division of Dorel. Schwinn bicycles, now a part of the Dorel empire, are still made with quality for dependability and performance, and they continue to lead the industry in innovation.

Discussion

1. What is the age of the target market for Schwinn bikes? One theory is that in locales where mountain bikes are more popular, the mean age of their customers is older than in locales where relatively little mountain biking is done. In an attempt to test this theory, a random sample of Colorado Springs customers is taken along with a random sample of customers in Alberta and British Columbia. The ages for these customers are given here. The customer is defined as "the person for whom the bike is primarily purchased." The shape of the population distribution of bicycle customer ages is unknown. Analyze the data and discuss the implications for Schwinn manufacturing and sales.

Colorado Springs	Alberta and B.C.
29	11
38	14
31	15
17	12
36	14
28	25
44	14
9	11
32	8
23	
35	

2. Suppose for a particular model of bike, the specified mass of a handlebar is 200 g and Schwinn uses three different suppliers of handlebars. Suppose Schwinn conducts a quality control study in which handlebars are randomly selected from each supplier and weighed. The results (in grams) are shown next. It is uncertain whether handlebar mass is normally distributed in the population. Analyze the data and discuss what the business implications are to Schwinn.

Supplier 1	Supplier 2	Supplier 3
200.76	197.38	192.63
202.63	207.24	199.68
198.03	201.56	203.07
201.24	194.53	195.18
202.88	197.21	189.11
194.62	198.94	
203.58		
205.41		

3. Quality technicians at Schwinn's manufacturing plant examine their finished products for paint flaws. Paint inspections are done on a production run of 75 bicycles. The inspection data are coded and the data analyzed using Minitab. If a bicycle's paint job contained no flaws, a 0 is recorded, and if it contained at least one

CASE (continued)

flaw, the code used is a 1. Inspectors want to determine whether the flawed bikes occur in a random fashion or in a nonrandom pattern. Study the Minitab output. Determine whether the flaws occur randomly. Report on the proportion of flawed bikes and discuss the implications of these results to Schwinn's production management.

```
Runs Test: Paint Flaw
Paint Flaw
```

```
K = 0.2533
The observed number of runs = 29
The expected number of runs = 29.3733
19 observations above K; 56 below
The test is significant at 0.9083.
Cannot reject at alpha = 0.05
```

Source: Adapted from Schwinn, available at <http://www.schwinnbike.com/can/eng/Heritage>.

USING THE COMPUTER

Minitab

- Five of the nonparametric statistics presented in this chapter can be accessed using Minitab. For each nonparametric technique, select **Stat** from the menu bar. From the **Stat** pull-down menu, select **Nonparametrics.** From the **Nonparametrics** pull-down menu, select the appropriate nonparametric technique from **Runs Test, Mann-Whitney, Kruskal-Wallis, Friedman,** and **1-Sample Wilcoxon.**
- To begin a runs test, select **Runs Test** from the **Nonparametrics** pull-down menu. Supply the location of the column with the data in the **Variables** space: check either **Above and below the mean** or **Above and below.** Minitab will default to **Above and below the mean** and will use the mean of the numbers to determine when the runs stop. Select **Above and below** if you want to supply your own value.
- To begin a Mann-Whitney *U* test, select **Mann-Whitney** from the **Nonparametrics** pull-down menu. Place the column location of the data from the first sample in **First**

Sample. Place the column location of the data from the second sample in **Second Sample.** Insert the level of confidence in **Confidence level.** In the slot beside **Alternative,** select the form of the alternative hypothesis. Choose from **not equal, less than,** and **greater than.**
- To begin a Kruskal-Wallis test, all observations from all treatment levels must be located in one column. Place the location of the column containing these observations in the space provided beside **Response.** Enter the treatment levels to match the observations in a second column. Place the location of the column containing these treatment levels in the space provided beside **Factor.**
- To begin a Friedman test, all observations must be located in one column. Place the location of the column containing these observations in the space provided beside **Response.** Enter the treatment levels to match the observations in a second column. Place the location of the column containing these treatment levels in the space provided beside **Treatment.** Enter the block levels to match the observations in a third column. Place the

location of the column containing these block levels in the space provided beside **Blocks.** You can store residuals and fits by clicking on **Store residuals** and **Store fits.** You cannot store the fits without storing the residuals.

- There is no Wilcoxon matched-pairs signed rank test in Minitab. You must manipulate Minitab to perform this test. Either enter the data from the two related samples in two columns and use the calculator under **Calc** on the main menu bar to subtract the two columns, thereby creating a third column of differences, or enter the differences in a column to begin with. Select **1-sample Wilcoxon.** In the space provided next to **Variables,** enter the location of the column containing the differences. Place the level of confidence in the box beside **Confidence interval.** Minitab will default to 95%. Minitab will default to a hypothesis test of a 0.0 median. To test any other value, check **Test median** and enter the new test value for the median. In the slot beside **Alternative,** select the form of the alternative hypothesis. Choose from **not equal, less than,** and **greater than.**

CHAPTER 18

STATISTICAL QUALITY CONTROL

Learning Objectives

This chapter presents basic concepts in quality control, with a particular emphasis on statistical quality control techniques. The key questions of the chapter are:

1. What is meant by the terms *quality, quality control,* and *total quality management*?

2. What are some important concepts in quality management?

3. What are some basic tools to solve quality-related problems?

4. What are $\bar{X}$ charts, R charts, p charts, and c charts?

Shutterstock

ITALY'S PIAGGIO MAKES A COMEBACK

Piaggio, founded in Genoa, Italy, in 1884 by a 20-year-old man named Rinaldo Piaggio, began as a luxury ship-fitting company. Expanding on its services and products by the year 1900, the company was also producing rail carriages, luxury coaches, truck bodies, and trains. During the First World War, Piaggio began producing airplanes and seaplanes and then expanded capacity by purchasing a new plant in Pisa in 1917 and taking over a small plant in Pontedera (in Tuscany) in 1921, making the Pontedera plant the company's centre for aeronautical production.

During the Second World War, the Pontedera plant was building state-of-the-art four-engine aircraft, but allied planes destroyed the plant because of its military importance. With the Pontedera plant gone, the state of Italian roads a disaster, and the Italian economy in shambles, Enrico Piaggio (Rinaldo's son and now CEO) decided to focus the company's

efforts on the personal mobility of the Italian people. Corradino D'Ascanio, Piaggio's ingenious aeronautical engineer, who had designed, constructed, and flown the first modern helicopter, was commissioned to design a simple, sturdy, economical vehicle for people to get around in that was both comfortable and elegant. Drawing from his aeronautical background, D'Ascanio, who did not like motorcycles, developed a completely new vehicle that had a front fork, like an airplane, allowing for easy wheel changing, and was housed in a unibody steel chassis. It was not noisy or uncomfortable like a motorcycle, and the steel frame protected the rider from road dirt

and debris. When Enrico Piaggio first saw the vehicle he said, "Sembra una Vespa!" ("It looks like a wasp!"), and, as a result, the vehicle became known as the Vespa.

By the end of 1949, 35,000 Vespas had been produced, and in 10 more years, over one million had been manufactured. Featured in such films as *Roman Holiday, The Talented Mr. Ripley,* and *Alfie,* the Vespa became popular around the world and known as a global symbol of Italy and Italian design. In 1959, Piaggio came under control of the powerful Agnelli family, owners of the carmaker Fiat SpA, and for the next two decades, the scooter-maker flourished. However, during the latter half of the 20th century, revolving-door management and millions of euros wasted on ill-conceived expansion plans left the company with crushing debt and vulnerable to competition from companies in the Pacific Rim. Losing money and market share, Piaggio was caught up in a downward spiral of increasing debt, bad quality, and inability to meet market demand. As the 21st century arrived, the company's status looked bleak, until 2003, when Italian industrialist Roberto Colaninno bought the company. Implementing a series of strategic moves and quality initiatives, Colaninno turned around the fortunes of Piaggio, now the fourth-largest manufacturer of scooters and motorcycles in the world, producing more than 600,000 vehicles annually. In a recent year, Piaggio had a revenue of $2.53 billion and a net income of almost $90 million.

Managerial and Statistical Questions

1. Was the decline of Piaggio driven by poor quality? If so, how?
2. What quality initiatives did Colaninno implement at Piaggio that helped turn the company around?
3. Were company workers consulted about ways to improve the product and the process?

Sources: Piaggio Vespa website at <http://www.vespacanada.com/company/history.cfm>; Gabriel Kahn, "Vespa's Builder Scoots Back to Profitability," *Wall Street Journal,* June 5, 2006, B1; <Piaggio.com>, 2009.

In the past three decades, institutions around the world have invested millions of dollars in improving quality, and in some cases, corporate cultures have been changed through the implementation of new quality philosophies. Much has been written and spoken about quality, and a great deal of research has been conducted on the effectiveness of various quality approaches. In order to study and explore the myriad of quality theories, approaches, tools, and concepts, it is important to first understand what quality is.

One major stumbling block to studying and implementing quality improvement methodologies is that quality means different things to different people. If you asked commuters whether their automobiles have quality, the response would vary according to each individual's perspective. One person's view of a quality automobile is one that goes 75,000 km without needing any major repair work. Other people perceive automobile quality as comfortable seats and extra electronic gadgetry. These people look for bells and whistles along with form-fitting, cushy seats in a quality car. Still other automobile consumers define automobile quality as the presence of numerous safety features.

In this chapter, we examine various definitions of quality and discuss some of the main concepts of quality and quality control. We explore some techniques for analyzing processes. In addition, we learn how to construct and interpret control charts.

18.1 INTRODUCTION TO QUALITY CONTROL

There are almost as many definitions of quality as there are people and products. However, one definition that captures the spirit of most quality efforts in the business world is that **quality** is *when a product delivers what is stipulated for it in its specifications.* From this point of view, quality is when the producer delivers what has been specified in the product description, as agreed upon by both buyer and seller. Philip B. Crosby, a well-known expert on quality, has said that "quality is conformance to requirements."[*] The product requirements must be met by the producer to ensure quality. This notion of quality is similar to the one based on specifications. Armand V. Feigenbaum, another well-known quality authority, says in his book *Total Quality Control* that "quality is a customer determination" as opposed to a management or designer determination.[†] He states that this determination is based on the customer's experience with the product or service and that it is always a moving target.

David A. Garvin, author of *Managing Quality,* claims that there are at least five types of quality: transcendent, product, user, manufacturing-based, and value.[‡] **Transcendent quality** *implies that a product has an "innate excellence."* It has *"uncompromising standards and high achievement."* Garvin says that this definition offers little practical guidance to business people. **Product quality** is *measurable in the product.* Consumers perceive differences in products, *and quality products have more attributes.* For example, a personal computer with more memory has more quality. Tires with more tread have more quality.

User quality means that the *quality of a product is determined by the consumer* and is in the eye of the beholder. One problem with user-based quality is that because there are widely varying individual preferences, there can be a plethora of views of quality for a given product or service. **Manufacturing-based quality** has to do with engineering and manufacturing practices. Once specifications are determined, quality is measured by the manufacturer's ability to target the requirements consistently with little variability. Most manufacturing-based definitions of quality have to do with conformance to requirements.

---

[*]Philip B. Crosby, *Quality Without Tears* (New York: McGraw-Hill, 1984).
[†]Armand V. Feigenbaum, *Total Quality Control,* 3rd ed. (New York: McGraw-Hill, 1991).
[‡]David A. Garvin, *Managing Quality* (New York: The Free Press, 1988).

Value quality is defined in costs and prices. From a certain point of view, value quality is based on cost-benefit analysis; that is, by how much did the benefit of the good or service outweigh the cost? Did the customer get his or her money's worth?

WHAT IS QUALITY CONTROL?

How does a company know whether it is producing a quality product? One way is to practise quality control. **Quality control** (sometimes referred to as quality assurance) is *the collection of strategies, techniques, and actions taken by an organization to assure itself that it is producing a quality product.*

From this point of view, quality control begins with product planning and design, where attributes of the product or service are determined and specified, and continues through product production or service operation until feedback from the final consumer is looped backed through the institution for product improvement. It is implied that all departments, workers, processes, and suppliers are in some way responsible for producing a quality product or service.

Quality control can be undertaken in two distinct ways: after-process control and in-process control. **After-process quality control** involves *inspecting the attributes of a finished product to determine whether the product is acceptable, is in need of rework, or is to be rejected and scrapped.* The after-process quality control method was the leading quality control technique for North American manufacturers for several decades until the 1980s. The after-process method emphasizes weeding out defective products before they reach the consumer. The problem with this method is that it does not generate information that can correct in-process problems or raw materials problems, nor does it generate much information about how to improve quality. Two main outcomes of the after-process methodology are (1) reporting the number of defects produced during a specific period of time and (2) screening defective products from consumers. Because North American companies dominated world markets in many areas for several decades during and after the Second World War, their managers had little interest in changing from the after-process method.

However, as Japan, other Asian nations, and Western European countries began to compete strongly in the world market in the late 1970s and 1980s, North American companies began to reexamine quality control methods. As a result, many North American companies, following the example of Japanese and European manufacturers, developed quality control programs based on in-process control. **In-process quality control** *techniques measure product attributes at various intervals throughout the manufacturing process in an effort to pinpoint problem areas.* This information enables quality control personnel in conjunction with production personnel to make corrections in operations as products are being made. This intervention in turn opens the door to opportunities for improving the process and the product.

TOTAL QUALITY MANAGEMENT

W. Edwards Deming, who has been referred to as the father of the quality movement, advocated that the achievement of quality is an organic phenomenon that begins with top managers' commitment and extends all the way to suppliers on one side and consumers on the other. Deming believed that quality control is a long-term total company effort. The effort called for by Deming is **total quality management (TQM).** TQM involves all members of the organization—from the CEO to the line worker—in improving quality. In addition, the goals and objectives of the organization come under the purview of quality control and can be measured in quality terms. Suppliers, raw materials, worker training, and opportunity for workers to make improvements are all part of TQM. The antithesis of TQM is when a company gives a quality control department total responsibility for improving product quality.

Deming presented a cause-and-effect explanation of the impact of TQM on a company. This idea has become known as the Deming chain reaction.[*] The chain reaction begins with improving quality. Improving quality will decrease costs because of less reworking, fewer mistakes, fewer delays and snags, and better use of machine time and materials. From the reduced costs comes an improvement in productivity because:

$$\text{Productivity} = \frac{\text{Output}}{\text{Input}}$$

A reduction of costs generates more output for less input and, hence, increases productivity. As productivity improves, a company is more able to capture the market with better quality and lower prices. This capability enables a company to stay in business and provide more jobs. As a note of caution, while Deming advocated that improved quality results in lower costs through efficiencies gained by streamlining and reducing waste, some managers have used it as an excuse to lay off workers in an effort to save money.

It is likely that Deming would have argued that such cost-cutting actually reduces quality and productivity due to an increase in operational errors, errors of omission, and a lack of attention to detail by a reduced staff that is overworked and stressed.

Deming listed 14 points that, if followed, can lead to improved TQM:[†]

1. Create constancy of purpose for improvement of product and service.
2. Adopt the new philosophy.
3. Cease dependence on mass inspection.
4. End the practice of awarding business on price tag alone.
5. Improve constantly and forever the system of production and service.
6. Institute training.
7. Institute leadership.
8. Drive out fear.
9. Break down barriers between staff areas.
10. Eliminate slogans.
11. Eliminate numerical quotas.
12. Remove barriers to pride of workmanship.
13. Institute a vigorous program of education and retraining.
14. Take action to accomplish the transformation.

The first point indicates the need to seek constant improvement in process, innovation, design, and technique. The second point suggests that to truly make changes, a new, positive point of view must be taken; in other words, the viewpoint that poor quality is acceptable must be changed. The third point is a call for change from after-process inspection to in-process inspection. Deming pointed out that after-process inspection has nothing to do with improving the product or the service. The fourth point indicates that a company should be careful in awarding contracts to suppliers and vendors. Purchasers should look more for quality and reliability in a supplier than for just low price. Deming called for long-term supplier relationships in which the company and supplier agree on quality standards.

Point 5 conveys the message that quality is not a one-time activity. Management and labour should be constantly on the lookout for ways to improve the product. Institute training, the sixth point, implies that training is an essential element in TQM. Workers need to learn how to do their jobs correctly and to learn techniques that will result in

---

[*]W. Edwards Deming, *Out of the Crisis* (Cambridge, MA: Massachusetts Institute of Technology Center for Advanced Engineering Study, 1986).
[†]Mary Walton, *The Deming Management Method* (New York: Perigee Books, 1986).

higher quality. Point 7, institute leadership, is a call for a new management based on showing, doing, and supporting rather than ordering and punishing. The eighth point results in establishing a safe work environment, where workers feel free to share ideas and make suggestions without the threat of punitive measures. Point 9, breaking down barriers, emphasizes reducing competition and conflicts between departments and groups. It is a call for more of a team approach—the notion that we're all in this together.

Deming did not believe that slogans help affect quality products, as stated in point 10. Quality control is not a movement of slogans. Point 11 indicates that quotas do not help companies make quality products. In fact, pressure to make quotas can result in inefficiencies, errors, and lack of quality. Point 12 says that managers must find ways to make it easier for workers to produce quality products; faulty equipment and poor-quality supplies do not allow workers to take pride in what is produced. Point 13 calls for total reeducation and training within a company about new methods and how to more effectively do one's job. Point 14 implies that rhetoric is not the answer; a call for action is necessary in order to institute change and promote higher quality.

QUALITY GURUS

Some other important and well-known quality gurus are Joseph Juran, Philip Crosby, Armand Feigenbaum, Kaoru Ishikawa, and Genichi Taguchi. Juran, a contemporary of Deming's, also assisted Japanese leaders in the 1950s in implementing quality concepts and tools so that they could produce products that would be attractive to world markets. Juran was particularly well-known for his "Juran Trilogy," which included quality planning, quality control, and quality improvement. Crosby, author of the popular book *Quality Is Free,* developed a zero-defects program to reduce defects in missile production in the U.S. in the late 1950s and early 1960s, and later he established a Quality College. Crosby bases his approach to quality on four basic tenets that he refers to as absolutes: (1) Quality means conformance to requirements. (2) Defect prevention is the only acceptable approach. (3) Zero defects is the only performance standard. (4) The cost of quality is the only measurement of quality. Feigenbaum has been a worldwide leader in quality management for over half a century. Feigenbaum published his widely-read text, *Total Quality Control,* in 1951 under the title *Quality Control: Principles, Practice, and Administration.* While Deming is often associated with TQM, it was Feigenbaum who actually coined the term *total quality control.* He originated the concept of *cost of quality* as a means of quantifying the benefits of a TQM approach, and he popularized the term *hidden factory,* which describes the part of plant capacity wasted due to poor quality. Ishikawa, a student of both Deming's and Juran's, is probably the most well-known figure in the Japanese quality movement. He has been credited with originating the concept of *quality circle* and championed what is now seen as Japan's company-wide approach to quality. Ishikawa emphasized data measurement and using statistical techniques in improving quality. He is known for developing the cause-and-effect or fishbone diagram that is sometimes referred to as the Ishikawa diagram. Taguchi, an important figure in the Japanese quality movement, wrote a two-volume book on experimental design that has been widely used in quality improvement efforts. In the 1970s, Taguchi developed the concept of the *quality loss function* and refined a set of cost-saving quality improvement techniques that later became known as Taguchi methods.

SIX SIGMA

Currently, a popular approach to TQM is Six Sigma. **Six Sigma** is a quality movement, a methodology, and a measurement. As a quality movement, Six Sigma is a major player throughout the world in both the manufacturing and service industries. As a methodology, it is used to evaluate the capability of a process to perform defect-free, where a defect is defined as anything that results in customer dissatisfaction. Six Sigma is customer focused and has the potential to achieve exponential quality improvement through the reduction of variation in system processes. Under the Six Sigma methodology, quality improvement projects are carefully defined so that they can be successfully completed within a relatively short time frame. Financials are applied to each completed project so that management can estimate how much the project saves the institution. On each project, intense study is used to determine root cause. In the end, a metric known as a *sigma level* can be assigned to represent the level of quality that has been attained, and this is the measurement aspect of Six Sigma.

The Six Sigma approach to quality is said to have begun in 1987 with Bill Smith, a reliability engineer at Motorola.[*] However, Six Sigma took off as a significant quality movement in the mid-1990s when Jack Welch, CEO of General Electric, ". . . went nuts about Six Sigma and launched it," calling it the most ambitious task the company had ever taken on.[†] "Six Sigma has taken the corporate world by storm and represents the thrusts of numerous efforts in manufacturing and service organizations to improve products, services, and processes."[‡] Six Sigma has been around for almost 20 years and has shown a sustained impact on quality improvement within a variety of companies in many industries. Six Sigma is derived from a previous quality scheme in which a process was considered to be producing quality results if $\pm 3\sigma$ or 99.74% of the products or attributes were within specification. (Note: The standard normal distribution table, Table A.5, produces an area of 0.4987 for a z score of 3. Doubling that and converting to a percentage yields 99.74%, which is the portion of a normal distribution that falls within $\mu \pm 3\sigma$.) Six Sigma methodology requires that $\pm 6\sigma$ of the product be within specification. The goal of Six Sigma methodology is to have 99.99966% of the product or attributes be within specification, or no more than 0.00034% = 0.0000034 out of specification. This means that no more than 3.4 of the product or attributes per million can be defective. Essentially, it calls for the process to approach a defect-free status.

Why Six Sigma? Several reasons highlight the importance of adopting a Six Sigma philosophy. First, in some industries the three sigma philosophy is simply unacceptable. For example, the three sigma goal of having 99.74% of the product or attribute be in specification in the prescription drug industry implies that it is acceptable to have 0.26% incorrectly filled prescriptions, or 2,600 out of every million prescriptions filled. In the airline industry, the three sigma goal implies that it is acceptable to have 2,600 unsatisfactory landings by commercial aircraft out of every million landings. In contrast, a Six Sigma approach would require that there be no more than 3.4 incorrectly filled prescriptions or 3.4 unsatisfactory landings per million, with a goal of approaching zero.

A second reason for adopting a Six Sigma approach is that it forces companies that adopt it to work much harder and more quickly to discover and reduce sources of variation in processes. It raises the bar of the quality goals of a firm, causing the company to place even more emphasis on continuous quality improvement. A third reason is that Six Sigma dedication to quality may be required to attain world-class status and be a top competitor in the international market.

Six Sigma contains a formalized problem-solving approach called the DMAIC process (Define, Measure, Analyze, Improve, and Control). At the beginning of each Six Sigma project, the project team carefully identifies the problem—not just the symptoms—at the Define stage. The scope of the project is limited so that it can be completed within four to six months. At the Measure stage, there is a heavy emphasis on metrics and measurement of current operating systems along with identifying variables and targeting data collection.

---

[*]James R. Evans and William M. Lindsay, *The Management and Control of Quality*, 5th ed. (Cincinnati, OH: South-Western Publishing, 2002).

[†]Jack Welch, *Jack: Straight from the Gut* (New York: Warner Books, 2001, pp. 329–330).

[‡]James R. Evans and William M. Lindsay, *An Introduction to Six Sigma & Process Improvement* (Cincinnati, OH: Thomson South-Western Publishing Company, 2005, p. 4).

During the Analyze stage, the focus is on analyzing data and collected information in an effort to determine what is occurring and uncovering root causes of problems. At the fourth stage, Improve, the project team generates ideas for solving problems and improving performance. Lastly, at the fifth stage, Control, the focus is on putting into motion those tools, standards, etc., that are needed to maintain the new quality that has been achieved through the Six Sigma project.

Another important aspect of Six Sigma as a methodology and a quality movement is the strong focus on the customer that is often referred to as critical to quality (CTQ). Maintaining a customer focus is vital to every stage of a Six Sigma project, keeping in mind that there are both internal and external customers. Six Sigma project team members work on things that are important to the customer and do not spend time on things that could be improved but are not important to the customer (not CTQ).

Under Six Sigma, most members of an organization are supposed to have at least some training in the methodology. Employees with minimal exposure to Six Sigma—perhaps only an introductory lecture—might be designated as "yellow belts" (named after the belt system in karate). Organizational members who have more extensive training and serve part time on Six Sigma teams are designated as "green belts." Fully trained employees having over 150 hours of training in Six Sigma, usually including at least one Six Sigma project, are called "black belts." Black belts work full time within an organization, usually directing several Six Sigma projects simultaneously. Master black belts are "experts" in Six Sigma. They have advanced training in statistical techniques and other Six Sigma tools and methods, and they work in the organization developing teams, training black belts, and providing technical direction.

DESIGN FOR SIX SIGMA

Companies using Six Sigma discovered that some processes, outcomes, and services, often designed before the Six Sigma era, contained so many flaws and problems that even the in-depth root analysis of the Six Sigma methodology could not solve some quality issues, and thus a complete redesign was necessary. In fact, history has shown that most processes can only achieve about a 5.0 sigma status with quality improvement. To actually achieve 6.0 sigma status, organizations often need to *design* for 6.0 sigma; that is, because of constraints or limitations built in by its original design, there may be a ceiling on how much a process or operation can be improved. **Design for Six Sigma (DFSS)**, an offshoot of Six Sigma, is a quality scheme that emphasizes designing the product or process right the first time, thereby allowing organizations the opportunity to reach even higher sigma levels through Six Sigma.

LEAN MANUFACTURING

Lean manufacturing is a quality management philosophy that focuses on the reduction of waste and the elimination of unnecessary steps in an operation or process. Whereas the tenets of lean manufacturing have existed in successful manufacturing circles for over a century, the Toyota Production System is generally credited with developing the notion of lean manufacturing as it exists today. Lean manufacturing requires a disciplined attitude in seeking out and eliminating waste in all areas of business, including supplier networks, customer relations, organization management, and design. Proponents of lean manufacturing claim it brings about an evaluation of the entire organization and restructures processes to reduce wasteful activities.

In particular, lean manufacturing focuses on seven types of waste: overproduction, waiting time, transportation, processing, inventory, motion, and scrap. Overproduction can include making more than is needed or making it earlier than is needed. Waiting includes products waiting for the next production step or people waiting for work to do.

Transportation waste can include moving products farther than is minimally required, and inventory waste can include having more inventory than is minimally required at any point in the process, including end product. Processing waste is doing more work than the customer values or needs, and motion waste is people moving around unnecessarily or wasting motion in performing their production or operation functions.

Some advocates of lean manufacturing claim that even if a process or service is operating at a Six Sigma level, it does not necessarily follow that the process or service is lean. That is, the quality of the process or service can be quite high, but there can still be waste in the system. Some critics of Six Sigma say that just improving the quality does not necessarily reduce the time that it takes to perform the process. With this in mind, a new approach to quality management has been developed by combining the investigative and variation reduction aspects of Six Sigma with the emphasis on increased efficiency of lean manufacturing, resulting in what some refer to as Lean Six Sigma.

SOME IMPORTANT QUALITY CONCEPTS

Of the several widely used techniques in quality control, seven in particular warrant discussion: benchmarking, just-in-time inventory systems, reengineering, failure mode and effects analysis, poka-yoke, quality circles, and Six Sigma teams.

BENCHMARKING

One practice used by North American companies to improve quality is benchmarking. **Benchmarking** is *a method by which a company attempts to develop and establish TQM from product to process by examining and emulating the best practices and techniques used in its industry.* The ultimate objective of benchmarking is to use a positive, proactive process to make changes that will affect superior performance. The process of benchmarking involves studying competitors and learning from the best in the industry.

An American pioneer in what is called competitive benchmarking was Xerox. Xerox was struggling to hold on to its market share against foreign competition. At one point, other companies could sell a machine for what it cost Xerox to make a machine. Xerox set out to find out why. The company instituted a benchmarking process in which the internal workings and features of competing machines were studied in depth. Xerox attempted to emulate and learn from the best of these features in developing its own products. In time, benchmarking was so successful within the company that top managers included benchmarking as a major corporate effort.[*]

JUST-IN-TIME INVENTORY SYSTEMS

Another technique used to improve quality control is the just-in-time system for inventory, which focuses on raw materials, subparts, and suppliers. Ideally, a **just-in-time (JIT) inventory system** means that *no extra raw materials or inventory of parts for production are stored.* Necessary supplies and parts needed for production arrive just in time. The advantage of this system is that holding costs, personnel, and space needed to manage inventory are reduced. Even within the production process, as subparts are assembled and merged, the JIT philosophy can be applied to smooth the process and eliminate bottlenecks.

A production facility is unlikely to become 100% JIT. One of the residual effects of installing a JIT system throughout the production process is that, as the inventory fat is

---

[*]Robert C. Camp, *Benchmarking* (Milwaukee, WI: Quality Press, ASQC, 1989).

trimmed from the production process, the pressure on the system to produce often discloses problems previously undetected. For example, one subpart being made on two machines may not be produced in enough quantity to supply the next step. Installation of the JIT system shows that this station is a bottleneck. The company might choose to add another machine to produce more subparts, change the production schedule, or develop another strategy. As the bottleneck is loosened and the problem is corrected, other areas of weakness may emerge. Thus, the residual effect of a JIT inventory system can be the opportunity for production and operations managers to work their way methodically through a maze of previously unidentified problems that would not normally be recognized.

A JIT inventory system typically changes the relationship between supplier and producer. Most companies using this system have fewer suppliers than they did before installing the system. The tendency is for manufacturers to give suppliers longer contracts under the JIT system. However, the suppliers are expected to produce raw materials and subparts to a specified quality and to deliver the goods as near to JIT as possible. JIT suppliers may even build production or warehouse facilities next to the producer's. In the JIT system, the suppliers become part of TQM.

JIT as a management philosophy has come to mean "…eliminating manufacturing wastes by producing only the right amount and combination of parts at the right place at the right time";[*] that is, JIT now generally signifies production with a minimum of waste.[†] The goal of JIT is to minimize "non-value-adding operations" and "nonmoving inventory" in a production process or operation.[‡] In this sense, some view JIT, also known as "lean production,"[‡] as the forerunner of what is now referred to as lean manufacturing. While some of the basic elements of JIT were used by Toyota in the 1950s, most historians give credit to Taiichi Ohno of Toyota for developing JIT in the 1970s, and Ohno is often referred to as the father of JIT.[‡]

There are several basic elements that underscore the JIT philosophy, including:[§]

1. Levelling the loads on work centres to smooth the flow of goods or services.
2. Reducing or even eliminating setup times.
3. Reducing lot sizes.
4. Reducing lead times.
5. Conducting preventive maintenance on machines and equipment to ensure that they work perfectly when needed.
6. Having a flexible workforce.
7. Requiring supplier quality assurance and implementing a zero-defects quality program.
8. Improving, eliminating, or reducing anything that does not add value to the product.
9. Striving for simplicity.
10. Making workers responsible for the quality of their output.

By levelling loads at workstations throughout the process, bottlenecks are reduced or eliminated, and there is a greater chance that goods/services will flow smoothly through the process.

REENGINEERING

A more radical approach to improving quality is reengineering. Whereas total quality approaches like Deming's 14 points call for continuous improvement, **reengineering** is *the*

---

[*]Quoted from the website for SEMICON FAREAST at <http://www.semiconfareast.com/jit.htm>.
[†]From the website <http://www.ifm.eng.cam.ac.uk/dstools/process/jit.html>.
[‡]<http://www.semiconfareast.com/jit.htm>.
[§]From the websites <http://www.ifm.eng.cam.ac.uk/dstools/process/jit.html> and <http://personal.ashland.edu/~rjacobs/m503jit.html>.

complete redesigning of the core business process in a company. It involves innovation and is often a complete departure from the company's usual way of doing business.

Reengineering is not a fine-tuning of the present process nor is it mere downsizing of a company. Reengineering starts with a blank sheet of paper and an idea about where the company would like to be in the future. Without considering the present limitations or constraints of the company, the reengineering process works backward from where the company wants to be in the future and then attempts to determine what it would take to get there. From this information, the company cuts or adds, reshapes, or redesigns itself to achieve the new goal. In other words, the reengineering approach involves determining what the company would be like if it could start from scratch and then redesigning the process to make it work that way.

Reengineering affects almost every functional area of the company, including information systems, financial reporting systems, the manufacturing environment, suppliers, shipping, and maintenance. Reengineering is usually painful and difficult for a company. Companies that have been most successful in implementing reengineering are those that faced big shifts in the nature of competition and that required major changes to stay in business.

Some recommendations to consider in implementing reengineering in a company are to (1) get the strategy straight first, (2) lead from the top, (3) create a sense of urgency, (4) design from the outside in, (5) manage the firm's consultant, and (6) combine top-down and bottom-up initiatives. Getting the strategy straight is crucial because the strategy drives the changes. The company must determine what business it wants to be in and how to make money in it. The company's strategy determines its operations.

The focus of reengineering is outside the company; the process begins with the customer. Current operations may have some merit, but time is spent determining the need of the marketplace and how to meet that need.

A company need not necessarily reengineer its entire operation. A specific process, such as billing, production, or distribution, can be reengineered. For example, a mortgage loan company may completely rethink and restructure the process for which a loan applicant gets approved. In health care, a hospital might radically redesign its admissions procedure to significantly reduce admissions time and stress for both the patient and the admissions officer. An integral part of the reengineering effort is to question basic assumptions and traditions, rethink the way business has been done, and reinvent the process so that significant improvements can be made.

FAILURE MODE AND EFFECTS ANALYSIS

Failure mode and effects analysis (FMEA) is a systematic way to identify the effects of a potential product or process failure and includes methodology for eliminating or reducing the chance of a failure occurring.[*] It is used to analyze potential reliability problems early in the development cycle, where it is easier to take actions to overcome these issues, thereby enhancing reliability through design. A crucial step in the FMEA analysis is anticipating what might go wrong with a product, and while anticipating every failure mode is not possible, a development team should formulate an extensive list of potential failure modes when implementing an FMEA analysis. FMEA was developed in the 1960s in the aerospace industry and is now used extensively in the automotive industry. It was developed as a preventative mechanism and is most useful when it is implemented before a product or process is released rather than later. Because FMEA helps engineers identify potential product or process failures, they can minimize the likelihood of those failures, track and manage risks associated with the product or process, and ensure that failures

---

[*]Pat Hammett, University of Michigan, "Failure Mode and Effects Analysis," PowerPoint presentation available at <http://www.fmeainfocentre.com/handbooks/umich.pdf>.

that do occur will not injure or seriously affect the customer. In this way, they can help provide reliable, safe, and customer-pleasing products and processes.[*]

The first step in an FMEA analysis is to select the process or product to be reviewed and describe its function. Most FMEA projects involve processes or products that are candidates for a high risk of error. Initially, investigators determine which uses of the product or process fall inside the intended use and which fall outside, since product failure often leads to litigation.[†] Next, they assemble a team made up of people who understand or use the product or process regularly.[‡] Using a block diagram or a flowchart showing the major components and how they are related, the team searches to identify locations, types, and severities of failure modes. Such failure modes might include cracking, fatigue, corrosion, electrical short, and spoilage. After identifying failure modes, a criticality index or risk priority number (RPN) is assigned to each. The RPN is calculated by multiplying the severity of the problem times the probability that it will occur times the detection rating. Severity has to do with the seriousness of the problem brought about by the failure. Occurrence is the frequency with which the failure happens. Detection is the likelihood that a failure can be discovered or noticed. Using the RPN, the failure mode items can be prioritized for action. The items with the highest scores receive the highest priorities and are acted on first. Such action could include inspections, testing, implementing quality control procedures, using different components or materials, limiting the operating range, redesigning the item, performing preventative maintenance, and including backup systems or redundancy.[*] After action is taken, an individual or a group is assigned the responsibility for implementing the actions by a target completion date. After actions are taken, an FMEA reassessment is taken for possible RPN revision.

Most FMEA efforts include the use of an FMEA worksheet or an FMEA data collection and analysis form. Shown below is one such example.[†]

PROCESS:

Function/ Task	Failure Mode	Effect	Severity Score	Occurrence Score	Detection Score	RPN = $S \cdot O \cdot D$	Recommended Action	Target Date

POKA-YOKE

Another common quality concept that can be used in continuous improvement is **poka-yoke**, which means "mistake proofing." Poka-yoke, pronounced POH-kah YOH-kay and developed by Japanese industrial engineer Shigeo Shingo in the early 1960s, uses devices, methods, or inspections in order to avoid machine error or simple human error. There are two main types of poka-yokes: (1) prevention-based poka-yokes and (2) detection-based poka-yokes. Prevention-based poka-yokes are mechanisms that sense that an error is about to occur and send some sort of signal of the occurrence or halt the process. Detection poka-yokes identify when a defect has occurred and stop the process so that the defect is not built in to the product or service and sent downstream.

In contrast to Deming, who believed that poor quality is generally not the fault of the worker (but rather equipment, training, materials, etc.), Shingo believed that "The causes of defects lie in worker errors, and defects are the results of neglecting those errors. It

---

[*]Kenneth Crow, DRM Associates, "Failure Modes and Effects Analysis (FMEA)." Document found at <http://www.npd-solutions.com/fmea/html>.

[†]Crow.

[‡]Donald E. Lighter and Douglas C. Fair, *Quality Management in Health Care: Principles and Methods*, 2nd ed. (Boston: Jones and Bartlett Publishers, 2004, p. 85).

follows that mistakes will not turn into defects if worker errors are discovered and eliminated beforehand."[*] As an example, suppose a worker is assembling a device that contains two push buttons. A spring must be placed under each push button in order for it to work. If either spring is not put in place, the associated push button will not work, and an error has been committed. If the worker does an on-the-spot inspection by looking at the device or by testing it, then the cost of fixing the device (rework) is minimal, both in terms of the time to fix it and the time lost due to inspection. If, on the other hand, the error is not identified and the device goes on down the assembly line and is incorporated as a part in a product, the cost of rework, scrap, repair, or warranty claim can become quite high. A simple poka-yoke solution might be that the worker first counts two springs out of the supply bin and places them both in a small dish before each assembly. If the worker is not paying attention, is daydreaming, or is forgetful, he or she merely needs to look at the dish to easily see if there is a leftover spring before sending the device on to the next station. Some other examples of poka-yoke include machines with limit switches connected to warning lights that go on if an operator improperly positions a part on a machine, computer programs displaying warning messages if a file is being closed but has not been saved, plugs on the back of a computer that have different sizes and/or shapes along with colour codes to prevent the connection of a plug into the wrong hole, electric hedge trimmers that force users to hold down two switches before the trimmers will work to make it harder for users to accidentally cut themselves, and a plate, which is only supposed to be screwed down in one position (orientation), that has screw holes in nonsymmetrical positions so that the holes only line up for mounting if the plate is in the proper position.

Shingo believed that most mistakes can be prevented if people make the effort to identify when and where errors happen and take corrective actions. Simple poka-yoke mechanisms, such as a device, a switch, a guide pin, a procedure, or a visual inspection, can go a long way in preventing errors that result in defects and thereby reduce productivity.

> **POINTS OF INTEREST**
> Even though Deming and Shingo believed the sources of errors to be different, the general agreement among quality experts is this: delivery of quality depends on processes and not on people. In the example at right, something needed fixing. Exhorting workers to work harder without fixing the process will not result in enhanced quality.

QUALITY CIRCLES AND SIX SIGMA TEAMS

In years past, the traditional business approach to decision making in North America allowed managers to decide what was best for the company and act upon that decision. In the past decade or so, the North American business culture underwent major changes as TQM was adopted. One aspect of TQM is team building. **Team building** occurs *when a group of employees are organized as an entity to undertake management tasks and perform other functions such as organizing, developing, and overseeing projects.*

The result of team building is that more workers take over managerial responsibilities. Fewer lines of demarcation separate workers from managers and union from nonunion. Workers are invited to work on a par with managers to remove obstacles that prevent a company from delivering a quality product. The old us versus them point of view is being replaced by a cooperative relationship between managers and workers in reaching common goals under team building.

One particular type of team that was introduced to North American companies by the Japanese is the quality circle. A **quality circle** is *a small group of workers,* usually from the same department or work area, and their supervisor, *who meet regularly to consider quality issues.* The size of the group ranges from 4 to 15 members, and they meet as often as once a week. The meetings are usually on company time and members of the circle are compensated. The supervisor may be the leader of the circle, but the members of the group determine the agenda and reach their own conclusions.

In contrast the Six Sigma approach to quality makes use of teams of various "belts" to work on Six Sigma projects. Such Six Sigma project teams are usually led by a black

---

[*]Shigeo Shingo, *Zero Quality Control: Source Inspection and the Poka-Yoke System* (University Park, IL: Productivity Press, 1986, p. 50).

belt, who is a company employee, works full time on Six Sigma projects, and has received extensive training in Six Sigma methodology. Virtually all Six Sigma team members possess at least a green belt and have at least some job-released time to work on the project. Somewhat in contrast to the traditional quality circle teams that come from a particular department or group, Six Sigma teams often include members from various functional groups in the organization, some of whom may come from different levels of the company. For example, it is not uncommon for hospital Six Sigma team membership to include physicians, nurses, pharmacists, technicians, administrators, and others in an attempt to uncover root cause, take targeted measurements, and brainstorm possible solutions.

STATISTICS IN BUSINESS TODAY

Six Sigma Focus at General Electric

General Electric's focus on quality began in the late 1980s with a movement called Work-Out®, which reduced company bureaucracy, opened its culture to new ideas, and helped create a learning environment that eventually led to Six Sigma. In the mid-1990s, GE established a goal of attaining Six Sigma quality by 2000. By 1999, GE had already invested more than $1 billion in its quality effort. Today at GE, Six Sigma defines the way it does business. GE continues to strive for greater quality by following a Six Sigma philosophy. In its push for Six Sigma status, GE engaged more than 5,000 employees in Six Sigma methodology in more than 25,000 completed projects.

GE's Six Sigma approach is data driven and customer focused. All of GE's employees are trained in the techniques, strategy, and statistical tools of Six Sigma. The focus of Six Sigma at GE is on reducing process variation and increasing process capability. The benefits delivered by this process include reduced cycle times, accelerated product designs, consistent efforts to eliminate variation, and increased probabilities of meeting customer requirements. The adoption of Six Sigma resulted in a culture in which quality thinking is embedded at every level in every operation throughout the company.

Why has GE pursued a Six Sigma philosophy? GE discovered that its customers were demanding better quality, and its employees thought they could be doing a better job. GE's competitors, such as Motorola, Texas Instruments, and Allied Signal, had proven that following a disciplined,

rigorous approach to quality significantly improved customer service and resulted in greater productivity. Internal process defects had been limiting GE's ability to achieve growth objectives. With increased globalization and information access, GE believes that products and services continually change the way its customers do business, and the highly competitive worldwide marketplace leaves no room for error in designing, producing, and delivering products. Six Sigma provides the philosophy and approach needed to meet these goals.

GE points out the difference between three sigma and Six Sigma: With three sigma, there are 1.5 misspelled words per page in a book in a small library; with Six Sigma, there is 1 misspelled word in all the books in a small library. In a post office with three sigma, 20,000 articles of mail are lost per hour; with Six Sigma, only 7 are lost per hour. GE also claims that Six Sigma can improve your golf score. If you played 100 rounds of golf per year, under a two sigma philosophy you would miss six putts per round. Under three sigma, you would miss one putt per round. Under Six Sigma, you would miss only one putt every 163 years!

Source: Adapted from General Electric, "Quality: GE's Evolution Towards Quality, What Is Six Sigma?" and "Achieving Quality for the Customer," available at <http://www.ge.com/commitment/quality.htm>; "Tip 'Six Sigma' Quality," accessed (formerly available) at <http://trailers.ge.com/getip/news/june.html>, and "What We Do," accessed (formerly available) at <http://www.crd.ge.com/whatwedo/sixsigma.html>.

18.2 PROCESS ANALYSIS

Much of what happens in the business world involves processes. A **process** is *a series of actions, changes, or functions that bring about a result.* Processes usually involve the manufacturing, production, assembling, or development of some output from a given input.

Generally, in a meaningful system, value is added to the input as part of the process. In the area of production, processes are often the main focus of decision makers. Production processes abound in the chemical, steel, automotive, appliance, computer, furniture, and clothing manufacture industries, as well as many others. Production layouts vary, but it is not difficult to picture an assembly line with its raw materials, parts, and supplies being processed into a finished product that becomes worth more than the sum of the parts and materials that went into it. However, processes are not limited to the area of production. Virtually all other areas of business involve processes. The processing of a cheque from the moment it is used for a purchase, through the financial institution, and back to the user is one example. The hiring of new employees by a human resources department involves a process that might begin with a job description and end with the training of a new employee. Many different processes occur within health care facilities. One process involves the flow of a patient from check-in at a hospital through an operation to recovery and release. Meanwhile, the dietary and foods department prepares food and delivers it to various points in the hospital as part of another process. The patient's paperwork follows still another process, and central supply processes medical supplies from the vendor to the floor supervisor.

Many tools have been developed over the years to assist managers and workers in identifying, categorizing, and solving problems in the continuous quality improvement process. Among these are the seven basic tools of quality developed by Kaoru Ishikawa in the 1960s.[*] Ishikawa believed that 95% of all quality-related problems could be solved using these basic tools,[†] which are sometimes referred to as the "seven old tools."[‡] The seven basic tools are as follows:

1. Flowchart or process map
2. Pareto chart
3. Cause-and-effect diagram (Ishikawa or fishbone chart)
4. Control chart
5. Check sheet or checklist
6. Histogram
7. Scatter chart or scatter diagram

FLOWCHARTS

One of the first activities that should take place in process analysis is the flowcharting of the process from beginning to end. A **flowchart** is *a schematic representation of all the activities and interactions that occur in a process.* It includes decision points, activities, input/output, start/stop, and a flow line. Figure 18.1 displays some of the symbols used in flowcharting.

The parallelogram represents input into the process or output from the process. In the case of the dietary/foods department at the hospital, the input includes uncooked food, utensils, plates, containers, and liquids. The output is the prepared meal delivered to the patient's room. The processing symbol is a rectangle that represents an activity. For the dietary/foods department, that activity could include cooking carrots or loading food carts. The decision symbol, a diamond, is used at points in the process where decisions are made that can result in different pathways. In some hospitals, the dietary/foods

---

[*]Jason Paster, April 2, 2001. Internet source found at <http://www.freequality.org/sites/www_freequality_freequality.org/Documents/knowledge/basicseventools.pdf>.
[†]MPR Associates, Inc., website at <http://www.devicelink.com/mddi/archive/98/04/012.html>.
[‡]Nancy R. Tague, *The Quality Toolbox,* 2nd ed. (Milwaukee, IL: ASQ Press, 2004, p. 15).

Figure 18.1

Flowchart Symbols

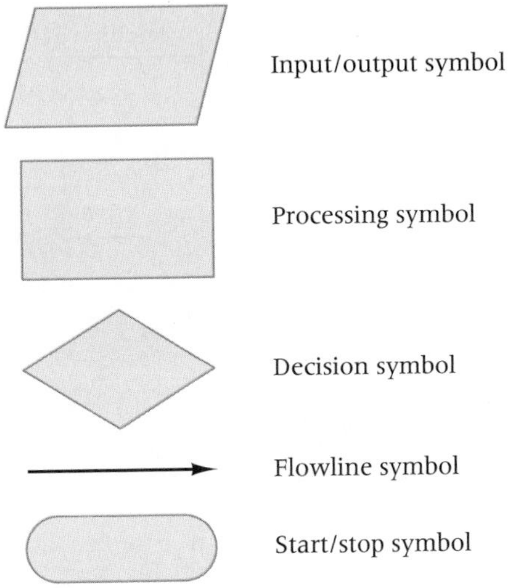

Input/output symbol

Processing symbol

Decision symbol

Flowline symbol

Start/stop symbol

department supports a hospital cafeteria as well as patient meals. At some point in the process, the decision must be made as to whether the food is destined for a patient room or the cafeteria. The cafeteria food may follow a general menu, whereas patient food may have to be individualized for particular health conditions. The arrow is the flow line symbol designating to the flowchart user the sequence of activities of the process. The flow line in the hospital food example would follow the pathway of the food from raw ingredients (vegetables, meat, flour, etc.) to the delivered product in patient rooms or in the cafeteria. The elongated oval represents the starting and stopping points in the process.

Particularly in nonmanufacturing settings, it is common that no one maps out the complete flow of sequential stages of various processes in a business. For example, one NASA subcontractor was responsible for processing the paperwork for change items on space projects. Change requests would begin at NASA and be sent to the subcontractor's building. The requests would be processed there and returned to NASA in about 14 days. Exactly what happened to the paperwork during the two-week period? As part of a quality effort, NASA asked the contractor to study the process. No one had taken a hard look at where the paperwork went, how long it sat on various people's desks, and how many different people handled it. The contractor soon became involved in process analysis.

As an example, suppose we want to flowchart the process of obtaining a home improvement loan of $10,000 from a bank. The process begins with the customer entering the bank. The flow takes the customer to a receptionist, who poses a decision dilemma. For what purpose has the customer come to the bank? Is it to get information, to cash a cheque, to deposit money, to buy a money order, to get a loan, or to invest money? Because we are charting the loan process, we follow the flow line to the loan department. The customer arrives in the loan department and is met by another receptionist who asks what type and size of loan the person needs. For small personal loans, the customer is given a form to submit for loan consideration with no need to see a loan officer. For larger loans, such as the home improvement loan, the customer is given a form to fill out and is assigned to see a loan officer. Small personal loans are evaluated and the customer is given a response immediately. If the answer is yes, word of the decision is conveyed to a teller who issues a cheque for the customer. For larger loans, the customer is interviewed by a loan officer, who then makes a decision. If the answer is yes, a contract is drawn up and signed. The customer is then sent to a teller, who has the cheque for the loan. Figure 18.2 provides a possible flowchart for this scenario.

Figure 18.2

Flowchart of Loan Process

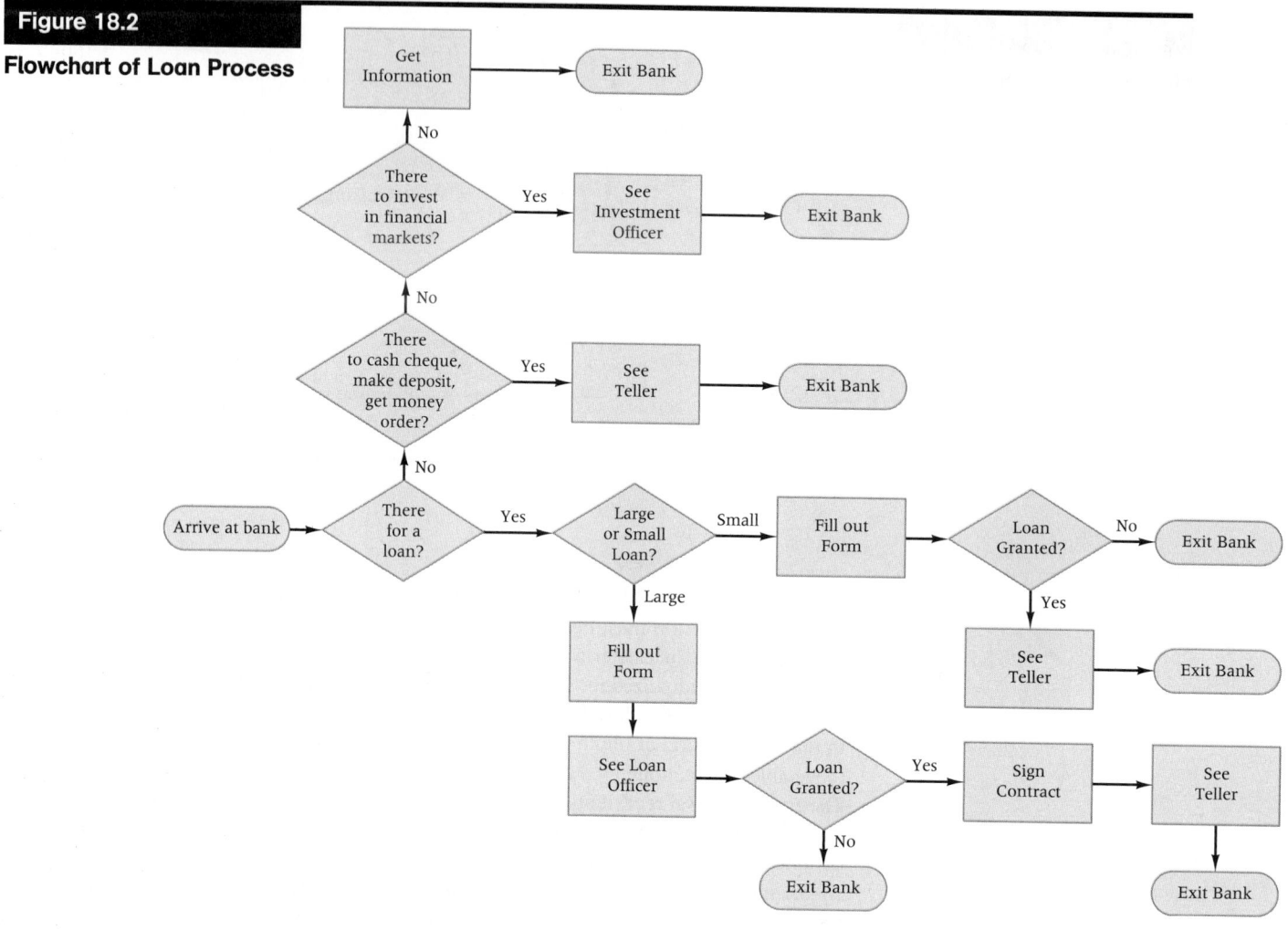

PARETO ANALYSIS

Once the process has been mapped by such techniques as the flowchart, procedures for identifying bottlenecks and problem causes can begin. One technique for displaying problem causes is Pareto analysis. **Pareto analysis** is *a quantitative tallying of the number and types of defects that occur with a product or service.* Analysts use this tally to produce *a vertical bar chart that displays the most common types of defects, ranked in order of occurrence from left to right.* The bar chart is called a **Pareto chart.** Pareto charts are presented and explained in greater detail in Section 2.2 of Chapter 2. Figure 18.3 contains a MINITAB Pareto chart depicting various potential sources of medication error in a hospital. Figure 18.4 redisplays Figure 2.8, which depicts the possible causes of motor problems.

CAUSE-AND-EFFECT (FISHBONE) DIAGRAMS

Another tool for identifying problem causes is the **cause-and-effect diagram,** sometimes referred to as a **fishbone,** or **Ishikawa, diagram.** This diagram was developed by Kaoru Ishikawa in the 1940s as a way to *display possible causes of a problem and the interrelationships among the causes.* The causes can be uncovered through brainstorming, investigating, surveying, observing, and other information-gathering techniques.

Figure 18.3

Pareto Chart of Medication Errors in a Hospital

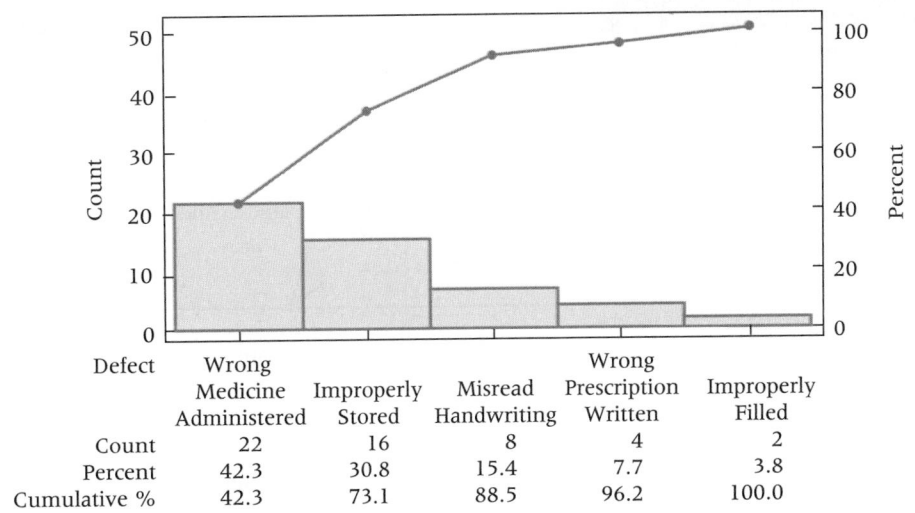

Defect	Wrong Medicine Administered	Improperly Stored	Misread Handwriting	Wrong Prescription Written	Improperly Filled
Count	22	16	8	4	2
Percent	42.3	30.8	15.4	7.7	3.8
Cumulative %	42.3	73.1	88.5	96.2	100.0

The name *fishbone diagram* comes from the shape of the diagram, which looks like a fish skeleton with the problem at the head of the fish and possible causes flaring out on both sides of the main "bone." Subcauses can be included along each "fishbone."

Suppose officials at the company producing the electric motor want to construct a fishbone diagram for the poor wiring problem shown as the major problem in Figure 18.4. Some of the possible causes of poor wiring might be raw materials, equipment, workers, or methods. Some possible raw material causes might be vendor problems (and their source of materials), transportation damage, or damage during storage (inventory). Possible causes of equipment failure might be out-of-date equipment, equipment that is out of adjustment, poor maintenance of equipment, or lack of effective tools. Poor wiring might also be the result of worker error, which can include lack of training or improper training, poor attitude, or excessive absenteeism that results in lack of consistency. Methods causes can include poor wiring schemes and inefficient plant layouts. Figure 18.5 presents a MINITAB fishbone diagram of this problem and its possible causes.

CONTROL CHARTS

A fourth diagnostic technique that has worldwide acceptance is the control chart. According to Armand V. Feigenbaum, a renowned expert on control charts, a **control chart** is *a graphical method for evaluating whether a process is or is not in a "state of statistical*

Figure 18.4

Pareto Chart for Electric Motor Problems

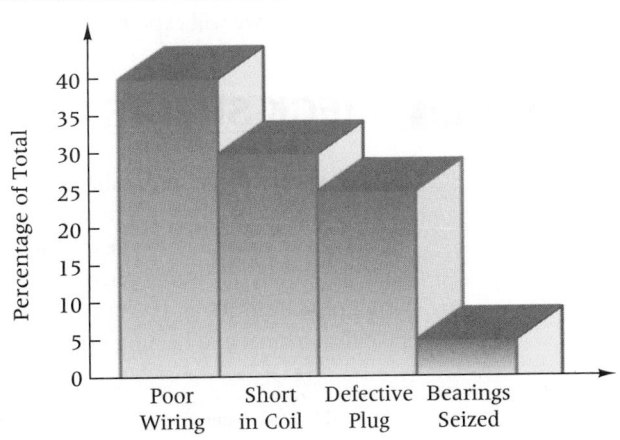

Figure 18.5

Cause-and-Effect Diagram for Electric Motor Problems

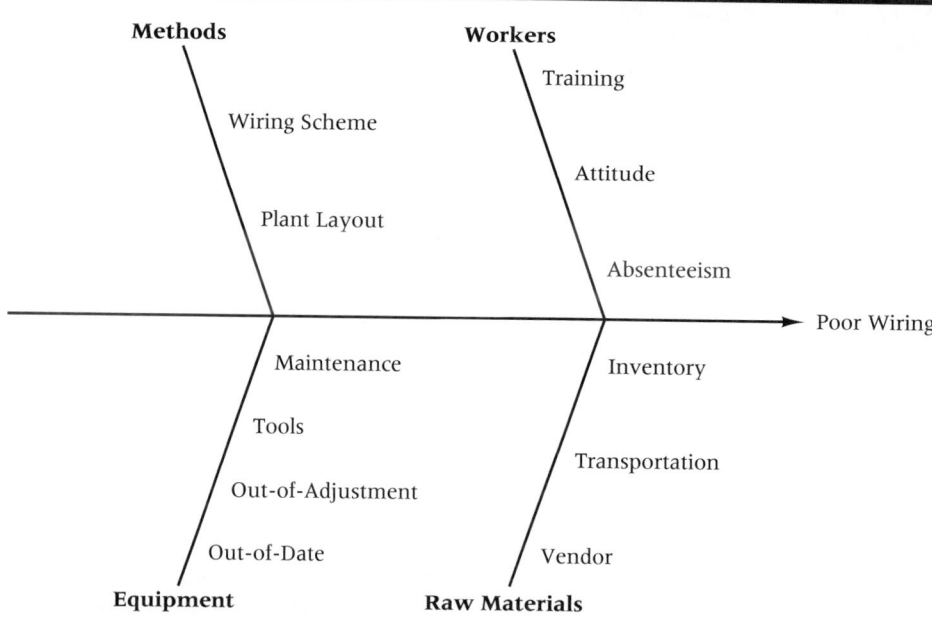

Figure 18.6

$\bar{x}$ Control Chart

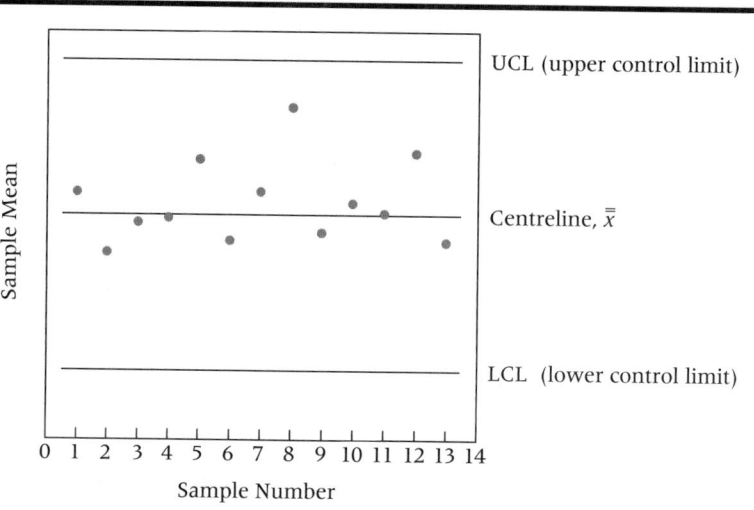

control." * Several kinds of control charts are used. Figure 18.6 is an $\bar{x}$ control chart. In the next section, we will explore control charts in more detail.

CHECK SHEETS OR CHECKLISTS

Check sheets, sometimes called checklists, come in a variety of forms but usually display the frequency of outcomes for some quality-related event or activity under study or being observed by using some type of matrix in which an observer records in a category each outcome from the event or activity. Most check sheets are simple forms consisting of multiple categories and columns for recording tallies and are used for collecting data in a logical format and helping organize data by category. Some advantages of using check

*Armand V. Feigenbaum, *Total Quality Control* (New York, McGraw-Hill, 1991).

sheets are that they are simple to use, they convert raw data into useful information, and the results may be interpreted on the form directly without additional processing.[*] Check sheets are especially useful in tracking problems and causes of problems and for providing hard evidence that supports fact rather than having to rely on opinion. They show how many times each particular item or value occurs, and their information is increasingly helpful as more data are collected. One of the side effects of using check sheets is that the person using them becomes very aware of the data being captured and can often see patterns building.[†]

In constructing a check sheet, there are several things to consider. First, decide what problem, activity, or event is being studied. Once the problem to study has been determined, it can be helpful to involve process workers in developing the check sheet categories. Once the problem has been identified and categories have been determined, the form can be designed. Check sheets should be user friendly, with all columns labelled clearly, and a format should be created that gives you the most information with the least amount of effort.[‡]

Shown below is an example of a check sheet that could be used to determine why patients in a hospital do not consume a meal within one hour of its delivery.[§] Assume that a team of nurses, aides, dietary personnel, patients, and others was assembled to identify possible causes for this problem.

Date:
Floor:
Shift: **Meal Consumption within 1 hour of delivery**

CHECK SHEET	MON	TUE	WED	THU	FRI	SAT	SUN	TOTAL
Menu Incorrect			I			I		2
Diet Order Changed	I			I			I	3
Wrong Order Delivered		I	I		I		I	4
Patient Asleep	II	III	I	II	III	II	III	16
Patient Out of Room	IIII	IIII	II	II	I	III	I	17
Doctor Making Rounds		I	III	II	I	I	I	9
Patient Not Hungry	I		II	I			I	5
Plate Warmer Broken	II	II	II	II			I	9
Nursing Unavailable	II	I	IIII	III	II	I	I	14
TOTAL	**12**	**12**	**16**	**13**	**8**	**8**	**10**	**79**

From this check sheet it can be gleaned that the top three reasons for meals not being consumed within one hour of delivery are patient asleep, patient out of the room, and nursing unavailable.

HISTOGRAM

Another important tool for quality improvement is the histogram. A **histogram** is a type of vertical bar chart used to depict a frequency distribution and was presented in Section 2.2 of Chapter 2 of this textbook. Most computer software packages, such as Excel, can produce a histogram from raw data. The histogram is a very useful tool in getting an initial overview of the data.

---

[*]James R. Evans and William M. Lindsay, *The Management and Control of Quality*, 5th ed. (Cincinnati, OH: South-Western Publishing, 2002, p. 609).
[†]Website at <http://syque.com/improvement/Check%20Sheet.htm>.
[‡]De La Salle University website at <http://quality.dlsu.edu.ph/tools/check_sheet.html>.
[§]Adapted from example shown at <http://mot.vuse.vanderbilt.edu/mt322/Check.htm>.

SCATTER CHART OR SCATTER DIAGRAM

Many times in the implementation of quality improvement techniques and in root-cause analysis, it is important to explore the relationship between two numerical variables. One graphical mechanism for examining the relationship between two variables is the **scatter chart**, sometimes referred to as a scatter diagram. A scatter chart is formally defined to be a two-dimensional graph plot of pairs of points from two numerical variables. Scatter charts are presented and discussed as scatter plots in Section 2.3 of Chapter 2 of this textbook. Often a scatter chart can aid the quality investigator in determining if there is a relationship between two variables, and if there is a relationship, what the direction of the relationship is. One note of caution about using the scatter chart as a tool is that even though there may appear to be a relationship between two variables (and indeed there may be a relationship between two variables), that does not mean that one variable causes the other variable to change or "drives" the other variable.

18.2 Problems

18.1   For each of the following scenarios, sketch the process with activities and decision points. Construct a flowchart by using the symbols depicted in Figure 18.1.
   a.   A customer enters the office of an insurance agent wanting to purchase auto insurance and leaves the office with a paid policy in hand.
   b.   A truckload of men's shirts enters a warehouse at the main distribution centre for a men's retail clothing company that has four stores in that area. The shirts are on the racks inside the stores ready for sale.
   c.   A couple enters a restaurant to enjoy dinner out. An hour and a half later, they leave, satisfied, having paid their bill. Construct the flowchart from the restaurant's point of view.

18.2   An airline company uses a central telephone bank and a semiautomated telephone process to take reservations. It has been receiving an unusually high number of customer complaints about its reservation system. The company conducted a survey of customers, asking them whether they had encountered any of the following problems in making reservations: busy signal, disconnection, poor connection, too long a wait to talk to someone, could not get through to an agent, connected with the wrong person. Suppose a survey of 744 complaining customers resulted in the following frequency tally.

Number of Complaints	Complaints
184	Too long a wait
10	Transferred to the wrong person
85	Could not get through to an agent
37	Got disconnected
420	Busy signal
8	Poor connection

Construct a Pareto chart from this information to display the various problems encountered in making reservations.

18.3   A bank has just sent out a monthly reconciliation statement to a customer with an error in the person's monthly income. Brainstorm to determine some possible causes of this error. Try to think of some possible reasons for the causes. Construct a fishbone diagram to display your results.

18.3 **CONTROL CHARTS**

Control charts have been in existence for about 80 years. Walter A. Shewhart is credited with developing control charts at Bell Laboratories in the 1920s. Shewhart and others, including one of his understudies at Bell Laboratories, W. Edwards Deming (mentioned earlier), were able to apply control charts to industrial processes as a tool to assist in controlling variation. The use of control charts failed to gain momentum after the Second World War because the success of North American manufacturers in the world market reduced the apparent need for such a tool. As Japanese and other international manufacturers became more competitive by using such tools, the control chart increased in popularity in North America.

Control charts are easy to use and understand. Often it is the line workers who record and plot product measurements on the charts. In more automated settings, sensors record chart values and send them to an information system, which compiles the charts. Control charts are used mainly to monitor product variation. The charts enable operators, technicians, and managers to see when a process gets out of control, which in turn improves quality and increases productivity.

VARIATION

If no variations occurred between manufactured items, control charts would be pointless. However, variation occurs for virtually any product or service. Variation can occur among units within a lot and can occur between lots. Among the reasons for product variation are differences in raw materials, differences in workers, differences in machines, changes in the environment, and wear and tear on machinery. Small variations can be caused by unnoticeable events, such as a passing truck that creates vibrations or dust that affects machine operation. Variations need to be measured, recorded, and studied so that out-of-control conditions can be identified and corrections can be made in the process.

TYPES OF CONTROL CHARTS

The two general types of control charts are (1) control charts for measurements and (2) control charts for attribute compliance. In this section, we discuss two types of control charts for measurements, $\bar{x}$ charts and R charts. We also discuss two types of control charts for attribute compliance, p charts and c charts.

Each control chart has a **centreline,** an **upper control limit (UCL),** and a **lower control limit (LCL).** Data are recorded on the control chart, and the chart is examined for disturbing patterns or for data points that indicate that a process is out of control. Once a process is determined to be out of control, measures can be taken to correct the problem causing the deviation.

$\bar{x}$ CHART

An $\bar{x}$ **chart** is *a graph of sample means computed for a series of small random samples over a period of time.* The means are average measurements of some product characteristic. For example, the measurement could be the volume of fluid in a litre container of rubbing alcohol, the thickness of a piece of sheet metal, or the size of a hole in a plastic part. These sample means are plotted on a graph that contains a centreline, the UCL, and the LCL.

$\bar{x}$ charts can be made from standards or without standards.[*] Companies sometimes have smoothed their process to the point where they have standard centrelines and control limits for a product. These standards are usually used when a company is producing products that have been made for some time and in situations where managers have little interest in monitoring the overall measure of location for the product. In this text, we will study only situations in which no standard is given. It is fairly common to compute $\bar{x}$ charts without existing standards—especially if a company is producing a new product, is closely monitoring proposed standards, or expects a change in the process. Many firms want to monitor the standards, so they recompute the standards for each chart. In the no-standards situation, the standards (such as mean and standard deviation) are estimated by using the sample data.

The centreline for an $\bar{x}$ chart is the average of the sample means, $\bar{\bar{x}}$. The $\bar{x}$ chart has a UCL that is three standard deviations of means above the centreline $(+3\sigma\bar{x})$. The lower boundary of the $\bar{x}$ chart, or the LCL, is three standard deviations of means below the centreline $(-3\sigma\bar{x})$. Recall the empirical rule presented in Chapter 3 stating that if data are normally distributed, approximately 99.7% of all values will be within three standard deviations of the mean. Because the shape of the sampling distribution of $\bar{x}$ is normal for large sample sizes regardless of the population shape, the empirical rule applies. However, because small samples are often used, an approximation of the three standard deviations of means is used to determine the UCL and the LCL. This approximation can be made using either sample ranges or sample standard deviations. For small sample sizes ($n \leq 15$ is acceptable, but $n \leq 10$ is preferred), a weighted value of the average range is a good approximation of the three-standard-deviation distance to the UCL and the LCL. The range is easy to compute (difference of extreme values) and is particularly useful when a wide array of nontechnical workers are involved in control chart computations. When sample sizes are larger, a weighted average of the sample standard deviations ($\bar{s}$) is a good estimate of the three standard deviations of means. The drawback of using the sample standard deviation is that it must always be computed, whereas the sample range can often be determined at a glance. Most control charts are constructed with small sample sizes; therefore, the range is more widely used in constructing control charts.

Table A.15 contains the weights applied to the average sample range or the average sample standard deviation to compute the UCL and the LCL. The value of A_2 is used for ranges and the value of A_3 is used for standard deviations. The following steps are used to produce an $\bar{x}$ chart.

1. Decide on the quality to be measured.
2. Determine a sample size.
3. Gather 20 to 30 samples.
4. Compute the sample average, $\bar{x}$, for each sample.
5. Compute the sample range, R, for each sample.
6. Determine the average sample mean for all samples, $\bar{\bar{x}}$, as:

$$\bar{\bar{x}} = \frac{\sum \bar{x}}{k}$$

   where k is the number of samples.
7. Determine the average sample range for all samples, $\bar{R}$, as:

$$\bar{R} = \frac{\sum R}{k}$$

   or determine the average sample standard deviation for all samples, $\bar{s}$, as:

$$\bar{s} = \frac{\sum s}{k}$$

---

[*]Armand V. Feigenbaum, *Total Quality Control* (New York, McGraw-Hill, 1991).

8. Using the size of the samples, n_i, determine the value of A_2 if using the range and A_3 if using standard deviations.
9. Construct the centreline, the UCL, and the LCL. For ranges:

$$\bar{\bar{x}} \text{ is the centreline}$$
$$\bar{\bar{x}} + A_2\bar{R} \text{ is the UCL}$$
$$\bar{\bar{x}} - A_2\bar{R} \text{ is the LCL}$$

For standard deviations:

$$\bar{\bar{x}} \text{ is the centreline}$$
$$\bar{\bar{x}} + A_3\bar{s} \text{ is the UCL}$$
$$\bar{\bar{x}} - A_3\bar{s} \text{ is the LCL}$$

Demonstration Problem 18.1

A manufacturing facility produces bearings. The diameter specified for the bearings is 5 mm. Every 10 minutes, six bearings are sampled and their diameters are measured and recorded. Twenty of these samples of six bearings are gathered. Use the resulting data and construct an $\bar{x}$ chart.

Sample 1	Sample 2	Sample 3	Sample 4	Sample 5
5.13	4.96	5.21	5.02	5.12
4.92	4.98	4.87	5.09	5.08
5.01	4.95	5.02	4.99	5.09
4.88	4.96	5.08	5.02	5.13
5.05	5.01	5.12	5.03	5.06
4.97	4.89	5.04	5.01	5.13

Sample 6	Sample 7	Sample 8	Sample 9	Sample 10
4.98	4.99	4.96	4.96	5.03
5.02	5.00	5.01	5.00	4.99
4.97	5.00	5.02	4.91	4.96
4.99	5.02	5.05	4.87	5.14
4.98	5.01	5.04	4.96	5.11
4.99	5.01	5.02	5.01	5.04

Sample 11	Sample 12	Sample 13	Sample 14	Sample 15
4.91	4.97	5.09	4.96	4.99
4.93	4.91	4.96	4.99	4.97
5.04	5.02	5.05	4.82	5.01
5.00	4.93	5.12	5.03	4.98
4.90	4.95	5.06	5.00	4.96
4.82	4.96	5.01	4.96	5.02

Sample 16	Sample 17	Sample 18	Sample 19	Sample 20
5.01	5.05	4.96	4.90	5.04
5.04	4.97	4.93	4.85	5.03
5.09	5.04	4.97	5.02	4.97
5.07	5.03	5.01	5.01	4.99
5.12	5.09	4.98	4.88	5.05
5.13	5.01	4.92	4.86	5.06

Solution

Compute the value of $\bar{x}$ for each sample and average these values, obtaining $\bar{\bar{x}}$:

$$\bar{\bar{x}} = \frac{\bar{x}_1 + \bar{x}_2 + \bar{x}_3 + \cdots + \bar{x}_{20}}{20}$$

$$= \frac{4.9933 + 4.9583 + 5.0566 + \cdots + 5.0233}{20}$$

$$= \frac{100.043}{20} = 5.002150 \text{ (the centreline)}$$

Compute the values of R and average them, obtaining $\bar{R}$:

$$\bar{R} = \frac{R_1 + R_2 + R_3 + \cdots + R_{20}}{20}$$

$$= \frac{0.25 + 0.12 + 0.34 + \cdots + 0.09}{20}$$

$$= \frac{2.72}{20} = 0.136$$

Determine the value of A_2 by using $n_i = 6$ (size of the sample) from Table A.15, giving $A_2 = 0.483$.

The UCL is:

$$\bar{\bar{x}} + A_2\bar{R} = 5.00215 + (0.483)(0.136) = 5.00215 + 0.06569 = 5.06784$$

The LCL is:

$$\bar{\bar{x}} - A_2\bar{R} = 5.00215 + (0.483)(0.136) = 5.00215 - 0.06569 = 4.93646$$

Using the standard deviation instead of the range, we have:

$$\bar{s} = \frac{\bar{s}_1 + \bar{s}_2 + \bar{s}_3 + \cdots + \bar{s}_{20}}{20}$$

$$= \frac{0.0905 + 0.0397 + 0.1136 + \cdots + 0.0356}{20}$$

$$= 0.0494$$

Next, determine the value of A_3 by using $n_i = 6$ (sample size) from Table A.15:

$$A_3 = 1.287$$

The UCL is:

$$\bar{\bar{x}} + A_3\bar{s} = 5.00215 + (1.287)(0.0494) = 5.00215 + 0.06358 = 5.06573$$

The LCL is:

$$\bar{\bar{x}} - A_3\bar{s} = 5.00215 - (1.287)(0.0494) = 5.00215 - 0.06358 = 4.93857$$

The following graph depicts the $\bar{x}$ control chart using the range (rather than the standard deviation) as the measure of dispersion to compute the LCL and the UCL. Observe that if the standard deviation is used instead of the range to compute the LCL and the UCL, because of the precision (or lack thereof) of this chart, there is little, if any, perceptible difference in the LCL and the UCL by the two methods.

Note that the sample means for samples 5 and 16 are above the UCL and the sample means for samples 11 and 19 are below the LCL. This result indicates that these four samples are out of control and alerts the production supervisor or worker to initiate further investigation of bearings produced during these periods. All other samples are within the control limits.

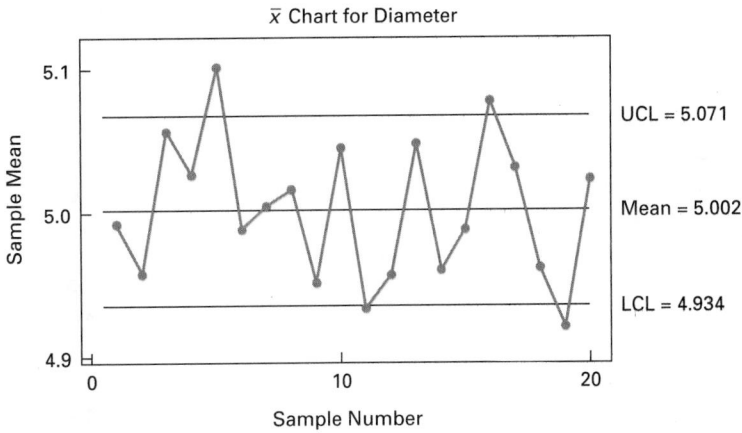

R CHARTS

An **R chart** is a plot of the sample ranges and is often used in conjunction with an $\bar{x}$ chart. Whereas $\bar{x}$ charts are used to plot the location values, $\bar{x}$, for each sample, R charts are used to plot the variation of each sample as measured by the sample range. The centreline of an R chart is the average range, $\bar{R}$. LCLs are determined by $D_3\bar{R}$, where D_3 is a weight applied to $\bar{R}$ reflecting sample size. The value of D_3 can be obtained from Table A.15. UCLs are determined by $D_4\bar{R}$, where D_4 is a value obtained from Table A.15, which also reflects sample size. The following steps lead to an R chart.

1. Decide on the quality to be measured.
2. Determine a sample size.
3. Gather 20 to 30 samples.
4. Compute the sample range, R, for each sample.
5. Determine the average sample range for all samples, $\bar{R}$, as:

$$\bar{R} = \frac{\sum R}{k}$$

where k is the number of samples.
6. Using the size of the samples, n_i, find the values of D_3 and D_4 in Table A.15.
7. Construct the centreline and control limits:

$$\text{Centreline} = \bar{R}$$
$$\text{UCL} = D_4\bar{R}$$
$$\text{LCL} = D_3\bar{R}$$

Demonstration Problem 18.2

Construct an R chart for the 20 samples of data in Demonstration Problem 18.1 on bearings.

Solution

Compute the sample ranges shown.

Sample	Range
1	0.25
2	0.12
3	0.34
4	0.1
5	0.07
6	0.05
7	0.03
8	0.09
9	0.14
10	0.18
11	0.22
12	0.11
13	0.16
14	0.21
15	0.06
16	0.12
17	0.12
18	0.09
19	0.17
20	0.09

Compute $\bar{R}$:

$$\bar{R} = \frac{0.25 + 0.12 + 0.34 + \cdots + 0.09}{20} = \frac{2.72}{20} = 0.136$$

For $n_i = 6$, $D_3 = 0$, and $D_4 = 2.004$ (from Table A.15):

$$\text{Centreline } \bar{R} = 0.136$$
$$\text{LCL} = D_3\bar{R} = (0)(0.136) = 0$$
$$\text{UCL} = D_4\bar{R} = (2.004)(0.136) = 0.2725$$

The resulting R chart for these data is shown next. Note that the range for sample 3 is out of control (beyond the UCL). The range of values in sample 3 appears to be unacceptable. Further investigation of the population from which this sample was drawn is warranted.

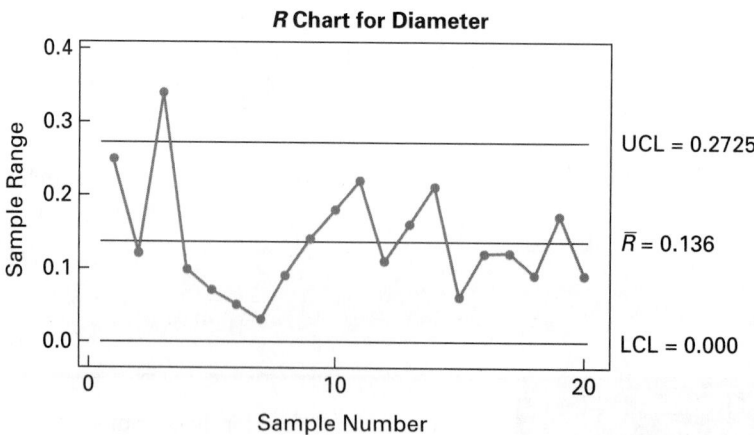

p CHARTS

When product attributes are measurable, $\bar{x}$ charts and R charts can be formulated from the data. Sometimes, however, product inspection yields no measurement—only a yes-or-no type of conclusion based on whether the item complies with the specifications. For this type of data, no measure is available from which to average or determine the range. However, attribute compliance can be depicted graphically by a p chart. A **p chart** *graphs the proportion of sample items in noncompliance for multiple samples.*

For example, suppose a company producing electric motors samples 40 motors three times a week for a month. For each group of 40 motors, it determines the proportion of the sample group that does not comply with the specifications. It then plots these sample proportions, $\hat{p}$, on a p chart to identify trends or samples with unacceptably high proportions of nonconformance. Other p chart applications include determining whether a can of paint has been manufactured with acceptable texture, a pane of glass contains cracks, or a tire has a defective tread.

Like the $\bar{x}$ chart and the R chart, a p chart contains a centreline. The centreline is the average of the sample proportions. The UCL and the LCL are computed from the average of the sample proportions plus or minus three standard deviations of proportions. The following are the steps for constructing a p chart.

1. Decide on the quality to be measured.
2. Determine a sample size.
3. Gather 20 to 30 samples.
4. Compute the sample proportion:

$$\hat{p} = \frac{n_{\text{non}}}{n}$$

   where
   n_{non} = the number of items in the sample in noncompliance
   n = the number of items in the sample
5. Compute the average proportion:

$$p = \frac{\Sigma\,\hat{p}}{k}$$

   where

   $\hat{p} = \dfrac{n_{\text{non}}}{n}$ = the sample proportion

   k = the number of samples
6. Determine the centreline, the UCL, and the LCL, when $q = 1 - p$:

$$\text{Centreline} = p$$

$$\text{UCL} = p + 3\sqrt{\frac{p \cdot q}{n}}$$

$$\text{LCL} = p - 3\sqrt{\frac{p \cdot q}{n}}$$

Demonstration Problem 18.3

A company produces bond paper. At regular intervals, samples of 50 sheets of paper are inspected. Suppose 20 random samples of 50 sheets of paper each are taken during a certain period of time, with the following numbers of sheets in noncompliance per sample. Construct a p chart from these data.

Sample	n	Out of Compliance
1	50	4
2	50	3
3	50	1
4	50	0
5	50	5
6	50	2
7	50	3
8	50	1
9	50	4
10	50	2
11	50	2
12	50	6
13	50	0
14	50	2
15	50	1
16	50	6
17	50	2
18	50	3
19	50	1
20	50	5

Solution

From the data, $n = 50$. The values of $\hat{p}$ follow.

Sample	$\hat{p}$ (out of compliance)
1	$4/50 = 0.08$
2	$3/50 = 0.06$
3	$1/50 = 0.02$
4	$0/50 = 0.00$
5	$5/50 = 0.10$
6	$2/50 = 0.04$
7	$3/50 = 0.06$
8	$1/50 = 0.02$
9	$4/50 = 0.08$
10	$2/50 = 0.04$
11	$2/50 = 0.04$
12	$6/50 = 0.12$
13	$0/50 = 0.00$
14	$2/50 = 0.04$
15	$1/50 = 0.02$
16	$6/50 = 0.12$
17	$2/50 = 0.04$
18	$3/50 = 0.06$
19	$1/50 = 0.02$
20	$5/50 = 0.10$

The value of p is obtained by averaging these $\hat{p}$ values:

$$p = \frac{\hat{p}_1 + \hat{p}_2 + \hat{p}_3 + \cdots + \hat{p}_{20}}{20}$$

$$= \frac{0.08 + 0.06 + 0.02 + \cdots + 0.10}{20} = \frac{1.06}{20} = 0.053$$

The centreline is $p = 0.053$.

The UCL is:

$$p + 3\sqrt{\frac{p \cdot q}{n}} = 0.053 + 3\sqrt{\frac{(0.053)(0.947)}{50}} = 0.053 + 0.095 = 0.148$$

The LCL is:

$$p - 3\sqrt{\frac{p \cdot q}{n}} = 0.053 - 3\sqrt{\frac{(0.053)(0.947)}{50}} = 0.053 - 0.095 = -0.042$$

To have −0.042 items in noncompliance is impossible, so the LCL is 0.

Following is the p chart for this problem. Note that all 20 proportions are within the quality control limits.

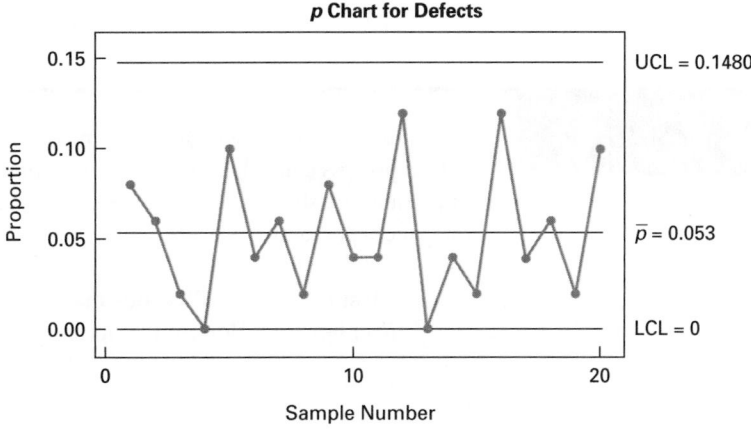

p Chart for Defects

c CHARTS

The c chart is less widely used than the $\bar{x}$, the R, or the p chart. Like the p chart, the c chart attempts to formulate information about defective items. However, whereas the p chart is a control chart that displays the proportion of items in a sample that are out of compliance with specifications, a **c chart** *displays the number of nonconformances per item or unit.* Examples of nonconformances could be paint flaws, scratches, openings drilled too large or too small, or shorts in electric wires. The c chart allows for multiple nonconforming features per item or unit. For example, if an item is a radio, there can be scratches (multiple) in the paint, poor soldering, bad wiring, broken dials, burned-out light bulbs, and broken antennae. A unit need not be an item such as a computer chip. It can be a bolt of cloth, 1 m of wire, or a 2 × 4 board. The requirement is that the unit remain consistent throughout the test or experiment.

In computing a c chart, a c value is determined for each item or unit by tallying the total nonconformances for the item or unit. The centreline is computed by averaging the c values for all items or units. Because in theory nonconformances per item or unit are rare, the Poisson distribution is used as the basis for the c chart. The long-run average for the Poisson distribution is λ, and the analogous long-run average for a c chart is $\bar{c}$ (the average of the c values for the items or units studied), which is used as the centreline value. UCLs and LCLs are computed by adding or subtracting three standard deviations of the mean, $\bar{c}$, from the centreline value, $\bar{c}$. The standard deviation of a Poisson distribution is the square root of λ; likewise, the standard deviation of $\bar{c}$ is the square root of $\bar{c}$. The UCL is thus determined by $\bar{c} + 3\sqrt{\bar{c}}$ and the LCL is given by $\bar{c} - 3\sqrt{\bar{c}}$. The following steps are used to construct a c chart.

1. Decide on nonconformances to be evaluated.
2. Determine the number of items of units to be studied. (This number should be at least 25.)
3. Gather items or units.
4. Determine the value of c for each item or unit by summing the number of nonconformances in the item or unit.
5. Calculate the value of $\bar{c}$:

$$\bar{c} = \frac{c_1 + c_2 + c_3 + \cdots + c_i}{i}$$

where

    i = number of items
    c_i = number of nonconformances per item

6. Determine the centreline, the UCL, and the LCL:

$$\text{Centreline} = \bar{c}$$

$$\text{UCL} = \bar{c} + 3\sqrt{\bar{c}}$$

$$\text{LCL} = \bar{c} - 3\sqrt{\bar{c}}$$

Demonstration Problem 18.4

A manufacturer produces gauges to measure oil pressure. As part of the company's statistical process control, 25 gauges are randomly selected and tested for nonconformances. The results are shown here. Use these data to construct a c chart that displays the nonconformances per item.

Item Number	Number of Nonconformances	Item Number	Number of Nonconformances
1	2	14	2
2	0	15	1
3	3	16	4
4	1	17	0
5	2	18	2
6	5	19	3
7	3	20	2
8	2	21	1
9	0	22	3
10	0	23	2
11	4	24	0
12	3	25	3
13	2		

Solution

Determine the centreline, the UCL, and the LCL:

$$\text{Centreline} = \bar{c} = \frac{2 + 0 + 3 + \cdots + 3}{25} = \frac{50}{25} = 2.0$$

$$\text{UCL} = \bar{c} + 3\sqrt{\bar{c}} = 2.0 + 3\sqrt{2.0} = 2.0 + 4.2 = 6.2$$

$$\text{LCL} = \bar{c} - 3\sqrt{\bar{c}} = 2.0 - 3\sqrt{2.0} = 2.0 - 4.2 = -2.2$$

The LCL cannot be less than zero; thus, the LCL is 0. The graph of the control chart is shown next. Note that none of the points are beyond the control limits and that there is a healthy deviation of points both above and below the centreline. This chart indicates a process that is relatively in control, with an average of two nonconformances per item.

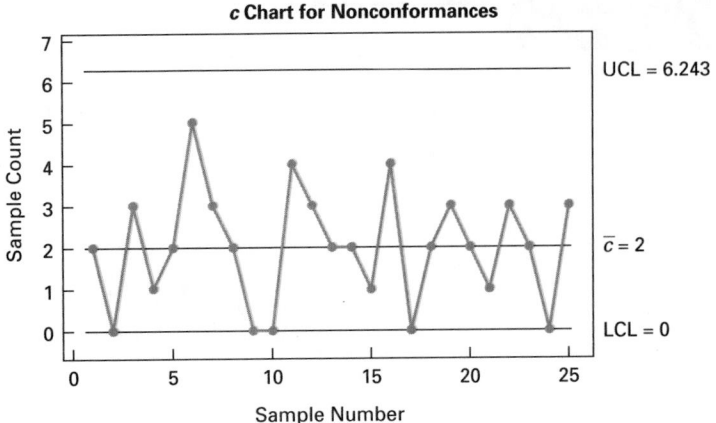

How can control charts be used to monitor processes? When is a process out of control? An evaluation of the points plotted on a control chart examines several things. Obviously, one concern is points that are outside the control limits. Control chart outer limits (UCL and LCL) are established at three standard deviations above and below the centreline. The empirical rule discussed in Chapter 3 and the z table value for $z = 3$ indicate that approximately 99.7% of all values should be within three standard deviations of the mean of the statistic. Applying this rule to control charts suggests that fewer than 0.3% of all points should be beyond the UCL and the LCL by chance. Thus, one of the more elementary items a control chart observer looks for is points outside the LCL and the UCL. If the system is in control, virtually no data points should be outside these limits. Workers responsible for process control should investigate samples in which sample members are outside the LCL and the UCL. In the case of the c chart, items that are above the UCL line contain an inordinate number of nonconformances in relation to the average. The occurrence of points beyond the control limits calls for further investigation.

Several other criteria can be used to determine whether a control chart is plotting a process that is out of control. In general, there *should* be random fluctuation above and below the centreline within the UCL and the LCL. However, a process can be out of control if too many consecutive points are above or below the centreline. Eight or more consecutive points on one side of the centreline are considered too many. In addition, if 10 of 11 or 12 of 14 points are on the same side of the centre, the process may be out of control.[*]

Another criterion for process control operators to look for is trends in the control charts. At any point in the process, is a trend emerging in the data? As a guideline, if six or more points are increasing or decreasing, the process may be out of control.[†] Such a trend can indicate that points will eventually deviate increasingly from the centreline (the gap between the centreline and the points will increase).

Another concern with control charts is an overabundance of points in the outer one third of the region between the centreline and the outer limits (LCL and UCL). By a rationalization similar to that imposed on the LCL and the UCL, the empirical rule and the table of z values show that approximately 95% of all points should be within two standard deviations of the centreline. With this in mind, fewer than 5% of the points should be in the outer one third of the region between the centreline and the outer control limits

---

[*]James R. Evans and William M. Lindsay, *The Management and Control of Quality*, 4th ed. (Cincinnati, OH: South-Western College Publishing, 1999).
[†]Richard E. DeVor, Tsong-how Chang, and John W. Sutherland, *Statistical Quality Design and Control* (New York: Macmillan, 1992).

Figure 18.7

Control Charts with Problems

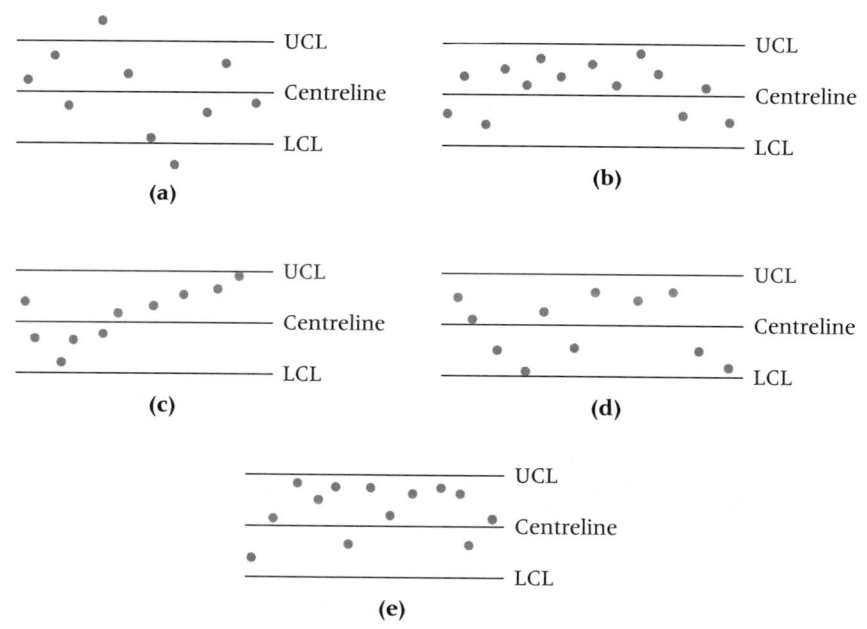

(because 95% should be within two thirds of the region). A rule to follow is that if two out of three consecutive points are in the outer one third of the chart, a control problem may be present. Likewise, because approximately 68% of all values should be within one standard deviation of the mean (empirical rule, z table for $z = 1$), only 32% should be in the outer two thirds of the control chart above and below the centreline. As a rule, if four out of five successive points are in the outer two thirds of the control chart, the process should be investigated.[*]

Another consideration in evaluating control charts is the location of the centreline. With each successive batch of samples, it is important to observe whether the centreline is shifting away from specifications.

The following list provides a summary of the control chart abnormalities that should be of concern to a statistical process controller.

1. Points are above the UCL and/or below the LCL.
2. Eight or more consecutive points are above or below the centreline. Ten out of 11 points are above or below the centreline. Twelve out of 14 points are above or below the centreline.
3. A trend of six or more consecutive points (increasing or decreasing) is present.
4. Two out of three consecutive values are in the outer one third.
5. Four out of five consecutive values are in the outer two thirds.
6. The centreline shifts from chart to chart.

Figure 18.7 contains several control charts, each of which has one of these types of problems. The chart in (a) contains points above and below the outer control limits. The one in (b) has eight consecutive points on one side of the centreline. The chart in (c) has seven consecutive increasing points. In (d), at least two out of three consecutive points are in the outer one third of the control chart. In (e), at least four out of five consecutive points are in the outer two thirds of the chart.

In investigating control chart abnormalities, several possible causes may be found. Some of them are listed here.[†]

---

[*]DeVor, Chang, and Sutherland; Evans and Lindsay.

[†]Eugene L. Grant and Richard S. Leavenworth, *Statistical Quality Control*, 5th ed. (New York, McGraw-Hill, 1980).

1. Changes in the physical environment
2. Worker fatigue
3. Worn tools
4. Changes in operators or machines
5. Maintenance
6. Changes in worker skills
7. Changes in materials
8. Process modification

The statistical process control person should be aware that control chart abnormalities can arise because of measurement errors or incorrect calculation of control limits. Judgment should be exercised so as not to overcontrol the process by readjusting to every oddity on a control chart.

18.3 Problems

18.4   A food-processing company makes potato chips, pretzels, and cheese chips. Although its products are packaged and sold by mass, the company has been taking sample bags of cheese chips and counting the number of chips in each bag. Shown here is the number of chips per bag for five samples of seven bags of chips. Use these data to construct an $\bar{x}$ chart and an R chart. Discuss the results.

Sample 1	Sample 2	Sample 3	Sample 4	Sample 5
25	22	30	32	25
23	21	23	26	23
29	24	22	27	29
31	25	26	28	27
26	23	28	25	27
28	26	27	25	26
27	29	21	31	24

18.5   A toy-manufacturing company has been given a large order for small plastic whistles that will be given away by a large fast-food hamburger chain with its kids' meal. Seven random samples of four whistles have been taken. The mass of each whistle has been ascertained in grams. The data are shown here. Use these data to construct an $\bar{x}$ chart and an R chart. What managerial decisions should be made on the basis of these findings?

Sample 1	Sample 2	Sample 3	Sample 4	Sample 5	Sample 6	Sample 7
4.1	3.6	4.0	4.6	3.9	5.1	4.6
5.2	4.3	4.8	4.8	3.8	4.7	4.4
3.9	3.9	5.1	4.7	4.6	4.8	4.0
5.0	4.6	5.3	4.7	4.9	4.3	4.5

18.6   A machine operator at a pencil-manufacturing facility gathered 10 different random samples of 100 pencils. The operator's inspection was to determine whether the pencils were in compliance or out of compliance with specifications. The results of this inspection are shown on the next page. Use these data to construct a p chart. Comment on the results of this chart.

Sample	Size	Number out of Compliance
1	100	2
2	100	7
3	100	4
4	100	3
5	100	3
6	100	5
7	100	2
8	100	0
9	100	1
10	100	6

18.7   A large manufacturer makes valves. Currently it is producing a particular valve for use in industrial engines. As a part of a quality control effort, the company engineers randomly sample seven groups of 40 valves and inspect them to determine whether they are in or out of compliance. Results are shown here. Use the information to construct a p chart. Comment on the chart.

Sample	Size	Number out of Compliance
1	40	1
2	40	0
3	40	1
4	40	3
5	40	2
6	40	5
7	40	2

18.8   A firm in Alberta manufactures light bulbs. Before the bulbs are released for shipment, a sample of bulbs is selected for inspection. Inspectors look for nonconformances such as scratches, weak or broken filaments, incorrectly bored turns, and insufficient outside contacts. A sample of 35 60-W bulbs has just been inspected, and the results are shown here. Use these data to construct a c chart. Discuss the findings.

Bulb Number	Number of Nonconformances	Bulb Number	Number of Nonconformances
1	0	19	2
2	1	20	0
3	0	21	0
4	0	22	1
5	3	23	0
6	0	24	0
7	1	25	0
8	0	26	2
9	0	27	0
10	0	28	0
11	2	29	1
12	0	30	0
13	0	31	0
14	2	32	0
15	0	33	0
16	1	34	3
17	3	35	0
18	0		

18.9   A soft drink bottling company just ran a long line of 355-ml soft drink cans filled with cola. A sample of 32 cans is selected by inspectors looking for nonconforming items. Among the things the inspectors look for are paint defects on the can, improper seal, incorrect volume, leaking contents, incorrect mixture of carbonation and syrup in the soft drink, and out-of-spec syrup mixture. The results of this inspection are given here. Construct a c chart from the data and comment on the results.

Can Number	Number of Nonconformances	Can Number	Number of Nonconformances
1	2	17	3
2	1	18	1
3	1	19	2
4	0	20	0
5	2	21	0
6	1	22	1
7	2	23	4
8	0	24	0
9	1	25	2
10	3	26	1
11	1	27	1
12	4	28	3
13	2	29	0
14	1	30	1
15	0	31	2
16	1	32	0

18.10   Examine the three control charts shown. Discuss any and all control problems that may be apparent from these control charts.

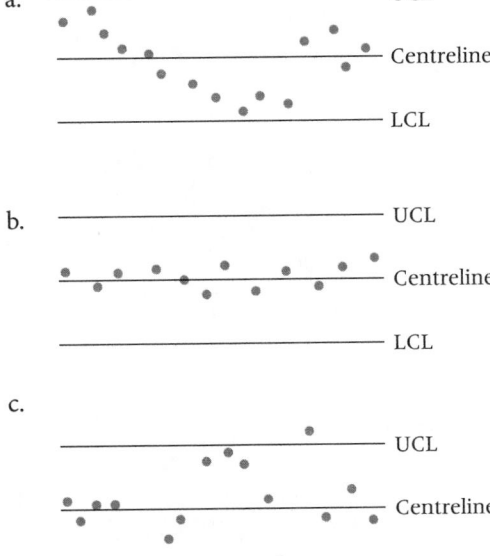

18.11 Study each of the following control charts and determine whether any of them indicate problems in the processes. Comment on each chart.

a.

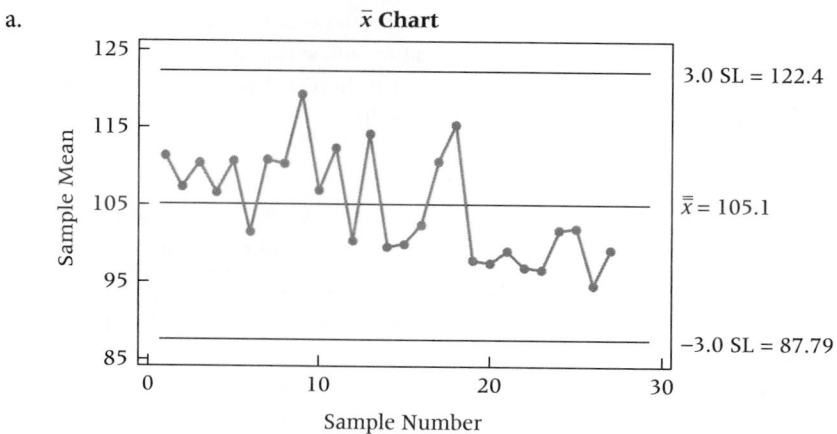

b.

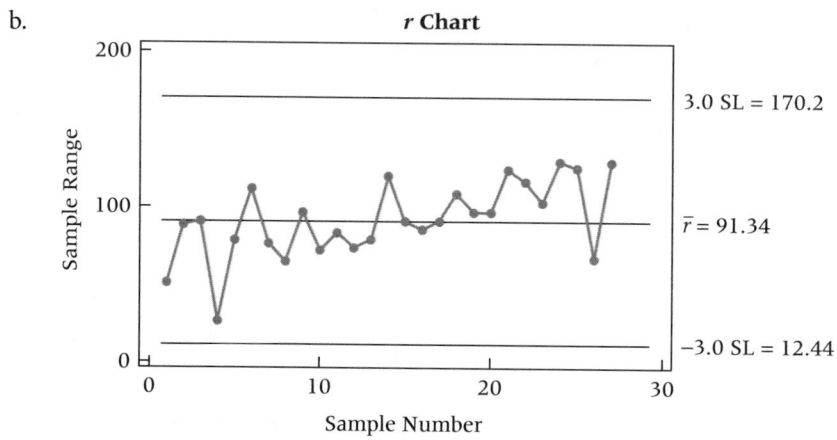

c.

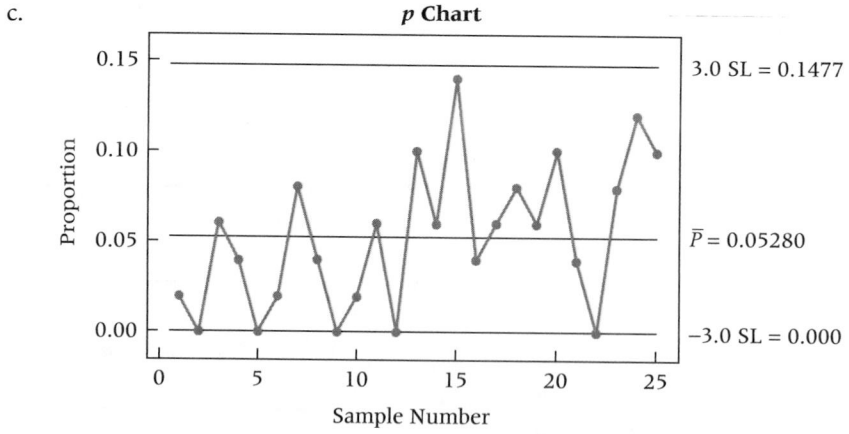

ITALY'S PIAGGIO MAKES A COMEBACK

After many years in decline and after several attempts were made to recapture its lustre, Piaggio was turned around under the ownership and leadership of Roberto Colaninno. How did he accomplish this? In 2002, one year before Colaninno took over the company, Piaggio had lost 129 million euros and was 577 million euros in debt. Being optimistic and focusing on Piaggio's assets, Colaninno insisted that the company wasn't dying but that "it just needed to be treated better." After making an initial investment of 100 million euros through his holding company for a third of Piaggio and the mandate to run it, he began his run at improving the company. He quickly hired a chief executive, Rocco Sabelli, who led an effort to redesign the factory and its assembly lines. Previously, each of several assembly lines had been set up to produce only one particular scooter model, but because demands for the different models varied according to their popularity, some assembly lines would have significant downtime while others would be running continuously, unable to keep up with the demand for strong-selling models. Under Sabelli, each assembly line was redesigned, refitted, and retooled so that any of Piaggio's scooter models could be made on any line with little changeover time. This created increased capacity for the production of hot-selling models to meet demand and, at the same time, effected a levelling of both manufacturing and human resources in the plant. Given that this was a radical departure from the way Piaggio had done business, one might say that Colaninno and Sabelli reengineered the company's manufacturing process. An even more dramatic example of reengineering took place following the Second World War when Piaggio transformed itself from an aeronautical production company to a scooter firm.

It has been a fairly common practice in Italian businesses for management to keep its distance from workers. In his first days on the job, Sabelli announced to all workers, including assembly-line workers, that they were to let him know personally about any problems or delays in the production process. Giving workers such access to management shortened the lines of communication so as to quickly improve the product and the process. Such an approach may be viewed, at least in spirit, as not unlike the quality circles introduced by the Japanese.

In a move that surprised many, Colaninno did not fire a single worker, thereby gaining the support of unions and reinforcing a notion argued by Deming that poor quality is usually more about such things as tools, training, design, process efficiency, and supplies than it is about the worker. Colaninno based bonuses for both blue-collar workers and management on profit margins and customer satisfaction—a common quality approach in which company employees are empowered to become responsible for product quality as measured by customer satisfaction, units sold, product warranty and repair claims, increased market share, and others. Colaninno also installed air conditioning in the factory, and productivity began to increase.

Company engineers were given deadlines for design projects in a manner similar to Six Sigma. As a result, the company recently rolled out two world firsts, including a gas-electric hybrid scooter and one with two wheels in front and one in the back for better road grip.

Why Statistics Is Relevant

Businesses today operate in a postindustrial era where quality is considered to be the cost of entry and not an optional extra. For a long time, this fact went unrecognized, until Japanese industrial goods started making inroads into other major markets. In today's highly competitive world, information travels fast through social media. So, it is imperative that businesses maintain and constantly improve the quality of products and services they offer. This is where statistics comes in. It is impossible to deliver quality without analyzing it quantitatively. Statistics offers simple methods to define, measure, and improve quality.

SUMMARY

1. Quality means different things to different people. According to one definition, a quality product delivers to the customer those attributes that have been agreed upon by both buyer and seller. Leading quality experts such as Philip B. Crosby, Armand V. Feigenbaum, and David A. Garvin suggest various divergent views on the notion of quality. Another accepted definition is "uniformity around a target value," which means low variability around what is specified.

Quality control is the collection of strategies, techniques, and actions an organization can use to ensure the production of a quality product. For decades, North American companies used after-process quality control, which essentially consisted of inspectors determining whether a product complied with its specifications. During the 1980s, North American companies joined Western European and Asian businesses in instituting in-process quality control, which enables the producer to determine weaknesses and flaws during the production process.

Total quality management (TQM) occurs when all members of an organization—from the CEO to the line worker—are involved in improving quality. One of the main proponents of TQM was W. Edwards Deming. Deming was known for his cause-and-effect explanation of TQM in a company, which is sometimes referred to as the Deming chain reaction. In addition, Deming presented 14 points that can lead to improved TQM. Some other well-known leaders in the quality movement are Joseph Juran, Philip Crosby, Armand Feigenbaum, Kaoru Ishikawa, and Genichi Taguchi.

In addition to TQM, some other major quality movements are Six Sigma, Design for Six Sigma (DFSS), and lean manufacturing. Six Sigma, besides being a quality movement, is also a methodology and a measurement. A goal of Six Sigma is no more than 3.4 defects per million opportunities. It is essentially a philosophy of zero defects achieved through root-cause analysis using a variety of statistical tools and methodologies in a team approach. DFSS is a quality scheme that emphasizes designing a product or process right the first time so that higher sigma levels of quality are possible. Lean manufacturing is a quality management philosophy that focuses on the reduction of waste and the elimination of unnecessary steps in an operation or process.

2. Some important quality concepts include benchmarking, just-in-time (JIT) inventory systems, reengineering, failure mode and effects analysis (FMEA), poka-yoke, quality circles, and Six Sigma teams. Benchmarking is a technique through which a company attempts to develop product and process excellence by examining and emulating the best practices and techniques used in the industry. JIT inventory systems are inventory systems that focus on raw materials, subparts, and suppliers. JIT is a philosophy of coordination and cooperation between supplier and manufacturer such that a part or raw material arrives just as it is needed. This approach saves on inventory and also serves as a catalyst for discovering bottlenecks and inefficiencies. It changes the manufacturer-supplier relationship. Reengineering is a radical approach to TQM in which the core business process is redesigned. FMEA is a systematic way of identifying the effects of potential product or process failure and includes methodology for eliminating or reducing the chance of failure. Poka-yoke means "mistake proofing," and it uses devices, methods, or inspections to avoid machine error or simple human error. Quality circles are small groups of workers who meet regularly to consider quality issues. Six Sigma teams, led by a black belt, attempt to uncover root causes of quality problems or opportunities and through the DMAIC process (Define, Measure, Analyze, Improve, and Control) seek to make significant improvements, resulting in substantial savings to the company.

3. Ishikawa developed seven basic tools of quality that he believed could be used to solve most quality-related problems. These are flowcharts, Pareto charts, cause-and-effect diagrams, control charts, check sheets, histograms, and scatter charts. Flowcharts are schematic representations of all activities that occur in a process. Pareto analysis is a method of examining types of defects that occur with a product. The result is usually a vertical bar chart that depicts the most common types of defects ranked in order of occurrence. The cause-and-effect (fishbone) diagram displays potential causes of quality problems. The diagram is shaped like a fish skeleton, with the head being the problem and the skeletal bones being the potential causes. A control chart is a graphic method of evaluating whether or not a process is in a state of statistical control. Check sheets are simple forms consisting of multiple categories and columns for recording the frequency of outcomes for some quality-related event or activity under study so that data can be presented in a logical format. A histogram is a type of vertical bar chart that is used to depict a frequency distribution. A scatter chart is a graphical mechanism for examining the relationship between two numerical variables.

4. Control charts are used to monitor product variation, thus enabling operators, technicians, and managers to see when a process gets out of control. The $\bar{x}$ chart and the R chart are two types of control charts for measurements. The $\bar{x}$ chart is a graph of sample means computed on a series of small random samples over time. The R chart is a plot of sample ranges. The $\bar{x}$ chart plots the measure of central tendency, whereas the R chart plots a measure of variability. The p chart and the c chart are two types of control charts for nonconformance. The p chart graphs the proportions of sample items that are in noncompliance. The c chart displays the number of nonconformances per item for a series of sampled items. All four types of control chart are plotted around a centreline and upper and lower control limits (UCLs and LCLs). The control limits are located three standard deviations from the centreline.

KEY TERMS

after-process quality control
benchmarking
c chart
cause-and-effect diagram
centreline
check sheet
control chart
Design for Six Sigma (DFSS)
Failure mode and effects
   analysis (FMEA)
fishbone diagram

flowchart
histogram
in-process quality control
Ishikawa diagram
just-in-time (JIT) inventory
   system
lean manufacturing
lower control limit (LCL)
manufacturing-based quality
p chart

Pareto analysis
Pareto chart
poka-yoke
process
product quality
quality
quality circle
quality control
R chart
reengineering

scatter chart
Six Sigma
team building
total quality management
   (TQM)
transcendent quality
upper control limit (UCL)
user quality
value quality
$\bar{x}$ chart

FORMULAS

$\bar{x}$ Charts

Centreline: $\bar{\bar{x}} = \dfrac{\sum \bar{x}}{k}$

UCL: $\bar{\bar{x}} + A_2\bar{R}$

LCL: $\bar{\bar{x}} - A_2\bar{R}$

or

UCL: $\bar{\bar{x}} + A_3\bar{s}$

LCL: $\bar{\bar{x}} - A_3\bar{s}$

R charts

Centreline: $\bar{R} = \dfrac{\sum R}{k}$

UCL: $D_4\bar{R}$

LCL: $D_3\bar{R}$

p charts

Centreline: $p = \dfrac{\sum \hat{p}}{k}$

UCL: $p + 3\sqrt{\dfrac{p \cdot q}{n}}$

LCL: $p - 3\sqrt{\dfrac{p \cdot q}{n}}$

c charts

Centreline: $\bar{c} = \dfrac{c_1 + c_2 + c_3 + \cdots + c_i}{i}$

UCL: $\bar{c} + 3\sqrt{\bar{c}}$

LCL: $\bar{c} - 3\sqrt{\bar{c}}$

KEY CONSIDERATIONS

Borderline ethical behaviour can occur in many areas of TQM. At the top, CEOs and other high-level managers can profess to the world that the company is committed to quality and not truly promote quality in the organization. Managers who use the quality movement only as a tool for attention and leverage and do not actually intend to implement the process may be defeating the purpose of having a quality control program.

Some of the specifics of quality control and statistical process control lend themselves to such behaviour. JIT systems can be used as an excuse to implement favouritism among suppliers. With the move to reduce the number of suppliers, contracting managers can be more selective in choosing suppliers. This practice can give contracting agents or purchasing agents more leverage in securing deals through unethical means.

JIT systems often encourage the supplier rather than the manufacturer to do the testing. This self-evaluation opens opportunity for the falsification of records and tests. It is hoped that such behaviour is uncovered by JIT systems that place pressure on suppliers to ship on-specification

parts and materials. The customer or user of the supplies in a JIT system is more likely to discover off-specification material than users in traditional systems.

Benchmarking could easily lend itself to violation of patent laws if a company is not careful. It could also encourage business espionage and unfair competitive practices. Benchmarking could create an atmosphere of continually seeking ways to steal competitive ideas and innovations.

Control charts present the same methodological challenges as any sampling process. Those workers constructing the charts have an opportunity to falsify data, selectively choose favourable items, or graphically misrepresent data to make a system look in control.

The implementation of a sound quality program in a company must be based on teamwork, mutual support, trust, and honesty. Nonrigorous procedures in quality control can set the process back for years, if not permanently. The intent in the quality movement is to bring out the best in people so as to optimize the quality of the product.

SUPPLEMENTARY PROBLEMS

Calculating the Statistics

18.12 Create a flowchart from the following sequence of activities: Begin. Flow to activity A. Flow to decision B. If Yes, flow to activity C. If No, flow to activity D. From C flow to activity E and to activity F. From F, flow to decision G. If Yes, flow to decision H. If No at G, stop. At H, if Yes, flow to activity I and on to activity J and then stop. If No at H, flow to activity J and stop. At D, flow to activity K, flow to L, and flow to decision M. If Yes at M, stop. If No at M, flow to activity N and then stop.

18.13 An examination of rejects shows at least 10 problems. A frequency tally of the problems follows. Construct a Pareto chart for these data.

Problem	Frequency
1	673
2	29
3	108
4	379
5	73
6	564
7	12
8	402
9	54
10	202

18.14 A brainstorm session on possible causes of a problem resulted in five possible causes: A, B, C, D, and E. Cause A has three possible subcauses, cause B has four, cause C has two, cause D has five, and cause E has three. Construct a fishbone diagram for this problem and its possible causes.

Testing Your Understanding

18.15 A bottled-water company has been randomly inspecting bottles of water to determine whether they are acceptable for delivery and sale. The inspectors are looking at water quality, bottle condition, and seal tightness. A series of 10 random samples of 50 bottles each is taken. Some bottles are rejected. Use the following information on the number of bottles from each batch that were rejected as being out of compliance to construct a p chart.

Sample	N	Number out of Compliance
1	50	3
2	50	11
3	50	7
4	50	2
5	50	5
6	50	8
7	50	0
8	50	9
9	50	1
10	50	6

18.16 A fruit juice company sells a plastic jug filled with 1.89 L of cranberry-apple juice. Inspectors are concerned about the consistency of volume of fill in these containers. Every two hours for three days of production, a sample of five containers is randomly selected and the volume of fill is measured. The results follow.

Sample 1	Sample 2	Sample 3	Sample 4
1.8939	1.8908	1.8924	1.8884
1.8908	1.8916	1.8861	1.8900
1.8916	1.8979	1.8900	1.8908
1.8892	1.8924	1.8908	1.8908
1.8932	1.8963	1.8892	1.8900

Sample 5	Sample 6	Sample 7	Sample 8
1.8876	1.8916	1.8908	1.8963
1.8892	1.8939	1.8900	1.8924
1.8916	1.8908	1.8900	1.8900
1.8908	1.8900	1.8876	1.8939
1.8900	1.8908	1.8916	1.8908

Sample 9	Sample 10	Sample 11	Sample 12
1.8900	1.8900	1.8908	1.8900
1.8916	1.8908	1.8892	1.8939
1.8924	1.8900	1.8916	1.8932
1.8908	1.8900	1.8924	1.8916
1.8908	1.8900	1.8908	1.8900

Use this information to construct $\bar{x}$ and R charts and comment on any samples that are out of compliance.

18.17 A metal-manufacturing company produces sheet metal. Statistical quality control technicians randomly select sheets to be inspected for blemishes and size problems. The number of nonconformances per sheet is tallied. Shown here are the results of testing 36 sheets of metal. Use the data to construct a *c* chart. What is the centreline? What is the meaning of the centreline value?

Sheet Number	Number of Nonconformances	Sheet Number	Number of Nonconformances
1	4	19	1
2	2	20	3
3	1	21	4
4	1	22	0
5	3	23	2
6	0	24	3
7	4	25	0
8	5	26	0
9	2	27	4
10	1	28	2
11	2	29	5
12	0	30	3
13	5	31	1
14	4	32	2
15	1	33	0
16	2	34	4
17	1	35	2
18	0	36	3

18.18   A manufacturing company produces cylindrical tubes for engines that are specified to be 1.20 cm thick. As part of the company's statistical quality control effort, random samples of four tubes are taken each hour. The tubes are measured to determine whether they are within thickness tolerances. Shown here are the thickness data in centimetres for nine samples of tubes. Use these data to develop an $\bar{x}$ chart and an *R* chart. Comment on whether or not the process appears to be in control at this point.

Sample 1	Sample 2	Sample 3	Sample 4	Sample 5
1.22	1.20	1.21	1.16	1.24
1.19	1.20	1.18	1.17	1.20
1.20	1.22	1.17	1.20	1.21
1.23	1.20	1.20	1.16	1.18

Sample 6	Sample 7	Sample 8	Sample 9
1.19	1.24	1.17	1.22
1.21	1.17	1.23	1.17
1.21	1.18	1.22	1.16
1.20	1.19	1.16	1.19

18.19   A manufacturer produces digital watches. Every two hours, a sample of six watches is selected randomly to be tested. Each watch is run for exactly 15 minutes and is timed by an accurate, precise timing device. Because of the variation among watches, they do not all run the same. Shown here are the data from eight

different samples given in minutes. Use these data to construct $\bar{x}$ and *R* charts. Observe the results and comment on whether the process is in control.

Sample 1	Sample 2	Sample 3	Sample 4
15.01	15.03	14.96	15.00
14.99	14.96	14.97	15.01
14.99	15.01	14.96	14.97
15.00	15.02	14.99	15.01
14.98	14.97	15.01	14.99
14.99	15.01	14.98	14.96

Sample 5	Sample 6	Sample 7	Sample 8
15.02	15.02	15.03	14.96
15.03	15.01	15.04	14.99
14.99	14.97	15.03	15.02
15.01	15.00	15.00	15.01
15.02	15.01	15.01	14.98
15.01	14.99	14.99	15.02

18.20   A company produces outdoor home thermometers. For a variety of reasons, a thermometer can be tested and found to be out of compliance with company specification. The company takes samples of thermometers on a regular basis and tests each one to determine whether it meets company standards. Shown here are data from 12 different random samples of 75 thermometers. Use these data to construct a *p* chart. Comment on the pattern of points in the chart.

Sample	n	Number out of Compliance
1	75	9
2	75	3
3	75	0
4	75	2
5	75	7
6	75	14
7	75	11
8	75	8
9	75	5
10	75	4
11	75	0
12	75	7

18.21   A plastics company makes thousands of plastic bottles for another company that manufactures saline solution for users of soft contact lenses. The plastics company randomly inspects a sample of its bottles as part of its quality control program. Inspectors look for blemishes on the bottle, size and thickness, ability to close, leaks, labelling problems, and so on. Shown here are the results of tests completed on 25 bottles. Use these data to construct a c chart. Observe the results and comment on the chart.

Bottle Number	Number of Nonconformances	Bottle Number	Number of Nonconformances
1	1	14	0
2	0	15	0
3	1	16	0
4	0	17	1
5	0	18	0
6	2	19	0
7	1	20	1
8	1	21	0
9	0	22	1
10	1	23	2
11	0	24	0
12	2	25	1
13	1		

18.22 A bathtub manufacturer closely inspects several tubs on every shift for nonconformances such as leaks, lack of symmetry, unstable base, and drain malfunctions. The following list gives the number of nonconformances per tub for 40 tubs. Use these data to construct a c chart of nonconformances for bathtubs. Comment on the results of this chart.

Tub	Number of Nonconformances	Tub	Number of Nonconformances
1	3	21	2
2	2	22	5
3	3	23	1
4	1	24	3
5	4	25	4
6	2	26	3
7	2	27	2
8	1	28	0
9	4	29	1
10	2	30	0
11	3	31	2
12	0	32	1
13	3	33	2
14	2	34	1
15	2	35	1
16	1	36	1
17	0	37	3
18	4	38	0
19	3	39	1
20	2	40	4

18.23 A glass manufacturer produces hand mirrors. Each mirror is supposed to meet company standards for such things as glass thickness, ability to reflect, size of handle, quality of glass, and colour of handle. To control for these features, the company quality people randomly sample 40 mirrors every shift and determine how many of the mirrors are out of compliance on at least one feature. Shown here are the data for 15 such samples. Use the data to construct a p chart. Observe the results and comment on the control of the process as indicated by the chart.

Sample	n	Number out of Compliance
1	40	2
2	40	0
3	40	6
4	40	3
5	40	1
6	40	1
7	40	5
8	40	0
9	40	4
10	40	3
11	40	2
12	40	2
13	40	6
14	40	1
15	40	0

Interpreting Charts

18.24 Study the chart on the size of a product that is supposed to measure 12 cm. Does the process appear to be out of control? Why or why not?

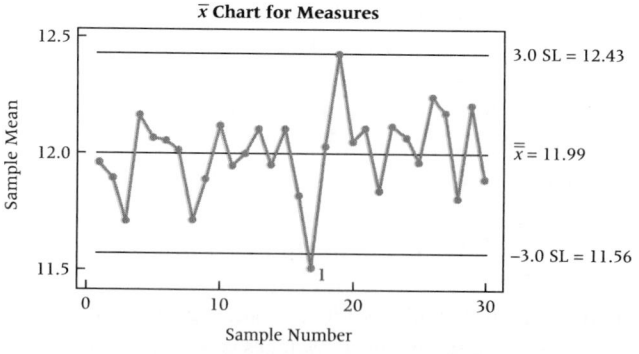

$\bar{x}$ Chart for Measures

3.0 SL = 12.43

$\bar{\bar{x}}$ = 11.99

−3.0 SL = 11.56

18.25 Study the *R* chart for the product and data used in Problem 18.24. Comment on the state of the production process for this item.

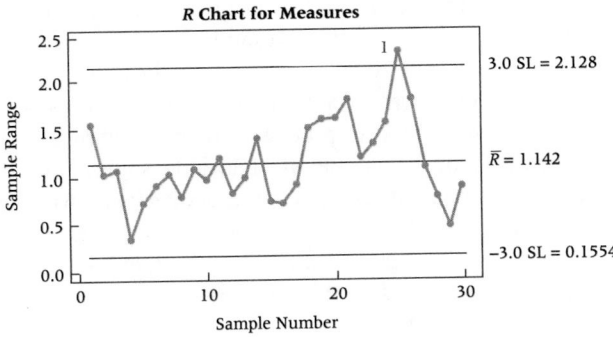

R Chart for Measures

18.26 Study the *p* chart for a manufactured item. The chart represents the results of testing 30 items at a time for compliance. Sixty different samples were taken for this chart. Discuss the results and the implications for the production process.

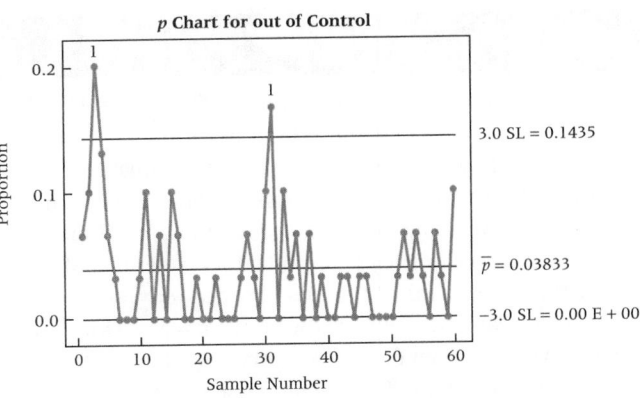

p Chart for out of Control

18.27 Study the *c* chart for nonconformances for a part produced in a manufacturing process. Comment on the results.

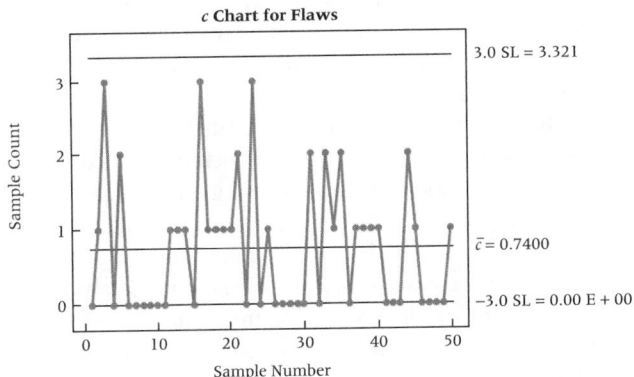

c Chart for Flaws

ANALYZING THE DATABASES

see www.wiley.com/canada/black

1. A hospital in the Canadian Hospitals Database takes weekly samples of patient account statements for 12 weeks with each sample containing 40 accounts. Auditors analyze the account statements, looking for nonconforming statements. Shown here are the results of the 12 samples. Use these data to construct a *p* chart for the proportion of nonconforming statements. What is the centreline? What are UCL and LCL? Comment on the control chart.

Sample	Number of Nonconforming Statements
1	1
2	0
3	6
4	3
5	0
6	2
7	8
8	3

(continued)

Sample	Number of Nonconforming Statements
9	5
10	2
11	2
12	1

2. A company in the Financial Database manufactures laptop computers. A supplier is shipping the company a particular part in lots of 5,000. The computer manufacturing company (consumer) is doing acceptance sampling with samples of size 25. If the supplier is actually producing lots with only 3% defective parts and if this proportion is acceptable to the consumer, what is the producer's risk if $c = 1$? (*C* stands for defective parts.) Suppose the supplier is actually producing the part in lots with 12% defective parts, which is unacceptable to the consumer. If *c* is still 1, what is the consumer's risk? Construct an OC curve for $n = 25$ and $c = 1$. Comment on the curve.

CASE

Catalyst Paper Introduces Microsoft Dynamics CRM

Catalyst Paper is a paper manufacturer in Richmond, British Columbia. This company is very successful and financially healthy, with sales of approximately $1.9 billion in 2008, and a workforce comprising more than 3,800 employees. Catalyst has become the leading telephone directory paper manufacturer, generating 2.4 million tonnes of paper per year.

Catalyst Paper seemed like the ideal company. However, in recent years it began dealing with many quality issues. These issues arose from the two enterprise resource planning (ERP) systems that the company was using. These systems were so complex and difficult to access that the salespeople were having a difficult time recording and retrieving client information. They therefore had to keep track of client information and sales requests by developing their own, easier-to-access paper folders and spreadsheets. This made the work very time-consuming and prone to errors.

Catalyst realized that this was a very inefficient way for such a successful company to be doing business. The current client information system was causing major problems, which caused incorrect ordering and production quantities of paper, which in turn had a negative impact on the company's sales and decreased customer satisfaction. Catalyst understood that it needed to improve the quality of its service by centralizing access to customer relationship management (CRM) information.

Catalyst needed a new CRM system in order to provide the employees with a centralized customer database with all the relevant customer information. This would allow the salespeople to promptly pull up the relevant customer information with no paper folder involved, therefore saving time, reducing the possibility of errors, and improving customer satisfaction.

Catalyst decided to implement the Microsoft Dynamics CRM. This system was integrated, and its ease of use made it an instant hit. A major benefit of this new system was salespeople being able to quickly access and assess customer information before the customer was called. Salespeople previously had to spend hours searching for and putting together information for each client. Now, the time spent assembling such information was reduced by 95%, which in turn resulted in an improvement of 5% in sales productivity.

Other benefits of Microsoft Dynamics CRM were speed and reliability, allowing salespeople to accurately quote customers the correct prices. The accuracy of a quote improved by 5%, and the time required to quote a customer improved by 10%. Overall, implementing the new Microsoft Dynamics CRM system has been very effective for Catalyst, both in improving sales and in customer satisfaction.

Discussion

1. As Catalyst Paper improved its quality with a more efficient CRM system, it also wanted to examine a specific process, such as the flow of troubleshooting, from the time the problem request was received until the problem was solved. Draw a flowchart for the process of troubleshooting by using the following outline, which includes some of the activities that might occur, as well as adding your own ideas.

   Troubleshooting flow: Customer calls customer support line and explains the problem. Customer service representative records problem in database and then notifies appropriate department of problem. Appropriate departmental employee reads details and familiarizes himself/herself with customer problem. Employee then collects client information and calls to speak to customer. Employee establishes rapport with customer and explains process of solving the issue and reassures customer that problem will be solved. Employee asks customer any pertinent questions. Once all information is collected, employee develops a schedule of what has to be done and when. Employee then begins assessing details about what work must be completed and by whom. If the problem is a one-person job, then the employee can take on the issue and fix the problem on his/her own. If the problem is serious and requires a team effort, an e-mail notice is sent out to other employees asking what task each of them is able to do to help solve the problem. Return e-mails must be kept track of to monitor which employee is in charge of which part of the problem. Employees are encouraged to voice any hesitations or concerns about the problem. Work is begun on resolving problem. Initial employee heading the troubleshooting task follows up every day to ensure work is on schedule. If any major disagreement or problem occurs during this process, employee addresses issue to departmental manager. Customer is updated on the status of the problem. Once problem is solved, employee in charge of troubleshooting the problem enters information in database and confirms to the customer that the problem has been solved.

2. It is very important for manufacturing companies to monitor their performance in order to ensure quality is being met. Companies are able to do this by using control charts. Think of the data that Catalyst can collect regarding all the quality issues that it must deal with on a regular basis. Based on your thinking, determine which variables can be used to ensure the quality characteristics of the manufacturing and sales processes of Catalyst. Then, based on these characteristics, discuss how the various control charts learned in this chapter can be used to monitor, control, and improve quality dimensions of Catalyst. In performing this analysis, ensure

that there is a discussion on the methods that can be used by the company to detect whether the manufacturing and sales processes are in control or not.

3. Should Catalyst rely solely on control charts to manage and improve the quality-control aspect of its operations, in general? Discuss other quality tools and methods that management can use to address the entire realm of quality issues, including after-process inspection.

References

"Catalyst Improves Underlying Financial Results in 2008," Website for data source: <http://www.newswire.ca/en/releases/archive/February2009/12/c7858.html>; "Paper Company Maximizes Sales Effectiveness through Centralized CRM", Microsoft Dynamics Customer Solution Case Study, April 2008, Website for data source: <http://www.ideaca.com/assets/case_studies/Case%20Study_Catalyst_Paper_CRM.pdf>

CHAPTER 19

DECISION ANALYSIS

Learning Objectives

This chapter describes how to use decision analysis to improve management decisions. The key questions of the chapter are:

1. What are the three types of decisions considered by mathematical and statistical approaches?

2. What is meant by decision alternatives, states of nature, and payoffs?

3. What are the four approaches to making decisions?

4. How can you calculate the expected monetary value associated with decision alternatives?

5. How can you assess the expected value of perfect information?

6. What is utility theory?

7. How can you revise probabilities with sample information?

J.P. Moczulski/Reuters

DECISION DILEMMA

DECISION MAKING AT THE CEO LEVEL

CEOs face major challenges in today's business world. As the international marketplace evolves, competition often increases. Technology continues to improve products and process. The political and economic climates both internationally and domestically shift constantly. In the midst of such dynamics, CEOs make decisions about investments, products, resources, suppliers, financing, and so on. Decision making may be the most important function of management. Successful companies are usually built around successful decisions. Even CEOs of successful companies feel the need to constantly improve the company's position.

In 1994, Ford Motor Company posted a record profit of more than $4 billion with 5 of the 10 best-selling vehicles in the U.S. Yet, CEO and chairman Alex Trotman made the decision to merge the North American and European operations into one global unit. The decision was implemented with Ford 2000, a program to design "world cars," with common components that can be sold worldwide with minor style changes to suit local tastes.

In the same year, George Fisher, CEO of Eastman Kodak Company, reversed a decade of diversification for Kodak and led the company in the direction of digital and electronic imaging. He implemented this thrust by aligning digital and electronic imaging with traditional products that emphasize paper and film.

Other CEOs have made tough decisions over the years. For example, in 2008, a Toronto Maple Leaf Foods plant was confirmed as being involved in the outbreak of the food-borne illness, caused by the bacterium *Listeria monocytogenes*. The CEO, Michael McCain, had to quickly decide how to handle the crisis and retain consumer confidence in Maple Leaf Foods products. In 2009 when the economic crisis affected coffee sales, Second Cup president and CEO Stacey Mowbray had to decide how many outlets the company needed to close.

CEOs of smaller companies also make tough decisions. The most critical decision-making period for a CEO is likely to be during growth phases. A study of 142 CEOs from small, private companies attempted to ascertain the types of decisions undertaken by top managers. Most of the companies in the study had experienced healthy growth in revenues over the four-year period preceding the study. CEOs in this study suggested that decisions made during growth phases are typically in the areas of expansion, personnel, finances, operations, and planning and control systems. According to respondents in the study, many of these decisions carry system-wide implications for the company, making the decisions quite critical.

CEOs responded that during a growth phase, decisions need to be made about how to handle new business. How is capacity to be expanded? Does the company build, lease, expand its present facility, relocate, automate, and so on? Risk is inevitably involved in undertaking most of these decisions. Will customer demand continue? Will competitors also increase capacity? How long will the increased demand continue? What is the lost opportunity if the company fails to meet customer demands?

According to the study, another critical area of decision making is personnel. What is the long-term strategy of the company? Should significant layoffs be implemented in an effort to become lean and mean? Does the firm need to hire personnel? How does management discover and attract talented managers? How can substandard personnel be released? In the area of production, how does management level personnel to match uneven product demand?

A third area of decision making that the study participants considered important incorporated systems, business, and finance. How can the company make operations and procedures more efficient? How are cash flow problems handled? Under what conditions does the company obtain financial backing for capital development?

In the area of marketing, decisions need to be made about pricing, distribution, purchasing, and suppliers. Should the company market overseas? What about vertical integration? Should the company expand into new market segments or with new product lines?

The CEOs in the study enumerated decision choices that represent exciting and sometimes risky opportunities for growing firms. The success or failure of such decision makers often lies in their ability to identify and choose optimal decision pathways for the company.

Managerial and Statistical Questions

1. In any given area of decisions, what choices or options are available to the manager?
2. What occurrences in nature, the marketplace, or the business environment might affect the outcome or payoff for a given decision option?
3. What are some strategies that can be used to help the decision maker determine which option to choose?
4. If risk is involved, can probabilities of occurrence be assigned to various states of nature within each decision option?
5. What are the payoffs for various decision options?
6. Does the manager's propensity toward risk enter into the final decision and, if so, how?

The main focus of this text has been business decision making. In this chapter, we discuss one last category of quantitative techniques for assisting managers in decision making. These techniques, generally referred to as **decision analysis**, are *particularly targeted at clarifying and enhancing the decision-making process* and can be used in such diverse situations as determining whether and when to drill oil wells, deciding whether and how to expand capacity, deciding whether to automate a facility, and determining what types of investments to make.

In decision analysis, decision-making scenarios are divided into the following three categories.

1. Decision making under certainty
2. Decision making under uncertainty
3. Decision making under risk

In this chapter, we discuss making decisions under each condition, as well as the concepts of utility and Bayesian statistics.

19.1 THE DECISION TABLE AND DECISION MAKING UNDER CERTAINTY

Many decision analysis problems can be viewed as having three variables: decision alternatives, states of nature, and payoffs.

Decision alternatives are *the various choices or options available to the decision maker in any given problem situation.* On most days, financial managers face the choices of whether to invest in blue chip stocks, bonds, commodities, guaranteed investment certificates (GICs), money markets, annuities, or other investments. Construction decision makers must decide whether to concentrate on one building job today, spread out workers and equipment to several jobs, or not work today. In virtually every possible business scenario, decision alternatives are available. A good decision maker identifies many options and effectively evaluates them.

States of nature are *the occurrences of nature that can happen after a decision is made that can affect the outcome of the decision and over which the decision maker has little or no control.*

These states of nature can literally be natural atmospheric and climatic conditions or they can be such things as the business climate, the political climate, the worker climate, or the condition of the marketplace, among many others. The financial investor faces such states of nature as the prime interest rate, the condition of the stock market, international monetary exchange rates, and so on. A construction company is faced with such states of nature as the weather, wildcat strikes, equipment failure, absenteeism, and supplier inability to deliver on time. States of nature are usually difficult to predict but are important to identify in the decision-making process.

The **payoffs** of a decision analysis problem are *the benefits or rewards that result from selecting a particular decision alternative.* Payoffs are usually given in terms of dollars. In the financial investment industry, for example, the payoffs can be small, modest, or large, or the investment can result in a loss. Most business decisions involve taking some chances with personal or company money in one form or another. Because for-profit businesses are looking for a return on the dollars invested, the payoffs are extremely important for a successful manager. The trick is to determine which decision alternative to choose in order to generate the greatest payoff. Suppose a CEO is examining various environmental decision alternatives. Positive payoffs could include increased market share, attracting and retaining quality employees, consumer appreciation, and governmental support. Negative payoffs might take the form of fines and penalties, lost market share, and lawsuit judgments.

DECISION TABLE

The concepts of decision alternatives, states of nature, and payoffs can be examined jointly by using a **decision table,** or **payoff table.** Table 19.1 shows the structure of a decision table. On the left side of the table are the various decision alternatives, denoted by d_i. Along the top row are the states of nature, denoted by s_j. In the middle of the table are the various payoffs for each decision alternative under each state of nature, denoted by $P_{i,j}$.

As an example of a decision table, consider the decision dilemma of the investor shown in Table 19.2. The investor is faced with the decision of where and how to invest $10,000 under several possible states of nature.

The investor is considering four decision alternatives.

1. Invest in the stock market
2. Invest in the bond market
3. Invest in GICs
4. Invest in a mixture of stocks and bonds

Because the payoffs are in the future, the investor is unlikely to know ahead of time what the state of nature will be for the economy. However, the table delineates three possible states of the economy.

1. A stagnant economy
2. A slow-growth economy
3. A rapid-growth economy

Table 19.1		State of Nature				
		s_1	s_2	s_3	$\cdots$	s_n
Decision Table	d_1	$P_{1,1}$	$P_{1,2}$	$P_{1,3}$	$\cdots$	$P_{1,n}$
	d_2	$P_{2,1}$	$P_{2,2}$	$P_{2,3}$	$\cdots$	$P_{2,n}$
	d_3	$P_{3,1}$	$P_{3,2}$	$P_{3,3}$	$\cdots$	$P_{3,n}$
Decision Alternative	$\cdot$	$\cdot$	$\cdot$	$\cdot$	$\cdot$	$\cdot$
	$\cdot$	$\cdot$	$\cdot$	$\cdot$	$\cdot$	$\cdot$
	$\cdot$	$\cdot$	$\cdot$	$\cdot$	$\cdot$	$\cdot$
	d_m	$P_{m,1}$	$P_{m,2}$	$P_{m,3}$	$\cdots$	$P_{m,n}$

where
s_j = state of nature
d_i = decision alternative
$P_{i,j}$ = payoff for decision i under state j

Table 19.2

Yearly Payoffs on an Investment of $10,000

		State of the Economy		
		Stagnant	Slow Growth	Rapid Growth
Investment Decision Alternative	Stocks	−$500	$700	$2,200
	Bonds	−$100	$600	$900
	GICs	$300	$500	$750
	Mixture	−$200	$650	$1,300

The matrix in Table 19.2 lists the payoffs for each possible investment decision under each possible state of the economy. Notice that the largest payoff comes with a stock investment under a rapid-growth economic scenario, with a payoff of $2,200 per year on an investment of $10,000. The lowest payoff occurs for a stock investment during stagnant economic times, with an annual loss of $500 on the $10,000 investment.

DECISION MAKING UNDER CERTAINTY

The most elementary of the decision-making scenarios is **decision making under certainty.** In making decisions under certainty, *the states of nature are known.* The decision maker needs merely to examine the payoffs under different decision alternatives and select the alternative with the largest payoff. In the preceding example involving the $10,000 investment, if it is known that the economy is going to be stagnant, the investor would select the decision alternative of GICs, yielding a payoff of $300. Indeed, each of the other three decision alternatives would result in a loss under stagnant economic conditions. If it is known that the economy is going to have slow growth, the investor would choose stocks as an investment, resulting in a $700 payoff. If the economy is certain to have rapid growth, the decision maker should opt for stocks, resulting in a payoff of $2,200. Decision making under certainty is almost the trivial case.

Concept Check

1. What is the meaning of the following terms: *decision alternatives, states of nature,* and *payoffs?*

19.2 DECISION MAKING UNDER UNCERTAINTY

In making decisions under certainty, the decision maker knows for sure which state of nature will occur, and he or she bases the decision on the optimal payoff available under that state. **Decision making under uncertainty** occurs *when it is unknown which states of nature will occur and the probability of a state of nature occurring is also unknown.* Hence, the decision maker has virtually no information about which state of nature will occur, and he or she attempts to develop a strategy based on payoffs.

Several different approaches can be taken to making decisions under uncertainty. Each uses a different decision criterion, depending on the decision maker's outlook. Each of these approaches will be explained and demonstrated with a decision table. Included are the maximax criterion, maximin criterion, Hurwicz criterion, and minimax regret.

In Section 19.1, we discussed the decision dilemma of the financial investor who wants to invest $10,000 and is faced with four decision alternatives and three states of nature. The data for this problem were given in Table 19.2. In decision making under certainty, we selected the optimal payoff under each state of the economy and then, on the basis of which state we were certain would occur, selected a decision alternative. Shown next are techniques to use when we are uncertain which state of nature will occur.

MAXIMAX CRITERION

The **maximax criterion** approach is an optimistic approach in which the decision maker bases action on a notion that the best things will happen. The decision maker *isolates the maximum payoff under each decision alternative and then selects the decision alternative that produces the highest of these maximum payoffs*. The name "maximax" means selecting the maximum overall payoff from the maximum payoffs of each decision alternative. Consider the $10,000 investment problem. The maximum payoff is $2,200 for stocks, $900 for bonds, $750 for GICs, and $1,300 for the mixture of investments. The maximax criterion approach requires that the decision maker select the maximum payoff of these four.

		State of the Economy			
		Stagnant	Slow Growth	Rapid Growth	Maximum
Investment Decision Alternative	Stocks	−$500	$700	$2,200	$2,200
	Bonds	−$100	$600	$900	$900
	GICs	$300	$500	$750	$750
	Mixture	−$200	$650	$1,300	$1,300

maximum of {$2,200, $900, $750, $1,300} = $2,200

Because the maximax criterion results in $2,200 as the optimal payoff, the decision alternative selected is the stock alternative, which is associated with the $2,200.

MAXIMIN CRITERION

The **maximin criterion** approach to decision making is a pessimistic approach. The assumption is that the worst will happen and attempts must be made to minimize the damage. The decision maker starts by examining the payoffs under each decision alternative and selects the worst, or minimum, payoff that can occur under that decision. Then, the decision maker *selects the maximum or best payoff of those minimums selected under each decision alternative*. Thus, the decision maker has maximized the minimums. In the investment problem, the minimum payoffs are −$500 for stocks, −$100 for bonds, $300 for GICs, and −$200 for the mixture of investments. With the maximin criterion, the decision maker examines the minimum payoffs for each decision alternative given in the last column and selects the maximum of those values.

		State of the Economy			
		Stagnant	Slow Growth	Rapid Growth	Minimum
Investment Decision Alternative	Stocks	−$500	$700	$2,200	−$500
	Bonds	−$100	$600	$900	−$100
	GICs	$300	$500	$750	$300
	Mixture	−$200	$650	$1,300	−$200

maximum of {−$500, −$100, $300, −$200} = $300

The decision is to invest in GICs because that investment alternative yields the highest, or maximum, payoff under the worst-case scenario.

HURWICZ CRITERION

The Hurwicz criterion is an approach somewhere between the maximax and the maximin approaches. The **Hurwicz criterion** approach selects the maximum and the minimum payoff from each decision alternative. A value called alpha (not the same as the probability of a Type I error), which is between 0 and 1, is selected as a weight of optimism. The nearer alpha is to 1, the more optimistic is the decision maker. The use of alpha values near 0 implies a more pessimistic approach. The maximum payoff under each decision alternative is multiplied by α and the minimum payoff (pessimistic view) under each decision alternative is multiplied by $1 - \alpha$ (weight of pessimism). These weighted products are summed for each decision alternative, resulting in a weighted value for each decision alternative. The maximum weighted value is selected, and the corresponding decision alternative is chosen. Following are the data for the investment example, along with the minimum and maximum values.

		State of the Economy				
		Stagnant	Slow Growth	Rapid Growth	Minimum	Maximum
Investment	Stocks	−$500	$700	$2,200	−$500	$2,200
Decision	Bonds	−$100	$600	$900	−$100	$900
Alternative	GICs	$300	$500	$750	$300	$750
	Mixture	−$200	$650	$1,300	−$200	$1,300

Suppose we are more optimistic than pessimistic and select $\alpha = 0.7$ for the weight of optimism. The calculations of weighted values for the decision alternative follow:

$$\text{Stocks: } (\$2,200)(0.7) + (-\$500)(0.3) = \$1,390$$
$$\text{Bonds: } (\$900)(0.7) + (-\$100)(0.3) = \$600$$
$$\text{GICs: } (\$750)(0.7) + (\$300)(0.3) = \$615$$
$$\text{Mixture: } (\$1,300)(0.7) + (-\$200)(0.3) = \$850$$

The Hurwicz criterion leads the decision maker to choose the maximum of these values, $1,390. The result under the Hurwicz criterion with $\alpha = 0.7$ is to choose stocks as the decision alternative. An advantage of the Hurwicz criterion is that it allows the decision maker the latitude to explore various weights of optimism. A decision maker's outlook might change from scenario to scenario and from day to day. In this case, if we had been fairly pessimistic and chosen an alpha of 0.2, we would have obtained the following weighted values:

$$\text{Stocks: } (\$2,200)(0.2) + (-\$500)(0.8) = \$40$$
$$\text{Bonds: } (\$900)(0.2) + (-\$100)(0.8) = \$100$$
$$\text{GICs: } (\$750)(0.2) + (\$300)(0.8) = \$390$$
$$\text{Mixture: } (\$1,300)(0.2) + (-\$200)(0.8) = \$100$$

Under this scenario, the decision maker would choose the GIC option because it yields the highest weighted payoff ($390) with $\alpha = 0.2$.

Table 19.3 displays the payoffs obtained by using the Hurwicz criterion for various values of alpha for the investment example. The circled values are the optimum payoffs and represent the decision alternative selection for that value of alpha. Note that for $\alpha = 0.0, 0.1, 0.2$, and 0.3, the decision is to invest in GICs. For $\alpha = 0.4$ to 1.0, the decision is to invest in stocks.

Figure 19.1 shows graphically the weighted values for each decision alternative over the possible values of alpha. The thicker line segments represent the maximum of these under each value of alpha. Notice that the graph reinforces the choice of GICs for $\alpha = 0.0$, 0.1, 0.2, and 0.3, and the choice of stocks for $\alpha = 0.4$ through 1.0.

Between $\alpha = 0.3$ and $\alpha = 0.4$, there is a point at which the line for weighted payoffs for GICs intersects the line for weighted payoffs for stocks. By setting the alpha expression with maximum and minimum values of the GIC investment equal to that of the stock investment, we can solve for the alpha value at which the intersection occurs. At this value of alpha, the weighted payoffs of the two investments under the Hurwicz criterion are

Table 19.3		Stocks		Bonds		GICs		Mixture	
Decision Alternatives for Various Values of Alpha		Max. 2,200	Min. −500	Max. 900	Min. −100	Max. 750	Min. 300	Max. 1,300	Min. −200
α	$1 - \alpha$								
0.0	1.0		−500		−100		(300)		−200
0.1	0.9		−230		0		(345)		−50
0.2	0.8		40		100		(390)		100
0.3	0.7		310		200		(435)		250
0.4	0.6		(580)		300		480		400
0.5	0.5		(850)		400		525		550
0.6	0.4		(1,120)		500		570		700
0.7	0.3		(1,390)		600		615		850
0.8	0.2		(1,660)		700		660		1,000
0.9	0.1		(1,930)		800		705		1,150
1.0	0.0		(2,200)		900		750		1,300

Note: Circled values indicate the choice for the given value of alpha.

Figure 19.1

Graph of Hurwicz Criterion Selections for Various Values of Alpha

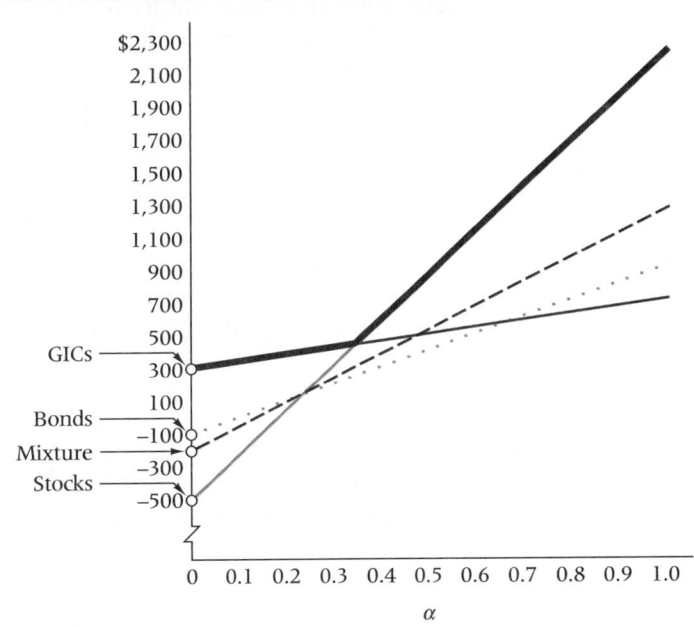

equal, and the decision maker is indifferent as to which one he or she chooses.

$$\text{Stocks Weighted Payoff} = \text{GICs Weighted Payoff}$$
$$2{,}200(\alpha) + (-500)(1 - \alpha) = 750(\alpha) + (300)(1 - \alpha)$$
$$2{,}200\alpha - 500 + 500\alpha = 750\alpha + 300 - 300\alpha$$
$$2{,}250\alpha = 800$$
$$\alpha = 0.3556$$

At $\alpha = 0.3556$, both stocks and GICs yield the same payoff under the Hurwicz criterion. For values less than $\alpha = 0.3556$, GICs are the chosen investment. For $\alpha > 0.3556$, stocks are the chosen investment. Neither bonds nor the mixture produces the optimum payoff under the Hurwicz criterion for any value of alpha. Notice that in Figure 19.1 the dark line segments represent the optimum solutions. The lines for both bonds and the mixture are beneath these optimum line segments for the entire range of α. In another problem with different payoffs, the results might be different.

MINIMAX REGRET

The strategy of **minimax regret** is based on lost opportunity. Lost opportunity occurs when a decision maker loses out on some payoff or portion of a payoff because he or she chose the wrong decision alternative. For example, if a decision maker selects decision alternative d_i, which pays $200, and the selection of alternative d_j would have yielded $300, the opportunity loss is $100 ($300 − $200 = $100).

In analyzing decision-making situations under uncertainty, an analyst can transform a decision table (payoff table) into an **opportunity loss table,** which can be used to apply the minimax regret criterion. Repeated here is the $10,000 investment decision table.

		State of the Economy		
		Stagnant	*Slow Growth*	*Rapid Growth*
Investment Decision Alternative	*Stocks*	−$500	$700	$2,200
	Bonds	−$100	$600	$900
	GICs	$300	$500	$750
	Mixture	−$200	$650	$1,300

Suppose the state of the economy turns out to be stagnant. The optimal decision choice would be GICs, which pay off $300. Any other decision would lead to an opportunity loss. The opportunity loss for each decision alternative other than GICs can be calculated by subtracting the decision alternative payoff from $300:

$$\text{Stocks: } \$300 - (-\$500) = \$800$$
$$\text{Bonds: } \$300 - (-\$100) = \$400$$
$$\text{GICs: } \$300 - \$300 = \$0$$
$$\text{Mixture: } \$300 - (-\$200) = \$500$$

The opportunity losses for the slow-growth state of the economy are calculated by subtracting each payoff from $700, because $700 is the maximum payoff that can be obtained from this state; any other payoff is an opportunity loss. These opportunity losses follow:

$$\text{Stocks: } \$700 - \$700 = \$0$$
$$\text{Bonds: } \$700 - \$600 = \$100$$
$$\text{GICs: } \$700 - \$500 = \$200$$
$$\text{Mixture: } \$700 - \$650 = \$50$$

The opportunity losses for a rapid-growth state of the economy are calculated similarly:

$$\text{Stocks: } \$2,200 - \$2,200 = \$0$$
$$\text{Bonds: } \$2,200 - \$900 = \$1,300$$
$$\text{GICs: } \$2,200 - \$750 = \$1,450$$
$$\text{Mixture: } \$2,200 - \$1,300 = \$900$$

Replacing payoffs in the decision table with opportunity losses produces the opportunity loss table, as shown in Table 19.4.

After the opportunity loss table is determined, the decision maker examines the lost opportunity, or regret, under each decision, and selects the maximum regret for consideration. For example, if the investor chooses stocks, the maximum regret or lost opportunity is $800. If the investor chooses bonds, the maximum regret is $1,300. If the investor chooses GICs, the maximum regret is $1,450. If the investor selects a mixture, the maximum regret is $900.

In making a decision based on a minimax regret criterion, the decision maker examines the maximum regret under each decision alternative and selects the minimum of these. The result is the stocks option, which has the minimum regret of $800. An investor who wants to minimize the maximum regret under the various states of the economy will choose to invest in stocks under the minimax regret strategy.

Table 19.4

Opportunity Loss Table

		State of the Economy		
		Stagnant	Slow Growth	Rapid Growth
Investment Decision Alternative	Stocks	$800	$0	$0
	Bonds	$400	$100	$1,300
	GICs	$0	$200	$1,450
	Mixture	$500	$50	$900

STATISTICS IN BUSINESS TODAY

The RadioShack Corporation Makes Decisions

In the 1960s, Charles Tandy founded and built a tight vertically integrated manufacturing and retailing company, the Tandy Corporation. RadioShack, a retail unit of the Tandy Corporation, has been one of the company's mainstays. However, RadioShack, along with the Tandy Corporation, has seen many changes over the years both because of decisions that management made and because of various states of nature that occurred.

In the early days, RadioShack was an outlet for Tandy products with a relatively narrow market niche. In the 1970s, the company made millions on the CB radio craze that hit the United States. In the early 1980s, RadioShack did well with an inexpensive personal computer. By the mid-1980s, the stores were becoming neglected, with much of the retailing profits being poured back into such unsuccessful manufacturing experiments as low-priced laptop computers and videodisc players.

In 1993, Tandy decided to sell its computer-making operations and reemphasize retailing by bringing in a new president for RadioShack. The resulting series of decisions resulted in a significant positive turnaround for RadioShack. The company placed more emphasis on telephones and cut a deal with the Sprint Corporation to make Sprint its exclusive wireless provider. Sprint, in turn, provided millions of dollars to update RadioShack stores. Since then, RadioShack has sold more wireless phones than most of its major rivals. In addition, RadioShack contracted to sell only Compaq computers and RCA audio and video equipment in its stores in exchange for these companies' investment in upgrading the retail outlet facilities. In 2000, RadioShack announced its alliance with Verizon Wireless, and the Tandy Corporation became the RadioShack Corporation. In 2001, RadioShack formed an alliance with Blockbuster. In 2002, RadioShack became the only U.S. retailer offering both DIRECTV and DISH Network. (In Canada, Radio Shack closed its nine company-owned retail stores in 2007.)

Since then, RadioShack Corporation has sold its Incredible Universe stores and its Computer City superstores. These moves left RadioShack with its 7,000 RadioShack stores as its main presence in the retail arena.

The fast-paced and ever-changing electronics industry presented many decision alternatives to RadioShack. In the early years, the corporation decided to sell mostly Tandy products in RadioShack stores. Then, the corporation opened a variety of types and sizes of retail stores, only to sell most of them later. At one point, Tandy invested heavily in manufacturing new items at the expense of retail operations, and then it sold its computer manufacturing operations and renewed its focus on retail. Currently, the corporation is putting most of its eggs in the RadioShack basket, with its exclusive agreements with Sprint, Compaq, and RCA and its emphasis on telephones, wireless service, and Internet service. RadioShack could have chosen other decision alternatives that may have led to different outcomes.

Some of the states of nature that occurred include the rise and fall of CB radios, the exponential growth in personal computers and wireless telephones, the development of the Internet as a market and as an outlet for goods and services, a strong U.S. economy, and a growing atmosphere of disgust by large electronics manufacturers with electronics superstores and their deeply discounted merchandise.

The payoffs from some of these decisions for the RadioShack Corporation have been substantial. Some decisions resulted in revenue losses, thereby generating still other decisions. The decision selections, the states of nature, and the resulting payoffs can make the difference between a highly successful company and one that fails.

Today, RadioShack operates more than 7,200 stores across the U.S. It is estimated that 94% of all Americans live or work within five minutes of a RadioShack store or dealer. RadioShack's mission is to demystify technology in every neighbourhood in the United States.

Demonstration Problem 19.1

A manufacturing company is faced with a capacity decision. Its present production facility is running at nearly maximum capacity. Management is considering the following three capacity decision alternatives.

1. No expansion
2. Add on to the present facility
3. Build a new facility

The managers believe that if a large increase occurs in demand for their product in the near future, they will need to build a new facility to compete and capitalize on more efficient technological and design advances. However, if demand does not increase, it might be more profitable to maintain the present facility and add no capacity. A third decision alternative is to add on to the present facility, which will suffice for a moderate increase in demand and will be cheaper than building an entirely new facility. A drawback of adding to the old facility is that if there is a large demand for the product, the company will be unable to capitalize on new technologies and efficiencies, which cannot be built into the old plant.

The following decision table shows the payoffs (in $ millions) for these three decision alternatives for four different possible states of demand for the company's product (less demand, same demand, moderate increase in demand, and large increase in demand). Use these data to determine which decision alternative would be selected by the maximax criterion and the maximin criterion. Use $\alpha = 0.4$ and the Hurwicz criterion to determine the decision alternative. Calculate an opportunity loss table and determine the decision alternative by using the minimax regret criterion.

		State of Demand			
		Less	No Change	Moderate Increase	Large Increase
Capacity Decision	No Expansion	$3	$2	$3	$6
	Add On	−$40	−$28	$10	$20
	Build a New Facility	−$210	−$145	−$5	$55

Solution

The maximum and minimum payoffs under each decision alternative follow.

	Maximum	Minimum
No Expansion	$6	−$3
Add On	$20	−$40
Build a New Facility	$55	−$210

Using the maximax criterion, the decision makers select the maximum of the maximum payoffs under each decision alternative. This value is the maximum of {$6, $20, $55} = $55, or the selection of the decision alternative of building a new facility and maximizing the maximum payoff ($55).

Using the maximin criterion, the decision makers select the maximum of the minimum payoffs under each decision alternative. This value is the maximum of {−$3, −$40, −$210} = −$3. They select the decision alternative of no expansion and maximize the minimum payoff (−$3).

Following are the calculations for the Hurwicz criterion with $\alpha = 0.4$:

$$\text{No Expansion: } \$6(0.4) + (-\$3)(0.6) = \$0.60$$
$$\text{Add On: } \$20(0.4) + (-\$40)(0.6) = -\$16.00$$
$$\text{Build a New Facility: } \$55(0.4) + (-\$210)(0.6) = -\$104.00$$

Using the Hurwicz criterion, the decision makers would select no expansion as the maximum of these weighted values ($0.60).

Following is the opportunity loss table for this capacity choice problem. Note that each opportunity loss is calculated by taking the maximum payoff under each state of nature and subtracting each of the other payoffs under that state from that maximum value.

		State of Demand			
		Less	No Change	Moderate Increase	Large Increase
Capacity Decision	No Expansion	$0	$0	$7	$49
	Add On	$37	$30	$0	$35
	Build a New Facility	$207	$147	$15	$0

Using the minimax regret criterion on this opportunity loss table, the decision makers first select the maximum regret under each decision alternative.

Decision Alternative	Maximum Regret
No Expansion	$49
Add On	$37
Build a New Facility	$207

Next, the decision makers select the decision alternative with the minimum regret, which is to add on, with a regret of $37.

Concept Check

1. What are the four major approaches to making decisions under uncertainty? Explain the basic criterion on which each approach is based.

19.2 Problems

19.1   Use the decision table given here to complete parts (a) through (d).

		State of Nature		
		s_1	s_2	s_3
Decision Alternative	d_1	250	175	−25
	d_2	110	100	70
	d_3	390	140	−80

a. Use the maximax criterion to determine which decision alternative to select.
b. Use the maximin criterion to determine which decision alternative to select.
c. Use the Hurwicz criterion to determine which decision alternative to select. Let $\alpha = 0.3$ and then let $\alpha = 0.8$ and compare the results.
d. Compute an opportunity loss table from the data. Use this table and a minimax regret criterion to determine which decision alternative to select.

19.2   Use the decision table given here to complete parts (a) through (d).

		State of Nature			
		s_1	s_2	s_3	s_4
Decision Alternative	d_1	50	70	120	110
	d_2	80	20	75	100
	d_3	20	45	30	60
	d_4	100	85	−30	−20
	d_5	0	−10	65	80

a. Use the maximax criterion to determine which decision alternative to select.
b. Use the maximin criterion to determine which decision alternative to select.
c. Use the Hurwicz criterion to determine which decision alternative to select. Let $\alpha = 0.5$.
d. Compute an opportunity loss table from the data. Use this table and a minimax regret criterion to determine which decision alternative to select.

19.3 Election results can affect the payoff from certain types of investments. Suppose a brokerage firm is faced with the prospect of investing $20 million a few weeks before the national election. They feel that if the Conservatives are elected, certain types of investments will do quite well; but if the Liberals are elected, other types of investments will be more desirable. To complicate the situation, a win for the NDP is likely to cause investments to behave in a different manner. Following are the payoffs for different investments under different political scenarios. Use the data to reach a conclusion about which decision alternative to select. Use both the maximax and the maximin criteria and compare the answers.

		Election Winner		
		Conservatives	*Liberals*	*NDP*
	A	$60	$15	−$25
Investment	B	$10	$25	$30
	C	−$10	$40	$15
	D	$20	$25	$5

19.4 The introduction of a new product into the marketplace is quite risky. The percentage of new product ideas that successfully make it into the marketplace is as low as 1%. Research and development costs must be recouped, along with marketing and production costs. However, if a new product is warmly received by customers, the payoffs can be great. Following is a payoff table (decision table) for the production of a new product under different states of the market. Notice that the decision alternatives are to not produce the product at all, to produce a few units of the product, and to produce many units of the product. The market may be not receptive to the product, somewhat receptive to the product, or very receptive to the product.
a. Use this matrix and the Hurwicz criterion to reach a decision. Let $\alpha = 0.6$.
b. Determine an opportunity loss table from this payoff table and use minimax regret to reach a decision.

		State of the Market		
		Not Receptive	*Somewhat Receptive*	*Very Receptive*
	Don't Produce	−50	−50	−50
Production Alternative	*Produce Few*	−200	300	400
	Produce Many	−600	100	1,000

19.3 DECISION MAKING UNDER RISK

In Section 19.1, we discussed making decisions in situations where it is certain which states of nature will occur. In Section 19.2, we examined several strategies for making decisions when it is uncertain which state of nature will occur. In this section, we examine decision making under risk. **Decision making under risk** occurs when *it is uncertain which states of nature will occur but the probability of each state of nature occurring has been determined.*

Table 19.5			State of the Economy		
Decision Table with State of Nature Probabilities			*Stagnant* (0.25)	*Slow Growth* (0.45)	*Rapid Growth* (0.30)
	Investment Decision Alternative	*Stocks*	−$500	$700	$2,200
		Bonds	−$100	$600	$900
		GICs	$300	$500	$750
		Mixture	−$200	$650	$1,300

Using these probabilities, we can develop some additional decision-making strategies. In preceding sections, we discussed the dilemma of how best to invest $10,000. Four investment decision alternatives were identified and three states of the economy seemed possible (stagnant economy, slow-growth economy, and rapid-growth economy). Suppose we determine that there is a 0.25 probability of a stagnant economy, a 0.45 probability of a slow-growth economy, and a 0.30 probability of a rapid-growth economy. In a decision table, or payoff table, we place these probabilities next to each state of nature. Table 19.5 is a decision table for the investment example shown in Table 19.2 with the probabilities given in parentheses.

DECISION TREES

Another way to depict the decision process is through the use of decision trees. **Decision trees** have a □ node to represent decision alternatives and a ○ node to represent states of nature. If probabilities are available for states of nature, they are assigned to the line segment following the state-of-nature node symbol, ○. Payoffs are displayed at the ends of the decision tree limbs. Figure 19.2 is a decision tree for the financial investment example given in Table 19.5.

EXPECTED MONETARY VALUE

One strategy that can be used in making decisions under risk is the **expected monetary value (EMV)** approach. A person who uses this approach is sometimes referred to as an **EMVer**. The EMV of each decision alternative is calculated by multiplying the probability of each state of nature by the state's associated payoff and summing these products across the states of nature for each decision alternative, producing an EMV for each decision alternative. The decision maker compares the EMVs for the decision alternatives and selects the alternative with the highest EMV.

As an example, we can compute the EMV for the $10,000 investment problem displayed in Table 19.5 and Figure 19.2 with the associated probabilities. We use the following calculations to find the EMV for the decision alternative *Stocks:*

$$\text{Expected Value for Stagnant Economy} = (0.25)(-\$500) = -\$125$$
$$\text{Expected Value for Slow-Growth Economy} = (0.45)(\$700) = \$315$$
$$\text{Expected Value for Rapid-Growth Economy} = (0.30)(\$2,200) = \$660$$

The EMV of investing in stocks is:

$$-\$125 + \$315 + \$660 = \$850$$

The calculations for determining the EMV for the decision alternative *Bonds* follow:

$$\text{Expected Value for Stagnant Economy} = (0.25)(-\$100) = -\$25$$
$$\text{Expected Value for Slow-Growth Economy} = (0.45)(\$600) = \$270$$
$$\text{Expected Value for Rapid-Growth Economy} = (0.30)(\$900) = \$270$$

Figure 19.2

Decision Tree for the Investment Example

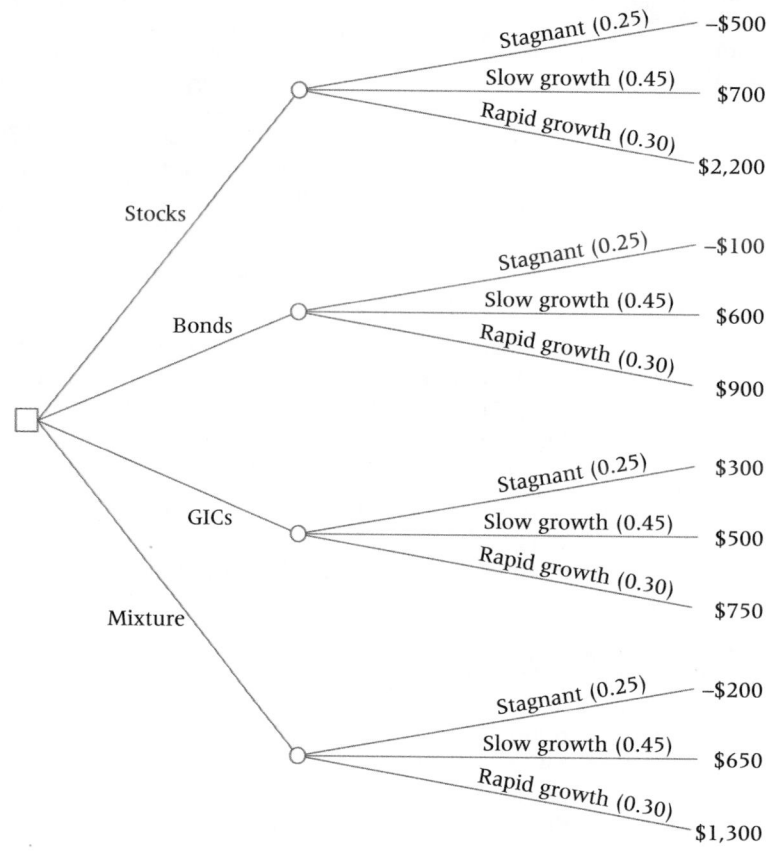

The EMV of investing in bonds is:

$$-\$25 + \$270 + \$270 = \$515$$

The EMV for the decision alternative *GICs* is found by the following calculations:

Expected Value for Stagnant Economy = (0.25)($300) = $75
Expected Value for Slow-Growth Economy = (0.45)($500) = $225
Expected Value for Rapid-Growth Economy = (0.30)($750) = $225

The EMV of investing in GICs is:

$$\$75 + \$225 + \$225 = \$525$$

The following calculations are used to find the EMV for the decision alternative *Mixture*:

Expected Value for Stagnant Economy = (0.25)(−$200) = −$50.00
Expected Value for Slow-Growth Economy = (0.45)($650) = $292.50
Expected Value for Rapid-Growth Economy = (0.30)($1,300) = $390.00

The EMV of investing in a mixture is:

$$-\$50 + \$292.50 + \$390 = \$632.50$$

A decision maker using EMV as a strategy will choose the maximum of the EMVs computed for each decision alternative:

$$\text{Maximum of } \{\$850, \$515, \$525, \$632.50\} = \$850$$

The maximum of the EMVs is $850, which is produced from a stock investment. An EMVer chooses to invest in stocks on the basis of this information.

This process of EMV can be depicted on decision trees like the one in Figure 19.2. Each payoff at the end of a branch of the tree is multiplied by the associated probability of

Figure 19.3

Expected Monetary Value for the Investment Example

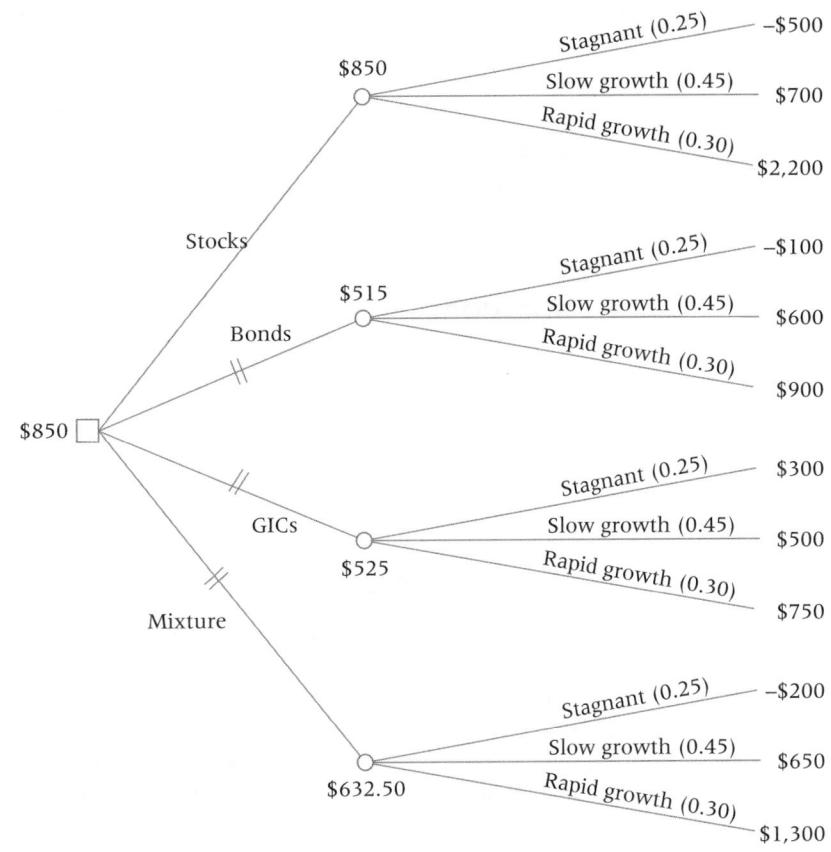

that state of nature. The resulting products are summed across all states for a given decision choice, producing an EMV for that decision alternative. These EMVs are displayed on the decision tree at the chance or state-of-nature nodes, ○.

The decision maker observes these EMVs. The optimal EMV is the one selected and is displayed at the decision node in the tree, □. The decision alternative pathways leading to lesser, or nonoptimal, monetary values are marked with a double vertical line symbol, ||, to denote rejected decision alternatives. Figure 19.3 depicts the EMV analysis on the decision tree in Figure 19.2.

The strategy of EMV is based on a long-run average. If a decision maker could play this game over and over with the probabilities and payoffs remaining the same, he or she could *expect* to earn an average of $850 in the long run by choosing to invest in stocks. The reality is that for any *one* occasion, the investor will earn a payoff of −$500, $700, or $2,200 on a stock investment, depending on which state of the economy occurs. The investor will not earn $850 at any *one* time on this decision, but he or she could average a profit of $850 if the investment continued through time. With an investment of this size, the investor will potentially have the chance to make this decision several times. Suppose, on the other hand, an investor has to decide whether to spend $5 million to drill an oil well. EMVs might not mean as much to the decision maker if he or she has only enough financial support to make this decision once.

POINTS OF INTEREST
Strictly speaking, it is not necessary to draw the tree diagram when we use decision trees. However, the tree diagram provides a powerful visual stimulus that makes the overall problem more understandable.

Demonstration Problem 19.2

Recall the capacity decision scenario presented in Demonstration Problem 19.1. Suppose probabilities have been determined for the states of demand such that there is a 0.10 probability that demand will be less, a 0.25 probability that there will be no change in demand, a 0.40 probability that there will be a moderate increase in demand, and a 0.25 probability that there will be a large increase in demand. Use the data presented in the problem, which are restated here, and the included probabilities to compute EMVs and reach a decision conclusion based on these findings.

		State of Demand			
		Less (0.10)	*No Change (0.25)*	*Moderate Increase (0.40)*	*Large Increase (0.25)*
	No Expansion	−$3	$2	$3	$6
Capacity Decision	*Add On*	−$40	−$28	$10	$20
	Build a New Facility	−$210	−$145	−$5	$55

Solution

The EMV for no expansion is:

$$(-\$3)(0.10) + (\$2)(0.25) + (\$3)(0.40) + (\$6)(0.25) = \$2.90$$

The EMV for adding on is:

$$(-\$40)(0.10) + (-\$28)(0.25) + (\$10)(0.40) + (\$20)(0.25) = -\$2.00$$

The EMV for building a new facility is:

$$(-\$210)(0.10) + (-\$145)(0.25) + (-\$5)(0.40) + (\$55)(0.25) = -\$45.50$$

The decision maker who uses the EMV criterion will select the no-expansion decision alternative because it results in the highest long-run average payoff, $2.90. It is possible that the decision maker will only have one chance to make this decision at this company. In such a case, the decision maker will not average $2.90 for selecting no expansion but rather will get a payoff of −$3.00, $2.00, $3.00, or $6.00, depending on which state of demand follows the decision. This analysis can be shown through the use of a decision tree.

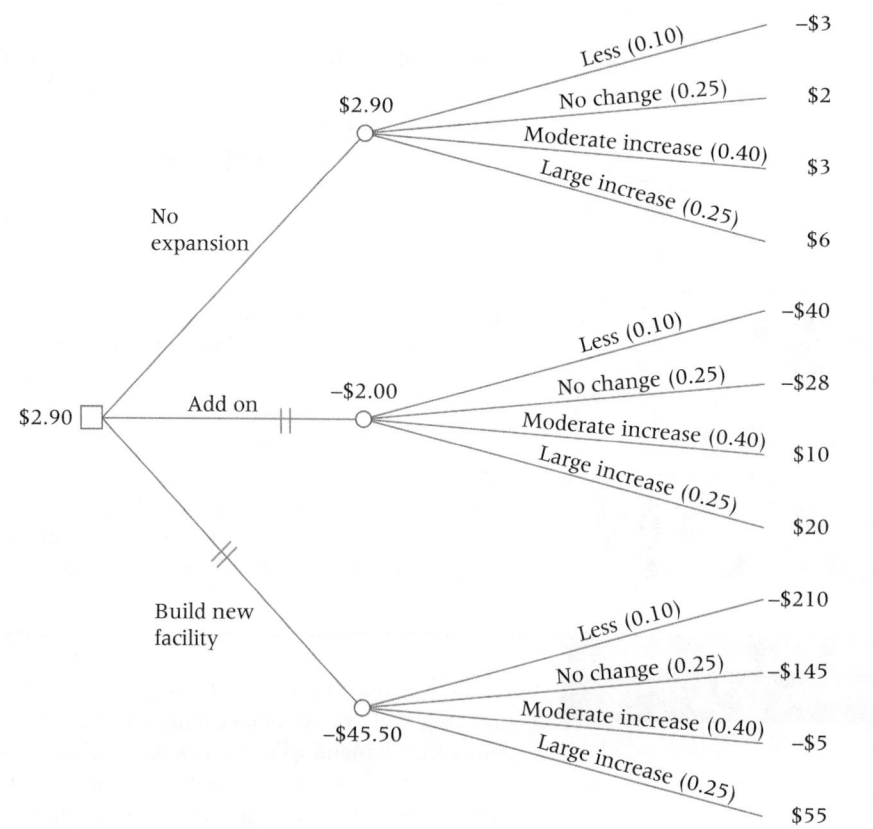

EXPECTED VALUE OF PERFECT INFORMATION

What is the value of knowing which state of nature will occur and when? The answer to this question can provide insight into how much it is worth to pay for market or business research. The **expected value of perfect information** is *the difference between the payoff that would occur if the decision maker knew which states of nature would occur and the expected monetary payoff from the best decision alternative when there is no information about the occurrence of the states of nature:*

Expected Value of Perfect Information = Expected Monetary Payoff with Perfect Information − Expected Monetary Payoff without Information

As an example, consider the $10,000 investment example with the probabilities of states of nature shown.

		State of the Economy		
		Stagnant (0.25)	Slow Growth (0.45)	Rapid Growth (0.30)
Investment	Stocks	−$500	$700	$2,200
Decision	Bonds	−$100	$600	$900
Alternative	GICs	$300	$500	$750
	Mixture	−$200	$650	$1,300

The following EMVs were computed for this problem:

Stocks: $850
Bonds: $515
GICs: $525
Mixture: $632.50

The investment of stocks was selected under the EMV strategy because it resulted in the maximum expected payoff of $850. This decision was made with no information about the states of nature. Suppose we could obtain information about the states of the economy; that is, we *know* which state of the economy will occur. Whenever the state of the economy is stagnant, we would invest in GICs and receive a payoff of $300. Whenever the state of the economy is slow growth, we would invest in stocks and earn $700. Whenever the state of the economy is rapid growth, we would also invest in stocks and earn $2,200. Given the probabilities of each state of the economy occurring, we can use these payoffs to compute an expected monetary payoff with perfect information:

Expected Monetary Payoff with Perfect Information
$$= (\$300)(0.25) + (\$700)(0.45) + (\$2,200)(0.30)$$
$$= \$1,050$$

The difference between this expected monetary payoff with perfect information ($1,050) and the expected monetary payoff with no information ($850) is the value of perfect information ($1,050 − $850 = $200). It would not be economically wise to spend more than $200 to obtain perfect information about these states of nature.

Demonstration Problem 19.3

Compute the value of perfect information for the capacity problem discussed in Demonstration Problems 19.1 and 19.2. The data are shown again here.

		State of Demand			
		Less (0.10)	No Change (0.25)	Moderate Increase (0.40)	Large Increase (0.25)
Capacity Decision	No Expansion	−$3	$2	$3	$6
	Add On	−$40	−$28	$10	$20
	Build a New Facility	−$210	−$145	−$5	$55

Solution

The EMV (payoff) under no information computed in Demonstration Problem 19.2 was $2.90 (recall that all figures are in millions of dollars). If the decision makers had perfect information, they would select no expansion for the state of less demand, no expansion for the state of no change, add on for the state of moderate increase, and build a new facility for the state of large increase. The expected payoff of perfect information is computed as:

$$(-\$3)(0.10) + (\$2)(0.25) + (\$10)(0.40) + (\$55)(0.25) = \$17.95$$

The expected value of perfect information is:

$$\$17.95 - \$2.90 = \$15.05$$

In this case, the decision makers might be willing to pay up to $15.05 million for perfect information.

UTILITY

As pointed out in the preceding section, EMV decisions are based on long-run averages. Some situations do not lend themselves to EMV analysis because these situations involve relatively large amounts of money and one-time decisions. Examples of these one-time decisions might be drilling an oil well, building a new production facility, merging with another company, ordering 100 new 737s, or buying a professional sports franchise. In analyzing the alternatives in such decisions, a concept known as utility can be helpful.

Utility is the degree of pleasure or displeasure a decision maker has in being involved in the outcome selection process given the risks and opportunities available. Suppose a person has the chance to enter a contest with a 50–50 chance of winning $100,000. If the person wins the contest, he or she wins $100,000. If the person loses, he or she receives $0. There is no cost to enter this contest. The expected payoff of this contest for the entrant is:

$$(\$100,000)(0.50) + (\$0)(0.50) = \$50,000$$

In thinking about this contest, the contestant realizes that he or she will never get $50,000. The $50,000 is the long-run average payoff if the game is played over and over. Suppose contest administrators offer the contestant $30,000 not to play the game. Would the player take the money and drop out of the contest? Would a certain payoff of $30,000 outdraw a 0.50 chance at $100,000? The answer to this question depends, in part, on the person's financial situation and on his or her propensity to take risks. If the contestant is a multimillionaire, he or she might be willing to take big risks and even refuse $70,000 to drop out of the contest, because $70,000 does not significantly increase his or her worth. On the other hand, a person on welfare who is offered $20,000 not to play the contest might take the money because $20,000 is worth a great deal to him or her. In addition, two different people on welfare might have different risk-taking profiles. One might be a risk taker who, in spite of a need for money, is not willing to take less than $70,000 or $80,000 to pull out of a contest. The same could be said for the wealthy person.

Utility theory provides a mechanism for determining whether a person is a risk taker, a risk avoider, or an EMVer for a given decision situation. Consider the contest just described. A person receives $0 if he or she does not win the contest and $100,000 if he or she does win the contest. How much money would it take for a contestant to be indifferent between participating in the contest and dropping out? Suppose we examine three possible contestants, X, Y, and Z.

X is indifferent between receiving $20,000 and a 0.50 chance of winning the contest. For any amount more than $20,000, X will take the money and not play the game. As we stated before, a 0.50 chance of winning yields an expected payoff of $50,000. Suppose we increase the chance of winning to 0.80, so that the expected monetary payoff is $80,000. Now X is indifferent between receiving $50,000 and playing the game and will drop out of the game for any amount more than $50,000. In virtually all cases, X is willing to take less money than the expected payoff to quit the game. X is referred to as a **risk avoider**. Many of us are risk avoiders. For this reason, we pay insurance companies to cover our lives, our homes, our businesses, our cars, and so on, even when we know the odds are in the insurance companies' favour. We see the potential to lose at such games as unacceptable, so we bail out of the games for less than the expected payoff and pay out more than the expected cost to avoid the game.

Y, on the other hand, loves such contests. It would take about $70,000 to get Y not to play the game with a 0.50 chance of winning $100,000, even though the expected payoff is only $50,000. Suppose Y were told that there was only a 0.20 chance of winning the game. How much would it take for Y to become indifferent to playing? It might take $40,000 for Y to be indifferent, even though the expected payoff for a 0.20 chance is only $20,000. Y is a **risk taker** and enjoys playing risk-taking games. It always seems to take more than the expected payoff to get Y to drop out of the contest.

Z is an EMVer. Z is indifferent between receiving $50,000 and having a 0.50 chance of winning $100,000. To get Z out of the contest if there is only a 0.20 chance of winning, the contest directors would have to offer Z about $20,000 (the expected value). Likewise, if there were an 0.80 chance of winning, it would take about $80,000 to get Z to drop out of the contest. Z makes a decision by going with the long-run averages even in one-time decisions.

Figure 19.4 presents a graph with the likely shapes of the utility curves for X, Y, and Z. This graph is constructed for the game using the payoff range of $0 to $100,000;

Figure 19.4

Risk Curves for Game Players

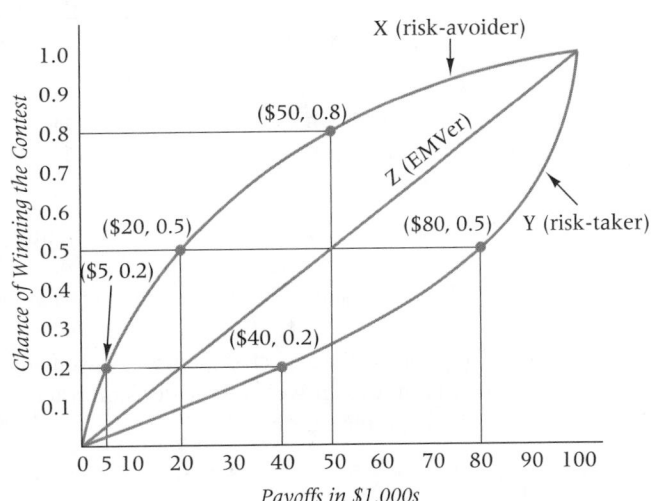

in-between values can be offered to the players in an effort to buy them out of the game. These units are displayed along what is normally the *x* axis. Along the *y* axis are the probabilities of winning the game, ranging from 0.0 to 1.0. A straight line through the middle of the values represents the EMV responses. If a person plays the game with a 0.50 chance of winning, he or she is indifferent to taking \$50,000 not to play and playing. For 0.20, it is \$20,000. For 0.80, it is \$80,000.

Notice in the graph that where the chance of winning is 0.50, contestant X is willing to drop out of the game for \$20,000. This point, (\$20,000, 0.50), is above the EMV line. When the chance is 0.20, X will drop out for \$5,000; for a chance of 0.80, X will drop out for \$50,000. Both of these points, (\$5,000, 0.20) and (\$50,000, 0.80), are also above the EMV line.

Y, in contrast, requires \$80,000 to be indifferent to a 0.50 chance of winning. Hence, the point (\$80,000, 0.50) is below the EMV line. Contest officials will have to offer Y at least \$40,000 for Y to become indifferent to a 0.20 chance of winning. This point, (\$40,000, 0.20), is also below the EMV line.

X is a risk avoider and Y is a risk taker. Z is an EMVer. In the utility graph in Figure 19.4, the risk avoider's curve is above the EMV line and the risk taker's curve is below the line.

As discussed earlier in the chapter, in making decisions under uncertainty, risk takers might be more prone to use the maximax criterion and risk avoiders might be more prone to use the maximin criterion. The Hurwicz criterion allows the user to introduce his or her propensity toward risk into the analysis by using alpha.

Much information has been compiled and published about utility theory. The objective here is to give you a brief introduction to it through this example, thus enabling you to see that there are risk takers and risk avoiders along with EMVers. A more detailed treatment of this topic is beyond the scope of this text.

POINTS OF INTEREST
Decision making involves uncertainty as well as risk. Uncertainty and risk are not the same. Uncertainty is not knowing how the future will unfold, while risk is the cost associated with an outcome.

Concept Check

1. What is meant by risk?
2. Explain the term *expected value of perfect information.*
3. What is utility?

19.3 Problems

19.5   Use the following decision table to construct a decision tree.

		State of Nature				
		s_1	s_2	s_3	s_4	s_5
	d_1	50	20	15	5	1
Decision	d_2	75	50	20	−5	−20
Alternative	d_3	15	12	10	8	6

19.6   Suppose the probabilities of the states of nature occurring for Problem 19.5 are $s_1 =$ 0.15, $s_2 = 0.25$, $s_3 = 0.30$, $s_4 = 0.10$, and $s_5 = 0.20$. Use these probabilities and EMVs to reach a conclusion about the decision alternatives in Problem 19.5.

19.7   How much is the expected monetary payoff with perfect information in Problem 19.5? From this answer and the decision reached in Problem 19.6, what is the value of perfect information?

19.8   Use the following decision table to complete parts (a) through (c).

		State of Nature		
		$s_1 (0.40)$	$s_2 (0.35)$	$s_3 (0.25)$
Decision Alternative	d_1	150	250	500
	d_2	100	200	400
	d_3	75	150	700
	d_4	125	450	650

a.   Draw a decision tree to represent this payoff table.
b.   Compute the EMV for each decision and label the decision tree to indicate what the final decision would be.
c.   Compute the expected payoff of perfect information. Compare this answer to the answer determined in part (b) and compute the value of perfect information.

19.9   A home buyer is completing an application for a home mortgage. He is given the option of locking in a mortgage loan interest rate or waiting 60 days until closing and locking in a rate on the day of closing. The buyer is not given the option of locking in at any time in between. If the buyer locks in at the time of application and interest rates go down, the loan will cost him $150 per month more (−$150 payoff) than it would have if he had waited and locked in later. If the buyer locks in at the time of application and interest rates go up, he has saved money by locking in at a lower rate. The amount saved under this condition is a payoff of +$200. If the buyer does not lock in at application and rates go up, he must pay more interest on the mortgage loan; the payoff is −$250. If the buyer does not lock in at application and rates go down, he has reduced the interest amount and the payoff is +$175. If the rate does not change at all, there is a $0 payoff for locking in at the time of application and also a $0 payoff for not locking in at that time. There is a probability of 0.65 that the interest rates will rise by the end of the 60-day period, a 0.30 probability that they will fall, and a 0.05 probability that they will remain constant.
a.   Construct a decision table from this information.
b.   Compute the EMVs from the table and reach a conclusion about the decision alternatives.
c.   Compute the value of perfect information.

19.10   A CEO faces a tough human resources decision. Because the company is currently operating in a budgetary crisis, the CEO will lay off 1,000 people, lay off 5,000 people, or lay off no one. One of the problems for the CEO is that she cannot foretell what the business climate will be like in the coming months. If the CEO knew there would be a rapid rise in demand for the company's products, she might be inclined to hold off on layoffs and attempt to retain the workforce. If the business climate worsens, however, big layoffs seem to be the reasonable decision. Shown here are payoffs for each decision alternative under each state of the business climate. Included in the payoffs is the cost (loss of payoff) to the company when workers are laid off. The probability of each state occurring is given. Use the table and the information given to compute the EMV for each decision alternative and make a recommendation based on these findings. What is the most the CEO should be willing to pay for information about the occurrence of the various states of the business climate?

		State of Business Climate		
		Improved (0.10)	About the Same (0.40)	Worsened (0.50)
Decision Alternative	No Layoffs	100	−300	−1,700
	Lay Off 1,000	−100	100	−700
	Lay Off 5,000	−200	300	600

19.11 A person has a chance to invest $50,000 in a business venture. If the venture works, the investor will reap $200,000. If the venture fails, the investor will lose his money. It appears that there is about a 0.50 probability of the venture working. Using this information, answer the following questions.

a. What is the EMV of this investment?

b. If this person decides not to undertake this venture, is he an EMVer, a risk avoider, or a risk taker? Why?

c. You would have to offer at least how much money to get a risk taker to quit pursuing this investment?

19.4 REVISING PROBABILITIES IN LIGHT OF SAMPLE INFORMATION

In Section 19.3, we discussed decision making under risk, in which the probabilities of the states of nature were available and included in the analysis. EMVs were computed on the basis of payoffs and probabilities. In this section, we include the additional aspect of sample information in the decision analysis. If decision makers opt to purchase or in some other manner garner sample information, the probabilities of states of nature can be revised. The revisions can be incorporated into the decision-making process, resulting—one hopes—in a better decision.

In Chapter 4, we examined the use of Bayes' rule in the revision of probabilities, in which we started with a prior probability and revised it on the basis of new information. Bayesian analysis can be applied to decision making under risk analysis to revise the prior probabilities of the states of nature, resulting in a clearer picture of the decision options. Usually the securing of additional information through sampling entails a cost. After the discussion of the revision of probabilities, we will examine the worth of sampling information. Perhaps the best way to explain the use of Bayes' rule in revising prior state-of-nature probabilities is by using an example.

Let us examine the revision of probabilities by using Bayes' rule with sampling information in the context of the $10,000 investment example discussed earlier in the chapter. Because the problem as previously stated is too complex to provide a clear example of this process, it is reduced here to simpler terms. The problem is still to determine how best to invest $10,000 for the next year. However, only two decision alternatives are available to the investor: bonds and stocks. Only two states of the investment climate can occur: no growth or rapid growth.

There is a 0.65 probability of no growth in the investment climate and a 0.35 probability of rapid growth. The payoffs are $500 for a bond investment in a no-growth state, $100 for a bond investment in a rapid-growth state, −$200 for a stock investment in a no-growth state, and $1,100 for a stock investment in a rapid-growth state. Table 19.6 presents the decision table (payoff table) for this problem.

Table 19.6			State of Nature	
Decision Table of the Investment Example			*No Growth (0.65)*	*Rapid Growth (0.35)*
	Decision Alternative	*Bonds*	$500	$100
		Stocks	–$200	$1,100

Figure 19.5

Decision Tree for the Investment Example

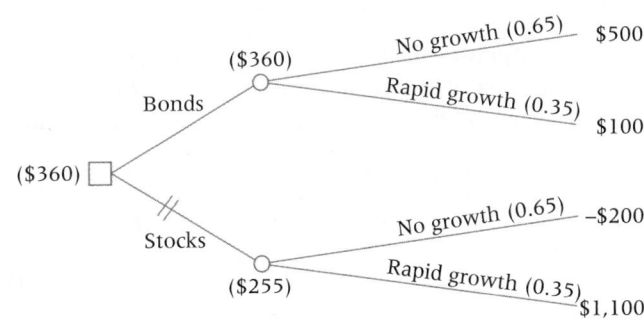

Figure 19.5 shows a decision tree with the decision alternatives, the payoffs, the states of nature, the probabilities, and the EMV of each decision alternative. The EMV for the bonds decision alternative is:

$$\text{EMV (bonds)} = \$500(0.65) + \$100(0.35) = \$360$$

The EMV for the stocks decision alternative is:

$$\text{EMV (stocks)} = -\$200(0.65) + \$1{,}100(0.35) = \$255$$

An EMVer would select the bonds decision alternative because the EMV is $360, which is higher than that of the stocks alternative ($255).

Suppose the investor has a chance to obtain some information from an economic expert about the future state of the investment economy. This expert does not have a perfect record of forecasting, but she has predicted a no-growth economy about 0.80 of the time when such a state actually occurred. She has been slightly less successful in predicting rapid-growth economies, with a 0.70 probability of success. The following table shows her success and failure rates in forecasting these two states of the economy.

	Actual State of the Economy	
	No Growth (s_1)	*Rapid Growth (s_2)*
Forecaster predicts no growth (F_1)	0.80	0.30
Forecaster predicts rapid growth (F_2)	0.20	0.70

When the state of the economy is no growth, the forecaster will predict no growth 0.80 of the time, but she will predict rapid growth 0.20 of the time. When the state of the economy is rapid growth, she will predict rapid growth 0.70 of the time and no growth 0.30 of the time. Using these conditional probabilities, we can revise prior probabilities of the states of the economy by using Bayes' rule, restated here from Chapter 4:

$$P(X_i \mid Y) = \frac{P(X_i) \cdot P(Y \mid X_i)}{P(X_1) \cdot P(Y \mid X_1) + P(X_2) \cdot P(Y \mid X_2) + \cdots + P(X_n) \cdot P(Y \mid X_n)}$$

Table 19.7	State of Economy	Prior Probabilities	Conditional Probabilities	Joint Probabilities	Revised Probabilities
Revision Based on a Forecast of No Growth (F_1)	No growth (s_1)	$P(s_1) = 0.65$	$P(F_1 \mid s_1)$ $= 0.80$	$P(F_1 \cap s_1)$ $= 0.520$	0.520/0.625 $= 0.832$
	Rapid growth (s_2)	$P(s_2) = 0.35$	$P(F_1 \mid s_2)$ $= 0.30$	$P(F_1 \cap s_2)$ $= 0.105$	0.105/0.625 $= 0.168$
				$P(F_1) = 0.625$	

Applying the formula to the problem, we obtain the revised probabilities shown in the following tables. Suppose the forecaster predicts no growth (F_1). The prior probabilities of the states of the economy are revised as shown in Table 19.7.

$P(F_1)$ is computed as follows:

$$P(F_1) = P(F_1 \cap s_1) + P(F_1 \cap s_2) = 0.520 + 0.105 + 0.625$$

$$P(s_1 \mid F_1) = \frac{P(F_1 \cap s_1)}{P(F_1)} = \frac{0.520}{0.625} = 0.832$$

$$P(s_2 \mid F_1) = \frac{P(F_1 \cap s_2)}{P(F_1)} = \frac{0.105}{0.625} = 0.168$$

The prior probabilities of the states of the economy are revised as shown in Table 19.8 for the case in which the forecaster predicts rapid growth (F_2). These revised probabilities can be entered into a decision tree that depicts the option of buying information and getting a forecast, as shown in Figure 19.6. Notice that the first node is a decision node to buy the forecast. The next node is a state-of-nature node, where the forecaster will predict either a no-growth economy or a rapid-growth economy. It is a state of nature because the decision maker has no control over what the forecast will be. As a matter of fact, the decision maker has probably paid for this independent forecast. Once a forecast is made, the decision maker is faced with the decision alternatives of investing in bonds or investing in stocks. At the end of each investment alternative branch is a state of the economy of either no growth or rapid growth. The four revised probabilities calculated in Tables 19.7 and 19.8 are assigned to these states of economy. The payoffs remain the same. The probability of the forecaster predicting no growth comes from the sum of the joint probabilities in Table 19.7. This value of $P(F_1) = 0.625$ is assigned a position on the first set of states of nature (forecast). The probability of the forecaster predicting rapid growth comes from summing the joint probabilities in Table 19.8. This value of $P(F_2) = 0.375$ is also assigned a position on the first set of states of nature (forecasts). The decision maker can make a choice from this decision tree after the EMVs are calculated. In Figure 19.6, the payoffs are the same as in the decision table without information. However, the probabilities of no-growth and

Table 19.8	State of Economy	Prior Probabilities	Conditional Probabilities	Joint Probabilities	Revised Probabilities
Revision Based on a Forecast of Rapid Growth (F_2)	No growth (s_1)	$P(s_1) = 0.65$	$P(F_2 \mid s_1)$ $= 0.20$	$P(F_2 \cap s_1)$ $= 0.130$	0.130/0.375 $= 0.347$
	Rapid growth (s_2)	$P(s_2) = 0.35$	$P(F_2 \mid s_2)$ $= 0.70$	$P(F_2 \cap s_2)$ $= 0.245$	0.245/0.375 $= 0.653$
				$P(F_2) = 0.375$	

Figure 19.6

Decision Tree for the Investment Example after Revision of Probabilities

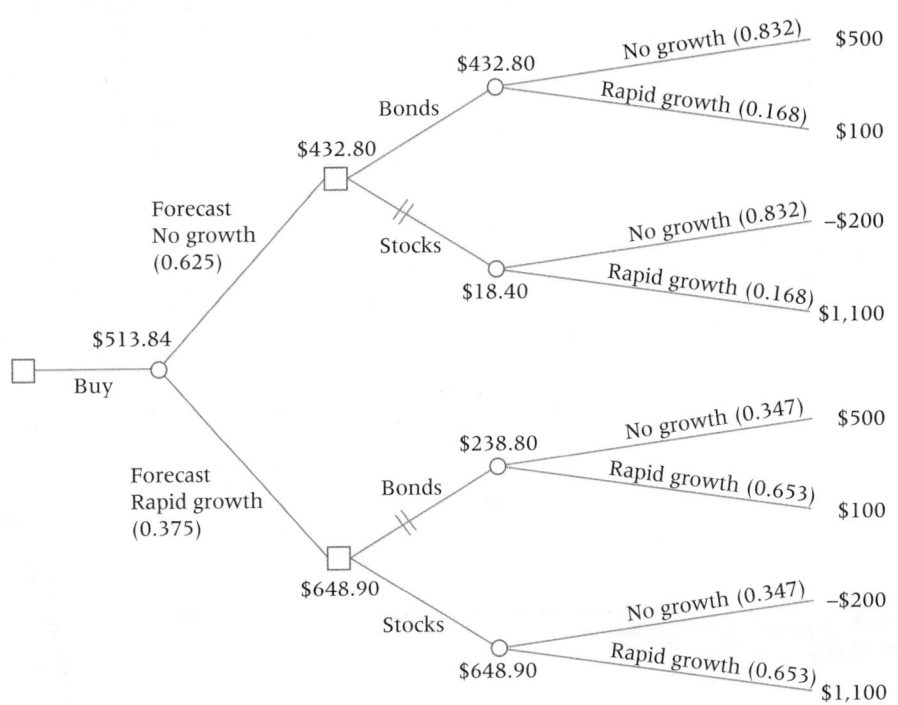

rapid-growth states have been revised. Multiplying the payoffs by these revised probabilities and summing them for each investment produces EMVs at the state-of-economy nodes. Moving back to the decision nodes preceding these values, the investor has the opportunity to invest in either bonds or stocks. The investor examines the EMVs and selects the investment with the highest value. For the decision limb in which the forecaster predicted no growth, the investor selects the bonds investment, which yields an EMV of $432.80 (as opposed to $18.40 from stocks). For the decision limb in which the forecaster predicted rapid growth, the investor selects the stocks investment, which yields an EMV of $648.90 (as opposed to $238.80 for bonds).

The investor is thus faced with the opportunity to earn an EMV of $432.80 if the forecaster predicts no growth or $648.90 if the forecaster predicts rapid growth. How often does the forecaster predict each of these states of the economy to happen? Using the sums of the joint probabilities from Tables 19.7 and 19.8, the decision maker gets the probabilities of each of these forecasts:

$$P(F_1) = 0.625 \text{ (no growth)}$$
$$P(F_2) = 0.375 \text{ (rapid growth)}$$

Entering these probabilities into the decision tree at the first probability node with the forecasts of the states of the economy and multiplying them by the EMV of each state yields an overall EMV of the opportunity:

EMV for Opportunity = $432.80(0.625) + $648.90(0.375) = $513.84

EXPECTED VALUE OF SAMPLE INFORMATION

The preceding calculations for the investment example show that the EMV of the opportunity is $513.84 with sample information, but it is only $360 without sample information, as shown in Figure 19.5. Using the sample information appears to profit the decision maker:

Apparent Profit of Using Sample Information = $513.84 − $360 = $153.84

How much did this sample information cost? If the sample information is not free, less than $153.84 is gained by using it. How much is it worth to use sample information? Obviously, the decision maker should not pay more than $153.84 for sample information because an expected $360 can be earned without the information. In general, the **expected value of sample information** is worth no more than *the difference between the EMV with the information and the EMV without the information.*

Expected Value of Sample Information	Expected Value of Sample Information = Expected Monetary Value with Information − Expected Monetary Value without Information

Suppose the decision maker had to pay $100 for the forecaster's prediction. The EMV of the decision with information shown in Figure 19.6 is reduced from $513.84 to $413.84, which is still superior to the $360 EMV without sample information. Figure 19.7 is the decision tree for the investment information with the options of buying the information or not buying the information included. The tree is constructed by combining the decision trees from Figures 19.5 and 19.6 and including the cost of buying information ($100) and the EMV with this purchased information ($413.84).

Figure 19.7

Decision Tree for the Investment Example–All Options Included

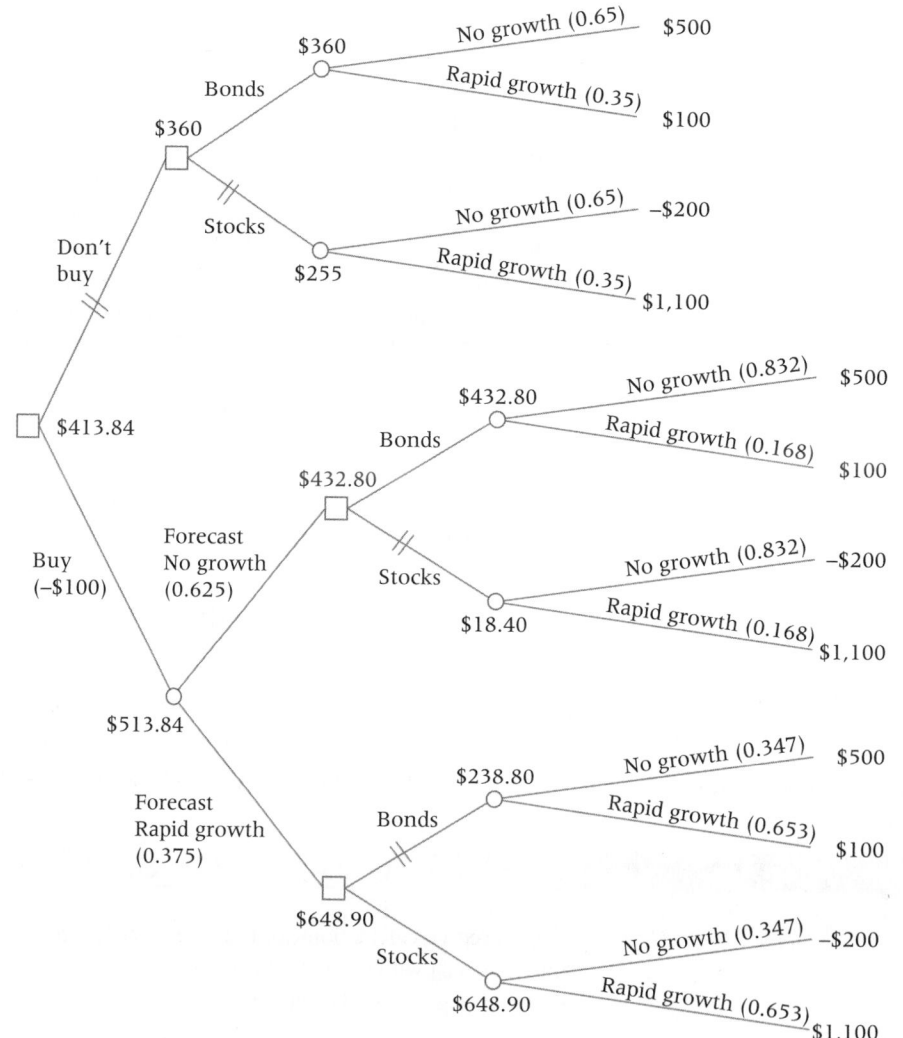

Demonstration Problem 19.4	In Demonstration Problem 19.1, the decision makers were faced with the opportunity to increase capacity to meet a possible increase in product demand. Here we reduced the decision alternatives and states of nature and altered the payoffs and probabilities. Use the following decision table to create a decision tree that displays the decision alternatives, the payoffs, the probabilities, the states of demand, and the expected monetary payoffs. The decision makers can buy information about the states of demand for $5 (recall that amounts are in millions of dollars). Incorporate this fact into your decision. Calculate the expected value of sampling information for this problem.

The decision alternatives are no expansion or build a new facility. The states of demand and prior probabilities are less demand (0.20), no change (0.30), or large increase (0.50).

		State of Demand		
		Less (0.20)	No Change (0.30)	Large Increase (0.50)
Decision	No Expansion	−$3	$2	$6
Alternative	New Facility	−$50	−$20	$65

The state-of-demand forecaster has historically not been accurate 100% of the time. For example, when the demand was less, the forecaster correctly predicted it 0.75 of the time. When there was no change in demand, the forecaster correctly predicted it 0.80 of the time. Sixty-five percent of the time the forecaster correctly predicted large increases when large increases occurred. Shown next are the probabilities that the forecaster will predict a particular state of demand under the actual states of demand.

		State of Demand		
		Less	No Change	Large Increase
	Less	0.75	0.10	0.05
Forecast	No Change	0.20	0.80	0.30
	Large Increase	0.05	0.10	0.65

Solution

The following figure is the decision tree for this problem when no sample information is purchased.

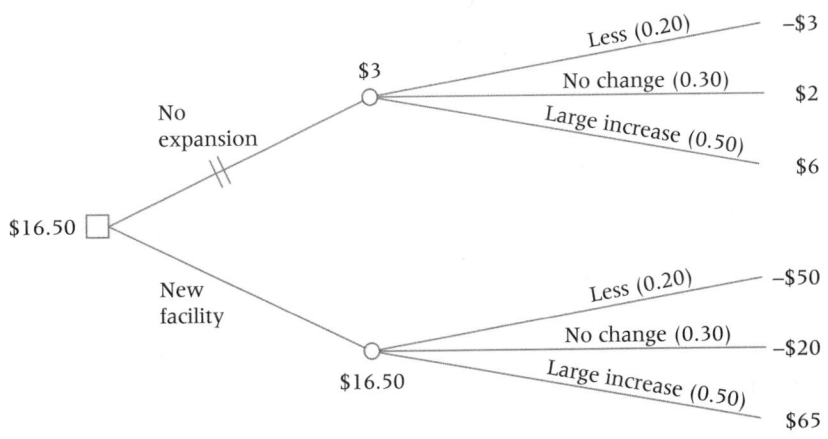

In light of sample information, the prior probabilities of the three states of demand can be revised. Shown here are the revisions for F_1 (forecast of less demand), F_2 (forecast of no change in demand), and F_3 (forecast of large increase in demand).

From these revised probabilities and other information, the decision tree containing alternatives and states using sample information can be constructed. The following figure is the decision tree containing the sample information alternative *and* the portion of the tree for the alternative of no sampling information.

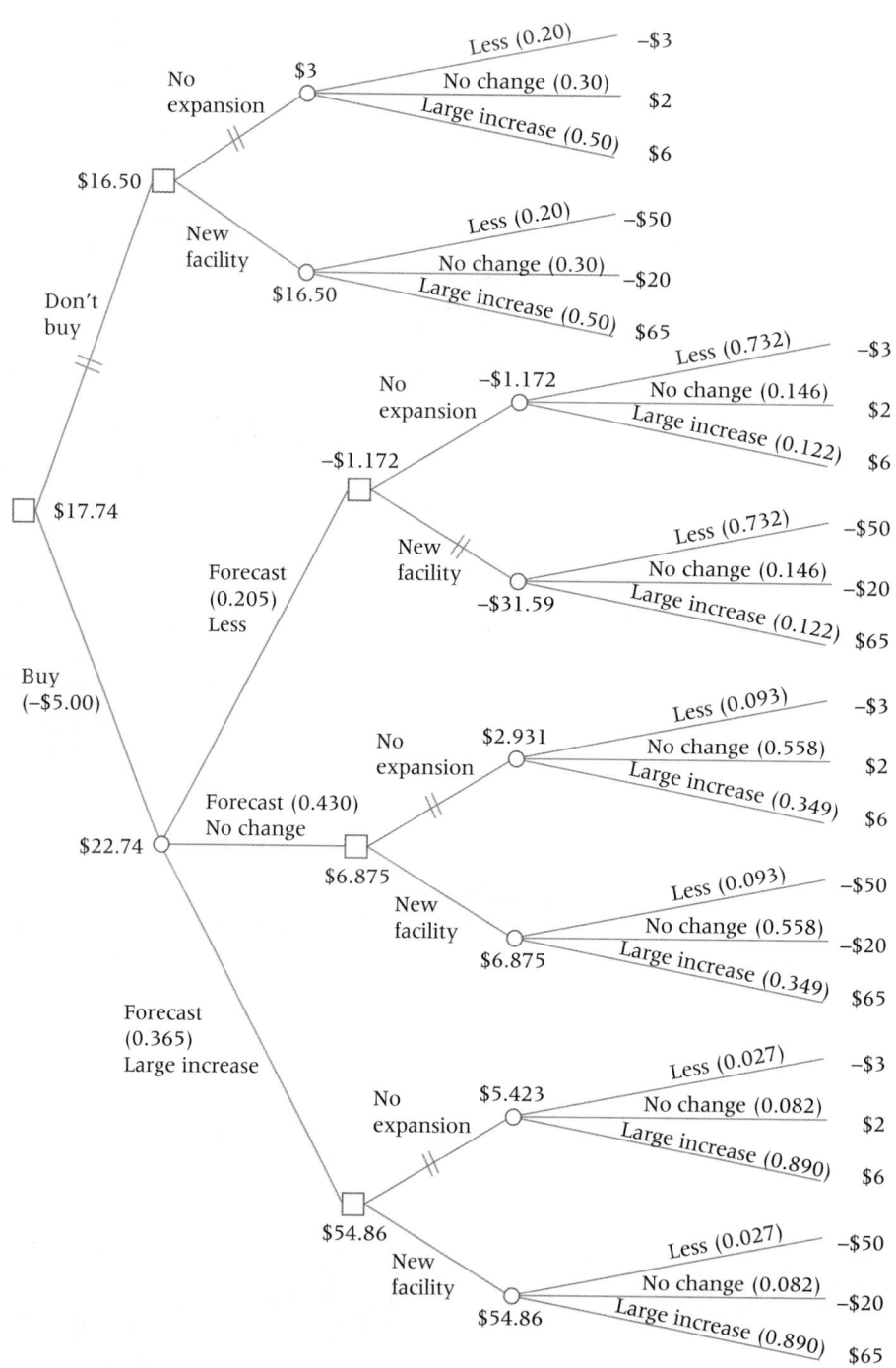

If the decision makers calculate the EMV after buying the sample information, they will see that the value is $17.74. The final EMV with sample information is calculated as follows:

EMV at Buy Node: $-\$1.172(0.205) + \$6.875(0.430) + \$54.86(0.365) = \$22.74$

However, the sample information cost $5. Hence, the net EMV at the buy node is:

$22.74 (EMV) − $5.00 (cost of information) = $17.74 (net EMV)

The worth of the sample information is:

EMV of Sample Information = EMV with Sample Information
− EMV without Sample Information
= $22.74 − $16.50 = $6.24

Concept Check

1. How does the expected value of sample information differ from the expected value of perfect information? Give an example of an instance where the expected value of sample information may be used.

19.4 Problems

19.12 Shown here is a decision table from a business situation. The decision maker has an opportunity to purchase sample information in the form of a forecast. With the sample information, the prior probabilities can be revised. Also shown are the probabilities of forecasts from the sample information for each state of nature. Use this information to answer parts (a) through (d).

		State of Nature	
		s_1 (0.30)	s_2 (0.70)
Alternative	d_1	\$350	−\$100
	d_2	−\$200	\$325

		State of Nature	
		s_1	s_2
Forecast	s_1	0.90	0.25
	s_2	0.10	0.75

a. Compute the EMV of this decision without sample information.
b. Compute the EMV of this decision with sample information.
c. Use a tree diagram to show the decision options in parts (a) and (b).
d. Calculate the value of the sample information.

19.13 a. A car rental agency faces the decision of buying a fleet of cars, all of which will be the same size. It can purchase a fleet of small cars, medium cars, or large cars. The smallest cars are the most fuel efficient and the largest cars are the greatest fuel users. One of the problems for the decision makers is that they do not know whether the price of fuel will increase or decrease in the near future. If the price increases, the small cars are likely to be most popular. If the price decreases, customers may demand the larger cars. Following is a decision table with these decision alternatives, the states of nature, the probabilities, and the payoffs. Use this information to determine the EMV for this problem.

		State of Nature	
		Fuel Decrease (0.60)	Fuel Increase (0.40)
Decision Alternative	Small Cars	−$225	$425
	Medium Cars	$125	−$150
	Large Cars	$350	−$400

b. The decision makers have an opportunity to purchase a forecast of the world oil markets that has some validity in predicting gasoline prices. The following matrix gives the probabilities of these forecasts being correct for various states of nature. Use this information to revise the prior probabilities and recompute the EMV on the basis of sample information. What is the expected value of sample information for this problem? Should the agency decide to buy the forecast?

		State of Nature	
		Fuel Decrease	Fuel Increase
Forecast	Fuel Decrease	0.75	0.15
	Fuel Increase	0.25	0.85

19.14 a. A small group of investors is considering planting a tree farm. Their choices are (1) don't plant trees, (2) plant a small number of trees, or (3) plant a large number of trees. The investors are concerned about the demand for trees. If demand for trees declines, planting a large tree farm would probably result in a loss. However, if a large increase in the demand for trees occurs, not planting a tree farm could mean a large loss in revenue opportunity. They determine that three states of demand are possible: (1) demand declines, (2) demand remains the same as it is, and (3) demand increases. Use the following decision table to compute an EMV for this decision opportunity.

		State of Demand		
		Decline (0.20)	Same (0.30)	Increase (0.50)
Decision Alternative	Don't Plant	$20	$0	$40
	Small Tree Farm	−$90	$10	$175
	Large Tree Farm	−$600	−$150	$800

b. Industry experts who believe they can forecast what will happen in the tree industry contact the investors. The following matrix shows the probabilities with which it is believed these experts can foretell tree demand. Use these probabilities to revise the prior probabilities of the states of nature and recompute the expected value of sample information. How much is this sample information worth?

		State of Demand		
		Decrease	Same	Increase
Forecast	Decrease	0.70	0.02	0.02
	Same	0.25	0.95	0.08
	Increase	0.05	0.03	0.90

19.15 a. Some oil speculators are interested in drilling an oil well. The rights to the land have been secured and they must decide whether to drill. The states of nature are that oil is present or that no oil is present. Their two decision alternatives are drill or don't drill. If they strike oil, the well will pay $1 million. If they have a dry hole, they will lose $100,000. If they don't drill, their payoffs are $0 when oil is present and $0 when it is not. The probability that oil is present is 0.11. Use this information to construct a decision table and compute an EMV for this problem.

b. The speculators have an opportunity to buy a geological survey, which sometimes helps in determining whether oil is present in the ground. When the geologists say there is oil in the ground, there actually is oil 0.20 of the time. When there is oil in the ground, 0.80 of the time the geologists say there is no oil. When there is no oil in the ground, 0.90 of the time the geologists say there is no oil. When there is no oil in the ground, 0.10 of the time the geologists say there is oil. Use this information to revise the prior probabilities of oil being present in the ground and compute the EMV based on sample information. What is the value of the sample information for this problem?

DECISION MAKING AT THE CEO LEVEL

The study of CEOs revealed that decision making takes place in many different areas of business. No matter what the decision concerns, it is critical for the CEO or manager to identify the decision alternatives. Sometimes decision alternatives are not obvious and can be identified only after considerable examination and brainstorming. Many different alternatives are available to decision makers in personnel, finance, operations, and so on. Alternatives can sometimes be obtained from worker suggestions and input. Others are identified through consultants or experts in particular fields. Occasionally, a creative and unobvious decision alternative is derived that proves to be the most successful choice.

Alex Trotman at Ford Motor, in a reorganization decision, chose the alternative of combining two operations into one unit. Other alternatives might have been to combine other operations into a unit (rather than the North American and European), create more units, or not reorganize at all. At Kodak, CEO George Fisher made the decision that the company would adopt digital and electronic imaging wholeheartedly. In addition, he determined that these new technologies would be interwoven with Kodak's paper and film products in such a manner as to be seamless. Fisher had other alternatives available, such as not entering the arena of digital and electronic imaging or entering it but keeping it separated from the paper and film operation. Maple Leaf Foods faced a crisis when cured meats manufactured in the Toronto plant were found to be contaminated, which resulted in serious illnesses leading to some fatalities. The CEO chose to close the plant briefly in August 2008, and recalled several products.

CEOs need to identify as many states of nature that can occur under the decision alternatives as possible. What might happen to sales? Will product demand increase or decrease? What is the political climate for environmental or international monetary regulation? What will occur next in the business cycle? Will there be inflation? What will the competitors do? What new inventions or developments will occur? What is the investment climate? Identifying as many of these states as possible helps the decision maker examine decision alternatives in light of those states and calculate payoffs accordingly.

Many different states of nature may arise that will affect the outcome of CEO decisions made in the 1990s. Ford Motor may find that the demand for a world car does not materialize, materializes so slowly that the company wastes its effort for many years, materializes as Trotman foresaw, or materializes even faster. The world economy might undergo a depression, a slowdown, constant growth, or even an accelerated rate of growth. Political conditions in countries of the world might make an American world car unacceptable. The governments of the countries that would be markets for such a car might cause the countries to become more a part of the world economy, stay about the same, slowly withdraw from the world scene, or become isolated.

States of nature can affect a CEO's decision in other ways. The rate of growth and understanding of technology is uncertain in many ways and can have a great effect on the decision to embrace digital and electronic imaging. Will the technology develop in time for the merging of these new technologies and the paper and film operations? Will there be suppliers who can provide materials and parts? What about the raw materials used in digital and electronic imaging? Will there be an abundance, a shortage, or an adequate supply of raw materials? Will the price of raw materials fluctuate widely, increase, decrease, or remain constant?

The decision maker should recognize whether he or she is a risk avoider or a risk taker. Does propensity toward risk vary by situation? Should it? How do the board of directors and shareholders view risk? Will the employees respond to risk taking or avoidance?

Successful CEOs may well incorporate risk taking, risk avoidance, and expected value decision making into their decisions. Perhaps the successful CEOs know when to take risks and when to pull back. In the case of Maple Leaf Foods, the CEO had to decide the extent of recall. Because consumer confidence is paramount where food products are concerned, Maple Leaf Foods broadened its recall to include a wide range of its products including Schneiders and McDonald's, as well as other products. Certainly, the decision by a successful company like Ford Motor, which had 5 of the top 10 vehicles at the time, to reorganize in an effort to make a world car is risk taking. Kodak's decision to embrace digital and electronic imaging and merge it with its paper and film operations is a risk-taking venture.

If successful, the payoffs from these CEO decisions could be great. The current success of Ford Motor may just scratch the surface if the company successfully sells its world car in the 21st century. On the other hand, the company could experience big losses or receive payoffs somewhere in between. The CEO of Maple Leaf Foods, Michael McCain, chose to go public and went on TV to reassure consumers stating "Tragically, our products have been linked to illness and loss of life. To those people who are ill, and to the families who have lost loved ones, I offer my deepest and sincerest sympathies". The CEO's decision not to leave crisis management entirely to PR agencies but to expand the product recall, face consumers head-on and take responsibility may, at least in part, be the reason why consumer confidence returned very quickly to Maple Leaf products.

CEOs are not always able to visualize all decision alternatives. However, creative, inspired thinking along with the brainstorming of others and an extensive investigation of the facts and figures can result in the identification of most of the possibilities. States of nature are unknown and harder to discern. However, awareness, insight, understanding, and knowledge of economies, markets, governments, and competitors can greatly aid a decision maker in considering possible states of nature that may affect the payoff of a decision along with the likelihood that such states of nature might occur. The payoffs for CEOs range from the loss of thousands of jobs including their own, loss of market share, and bankruptcy of the company, to worldwide growth, record stockholder dividends, and fame.

Why Statistics Is Relevant

Modern societies and businesses always operate under a great deal of uncertainty: What will the unemployment level be next year? Will the rate of inflation go up or down? How many beds will a hospital need to avoid turning away patients? How will my business be affected if the new product fails? Will the stock market go up? If we know the answer to these questions, we can plan for the future confidently (and make a lot of money in the stock market). But this is not the case. A decision maker has to decide without having access to what may happen in the future.

Even though the decision maker has no way of knowing the future, the decision has to be optimal in the sense that no matter what decision is taken, it is the one that is likely to decrease risk, increase the rewards, or both, given the level of uncertainty.

Decision theory provides a means of achieving these objectives. It does not eliminate risk but provides a means of assessing the consequences of different courses of action so the decision maker can achieve his or her objective of minimizing potential losses, maximizing potential gains, or optimizing both.

SUMMARY

1. Decision analysis is a branch of quantitative management in which mathematical and statistical approaches are used to assist decision makers in reaching judgments about alternative opportunities. Three types of decisions are (1) decisions made under certainty, (2) decisions made under uncertainty, and (3) decisions made with risk.

2. Decision alternatives are the options open to decision makers from which they can choose. States of nature are situations or conditions arising after the decision has been made, over which the decision maker has no control. Payoffs are the gains or losses that the decision maker will reap from various decision alternatives. These three aspects (decision alternatives, states of nature, and payoffs) can be displayed in a decision table or payoff table.

3. Decision making under certainty is the easiest of the three types of decisions to make. In this case, the states of nature are known, and the decision maker merely selects the decision alternative that yields the highest

payoff. Decisions are made under uncertainty when the likelihoods of the states of nature occurring are unknown. Four approaches to making decisions under uncertainty are the *maximax* criterion, the *maximin* criterion, the *Hurwicz* criterion, and *minimax* regret.

The maximax criterion is an optimistic approach based on the notion that the best possible outcomes will occur. In this approach, the decision maker selects the maximum possible payoff under each decision alternative and then selects the maximum of these. Thus, the decision maker is selecting the maximum of the maximums. The maximin criterion is a pessimistic approach. The assumption is that the worst case will happen under each decision alternative. The decision maker selects the minimum payoffs under each decision alternative and then picks the maximum of these as the best solution. Thus, the decision maker is selecting the best of the worst cases, or the maximum of the minimums.

The Hurwicz criterion is an attempt to give the decision maker an alternative to maximax and maximin that is somewhere between an optimistic and a pessimistic approach. With this approach, decision makers select a value called alpha between 0 and 1 to represent how optimistic they are. The maximum and minimum payoffs for each decision alternative are examined. The alpha weight is applied to the maximum payoff under each decision alternative and $1 - \alpha$ is applied to the minimum payoff. These two weighted values are combined for each decision alternative, and the maximum of these weighted values is selected.

Minimax regret is calculated by examining opportunity loss. An opportunity loss table is constructed by subtracting each payoff from the maximum payoff under each state of nature. This step produces a lost opportunity under each state.

The maximum lost opportunity from each decision alternative is determined from the opportunity table. The minimum of these values is selected, and the corresponding decision alternative is chosen. In this way, the decision maker has reduced or minimized the regret, or lost opportunity.

4. In decision making with risk, the decision maker has some prior knowledge of the probability of each occurrence of each state of nature. With these probabilities, a weighted payoff referred to as expected monetary value (EMV) can be calculated for each decision alternative. A person who makes decisions based on these EMVs is called an EMVer. The EMV is essentially the average payoff that would occur if the decision process were to be played out over a long period of time with the probabilities holding constant.

5. The expected value of perfect information can be determined by comparing the EMV if the states of nature are known to the EMV with no such information. The difference in the two is the expected value of perfect information.

6. Utility refers to a decision maker's propensity to take risks. People who avoid risks are called risk avoiders. People who are prone to take risks are referred to as risk takers. People who use EMV generally fall between these two categories. Utility curves can be sketched to ascertain or depict a decision maker's tendency toward risk.

7. By using Bayes' theorem, the probabilities associated with the states of nature in decision making under risk can be revised when new information is obtained. This information can be helpful to the decision maker. However, it usually carries a cost for the decision maker. This cost can reduce the payoff of decision making with sample information. The EMV with sample information can be compared to the EMV without it to determine the value of sample information.

KEY TERMS

decision alternatives	decision table	expected value of sample	payoffs
decision analysis	decision trees	information	payoff table
decision making under	EMVer	Hurwicz criterion	risk avoider
certainty	expected monetary value	maximax criterion	risk taker
decision making under risk	(EMV)	maximin criterion	states of nature
decision making under	expected value of perfect	minimax regret	utility
uncertainty	information	opportunity loss table	

FORMULA

Bayes' Rule

$$P(X_i \mid Y) = \frac{P(X_i) \cdot P(Y \mid X_i)}{P(X_1) \cdot P(Y \mid X_1) + P(X_2) \cdot P(Y \mid X_2) + \cdots + P(X_n) \cdot P(Y \mid X_n)}$$

KEY CONSIDERATIONS

Methodological considerations occasionally arise in decision analysis situations. The techniques presented in this chapter can aid the decision maker in selecting from among decision alternatives in light of payoffs and expected values. Payoffs do not always reflect all costs. The decision maker needs to decide whether to consider other factors not in the decision criteria in examining decision alternatives. For example, some decision alternatives are environmentally damaging in the form of ground, air, or water pollution. Other choices endanger the health and safety of workers. In the area of human resources, some decision alternatives include eliminating jobs and laying off workers. Should the issues involved in these decisions be factored into payoffs? For example, what effects would a layoff have on families and communities? Does a business have any social obligation toward its workers and its

community that should be taken into consideration in payoffs? Does a decision alternative involve producing a product that is detrimental to a customer or a customer's family? States of nature are usually beyond the control of the decision maker; therefore, it seems unlikely that methodological issues would be connected with a state of nature. However, obtaining sample or perfect information under which to make decisions about states of nature has the usual potential for methodological mistakes in sampling.

In many cases, payoffs other than the dollar values assigned to a decision alternative should be considered. In using decision analysis for optimal effectiveness, the decision maker should attempt to factor into the payoffs the cost of pollution, safety features, human resource loss, and so on.

SUPPLEMENTARY PROBLEMS

Calculating the Statistics

19.16 Use the following decision table to complete parts (a) through (d).

		State of Nature	
		s_1	s_2
Decision Alternative	d_1	50	100
	d_2	−75	200
	d_3	25	40
	d_4	75	10

a. Use the maximax criterion to determine which decision alternative to select.
b. Use the maximin criterion to determine which decision alternative to select.
c. Use the Hurwicz criterion to determine which decision alternative to select. Let $\alpha = 0.6$.
d. Compute an opportunity loss table from these data. Use this table and a minimax regret criterion to determine which decision alternative to select.

19.17 Use the following decision table to complete parts (a) through (c).

		State of Nature			
		s_1 (0.30)	s_2 (0.25)	s_3 (0.20)	s_4 (0.25)
Decision Alternative	d_1	400	250	300	100
	d_2	300	−100	600	200

a. Draw a decision tree to represent this decision table.
b. Compute the EMV for each decision and label the decision tree to indicate what the final decision would be.
c. Compute the expected payoff of perfect information. Compare this answer to the answer determined in part (b) and compute the value of perfect information.

19.18 Shown here is a decision table. A forecast can be purchased by the decision maker. The forecaster is not correct 100% of the time. Also given is a table containing the probabilities of the forecaster being correct under different states of nature. Use the first table to compute the EMV of this decision without sample information. Use the second table to revise the prior probabilities of the various decision alternatives. From this and the first table, compute the EMV with sample information. Construct a decision tree to represent the options, the payoffs, and the expected monetary values. Calculate the value of sample information.

		State of Nature	
		s_1 (0.40)	s_2 (0.60)
Decision Alternative	d_1	$200	$150
	d_2	−$75	$450
	d_3	$175	$125

	State of Nature	
	s_1	s_2
Forecast s_1	0.90	0.30
s_2	0.10	0.70

Testing Your Understanding

19.19 Managers of a manufacturing firm decided to add picture frames to its list of production items. However, they have not decided how many to produce because they are uncertain about the level of demand. Shown here is a decision table that has been constructed to help the managers in their decision situation. Use this table to answer parts (a) through (c).

		State of Demand		
		Small	Moderate	Large
Decision Alternative (Produce)	Small Number	$200	$250	$300
	Modest Number	$100	$300	$600
	Large Number	–$300	$400	$2,000

a. Use maximax and maximin criteria to evaluate the decision alternatives.

b. Construct an opportunity loss table and use minimax regret to select a decision alternative.

c. Compare the results of the maximax, maximin, and minimax regret criteria in selecting decision alternatives.

19.20 Some companies use production learning curves to set pricing strategies. They price their product lower than the initial cost of making the product; after some period of time, the learning curve takes effect and the product can be produced for less than its selling price. In this way, the company can penetrate new markets with aggressive pricing strategies and still make a long-term profit.

A company is considering using the learning curve to set its price on a new product. There is some uncertainty as to how soon, if at all, the production operation will learn to make the product more quickly and efficiently. If the learning curve does not drop enough or the initial price is too low, the company will be operating at a loss on this product. If the product is priced too high, the sales volume might be too low to justify production. Shown here is a decision table that contains as its states of nature several possible learning-curve scenarios. The decision alternatives are three different pricing strategies.

a. Use this table and the Hurwicz criterion to make a decision about the pricing strategies with each given value of alpha.

		State of Nature		
		No Learning	Slow Learning	Fast Learning
Decision Alternative	Price Low	–$700	–$400	$1,200
	Price Medium	–$300	–$100	$550
	Price High	$100	$125	$150

i. $\alpha = 0.10$
ii. $\alpha = 0.50$
iii. $\alpha = 0.80$

b. Compare and discuss the decision choices in part (a).

19.21 An entertainment company owns two amusement parks in British Columbia. They are faced with the decision of whether to open the parks in the winter. If they choose to open the parks in the winter, they can leave the parks open during regular hours (as in the summer) or they can open only on the weekends. To some extent, the payoffs from opening the parks hinge on the type of weather that occurs during the winter season. Following are the payoffs for various decision options about opening the park for two different weather scenarios: mild weather and severe weather. Use the information to construct a decision tree. Determine the EMV and the value of perfect information.

		State of the Weather	
		Mild (0.75)	Severe (0.25)
Decision Alternative	Open Regular Hours	$2,000	–$2,500
	Open Weekends Only	$1,200	–$200
	Not Open at All	–$300	$100

19.22 A Canadian manufacturing company has decided to consider producing a particular model of one of its products just for sale in Germany. Because of the German requirements, the product must be made specifically for German consumption and cannot be sold in Canada. Company officials believe the market for the product is highly price sensitive. Because the product will be manufactured in Canada and exported to Germany, the biggest variable factor in being price competitive is the exchange rate between the two countries. If the Canadian dollar is strong, German consumers will have to pay more for the product in euros. If the Canadian dollar becomes weaker against the euro, Germans can buy more Canadian products for their money. The company officials are faced with decision alternatives of whether to produce the product. The states of the exchange rates are Canadian dollar weaker, Canadian dollar stays the same, and Canadian dollar stronger. The probabilities of these states occurring are 0.35, 0.25, and 0.40, respectively. Some negative payoffs will result from not producing the product because of sunk development and market research costs and because of lost market opportunity. If the product is not produced, the payoffs are –$700 when the dollar gets weaker, –$200 when the dollar remains about the same, and $150 when the dollar gets stronger. If the product is produced, the payoffs are $1,800 when the dollar gets weaker, $400 when the exchange rates stay about the same, and –$1,600 when the dollar gets stronger.

Use this information to construct a decision tree and a decision table for this decision-making situation. Use the probabilities to compute the EMVs of the decision alternatives. On the basis of this information, which decision choice should the company make? Compute the EMV of perfect information and the value of perfect information.

19.23   a.   A small retailer began as a mom-and-pop operation selling crafts and consignment items. During the past two years, the store's volume grew significantly. The owners are trying to decide whether to purchase an automated checkout system. The store's present manual system is slow. They are concerned about lost business due to inability to ring up sales quickly. The automated system would also offer some accounting and inventory advantages. The problem is that the automated system carries a large fixed cost, and the owners feel that sales volume would have to grow to justify the cost.

The following decision table contains the decision alternatives for this situation, the possible states of future sales, prior probabilities of those states occurring, and the payoffs. Use this information to compute the expected monetary payoffs for the alternatives.

		State of Sales		
		Reduction (0.15)	Constant (0.35)	Increase (0.50)
Decision Alternative	Automate	–$40,000	–$15,000	$60,000
	Don't Automate	$5,000	$10,000	–$30,000

b.   For a fee, the owners can purchase a sales forecast for the near future. The forecast is not always perfect. The probabilities of these forecasts being correct for particular states of sales are shown here. Use these probabilities to revise the prior state probabilities. Compute the EMV on the basis of sample information. Determine the value of the sample information.

		State of Sales		
		Reduction	Constant	Increase
Forecast	Reduction	0.60	0.10	0.05
	Constant	0.30	0.80	0.25
	Increase	0.10	0.10	0.70

19.24   a.   A city is considering airport expansion. In particular, the mayor and city council are trying to decide whether to sell bonds to construct a new terminal. The problem is that at present demand for gates is not strong enough to warrant construction of a new terminal. However, a major airline is investigating several cities to determine which it will choose for its new headquarters. If this city is selected, the new terminal will easily pay for itself. The decision to build the terminal must be made by the city before the airline will say whether the city has been chosen. Shown here is a decision table for this dilemma. Use this information to compute EMVs for the alternatives and reach a conclusion.

		State of Nature	
		City Chosen (0.20)	City Not Chosen (0.80)
Decision Alternative	Build Terminal	$12,000	–$8,000
	Don't Build Terminal	–$1,000	$2,000

b. An airline industry expert indicates that she will sell the city decision makers her best guess as to whether the city will be chosen. The probabilities of her being right or wrong are given.

		State of Nature	
		City Chosen	City Not Chosen
Forecast	City Chosen	0.45	0.40
	City Not Chosen	0.55	0.60

ANALYZING THE DATABASES

see www.wiley.com/college/black

1. Suppose you are the CEO of a financial company. You are considering expansion of the physical facility. What are some decision alternatives to consider? What are some states of nature that can occur in this decision-making environment (a publicly traded company). What are some decisions that you might make in which you would consider decision alternatives? Name three arenas in which you would be making substantial strategic decisions (e.g., marketing, finance, production, and human resources). Delineate at least three decision alternatives in each of these arenas. Examine and discuss at least two states of nature that could occur under these decision alternatives in each arena.

CASE

Fletcher-Terry: On the Cutting Edge

The Fletcher-Terry Company is a worldwide leader in the development of glass-cutting tools and accessories for professional glaziers, glass manufacturers, glass artisans, and professional framers. The company can trace its roots back to 1868. For many decades, Fletcher-Terry had much success making its traditional product lines of hand-held glass cutters and cutting wheels for the glass, glazing, and hardware markets. However, by the 1980s, Fletcher-Terry was facing a crisis. Its two largest customers, distributors of cutting devices, decided to introduce their own private-label cutters made overseas. By the end of 1982, Fletcher-Terry's sales of hand-held glass cutters were down 45%.

Fletcher-Terry responded by investing heavily in technology with the hope that automation would cut costs; however, the technology never worked. The company then decided to expand its line of offerings by creating private lines through imports, but the U.S. dollar weakened and any price advantage was lost. Eventually, Fletcher-Terry had to write off this line with a substantial loss.

Company managers realized that if they did not change the way they did business, the company would not survive. They began a significant strategic planning process in which they set objectives and redefined the mission of the company. Among the new objectives were to increase market share where the company was already strong, penetrate new markets with new products, provide technological expertise for product development, promote greater employee involvement and growth, and achieve a sales growth rate twice that of the gross domestic product.

To accomplish these objectives, the company invested in plant and process improvements that reduced costs and improved quality. Markets were researched for both old and new products, and marketing efforts were launched to reestablish the company's products as being "the first choice of professionals." A participatory management system was implemented that encouraged risk taking and creativity among employees.

Following these initiatives, sales growth totalled 82.5% from 1987 and 1993. Fletcher-Terry expanded its offerings with bevel mat cutters, new fastener tools, and a variety of hand tools essential to professional picture framers, and graduated from being a manufacturer of relatively simple hand tools to being a manufacturer of mechanically complex equipment and tools. Today, Fletcher-Terry maintains a leadership position in its industry through dedicated employees who are constantly exploring new ideas to help customers become more productive. Because of its continuous pursuit of quality, the company earned the Ford Q-101 Quality Supplier Award. In August of 2001, Fletcher-Terry introduced its FramerSolutions.com online business-to-business custom mat-cutting service especially designed for professional picture framers. The mission of Fletcher-Terry is to develop innovative tools and equipment for the markets they serve worldwide and make customer satisfaction its number one priority.

CASE (continued)

Discussion

1. Fletcher-Terry managers have been involved in many decisions over the years. Of particular importance were the decisions made in the 1980s when the company was struggling to survive. Several states of nature took place in the late 1970s and 1980s over which managers had little or no control. Suppose the Fletcher-Terry management team wants to reflect on their decisions and the events that surrounded them, and they ask you to make a brief report summarizing the situation. Delineate at least five decisions that Fletcher-Terry probably had to make during that troublesome time. Using your knowledge of the economic situation both in the U.S. and in the rest of the world in addition to information given in the case, present at least four states of nature during that time that had significant influence on the outcomes of the managers' decisions.

2. At one point, Fletcher-Terry decided to import its own private line of cutters. Suppose that before taking such action, the managers had the following information available. Construct a decision table and a decision tree by using this information. Explain any conclusions reached.

   Suppose the decision for managers was to import or not import. If they imported, they had to worry about the purchasing value of the dollar overseas. If the value of the dollar went up, the company could profit $350,000. If the dollar maintained its present position, the company would still profit by $275,000. However, if the value of the dollar decreased, the company would be worse off with an additional loss of $555,000. One business economic source reported that there was a 25% chance that the dollar would increase in value overseas, a 35% chance that it would remain constant, and a 40% chance that it would lose value overseas. If the company decided not to import its own private label, it would have a $22,700 loss no matter what the value of the dollar was overseas. Explain the possible outcomes of this analysis to the management team in terms of EMV, risk aversion, and risk taking. Bring common sense into the process and give your recommendations on what the company should do given the analysis. Keep in mind the company's situation and the fact that it had not yet tried any solution. Explain to company officials the expected value of perfect information for this decision.

References

Adapted from "Fletcher-Terry: On the Cutting Edge," Real-World Lessons for America's Small Businesses: Insights from the Blue Chip Enterprise Initiative. Published by *Nation's Business* magazine on behalf of Connecticut Mutual Life Insurance Company and the U.S. Chamber of Commerce in association with The Blue Chip Enterprise Initiative, 1994. See also Fletcher-Terry, available at <http://www.fletcher-terry.com/>.

Table A.1

Random Numbers

12651	61646	11769	75109	86996	97669	25757	32535	07122	76763
81769	74436	02630	72310	45049	18029	07469	42341	98173	79260
36737	98863	77240	76251	00654	64688	09343	70278	67331	98729
82861	54371	76610	94934	72748	44124	05610	53750	95938	01485
21325	15732	24127	37431	09723	63529	73977	95218	96074	42138
74146	47887	62463	23045	41490	07954	22597	60012	98866	90959
90759	64410	54179	66075	61051	75385	51378	08360	95946	95547
55683	98078	02238	91540	21219	17720	87817	41705	95785	12563
79686	17969	76061	83748	55920	83612	41540	86492	06447	60568
70333	00201	86201	69716	78185	62154	77930	67663	29529	75116
14042	53536	07779	04157	41172	36473	42123	43929	50533	33437
59911	08256	06596	48416	69770	68797	56080	14223	59199	30162
62368	62623	62742	14891	39247	52242	98832	69533	91174	57979
57529	97751	54976	48957	74599	08759	78494	52785	68526	64618
15469	90574	78033	66885	13936	42117	71831	22961	94225	31816
18625	23674	53850	32827	81647	80820	00420	63555	74489	80141
74626	68394	88562	70745	23701	45630	65891	58220	35442	60414
11119	16519	27384	90199	79210	76965	99546	30323	31664	22845
41101	17336	48951	53674	17880	45260	08575	49321	36191	17095
32123	91576	84221	78902	82010	30847	62329	63898	23268	74283
26091	68409	69704	82267	14751	13151	93115	01437	56945	89661
67680	79790	48462	59278	44185	29616	76531	19589	83139	28454
15184	19260	14073	07026	25264	08388	27182	22557	61501	67481
58010	45039	57181	10238	36874	28546	37444	80824	63981	39942
56425	53996	86245	32623	78858	08143	60377	42925	42815	11159
82630	84066	13592	60642	17904	99718	63432	88642	37858	25431
14927	40909	23900	48761	44860	92467	31742	87142	03607	32059
23740	22505	07489	85986	74420	21744	97711	36648	35620	97949
32990	97446	03711	63824	07953	85965	87089	11687	92414	67257
05310	24058	91946	78437	34365	82469	12430	84754	19354	72745
21839	39937	27534	88913	49055	19218	47712	67677	51889	70926
08833	42549	93981	94051	28382	83725	72643	64233	97252	17133
58336	11139	47479	00931	91560	95372	97642	33856	54825	55680
62032	91144	75478	47431	52726	30289	42411	91886	51818	78292
45171	30557	53116	04118	58301	24375	65609	85810	18620	49198
91611	62656	60128	35609	63698	78356	50682	22505	01692	36291
55472	63819	86314	49174	93582	73604	78614	78849	23096	72825
18573	09729	74091	53994	10970	86557	65661	41854	26037	53296
60866	02955	90288	82136	83644	94455	06560	78029	98768	71296
45043	55608	82767	60890	74646	79485	13619	98868	40857	19415
17831	09737	79473	75945	28394	79334	70577	38048	03607	06932
40137	03981	07585	18128	11178	32601	27994	05641	22600	86064
77776	31343	14576	97706	16039	47517	43300	59080	80392	63189
69605	44104	40103	95635	05635	81673	68657	09559	23510	95875
19916	52934	26499	09821	97331	80993	61299	36979	73599	35055
02606	58552	07678	56619	65325	30705	99582	53390	46357	13244
65183	73160	87131	35530	47946	09854	18080	02321	05809	04893
10740	98914	44916	11322	89717	88189	30143	52687	19420	60061
98642	89822	71691	51573	83666	61642	46683	33761	47542	23551
60139	25601	93663	25547	02654	94829	48672	28736	84994	13071

Table A.2

Binomial Probability Distribution

n = 1

Probability

x	.1	.2	.3	.4	.5	.6	.7	.8	.9
0	.900	.800	.700	.600	.500	.400	.300	.200	.100
1	.100	.200	.300	.400	.500	.600	.700	.800	.900

n = 2

Probability

x	.1	.2	.3	.4	.5	.6	.7	.8	.9
0	.810	.640	.490	.360	.250	.160	.090	.040	.010
1	.180	.320	.420	.480	.500	.480	.420	.320	.180
2	.010	.040	.090	.160	.250	.360	.490	.640	.810

n = 3

Probability

x	.1	.2	.3	.4	.5	.6	.7	.8	.9
0	.729	.512	.343	.216	.125	.064	.027	.008	.001
1	.243	.384	.441	.432	.375	.288	.189	.096	.027
2	.027	.096	.189	.288	.375	.432	.441	.384	.243
3	.001	.008	.027	.064	.125	.216	.343	.512	.729

n = 4

Probability

x	.1	.2	.3	.4	.5	.6	.7	.8	.9
0	.656	.410	.240	.130	.063	.026	.008	.002	.000
1	.292	.410	.412	.346	.250	.154	.076	.026	.004
2	.049	.154	.265	.346	.375	.346	.265	.154	.049
3	.004	.026	.076	.154	.250	.346	.412	.410	.292
4	.000	.002	.008	.026	.063	.130	.240	.410	.656

n = 5

Probability

x	.1	.2	.3	.4	.5	.6	.7	.8	.9
0	.590	.328	.168	.078	.031	.010	.002	.000	.000
1	.328	.410	.360	.259	.156	.077	.028	.006	.000
2	.073	.205	.309	.346	.313	.230	.132	.051	.008
3	.008	.051	.132	.230	.313	.346	.309	.205	.073
4	.000	.006	.028	.077	.156	.259	.360	.410	.328
5	.000	.000	.002	.010	.031	.078	.168	.328	.590

n = 6

Probability

x	.1	.2	.3	.4	.5	.6	.7	.8	.9
0	.531	.262	.118	.047	.016	.004	.001	.000	.000
1	.354	.393	.303	.187	.094	.037	.010	.002	.000
2	.098	.246	.324	.311	.234	.138	.060	.015	.001
3	.015	.082	.185	.276	.313	.276	.185	.082	.015
4	.001	.015	.060	.138	.234	.311	.324	.246	.098
5	.000	.002	.010	.037	.094	.187	.303	.393	.354
6	.000	.000	.001	.004	.016	.047	.118	.262	.531

(continued)

Table A.2

Binomial Probability Distribution (*Continued*)

$n = 7$

Probability

x	.1	.2	.3	.4	.5	.6	.7	.8	.9
0	.478	.210	.082	.028	.008	.002	.000	.000	.000
1	.372	.367	.247	.131	.055	.017	.004	.000	.000
2	.124	.275	.318	.261	.164	.077	.025	.004	.000
3	.023	.115	.227	.290	.273	.194	.097	.029	.003
4	.003	.029	.097	.194	.273	.290	.227	.115	.023
5	.000	.004	.025	.077	.164	.261	.318	.275	.124
6	.000	.000	.004	.017	.055	.131	.247	.367	.372
7	.000	.000	.000	.002	.008	.028	.082	.210	.478

$n = 8$

Probability

x	.1	.2	.3	.4	.5	.6	.7	.8	.9
0	.430	.168	.058	.017	.004	.001	.000	.000	.000
1	.383	.336	.198	.090	.031	.008	.001	.000	.000
2	.149	.294	.296	.209	.109	.041	.010	.001	.000
3	.033	.147	.254	.279	.219	.124	.047	.009	.000
4	.005	.046	.136	.232	.273	.232	.136	.046	.005
5	.000	.009	.047	.124	.219	.279	.254	.147	.033
6	.000	.001	.010	.041	.109	.209	.296	.294	.149
7	.000	.000	.001	.008	.031	.090	.198	.336	.383
8	.000	.000	.000	.001	.004	.017	.058	.168	.430

$n = 9$

Probability

x	.1	.2	.3	.4	.5	.6	.7	.8	.9
0	.387	.134	.040	.010	.002	.000	.000	.000	.000
1	.387	.302	.156	.060	.018	.004	.000	.000	.000
2	.172	.302	.267	.161	.070	.021	.004	.000	.000
3	.045	.176	.267	.251	.164	.074	.021	.003	.000
4	.007	.066	.172	.251	.246	.167	.074	.017	.001
5	.001	.017	.074	.167	.246	.251	.172	.066	.007
6	.000	.003	.021	.074	.164	.251	.267	.176	.045
7	.000	.000	.004	.021	.070	.161	.267	.302	.172
8	.000	.000	.000	.004	.018	.060	.156	.302	.387
9	.000	.000	.000	.000	.002	.010	.040	.134	.387

$n = 10$

Probability

x	.1	.2	.3	.4	.5	.6	.7	.8	.9
0	.349	.107	.028	.006	.001	.000	.000	.000	.000
1	.387	.268	.121	.040	.010	.002	.000	.000	.000
2	.194	.302	.233	.121	.044	.011	.001	.000	.000
3	.057	.201	.267	.215	.117	.042	.009	.001	.000
4	.011	.088	.200	.251	.205	.111	.037	.006	.000
5	.001	.026	.103	.201	.246	.201	.103	.026	.001
6	.000	.006	.037	.111	.205	.251	.200	.088	.011
7	.000	.001	.009	.042	.117	.215	.267	.201	.057
8	.000	.000	.001	.011	.044	.121	.233	.302	.194
9	.000	.000	.000	.002	.010	.040	.121	.268	.387
10	.000	.000	.000	.000	.001	.006	.028	.107	.349

Table A.2

Binomial Probability Distribution (*Continued*)

n = 11

	Probability								
x	.1	.2	.3	.4	.5	.6	.7	.8	.9
0	.314	.086	.020	.004	.000	.000	.000	.000	.000
1	.384	.236	.093	.027	.005	.001	.000	.000	.000
2	.213	.295	.200	.089	.027	.005	.001	.000	.000
3	.071	.221	.257	.177	.081	.023	.004	.000	.000
4	.016	.111	.220	.236	.161	.070	.017	.002	.000
5	.002	.039	.132	.221	.226	.147	.057	.010	.000
6	.000	.010	.057	.147	.226	.221	.132	.039	.002
7	.000	.002	.017	.070	.161	.236	.220	.111	.016
8	.000	.000	.004	.023	.081	.177	.257	.221	.071
9	.000	.000	.001	.005	.027	.089	.200	.295	.213
10	.000	.000	.000	.001	.005	.027	.093	.236	.384
11	.000	.000	.000	.000	.000	.004	.020	.086	.314

n = 12

	Probability								
x	.1	.2	.3	.4	.5	.6	.7	.8	.9
0	.282	.069	.014	.002	.000	.000	.000	.000	.000
1	.377	.206	.071	.017	.003	.000	.000	.000	.000
2	.230	.283	.168	.064	.016	.002	.000	.000	.000
3	.085	.236	.240	.142	.054	.012	.001	.000	.000
4	.021	.133	.231	.213	.121	.042	.008	.001	.000
5	.004	.053	.158	.227	.193	.101	.029	.003	.000
6	.000	.016	.079	.177	.226	.177	.079	.016	.000
7	.000	.003	.029	.101	.193	.227	.158	.053	.004
8	.000	.001	.008	.042	.121	.213	.231	.133	.021
9	.000	.000	.001	.012	.054	.142	.240	.236	.085
10	.000	.000	.000	.002	.016	.064	.168	.283	.230
11	.000	.000	.000	.000	.003	.017	.071	.206	.377
12	.000	.000	.000	.000	.000	.002	.014	.069	.282

n = 13

	Probability								
x	.1	.2	.3	.4	.5	.6	.7	.8	.9
0	.254	.055	.010	.001	.000	.000	.000	.000	.000
1	.367	.179	.054	.011	.002	.000	.000	.000	.000
2	.245	.268	.139	.045	.010	.001	.000	.000	.000
3	.100	.246	.218	.111	.035	.006	.001	.000	.000
4	.028	.154	.234	.184	.087	.024	.003	.000	.000
5	.006	.069	.180	.221	.157	.066	.014	.001	.000
6	.001	.023	.103	.197	.209	.131	.044	.006	.000
7	.000	.006	.044	.131	.209	.197	.103	.023	.001
8	.000	.001	.014	.066	.157	.221	.180	.069	.006
9	.000	.000	.003	.024	.087	.184	.234	.154	.028
10	.000	.000	.001	.006	.035	.111	.218	.246	.100
11	.000	.000	.000	.001	.010	.045	.139	.268	.245
12	.000	.000	.000	.000	.002	.011	.054	.179	.367
13	.000	.000	.000	.000	.000	.001	.010	.055	.254

(continued)

Table A.2

Binomial Probability Distribution (*Continued*)

n = 14

Probability

x	.1	.2	.3	.4	.5	.6	.7	.8	.9
0	.229	.044	.007	.001	.000	.000	.000	.000	.000
1	.356	.154	.041	.007	.001	.000	.000	.000	.000
2	.257	.250	.113	.032	.006	.001	.000	.000	.000
3	.114	.250	.194	.085	.022	.003	.000	.000	.000
4	.035	.172	.229	.155	.061	.014	.001	.000	.000
5	.008	.086	.196	.207	.122	.041	.007	.000	.000
6	.001	.032	.126	.207	.183	.092	.023	.002	.000
7	.000	.009	.062	.157	.209	.157	.062	.009	.000
8	.000	.002	.023	.092	.183	.207	.126	.032	.001
9	.000	.000	.007	.041	.122	.207	.196	.086	.008
10	.000	.000	.001	.014	.061	.155	.229	.172	.035
11	.000	.000	.000	.003	.022	.085	.194	.250	.114
12	.000	.000	.000	.001	.006	.032	.113	.250	.257
13	.000	.000	.000	.000	.001	.007	.041	.154	.356
14	.000	.000	.000	.000	.000	.001	.007	.044	.229

n = 15

Probability

x	.1	.2	.3	.4	.5	.6	.7	.8	.9
0	.206	.035	.005	.000	.000	.000	.000	.000	.000
1	.343	.132	.031	.005	.000	.000	.000	.000	.000
2	.267	.231	.092	.022	.003	.000	.000	.000	.000
3	.129	.250	.170	.063	.014	.002	.000	.000	.000
4	.043	.188	.219	.127	.042	.007	.001	.000	.000
5	.010	.103	.206	.186	.092	.024	.003	.000	.000
6	.002	.043	.147	.207	.153	.061	.012	.001	.000
7	.000	.014	.081	.177	.196	.118	.035	.003	.000
8	.000	.003	.035	.118	.196	.177	.081	.014	.000
9	.000	.001	.012	.061	.153	.207	.147	.043	.002
10	.000	.000	.003	.024	.092	.186	.206	.103	.010
11	.000	.000	.001	.007	.042	.127	.219	.188	.043
12	.000	.000	.000	.002	.014	.063	.170	.250	.129
13	.000	.000	.000	.000	.003	.022	.092	.231	.267
14	.000	.000	.000	.000	.000	.005	.031	.132	.343
15	.000	.000	.000	.000	.000	.000	.005	.035	.206

Table A.2

Binomial Probability Distribution (*Continued*)

					n = 16				
					Probability				
x	.1	.2	.3	.4	.5	.6	.7	.8	.9
0	.185	.028	.003	.000	.000	.000	.000	.000	.000
1	.329	.113	.023	.003	.000	.000	.000	.000	.000
2	.275	.211	.073	.015	.002	.000	.000	.000	.000
3	.142	.246	.146	.047	.009	.001	.000	.000	.000
4	.051	.200	.204	.101	.028	.004	.000	.000	.000
5	.014	.120	.210	.162	.067	.014	.001	.000	.000
6	.003	.055	.165	.198	.122	.039	.006	.000	.000
7	.000	.020	.101	.189	.175	.084	.019	.001	.000
8	.000	.006	.049	.142	.196	.142	.049	.006	.000
9	.000	.001	.019	.084	.175	.189	.101	.020	.000
10	.000	.000	.006	.039	.122	.198	.165	.055	.003
11	.000	.000	.001	.014	.067	.162	.210	.120	.014
12	.000	.000	.000	.004	.028	.101	.204	.200	.051
13	.000	.000	.000	.001	.009	.047	.146	.246	.142
14	.000	.000	.000	.000	.002	.015	.073	.211	.275
15	.000	.000	.000	.000	.000	.003	.023	.113	.329
16	.000	.000	.000	.000	.000	.000	.003	.028	.185

					n = 17				
					Probability				
x	.1	.2	.3	.4	.5	.6	.7	.8	.9
0	.167	.023	.002	.000	.000	.000	.000	.000	.000
1	.315	.096	.017	.002	.000	.000	.000	.000	.000
2	.280	.191	.058	.010	.001	.000	.000	.000	.000
3	.156	.239	.125	.034	.005	.000	.000	.000	.000
4	.060	.209	.187	.080	.018	.002	.000	.000	.000
5	.017	.136	.208	.138	.047	.008	.001	.000	.000
6	.004	.068	.178	.184	.094	.024	.003	.000	.000
7	.001	.027	.120	.193	.148	.057	.009	.000	.000
8	.000	.008	.064	.161	.185	.107	.028	.002	.000
9	.000	.002	.028	.107	.185	.161	.064	.008	.000
10	.000	.000	.009	.057	.148	.193	.120	.027	.001
11	.000	.000	.003	.024	.094	.184	.178	.068	.004
12	.000	.000	.001	.008	.047	.138	.208	.136	.017
13	.000	.000	.000	.002	.018	.080	.187	.209	.060
14	.000	.000	.000	.000	.005	.034	.125	.239	.156
15	.000	.000	.000	.000	.001	.010	.058	.191	.280
16	.000	.000	.000	.000	.000	.002	.017	.096	.315
17	.000	.000	.000	.000	.000	.000	.002	.023	.167

(continued)

Table A.2

Binomial Probability Distribution (*Continued*)

n = 18

Probability

x	.1	.2	.3	.4	.5	.6	.7	.8	.9
0	.150	.018	.002	.000	.000	.000	.000	.000	.000
1	.300	.081	.013	.001	.000	.000	.000	.000	.000
2	.284	.172	.046	.007	.001	.000	.000	.000	.000
3	.168	.230	.105	.025	.003	.000	.000	.000	.000
4	.070	.215	.168	.061	.012	.001	.000	.000	.000
5	.022	.151	.202	.115	.033	.004	.000	.000	.000
6	.005	.082	.187	.166	.071	.015	.001	.000	.000
7	.001	.035	.138	.189	.121	.037	.005	.000	.000
8	.000	.012	.081	.173	.167	.077	.015	.001	.000
9	.000	.003	.039	.128	.185	.128	.039	.003	.000
10	.000	.001	.015	.077	.167	.173	.081	.012	.000
11	.000	.000	.005	.037	.121	.189	.138	.035	.001
12	.000	.000	.001	.015	.071	.166	.187	.082	.005
13	.000	.000	.000	.004	.033	.115	.202	.151	.022
14	.000	.000	.000	.001	.012	.061	.168	.215	.070
15	.000	.000	.000	.000	.003	.025	.105	.230	.168
16	.000	.000	.000	.000	.001	.007	.046	.172	.284
17	.000	.000	.000	.000	.000	.001	.013	.081	.300
18	.000	.000	.000	.000	.000	.000	.002	.018	.150

n = 19

Probability

x	.1	.2	.3	.4	.5	.6	.7	.8	.9
0	.135	.014	.001	.000	.000	.000	.000	.000	.000
1	.285	.068	.009	.001	.000	.000	.000	.000	.000
2	.285	.154	.036	.005	.000	.000	.000	.000	.000
3	.180	.218	.087	.017	.002	.000	.000	.000	.000
4	.080	.218	.149	.047	.007	.001	.000	.000	.000
5	.027	.164	.192	.093	.022	.002	.000	.000	.000
6	.007	.095	.192	.145	.052	.008	.001	.000	.000
7	.001	.044	.153	.180	.096	.024	.002	.000	.000
8	.000	.017	.098	.180	.144	.053	.008	.000	.000
9	.000	.005	.051	.146	.176	.098	.022	.001	.000
10	.000	.001	.022	.098	.176	.146	.051	.005	.000
11	.000	.000	.008	.053	.144	.180	.098	.017	.000
12	.000	.000	.002	.024	.096	.180	.153	.044	.001
13	.000	.000	.001	.008	.052	.145	.192	.095	.007
14	.000	.000	.000	.002	.022	.093	.192	.164	.027
15	.000	.000	.000	.001	.007	.047	.149	.218	.080
16	.000	.000	.000	.000	.002	.017	.087	.218	.180
17	.000	.000	.000	.000	.000	.005	.036	.154	.285
18	.000	.000	.000	.000	.000	.001	.009	.068	.285
19	.000	.000	.000	.000	.000	.000	.001	.014	.135

Table A.2

Binomial Probability Distribution (*Continued*)

n = 20

x	.1	.2	.3	.4	.5	.6	.7	.8	.9
0	.122	.012	.001	.000	.000	.000	.000	.000	.000
1	.270	.058	.007	.000	.000	.000	.000	.000	.000
2	.285	.137	.028	.003	.000	.000	.000	.000	.000
3	.190	.205	.072	.012	.001	.000	.000	.000	.000
4	.090	.218	.130	.035	.005	.000	.000	.000	.000
5	.032	.175	.179	.075	.015	.001	.000	.000	.000
6	.009	.109	.192	.124	.037	.005	.000	.000	.000
7	.002	.055	.164	.166	.074	.015	.001	.000	.000
8	.000	.022	.114	.180	.120	.035	.004	.000	.000
9	.000	.007	.065	.160	.160	.071	.012	.000	.000
10	.000	.002	.031	.117	.176	.117	.031	.002	.000
11	.000	.000	.012	.071	.160	.160	.065	.007	.000
12	.000	.000	.004	.035	.120	.180	.114	.022	.000
13	.000	.000	.001	.015	.074	.166	.164	.055	.002
14	.000	.000	.000	.005	.037	.124	.192	.109	.009
15	.000	.000	.000	.001	.015	.075	.179	.175	.032
16	.000	.000	.000	.000	.005	.035	.130	.218	.090
17	.000	.000	.000	.000	.001	.012	.072	.205	.190
18	.000	.000	.000	.000	.000	.003	.028	.137	.285
19	.000	.000	.000	.000	.000	.000	.007	.058	.270
20	.000	.000	.000	.000	.000	.000	.001	.012	.122

n = 25

x	.1	.2	.3	.4	.5	.6	.7	.8	.9
0	.072	.004	.000	.000	.000	.000	.000	.000	.000
1	.199	.024	.001	.000	.000	.000	.000	.000	.000
2	.266	.071	.007	.000	.000	.000	.000	.000	.000
3	.226	.136	.024	.002	.000	.000	.000	.000	.000
4	.138	.187	.057	.007	.000	.000	.000	.000	.000
5	.065	.196	.103	.020	.002	.000	.000	.000	.000
6	.024	.163	.147	.044	.005	.000	.000	.000	.000
7	.007	.111	.171	.080	.014	.001	.000	.000	.000
8	.002	.062	.165	.120	.032	.003	.000	.000	.000
9	.000	.029	.134	.151	.061	.009	.000	.000	.000
10	.000	.012	.092	.161	.097	.021	.001	.000	.000
11	.000	.004	.054	.147	.133	.043	.004	.000	.000
12	.000	.001	.027	.114	.155	.076	.011	.000	.000
13	.000	.000	.011	.076	.155	.114	.027	.001	.000
14	.000	.000	.004	.043	.133	.147	.054	.004	.000
15	.000	.000	.001	.021	.097	.161	.092	.012	.000
16	.000	.000	.000	.009	.061	.151	.134	.029	.000
17	.000	.000	.000	.003	.032	.120	.165	.062	.002
18	.000	.000	.000	.001	.014	.080	.171	.111	.007
19	.000	.000	.000	.000	.005	.044	.147	.163	.024
20	.000	.000	.000	.000	.002	.020	.103	.196	.065
21	.000	.000	.000	.000	.000	.007	.057	.187	.138
22	.000	.000	.000	.000	.000	.002	.024	.136	.226
23	.000	.000	.000	.000	.000	.000	.007	.071	.266
24	.000	.000	.000	.000	.000	.000	.001	.024	.199
25	.000	.000	.000	.000	.000	.000	.000	.004	.072

Table A.3

Poisson Probabilities

					λ					
x	.005	.01	.02	.03	.04	.05	.06	.07	.08	.09
0	.9950	.9900	.9802	.9704	.9608	.9512	.9418	.9324	.9231	.9139
1	.0050	.0099	.0196	.0291	.0384	.0476	.0565	.0653	.0738	.0823
2	.0000	.0000	.0002	.0004	.0008	.0012	.0017	.0023	.0030	.0037
3	.0000	.0000	.0000	.0000	.0000	.0000	.0000	.0001	.0001	.0001

x	.1	.2	.3	.4	.5	.6	.7	.8	.9	1.0
0	.9048	.8187	.7408	.6703	.6065	.5488	.4966	.4493	.4066	.3679
1	.0905	.1637	.2222	.2681	.3033	.3293	.3476	.3595	.3659	.3679
2	.0045	.0164	.0333	.0536	.0758	.0988	.1217	.1438	.1647	.1839
3	.0002	.0011	.0033	.0072	.0126	.0198	.0284	.0383	.0494	.0613
4	.0000	.0001	.0003	.0007	.0016	.0030	.0050	.0077	.0111	.0153
5	.0000	.0000	.0000	.0001	.0002	.0004	.0007	.0012	.0020	.0031
6	.0000	.0000	.0000	.0000	.0000	.0000	.0001	.0002	.0003	.0005
7	.0000	.0000	.0000	.0000	.0000	.0000	.0000	.0000	.0000	.0001

x	1.1	1.2	1.3	1.4	1.5	1.6	1.7	1.8	1.9	2.0
0	.3329	.3012	.2725	.2466	.2231	.2019	.1827	.1653	.1496	.1353
1	.3662	.3614	.3543	.3452	.3347	.3230	.3106	.2975	.2842	.2707
2	.2014	.2169	.2303	.2417	.2510	.2584	.2640	.2678	.2700	.2707
3	.0738	.0867	.0998	.1128	.1255	.1378	.1496	.1607	.1710	.1804
4	.0203	.0260	.0324	.0395	.0471	.0551	.0636	.0723	.0812	.0902
5	.0045	.0062	.0084	.0111	.0141	.0176	.0216	.0260	.0309	.0361
6	.0008	.0012	.0018	.0026	.0035	.0047	.0061	.0078	.0098	.0120
7	.0001	.0002	.0003	.0005	.0008	.0011	.0015	.0020	.0027	.0034
8	.0000	.0000	.0001	.0001	.0001	.0002	.0003	.0005	.0006	.0009
9	.0000	.0000	.0000	.0000	.0000	.0000	.0001	.0001	.0001	.0002

x	2.1	2.2	2.3	2.4	2.5	2.6	2.7	2.8	2.9	3.0
0	.1225	.1108	.1003	.0907	.0821	.0743	.0672	.0608	.0550	.0498
1	.2572	.2438	.2306	.2177	.2052	.1931	.1815	.1703	.1596	.1494
2	.2700	.2681	.2652	.2613	.2565	.2510	.2450	.2384	.2314	.2240
3	.1890	.1966	.2033	.2090	.2138	.2176	.2205	.2225	.2237	.2240
4	.0992	.1082	.1169	.1254	.1336	.1414	.1488	.1557	.1622	.1680
5	.0417	.0476	.0538	.0602	.0668	.0735	.0804	.0872	.0940	.1008
6	.0146	.0174	.0206	.0241	.0278	.0319	.0362	.0407	.0455	.0504
7	.0044	.0055	.0068	.0083	.0099	.0118	.0139	.0163	.0188	.0216
8	.0011	.0015	.0019	.0025	.0031	.0038	.0047	.0057	.0068	.0081
9	.0003	.0004	.0005	.0007	.0009	.0011	.0014	.0018	.0022	.0027
10	.0001	.0001	.0001	.0002	.0002	.0003	.0004	.0005	.0006	.0008
11	.0000	.0000	.0000	.0000	.0000	.0001	.0001	.0001	.0002	.0002
12	.0000	.0000	.0000	.0000	.0000	.0000	.0000	.0000	.0000	.0001

Table A.3

Poisson Probabilities
(*Continued*)

					λ					
x	**3.1**	**3.2**	**3.3**	**3.4**	**3.5**	**3.6**	**3.7**	**3.8**	**3.9**	**4.0**
0	.0450	.0408	.0369	.0334	.0302	.0273	.0247	.0224	.0202	.0183
1	.1397	.1304	.1217	.1135	.1057	.0984	.0915	.0850	.0789	.0733
2	.2165	.2087	.2008	.1929	.1850	.1771	.1692	.1615	.1539	.1465
3	.2237	.2226	.2209	.2186	.2158	.2125	.2087	.2046	.2001	.1954
4	.1733	.1781	.1823	.1858	.1888	.1912	.1931	.1944	.1951	.1954
5	.1075	.1140	.1203	.1264	.1322	.1377	.1429	.1477	.1522	.1563
6	.0555	.0608	.0662	.0716	.0771	.0826	.0881	.0936	.0989	.1042
7	.0246	.0278	.0312	.0348	.0385	.0425	.0466	.0508	.0551	.0595
8	.0095	.0111	.0129	.0148	.0169	.0191	.0215	.0241	.0269	.0298
9	.0033	.0040	.0047	.0056	.0066	.0076	.0089	.0102	.0116	.0132
10	.0010	.0013	.0016	.0019	.0023	.0028	.0033	.0039	.0045	.0053
11	.0003	.0004	.0005	.0006	.0007	.0009	.0011	.0013	.0016	.0019
12	.0001	.0001	.0001	.0002	.0002	.0003	.0003	.0004	.0005	.0006
13	.0000	.0000	.0000	.0000	.0001	.0001	.0001	.0001	.0002	.0002
14	.0000	.0000	.0000	.0000	.0000	.0000	.0000	.0000	.0000	.0001

x	**4.1**	**4.2**	**4.3**	**4.4**	**4.5**	**4.6**	**4.7**	**4.8**	**4.9**	**5.0**
0	.0166	.0150	.0136	.0123	.0111	.0101	.0091	.0082	.0074	.0067
1	.0679	.0630	.0583	.0540	.0500	.0462	.0427	.0395	.0365	.0337
2	.1393	.1323	.1254	.1188	.1125	.1063	.1005	.0948	.0894	.0842
3	.1904	.1852	.1798	.1743	.1687	.1631	.1574	.1517	.1460	.1404
4	.1951	.1944	.1933	.1917	.1898	.1875	.1849	.1820	.1789	.1755
5	.1600	.1633	.1662	.1687	.1708	.1725	.1738	.1747	.1753	.1755
6	.1093	.1143	.1191	.1237	.1281	.1323	.1362	.1398	.1432	.1462
7	.0640	.0686	.0732	.0778	.0824	.0869	.0914	.0959	.1002	.1044
8	.0328	.0360	.0393	.0428	.0463	.0500	.0537	.0575	.0614	.0653
9	.0150	.0168	.0188	.0209	.0232	.0255	.0281	.0307	.0334	.0363
10	.0061	.0071	.0081	.0092	.0104	.0118	.0132	.0147	.0164	.0181
11	.0023	.0027	.0032	.0037	.0043	.0049	.0056	.0064	.0073	.0082
12	.0008	.0009	.0011	.0013	.0016	.0019	.0022	.0026	.0030	.0034
13	.0002	.0003	.0004	.0005	.0006	.0007	.0008	.0009	.0011	.0013
14	.0001	.0001	.0001	.0001	.0002	.0002	.0003	.0003	.0004	.0005
15	.0000	.0000	.0000	.0000	.0001	.0001	.0001	.0001	.0001	.0002

(*continued*)

Table A.3

Poisson Probabilities
(*Continued*)

					λ					
x	5.1	5.2	5.3	5.4	5.5	5.6	5.7	5.8	5.9	6.0
0	.0061	.0055	.0050	.0045	.0041	.0037	.0033	.0030	.0027	.0025
1	.0311	.0287	.0265	.0244	.0225	.0207	.0191	.0176	.0162	.0149
2	.0793	.0746	.0701	.0659	.0618	.0580	.0544	.0509	.0477	.0446
3	.1348	.1293	.1239	.1185	.1133	.1082	.1033	.0985	.0938	.0892
4	.1719	.1681	.1641	.1600	.1558	.1515	.1472	.1428	.1383	.1339
5	.1753	.1748	.1740	.1728	.1714	.1697	.1678	.1656	.1632	.1606
6	.1490	.1515	.1537	.1555	.1571	.1584	.1594	.1601	.1605	.1606
7	.1086	.1125	.1163	.1200	.1234	.1267	.1298	.1326	.1353	.1377
8	.0692	.0731	.0771	.0810	.0849	.0887	.0925	.0962	.0998	.1033
9	.0392	.0423	.0454	.0486	.0519	.0552	.0586	.0620	.0654	.0688
10	.0200	.0220	.0241	.0262	.0285	.0309	.0334	.0359	.0386	.0413
11	.0093	.0104	.0116	.0129	.0143	.0157	.0173	.0190	.0207	.0225
12	.0039	.0045	.0051	.0058	.0065	.0073	.0082	.0092	.0102	.0113
13	.0015	.0018	.0021	.0024	.0028	.0032	.0036	.0041	.0046	.0052
14	.0006	.0007	.0008	.0009	.0011	.0013	.0015	.0017	.0019	.0022
15	.0002	.0002	.0003	.0003	.0004	.0005	.0006	.0007	.0008	.0009
16	.0001	.0001	.0001	.0001	.0001	.0002	.0002	.0002	.0003	.0003
17	.0000	.0000	.0000	.0000	.0000	.0001	.0001	.0001	.0001	.0001

x	6.1	6.2	6.3	6.4	6.5	6.6	6.7	6.8	6.9	7.0
0	.0022	.0020	.0018	.0017	.0015	.0014	.0012	.0011	.0010	.0009
1	.0137	.0126	.0116	.0106	.0098	.0090	.0082	.0076	.0070	.0064
2	.0417	.0390	.0364	.0340	.0318	.0296	.0276	.0258	.0240	.0223
3	.0848	.0806	.0765	.0726	.0688	.0652	.0617	.0584	.0552	.0521
4	.1294	.1249	.1205	.1162	.1118	.1076	.1034	.0992	.0952	.0912
5	.1579	.1549	.1519	.1487	.1454	.1420	.1385	.1349	.1314	.1277
6	.1605	.1601	.1595	.1586	.1575	.1562	.1546	.1529	.1511	.1490
7	.1399	.1418	.1435	.1450	.1462	.1472	.1480	.1486	.1489	.1490
8	.1066	.1099	.1130	.1160	.1188	.1215	.1240	.1263	.1284	.1304
9	.0723	.0757	.0791	.0825	.0858	.0891	.0923	.0954	.0985	.1014
10	.0441	.0469	.0498	.0528	.0558	.0588	.0618	.0649	.0679	.0710
11	.0244	.0265	.0285	.0307	.0330	.0353	.0377	.0401	.0426	.0452
12	.0124	.0137	.0150	.0164	.0179	.0194	.0210	.0227	.0245	.0263
13	.0058	.0065	.0073	.0081	.0089	.0099	.0108	.0119	.0130	.0142
14	.0025	.0029	.0033	.0037	.0041	.0046	.0052	.0058	.0064	.0071
15	.0010	.0012	.0014	.0016	.0018	.0020	.0023	.0026	.0029	.0033
16	.0004	.0005	.0005	.0006	.0007	.0008	.0010	.0011	.0013	.0014
17	.0001	.0002	.0002	.0002	.0003	.0003	.0004	.0004	.0005	.0006
18	.0000	.0001	.0001	.0001	.0001	.0001	.0001	.0002	.0002	.0002
19	.0000	.0000	.0000	.0000	.0000	.0000	.0001	.0001	.0001	.0001

Table A.3

Poisson Probabilities
(*Continued*)

x						λ				
	7.1	7.2	7.3	7.4	7.5	7.6	7.7	7.8	7.9	8.0
0	.0008	.0007	.0007	.0006	.0006	.0005	.0005	.0004	.0004	.0003
1	.0059	.0054	.0049	.0045	.0041	.0038	.0035	.0032	.0029	.0027
2	.0208	.0194	.0180	.0167	.0156	.0145	.0134	.0125	.0116	.0107
3	.0492	.0464	.0438	.0413	.0389	.0366	.0345	.0324	.0305	.0286
4	.0874	.0836	.0799	.0764	.0729	.0696	.0663	.0632	.0602	.0573
5	.1241	.1204	.1167	.1130	.1094	.1057	.1021	.0986	.0951	.0916
6	.1468	.1445	.1420	.1394	.1367	.1339	.1311	.1282	.1252	.1221
7	.1489	.1486	.1481	.1474	.1465	.1454	.1442	.1428	.1413	.1396
8	.1321	.1337	.1351	.1363	.1373	.1381	.1388	.1392	.1395	.1396
9	.1042	.1070	.1096	.1121	.1144	.1167	.1187	.1207	.1224	.1241
10	.0740	.0770	.0800	.0829	.0858	.0887	.0914	.0941	.0967	.0993
11	.0478	.0504	.0531	.0558	.0585	.0613	.0640	.0667	.0695	.0722
12	.0283	.0303	.0323	.0344	.0366	.0388	.0411	.0434	.0457	.0481
13	.0154	.0168	.0181	.0196	.0211	.0227	.0243	.0260	.0278	.0296
14	.0078	.0086	.0095	.0104	.0113	.0123	.0134	.0145	.0157	.0169
15	.0037	.0041	.0046	.0051	.0057	.0062	.0069	.0075	.0083	.0090
16	.0016	.0019	.0021	.0024	.0026	.0030	.0033	.0037	.0041	.0045
17	.0007	.0008	.0009	.0010	.0012	.0013	.0015	.0017	.0019	.0021
18	.0003	.0003	.0004	.0004	.0005	.0006	.0006	.0007	.0008	.0009
19	.0001	.0001	.0001	.0002	.0002	.0002	.0003	.0003	.0003	.0004
20	.0000	.0000	.0001	.0001	.0001	.0001	.0001	.0001	.0001	.0002
21	.0000	.0000	.0000	.0000	.0000	.0000	.0000	.0000	.0001	.0001

x	8.1	8.2	8.3	8.4	8.5	8.6	8.7	8.8	8.9	9.0
0	.0003	.0003	.0002	.0002	.0002	.0002	.0002	.0002	.0001	.0001
1	.0025	.0023	.0021	.0019	.0017	.0016	.0014	.0013	.0012	.0011
2	.0100	.0092	.0086	.0079	.0074	.0068	.0063	.0058	.0054	.0050
3	.0269	.0252	.0237	.0222	.0208	.0195	.0183	.0171	.0160	.0150
4	.0544	.0517	.0491	.0466	.0443	.0420	.0398	.0377	.0357	.0337
5	.0882	.0849	.0816	.0784	.0752	.0722	.0692	.0663	.0635	.0607
6	.1191	.1160	.1128	.1097	.1066	.1034	.1003	.0972	.0941	.0911
7	.1378	.1358	.1338	.1317	.1294	.1271	.1247	.1222	.1197	.1171
8	.1395	.1392	.1388	.1382	.1375	.1366	.1356	.1344	.1332	.1318
9	.1256	.1269	.1280	.1290	.1299	.1306	.1311	.1315	.1317	.1318
10	.1017	.1040	.1063	.1084	.1104	.1123	.1140	.1157	.1172	.1186
11	.0749	.0776	.0802	.0828	.0853	.0878	.0902	.0925	.0948	.0970
12	.0505	.0530	.0555	.0579	.0604	.0629	.0654	.0679	.0703	.0728
13	.0315	.0334	.0354	.0374	.0395	.0416	.0438	.0459	.0481	.0504
14	.0182	.0196	.0210	.0225	.0240	.0256	.0272	.0289	.0306	.0324
15	.0098	.0107	.0116	.0126	.0136	.0147	.0158	.0169	.0182	.0194
16	.0050	.0055	.0060	.0066	.0072	.0079	.0086	.0093	.0101	.0109
17	.0024	.0026	.0029	.0033	.0036	.0040	.0044	.0048	.0053	.0058
18	.0011	.0012	.0014	.0015	.0017	.0019	.0021	.0024	.0026	.0029
19	.0005	.0005	.0006	.0007	.0008	.0009	.0010	.0011	.0012	.0014
20	.0002	.0002	.0002	.0003	.0003	.0004	.0004	.0005	.0005	.0006
21	.0001	.0001	.0001	.0001	.0001	.0002	.0002	.0002	.0002	.0003
22	.0000	.0000	.0000	.0000	.0001	.0001	.0001	.0001	.0001	.0001

(continued)

Table A.3

Poisson Probabilities
(*Continued*)

					λ					
x	9.1	9.2	9.3	9.4	9.5	9.6	9.7	9.8	9.9	10.0
0	.0001	.0001	.0001	.0001	.0001	.0001	.0001	.0001	.0001	.0000
1	.0010	.0009	.0009	.0008	.0007	.0007	.0006	.0005	.0005	.0005
2	.0046	.0043	.0040	.0037	.0034	.0031	.0029	.0027	.0025	.0023
3	.0140	.0131	.0123	.0115	.0107	.0100	.0093	.0087	.0081	.0076
4	.0319	.0302	.0285	.0269	.0254	.0240	.0226	.0213	.0201	.0189
5	.0581	.0555	.0530	.0506	.0483	.0460	.0439	.0418	.0398	.0378
6	.0881	.0851	.0822	.0793	.0764	.0736	.0709	.0682	.0656	.0631
7	.1145	.1118	.1091	.1064	.1037	.1010	.0982	.0955	.0928	.0901
8	.1302	.1286	.1269	.1251	.1232	.1212	.1191	.1170	.1148	.1126
9	.1317	.1315	.1311	.1306	.1300	.1293	.1284	.1274	.1263	.1251
10	.1198	.1210	.1219	.1228	.1235	.1241	.1245	.1249	.1250	.1251
11	.0991	.1012	.1031	.1049	.1067	.1083	.1098	.1112	.1125	.1137
12	.0752	.0776	.0799	.0822	.0844	.0866	.0888	.0908	.0928	.0948
13	.0526	.0549	.0572	.0594	.0617	.0640	.0662	.0685	.0707	.0729
14	.0342	.0361	.0380	.0399	.0419	.0439	.0459	.0479	.0500	.0521
15	.0208	.0221	.0235	.0250	.0265	.0281	.0297	.0313	.0330	.0347
16	.0118	.0127	.0137	.0147	.0157	.0168	.0180	.0192	.0204	.0217
17	.0063	.0069	.0075	.0081	.0088	.0095	.0103	.0111	.0119	.0128
18	.0032	.0035	.0039	.0042	.0046	.0051	.0055	.0060	.0065	.0071
19	.0015	.0017	.0019	.0021	.0023	.0026	.0028	.0031	.0034	.0037
20	.0007	.0008	.0009	.0010	.0011	.0012	.0014	.0015	.0017	.0019
21	.0003	.0003	.0004	.0004	.0005	.0006	.0006	.0007	.0008	.0009
22	.0001	.0001	.0002	.0002	.0002	.0002	.0003	.0003	.0004	.0004
23	.0000	.0001	.0001	.0001	.0001	.0001	.0001	.0001	.0002	.0002
24	.0000	.0000	.0000	.0000	.0000	.0000	.0000	.0001	.0001	.0001

Table A.4

The e^{-x} Table

x	e^{-x}	x	e^{-x}	x	e^{-x}	x	e^{-x}
0.0	1.0000	3.0	0.0498	6.0	0.00248	9.0	0.00012
0.1	0.9048	3.1	0.0450	6.1	0.00224	9.1	0.00011
0.2	0.8187	3.2	0.0408	6.2	0.00203	9.2	0.00010
0.3	0.7408	3.3	0.0369	6.3	0.00184	9.3	0.00009
0.4	0.6703	3.4	0.0334	6.4	0.00166	9.4	0.00008
0.5	0.6065	3.5	0.0302	6.5	0.00150	9.5	0.00007
0.6	0.5488	3.6	0.0273	6.6	0.00136	9.6	0.00007
0.7	0.4966	3.7	0.0247	6.7	0.00123	9.7	0.00006
0.8	0.4493	3.8	0.0224	6.8	0.00111	9.8	0.00006
0.9	0.4066	3.9	0.0202	6.9	0.00101	9.9	0.00005
1.0	0.3679	4.0	0.0183	7.0	0.00091	10.0	0.00005
1.1	0.3329	4.1	0.0166	7.1	0.00083		
1.2	0.3012	4.2	0.0150	7.2	0.00075		
1.3	0.2725	4.3	0.0136	7.3	0.00068		
1.4	0.2466	4.4	0.0123	7.4	0.00061		
1.5	0.2231	4.5	0.0111	7.5	0.00055		
1.6	0.2019	4.6	0.0101	7.6	0.00050		
1.7	0.1827	4.7	0.0091	7.7	0.00045		
1.8	0.1653	4.8	0.0082	7.8	0.00041		
1.9	0.1496	4.9	0.0074	7.9	0.00037		
2.0	0.1353	5.0	0.0067	8.0	0.00034		
2.1	0.1225	5.1	0.0061	8.1	0.00030		
2.2	0.1108	5.2	0.0055	8.2	0.00027		
2.3	0.1003	5.3	0.0050	8.3	0.00025		
2.4	0.0907	5.4	0.0045	8.4	0.00022		
2.5	0.0821	5.5	0.0041	8.5	0.00020		
2.6	0.0743	5.6	0.0037	8.6	0.00018		
2.7	0.0672	5.7	0.0033	8.7	0.00017		
2.8	0.0608	5.8	0.0030	8.8	0.00015		
2.9	0.0550	5.9	0.0027	8.9	0.00014		

Areas of the Standard Normal Distribution

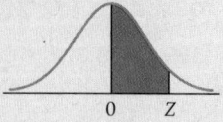

The entries in this table are the probabilities that a standard normal random variable is between 0 and z (the shaded area).

z	0.00	0.01	0.02	0.03	0.04	0.05	0.06	0.07	0.08	0.09
0.0	.0000	.0040	.0080	.0120	.0160	.0199	.0239	.0279	.0319	.0359
0.1	.0398	.0438	.0478	.0517	.0557	.0596	.0636	.0675	.0714	.0753
0.2	.0793	.0832	.0871	.0910	.0948	.0987	.1026	.1064	.1103	.1141
0.3	.1179	.1217	.1255	.1293	.1331	.1368	.1406	.1443	.1480	.1517
0.4	.1554	.1591	.1628	.1664	.1700	.1736	.1772	.1808	.1844	.1879
0.5	.1915	.1950	.1985	.2019	.2054	.2088	.2123	.2157	.2190	.2224
0.6	.2257	.2291	.2324	.2357	.2389	.2422	.2454	.2486	.2517	.2549
0.7	.2580	.2611	.2642	.2673	.2704	.2734	.2764	.2794	.2823	.2852
0.8	.2881	.2910	.2939	.2967	.2995	.3023	.3051	.3078	.3106	.3133
0.9	.3159	.3186	.3212	.3238	.3264	.3289	.3315	.3340	.3365	.3389
1.0	.3413	.3438	.3461	.3485	.3508	.3531	.3554	.3577	.3599	.3621
1.1	.3643	.3665	.3686	.3708	.3729	.3749	.3770	.3790	.3810	.3830
1.2	.3849	.3869	.3888	.3907	.3925	.3944	.3962	.3980	.3997	.4015
1.3	.4032	.4049	.4066	.4082	.4099	.4115	.4131	.4147	.4162	.4177
1.4	.4192	.4207	.4222	.4236	.4251	.4265	.4279	.4292	.4306	.4319
1.5	.4332	.4345	.4357	.4370	.4382	.4394	.4406	.4418	.4429	.4441
1.6	.4452	.4463	.4474	.4484	.4495	.4505	.4515	.4525	.4535	.4545
1.7	.4554	.4564	.4573	.4582	.4591	.4599	.4608	.4616	.4625	.4633
1.8	.4641	.4649	.4656	.4664	.4671	.4678	.4686	.4693	.4699	.4706
1.9	.4713	.4719	.4726	.4732	.4738	.4744	.4750	.4756	.4761	.4767
2.0	.4772	.4778	.4783	.4788	.4793	.4798	.4803	.4808	.4812	.4817
2.1	.4821	.4826	.4830	.4834	.4838	.4842	.4846	.4850	.4854	.4857
2.2	.4861	.4864	.4868	.4871	.4875	.4878	.4881	.4884	.4887	.4890
2.3	.4893	.4896	.4898	.4901	.4904	.4906	.4909	.4911	.4913	.4916
2.4	.4918	.4920	.4922	.4925	.4927	.4929	.4931	.4932	.4934	.4936
2.5	.4938	.4940	.4941	.4943	.4945	.4946	.4948	.4949	.4951	.4952
2.6	.4953	.4955	.4956	.4957	.4959	.4960	.4961	.4962	.4963	.4964
2.7	.4965	.4966	.4967	.4968	.4969	.4970	.4971	.4972	.4973	.4974
2.8	.4974	.4975	.4976	.4977	.4977	.4978	.4979	.4979	.4980	.4981
2.9	.4981	.4982	.4982	.4983	.4984	.4984	.4985	.4985	.4986	.4986
3.0	.4987	.4987	.4987	.4988	.4988	.4989	.4989	.4989	.4990	.4990
3.1	.4990	.4991	.4991	.4991	.4992	.4992	.4992	.4992	.4993	.4993
3.2	.4993	.4993	.4994	.4994	.4994	.4994	.4994	.4995	.4995	.4995
3.3	.4995	.4995	.4995	.4996	.4996	.4996	.4996	.4996	.4996	.4997
3.4	.4997	.4997	.4997	.4997	.4997	.4997	.4997	.4997	.4997	.4998
3.5	.4998									
4.0	.49997									
4.5	.499997									
5.0	.4999997									
6.0	.499999999									

Critical Values from the *t* Distribution

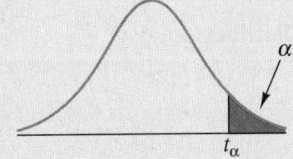

	Values of α for one-tailed test and α/2 for two-tailed test					
df	$t_{.100}$	$t_{.050}$	$t_{.025}$	$t_{.010}$	$t_{.005}$	$t_{.001}$
1	3.078	6.314	12.706	31.821	63.656	318.289
2	1.886	2.920	4.303	6.965	9.925	22.328
3	1.638	2.353	3.182	4.541	5.841	10.214
4	1.533	2.132	2.776	3.747	4.604	7.173
5	1.476	2.015	2.571	3.365	4.032	5.894
6	1.440	1.943	2.447	3.143	3.707	5.208
7	1.415	1.895	2.365	2.998	3.499	4.785
8	1.397	1.860	2.306	2.896	3.355	4.501
9	1.383	1.833	2.262	2.821	3.250	4.297
10	1.372	1.812	2.228	2.764	3.169	4.144
11	1.363	1.796	2.201	2.718	3.106	4.025
12	1.356	1.782	2.179	2.681	3.055	3.930
13	1.350	1.771	2.160	2.650	3.012	3.852
14	1.345	1.761	2.145	2.624	2.977	3.787
15	1.341	1.753	2.131	2.602	2.947	3.733
16	1.337	1.746	2.120	2.583	2.921	3.686
17	1.333	1.740	2.110	2.567	2.898	3.646
18	1.330	1.734	2.101	2.552	2.878	3.610
19	1.328	1.729	2.093	2.539	2.861	3.579
20	1.325	1.725	2.086	2.528	2.845	3.552
21	1.323	1.721	2.080	2.518	2.831	3.527
22	1.321	1.717	2.074	2.508	2.819	3.505
23	1.319	1.714	2.069	2.500	2.807	3.485
24	1.318	1.711	2.064	2.492	2.797	3.467
25	1.316	1.708	2.060	2.485	2.787	3.450
26	1.315	1.706	2.056	2.479	2.779	3.435
27	1.314	1.703	2.052	2.473	2.771	3.421
28	1.313	1.701	2.048	2.467	2.763	3.408
29	1.311	1.699	2.045	2.462	2.756	3.396
30	1.310	1.697	2.042	2.457	2.750	3.385
40	1.303	1.684	2.021	2.423	2.704	3.307
50	1.299	1.676	2.009	2.403	2.678	3.261
60	1.296	1.671	2.000	2.390	2.660	3.232
70	1.294	1.667	1.994	2.381	2.648	3.211
80	1.292	1.664	1.990	2.374	2.639	3.195
90	1.291	1.662	1.987	2.368	2.632	3.183
100	1.290	1.660	1.984	2.364	2.626	3.174
150	1.287	1.655	1.976	2.351	2.609	3.145
200	1.286	1.653	1.972	2.345	2.601	3.131
∞	1.282	1.645	1.960	2.326	2.576	3.090

Table A.7

Percentage Points of the F Distribution

| v_1 | | | | | $\alpha = .10$ | | | | |

Numerator Degrees of Freedom

v_2	1	2	3	4	5	6	7	8	9
1	39.86	49.50	53.59	55.83	57.24	58.20	58.91	59.44	59.86
2	8.53	3.00	9.16	9.24	9.29	9.33	9.35	9.37	9.38
3	5.54	5.46	5.39	5.34	5.31	5.28	5.27	5.25	5.24
4	4.54	4.32	4.19	4.11	4.05	4.01	3.98	3.95	3.94
5	4.06	4.78	3.62	3.52	3.45	3.40	3.37	3.34	3.32
6	3.78	3.46	3.29	3.18	3.11	3.05	3.01	2.98	2.96
7	3.59	3.26	3.07	2.96	2.88	2.83	2.78	2.75	2.72
8	3.46	3.11	2.92	2.81	2.73	2.67	2.62	2.59	2.56
9	3.36	3.01	2.81	2.69	2.61	2.55	2.51	2.47	2.44
10	3.29	2.92	2.73	2.61	2.52	2.46	2.41	2.38	2.35
11	3.23	2.86	2.66	2.54	2.45	2.39	2.34	2.30	2.27
12	3.18	2.81	2.61	2.48	2.39	2.33	2.28	2.24	2.21
13	3.14	2.76	2.56	2.43	2.35	2.28	2.23	2.20	2.16
14	3.10	2.73	2.52	2.39	2.31	2.24	2.19	2.15	2.12
15	3.07	2.70	2.49	2.36	2.27	2.21	2.16	2.12	2.09
16	3.05	2.67	2.46	2.33	2.24	2.18	2.13	2.09	2.06
17	3.03	2.64	2.44	2.31	2.22	2.15	2.10	2.06	2.03
18	3.01	2.62	2.42	2.29	2.20	2.13	2.08	2.04	2.00
19	2.99	2.61	2.40	2.27	2.18	2.11	2.06	2.02	1.98
20	2.97	2.59	2.38	2.25	2.16	2.09	2.04	2.00	1.96
21	2.96	2.57	2.36	2.23	2.14	2.08	2.02	1.98	1.95
22	2.95	2.56	2.35	2.22	2.13	2.06	2.01	1.97	1.93
23	2.94	2.55	2.34	2.21	2.11	2.05	1.99	1.95	1.92
24	2.93	2.54	2.33	2.19	2.10	2.04	1.98	1.94	1.91
25	2.92	2.53	2.32	2.18	2.09	2.02	1.97	1.93	1.89
26	2.91	2.52	2.31	2.17	2.08	2.01	1.96	1.92	1.88
27	2.90	2.51	2.30	2.17	2.07	2.00	1.95	1.91	1.87
28	2.89	2.50	2.29	2.16	2.06	2.00	1.94	1.90	1.87
29	2.89	2.50	2.28	2.15	2.06	1.99	1.93	1.89	1.86
30	2.88	2.49	2.28	2.14	2.05	1.98	1.93	1.88	1.85
40	2.84	2.44	2.23	2.09	2.00	1.93	1.87	1.83	1.79
60	2.79	2.39	2.18	2.04	1.95	1.87	1.82	1.77	1.74
120	2.75	2.35	2.13	1.99	1.90	1.82	1.77	1.72	1.68
∞	2.71	2.30	2.08	1.94	1.85	1.77	1.72	1.67	1.63

Denominator Degrees of Freedom

Table A.7

Percentage Points of the F Distribution (Continued)

				$\alpha = .10$							v_1
				Numerator Degrees of Freedom							
10	12	15	20	24	30	40	60	120	∞		v_2
60.19	60.71	61.22	61.74	62.00	62.26	62.53	62.79	63.06	63.33		1
9.39	9.41	9.42	9.44	9.45	9.46	9.47	9.47	9.48	9.49		2
5.23	5.22	5.20	5.18	5.18	5.17	5.16	5.15	5.14	5.13		3
3.92	3.90	3.87	3.84	3.83	3.82	3.80	3.79	3.78	3.76		4
3.30	3.27	3.24	3.21	3.19	3.17	3.16	3.14	3.12	3.10		5
2.94	2.90	2.87	2.84	2.82	2.80	2.78	2.76	2.74	2.72		6
2.70	2.67	2.63	2.59	2.58	2.56	2.54	2.51	2.49	2.47		7
2.54	2.50	2.46	2.42	2.40	2.38	2.36	2.34	2.32	2.29		8
2.42	2.38	2.34	2.30	2.28	2.25	2.23	2.21	2.18	2.16		9
2.32	2.28	2.24	2.20	2.18	2.16	2.13	2.11	2.08	2.06		10
2.25	2.21	2.17	2.12	2.10	2.08	2.05	2.03	2.00	1.97		11
2.19	2.15	2.10	2.06	2.04	2.01	1.99	1.96	1.93	1.90		12
2.14	2.10	2.05	2.01	1.98	1.96	1.93	1.90	1.88	1.85		13
2.10	2.05	2.01	1.96	1.94	1.91	1.89	1.86	1.83	1.80		14
2.06	2.02	1.97	1.92	1.90	1.87	1.85	1.82	1.79	1.76		15
2.03	1.99	1.94	1.89	1.87	1.84	1.81	1.78	1.75	1.72		16
2.00	1.96	1.91	1.86	1.84	1.81	1.78	1.75	1.72	1.69		17
1.98	1.93	1.89	1.84	1.81	1.78	1.75	1.72	1.69	1.66		18
1.96	1.91	1.86	1.81	1.79	1.76	1.73	1.70	1.67	1.63		19
1.94	1.89	1.84	1.79	1.77	1.74	1.71	1.68	1.64	1.61		20
1.92	1.87	1.83	1.78	1.75	1.72	1.69	1.66	1.62	1.59		21
1.90	1.86	1.81	1.76	1.73	1.70	1.67	1.64	1.60	1.57		22
1.89	1.84	1.80	1.74	1.72	1.69	1.66	1.62	1.59	1.55		23
1.88	1.83	1.78	1.73	1.70	1.67	1.64	1.61	1.57	1.53		24
1.87	1.82	1.77	1.72	1.69	1.66	1.63	1.59	1.56	1.52		25
1.86	1.81	1.76	1.71	1.68	1.65	1.61	1.58	1.54	1.50		26
1.85	1.80	1.75	1.70	1.67	1.64	1.60	1.57	1.53	1.49		27
1.84	1.79	1.74	1.69	1.66	1.63	1.59	1.56	1.52	1.48		28
1.83	1.78	1.73	1.68	1.65	1.62	1.58	1.55	1.51	1.47		29
1.82	1.77	1.72	1.67	1.64	1.61	1.57	1.54	1.50	1.46		30
1.76	1.71	1.66	1.61	1.57	1.54	1.51	1.47	1.42	1.38		40
1.71	1.66	1.60	1.54	1.51	1.48	1.44	1.40	1.35	1.29		60
1.65	1.60	1.55	1.48	1.45	1.41	1.37	1.32	1.26	1.19		120
1.60	1.55	1.49	1.42	1.38	1.34	1.30	1.24	1.17	1.00		∞

Denominator Degrees of Freedom

(continued)

Table A.7

Percentage Points of the F Distribution (Continued)

v_2	1	2	3	4	5	6	7	8	9
1	161.45	199.50	215.71	224.58	230.16	233.99	236.77	238.88	240.54
2	18.51	19.00	19.16	19.25	19.30	19.33	19.35	19.37	19.38
3	10.13	9.55	9.28	9.12	9.01	8.94	8.89	8.85	8.81
4	7.71	6.94	6.59	6.39	6.26	6.16	6.09	6.04	6.00
5	6.61	5.79	5.41	5.19	5.05	4.95	4.88	4.82	4.77
6	5.99	5.14	4.76	4.53	4.39	4.28	4.21	4.15	4.10
7	5.59	4.74	4.35	3.12	3.97	3.87	3.79	3.73	3.68
8	5.32	4.46	4.07	3.84	3.69	3.58	3.50	3.44	3.39
9	5.12	4.26	3.71	3.63	3.48	3.37	3.29	3.23	3.18
10	4.96	4.10	3.71	3.48	3.33	3.22	3.14	3.07	3.02
11	4.84	3.98	3.59	3.36	3.20	3.09	3.01	2.95	2.90
12	4.75	3.89	3.49	3.26	3.11	3.00	2.91	2.85	2.80
13	4.67	3.81	3.41	3.18	3.03	2.92	2.83	2.77	2.71
14	4.60	3.74	3.34	3.11	2.96	2.85	2.76	2.70	2.65
15	4.54	3.68	3.29	3.06	2.90	2.79	2.71	2.64	2.59
16	4.49	3.63	3.24	3.01	2.85	2.74	2.66	2.59	2.54
17	4.45	3.59	3.20	2.96	2.81	2.70	2.61	2.55	2.49
18	4.41	3.55	3.16	2.93	2.77	2.66	2.58	2.51	2.46
19	4.38	3.52	3.13	2.90	2.74	2.63	2.54	2.48	2.42
20	4.35	3.49	3.10	2.87	2.71	2.60	2.51	2.45	2.39
21	4.32	3.47	3.07	2.84	2.68	2.57	2.49	2.42	2.37
22	4.30	3.44	3.05	2.82	2.66	2.55	2.46	2.40	2.34
23	4.28	3.42	3.03	2.80	2.64	2.53	2.44	2.37	2.32
24	4.26	3.40	3.01	2.78	2.62	2.51	2.42	2.36	2.30
25	4.24	3.39	2.99	2.76	2.60	2.49	2.40	2.34	2.28
26	4.23	3.37	2.98	2.74	2.59	2.47	2.39	2.32	2.27
27	4.21	3.35	2.96	2.73	2.57	2.46	2.37	2.31	2.25
28	4.20	3.34	2.95	2.71	2.56	2.45	2.36	2.29	2.24
29	4.18	3.33	2.93	2.70	2.55	2.43	2.35	2.28	2.22
30	4.17	3.32	2.92	2.69	2.53	2.42	2.33	2.27	2.21
40	4.08	3.23	2.84	2.61	2.45	2.34	2.25	2.18	2.12
60	4.00	3.15	2.76	2.53	2.37	2.25	2.17	2.10	2.04
120	3.92	3.07	2.68	2.45	2.29	2.18	2.09	2.02	1.96
∞	3.84	3.00	2.60	2.37	2.21	2.10	2.01	1.94	1.88

v_1 — $\alpha = .05$

Numerator Degrees of Freedom

Denominator Degrees of Freedom

Table A.7

Percentage Points of the F Distribution (Continued)

				$\alpha = .05$						v_1
				Numerator Degrees of Freedom						
10	12	15	20	24	30	40	60	120	∞	v_2
241.88	243.90	245.90	248.00	249.10	250.10	251.10	252.20	253.30	254.30	1
19.40	19.41	19.43	19.45	19.45	19.46	19.47	19.48	19.49	19.50	2
8.79	8.74	8.70	8.66	8.64	8.62	8.59	8.57	8.55	8.53	3
5.96	5.91	5.86	5.80	5.77	5.75	5.72	5.69	5.66	5.63	4
4.74	4.68	4.62	4.56	4.53	4.50	4.46	4.43	4.40	4.36	5
4.06	4.00	3.94	3.87	3.84	3.81	3.77	3.74	3.70	3.67	6
3.64	3.57	3.51	3.44	3.41	3.38	3.34	3.30	3.27	3.23	7
3.35	3.28	3.22	3.15	3.12	3.08	3.04	3.01	2.97	2.93	8
3.14	3.07	3.01	2.94	2.90	2.86	2.83	2.79	2.75	2.71	9
2.98	2.91	2.85	2.77	2.74	2.70	2.66	2.62	2.58	2.54	10
2.85	2.79	2.72	2.65	2.61	2.57	2.53	2.49	2.45	2.40	11
2.75	2.69	2.62	2.54	2.51	2.47	2.43	2.38	2.34	2.30	12
2.67	2.60	2.53	2.46	2.42	2.38	2.34	2.30	2.25	2.21	13
2.60	2.53	2.46	2.39	2.35	2.31	2.27	2.22	2.18	2.13	14
2.54	2.48	2.40	2.33	2.29	2.25	2.20	2.16	2.11	2.07	15
2.49	2.42	2.35	2.28	2.24	2.19	2.15	2.11	2.06	2.01	16
2.45	2.38	2.31	2.23	2.19	2.15	2.10	2.06	2.01	1.96	17
2.41	2.34	2.27	2.19	2.15	2.11	2.06	2.02	1.97	1.92	18
2.38	2.31	2.23	2.16	2.11	2.07	2.03	1.98	1.93	1.88	19
2.35	2.28	2.20	2.12	2.08	2.04	1.99	1.95	1.90	1.84	20
2.32	2.25	2.18	2.10	2.05	2.01	1.96	1.92	1.87	1.81	21
2.30	2.23	2.15	2.07	2.03	1.98	1.94	1.89	1.84	1.78	22
2.27	2.20	2.13	2.05	2.01	1.96	1.91	1.86	1.81	1.76	23
2.25	2.18	2.11	2.03	1.98	1.94	1.89	1.84	1.79	1.73	24
2.24	2.16	2.09	2.01	1.96	1.92	1.87	1.82	1.77	1.71	25
2.22	2.15	2.07	1.99	1.95	1.90	1.85	1.80	1.75	1.69	26
2.20	2.13	2.06	1.97	1.93	1.88	1.84	1.79	1.73	1.67	27
2.19	2.12	2.04	1.96	1.91	1.87	1.82	1.77	1.71	1.65	28
2.18	2.10	2.03	1.94	1.90	1.85	1.81	1.75	1.70	1.64	29
2.16	2.09	2.01	1.93	1.89	1.84	1.79	1.74	1.68	1.62	30
2.08	2.00	1.92	1.84	1.79	1.74	1.69	1.64	1.58	1.51	40
1.99	1.92	1.84	1.75	1.70	1.65	1.59	1.53	1.47	1.39	60
1.91	1.83	1.75	1.66	1.61	1.55	1.50	1.43	1.35	1.25	120
1.83	1.75	1.67	1.57	1.52	1.46	1.39	1.32	1.22	1.00	∞

Denominator Degrees of Freedom

(continued)

Table A.7

Percentage Points of the F Distribution (Continued)

v_2 \ v_1	1	2	3	4	5	6	7	8	9
1	647.79	799.48	864.15	899.60	921.83	937.11	948.20	956.64	963.28
2	38.51	39.00	39.17	39.25	39.30	39.33	39.36	39.37	39.39
3	17.44	16.04	15.44	15.10	14.88	14.73	14.62	14.54	14.47
4	12.22	10.65	9.98	9.60	9.36	9.20	9.07	8.98	8.90
5	10.01	8.43	7.76	7.39	7.15	6.98	6.85	6.76	6.68
6	8.81	7.26	6.60	6.23	5.99	5.82	5.70	7.60	5.52
7	8.07	6.54	5.89	5.52	5.29	5.12	4.99	4.90	4.82
8	7.57	6.06	5.42	5.05	4.82	4.65	4.53	4.43	4.36
9	7.21	5.71	5.08	4.72	4.48	4.32	4.20	4.10	4.03
10	6.94	5.46	4.83	4.47	4.24	4.07	3.95	3.85	3.78
11	6.72	5.26	4.63	4.28	4.04	3.88	3.76	3.66	3.59
12	6.55	5.10	4.47	4.12	3.89	3.73	3.61	3.51	3.44
13	6.41	4.97	4.35	4.00	3.77	3.60	3.48	3.39	3.31
14	6.30	4.86	4.24	3.89	3.66	3.50	3.38	3.29	3.21
15	6.20	4.77	4.15	3.80	3.58	3.41	3.29	3.20	3.12
16	6.12	4.69	4.08	3.73	3.50	3.34	3.22	3.12	3.05
17	6.04	4.62	4.01	3.66	3.44	3.28	3.16	3.06	2.98
18	5.98	4.56	3.95	3.61	3.38	3.22	3.10	3.01	2.93
19	5.92	4.51	3.90	3.56	3.33	3.17	3.05	2.96	2.88
20	5.87	4.46	3.86	3.51	3.29	3.13	3.01	2.91	2.84
21	5.83	4.42	3.82	3.48	3.25	3.09	2.97	2.87	2.80
22	5.79	4.38	3.78	3.44	3.22	3.05	2.93	2.84	2.76
23	5.75	4.35	3.75	3.41	3.18	3.02	2.90	2.81	2.73
24	5.72	4.32	3.72	3.38	3.15	2.99	2.87	2.78	2.70
25	5.69	4.29	3.69	3.35	3.13	2.97	2.85	2.75	2.68
26	5.66	4.27	3.67	3.33	3.10	2.94	2.82	2.73	2.65
27	5.63	4.24	3.65	3.31	3.08	2.92	2.80	2.71	2.63
28	5.61	4.22	3.63	3.29	3.06	2.90	2.78	2.69	2.61
29	5.59	4.20	3.61	3.27	3.04	2.88	2.76	2.67	2.59
30	5.57	4.18	3.59	3.25	3.03	2.87	2.75	2.65	2.57
40	5.42	4.05	3.46	3.13	2.90	2.74	2.62	2.53	2.45
60	5.29	3.93	3.34	3.01	2.79	2.63	2.51	2.41	2.33
120	5.15	3.80	3.23	2.89	2.67	2.52	2.39	2.30	2.22
∞	5.02	3.69	3.12	2.79	2.57	2.41	2.29	2.19	2.11

$\alpha = .025$

Numerator Degrees of Freedom

Denominator Degrees of Freedom

Table A.7

Percentage Points of the F Distribution (Continued)

					$\alpha = .025$						v_1
				Numerator Degrees of Freedom							
10	12	15	20	24	30	40	60	120	∞		v_2
968.63	976.72	984.87	993.08	997.27	1001.40	1005.60	1009.79	1014.04	1018.00		1
39.40	39.41	39.43	39.45	39.46	39.46	39.47	39.48	39.49	39.50		2
14.42	14.34	14.25	14.17	14.12	14.08	14.04	13.99	13.95	13.90		3
8.84	8.75	8.66	8.56	8.51	8.46	8.41	8.36	8.31	8.26		4
6.62	6.52	6.43	6.33	6.28	6.23	6.18	6.12	6.07	6.02		5
5.46	5.37	5.27	5.17	5.12	5.07	5.01	4.96	4.90	4.85		6
4.76	4.67	4.57	4.47	4.41	4.36	4.31	4.25	4.20	4.14		7
4.30	4.20	4.10	4.00	3.95	3.89	3.84	3.78	3.73	3.67		8
3.96	3.87	3.77	3.67	3.61	3.56	3.51	3.45	3.39	3.33		9
3.72	3.62	3.52	3.42	3.37	3.31	3.26	3.20	3.14	3.08		10
3.53	3.43	3.33	3.23	3.17	3.12	3.06	3.00	2.94	2.88		11
3.37	3.28	3.18	3.07	3.02	2.96	2.91	2.85	2.79	2.72		12
3.25	3.15	3.05	2.95	2.89	2.84	2.78	2.72	2.66	2.60		13
3.15	3.05	2.95	2.84	2.79	2.73	2.67	2.61	2.55	2.49		14
3.06	2.96	2.86	2.76	2.70	2.64	2.59	2.52	2.46	2.40		15
2.99	2.89	2.79	2.68	2.63	2.57	2.51	2.45	2.38	2.32		16
2.92	2.82	2.72	2.62	2.56	2.50	2.44	2.38	2.32	2.25		17
2.87	2.77	2.67	2.56	2.50	2.44	2.38	2.32	2.26	2.19		18
2.82	2.72	2.62	2.51	2.45	2.39	2.33	2.27	2.20	2.13		19
2.77	2.68	2.57	2.46	2.41	2.35	2.29	2.22	2.16	2.09		20
2.73	2.64	2.53	2.42	2.37	2.31	2.25	2.18	2.11	2.04		21
2.70	2.60	2.50	2.39	2.33	2.27	2.21	2.14	2.08	2.00		22
2.67	2.57	2.47	2.36	2.30	2.24	2.18	2.11	2.04	1.97		23
2.64	2.54	2.44	2.33	2.27	2.21	2.15	2.08	2.01	1.94		24
2.61	2.51	2.41	2.30	2.24	2.18	2.12	2.05	1.98	1.91		25
2.59	2.49	2.39	2.28	2.22	2.16	2.09	2.03	1.95	1.88		26
2.57	2.47	2.36	2.25	2.19	2.13	2.07	2.00	1.93	1.85		27
2.55	2.45	2.34	2.23	2.17	2.11	2.05	1.98	1.91	1.83		28
2.53	2.43	2.32	2.21	2.15	2.09	2.03	1.96	1.89	1.81		29
2.51	2.41	2.31	2.20	2.14	2.07	2.01	1.94	1.87	1.79		30
2.39	2.29	2.18	2.07	2.01	1.94	1.88	1.80	1.72	1.64		40
2.27	2.17	2.06	1.94	1.88	1.82	1.74	1.67	1.58	1.48		60
2.16	2.05	1.94	1.82	1.76	1.69	1.61	1.53	1.43	1.31		120
2.05	1.94	1.83	1.71	1.64	1.57	1.48	1.39	1.27	1.00		∞

Denominator Degrees of Freedom

(continued)

Table A.7

Percentage Points of the F Distribution (*Continued*)

v_2	1	2	3	4	5	6	7	8	9
1	4052.18	4999.34	5403.53	5624.26	5763.96	5858.95	5928.33	5980.95	6022.40
2	98.50	99.00	99.16	99.25	99.30	99.33	99.36	99.38	99.39
3	34.12	30.82	29.46	28.71	28.24	27.91	27.67	27.49	27.34
4	21.20	18.00	16.69	15.98	15.52	15.21	14.98	14.80	14.66
5	16.26	13.27	12.06	11.39	10.97	10.67	10.46	10.29	10.16
6	13.75	10.92	9.78	9.15	8.75	8.47	8.26	8.10	7.98
7	12.25	9.55	8.45	7.85	7.46	7.19	6.99	6.84	6.72
8	11.26	8.65	7.59	7.01	6.63	6.37	6.18	6.03	5.91
9	10.56	8.02	6.99	6.42	6.06	5.80	5.61	5.47	5.35
10	10.04	7.56	6.55	5.99	5.64	5.39	5.20	5.06	4.94
11	9.65	7.21	6.22	5.67	5.32	5.07	4.89	4.74	4.63
12	9.33	6.93	5.95	5.41	5.06	4.82	4.64	4.50	4.39
13	9.07	6.70	5.74	5.21	4.86	4.62	4.44	4.30	4.19
14	8.86	6.51	5.56	5.04	4.69	4.46	4.28	4.14	4.03
15	8.68	6.36	5.42	4.89	4.56	4.32	4.14	4.00	3.89
16	8.53	6.23	5.29	4.77	4.44	4.20	4.03	3.89	3.78
17	8.40	6.11	5.19	4.67	4.34	4.10	3.93	3.79	3.68
18	8.29	6.01	5.09	4.58	4.25	4.01	3.84	3.71	3.60
19	8.18	5.93	5.01	4.50	4.17	3.94	3.77	3.63	3.52
20	8.10	5.85	4.94	4.43	4.10	3.87	3.70	3.56	3.46
21	8.02	5.78	4.87	4.37	4.04	3.81	3.64	3.51	3.40
22	7.95	5.72	4.82	4.31	3.99	3.76	3.59	3.45	3.35
23	7.88	5.66	4.76	4.26	3.94	3.71	3.54	3.41	3.30
24	7.82	5.61	4.72	4.22	3.90	3.67	3.50	3.36	3.26
25	7.77	5.57	4.68	4.18	3.85	3.63	3.46	3.32	3.22
26	7.72	5.53	4.64	4.14	3.82	3.59	3.42	3.29	3.18
27	7.68	5.49	4.60	4.11	3.78	3.56	3.39	3.26	3.15
28	7.64	5.45	4.57	4.07	3.75	3.53	3.36	3.23	3.12
29	7.60	5.42	4.54	4.04	3.73	3.50	3.33	3.20	3.09
30	7.56	5.39	4.51	4.02	3.70	3.47	3.30	3.17	3.07
40	7.31	5.18	4.31	3.83	3.51	3.29	3.12	2.99	2.89
60	7.08	4.98	4.13	3.65	3.34	3.12	2.95	2.82	2.72
120	6.85	4.79	3.95	3.48	3.17	2.96	2.79	2.66	2.56
∞	6.63	4.61	3.78	3.32	3.02	2.80	2.64	2.51	2.41

$\alpha = .01$

Numerator Degrees of Freedom (v_1)

Denominator Degrees of Freedom

Table A.7

Percentage Points of the *F* Distribution (*Continued*)

				$\alpha = .01$							v_1
				Numerator Degrees of Freedom							
10	12	15	20	24	30	40	60	120	∞		v_2
6055.93	6106.68	6156.97	6208.66	6234.27	6260.35	6286.43	6312.97	6339.51	6366.00		1
99.40	99.42	99.43	99.45	99.46	99.47	99.48	99.48	99.49	99.50		2
27.23	27.05	26.87	26.69	26.60	26.50	26.41	26.32	26.22	26.13		3
14.55	14.37	14.20	14.02	13.93	13.84	13.75	13.65	13.56	13.46		4
10.05	9.89	9.72	9.55	9.47	9.38	9.29	9.20	9.11	9.02		5
7.87	7.72	7.56	7.40	7.31	7.23	7.14	7.06	6.97	6.88		6
6.62	6.47	6.31	6.16	6.07	5.99	5.91	5.82	5.74	5.65		7
5.81	5.67	5.52	5.36	5.28	5.20	5.12	5.03	4.95	4.86		8
5.26	5.11	4.96	4.81	4.73	4.65	4.57	4.48	4.40	4.31		9
4.85	4.71	4.56	4.41	4.33	4.25	4.17	4.08	4.00	3.91		10
4.54	4.40	4.25	4.10	4.02	3.94	3.86	3.78	3.69	3.60		11
4.30	4.16	4.01	3.86	3.78	3.70	3.62	3.54	3.45	3.36		12
4.10	3.96	3.82	3.66	3.59	3.51	3.43	3.34	3.25	3.17		13
3.94	3.80	3.66	3.51	3.43	3.35	3.27	3.18	3.09	3.00		14
3.80	3.67	3.52	3.37	3.29	3.21	3.13	3.05	2.96	2.87		15
3.69	3.55	3.41	3.26	3.18	3.10	3.02	2.93	2.84	2.75		16
3.59	3.46	3.31	3.16	3.08	3.00	2.92	2.83	2.75	2.65		17
3.51	3.37	3.23	3.08	3.00	2.92	2.84	2.75	2.66	2.57		18
3.43	3.30	3.15	3.00	2.92	2.84	2.76	2.67	2.58	2.49		19
3.37	3.23	3.09	2.94	2.86	2.78	2.69	2.61	2.52	2.42		20
3.31	3.17	3.03	2.88	2.80	2.72	2.64	2.55	2.46	2.36		21
3.26	3.12	2.98	2.83	2.75	2.67	2.58	2.50	2.40	2.31		22
3.21	3.07	2.93	2.78	2.70	2.62	2.54	2.45	2.35	2.26		23
3.17	3.03	2.89	2.74	2.66	2.58	2.49	2.40	2.31	2.21		24
3.13	2.99	2.85	2.70	2.62	2.54	2.45	2.36	2.27	2.17		25
3.09	2.96	2.81	2.66	2.58	2.50	2.42	2.33	2.23	2.13		26
3.06	2.93	2.78	2.63	2.55	2.47	2.38	2.29	2.20	2.10		27
3.03	2.90	2.75	2.60	2.52	2.44	2.35	2.26	2.17	2.06		28
3.00	2.87	2.73	2.57	2.49	2.41	2.33	2.23	2.14	2.03		29
2.98	2.84	2.70	2.55	2.47	2.39	2.30	2.21	2.11	2.01		30
2.80	2.66	2.52	2.37	2.29	2.20	2.11	2.02	1.92	1.80		40
2.63	2.50	2.35	2.20	2.12	2.03	1.94	1.84	1.73	1.60		60
2.47	2.34	2.19	2.03	1.95	1.86	1.76	1.66	1.53	1.38		120
2.32	2.18	2.04	1.88	1.79	1.70	1.59	1.47	1.32	1.00		∞

Denominator Degrees of Freedom

(continued)

Table A.7

Percentage Points of the *F* Distribution (*Continued*)

$\alpha = .005$

Numerator Degrees of Freedom

v_2 \ v_1	1	2	3	4	5	6	7	8	9
1	16212.46	19997.36	21614.13	22500.75	23055.82	23439.53	23715.20	23923.81	24091.45
2	198.50	199.01	199.16	199.24	199.30	199.33	199.36	199.38	199.39
3	55.55	49.80	47.47	46.20	45.39	44.84	44.43	44.13	43.88
4	31.33	26.28	24.26	23.15	22.46	21.98	21.62	21.35	21.14
5	22.78	18.31	16.53	15.56	14.94	14.51	14.20	13.96	13.77
6	18.63	14.54	12.92	12.03	11.46	11.07	10.79	10.57	10.39
7	16.24	12.40	10.88	10.05	9.52	9.16	8.89	8.68	8.51
8	14.69	11.04	9.60	8.81	8.30	7.95	7.69	7.50	7.34
9	13.61	10.11	8.72	7.96	7.47	7.13	6.88	6.69	6.54
10	12.83	9.43	8.08	7.34	6.87	6.54	6.30	6.12	5.97
11	12.23	8.91	7.60	6.88	6.42	6.10	5.86	5.68	5.54
12	11.75	8.51	7.23	6.52	6.07	5.76	5.52	5.35	5.20
13	11.37	8.19	6.93	6.23	5.79	5.48	5.25	5.08	4.94
14	11.06	7.92	6.68	6.00	5.56	5.26	5.03	4.86	4.72
15	10.80	7.70	6.48	5.80	5.37	5.07	4.85	4.67	4.54
16	10.58	7.51	6.30	5.64	5.21	4.91	4.69	4.52	4.38
17	10.38	7.35	6.16	5.50	5.07	4.78	4.56	4.39	4.25
18	10.22	7.21	6.03	5.37	4.96	4.66	4.44	4.28	4.14
19	10.07	7.09	5.92	5.27	4.85	4.56	4.34	4.18	4.04
20	9.94	6.99	5.82	5.17	4.76	4.47	4.26	4.09	3.96
21	9.83	6.89	5.73	5.09	4.68	4.39	4.18	4.01	3.88
22	9.73	6.81	5.65	5.02	4.61	4.32	4.11	3.94	3.81
23	9.63	6.73	5.58	4.95	4.54	4.26	4.05	3.88	3.75
24	9.55	6.66	5.52	4.89	4.49	4.20	3.99	3.83	3.69
25	9.48	6.60	5.46	4.84	4.43	4.15	3.94	3.78	3.64
26	9.41	6.54	5.41	4.79	4.38	4.10	3.89	3.73	3.60
27	9.34	6.49	5.36	4.74	4.34	4.06	3.85	3.69	3.56
28	9.28	6.44	5.32	4.70	4.30	4.02	3.81	3.65	3.52
29	9.23	6.40	5.28	4.66	4.26	3.98	3.77	3.61	3.48
30	9.18	6.35	5.24	4.62	4.23	3.95	3.74	3.58	3.45
40	8.83	6.07	4.98	4.37	3.99	3.71	3.51	3.35	3.22
60	8.49	5.79	4.73	4.14	3.76	3.49	3.29	3.13	3.01
120	8.18	5.54	4.50	3.92	3.55	3.28	3.09	2.93	2.81
∞	7.88	5.30	4.28	3.72	3.35	3.09	2.90	2.74	2.62

Denominator Degrees of Freedom

Table A.7

Percentage Points of the F Distribution (Continued)

				α = .005						v_1
				Numerator Degrees of Freedom						
10	12	15	20	24	30	40	60	120	∞	v_2
24221.84	24426.73	24631.62	24836.51	24937.09	25041.40	25145.71	25253.74	25358.05	25465.00	1
199.39	199.42	199.43	199.45	199.45	199.48	199.48	199.48	199.49	199.50	2
43.68	43.39	43.08	42.78	42.62	42.47	42.31	42.15	41.99	41.83	3
20.97	20.70	20.44	20.17	20.03	19.89	19.75	19.61	19.47	19.32	4
13.62	13.38	13.15	12.90	12.78	12.66	12.53	12.40	12.27	12.14	5
10.25	10.03	9.81	9.59	9.47	9.36	9.24	9.12	9.00	8.88	6
8.38	8.18	7.97	7.75	7.64	7.53	7.42	7.31	7.19	7.08	7
7.21	7.01	6.81	6.61	6.50	6.40	6.29	6.18	6.06	5.95	8
6.42	6.23	6.03	5.83	5.73	5.62	5.52	5.41	5.30	5.19	9
5.85	5.66	5.47	5.27	5.17	5.07	4.97	4.86	4.75	4.64	10
5.42	5.24	5.05	4.86	4.76	4.65	4.55	4.45	4.34	4.23	11
5.09	4.91	4.72	4.53	4.43	4.33	4.23	4.12	4.01	3.90	12
4.82	4.64	4.46	4.27	4.17	4.07	3.97	3.87	3.76	3.65	13
4.60	4.43	4.25	4.06	3.96	3.86	3.76	3.66	3.55	3.44	14
4.42	4.25	4.07	3.88	3.79	3.69	3.59	3.48	3.37	3.26	15
4.27	4.10	3.92	3.73	3.64	3.54	3.44	3.33	3.22	3.11	16
4.14	3.97	3.79	3.61	3.51	3.41	3.31	3.21	3.10	2.98	17
4.03	3.86	3.68	3.50	3.40	3.30	3.20	3.10	2.99	2.87	18
3.93	3.76	3.59	3.40	3.31	3.21	3.11	3.00	2.89	2.78	19
3.85	3.68	3.50	3.32	3.22	3.12	3.02	2.92	2.81	2.69	20
3.77	3.60	3.43	3.24	3.15	3.05	2.95	2.84	2.73	2.61	21
3.70	3.54	3.36	3.18	3.08	2.98	2.88	2.77	2.66	2.55	22
3.64	3.47	3.30	3.12	3.02	2.92	2.82	2.71	2.60	2.48	23
3.59	3.42	3.25	3.06	2.97	2.87	2.77	2.66	2.55	2.43	24
3.54	3.37	3.20	3.01	2.92	2.82	2.72	2.61	2.50	2.38	25
3.49	3.33	3.15	2.97	2.87	2.77	2.67	2.56	2.45	2.33	26
3.45	3.28	3.11	2.93	2.83	2.73	2.63	2.52	2.41	2.29	27
3.41	3.25	3.07	2.89	2.79	2.69	2.59	2.48	2.37	2.25	28
3.38	3.21	3.04	2.86	2.76	2.66	2.56	2.45	2.33	2.21	29
3.34	3.18	3.01	2.82	2.73	2.63	2.52	2.42	2.30	2.18	30
3.12	2.95	2.78	2.60	2.50	2.40	2.30	2.18	2.06	1.93	40
2.90	2.74	2.57	2.39	2.29	2.19	2.08	1.96	1.83	1.69	60
2.71	2.54	2.37	2.19	2.09	1.98	1.87	1.75	1.61	1.43	120
2.52	2.36	2.19	2.00	1.90	1.79	1.67	1.53	1.36	1.00	∞

Table A.8

The Chi-Square Table

Values of χ^2 for Selected Probabilities

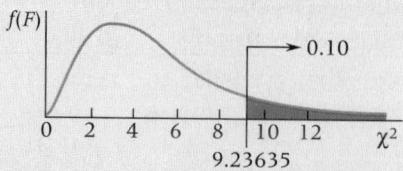

Example: df (Number of degrees of freedom) = 5, the tail above $\chi^2 = 9.23635$ represents 0.10 or 10% of area under the curve.

Degrees of Freedom	Area in Upper Tail									
	.995	.99	.975	.95	.9	.1	.05	.025	.01	.005
1	0.0000393	0.0001571	0.0009821	0.0039322	0.0157907	2.7055	3.8415	5.0239	6.6349	7.8794
2	0.010025	0.020100	0.050636	0.102586	0.210721	4.6052	5.9915	7.3778	9.2104	10.5965
3	0.07172	0.11483	0.21579	0.35185	0.58438	6.2514	7.8147	9.3484	11.3449	12.8381
4	0.20698	0.29711	0.48442	0.71072	1.06362	7.7794	9.4877	11.1433	13.2767	14.8602
5	0.41175	0.55430	0.83121	1.14548	1.61031	9.2363	11.0705	12.8325	15.0863	16.7496
6	0.67573	0.87208	1.23734	1.63538	2.20413	10.6446	12.5916	14.4494	16.8119	18.5475
7	0.98925	1.23903	1.68986	2.16735	2.83311	12.0170	14.0671	16.0128	18.4753	20.2777
8	1.34440	1.64651	2.17972	2.73263	3.48954	13.3616	15.5073	17.5345	20.0902	21.9549
9	1.73491	2.08789	2.70039	3.32512	4.16816	14.6837	16.9190	19.0228	21.6660	23.5893
10	2.15585	2.55820	3.24696	3.94030	4.86518	15.9872	18.3070	20.4832	23.2093	25.1881
11	2.60320	3.05350	3.81574	4.57481	5.57779	17.2750	19.6752	21.9200	24.7250	26.7569
12	3.07379	3.57055	4.40378	5.22603	6.30380	18.5493	21.0261	23.3367	26.2170	28.2997
13	3.56504	4.10690	5.00874	5.89186	7.04150	19.8119	22.3620	24.7356	27.6882	29.8193
14	4.07466	4.66042	5.62872	6.57063	7.78954	21.0641	23.6848	26.1189	29.1412	31.3194
15	4.60087	5.22936	6.26212	7.26093	8.54675	22.3071	24.9958	27.4884	30.5780	32.8015
16	5.14216	5.81220	6.90766	7.96164	9.31224	23.5418	26.2962	28.8453	31.9999	34.2671
17	5.69727	6.40774	7.56418	8.67175	10.08518	24.7690	27.5871	30.1910	33.4087	35.7184
18	6.26477	7.01490	8.23074	9.39045	10.86494	25.9894	28.8693	31.5264	34.8052	37.1564
19	6.84392	7.63270	8.90651	10.11701	11.65091	27.2036	30.1435	32.8523	36.1908	38.5821
20	7.43381	8.26037	9.59077	10.85080	12.44260	28.4120	31.4104	34.1696	37.5663	39.9969
21	8.03360	8.89717	10.28291	11.59132	13.23960	29.6151	32.6706	35.4789	38.9322	41.4009
22	8.64268	9.54249	10.98233	12.33801	14.04149	30.8133	33.9245	36.7807	40.2894	42.7957
23	9.26038	10.19569	11.68853	13.09051	14.84795	32.0069	35.1725	38.0756	41.6383	44.1814
24	9.88620	10.85635	12.40115	13.84842	15.65868	33.1962	36.4150	39.3641	42.9798	45.5584
25	10.51965	11.52395	13.11971	14.61140	16.47341	34.3816	37.6525	40.6465	44.3140	46.9280
26	11.16022	12.19818	13.84388	15.37916	17.29188	35.5632	38.8851	41.9231	45.6416	48.2898
27	11.80765	12.87847	14.57337	16.15139	18.11389	36.7412	40.1133	43.1945	46.9628	49.6450
28	12.46128	13.56467	15.30785	16.92788	18.93924	37.9159	41.3372	44.4608	48.2782	50.9936
29	13.12107	14.25641	16.04705	17.70838	19.76774	39.0875	42.5569	45.7223	49.5878	52.3355
30	13.78668	14.95346	16.79076	18.49267	20.59924	40.2560	43.7730	46.9792	50.8922	53.6719
40	20.70658	22.16420	24.43306	26.50930	29.05052	51.8050	55.7585	59.3417	63.6908	66.7660
50	27.99082	29.70673	32.35738	34.76424	37.68864	63.1671	67.5048	71.4202	76.1538	79.4898
60	35.53440	37.48480	40.48171	43.18797	46.45888	74.3970	79.0820	83.2977	88.3794	91.9518
70	43.27531	45.44170	48.75754	51.73926	55.32894	85.5270	90.5313	95.0231	100.4251	104.2148
80	51.17193	53.53998	57.15315	60.39146	64.27784	96.5782	101.8795	106.6285	112.3288	116.3209
90	59.19633	61.75402	65.64659	69.12602	73.29108	107.5650	113.1452	118.1359	124.1162	128.2987
100	67.32753	70.06500	74.22188	77.92944	82.35813	118.4980	124.3221	129.5613	135.8069	140.1697

Table A.9

Critical Values for the Durbin-Watson Test

Entries in the table give the critical values for a one-tailed Durbin-Watson test for autocorrelation. For a two-tailed test, the level of significance is doubled.

Significant Points of d_L and d_U: $\alpha = .05$
Number of Independent Variables

k	1		2		3		4		5	
n	d_L	d_U	d_L	d_U	d_L	d_U	d_L	d_U	d_L	d_U
15	1.08	1.36	0.95	1.54	0.82	1.75	0.69	1.97	0.56	2.21
16	1.10	1.37	0.98	1.54	0.86	1.73	0.74	1.93	0.62	2.15
17	1.13	1.38	1.02	1.54	0.90	1.71	0.78	1.90	0.67	2.10
18	1.16	1.39	1.05	1.53	0.93	1.69	0.82	1.87	0.71	2.06
19	1.18	1.40	1.08	1.53	0.97	1.68	0.86	1.85	0.75	2.02
20	1.20	1.41	1.10	1.54	1.00	1.68	0.90	1.83	0.79	1.99
21	1.22	1.42	1.13	1.54	1.03	1.67	0.93	1.81	0.83	1.96
22	1.24	1.43	1.15	1.54	1.05	1.66	0.96	1.80	0.86	1.94
23	1.26	1.44	1.17	1.54	1.08	1.66	0.99	1.79	0.90	1.92
24	1.27	1.45	1.19	1.55	1.10	1.66	1.01	1.78	0.93	1.90
25	1.29	1.45	1.21	1.55	1.12	1.66	1.04	1.77	0.95	1.89
26	1.30	1.46	1.22	1.55	1.14	1.65	1.06	1.76	0.98	1.88
27	1.32	1.47	1.24	1.56	1.16	1.65	1.08	1.76	1.01	1.86
28	1.33	1.48	1.26	1.56	1.18	1.65	1.10	1.75	1.03	1.85
29	1.34	1.48	1.27	1.56	1.20	1.65	1.12	1.74	1.05	1.84
30	1.35	1.49	1.28	1.57	1.21	1.65	1.14	1.74	1.07	1.83
31	1.36	1.50	1.30	1.57	1.23	1.65	1.16	1.74	1.09	1.83
32	1.37	1.50	1.31	1.57	1.24	1.65	1.18	1.73	1.11	1.82
33	1.38	1.51	1.32	1.58	1.26	1.65	1.19	1.73	1.13	1.81
34	1.39	1.51	1.33	1.58	1.27	1.65	1.21	1.73	1.15	1.81
35	1.40	1.52	1.34	1.58	1.28	1.65	1.22	1.73	1.16	1.80
36	1.41	1.52	1.35	1.59	1.29	1.65	1.24	1.73	1.18	1.80
37	1.42	1.53	1.36	1.59	1.31	1.66	1.25	1.72	1.19	1.80
38	1.43	1.54	1.37	1.59	1.32	1.66	1.26	1.72	1.21	1.79
39	1.43	1.54	1.38	1.60	1.33	1.66	1.27	1.72	1.22	1.79
40	1.44	1.54	1.39	1.60	1.34	1.66	1.29	1.72	1.23	1.79
45	1.48	1.57	1.43	1.62	1.38	1.67	1.34	1.72	1.29	1.78
50	1.50	1.59	1.46	1.63	1.42	1.67	1.38	1.72	1.34	1.77
55	1.53	1.60	1.49	1.64	1.45	1.68	1.41	1.72	1.38	1.77
60	1.55	1.62	1.51	1.65	1.48	1.69	1.44	1.73	1.41	1.77
65	1.57	1.63	1.54	1.66	1.50	1.70	1.47	1.73	1.44	1.77
70	1.58	1.64	1.55	1.67	1.52	1.70	1.49	1.74	1.46	1.77
75	1.60	1.65	1.57	1.68	1.54	1.71	1.51	1.74	1.49	1.77
80	1.61	1.66	1.59	1.69	1.56	1.72	1.53	1.74	1.51	1.77
85	1.62	1.67	1.60	1.70	1.57	1.72	1.55	1.75	1.52	1.77
90	1.63	1.68	1.61	1.70	1.59	1.73	1.57	1.75	1.54	1.78
95	1.64	1.69	1.62	1.71	1.60	1.73	1.58	1.75	1.56	1.78
100	1.65	1.69	1.63	1.72	1.61	1.74	1.59	1.76	1.57	1.78

J. Durbin and G. S. Watson, "Testing for Serial Correlation in Least Square Regression II," *Biometrika*, vol. 38, 1951, pp. 159–78, by permission of Oxford University Press.

(continued)

Table A.9

Critical Values for the Durbin-Watson Test
(*Continued*)

Significant Points of d_L and d_U: $\alpha = .01$
Number of Independent Variables

k	1		2		3		4		5	
n	d_L	d_U	d_L	d_U	d_L	d_U	d_L	d_U	d_L	d_U
15	0.81	1.07	0.70	1.25	0.59	1.46	0.49	1.70	0.39	1.96
16	0.84	1.09	0.74	1.25	0.63	1.44	0.53	1.66	0.44	1.90
17	0.87	1.10	0.77	1.25	0.67	1.43	0.57	1.63	0.48	1.85
18	0.90	1.12	0.80	1.26	0.71	1.42	0.61	1.60	0.52	1.80
19	0.93	1.13	0.83	1.26	0.74	1.41	0.65	1.58	0.56	1.77
20	0.95	1.15	0.86	1.27	0.77	1.41	0.68	1.57	0.60	1.74
21	0.97	1.16	0.89	1.27	0.80	1.41	0.72	1.55	0.63	1.71
22	1.00	1.17	0.91	1.28	0.83	1.40	0.75	1.54	0.66	1.69
23	1.02	1.19	0.94	1.29	0.86	1.40	0.77	1.53	0.70	1.67
24	1.04	1.20	0.96	1.30	0.88	1.41	0.80	1.53	0.72	1.66
25	1.05	1.21	0.98	1.30	0.90	1.41	0.83	1.52	0.75	1.65
26	1.07	1.22	1.00	1.31	0.93	1.41	0.85	1.52	0.78	1.64
27	1.09	1.23	1.02	1.32	0.95	1.41	0.88	1.51	0.81	1.63
28	1.10	1.24	1.04	1.32	0.97	1.41	0.90	1.51	0.83	1.62
29	1.12	1.25	1.05	1.33	0.99	1.42	0.92	1.51	0.85	1.61
30	1.13	1.26	1.07	1.34	1.01	1.42	0.94	1.51	0.88	1.61
31	1.15	1.27	1.08	1.34	1.02	1.42	0.96	1.51	0.90	1.60
32	1.16	1.28	1.10	1.35	1.04	1.43	0.98	1.51	0.92	1.60
33	1.17	1.29	1.11	1.36	1.05	1.43	1.00	1.51	0.94	1.59
34	1.18	1.30	1.13	1.36	1.07	1.43	1.01	1.51	0.95	1.59
35	1.19	1.31	1.14	1.37	1.08	1.44	1.03	1.51	0.97	1.59
36	1.21	1.32	1.15	1.38	1.10	1.44	1.04	1.51	0.99	1.59
37	1.22	1.32	1.16	1.38	1.11	1.45	1.06	1.51	1.00	1.59
38	1.23	1.33	1.18	1.39	1.12	1.45	1.07	1.52	1.02	1.58
39	1.24	1.34	1.19	1.39	1.14	1.45	1.09	1.52	1.03	1.58
40	1.25	1.34	1.20	1.40	1.15	1.46	1.10	1.52	1.05	1.58
45	1.29	1.38	1.24	1.42	1.20	1.48	1.16	1.53	1.11	1.58
50	1.32	1.40	1.28	1.45	1.24	1.49	1.20	1.54	1.16	1.59
55	1.36	1.43	1.32	1.47	1.28	1.51	1.25	1.55	1.21	1.59
60	1.38	1.45	1.35	1.48	1.32	1.52	1.28	1.56	1.25	1.60
65	1.41	1.47	1.38	1.50	1.35	1.53	1.31	1.57	1.28	1.61
70	1.43	1.49	1.40	1.52	1.37	1.55	1.34	1.58	1.31	1.61
75	1.45	1.50	1.42	1.53	1.39	1.56	1.37	1.59	1.34	1.62
80	1.47	1.52	1.44	1.54	1.42	1.57	1.39	1.60	1.36	1.62
85	1.48	1.53	1.46	1.55	1.43	1.58	1.41	1.60	1.39	1.63
90	1.50	1.54	1.47	1.56	1.45	1.59	1.43	1.61	1.41	1.64
95	1.51	1.55	1.49	1.57	1.47	1.60	1.45	1.62	1.42	1.64
100	1.52	1.56	1.50	1.58	1.48	1.60	1.46	1.63	1.44	1.65

Table A.10

Critical Values of the Studentized Range (q) Distribution

$\alpha = .05$

Degrees of Freedom	Number of Populations																		
	2	3	4	5	6	7	8	9	10	11	12	13	14	15	16	17	18	19	20
1	18.0	27.0	32.8	37.1	40.4	43.1	45.4	47.4	49.1	50.6	52.0	53.2	54.3	55.4	56.3	57.2	58.0	58.8	59.6
2	6.08	8.33	9.80	10.9	11.7	12.4	13.0	13.5	14.0	14.4	14.7	15.1	15.4	15.7	15.9	16.1	16.4	16.6	16.8
3	4.50	5.91	6.82	7.50	8.04	8.48	8.85	9.18	9.46	9.72	9.95	10.2	10.3	10.5	10.7	10.8	11.0	11.1	11.2
4	3.93	5.04	5.76	6.29	6.71	7.05	7.35	7.60	7.83	8.03	8.21	8.37	8.52	8.66	8.79	8.91	9.03	9.13	9.23
5	3.64	4.60	5.22	5.67	6.03	6.33	6.58	6.80	6.99	7.17	7.32	7.47	7.60	7.72	7.83	7.93	8.03	8.12	8.21
6	3.46	4.34	4.90	5.30	5.63	5.90	6.12	6.32	6.49	6.65	6.79	6.92	7.03	7.14	7.24	7.34	7.43	7.51	7.59
7	3.34	4.16	4.68	5.06	5.36	5.61	5.82	6.00	6.16	6.30	6.43	6.55	6.66	6.76	6.85	6.94	7.02	7.10	7.17
8	3.26	4.04	4.53	4.89	5.17	5.40	5.60	5.77	5.92	6.05	6.18	6.29	6.39	6.48	6.57	6.65	6.73	6.80	6.87
9	3.20	3.95	4.41	4.76	5.02	5.24	5.43	5.59	5.74	5.87	5.98	6.09	6.19	6.28	6.36	6.44	6.51	6.58	6.64
10	3.15	3.88	4.33	4.65	4.91	5.12	5.30	5.46	5.60	5.72	5.83	5.93	6.03	6.11	6.19	6.27	6.34	6.40	6.47
11	3.11	3.82	4.26	4.57	4.82	5.03	5.20	5.35	5.49	5.61	5.71	5.81	5.90	5.98	6.06	6.13	6.20	6.27	6.33
12	3.08	3.77	4.20	4.51	4.75	4.95	5.12	5.27	5.39	5.51	5.61	5.71	5.80	5.88	5.95	6.02	6.09	6.15	6.21
13	3.06	3.73	4.15	4.45	4.69	4.88	5.05	5.19	5.32	5.43	5.53	5.63	5.71	5.79	5.86	5.93	5.99	6.05	6.11
14	3.03	3.70	4.11	4.41	4.64	4.83	4.99	5.13	5.25	5.36	5.46	5.55	5.64	5.71	5.79	5.85	5.91	5.97	6.03
15	3.01	3.67	4.08	4.37	4.59	4.78	4.94	5.08	5.20	5.31	5.40	5.49	5.57	5.65	5.72	5.78	5.85	5.90	5.96
16	3.00	3.65	4.05	4.33	4.56	4.74	4.90	5.03	5.15	5.26	5.35	5.44	5.52	5.59	5.66	5.73	5.79	5.84	5.90
17	2.98	3.63	4.02	4.30	4.52	4.70	4.86	4.99	5.11	5.21	5.31	5.39	5.47	5.54	5.61	5.67	5.73	5.79	5.84
18	2.97	3.61	4.00	4.28	4.49	4.67	4.82	4.96	5.07	5.17	5.27	5.35	5.43	5.50	5.57	5.63	5.69	5.74	5.79
19	2.96	3.59	3.98	4.25	4.47	4.65	4.79	4.92	5.04	5.14	5.23	5.31	5.39	5.46	5.53	5.59	5.65	5.70	5.75
20	2.95	3.58	3.96	4.23	4.45	4.62	4.77	4.90	5.01	5.11	5.20	5.28	5.36	5.43	5.49	5.55	5.61	5.66	5.71
24	2.92	3.53	3.90	4.17	4.37	4.54	4.68	4.81	4.92	5.01	5.10	5.18	5.25	5.32	5.38	5.44	5.49	5.55	5.59
30	2.89	3.49	3.85	4.10	4.30	4.46	4.60	4.72	4.82	4.92	5.00	5.08	5.15	5.21	5.27	5.33	5.38	5.43	5.47
40	2.86	3.44	3.79	4.04	4.23	4.39	4.52	4.63	4.73	4.82	4.90	4.98	5.04	5.11	5.16	5.22	5.27	5.31	5.36
60	2.83	3.40	3.74	3.98	4.16	4.31	4.44	4.55	4.65	4.73	4.81	4.88	4.94	5.00	5.06	5.11	5.15	5.20	5.24
120	2.80	3.36	3.68	3.92	4.10	4.24	4.36	4.47	4.56	4.64	4.71	4.78	4.84	4.90	4.95	5.00	5.04	5.09	5.13
∞	2.77	3.31	3.63	3.86	4.03	4.17	4.29	4.39	4.47	4.55	4.62	4.68	4.74	4.80	4.85	4.89	4.93	4.97	5.01

Reprinted by permission of the *Biometrika* Trustees from *Biometrika Tables for Statisticians,* E. S. Pearson and H. O. Hartley, vol. 1, 3d edition, pp. 176–77. Copyright © 1966, *Biometrika* Trustees. Used with permission.

(continued)

Table A.10

Critical Values of the Studentized Range (q) Distribution (*Continued*)

Degrees of Freedom	\multicolumn{19}{c}{$\alpha = .01$ — Number of Populations}

Degrees of Freedom	2	3	4	5	6	7	8	9	10	11	12	13	14	15	16	17	18	19	20
1	90.0	135.	164.	186.	202.	216.	227.	237.	246.	253.	260.	266.	272.	277.	282.	286.	290.	294.	298.
2	14.0	19.0	22.3	24.7	26.6	28.2	29.5	30.7	31.7	32.6	33.4	34.1	34.8	35.4	36.0	36.5	37.0	37.5	37.9
3	8.26	10.6	12.2	13.3	14.2	15.0	15.6	16.2	16.7	17.1	17.5	17.9	18.2	18.5	18.8	19.1	19.3	19.5	19.8
4	6.51	8.12	9.17	9.96	10.6	11.1	11.5	11.9	12.3	12.6	12.8	13.1	13.3	13.5	13.7	13.9	14.1	14.2	14.4
5	5.70	6.97	7.80	8.42	8.91	9.32	9.67	9.97	10.2	10.5	10.7	10.9	11.1	11.2	11.4	11.6	11.7	11.8	11.9
6	5.24	6.33	7.03	7.56	7.97	8.32	8.61	8.87	9.10	9.30	9.49	9.65	9.81	9.95	10.1	10.2	10.3	10.4	10.5
7	4.95	5.92	6.54	7.01	7.37	7.68	7.94	8.17	8.37	8.55	8.71	8.86	9.00	9.12	9.24	9.35	9.46	9.55	9.65
8	4.74	5.63	6.20	6.63	6.96	7.24	7.47	7.68	7.87	8.03	8.18	8.31	8.44	8.55	8.66	8.76	8.85	8.94	9.03
9	4.60	5.43	5.96	6.35	6.66	6.91	7.13	7.32	7.49	7.65	7.78	7.91	8.03	8.13	8.23	8.32	8.41	8.49	8.57
10	4.48	5.27	5.77	6.14	6.43	6.67	6.87	7.05	7.21	7.36	7.48	7.60	7.71	7.81	7.91	7.99	8.07	8.15	8.22
11	4.39	5.14	5.62	5.97	6.25	6.48	6.67	6.84	6.99	7.13	7.25	7.36	7.46	7.56	7.65	7.73	7.81	7.88	7.95
12	4.32	5.04	5.50	5.84	6.10	6.32	6.51	6.67	6.81	6.94	7.06	7.17	7.26	7.36	7.44	7.52	7.59	7.66	7.73
13	4.26	4.96	5.40	5.73	5.98	6.19	6.37	6.53	6.67	6.79	6.90	7.01	7.10	7.19	7.27	7.34	7.42	7.48	7.55
14	4.21	4.89	5.32	5.63	5.88	6.08	6.26	6.41	6.54	6.66	6.77	6.87	6.96	7.05	7.12	7.20	7.27	7.33	7.39
15	4.17	4.83	5.25	5.56	5.80	5.99	6.16	6.31	6.44	6.55	6.66	6.76	6.84	6.93	7.00	7.07	7.14	7.20	7.26
16	4.13	4.78	5.19	5.49	5.72	5.92	6.08	6.22	6.35	6.46	6.56	6.66	6.74	6.82	6.90	6.97	7.03	7.09	7.15
17	4.10	4.74	5.14	5.43	5.66	5.85	6.01	6.15	6.27	6.38	6.48	6.57	6.66	6.73	6.80	6.87	6.94	7.00	7.05
18	4.07	4.70	5.09	5.38	5.60	5.79	5.94	6.08	6.20	6.31	6.41	6.50	6.58	6.65	6.72	6.79	6.85	6.91	6.96
19	4.05	4.67	5.05	5.33	5.55	5.73	5.89	6.02	6.14	6.25	6.34	6.43	6.51	6.58	6.65	6.72	6.78	6.84	6.89
20	4.02	4.64	5.02	5.29	5.51	5.69	5.84	5.97	6.09	6.19	6.29	6.37	6.45	6.52	6.59	6.65	6.71	6.76	6.82
24	3.96	4.54	4.91	5.17	5.37	5.54	5.69	5.81	5.92	6.02	6.11	6.19	6.26	6.33	6.39	6.45	6.51	6.56	6.61
30	3.89	4.45	4.80	5.05	5.24	5.40	5.54	5.65	5.76	5.85	5.93	6.01	6.08	6.14	6.20	6.26	6.31	6.36	6.41
40	3.82	4.37	4.70	4.93	5.11	5.27	5.39	5.50	5.60	5.69	5.77	5.84	5.90	5.96	6.02	6.07	6.12	6.17	6.21
60	3.76	4.28	4.60	4.82	4.99	5.13	5.25	5.36	5.45	5.53	5.60	5.67	5.73	5.79	5.84	5.89	5.93	5.98	6.02
120	3.70	4.20	4.50	4.71	4.87	5.01	5.12	5.21	5.30	5.38	5.44	5.51	5.56	5.61	5.66	5.71	5.75	5.79	5.83
∞	3.64	4.12	4.40	4.60	4.76	4.88	4.99	5.08	5.16	5.23	5.29	5.35	5.40	5.45	5.49	5.54	5.57	5.61	5.65

Table A.11

Critical Values of R for the Runs Test: Lower Tail

n_1 \ n_2	2	3	4	5	6	7	8	9	10	11	12	13	14	15	16	17	18	19	20
2											2	2	2	2	2	2	2	2	2
3					2	2	2	2	2	2	2	2	2	3	3	3	3	3	3
4			2	2	2	3	3	3	3	3	3	3	3	3	4	4	4	4	4
5			2	2	3	3	3	3	3	4	4	4	4	4	4	4	5	5	5
6		2	2	3	3	3	3	4	4	4	4	5	5	5	5	5	5	6	6
7		2	2	3	3	3	4	4	5	5	5	5	5	6	6	6	6	6	6
8		2	3	3	3	4	4	5	5	5	6	6	6	6	6	7	7	7	7
9		2	3	3	4	4	5	5	5	6	6	6	7	7	7	7	8	8	8
10		2	3	3	4	5	5	5	6	6	7	7	7	7	8	8	8	8	9
11		2	3	4	4	5	5	6	6	7	7	7	8	8	8	9	9	9	9
12	2	2	3	4	4	5	6	6	7	7	7	8	8	8	9	9	9	10	10
13	2	2	3	4	5	5	6	6	7	7	8	8	9	9	9	10	10	10	10
14	2	2	3	4	5	5	6	7	7	8	8	9	9	9	10	10	10	11	11
15	2	3	3	4	5	6	6	7	7	8	8	9	9	10	10	11	11	11	12
16	2	3	4	4	5	6	6	7	8	8	9	9	10	10	11	11	11	12	12
17	2	3	4	4	5	6	7	7	8	9	9	10	10	11	11	11	12	12	13
18	2	3	4	5	5	6	7	8	8	9	9	10	10	11	11	12	12	13	13
19	2	3	4	5	6	6	7	8	8	9	10	10	11	11	12	12	13	13	13
20	2	3	4	5	6	6	7	8	9	9	10	10	11	12	12	13	13	13	14

All values in table correspond to $\alpha = .025$.

Source: Adapted from F. S. Swed and C. Eisenhart, *Ann. Math. Statist.,* vol. 14, 1943, pp. 83–86.

Table A.12

Critical Values of R for the Runs Test: Upper Tail

n_1 \ n_2	2	3	4	5	6	7	8	9	10	11	12	13	14	15	16	17	18	19	20
2																			
3																			
4				9	9														
5			9	10	10	11	11												
6			9	10	11	12	12	13	13	13	13								
7				11	12	13	13	14	14	14	14	15	15	15					
8				11	12	13	14	14	15	15	16	16	16	16	17	17	17	17	17
9					13	14	14	15	16	16	16	17	17	18	18	18	18	18	18
10					13	14	15	16	16	17	17	18	18	18	19	19	19	20	20
11					13	14	15	16	17	17	18	19	19	19	20	20	20	21	21
12					13	14	16	16	17	18	19	19	20	20	21	21	21	22	22
13						15	16	17	18	19	19	20	20	21	21	22	22	23	23
14						15	16	17	18	19	20	20	21	22	22	23	23	23	24
15						15	16	18	18	19	20	21	22	22	23	23	24	24	25
16							17	18	19	20	21	21	22	23	23	24	25	25	25
17							17	18	19	20	21	22	23	23	24	25	25	26	26
18							17	18	19	20	21	22	23	24	25	25	26	26	27
19							17	18	20	21	22	23	23	24	25	26	26	27	27
20							17	18	20	21	22	23	24	25	25	26	27	27	28

All values in table correspond to $\alpha = .025$.

Table A.13

p-Values for Mann-Whitney *U* Statistic Small Samples ($n_1 \le n_2$)

$n_2 = 3$	U_0	n_1 1	2	3
	0	.25	.10	.05
	1	.50	.20	.10
	2		.40	.20
	3		.60	.35
	4			.50

$n_2 = 4$	U_0	n_1 1	2	3	4
	0	.2000	.0667	.0286	.0143
	1	.4000	.1333	.0571	.0286
	2	.6000	.2667	.1143	.0571
	3		.4000	.2000	.1000
	4		.6000	.3143	.1714
	5			.4286	.2429
	6			.5714	.3429
	7				.4429
	8				.5571

$n_2 = 5$	U_0	n_1 1	2	3	4	5
	0	.1667	.0476	.0179	.0079	.0040
	1	.3333	.0952	.0357	.0159	.0079
	2	.5000	.1905	.0714	.0317	.0159
	3		.2857	.1250	.0556	.0278
	4		.4286	.1964	.0952	.0476
	5		.5714	.2857	.1429	.0754
	6			.3929	.2063	.1111
	7			.5000	.2778	.1548
	8				.3651	.2103
	9				.4524	.2738
	10				.5476	.3452
	11					.4206
	12					.5000

Table A.13

p-Values for Mann-Whitney *U* Statistic Small Samples ($n_1 \leq n_2$) (*Continued*)

$n_2 = 6$	U_0	1	2	3	4	5	6
	0	.1429	.0357	.0119	.0048	.0022	.0011
	1	.2857	.0714	.0238	.0095	.0043	.0022
	2	.4286	.1429	.0476	.0190	.0087	.0043
	3	.5714	.2143	.0833	.0333	.0152	.0076
	4		.3214	.1310	.0571	.0260	.0130
	5		.4286	.1905	.0857	.0411	.0206
	6		.5714	.2738	.1286	.0628	.0325
	7			.3571	.1762	.0887	.0465
	8			.4524	.2381	.1234	.0660
	9			.5476	.3048	.1645	.0898
	10				.3810	.2143	.1201
	11				.4571	.2684	.1548
	12				.5429	.3312	.1970
	13					.3961	.2424
	14					.4654	.2944
	15					.5346	.3496
	16						.4091
	17						.4686
	18						.5314

(n_1 header spans columns 1–6)

$n_2 = 7$	U_0	1	2	3	4	5	6	7
	0	.1250	.0278	.0083	.0030	.0013	.0006	.0003
	1	.2500	.0556	.0167	.0061	.0025	.0012	.0006
	2	.3750	.1111	.0333	.0121	.0051	.0023	.0012
	3	.5000	.1667	.0583	.0212	.0088	.0041	.0020
	4		.2500	.0917	.0364	.0152	.0070	.0035
	5		.3333	.1333	.0545	.0240	.0111	.0055
	6		.4444	.1917	.0818	.0366	.0175	.0087
	7		.5556	.2583	.1152	.0530	.0256	.0131
	8			.3333	.1576	.0745	.0367	.0189
	9			.4167	.2061	.1010	.0507	.0265
	10			.5000	.2636	.1338	.0688	.0364
	11				.3242	.1717	.0903	.0487
	12				.3939	.2159	.1171	.0641
	13				.4636	.2652	.1474	.0825
	14				.5364	.3194	.1830	.1043
	15					.3775	.2226	.1297
	16					.4381	.2669	.1588
	17					.5000	.3141	.1914
	18						.3654	.2279
	19						.4178	.2675
	20						.4726	.3100
	21						.5274	.3552
	22							.4024
	23							.4508
	24							.5000

(n_1 header spans columns 1–7)

(continued)

Table A.13

p-Values for Mann-Whitney *U* Statistic Small Samples ($n_1 \leq n_2$) (*Continued*)

					n_1				
$n_2 = 8$	U_0	1	2	3	4	5	6	7	8
	0	.1111	.0222	.0061	.0020	.0008	.0003	.0002	.0001
	1	.2222	.0444	.0121	.0040	.0016	.0007	.0003	.0002
	2	.3333	.0889	.0242	.0081	.0031	.0013	.0006	.0003
	3	.4444	.1333	.0424	.0141	.0054	.0023	.0011	.0005
	4	.5556	.2000	.0667	.0242	.0093	.0040	.0019	.0009
	5		.2667	.0970	.0364	.0148	.0063	.0030	.0015
	6		.3556	.1394	.0545	.0225	.0100	.0047	.0023
	7		.4444	.1879	.0768	.0326	.0147	.0070	.0035
	8		.5556	.2485	.1071	.0466	.0213	.0103	.0052
	9			.3152	.1414	.0637	.0296	.0145	.0074
	10			.3879	.1838	.0855	.0406	.0200	.0103
	11			.4606	.2303	.1111	.0539	.0270	.0141
	12			.5394	.2848	.1422	.0709	.0361	.0190
	13				.3414	.1772	.0906	.0469	.0249
	14				.4040	.2176	.1142	.0603	.0325
	15				.4667	.2618	.1412	.0760	.0415
	16				.5333	.3108	.1725	.0946	.0524
	17					.3621	.2068	.1159	.0652
	18					.4165	.2454	.1405	.0803
	19					.4716	.2864	.1678	.0974
	20					.5284	.3310	.1984	.1172
	21						.3773	.2317	.1393
	22						.4259	.2679	.1641
	23						.4749	.3063	.1911
	24						.5251	.3472	.2209
	25							.3894	.2527
	26							.4333	.2869
	27							.4775	.3227
	28							.5225	.3605
	29								.3992
	30								.4392
	31								.4796
	32								.5204

Table A.13

***p*-Values for Mann-Whitney *U* Statistic Small Samples ($n_1 \le n_2$) (*Continued*)**

$n_2 = 9$ U_0	1	2	3	4	5	6	7	8	9
0	.1000	.0182	.0045	.0014	.0005	.0002	.0001	.0000	.0000
1	.2000	.0364	.0091	.0028	.0010	.0004	.0002	.0001	.0000
2	.3000	.0727	.0182	.0056	.0020	.0008	.0003	.0002	.0001
3	.4000	.1091	.0318	.0098	.0035	.0014	.0006	.0003	.0001
4	.5000	.1636	.0500	.0168	.0060	.0024	.0010	.0005	.0002
5		.2182	.0727	.0252	.0095	.0038	.0017	.0008	.0004
6		.2909	.1045	.0378	.0145	.0060	.0026	.0012	.0006
7		.3636	.1409	.0531	.0210	.0088	.0039	.0019	.0009
8		.4545	.1864	.0741	.0300	.0128	.0058	.0028	.0014
9		.5455	.2409	.0993	.0415	.0180	.0082	.0039	.0020
10			.3000	.1301	.0559	.0248	.0115	.0056	.0028
11			.3636	.1650	.0734	.0332	.0156	.0076	.0039
12			.4318	.2070	.0949	.0440	.0209	.0103	.0053
13			.5000	.2517	.1199	.0567	.0274	.0137	.0071
14				.3021	.1489	.0723	.0356	.0180	.0094
15				.3552	.1818	.0905	.0454	.0232	.0122
16				.4126	.2188	.1119	.0571	.0296	.0157
17				.4699	.2592	.1361	.0708	.0372	.0200
18				.5301	.3032	.1638	.0869	.0464	.0252
19					.3497	.1942	.1052	.0570	.0313
20					.3986	.2280	.1261	.0694	.0385
21					.4491	.2643	.1496	.0836	.0470
22					.5000	.3035	.1755	.0998	.0567
23						.3445	.2039	.1179	.0680
24						.3878	.2349	.1383	.0807
25						.4320	.2680	.1606	.0951
26						.4773	.3032	.1852	.1112
27						.5227	.3403	.2117	.1290
28							.3788	.2404	.1487
29							.4185	.2707	.1701
30							.4591	.3029	.1933
31							.5000	.3365	.2181
32								.3715	.2447
33								.4074	.2729
34								.4442	.3024
35								.4813	.3332
36								.5187	.3652
37									.3981
38									.4317
39									.4657
40									.5000

(continued)

Table A.13

p-Values for Mann-Whitney *U* Statistic Small Samples ($n_1 \leq n_2$) (*Continued*)

$n_2 = 10$ U_0	1	2	3	4	5	6	7	8	9	10
						n_1				
0	.0909	.0152	.0035	.0010	.0003	.0001	.0001	.0000	.0000	.0000
1	.1818	.0303	.0070	.0020	.0007	.0002	.0001	.0000	.0000	.0000
2	.2727	.0606	.0140	.0040	.0013	.0005	.0002	.0001	.0000	.0000
3	.3636	.0909	.0245	.0070	.0023	.0009	.0004	.0002	.0001	.0000
4	.4545	.1364	.0385	.0120	.0040	.0015	.0006	.0003	.0001	.0001
5	.5455	.1818	.0559	.0180	.0063	.0024	.0010	.0004	.0002	.0001
6		.2424	.0804	.0270	.0097	.0037	.0015	.0007	.0003	.0002
7		.3030	.1084	.0380	.0140	.0055	.0023	.0010	.0005	.0002
8		.3788	.1434	.0529	.0200	.0080	.0034	.0015	.0007	.0004
9		.4545	.1853	.0709	.0276	.0112	.0048	.0022	.0011	.0005
10		.5455	.2343	.0939	.0376	.0156	.0068	.0031	.0015	.0008
11			.2867	.1199	.0496	.0210	.0093	.0043	.0021	.0010
12			.3462	.1518	.0646	.0280	.0125	.0058	.0028	.0014
13			.4056	.1868	.0823	.0363	.0165	.0078	.0038	.0019
14			.4685	.2268	.1032	.0467	.0215	.0103	.0051	.0026
15			.5315	.2697	.1272	.0589	.0277	.0133	.0066	.0034
16				.3177	.1548	.0736	.0351	.0171	.0086	.0045
17				.3666	.1855	.0903	.0439	.0217	.0110	.0057
18				.4196	.2198	.1099	.0544	.0273	.0140	.0073
19				.4725	.2567	.1317	.0665	.0338	.0175	.0093
20				.5275	.2970	.1566	.0806	.0416	.0217	.0116
21					.3393	.1838	.0966	.0506	.0267	.0144
22					.3839	.2139	.1148	.0610	.0326	.0177
23					.4296	.2461	.1349	.0729	.0394	.0216
24					.4765	.2811	.1574	.0864	.0474	.0262
25					.5235	.3177	.1819	.1015	.0564	.0315
26						.3564	.2087	.1185	.0667	.0376
27						.3962	.2374	.1371	.0782	.0446
28						.4374	.2681	.1577	.0912	.0526
29						.4789	.3004	.1800	.1055	.0615
30						.5211	.3345	.2041	.1214	.0716
31							.3698	.2299	.1388	.0827
32							.4063	.2574	.1577	.0952
33							.4434	.2863	.1781	.1088
34							.4811	.3167	.2001	.1237
35							.5189	.3482	.2235	.1399
36								.3809	.2483	.1575
37								.4143	.2745	.1763
38								.4484	.3019	.1965
39								.4827	.3304	.2179
40								.5173	.3598	.2406
41									.3901	.2644
42									.4211	.2894
43									.4524	.3153
44									.4841	.3421
45									.5159	.3697
46										.3980
47										.4267
48										.4559
49										.4853
50										.5147

Table A.14

Critical Values of *T* for the Wilcoxon Matched-Pairs Signed Rank Test (Small Samples)

1-SIDED	2-SIDED	n = 5	n = 6	n = 7	n = 8	n = 9	n = 10
$\alpha = .05$	$\alpha = .10$	1	2	4	6	8	11
$\alpha = .025$	$\alpha = .05$		1	2	4	6	8
$\alpha = .01$	$\alpha = .02$			0	2	3	5
$\alpha = .005$	$\alpha = .01$				0	2	3

1-SIDED	2-SIDED	n = 11	n = 12	n = 13	n = 14	n = 15	n = 16
$\alpha = .05$	$\alpha = .10$	14	17	21	26	30	36
$\alpha = .025$	$\alpha = .05$	11	14	17	21	25	30
$\alpha = .01$	$\alpha = .02$	7	10	13	16	20	24
$\alpha = .005$	$\alpha = .01$	5	7	10	13	16	19

1-SIDED	2-SIDED	n = 17	n = 18	n = 19	n = 20	n = 21	n = 22
$\alpha = .05$	$\alpha = .10$	41	47	54	60	68	75
$\alpha = .025$	$\alpha = .05$	35	40	46	52	59	66
$\alpha = .01$	$\alpha = .02$	28	33	38	43	49	56
$\alpha = .005$	$\alpha = .01$	23	28	32	37	43	49

1-SIDED	2-SIDED	n = 23	n = 24	n = 25	n = 26	n = 27	n = 28
$\alpha = .05$	$\alpha = .10$	83	92	101	110	120	130
$\alpha = .025$	$\alpha = .05$	73	81	90	98	107	117
$\alpha = .01$	$\alpha = .02$	62	69	77	85	93	102
$\alpha = .005$	$\alpha = .01$	55	61	68	76	84	92

1-SIDED	2-SIDED	n = 29	n = 30	n = 31	n = 32	n = 33	n = 34
$\alpha = .05$	$\alpha = .10$	141	152	163	175	188	201
$\alpha = .025$	$\alpha = .05$	127	137	148	159	171	183
$\alpha = .01$	$\alpha = .02$	111	120	130	141	151	162
$\alpha = .005$	$\alpha = .01$	100	109	118	128	138	149

1-SIDED	2-SIDED	n = 35	n = 36	n = 37	n = 38	n = 39	
$\alpha = .05$	$\alpha = .10$	214	228	242	256	271	
$\alpha = .025$	$\alpha = .05$	195	208	222	235	250	
$\alpha = .01$	$\alpha = .02$	174	186	198	211	224	
$\alpha = .005$	$\alpha = .01$	160	171	183	195	208	

1-SIDED	2-SIDED	n = 40	n = 41	n = 42	n = 43	n = 44	n = 45
$\alpha = .05$	$\alpha = .10$	287	303	319	336	353	371
$\alpha = .025$	$\alpha = .05$	264	279	295	311	327	344
$\alpha = .01$	$\alpha = .02$	238	252	267	281	297	313
$\alpha = .005$	$\alpha = .01$	221	234	248	262	277	292

1-SIDED	2-SIDED	n = 46	n = 47	n = 48	n = 49	n = 50	
$\alpha = .05$	$\alpha = .10$	389	408	427	446	466	
$\alpha = .025$	$\alpha = .05$	361	379	397	415	434	
$\alpha = .01$	$\alpha = .02$	329	345	362	380	398	
$\alpha = .005$	$\alpha = .01$	307	323	339	356	373	

From E. Wilcoxon and R. A. Wilcox, "Some Rapid Approximate Statistical Procedures," 1964. Reprinted by permission of Lederle Labs, a division of the American Cyanamid Co.

Table A.15

Factors for Control Charts

| Number of Items In Sample | AVERAGES | | | | RANGES | |
| | Factors for Control Limits | | Factors for Central Line | | Factors for Control Limits | |
n	A_2	A_3	d_2	D_3	D_4
2	1.880	2.659	1.128	0	3.267
3	1.023	1.954	1.693	0	2.575
4	0.729	1.628	2.059	0	2.282
5	0.577	1.427	2.326	0	2.115
6	0.483	1.287	2.534	0	2.004
7	0.419	1.182	2.704	0.076	1.924
8	0.373	1.099	2.847	0.136	1.864
9	0.337	1.032	2.970	0.184	1.816
10	0.308	0.975	3.078	0.223	1.777
11	0.285	0.927	3.173	0.256	1.744
12	0.266	0.886	3.258	0.284	1.716
13	0.249	0.850	3.336	0.308	1.692
14	0.235	0.817	3.407	0.329	1.671
15	0.223	0.789	3.472	0.348	1.652

Adapted from American Society for Testing and Materials, *Manual on Quality Control of Materials*, 1951, Table B2, p. 115. Copyright ASTM INTERNATIONAL. Reprinted with permission.

ANSWERS TO SELECTED ODD-NUMBERED QUANTITATIVE PROBLEMS

Chapter 1

1.5.
a. ratio
b. ratio
c. ordinal
d. nominal
e. ratio
f. ratio
g. nominal
h. ratio

1.7.
a. 900 electric contractors
b. 35 contractors
c. average score for 35 participants
d. average score for all 900 electric contractors

Chapter 2

No answers given

Chapter 3

3.1. $\Sigma x = 333.6$
3.3. 294
3.5. 4

3.7. 107, 127, 145, 114, 127.5, 143.5
3.9. 3,444,391.5, 6,257,698.5, 2,617,725, 3,911,814, 6,267,891, 9,349,818
3.11.
a. 8
b. 2.0408
c. 6.2041
d. 2.4908
e. 4
f. 0.69, −0.92, −0.11, 1.89, −1.32, −0.52, 0.29
3.13.
a. 4.598
b. 4.598
3.15. 58,631.295, 242.139
3.17.
a. .75
b. .84
c. .609
d. .902
3.19.
a. 2.667
b. 11.06
c. 3.326
d. 5
e. −0.85
f. 37.65%
3.21. Between 113 and 137
Between 101 and 149
Between 89 and 161

3.23. 2.236
3.25. 95%, 2.5%, .15%, 16%
3.27. 4.64, 3.59, 1
3.29. 185.694, 13.627
3.31.
a. 44.8969
b. 44.818
c. 39
d. 187.189
e. 13.682
3.33.
a. 101,250
b. 75,000
c. 25,000
d. 8,373,437,500
e. 91,506.49
3.35. skewed right
3.37. 0.726; positively skewed
3.39. no mild or extreme outliers. negatively skewed
3.41. 2.5, 2, 2, 7, 1, 3 2
3.43. 6345.2, 5488.5, 4524, 6299.5, 10,441, 4485.5, 7741.5, 7769, 3256
3.45.
a. 2425,1965
b. 5208, 1335
c. 2,023,272.55, 1422.42
d. −0.63, 2.72
e. 0.97

3.47. **a.** 33,412, 33.75, 32.5
        b. 58.483, 7.647
3.49. 10.78%, 6.43%
3.51. **a.** 392 to 446, 365 to 473,
             338 to 500
        b. 79.7%
        c. −0.704
3.53. skewed right, median
3.55. 21.93, 18.14

Chapter 4

4.1.   15, .60
4.3.   {4, 8, 10, 14, 16, 18, 20, 22,
           26, 28, 30}
4.5.   20, combinations, .60
4.7.   **a.** 38,760
        b. 720
4.9.   **a.** .7167
        b. .5000
        c. .6500
        d. .5167
4.11. not solvable
4.13. **a.** .86
        b. .31
        c. .14
4.15. **a.** .2807
        b. .0526
        c. .0000
        d. .0000
4.17. **a.** .0122
        b. .0144
4.19. **a.** .90
        b. .053
        c. .047
        d. .396
        e. .504
        f. .396
        g. .504
4.21. **a.** .039
        b. .571
        c. .129
4.23. **a.** .2286
        b. .2297
        c. .3231
        d. .0000
4.25. not independent
4.27. **a.** .4054
        b. .3261

c. .4074
d. .32
4.29. **a.** .07
        b. .3088
        c. .3919
        d. .9504
4.31. .0538, .5161, .4301
4.33. .7941, .2059
4.35. **a.** .4211
        b. .6316
        c. .2105
        d. .1250
        e. .5263
        f. .0000
        g. .6667
        h. .0000
4.37. **a.** .08974
        b. .0000; A & B are
             mutually exclusive
        c. .28205
        d. .0000; mutually
             exclusive
        e. .36364
        f. .38095
        g. .4615
        h. .02513
4.39. **a.** .91
        b. .09
        c. .3462
        d. .13
4.41. **a.** .032
        b. .00629
        c. .20
        d. .03366
        e. .7607
4.43. **a.** .43
        b. .189
        c. .6143
        d. .699
4.45. **a.** .312
        b. .572
        c. .9176
        d. .22
        e. .9533
4.47. **a.** .21
        b. .00; mutually
             exclusive
        c. .00
        d. .81

4.49. **a.** .38
        b. .21
        c. .0000
        d. .5190
4.51. .3291, .0623
4.53. .13248, .12572, .16621, .57559,
        .26154

Chapter 5

5.1.   2.666, 1.8364, 1.3552
5.3.   0.956, 1.1305
5.5.   **a.** .0036
        b. .1147
        c. .3822
        d. .5838
5.7.   **a.** 14, 2.05
        b. 24.5, 3.99
        c. 50, 5
5.9.   **a.** .1356
        b. .0032
        c. .113
5.11. **a.** .585
        b. .009
        c. .013
5.13. **a.** .1032
        b. .000
        c. .0352
        d. .348
5.15. **a.** .0538
        b. .1539
        c. .4142
        d. .0672
        e. .0244
        f. .3702
5.17. **a.** 6.3, 2.51
        b. 1.3, 1.14
        c. 8.9, 2.98
        d. 0.6, .775
5.19. 3.5
        a. .0302
        b. .1424
        c. .0817
        d. .42
        e. .1009
5.21. **a.** .5488
        b. .3293
        c. .1220

d. .8913

e. .1912

5.23. **a.** .3012

b. .0000

c. .0336

5.25. **a.** .0104

b. .0000

c. .1653

d. .9636

5.27. **a.** .5091

b. .2937

c. .4167

d. .0014

5.29. **a.** .3756

b. .0002

c. .1486

5.31. **a.** .4286

b. .0714

c. .1143

5.33. .0474

5.35. **a.** .124

b. .849

c. .090

d. .000

5.37. **a.** .1607

b. .7626

c. .3504

d. .5429

5.39. .111, .017, 5, .180, .125, .000, .056, 8, 8

5.41. **a.** .2644

b. .0694

c. .0029

d. .7521

5.43. **a.** 3.52

b. .1098

5.45. **a.** .0687

b. .020

c. .1032

d. 2.28

5.47. .174

5.49. .5488, .0232, .3012

5.51. **a.** .0002

b. .0595

c. .2330

5.53. **a.** .0907

b. .0358

c. .1517

d. .8781

5.55. **a.** .2650

b. .0136

c. .0067

5.57. **a.** .3611

b. .7922

c. .0817

5.59. **a.** .0215

b. .1317

c. .7907

Chapter 6

6.1. **a.** 0.25

b. 220, 11.547

c. .250

d. .375

e. .625

6.3. 2.97, 0.098, .2941

6.5. 981.5, .000294, .2353, .0000, .2353

6.7. **a.** .7088

b. .0099

c. .5042

d. .1030

e. .6772

f. .1093

6.9. **a.** .0139

b. .7172

c. .2366

d. .0392

6.11. **a.** .9050

b. .0132

c. .1308

d. 17,293.23

e. $25,440

6.13. 2100, 2558

6.15. 6.66

6.17. **a.** $P(x \leq 16.5 \mid \mu = 21$ and $\sigma = 2.51)$

b. $P(10.5 \leq x \leq 20.5 \mid \mu = 12.5$ and $\sigma = 2.5)$

c. $P(21.5 \leq x \leq 22.5 \mid \mu = 24$ and $\sigma = 3.10)$

d. $P(x > 14.5 \mid \mu = 7.2$ and $\sigma = 1.99)$

6.19. **a.** .1170, .120

b. .4090, .415

c. .1985, .196

d. fails test

6.21. .0495

6.23. **a.** .0475

b. .6733

c. .0268

d. .0801

6.27. **a.** .0012

b. .8700

c. .0011

d. .9918

6.29. **a.** .0000

b. .0000

c. .0872

d. .41 minutes

6.31. 70, .00079, .9425

6.33. 15, 15, .1254

6.35. **a.** .1587

b. .0013

c. .6915

d. .9270

e. .0000

6.37. **a.** .0202

b. .9817

c. .1849

d. .4449

6.39. .0071

6.41. .1131, .2912, .1543

6.43. .5319, 41.5, .0213

6.45. **a.** .2119

b. .6284

c. .3617

d. .0028

6.47. **a.** .2236

b. .0537

c. .9972

d. .5054

6.49. **a.** .0009

b. .8790

c. .3458

6.51. **a.** .3594

b. .2887

c. .9761

6.53. $11,428.57

6.55. .5488, .2592, 1.67 months

6.57. 1940, 2018.75, 2269

6.59. .0367, .0166

Chapter 7

7.7. 825

7.13. a. .0548
b. .7881
c. .0082
d. .8575
e. .1664

7.15. 11.11

7.17. a. .9772
b. .2385
c. .1469
d. .1230

7.19. .0000

7.21. a. .0885
b. .0060
c. .0000
d. 7.0699

7.23. a. .1492
b. .9404
c. .6985
d. .1445
e. .0000

7.25. .26

7.27. a. .9960
b. .00003
c. .1190

7.29. a. .1020
b. .7568
c. .7019

7.31. 55, 45, 90, 25, 35

7.37. a. .3156
b. .00003
c. .1736

7.41. a. .0021
b. .9265
c. .0281

7.43. a. .0154
b. .1271
c. .4368
d. .0274
e. .00003

7.45. a. .8534
b. .0256
c. .0007

7.49. .4682, .0000, .0034

7.51. .9394

Chapter 8

8.1. a. $24.11 \leq \mu \leq 25.89$
b. $113.17 \leq \mu \leq 126.03$
c. $3.136 \leq \mu \leq 3.702$
d. $54.55 \leq \mu \leq 58.85$

8.3. $45.92 \leq \mu \leq 48.08$

8.5. $66, 62.75 \leq \mu \leq 69.25$

8.7. $5.3, 5.13 \leq \mu \leq 5.47$

8.9. $2.852 \leq \mu \leq 3.760$

8.11. $24.511, 1.497, 23.014 \leq \mu \leq 26.008$

8.13. $42.18 \leq \mu \leq 49.06$

8.15. $120.6 \leq \mu \leq 136.2, 128.4$

8.17. $15.631 \leq \mu \leq 16.545, 16.088$

8.19. $2.26886 \leq \mu \leq 2.45346, 2.36116, .0923$

8.21. $36.77 \leq \mu \leq 62.83$

8.23. $7.53 \leq \mu \leq 14.67$

8.25. a. $.316 \leq p \leq .704$
b. $.777 \leq p \leq .863$
c. $.456 \leq p \leq .504$
d. $.246 \leq p \leq .394$

8.27. $.38 \leq p \leq .56$
$.36 \leq p \leq .58$
$.33 \leq p \leq .61$

8.29. $.4287 \leq p \leq .5113$
$.2488 \leq p \leq .3112$

8.31. a. .266
b. $.247 \leq p \leq .285$

8.33. $.5935 \leq p \leq .6665$

8.35. a. $18.46 \leq \sigma^2 \leq 189.73$
b. $0.64 \leq \sigma^2 \leq 7.46$
c. $645.45 \leq \sigma^2 \leq 1923.10$
d. $12.61 < cr^2 \leq 31.89$

8.37. $9.71 \leq \sigma^2 \leq 46.03, 18.49$

8.39. $14,084,038.51 \leq \sigma^2 \leq 69,553,848.45$

8.41. a. 2522
b. 601
c. 268
d. 16,577

8.43. 106

8.45. 1,083

8.47. 97

8.49. $12.03, 11.78 \mu \leq 12.28$,
$11.72 \leq \mu \leq 12.34$,
$11.58 \leq \mu \leq 12.48$

8.51. $29.133 \leq \sigma^2 \leq 148.235$,
$25.911 \leq \sigma^2 \leq 182.52$

8.53. $9.19 \leq \mu \leq 12.34$

8.55. $2.307 \leq \sigma^2 \leq 15.374$

8.57. $36.231 \leq \mu \leq 38.281$

8.59. $.542 \leq p \leq .596$

8.61. $5.892 \leq \mu \leq 7.542$

8.63. $.726 \leq p \leq .814$

8.65. $34.11 \leq \mu \leq 53.29$,
$101.44 \leq \sigma^2 \leq 821.35$

8.67. $-0.20 \leq \mu \leq 5.16, 2.48$

8.69. 543

8.71. $.00013 \leq \sigma^2 \leq .00037$

Chapter 9

9.1. a. $z = 2.77$, reject
b. .0028, reject
c. 22.115, 27.885

9.3. a. $z = 1.59$, reject
b. .0559, reject
c. 1212.04

9.5. $z = 1.84$, fail to reject

9.7. $z = 1.46$, fail to reject

9.9. $z = -5.46$, reject

9.11. $t = 0.56$, fail to reject

9.13. $t = 2.44$, reject

9.15. $t = 1.59$, fail to reject

9.17. $t = -3.31$, reject

9.19. $t = -2.02$, fail to reject

9.21. fail to reject

9.23. $z = -1.66$, fail to reject

9.25. $z = -1.89$, fail to reject

9.27. $z = 1.23$, fail to reject,
$z = 1.34$, fail to reject

9.29. $z = -3.11$, reject

9.31. a. $\chi^2 = 22.4$, fail to reject
b. $\chi^2 = 42$, reject
c. $\chi^2 = 0.64$, reject
d. $\chi^2 = 2.4$, reject

9.33. $\chi^2 = 21.7$, fail to reject

9.35. $\chi^2 = 17.34$, reject

9.37. a. $\beta = .8159$
b. $\beta = .7422$
c. $\beta = .5636$
d. $\beta = .3669$

9.39. a. $\beta = .3632$
b. $\beta = .0122$
c. $\beta = .0000$

9.41. $z = 3.21$, reject

9.43. a. $z = 0.85$, fail to reject
b. $z = -2.05$, reject

9.45. a. $\beta = .1003$,
b. $\beta = .6255$

9.47. $z = 1.46$, fail to reject

9.49. $\chi^2 = 0.62$, fail to reject

9.51. a. $z = 1.38$, fail to reject
b. $z = -2.52$, $\beta = .0059$

9.53. $z = 1.53$, fail to reject,
$z = 0.74$, $\beta = .7704$

9.55. $z = 0.77$, fail to reject, 0.01,
$z = 0.79$, $\beta = .7852$

9.57. $\chi^2 = 47.01$, reject

9.59. a. $z = -1.43$, fail to reject
b. $\beta = .3156$

9.61. $t = -2.60$, reject

Chapter 10

10.1. a. $z = -1.01$, fail to reject
b. -2.41
c. $.1562$

10.3. a. $z = 5.48$, reject
b. $4.04 \leq \mu \leq 10.02$

10.5. $-1.86 \leq \mu \leq -0.54$

10.7. $z = -2.32$, fail to reject

10.9. $z = 227$, reject

10.11. $t = -1.05$, fail to reject

10.13. $t = 4.64$, reject

10.15. $6887.76 \leq \mu_1 - \mu_2 \leq$
$11,112.24$

10.17. $t = 2.06$, reject

10.19. $t = 5.15$, reject

10.21. $t = 3.31$, reject

10.23. $26.29 \leq D \leq 54.83$

10.25. $-3415.6 \leq D \leq 6021.2$

10.27. $0.1685 \leq D \leq 1.2825$

10.29. $63.71 \leq D \leq 86.29$

10.31. a. $z = 0.75$, fail to reject
b. $z = 4.83$, reject

10.33. $zx = -3.35$, reject

10.35. $z = -0.94$, fail to reject

10.37. $z = 2.35$, reject

10.39. $F = .5548$, fail to reject

10.41. $F = 0.8408$, fail to reject

10.43. $F = 1.53$, fail to reject

10.45. $z = -2.38$, reject

10.47. $t = 0.85$, fail to reject

10.49. $t = -5.26$, reject

10.51. $z = -1.20$, fail to reject

10.53. $F = 1.24$, fail to reject

10.55. $-3.201 \leq D \leq 2.313$

10.57. $F = 1.31$, fail to reject

10.59. $t = 3.12$, reject

10.61. $z = 6.78$, reject

10.63. $3.553 \leq D \leq 5.447$

10.65. $t = 6.71$, reject

10.67. $.142 \leq p_1 - p_2 \leq .250$

10.69. $z = 8.86$, reject

10.71. $t = 4.52$, reject

Chapter 11

11.5. $F = 11.07$, reject

11.7. $F = 13.00$, reject

11.9. 4, 50, 54, 145.8975, 19.4436,
$F = 7.50$, reject

11.11. $F = 10.10$, reject

11.13. $F = 11.76$ reject

11.15. 4 levels; sizes 18, 15, 21, and
11; $F = 2.95$, $p = .04$; means =
226.73, 238.79, 232.58, and
239.82.

11.17. HSD = 0.896, groups 3 & 6
significantly different

11.19. HSD = 1.586, groups 1 & 2
significantly different

11.21. HSD = 10.27, groups 1 & 3
significantly different

11.23. $HSD_{1,3} = .0381$, groups 1 & 3
significantly different

11.25. $HSD_{1,3} = 1.763$, $HSD_{2,3} =$
1.620, groups 1 & 3 and 2 &
3 significantly different

11.29. $F = 1.48$, fail to reject

11.31. $F = 3.90$, fail to reject

11.33. $F = 15.37$, reject

11.37. 2, 1, 4 row levels, 3 column
levels, yes
$df_{row} = 3$, $df_{col.} = 2$, $df_{int} = 6$,
$df_{error} = 12$, $df_{total} = 23$

11.39. $MS_{row} = 1.047$, $MS_{col.} =$
1.281, $MS_{int} = 0.258$,
$MS_{error} = 0.436$,
$F_{row} = 2.40$, $F_{col.} = 2.94$,
$F_{int.} = 0.59$,
fail to reject any hypothesis

11.41. $F_{row} = 87.25$, reject;
$F_{col.} = 63.67$, reject;
$F_{int.} = 2.07$, fail to reject

11.43. $F_{row} = 34.31$, reject;
$F_{col.} = 14.20$, reject;
$F_{int} = 3.32$, reject

11.45. no significant interaction
or row effects; significant
column effects.

11.47. $F = 8.82$, reject; HSD = 3.33
groups 1 & 2, 2 & 3, and
2 & 4 significantly
different.

11.49. $df_{treat.} = 5$, $MS_{treat} = 42.0$,
$df_{error} = 36$, $MS_{error} = 18.194$,
$F = 2.31$

11.51. 1 treatment variable, 3
levels; 1 blocking variable, 6
levels; $df_{treat.} = 2$, $df_{block} = 5$,
$df_{error} = 10$

11.53. $F_{treat.} = 31.49$, reject; $F_{blocks} =$
43.20, reject; HSD = 8.757,
no pairs significant

11.55. $F_{rows} = 38.21$, reject;
$F_{col.} = 0.23$, fail to reject;
$F_{inter.} = 1.30$, fail to reject

11.57. $F = 7.38$, reject

11.59. $F = 0.46$, fail to reject

11.61. $F_{treat} = 13.64$, reject

Chapter 12

12.1. -0.927

12.3. -0.37

12.5. 0.975, 0.985, 0.957

12.7. $\hat{y} = 144.414 - 0.898x$

12.9. $\hat{y} = 15.460 - 0.715x$

12.11. $\hat{y} = 378.2 - 0.0005x$

12.13. 48.1694, 32.0489, 57.3811,
41.2606, 25.1401, -1.1694,
3.9511, -1.3811, 2.7394,
-4.1401

12.15. 18.6597, 37.5229, 51.8948,
62.6737, 86.0281, 118.3648,
122.8561, 6.3403, -8.5229,
-5.8948, 7.3263, 1.9720,
-6.3648, 5.1439

12.17. 4.0259, 11.1722, 9.7429, 12.6014, 10.4576, 0.9741, 0.8278, −0.7429, 2.3986, −3.4576

12.19. 4.7244, −0.9836, −0.3997, −6.7537, 2.7683, 0.6442, no apparent violation of assumptions

12.21. Error terms appear to be non independent

12.25. SSE = 272.0, s_e = 7.376

12.27. SSE = 19.8885, s_e = 2.575

12.29. 4.391

12.31. 40.526

12.33. r^2 = .972

12.35. r^2 = .685

12.37. SSE = 0.6031; r^2 = 0.2592, Real GDP is not a good predictor of Long-Term Interest Rates

12.39. t = −13.18, reject

12.41. t = −2.56, fail to reject

12.43. t = 2.874

12.45. 38.523 ≤ y ≤ 70.705, 10.447 ≤ y ≤ 44.901

12.47. 0.97 ≤ $E(y_{10})$ ≤ 15.65

12.49. Trend line: Long-term interest rate = 3.3371 + 0.015071 (Recoded Month); Forecast for December 2009 = 3.46

12.51. r = −.940

12.53. a. $\hat{y}$ = −11.335 + 0.355 x
 b. 7.48, 5.35, 3.22, 6.415, 9.255, 10.675, 4.64, 9.965, −2.48, −0.35, 3.78, −2.415, 0.745, 1.325, −1.64, 1.035
 c. SSE = 32.4649
 d. s_e = 2.3261
 e. r^2 = .608
 f. t = 3.05, reject

12.55. a. 20.92 ≤ $E(y_{60})$ ≤ 26.8
 b. 20.994 ≤ y ≤ 37.688

12.57. r^2 = .826

12.59. $\hat{y}$ = −0.863565 + 0.92025x; r^2 = .405

12.61. r = −.489

12.63. r^2 = .90605, s_e = 21.12266

12.65. r^2 = .2406, s_e = 1337.5556, t = −1.26, fail to reject

Chapter 13

13.1. $\hat{y}$ = 25.0287 − 0.0497x_1 + 1.9282x_2, 28.586

13.3. $\hat{y}$ = 121.62 − 0.174x_1 + 6.02x_2 + 0.00026x_3 + 0.0041x_4, 4

13.5. Per capita consumption = −7,655.99 + 116.66 paper consumption − 265.09 fish consumption + 45.63 gasoline consumption

13.7. 9, only t = 2.73 for x_1, significant at α = .05

13.9. Per capita consumption = − 7,655.99 + 116.66 paper consumption − 265.09 fish consumption + 45.63 gasoline consumption; F = 14.32 with p-value = .0023; t = 2.66 with p-value = .033 for gasoline consumption. The p-values of the t statistics for the other two predictors are insignificant.

13.11. $\hat{y}$ = 3.98077 + 0.07322x_1 − 0.03232x_2 − 0.00389x_3, F = 100.47 significant at α = .000 001, t = 3.50 for x_1 significant at p-value = .005

13.13. 3 predictors, 15 observations, $\hat{y}$ = 657.053 + 5.7103x_1 − 0.4169x_2 − 3.4715x_3, F = 8.96 with p = .0027, x_1 significant at α = .01, x_3 significant at α = .05

13.15. s_e = 9.722, R^2 = .515, adjusted R^2 = .404

13.17. S = 6.490, R^2 = .0056, adjusted R^2 = −.243

13.19. model with x_1, x_2: s_e = 6.333, R^2 = .963, adjusted R^2 = .957

model with x_1 : s_e = 6.124, R^2 = .963, adjusted R^2 = .960

13.21. lack of homogeneity error of variance

13.23. 2, $\hat{y}$ = 203.3937 + 1.1151x_1 − 2.2115x_2, F = 24.55, R^2 = 66.3%

13.25. y = 362.3054 − 4.74552x_1 − 13.8997x_2 + 1.874297x_3; F = 16.05, s_e = 37.07; R^2 = .858; adjusted R^2 = .804; x_1 only significant predictor

13.27. Treasury Rate = − 1.3128+ 0 Bank Rate + 0.9015 Prime Rate, F = 689.8266 with p = .000 00836 (significant), R^2 = 0.993; adjusted R^2 = 0.991; t test for Prime Rate is significant

13.29. Exchange rate(C$ per US$) = 1.949 + 0.0000 (Price Index) −1.0406 (Relative Unit Labour Cost) + 0.0000 (PPI-Mfg) + 0.5442 (CPI)

Chapter 14

14.1. Simple Model: $\hat{y}$ = −147.27 + 27.128x, F = 229.67 with p = .000, s_e = 27.27, R^2 = .97, adjusted R^2 = .966 Quadratic Model: y = −22.01 + 3.385x_1 + 0.9373x_2, F = 578.76 with p = .000, s_e = 12.3, R^2 = .995, adjusted R^2 = .993, for x_1: t = 0.75, for x_2: t = 5.33

14.3. Simple Model: $\hat{y}$ = −1456.6 +71.017x; R^2 = .928; adjusted R^2 = .910; Quadratic Model: $\hat{y}$ = 1012 − 14.06 x + 0.6115 x^2, R^2 = .947; adjusted R^2 = .911, $t(x)$ = −0.17, $t(x^2)$ = 1.03, no significant predictor

14.5. $\hat{y} = -28.61 - 2.68x_1 + 18.25x_2 - 0.2135x_1^2 - 1.533x_2^2 + 1.226x_1x_2$; $F = 63.43$; $s_e = 4.669$, $R^2 = .958$; adjusted $R^2 = .943$; no significant t ratios. Model with no interaction term: $R^2 = .957$

14.7. $\hat{y} = 13.619 - 0.01201x_1 + 2.988x_2$, $F = 8.43$ significant at $\alpha = .01$, $t = 3.88$ for x_2, (dummy variable) significant at $\alpha = .01$, $s_e = 1.245$, $R^2 = .652$, adj. $R^2 = .575$

14.9. x_1 and x_2 are significant predictors at $\alpha = .05$

14.11. Price $= 3.4394 - 0.0195$ Hours $+ 9.113$ ProbSeat $+ 10.528$ Location, $F = 6.58$ significant at $\alpha = .01$, $t = 3.95$ for Location (dummy variable) significant at $\alpha = .01$, $s_e = 3.94$, $R^2 = .664$, adj. $R^2 = .563$

14.13. Step 1: x_2 entered, $t = -7.53$, $r^2 = .794$
Step 2: x_3 entered, $t_2 = -4.60$, $t_3 = 2.93$, $R^2 = .876$

14.15. 4 predictors, x_4 and x_5 are not in model.

14.17. Step 1: Durability in the model, $t = 3.32$, $r^2 = .379$, $s_e = 15.48$

14.19.

	y	x_1	x_2	x_3
y	–	−.653	−.891	.821
x_1	−.653		.650	−.615
x_2	−.891	.650		−.688
x_3	.821	−.615	−.688	

14.21.

	Value	Durability	Service
Value	–	.559	.553
Durability	.559		.364
Service	.553	.364	

14.23. $\hat{y} = 564 - 27.99\,x_1 - 6.155\,x_2 - 15.90\,x_3$, $R^2 = .809$, adjusted $R^2 = .738$, $s_e = 42.88$, $F = 11.32$ with $p = .003$, x_2 only significant predictor x_1 is a nonsignificant indicator variable

14.25. The procedure stopped at step 1 with only log x in the model, $= -13.20 + 11.64$ log x_1, $R^2 = .9617$

14.27. The procedure went 2 steps, step 1: silver entered, $R^2 = .5244$, step 2: aluminum entered, $R^2 = .8204$, final model: gold $= -50.07 + 18.9$ silver $+ 3.59$ aluminum

14.29. The procedure went 5 steps, step 1: bread entered, $R^2 = .9919$, step 2: coffee entered, $R^2 = .9975$, step 3: chicken entered, $R^2 = .9980$, step 4: beef entered, $R^2 = .9998$, step 5: eggs entered, $R^2 = .999999505$, final model: Price Index $= 100.011 + 1.000$ Bread $+ 1.002$ Coffee $+ 1.000$ Chicken $+ 0.997$ Beef $+ 0.995$ Eggs

14.31. The procedure went 1 step, step 1: Familiarity entered, $R^2 = .6167$, $t = 6.71$, Satisfaction and Proximity did not enter into the analysis.

Chapter 15

15.1. MAD $= 1.367$, MSE $= 2.27$

15.3. MAD $= 3.583$, MSE $= 15.765$

15.5. **a.** 44.75, 52.75, 61.50, 64.75, 70.50, 81
b. 53.25, 56.375, 62.875, 67.25, 76.375, 89.125

15.7. $\alpha = .3$: 9.4, 9, 8.7, 8.8, 9.1, 9.7, 9.9, 9.8

$\alpha = .7$: 9.4, 8.6, 8.1, 8.7, 9.5, 10.6, 10.4, 9.8

15.9. $\alpha = .2$: 332.0, 404.4, 427.1, 386.1, 350.7, 315.0, 325.2, 362.6, 423.5, 453, 477.4, 554.9
$\alpha = .9$: 332.0, 657.8, 532.0, 253.0, 213.4, 176.1, 347.0, 495.5, 649.9, 578.9, 575.4, 836;
$MAD_{\alpha=2} = 190.8$;
$MAD_{\alpha=9} = 168.6$

15.11. Simple regression model: Consumer Price Index $= -4409.2 + 2.2623$ Year, $R^2 = 0.97$. $s_e = 2.43$, $F = 668.56$
Quadratic Model: Consumer Price Index $= -162020 + 160.43$ Year $- 0.03968$ Year^2, $R^2 = 0.98$, $s_e = 2.06$, $F = 467$

15.13. T*C: 1.856, 1.860, 1.861, 1,865, 1.872, 1.879, 1.885, 1.886, 1.882, 1.877, 1.877, 1.883
S*I: 98.94, 101.44, 102.06, 105.75, 101.83, 97.71, 103.89, 99.52, 97.02, 99.35, 96.76, 101.79

15.15. $D = 1.457$, inconclusive

15.17. $D = 0.494$, significant autocorrelation

15.19. Model with 1 lagged variable: Crude Oil Production $= -1.604 + 1.037$ Lag 1, $F = 829.67$, $p = .000$, $R^2 = 97.2\%$, adjusted $R^2 = 97.1\%$, $s_e = 3.82$
Model with 2 lagged variables: Housing Starts $= 0.983 + 1.242$ Lag1 $- 0.233$ Lag2, $F = 405.94$, $p = .000$, $R^2 = 97.4\%$, adjusted $R^2 = 97.1\%$, $s_e = 3.78$; Both models are very strong.

15.21. **a.** 100.0, 139.9, 144.0, 162.6, 200.0, 272.8, 310.7, 327.1, 356.6, 376.9, 388.8, 398.9

b. 32.2, 45.0, 46.4, 52.3, 64.4, 87.8, 100.0, 105.3, 114.8, 121.3, 125.1, 128.4

15.23. 103.2, 124.7

15.25. 121.6, 127.4, 131.4

15.27. **a.** Linear: $= 9.96 - 0.14$ Month, $R^2 = 90.9\%$, Quadratic: $= 10.4 - 0.252$ Month $+ .00445$ $Month_2$, $R^2 = 94.4\%$
b. MAD $= .3385$
c. MAD $(\alpha = .3) = .4374$, MAD $(\alpha = .7) = .2596$
d. $\alpha = .7$ did best
e. 100.28, 101.51, 99.09, 99.12

15.29. 100, 104.8, 114.5, 115.5, 114.1

15.31. $MAD_{movavg.} = 540.44$, $MAD_{\alpha=.2} = 846.43$

15.33. Deasonalized data for 2009 = 5422, 3391, 3685, 3172, 4034, 3506, 6227, 3955, 3170, 3618, 3776, 2842

15.35. Laspeyres: 105.2, 111.0; Paasche: 105.1, 110.8

15.37. $MSE_{ma} = 0.2285$; $MSE_{wma} = 0.1599$

15.39. 98.07, 103.84, 97.04, 101.05

15.41. Linear Model: $\hat{y} = 53.41032 + 0.532488\,x$, $R^2 = 55.7\%$, $F = 27.65$ with $p = .000$, $s_e = 3.43$; Quadratic Model:
$\hat{y} = 47.68663 + 1.853339\,x$ $-0.052834\,x^2$, $R^2 = 76.6\%$, $F = 34.37$ with $p = .000$, $s_e = 2.55$; Quadratic Model is stronger

15.43. $D = 1.443$, accept the null hypothesis, no autocorrelation is present

Chapter 16

16.1. $\chi^2 = 18.095$, reject.

16.3. $\chi^2 = 2.004$, fail to reject, $\lambda = 0.9$; Insufficient evidence to reject as Poisson distributed.

16.5. $\chi^2 = 198.48$, reject.

16.7. $\chi^2 = 2.45$, fail to reject

16.9. $\chi^2 = 3.398$, fail to reject

16.11. $\chi^2 = 0.00$, fail to reject

16.13. $\chi^2 = 34.97$, reject

16.15. $\chi^2 = 6.43$, reject

16.17. $\chi^2 = 3.93$, fail to reject

16.19. $\chi^2 = 1.652$, fail to reject

16.21. $\chi^2 = 14.91$, reject

16.23. $\chi^2 = 7.25$, fail to reject

16.25. $\chi^2 = 59.63$, reject

16.27. $\chi^2 = 54.63$, reject

Chapter 17

17.1. $R = 11$, fail to reject

17.3. $\alpha/2 = .025$, p-value $= .0264$, fail to reject

17.5. $R = 27$, $z = -1.08$, fail to reject

17.7. $U = 26.5$, p-value $= .6454$, fail to reject

17.9. $U = 11$, p-value $= .0156$, fail to reject

17.11. $z = -3.78$, reject

17.13. $z = -2.59$, reject

17.15. $z = -3.20$, reject

17.17. $z = -1.75$, reject

17.19. $K = 21.21$, reject

17.21. $K = 2.75$, fail to reject

17.23. $K = 18.99$, reject

17.25. $\chi_r^2 = 13.8$, reject

17.27. $\chi_r^2 = 14.8$, reject

17.29. 4, 5, $S = 2.04$, fail to reject

17.31. $r_s = .893$

17.33. $r_s = -.95$

17.35. $r_s = -.398$

17.37. $r_s = -.855$

17.39. $U = 20$, p-value $= .2344$, fail to reject

17.41. $K = 7.75$, fail to reject

17.43. $r_s = -.81$

17.45. $z = -0.40$, fail to reject

17.47. $z = 0.96$, fail to reject

17.49. $U = 45.5$, p-value $= .739$, fail to reject

17.51. $z = -1.91$, fail to reject

17.53. $R = 21$, fail to reject

17.55. $z = -2.43$, reject

17.57. $K = 17.21$, reject

17.59. $K = 11.96$, reject

Chapter 18

18.5. $\bar{\bar{x}} = 4.51$, UCL $= 5.17$, LCL $= 3.85$
$\bar{R} = 0.90$, UCL $= 2.05$, LCL $= 0$

18.7. $p = .05$, UCL $= .1534$, LCL $= .000$

18.9. $\bar{c} = 1.34375$, UCL $= 4.82136$, LCL $= .000$

18.11. Chart 1: nine consecutive points below centerline, four out of five points in the outer 2/3 of the lower region; Chart 2: eight consecutive points above the centerline; Chart 3: in control

18.13. 26.96, 1.16, 4.33, 15.18, 2.92, 22.60, 0.48, 16.11, 2.16, 8.09

18.15. $p = .104$, LCL $= 0.000$, UCL $= .234$

18.17. $\bar{c} = 2.13889$, UCL $= 6.52637$, LCL $= .00000$

18.19. For $\bar{x}$ Chart: $\bar{\bar{x}} = 14.99854$, UCL $= 15.02269$, LCL $= 14.97439$; For R Chart: $\bar{R} = .05$, UCL $= .1002$, LCL $= .0000$

18.21. $\bar{c} = 0.64$, UCL $= 3.04$, LCL $= .00000$

18.23. $p = 0.06$, LCL $= 0.0005$, UCL $= .17265$

Chapter 19

19.1. **a.** 390
b. 70
c. 82, 296
d. 140

19.3. 60, 10

19.7. 31.75, 6.50

19.9. Lock in $= 85, 182.5, 97.5$

19.11. **a.** 75,000

b. Avoider

c. >75,000

19.13. 244.275, 194.275

19.15. 21,012.32, 12.32

19.17. **b.** 267.5, 235

c. 352.5, 85

19.19. **a.** 2000, 200

b. 500

19.21. 875, 650

19.23. Reduction: .60, .2333, .1667

Constant: .10, .6222, .2778

Increase: .0375, .0875, .8750;

21,425.55, 2675.55

GLOSSARY

A

a posteriori A term referring to after the experiment; pairwise comparisons made by the researcher *after* determining that there is a significant overall *F* value from ANOVA. Also called *post hoc*.

a priori A term referring to something determined before, or prior to, an experiment.

adjusted R^2 A modified value of R^2 in which the degrees of freedom are taken into account, thereby allowing the researcher to determine whether the value of R^2 is inflated for a particular multiple regression model.

after-process quality control A type of quality control in which product attributes are measured by inspection after the manufacturing process is completed to determine whether the product is acceptable.

all possible regressions A multiple regression search procedure in which all possible multiple linear regression models are determined from the data using all variables.

alpha (α) The probability of committing a Type I error. Also called the *level of significance*.

alternative hypothesis The hypothesis that complements the *null hypothesis*; usually it is the hypothesis that the researcher is interested in proving.

analysis of variance (ANOVA) A technique for statistically analyzing the data from a completely randomized design; uses the *F* test to determine whether there is a significant difference in two or more independent groups.

arithmetic mean The average of a group of numbers.

autocorrelation A problem that arises in regression analysis when the data occur over time and the error terms are correlated. Also called *serial correlation*.

autoregression A multiple regression forecasting technique in which the independent variables are time-lagged versions of the dependent variable.

averaging models Forecasting models in which the forecast is the average of several preceding time periods.

B

backward elimination A step-by-step multiple regression search procedure that begins with a full model containing all predictors. A search is made to determine if there are any nonsignificant independent variables in the model. If there are no nonsignificant predictors, then the backward process ends with the full model. If there are nonsignificant predictors, then the predictor with the smallest absolute value of *t* is eliminated and a new model is developed with the remaining variables. This procedure continues until only variables with significant *t* values remain in the model.

Bayes' rule An extension of the conditional law of probabilities discovered by Thomas Bayes that can be used to revise probabilities.

benchmarking A quality control method in which a company attempts to develop and establish total quality management from product to process by examining and emulating the best practices and techniques used in their industry.

beta (β) The probability of committing a Type II error.

bimodal Data sets that have two modes.

binomial distribution Widely known discrete distribution in which there are only two possibilities on any one trial.

bivariate regression Simple, linear regression.

blocking variable A variable that the researcher wants to control but is not the treatment variable of interest.

947

box and whisker plot A diagram that uses the upper and lower quartiles along with the median and the two most extreme values to depict a distribution graphically; sometimes called a box plot.

C

c chart A quality control chart for attribute compliance that displays the number of nonconformances per item or unit.

categorical data Non numerical data that are frequency counts of categories from one or more variables.

cause-and-effect diagram A tool for displaying possible causes for a quality problem and the interrelationships among the causes. Also called a *fishbone diagram* or an *Ishikawa diagram*.

census A process of gathering data from the whole population for a given measurement of interest.

central limit theorem A theorem that states that regardless of the shape of a population, the distributions of sample means and proportions are normal if sample sizes are large.

centreline The middle horizontal line of a control chart, often determined either by a product or service specification or by computing an expected value from sample information.

Chebyshev's theorem A theorem stating that at least $1 - 1/k^2$ values will fall within $\pm k$ standard deviations of the mean regardless of the shape of the distribution.

check sheet Simple forms consisting of multiple categories and columns for recording tallies for displaying the frequency of outcomes for some quality-related event or activity.

chi-square distribution A continuous distribution determined by the sum of the squares of k independent random variables.

chi-square goodness-of-fit test A statistical test used to analyze probabilities of multinomial distribution trials along a single dimension; compares expected, or theoretical, frequencies of categories from a population distribution with the observed, or actual, frequencies from a distribution.

chi-square test of independence A statistical test used to analyze the frequencies of two variables with multiple categories to determine whether the two variables are independent.

class mark Another name for *class midpoint*; the midpoint of each class interval in grouped data.

class midpoint For any given class interval of a frequency distribution, the value halfway across the class interval; the average of the two class endpoints.

classical method The method of assigning probabilities based on rules and laws.

classification variable The independent variable of an experimental design that was present prior to the experiment and is not the result of the researcher's manipulations or control.

classifications The subcategories of the independent variable used by the researcher in the experimental design. Also called *levels*.

cluster sampling A type of random sampling in which the population is divided into nonoverlapping areas or clusters and elements are randomly sampled from the areas or clusters. Also called area sampling.

coefficient of correlation (r) A statistic developed by Karl Pearson to measure the linear correlation of two variables.

coefficient of determination (r^2) The proportion of variability of the dependent variable accounted for or explained by the independent variable in a regression model.

coefficient of multiple determination (R^2) The proportion of variation of the dependent variable accounted for by the independent variables in the regression model.

coefficient of skewness A measure of the degree of skewness that exists in a distribution of numbers; compares the mean and the median in light of the magnitude of the standard deviation.

coefficient of variation (CV) The ratio of the standard deviation to the mean, expressed as a percentage.

collectively exhaustive events A list containing all possible elementary events for an experiment.

combinations A counting method used to determine the number of possible ways n things can happen from N total possibilities when sampling without replacement.

complement of a union The only possible case other than the union of sets X and Y; the probability that neither X nor Y is in the outcome.

complementary events Two events, one of which comprises all the elementary events of an experiment that are not in the other event.

completely randomized design An experimental design wherein there is one treatment or independent variable with two or more treatment levels and one dependent variable. This design is analyzed by analysis of variance.

concomitant variables Variables that are not being controlled by the researcher in the experiment but can have an effect on the outcome of the treatment being studied. Also called *confounding variables*.

conditional probability The probability of the occurrence of one event given that another event has occurred.

confidence interval A range of values within which the analyst can declare, with some confidence, the population parameter lies.

confounding variables Variables that are not being controlled by the researcher in the experiment but can have an effect on the outcome of the treatment being studied. Also called *concomitant variables*.

contingency analysis Another name for the *chi-square test of independence*.

contingency table A two-way table that contains the frequencies of responses to two questions. Also called a *raw values matrix*.

continuous distribution Distribution constructed from continuous random variables.

continuous random variable Variable that takes on values at every point over a given interval.

control chart A quality control graph that contains an upper control limit, a lower control limit, and a centreline; used to evaluate whether a process is or is not in a state of statistical control.

convenience sampling A nonrandom sampling technique in which items for the sample are selected for the convenience of the researcher.

correction for continuity A correction made when a binomial distribution problem is approximated by the normal distribution because a discrete distribution problem is being approximated by a continuous distribution.

correlated *t* test A *t* test to test the differences in two related or matched samples; sometimes called the *matched-pairs test* or the t *test for related measures*.

correlation A measure of the degree of relatedness of two or more variables.

critical value The value that divides the nonrejection region from the rejection region.

critical value method A method of testing hypotheses in which the sample statistic is compared with a critical value in order to reach a conclusion about rejecting or failing to reject the null hypothesis.

cumulative frequency A running total of frequencies through the classes of a frequency distribution.

cycles Patterns of highs and lows through which data move over time periods usually of more than a year.

cyclical effects The rise and fall of time-series data over periods longer than one year.

D

decision alternatives The various choices or options available to the decision maker in any given problem situation.

decision analysis A category of quantitative business techniques particularly targeted at clarifying and enhancing the decision-making process.

decision making under certainty A decision-making situation in which the states of nature are known.

decision making under risk A decision-making situation in which it is uncertain which states of nature will occur but the probability of each state of nature occurring has been determined.

decision making under uncertainty A decision-making situation in which the states of nature that may occur are unknown and the probability of a state of nature occurring is also unknown.

decision table A matrix that displays the decision alternatives, the states of nature, and the payoffs for a particular decision-making problem. Also called a *payoff table*.

decision trees A flowchart-like depiction of the decision process that includes the various decision alternatives, the various states of nature, and the payoffs.

decomposition Breaking down the effects of time-series data into the four component parts of trend, cyclical, seasonal, and irregular.

degrees of freedom (df) A mathematical adjustment made to the size of the sample; used along with α to locate values in statistical tables.

dependent samples Two or more samples selected in such a way as to be dependent or related; each item or person in one sample has a corresponding matched or related item in the other samples. Also called related samples.

dependent variable In regression analysis, the variable that is being predicted.

descriptive statistics Statistics that have been gathered on a group to describe or reach conclusions about that same group.

deseasonalized data Time-series data in which the effects of seasonality have been removed.

Design for Six Sigma (DFSS) A quality scheme, an offshoot of Six Sigma, that places an emphasis on designing a product or process right the first time thereby allowing organizations the opportunity to reach even higher sigma levels through Six Sigma.

deterministic model Mathematical models that produce an "exact" output for a given input.

deviation from the mean The difference between a number and the average of the set of numbers of which the number is a part.

discrete distribution Distribution constructed from discrete random variables.

discrete random variable Random variable in which the set of all possible values is at most a finite or a countably infinite number of possible values.

disproportionate stratified random sampling A type of stratified random sampling in which the proportions of items selected from the strata for the final sample do not reflect the proportions of the strata in the population.

dummy variable Another name for a *qualitative* or *indicator variable*; usually coded as 0 or 1 and represents whether or not a given item or person possesses a certain characteristic.

Durbin-Watson test A statistical test for determining whether significant autocorrelation is present in a time-series regression model.

E

elementary events Events that cannot be decomposed or broken down into other events.

empirical rule A guideline that states the approximate percentage of values that fall within a given number of standard deviations of a mean of a set of data that are normally distributed.

EMVer A decision maker who bases his or her decision on the expected monetary value of the decision alternative.

error of an individual forecast The difference between the actual value and the forecast of that value.

error of estimation The difference between the statistic computed to estimate a parameter and the parameter. Also called error of the interval.

event An outcome of an experiment.

expected monetary value (EMV) A value of a decision alternative computed by multiplying the probability of each state of nature by the state's associated payoff and summing these products across the states of nature.

expected value The long-run average of occurrences; sometimes called the *mean value*.

expected value of perfect information The difference between the payoff that would occur if the decision maker knew which states of nature would occur and the expected monetary payoff from the best decision alternative when there is no information about the occurrence of the states of nature.

expected value of sample information The difference between the expected monetary value with information and the expected monetary value without information.

experiment A process that produces outcomes.

experimental design A plan and a structure to test hypotheses in which the researcher either controls or manipulates one or more variables.

exponential distribution A continuous distribution closely related to the Poisson distribution that describes the times between random occurrences.

exponential smoothing A forecasting technique in which a weighting system is used to determine the importance of previous time periods in the forecast.

F

F distribution A distribution based on the ratio of two random variances; used in testing two variances and in analysis of variance.

F value The ratio of two sample variances, used to reach statistical conclusions regarding the null hypothesis; in ANOVA, the ratio of the treatment variance to the error variance.

factorial design An experimental design in which two or more independent variables are studied simultaneously and every level of each treatment is studied under the conditions of every level of all other treatments. Also called a factorial experiment.

factors Another name for the *independent variables* of an experimental design.

failure mode and effects analysis (FMEA) A systematic way for identifying the effects of potential product or process failure. It includes methodology for eliminating or reducing the chance of a failure occurring.

finite correction factor A statistical adjustment made to the *z* formula for sample means; adjusts for the fact that a population is finite and the size is known.

first-differences approach A method of transforming data in an attempt to reduce or remove autocorrelation from a time-series regression model; results in each data value being subtracted from each succeeding time period data value, producing a new, transformed value.

fishbone diagram A display of possible causes of a quality problem and the interrelationships among the causes. The problem is diagrammed along the main line of the "fish" and possible causes are diagrammed as line segments angled off in such a way as to give the appearance of a fish skeleton. Also called an *Ishikawa diagram* or a *cause-and-effect diagram*.

flowchart A schematic representation of all the activities and interactions that occur in a process.

forecasting The art or science of predicting the future.

forecasting error A single measure of the overall error of a forecast for an entire set of data.

forward selection A multiple regression search procedure that is essentially the same as stepwise regression analysis except that once a variable is entered into the process, it is never deleted.

frame A list, map, directory, or some other source that is being used to represent the population in the process of sampling.

frequency distribution A summary of data presented in the form of class intervals and frequencies.

frequency polygon A graph constructed by plotting a dot for the frequencies at the class midpoints and connecting the dots.

Friedman test A nonparametric alternative to the randomized block design.

G

grouped data Data that have been organized into a frequency distribution.

H

heteroscedasticity The condition that occurs when the error variances produced by a regression model are not constant.

histogram A type of vertical bar chart constructed by graphing line segments for the frequencies of classes across the class intervals and connecting each to the *x* axis to form a series of rectangles.

homoscedasticity The condition that occurs when the error variances produced by a regression model are constant.

Hurwicz criterion An approach to decision making in which the maximum and minimum payoffs selected from each decision alternative are used with a weight, α, between 0 and 1 to determine the alternative with the maximum weighted average. The higher the value of α, the more optimistic the decision maker.

hypergeometric distribution A distribution of probabilities of the occurrence of *x* items in a sample of *n* when there are *A* of that same item in a population of *N*.

hypothesis A tentative explanation of a principle operating in nature.

hypothesis testing A process of testing hypotheses about parameters by setting up null and alternative hypotheses, gathering sample data, computing statistics from the samples, and using statistical techniques to reach conclusions about the hypotheses.

I

independent events Events such that the occurrence or nonoccurrence of one has no effect on the occurrence of the others.

independent samples Two or more samples in which the selected items are related only by chance.

independent variable In regression analysis, the predictor variable.

index number A ratio, often expressed as a percentage, of a measure taken during one time frame to that same measure taken during another time frame, usually denoted as the base period.

indicator variable Another name for a *dummy* or *qualitative variable*; usually coded as 0 or 1 and represents whether or not a given item or person possesses a certain characteristic.

inferential statistics Statistics that have been gathered from a sample and used to reach conclusions about the population from which the sample was taken.

in-process quality control A quality control method in which product attributes are measured at various intervals throughout the manufacturing process.

interaction What occurs when the effects of one treatment in an experimental design vary according to the levels of treatment of the other effect(s).

interquartile range The range of values between the first and the third quartile.

intersection The portion of the population that contains elements that lie in both or all groups of interest.

interval estimate A range of values within which it is estimated with some confidence the population parameter lies.

interval-level data Next to highest level of data. These data have all the properties of ordinal-level data, but in addition, intervals between consecutive numbers have meaning.

irregular fluctuations Unexplained or error variation within time-series data.

Ishikawa diagram A tool developed by Kaoru Ishikawa as a way to display possible causes of a quality problem and the interrelationships of the causes. Also called a *fishbone diagram* or a *cause-and-effect diagram*.

J

joint probability The probability of the intersection occurring, or the probability of two or more events happening at once.

judgment sampling A nonrandom sampling technique in which items selected for the sample are chosen by the judgment of the researcher.

just-in-time inventory system An inventory system in which little or no extra raw materials or parts for production are stored.

K

Kruskal-Wallis test The nonparametric alternative to one-way analysis of variance; used to test whether three or more samples come from the same or different populations.

kurtosis The amount of peakedness of a distribution.

L

lambda (λ) The symbol that denotes the long-run average of a Poisson distribution.

Laspeyres price index A type of weighted aggregate price index in which the quantity values used in the calculations are from the base year.

lean manufacturing A quality management philosophy that focuses on the reduction of wastes and the elimination of unnecessary steps in an operation or process.

least squares analysis The process by which a regression model is developed based on calculus techniques that attempt to produce a minimum sum of the squared error values.

leptokurtic Distributions that are high and thin.

level of significance The probability of committing a Type I error. Also called *alpha*.

levels The subcategories of the independent variable used by the researcher in the experimental design. Also called *classifications*.

lower control limit (LCL) The bottom-end line of a control chart, usually situated approximately three standard deviations of the statistic below the centreline; data points below this line indicate quality control problems.

M

Mann-Whitney *U* test A nonparametric counterpart of the *t* test used to compare the means of two independent populations.

manufacturing-based quality A view of quality in which the emphasis is on the manufacturer's ability to target consistently the requirements for the product with little variability.

marginal probability A probability computed by dividing a subtotal of the population by the total of the population.

matched-pairs test A *t* test to test the differences in two related or matched samples; sometimes called the t *test for related measures* or the *correlated* t *test*.

maximax criterion An optimistic approach to decision making under uncertainty in which the decision alternative is chosen according to which alternative produces the maximum overall payoff of the maximum payoffs from each alternative.

maximin criterion A pessimistic approach to decision making under uncertainty in which the decision alternative is chosen according to which alternative produces the maximum overall payoff of the minimum payoffs from each alternative.

mean absolute deviation (MAD) The average of the absolute values of the deviations around the mean for a set of numbers.

mean square error (MSE) The average of all errors squared of a forecast for a group of data.

mean value The long-run average of occurrences. Also called the *expected value*.

measures of central tendency One type of measure that is used to yield information about the centre of a group of numbers.

measures of shape Tools that can be used to describe the shape of a distribution of data.

measures of variability Statistics that describe the spread or dispersion of a set of data.

median The middle value in an ordered array of numbers.

mesokurtic Distributions that are normal in shape—that is, not too high or too flat.

metric data Interval- and ratio-level data. Also called quantitative data.

minimax regret A decision-making strategy in which the decision maker determines the lost opportunity for each decision alternative and selects the decision alternative with the minimum of lost opportunity or regret.

mn counting rule A rule used in probability to count the number of ways two operations can occur if the first operation has m possibilities and the second operation has n possibilities.

mode The most frequently occurring value in a set of data.

moving average The result of using an average of data from previous time periods to forecast the value for ensuing time periods and this average is modified at each new time period by including more recent values not in the previous average and dropping out values from the more distant time periods that were in the average. It is continually updated at each new time period.

multicollinearity A problematic condition that occurs when two or more of the independent variables of a multiple regression model are highly correlated.

multimodal Data sets that contain more than two modes.

multiple comparisons Statistical techniques used to compare pairs of treatment means when the analysis of variance yields an overall significant difference in the treatment means.

multiple regression Regression analysis with one dependent variable and two or more independent variables or at least one nonlinear independent variable.

mutually exclusive events Events such that the occurrence of one precludes the occurrence of the other.

N

naive forecasting models Simple models in which it is assumed that the more recent time periods of data represent the best predictions or forecasts for future outcomes.

nominal-level data The lowest level of data measurement; used only to classify or categorize.

nonlinear regression model A multiple regression model in which the model is nonlinear, such as a polynomial model, logarithmic model, and exponential model.

nonmetric data Nominal- and ordinal-level data. Also called qualitative data.

nonparametric statistics A class of statistical techniques that make few assumptions about the population and are particularly applicable to nominal- and ordinal-level data.

nonrandom sampling Sampling in which not every unit of the population has the same probability of being selected into the sample.

nonrandom sampling techniques Sampling techniques used to select elements from the population by any mechanism that does not involve a random selection process.

nonrejection region Any portion of a distribution that is not in the rejection region. If the observed statistic falls in this region, the decision is to fail to reject the null hypothesis.

nonsampling errors All errors other than sampling errors.

normal distribution A widely known and much-used continuous distribution that fits the measurements of many human characteristics and many machine-produced items.

null hypothesis The hypothesis that assumes the status quo—that the old theory, method, or standard is still true; the complement of the *alternative hypothesis*.

O

observed significance level Another name for the p *value* method of testing hypotheses.

observed value A statistic computed from data gathered in an experiment that is used in the determination of whether or not to reject the null hypothesis.

ogive A cumulative frequency polygon; plotted by graphing a dot at each class endpoint for the cumulative or decumulative frequency value and connecting the dots.

one-tailed test A statistical test wherein the researcher is interested only in testing one side of the distribution.

one-way ANOVA The process used to analyze a completely randomized experimental design. This process involves computing a ratio of the variance between treatment levels of the independent variable to the error variance. This ratio is an F value, which is then used to determine whether there are any significant differences between the means of the treatment levels.

operating characteristic (OC) curve In hypothesis testing, a graph of Type II error probabilities for various possible values of an alternative hypotheses.

opportunity loss table A decision table constructed by subtracting all payoffs for a given state of nature from the maximum payoff for that state of nature and doing this for all states of nature; displays the lost opportunities or regret that would occur for a given decision alternative if that particular state of nature occurred.

ordinal-level data Next-higher level of data from nominal-level data; can be used to order or rank items, objects, or people.

outliers Data points that lie apart from the rest of the points.

P

p chart A quality control chart for attribute compliance that graphs the proportion of sample items in noncompliance with specifications for multiple samples.

p value A method of testing hypotheses in which there is no preset level of α. The probability of getting a test statistic at least as extreme as the observed test statistic is computed under the assumption that the null hypothesis is true. This probability is called the p value, and it is the smallest value of α for which the null hypothesis can be rejected.

Paasche price index A type of weighted aggregate price index in which the quantity values used in the calculations are from the year of interest.

parameter A descriptive measure of the population.

parametric statistics A class of statistical techniques that contain assumptions about the population and that are used only with interval- and ratio-level data.

Pareto analysis A quantitative tallying of the number and types of defects that occur with a product or service, often recorded in a Pareto chart.

Pareto chart A vertical bar chart in which the number and types of defects for a product or service are graphed in order of magnitude from greatest to least.

partial regression coefficient The coefficient of an independent variable in a multiple regression model that represents the increase that will occur in the value of the dependent variable from a 1-unit increase in the independent variable if all other variables are held constant.

payoff table A matrix that displays the decision alternatives, the states of nature, and the payoffs for a particular decision-making problem. Also called a *decision table*.

payoffs The benefits or rewards that result from selecting a particular decision alternative.

Pearson product-moment correlation coefficient A measure of the linear correlation of two variables.

percentiles Measures of central tendency that divide a group of data into 100 parts.

permutation Permutations are distinct sequences of k objects that could be selected from a set of objects, in which order matters.

pie chart A circular depiction of data where the area of the whole pie represents 100% of the data being studied and slices represent a percentage breakdown of the sublevels.

platykurtic A term to describe distributions that are flat and spread out.

point estimate An estimate of a population parameter constructed from a statistic taken from a sample.

Poisson distribution A discrete distribution that is constructed from the probability of occurrence of rare events over an interval; focuses only on the number of discrete occurrences over some interval or continuum.

poka-yoke A quality concept (meaning "mistake proofing") that uses devices, methods, or inspections in order to avoid machine error or simple human error.

population A collection of persons, objects, or items of interest.

post hoc A term referring to after the experiment; pairwise comparisons made by the researcher *after* determining that there is a significant overall F value from ANOVA. Also called *a posteriori*.

power The probability of rejecting a false null hypothesis.

power curve A graph that plots the power values against various values of the alternative hypothesis.

precision The error portion of the confidence interval that is added and/or subtracted from the point estimate to form the confidence interval. Also called bounds.

prediction interval A range of values used in regression analysis to estimate a single value of y for a given value of x.

probabilistic model A model that includes an error term that allows for various values of output to occur for a given value of input.

probability matrix A two-dimensional table that displays the marginal and intersection probabilities of a given problem.

process A series of actions, changes, or functions that bring about a result.

product quality A view of quality in which quality is measurable in the product based on the fact that there are perceived differences in products and that quality products possess more attributes.

proportionate stratified random sampling A type of stratified random sampling in which the proportions of the items selected for the sample from the strata reflect the proportions of the strata in the population.

Q

quadratic regression model A multiple regression model in which the predictors are a variable and the square of the variable.

qualitative variable Another name for a *dummy* or *indicator variable*; represents whether or not a given item or person possesses a certain characteristic and is usually coded as 0 or 1.

quality What a product achieves when it delivers what is stipulated in its specifications.

quality circle A small group of workers consisting of supervisors and six to 10 employees who meet frequently and regularly to consider quality issues in their department or area of the business.

quality control The collection of strategies, techniques, and actions taken by an organization to ensure the production of quality products.

quartiles Measures of central tendency that divide a group of data into four subgroups or parts.

quota sampling A nonrandom sampling technique in which the population is stratified on some characteristic and then elements selected for the sample are chosen by nonrandom processes.

R

R chart A plot of sample ranges used in quality control.

random sampling Sampling in which every unit of the population has the same probability of being selected for the sample.

random variable A variable that contains the outcomes of a chance experiment.

randomized block design An experimental design in which there is one independent variable of interest and a second variable, known as a blocking variable, that is used to control for confounding or concomitant variables.

range The difference between the largest and the smallest values in a set of numbers.

ratio-level data Highest level of data measurement; contains the same properties as interval-level data, with the additional property that zero has meaning and represents the absence of the phenomenon being measured.

rectangular distribution A relatively simple continuous distribution in which the same height is obtained over a range of values. Also called the *uniform distribution*.

reengineering A radical approach to total quality management in which the core business processes of a company are redesigned.

regression analysis The process of constructing a mathematical model or function that can be used to predict or determine one variable by any other variable.

rejection region The portion of a distribution in which a computed statistic lies that will result in the decision to reject the null hypothesis.

relative frequency The proportion of the total frequencies that fall into any given class interval in a frequency distribution.

relative frequency of occurrence method The method of assigning probability based on cumulated historical data.

repeated measures design A randomized block design in which each block level is an individual item or person, and that person or item is measured across all treatments.

research hypothesis A statement of what the researcher believes will be the outcome of an experiment or a study.

residual The difference between the actual y value and the y value predicted by the regression model; the error of the regression model in predicting each value of the dependent variable.

residual plot A type of graph in which the residuals for a particular regression model are plotted along with their associated values of x.

response plane A plane fit in a three-dimensional space and that represents the response surface defined by a multiple regression model with two independent first-order variables.

response surface The surface defined by a multiple regression model.

response variable The dependent variable in a multiple regression model; the variable that the researcher is trying to predict.

risk avoider A decision maker who avoids risk whenever possible and is willing to drop out of a game when given the chance even when the payoff is less than the expected monetary value.

risk taker A decision maker who enjoys taking risk and will not drop out of a game unless the payoff is more than the expected monetary value.

robust A term that describes a statistical technique that is relatively insensitive to minor violations in one or more of its underlying assumptions.

runs test A nonparametric test of randomness used to determine whether the order or sequence of observations in a sample is random.

S

sample A portion of the whole.

sample proportion The quotient of the frequency at which a given characteristic occurs in a sample and the number of items in the sample.

sample-size estimation An estimate of the size of sample necessary to fulfill the requirements of a particular level of confidence and to be within a specified amount of error.

sample space A complete roster or listing of all elementary events for an experiment.

sampling error Error that occurs when the sample is not representative of the population.

scatter plot (chart) A plot or graph of the pairs of data from a simple regression analysis.

search procedures Processes whereby more than one multiple regression model is developed for a given database, and the models are compared and sorted by different criteria, depending on the given procedure.

seasonal effects Patterns of data behaviour that occur in periods of time of less than one year, often measured by the month.

serial correlation A problem that arises in regression analysis when the error terms of a regression model are correlated due to time-series data. Also called *autocorrelation*.

set notation The use of braces to group numbers that have some specified characteristic.

simple average The arithmetic mean or average for the values of a given number of time periods of data.

simple average model A forecasting averaging model in which the forecast for the next time period is the average of values for a given number of previous time periods.

simple index number A number determined by computing the ratio of a quantity, price, or cost for a particular year of interest to the quantity price or cost of a base year, expressed as a percentage.

simple random sampling The most elementary of the random sampling techniques; involves numbering each item in the population and using a list or roster of random numbers to select items for the sample.

simple regression Bivariate, linear regression.

Six Sigma A total quality management approach that measures the capability of a process to perform defect-free work, where a defect is defined as anything that results in customer dissatisfaction.

skewness The lack of symmetry of a distribution of values.

smoothing techniques Forecasting techniques that produce forecasts based on levelling out the irregular fluctuation effects in time-series data.

snowball sampling A nonrandom sampling technique in which survey subjects who fit a desired profile are selected

based on referral from other survey respondents who also fit the desired profile.

Spearman's rank correlation A measure of the correlation of two variables; used when only ordinal-level or ranked data are available.

standard deviation The square root of the variance.

standard error of the estimate (s_e) A standard deviation of the error of a regression model.

standard error of the mean The standard deviation of the distribution of sample means.

standard error of the proportion The standard deviation of the distribution of sample proportions.

standardized normal distribution z distribution; a distribution of z scores produced for values from a normal distribution with a mean of 0 and a standard deviation of 1.

states of nature The occurrences of nature that can happen after a decision has been made that can affect the outcome of the decision and over which the decision maker has little or no control.

stationary A term to describe time-series data that contain no trend, cyclical, or seasonal effects.

statistic A descriptive measure of a sample.

statistical hypothesis A formal hypothesis structure set up with a null and an alternative hypothesis to scientifically test research hypotheses.

statistics A science dealing with the collection, analysis, interpretation, and presentation of numerical data.

stem and leaf plot A plot of numbers constructed by separating each number into two groups, a stem and a leaf. The leftmost digits are the stems and the rightmost digits are the leaves.

stepwise regression A step-by-step multiple regression search procedure that begins by developing a regression model with a single predictor variable and adds and deletes predictors one step at a time, examining the fit of the model at each step until there are no more significant predictors remaining outside the model.

stratified random sampling A type of random sampling in which the population is divided into various non-overlapping strata and then items are randomly selected into the sample from each stratum.

subjective method A method of assigning probabilities based on the intuition or reasoning of the person determining the probability.

substantive result What occurs when the outcome of a statistical study produces results that are important to the decision maker.

sum of squares of error (SSE) The sum of the residuals squared for a regression model.

sum of squares of *x* The sum of the squared deviations about the mean of a set of values.

systematic sampling A random sampling technique in which every *k*th item or person is selected from the population.

T

***t* distribution** A distribution that describes the sample data in small samples when the standard deviation is unknown and the population is normally distributed.

***t* test for related measures** A *t* test to test the differences in two related or matched samples; sometimes called the *matched-pairs test* or the *correlated* t *test*.

***t* value** The computed value of *t* used to reach statistical conclusions regarding the null hypothesis in small-sample analysis.

team building The organization of a group of employees as an entity to undertake management tasks and perform other functions such as organizing, developing, and overseeing projects.

time-series data Data gathered on a given characteristic over a period of time at regular intervals.

total quality management (TQM) A program that occurs when all members of an organization are involved in improving quality; all goals and objectives of the organization come under the purview of quality control and are measured in quality terms.

transcendent quality A view of quality that implies that a product has an innate excellence, uncompromising standards, and high achievement.

treatment variable The independent variable of an experimental design that the researcher either controls or modifies.

trend Long-run general direction of a business climate over a period of several years.

Tukey-Kramer procedure A modification of the Tukey HSD multiple comparison procedure; used when there are unequal sample sizes.

Tukey's four-quadrant approach A graphical method using the four quadrants for determining which expressions of Tukey's ladder of transformations to use.

Tukey's HSD test In analysis of variance, a technique used for pairwise a posteriori multiple comparisons to determine if there are significant differences between the means of any pair of treatment levels in an experimental design. This test requires equal sample sizes and uses a *q* value along with the mean square error in its computation.

Tukey's ladder of transformations A process used for determining ways to recode data in multiple regression analysis to achieve potential improvement in the predictability of the model.

two-stage sampling Cluster sampling done in two stages: A first round of samples is taken and then a second round is taken from within the first samples.

two-tailed test A statistical test wherein the researcher is interested in testing both sides of the distribution.

two-way ANOVA The process used to statistically test the effects of variables in factorial designs with two independent variables.

Type I error An error committed by rejecting a true null hypothesis.

Type II error An error committed by failing to reject a false null hypothesis.

U

ungrouped data Raw data, or data that have not been summarized in any way.

uniform distribution A relatively simple continuous distribution in which the same height is obtained over a range of values. Also called the *rectangular distribution*.

union A new set of elements formed by combining the elements of two or more other sets.

union probability The probability of one event occurring or the other event occurring or both occurring.

unweighted aggregate price index number The ratio of the sum of the prices of a market basket of items for a particular year to the sum of the prices of those same items in a base year, expressed as a percentage.

upper control limit (UCL) The top-end line of a control chart, usually situated approximately three standard deviations of the statistic above the centreline; data points above this line indicate quality control problems.

user quality A view of quality in which the quality of the product is determined by the user.

utility The degree of pleasure or displeasure a decision maker has in being involved in the outcome selection process given the risks and opportunities available.

V

value quality A view of quality having to do with price and costs and whether the consumer got his or her money's worth.

variance The average of the squared deviations about the arithmetic mean for a set of numbers.

variance inflation factor (VIF) A statistic computed using the R^2 value of a regression model developed by predicting one independent variable of a regression analysis by other independent variables; used to determine whether there is multicollinearity among the variables.

W

weighted aggregate price index number A price index computed by multiplying quantity weights and item prices and summing the products to determine a market basket's worth in a given year and then determining the ratio of the market basket's worth in the year of interest to the same value computed for a base year, expressed as a percentage.

weighted moving average A moving average in which different weights are applied to the data values from different time periods.

Wilcoxon matched-pairs signed rank test A nonparametric alternative to the t test for two related or dependent samples.

X

x chart A quality control chart for measurements that graphs the sample means computed for a series of small random samples over a period of time.

Z

z distribution A distribution of z scores; a normal distribution with a mean of 0 and a standard deviation of 1.

z score The number of standard deviations a value (x) is above or below the mean of a set of numbers when the data are normally distributed.

INDEX